D1595393

SOME
SOUTH CAROLINA
COUNTY
RECORDS
Vol. 2

The Rev. Silas Emmett Lucas Jr.

Editor

All rights reserved. No part of this publication may be reproduced,
stored in a retrieval system, transmitted in any form,
posted on to the web in any form or by any means
without the prior written permission of the publisher.

Please direct all correspondence and orders to:

www.southernhistoricalpress.com
or
SOUTHERN HISTORICAL PRESS, Inc.
PO BOX 1267
375 West Broad Street
Greenville, SC   29601
southernhistoricalpress@gmail.com

ISBN #0-89308-648-7

Printed in the United States of America

PREFACE

In 1976 Southern Historical Press published a small book entitled *Some South Carolina County Records, Volume 1,* containing 162 pages, compiled by Brent Holcomb. We had anticipated doing several volumes of this series, but somehow other things prevented us from returning to the project.

The publisher of this book is also editor of the *Georgia Genealogical Magazine,* which he has edited since 1970, and over those nineteen years he has run a small section of South Carolina county records in each issue. It is my feeling and experience that people who buy genealogical books from Southern Historical Press generally do not subscribe to the *GGM,* and likewise, people who subscribe to the magazine by and large generally do not buy genealogy books.

In going back over the contents of the *GGM* for these nineteen years, we have found this wealth of South Carolina genealogical source material that really needed to be brought to the attention of the public at large. It was with this in mind that we have taken the bulk of the South Carolina material appearing in the *Georgia Genealogical Magazine* and compiled it into book form as found herein.

> The Rev. Silas Emmett Lucas, Jr.
> Editor and Publisher

CONTENTS

SETTLERS FROM OLD NINETY SIX
SOUTH CAROLINA TO GEORGIA AND ALABAMA

The following unpublished typescript of migrations to Georgia and Alabama was prepared by G. L. Summer (in 1948?). The original is in the Georgia Historical Society and is reproduced here with permission.

List of pioneers and families, with other historical data, who moved from the old Ninety Six District, South Carolina (Counties of Newberry, Union, Laurens, Abbeville, Edgefield, and Spartanburg), between the years 1780 and 1850, to Georgia.

Compiled by G. L. Summer

HENRY L. CUNNINGHAM, ROBERT H. PARRIS and wife, MARGARET H. (CUNNINGHAM) PARRIS, moved to Forsythe, Ga. Claim filed by WM. D. CUNNINGHAM, of Hamburg, S. C. in the estate of ROBERT F. CUNNINGHAM, of Hamburg, S. C.

ROBERT SUMMERS and his wife, SARAH STEELE SUMMERS, went to Jasper County, Ga. DAVID STEELE is named as brother of SARAH STEELE SUMMERS.

BENJAMIN F. PARTAIN and wife, SARAH (JENNINGS) PARTAIN (daughter of JOHN JENNINGS), moved to Walker County, Ga. HIRAM JENNINGS went to Walker County, and SPEER PARTAIN went to Harris County.

JAMES W. and ELIZABETH REYNOLDS moved to Meriweather County.

JAMES W. THORNBURG and wife, MARY ANN (FERGUSON) THORNBURG, to Baker County. She was a daughter of WM. H. FERGUSON and a grand-daughter of WM. FERGUSON.

JESSE HUNTER removed to Green County.

MARK TRAVERS moved at an early period.

The following pioneers and some of their descendants moved into Georgia: GEORGE EICHLEBERGER, PETER LESTER, JOHN SLIGH, HUGH O'NEALL, JAMES BOWERS, DR. MITCHEL SUBER (went to Oglethorpe), GEORGE HENRY SUMMER (to Jefferson County), BRADFORD BOYD (son of SAMUEL BOYD), STEPHEN SHELL, THOMAS T. CURETON (to Newton County), SHADRACH VAN SANT, MARTIN SIGLEY, JOHN KINARD, WILLIAM SUMMER (his gr-sons, ELIAS, NELSON and ADAM), ABRAM GILBERT, (later went to Alabama), BURR GOGGANS, BENJ. GREGORY (to Newton County), THENEY GATES (went to Jefferson County), Descendants of CHARLES FLOYD, HARRISON REESE, JOHN BUCHANAN, THOMAS DURRETT, LEWIS HOGGE, JONAS BEARD, and GEO. LEITNER.

WILLIAM MC AMIE and wife, SARAH, went to Twiggs County. JAMES BONDS settled in Gwinnett County.

The following pioneers or their descendants settled in Georgia: JOSEPH YOUNG, JAMES MC CLURE, JOHN MC MORRIS, WM. WATKINS, JOSEPH SIBLEY (settled near Augusta), JAMES HOUSTON and wife, MARY A. DAVENPORT HOUSTON, went into Glynn County, WILLIAM BROWN, to Newton County, GILES ELMORE, and WILLIAM B. SPEARMAN who moved just after the Civil War.

THOMAS C. REEDER and wife, MARY TEAGUE (FOWLER) REEDER, WM. B. SPEARMAN was a member of Co. A, 4th Bat. S. C. Vols. Civil War. FRED S. CURETON went to Moreland, Ga. after the Civil War. He was a member of Co. A., 4th Bat. S. C. Vols. CHARLES BANKS and wife, BETSEY, and their children: ALBERT E. and MARIE BANKS. LEVI RICHARDSON and wife, SALLY, who afterwards migrated to Alabama. ISHAM CORLEY and wife, PATSY, and YOUNG KING and wife, DELILA.

HENRY THOMPSON went to Newton County. Certificate of marriage to WINNIE BROWN is dated Feb. 4th, 1830.

1

ELI LOFTIN, MRS. JOHN ECTOR, E. H. GRAY (to Meriweather County), ISAAC and FRANCES VOLUNTINE (to Richmond County), JAMES A. CROME (to Union Point), ABRAHAM COX and MARY COX (to Jones County), JOSEPH WALLACE (to Randolph County), Descendants of GEO. GRAY and WM. BROWN (in Newton County), ABRAM HOLLAND (went to Laurens Dist.), J. H. CRISP and family (moved within recent years), ALEXANDER G. SAXON (to Franklin County), WM. A. MITCHEL (to Augusta).

The following pioneers or their descendants went into Georgia: PATRICK MC DOWELL, HENRY DOMINICK, DRURY VAUGHN, BENJAMIN RICHARDSON, JAMES HARRIS, FRED WYSE, WM. MORGAN and wife, SARAH (SHEPPARD) MORGAN (to Coweta County), THOMAS A. SULLIVAN and wife, SOPHRONIA CAROLINE (DAL-RYMPLE) SULLIVAN, moved to Cass Co., WM. MOORE into Elbert County, and ELIJAH MOORE. WILLIAM GRAY (to Jones County), ABRAHAM PATRICK CAR-MICHAEL (to Coweta County), CALEB BURTON (to Franklin County), EDMUND STEPHENS and wife, JANE (GRIFFIN) STEPHENS, ROBERT F. GRIFFIN, STEPHEN HEARD (to Wilkes County), PETER GILLIAM (to Clark County), WM. B. HODGES and MRS. SALLY MORROW (to Newton County, HENRY W. SHELL (to Newton County), JAMES WATKINS, GEORGE MC COLLUM and wife, ELIZABETH, and DR. NATHAN RENWICK (he settled in Troup County), JAMES COCHRAN (to Hall County), JOHN HAMPTON (to Jackson County), WM. WADLINGTON (to Ogle-thorpe), WILLIAM MALONE (to Oglethorpe), THOMAS MATHIS, ADAM POOLE or some of his descendants, JAMES RUSSEL and wife, MARY (NANCE) RUSSELL, SILAS BRUNSON and JACOB SLAPPY (they went to Augusta), descendants of GEO. SLIGH, GEORGE SUBER and his wife, ELIZABETH, settled in Jones County.

Some of the descendants of JOHN PAYSINGER live near Augusta (they moved at a later period), JOHN BLALOCK, BENJAMIN WATTS (into Chatham County), JANE W. JOYNER (to Wilkes County), ROBERT WATTS (buried at Savannah, his native city).

DANIEL MOORE went to Haversham County, JAMES CRUMLEY to Dawson County, WM. SMITH CRUMLEY to Nancheta Valley, PENNINGTON KING or his descendants to Jones County, JOSEPH ETHERIDGE went from Laurens County, S. C.

THOMAS LAKE's descendants, ENOCH M. LAKE, JAMES P. BRYAN, JOHN GIRA-DEAU LEGARE and his wife, went to Dawson, Ga. MRS. A. L. PATTERSON was living in Burke County. ROBERT BOYD, THOMAS RUTHERFORD, JOHN DUN-CAN, HENRY BLACK and others went at the period just before the beginning of the Civil War.

Some descendants of Major ROBERT GILLAM, A Rev. War Officer. Some descendants of JOHN SATTERWHITE, DANIEL MC KEE, MICHAEL MC KEE, MRS. ANNE FINLEY, SOLOMON WALDROP (he settled in Jasper County), MRS. JANE PRESS-LY (to Clarke County), JOHN CLELAND and wife, PERMELIA THOMAS CLELAND, moved to DeKalb County, ANNE THOMAS to DeKalb County, MRS. MARGARET A. (RUSSELL) BROWN (to Coweta County), ROBERT Y. BROWN (to Coweta Co.) JOHN TOLBERT and wife, MARY (RUSSELLS) TOLBERT (to Coweta County), JAMES RUSSELL (to Coweta County), ROBERT RUSSELL (to Coweta County), ELIJAH ELMORE (to Coweta County), RUTHA MC CULLOUGH (to Coweta County), THOMAS ENTRIKEN (to Coweta County), WM. L. HEIRS (to Heard County), ZODIC LEVY (to Cobb County).

HARMON ROBERTS, SAMUEL HOGG, MRS. J. D. HOUSTON (to Brunswick), descendants of ABRAM YOUNG, GEORGE SUBER and wife, ELIZABETH E. SUBER, went into Jones County, DAVID DOMINICK into Coweta County, JAMES F. DOMINICK into Coweta County, YOUNG BROWN, JAMES BROWN and wife, MELVINA (HAYNES) BROWN, THOMAS EDWARD KINARD, JOHN T. SWANN and wife, HARRIET N. SWANN, into Decatur (she was sister of THOMAS B. CALMES). Rev. MONROE J. EPTING went at later period to Savannah, and Rev. HENRY P. COUNTS went to Harolson, Ga. at a later period.

JOHN HUDSON and his wife, SARAH ELIZABETH (MORGAN) HUDSON, went from Laurens, S. C. THOMPSON EARLE settled in Baker Co., GEORGE W. GARMANY went to Savannah. WM. BURTON settled in Twiggs County. WM. PAGE and wife, HESTER HANCOCK PAGE.

MICHAEL HENTZ whose son JOHN was a member of Ga. State Legislature

Cont'd from page 2:
and husband of the authoress, CAROLINE LEE HENTZ. AUGUSTUS YOUNG and
WM. BEDENBAUGH, HIRAM G. WALDROP (to Coweta County), EPHRIAM LYLES
(to Twiggs County), THOS. GILL and wife, HANNAH. JACKSON WALKER (to
Putnam County), HARRIET WALKER (to Putnam County), AARON SUTTON (to
Monroe County), JACOB CHAPMAN (to Butts County), JOHN ROGERS and his
wife, MARY ANN (CHAPMAN) ROGERS (they settled in Henry County), SARAH
ETHERIDGE went into Gwinnett County), PENELOPE PADGETT and NELOPY PADG-
ETT went to Barbour County, EDWARD WHITE and wife, SUSAN (to Walton
County), JORDON HUNT and wife, MARTHA (CLARY) HUNT, to Upson County.
SILAS DABBS and wife, LUCY (BODIE) DABBS (to Harris County), WM. PINK-
NEY HUNNICUTT (to Gwinnett County), JOSHUA WATSON (to Washington, Ga.)

JOEL WAISTECOATE (to Effingham County), WM SPENCER, ROBERT and REUBEN
TAYLOR (to Effingham County), DANIEL FORD and wife, AGATHA (WALKER)
FORD, ELIJAH WALKER, JOEL TUCKER, WOODSON LIGEN (to Augusta), sons
of HARRISON JONES, SR. viz: WILLIAM, RICHARD, WELDON, HARRISON, and
JOHN P. JONES. WM. G. WRIGHT (to Columbia County), VERLINDA BISHOP
(to Meriweather County), JOHN LEAKE (to Cass County), MRS. DORCAS LEAKE
(to Cass County), WM. G. VINSON and wife, LYDIA (GRAYDON) VINSON (to
Crawford County), JOHN TERRY (to Forsythe County), STEPHEN TERRY (to
Forsythe County), TULLEY E. MOSELEY (to Forsythe County).

Some heirs of THOMAS HILTON settled in Cass County, viz: WM. BROWN,
ENSLEY HILTON, STORGER HILTON, SARAH BROWNLET, MARTHA CHILDRESS, etc.

WILLIAM WILLIAMSON (to Walton County), BRYANT T. LEAKE and wife, MARTHA
(COOK) LEAKE (to Cass County), ROBERT DUNLAP or some of his descendants,
JAMES M. OWENS and his wife, ELIZA ELIZABETH CRAWFORD OWENS (to Cass
County), JAMES M. DAVIS and wife, MATILDA (GOGGANS) DAVIS (to Monroe
County), JOSEPH BEAVERS and wife, LUCINDA (CALHOUN) BEAVERS (went to
Chattooga County). (Mrs. LUCINDA BEAVERS was a grand-daughter of HULET
SULLIVAN), JESSE GRAY, WALKER GRAY, THOMAS GRAY, JOHN BOGAN and his
wife, REBECCA (FARROW) BOGAN (to Jasper County), MRS. MARTHA FUREY
(to Richmond County), JOHN KENNEDY (to Cass County), JOHN BUIS (or
BUIST), ZADOCK FORD (to Gwinnett County), WM. W. CAMP (to Campbell
County), LANGLEY B. CAMP (to Campbell County), LEWIS MATHIS, THOMAS
RUSSELL and wife, POLLY (BISHOP) RUSSELL.

From Union District are some of those who moved into Georgia: ANDREW
TORRENCE, JOHN SIMPSON, NEWTON FOOTE (to Elbert County), MRS. PEGGY
KINCHELD JOHNSON (to Elbert County), JOHN HUMPHRIES (he went first
to Columbus), MRS. MARY WHITE TAYLOR and THOMAS TAYLOR (to Prince Co.),
LEANDER SMITH (to Habersham County), JAMES ROBINSON (late of Green
County), HENRY SANFORD (of Green County), ROBERT B. GILLIAM and wife,
MARY W. MURPHY GILLIAM, MRS. MILLY W. JACKSON, AMOS DUNCAN, JOHN ASHBY,
(went to Lumpkin County), JOHN ASHBY (to Clarksville), JEPTHA M. MURPHY,
HIRAM CUMMINGS and wife, ELIZABETH (JACKSON) CUMMINGS.

From Abbeville District are the following:
NATHANIEL STINCHCOURT and wife, SUSAN SARAH (OLIVER) STINCHCOURT, (to
Lafayette County), SARAH TERRELL (to Elbert County), JAMES RED to Burke
County, JOHN LINDSEY (to Wilkes County), LE ROY POPE (to Petersburgh),
WM. GRIFFIN (later went to Va.), JAMES BROOKS (to Franklin County),
JAMES REID (to Savannah), JOSEPH ASHTON (to Richmond County), JOSEPH
ASHTON's widow, LUCY ASHTON, married CHARLES STOVALL according to a
certificate of marriage. WM. SAMPLES (to Putnam County), WALTER ADAIR
(to Franklin County), JAMES COLLIER (to Richmond County), ROBERT KEY
(to Elbert County), MRS. SARAH WADE (widow of PLEASANT WADE), MRS.
WILLIAM WALTON (to Lincoln County), JOHN B. CALLAHAM (to Elbert County),
JOHN M. DAVENPORT (to Morgan County, afterward removed to Burke County).
JAMES CARUTHERS or his descendants, ISAAC S. WHITTEN (to Hancock County),
ISAAC S. WHITTEN married MRS. MARTHA F. MERIWEATHER, SAMUEL YOUNG and
wife, MARGARET YOUNG (to Cobb County), MRS. AMELIA (SIMS) GRIFFIN (to
Lincoln County), MRS. LUCINDA (SIMS) WALKER (to Lincoln County), MRS.
JAMES (SIMS) STOVALL (to Lincoln County), NATHAN and RICHARD GRIFFIN
went into Lee County, NATHAN SIMMS to Elbert County. BENJAMIN HARRIS
to Richmond County, MARY BOWERS to Richmond County, LUD HARRIS to Richmond County, WILLIAM HAMMOND went to Augusta. THOMAS HART and wife,

Cont'd from page 3:
CELIA (SNEAD) HART, GARLAND SNEAD, NATHANIEL SNEAD, WILLIAM LAMKIN, WILLIAM NICHOLS, JOHN C. TOLBERT, BENJAMIN MARTIN.

CHARLES GOODWIN settled at "Silver Bluff" near Augusta. LEWIS HOLLOWAY's descendants (he was son of a Va. pioneer), JAMES BILBO (to Screven County), NATHANIEL LUNDY (to Screven County), THOMAS HOLLOWAY, JOHN FOX (to Augusta), descendants of HUGH MIDDLETON, ELISHA BROWN (to Columbia County), MRS. MARY ATTAWAY, ROBERT ATTAWAY, GEORGE PEARSON (he settled in Augusta), ROBERT GRANT, JOHN JENKINS, ABNER REID (he went to Augusta), JOHN LAMAR, WILLIAM W. OLDS (Columbia County). MRS. NANCY MOSELEY (daughter of THOMAS BUTLER) settled in Wilkes County. ROBERT and JOHN BOLTON (to Savannah), DR. JAMES BRADLEY (to Oglethorpe), JOHN BRADLEY (to Oglethorpe), MATHIAS ARDIS or his descendants settled in Oglethorpe.

Co-Partnership between GREEN B. MARSHALL of Augusta and BERNIE MC KINNIE of Savannah for making brick. Year 1817 - contract for seven years for operations at "Meadows Gardens" in South Carolina.

ASA HOLSTON (to Meriweather County). In the year 1834 he deeded a slave to four daughters, viz: ELIZA, MARY, CAROLINE, and EMILY.

GEORGE W. YARBROUGH, RICHARD BULLOCK and wife, URSULA BULLOCK (to Augusta), JOSHUA KEY (to Augusta), MRS. MARTHA (KEY) JARRETT (to Jackson County), HUGH NESBITT (to Augusta), DAVID CLARK (to Richmond County), BENNETT H. CRAWFORD (to Jasper County). Descendants of WM. YELDELL, JAMES LUMPKIN (to Columbia County), MRS. ELIZABETH HANCOCK (widow of JESSE HANCOCK) to Richmond County. SARAH L. BREITHAUGHT (child of CHRISTIAN BREITHAUGHT) to Bibb County, BENJAMIN WALL settled in Chatham County.

Some of the following families removed from Georgia into Alabama, who were originally from South Carolina: HALL, HILL, BURNETT, CLISBY, TULIS, SUMMER, CHADWICK, KING, BEARD, ABRAMS, DURRETT, MC CRARY, TERRY, SPENCE, GLENN, LANGFORD, GRAY, GILBERT, GORES, SUMMERS, FLOYD, HENDERSON, LYLES, HODGES, MC MERRIES, GRENSHAW, BELK, THOMPSON. There were probably others.

The above names and data were compiled by G. Leland Summer, Newberry, South Carolina. Found in old County Court House records, libraries, family records, church records, etc. and were accumulated over a period of several years.

List of names of early pioneers or their families who migrated to Alabama from the Ninety Six District of South Carolina between the years 1780 and 1850.

ADKINSON, JOHN and wife, SARAH, to Russell County.
ADAMS, WILLIAM S. moved to Crocketville.
ABRAMS, WILLIAM, settled in Picken County.
ALBERSON, ELIJAH, and wife, CLARY (GRIFFIN) ALBERSON, to Marion County.
ADAMS, WILLIAM, went to Chambers County. LUCINDA ADAMS to Chambers County.
AULL, REV. HERMAN, died in South Carolina, had descendants who moved to Alabama.
ALLEN, WADE, to Montgomery County.
ANDERSON, GEORGE and wife, NARCISSA (SONDLEY) ANDERSON.
BUCKABOO, ABNER A., to Chambers County, also SARAH BUCKABOO (widow of WM. BUCKABOO, and children: ROBERT F., BENJ. W., SUSANNAH J. and SEABORN), to Chambers County.
BURNETT, MRS. JULIAN A. (formerly JULIAN ADAMS), went to Tallapoosa County, as did JEREMIAH BURNETT.
BLAIR, GEORGE W. and wife, MARTHA BLAIR (she was a daughter of THOS. H. and ESTHER RAWLES), went to Russell County. C. C. BLAIR settled in Russell County.
BUSH, LEWIS and wife, ELIZABETH (CHADWICK) BUSH, to Russell County.
BRANDAWAY, NANCY, went to Jackson County.
BOYD, AARON and wife, LUDY, to Tuscaloosa County.
BOWERS, JAMES L. and wife, MARY ANN, to Monroe County.
BELK, JEREMIAH and wife, JANE BELK.

4

BARTON, WILLOUGHBY and ABSOLOM, moved to Richmond County.
BEASLEY, WILLIAM and wife, REBECCA BEASLEY, to Barbour County.
BEVIS, THOMAS, to Lauderdale County.
BOWIE, SIDNEY J. (Lawyer and Congressman) to Birmingham.
BOWIE, ALEXANDER (Chancellor).
BROWN, GREEN B. and wife, EMOLINE (TATE) BROWN, to Pickens County.
BROCK, ELIAS and wife, HANNAH, to Talledega County.
BROCK, DR. JAMES and JOHN BROCK, to Talledega County.
BERKE, JAMES J. and wife, CHARLOTTE (LUKE) BERKE, to Tallapoosa County.
BOLT, JAMES, moved to Randolph County.
BALLENTINE, JAMES D., went to Tallapoosa County.
BALLENTINE, JAMES A., EDWIN D., MARY ANN, and ZACARIAH (children of LEMUEL BALLENTINE, son of JAMES D.) all moved to Tallapoosa County.
BRYANT, WILLIAM T. and wife, CATHERINE, and sons, ELISHA, JOSEPH and WILLIAM, to Green County.
BROWN, MARY A. W., to Sumpter County.
BEDENBAUGH, DANIEL
CLISBY, JOHN and EMILY D. CLISBY (heirs of MRS. MARY TILLMAN), moved to Coosa County.
CHAPMAN, BENJAMIN and wife, ELIZABETH CAROLINA (DE SHARGO) CHAPMAN, marriage license dated July 9, 1838, lived in Tallapoosa County.
CHADWICK, ELIAS and JOHN, WILLIAM, and ELIZABETH (CHADWICK) BUSH, to Russell County.
COTTER, JOHN and wife, MARY ANN (JONES) COTTER, daughter of JOSEPH P. and MARY JONES, went to Chambers County.
CROMER, HILLIARD, to Talledega County (he returned to South Carolina and married) left S. C. with the LAKES and others.
CROMER, CHRISTIAN, SIMON and PHILLIP.
CRENSHAW, ANDERSON, lawyer, to Butler County. Became a distinguished Jurist of Alabama. His parents are buried in Newberry County, South Carolina, at old Bethel Cemetery on Kings Creek. Dr. ABNER CRENSHAW, brother of Judge ANDERSON CRENSHAW.
CHANDLER, ISRAEL, his descendants left for Alabama with the GILBERTS.
CALDWELL, DAN, went to Chambers County.
CANNON, DANIEL, to Lauderdale County.
CORLEY, ALLEN B. and wife, WINNEY (BLADDON) CORLEY, to Washington County.
COBURN, THOMAS S. and wife, ELLEN (BODIE) COLBURN, to Loundes County.
CALLOWAY, MELTON and wife, MASSEY CALLOWAY, to Green County.
COOKE, HENRY to Perry County.
COOKE, MICHAEL to Sumpter County.
BOLAND - descendants of JOHN BOLAND, emigrant.
CUNNINGHAM, JOHN, moved to Tuscaloosa County.
COATE, descendants of JOHN COATE, to Clarke County. (He was one of the original proprietors of the lands on which the city of Newberry, S. C. was located).
BLACKBURN, JOHN E., RANSOME, MARTHA L. and NANCY E., to Sumpter County.
CHAPMAN, MARCUS and CHEVIS M. went from Union District. STEPHEN R. CHAPMAN.
CULPEPPER, JOSEPH B., went to Culpepper County.
CULPEPPER, JOHN and wife, ANN ELIZABETH CULPEPPER.
COLLIER, EDWARD and wife, to Springfield.
BENNETT, JORIAL.
CROCKER, some descendants of JACOB CROCKER.
CLIFFORD, THOMAS, to Montgomery County.
COOPER, CAMPBELL and wife, MARTHA (DOBY) COOPER, to Russell County. Some descendants of JAMES COOPER.
COOPER, REUBEN and wife, SUSAN (DOBY) COOPER, to Russell County.
COLLINS, JAMES and wife.
COLLINS, MATTHEW. Also, MRS. FRANCIS (COLLINS) JOHNSON.
BEARD, WM. B. S., went to Tuscaloosa County.
CASEY, MRS. ELIZABETH, widow of Gen. LEVI CASEY, to Lauderdale County.
DAY, MASON, Guardian of his three children: THOMAS, CAROLINE J., and LUCILE J. DAY.
DUCKETT, JOSIAS, moved to Perry County in year 1827.
DURRETT, THOMAS, went to Tuscaloosa County. Also BENJ. DURRETT.
DAVENPORT, FRANCIS and JESSE G., went to Butler County.
DAVIS, J. H., to Randolph County. JAMES M. DAVIS, to Tallapoosa County.
DUNLAP, ROBERT. JACOB G. DANNER went to Sumpter County.
DOBBINS, WASHINGTON, moved to Perry County, married KEZIAH KELLER, daughter of GEORGE and ELIZABETH KELLER.

DUNCAN, WILLIAM
DUCKETT, MARY (heir of BARUCH O'DELL), went to Sumpter County.
DUCKETT, some descendants of Capt. THOS. DUCKETT.
DAWSON, SAMUEL G., to Chambers County.
DAVENPORT, BERLEY, to Butler County.
DAY, SIMON and wife, SOPHIA (BODIE) DAY, to Dallas County.
EASTLAND, ELIJAH. EZEKIAH EASTLAND, son of THOMAS EASTLAND.
EARGLE, JOSEPH, to Pickens County.
EICHLEBERGER, some descendants of Capt. EICHELBERGER. JOHN EICHLEBERGER,
JR. moved to Gilbertsboro.
EDWARDS, JOHN S., to Jasper County.
EDWARDS, LYLLETON.
FRYER, GEO. W. and wife, MATILDA (JOHNSON) FRYER, to Barbour County.
FELTMAN, JACOB and wife, MARY, to Tuscaloosa County.
FLOYD, some descendants of Capt. JOHN FLOYD. JACK FLOYD lived at Opelika.
FAIR, General E. Y. moved to Selma.
FERNANDEZ, WILLIAM.
FOUNTAIN, WILLIAM M., Morgan County.
GARY, some descendants of WM. GARY.
GARY, JOHN H., moved to Sumpter County.
GARMANY, WILLIAM and wife, NANCY (SHEPPEARD) GARMANY, to Cherokee Co.
GOREE, NATHAN, to Dallas County.
GOREE, CLAIBORNE and wife, JUDITH, went to Dallas County.
GOREE, EPHRIAM, to Montgomery Co. SILAS and JAMES GOREE.
GLASS, THOMAS, JR., descendant of Capt. WM. F. HOUSEAL of the Rev.
War.
GILBERT, THOMAS, to Gilbertsboro.
GOREE, JAMES LYLES, went to Marion Co. (he was a descendant of Capt.
JAMES LYLES of the Rev. War).
GILBERT, BOOKTER, went from Laurens Dist., S. C. to Clark Co., Ala.
GRAY, SIMON P., a lawyer, went to Monroe County.
GRIFFIN, REBECCA, to Marion Co. RICHARD GRIFFIN, to Madison Co.
GREER, JOSEPH and wife, JANE, to Chambers County.
GOGGANS, some descendants of DANIEL GOGGANS, Rev. War Patriot.
GODFREY, MRS. AMY, to Tallapoosa County.
GOGGANS, LUCINDA T., to Tallapoosa Co. Also, SAMUEL GOGGANS.
GRAYDON, SAMUEL, to Tallapoosa County.
GRAY, JACOB and wife, CHARLOTTE REBECCA (TODD) GRAY.
GOODWIN, JULIUS, to Bibb County.
GRIFFIN, ISAAC, died in Alabama in 1827.
GOGGANS, ABRAM, to Madison County.
GILBERT, DAVID, went to Limestone County.
HALL, JOHN W. and wife, CLEMENTINE HALL, (she was relict of JOSHUA
JOHNSON, deceased, of Rutherford County, Tennessee).
HILL, WILLIAM and ELIZA, to Bibb County.
HALL, SAMUEL and wife, NANCY (DARBY) HALL, to Pickens County.
HENDERSON, some descendantss of Capt. JOHN HENDERSON.
HODGES, JAMES A., went to Tuscaloosa County.
HOMER, WM. E. LAWSON and wife.
HAMRICK, A. W.
HANCOCK, DR. LANA, a physician, connected with the GOREE and SIMS fam-
ilies of old Ninety Six Dist., S. C.
HUTCHINSON, ABNER and wife, SARAH, to Chambers County.
HUNTER, STARKE, to Connent (Conecuh?) County.
HAGOOD, MARK, to St. Clair County.
HOUSTON, WILLIAM.
HUNTER, NATHAN and wife, AMANDA (MILLS) HUNTER.
HANNA, JOHN and WILLIAM. JAMES HANNA went to Chambers County.
HUDSON, WILLIAM and ROBERT, to Sumpter County.
HAVARD, JOHN and wife, MARY (RILEY) HAVARD.
HAGOOD, MRS. ELIZABETH DAWSON, to Chambers County.
HUMPHRIES, MRS. MARGARET, some of her children moved to Russell Co.
HAWKINS, PETER.
JOHNSON, some descendants of JOHN JOHNSTON.
JOHNSTONE, DR. BURR. DR. JOHN FOOTE JOHNSTONE went to Montgomery.
JOHNSON, JOSEPH, to Marion County.
JONES, FREEMAN, MRS. MALISSA R. JONES, to Lowndes County.
JEANS, JAMES A. and ELBERT P. JEANS.
JOHNSON, MRS. FRANCES COLLINS.

JONES, MRS. REBECCA (WALDRON).
KILCREASE, JOHN L. and wife, SUSAN (HILL) KILCREASE, to Maury County.
KING, DR. JACOB H., to Talladega County.
KELLER, some descendants of GEORGE KELLER.
KINGSMORE, MRS. E. M., moved at a later time to Birmingham.
KOONE, some descendants of ADAM KOONE.
KOONE, MARTHA DUNCAN. SILAS KOONE.
KELLY, GEO. W. and wife, MARY A., to Coosa County.
KERR, CHARLES J., to Dallas County.
KYSER, GEORGE.
KENNEDY, MRS. LUCY (HUFF).
KENNER, SAMUEL B., moved to Marion Co., (member of S. C. Legislature).
LACY, WM. B., settled in Chambers County.
LAVENDER, ROBERT, to Pickens County.
LESTER, PETER.
LE GRONNE, JOHN and GEORGE.
LANGFORD, DR. WM. B., settled in Lauderdale County.
LOWE, MRS. JOHN SCOTT, to Jasper County.
LYLES, some descendants of Capt. EPHRIAM LYLES of the Revolution; descendants of Col. JAMES LYLES of the Rev. War.
LEE, JARED C., JR., went to Birmingham. HONORIAS P. LEE was killed in Confederate Army, name on monument at Selma, Ala.
LINDSEY, WILLIAM and wife, WINNEY (ROGERS) LINDSEY, to Wilcox County.
LESTER, ALFRED and SMITH LESTER. Some descendants of JAMES LESTER, SR.
LITTLETON, MARK.
LOVE, ROBERT and family.
LINDLEY, DAVID.
LINVILLE, LEWIS, to Chambers County.
LEWIS, WILLIAM and wife, REBECCA (RILEY) LEWIS.
LAMAR, JOHN.
LEWERY, MICHAEL, to Walker County.
MATHIS (or MATHEWS), LEWIS D., to Montgomery Co. (Heir of HENRY MATHIS).
MARS, JOHN.
MORRIS, JOSHUA, DOCTOR, JOHN, JOSEPH, WM. HENRY. and PLEASANT, JR.
MOSELEY, EDWARD, to Montgomery County.
MITCHEL, HARRIS and wife, SALLY (WALKER) MITCHEL.
MITCHEL, WM. and wife, POLLY (LINDLEY) MITCHEL.
MILLS, some descendants of WM. MILLS.
MOORE, HENRY, also some descendants of THOS. MOORE.
MEADORS, RACHEL, to Chambers County.
MAYES, JAMES THOS., JR., moved at later period.
MAYES, ANDREW, to Dallas County.
MEEK, MRS. NANCY E., wife of WM. H. MEEK, to Green County.
MICKEL, WILLIAM, to Clark County.
MYRICK, JOHN.
MC CRARY, THOMAS and JAMES, heirs of MRS. ANN MC CRARY, deceased, settled in Barbour County.
MC CRACKIN, JAMES, to Pickens County.
MC MERRIES, JAMES, (connected with the CALDWELL families).
MC CAUGHRIN, S. J. and wife, moved at later time.
MC CANN, EDWARD, to Hayneville, Lowndes County.
MC DANIEL, SARA ANN FRANCES, wife of RICHARD S. HOBSON.
MC MEEKINS, ALEXANDER and wife, MARGARET, to Russell County.
MC MEEKIN, ISOM and wife, REBECCA, to Russell County.
MC CRACKIN, MRS. ELIZABETH (JOHNSON), to Barbour County.
NELSON, ISAAC B. and wife, ELIZABETH (COUNTS) NELSON, to Livingstone County. (Daughter of JOHN COUNTS).
NANCE, MARY and SARAH ANN. ROBERT RUTHERFORD NANCE.
OLIVER, JOHN C. and JAMES, to Madison County.
O'NEALL, EDWARD and wife, REBECCA, to Madison County.
POOLE, WM. and wife, ELIZABETH (SPARKS) POOLE, Shelby County.
PETERSON, DAVID.
PITTS, REUBEN, OBEDIAH, wife of OBEDIAH, NANCY (GRIFFIN) PITTS. ABNER, REUBEN, DRAYTON and PERMELIA PITTS, to Russell County.
PICKENS, MRS. CAROLINE (HENDERSON), wife of former Governor Pickens.
QUARLES, WILLIAM G. and wife, ELIZABETH (SULLIVAN) QUARLES, to Lowndes County. Est. of her sister, ELLEN SULLIVAN. R. G. QUARLES and wife moved to Springfield.

7

PRESSLEY, MRS. MARY (TATE), to Pickens County.
PRATT, JOHN P., to Pickens County.
POWELL, MRS. SARAH, to Fayette County.
POOL, GABRIEL and wife, ELIZABETH (GRADON) POOL to Lauderdale County.
PEARSON, REUBEN to Dallas County. MARY G., THOMAS J. and NANCY G. PEARSON.
PICKENS, Gov. ISRAEL of Alabama granted Power of Attorney dated April 17th, 1826, estate of JOHN LEONARD, to people living in Monroe County, viz: WM. M. FOUNTAIN, MARY G. PEARSON, THOMAS J. PEARSON and NANCY G. PEARSON.
POPE, Rev. GEORGE.
PITTS, DANIEL.
RAMAGE, ROBERT and wife, MARY, to Chambers County.
RISER, some descendants of MARTIN RISER.
RAINY, THOMAS, to Chambers County.
ROBERTSON, JAMES M., to Springfield.
REYNOLDS, BENJAMIN and wife, SARAH (MOSLEY) REYNOLDS, to Montgomery County.
REYNOLDS, JOHN and wife, ANN (POW) REYNOLDS.
RICHARDSON, LEVI and wife, MARTHA, to Lauderdale County.
RISER, GEORGE (grand-son of Rev. War Patriot).
STILL, FRANCES ANN (daughter of JOHN and ELIZABETH STILL).
STILL, WILLIAM CASON, (son of JOHN and ELIZABETH STILL), settled in Chambers County.
SPIKES, WILLIAM and wife, ANN (GITTY) SPIKES, to Chambers County.
SUMMERS, JOHN, to Jackson County. ELIJAH SUMMERS to Clark County.
SPARKS, JOSEPH and JESSE, to Shelby County.
SCHOPPERT, PHILLIP.
SPENCE, TABITHA, and some descendants of JAMES SPENCE.
STOCKMAN, JOHN. Also PETER STOCKMAN.
SUMMER, JOHN. Also some descendants of NICHOLAS SUMMER. Major HENRY SUMMER practiced law at Talledega for a short time and returned to South Carolina. (He was an honor graduate of the University of South Carolina).
SMYLEY, Capt. JOHN.
SAWYER, MRS. ELIZA, widow, and her two children, WILLIAM and POLLY.
SIMS, WILLIAM, some of his descendants.
SIMS, NATHAN, some of his descendants. D. THOMPSON SIMS to Pickens County.
SHEPPARD, SIMEON and YOUNG R. SHEPPARD, to Cherokee County.
SAXON, BENJAMIN THOMPSON, lawyer of Newberry, S. C., where he died and lies buried at old "Village Cemetery". He was born at Madison Co., Ala. but was a descendant of a pioneer family of old Laurens District, S. C.
SATTERWHITE, THOMAS, to Limestone County.
STEPHENS, DAVID, to Shelby County.
SPEER, JOHN and wife, FRANCES SPEER.
SATTERWHITE, THERESA, to Madison County. She was a daughter of DRURY SATTERWHITE.
SPEARMAN, MRS. SUSANNAH, widow of EDMUND SPEARMAN; FRANK SPEARMAN.
SHEPPARD, JAMES, settled at Eutaw.
STARKE, TURNER. He went to Mobile.
SCHUMPERT, JACOB. Some of his descendants moved at a later time, including Dr. JOHN I. SCHUMPERT.
SHAW, ROBERT, settled in Chambers County.
SHELBY, MRS. ELIZABETH DUNCAN.
STEWARD, JAMES W., to Lauderdale County.
SHEPPARD, LEWIS A. and wife, SUSANNAH C. SHEPPARD, to Chambers County.
SCHUMPERT, AMOS K.
SONDLEY, GEORGE. Some of his descendants.
SUMMERS, Rev. JOSEPH, died in Newberry County, S. C. Some of his descendants went to Clark County, Ala. and other sections. He was a Quaker minister from Maryland before the Rev. War, and was connected with the family of Lt. Col. PHILEMON WATERS of the Revolution. Local history states that he wore his beard almost touching the ground, a Quaker fashion in early times.
SWANN, THOMAS J. and wife, SARAH ANN (GOGGANS) SWANN, to Tallapoosa County.
STALWORTH, JAMES and wife, MARIA (POPE) STALWORTH.

8

STOCKMAN, JOHN and wife, REBECCA (POW) STOCKMAN.
SPANN, WILLIAM and PHILLIP, sons of HENRY SPANN and wife, MARY (POW) SPANN.
SPENCER, SHEPPARD, JR. and wife, ELIZABETH, to Sumpter County.
SHELTON, SAMUEL W.
TOMPKINS, THOMAS J., to Bibb County.
THORNTON, JOB, and daughter, MARTHA THORNTON, to Pike County.
TULLIS, ELIZABETH W., to Coosa County. She was a daughter of WILLIAM and REBECCA RAINEY. NEWELL TULLIS went to Coosa County.
TERRY, FRANCIS A. and MOSES P. TERRY, minor heirs of estate of JANE TERRY and STEPHEN TERRY. Went to Bibb County.
THOMSON, WILLIAM, to Alabama about 1852.
THOMAS, SAMUEL and wife, DELILA (PRATER) THOMAS.
TOOD, ROBERT, JR. (Now spelled TODD).
TUCKER, WILLIAM, to Sumpter County.
THOMPSON, MRS. REBECCA (HUFF)
UTZ, JAMES, some of his descendants went to Alabama or Mississippi.
VARDAMAN, THOMAS.
WILLIAMSON, WILLIAM and wife, DORCAS, to Talledega County.
WRENN, MACK, to Coosa County.
WHITTEN, MRS. NARCISSA, to Pickens County.
WYSE, FREDERICK. Some of his descendants went to Alabama or Mississippi.
WATKINS, GEORGE, to Lauderdale County.
WEST, JOHN. Some of his descendants moved to Alabama.
WORTHINGTON, JOHN. Some of his descendants moved to Alabama.
WORTHINGTON, BENJAMIN. Some of his descendants moved to Alabama.
WAITS, JAMES, settled at Gravelly Springs, Ala., near Florence. S. K. WAITS went to Coosa County. SAMUEL T. WAITS moved to Talledega County and LEVI WAITS to Talledega County.
WALLACE, HUGH, to Columbus County. Also, descendants of JOHN WALLACE.
WATTS, SAMUEL, to Cedar Bluff.
WATTS, MRS. TEMPERANCE and her son, THOMAS J. WATTS, to Columbus Co.
WHITEHEAD, JACOB and wife, SARAH (HESTER) to Henry County.
WARE, EDMUND P., moved to Pickens County.
WERTZ, some descendants of JOHN and HENRY WERTZ.
WOFFORD, JAMES. MRS. SARAH WOFFORD and MRS. JANE WOFFORD.
WILSON. Some heirs of JAMES WILSON to St. Claire County. MRS. SARAH WILSON, wife of JAMES WILSON, to St. Claire Co.
WATSON, ALBERT N., AMAZIAH, WILLIAM WILEY, LILLIE A., and MARTHA JANE WATSON, to Tuscaloosa County.
WRIGHT, JACOB, to Talledega County.
WILLIAMS, JOHN D. and wife, HARRIET (POPE) WILLIAMS.
WELLS, some descendants of WM. WELLS.
WHITE, some descendants of JOHN WHITE.
YOUNG, some descendants of JAMES YOUNG.
YOUNG, ROBERT and wife, NANCY (POOL) YOUNG, to Maringo County.
YOUNGBLOOD, MANLY and wife, BERENA (WELLS) to Pike County at early period.
ZEIGLAR, some descendants of WM. ZEIGLAR.

Some old Ninety Six District families branches of whom moved from Georgia into Alabama, viz: ADAIR, ADKINS, AIKEN, BOYD, BONDS, BUCHANAN, BROWN, BRUNSON, BISHOP, CARTER, CURETON, CHAPMAN, COX, COLLIER, COLLINS, DABBS, DAVIS, DOMINICK, DUNCAN, GRAY, GREGORY, GOREE, GARY, HUNTER, HENTZ, HOLLAND, HUDSON, HILTON, GILLIAM, JENNINGS, KENNEDY, KINARD, LEE, KEY, LESTER, LYLES, LAKE, LINDSAY, MALONE, MATHEWS, MILES, MURPHY, O'NEALL, OWENS, OWNES, QUADDLEBAUM, REYNOLDS, REESE, REEDER, RICHARDSON, ROGERS, RED, REID, PAYSINGER, SHELL, SUBER, SAXON, SUMMER, SUMMERS, SWANN, SIMPSON, SANDERS, SMITH, SAMPLES, TAYLOR, WATKINS, WALLACE, WAITS, WATTS, WATSON, WADE, WHITTEN, YOUNG.

(Records from Newberry Co., S. C.)

Page 1:   Indenture dated 19 Nov. 1786 bet. MICHIAL DICKSON of Camden
            District Craven County of one part and JOHN SERVICE, Weaver,
of the other part. By a certain grant bearing date 23 Jan. 1773 & in
the 13th. year of his Majestys Reign under the hand of the right Honorable Lord Charles Greenvel Montague, Capt. General and Governor over
the province of S. C. did grant unto MICHIAL DIXON 100 acres land,
50 acres of the sd. tract MICHAIL DIXON and SARAH his wife sold unto
JOHN SERVICE situate on waters of Bull Run in Craven County. Sum of
62 lbs., 10 shillings. Signed: MICHIAL DICKSON, SARAH (X) DICKSON.
Wit: WILLIAM BOYD, JOHN MILLER, JAMES MC QUISTION.

Page 4:   Indenture dated 16 May 1781 bet. JOHN WALKER and JANE his
            wife of Camden Dist. Craven County of the one part and JOHN
SERVICE of Camden Dist. Craven Co. of the one part, Weaver, certain
grant dated 19 Nov. 1772 in the 17th. year of his Excellency Lord Chas.
Greenvelle Montgue Capt. Gen. did grant unto JOHN WALKER and JANE his
wife a plantation of 100 acres in Craven County on a small branch of
Hickory Creek bounded south by land surveyed for MICHAIL DICKSON east
by JOHN WALKER and other sides vacant land. Signed: JOHN (X) WALKER,
JANE (X) WALKER. Wit: WILLIAM BOYD, JOHN CAMPBELL, JOHN MC LOTTEY(?)

Page 7:   Indenture dated 8 August 1779 in 3rd. year of Free States
            bet. PETER WILEY of the Parrish of St. Marks, Weaver, of
the one part and FRANCIS WILEY, planter, of the other part. By a grant
bearing date 13 May 1768 and in the 8th. year of his Excellency Lord
Chas. Greenvelle Montague did grant unto PETER WILEY a plantation of
250 acres on a small branch of Rocky Creek in Craven County bounded
N.E. by land surveyed for PHILIP WALKER and all other sides vacant
land. Two thousand lbs. pd. by sd. FRANCIS WILEY. Signed: PETER WYLIE.
Wit: ALEXANDER GASTON, WILLIAM WYLIE.

Page 10:   Indenture dated 7 Aug. 1779 bet. PETER WYLIE of St. Marks,
            Weaver, of the one part and FRANCIS WYLIE of the Parrish
afsd., planter of the other part. For 10 shillings pd. by FRANCIS WILEY
did sell unto FRANCIS WYLIE 250 acres on a small branch of Rockey Creek
in Craven County. Signed: PETER WYLIE. Wit: ALEXANDER GASTON, WILLIAM
WYLIE.

Page 12:   Indenture dated 7 June 1783 bet. FRANCIS WYLIE of the Parrish
            of St. Marks, planter, of the one part and WILLIAM WYLIE,
Yeoman, of the Parrish afsd. of the other part, grant bearing date
30 May 1768 & in the 8th. year of the British King did grant unto FRAN-
CIS WYLIE 100 acres on a small branch of Rocky Creek, bounded S.E.
by land surveyed for ROBERT MC LARRY(?) all other sides vacant land.
Signed: FRANCIS WYLIE. Wit: DAVID MORROW, JAMES WYLIE.

Page 15:   Indenture dated 16 June 1783 bet. FRANCIS WYLIE of the Par-
            rish of St. Marks, planter, of the one part and WILLIAM
WYLIE of the Parrish afsd., Yeoman, of the other part in sum of 10
shillings pd. by WILLIAM WYLIE do sell to WILLIAM WYLIE 100 acres on
a small branch of Rocky Creek bounded S.E. by land surveyed for ROBERT
MC HARRY(?) & all other sides vacant. Signed: FRANCIS WYLIE. Wit: DAVID
MORROW, JAMES WYLIE.

Page 17:   Know all men by these presents that we WILLIAM GASTON, JAMES
            GASTON, JOSEPH GASTON, MARTHA GASTON, JOSEPH GASTON, JR.,
JOHN GASTON, ALEXANDER WALKER and EASTHER WALKER all of Chester County,
planters, do appoint HUGH GASTON of Chester County our Attorney to
sell, make and convey 2 tracts of land in Georgia in Washington County
the warrants of survey granted unto ALEXANDER GASTON and DAVID GASTON.
Signed: WILLIAM GASTON, JOHN GASTON, JAMES GASTON, JOSEPH GASTON, JR.,
JOSEPH GASTON, MARTHA GASTON, ALEXANDER WALKER, EASTHER WALKER. No
witnesses names given.

Page 18:   Indenture dated 26 Feb. 1780 bet. DAVID MORROW and MARY
            his wife of Camden Dist. of one part and JOHN GREEN of the

Cont'd from page 10:
other part, for the sum of three thousand lbs. on both sides of South
Fork of Fishing Creek. Signed: DAVID (X) MORROW, MARY (X) MORROW. Wit:
WILLIAM JONES, JOHN MILLS, JONATHAN JONES.

Page 22:   Indenture dated 19 Jan. 1785 bet. JOHN GREEN and MARY his
            wife of Craven County of the one part and JAMES LANGSTON
Merchant of the other part for the sum of 100 lbs., 50 acres gtd. to
DAVID MORROW and by him conveyed to JOHN GREEN. Signed: JOHN GREEN,
MARY (X) GREEN. Wit: JOHN SIMPSON, WILLIAM JONES, JONATHAN JONES. Proved
20 Oct. 1785.

Page 24:   Indenture dated 19 Jan. 1785 bet. JONATHAN JONES and BARSHEBA
            his wife of the Parrish of St. Marks, Yeoman of one part
and (LANGSBEEY? not clear) of St. Marks of the other part, merchant.
A certain grant bearing date 10 May 1768 by Charles Greenvelle Montague
Capt. Gen. over S. C. did grant unto ROBERT CLOVER 250 acres on JAMES
MC CLURE spring branch waters of the South Fork of Fishing Creek Craven
Co. bounded all sides on vacant land, sd. tract conveyed to HENRY CULP
21 Sept. 1768. Signed: JONATHAN JONES, BARSHEBA (B) JONES. Wit: WILLIAM
JONES, JOHN GREEN, JOHN SIMPSON. Pro. 20 Oct. 1785.

Page 27:   Indenture dated 7 Sept. 1785 bet. ISAAC EOLLY (this last
            name was not clear) of Chester Co., Planter and JAMES LANGS-
BEY, Merchant of the other part "sum of lbs." to sd. ISAAC EOLL(?)
pd. by JAMES LANGSBEY a tract of 200 acres lying on south fork of Fishing Creek orig. gtd. to JOHN MC ELLELLY by patent dated 9 April 1770
and registered in Book No. 6 North Carolina, Tryon County and being
surveyed from sd. MC ELLELLY to JOHN PENNY by an instrument of writing
dated 13 Oct. 1771 and from sd. PENNY unto MOSES ALEXANDER by date
18 Oct. 1771 and left by MOSES ALEXANDER to his son and heir the sd.
NATHANIEL ALEXANDER conveyed to ISAAC EOFF(?) by deed 26 March 1784.
Signed: ISAAC EOLL(?) Wit: JOHN MILLS, WILLIAM JONES, BERSHEBA (B)
JONES. Proved 20 Oct. 1785.

Page 30:   Indenture dated 23 Oct. 1784 COL. EDWARD LACEY and JANE
            his wife of Camden Dist. of one part and JAMES MC NEEL of
the other part for sum of 105 lbs. do sell to JAMES MC NEEL 440 acres
with a dwelling house about 40 acres cleared ground thereon lying on
Susey branch being a fork of Turkey Creek of Broad River bounded by
GEORGE SADLER, on the east by Col. PATRICK MC GRIFF, 440 acres to ED-
WARD LACEY by Gov. TYRON formerly of N. C. 29 April 1768. Signed: ED-
WARD LACEY, JANE LACEY. Wit: PAT MC GRIFF, ABRAHAM REEVE. Proved 20
Oct. 1785.

Page 32:   Indenture dated 24 Dec. 1784 bet. JOSEPH BROWN of Camden
            Dist. of one part and THOMAS RODEN of the other part, 50
lbs. pd. by THOMAS RODEN, sd. JOSEPH BROWN do sell to THOMAS RODEN
200 acres which was gtd. to BROWN by patent 16 Jan. 1772 sit. in Craven
Co. on small branch leading into Sandy River all other sides by vacant
land. SARAH BROWN, wife of JOSEPH BROWN. Signed: JOSEPH BROWN, SARAH
BROWN. Wit: WILLIAM RODEN, JAMES BROWN, SARAH BROWN. Proved 17 Jan.
1786.

Page 33:   Indenture dated 15 Dec. 1785 bet. ARCHIBALD ELLIOTT, planter,
            of one part and WILLIAM ELLIOTT, son of ARCHIBALD ELLIOTT
of the other part of Chester Co. give 152 acres lying on both sides
of the south fork of Fishing Creek bounded on the east by ARCHIBALD
ELLIOTT and ROBERT GILLS lands, on the N. by Rev. JOHN SIMPSON's land
and on W. on ALEXANDER and SAMUEL BROWN's lands, on the south by GEORGE
CRAIG's land being part of land gtd. unto DAVID LEEVES(?). Signed:
ARCHIBALD (X) ELLIOTT. Wit: HIGH DODS, WILLIAM (last name not clear).
Proved 17 Jan. 1786.

Page 35:   Indenture dated 10 Jan. 1783 bet. ALEXANDER BROWN of Camden
            Dist., Planter of the one part and SAMUEL BROWN of sd. Dist.
son to ALEXANDER BROWN of the other part, do give to SAMUEL BROWN tract
of land lying on the south side of the south fork of Fishing Creek
bet. lands of ALEXANDER BROWN, WILLIAM ELLIOTT, GEORGE CRAIG, JONATHAN

11

Cont'd from page 11:
JONES and JOHN MILLS cont. 130 acres. Signed: ALEXANDER BROWN. Wit:
ALEXANDER BROWN, JR., (I. or J.?) MC FARLIN. Proved 17 Jan. 1786.

Page 37:   Indenture dated 11 June 1785 bet. JAMES FERGUSON, SR., plant-
            er of Chester Co. of one part and ROBERT FERGUSON, Yeoman
of the other part, whereas by a cert. grant 10 May 1768 in 8th. year
of Reign of George 3rd. King, did grant unto JAMES FORGUSON, SR., 500
acres on the S.W. side of Cataba River bet. Fishing Creek and Rocky
Creek bounded on all sides by vacant land, for the sum of 200 lbs.
pd. by ROBERT FORGUSON. Signed: JAMES FORGUSON. Wit: WILLIAM WILEY,
ABRAHAM FORGUSON. Proved 17 Jan. 1786.

Page 40:   Indenture dated 11 June 1785 bet. JAMES FORGUSON, SR. of
            Chester Co., Planter of the one part and ABRAHAM FORGUSON,
shoemaker of the other part. Whereas by a cert. grant 10 May 1768 in
8th. year of George the 3rd. then King, did grant unto JAMES FORGUSON,
SR. 200 acres on S.W. side of Cataba River bet. Fishing Creek bounded
all sides on vacant land. Signed: JAS. FORGUSON. Wit: WILLIAM WILEY,
ROBERT FORGUSON. Proved 17 Jan. 1786.

Page 43:   Indenture dated 1 Ovt. 1785 bet. WILLIAM MC FADEN of Chester
            Co. of the one part and GEORGE LEWIS of the other part.
Wherein by a cert. grant dated 24 Jan. 1770 the 10th. year of George
the 3rd. then King did grant unto WILLIAM MC FADDEN 200 acres in Craven
Co. now Chester on the West side of Fishing Creek bounded all sides
by vacant land. Signed: WILLIAM MC FADDEN, ANN (X) MC FADDEN. Wit:
WILLIAM WILEY, THOMAS DUGAN, ROBERT FORGUSON.

Page 46:   Know that I GEORGE MORRIS for the sum of 30 lbs. paid him
by JOHN MORRIS do sell unto JOHN MORRIS one red cow and calf marked
with a cross in each ear and also a split in each ear. Dated: 21 Dec.
1785. Signed: GEORGE MORRIS. Wit: JOHN ___(?)__ and THOMAS STROUD.
Proved 17 Jan. 1786.

Page 47:   PETER PETREE, planter of Chester Co. for me here unto do
            appoint Col. ARCHIBALD LITTLE of Orange Co., N. C. my attor-
ney to recover of AMOS TIMS, planter of the county of Granville, N.
C., all sums of money now due and owing unto me. Dated: 10 Jan. 1786.
Signed: PETER PETREE. Wit: JAMES STEWART, HAZEL HARDWICK. Proved 18
Jan. 1786 at the house of JOHN WALKER. Present were JOSEPH BROWN, DAVID
HOPKINS, JAMES KNOX, ANDREW HEMPHILL.

Page 49:   Indenture dated 31 Oct. 1777 bet. ARCHIBALD ELLIOTT of Par-
            rish of St. Marks, yeoman of the one part and JOSEPH WALKER
of the Parrish afsd. of the other part. By a certain grant 31 Aug.
1753 did grant unto JAMES MC CULLOUGH 400 acres lying and being in
Anson Co., N. C. but now by the continuation of the boundry line in
S. C. and Craven Co. on South side of Fishing Creek upon a great branch
thereof bet. the middle path. May more fully appear JAS. MC CULLOUGH
being due ALEXANDER MC CULLOUGH eldest son and Exor. & heir at law
of the estate of JAS. MC CULLOUGH, dec'd. Signed: ARCHIBALD (A) ELLIOTT.
Wit: HUGH WHITESIDE, SAMUEL LORD (LAND?), JOHN GASTON. Proved 18 Jan.
1786.

Page 52:   Indenture dated 30 Oct. 1777 bet. ARCHIBALD ELLIOTT of the
            Parrish of St. Marks, yeoman of the one part and JOSEPH
WALKER of the Parish afsd., planter of the other part. Witness that
ARCHIBALD ELLIOTT for the sum of 10 shillings pd. by JOSEPH WALKER
do sell unto JOSEPH WALKER 100 acres lying in Craven Co. on S. side
of Fishing Creek upon a Great Branch bet. the middle path and the 2nd
path including the old Indian Camps. Signed; ARCHIBALD ELLIOTT. Wit:
HUGH WHITESIDE, SAMUEL LORD (LAND?), JOHN GASTON. Proved 18 Jan. 1786.

Page 54:   Indenture dated 28 May 1776 bet. JOHN COMBEST and AGNES
            his wife of the Parish of St. Marks, planter of the one
part and PETER CULP of the Parish afsd., planter of the other part.
By a cert. grant bearing date 19 Aug. 1774 did grant unto JOHN COMBEST
50 acres in Craven Co. on both sides of Fishing Creek, W. by PETER

Cont'd from page 12:
CULP and East by vacant land, N.E. by JOHN LOTT's land. Signed: JOHN
COMBEST, ANN (X) COMBEST. Wit: NICHOLAS BISHOP, JOHN CARTER. Proved
28 Dec. 1785.

Page 59:   Indenture dated 10 Jan. 1785 bet. JOHN MOULTREY of Craven
             Co. and WILLIAM SHAW of Guilford Co., N. C. of the other
part, for the sum of 100 lbs. pd. by WILLIAM SHAW do convey unto WM.
SHAW 250 acres lying on the East side of Broad River and branch called
Sandy, N.W. on JOHN WALKER's land, N.E. on land of HAZEL HADRIDGE,
S.W. on land of AMOS TIMS, all other by vacant land. Was granted Mar.
19, 1773 by WM. BULL. (No signature shown). Wit: JAMES (TATE?), CHARLES
MC CLURE, JAMES HOUSTON, THOMAS DICK.

Page 61:   NATHANIEL SAMPLE of Camden Dist. "me here unto moving" do
             appoint PHILLIP WALKER, Esq. of sd. Dist. my attorney to
sure demand of JOHN MC GLAMERY debts owing to me. Dated 5 April 1783.
Signed: NATHANIEL SAMPLE. Wit: Capt. ROBERT COOPER. Proved 17 July
1783.

Page 62:   Indenture dated 22 Oct. 1783 bet. ARCHIBALD ELLIOTT and
             SARAH his wife of one part, planter and Rev. JOHN SIMPSON
of the other part V.D.M. for sum of 200 lbs. pd. ARCHIBALD and SARAH
ELLIOTT by JOHN SIMPSON, "causes us there unto moving". ARCHIBALD and
SARAH his wife do convey unto JOHN SIMPSON 269 acres lying on waters
of the south fork of Fishing Creek, co. of Craven joining ALEXANDER
BROWN by patent dated 1772 from DAVID LEWIS. Signed: ARCHIBALD (X)
ELLIOTT, SARAH (B) ELLIOTT. Wit: WILLIAM ELLIOTT, DANIEL COOKE. Proved
15 Nov. 1783.

Page 66:   Indenture dated 15 Feb. 1785 bet. ISAAC SMITH and MARY his
             wife of Camden Dist. of one part and DAVID CARR of same
Dist. of the other part. By a cert. grant dated 15 April 1767 did grant
to ISAAC SMITH 250 acres surveyed him 9 Jan. 1767 in Craven Co. on
both sides of Fishing Creek bounding lands of PHILLIP WALKER and between
that and JOHN LATTA's land, "crossing a little below the shoals below
LATTA's line". Signed: ISAAC SMITH, MARY (O) SMITH. Wit: DAVID HUNTER,
ROBERT SCOTT.

Page 69:   Deed made 5 Aug. 1782 bet. JOHN MILES (or MILLS?) of Camden
             Dist. of one part and CHARLES MILES(?) of the other part,
JOHN MILES for sum of 1 thousand lbs. pd. by CHAS. MILES(?) do sell
138 acres in Craven County on North side of Broad River on a branch
called Turkey Creek being part of 200 acres granted to JAMES MILES(?)
by patent bearing date 20 April 1763. Wit: WILLIAM GIVIN, WILLIAM MILES,
RICHARD MILES. Signed: JOHN MILES. Proved 5 Aug. 1782.

Page 71:   Deed made 16 Aug. 1785 bet. JOHN HENDERSON of Camden Dist.
             planter of one part and ARCHABALD MC QUISTON, shoe maker
of the other part and by a certain grant 7 May 1771 did grant unto
JOHN HENDERSON 100 acres in Craven County and branch of Rocky Creek
called Bull Run, all other sides by vacant land. Wit: DAVID MC QUIS-
TION, HUGH MC QUISTION, JAMES WILSON. Signed: JOHN HENDERSON. Proven
18 Jan. 1786.

Page 74:   Deed made 4 May 1785 bet. DAVID HOPKINS of Camden Dist.
             of one part and JAMES TIMS of the other part for 100 lbs.
did sell to JAMES TIMS 100 acres surveyed 10 April 1773 on a warrant
granted to me 6 April 1773 on waters of Sandy River on land bounding
MOSES BOND, and on all other sides by vacant land. Wit: JEREMIAH KINGS-
LEY, JAMES DOUGHTREY, THOMAS HUMPRES. Signed: DAVID HOPKINS. Proved
19 Jan. 1786.

Page 75:   Deed made between JOHN IMBEY (JIMBEY?) of Chester County
             of one part and ANN MILLER (otherwise HART), widow of the
other part for the sum of 14 lbs. 5 Sterling and 8 pence to JOHN IMBEY
paid by ANN HART doth convey 100 acres lying on waters of Dry Fork
of Fishing Creek in Craven Co. otherwise Chester Co. on the Seludy
Road that goes to the Fish Dam Ford on Broad River, bounded N.E. by

Cont'd from page 13:
RICHARD BERRILL land, other sides by vacant land the same being granted
to JOHN IMBEY 8 Dec. 1774. Wit: JOHN MILES, WILLIAM BOYD, DAVID BOYD.
Signed: JOHN (X) IMBEY(?). Proved 21 Jan. 1786.

Page 77:   Deed made 11 June 1785 between JAMES FURGUSON, SR., planter
            of Chester County of one part and ROBERT FURGUSON, yeoman
of the other part. By a grant 10 May 1786 (must be a mistake, P.Y.)
did grant unto JAMES FURGUSON, SR., 500 acres on the S.W. side of Cataba
river between Fishing Creek and Rocky Creek, bounded by vacant land.
"For the sum of 200 lbs." Wit: WILLIAM WILEY, ABRAHAM FURGUSON. Signed:
JAMES FURGUSON.

Page 79:   Deed made 28 May 1776 bet. JOHN COMBEST & AGNES his wife
            St. Marks Parish. planter of one part and PETER CULP of
Parish of the other part. By a grant dated 19 Aug. 1774 did grant unto
JOHN COMBEST 50 acres in Craven County on both sides of Fishing Creek
West by PETER CULP's land other sides by vacant land. Wit: NICHOLAS
BISHOP, JOHN CARTER. Signed: JOHN COMBEST, ANN (X) COMBEST.

Page 81:   Deed made 27 May 1776 between JOHN COMBEST and AGNES his
            wife of St. Marks Parish, planter of one part and PETER
CULP, planter of the other part. For sum of 10 shillings paid by PETER
CULP do sell (number of acres not given, P.Y.) situate in Craven County
on both sides of Fishing Creek West by PETER CULP's land N.E. by vacant
land N.E. by JOHN LATTA's land. Wit: NICHOLAS BISHOP, JOHN CARTER.
Signed: JOHN COMBEST, ANN (X) COMBEST. Proved 18 Jan. 1786.

Page 83:   Deed made 8 April 1786 between THOMAS RODEN of Camden Dist.
            of one part and WILLIAM HEAD, SR., planter of the other
part. For sum of 2 lbs. pd. by WILLIAM HEAD doth sell 100 acres being
part of a grant of 800 acres which was granted to JOSEPH BROWN the
16th Jan. 1772 lying on the east side of JOHN MOBERLEY's land. (Location
of land not given, P.Y.) Wit: ENOCH PEARSON, EZEKEL SANDERS, THOMAS
(X) SAUNDERS. Signed: THOMAS RODEN, MARY (M) RODEN. Proven 18 April
1786.

Page 85:   Deed made 29 June 1786 between DAVID BOYD and MARGRET his
            wife of Chester County and Camden Dist. of one part and
WILLIAM BOYD of same county of the other part. By a certain grant 13
May 1768 did grant unto MARGARET WYLIE, wife of DAVID BOYD 100 acres
in Craven County now Chester County on a branch of Rocky Creek bounded
E. on land surveyed for JANE MC CARTNEY, all other sides vacant. Wit:
WILLIAM BOYD, SAMUEL BOYD, JOHN BOYD. Signed: DAVID BOYD, MARGARET
(X) BOYD.

Page 88:   Deed made 30 June 1786 bet. DAVID BOYD and MARGARET his
            wife of Chester County and Camden Dist. of one part and
WILLIAM BOYD of the other part. For 1 shilling and 6 pence sterling
for 100 acres in Chester County on a branch of Rocky Creek bounded
E by JANE MC CARTNEY, all other sides vacant. Wit: WILLIAM BOYD, SAMUEL
BOYD, JOHN BOYD. Signed: DAVID BOYD, MARGARET (X) BOYD.

Page 90:   Deed made 15 April 1786 bet. JOHN MILES of Chester County
            of one part and WILLIAM MILES of the other part. For sum
of 76 lbs. pd by WILLIAM MILES do sell all that tract lying on the
east side of Turkey Creek joining and between MATTHEW FLOID's and JAMES
MILES' lands. 76 acres. Wit: JO PALMER, JOHN MARTIN. Signed: JOHN MILES.

Page 92:   Deed made 5 Aug. 1782 bet. JOHN MILES of Camden Dist. of
            one part and CHARLES MILES of the other part. For one thous-
and lbs. pd. by CHARLES MILES do grant 138 acres in Craven County on
north side of Broad River on a branch of Turkey Creek being part of
200 acres granted to JAMES MILES. Wit: WILLIAM GIVIN, WILLIAM MILES,
RICHARD MILES. Signed: JOHN MILES.

Page 95:   Deed made 15 April 1786 bet. JOHN MILES of Chester County
            of one part and WILLIAM MILES of the other for 100 lbs.
pd. by WILLIAM MILES, land lying on a branch of Turkey Creek bounded

Cont'd from page 14:
E. on JAMES MILES, S on WILLIAM MINTERS, N.W. on JOSEPH FEAMSTER and
JAMES MILES, all other sides vacant. Wit: JO PALMER, JOHN MARTIN. Signed:
JOHN MILES.

Page 97:   Deed made (no date given, P.Y.) 1786 bet. JOHN MILES of
            Chester County of one part and WILLIAM MILES of other part
for sum of 100 lbs. pd. by WILLIAM MILES, land lying on Turkey Creek,
bounded all sides by vacant land. 100 acres. Wit: JO PALMER, JOHN MAR-
TIN. Signed: JOHN MILES.

Page 99:   Deed made 2 Nov. 1785 bet. ROBERT MILLER of Camden Dist.
            Chester County of one part and ELIZABETH MILLER, SR. of
the other part for sum of 60 lbs. pd. by ELIZABETH MILLER 200 acres
being the one half of 400 acres in Craven County ona small branch bounded N.W. by land surveyed for JOHN MILLS all other sides vacant, land
surveyed for JOSIAS MILLER now dec'd. therefore the right and title
falls to his son ROBERT MILLER. Wit: SAMUEL MILLER, THOS. (X) MILLER,
ARCHIBALD MC QUESTION. Signed: ROBERT MILLER.

Page 101:   Deed made 1 Nov. 1785 bet. ROBERT MILLER of Camden Dist.
            of one part and ELIZABETH MILLER, SR. of the other part
for the sum of 10 shillings pd. by ELIZABETH MILLER do sell 200 acres
being one half of 400 acres in Craven County now Chester County on
a small branch of Rocky Creek bounded N.W. by land surveyed for JOHN
MILLS all other sides by vacant land surveyed for JOSIAS MILLER, now
dec'd. which falls by law to his son ROBERT MILLER, who sold one half
of 400 acres to ELIZABETH MILLER, SR. Wit: SAMUEL MILLER, THOMAS (X)
MILLER, RICHARD MC QUISTON. Signed: ROBERT MILLER. Proved 19 Apr. 1786.

Page 103:   Deed made 11 Nov. 1785 bet. JOHN MC FADDEN of Chester County
            of one part and THOMAS DUGAN of the other part. By a grant
dated 18 May 1771 did grant unto JOHN MC FADDEN 331 acres lying on
Fishing Creek in Craven County now Chester, bounding N.W. on JOHN
MATHIES land and other sides on land of JACOB BECCKLEY, ROBERT MARTIN,
ANDREW & THOMAS MARTIN. For 200 lbs. Wit: WILLIAM WILEY, ROBERT FURGU-
SON. Signed: JOHN MC FADDEN. Proved 19 April 1786.

Page 105:   Deed made 3 Jan. 1786 bet. JOHN GILL and SARAH his wife
            of Chester Co., planter of one part and JOSIAH PORTER, plant-
er of the other part for sum of 62 lbs. 10 shillings, do sell to JOSIAH
PORTER 200 acres in Chester Co. on Crafts branch on South fork of Fishing Creek, EDWARD CRAFT's corner, SAMUEL PORTER's corner, near the
line of a survey bearing date 25 April 1767 under the hand of WILLIAM
TRION, Esq. Governor of North Carolina. Wit: SAMUEL PORTER, JAMES GILL,
ROBERT GILL. Signed: JOHN GILL, SARAH GILL.

Page 108:   Deed made 12 April 1786 bet. THOMAS FRANKLYN and PERCILLA
            his wife, of Chester Co., planter of one part and WILLIAM
TRUSSELL of the other part, sadler, by a grant bearing date 21 Jan.
1785 did grant unto THOMAS FRANKLYN, SR. 138 acres lying in Camden
Dist., Chester Co. on waters of Sandy River hath sold to WILLIAM TRUS-
SELL 100 acres for 22 lbs. Wit: RICHARD EVANS, JOHN FRANKLYN, JAMES
(X) TRUSSELL. Signed: THOMAS FRANKLYN, PERCILLA FRANKLYN.

Page 113:   Deed made 15 Oct. 1784 bet. ISAAC KELOUGH and MARY his wife
            of one part and DAVID WILLIAMS of the other part for 71
lbs. 7 shillings and 6 pence do sell to DAVID WILLIAMS 257 acres lying
on Turkey Creek where on ISAAC KELOUGH now dwells and was granted to
MOSES MC CARTER by patent 4 May 1769 joining SETH JOHNSTON's corner
near JOHN MC KNITT ALEXANDER's land. Wit: JAMES MC NEEL, WILLIAM BURRISS.
Signed: ISAAC KELOUGH, MARY (X) KELOUGH. Proved 20 May 1785.

Page 114:   Deed made 3 June 1774 bet. WILLIAM MC CLURE of St. Marks
            Parrish, student, of one part and JOHN MC CLURE, planter,
of the other part. By a grant bearing date 8 Feb. 1768 did grant to
JAMES MC CLURE 100 acres lying on Rocky Creek, Craven County, for 175
lbs. paid by JOHN MC CLURE that plantation of 100 acres left to WIL-
LIAM MC CLURE by his father, JAMES MC CLURE. Wit: HUGH KNOX, JOHN KNOX,
JAMES MC CLURE. Signed: WILLIAM MC CLURE.

Page 117: Deed made 3 June 1774 bet. WILLIAM MC CLURE of St. Marks
          Parish, student of one part and JOHN MC CLURE, planter of
the other part. Grant bearing date 3 May 1764 did grant unto JAMES
MC CLURE 100 acres on waters of Rockey Creek a branch of Catabaw river
in Craven Co. bounded all sides by vacant land. Wit: JOHN KNOX, HUGH
KNOX, JAMES MC CLURE. Signed: WILLIAM MC CLURE.

Page 120: Deed made 30 Sept. 1785 bet. THOMAS FRANKLYN of Chester
          County, planter of one part and JACOB DUNGAN, of the other
part, planter. By grant dated 21 Jan. 1785 did grant unto THOMAS FRANK-
LYN 150 acres in Chester Co. situated in Camden Dist. on waters of
Sandy River for 28 lbs. 11 shillings and 5 pence, pd. by JACOB DUNGAN.
Wit: WILLIAM BOYD, JOHN WEIR, THOMAS B. FRANKLYN. Signed: THOMAS FRANK-
LYN.

Page 122: Deed made 29 Sept. 1785 bet. THOMAS FRANKLYN of Chester
          County of one part, planter, and JACOB DUNGAN of the other
part, planter, for the sum of 1 shilling pd. by JACOB DUNGAN to sell
150 acres of land in Chester County situate in Camden Dist. on waters
of Sandy River. Wit: WILLIAM BOYD, JOHN WEIR, THOMAS FRANKLYN. Signed:
JOHN FRANKLYN (written John here, P.Y.) Proved 6 July 1786.

Page 124: Deed made 2 Sept. 1774 bet. JOHN GILL and SARAH his wife
          of St. Marks Parish, yeoman, of one part and CHRISTOPHER
STREIGHT, blacksmith, of the other part. By a grant dated 25 April
1767 did grant unto JOHN GILL 500 acres formerly lying and being in
the County of Mecklinburgh, North Carolina upon Crafts branch of South
fork of Fishing Creek but now by extention of the boundery line in Craven
County for the sum of 100 lbs. pd. by CHRISTOPHER STREIGHT 500 acres
of land. Wit: GEORGE GILL, JAMES COOPER. Signed: JOHN GILL, SARAH GILL.

Page 127: Deed made 1 Sept. 1770 bet. JOHN GILL and SARAH, his wife
          of St. Marks Parish, yeoman, of one part and CHRISTOPHER
STREIGHT, blacksmith, of the other part for the sum of 10 shillings
pd. by CHRISTOPHER STREIGHT do sell 67 acres in Craven County on water
of Fishing Creek. Wit: GEORGE GILL, JAMES COOPER. Signed: JOHN GILL,
SARAH GILL.

Page 129: Deed made 16 May 1786 bet. ROBERT GILL, SR. of Chester Co.,
          planter, of one part and CHRISTOPHER STREIGHT, blacksmith,
of the other part for the sum of 1 lb. 1 shilling and 9 pence pd. by
CHRISTOPHER STREIGHT do sell 1 acre situate in Chester Co. on Saludy
Road being part of land granted to SUSANAH GLOVER containing 150 acres
on South Fork of Fishing Creek by patent dated 10 July 1766 which was
afterwards conveyed by STEPHEN TERRY and SUSANNAH, his wife to JAMES
MC CLURE and conveyed by MC CLURE to ROBERT GILL. Wit: JAMES PAGAN,
ISIAH PORTER, GEORGE GILL. Signed: ROBERT GILL. Proved 5 July 1786.

Page 131: Know that I JESSE CRANSHAW of Wilkes County, Georgia for
          the sum of 100 lbs. have sold unto Col. EDWARD LACEY, 1
negro boy 8 years named Dick country born formerly part of estate of
Major WILLIAM (not plain, P.Y.) Wit: WILLIAM SMITH, JAMES ADAIR. Signed:
JESSE CRANSHAW.
          Be it remembered that at any time or as soon as the within
JESSE CRANSHAW shall come into Chester Co. in S. C. and settle account
due him by EDWARD LACEY & Co. Proved 7 July 1786.

Page 133: Deed made 4 Jan. 1785 bet. ALEXANDER MOORE, Esq., Sheriff
          of Camden Dist. of one part and WILLIAM IRVING of Fishing
Creek, planter, of the other part Witness that GEORGE WADE in the Court
of Common Pleas did impliad(?) JOHN FONDREEN....Wit: CHARLES MC CLURE,
JAMES YOUNG. Signed: ALEXANDER MOORE. Proved 1786.

Page 135: Deed made 13 Jan. 1783 bet. ALEXANDER BROWN of Camden Dist.
          planter of one part and SAMUEL BROWN, son to ALEXANDER BROWN
of the other part. For love ...confirm unto sd. SAMUEL BROWN 130 acres
on South Fork of Fishing Creek between lands of ALEXANDER BROWN, WILLIAM
ELLIOTT, GEORGE CRAIG, JONATHAN JONES & JOHN ___(?). Wit: ALEXANDER
BROWN, JR., JAMES MC FARLIN. Signed: ALEXANDER BROWN.

Page 137: Know that I ELIJAH BROWN of Camden Dist. for the sum of
151 lbs. pd by bond and bail by JOHN MILLS, JR. do sell
a negro fellow named Guy. Dated 29 Sept. 1784. Wit: GEORGE GILL, WILLEY
L. BROWN. Signed: ELIJAH BROWN.

Page 183: Know that I ISAAC BALL of Wilkes County, Georgia administra-
tor of the estate of JAMES ARMSTRONG, dec'd, late of Camden
Dist. do appoint my trusty friend JOHN BLANTON of Burke County, North
Carolina my attorney to sue for a negro man named Scipio about 28 years
of age being feloniously taken by a certain JAMES SIMMERAL of Camden
Dist. from HUGH ARMSTRONG, son of JAMES ARMSTRONG, dec'd. about April
1782. Dated 11 April 1784. Wit: JOHN WALLACE, RICHARD BALL, WILLIAM
PHILLIPS. Signed: ISAAC BALL. Proved 4 July 1786.

Page 140: Know that I JOHN WALKER of Chester Co. Exor. of CHARLES
WALKER, dec'd. do appoint JAMES RAMSEY my attorney who re-
sides in Rockbridge County, Virginia to collect money due on a bond
on MICHAEL BOWYER of Augusta County in Stantown amounting to 35 lbs.
Dated 6 Sept. 1786. Wit: RICHARD TALIAFERO, HUGH BONNER. Signed: JOHN
(X) WALKER.

Page 141: Deed made 10 May 1786 bet. ADAM MC COOL of one part and
ADAM MC COOL of the other part (written this way, P.Y.)
of 120 acres granted to ADAM MC COOL by WILLIAM TRYON, Esq. Governor
of North Carolina. Chester County. Dated 25 April 1767. Wit: JACOB
BROWN, JOHN MC COOL. Signed: ADAM MC COOL. Proved 1 Oct. 1786.

Page 148: Deed made 10 Oct. 1785 bet. JEAN WILSON and JAMES WILSON
of Rocky Creek Craven County Camden District of one part
and HAMTON STROUD of the other part for the sum of 5 lbs., 50 acres
being part of land belonging to WILLIAM WILSON, dec'd. husband to JEAN
and father to JAMES WILSON lying on north side of Rocky Creek joining
to THOMAS DYES land and now in possession of JAMES MORRIS. Wit: ROBERT
ROBISON, SAMUEL (X) STRANGE, MARY (X) WILSON. Signed: JEAN (X) WILSON,
JAMES (X) WILSON.

Page 144: Inventory made 10 Oct. 1785 bet. JEAN WILSON and JAMES WILSON
of Rocky Creek Craven Co. and Camden Dist. of one part and
HAMPTON STROUD of Rocky Creek of other part. For and in consideration
of 3 cows and calves given by STROUD do give 50 acres being part of
WILLIAM WILSON's land, dec'd husband to JANE and father to JAMES WILSON,
lying on north side of Big Rocky Creek and now in possession of JAMES
MORRIS . Wit: ROBERT ROBISON, SAMUEL (X) STRANGE, MARY (X) WILSON.
Signed: JEAN (X) WILSON, JAMES (X) WILSON.

Page 147: Deed made 20 March 1784 bet. ARCHIBAL ELLIOTT and SARAH
his wife of Craven Co., planter of one part and ROBERT GILL
planter of the other part. For the sum of 300 lbs. pd. by ROBERT GILL
have granted to ROBERT GILL 150 acres lying on both sides of South
Fork of Fishing Creek in Craven County bounding east by ARCHIBALD ELLI-
OTT's land, north by Rev. M.(?) SIMPSON's, on west by WILLIAM ELLIOTT,
south by ELIZABETH WILSON's land. 80 acres of land part of tract granted
to JAMES MC CULLOCH under the hand of MATTHEW ROWAN, Esq. Commander
over the province of North Carolina the 31 Aug. 1753 and conveyed by
deeds of lease and release under the hand of ALEXANDER MC CULLOCH,
Exor. of sd. JAMES MC CULLOCH, dec'd. unto ARCHIBALD ELLIOTT 24 Nov.
1762. Wit: JAMES MC FARLAN, SAMUEL KELSEY. Signed: ARCHIBALD (X) ELLIOTT
& SARAH (X) ELLIOTT.

Page 151: Deed made 12 March 1784 bet. WILLIAM ELLIOTT of Craven Co.
planter of one part and ROBERT GILL of the other part for
10 shillings pd. by ROBERT GILL have granted to ROBERT GILL 9 acres
on So. Fork of Fishing Creek part of 150 acres conveyed by ARCHIBALD
ELLIOTT, father of WILLIAM ELLIOTT. Wit: JAS. MC FARLAN, SAMUEL KELSEY.
Signed: WILLIAM ELLIOTT.

Page 153: Deed made 29 Jan. 1780 bet. SAMUEL MC KINNEY of the Parish
of St. Marks, yeoman, of one part and GEORGE KELSEY of Parish
afsd., yeoman, of the other part. By grant dated 29 April 1768 by WM.

Cont'd from page 17:
TRYON, Esq. Governor of North Carolina did grant unto JAMES SMITH, 200 acres lying in Mecklinburg County, North Carolina at the date of the grant but by the continuation of the boundry line now in Craven County, S. C. on the west side of Catawba River and north side of the main Fishing Creek on both sides of the Cain River and on both sides of the Waggon Road. Wit: HUGH WHITESIDE, JOHN MILLS, SAMUEL KELSEY. Signed: SAMUEL (X) MC KINNEY. Proved 3 Oct. 1786.

Page 156: Deed made 10 Dec. 1782 bet. ARTHUR HICKLIN of Camden Dist. Craven Co. of one part and JOHN SMITH of Camden Dist. Craven Co. of the other part. By grant dated 1 Aug. 1758 did grant unto CASPER SLEGER(?) 150 acres on South Branch of Rocky Creek Craven Co. bounded all sides by vacant land, which CASPER SLEGER(?) did convey unto ANDREW ROGERS the sd. ANDREW ROGERS did convey unto his son ARTHUR ROGERS then the sd. ROGERS did convey the plantation unto ARTHUR HICKLIN, sd. HICKLIN did convey unto JOHN SMITH. Wit: WILLIAM HICKLIN, JAMES PADEN, ALEXANDER KINNEY. Signed: ARTHUR (X) HICKLIN.

Page 159: Deed made 9 Dec. 1782 bet. ARTHUR HICKLIN of Camden Dist. Craven Co. of one part and JOHN SMITH of Camden Dist. Craven Co. of the other part for the sum of 10 shillings pd. by JOHN SMITH did sell 150 acres on So. Branch of Rocky Creek bounded all sides by vacant land. Wit: WILLIAM HICKLIN, JAMES PADEN, ALEXANDER KENNY. Signed: ARTHUR (X) HICKLIN. Proved 2 Oct. 1786.

Page 161: Deed made 3 Nov. 1784 bet. JOHN EVANS of Sumpter Co.,S.C. planter of one part and RICHARD EVANS of Sumpter Co. the other part did grant unto OWEN EVANS, dec'd. 100 acres in Craven Co. now Sumpter Co. on a branch of Sandy River of Broad River bounded all sides by vacant land, which sd. OWEN EVANS by his will did will to his son JOHN EVANS. Wit: THOMAS CHAMBERS, OWEN EVANS, WILLIAM BOYD. Signed: JOHN EVANS.

Page 163: Deed made 2 Nov. 1784 bet. JOHN EVANS of Sumpter Co., S.C. planter of one part and RICHARD EVANS of Sumpter Co. of the other part for the sum of 1 shilling and 6 pence sterling pd. by RICHARD EVANS doth sell 100 acres in Craven Co. now Sumpter Co. on a branch of Sandy River of the waters of Broad River bounded all sides by vacant land. Wit: THOMAS CHAMBERS, OWEN EVANS, WILLIAM BOYD. Signed: JOHN EVANS. Proved 2 Oct. 1786.

Page 166: Deed made 3 Oct. 1786 bet. JAMES KNOX and ELIZABETH, his wife of Camden Dist. Chester Co. of one part and ROBERT CHERRY of same dist. of the other part, hatter. By grant dated 6 April 1768 did grant to JAMES KNOX 450 acres surveyed to him by JOHN GASTON on waters of Rocky Creek bounded SE by DAVID HUNTER and all other sides by (vacant) land. "For 30 English quineas paid by ROBERT CHERRY." Wit: WILLIAM KNOX, DAVID HUNTER. Signed: JAMES KNOX, ELIZABETH KNOX.

Page 169: Know that we HAZEL HARDWICK and MARY HARDWICK his wife of Camden Dist. Chester Co. for the sum of 200 lbs. pd. by RICHARD TALIAFERRO of the same county, planter, do sell 442 acres lying on waters of Sandy River bounded W by WILLIAM BRITAINS, S by CHRIST-OPHER LOVINGS, E by vacant land, N by some person unknown. No witness name given. Signed: HAZEL HARDWICK, MARY HARDWICK.

Page 171: Know that we HAZEL HARDWICK and MARY HARDWICK of Chester Co. for the sum of 100 lbs. pd. by RICHARD TALIAFERRO, plant-er do sell 390 acres on waters of Sandy River. Dated 30 Sept. 1786. No witness given. Signed: HAZEL HARDWICK, MARY HARDWICK. Proved 30 Sept. 1786.

Page 173: Deed made 15 July 1786 bet. JAMES LANGSBY and ELIZABETH his wife of Chester Co., merchant of one part and WILLIAM JONES, blacksmith of the other part for the sum of 50 lbs. for 50 acres pd. by WILLIAM JONES. Wit: JOHN SIMPSON. JONATHAN JONES. Signed: JAMES LANGSBEE, ELIZABETH (X) LANGSBEE.
Proved 2 Oct. 1786.

18

Page 175: Deed made 15 July 1786 bet. JAMES LANGSBEE and ELIZABETH his wife of one part, merchant and WILLIAM JONES of Chester Co. of the other part. By grant bearing date 10 May 1768 did grant to ROBERT GLOVER 250 acres on JAMES MC CLURE spring branch waters of South Fork of Fishing Creek in Craven County all other sides by vacant land, land conveyed to HENRY CULP the 21st Sept. 1768. Wit: JOHN SIMPSON, JONATHAN JONES. Signed: JAMES LANGSBY, ELIZABETH LANGSBY.

Page 178: Deed made 15 July 1786 bet. JAMES LANGSBY of Chester Co., Merchant of one part and WILLIAM JONES, blacksmith of the other part. For the sum of 80 lbs. pd. by WILLIAM JONES 2 acres lying on S. Fork of Fishing Creek, Chester Co. joining SAMUEL MORROW's line. Wit: JOHN SIMPSON, JONATHAN JONES. Signed: JAMES LANGSBY. Proved 2 Oct. 1786.

Page 181: Deed made 5 May 1786 bet. WILLIAM JONES of Chester Co., blacksmith of one part and JONATHAN JONES his son of Chester Co. of the other part. By a grant dated 26 July 1774 did grant unto JOHN BROWN 150 acres on S. side of So. Fork of Fishing Creek in Craven Co. bounded SE by JOHN MC LILLIE's land, and JOHN MILLER's land, SW on AUGUSTEEN CULP's land, sd. land being conveyed by JOHN BROWN unto WILLIAM JONES and CATHARINE his wife for the sum of 50 lbs. Wit: JOHN HAYS, SAMUEL KNOX. Signed: WILLIAM JONES, CATHARINE JONES. Proved 2 Oct. 1786.

Page 184: Deed made 6 Dec. 1784 bet. DANIEL PRICE, SR., planter of Camden Dist. of one part and WALTHALL BURTON, planter of the other part for the sum of 50 lbs. pd. by WALTHALL BURTON have sold 200 acres on Flinthams Creek bounded SE by WILLIAM STONE's land, SW by WILLIAM STONE's land, S by vacant land. By a certain grant 16 Dec. 1786 (must be a mistake here, P.Y.) granted to GEORGE FLINN it being sold and conveyed to DANIEL PRICE. Wit: JAMES HUEY, JOHN PRATT. Signed: DANIEL PRICE.

Page 185: Deed made 6 Dec. 1784 bet. DANIEL PRICE, SR. of Camden Dist. planter of one part and WALTHALL BURTON of the other part for the sum of 100 lbs. pd. by WALTHALL BURTON 200 acres in Craven Co. bounded by vacant land at the time of running out as appears by grant 16 Dec. 1766. Wit: JAMES HUEY, JOHN PRATT. Signed: DANIEL PRICE.

Page 187: Deed made 4 Oct. 1786 bet. WALTHALL BURTON, planter of Camden Dist. of one part and GEORGE HEAD, planter of the other part, for the sum of 200 lbs. pd. by GEORGE HEAD do sell a tract of land on a branch of Broad River called Flinthams Creek, SE by WILLIAM STONE's land, SW by WILLIAM STONE's land, SW by vacant land for 400 acres. By grant dated 3 June 1766 granted to DANIEL PRICE and GEORGE KEWN and sold and conveyed to WALTHALL BURTON by special deed. Wit: WILLIAM HEAD, JOHN WADE. Signed: WALTHALL BURTON.

Page 169: Deed made 7 Nov. 1786 bet. ALLEN BURTON, planter of Camden Dist. of one part and JOHN COLLIN, planter of the other part for 100 lbs. pd. by JOHN COLLIN (or COLVIN) (written this way here, P.Y.) do sell 150 acres in Camden Dist. on waters of Sandy River as appears by grant dated 21 Jan. 1785. Wit: THOMAS JENKINS, JAMES (X) CARSON, BENJAMIN BURTON. Signed: ALLEN BURTON.

Page 191: Deed made 19 Feb. 1777 bet. DANIEL MC DONALD, planter of Camden Dist. of one part and WILLIAM MC DONALD, planter of the other part for the sum of 10 shillings pd. by WILLIAM MC DONALD do sell 250 acres situate on Wateree River in Craven Co. bounded SE by sd. river, NW on vacant land when surveyed and part on JOHN GIPSON land, SW on vacant land first surveyed for THOMAS HAYNES 22 Sept. 1749 and granted to SAMUEL WAGGONER 18 April 1756. Wit: GLUS CUSTON, JESSE TILMAN, WILLIAM (X) WOOD. Signed: DANIEL MC DONALD.

Page 193: Deed made 18 Feb. 1777 bet. DANIEL MC DONALD, planter of Camden Dist. Craven Co. of one part and WILLIAM MC DONALD, planter of other part. For the sum of 5 thousand lbs. pd. by WILLIAM MC DONALD. (Location not given, P.Y.) Wit: GLUS TILMAN, JESSE TILMAN, WILLIAM (X) WOOD. Signed: DANIEL MC DONALD.

19

Page 205: Deed made 18 July 1785 bet. JOHN BELL of Craven Co. Camden
          Dist., planter of one part and CHARLES ARTERBURY of other
part for 150 lbs. pd. by CHARLES ARTERBURY 100 acres in Craven Co.
in a place called Welches Fork on a small branch of Sandy River, bounded
all sides by vacant land. Wit: JAMES KNOX, JOHN ADAIR. Signed: JOHN
BELL.

Page 208: Deed made 17 July 1785 bet. JOHN BELL of Craven Co., Camden
          Dist. of one part and CHARLES ARTERBERRY, planter of the
other part. For sum of 10 shillings pd. by CHARLES ARTERBURY do sell
100 acres in Craven Co. in a place called Welches Fork on a small branch
of Sandy River. Wit: JAMES KNOX, JOHN ADAIR. Signed: JOHN BELL.

Page 210: Deed made 20 Jan. 1784 bet. TURNER KENDRICK of Camden Dist.,
          planter of one part and GEORGE BISHOP, JR. of the other
part. By a grant dated 4 May 1775 did grant unto DAVID MC CRUTH(?)
100 acres in Camden Dist. on north side of Broad River on Susys Bowls
branch of Turkey Creek bounded south on TURNER KENDRICK's all other
sides vacant land. Wit: GEORGE BISHOP, WILLIAM BISHOP. Signed: TURNER
KENDRICK.

Page 213: Deed made 2 Jan. 1786 bet. ELIZABETH STRAIN of Chester Co.
          of one part and AGNES BROWN natural daughter of ELIZABETH
STRAIN of the other part. For love and affection which she has and
beareth unto AGNES BROWN doth grant unto her a young negro wench about
eleven years of age named Phillis, likewise a cow and calf. Wit: DAVID
STRAIN, SAMUEL BROWN. Signed: ELIZABETH STRAIN.

Page 215: Deed made 9 Nov. 1786 bet. ALLEN BURTON of Camden Dist.,
          planter of one part and THOMAS JENKINS, planter of the other
part for the sum of 100 lbs. pd. by THOMAS JENKINS 378 acres in Camden
Dist. on waters of Sandy River. Wit: JAMES (X) CARSON, JOHN COLVIN,
BENJAMIN BURTON. Signed: ALLEN BURTON.

Page 216: Deed made 2 Jan. 1787 bet. WILLIAM YOUNG of Chester Co.
          of one part and ROBERT SMITH of the other part for the sum
of 5 lbs. pd. by ROBERT SMITH have sold 23 acres being part of land
laid out for MANNIN GORE and released to WILLIAM YOUNG 21 Jan. 1785.
(Location not given, P.Y.) (No witness given, P.Y.) Signed: WILLIAM
(X) YOUNG.

Page 218: Deed made 14 Nov. 1786 bet. HAZEL HARDWICK of Chester Co.
          and Camden Dist. of one part and LEONARD PRATT and JOHN
PRATT with SARAH PRATT the sd. JOHN's wife of the other part. For the
sum of 46 lbs. 13 shillings and 4 pence pd. by the sd. HAZEL HARDWICK
do sell 250 acres land on waters of Sandy River. Wit: RICHARD TALIAFER-
RO, JOHN COLVIN, JAMES GORE. Signed: LEONARD PRATT, JOHN PRATT, SARAH
PRATT.

Page 220: Deed made 2 Jan. 1787 bet. JOHN HUMPHRIES of Chester Co.
          of one part and ROBERT SMITH of the other part. For the
sum of 40 lbs. Virginia money pd. by ROBERT SMITH do sell land being
part of a tract laid out for AMBROS NIX and lying on land laid out
for THOMAS RODEN and thence laid out to CHARLES HUMPHRIES. (No witness
given, P.Y.) Signed: JOHN (X) HUMPHRIS.

Page 222: Deed made 10 Feb. 1786 bet. THOMAS REAVES living in the
          State of Georgia on Brier Creek, planter of one part and
JOHN FINDLY of the Waxsaws Lancaster Co., planter of the other part.
For the sum of 85 lbs. for 140 acres on a branch of Wateree River called
Fishing Creek. Grant was granted to ALEXANDER MC COWN where THOMAS
REAVES formerly lived, laid off by WILLIAM CARSON 140 acres. Wit: JOHN
MC COWN, ROBERT ROBINSON, ROBERT THOMPSON. Signed: THOMAS (X) REAVES.

Page 228: Deed made 16 July 1786 bet. DAVID MC CALLA and MARY his
          wife of Chester Co., yeoman of one part and WILLIAM LEWIS,
yeoman of the other part. By a certain grant dated 3 April 1786 did
grant unto DAVID MC CALLA 125 acres on a branch of Rocky Creek in Chester Co. bounded E by lands of JOHN BURNS, N by WILLIAM MILLINGS, E by

20

Cont'd from page 20:
MARY BIGHAM's and S by JOHN BIGHAM. Wit: MICHAEL DICKSON, WILLIAM MOR-
RAY, SAMUEL ADAMS. Signed: DAVID MC CALLA, MARY MC CALLA.

Page 231: Deed made 15 July 1786 bet. DAVID MC CALLA and MARY his
            wife of Chester Co., yeoman of one part and WILLIAM LEWIS,
yeoman of the other part. For the sum of 10 shillings have sold 125
acres situate on a branch of Rocky Creek in Chester Co. bounded E by
JOHN BURNS, N by WILLIAM MILLINGS, W by MARY BIGHAM, S by JOHN BIGHAM.
Wit: MICHAEL DICKSON, WILLIAM MORROW, SAMUEL ADAMS. Signed: DAVID MC
CALLA, MARY MC CALLA.

Page 234: Deed made 5 April 1787 bet. DAVID MC CALLA of Chester Co.
            of one part and PETER COONROOD of the other part for the
sum of 10 lbs. do sell to PETER COONROOD 308 acres lying on waters
of Sandy River bounded NE on one DOUGLAS land S on vacant land to the
SW on JOHN FERGUSON and WILLIAM FERGUSON land, sd. tract was surveyed
for JOHN ADAIR and granted to JAMES NEILSON. Wit: EDWARD LACEY, PATRICK
MC GRIFF, JOHN MILLS. Signed: DAVID MC CALLA. Proved 3 July 1787.

Page 235: Deed made 7 April 1787 bet. JOSEPH MC KINNEY of Chester
            Co., yeoman of one part and SAMUEL LUSK of York County of
the other part. By grant dated 18 May 1773 did grant to JOSEPH MC KINNEY
100 acres in Chester Co. on Neelys Branch of Fishing Creek for the
sum of 40 lbs. Wit: HUGH WHITESIDE, JOHN (X) MC GLAMERY, PATRICK (X)
MC KINNEY. Signed: JOSEPH (X) MC KINNEY.

Page 238: Deed made 5 Oct. 1786 bet. MICHAEL DICKSON, planter of Camden
            Dist. of one part and DAVID MC DILL, planter of the other
part. By grant dated 16 April 1765 under the hand of William Tryon,
Governor of N. C. did grant unto MICHAEL DICKSON 300 acres situated
bet. Catawba River of Broad River on both sides of Rocky Creek at the
ford of the Saludy Road being land surveyed for JOHN FONDREN. Wit:
CHARLES MILLER, SAMUEL H. DICKSON, JOHN MC DILL. Signed: MICHAEL DICKSON

Page 242: Deed made 4 Oct. 1786 bet. MICHAEL DICKSON of Camden Dist.
            of one part and DAVID MC DILL of the other part for 10 shill-
ings pd. by DAVID MC DILL did sell 100 acres part of a tract of 300
acres situated on Rocky Creek at and below the ford of the Saludy Road
bet. Catawba river and Broad river, bounded all sides by vacant land.
Wit: CHARLES MILLER, SAMUEL H. DICKSON, JOHN MC DILL. Signed: MICHAEL
DICKSON.

Page 244: Deed made 3 April 1787 bet. DAVID PRUIT of Union County
            96 Dist. of one part and OWEN EVANS of Chester Co. and Camden
Dist. of the other part. For the sum of 300 lbs. pd. by OWEN EVANS
400 acres granted RICHARD WARIN dated 23 Dec. 1771 on a branch of Sandy
River called Cany Fork. Wit: WILLIAM BOYD, JOHN EVAN, RICHARD EVANS.
Signed: DAVID (X) PRUIT.

Page 245: Deed made 13 April 1787 bet. JOHN EVINS of Chester County of
            one part and JAMES MC CARTER of Abbeville Co. of the other
part for 40 lbs. do sell to JAMES MC CARTER 196 acres situated in Camden
Dist. on a branch of Sandy River joining JAMES FERGUSON's land and
JAMES WILKEY's land, GEORGE WIER's land, being part of 532 acres granted
to JOHN EVANS. 5 June 1786. Wit: RICHARD EVANS, OWEN EVANS, AGNES (X)
EVANS. Signed: JOHN EVANS.

Page 247: Deed made 13 March 1787 bet. JOHN GRISHAM of one part, plant-
            er of Chester Co. and DAVID GRISHAM, planter of the other
part for sum of one shilling 6 pence do sell to DAVID GRISHAM 100
acres lying on waters of Flintams Creek of Sandy River which was granted
to JOHN GRISHAM 5 Dec. 1785. Wit: ROBERT LEMOND, JEREMIAH GRISHAM,
ALEXANDER JOHNSTON. Signed: JOHN (X) GRISHAM, ELENOR (X) GRISHAM.

Page 249: Deed made 13 March 1787 bet. ROBERT LEMMON, planter of Camden
            Dist., Chester Co. of one part and JEREMIAH GRISHAM of the
other part for sum of 10 lbs. pd. by JEREMIAH GRISHAM have sold 155
acres situate in Camden Dist. on a branch of Broad River called Sandy

Cont'd from page 21:
Creek alias Stone Creek, part of land granted to ROBERT LEMMON 2 Oct. 1786. Wit: DAVID (X) GRISHAM, ALEXANDER JOHNSTON. Signed: ROBERT LEMMOND, UNITY (X) LEMMOND.

Page 251: Know all men that we WILLIAM MILLER and ANN HEART of Chester Co. for the sum of 77 lbs. pd. by JOHN LATTA do sell to JOHN LATTA a negro woman named Dolly. Wit: JOHN MILLS, JR., NICHOLAS BISHOP, JOHN MILLS, SR. Signed: WILLIAM MILLER, ANN (X) HEART.

Page 252: Deed made (no day given, P.Y.) bet. HAMPTON STROUD of Rock Creek Chester Co., planter of one part and EDWARD STEDMAN of Fishing Creek of the other part for the sum of 14 lbs. 5 shillings and 8 pence pd. by EDWARD STEDMAN, for divers other causes him unto moving, have sold 50 acres in the actual possession of sd. EDWARD STEDMAN. Wit: ELIJAH BANKSTON, SAMUEL FERGUSON, THOMAS (X) STROUD. Signed: HAMPTON (X) STROUD, MARY (X) STROUD.

Page 253: Deed made 31 Oct. 1786 bet. HAMPTON STROUD of Rocky Creek Chester Co., planter of one part and EDWARD STEDMAN of Fishing Creek of the other part for the sum of 5 lbs. pd. by EDWARD STEDMAN and for divers other causes him thereunto moving do sell 50 acres lying on Rocky Creek and on the W by THOMAS DYES land, N by more of DYES land, E by JOHN SMITH. Wit: ELIJAH BANKSTON, SAMUEL FERGUSON, THOMAS (X) STROUD. Signed: HAMPTON (X) STROUD, MARY (X) STROUD.

Page 255: Deed made 29 Nov. 1780 bet. JOHN WALL being the heir of BIRD WALL, dec'd. of one part and WILLIAM WALL and CHARLES WALL of Chester Co. of the other part did grant to BIRDWELL WALL 100 acres on Rocky Creek 12 June 1771 north side of Cawtaba River NW on BENJAMIN STREET and WILLIAM WALL land, all other sides by vacant land. Wit: ELIJAH (X) GIBSON, ABRAM (X) GIBSON, ISOM LOWRY. Signed: JOHN (X) WALL.

Page 257: Deed made 28 Nov. 1786 bet. JOHN WALL, dec'd. of one part and WILLIAM WALL and CHARLES WALL of Chester Co. of the other part do sell 150 acres lying on the Catawba River on SW side thereof in Craven Co. bounded NW part of it to the river by land laid out to ABRAHAM STOVER, other 2 sides by vacant land. Wit: ELIJAH (X) GIBSON, ABRAM (X) GIBSON, ISOM LOWRY. Signed: JOHN (X) WALL.

Page 257: Deed made 28 Nov. 1786 bet. JOHN WALL of one part and WILLIAM & CHARLES WALL of the other part of Chester Co. and sd. JOHN WALL, dec'd. for sum of 2 shillings pd. by WILLIAM & CHARLES WALL 150 acres lying on Catawba River. Wit: ELIJAH (X) GIBSON, ABRAHAM (X) GIBSON, ISOM LOWRY. Signed: JOHN (X) GIBSON.

Page 259: Deed made 29 (month not given, P.Y.) 1786 bet. JOHN WALL of one part and WILLIAM and CHARLES WALL of the other part of Chester Co. by a grant dated 27 Sept. 1769 grant unto WILLIAM & CHARLES WALL 150 acres lying on Catawba River on the SW side of Craven Co., NW side part of it near to the river by land of ABRAHAM STOVER and the other part by vacant land. Wit: ELIJAH (X) GIBSON, ABRAHAM (X) GIBSON, ISOM LOWREY. Signed: JOHN (X) WALL.

Page 264: Deed made 11 April 1780 bet. PHILIP WALKER and MARTHA WALKER his wife of Rocky Creek Camden Dist., planter of one part and THOMAS MORRISON, weaver of the other part. By grant dated 1 June 1767 did grant to PHILIP WALKER 100 acres lying on a branch of Catawba River called Rocky Creek bounded SE by JOHN MC DONALD and all other sides by vacant land. Wit: ROBERT MORRISON, SAMUEL WARE, ALEXANDER ROSEBOROUGH. Signed: PHILIP (X) WALKER, MARTHA WALKER.

Page 266: Deed made 11 Sept. 1786 bet. JOHN CULP of Mackelan Burgh County, North Carolina of one part and BENJAMIN CULP of Chester Co. of the other part. By a grant dated 19 Nov. 1772 did grant unto JOHN CULP 150 acres in the State of S. C. on waters of Fishing Creek bounded SE by ARCHIBALD ELLIOTT and all other sides by vacant land. Wit: WILLIAM WILEY, ANDREW LOCKHARD, JOHN WILEY, JR. S:JOHN (X)

Page 269: Deed made 31 March 1787 bet. WILLIAM HICKLIN, planter of
          Lancaster Co. of one part and JAMES BURNS of Chester Co.
of the other part for sum of 40 shillings pd. by JAMES BURNS did sell
100 acres lying in Chester Co. on Bull Run bounded N. by JOHN MC LILLY,
NE by BENJAMIN ELLIS, E by JAMES BURNS, W by vacant land, the same
being obtained by a Bounty Warrant Jan. 12, 1768 by JOHN WAUGH, thence
sold to JAMES NICHOLS. Wit: JAMES PADEN, ROBERT BOYD. Signed: WILLIAM
HICKLIN.

Page 272: Deed made 30 March 1787 bet. WILLIAM HICKLIN of Lancaster
          Co., planter of one part and JAMES BURNS of Chester Co.
of the other part for sum of 40 shillings pd. by JAMES BURNS, do grant
unto JAMES BURNS 100 acres in Chester Co. on Bull Run. Wit: JAMES PADEN,
ROBERT BOYD. Signed: WILLIAM HICKLIN.

Page 274: Deed made 11 Nov. 1785 bet. ISAAC EVINS of Craven Co. Camden
          Dist., planter of one part and WILLIAM BOYD of same Co.
of the other part, for the sum of 25 lbs. pd. by WILLIAM BOYD do sell
100 acres granted by William Bull, Lt. Governor of S. C. unto ISAAC
EVINS 1 Dec. 1769 on a branch of Rocky Creek, SW on land surveyed for
RICHARD STOREY, other sides by vacant land. Wit: JOHN BELL, JOHN BURNS,
SUSANNA (X) GLOVER. Signed: ISAAC EVINS.

Page 275: Deed made 11 Nov. 1785 bet. ISAAC EVINS of Craven Co. Camden
          Dist. of one part and WILLIAM BOYD, planter of the other
part, for the sum of 100 lbs. do sell to WILLIAM BOYD 100 acres granted
by William Bull, Lt. Gov. to ISAAC EVINS 1 Dec. 1769 lying on a branch
of Rocky Creek bounding SW by land surveyed for RICHARD STOREY all
other sides by vacant land. Wit: JOHN BURNS, JOHN BELL, SUSANNA(X)
GLOVER. Signed: ISAAC EVINS.

Page 277: Deed made 9 Oct. 1785 bet. JOHN CARTER of Chester Co. of
          one part and JAMES BISHOP, planter of the other part, the
sd. JOHN CARTER by a certain grant dated 2 May 1770 by Wm. Bull, Gov.
of S. C. did grant 200 acres between Catawba River and Broad River
on Rocky Creek where the road from the South fork of Catawba River
to Charles Town, all other sides by vacant land. Said tract was given
to the sd. JOHN CARTER by the will of JACOB CARTER, dec'd. Wit: JOHN
DICKSON, CHARLES MILLER, WILLIAM MILLER. Signed;JOHN CARTER.

Page 280: Deed made 10 Oct. 1785 bet. JOHN CARTER of Chester Co.,
          planter of one part and JAMES BISHOP, planter of the other
part, for 10 shillings pd. by JAMES BISHOP do sell 111 acres of land
being part of 200 acres on Rocky Creek where the south fork road to
Charleston crosses the creek between Catawba river and Broad river.
Wit: JOHN DICKSON, CHARLES MILLER, WILLIAM MILLER. Signed: JOHN CARTER.

Page 282: Deed made 2 Sept. 1784 bet. WILLIAM LORD and SARAH his wife
          of Sumpter Co. of one part and ANN HERBISON of the other
part, by a certain grant dated 7 April 1770 did grant unto ABRAHAM
DY 300 acres in Craven Co. now Sumpter Co. on a branch of Rocky Creek.
Wit: WILLIAM BOYD, PATRICK HERBISON, ROBERT MARTIN. Signed: WILLIAM
LORD, SARAH (X) LORD.

Page 285: Deed made 1 Sept. 1784 bet. WILLIAM LORD and SARAH his wife
          of Sumpter Co. of one part and ANN HERBISON of other part,
for 1 shilling and 5 pence doth sell to ANN HERBISON 150 acres being
part of a tract of 300 acres lying in Craven Co. now Sumpter Co. on
a branch of Rocky Creek made to ABRAHAM DIE by grant dated 7 April
1770. Wit: WILLIAM BOYD, PATRICK (X) HERBISON, ROBERT MARTIN. Signed:
WILLIAM LORD, SARAH (X) LORD.

Page 287: Deed made 7 Aug. 1787 bet. BENJAMIN STREET of Camden Dist.
          in Chester Co., doctor and MARY his wife of one part and
ABNER WILKS of the other part. By a grant dated 15 Feb. 1769 did grant
unto JOHN RENNELS, planter 300 acres on both sides of Hogs branch bounded NW on WILLIAM SANDIFER land, SW on JAMES MONTGOMERY land, all other
sides by vacant land. Wit: FRANCIS WILKS, JONATHAN HAND, DAVID EAKINS.
Signed: BENJAMIN STREET, MARY STREET.

Page 289: Deed made 7 Aug. 1787 bet. BENJAMIN STREET of Camden Dist.
           in Chester Co. of one part and ABNER WILKS of the other
part for 10 shillings pd. by ABNER WILKS, do sell 150 acres lying on
the south side of Hogs branch being part of 300 acres granted to JOHN
RENNELS. Wit: FRANCIS WILKS, JONATHAN HAND, DAVID EAKENS. Signed: BENJA-
MIN STREET, MARY (X) STREET. (The above Mary Street did not sign with
a cross mark in the middle of the page, P.Y.)

Page 291: Deed made 28 June 1787 bet. WILLIAM HOGAN of Chester Co.
           of one part and JAMES DILLARD of the other part for 100
lbs. pd. by JAMES DILLARD to sell 160 acres lying on south side of
Sandy River originally granted to JOHN DAVIS 1 June 1767 containing
200 acres and conveyed from sd. DAVIS to sd. HOGAN by deed of lease
and release. Wit: T.(?) LEWIS, WILLIAM HALL, JAMES DILLARD, JR. Signed:
WILLIAM HOGAN.

Page 293: Deed made 28 June 1787 bet. WILLIAM HOGAN of Chester Co.
           of one part and JAMES DILLARD of the other part for sum
of 10 shillings pd. by JAMES DILLARD do sell 160 acres being part of
a tract lying on south side of Sandy River originally granted to JOHN
DAVIS by a grant containing 200 acres dated 1 June 1767 and conveyed
from JOHN DAVIS to WILLIAM HOGAN. Wit: T.(?) LEWIS, WILLIAM HALL, JAMES
DILLARD, JR. Signed: WILLIAM HOGAN. (same as above p. 291)

Page 295: Deed made 24 May 1787 bet. DAVID HOPKINS of Chester Co.
           of one part and EDWARD GRIMES, a free negro, of other part
for 13 lbs. do agree to give EDWARD GRIMES clothes, meat, drink, washing and lodging fitting for such servant. Wit: JAMES GLENN, JR., JOHN
(X) HARPER. Signed: EDWARD (X) GRIMES, DAVID HOPKINS.

Page 296: Deed made 3 Sept. 1783 bet. ELISHA DYE and RICHARD DYE of
           Sumpter Co., planters of one part and ROBERT JAMISON, planter
of the other part. By a grant dated 7 Apr. 1770 by Wm. Bull, Gov. of
S. C. did grant unto ABRAM DYE now dec'd. 300 acres lying on Bullskin
Run waters of Rocky creek. Wit: JAMES HANNA, WILLIAM MC CULLOCK. Signed:
ELISHA DYE, RICHARD (X) DYE.

Page 299: Deed made 3 Sept. 1787 bet. PHILIP WALKER of Chester Co.
           of one part and JOHN MC GLAMARY, yeoman of the other part.
By grant dated 21 Dec. 1763 under the hand of Arthur Dobbs, Gov. of
N. C. did grant unto MARY SMITH, widow, 300 acres then in Mecklinburg
co., N.C. but by the continuation of the boundery line now in the state
of S. C. Chester Co. on the north side of Fishing Creek, the tract
of land conveyed to MARY SMITH alias MORRIS and her husband ROBERT
MORRIS. No witness given. Signed: PHILIP WALKER.

Page 301: Know that I JOHN REDFORD of Mecklinburg Co., N. C. do own
           and confess that I have spoken certain fallen and scandos
(sic) words concerning ISAAC PRITCHART and JEAN his wife which I do
in like manner confess that I never had any reason to suspect ISAAC
PRITCHART nor JEAN his wife of being guilty of anything etc. Wit: J.
MILLS, ACH DAVIE. Signed: JOHN (X) REDFORD.

Page 302: Deed made 4 Nov. 1786 bet. WILLIAM BOYD, Surveyor of S.
           C. of Camden Dist. of one part and JOHN SERVIS, weaver of
the other part, for the sum of 10 shillings pd. by JOHN SERVIS 100
acres lying on Rocky Creek bounded by JAIN MC CARTNEY and JOHN COMBEST
including the forks of the grassy runs below the waggon roads between
Catawba and Broad river in Chester Co. Wit: HUGH STUART, SAMUEL CROOK,
GEORGE W. KENNEDY. Signed: WILLIAM BOYD.

Page 304: Deed made 8 May 1787 bet. JOHN JAGGORS of one part and WIL-
           LIAM HALL of the other part, for 50 lbs. from WILLIAM HALL
have sold 164 acres being part of 474 acres granted to JOHN JAGGORS
on the NW side of Sandy River beginning at a beach on Sandy River.
Wit: T.(?) LEWIS, NATHAN JAGGORS, JAMES (X) MINIS. Signed: JOHN JAGGORS.

Page 307: Deed made 7 May 1787 bet. JOHN JAGGORS of S.C. of one part
           and WILLIAM HALL of the other part for 10 shillings pd.

Cont'd from page 24:
by WILLIAM HALL have sold 164 acres being part of 474 acres on NW side
of Sandy River. Wit: T.(?) LEWIS, NATHAN JAGGORS, JAMES (X) MINIS.
Signed: JOHN JAGGORS.

Page 308: Deed made 17 Sept. 1787 bet. JAMES BURNS of Chester Co.,
          planter of one part and ROBERT BOYD of the other part for
the sum of 50 lbs. pd. by ROBERT BOYD do sell 100 acres lying on a
branch of Rocky Creek called Bull Run bounding N by JOHN MC ALILYS,
NE by BENJAMIN ELLIS land to the E by JAMES BURNS land, W by vacant
land, the same being obtained by a warrant dated 12 Jan. 1768 by JOHN
WAUGH then sold to JAMES NICHOLS and conveyed by JAMES NICHOLS to WIL-
LIAM HICKLIN then conveyed to JAMES BURNS. Wit: JAMES WILLIAMSON, ROBERT
MORRISON. Signed: JAMES BURNS.

Page 311: Deed made 26 March 1787 bet. ALEXANDER DONALD of one part
          and FERDINAND HOPKINS of Chester Co. of the other part,
that FERDINAND HOPKINS for the sum of 100 lbs. to him in hand pd. by
the sd. ALEXANDER DONALD have sold 86 acres granted 9 Oct. 1784 on
the south fork of Sandy River on the north side of the old Saludy Road
bounding SE on land laid out to JAMES FLITCHALL, NW on THOMAS JENKINS,
SW on vacant land. Wit: (name not plain, P.Y.), JEREMIAH KINGSLEY.
Signed: FERDINAND HOPKINS.

Page 312: Deed made 2 Jan. 1780 bet. WILLIAM MC CAW and ANN his wife
          of Camden Dist., planter of one part and SAMUEL WIER of
the other part. By grant dated 14 Sept. 1771 did grant to WILLIAM MC
CAW 450 acres and for 50 lbs. pd. by SAMUEL WIER land lying on waters
of Rocky Creek in Camden Dist. Wit: JAMES GRIER (or GLUS?) (not positive, P.Y.), JAMES BANKHEAD. Signed: WILLIAM MC CAW, ANN (X) MC CAW.

Page 315: Know that I MARY HAMBLETON of Chester Co. for the sum of
          100 lbs. pd. by JOHN MC GLAMARY, yeoman, do sell 1 sorrel
horse, 1 black mare, and bay mare and 2 year old fillys, 10 head of
neat cattle, etc. Wit: DANIEL COOKE, THOMAS WHITE. Signed: MARY (X)
HAMBLETON.

Page 316: Deed made 25 June 1787 bet. JOHN GRISHAM of Camden Dist.,
          planter of one part and ISAAC TAYLOR, planter of the other
part, for 350 lbs. pd. by ISAAC TAYLOR do sell one certain tract lying
on a branch of Broad River called Sandy Creek or otherwise Stones Creek
bounding NW on land surveyed for LUCY COLLINS, all other sides by vacant
land. Wit: THOMAS BAKER FRANKLIN, WILLIAM (X) GRISSOM. Signed: JOHN
(X) GRISSOM (written this way, P.Y.)

Page 318: Deed made 3 Oct.1787 bet. Col. PATRICK MC GRIFF, planter
          of one part and JAMES LAY of the other part, both of Chester
Co. for the sum of 100 lbs. pd. by JAMES LAY have sold 100 acres, by
patent granted to PATRICK MC GRIFF 2 Oct. 1786. (no witness given,
P.Y.) Signed: PATRICK MC GRIFF.

Page 319: Deed made 22 Sept. (no year given) bet. ALEXANDER BROWN
          and SAMUEL BROWN his son, planters of Chester Co. of one
part and GEORGE GILL, JR. of the other part. For 106 lbs. pd. by GEORGE
GILL, JR. do sell 150 acres lying on the south side of the fork of
Fishing Creek. Wit: WILLEY S. BROWN, WILLIAM WYLIE, SAMUEL H. DICKSON.
Signed: ALEXANDER BROWN, SAMUEL BROWN.

Page 322: Deed made 2 Jan. 1780 bet. THOMAS HUSTON, planter and AGNES
          his wife of Camden Dist. of one part and SAMUEL WIER, planter
of the other part. By grant dated 13 Aug. 1762 did grant to HUGH MC
DONALD 150 acres on both sides of Rocky Creek in Craven Co. bounded
all sides by vacant land when surveyed and conveyed from HUGH MC DONALD
to GEORGE WIER 31 March 1764. Wit: JAMES GREER, ELENOR HUSTON. Signed:
THOMAS HUSTON, AGNES (X) HUSTON.

Page 325: Deed made 31 Aug. (year not given) bet. PATRICK MC GRIFF
          of one part and THOMAS MC GRIFF of the other part both of
Camden Dist. for sum of 50 lbs. pd. by THOMAS MC GRIFF do sell 100
acres granted by patent to Mr. KIRKPATRICK 1 Sept. 1768. Wit: EDWARD

Cont'd from page 25:
LACEY, RICHARD MILES, HUGH STUART. Signed: PATRICK MC GRIFF.

Page 327: Deed made 10 Dec. 1783 bet. KATHARINE BROWN of Camden Dist.,
widow of one part and WILLIAM BROWN of the other part for
the sum of 100 lbs. pd. by WILLIAM BROWN do sell 116 acres being of
a tract of 350 acres granted to sd. KATHARINE BROWN 23 Jan. 1773. Wit:
JAMES ADARE, JOHN WALKER, TURNER KENDRICK. Signed: KATHARINE (X) BROWN.

Page 328: Deed made 5 Jan. 1788 bet. RICHARD TALIAFERRO of Chester
Co. of one part and WILLIAM BRITAIN of the other part for
the sum of 20 shillings pd. by WILLIAM BRITAIN have sold one acre of
land whereon the Britain Grist mill stands. (no witness given). Signed:
RICHARD TALIAFERRO.

Page 329: Deed made 2 Jan. 1788 bet. THOMAS CROSBY of Chester Co.
of one part and THOMAS LEWIS of Greenville Co. of the other
part for the sum of 50 lbs. pd. do convey unto the sd. THOMAS LEWIS
90 acres situate in Camden part in the county of Chester and part in
Fairfield county on the south side of Sandy River bounded SE on JAMES
DILLARD, SW on lands of the heirs of AMOS DAVIS, dec'd, NW on RICHARD
CROSBY land granted to THOMAS CROSBY 21 Jan. 1785. Wit: ALLEN DE GRAF-
FINREID. Signed: THOMAS CROSBY.

Page 331: Deed made 5 Jan. 1788 bet. RICHARD DAVIS of Chester Co.,
planter of one part and ALLEN DE GRAFFENREID, merchant of
the other part for the sum of 5 shillings doth convey to ALLEN DE GRAF-
FENREID 300 acres being half of a tract of 600 acres originally granted
to JOHN HITCHCOCK from the state of North Carolina by date 3 Feb. 1754
and from sd. JOHN HITCHCOCK to ANN DAVIS, wife of RICHARD DAVIS. Wit:
JOHN PRATT, THOMAS CROSBY. Signed: RICHARD (X) DAVIS, ANN (X) DAVIS.

Page 333: Deed made 7 Jan. 1788 bet. RICHARD DAVIS of Chester Co.
and ALLEN DE GRAFFENREID of the other part for sum of 100
lbs. do convey to sd. ALLEN DE GRAFFENREID 300 acres being the half
of a tract of 300 acres originally granted to JOHN HITCHCOCK from North
Carolina by a grant dated 3 Feb. 1754. Wit: JOHN PRATT, THOMAS CROSBY.
Signed: RICHARD (X) DAVIS, ANN (X) DAVIS.

Page 336: Deed made 3 Jan. 1788 bet. JAMES NEELY of Chester Co., yeoman
of one part and THOMAS NEELY, yeoman of the other part by
a grant dated 26 July 1774 did grant unto JAMES NEELY 220 acres in
Craven Co. on a branch of Fishing Creek, bounding NW by WILLIAM MC
KINEY land, for the sum of 10 lbs. pd. by THOMAS NEELY. No witness
given. Signed: JAMES NEELY.

Page 339: Deed made 16 Aug. 1787 bet. MAJOR GRISHAM of Chester Co.
of one part and THOMAS BAKER FRANKLIN of the other part
that the sd. MAJOR GRISHAM and FANNEY his wife for the sum of 10 lbs.
pd. by THOMAS BAKER FRANKLIN do sell 50 acres which was granted to
sd. MAJOR GRISHAM by patent bearing date 20 Aug. 1786. Wit: PATRICK
MC GRIFF, EDMOND NUNN, JAMES NUNN. (written both Major and Mager Grisham,
P.Y.) Signed: MAGER (X) GRISHAM, FANNY (X) GRISHAM.

Page 344: Deed made 2 Jan. 1788 bet. HUGH KELSEY of Chester Co. of
one part and ROBERT KELSEY, waggon maker of the other part.
By a grant dated 6 Feb. 1773 did grant unto ROBERT KELSEY 100 acres
in Craven Co. on a branch of Rocky Creek bounded SW by HENRY SMITH,
all other sides by vacant land, the above named THOMAS KELSEY died
intestate and HUGH KELSEY is his elder brother and heir to the sd.
tract of land. No witness given. Signed: HUGH KELSEY.

Page 347: Deed made 3 Aug. 1787 bet. JOHN DOUGHARTY of Chester Co.
of one part and THOMAS BAKER FRANKLIN of the other part
for the sum of 10 lbs. pd. by FRANKLIN do convey 100 acres situated
on a branch of Sandy River, bounding south on THOMAS B. FRANKLIN, NE
on WILLIAM TRUSELL. Wit: JOHN PRATT, JAMES GORE, JOHN FRANKLIN. Signed:
JOHN DOUGHARTY.

Page 349: Deed made 14 Sept. 1787 bet. THOMAS FRANKLIN of Camden Dist.

Cont'd from page 26:
of one part and ROBERT DUNLAY, farmer of the other part
for the sum of 2 shillings pd. by ROBERT DUNLAP doth sell 100 acres
in Camden Dist. on waters of Sandy River. No witness given. Signed:
THOMAS BAKER FRANKLIN.

Page 351: Deed made 15 Sept. 1787 bet. THOMAS FRANKLIN of Camden Dist.
of one part and ROBERT DUNLAP, farmer of the other part.
By a grant dated 3 April 1786 did grant unto JOHN DOUGHARTY 100 acres
in Camden Dist. on waters of Sandy River. No witness given. Signed:
THOS. B. FRANKLIN.

Page 354: Deed made 14 May 1777 bet. MARY HANNAH of St. Marks Parish
Craven Co., young woman of one part and WILLIAM MILLER,
planter of the other part. By a grant dated 8 Dec. 1774 grant to
MARY HANNAH 100 acres in Craven Co. on waters of Rocky Creek bounded
NE by NICHOLAS BISHOP, SE by WILLIAM MILLER and the other sides by
vacant land. MARY HANNAH for the sum of 200 lbs. pd. by WILLIAM MILLER
do convey 100 acres. Wit: WILLIAM BOYD, JOHN MC QUESTON, AGNES (X)
HANNAH. Signed: MARY (X) HANNAH.

Page 357: Deed made 20 Aug. 1787 bet. THOMAS HUMPHREYS and MARY his
wife of Chester Co. of one part and GEORGE BLISSET of the
other part. That the sd. THOMAS and MARY HUMPHREYS his wife for the
sum of 50 lbs. do sell 100 acres being part of a tract granted to
THOMAS HUMPHREYS dated 6 Feb. 1786, E on WILLIAM NUNN's line, NE on
WASHINGTON HOPKINS line, SW on JOHN TERRY's land. Wit: FRANCIS NUNN,
ALEXANDER DONALD, THOMAS JENKINS. Signed: THOMAS HUMPHREYS, MARY (X)
HUMPHREYS.

Page 359: Deed made 9 Jan. 1788 bet. DAVID BOYD and MARGARET his wife
of Chester Co. of one part and WILLIAM BOYD, young man of
the other part. By a grant dated 15 Nov. 1774 did grant unto DAVID
BOYD 350 acres lying on Stamps branch between the main and south forks
of Fishing Creek then in Craven Co. but now in Chester Co. bounded
NE with SAMUEL WARRY's land, S with JAMES GILL's land, all other sides
vacant land. Wit: WILLIAM BOYD, JOHN BOYD, ANON(?) BOYD. Signed: DAVID
BOYD, MARGARET (X) BOYD.

Page 362: Deed made 4 Jan. 1788 bet. SAMUEL MC CANE(?) of Chester
Co. of one part and JOHN SIMPSON, Minister of the same place
of the other part for the sum of 30 lbs. proclamation money pd. by
JOHN SIMPSON do grant 32 acres situate in Camden Dist. on waters of
the S. fork of Fishing Creek joining and between the lands of JOHN
SIMPSON, CHRISTOPHER STRONG & ALEXANDER BROWN part of a tract originally
granted to SAMUEL MC CANCE(?) granted 23 Oct. 1764. No witness given.
Signed: SAMUEL MC CANCE(?).

Page 364: Deed made 4 Jan. 1788 bet. Col. DAVID HOPKINS of Chester
Co. of one part and CALEB DAVIS of the other part for the
sum of 100 lbs. pd. by CALEB DAVIS 160½ acres being one half of a tract
of 371 acres granted to Col. HOPKINS. Wit: JAMES FRASER, JEREMIAH DAVIS.
Signed: DAVID HOPKINS.

Page 365: Deed made 8 June 1780 bet. DAVID HOPKINS, Esq. and his wife,
MARY of Camden Dist. of one part and FERDINAND HOPKINS of
the State of Virginia and County of Cumberland of the other part. Witness that DAVID and MARY HOPKINS his wife for the sum of 5 thousand
lbs. pd. by FERDINAND HOPKINS have granted 2 tracts of land. First
1 tract situate in Camden Dist. on the north side of Broad River originally granted by the Hon. Mathew Rowan, Esq. of N. C. the 28 June 1752
to JOHN SMITH and conveyed by the sd. JOHN SMITH to MARK EDWARDS, SR.
and then conveyed by MARK EDWARDS, SR. to DAVID HOPKINS, Esq. on the
north side of Broad River. Wit: NATHANIEL ABNEY, JAMES JARRARD. Signed:
DAVID HOPKINS, MARY HOPKINS.

Page 368: Deed made 3 Jan. 1788 bet. JAMES MC CLURE and JANE his wife
planter of one part of Chester Co. and RICHARD GLADNEY of
Fairfield Co. of the other part. By a certain tract of 200 acres surv'd

27

Cont'd from page 27:
for DAVID HUNTER, dated 7 Oct. 1767 situate in Chester Co. on waters
of Fishing Creek and on the waters of Rocky Creek bounding on all sides
by vacant land and whereas sd. JAMES MC CLURE, SR. did purchase from
sd. DAVID HUNTER and sd. JAMES MC CLURE, SR. by his last will did bequeath unto his son the above named JAMES MC CLURE 200 acres of land
and whereas JAMES MC CLURE for the sum of 12 lbs. pd. by RICHARD GLAD-
NEY. No witness given. Signed: JAMES MC CLURE.

Page 370: Deed made 10 Nov. 1787 bet. JOHN TURNER of Fairfield Co.
of one part and JOHN HOLEMAN of the other part, by a grant
dated 19 Feb. 1767 did grant unto JAMES COBB 100 acres situate on the
north side of Broad River in Craven Co. bounded NE by land surveyed
for JOHN LEE, all other sides by vacant land, for the sum of 50 lbs.
pd. by JOHN HOLEMAN 100 acres. Wit: RICHARD TALIAFERRO, JOHN BELL.
Signed: JOHN TURNER.

Page 375: Deed made 25 Jan. 1785 bet. JOHN OWEN of Craven Co. of one
part and JAMES GILL of the other part. For the sum of 150
lbs. pd. by JAMES GILL doth sell 2 tracts of land the first containing
100 acres between Rocky Creek and south fork of Fishing Creek in Craven
Co. bounded SE on ROBERT KNOX land and vacant land, NW on RICHARD KER-
REL land, all other sides vacant, the same granted to JOSEPH GALBRETH
by patent dated 12 Aug. 1768. The second tract of 82 acres situate
on Carrels branch of Fishing Creek bounded SE and SW on land laid out
to RICHARD CARRELL other sides on vacant land the same being granted
to JOHN ANTHONY 15 March 1771 which tracts were conveyed to sd. JOHN
OWEN. Wit: ELIJAH BROWN, WILLEY S. BROWN, JOSIAH PORTER. Signed: JOHN
OWEN.

Page 377: Deed made 20 Oct. 1783 bet. JOHN STONE and MOSES STONE and
JACOB STONE of Craven Co., planters of one part and DENNIS
CARRIL and WILLIAM STONE, planters of the other part. For the sum of
200 lbs. pd. JOHN STONE, MOSES STONE, JACOB STONE by the sd. DENNIS
CARRIL 200 acres situate on Sandy Creek a branch of Broad river bounding
north by JOHN COLVIN and part vacant land on part of land laid out
to DANIEL PRICE. Signed: JOHN (X) STONE, MOSES (X) STONE, JACOB (X)
STONE.

Page 380: Deed made 19 Oct. 1783 bet. JOHN STONE, MOSES STONE, JACOB
STONE of Craven Co., planters of one part and DENNIS CARRIL
and WILLIAM STONE, planters of the other part. For 10 shillings do
sell 202 acres situate on Sandy Creek a branch of Broad river, bounding
north on land held by JOHN COLVIN and part vacant land laid out to
DANIEL PRICE. Wit: CAIN CARRELL, WILLIS CARRELL, THOMAS (X) FRANKLAND.
Signed: JOHN (X) STONE, MOSES (X) STONE, JACOB (X) STONE.

Page 382: Deed made 11 April 1772 bet. RICHARD CARRELL of the Parish
of St. Marks, planter of the first part and JOHN WALKER
of the Parish of St. Marks of the other part by a certain grant dated
17 June 1763 did grant unto RICHARD CARRELL 150 acres lying on a branch
of Fishing Creek in the Parish of St. Marks in the City of Craven.
Signed: RICHARD (X) CARRELL. Wit: WM. DICKSON, WM. BOONE, WM. BARRY.

Page 385: Deed made 11 April 1772 bet. RICHARD CARROL of St. Marks
Parish, planter of one part and JOHN WALKER of the same
Parish, planter of the other part. By a grant dated 15 Feb. 1769 did
grant to RICHARD CARROLL 300 acres lying on a branch of Fishing Creek
and on the Saludy Road in the Parish of St. Marks in Craven Co. bounded
on a tract of land of an Elder DALE containing 150 acres granted to
sd. RICHARD CARROL. Wit: WILLIAM DICKSON, WILLIAM BROWN, WILLIAM DICK-
SON, JR., WILLIAM BERRY. Signed: RICHARD (X) CARROL. (Name written
with an X here. Above deed did not have an X mark. P.Y.)

Page 387: Deed made 12 Nov. 1787 bet. WILLIAM ADIR and MARY his wife
of Camden Dist. County of Chester of first part and CLAUDIAS
CHARVIN of the other part witness that WILLIAM ADIR the sum of 235
pounds of money paid to him by CLAUDIAS CHARVIN do grant and sell unto
CHARVIN his heirs and assigns forever all that tract of land lying
on the south fork of Fishing Creek containing 280 acres it being the

Cont'd from page 28:
lowest half of the tract of 560 acres granted 29 March 1753 to ABRAHAM
KIRKENDALL all conveyed to WILLIAM ADIR and MARY his wife by the sd.
ABRAHAM KIRKENDALL date 15 May 1754. Signed: WILLIAM ADIR, MARY ADIR.
Wit: JO. PALMER, JOHN WILLIAMS, EDWARD LACEY, JAMES MC NEIL.

Page 390: Deed made 1 June 1780 bet. MICHAEL DICKSON of Camnden Dist.,
         planter of the first part and WILLIAM MILLER, yeoman of
the other part witness that MICHAEL DICKSON in consideration of the
sum of 10 shillings to him and in hand paid WILLIAM MILLER. MICHAEL
DICKSON do sell WILLIAM MILLER a tract of land 150 acres lying on Rocky
Creek. Signed: MICHAEL DICKSON. Wit: THOMAS CAMRON, CHARLES MILLER,
JAMES MC CAW. (Note: name written MILLER, MILLIN, MILLAN)

Page 392: Deed made 2 June 1780 bet. MICHAEL DICKSON of Camden Dist.
         planter of the first part and WILLIAM MILLAN of the other
part by a certain grant dated 16 April 1765 in the fifth year of King
George III did give to MICHAEL DICKSON 300 acres on both sides of Rocky
Creek (then Mecklenburg County, North Carolina between Catawba River
and Broad River at the board of the Saluda Road now in the district
of Camden.) Signed: MICHAEL DICKSON. Wit: THOMAS CAMRON, CHARLES MILLIN,
JAMES MC CAW.

Page 395: Deed made 3 Feb. 1783 bet. JOHN PUGH of Camden Dist. and
         THOMAS WALLACE of the Dist. aforesaid. JOHN PUGH in consider-
ation of 500 pounds to him in hand paid of the State of aforesaid by
the above named THOMAS WALLACE conveyed and made over unto the sd.
WALLACE his heirs and assigns forever did bargain and sell unto the
sd. THOMAS WALLACE a tract of land lying on head of Sandy River granted
to JOHN PUGH by his Excellency William Tryon Governor of N. C. 100
acres being part of a tract of 300 acres. Signed: JOHN PUGH. Wit: JAMES
PEGAN, JOHN (X) WEEK.

Page 397: Deed made 1 Dec. 1787 bet. JAMES MC CLUER of Chester Co.
         of the first part and ROBERT MILLER and MARY MILLER and
HENRY MILLER, planters and spinner of the other part in consideration
of the sum of 15 pounds sterling to the sd. ROBERT MILLER, MARY MILLER,
HENRY MILLER, in hand pd. by the sd. JAMES MC CLUER hath bargain do
give grant convey unto the sd. JAMES MC CLUER his heirs and assigns
forever 25 acres situate in Chester Co. on waters of Rocky Creek being
part of a tract of land which formerly contained 150 acres. Signed:
ROBERT MILLER, MARY (X) MILLER, HENRY MILLER. Wit: SAMUEL LOWRY, ANDREW
MILLER.

Page 399: Deed made 9 Nov. 1787 bet. JOHN TURNER of Fairfield County
         of first part and JOHN HALMAN of the other part of a certain
grant dated 18 June 1763 did grant unto JOHN LEE a plantation on a
tract of land containing 50 acres lying in Craven Co. on the waters
of Rocky Creek bounded at that time all sides by vacant land granted
released and conveyed to the sd. JOHN HALLMAN his heirs and assigns
forever. Signed: JOHN TURNER (L.S.) Wit: RICH. D. TALIAFERRO, JOHN
BELL.

Page 402: Deed made 9 Nov. 1787 bet. JOHN TURNER of Fairfield Co.
         of the first part and JOHN HALLMAN of the other part that
JOHN TURNER in consideration of the sum of 1 shilling six pence ster-
ling to him in hand paid by the sd. JOHN HALLMAN that the sd. JOHN
TURNER has so bargain and sell unto JOHN HALLMAN 50 acres lying in
Craven Co. on the waters of Rocky Creek at that time bounded on all
sides by vacant land. Signed: JOHN TURNER. Wit: RICHARD TALIAFERRO,
JOHN BELL.

Page 403: Deed made 3 Jan. 1788 bet. JAMES MC CLURE and JEAN his wife
         of Chester Co., planter of the first part and RICHARD GLADNEY
of Fairfield Co. of the other part witness that JAMES MC CLURE and
JEAN his wife for the sum of 10 shillings to him pd. by the sd. RICHARD
GLADNEY do bargain and sell unto RICHARD GLADNEY a tract of land of
100 acres being the half of 200 acres situate lying in Chester Co.
on the waters of Fishing Creek and Rocky Creek on all sides by vacant

Cont'd from page 29:
land. Signed: JAMES MC CLURE. No witness.

Page 405: Deed made 29 Aug. 1787 bet. WILLIAM HUMPHRES of Camden Dist.
in Chester Co. in the state of S. C. of the first part and
JOHN HAIS of the other part witness that WILLIAM HUMPHRES in consideration of 80 pounds sterling paid to him by the sd. JOHN HAYS acknowledged
that WILLIAM HUMPHRES doth grant unto the sd. JOHN HASE 100 acres which
was part of 200 acres granted to JOSEPH BROWN in Chester County on
a small branch leading into Sandy River surveyed 28 March 1767 for
JOHN WILKESON. Signed: WILLIAM HUMPHRES, LUCY HUMPHRES. Wit: ABNER
WILKS, DANIEL JAGGERS, NATHAN JAGGERS.

Page 407: Deed made 10 Jan. 1787 bet. Doctor CLAUDIAS CHARVIN of Chester County of the first part and DANIEL WILLIAM of York
County, Gentleman, of the other part whereas DANIEL WILLIAM hath become
bound with CLAUDIAS CHARVIN unto WILLIAM ADAIR by several bonds payment
of several sums of money he said CLAUDIAS CHARVIN hath granted unto
DANIEL WILLIAMS 280 acres being part of a tract of 570 acres originally
granted to ABRAHAM KIRKENDALL situate in Chester Co. on the south fork
of Fishing Creek. Signed: CLAUDIAS CHARVIN. No witness.

Page 408: To all people and etc. I JOHN SMITH of the county of Chester
greetings - know ye that I JOHN SMITH for and in consideration of the natural love and affection I bear for my son MOSES SMITH
and for other good causes me these and to moving have truly given and
granted and by these presents do give and grant unto MOSES SMITH the
negro man named Fortune and the negro boy named Richard, two cows and
calves and further I do give unto my son MOSES SMITH a small negro
girl named Dinna. Signed: JOHN SMITH. Wit: S. M. BOYD, ANDREW HEMPHILL.

Page 409: I, JOHN SMITH of Chester County greeting - know ye that
I the sd JOHN SMITH for the natural love and affection I
have for my son JOSHUA SMITH and also for other good causes and consideration and me in moving have given and granted JOSHUA SMITH the negro
man named Abram, negro boy Capt., the negro girl named Sibbina and
the young negro boy named Jack. The mare called Liberty. Signed: JOHN
SMITH. Wit: S. M. BOYD, ANDREW HEMPHILL.

Page 411: Deed made 5 April 1788 bet. WILLIAM ARMOUR of Camden Dist.
of first part and JOHN HEREN of the other part for the sum
of 50 pounds of S. C. pd. to WILLIAM ARMOUR the sd. ARMOUR hath granted
unto JOHN HEREN in his actual possession now being by virtue of bargain
and sell to him thereof made for one whole year and to his heirs and
assigns 150 acres in Camden Dist. on the waters of Sandy River and
all the estate title interest use trust possessed what soever of the
sd. WILLIAM ARMOUR, his wife MARY ARMOUR of every part thereof. Signed:
WILLIAM (X) ARMOUR, MARY (X) ARMOUR. Wit: ROBERT COLLINS, SR., ROBERT
(R) COLLINS, JR.

Page 414: Deed made 4 April 1788 bet. WILLIAM ARMOUR of Camden Dist.
of first part and JOHN HEREN of the state aforesaid of the
other part for and in consideration of 10 shillings of money paid by
the sd. JOHN HEREN pd. to sd. WILLIAM ARMOUR he the sd. ARMOUR hath
sold and with a consent of his wife unto the sd. HEREN 150 acres situate
in Camden Dist. on waters of Sandy River. Signed: WILLIAM (A) ARMOUR,
MARY (X) ARMOUR. Wit: ROBERT COLLINS, SR., ROBERT (R) COLLINS, JR.

Page 416: Deed made 13 August 1785 bet. THOMAS RODEN of South Carolina
and the District of Camden of first part and JOHN MOBERLY,
planter of the other part witness at THOMAS RODEN in consideration
of 44 pounds and five shillings sterling now to him paid by the sd.
JOHN MOBERLY doth sell unto JOHN MOBERLY his heirs and assigns 88½
acres as being part of a grant of 200 acres which was granted to JOSEPH
BROWN bearing date 16 January 1772. Signed: THOMAS RODEN, MARY (M)
RODEN. Wit: MOSES HILL, WILLIAM RODEN, LEWIS (X) ROBERT.

Page 418: Deed made 5 February 1787 bet. JOHN DOUGHERTY of Camden
Dist. of the one part and THOMAS RODEN of the other part

Cont'd from page 30:
in consideration of sum of 40 pounds money pd to the sd. JOHN DOUGHERTY
do sell unto THOMAS RODEN in his actual possession 100 acres of land
in Camden Dist. on Welshes Fork the waters of Sandy River bounded all
sides by vacant land when surveyed. Granted to sd. JOHN DOUGHERTY 21
January 1785. Signed: JOHN DOUGHERTY, AGEY (X) DOUGHERTY. Wit: WM.
(A) ARMOUR, MOSES (X) STONE.

Page 419: Deed made 24 February 1787 bet. JOHN DOUGHERTY of Camden
          Dist. of one part and THOMAS RODEN of the other part for
sum of 10 shillings paid by the sd. THOMAS RODEN pd. to the sd. JOHN
DOUGHERTY the receipt of is hereby acknowledged do sell of consent
of wife AGNES DOUGHERTY unto the sd. THOMAS RODEN 100 acres in Camden
District on Welshes Fork the waters of Sandy River bounded all sides
by vacant land when surveyed. Signed: JOHN DOUGHERTY, AGEY (X) DOUGHERTY.
Wit: WM. (A) ARMOUR, MOSES (X) STONE.

Page 423: Deed made 6 February 1787 bet. JOHN DOUGHERTY of state of
          South Carolina Camden District of one part and THOMAS RODEN
of the other part for sum of 10 pounds paid to JOHN DOUGHERTY he the
said JOHN DOUGHERTY hath sold unto the said THOMAS RODEN 100 acres
of land situate in Camden District on waters of Sandy River bounded
on ISAAC TAYLOR and ROBERT LEMON bounded on vacant land. Signed: JOHN
DOUGHERTY, AGEY (X) DOUGHERTY. Wit: WILLIAM (X) ARMOUR, MOSES (X) STONE,
WM. (W) GRISHAM.

Page 426: Deed made 25 February 1787 bet. JOHN DOUGHERTY of Camden
          Dist. of one part and THOMAS RODEN of the other part for
the sum of 10 shillings money of the sd. state by the sd. THOMAS RODEN
will and truly paid to the sd. JOHN DOUGHERTY he the sd. DOUGHERTY
hath sold with consideration of wife AGNES DOUGHERTY unto THOMAS RODEN
100 acres in Camden District on waters of Sandy River. Signed: JOHN
DOUGHERTY, AGEY (X) DOUGHERTY. Wit: WM. (A) ARMOUR, MOSES (X) STONE,
WM. (W) GRISHAM.

Page 428: Deed made 9 February 1788 bet. PETER WILEY of Chester Co.
          of one part and GEORGE AGNEW of the other part for and by
a certain grant bearing date 26 Sept. 1772 did give and grant CALEB
SMITH 100 acres and by the sd. CALEB SMITH for the consideration of
sum of 100 pounds have granted confirmed the sd. plantation of tract
of 100 acres DAVID NICKEL and by the sd. NICKEL for and in consideration of the sum of 240 pounds have granted and confirmed an indenture
bearing date 1 January 1783 unto PETER WILEY containing 100 acres.
Lying on both sides of big Rocky Creek. Signed: PETER (X) WILEY. Wit:
JAMES STINSON, EDWARD STUDMAN.

Page 431: Deed made 8 February 1788 bet. PETER WILEY of Fairfield
          County of one part and GEORGE AGNEW of Chester County of
other part witness that PETER WILEY in consideration of sum of 10 shillings to him in hand paid by the said GEORGE AGNEW he the sd WILEY doth
sell unto AGNEW 100 acres of land lying and being on Big Rocky Creek.
Signed: PETER (X) WILEY. Wit: JAMES STINSON, EDWARD STUDMAN.

Page 433: Deed made 20 November 1787 bet. EDWARD FRANKLIN and RACHEL
          FRANKLIN his wife of Camden District County of Chester of
one part and ANDERSON THOMAS of the other part witness that the sd.
EDWARD FRANKLIN and RACHEL FRANKLIN his wife in consideration of 1000
pounds to them in hand paid doth grant unto ANDERSON THOMAS and to
his heirs and assigns forever. Signed: EDWARD (X) FRANKLIN , RACHEL
FRANKLIN. Wit: JOHN DOYLE, WILLIAM (X) DOYLE, OWEN (X) FRANKLIN.

Page 439: Deed made 5 April 1788 bet. ROBERT GORRELL and AGNES his
          wife of Chester County of one part and REUBEN LACEY of the
other part do sell unto REUBEN LACEY his heirs and assigns 50 acres
known by the name of Gorrells Old Field lying on the road leading from
Loves Ford on Broad River to the Nation ford on Catawba River on waters
of Turkey Creek bounded by vacant land on all sides. Signed: ROBERT
GORRELL, AGNES GORRELL. Wit: WM. MILES, WIL GORRELL, EDWARD LACEY.

Page 441: Deed made 9 April 1788 bet. WILLIAM BROWN of York County of one part and JOHN WALKER late of the County of Chester of the other part witness that WILLIAM BROWN for and in consideration of 60 pounds to him in hand paid by the sd. JOHN WALKER receipt of which is hereby acknowledged he the sd. WILLIAM BROWN hath granted and by these presence do sell unto JOHN WALKER and his heirs 116 acres situate in the state aforesaid on waters of Turkey Creek in the county of Chester being part of 350 acres granted to KATHARINE BROWN dated 23 January 1773 the sd. 116 acres conveyed to WILLIAM BROWN by the sd. KATHARINE BROWN. Signed: WM. BROWN. Wit: EDW. LACEY, JOHN BELL, PAT MC GRIFF.

Page 443: Deed made 13 April 1776 bet. JOHN LAND of the Parish of St. Mark in County of Craven of one part and SAMUEL GRIFFIN of the parish county of the other part by a certain grant dated 16 January 1772 did grant unto JOHN LAND a planter 100 acres in Chester County of foresaid near the head of Sandy River bounded all sides by vacant land. Signed: JOHN LAND. Wit: RALPH (X) GRIFFIN, GEORGE MORRACE, ANDREW HEMPHILL.

Page 445: Deed made 12 April 1776 bet. JOHN LAND of Parish of St. Mark county of Craven in province of South Carolina of one part and SAMUEL GRIFFIN of county and parish aforesaid of other part. Witness for sum of 10 shillings paid by SAMUEL GRIFFIN the receipt whereof is hereby acknowledged. He the sd. JOHN LAND doth sell unto SAMUEL GRIFFIN 100 acres in County of Craven by a certain grant bearing date 16 January 1772 did grant unto JOHN LAND 100 acres near head of Sandy River bounded on all sides by vacant land. Signed: JOHN LAND. Wit: RALPH (X) GRIFFIN, GEORGE MORRIS, ANDREW HEMPHILL.

Page 448: Deed made 9 April 1788 bet. JOHN MILLS, Esq. Coroner of Chester County of one part and JAMES NORTON of the other part witness that JAMES NORTON in the County Court of Chester did implead JOHN ALLAN administrator of estate of THOMAS BURNS, deceased, on an action of death. In July Court 1787 did obtain judgement in the same court for his debt and cost seemed to be levied off the goods and chattels of the sd. JOHN ALLAN whereas JOHN MILL Coroner did seize and after due and legal notice given exposed to public sale on 15 Oct. last a certain tract of land containing about 100 acres on Rocky Creek and bounded on all sides by vacant land when originally granted to THOMAS BURNS the 19th September 1758. Signed: JOHN MILLS, Coroner Chester County. Wit: DAVID HUNTER, WILLIAM MOORE.

Page 450: Deed made 9 April 1788 bet. WILLIAM YOUNG of South Carolina Camden District Chester County of one part and EZEKIAL SANDERS of the other part witness that sd. YOUNG of the the sum of 50 pounds whereof the receipt he the sd. YOUNG did hereby acknowledge do sell and make over to EZEKIAL SANDERS his heirs and assigns 377 acres. Signed: WILLIAM (X) YOUNG, ELENDER (+) YOUNG. Wit: W. EMERY, THOMAS (X) SANDERS, CHAS. DE GRAFFENREID.

Page 452: Deed made 19 April 1788 bet. WILLIAM YOUNG of Camden Dist. Chester County of one part and CHRISTOPHER DE GRAFFENREID of the other part witness at the sd. YOUNG of the sum of 70 pounds pd. by the sd. DE GRAFFENREID the sd. YOUNG hath granted and confirmed to sd. CHRISTOPHER DE GRAFFENREID his heirs and assigns one certain tract of land lying in Chester County Camden District containing 250 acres beginning at Starns Branch. Signed: WILLIAM (+) YOUNG, ELENDER (+) YOUNG (looks like his and hers for Elender). Wit: WM. EMBRY, THOMAS (+) SANDERS, EZEKL (X) SANDERS.

Page 453: Deed made 10 April 1788 bet. NATHAN JAGGERS of Chester Co. of one part and JOHN JAGGERS of the other part for the sum of 100 pounds pd. by JOHN JAGGERS doth discharge himself of the ..... to the sd. JOHN JAGGERS his heirs executors and everyone of them forever by these presence that the sd. NATHAN JAGGERS doth confirm unto the sd. JOHN JAGGERS for one whole year for the consideration of 100 pounds. Signed: NATHAN JAGGERS. Wit: PETER SEELEY, SARAH SEELEY, ELENDER (X) SEELEY.

Page 457:   Deed made 9 April 1788 bet. NATHAN JAGGERS of Chester County
            of one part and JOHN JAGGERS of the other part witness for
sum of 100 pounds to me in hand paid by sd JOHN JAGGERS the receipt
whereof is hereby acknowledged doth sell unto JOHN JAGGERS his heirs
executors and assigns 130 acres in Chester County lying on North side
of Big Rocky Creek. Signed: NATHAN GAGGERS (His (G) mark) Wit: PETER
SEELEY, ELENDER (+) SEELEY, SARAH SEELEY.

Page 459:   Deed made 9 April 1788 bet. WILLIAM YOUNG of Camden District
            Chester County of one part and JOHN YOUNG of the other part
witness that said WILLIAM YOUNG for sum of 23 pounds paid by the sd.
JOHN YOUNG he the sd. WILLIAM YOUNG doth sell unto JOHN YOUNG his heirs
and assigns forever 100 acres lying in Chester County to a branch called
Stuns Branch. Signed: WILLIAM (+) YOUNG, ELENDER (+) YOUNG. Wit: W.
EMBRY, CHR. S. D. GRAFFENREID, EZEKIEL SANDERS.

Page 461:   Deed made 6 March 1788 bet. JOHN MORRYS and MARY his wife
            of Chester County of one part and BENJAMIN MORRIS of the
other part did grant unto THOMAS MORRIS 350 acres lying on waters of
Rocky Creek then Craven County bounded on lines with WILLIAM STROUD's
land at another side ALEXANDER RATTERUY(?) land and all other sides
by vacant land this indenture witness that JOHN MORRIS and MARY MORRIS
his wife being the right lawful heirs of THOMAS MORRIS, deceased and
having the full right and claim of 350 acres of land by heirship doth
for 100 pounds to him paid by the sd. BENJAMIN MORRIS have granted
unto BENJAMIN MORRIS now in his actual possession 300 acres being part
of the foresaid 350 acres. Signed: JOHN (X) MORRISS, MARY (X) MORRISS.
Wit: ANDREW HEMPHILL, BENJAMIN SMITH, JOHN FURGURSON. (Note: surname
is spelled MORRYS, MORRIS, MORRISS).

Page 464:   Deed made 5 March 1788 bet. JOHN MORRISS and MARY MORRISS
            his wife of one part in County of Chester and BENJAMIN MORRIS
of other part witness that JOHN MORRISS and MARY his wife for the sum
of 10 shillings paid by BENJAMIN MORRIS is hereby acknowledged by sd.
JOHN MORRISS and MARY his wife doth sell unto BENJAMIN MORRIS 300 acress
being part of 350 acres granted unto THOMAS MORRISS. Signed: JOHN (X)
MORRISS, MARY (+) MORRISS. Wit: ANDREW HEMPHILL, BENJAMIN SMITH, JOHN
FURGUSON.

Page 467:   Deed made 26 January 1788 bet. JAMES JACK and MARGARET his
            wife of one part and JOHN HAYS, blacksmith of the other
part for sum of 15 pounds to sd. JAMES JACK and MARGARET his wife paid
by sd. HAYS the payment whereof his hereby acknowledged and for other
good causes and consideration us moving be the sd. JAMES JACK and MARY
his wife did convey unto the sd. JOHN HAYS 100 acres the same being
originally given unto JOSEPH MITCHEL of Mecklenburg, North Carolina
lying on Branch of South fork Fishing Creek between the lands of BROWN
and MILLER. Signed: JAMES JACK. Wit: JOHN DOWNING, ROBERT LUSK.

Page 473:   Deed made 6 May 1780 bet. JAMES BURCHAM, blacksmith of Camden
            District of one part and JAMES BLAIR of the other part by
a certain grant dated 26 July 1774 did grant unto ROBERT MC FADDEN
350 acres in Craven County on a small branch of Fishing creek bounded
NW on land of JAMES FERGUSON, all other sides by vacant land. Signed:
JAS. BURCHAM. Wit: WM. WILEY, WILLIAM HADDEN.

Page 478:   Deed made 25 December 1787 bet. ROBERT PATTON, Esq. and
            SARAH his wife of one part and WILLIAM RICHARDSON DAVIS,
Esq. of state of North Carolina of other part witness that ROBERT PATTON
and SARAH his wife in consideration of sum of 450 pounds paid by WILLIAM
R. DAVIS they the sd. ROBERT PATTON and SARAH his wife hath granted
unto sd. WILLIAM RICHARDSON DAVIS and his heirs all that tract of land
lying in South Carolina formally in the province of North Carolina
and County of Anson on West side of Catawba River granted and surveyed
for JAMES PATTON near his own land. Signed: ROBERT PATTON, SARAH PATTON.
Wit: SAML. LOWRIE, WILLEY BROWN, JOSEPH DAVIS.

Page 481:   Deed made 25 December 1787 bet. ROBERT PATTON, Esq. and
            SARAH his wife of Camden District of one part and WILLIAM

Cont'd from page 33:
RICHARDSON DAVIS, Esq. North Carolina of the other part for the sum
of 100 pounds to sd ROBERT PATTON and SARAH his wife paid by WILLIAM
RICHARDSON DAVIS by the sd. ROBERT PATTON and SARAH his wife do grant
unto DAVIS and his heirs 100 acres in Craven County on West side of
Catawba River, N Patton lands belonging to JAMES PATTON and ROBERT
PATTON as appears by a grant obtained by PRUDENCE PATTON from the Gover-
nor of South Carolina. Signed: ROBERT PATTON, SARAH PATTON. Wit: SAML.
LOWRIE, WILLEY BROWN, JOSEPH DAVIS.

Page 489: Deed made 5 January 1788 bet. PLEASANT WILLIAM FARGUSON
           and MARY FARGUSON widow of JAMES FARGUSON of Chester County
of one part and JOHN FARGUSON of other part did grant unto JAMES FAR-
GUSON 200 acres in Craven County now Chester County on SW side of the
Catawba River on the head of two small branches of Rocky Creek bounded
on all sides by vacant land. Signed: PLEASANT WM. FARGUSON, MARY (+)
FARGUSON. Wit: WILLIAM WYLEY, JAMES ADAM.

Page 492: Deed made 15 February 1788 bet. WILLIAM FORD, SR. of Chester
           County of one part and WILLIAM FORD, JR. his son of the
other part witness that WILLIAM FORD, SR. for natural love and affection
which he hath to WILLIAM FORD his son and for the better maintenance
and livelihood of him the sd. WILLIAM FORD, JR. doth grant to sd. WIL-
LIAM FORD, JR. 200 acres late the property of WILLIAM STORMENT's line
on little Rocky Creek and in the occupation of GINNENS ALLEN. Signed:
WILLIAM FORD, SR. Wit: JAMES (X) MORRIS, MARY (+) FORD.

Page 494: Know that I SAMUEL HUGHEY of Chester County for the sum
           of 100 pounds paid to me by MARK EDWARDS, SR do sell unto
MARK EDWARDS one sorrel mare and two bay geldings and etc. Signed:
SAM HUGHEY. Wit: EZEKIEL SANDERS, JAMES EDWARD, WILLIAM SHARPE.

Page 495: Deed made 16 April 1788 bet. DAVIS HOPKINS, Esq. of Chester
           County of one part and NATHAN SIMS of other part witness
that DAVIS HOPKINS for 200 pounds paid money in to his hand paid of
so secured to be paid by NATHAN SIMS 150½ acres being part of a tract
of 321 acres granted to DAVIS HOPKINS, Esq. situate in the District
of Camden on waters of Sandy River. Signed: D. HOPKINS. Wit: JAMES
GLENN, THOMAS GLENN.

Page 496: Deed made 24 August 1787 bet. WILLIAM ARNOLD and AGNES his
           wife of County of York one part and JOHN FEARES* of Chester
County, blacksmith of other part for the sum of 70 pounds in hand paid
unto WILLIAM ARNOLD and AGNES his wife by the sd. JOHN FAIRESS* do
grant unto JOHN PARRISS* his heirs and etc. a certain tract of land
in Chester county on waters of Fishing Creek and join lands of DAVID
HUNTER on N and the W originally SAMUEL HAMLETON. Signed: WILLIAM ARNOLD
and AGNES (+) ARNOLD. Wit: DAVID HUNTER, ELIJAH BROWN, LEWIS THOMPSON.
(*surname spelled each of three ways).

Page 502: Deed made 5 February 1788 bet. CHRISTOPHER MORGAN and MARTHA
           his wife, planter of Chester County of one part and GEORGE
MORRISS, planter of the other part witness that for 26 pounds to the
sd. CHRISTOPHER MORGAN and MARTHA his wife doth hereby acknowledge
and discharge the sd. GEORGE MORRISS his heirs and etc. doth convey
unto GEORGE MORRISS for sd. CHRISTOPHER MORGAN and MARTHA his wife
for one whole year for consideration of 10 shillings 50 acres being
a part of ......DARRELL of a tract of land lying on Rocky Creek given
and granted unto HUGH MONTGOMERY and convey unto a certain MOSES REAVES
(part of above is missing). Signed: CHRISTOPHER (X) MORGAN. Wit: ANDREW
HEMPHILL, ROBERT HEMPHILL.

Page 505: Deed made 8 July 1788 bet. JOHN COUPER*, SR of Mecklenburg
           County and THOMAS GERRET of Rock Creek in Chester County
planter of other part whereas by certain grant JOHN COUPER, SR. 200
acres on waters of Rocky Creek then in Craven County now Chester County
bounded on land of CHARLES KITCKINGS, JOHN WEIR, THOMAS MORTAN and
vacant land. Signed: JOHN (his mark a written "L") COUPER* Wit: JOHN
MILLS, JAMES KELL, ROBERT JAMESON. (* spelled both ways).

Page 509: Deed made 16 June 1788 bet. ROBERT LEMONS of Camden Dist.,
          planter of one part and GEORGE HEAD, planter of the other
part witness that ROBERT LEMONS for the sum of 100 pounds paid in hand
are assumed to be by GEORGE HEAD his heirs etc. do bargain to sd. GEORGE
HEAD one certain tract of land lying on waters of Sandy River. Signed:
ROBERT LEMONS. Wit: JAS. HUEY, JOSEPH TIMMS, GOO. MC LOAN(?)

Page 511: Know that we JOHN MILLS, JR. and EDWARD LACEY and JOHN WALKER
           are bound unto the treasurers of the state of South Carolina
of 1000 pounds in JOHN MILLS made default in the underwritten condition.
The condition of the above obligation is such that if JOHN MILLS shall
well and truly abide by absence and perform his duty as a general tax
collector of Chester County. Signed: JOHN MILLS, EDWARD LACEY, JOHN
(J) WALKER. No witness.

Page 512: Deed made 15 May 1787 bet. SAMUEL CARTER of Camden District
           of one part and RANDEL CARTER of other part for the sum
of 40 pounds paid to sd. SAMUEL CARTER hath conveyed unto sd. RANDEL
CARTER 107 acres of land situate in Camden District on waters of Sandy
River it being part of a tract granted to sd. SAMUEL CARTER. Signed:
SAMUEL CARTER, ELIZABETH (X) CARTER. Wit: WILLIAM CARTER, MOSES HILL,
JOHN SEOF(?)

Page 518: Deed made 9 July 1788 bet. JAMES RAMSEY of Chester County
           of one part, planter and JAMES MC CLIHIN(?) of other part,
planter for the sum of 5 pounds to JAMES RAMSEY in hand pd. by JAMES
MC CLIKINA(?) doth grant unto JAMES MC CLIKINA his heirs 20 acres lying
in Chester County on South fork of Fishing Creek join and between lands
granted WILLIAM JONES and JOHN PRICE. Signed: JAMES RAMSEY. Wit: JOHN
PRICE, THOS. MOORE.

Page 520: Deed made 9 July 1788 bet. JAMES MC CLEHENA and WILLIAM
           MC CLEHENA of Chester County of one part, planters and JAMES
RAMSEY of other part for the sum of 5 pounds to sd. JAMES MC CLEHENA
and WILLIAM MC CLEHENA in hand pd. by JAMES RAMSEY have bargained and
doth grant to sd. JAMES RAMSEY his heirs and assigns 20 acres in Chester
County on South fork of Fishing creek join and between lands granted
to JOHN PRICE and WILLIAM JONES. Signed: JAMES MC CLEHENA, WILLIAM
MC CLEHENA. Wit: JOHN PRICE, THOS. MOORE.

Page 531: Deed made 7 September 1787 bet. JOHN CARSON of Rocky Creek
           Chester County, planter of one part and ANDREW STEVENSON,
planter of other part by a certain grant did give and grant unto JOHN
CARSON 100 acres in Craven County but now Chester County on a small
branch of Rocky Creek and to North East by land surveyed for DUGALL
BALLANTINE South East for MARY HARBISON all other sides by vacant land.
Signed: JOHN CARSON, ELIZABETH CARSON. Wit: JAMES MC LONSON, JAMES
KILL(?), SARAH (X) MISKELLY.

Page 537: Deed made 4 July 1788 bet. PETER LEMBY of Fairfield County
           of one part and JAMES MANNIN GORE of Chester County of the
other part do bargain unto JAMES MANNIN GORE 294 acres situate on deep
lick creek of Sandy River in Chester County granted to PETER LEMBY
5 September 1785. Signed: PETER (PL) LEMBY. Wit: THMAS LEWIS, ELIJAH
MAJOR.

Page 539: Deed made 28 June 1788 bet. DAVID HOPKINS of Chester County
           of one part and JOHN RICHARDSON of Fairfield County of the
other part witness that DAVID HOPKINS for 20 pounds sterling to him
paid in hand by JOHN RICHARDSON do confirm unto JOHN RICHARDSON his
heirs and assigns one certain tract of land situate on branches of
Jones Creek. Signed: DAVID HOPKINS. Wit: PAUL C. ABNEY, T. (?) WATSON.

Page 540: Deed made 5 February 1787 bet. JOHN WILKISON of Orangeburg
           District of one part and JAMES ADAIR of Camden District
of other part do convey 200 acres lying on Sandy River in Chester County
by letter granted 13 October 1772 to Mr. JOHN HITCHCOCK. Signed: JOHN
WILKISON. Wit: JOHN PRISCOUT(?), ENOCH T. SEAL, JAMES FOWLER.

Page 542: Deed made 4 October 1788 bet. JAMES SHEPHERD of Wilkes County Georgia of one part and JOHN TERRY of Chester County of other part witness that JAMES SHEPHERD for the sum of 400 pounds paid by JOHN TERRY do sell unto JOHN TERRY 450 acres situate in Chester County on waters of Sandy River unto sd. JOHN TERRY his heirs/assigns forever it being a tract granted dated to DAVID MORROW and by his conveyed to WILLIAM REY and from the sd. REY to JOHN WARREN and from sd. WARREN to JAMES SHEPHERD. Signed: JAMES SHEPHERD. Wit: WM. GASSAWAY MORROW, GEORGE (X) BLISITT.

Page 544: Deed made 6 August 1788 bet. PATRICK HAMBLETON of Chester County, yeoman of one part and DANIEL COOK of County and state aforesaid, taylor, of the other part. Signed: PATRICK (X) HAMBLETON (also written HARBISON). Wit: THOS. WHITESIDE, ANTHONY MC MANS.

Page 547: Know all men JOHN LOVE of Camden District of South Carolina, taylor, am firmly bound to ADAM MC COOL, WILLIAM GASTON and JAMES LOVE they and each of them in the just sum of 5000 pounds sterling unto them their heirs and assigns, etc. the payment whereof will truly be made. Signed: JOHN LOVE. Wit: MARGARET (M) DAVID, JANE LOVE.

Page 548: Deed made 17 July 1788 bet. JAMES DOUGHARTY of Orangeburg District of one part and JOHN COLSON of Chester County of the other part witness that JAMES DOUGHARTY for 50 pounds sterling money in hand paid doth sell unto the sd. JOHN COLSON his heirs, etc. 500 acres on Welshes fork of Sandy River and was granted to sd. JOHN DOUGHARTY. Signed: JOHN DOUGHARTY. Wit: THOS. JENKINS, JOHN (X) COLVIN, JR.

Page 549: Know that I, ALEXANDER BROWN of Fishing Creek in Chester County, planter do appoint my trusted friend JOHN MILLS, JR. of Chester County my attorney for me and in my name to demand or receive from all and every person or persons in the sd. county and state what money or other property due me in my name and in the name of ALEXANDER BROWN, SR. in sd. county of late, etc. Signed: ALEXANDER BROWN. Wit: MICHAEL DICKSON, JOSEPH LYNN.

Page 551: Deed made 2 October 1779 bet. DANIEL COOK of Camden District Craven County, taylor, of one part and JOSEPH BOOTH, planter of the other part did grant unto DANIEL COOK 100 acres in Craven County on the waters of Fishing Creek and is sd. to be bounded South West by WILLIAM MC FADDEN land, South East by vacant land, North West survey for CHARLES STRONG and North East by an old land and all other sides by vacant land. Signed: DANL. COOK. Wit: ROBERT MARTIN, WILLIAM LORD.

Page 544: Deed made (?) September 1788 bet. HUGH GASTON and his wife MARTHA of Chester County, planter of one part and JERRED EDWARDS of other part did grant unto HUGH GASTON 100 acres now County of Chester on Fishing Creek joining lands of JERRED EDWARDS, deceased. Signed: HUGH GASTON, MARTHA GASTON. No witness.

Page 556: Deed made 2 September 1788 bet. JOHN SADLER of one part and JOHN OWIN of the other part witness that JOHN SADLER for the sum of 40 pounds paid by JOHN OWIN is hereby acknowledged for other good causes moving have granted bargained sold and confirmed and make over all that part of land to JOHN SADLER by William Tryon, Governor of North Carolina containing 300 acres except 200 acres made over to JOHN PUGH by a deed where he now lives remain part of 100 acres WILLIAM BANK formerly lived in Chester County. Signed: JOHN SADLER, MARY SADLER. Wit: DAVID OWIN, WILLIAM SADLER.

End of Deed Book A

Page 1:   Indenture made 21 March 1785 bet. WILLIAM COLLINS of Rocky
            Creek Craven County Camden District, blacksmith of one part
and JAMES KELL, weaver of the other part by a certain grant dated 18
August 1763 in the third year of King of Britain do grant unto JOHN
WALKER a plantation a part of land containing 50 acres situated on
Rocky Creek a branch of Catawba River fallen in on the west thereof
bounded on all sides on vacant land. The sd. 50 acres as aforesaid
to WILLIAM COLLINS by lease and release in the year 1776 "Therefore
and unto belonging here in before granted unto the sd. JAMES KELL his
heirs and assigns forever and he the sd. WILLIAM COLLINS doth hereby
for himself his heirs etc. do agree with sd. JAMES KELL his heirs and
assigns." Wit: JOHN BELL, JOHN KELL, ELIJAH DAVIS. Signed: WILLIAM
COLLINS.

Page 3:   Indenture made 18 September 1788 bet. ADAM WILLIAMSON of
            Chester County of one part and HANNAH EVANS of the other
part witness that ADAM WILLIAMSON in the sum of fifty five pounds sterling paid by HANNAH EVANS her heirs and assigns 227 acres situated
in Camden District on waters of Sandy River east side of Broad River
joining land granted to OWEN EVANS and joining land granted to JAMES
FORGESSON likewise joining land belonging to JAMES MC CARTER being
part of a tract of land containing 532 acres laid out unto JOHN EVANS
grant being dated 5 June 1786. Wit: MARY EVANS, OWEN EVANS, ELIZABETH
EVANS. Signed: ADAM WILLIAMSON.

Page 4:   Indenture made 24 March 1787 bet. JOHN EVANS of Chester
            County of one part and ADAM WILLIAMSON of the other part
witnessed that sd. JOHN EVANS for the sum of fifty pounds sterling
money paid by sd. ADAM WILLIAMSON do sell unto ADAM WILLIAMSON his
heirs and assigns 227 acres situated in Camden District on waters of
Sandy River east side of Broad River joining land to OWEN EVANS joining land granted to JAMES FERGUSON likewise joining land belonging
to JAMES MC CARTER being a part of a tract containing 532 acres land
conveyed unto sd. JOHN EVANS grant dated 5 June 1786. Wit: OWEN EVANS,
AGNES (X) EVANS, ELIZABETH EVANS. Signed: JOHN EVANS.

Page 5:   Indenture made 6 October 1788 bet. JAMES HUEY of Chester
            County of one part and MAJOR GRISHAM of the other part wit-
nessed that sd. JAMES HUEY and SARAH HUEY his wife for the sum of two
hundred pounds paid by sd. MAJOR GRISHAM to the sd. JAMES HUEY and
SARAH HUEY do grant unto sd. MAJOR GRISHAM his assigns etc. 100 acres
which was granted to EDWARD WILSON and from sd. WILSON to DENNIS CARROLL
and from CARROLL to JOHN WOOD, JR. and from WOOD to JAMES HUEY and
SARAH HUEY to MAJOR GRISHAM the sd. acres situated on waters of Sandy
River. Wit: ELIJAH NUNN, JOHN FRANKLIN, JOHN (R) ROGERS. Signed: JAMES
HUEY, SARAH HUEY.

Page 6:   Indenture made 12 July 1788 bet. JOHN HAYES of Chester Co.
            of one part and JAMES HAYES of other part in consideration
of one hundred pounds paid by sd. JAMES HAYES the sd. HAYES hereby
acknowledges to have sold and conveyed unto JAMES HAYES his assigns,
etc. one hundred acres being a part of 200 acres granted to JOSEPH
BROWN in Chester County on Rocky Branch River into Sandy River survey
28 March 1767 by JOHN WILLIAMSON. Wit: EDMOND LEA, JACOB DUNNIGAN,
THOMAS GORE. Signed: JOHN (N) HAYES.

Page 7:   Indenture made 17 September 1780 bet. JOHN LOVE of Chester
            County of one part and JAMES LOVE, JR. of the other part
witnessed that JOHN LOVE for the sum of five pounds sterling money
to him in hand pd. by sd. JAMES LOVE his assigns etc. a tract of land
on Broad River and Turkey Creek being part of three tracts of land
granted to JOHN LOVE 4 December 1771, 5 June 1787, 29 April 1768 by
Governor of South Carolina containing 138 acres beginning at mouth
of Turkey Creek down Broad River to a black oak tree. Wit: WILLIAM
GASTON, CALEB BALDWIN, WILLIAM LOVE. Signed: JOHN LOVE.

Page 8:   Indenture made 17 September 1788 bet. JOHN LOVE of Chester

Cont'd from page 37:
County of one part and JOHN JAMES LOVE of the other part
in consideration of the sum of five pounds paid by JOHN JAMES LOVE
doth grant to JOHN JAMES LOVE his assigns etc. a tract of land bounded
on waters of Turkey Creek being part of two tracts of land granted
to sd. JOHN LOVE by Governor of North Carolina 15 February 1764, the
other by the Governor of South Carolina in 1768 containing 84 acres.
Wit: WILLIAM GASTON, CALEB BALDWIN, JAMES LOVE. Signed: JOHN LOVE

Page 9:   Indenture made 31 March 1788 bet. ROBERT HARPER and MARGARET
his wife of Chester County State of South Carolina, silversmith of one part and JOHN HAYES of county and state aforesaid of the
other part for the sum of ten pounds to sd. ROBERT HARPER and MARGARET
his wife. No witnesses. Signed: ROBERT HARPER.

Page 10:   Indenture made 31 March 1788 bet. ROBERT HARPER and MARGARET
his wife of Chester County, silversmith of one part and
JOHN HAYES, silversmith of the other part in consideration of ten pounds
sterling to sd. ROBERT HARPER and MARGARET his wife in hand pd. by
JOHN HAYES doth grant and convey unto sd. JOHN HAYES his heirs forever
14 acres half situated in South Fork of Fishing Creek being part of
142 acres granted to sd. ROBERT HARPER 1 September 1785. No witnesses.
Signed: ROBERT HARPER.

Page 12:   Indenture made 22 April 1788 bet. JOHN HAYES, blacksmith
of Chester County of one part and ROBERT HARPER of sd. county
of the other part for consideration of ten shillings to sd. JOHN HAYES
pd. by ROBERT HARPER for other good causes and considerations him hereunto moving the sd. JOHN HAYES doth grant unto ROBERT HARPER his heirs
and assigns 51 acres situated and lying on waters of South Fork of
Fishing Creek north side of sd. creek Chester County. Wit: JOHN MILLS,
MARY MILLS. Signed: JOHN HAYES.

Page 14:   Indenture made 18 December 1779 bet. JAMES FLETCHALL of
Camden District of one part and JOSEPH DAVIS of the other
part in sum of 406 pounds and 5 shillings doth acquiesce and forever
discharge and release him sd. JOSEPH DAVIS his heirs, etc. doth grant
and confirm to him the sd. JOSEPH DAVIS his heirs, etc. all that parcel
of land lying on South of lower side of South Fork of Sandy River in
the aforesaid District granted to JAMES FLETCHALL by certain grant
dated 22 October 1768. Wit: ROBERT (X) SAUNDERS, THOMAS (X) GORE. Signed
by: JAMES FLETCHALL.

Page 15:   Know all men that I, JOHN RAST of Orangeburg District, a
planter, do sell a negro man named Abram unto JOHN FRANKLYN
of Charleston District and do defend the sd. negro man against all
and any claims wherein and agree to give up my right of ownership to
sd. negro man to JOHN FRANKLYN and his heirs forever, dated 6 May 1788.
Signed: JOHN (X) RAST.

Page 15:   Know all men that I, MANUEL POWELL of Camden District, a
planter, am held and firmly bound unto ISOM and JOSEPH POWELL
in the sum of 5000 pounds dated 8 December 1777. The above bonded MANUEL
POWELL shall well and truly make a title to sd. ISOM & JOSEPH POWELL
for a certain plantation lying on south side of Rocky Creek and both
sides of Turkey Branch bounded by WILLIAMSON land and MOSES REAVES
late the property of DAVIS POWELL, deceased. Wit: HUGH MONTGOMERY,
WILLIAM HARDIN, JOHN MONTGOMERY. Signed: MANUEL (X) POWELL.

Page 16:   Indenture made 16 July 1788 bet. MARTHA LAMANDS and ROBERT
LAMANDS of one part and SAMUEL LACEY of the other part for
the sum of 30 pounds sterling paid by sd. LACEY to sd. MARTHA & ROBERT
LAMANDS have granted and confirmed to sd. SAMUEL LACEY his heirs for-
ever 300 acres of land lying in Chester County on waters of Sealy's
fork on Sandy River and grant patton(sic) to JAMES LAMANDS 5 May 1773.
Wit: JAMES FOWLER, JOHN GILL, AGNES GILL. Signed: MARTHA (X) LAMANDS,
ROBERT LAMANDS.

Page 17:   Know that I, JOHN CARSON of Chester County for good causes

38

Cont'd from page 38:
hereto moving have appointed PHILIP WALKER of Chester County
my attorney to ask and receive from all persons indebted to me and
ANDREW STEVENSON on bond in the hand of WILLIAM ARCHER. Wit: JON MC
DONALD, L. R. ISBELL. Signed: JOHN CARSON.

Page 19: Indenture made 9 October 1786 bet. THOMAS BAKER FRANKLIN
of Chester County of one part and JOHN HAYES of the other
part witnessed that THOMAS BAKER FRANKLIN for the sum of 40 pounds
sterling pd. by sd. HAYES 150 acres lying on east and north and west
sides of sd. plantation. Wit: WILLIAM BOYD, JOHN FRANKLIN, ABRAHAM
(A) MILLER. Signed: THOMAS BAKER FRANKLIN.

Page 20: Know that I, EDWARD LACEY, Sheriff of Chester County by
virtue of two executives put into my hand suits of FIELDING
WOODRUFF and JOHN EWART viz. THOMAS MOORE have leveyed on an agreeable
to law by public sale 10 July past sold to JOHN WALKER, JR. a negro
boy Prince taken for property of sd. MOORE for 30 pounds sterling dated
8 October 1788. No witnesses. Signed: EDWARD LACEY.

Page 21: Indenture made 2 December 1788 bet. ZACHARIAH ROBERTS of
Chester County Camden District of one part and ALLEN DE-
GRAFFENREID of the other part for the sum of 100 pounds from sd. DE-
GRAFFENREID to sd. ROBERTS the sd. ROBERTS hath granted to these presence do sell and convey unto sd. DEGRAFFENREID in his actual possession
by virtue of bargain and sell to him hereof made by sd. ROBERTS for
one whole year. 300 acres more or less being half of a tract of land
containing 600 acres originally granted to JOHN HITCHCOCK from North
Carolina bearing date 3 February 1754 and from sd. HITCHCOCK to MARY
his wife of sd. ROBERTS to her and her heirs forever. Wit: WM. EMBRIE,
RICHD. DAVIS, ZEPH ROBERT. Signed: ZACHARIAH ROBERTS, MARY ROBERTS.

Page 23: Indenture made 6 January 1789 bet. THOMAS HUSTON of Chester
County of one part and ELLIOTT LEE of the other part witnessed that sd. THOMAS HUSTON in consideration of sum of 200 pounds money
pd. by sd. ELLIOTT LEE the sd. THOMAS HUSTON doth acknowledge sd. sum
and by these presence doth grant unto sd. ELLIOTT LEE his heirs and
assigns forever a tract parcel of land containing 150 acres situated
and being on Saluda Road in the dry fork of Saluda Creek in Craven
County now Chester County bounding 2 lines on ROBERT WALKER's land
on other side vacant. Wit: J. A. Y. ARILY, SAML. BROWN. Signed: THOMAS
HUSTON.

Page 24: Indenture made 28 December 1788 bet. MICHAEL HART of the
State of North Carolina County of Lincoln (yeoman) of one
part and WILLIAM SLEEKER, JR. son of GEORGE SLEEKER, deceased of the
other part and EDWARD WHITE and AGNES SLEEKER executrix of sd. GEORGE
SLEEKER to their care do confer unto sd. WILLIAM SLEEKER, JR. 200 acres
of land. Wit: ROBERT WHITE, THOMAS NEELY. Signed: MICHAEL (X) HART.

Page 26: Indenture made 17 March 1786 bet. MARGARET BARNET widow
and executrix of JOHN BARNET, deceased of Camden District
of one part and STETH FENNALL, planter of the other part witnessed
by a certain grant dated 25 September 1754 under the hand of Honorable
Mathew Rowan Commissioner over the State of North Carolina did grant
unto CASPER SLEAGER 768 acres sd. traact conveyed unto ARCHIBALD ELLIOTT
and released to WILLIAM MC KINNEY 150 acres sold and released 150 acres
to JOHN BARNET, deceased to REBECCA BARNET, deceased by bond to make
a right to sd. 150 acres of land sd. REBECCA BARNET, deceased will
sd. land to her son WILLIAM BARNET who sold the same to SETH FENNALL.
Wit: WILLIAM WILEY, BENJAMIN RIVES, JOHN (IS) STUDM.T(?) Signed: MAR-
GARET BARNET.

Page 29: Indenture made 6 January 1789 bet. THOMAS JENKINS of Chester
County of one part and JOHN SEALY of the other part witnessed
that THOMAS JENKINS for sum of 85 pounds to be pd. by sd. JOHN SEALY
his heirs and etc. do confirm unto JOHN SEALY his heirs and assigns
100 acres bounded to south west by JOHN SEALY land all other sides
vacant land as approved by a certain grant dated 3 June 1766. No wit-

Cont'd from page 39:
nesses shown. Signed: THOMAS JENKINS.

Page 30:   Indenture made 29 December 1788 bet. GEORGE BISHOP of one
            part of Chester County and JOHN ABERNATHY late of York County
of the other part witnessed that sd. GEORGE BISHOP for the sum of 45
pounds in hand pd. hath conveyed and made over unto sd. JOHN ABERNATHY
his heirs and assigns forever all that land containing 79 acres being a tract of land granted to DAVID MC CREIGHT bearing date 4 May
1775. Wit: WM. LILES, EDWARD LACEY, GEORGE SADLER. Signed: GEORGE (+)
BISHOP.

Page 31:   Indenture made 6 December 1788 bet. JOHN MC COOLL of Union
            county, planter of one part and BENJAMIN LOVE of Chester
County, planter of the other part witness that sd. MC COOLL for the
sum of 10 shillings paid by sd. LOVE he sd. JOHN MC COOLL hath sold
and by these presence doth sell unto sd. BENJAMIN LOVE all that plantation containing 150 acres lying on Turkey Creek in Chester County.
Wit: WILLIAM LOVE, RICHARD LOVE, GARD'R. JAMISON. Signed: JOHN MC COOLL.

Page 33:   Indenture made 29 November 1788 bet. JOHN NUNN of Chester
            County of one part and MAJOR GRISHAM of the other part wit-
nessed that JOHN NUNN for the sum of 10 pounds sterling to him paid
by sd. MAJOR GRISHAM his heirs and etc. doth confirm to sd. GRISHAM
his heirs and etc. one certain tract of land lying on waters Stones
Creek of Sandy River containing 41 acres being part of a tract containing 241 acres. Wit: SARAH BRATT, JAMES HARDWICK, ANN (X) KITCHENS.
Signed: JOHN NUNN, ELIZA (X) NUNN.

Page 35:   Indenture made 28 June 1787 bet. WILLIAM HOGAN of Chester
            County of one part and JAMES DILLARD of the other part where-
as the sd. WILLIAM HOGAN doth sell unto JAMES DILLARD all that plantation 160 acres lying on south side of Sandy River original grant
to JOHN DAVIS by grant dated 1 June 1767 containing 200 acres and conveyed to sd. DAVIS to sd. HOGAN by deed granted 1 December 1784. Wit:
T. LEWIS, WILLIAM HALL, JAMES DILLARD, JR. Signed: WILLIAM HOGAN.

Page 38:   Indenture made 6 October 1785 bet. JAMES NEELY and his wife
            MARTHA of Chester County, planter of one part and ISOM FIELD-
ING of the other part whereas by a certain grant dated 1 September
in year of our Lord 1768 did grant unto WILLIAM GASTON 100 acres on
waters of Fishing Creek in Craven County now Chester County bounded
north west by ELIZABETH CRAIG's land all other sides vacant land. Wit:
THOMAS FARRELL, STETH FENNELL, WILLIAM WILEY. Signed: JAMES NEELEY.

Page 40:   Indenture made 22 December 1788 bet. JAMES HAYS of Chester
            County of one part and JOHN RODEN of the other part witness-
ed that JAMES HAYS for 100 pounds sterling money to him pd. by sd.
JOHN RODEN doth sell unto JOHN RODEN his heirs and assigns forever
100 acres which was part of 200 acres granted to JOSEPH BROWN. Wit:
FRANCIS WILKS, GREENBERRY RODEN, ABART LEE. Signed: JAMES HAYS, PEN-
NESSO (X) HAYS.

Page 41:   Indenture made 5 September 1788 bet. ALEXANDER BROWN, attor-
            ney for ALEXANDER BROWN, SR. late of this place Chester
County,yeoman of one part and JOSEPH LYON, school master of the other
part whereas by a grant dated 29 April 1768 and in the eighth year
of his majesty's reign under the hand of William Tryon, Esq. Governor
over North Carolina did grant unto ALEXANDER BROWN, SR., 290 acres
in Mecklenburg County, North Carolina lying both sides of south fork
of Fishing Creek between lines of GEORGE CRAIG, HENRY CULP, WILLIAM
MILLER, JOHN BOYD and DAVID LEWIS. Wit: JOHN SIMPSON, WILLIAM ELLIOTT.
Signed: ALEXANDER BROWN.

Page 43:   Know that I, ALEXANDER BROWN of Camden District for causes
            me here into moving do appoint ALEXANDER BROWN, JR. of Camden
District my well beloved son my lawful attorney to make all my interest
right and property of certain tract of land whereon I formerly lived.
Wit: WILLIAM MOORE. Signed: ALEXANDER BROWN.

Page 44:   Indenture made 21 August 1777 bet. ALEXANDER PORTER of Meck-
             lenburg County in the province of North Carolina of one
part and JOHN BELL of Craven County, planter of the other part whereas
by a grant dated 4 May 1775 did grant unto ALEXANDER PORTER 100 acres
lying on North fork of Rocky Creek in Craven County. Wit: JAMES BIGHAM,
SAMUEL BIGHAM. Signed: ALEXANDER PORTER.

Page 46:   Indenture made 8 September 1776 bet. ELIZABETH STEEN of
             Craven County Parish of St. Marks, spinner of one part and
WILLIAM MILLEN(?), weaver of the other part witness that ELIZABETH
STEEN do sell unto WILLIAM MILLEN 100 acres lying in Craven County.
Wit: MICHAEL DICKSON, CHARLES MILLER, JOHN COMBEST. Signed: ELIZABETH
(X) STEEN.

Page 48:   Indenture made 9 September 1776 bet. ELIZABETH STEEN of
             Craven County Parish of St. Marks in Camden District, spinner
of one part and WILLIAM MILLEN(?), weaver of the other part whereas
by a certain grant dated 1 March 1775 did grant unto ELIZABETH STEEN
100 acres on branch of Rocky Creek bounded on all sides by vacant land
now witnessed that sd. ELIZABETH STEEN for the sum of 50 pounds paid
by W. MILLEN. Wit: MICHAEL DICKSON, CHARLES MILLER, JOHN COMBEST. Signed
by: ELIZABETH (X) STEEN.

Page 50:   Know that we ROBERT GORRELL, EDWARD LACEY and JOHN PRATT
             of a bond unto the justices of Chester County in the sum
of 100 pounds dated 6 January 1789. Signed: ROBT. GORRELL, EDW. D.
LACEY, JOHN PRATT.

Page 51:   Know that we THOMAS B. FRANKLYN and PATRICK MC GRIFF and
             JAMES GORE abound unto the justices of Chester County in
the sum of 100 pounds money to payment whereof will truly to be made
unto sd. justices their heirs, etc. dated 6 January 1789. Signed: THOMAS
B. FRANKLYN, PATRICK MC GRIFF, JAMES GORE.

Page 52:   Know that we JOHN HAYS, JAMES TRUSSELL of Chester County
             abound unto THOMAS B. FRANKLYN in the sum of 1000 pounds
money to be paid to sd. THOMAS B. FRANKLYN his heirss etc. dated 1
December 1788. (spelled both FRANKLIN & FRANKLYN). Wit: H. CASON, JOHN
FRANKLIN. Signed: JOHN (X) HAYES, JAMES (X) TRUSSELL.

Page 53:   Know that we THOMAS JENKINS, EDWARD LACEY, RICHARD TALIA-
             FERRO, are bond unto justices of Craven County in the sum
of 100 pounds money of South Carolina to payment whereof will and truly
be made unto sd. justices their heirs and successors dated 7 January
1789 whereas THOMAS JENKINS hath obtained license from the Court of
Chester to Tavern at his house in sd. county for space of one year
from date hereof if therefore THOMAS JENKINS shall keep good wholesome
diet, clean lodging, stables and passage for horses, in that case may
and provided also keeping up in his house rates of liquors, diets,
etc. Signed: THOMAS JENKINS, EDWARD LACEY, R. TALIAFERRO.

Page 53:   These may serve to contract that I, SAMUEL MORRIS of 96
             District have bargained and forever acquit any manner of
claim or claims unto EDWARD LACEY of Camden District his heirs and
assigns to a negro wench name Jude about 24 years of age yellow com-
plected has lost part of four fingers off her right hand also the child
she now has named Isaac. Wit: WILLIAM MILLES, JAMES MC NEALE. Signed:
SAMUEL MORRIS.

Page 54:   Know that we THOMAS BRAGG, EDWARD LACEY and R. TALIAFERRO
             are bound to the justices of Chester County of sum of 100
pounds will and truly to be made unto sd. justices their heirs or successors dated 7 Jan. 1789 whereas THOMAS BRAGG hath obtained license
from Court of Chester County to keep Tavern at his house in sd. county
for space of one year the sd. THOMAS BRAGG shall keep good wholesome
diet, clean lodging, stables and pasturage for horses and act up in
every respect. Signed: THOMAS BRAGG, EDWARD LACEY, RICHARD TALIAFERRO.

Page 55:   Indenture made 3 July 1784 bet. PATRICK HAMILTON of Craven
             County, weaver of one part and PETER ROBINSON, Inn Keeper

41

Cont'd from page 41:
of the other part witnessed for sum of 50 guineas sterling paid by
sd. PETER ROBINSON do grant unto sd. PETER ROBINSON his heirs and assigns forever 300 acres bounded on waters of Fishing Creek joining
SAMUEL HAMILTON land all sides vacant land as appear by a plantation
annexed to original grant the same to be granted as bounty to PATRICK
HAMILTON 1 September 1768. Wit: MICHAEL STEDMAN, WILLIAM SMITH.

Page 57:   Indenture made 25 October 1788 bet. JOHN HAYS of Chester
            County of one part and JAMES TRUSSELL of other part witnes-
sed that JOHN HAYS for the sum of 100 pounds to me in hand pd. by JAMES
TRUSSELL I the sd. JOHN HAYS hath sold unto sd. TRUSSELL his heirs
and etc. Wit: JOHN TRUSSELL, ABSALOM HUMPHREYS, JOHN (+) RAMSEY. Signed:
JOHN (X) HAYES. (spelled both HAYS & HAYES).

Page 58:   Indenture made 22 March 1789 bet. SAMUEL NEELY, yeoman of
            Chester County of one part and JOHN CHAMBERS of York County
of the other part whereas by a certain grant dated 21 October 1758
under the hand of his excellency Arthur Dobbs, Esq. in chief of our
province of North Carolina did grant unto WILLIAM NEELY 400 acres suppose at time of survey to be situated in North Carolina Anson County
by by the continuation of the boundary line now in the State of South
Carolina Chester County on both sides of Fishing Creek west side of
Catawba River. No witnesses. Signed: SAMUEL NEELY.

Page 60:   Indenture made 28 October 1787 bet. LEONARD PRATT of Chester
            County of one part and WILLIAM WATSON of the other part
witness that sd. LEONARD PRATT for the sum of 10 pounds sterling to
him in hand paid by sd. WILLIAM WATSON do confer unto WILLIAM WATSON
his heirs one certain tract containing 100 acres according to a grant
dated 9 September 1774 sd land situated on Martins Branch of Sandy
River. Wit: JOHN PRATT, JOHN WATSON. Signed: LEONARD (+) PRATT.

Page 61:   Indenture made 24 March 1789 bet. GEORGE KELSEY of Chester
            County, planter of one part and WILLIAM WHITESIDE, wheel-
wright of the other part by a grant dated 29 April 1768 under the hand
of William Tryon, Governor over North Carolina did grant unto JAMES
SMITH a planter 200 acres supposed at time of survey to be in North
Carolina, Mecklenburg County but now in State of South Carolina on
west side of Catawba River and north side of main Fishing Creek on
both sides of the Rainey Run and both sides of the Wagon Road. Wit:
HUGH WHITESIDE, WM. NEELY, JAS. NEELY. Signed: GEORGE KELSEY.

Page 62:   Indenture made 16 May 1788 bet. THOMAS LEONARD of Chester
            County of one part and WILLIAM CROOK, planter of the other
part witnessed that THOMAS LEONARD for the sum of 10 shillings pd.
to WILLIAM CROOK do acknowledge he the sd. THOMAS LEONARD doth sell
unto WILLIAM CROOK all that plantation of 114 acres and half being
part of a tract of 346 acres and lying on waters of Fishing Creek.
Wit: JOHN MC CREARY, JOHN STEEL. Signed: THOMAS LEONARD.

Page 65:   Indenture made 17 May 1788 bet. THOMAS LEONARD of Chester
            County, planter of one part and WILLIAM CROOK, planter of
the other part by a certain grant dated 23 June 1774 did grant unto
DAVICE LEONARD 346 acres lying in Craven County on a draft of Fishing
Creek north west on CASPER SLEEKER's north east on ARCHIBALD CLARK's
south east on DR. EMER's land. Wit: JOHN MC CREARY, JOHN STEEL. Signed:
THOMAS LEONARD.

Page 67:   Indenture made 1 January 1789 bet. EDWARD LACEY, Esq., High
            Sheriff of Chester County of one part and WILLIAM MC KINNEY
of the other part whereas WILLIAM MC KINNEY in County Court of Fairfield
did implead PETER ROBISON off of a plea of debt 1787. No witnesses.
Signed: EDWARD LACEY.

Page 69:   Indenture made 1 July 1788 bet. JOHN LONG of Camden District
            of one part and DRURY GOING of the other part witnessed
that JOHN LONG for the sum of 50 pounds paid by sd. DRURY GOING his
heirs forever all that tract of land lying on waters of Turkey Creek.
Wit: ALEXANDER TOMBS, DAVID TOMBS, JOB GOING. Signed: JOHN LONG.

Page 70:   Indenture made 8 January 1789 bet. WILLIAM BORROW of Fair-
            field County, executor of the estate of WILLIAM BORROW,
deceased of one part and ALEXANDER STEVENSON of York County of the
other part witnessed that WILLIAM BORROW for the sum of 60 pounds pd.
by ALEXANDER STEVENSON. Wit: EDWARD LACEY, JANE LACEY, ROBERT (X) CONLEY.
Signed: WILLIAM BORROW, Executor.

Page 71:   Indenture made 14 February 1789 bet. ELIJAH NUNN of Chester
            County of one part and EDMUND LEE of the other part witnessed
ELIJAH NUNN for the sum of 85 pounds paid by the sd. EDMUND LEE do
grant unto EDMUND LEE 100 acres it being part of a tract of land granted
to JOSEPH BROWN 16 January 1772 and to JOHN MOBERLEY 1787 and transferred from MOBERLEY to ELIJAH NUNN and from NUNN to EDMUND LEE the
sd. 100 acres lying on branch of Sandy River known by the name of Stamp
Branch. Wit: JOHN WRIGHT, JOHN JAGGERS. Signed: ELIJAH NUNN.

Page 73:   Indenture made 1789 bet. WILLIAM GASTON of Chester County
            of one part and DRURY GOING of the other part witnessed
that WILLIAM GASTON for the sum of 3 pounds 14 shillings and 4 pence
pd by the sd DRURY GOING doth grant to DRURY GOING his heirs and assigns forever a tract of land lying on Mill Creek in Chester County
being part of a tract granted to WILLIAM GASTON 3 September 1787 containing 200 acres. No witnesses. Signed: WILLIAM GASTON.

Page 74:   Know that I, HUGH COOPER of Chester County and good causes
            me here to moving do appoint my trusted friend ROBERT COOPER,
blacksmith my attorney to demand ROBERT BORROW of North Carolina the
full damages sustained by me the sd. BARROW taken and detaining of
2 of my horses from July 1780 giving by these presence granting unto
my sd. attorney. Wit: HUGH WHITESIDE, J.P. Signed: HUGH COOPER.

Page 74:   Indenture made 27 December 1782 bet. DANIEL COLLSON of Camden
            District in Craven County, miller of one part and WILLIAM
MC DONALD, planter of the other part witnessed that DANIEL COLLSON
for the sum of 10 shillings paid to DANIEL COLLSON and pd. by sd. WIL-
LIAM MC DONALD 100 acres granted originally to ARTHUR HECKLIN, JR.
and transferred by the sd. ARTHUR HECKLIN, JR. and DANIEL COLLSON by
deed of gift. Wit: W. HOWELL, THOS. HOWELL. Signed: DANIEL COLLSON.

Page 76:   Indenture made 28 December 1782 bet. DANIEL COLLSON of Camden
            District in Craven County, miller of one part and WILLIAM
MC DONALD, planter of the other part for the sum of 300 pounds to sd.
COLLSON in hand pd. by MC DONALD containing 100 acres situated in Craven
County original grant to ARTHUR HECKLIN, JR. 23 October 1765 and the
sd. HECKLIN, JR. did transfer 100 acres by deed of gift 30 May 1774
unto DAVID COLLSON his heirs and etc. bounding north east by FREDERICK
FORD, south east by vacant land, south west by JOHN LEONARD land, west
by land of BENJAMIN EVERITT. Wit: WM. HOWELL, THOS. HOWELL. Signed:
DANIEL COLLSON.

Page 77:   Know that I, ROBERT GORRELL of Chester County for good cause
            me hereunto moving do appoint my trusted friend RALPH GORRELL
of North Carolina one state of Guilford and also trusted friend JOHN
CUNNINGHAM of the Kingdom of Ireland and city of Londonderry, merchant,
my lawful attorney for me in my name to ask and demand from JOHN CALHOUN
late of Charleston, South Carolina 159 pounds Irish money. No witnesses.
Signed: ROBERT GORRELL.

Page 78:   Indenture made 16 December 1788 bet. CHRISTOPHER STRAIGHT
            of Chester County, blacksmith of one part and GEORGE STRAIGHT
a planter of the other part by a certain grant dated 28 October 1763
under the hand of Wm. Tryon of N. C. did grant to JAMES MOORE a plantation of 300 acres lying in County of Mecklenburg, North Carolina
at time of survey but by the continuation of boundary line now in York
County. No witnesses. Signed: CHRISTOPHER STRAIGHT.

Page 80:   Indenture made 22 August 1786 bet. WILLIAM HENRY of North
            Carolina Mecklenburg County, yeoman of one part and WILLIAM
FARRISS of Chester County of the other part by a certain grant dated

Cont'd from page 43:
22 April 1767 under the hand of Wm. Tryon, Esq. Governor over North Carolina did grant unto WILLIAM HENRY 190 acres lying between the south and north Fork of Fishing Creek boundary on land of SAMUEL MC CANCE, land of SAMUEL NEELEY, HUGH WHITESIDE, WILLIAM NEELEY and ARCHIBALD ELLIOTT land in Chester County. Wit: WILLIAM WHITESIDE, THOMAS WHITE-SIDE. Signed: WILLIAM HENRY.

Page 82:   Indenture made 23 March 1789 bet. SAMUEL NEELEY of Chester
            County of one part and JOHN LATTA of the other part whereas
by a certain grant dated 21 October 1758 under the hand of his excellency Arthur Dobbs, Esq. over the province of North Carolina did grant
unto WILLIAM NEELEY 400 acres situated at the time of survey in Anson
County, North Carolina but now by the continuation of the boundary
line in South Carolina Chester County both sides of Fishing Creek north
west side of Catawba River. No witnesses. Signed: SAMUEL NEELEY.

Page 83:   Indenture made 23 February 1789 bet. CLAUDIUS CHARVIN of
            Chester County of one part and DANIEL WILLIAMS of York County
of the other part for the sum of 260 pounds that the sd. WILLIAMS stand
security for CHARVIN unto WILLIAM ADAIR on 3 different bonds hath sold
unto DANIEL WILLIAMS 1 negro wench name of Jine etc. Wit: GEORGE PURVIS,
JOSEPHUS (name not plain), DAVID ADRIAN. Signed: CLAUDIUS CHARVIN.

Page 85:   Indenture made 10 June 1789 bet. ISAAC MC FADDEN and his
            wife of Chester County of one part and JOHN FARGUSON of
the other part by a certain grant dated 26 July 1774 did grant unto
ROBERT MC FADDEN, deceased, 350 acres lying on small trunk of Fishing
Creek in Craven County now Chester County bounded north west on land
of JAMES FARGUSON, JR. north west on land of JOHN FARGUSON, all other
sides by vacant land. This indenture witness that the sd. ISAAC MC
FADDEN and ELIZABETH his wife for the sum of 50 pounds pd. by the sd.
JOHN FARGUSON do release to the sd. JOHN FARGUSON 246 acres of the
foresaid tract of 350 acres, 104 acres being released to JAMES BLAIR
dated 6 May 1780. Wit: DAVID HUNTER, RALPH MC FADDEN, CANDER MC FADDEN.
Signed: ISAAC MC FADDEN, ELIZABETH (X) MC FADDEN.

Page 87:   Indenture made 19 May 1789 bet. JAMES HARP of Newberry Co.
            of one part and WILLIAM EMBRY of Chester County of the other
part witnessed that sd. JAMES HARP for the sum of 50 pounds pd by WIL-
LIAM EMBRY his heirs and assigns forever all that tract of land lying
in County of Chester. Wit: ALLEN ROBISON, TOBIAS (X) HARP, WILLIAM
(X) CALLOM. Signed: JAMES (X) HARP.

Page 88:   Indenture made 25 June 1789 bet. ADAM MC COOL of Chester
            County of one part and WILLIAM LOVE of the other part by
a certain grant dated 1 December 1772 did grant unto ADAM MC COOL 250
acres lying on both sides of little Turkey Creek north side of Broad
River. Wit: THOMAS BRANDON, JAMES BARROW, ADAM MC COOL. Signed: ADAM
MC COOL.

Page 89:   Indenture made 30 January 1788 bet. DAVID HOPKINS, Esq.
            of Chester County of one part and WILLIAM BRITAIN of the
other part witnessed that DAVID HOPKINS, Esq. for the sum of 50 pounds
do sell and make over unto sd. WILLIAM BRITAIN 100 acres situate on
the branch of Sandy River. Wit: FER. D. HOPKINS, JAMES FRASER. Signed:
DAVID HOPKINS.

Page 90:   Indenture made 5 January 1786 bet. RICHARD WHITAKER of York
            County of one part and JAMES HARP of 96 District of the
other part for the sum of 200 pounds pd to sd RICHARD WHITAKER by JAMES
HARP he the sd WHITAKER has granted and sold unto sd HARP his executors
and assigns 125 acres on the waters of Broad River joining JOHN WOODS
land etc. Wit: DAVID PATRICK, WILLIAM PATRICK. Signed: RICHARD (R)
WHITAKER.

Page 93:   Indenture made 25 January 1786 bet. RICHARD WHITAKER of
            Camden District York County of one part and JAMES HARP of
96 District of the other part witnessed that the sd. WHITAKER for the

Cont'd from page 44:
sum of 200 pounds paid by JAMES HARP doth acquit and discharge the
sd. HARP his heirs and assigns for these presence he the sd WHITAKER
doth grant to sd. HARP in his actual possession do grant 125 acres
being part of land grant to RICHARD WHITAKER 21 January 1785 situated
on Broad River joining land of JOHN WOODS. Wit: DAVID PATRICK, WILLIAM
PATRICK. Signed: RICHARD (R) WHITAKER.

Page 94:   Indenture made 5 July 1785 bet. RICHARD WHITAKER of York
             County Camden District of one part and JOHN WOODS of Lincoln
County, North Carolina of the other part witnessed that RICHARD WHITAKER
for the sum of 50 pounds paid by JOHN WOODS do confer unto the sd WOODS
his heirs and assigns a tract of land lying in Chester County on waters
of bushy fork of Sandy River. Wit: ALEXANDER EKANS, THOMAS BARNETT,
JOHN FEARISK. Signed: RICHARD (R) W. WHITAKER.

Page 95:   Indenture made 17 June 1789 bet. WILLIAM ROBERSON of Guilford
             County, North Carolina of one part for the sum of 20 pounds
to the sd WILLIAM ROBERSON pd by WILLIAM MASSEY do sell to sd MASSEY
59 acres in Chester County on north side of Fishing Creek and is bounded
north west with LAWRENCE GALAHER on Fishing Creek and JOHN MC COWN
land. Indenture made first from ALEXANDER MC COWN to JOHN MC COWN and
from JOHN MC COWN to JOSIAH EDWARDS. Wit: JAMES MASSEY, WILLIAM MASSEY,
WILLIAM HUNT. Signed: WILLIAM ROBERTSON. (Spelled both ways)

Page 97:   Indenture made 8 June 1789 bet. WILSON HENDERSON of one
             part and WILLIAM BRITAIN of other part witnessed that sd
WILSON HENDERSON for sum of 10 pounds money to him in hand paid has
sold unto WILLIAM BRITAIN 10 acres lying in Chester County on waters
of Sandy River. Wit: RICHARD TALIAFERRO. Signed: WILSON HENDERSON.

Page 98:   Indenture made 1 July 1789 bet. JOSIAH HILL of Chester Co.
             of one part and JAMES ADARE of the other part witnessed
that JOSIAH HILL for the sum of 10 pounds pd by JAMES ADARE doth sell
unto ADARE 250 acres lying in Chester County on waters of Mill Creek
being part of the tract of 12,700 acres granted to sd JOSIAH HILL on
and bounded on corner of JEAN YOUNG on WILLIAM MINTER's line. Wit:
W. PALMER, RICHD. MILES. Signed: JOSIAH HILL.

Page 99:   Indenture made 1 July 1789 bet. JOSIAH HILL of Chester County
             of one part and JAMES ADARE of other part witnessed that
the sd. JOSIAH HILL for sum of 10 pounds paid by JAMES ADARE do sell
unto JAMES ADARE 150 acres lying in Chester County on waters of Sandy
River being part of tract of 12,700 acres granted to sd HILL the 7th
day July 1786. Wit: W. PALMER, RICHARD MILES. Signed: JOSIAH HILL.

Page 101:   Indenture made 4 July 1789 bet. WILLIAM GASTON, Esq. and
             JOHN LOVE both of Chester County of one part and ADAM MC
COOL of the other part witnessed that WILLIAM GASTON and JOHN LOVE
for sum of 5 pounds paid by A. MC COOL do grant unto ADAM MC COOL a
tract of land lying on Turkey Creek being part and partial of a larger
bit of land granted WILLIAM LOVE 3 September 1753 by Mathew Rowen,
Governor of N. C. containing 800 acres, 438 acres being since granted
to sd WILLIAM GASTON by William Bull, Governor of S. C. Wit: JAMES
BELL, JAMES BARRON, JOHN BRANDON. Signed: WILLIAM GASTON, JOHN LOVE.

Page 102:   Indenture made 5 October 1789 bet. WILLIAM CLARK of one
             part and JAMES MITCHELL of the other part witnessed that
WILLIAM CLARK for sum of 100 pounds pd by JAMES MITCHELL the receipt
hereof is hereby acknowledged and for other good causes him moving.
Do confer 300 acres in Chester Co. of a Branch of Broad River called
WILLIAM WILSON creek on north side of sd river. Wit: ALEXANDER STEVEN-
SON, SAMUEL LACEY. Signed: WILLIAM (X) CLARK.

Page 104:   Indenture made 2 April 1780 bet. JOHN SADLER and MARY his
             wife of Camden Dist. and JOHN PUGH of the Dist. and State
aforesaid witnessed that JOHN SADLER and MARY his wife condition 10,000
pounds of money paid by JOHN PUGH. The sd SADLER and wife hath confer
over unto sd PUGH one tract of land lying on head of Sandy River granted

Cont'd from page 45:
JOHN SADLER by William Tryon, Governor of North Carolina containing
100 acres being part of 300 acres of which 100 bounded by a line of
mark trees to WILLIAM BANKS. Wit: ROBERT COLLINS, ISAAC SADLER, JOHN
GILLIAN. Signed: JOHN SADLER, MARY (X) SADLER.

Page 105: Indenture made 27 December 1788 bet. JOHN RICHARDSON of
         Fairfield County of one part and ROBERT COLLINS of Chester
County of the other part witnessed that JOHN RICHARDSON for sum of
35 pounds paid by ROBERT COLLINS, JR. doth confer unto ROBERT COLLINS,
JR. situate on branch of Jonises Creek bounded north west on land of
DAVID HOPKINS, Esq. all other sides vacant land survey 6 July 1773
on a warrant granted to EPHRIAM MITCHEL, Esq. the 6th April 1773 con-
taining 100 acres. Wit: EDWARD WATTS, ROBERT COLLINS, SR., SAML. MC
MILLAN. Signed: JOHN (X) RICHARDSON, JEAN (X) RICHARDSON.

Page 106: Indenture made 3 October 1789 bet. THOMAS JENKINS of Chester
         County of one part and WILLIAM MOBBERLY of other part wit-
nessed that THOMAS JENKINS for sum of 80 pounds paid by the sd WILLIAM
MOBBERLY do confer unto sd MOBBERLY 100 acres on Sandy Creek. Wit:
WILLIAM JENKINS, PAT MC GRIFF, BARNETT ALLEN. Signed: THOMAS JENKINS.

Page 107: Indenture made 5 July 1784 bet. MOSES MC COWN and FRANK
         his wife of Camden District, S. C., planter of one part and
JAMES MC COWN, JR. and MARY MC COWN, planters of other part whereas
by two certain grant, granted the one for 200 acres granted unto JAMES
MC COWN, SR. the sd land being on the conjunction of Catawba River
the mouth of Fishing Creek was granted formerly to JAMES BRADLEY. Wit:
DAVID HUNTER, HUGH MC WATERS. Signed: MOSES MC COWN, FRANK (X) MC COWN.

Page 110: Indenture made 4 July 1784 bet. MOSES MC COWN and FRANK
         his wife of Camden Dist. of one part and JAMES MC COWN and
MARY MC COWN of this Dist. of the other part. Witnessed that the sd
MOSES MC COWN and FRANK his wife for sum of 5 shillings sterling pd
by JAMES MC COWN and MARY MC COWN doth sell unto sd JAMES MC COWN and
MARY MC COWN 2 plantations of land containing 400 acres, the same being
held by 2 original grants each containing 200 acres one was originally
granted to JAMES MC COWN, SR. and was conveyed from sd JAMES MC COWN
to sd MOSES MC COWN situate on waters of Fishing Creek and Catawba
River joining land formerly granted to JAMES BRADLEY other 200 acres
of land of aforesd lying on Fishing Creek about 2 miles up sd creek
from the river, other adjoining land of ALEXANDER MC COWN original
title being obtained by ROBERT SWAN and conveyed by sd SWAN to sd MOSES
MC COWN. Wit: DAVID HUNTER, HUGH MC WATERS. Signed: MOSES MC COWN,
FRANK (X) MC COWN.

Page 112: Indenture made 4 September 1789 bet. JOSIAH HILL of Chester
         County of one part and JOHN PEW of other part witnessed
that JOSIAH HILL for sum of 10 pounds sterling money paid by JOHN PEW
do sell unto JOHN PEW his heirs and assigns forever all that tract
of land containing 100 acres of land and situated in Camden Dist. being
part of tract of 12,700 acres of land granted to sd JOSIAH HILL the
6th day Nov. 1786 bounded south east by land of JOHN PEW, south west
and north west on JOSIAH HILL land and north east on JOHN PARKER's
land. Wit: EDWARD LACEY, SAMUEL LACEY, SAMUEL LACEY, JR. Signed: JOSIAH
HILL.

Page 113: Indenture made 12 May 1776 bet. WILLIAM EMBRY of one part
         of Craven Co. and JAMES THOMAS of 96 Dist. of the other
part witnessed that the sd JAMES THOMAS for sum of 125 pounds money
pd by sd WILLIAM EMBRY doth sell unto WILLIAM EMBRY and his heirs and
assigns forever a parcel of land in Craven Co. on north east side of
Broad River being on JOHN HITCHCOCK's line. Wit: JOHN STARN, THOMAS
HUGHES, RICHARD __(?). Signed: JAMES THOMAS.

Page 114: Indenture made 9 June 1789 bet. JOHN STEEL of Chester County
         of one part and THOMAS STEEL of other part witnessed that
the sd JOHN STEEL he being the heir of CATHARINE STEEL, deceased for
sum of 10 shillings sold unto THOMAS STEEL now in his actual possession

Cont'd from page 46:
a tract of land containing 200 acres it being a part of a tract of
400 acres originally granted unto CATHARINE STEEL lying on both sides
of Fishing Creek north west on JOHN LENNARD land north west on vacant
land northwest on WILLIAM GASTON's land. Wit: GEORGE MORRIS, THOMAS
BELL. Signed: JOHN STEEL.

Page 115: Indenture made 10 June 1789 bet. JOHN STEEL the heir of
          CATHARINE STEEL widow deceased of Chester Co. of one part
and THOMAS STEEL of other part witnessed that sd JOHN STEEL for sum
of 100 pounds hath granted unto THOMAS STEEL now in his actual possession 200 acres being part of 400 acres originally granted unto CATHARINE
STEEL and sd 200 acres being part of the divide left to him lying on
both sides of Fishing Creek. Wit: GEORGE MORRIS, THOMAS BELL. Signed:
JOHN STEEL.

Page 117: Indenture made 27 November 1788 bet. ROBERT TINDEL, THOMAS
          EAKINS, planters of Chester Co. of one part and JOHN CALD-
WELL of the other part witnessed that ROBERT TINDEL and THOMAS EAKINS
for sum of 15 pounds release unto JOHN CALDWELL his heirs and assigns
forever all that tract of land lying in Chester Co. on waters of JACK
LOVE's branch containing 100 acres. Wit: JAMES JOHNSTON, JAMES MC CALLA,
STAFFD. CURRY. Signed: ROBERT TINDALL, THOMAS EAKINS.

Page 119: Know that I, HANNAH BISHOP of Chester County, widow, for
          causes me hereunto moving do appoint my trusty and loving
friend JOHN CARTER of county aforesd, planter, for me in my name to
receive from the executor of last will and testament of my father THOMAS
BRACKEN, late of State of Pennsylvania, deceased, all such legacies
has been devised to me. Dated 6 April 1790. Wit: WILLIAM HUGHES, JO.
BROWN. Signed: HANNAH BISHOP.

Page 119: Indenture made 22 September 1789 bet. JONATHAN JONES and
          BARSHEBA his wife of Chester Co. of one part and JAMES LANGS-
BY of the other part for sum of 10 shillings to them in hand pd by
sd JAMES LANGSBY, and they the sd JONATHAN JONES and BATHSHEBA his
wife do sell unto JAMES LANGSBY 114 acres situated in Camden Dist.
on south side of Catawba River on McClures branch which runs into the
south fork of Fishing Creek. Wit: JOHN HARDIN, JOSEPH (X) JONES. Signed:
JONATHAN JONES, BATHSHEBA (X) JONES.

Page 121: Indenture made 23 September 1789 bet. JONATHAN JONES and
          BATHSHEBA his wife of Chester Co. and State of S. C. of
one part and JAMES LANGSBY of the other part by a certain grant dated
2 Oct. 1786 did grant unto JONATHAN JONES 114 acres situated in Dist.
of Camden on south side of Catawba River on McClures branch which runs
into the south fork of Fishing Creek. Wit: JOHN HARDIN, JOSEPH (X)
JONES. Signed: JONATHAN JONES, BATHSHEBA (X) JONES.

Page 123: Indenture made 18 July 1789 bet. CHRISTOPHER DEGRAFFENREID
          of York County of one part and AMBROSE NIX of Chester County
of the other part witnessed that sd DEGRAFFENREID for sum of 100 pounds
pd by sd NIX doth grant to sd NIX his heirs and assigns forever 250
acres lying in Chester Co. being on Starnes branch. Wit: WILLIAM EMBRY,
JOHN (+) NIX, THOS. (X) SAUNDERS. Signed: CHRISTOPHER DEGRAFFENREID.

Page 124: Indenture made 13 May 1776 bet. WILLIAM EMBRY of one part
          of Craven County and JAMES THOMAS of the other part of 96
District for sum of 125 pounds to JAMES THOMAS in hand pd by WILLIAM
EMBRY doth clearly acquit and discharge WILLIAM EMBRY his heirs and
everyone of them all that partial line in Craven Co. north east side
of Broad River boundary on JOHN HITCHCOCK's line. Wit: JOHN STARN,
THOS. HUGHES, RICHARD HUSE. Signed: JAMES THOMAS.

Page 126: Indenture made 23 September 1789 bet. JAMES SHARP of Orange-
          burg Dist., planter of one part and WILLIAM SHARP of Camden
Dist. of the other part. For sum of 10 shillings paid by WILLIAM SHARP
do sell unto WILLIAM SHARP his heirs and etc. 200 acres situated in
Camden Dist. of Chester Co. state aforesd on creek called Sandy River

Cont'd from page 47:
all sides being vacant at time of original survey. Wit: EDWARD (B)
BOWLIN, THOMAS C. WARNER. Signed: JAMES SHARP.

Page 127: Indenture made 23 September 1789 bet. JAMES SHARP of Orangeburg Dist., planter of the other part for sum of 200 pounds
do sell unto WILLIAM SHARP 200 acres situated in Camden Dist. Chester
Co. and on a creek called Sandy Creek all sides being vacant at time
of original survey. Wit: EDWARD (B) BOWLIN, THOMAS C. WARNER. Signed:
JAMES SHARP.

Page 129: Indenture made 14 July 1787 bet. JOHN DAUGHERTY of one part
and HUGH MC KOWN of the other part for sum of 10 shillings
paid by HUGH MC KOWN do sell unto HUGH MC KOWN 100 acres lying in Chester County on head waters of Sandy River bounded south east by AMOS
DAVIS, south east by old survey north east vacant land. Wit: JAMES
CORRY, DAVID (X) GRISSOM, JAMES (X) MC KOWN. Signed: JOHN DAUGHERTY.

Page 130: Indenture made 15 July 1787 bet. JOHN DOUGHERTY of Chester
county of one part and HUGH MC KOWN, planter of the other
part for sum of 10 pounds pd by JOHN DOUGHERTY doth acquit and discharge
the sd MC KOWN his heirs etc. Wit: JAMES CORRY, DAVID (X) GRISSOM,
JAMES (X) MC KOWN. Signed: JOHN DOUGHERY.

Page 134: Indenture made 11 November 1789 bet. WILLIAM BRITIAN and
JEAN his wife of Chester Co. of one part and AMBROSE LEE
of the other part witnessed that WILLIAM BRITIAN and JEAN his wife
for sum of 100 pounds pd by sd AMBROSE LEE doth sell unto LEE his heirs
etc. 100 acres lying on waters of Sandy River. Wit: RICHARD TALIAFERRO,
WILLIAM SHARP. Signed: WILLIAM BRITIAN.

Page 135: Indenture made 2 November 1789 bet. JOHN CALVIN of Chester
County planter of one part and MARTIN ELOM planter of the
other part for sum of 70 pounds pd, do sell unto MARTIN ELOM a tract
of land lying in Chester Co. on Welshes fork of Sandy River containing
500 acres boundary on JAMES SHARP land and JOHN DOUGHERTY land. Wit:
JOHN PRATT, WILLIAM SHARP, ANN (X) KETCHINGS. Signed: JOHN CALVIN.

Page 136: Indenture made 27 November 1789 bet. JOSEPH DAVIS of Camden
Dist. of Chester Co. of one part and ALLEN DEGRAFFENREID
of the other part for sum of 50 pounds pd by sd DEGRAFFENREID do sell
unto sd ALLEN DEGRAFFENREID 30 acres lying in Chester Co. on south
fork of Sandy River. Wit: THOMAS (+) WILKS, JOHN (+) NIX, WM. HUGHES.
Signed: JOSEPH DAVIS.

Page 137: Indenture made 17 October 1789 bet. AMOS TIMMS of Granville
County and state of North Carolina of one part and JAMES
ALLISON of Chester County of the other part for sum pd by sd JAMES
ALLISON 200 acres being a tract of land granted to AMOS TIMMS and trans-
ferred from AMOS TIMMS to JAMES ALLISON lying in Chester County. Wit:
JOSEPH TIMMS, JOHN TIMMS, JAMES (X) GILCHRIST. Signed: AMOS TIMMS.

Page 139: Indenture made 7 September 1789 bet. THOMAS BAKER FRANKLIN
of Chester Co. planter of one part and JOHN FRANKLIN planter
of the other part witnessed that THOMAS BAKER FRANKLIN for sum of 50
pounds pd for 271 acres lying on Hintons Creek of Sandy River being
part of four different tracts granted to THOMAS BAKER FRANKLIN 24 Nov.
1767 containing 100 acres etc. Wit: PAT'K. MC GRIFF, ALEX JOHNSTON,
JAMES GORE. Signed: THOMAS BAKER FRANKLIN.

Page 141: Indenture made 21 August 1789 bet. JOHN MC FADDEN and MARY
his wife of Chester Co. of one part and WILLIAM MC DONALD
of the other part witnessed that JOHN & MARY MC FADDEN for sum of 30
pounds pd by MC DONALD hath sold unto WILLIAM MC DONALD 100 acres lying
in Chester County on waters of Fishing Creek on west bounded by JOHN
WHITE's land, north east by vacant land and south west by CATHERINE
STALLE's (STEEL?) land. Wit: WILLIAM CROOK, ANDREW LOCKART, JOHN GORDON.
Signed: JOHN MC FADDEN, MARY MC FADDEN.

Page 143: Indenture made 26 July 1789 bet. MAJOR GRESHAM of Chester

Cont'd from page 48:
County of one part and JOHN RANEY of the other part witnessed that MAJOR GRESHAM from the sum of 50 pounds pd by JOHN RANEY do
sell unto JOHN RANEY 100 acres being a tract of land granted to MAJOR
GRESHAM dated 5 December 1785 lying on Bear branch of Sandy River and
beginning at a post oak on ELIJAH NUNN's line. Wit: ELIJAH NUNN, THOS.
BAKER FRANKLIN, WILLIAM RANEY. Signed: MAJOR GRESHAM.

Page 144: Indenture made 15 December 1789 bet. RICHARD' EVANS of Chester
County of one part and MARY EVANS of the other part witness-
ed that RICHARD EVANS in consideration of sum of 20 pounds to him in
hand pd hath sold unto MARY EVANS or her heirs 100 acres situated in
Camden District on branch of Sandy River. Wit: ADAM WILLIAMSON, ELIZA-
BETH EVANS. Signed: RICHARD EVANS.

Page 145: Indenture made 6 July 1789 bet. MAJOR GRESHAM of Chester
County of one part and JOHN RANEY of the other part for
sum pd by JOHN RANEY, MAJOR GRESHAM do hereby acknowledge that the
sd GRESHAM hath sold unto JOHN RANEY all that tract of land containing
50 acres situated in Chester Co. on a branch leading into Bear Branch
beginning on JOHN HOPKIN's land. Wit: ELIJAH NUNN, THOMAS BAKER FRANK-
LIN, WILLIAM RANEY. Signed: MAJOR GRESHAM.

Page 147: Indenture made 14 November 1789 bet. JAMES BROWN and ANN
his wife of Chester County of one part and JOSEPH FENNESTER
of York Co. of the other part witnessed that JAMES and ANN BROWN his
wife for sum of 50 pounds pd by JOSEPH FENNESTER a tract of land lying
on Bales Branch and being part of a tract of 200 acres granted to JAMES
BROWN 7 Nov. 1785. Wit: JAMES FEENSTER, JEAN BROWN, JAMES ADARE. Signed:
JAS. BROWN, ANN BROWN.

Page 148: Indenture made 13 March 1790 bet. JAMES TIMMS and PATTY
TIMMS his wife of Camden Dist. of Chester Co. of one part
and JAMES FRASIER of the other part witnessed that JAMES TIMMS and
PATTY TIMMS for sum of 40 pounds pd by JAMES FRASIER do sell one certain tract of land containing 231 acres being part of a tract of land
containing 335 acres granted to sd JAMES TIMMS on 6 Nov. 1786 lying
on Sealeys Creek. Wit: JEREMIAH KINGSLEY, AMBROSE (X) LEE. Signed:
JAMES TIMMS, PATTY (X) TIMMS.

Page 149: Indenture made 10 May 1790 bet. JOSEPH BREVARD, Esq. of
Camden Dist. of one part and Capt. EDWARD ALLEN of the town
of Salem in the Commonwealth of Massachusetts of the other part witnessed that whereas DAVID HOPKINS of Chester Co. Esq. was seized in
his demesne as a fee of some other good estate and inheritance to him
and his heirs forever of and in a certain tract of land particularly
mentioned here in state aforesd on NE side of Broad river first one
tract of 650 acres being two different tracts of one survey one of
350 acrs originally granted to JAMES MOORE by a grant bearing date
4 Nov. 1762. Bounded at the time of original survey on all sides by
vacant land the other 300 acres originally to DAVID HOPKINS by grant
bearing date 19 Nov. 1772. Bounded at time of original survey to the
NE to land belonging to MARK EDWARDS to NW by the Broad river and SE
by JOHN HITCHCOCK's land. Sheriff of Camden Dist., S. C. Signed: JOSEPH
BREVARD.

Page 152: Know by these presence that I, JOSEPH BREVARD, Esq., Sheriff
of Camden District by virtue of a certain writ of fiene-
facias out of the Court of Common Pleas of sd state under the hand
of __(?)__ BURKE, Esq. dated at Charleston 17 March 1789 commanded
then of either of the goods chattels and land of DAVID HOPKINS and
JOHN WINN a certain sum of 906 pounds which JOHN MANSON and THOMAS
MANSON for them cost and charges by them expended in about prosecuting
their suit etc. Wit: JOHN & THOMAS MANSON, DAVID BS HOPKINS, JOHN WINN.

Page 155: Indenture made 19 February 1790 bet. WILLIAM KIRKLAND, JR
of Camden Dist. of one part and JOHN TAYLOR of Chester Co.
of the other part. Doth witness that WILLIAM KIRKLAND, JR. for sum
of 10 shillings pd by JOHN TAYLOR doth sell unto sd TAYLOR 277 acres

Cont'd from page 49:
according to a grant granted to sd WILLIAM KIRKLAND certified 25 Nov.
1785 the sd land lying on Sandy River and waters of Broad River in
Chester in Camden District. Wit: EZEKIEL SANDERS, ELEAZER GORE. Signed:
WILLIAM KIRKLAND.

Page 156: Indenture made 15 September 1789 bet. RICHARD TALIAFERRO
         and MILLEY his wife of Chester County of one part and JOHN
WRIGHT of the other part witnessed that RICHARD and MILLEY TALIAFERRO
for the sum of 92 English Guineas pd them have sold unto JOHN WRIGHT
a tract of land which was granted to HAZEL HARDWICK and from him conveyed to RICHARD TALIAFERRO 162 acres. Wit: WILLIAM BOYD, EDMUND LEE.
Signed: RICHARD TALIAFERRO, MILLEY TALIAFERRO.

Page 157: Indenture made 1 April 1790 bet. ROBERT CHERRY and LETTUCE
         his wife of Chester Co. of one part and HUGH MC CLURE of
the other part by a certain grant dated 6 April 1768 did grant unto
JAMES KNOX 450 acres dated 28 May 1767 in Chester Co. on waters of
Rocky Creek bounded on SE by DAVID HUNTER and the sd tract of 450 acres
was conveyed by JAMES KNOX to ROBERT CHERRY by a deed dated 3 October
1786. Wit: JOHN MC COLLOUGH, THOMAS PORTER, JOHN CHERRY. Signed: ROBERT
CHERRY, LETTUCE (X) CHERRY.

Page 159: Indenture made 14 September 1789 bet. MOSES DUKES of Fair-
         field County of one part and WILLIAM DUNAVANT of Lancaster
Co. of the other part for the sum of 10 shillings pd by DUNAVANT do
sell unto sd DUNAVANT 370 acres of land on the north side of Wateree
River bounded at time of survey by vacant land originally granted to
JOSEPH BRADLEY. Wit: DUNAVANT J.P.(?), WILLIAM WILSON. Signed: MOSES
DUKES.

Page 160: Indenture made 15 September 1789 bet. MOSES DUKE of Fair-
         field Co. of one part and WILLIAM DUNAVANT of Lancaster
Co. of the other part for the sum of 16503(?) pounds pd do grant unto
WILLIAM DUNAVANT 320 acres situated on the south side of Wateree River
bounded on vacant land originally granted to JOSEPH BRADLEY 4 Nov.
1762. Wit: WILLIAM WILSON. Signed: MOSES DUKE.

Page 162: Indenture made 25 Jan. 1790 bet. JOHN FRANKLIN of Chester
         Co. of one part and WILLIAM SHAW of the other part for the
sum of 100 pounds pd by WILLIAM SHAW do sell unto sd SHAW 17 acres
being part of a tract of land which was granted to JOHN FRANKLIN 24
Dec. 1772. Wit: SAMUEL CRAIG, WILLIAM (X) RAINEY. Signed: JOHN FRANKLIN

Page 164: Indenture made 15 Sept. 1789 bet. RICHARD TALIAFERRO and
         MILLEY his wife of Chester Co. of one part and EDMOND LEE
of the other part. Witnessed that RICHARD TALIAFERRO and MILLEY his
wife for the sum of 92 English Guineas pd have sold to sd LEE a certain
tract of land which was granted to HAZEL HARDWICK and from him conveyed
to sd TALIAFERRO. Wit: WILLIAM BOYD, JOHN WRIGHT. Signed: RICHARD TALIA-
FERRO, MILLEY TALIAFERRO.

Page 165: Indenture made 26 Nov. 1782 bet. SAMUEL CALDWELL and his
         wife MARGARET of Camden Dist. planters of one part and THOMAS
MORRISON, weaver of the other part by a certain grant dated 1 Sept.
1768. Did grant unto SAMUEL CALDWELL 100 acres of land on waters of
Rocky Creek in Craven Co. bounded NW by EDWARD HENDERSON, the other
sides by vacant land. Wit: WILLIAM MC CLINTOCK, JAMES (X) STUART. Signed
bu: SAMUEL CALDWELL, MARGARET (X) CALDWELL.

Page 167: Indenture made 6 Apr. 1788 bet. JOHN YARBROUGH, SR. of one
         part and LITTLETON RANDOLPH ISBELL of the other part witness
that JOHN YARBROUGH, SR. for sum of 10 pounds sold unto sd ISBELLS
50 acres being part of a grant originally granted to JOHN LAND of 250
acres. Wit: JON'A. HEMPHILL, DANIEL MUSE, SR., WILLIAM YARBROUGH. Signed
by JOHN YARBROUGH, SR.

Page 168: Indenture made 7 Apr. 1788 bet. JOHN YARBROUGH, SR. of one
         part and LITTLETON RANDOLPH ISBELLS of the other part. Do

Cont'd from page 50:
witness that JOHN YARBROUGH, SR. for sum of 100 pounds sold unto sd
LITTLETON RANDOLPH ISBELLS,now in his actual possession 50 acres. Lying
in Chester Co. on the north side of Rocky Creek. Wit: JON'A. HEMPHILL,
DANIEL MUSE, SR., WILLIAM YARBROUGH. Signed: JOHN YARBROUGH.

Page 170: Indenture made 18 May 1789 bet. JAMES HEMPHILL, SR. of Chest-
er Co. of one part and ANDREW HEMPHILL of the other part.
Witness that JAMES HEMPHILL for sum of 32 pounds do grant unto ANDREW
HEMPHILL in his actual possession 150 acres. Wit: CHARLES WALL, WILLIAM
(X) WALL, JESSIE BANDY. Signed: JAMES HEMPHILL.

Page 172: Indenture made 25 Feb. 1790 bet. DANIEL COMER and ELIZABETH
his wife of Union Co. of one part and ALLEN DE GRAFFENREID
of Chester Co. of the other part. Witnessed that for the sum of 5 shillings from the sd. DE GRAFFENREID to the sd. COMER hath sold unto the
sd DE GRAFFENREID 300 acres on the waters of Sandy River. Wit: W. EMBRY,
THOS. BRANDON, ARCHIBALD RIDDLE. Signed: DANIEL COMER, ELIZABETH (+)
COMER.

Page 173: Indenture made 26 Feb. 1790 bet. DANIEL COMER and ELIZABETH
his wife of Union Co. of one part and ALLEN DE GRAFFENREID
of Chester Co. for the sum of 100 pounds from the sd DE GRAFFENREID
to the sd COMER. Do sell unto the sd DE GRAFFENREID 300 acres lying
on Sandy River. Wit: W. EMBRY, THOS. BRANDON, ARCHIBALD RIDDLE. Signed:
DANIEL COMER, ELIZABETH (X) COMER.

Page 175: Indenture made 3 July 1789 bet. JAMES POTTS of Charleston,
cooper, of one part and WILLIAM ANDERSON of Chester Co.,
planter of the other part. Witness that JAMES POTTS for the sum of
50 pounds pd to WILLIAM ANDERSON do grant unto sd ANDERSON in his actual
possession 100 acres lying on east side of Broad River near a creek
called Turkey Creek waters of sd Broad River. Wit: GEO. LESLIE, JAMES
MITCHELL. Signed: JAMES (X) POTTS.

Page 177: Indenture made 24 Mar. 1790 bet. JOHN SEELY and PETER SEELY
both of Chester Co. 1 shilling sterling for 200 acres on
North branch of Sandy River as appears by grant dated 19 Sept. 1758.
Wit: ASA DARBY, SARAH SEELY, SAMUEL SEELY. Signed: JOHN SEELY, JANE
(X) SEELY. Seal.

Page 179: Indenture made 12 Oct. 1789 bet. ALEXANDER BROWN and JAMES
BROWN both of Chester Co. 100 pounds for 116 acres on
waters of Turkey Creek part of a grant to CATHERINE BROWN dated 23
Jan. 1773 transferred by will of sd. CATHERINE BROWN to sd. ALEXANDER
BROWN. Wit: WILLIAM GIVEN, DAVID PATTERSON, C. BRACKFIELD. Signed:
ALEXANDER BROWN. Seal.

Page 180: Indenture made 2 Jan. 1778 bet. ROBERT LAIRD and ELIZABETH
his wife of Craven Co., Camden Dist. and St. Mark Parish
to REESE HUGHES of same Co., Dist. and Parish. 200 pds. good money
for 100 acres on east side of Rocky Creek, originally granted to MICAM
FISHER of North Carolina in 1752, 285 acres in Craven Co., S. C. on
both sides of Rocky Creek. FISHER sold sd. tract to STEPHEN WHITE,
a blacksmith in 1759, STEPHEN WHITE and wife AGNES to LODOWICK LAIRD,
24 Aug. 1764, sd. LODOWICK LAIRD to ROBERT LAIRD his son. Wit: JOHN
KEEL, WILLIAM LAIRD, JOSIAH HUGHES. Signed: ROBERT LAIRD, ELIZ. (X)
LAIRD. Seal.

Page 180: Indenture made 6 Apr. 1790 bet. JAMES MC GAUGHEY and his
wife JEAN to JOHN MILLS, JR. both of Chester Co., 56 pd.
6 shillings 8 pence sterling for 100 acres on south fork of Fishing
Creek. Original granted to SAMUEL MORROW, 10 Sept. 1765. MORROW did
lease and release to JAMES MC GAUGHEY, 27 Apr. 1771. Wit: JAMES PEGAN,
JAMES GRAHAM. Signed: JAMES MC GAUGHEY, JENNET (X) MC GAUGHEY.

Page 185: Indenture made 12 Nov. 1788 bet. THOMAS STROUD of Chester
Co. and JOHN BARBER of Fairfield Co. 50 pds. sterling for
100 acres on Big Rocky Creek. Originally granted to JAMES JACK and

Cont'd from page 51:
JEAN JACK released by them to ARTHUR SCOTT and JEAN his wife on 6 Dec.
1773, ARTHUR & JEAN SCOTT unto THOMAS STROUD, 16 Jan. 1779. Wit: SAMUEL
FERGUSON, GEORGE (X) EGGNEW, ANDW. HEMPHILL. Signed: THOMAS (X) STROUD.
Seal.

Page 188: Indenture made 26 Nov. 1789 bet. ALEXANDER MC COWN, SR.
JOHN MC COWN both of Chester Co., 160 pds. sterling for
100 acres on south side of Fishing Creek, originally granted to JOSEPH
BRADLEY 4 Nov. 1762, from BRADLEY to ALEXANDER MC COWN 5 Dec. 1772.
Wit: ANDW. HEMPHILL, JOHN STEEL. Signed: ALEXANDER (X) MC KOWN.

Page 193: Bond of DANIEL COMER and THOS. BRANDON both of Union Co.
are held and bound unto THOMAS JENKINS of Chester Co. in
the sum of four thousand pounds sterling, dated 28 May 1789. Conditions
are THOMAS JENKINS and other heirs of RICHARD JENKINS, dec'd. who signed
a security bond for THOMAS FLETCHALL who was to administer the estate
of EDWARD FLETCHALL, dec'd. Wit: EDWARD LACEY, J.P., JOHN PRATT, J.P.
Signed: DANIEL COMER, Seal. THOS. BRANDON, Seal.

Page 194: Signed at Pendleton Co. on 16 Apr. 1790. MARY ROBERTS, wife
of ZACHARIAH ROBERTS signed her dower release and all right
of inheritance of land sold to ALLEN DE GRAFFENREID. Wit: W. EMBRY,
RT. MAXWELL. Reg. in Chester Co., 22 Apr. 1790.

Page 195: Signed in Pendleton Co. on 16 Apr. 1790 ANN DAVIS wife of
Richard Davis. Signs dower release and all rights of inheri-
tance of land sold to ALLEN DE GRAFFENREID. Wit: W. EMBRY, RT. MAXWELL,
ANDW. PICKENS, J.P. ROBERT ANDERSON, J.P. Signed: ANN (X) DAVIS.

Page 196: Indenture made 1 July 1790 bet. ROBERT MILLER and JAMES
MC CLURE both of Chester Co. 5 pds. sterling for 56 acres
on waters of Rockey Creek part of MILLER patent dated 6 Feb. 1773.
Wit: HUGH MC CLURE, DAVID DVS(?). Signed: ROBERT MILLER. Seal.

Page 198: Indenture made 6 Apr. 1790 bet. THOMAS MORRISON and wife
ELIZABETH and ALEXANDER ROSEBOROUGH and ROBERT MILLER both
of Chester Co. 5 shillings for 3 acres on Rockey Creek. To be laid
off circumvoleing(?) the Meeting House, for the use and benefit of
the Associate Reform Synod, to be laid off square. Part of a grant
dated 1 Sept. 1768 to SAMUEL CALDWELL for 100 acres, CALDWELL to THOMAS
MORRISON 26 Nov. 1782. Wit: CHRISTOPHER STRONG, WILLIAM ELLIOTT. Signed:
THOMAS (X) MORRISON, ELIZABETH (X) MORRISON. Seal.

Page 200: A mortgage bond JAMES FLETCHALL of Camden Dist. borrowed
1000 dollars from Capt. DAVID HOPKINS, 2 Apr. 1779. Obligation is that JAMES FLETCHALL bind two tracts of land being on the South
fork of Sandy River, one part known as the plantation where Mrs. MARY
DAVIS now lives, being land given him by his father THOMAS FLETCHALL,
adj. AMBROSE NIX's line. Wit: LEVY SMITH, JAMES GARRATTE. Signed: JAMES
FLETCHALL. Seal. Wit: In Union Co. 28 day --- 1789 CHARLES JONES, J.P.

Page 201: Indenture made 21 Oct. 1789 bet. WILLIAM MILES and BENJAMIN
WRING both of Chester Co. 5 shillings MILES signs a lease
and release to five tracts of land. Wit: NANCY ANDERSON, JOHN WINN.
Signed: WILLIAM MILES.

Page 202: Indenture made 22 Oct. 1789 bet. WILLIAM MILES of Chester
Co. and BENJAMIN WARING of Claremont Co. BENJAMIN WARING
at the express request and solicitation of WILLIAM MILES did enter
into a joint bond or obligation with him and DANIEL HUGER and JOHN
WINN, whereby they were bound unto SMITH, DESAUSSURE & DARRELL in the
penal sum of 6,910 pds. dated 16 July 1784. For five tracts of land
in Chester Co. on waters of Sandy River and Susey Creek, viz: one tract
of 100 acres granted to JOHN MILES, 19 Aug. 1774, adj. WILLIAM MINTER,
JOSEPH FEMSTER and JAMES MILES. One tract of 100 acres granted to DANIEL
NARSHAW, 21 Mar. 1768, adj. WM. GIVENS, JNO. MILES, RICHARD MILES and
HUGH SIMPSON. One other tract of 400 acres granted ZEPH. JOHNSTON,
WM. GIVENS, MOSES MC CARTY and WILLIAM MINTER. One other tract of 200

Cont'd from page 52:
acres granted to THOS. ROBINSON, 4 May 1775 adj. Col. LACEY and ROBERT
GORRELL. One other tract of 400 acres adj. to the last tract and ROBT.
GORRELL granted to JOSIAH HILL. Total of 1200 acres. Wit: NANCY ANDERSON
and JOHN WINN. Signed: WILLIAM MILES. Seal.

Page 204: A power of attorney from WILLIAM ARMER of Chester County
to THOMAS LEWIS of same county, to be my lawful attorney
in the state of North Carolina. Dated 5 Aug. 1789. Wit: PAT GRIFF,
RICHD. TALIAFERRO. Signed: WM. (X) ARMER. Seal.

Page 205: Bill of sale DANIEL COOK of Chester Co. to JOHN MC GLAMORY
of same Co. sold one negro boy age 16 years for 60 pds.
sterling. Dated 29 Dec. 1789. Wit: HUGH WHITESIDE, SR., HUGH WHITE-
SIDE. Signed: DANIEL COOK, Seal.

Page 206: Bill of Sale of PETER ROBESON to JOHN LATTO, SR. and JAMES
SMITH all of Chester Co. for 17 pds. sterling for horses,
cattle and household furniture. Dated 28 Dec. 1789. Wit: HUGH WHITESIDE,
DANIEL COOK. Signed: PETER ROBESON, Seal.

Page 207: Deed or bond from DAVID HOPKINS of Camden Dist. unto JAMES
GLENN of Cumberland Co., VA dated 12 Apr. 1783. One thousand
pds. sterling bond is on two tracts of land on Broad River, one where
GEORGE VAUGHN now lives, adj. WILLIAM CROSBY and JOHN CROSBY.
One other tract on the other side of the Broad River, adj. ELIS. HOL-
LINGSWORTH, THOMAS SHOCKLEY and WILLIAM SEAMATER. Wit: BERNARD GLENN,
FERDENN HOPKINS, UNIS LION. Signed: DAVID HOPKINS, Seal. Reg. in 1790
CHARLES SIMS, J.P.

Page 208: A land line dispute bet. JAMES BINGHAM and RUA HUGHS both
of Chester Co. planters dated 2 Oct. 1789 on Rockey Creek
of sd. county. ALEXANDER JOHNSON, WILLIAM BOYD and PHILLIP PEARSON
surveyors, JOHN WINN, JAMES CRAGE, JOSEPH BROWN and EDWARD LACY, Esqrs.
arbitrators; seals.

Page 210: This indent is to certify that the sale of land held 21
Dec. 1789 for 300 acres held at the seet(?) of PHILLIP WALKER
by EDWARD LACEY, sheriff, purchased by JOHN CAMBELL. This settles all
claims to sd. land. Signed: ALEXANDER CAMBELL, Seal.

Page 210: This indenture made 17 Nov. 1787 bet. LITTLETON ISBELL and
HUGH RANDOLPH both of Chester Co. 50 pds. sterling for 150
acres near Little Rockey Creek, adj. on south JOHN BISHOP, on east
by a tract formerly JOHN MORTON's, on west PETER SANDEFUR, on north
by ISAIK GRIMMES. Wit: SERA (X) FEATHERSTONE, A. HEMPHILL. Signed:
LITTLE ISBELL, Seal.

Page 212: Indenture made 5 Apr. 1790 bet. WILLIAM WHITESIDE and GEORGE
RELSEY, both of Chester Co. for 16 pds. sterling 100 acres
of land adj. RILSEY own land. With horses, cattle, cows and calves.
This deed or bill of sale is to be void if payment of 16 pds. sterling
and lawful interest is paid by 1 May 1795. Wit: HUGH WHITESIDE. Signed:
WILLIAM WHITESIDE, Seal.

Page 214: Bill of sale dated 1 Oct. 1789 bet. ALEXANDER MC COWN, SR.
and SARAH MC COWN both of Chester Co. for 20 pds. one negro
boy named Derry about five years old and two cows and calves. Wit:
ANDREW HEMPHILL, JOHN STEEL. Signed: ALEXANDER MC COWN, Seal.

Page 216: Bill of sale dated 13 Dec. 1789 bet. ALEXANDER MC COWN,
SR. and JAMES MC KOWN both of Chester Co. 60 pds. sterling
for one negro man named Buster. Wit: ANDREW HEMPHILL, JOHN STEEL. Signed
by: ALEXANDER MC KOWN, Seal.

Page 217: Bill of sale dated 2 Oct. 1789 bet. ALEXANDER MC KOWN, SR.
and NANCY MC KOWN both of Chester Co. 20 pds. sterling for
one negro girl named Dina age nine years old. Wit: ANDREW HEMPHILL,
JOHN STEEL. Signed: ALEXANDER MC KOWN, Seal.

Page 219: Bill of sale dated 1 Oct. 1789 bet. ALEXANDER MC KOWN, SR.
           and ELIZABETH MC KOWN both of Chester Co. 20 pds. sterling
for one negro girl named Patty about seven years old and two black
and white cows and calves. Wit: ANDR. HEMPHILL, JOHN STEEL. Signed:
ALEXANDER MC KOWN, Seal.

Page 220: Bill of sale dated 30 Dec. 1789 bet. ALEXANDER MC KOWN,
           SR. and JAMES MC COWN both of Chester Co. 60 pds. sterling
for one negro woman named Phillis (age not given). Wit: ANDR. HEMPHILL,
JOHN STEEL. Signed: ALEXANDER MC KOWN, Seal.

Page 222: Indenture made 7 July 1790 bet. MARY GASTON alias MC CLURE
           and SAMUEL LOWERY both of Chester Co. 5 pds. sterling for
100 acres of land on the drafts of the South fork of Fishing Creek,
bounding NE by JONATHAN JONES, SE by JOHN MC CLURE, SW by STROUNG,
NW by JAMES KNOX, other sides by JAMES MC CLURE, dec'd. The sd land
granted to MARY GASTON alias MC CLURE by patent dated 1 Dec. 1772.
Wit: SAMUEL LOWERY, JOHN MC CREARY. Signed: MARY MC CLURE, Seal.

Page 225: Indenture made 7 Oct. 1790 bet. OWEN EVANS of Pendleton
           Co., Ninety Six Dist. and JOSHUA RIPAULT of county and dist.
unknown, 85 pds. sterling for 200 acres on branch of Sandy River called
Cany Fork. First granted to RICHARD WARING dated 23 Dec. 1771 adj.
BENJAMIN CARTER line, EDMUND RUSSELL line, WILLIAM BOYD line. Wit:
GEORGE WARE, ADAM WILLIAMSON. Signed: OWEN EVANS, Seal.

Page 226: Indenture made 21 May 1790 bet. ELIJAH NUN and JOHN WRIGHT,
           both of Chester Co. 45 pds. for 90 acres on Sandy River.
Wit: FRANCIS WILKS, GREENBERY ROADEN, HEZEKIAH PONDER. Signed: ELIJAH
NUN(NUNN), Seal.

Page 228: Indenture made 21 May 1790 bet. ELIJAH NUNN and FRANCES
           his wife and JOHN WRIGHT all of Chester Co. 200 pds. for
245 acres on the waters of Sandy River. Wit: FRANCIS WILKS, GREENBERY
RODEN, HEZEKIAH PONDER. Signed: ELIJAH NUNN, Seal and FRANCES NUNN,
Seal.

Page 230: Indenture made 29 Dec. 1789 bet. WILLIAM HEAD, SR. and WIL-
           LIAM WATSON both of Craven Co. 100 pds. for 900 acres on
Martains branch and Fishing Hole branch adj. ASHFORD JENKIN's land,
on the south side of Sandy River. Granted to WM. HEAD, SR. 5 Mar. 1787.
Wit: JOHN WATSON, ELI CORNWELL, ROBERT (X) WATSON. Signed: WM. HEAD,
SR., Seal.

Page 232: Indenture made 1 Mar. 1773 bet. GASPER SLECKER and ELIZABETH
           his wife and GEORGE SLECKER both of Craven Co. 140 pds.
for 150 acres, part of a tract of 300 acres granted by the King dated
23 Jan. 1773 land on the drafts of Fishing Creek. Wit: ABRAHAM (X)
ADAMS, WILLIAM (X) SLEGER. Signed: GASPER SLEGER, Seal, ELIZABETH (X)
SLEGER.

Page 235: Indenture made 4 Aug. 1790 bet. WILLIAM WALL and CHARLES
           WALL both of Chester Co. 100 pds. sterling for 150 acres
lying on SW side of Catawba River. Bounding on NW by the River and
land of ABRAHAM STOVER. Land granted and release by JOHN WALL an heir
of WILLIAM WALL, dec'd. Dated 29 Nov. 1786. Land originally granted
unto WILLIAM WALL, dec'd. Wit: ANDR. HEMPHILL, HARDY (X) STROUD. Signed:
WILLIAM WALL, Seal.

Page 238: Indenture made 30 Sept. 1790 bet. ANDERSON THOMAS and SUSAN-
           NAH his wife of Fairfield Co., Camden Dist. and EDWARD MAHAN
of Chester Co. 20 pds. for a tract of land suppose to be 50 acres,
on the waters of Sandy River, adj. Capt. THOMAS line. Wit: WILLIAM
(X) JOHNSON, EDWARD (X) HOLSEY. Signed: ANDERSON THOMAS and SUSANNAH
(X) THOMAS, Seal.

Page 240: Bill of sale from GEORGE KENNEDY to JOHN SERVISE both of
           Chester Co. 21 pds. sterling for a horse, nine head of cattle
marked with the mark of JOHN COMBERT, dec'd. and sundry household ef-

Cont'd from page 54:
fects. Dated 10 Jan. 1789. Wit: JOHN MILLS, JR., JOHN GILLS, JR. Signed:
GEORGE KENNEDY, Seal.

PAge 241: A mortgage made 6 Aug. 1785 bet. PETER JOHNSON of Mecklen-
            burg state of North Carolina and EDWARD LACEY, JR. of Chester
Co. sum of 500 pds. money of S. C. Condition of obligation is that
EDWARD LACEY, JR. may sell two tracts of land in the name of JOHN KIRK-
CONNELL land by patent from N. C. One tract on Owens branch of Sandy
River, the other on Suley branch of Turkey Creek. Both tracts 200 acres.
Wit: PAT. MC GUFF, EDW. BLAND. Signed: PETER JOHNSON.

Page 242: Indenture made 5 Aug. 1790 bet. ELIZABETH HENDERSON a poor
            girl of Chester Co. and with consent of JAMES RAGEN and
THOMAS GARRET overseers of the poor and PHILLIP WALKER planter of Chester Co. Sd. ELIZABETH HENDERSON to serve lawfully and faithful until
age 18 or marriage. Sd. WALKER is to supply all needs, to teach to
read the New Testament in English. Wit: JAMES RAGEN, THOMAS (X) GARRET,
WALKER (X) BROWN. Signed: ELIZABETH (X) HENDERSON and PHILLIP WALKER,
Seal.

PAge 245: Power of Attorney from JEREMIAH JAGGARS made 20 Mar. 1788
            at Granby town, Orangeburgh Dist. Do constitute and appoint
my trusty and loving brother NATHAN JAGGARS of Chester Co. to make
a deed for a tract of land lying on the north side of Rockey Creek
to JOHN JAGGARS. Land first granted to BENJAMIN STREET. Wit: THOMAS
HUGHES. Signed: JEREMIAH JAGGARS, Seal.

Page 245: Deed of gift from ELIZABETH MC COLPIN to grand-daughter
            MARY WATSON of Chester Co., dated 30 Sept. 1790. Do hereby
give and grant unto MARY one brown bay mare about thirteen and one
half hands high, six years old last spring, and a colt of the same
about 14 months old. Wit: JOSHUA GORE, JOSEPH WATSON. Signed: ELIZABETH
(X) MC COLPIN, Seal.

Page 246: Indenture made 16 Dec. 1786 bet. GEORGE SLEEKER and SUFFIAH
            ADAMS both of Chester Co. 20 pds. sterling for 150 acres
on waters of Fishing Creek, adj. CASPER SLEEKER and sd. SUFFIAH ADAMS
own land. Wit: CASPER SLEEKER, ELIZABETH (X) SLEGER. Signed: GEORGE
(X) SLEGER and AGNES (X) SLEGER, Seal.

Page 248: Indenture made 7 Aug. 1790 bet. EDWARD LACEY, high sheriff
            of Chester Co. and JAMES ADAIR, saddler of Chester Co. JOSEPH
BROWN did implea JOHN WALKER for damage in the county court of July
1788, and obtained damage in same. JOHN WALKER received damage in same
court from JOSEPH BROWN. Each damages was 20 pds. JAMES ADAIR was last
bidder in the sum of 40 pds. for 590 acres on hold branch, a water
of Turkey Creek. Wit: JO. BROWN, JO. PALMER, THOS. HAIL. Signed: EDWARD
LACEY, Seal.

Page 249: Indenture made 4 Sept. 1790 bet. ROBERT KELSEY, yeoman and
            HUGH KELSEY of Chester Co. 20 pds. for 100 acres part of
a grant to ROBERT KELSEY 17 Mar. 1775 lying on a small branch of Rockey
Creek, adj. JACOB CARTER and vacant land to MICHAEL DIXON's line. No
witnesses. Signed: ROBERT (X) KELSEY, Seal.

Page 252: Indenture made 22 Mar. 1790 bet. RICHARD TALIAFERRO and
            MILLEY his wife of Chester Co. and CHARLES TALIAFERRO, JR.
of Amherst Co., VA 80 pds. sterling for 390 acres on waters of Sandy
River. Originally granted to HAZEL HARDWICK and conveyed to RICHARD
TALIAFERRO adj. north JOHN MC COMBS, east JAMES ALLISON, south WILLIAM
SHAWFF on west by RICHARDS. Wit: CHRISTOPHER (X) LOVING, JR., WILLIAM
(X) RANEY. Signed: RICHD. TALIAFERRO, MILLEY TALIAFERRO. Seal.

Page 254: Indenture made 22 Sept. 1790 bet. BENJAMIN STREAT, Doctor
            of Physic and EAKE BROWN, yeoman both of Chester Co. 50
pds. sterling for 100 acres on Turkey Branch of Rockey River. Original
granted to WILLIAM LAND on 3 Apr. 1772. Wit: ANDW. HEMPHILL, WM. CLEM-
INGS. Signed: BENJAMIN STREAT, Seal.

Page 258: Indenture made 15 May 1790 bet. JOHN MC COLPINE of Chester
          Co. and MANNIN GORE of Newberry Co. 100 pds. sterling for
300 acres on the waters of Sandy River. Originally granted to JAMES
STEPP, 26 July 1774. Wit: ELIJAH NUNN, JOSEPH WATSON. Signed: JOHN
MC COLPINE, Seal.

Page 260: Indenture made 15 May 1790 bet. MANNIN GORE of Newberry
          Co. and JOHN HUMPHRIS of Chester Co. 100 pds. for 300 acres
on waters of Sandy River, originally granted to JAMES STEPP from STEPP
to MC COLPINE, MC COLPINE to GORE. Wit: ELIJAH NUNN, JOSEPH WATSON.
Signed: MANNIN GORE, Seal.

Page 261: Indenture made 4 Oct. 1790 bet. PETER KOONROD and JACOB
          BRAKEFIELD both of Chester Co., 10 pds. for 180 & 1/2 acres
on the waters of Sandy River. Originally granted to JAMES NICHOLSON &
from NICHOLSON to JOHN ADAIR, Esq., from ADAIR to DAVID MC CALLAS,
from MC CALLAS to PETER KOONROD. Wit: ROBERT OWENS, HENRY SMITH, THOMAS
(X) MC GRIFF. Signed: PETER (X) KOONROD, Seal.

Page 263: Indenture made 16 Nov. 1787 bet. LITTLETON ISBELL and HUGH
          RANDOLPH both of Chester Co. 10 pds. sterling for 150 acres
on Hedge Branch near Rockey River, adj. E. by JOHN MORTANS, W. by PETER
SANDEFUR, S. by JOHN BISHOP, N. by ISAAC GAINERS. Wit: THOMAS LAND,
SARAH (X) FEATHERSTONE, ANDWR. HEMPHILL. Signed: LITTLETON ISBELL,
Seal.

Page 264: Indenture made 7 Apr. 1789 bet. JAMES WYLIE and wife SARAH
          and RALPH MC FADDEN both of Chester Co. 50 pds. sterling
for 100 acres on Fishing Creek and on road leading from SAL and WIL-
LIAM NEELY. Originally granted to SARAH CAMPBELL now wife of JAMES
WYLIE dated 6 Apr. 1768. Wit: JAMES KNOX, FRED HOPKINS, I. M. MC LIN-
TOCK, GAY MC FADDEN. Signed: JAMES WYLIE, SARAY (X) WYLIE, Seal.

Page 267: Indenture made 30 Nov. 1790 bet. MARTIN ELAM of Chester
          Co. and ANDERSON THOMAS of Fairfield Co. 50 pds. sterling
for 490 acres on Welches fork of Sandy River, adj. JAMES SHARP's land,
JOHN DAUGHERTY land, it being part of a 500 acres grant to JAMES DAUGHER-
TY dated 6 Feb. 1786. Wit: WM. JENKINS, WM. (X) ARMER. Signed: MARTIN
ELAM, Seal.

Page 268: License of ALLEN DEGRAFFENREID to keep a public tavern in
          his house. Dated 4 Jan. 1790. Bondsmen: JOSEPH TIMS, JAMES
GORE. RICHD. TALIAFERRO, Clerk Chester Co.

Page 269: Bill of sale for cattle and household goods. Dated 12 Nov.
          1790 bet. PATRICK HAMBLETON and DANIEL COOK. Sum of 15
pds. sterling money. Wit: HUGH WHITESIDE, SR., HUGH WHITESIDE. Signed:
PATRICK HAMBLETON, Seal.

Page 271: Indenture made 10 Nov. 1787 bet. ROBERT FARGUSON and wife
          ELIZABETH and WILLIAM WILIE both of Chester Co. 300 pds.
sterling for 75 acres originally granted to EDWARD WHITE, 10 Jan. 1771
on both sides of Fishing Creek, adj. JOHN MC FADDEN land, JAMES FORGASON
and ANDREW MARTAIN. Wit: ROBERT MC FADDEN, THOMAS DUGON, JOHN WILEY.
Signed: ROBERT FARGASON, ELIZABETH (X) FARGASON, Seal.

Page 274: Indenture made 5 Jan. 1791 bet. SAMUEL WIER and wife ELIZA-
          BETH and DANIEL ELLIOT, blacksmith, both of Chester Co.
sum of (?) for 200 acres on Fishing Creek, on west side of Catawba
River. Originally granted to BENJAMIN COOK, 27 Nov. 1771, adj. east
side HENRY CRAWFORD, on north COLDWELL land, WILLIAM COOK by lease
and release to WILLIAM FURGASON, 20 Jan. 1772. FURGASON to SAMUEL WIER.
Wit: CHAS. CARR, DAVID SHAN, EBENEZER ELLIOT. Signed: SAMUEL WIER.

Page 277: Indenture made 3 Oct. 1785 bet. ABRAHAM MYERS and THOMAS
          MORRIS both of Chester Co. 500 pds. for 150 acres on (?)
fork of Sandy River, adj. JONATHAN MAYFIELD land. Wit: ELISHA GORE,
MICHAEL (X) WILKINSON. Signed: ABRAHAM MYERS, SARAH (X) MYERS, Seal.

Page 278: Indenture made 27 Oct. 1790 bet. JOHN SMITH of Richmond

Cont'd from page 56:
County, GA and NEWMAN MILCOLLUM of Chester Co. 80 pds. ster-
ling for 100 acres on a small branch of Sandy River called Bresly Fork.
Wit: WILLIAM LEE, J.P., FRANCES WILKS, JAMES MASON. Signed: JOHN SMITH,
ELIZABETH SMITH, Seal.

Page 280:   Indenture made 18 Oct. 1788 bet. ALEXANDER MOORE of York
            Co. and ISAAC PIRCHARD of Chester Co. 30 pds. paid by ROBERT
NUNN for 100 acres in the fork of big and little Rockey Creek, adj.
GEORGE MORROW on south, PETER NANTR(?) on east, PHILLIP WALKER on north.
Wit: JOHN MOORE, JOHN LINN. Signed: ALEXANDER MOORE, Seal.

Page 282:   Deed of gift from RICE HUGHES, SR. unto his son CAGER HUGHES,
            dated 9 Aug. 1789. CAGER HUGHES is to get all negroes, horses,
cattle, hogs, plows and tools of all kinds, beds, tables, chests and
all in the house. RICE HUGHES, SR. to keep all land. Wit: JOHN HILL,
MESSAY (X) LAIRD. Signed: RICE HUGHES, Seal. (N.B.- the above assignment is not made and given from any fraudulent assign.)

Page 283:   Indenture made 4 Dec. 1782 bet. BLARKLEY SHOOMAKE and ROBERT
            ROBINSON, JR. both of Chester Co. 20 pds. for 200 acres
on Rockey Creek, adj. on south by BENJAMIN STREAT, other sides by vacant
land. Wit: JOHN ROBINSON, JAMES MC CREIGHT, MATTHEW MC CREIGHT. Signed:
BLARKLEY SHOOMAKE, Seal.

Page 287:   Indenture made bet. JOHN READEN and ELIJAH NUNN dated 27
            Dec. 1790, 40 pds. sterling for 124 acres. Originally granted
to READEN, 15 Oct. 1784. No water courses given. Wit: ABNER QILKS,
GREENBERRY RODEN. Signed: JOHN (I) ROADEN, Seal.

Page 278:   Indenture made bet. HANNAH EVANS of Pendleton Co. and JOHN
            ORR of Chester Co. dated 11 Oct. 1790, 25 pds. sterling
for 100 acres, part of a grant to JOHN EVANS dated 5 June 1786 on waters
of Sandy River, adj. widow FARGUSON line. HUGH STUART line, and ARCH-
ABLE SHELL line. Wit: HUGH STUART, WILL BOYD, ARCH. BELL. Signed: HANNAH
(X) EVANS, Seal.

Page 290:   Bill of sale from ROBERT COLLINS of Fairfield Co. unto JOHN
            HERRING of Chester Co. dated 13 July 1790 for 125 pds. ster-
ling sells one negro man named Hagar, four horses, one mare, six head
cattle, thirteen head hogs, one note on WILLIAM ALLEN, one note on
WM. GORMAN for 13 acres of tobacco. All household goods, and farm tools.
Wit: WILLIAM MALONE, ARON (X) GORE, NANCY (X) FRANKLIN. Signed: ROBERT
COLLINS, SR., Seal. (N.B.- GORE may be GOSE)

Page 292:   Indenture made bet. ROBERT BROWN and JOHN ADAMS both of
            St. Mark parish Craven Co.. dated 7 Dec. 1768. This is a
lease and release, 100 pds. for 100 acres with vacant land on all sides,
originally granted to ROBERT BROWN on 20 Aug. 1767, lying on the Sandy
fork of Rockey River. Wit: PETER CULP, ARCH (X) EAYLOTT, EDWARD CROFT.
Signed: ROBERT BROWN, wife MARGARET (X) BROWN. Seal. (N.B.- this deed
was proved by oath of PETER CULP before ZACHARY ISBELL, 7 Jan. 1769.)

Page 298:   Indenture made bet. JOHN ADAMS planter and JAMES BLAIR a
            saddler both of Chester Co., Camden Dist. dated 10 Sept.
1785, 52 pds. sterling for 100 acres lying on the fork of Rockey River,
that I, JOHN ADAMS, purchased from ROBERT BROWN, 7 Dec. 1768. Wit:
JOHN KELL, ROBERT MILLER. Signed: JOHN ADAMS, Seal.

Page 303:   Indenture made bet. JAMES KNOX and HUGH WHITESIDE both of
            Chester Co., Esqrs. and ALEXANDER CRAFORD, yeoman of same
Co. 80 pds. sterling for 68 acres on Catawba River, part of a grant
for 450 acres to WILLIAM TAYLOR, dec'd. dated 8 Mar. 1763. Sd. WILLIAM
TAYLOR, dec'd. did appoint CORNELUS ANDERSON and SAMUEL DUNLAP executors of his last Will and Testament. The former being dead and the
latter refusing to act. JAMES KNOX and HUGH WHITESIDE by court order
were appointed. No Witnesses. Signed: JAMES KNOX, HUGH WHITESIDE, Seals.

Page 306:   Indenture made 2 Jan. 1791 bet. SAMUEL WIER and EBENEZER

57

Cont'd from page 57:
        ELLIOTT both of Chester Co. 10 shillings sterling for 100
acres. Originally granted to JAMES HENRY by Wm. Tryon, Gov. of N. C.
on 5 Apr. 1767, lying on a ridge between Fishing and Rockey Creeks
on both sides of Henry run near a spring. Grant recorded in N. C. when
new state line was run sd. land fell in S. C., Chester Co. Wit: CHAS.
ORR, DAVID STRAIN, DANIEL ELLIOTT. Signed: SAMUEL WIER, Seal.

Page 310: Bill of sale bet. MARTAIN ELAM of Chester Co. and ANDERSON
        THOMAS of Fairfield Co., dated 10 Nov. 1790, 57 pds. and
8 shillings for one negro named Sarah, one negro named Simon, one negro
named Grace, one negro named Hannah, one negro named Samuel, three
horses, cattle, sheep, hogs, household goods, guns, tools, and farm
plows. Wit: WM. JENKINS, WM. (X) ARMER. Signed: MARTAIN ELAM, Seal.

Page 312: Indenture made bet. HUGH MILLIN, Esq. Sheriff of Camden
        Dist. and PHILLIP FOX of Chester Co. dated 29 Dec. 1790.
Whereas JOHN HARTH of Charleston City did impead(?) WILLIAM JONES who
was security for JAMES LONGESBAY on an auction of debt in April court
1786. Sd. sheriff did sell 250 acres of land lying on South fork of
Fishing Creek to PHILLIP FOX for 58 pds. sterling. Wit: JOHN (X) MILLS,
JNO. D. TINKLER. Signed: HUGH MILLING, late sheriff of Camden Dist.

Page 315: Indenture made bet. JOHN FRANKLIN and MORNING his wife and
        ROBERT KENNEDY both of Chester Co., dated 20 Apr. 1790.
70 pds. sterling for 106 acres on Flan Shan branch of Sandy River.
Originally granted unto JOHN FRANKLIN, 24 Dec. 1772 and by last will
and testament of THOMAS FRANKLIN unto his son JOHN FRANKLIN. Adj. WIL-
LIAM TRUSSEL, CLABORN WRIGHT, JOHN & THOMAS BAKER. Wit: JOHN WILLSON,
SAMUEL CRAIG, JOHN KENNEDY. Signed: JOHN FRANKLIN, MORNING (X) FRANKLIN.

Page 321: Indenture made bet. DAVID VENTERS and MARY his wife of York
        Co. and ISAAC MC FADDEN of Chester Co. dated 23 Oct. 1790,
20 pcs. of S. C. money for 220 acres on the waters of Neal Creek. Adj.
JAMES ROBINSON, JAMES DUNN, WILLIAM WILEY, JOHN DODS and ISAAC MC FAD-
DEN own land. Wit: JNO. MC CENAHAN, JOHN DODS, DAVID FARREL. Signed:
DAVID VANTURY, MARY (X) VANTURY, Seal.

Page 324: Indenture made bet. WILLIAM PATTON and JEAN his wife of
        Union Co. and JOHN DODS of Chester Co. dated 25 Oct. 1790,
20 pds. sterling for 150 acres near the trading path on the south side
of Catawba River. Adj. on north ROBERT PATTON, on west ISAAC MC FADDEN,
on south WILLIAM WILEY, on east WILLIAM HUMPHRIES. This tract a part
of 386 acres granted unto WILLIAM PATTON, 21 Mar. 1753 by Mathew Rowan,
Esq., Gov. of N. C. The land was then in N. C. now in S. C. Wit: ALEXAN-
DER EAKIN, ROBERT PATTON, WILLIAM PATTON. Signed: WILLIAM PATTON &
JEAN (X) PATTON, Seal.

Page 327: Indenture made bet. WILLIAM BRITAIN and JEAN his wife and
        OWIN LEE both of Chester Co. dated 3 July 1790, 100 pds.
sterling for 98½ acres on the waters of Sandy River. Wit: RICHD. TALIA-
FERRO. Signed: WILLIAM BRITAIN, Seal.

Page 328: Bill of sale from LEAKIN DAUSEY of the state of Georgia
        unto PHILLIP WALKER for 55 gold guineas, one negro boy about
17 years old name Ceaser, dated 6 Jan. 1790. Wit: SAMUEL FURGUSON,
GEORGE MORRIS. Signed: LEAKIN DOSEY, Seal.

Page 330: Indenture made bet. ANDREW HEMPHILL and ISBELL his wife
        and DANIEL GREEN (stiller) both of Chester Co., dated 5
Feb. 1791, 30 pds. sterling for 150 acres (no water course given),
adj. SE by WILLIAM FURGUSON line. Originally granted unto JAMES HEMP-
HILL, SR. Wit: WILLIAM STEENSON, ROBERT BREADY. Signed: ANDREW HEMPHILL
and ISBELL (X) HEMPHILL, Seals.

Page 334: Indenture made bet. JAMES BLAIR and MARGARET his wife (sad-
        dler) and FRANCES HENDERSON both of Chester Co. and St.
Mark parish. Dated 29 Dec. 1790. 100 pds. sterling for 100 acres on
the Sandy fork of Rockey River. Originally granted unto ROBERT   BROWN,

Cont'd from page 58:
20 Aug. 1767. BLAIR bought land from JOHN ADAMS in 1785. Wit: FRANCES
(X) HENDERSON, PHILLIP WALKER. Signed: JAMES & MARGARET BLAIR.

Page 339: Bill of sale dated 20 Oct. 1783 bet. PATRICK MC GRIFF and
          EDWARD LACEY for one negro woman named Jude about 18 years
old, she being stout, well made and county born, for 100 pds. sterling.
Wit: JOHN (X) PEW, JOHN ADAIR. Signed: PATK. MC GRIFF, Seal.

Page 341: Indenture made bet. JOHN COOPER, JR. and JOHN MORRIS both
          of Chester Co., dated 1 Dec. 1776, 200 pds. lawful money
of S. C. for 100 acres near Rockey Creek and between it and the Beaver
Dam branch. Adj. NATHAN SCOT land, JOHN DIES land, THOMAS MORRIS land.
Originally granted unto JOHN COOPER, 14 Oct. 1774. Wit: JOHN KELL,
GEORGE MORRSE. Signed: JOHN COOPER, JR., Seal.

Page 346: Bill of sale dated 10 Nov. 1790, York County bet. DANIEL
          WILLIAMS and JAMES MC NEIL and ARCHIBALD GILL of Chester
Co., 31 pds. sterling for one negro boy about 11 or 12 years old, American born, and free of any impairments whatever. Wit: SAMUEL MC NEIL,
JAMES HETHERINGTON. Signed: DANIEL WILLIAMS, JAMES MC NEIL, Seal. Proved
5 Apr. 1791, Chester Co., S. C.

Page 347: Bill of sale dated 10 Nov. 1790, York Co. bet. DANIEL WILL-
          IAMS, JAMES MC NEIL and ARCHIBALD GILL of Chester Co. 31
pds. 9 shillings sterling for one young American born negro girl about
10 years old named Amelia to be sound and free of any impairments whatsoever. Wit: JAMES HETHERINGTON, SAMUEL MC NEIL. Signed: DANIEL WIL-
LIAMS, JAMES MC NEIL. Proved in Chester Co. 5 Apr. 1791.

Page 349: Indenture made bet. ISAM FIELDING and his wife ELIZABETH
          and DAVID HYATT both of Chester Co., dated 20 Mar. 1791,
20 pds. sterling for 100 acres of land on the waters of Fishing Creek,
adj. N.W. by ELIZABETH CRAG land, all other sides vacant land. Originally granted unto WM. GASTON, late, dated 1 Sept. 1768. GASTON sold sd
land to JAMES NEALY dated 18 Jan. 1769. Wit: BENJAMIN RIEVES, WILLIAM
PEACE, WILLIAM (X) HARPER. Signed: ISAM (X) FIELDING, ELIZABETH (X) FI-
ELDING.

Page 353: Indenture made bet. THOMAS LEONARD of Chesterfield Co. and
          JOSHUA CROOK of Chester Co. dated 29 Nov. 1790, 75 pds.
sterling for 231½ acres on Fishing Creek, adj. WM. CROOK's line, CASPER
SLECKER land. Originally granted unto DAVID LEONARD 23 June 1774. DAVID
LEONARD died intestate, son THOMAS LEONARD became heir to all his land.
Wit: JOHN MC CREARY, ALEXANDER WALKER, SOLOMON CROOK. Signed: THOMAS
LEONARD, Seal.

Page 355: Indenture made bet. PETER JONES, Sheriff of Chester Co.
          and JAMES WYLIE of Chester Co. Dated 28 Feb. 1791. ABRAHAM
WRIGHT did implead ARCHIBALD CLARK in Oct. Court of 1790 for his debt
and cost on CLARKS goods and chattles, PETER JONES, Sheriff sold to
JAMES WYLIE 200 acres for 7 pds. sterling, land on Fishing Creek on
a ridge between it and Catawba River. Originally granted unto ARCHIBALD
CLARK, 27 Nov. 1770. Wit: ABRAHAM WRIGHT, JAMES MC CLINTOCK. Signed:
PETER JONES, Sheriff, Seal.

Page 358: Indenture made bet. BENJAMIN RIVES and WILLIAM HARPER both
          of Chester Co. dated 15 Jan. 1791, 5 pds. sterling for 161
acres on west side of Catawba River, adj. SHROD WILLS, WILSON HENDER-
SON, WILLIAM SHADRIT. Wit: WILSON HENDERSON, JACOB COOPER, THOMAS NEALY.
Signed: BENJAMIN RIVES, Seal.

Page 360: Indenture made bet. BENJAMIN ROADEN and THOMAS MORRISES
          both of Chester Co. dated 25 Jan. 1783, 50 pds. S. C. money
for 75 acres on waters of Buffalo fork of Sandy River and HENRY COBEL's
branch, adj. ROBIN MAKFIELD, WILLIAM ROADEN and THOMAS MORRISES line.
Wit: ELISHA MAYFIELD, JESSEE (X) OBRIANT. Signed: WILLIAM RODEN, MARY
(X) RODEN, Seal.

Page 361: Indenture made bet. ROBERT GILL and SAMUEL KELLEY both of

Cont'd from page 59:
Chester Co., dated 13 Mar. 1791, 28 pds. sterling for 200
acres on the waters of Fishing Creek. Originally granted unto GEORGE
GLOVER dated 25 Sept. 1766, he died intestate, wife and eldest son
ROBERT being made administrator, by lease and release dated 1 May 1770
conveyed unto ROBERT GILL. Wit: JOHN MILLS, PHILLIP FOX. Signed: ROBERT
GILL, Seal.

Page 365:   Bill of sale dated 3 Jan. 1791 bet. THOMAS MORRISE and HUGH
            MC CLURE both of Chester Co. for 10 pds. 1 gray mare, and
colt, two cows. Wit: JOHN KNOX, JOHN JOHNSTON. Signed: THOS. MORRISE.

Page 366:   Indenture made bet. JONATHAN JONES, yeoman and   WILLIAM
            JONES both of Chester Co. dated 28 Mar. 1791, 50 pds. sterl-
ing for 143 acres on Sandy River and east side of Broad River. Wit:
WILLIAM WHITESTONE, THOMAS WHITESTONE, JOSEPH JONES. Signed: JONATHAN
JONES, and wife BETHSHEBA (X) JONES, Seal.

Page 370:   Indenture made bet.' JONATHAN JONES and wife BETHSHEBA and
            WILLIAM JONES both of Chester Co. dated 2 Oct. 1786, 30
pds. sterling for 292 acres on waters of Sandy River the east side
of river, adj. JONATHAN JONES, JR. land, part of widow MORROW's land,
and on JAMES ADAIR line. Wit: WM. WHITESIDE, THOMAS WHITESIDE, JOSEPH
JONES. Signed: JONATHAN JONES, BETHSHEBA (X) JONES, Seal.

Page 374:   Indenture made bet. NATHAN BRISCO of Rutherford Co., N.
            C. and JOHN N. BELL, yeoman of Camden Dist., dated 25 Feb.
1791, 25 hundred weight of tobacco for 100 acres on North side of Broad
River on a branch of Turkey Creek, called Susy Bell Creek. Wit: JOHN
ROBINS. Signed: NATHAN BRISCO, Seal.

Page 376:   Indenture made 27 Jan. 1791 bet. ELIZABETH LONRIE a poor
            girl with THOMAS GARRET & JOHN JARRIS overseer of the poor
of Chester Co. and WILLIAM MOORE of same county. ELIZABETH LONRIE binds
herself unto WILLIAM MOORE to learn housekeeping until she is 18 years
old or day of marriage. Her age not given. Wit: THOMAS WHITESIDE, HUGH
WHITESIDE. Signed: ELIZABETH (X) LONRIE and WILLIAM MOORE, Seals.

Page 378:   I, WILLIAM MOORE do bind myself, my heirs, etc. to give
            the within named girl ELIZABETH LONRIE when she arrives
at the age of 18 years old a decent suite of clothing, a feather bed
and furniture to be of value in the amount of 12 pds. Also one spinning wheel and in the time of her apprenticeship to be taught to read
English distinctly. Signed: WILLIAM MOORE, Seal.

Page 378:   Indenture made bet. JONATHAN JONES, SR. and wife BETHSHEBA
            and JONATHAN JONES, JR. both of Chester Co., dated 23 Apr.
1790, 100 pds. sterling for 193 acres adj. PAUL FERGUSON line, JONATHAN
JONES, SR. line, ANDREW MORRISON line. Wit: HUGH WHITESIDE, WM. WHITE-
SIDE, WM. JONES. Signed: JONATHAN JONES & BETHSHEBA (X) JONES, Seal.

Page 382:   Indenture made bet. BENJAMIN RIVES and wife MARY and SHAROD
            WILLS both of Chester Co., dated 15 Jan. 1791, 5 pds. ster-
ling for 100 acres it being part of a tract of 396 acres granted unto
sd. RIVES on the west side of Catawba River, adj. on east by ADKINS
land, on south by WILLIAM HENDERSON land, on west by RIVES land. Wit:
WILSON HENDERSON, JACOB COOPER, THOMAS NEELY. Signed: BENJAMIN RIVES,
MARY (O) RIVES, Seals.

Page 384:   Indenture made bet. PETER JONES, Esq., Sheriff and ROBERT
            WALKER both of Chester Co., dated 2 Jan. 1791, 9 pds. and
16 shillings for 100 acres on the north side of Rockey River, adj.
PETER NANUS, PHILLIP WALKER, ROBERT WALKER and ROBERT MILLER. JOHN
MILLS, Esq. has a power of attorney from CHARLES HAMPTON of Charles
Town who did implead ROBERT MC CLAND for debt of 3 pds. 2 shillings,
2 pence, in the Chester Co. Court. Levied on the goods, chattels, land
and tenements. Wit: SAML. LONRIE, JOHN WALKER, JR. Signed: PETER JONES,
Sheriff, Seal.

Page 386:   Indenture made bet. ROBERT FROST and wife RUTH and EDWARD

Cont'd from page 60:
              HENDERSON both of Chester Co., dated 13 Oct. 1781, 200 pds.
current money of S. C. for 150 acres on a branch of Sandy River called
Suley Creek. Wit: JNO. MAYFIELD, SOVILLEN BOND, ISAM BOND. Signed:
ROBERT FROST, RUTH (X) FROST.

Page 390: Indenture made bet. JOHN HITCHCOCK of Broad River and ARCHA-
           BALD KELL of Rockey River both of Chester Co., dated 3 May
1780. 160 pds. current money of S. C. for 200 acres being one half
of a grant of 400 acres given unto JOHN HITCHCOCK, 7 Nov. 1770 on a
branch of Sandy Creek of Broad River, adj. JOHN HUNTER. Wit: ZACHARIAH
ROBERTS, JOHN HUNTER. Signed: JOHN HITCHCOCK, Seal.

Page 395: Indenture made bet. THOMAS WALLACE and JOHN PUGH both of
           Chester Co., dated 23 Apr. 1790, 500 pds. S. C. money for
100 acres lying on the head of Sandy River, being part of a tract of
300 acres granted by Gov. Wm. Tryon of N. C. (two places in this deed
can't be read because of ink smears). Wit: GEO. GILL, PAT. MC RIFF.
Signed: THOMAS WALLACE, Seal.

Page 397: Indenture made bet. RICHARD SMITH and WILLIAM MOORE both
           of Chester Co., dated 6 Aug. 1789, 50 pds. sterling for
100 acres lying on Rockey Creek, adj. south by GEORGE MORRISON, on
east by PETER NANCE land, on north by PHILLIP WALKER land. Wit: ELYAH
DAVIS, JOHN DAVIS, DINAH DAVIS. Signed: RICH. SMITH, Seal.

Page 398: Indenture made bet. DANIEL TRAVERSE and wife SARAH of Chester
           Co. and WILLIAM BECK of York Co., dated 8 Oct. 1789, 60
pds. sterling for 150 acres on a branch of Turkey Creek, originally
granted unto DANIEL TRAVERSE, 1 Mar. 1775. Adj. on south by JAMES ANDER-
SON. Wit: JAMES ADAIR, CHRISTOPHER (X) LEVIN, JAMES MC NEEL. Signed:
DANIEL TRAVERSE, SARAH (X) TRAVERSE, Seal.

Page 400: Deed of gift from DANIEL CURRY to well beloved son DAVID
           CURRY both of Chester Co., dated 15 June 1790. For love
and goodwill DAVID to get one negro named Grace, one horse value of
15 pds., cows and calf. Wit: JOHN ASHFORD GORE, ELEAZAR GORE. Signed:
DANIEL (X) CURRY.

Page 401: Deed of gift from DANIEL CURRY to well beloved daughter
           ANNE CURRY both of Chester Co., dated 15 June 1790, for
love and goodwill ANNE to get one negro named Mary. Wit: JOHN ASHFORD
GORE, ELEAZAR GORE. Signed: DANIEL (X) CURRY, Seal.

Page 401: Deed of gift from DANIEL CURRY to well beloved daughter
           MARY CURRY both of Chester Co. dated 15 June 1790 for love
and goodwill MARY to get one negro named Siller. Wit: JOHN ASHFORD
GORE, ELEAZAR GORE. Signed: DANIEL (X) CURRY, Seal.

Page 402: Deed of gift from DANIEL CURRY to well beloved wife BESTORE,
           horses, cattle, hogs, and household goods. Dated 15 June
1790. Wit: THOMAS GORE, JOHN ASHFORD GORE. Signed: DANIEL (X) CURRY.

Page 402: Deed of gift from DANIEL CURRY to well beloved son JOHN
           CURRY both of Chester Co. dated 15 June 1790. For love and
goodwill JOHN to get one negro named Polley about thirty years old.
Wit: JOHN ASHFORD GORE, ELEAZAR GORE. Signed: DANIEL (X) CURRY.

Page 403: Indenture made bet. JAMES ADAIR of Chester Co. and HERMON
           KOLB of York Co. dated 31 Mar. 1790, 20 pds. 8 shillings
for 150 acres on waters of Sandy River. Wit: ROBERT FOWLER (torn) __
ROBERTS, (torn)__ MOFFETT. Signed: JAMES ADAIR, ANNA ADAIR, Seal.

Page 405: A power of attorney from JOHN ROBINSON of Newberry Co. to
           trusty friend WILLIAM THOMAS LITON of Chester Co. dated
13 ___? 1790 to use, ask, demand, recover and receive in my name from
the estate of THOMAS REAVER, dec'd. Wit: HUGH THOMAS, JOHN CATON, KATH-
ERINE (X) CATON. Signed: JOHN (X) ROBINSON, Seal. Proved in Chester
Co. bef. CHARLES SIMS, J.P. on oath of HUGH THOMAS, 1 May 1799.

Page 407: Indenture made bet. JAMES KNOX and HUGH WHITESIDE, Esq. of Chester Co. and PETER CULP, yeoman of Chester Co., dated 29 June 1790, 12 pds. sterling for 100 acres on the north fork of Fishing Creek, originally granted unto WILLIAM TAYLOR, 11 Aug. 1774, adj. when granted on NW by BENJAMIN CULP, on SW by WILLIAM TAYLOR owen(?) land. Sd. TAYLOR by last will and testament ordered land to be sold, appointing CORNELUS ANDERSON and SAMUEL DUNLAP, ANDERSON being dead and DUNLAP refusing to act. Court appointed KNOX & WHITESIDE to be executors. Wit: JOHN MILLS, HUGH KNOX, DAVID STRAIN. Signed: JAMES KNOX, HUGH WHITESIDE.

Page 410: Indenture made bet. JOHN MC COLPIN and ASA DERBY both of Chester Co. dated 8 May 1790, 50 pds. sterling for 150 acres (no water ways given). Originally granted unto JAMES STEPP, 26 July 1774, adj. NW on JOHN TAYLOR land, on S by JOHN HUMPHRIES, NE by JOHN SEALY land. Wit: ROBERT FROST, JAMES SANDERS. Signed: JOHN MC COLPIN, NANCY (X) MC COLPIN, Seals.

Page 412: Power of Attorney from JOHN ADAIR of the district of Kentucky State of Virginia unto WILLIAM MILES of Chester Co. to act, sue, recover and receipt of one sorrel horse from JOHN DOWNING of Chester Co., dated 16 Mar. 1789. Wit: JOHN WILLIAMS, JOHN MILES. Signed: JOHN ADAIR, Seal.

Page 413: I, HAZEL HARDWICK of Chester Co. am bound, held unto PETER PETICE both of Chester Co. dated 10 Dec. 1789. In the sum of 50 pds. sterling. Conditions are that PETER PETICE to have possession of 50 acres of land adj. JESSE TIMMS line, Charles town road, and PETER PETICE land. Sd. PETICE not to sell or rent sd. land until HAZEL PETICE (?) comes of full age of 21 years, then HAZEL HARDWICK is to cause to be made a good and lawful right to sd. land. Wit: ELYAH NUNN, JOHN PRATT, SARAH PRATT. Signed: HAZEL HARDWICK, Seal.

Page 414: We, DAVID HOPKINS, FERDENAN and NEWTON HOPKINS are held and bound unto DAVID PRUIT all of Chester Co., dated 10 Oct. 1786. In the sum of 100 pds. for their rights to 300 acres of land granted unto WASHINGTON HOPKINS, 21 Jan. 1785 on the waters of Sandy River. Wit: THOMAS GLENN, JOSEPH (X) HUGHEY. Signed: D. HOPKINS, F. HOPKINS, N. HOPKINS, Seals.

Page 415: I do sign over my rights and title of the within bond containing one hundred pds. sterling unto JOHN WIER his heirs, etc. Wit: WILL BOYD, JOHN CUGAN, HANNAH BOYD. Signed: DAVID (X) PRUIT.

Page 415: Indenture made bet. JOHN FLINTHEN of Orange Co., N. C. to JAMES HUEY of Chester Co., dated 25 Nov. 1789. 100 pds. sterling for 100 acres on the north side of Broad River on a branch called Flinthen creek. Originally granted unto EDWARD FLINTHEN, 27 June 1766. Wit: JAMES GORE, JOHN CALVIN. Signed: JOHN FLINTHEN, Seal.

Page 417: Indenture made bet. JOHN FLINTHEN of Orange Co., N. C. and JAMES HUEY of Chester Co., dated 25 Nov. 1789. 200 pds. sterling for 200 acres on the Broad River and East Sandy River adj. E by WILLIAM STONE, on W by JOHN LYON. Part was granted unto EDWARD FLINTHEN, 2 Sept. 1766, the other part granted unto DANIEL PRICE, 31 Oct. 1765. Wit: JOHN PRATT, JAMES CALVIN. Signed: JOHN FLINTHEN, Seal.

Page 418: Indenture made bet. JOHN GRISHAM of Chesterfield Co. and JEREMIAH GRISHAM of Chester Co., dated 29 Aug. 1788. 75 pds. sterling for 100 acres on the waters of Sandy River and Stones Creek. Originally granted to JOHN GRISHAM, 15 Sept. 1784. Wit: JOHN DAUGHERTY, ISAAC WAGNER, NICHOLAS (X) SHEETS. Signed: JOHN (X) GRISHAM.

Page 420: Indenture made bet. JAMES STAPP of Lincoln Co., VA and JOHN MC COLPIN of Chester Co. dated 29 Sept. 1789. 100 pds. sterling for 600 acres on a branch of Sandy River, adj. SE by JOHN SEALEY, SW, NW by MAC. & WM. FERGUSON and NE by STEWART BROWN. Wit: ISAAC VANMATNE, EDWARD (X) HALSEY. Signed: JAMES STAPP, Seal.

Page 422: Indenture made bet. JOHN STARN and wife MARY and WILLIAM
YOUNG, both of Chester Co., dated 3 Apr. 1790. 10 pds. ster-
ling for 100 acres on Bressley Fork. Wit: W. ENLY, JAMES (X) YOUNG,
JOHN YOUNG. Signed: JOHN STARN, MARY STARN, Seals.

Page 424: Indenture made bet. WILLIAM RANEY and wife MARY and CLAYBORN
WRIGHT both of Chester Co., dated 28 June 1790. 100 pds.
sterling for 100 acres on Sandy River, adj. NOTLEY COATES line, SAMUEL
CRAEG's line, WILLIAM TRUSSEL line, JOHN FRANKLIN line. Wit: ONRA LEA,
RICH. WRIGHT. Signed: WILLIAM (X) RANEY, MARY (X) RANEY, Seals.

Page 426: Indenture made bet. JOHN FRANKLIN and MOURNING his wife
and WILLIAM RANEY both of Chester Co., dated 28 June 1790.
100 pds. sterling for 100 acres on the waters of Sandy River, adj.
NOTLEY COATES line, SAMUEL CRAEGS line, WILLIAM TRUSSELLS line. Wit:
PETER DORAN, CLAYBORN WRIGHT. Signed: JOHN FRANKLIN, MOURNING (X) FRANK-
LIN, Seals.

Page 428: Bill of sale from JAMES MINNES to NATHAN JAGGARS. Dated
20 Apr. 1788. 150 pds. sterling, MINNES sells part of his
property to wit.-one negro woman named Juda, one sorl(sic) horse about
11 yrs. old and fourteen hands high also one bay mare named Ball same
height, fifteen yrs. old. Likewise GABRIEL BROWN note or whatever may
be received by law for the same, also household furniture and farm
tools. Wit: WILLIAM MINNES, BENJAMIN STUART. Signed: JAMES MINNES,
Seal.

Page 429: Indenture made bet. JOHN MC FADDEN and wife MARY and MOSES
SMITH, both of Chester Co., dated 4 Sept. 1789. By lease
and release for 100 pds. sterling for 100 acres on Rockey River on
the South side of Waterree River. Originally granted unto JOHN MC FADDEN
7 Oct. 1762. Wit: EDWARD STUDMAN, JOSHUA SMITH. Signed: JOHN MC FADDEN,
MARY MC FADDEN, Seal.

Page 435: Indenture made bet. RICH. TALIAFERRO and MILLEY his wife
of Chester Co. and CHARLES TALIAFERRO, JR. of Amherst Co.,
of Va. dated 8 July 1790. 90 pds. sterling for 390 acres on waters
of Sandy River. No witnesses. Signed: RICH. TALIAFERRO, MILLEY TALIA-
FERRO, Seals.

Page 436: Indenture: that PATRICK FINLEY, a single man, hath put himself an apprentice to THOMAS CABAN, tanner, to learn his
art, trade, or mystery and after the manner of an apprentice for and
during the full term of three years. He shall faithfully serve his
surety. Keep his lawfully commands every where, gladly obey, he shall
do no damage to his sd. master nor see it done by others, without letting or giving him notice thereof to his sd. master. He shall not waste
sd. masters goods nor lend them unlawfully to others. He shall not
commit fornication nor contract matrimony with the sd. term. He shall
not buy or sell, he shall not absent himself day nor night from his
sd. masters service without his leave. But in all things behave himself
as a faithful apprentice aught to do during the sd. term. The sd. master
shall use the utmost endeaver to teach or cause to be taught and instruct the sd. apprentice in his trade and mystery. Provide for him
the sd. apprentice sufficient meat, drink, washing and lodging fitting
for an apprentice during the sd. term. Also lend him in the sd. term
six wearing shirts, three hunting shirts, six pair of overalls, and
a full suit of home spun cloath, one fine shirt, two felt hats, and
at the expiration of the aforesd. term, the sd. master to give him
a horse, saddle, bridle and saddle bags, to be valued at fifteen pds.
The sd. master is also to give sd. apprentice one pair of leather breach-
ers and three pair of wolling stockings. For the true performance of
all and every the sd. covenents and agreements either of the sd. parties
bind themselfs to the other by these presents. In witness whereof they
have enterchangeable put their hand and seal -- This 24 day March 1790.
Wit: EDW. LACEY, WM. GRAHAM, ROBT. HELSEY, JOHN HUTTON. Signed: WIL-
LIAM (X) FINLEY and THOMAS CABAN. (In the first, PATRICK is used, then
signed by WILLIAM FINLEY)

(Pages 438 to 444 contain three letters from Col. DAVID HOPKINS, Esq.

63

Cont'd from page 63:
                    and Capt. CHARLES SIMS, about the removal of their slaves
to the state of Virginia. Every effort has been made to transcribe
same, from the microfilm as they are. There are some ink blurs that
obliterated all words.)

Page 438:   Dear Sons: Tyger River, Mrs. ANDERSON's, Nov. 9, 1780. Last
            Tuesday night or rather Wednesday morning we were attacted
by the British part of Tarlton core commanded by Maj. WINS at the Fish
dam pond on Broad River, we kept the ground tho with difficulty as
we had a number of tories amungst us. I am doubtfull, I have lost my
favorite boy Morrise when the action commensed, he was lying at a fire
some distance from me and attempted to get to me and fell in with the
British cavalry where he was shot and bayoneted in such a manner that
I believe there is very little hope of his recovery which is a lost
I particular feel as I am now destetute of servent. Only at will of
others, I have boys that are very obligeing but under slinder restri-
bution, the enemy has covered the greatest part of the State. Tho I
think our move to the fish dam is much in our favour as it put it,
in our power to remove the properity taken by the enemy and negros
taken to the sister states where perhaps --- for by --- or to him or
them he may direct it to and as I have been so unfortunate as to loose
my all except my lands and have now --- my negros, I prevailed on Capt.
CHARLES SIMS to take the negros with him to Virginia and have his positive promise to deliver them to you two at Mr. JAMES GLENNS in Cumberland Co., Va. I have furnished him with three valuable beast in order
to carry the baggage and young negros which I expect you will reason
with the negros. There is in number 17 a list of their names I have
inclosed to you and if it is in your power to secure them from the
enemy or dispose of them if you find it adviseable for I look on it
to be so much dragged out of the fury, and all your own if you can
save them. Therefor do what you think best and as I have property here
I have not the least idea of it however I hope it may not be the case
in Virginia where you are, and as you have able advisers I would earn-
estly recommend to you not to neglect that part as you are both young
and never had an opportunity of being acquainted with the course of
the world. There is Capt. WM. THOMPSON, Mr. DAVID ANDERSON, Mr. MATTHEW
SIMS, Mr. NATHAN GLENN, or Mr. JAMES GLENN all who are near relations
and to be confied in and who will cheerfullness give you the best coun-
sull. I have nothing more at present that I now recollect, and haste
oblige me to conclude as we are now under marching orders I shall write
to you by every opportunity and hope you will not neglect doing the
same by me. This from your loving father till death. D. HOPKINS
Mr. FERDINAND HOPKINS
Mr. NEWTON HOPKINS

The names of then negros sent by Capt. CHARLES SIMS to my sons FERDI-
NAND and NEWTON HOPKINS now in the State of Virginia, Cumberland County.
9 day Nov.1780.

1. Daniel	5. Betty	9. Jacob	13. Jinney
2. Tanner	6. Robin	10. Milley	14. Harvy
3. ----	7. Cloe	11. Isaac	15. Phillis
4. ----	8. Lucey	12. Dick	16. Marge
			17. Morris

Page 440:   The property of FERDINAND and NEWTON HOPKINS in case they
            or either of them can save or dispose of them agreeable
to the contents of my letter, which has the inclosed DAVID HOPKINS,
Mr. FERDINAND HOPKINS and NEWTON HOPKINS. State of Virginia Cumberland
County, Mr. JAS. GLENN's home, by Capt. SIMS.

Personally appeared CHARLES SIMS, Esq. One of the justices of Union
County who being sworn maketh oath that dureing the British being in
the neighbourhood of Lile's ford and Sherves ferry. He being then a
prisoner of war to the British on parole he went to the quarters of
Gen. Sumpter on Tiger River and there obtained a certificate for the
removal of his negroes and those of Col. DAVID HOPKINS to the State
of Virginia, and when the negroes of Col. DAVID HOPKINS were given
to him they having been taken by British, and retaken it was the express

64

Cont'd from page 64:
orders of and request of Col. HOPKINS to the deponent, to deliver the
sd. negroes being in number seventeen or there about to his sons FERDI-
NAND HOPKINS and NEWTON HOPKINS and that he freely and voluntarily
and positively give them the said negroes to all intent and purposes
the subseance of which disterbation is mentioned in a letter rote by
the said Col. HOPKINS, dated Nov. 9, 1780 and to signing of which the
deponent also swears.

Signed: CHARLES SIMS

Sworn before me this
6th August 1781 -- R. BREMAN, J.P.

Page 441:   South Carolina   Fort Lacey   Dec. 20th, 1780
            My dear sons I find these are much worse than when you left
South Carolina. At last the enemy has had possession of all I possessed
and am told, had come to a conclusion of the division of the negroes
and plantation and were under cover of the British which made them
think all quite safe. They had taken of only five of the negroes and
they on FARGUSON's defeate were left to themselves and chose to come
home and Tuesday evening the 7th of last month Gen. Sumpter arrived
at the Fish dam pond on Broad River and the next morning about one
o'clock we were attacted by the British part of Tarlton's core, their
number from the best information was about two hundred and sixty our
number consisted of about three hundred or upwards, they attacted us
with their cavalry in front however, after they left in about an hour
the enemy sees cause to quit the ground with the loss of twenty seven
killed, wounded and taken and commanding officer Maj. WINGO wounded
and taken amongst the rest, they had seven killed on the ground and
four died of their wounds. The evening we left three killed and six
wounded. My boy who I so much esteemed I believe is mortaly wounded
as he is shot between the body and shoulder and bayoneted in three
different places on the body. The next day we advanced as far as Tyger
River and after crossing it incamped on the South side when we has
our neighborhood under CARY, which abandoned a small party for those
who had recovered or had property that they wished out of the way of
the enemy to make a venture. Capt. CHARLES SIMS concluded to rest his
negroes for the time. I prevailed on him to try to   )
)take them to
)you happen
)there possible
till he could see you which he said he would be sure to do if he got
his negroes in safe as he should go by your uncle GLENN's where you
board. I also told him to be sure to tell you that if you could possibly
save the negroes from the enemy that all and every of them should be
your absolute right and property. I am informed that Capt. SIMS has
left the negroes on the Yadkins River opposite the Movarian town if
it should be the case, perhaps he may leave his negroes on the way
in, stay with the so long that you may lose yours, therefore, I have
this opportunity by Mr. STOGDEN who tells me he is going into Virginia
immediately and with all the speed he possibly can, and through the
neighbourhood where you are, he has promised me either to call at Mr.
GLEEN's and deliver this letter to you with his own hand, or be sure
to send it to you by a safe hand, and if it should be the first account
you have had of the negros I would recommend you both to push immediately to where the negroes are and run them with all speed into Virginia, and the most safest part you can be informed of as I would wish
you to save them if possible, as they have been taken and retaken and
it will ___ ___ certainly be so much saved to yourself ___ and if it
should so happen that you should secure the negroes and we gain our
independency I would wish you to make an equal division with your brother and sister as if it should be the will of Providence that I survive the wounds I have ___
in our faviour (
believe it   (
all my rights (
and every of the negroes I did formerly or do now own to you as aforesaid all the other part of my estate except my lands has fell into
the hands of the enemy. They drove off at one time between ninety and
a hundred head of cattle, ___ ___. They have also got all my sheep

Cont'd from page 65:
and the greatest part of my hoggs, plantation tools, household furniture
and many other articles of value, so that I am properly ___ soldier
and determined to see ___
cause or further the attempt the ___
news. I have omited which was the ___
Black Stock on Tyger River ___
Five days after I saw Capt. SIMS ___
attacted us about an hour and a haf ___
the evening action continued until ___
down when we beat them off the groun ____
four killed and Gen. Sumpter badley wounded Capt. GABARIAL BROWN was
killed, to my left hand and Gen. Sumpter was to my right it both happen-
ed from one platoon from the enemy on their retreat it is supposed
they had sixty or seventy men killed and wounded. Gen. Sumpter is on
the recovery. I have nothing more particular at present but am with
sincere respect your loving father till death?....DAVID HOPKINS

Mr. FERDINAND HOPKINS and NEWTON HOPKINS)
in the State of Virginia, Cumberland)   N.B. We were so scarce of paper
County Gunney Creek -- Mr. GLEEN)   in camp at the time Capt. Sims
                                         started for Virginia I could
                                         scarsely get enough to send
a list of the negroes which were only seventeen. I amas? a Boy. D.
HOPKINS
Mr. FERDINAND HOPKINS & NEWTON HOPKINS in the State of Virginia, Cumberland County Gunney Creek. Mr. JAMES GLEEN in hand by Mr. STOGDEN.

Page 445: Deed of gift from DOROTHY MOORE to DOROTHY MOORE, JR. both
          of Chester Co. Dated 4 July 1789, for love and goodwill
that I have for my daughter. I give one negro woman named Rachel, two
feather beds and furniture, one cow and calf, all real and personal
property I may have. Wit: THOS. JENKINS, WM. JENKINS, JOHN HUMPHRIES.
Signed: (smeared) MOORE.

Page 446: Deed of gift from RUE HUGHES to JOSIAH HUGHES both of Chester
          Co. Dated 16 Sept. 1778, for love and goodwill that I bear
for my son JOSIAH HUGHES the land I bought from ROBERT LAIRD containing
250 acres on the NE side of Rockey Creek. Wit: JOHN KELL, RUE HUGHES,
JR. Signed: RUE HUGHES.

Page 447: Indenture made bet. SAMUEL HAMBLETON and LILLES his wife,
          yeoman and DANIEL COOK, taylor, both of Chester Co. Dated
4 Nov. 1789. 40 pds. sterling, for 100 acres of land on the waters
of Fishing Creek originally granted unto JOHN HAMBLETON, 21 Jan. 1785.
Wit: JOHN MILLS, WILLIAM MILLER. Signed: SAMUEL (H) HAMBLETON, LILLES
(L) HAMBLETON.

Page 450: Indenture made bet. SAMUEL HAMBLETON, yeoman and DANIEL
          COOK, taylor, both of Chester Co. Dated 4 June 1789 60 pds.
sterling for 250 acres on waters of Fishing Creek. Adj. S by WM. WEST
line, and NATHAN SEMPLE land, on W by JOHN MC KENNEY land. Wit: JOHN
MILLS, CHAS. ORR, WILLIAM MILLER. Signed: SAMUEL (H) HAMBLETON, LILLES
(L) HAMBLETON, Seal.

Page 454: State of South Carolina) This day came JAMES THOMAS personal
          Chester County   ) ly before me DAVID HOPKINS, Esq.....
one of the Justices assigned to keep the peace for sd county and first
being duly sworn on the Holy Evangable of Almity God. Deponst and saith
that he verely believes he was the son of DANIEL THOMAS, SR., dec'd
and brother to WILLIAM THOMAS, dec'd and late resident of Fairfax Co.
in the State of Virginia and that DANIEL THOMAS, SR., dec'd his father
departed this life in the year of our Lord, one thousand seven hundred
and eighty in the month of October in the same year, leaving behind
him three sons and three daughters, the eldest of which is WILLIAM
THOMAS and that his father died intestate leaving him no will at all
and never made any distribtion in any manner whatsoever of his property
in his life time. And that he very well remember that his father in

Cont'd from page 66:
his life time and before he left the State of Virginia surveyed two
tracts of land in Hampshire County on George run a branch of Patterson
Creek in the State of Virginia and that not to his knowledge know of
his father desposing of the sd land in any manner. Signed: JAMES THOMAS,
W. FURGUSON. Subscribed before me the 3d day of July 1790. D. HOPKINS,
J.P.

Page 455: State of South Carolina) This day came CATHERINE THOMAS
        Chester County   ) of the County and State aforesd
the former wife and now widow of DANIEL THOMAS, dec'd. before me DAVID
HOPKINS, Esq. one of the Justices assigned to keep the peace for sd.
county. And first being sworn on the Holy Evangalist of Almighty God,
deponith saith that in the year of our Lord one thousand seven hundred
and thirty six she in the month of September in the same year was married to DANIEL THOMAS, SR., dec'd. then living in Westmoreland County
and state of Virginia and in the year of our Lord one thousand seven
hundred and thirty seven day in and upon the twenty fifth day of May in
the same year she bore a son by the sd. DANIEL THOMAS, dec'd. Whose
name was called WILLIAM and that she knows the sd. WILLIAM to be the
eldest son and lawful heir of the sd. DANIEL THOMAS, SR., dec'd. and
the sd. WILLIAM THOMAS, eldest son of DANIEL THOMAS, SR., dec'd. is
now living in the county and state aforesaid on Broad River. And further
sayeth not. Signed: KATHERINE (N) THOMAS. Subscribed and sworn before
me this third day of July 1790. D. HOPKINS, J.P.

Page 456: Indenture made bet. LAWRENCE GALLAHER and ALEXANDER MC COWEN
        both of Chester Co. Dated 3 Oct. 1771, 200 pds. current
money of S. C. for 100 acres on a branch of Watereé River called Fishing Creek. Adj. NE by ARCHABALD MC DOWELL, other sides vacant land.
Wit: THOMAS JONES, WILLIAM LONG, WILLIAM BOYKIN. Signed: LAWRENCE (A)
GALLAHER, Seal.

Page 461: Indenture made bet. JOHN HAGANS and JAMES KNOX a practition-
        er of Physick, both of Chester Co. Dated 14 Oct. 1789. JAMES
HAGANS stands justly indebted to JAMES KNOX in the sum of the whole
to thirty five pds. six shillings, three pence sterling. In two notes,
one for thirty pds., and one for five pds., six shillings and three
pence. To be pd. by 27 Mar. 1793. Notes secured by two tracts of land.
One of 250 acres on the Catawba River, originally granted unto GASPER
CULP 5 Feb. 1754 by Matthew Rowan, Gov. of N. C. Who sold to JOHN LANCE,
who sold to JOHN WALKER, who sold to JOHN HAGANS. Likewise a tract
of fourteen acres granted unto ISAAC TAYLOR, who sold to GEORGE SLEGER,
JR. who sold to JOHN WALKER, who sold to JOHN HAGANS. Land adj. MATHEW
PATTON and the river. Also four horses, six head of black cattle twenty
head of hogs, and all household furniture. Wit: DANL. HARPER, SAML.
HERRON, JOHN JOHNSTON. Signed: JOHN HAGANS, Seal.

Page 464: Power of attorney from HANNAH BISHOP, widow of Chester Co.
        Do make my trusty and loving friend DAVID PORTER of the
County of York, he to use my name and receive from the estate of my
father THOMAS BRAKEN of the State of Pennsylvania, what is derived
from his last will and testament. Dated 25 June 1791. Signed: HANNAH
BISHOP, Seal.

Page 465: Deed of gift from WILLIAM SHARP to ANN HEAD both of Chester
        Co. Dated 4 Apr. 1791. I, WILLIAM SHARP of and in considera-
tion of natural affection and divers other good causes do give and
grant unto ANN HEAD one sorrel horse about fourteen hands high, also
one brown bay filley two years old. Also one cow and yearling and one
feather bed and furniture. Wit: WILLIAM (X) COLERN, NUOLAS (X) COLERN,
SARAH (X) WOOD. Signed: WILLIAM SHARP, Seal.

Page 466: Indenture made bet. ANTHANY MC MEANS and PHEBIE his wife
        to JAMES LUSK, yeoman, both of Chester Co. dated 7 Sept.
1790. 30 pds. sterling for 100 acres (no water course given). Wit:
JOHN FARRIS, SAMUEL LUSK, CALEB FARRIS. Signed: ANTHANY (X) MC MEANS,
PHEBE (X) MC MEANS.

Page 468: Indenture made bet. ELEAZER GORE and his wife ELIZABETH
        to PHILLIP KNOWLAND, son of SAMSON KNOWLAND both of Chester
Co. Dated 2 Dec. 1789. 100 pds. sterling for two tracts of land. One
on main Sandy River of 50 acres originally granted to ZACHARIAH ISBELL,
8 Mar. 1769, from ISBELL to JAMES GORE, and from ELEAZER GORE to PHILLIP
KNOWLAND. Also one tract of 48 acres granted to ISBELL 17 Dec. 1766,
from ISBELL to JAMES GORE, and to ELEAZER GORE. Wit: JOSHUA GORE, SAMP-
SON NOLAND, WILLIAM BRITAIN. Signed: ELEAZER GORE, ELIZABETH GORE,
Seal.

Page 470: Indenture made bet. AMOS TIMMS and wife FANNY of Craven
        Co. and PETER NOWLAND of Granville Co., N. C. Dated 9 Sept.
1782. 277 pds. ten shillings and nine pence and half penny money of
North Carolina. For 100 acres on Sandy Creek on north side of Broad
River. Wit: HENRY (X) NOWLAND, JOSEPH TIMMS, PIERCE NOWLAND. Signed:
AMOS TIMMS, FRANCES (X) TIMMS.

Page 472: Indenture made bet. JAMES TURNER and wife SUSSANAH, weaver
        to PATRICK MEGERETY, taylor both of Chester Co. Dated 5
Oct. 1771, 150 pds. for 200 acres on Beaver Dam branch of Rockey Creek.
Originally granted to JAMES TURNER 14 June 1768. With vacant land on
all sides. Wit: FRANCIS (X) HENDERSON, ROBERT GASTON. Signed: JAMES
(X) TURNER, SUSSANAH (X) TURNER.

Page 475: Indenture made bet. WILLIAM PAUL and JAMES PAUL to WILLIAM
        GASTON, all of Chester Co. Dated 15 Sept. 1789. 7 pds. 2
shillings, ten pence for 50 acres being part of a tract of 300 acres
granted to HENRY WINUSE(?) on 3 Apr. 1772. Lying on a branch called
River Dam on the north side of Rockey Creek. Adj. ROBERT FUTHERTON,
JAMES FURGUSON and AMOS TURNER, SARI KNOWLAN, JAMES BUNSLEY. Wit:MEHAM
FERGUSON, WILLIAM FUTTERTON. Signed: WILLIAM PAUL, JAMES PAUL.

Page 480: Indenture made bet. EDWARD HENDERSON and ANNA his wife to
        ROBERT FROST both of Chester Co. Dated 15 Oct. 1781. 200
pds. for 100 acres on a branch of Sandy River. Adj. JOHN BOND, dec'd.
Wit: JNO. MAYFIELD, SEVILLER BOND, ISOM BOND. Signed: EDWARD HENDERSON,
ANNA (X) HENDERSON, Seals.

Page 484: Indenture made bet. AMOS TIMMS and FANNY his wife of Chester
        Co. and PETER NOLAND of Granville Co., N. C. Dated 9 Sept.
1782. 200 pds. money of N. C. for 150 acres on Sandy Creek on the north
side of Broad River. Wit: HENRY NOLAND, PIERCE NOLAND, JOSEPH TIMMS.
Signed: AMOS TIMMS, FANNY (X) TIMMS, Seals.

Page 486: Indenture made bet. JAMES NUHOLSON of Charleston City and
        DAVID MC CALLA of Camden Dist. Dated 25 Nov. 1786. 50 pds.
sterling for 380 acres on the waters of Sandy River. Adj. SW by DOUGLESS
land, on W by JOHN FURGUSON and WILLIAM FURGUSON land, on NW by LEWIS
land. Land surveyed for JAMES ADAIR and granted unto JAMES NUHOLSON
on 3rd April last. Wit: WILLIAM WYLEY, JOHN MC CRARY. Signed: JAMES
NUHOLSON, Seal.

Page 490: Indenture made bet. ADAM FERGUSON and CHARLES HUMPHRES both
        of Camden Dist. Dated 5 Oct. 1782. 500 pds. money of S.
C. for 100 acres on the drafts of Sandy River. Adj. on NE by JAMES
FERGUSON land. Originally granted 11 Feb. 1773. Wit: ASA DERBY, EDWARD
HENDERSON, ROBERT (X) PROCTER. Signed: ADAM FERGUSON & ELIZABETH (X)
FERGUSON, Seals. This deed was attested bef. DAVID HOPKINS, J.P. It
is stated that ELIZABETH is the wife of ADAM FERGUSON on 2 Jan. 1784.

Page 491: Indenture made bet. MARTIN ELAIN and THOMAS RODEN both of
        Chester Co. Dated 27 May 1790. 2 pds. sterling money for
10 acres, being part of 500 acres granted unto JAMES DAUGHERTY, from
DAUGHERTY to JOHN COLVIN 10 July 1788, from COLVIN to MARTIN ELAIN
2 Nov. 1789. Wit: LEWIS (X) ROBERTS, ABRAHAM PAGIT. Signed: MARTIN
ELAIN, Seal.

Page 493: In pursuant of a resolution of the Honourable the Privy
        Council and an order of mine of the seventeenth of Feb.

68

Cont'd from page 68:
last found therein it return having been made to me of the votes of
the inhabitants of the County of Chester by which it appear that a
great majority of the votes were in favor of HUGH STEWART's plantation
as a proper place for fixing the public building of the sd County by
virtue of the power in me vested. I do hereby determine that the public
building for the county of Chester shall be built at the plantation
of HUGH STEWART in the sd county on the cross roads formed by the Saluda
Road and the Turkey Creek Charleston Road which all concerned are to
take notice and govern themselves accordingly. Given under my hand
this sixteenth day of May one thousand seven hundred and ninety one.
CHARLES PINCKNEY.

Page 493: Indenture made bet. HENRY HUNTER, Sheriff of Camden Dist.
and JOHN ELLISON of the same dist. Dated 1 Mar. 1789. Witnesseth that MOSES MC COWN of the same dist. was seized in his demesne
and charged with the unlawful taking and carrying away the goods and
chattels which were of ROBERT KING's, dec'd. during his life time.
Whereas HENRY KING as adm. of the estate of ROBERT KING, dec'd. did
receive from the court of common pleas a judgement of 43 pds. from
the sd. MOSES MC COWN. The sd. sheriff to take the land and 10 shill-
ings and 8 pence belonging to MOSES MC COWN and sell at public outcry.
The land is 200 acres on Fishing Creek adj. on E by land of JOHN LIN-
LUY, on the S by JOSEPH KERSHAW, Esq., on W by vacant land, on the
N by JOHN LENNARD's land. Sale held on the ___ day of Aug. last past,
JOHN ELLISON being the highest and last bidder of the sum of 50 pds.
Wit: JNO. BREVARD, JOHN MC GEE, JOHN SIMMISON. Signed: HENRY HUNTER,
Sheriff C.D. seal. Attested to bef. JAMES KERSHAW, J.P. By JOSEPH BREV-
ARD, 2 Mar. 1789.

Page 496: Personally appeared PRISCILLAR FRANKLIN bef. me JOHN PRATT
one of the Justices of the Co. of Chester and after being
duly sworn as the law directs deponent and sayeth she saw JOHN FRANKLIN
let PHILLIP RILEY have a note in hand on JOHN COLVIN and that sd. RILEY
took the sd. note and was to have all rights and not look to FRANKLIN
for it. If he not recover it from COLVIN. Sworn to this 27 Aug. 1791.
Signed: PRISCILLAR (X) FRANKLIN. Signed bef. me JOHN PRATT, J.P.

Page 497: Indenture made bet. JOSIAH HILL and SAMUEL LOWRIE, Esq.
both of Camden Dist. Dated 4 Aug. 1790. 10 pds. for 100
acres on Sandy River being part of a grant of twenty thousand and seven
hundred acres granted unto HILL in 1780. Beginning at JOHN CARSON corner
on JOHN PEW line and run the sd line to the cross in the wagon road
on JAMES LEMON's line. Wit: PAT MC GRIFF, JOHN OWENS. Signed: JOSIAH
HILL, Seal.

Page 498: Indenture made bet. JOHN HUNTER and ARCHIBALD KELL both
of Chester Co. Dated 7 Jan. 1791, 3 pds. 13 shillings for
102 acres on waters of Sandy River, being one half of a grant for two
hundred and four acres granted unto JOHN HUNTER on 5 Jan. 1789. Wit:
JOHN KELL, ALEXANDER KELL. Signed: JOHN HUNTER, Seal.

Page 500: Power of attorney from THOMAS GORE of Wake Co. in N. C.
unto JAMES GORE of Chester Co., S. C. Dated 25 May 1791.
For diver good causes and consideration JAMES GORE is to ask, demand,
sue, etc. all sum and sums, due me in the state of South Carolina for
service done in the third regiment commanded by Col. WILLIAM THOMPSON .
To make use of all lawfully acts, and things whatsoever in my name.
Wit: JOHN PRATT. Signed: THOMAS (X) GORE, Seal. THOMAS PRATT, Esq.
attested to the same bef. me, ELYAH NUNN, J.P. Dated 18 July 1791.

Page 501: Indenture made bet. JOHN MC FADEN, yeoman and THOMAS WALKER,
blacksmith. Both of Chester Co. Dated 29 Aug. 1791. 27 pds.
10 shillings for 100 acres on Fishing Creek adj. ROBERT MC FADEN land,
other sides vacant when surveyed. Originally granted to JOHN MC FADEN
on 26 July 1774. Wit: THOMAS NEELY, ABRAHAM WALKER, JOHN MC CRARY.
Signed: JOHN MC FADEN, MARY (X) MC FADEN, Seal. When ABRAHAM WALKER
attested to the deed it is stated MARY is the wife of JOHN MC FADEN.
23 Sept. 1791.

Page 503: Indenture made bet. ROBERT MC FADEN, yeoman and THOMAS WALKER
blacksmith both of Chester Co. Dated 29 Aug. 1791. 27 pds.
10 shillings for 100 acres on Fishing Creek adj. JOHN MC FADEN land
and all other sides vacant when surveyed. Originally granted to ROBERT
MC FADEN 26 July 1774. Wit: THOMAS NEELY, ABRAHAM WALKER, JOHN MC CRARY.
Signed: ROBERT MC FADEN, ESTER (X) MC FADEN, seal. When ABRAHAM WALKER
attested to the deed it is stated that ESTER is the wife of ROBERT
MC FADEN. 23 Sept. 1791.

Page 505: Power of attorney from TABITHA WADE to JEREMIAH DAVIS. Dated
12 Sept. 1791. For divers consideration and good causes
I do constitute and appoint my trusty friend JEREMIAH DAVIS of Chester
Co. my true and lawful attorney to ask, demand, recover, receive of
and from the estate of WILLIAM MUNROE in the county of Charles in the
State of Maryland. Granting to my sd. attorney my sole and full power
and authority to take, persue and follow such legal courses for recover
and receiving, obtaining same as I myself might or could do. Signed:
TABITHA (X) WADE. Attested bef. ELIJAH NUNN, J.P. 12 Sept. 1791.

Page 506: Indenture made bet. PHILIP SANDERFUR & ELIZABETH his wife
of York Co. and SAMUEL IRVING of York Co. Dated 5 June 1787.
Sum of 125 guineas for 250 acres on the fork of Rockey Creek adj. NW
JOHN MORROW, NE JOHN MC COWN, S WILLIAM WILEY, SW on CAMBERT's land.
Wit: ROBERT GREEN, JOHN SHAW, JNO. GORDEN, JR. Signed: PHILIP SANDERFUR.
Attested bef. JOSEPH PALMER, J.P. by ROBERT GREER, 25? Aug. 1791.

Page 508: Indenture made bet. THOMAS BAKER FRANKLIN and MAJOR GRISHAM
both of Chester Co. dated 5 Nov. 1791. Sum of 50 pds. sterling for twenty one and one fifth acres on waters of Sandy River. No
other water courses given. Wit: ROBERT LEMON, JOHN COLVIN, WILLIAM
RIVERS. Signed: THOMAS BAKER FRANKLIN, NANCY (X) FRANKLIN.

Page 509: Indenture made bet. JAMES CARR of the State of Virginia,
yeoman and JOHN KNOX of the Dist. of Camden, weaver, dated
14 Aug. 1779. Sum of 50 pds. for 150 acres on Beaverdam fork of Rockey
River adj. NW on THOMAS LAND, SW on JANE BIGHAM land, SE on JOHN GASTON,
JR. land, NE on JOHN LINNIN originally granted to JAMES CARR 11 Aug.
1774. Wit: JOHN GASTON, JR., EBENEZER GASTON. Signed: JAMES CARR, seal.
Attested bef. PHILIP WALKER, J.P. by JOHN GASTON, 6 Jan. 1792.

Page 512: Indenture made bet. JOHN KNOX of Kentucky, Madison Co. and
Mr. JAMES MC GARA, Minister of Rockey River in Chester Co.,
dated 29 Oct. 1791. Sum of 55 pds. sterling for 150 acres on Beaverdam
fork of Rockey River adj. NW on THOMAS LAND, SW on JANE BIGHAM, SE
on JOHN GASTON, JR., NE on JOHN LINNIN. Orig. granted to JAMES CARR
11 Aug. 1774. Wit: JAMES KELL, ADAM EAGOR. Signed: JOHN KNOX, seal.
Attested bef. PHILIP WALKER, J.P. by JAMES KELL, 25 Jan. 1792.

Page 514: Indenture made bet. WILLIAM NYBET and ELIZABETH his wife
and JAMES NYBET both of Chester Co. dated 10 Nov. 1789.
Sum of 90 pds. for 104 acres on Rockey Creek, orig. granted to PHILIP
WALKER 1 Aug. 1752 with vacant land on all sides. WALKER sold to GEORGE
MOORE, from MOORE to WILLIAM NYBET. Signed: WILLIAM NESBET & ELIZABETH
(X) NESBET. Attested bef. PHILIP WALKER, J.P. by JAMES KELL, 26 Mar.
1792.

Page 516: Bill of sale from CHARLES KITCHEN of Laurens Co. to THOMAS
GARTHER of Rockey Creek Chester Co. dated 10 Oct. 1791.
Sum of 50 pds. for one negro woman named Ester and her two mulatto
boys named Henry and Ben. Wit: HENRY DYE, JOHN DYE. Signed: CHARLES
KITCHEN, seal. Attested bef. PHILIP WALKER, J.P. by JOHN DYE, 24 Jan.
1792.

Page 517:; Bill of sale from CHARLES KITCHEN of Laurens Co. to THOMAS
GATHER OF Chester Co. dated 1 Sept. 1791, sum of 35 pds.
money of S. C. for one negro woman named Dinah. Wit: HENRY DYE, JOHN
DYE. Signed: CHARLES KITCHEN. Attested bef. PHILIP WALKER, J.P. by
JOHN DYE, 24 Jan. 1792.

Page 517: Indenture made bet. ROBERT WILLIAM and JEAN AGNEW both of

70

Cont'd from page 70:
Chester Co. dated 6 Dec. 1791. Sum of 50 pds. sterling for 100 acres being part of a tract of 400 acres on Rockey Creek adj. JOHN MORISE, JOHN BASLIS land. Wit: JOHN RICHMOND, THOMAS STROUD, JOHN CONNERY. Signed: ROBERT WILLIAMS, ELIZABETH (X) WILLIAMS. Attested bef. PHILIP WALKER, J.P. by JOHN CONNERY dated 6 Jan. 1792. (Here it is stated that ELIZABETH is ROBERT WILLIAMS wife.)

Page 520: Indenture made bet. ROBERT DUKE and JOHN LEONARD both of Chester Co. dated 4 Jan. 1779. Sum of 100 pds. lawful money of S. C. for 300 acres on Fishing Creek and Catawba River adj. THOMAS STEEL line, ARTHUR HUKLIN, JR. and ROBERT LANDRUN line. Wit: INZ (X) DUKE, ALEXANDER MC NEAL. Signed: ROBERT DUKE, seal. Attested bef. JOHN GASTON by ALEXANDER MC NEAL. Dated 12 Jan. 1779.

Page 522: Indenture made bet. ROBERT WILLIAMS, blacksmith and HARDY STROUD both of Chester Co. dated 31 Dec. 1791. Sum of 7 pds. for 100 acres on the north side of Rockey Creek, adj. WM. STINSON, GEO. AGNEW. Wit: JOHN CONNERY, WM. LENOX. Signed: ROBT. (X) WILLIAMS, ELIZABETH (X) WILLIAMS, seal.

Page 525: Indenture made bet. JOHN LEONARD of Richmond Co., state of Georgia and WM. MC DONALD of Chester Co. dated 22 Feb. 1790. Sum of 100 pds. good and lawful money for 300 acres on the waters of Fishing Creek adj. on NE by THOMAS STEEL and ARTHUR HUKLAND's land, SE by BENJAMIN COOK, SW by ROBERT DUKE. Orig. granted to ROBERT DUKE 23 June 1774, sold to JOHN LEONARD, 14 Jan. 1779. Wit: FEDR. KUMBALL, JR., ROB. MC KANN, ROBT. BURNETT. Signed: JOHN LEONARD, seal.

Page 526: Indenture made bet. JOHN KATURY and WM. MC DONALD both of Chester Co. dated 25 Oct. 1791. Sum of 95 pds. 10 shillings for 191 acres on waters of Wateree River on north side, adj. SAMUEL WAGONER and JOHN MC CENNELL. Orig. granted to JOHN KATURY father, ALEX KATURY, 30 Oct. 1776. Wit: MOSES MC COUN, MIDA MC DONALD. Signed: JOHN (X) KATURY. (Be it remembered that this day the above date ELIZABETH STROUD (formerly KATURY) volunterily renounced all claim to dower in the above plantation, signed ELIZABETH (X) STROUD KATURY Signed: JAMES KNOX, J.P. Attested bef. JAMES KNOX, J.P. by MIDDLETON MC DONALD, dated 22 Jan. 1792.

Page 527: Indenture made bet. JOHN WILSON of Chester Co. and CLAYTON ROGERS of the same co. dated 10 June 1773. Sum of 150 pds. current money for 150 acres on a branch of Turkey Creek waters of Broad River, adj. land claimed by JAMES RIGHT, vacant land on all other sides. Orig. granted to JOHN WILSON 3 July 1772. Wit: WM. KIRKPATRICK, ISAAC SADLER, FRANCIS RAY. Signed: JOHN WILSON, ELIZABETH (X) WILSON, seal. Attested bef. JNO. MILL, J.P. by FRANCIS RAY, dated 25 Jan. 1792. Here it is stated that ELIZABETH was the wife of JOHN WILSON.

Page 530: An account of JOHN RENOLDS to JOHN MC COWN. Dated Nov. - 1774 for corage (?) of tobacco to Charleston and other items, sum of 9 pds. 1 shilling 6 pence the account attested bef. ANDREW HEMPHILL, J.P. 9 Apr. 1787 also MC COWN sells the account the same day to THOMAS STROUD. Wit: ANDREW HEMPHILL, JOHN (X) MORROSS.

Page 530: Note from BENJAMIN SMITH to JOHN RUNOLDS both of Camden Dist. in the sum of 500 pds. Note secured by a title to 600 acres of land on Cold Water Creek. Being part of the land bought from JOHN BROWN, adj. JAMES MACKEY, MARTIN (X) RUNOLDS. Signed: BENJ. (X) HAGIN. No date of record.

Page 531: Note on BENJAMIN HAGIN to JOHN RUNOLDS is sold to THOMAS DYER on 19 Mar. 1785. On 1 Jan. 1788 the same note is sold from DYER to THOMAS STROUD.

Page 532: A lease and release from JOHN WILSON and wife ELIZABETH unto CLAYTON ROGERS for 10 shillings. (This is the same land sold and recorded on page 527.)

71

Page 533: Indenture made bet. JAMES KNOX, Esq., Doctor and HUGH MC-
           KELVEY both of Chester Co. Dated 17 Sept. 1791. Sum of 16
guineas for 100 acres on a lease and release for one year. Land on
Rockey River, adj. FRANCIS FREDRICK land, vacant on all other sides.
Wit: THOMAS MC CULLEY, JAMES NESBIT. Signed: JAMES KNOX, seal.

Page 535: Indenture made bet. RICHARD ATKINS and JAMES WALKER both
           of Chester Co. Dated 10 Feb. 1791. Sum of 20 pds. for 150
acres on waters of Catawba River bet. the sd. river and Fishing Creek.
Part of a tract granted CULP. Wit: JOHN MEFREARY, ALEXANDER CRAWFORD,
JOHN WALKER. Signed: RICHARD ATKINS, seal.

Page 537: Indenture made bet. JOHN STUDMANT and his wife HANNAH of
           Fairfield Co. and PAUL GUTTREY of Chester Co. Dated 18 Jan.
1792. Sum of 500 pds. lawful and current money for 190 acres on Turkey
Creek fork of Fishing Creek. Orig. granted to JOHN MC KENNY 11 Aug.
1774. JOHN sold the land to WM. MC KENNEY his grant 2 Apr. 1777. Rec.:
2 May 1787. This land adj. JOHN MC FABIN, WM. MC KENNEY, HENRY CULP,
AUGUSTUS CULP, JAMES NEELEY. On 20 Nov. 1782 WM. MC KENNEY by a will
did give to his daughter HANNAH 150 acres she by then married to JOHN
STUDMANT, they also rec'd 40 acres from the estate of WM. MC KENNEY,
dec'd. Wit: DAVID BELL, WM. WILEY. Signed: JOHN (X) STUDMANT, HANNAH
(X) STUDMANT. Attested bef. JOHN BELL, J.P. by DAVID BELL. 18 Jan.
1792.

Page 539: Indenture made bet. WILLIAM WHITE and JEAN his wife and
           JAMES KENEDY both of Chester Co. Dated 4 Dec. 1786. Sum
of 27 pds. sterling for 200 acres on north side of Broad River on Bullock Creek road, adj. JOSEPH COBB, BENJAMIN ELLIS, HUGH BANNERS, JAMES
WILKES. Orig. granted to JOHN WHITE, dec'd. 1768, WILLIAM WHITE being
the lawful heir of JOHN WHITE. Wit: WM. BOYD, JAMES WILSON, JAMES WILK-
INGS. Signed: WILLIAM (X) WHITE, JANE (X) WHITE. Attested bef. JOHN
BELL, Esq. by JAMES WILKINGS on 16 Apr. 1791.

Page 540: Bond from JOHN GASTON to Mr. JAMES MC GARRAH, Minister,
           in the sum of 150 pds. sterling. Dated 29 Oct. 1791. Wit:
JAMES KELL, ADAM EDGER. Signed: JOHN GASTON, seal. (N.B. The above
land is secured by 150 acres of land on Rockey Creek. The land first
being given to JAMES CARR, then sold to JOHN KNOX, JR.) Attested bef.
PHILIP WALKER, J.P.

Page 541: Indenture made bet. DRURY GOING and ASSA TINDALL both of
           Chester Co. Dated 11 Oct. 1791. For love and affection I
bear for my son-in-law ASSA TINDALL and for his better support, I give,
grant and convey 100 acres on a branch of Turkey Creek, waters of Broad
River, adj. JAMES KIRKPATRICK, CLAYTON ROGERS. All other sides vacant.
Orig. granted to JOHN LONG on 6 June 1785. Wit: BUTTRICK ROGERS, SARAH
ROGERS, ISAAC ROGERS. Signed: DRURY (X) GOING, seal. Attested bef.
CLAYTON ROGERS, J.P. by ISAAC ROGERS, 24 Jan. 1792.

Page 542: Indenture made bet. DRURY GOING of Chester Co. and ROBERT
           ELLIOTT of Union Co. Dated 13 Jan. 1792. Sum of 1000 pds.
lawful money for two tracts of land, one containing 250 acres on Broad
River where GOING now lives. This tract adj. ARON LOCQUERTS (LOCKART)
land. The other tract of 100 acres including ELLIOTT old field. This
tract adj. JOSEPH ROBERSON. The 250 acres tract was granted to BENJAMIN
LOVE 3 Feb. 1754 from LOVE to ROBERT ELLIOTT, who sold to DRURY GOING.
The 100 acres tract granted to MARY MC MULLOUGH 23 Jan. 1752, from
MC MULLOUGH to ROBERT ELLIOTT who sold to DRURY GOING. GOING sells
both tracts back to ELLIOTT. Wit: JOB GOING, JOHN HILL, ISAAC GOING.
Signed: DRURY (X) GOING. Attested bef. WM. GASTON, J.P. by JOB GOING.
10 Feb. 1792.

Page 544: Bill of sale from MOSES LEABERRY to JOHN N. BELL both of
           Chester Co. Dated 23 Jan. 1792. Sum of 3 pds. sterling for
one gray horse about thirteen hands high and eight years old. Wit:
JOHN ROBINS. Signed: MOSES (X) LEABERRY, seal.

Page 544: Bill of sale from MOSES LEABERRY to THOMAS ROBINS both of

72

Cont'd from page 72:
           Chester Co. Dated 24 Jan. 1792. Sum of 1 pd. 15 shillings
8 pence for one sorrel mare about fifteen years old, one pot & skillet,
one cotton wheel & cards, one fatted hog. Wit: JOHN (X) BELL, VALETINE
BELL. Signed: MOSES (X) LEABERRY, seal.

Page 544: Indenture made bet. JOHN HUMPHRES and JOHN RODEN both of
           Chester Co. Dated 26 Sept. 1791. Sum of 50 pds. sterling
for 60 acres being part of a grant of 300 acres on branch of Sandy
River called Rockey branch adj. THOMAS RODEN, CHARLES HUMPHRES. Wit:
AARON ALLEN (X) SHARP, JOSEPH WATSON. Signed: JOHN (X) HUMPHRES, ELIZA-
BETH (X) HUMPHRES. Attested bef. JOHN PRATT, J.P. by AARON ALLEN SHARP.
ELIZABETH is sd to be wife of JOHN.

Page 546: Indenture made bet. JAMES MOFFET of Wilkes Co., state of
           Georgia, and MOSES CANTZEN of Lancaster Co., S. C. Dated
20 Jan. 1791. Sum of 50 pds. sterling for 400 acres on waters of Sandy
River south branch, granted to JAMES MOFFET 22 Aug. 1768. Wit: WM.
FERRELL, JACOB (X) JORDEN, SAMUEL HUNTER. Signed: JAMES MOFFET. Attested
bef. ROBERT DUNLAP, T.L.C. by WM. FERRELL, 19 Jan. 1792.

Page 549: Indenture made bet. CHARLES SPRADLING and MARTHA his wife
           and JOHN BELL both of Chester Co. Dated 10 Nov. 1778. Sum
of 2200 pds. lawful money "for 420 acres more or less being the North
East quarter and West end of the original tract laid off in the form
of a carpenture square." This being a part of a grant given to JOHN
GORDIN on 25 Dec. 1754 by Mathew Rowan, Gov. of N. C. for 640 acres
on the head waters of Broad River on the north side, dividing it and
the Catawba River. After the death of JOHN GORDIN, his wife RUTH sold
to SPRADLING. Wit: ALEXANDER TURNER, WM. BOYLE, JOHN TURNER. Signed:
CHARLES (cs) SPRADLING, MARTHA (X) SPRADLING. Attested bef. PHIL. PEAR-
SON, J.P. by Captain JOHN TURNER. 7 May 1784.

Page 552: A lease and release from CHARLES SPRADLING and JOHN BELL
           both of Chester Co. Dated 9 Nov. 1778. Sum of 10 shillings
for one year on the above land of 420 acres. Same witnesses.

Page 553: Indenture made bet. ROBERT ELLIOTT and JEAN his wife of
           Union Co. and DRURY GOINGS of Chester Co. Dated 14 Jan.
1792. Sum of 1000 pds. for 350 acres on the Broad River. (This is the
same land that was sold to ELLIOTT on page 542 from GOINGS, dates are
different.) Attested bef. WM. GASTON, J.P. by JOB GOINGS. 23 Jan. 1791.

Page 556: Bill of sale from CHARLES KITCHEN of Laurens Co. and THOMAS
           GATHER of Chester Co. Dated 1 Sept. 1791. Sum of 30 pds.
sterling KITCHEN does bargain, sell and deliver one negro woman named
Philis. Wit: JOHN KITCHEN. Signed: CHARLES KITCHEN, seal.

Page 557: Indenture made bet. PATRICK MC GRIFF and GEORGE SADLER both
           of Chester Co. Dated 7 May 1791. Sum of 50 pds. for 129
acres where the sd. SADLER now lives. Orig. granted to PATRICK MC GRIFF
for 200 acres by a survey of NAT ALEXANDER on 3 Apr. 1786. MC GRIFF
holding out 71 acres for himself. Wit: EDWARD LAUY, MILES _____. Signed:
PATRICK MC GRIFF.

Page 558: Indenture made bet. EDWARD WHITE, cordwinder and ELIZABETH
           his wife and WILLIAM MC KINNY both of Chester Co. Dated
9 July 1773 sum of 100 pds. for 100 acres on Fishing Creek. Part of
a grant of 250 acres given to EDWARD WHITE on 10 Jan. 1771 adj. JOHN
MC FADIN, JAMES FERGUSON, WM. MC FADIN, ANDREW MARTAIN. Wit: THOMAS
FULTON, ANDREW LOCQUERT (LOCKART). Signed: EDWARD WHITE, ELIZABETH
(X) WHITE. Attested bef. JAMES PATTON, J.P. by ANDREW LOCKART on 11
Jan. 1774.

Page 560: Indenture made bet. JAMES FERGUSON and AGNES his wife to
           WILLIAM MC KINNEY both of Chester Co. Dated 9 Sept. 1771.
Sum of 150 pds. lawful money of S. C. for 140 acres on the north side
of Fishing Creek, sd. creek to be the dividing line. Land orig. granted
to JAMES FERGUSON 12 Dec. 1768 adj. JARNL. KNOX, WILLIAM MC KAY, THOMAS

Cont'd from page 73:
MARTIN. Wit: EDWARD WHITE, WILLIAM WILEY, ABRAHAM FERGUSON. Signed: JAMES FERGUSON, AGNES (X) FERGUSON. Seal. Attested bef. JOHN GASTON, J.P. by WILLIAM WILEY, 11 Sept. 1771.

Page 563: Indenture made bet. JEREMIAH THOMAS and MARY his wife and JOHN DONALD both of Chester Co. Dated 31 Jan. 1791. Sum of 50 pds. money of S. C. for 68 acres and one half of the spring. Orig. granted to MOSES BOND 12 July 1766. Wit: JAMES DONOLD, WM. BOYD. Signed: JEREMIAH THOMAS, MARY (X) THOMAS. Seal. Attested bef. ELIJAH NUNN, J.P. by JAMES DONOLD on 25 Jan. 1792.

Page 565: Indenture made bet. WILLIAM MC GARITY and FRANCIS HENDERSON both of Rockey Creek in Chester Co. Dated 20 Jan. 1792. Sum of 10 pds. for 40 acres on waters of Rockey Creek, adj. WILLIAM MC GARITY, JAMES BIGHAM and FRANCIS HENDERSON. Wit: WM. DONALDSON, THOMAS MC CULLEY. Signed: WILLIAM (X) MC GARITY, seal. Attested bef. PHILIP WALKER, J.P. by THOMAS MC CULLEY. 25 Jan. 1792.

Page 566: Bill of sale from JONATHAN JONES of Chester Co. In the sum of 65 pds. pd. by WILLIAM PATTON of York Co. for one negro woman named Rose and her child named Judey. Dated 5 Nov. (year not given). Wit: HUGH WHITESIDE, THOMAS WHITESIDE. Signed: JONATHAN JONES, seal. Attested bef. HUGH WHITESIDE, J.P. by THOMAS WHITESIDE, 21 Jan. 1792.

Page 567: A bond, PHILLIP WALKER, yeoman is held and firmly bound unto SAMUEL WIER, yeoman both of Chester Co. in the sum of 1000 pds. current money of S. C. This bond is secured by 100 acres of land on Rockey River, after 10 months. Wit: PHILIP WALKER, Esq. Signed: PHILIP (X) WALKER, seal. Dated 14 Jan. 1782. On 3 Jan. 1787 SAMUEL WIER assigned this bond unto SAML. HAMBLETON. Wit: JAMES KNOX.

Pagr 567: A gift from THOMAS GATHER to the heirs of FRANCES KITCHEN, the wife of CHARLES KITCHEN, four negroes, two males and two females, by name males Henry and Ben, females Esther and Dinah. Dated 23 Jan. 1792. Wit: JOHN (X) DYE, THOS. MORRIS. Signed: THOMAS (X) GATHER, seal. Attested bef. PHILIP WALKER, J.P. Here the heir is named as JOHN KITCHEN. Signed: JOHN (X) GATHER.

Page 568: Power of attorney from NATHAN SIMS to his trusty son MATTHEW SIMS to use my name to ask, demand, recover, receive from the estate of WILLIAM HUGHES, dec'd. for me or my wife. Wit: DANIEL GREEN, DAVID SIMS. Signed: NATHAN SIMS, seal. Attested bef. JOHN PRATT, J.P. by DAVID SIMS, 5 Dec. 1791.

Page 569: State of North Carolina)   "Know all men by these present Cumberland County   )   that we JAMES CAMPBELL and ALEX-ANDER CAMPBELL being heirs at law of the Reverend JAMES CAMPBELL and that our brother dec'd. do constitute and appoint our trusty and well beloved friend ROBERT JAMESON to sell make over and convey all the estate real or personal now belonging to the sd JAMES CAMPBELL in the State of South Carolina for our use and all his acts legally here upon we will confirm." Wit: JOHN CLARK. Signed: JAMES CAMPBELL, ALEXANDER CAMPBELL. Dated 10 Feb. 1789. Attested bef. PHILIP WALKER, J.P. by JOHN CLARK, 25 Jan. 1792.

Page 570: Bill of sale from JOHN SEALY unto PETER SEALY for the sum of 4 shillings sterling, hath bargain and sell four negroes, one woman named Sarah, one girl named Mariah, the youngest child of Sarah, also two boys, one named Jacob, the other Juners, the son of Hannah. Wit: SAMUEL (X) SEALY, JEREMIAH TERRY. Signed: JOHN SEALY, seal. Dated 12 Sept. 1791. Attested bef. JOHN PRATT, J.P. by SAMUEL SEALY. 21 Jan. 1792.

Page 571: Indenture made bet. HUGH WILSON of York Co. and ROBERT WILSON of York Co., 24 Jan. 1792. Sum of 10 shillings current money for 50 acres on the north side of Broad River, adj. JOSEPH ROBERSON, FRANCIS KILPATRICK, ROBERT BLACK & DRURY GOINGS. Orig. granted to HUGH

Cont'd from page 74:
WILSON, 20 Nov. 1771 by JOSIAH MARTIN, Gov. of N. C. Wit: JAMES JAMESON,
JEAN (X) KENDAY, JOSEPH JAMESON. Signed: HUGH WILSON, seal. Attested
bef. JOSEPH BROWN, J.P. by JAMES JAMESON, 14 Apr. 1792.

Page 572: Indenture made bet. WILLIAM SHARP and JOHN BELL, Esq. both
of Chester Co., 1 Oct. 1790. Sum of 200 pds. sterling for
200 acres on Sandy Creek a branch of Broad River. Vacant land on all
sides when surveyed. Orig. granted to JAMES SHARP 6 Apr. 1762. Conveyed
to WILLIAM SHARP by a lease and release 23 Dec. 1789. Wit: WILLIAM
MC QUESTON, ROBERT MURDOCK, ROBERT ANDREW. Signed: WILLIAM SHARP, seal.
Attested bef. JOHN PRATT, J.P. by WILLIAM MC QUESTON, 19 Apr. 1792.

Page 574: Indenture made bet. ADAM EDGER of Rockey Creek and JAMES
MC QUSTON, HUGH MILLING & JOHN KELL all of Chester Co. 8
Nov. 1791. Sum of 1 pd. 10 shillings, 4 pence sterling for two acres,
18 poles and perches more or less. To including the spring of water,
meeting house and study house. The land is to be used for the reform
Presbyterian Congregation. Wit: THOS. DONILLY, WILLIAM EDGAR. Signed:
ADAM EDGER, seal. Attested bef. ELIJAH NUNN, J.P. by THOS. DONILLY,
27 Jan. 1792.

Page 578: Indenture made bet. ANDREW GRAHAM and MARGARET his wife
and LARD (LORD) BURNES both of Chester Co., 5 Jan. 1791.
Sum of 50 pds. for 100 acres on Rockey Creek, adj. JAMES KNOX, FRANCIS
HENDERSON, BENJAMIN MITCHELL and LARD's own land. Wit: SAMUEL HENDERSON,
MARGARET (X) MC CONNELL. Signed: ANDREW GRAHAM, MARGARET (X) GRAHAM.

Page 578: Indenture made bet. GEORGE CHERRY and JENNETT his wife and
JOHN JOHNSTONE both of Rockey Creek in Chester Co., 9 May
1789. Sum of 12 pds. sterling for 100 acres on Rockey Creek. Orig.
granted to GEORGE CHERRY 26 July 1774. Wit: JAMES YOUNG, WILLIAM KIRK-
PATRICK. Signed: :GEORGE CHERRY, JENNETT (X) CHERRY. Attested bef ANDREW
HEMPHILL, J.P. by THOS. MC CULLEY, 26 Jan. 1792.

Page 580: Indenture made bet. WILLIAM MILLER and MARGARET his wife
and ROBERT MORRISON both of Chester Co., 15 Sept. 1791.
Sum of 30 pds. sterling for 200 acres on North Fork of Rockey River.
Adj. ROBERT BRADFORD, JAMES CRAWFORD, JAMES WILEY & THOMAS BLAIR. Orig.
granted to WILLIAM MILLER 7 Jan. 1788. Wit: WM. WEIR, WM. BOYD. Signed:
WILLIAM MILLER, MARGARET MILLER, seal.

Page 583: Indenture made bet. PHILIP COHOON & MARTHA his wife of Wash-
ington County, state of Georgia and JAMES WOOD of Chester
Co., 15 Dec. 1791. Sum of 80 pds. sterling for 200 acres on the south
side of Catawba River on Fishing Creek. Orig. granted to GEORGE HUDSON
in 1767, from GEORGE HUDSON to WILLIAM HUDSON and from his heirs to
PHILIP COHOON. Wit: SOLOMON WOOD, J.P., JAMES COHOON, JOHN MC CULLY.
Signed: PHILIP COHOON, MARTHA (X) COHOON. Attested bef. JAMES KNOX,
J.P. by JAMES COHOON, 28 Dec. 1791.

Page 584: Indenture made bet. CHARLES ORR, attorney in fact for DANIEL
HARPER of Lancaster Co. and WILLIAM ORR & JOHN ORR of Lancaster Co., 20 Oct. 1787. For divers causes and eighty consideration
for 100 acres on Sandy River. Orig. granted to DANIEL HARPER 6 Dec.
1768. "By virtue of the power invested in the sd. CHARLES ORR by the
sd. DANIEL HARPER and also as it was their property by virtue of promise
made by the sd. DANIEL HARPER to their father when on his death bed,
he the grandfather to the sd. WM. & JOHN ORR." Wit: DAVID HUNTER, JAMES
NORTON. Signed: CHARLES ORR, seal.

Page 586: Indenture made bet. ARCHEBALD ELLIOTT, JR. and ARCHEBALD
ELLIOTT, JR.(?) both of Chester Co. 10 Mar. 1792. Sum of
50 pds. sterling for 250 acres on the south fork of Fishing Creek adj.
ROBERT GILL, dec'd., HUGH DOBBS, JOSEPH WALKER. Wit: HUGH WHITESIDE,
GEORGE HILL, THOMAS WHITESIDE. Signed: ARCHEBALD (ae) ELLIOTT. Attested
bef. HUGH WHITESIDE, J.P. by GEORGE HILL 26 Mar. 1792. (In some places
the grantor does not add the Junior to his name.)

Page 588: Indenture made bet. ROBERT JAMESON and GARDNER MILLER both

75

Cont'd from page 75:
              of Chester Co., dated 6 Jan. 1792. Sum of 40 pds. sterling
for 150 acres on Bullock a branch of Rockey Creek. Orig. granted to
JASPER ROGERS 10 July 1766 who sold to REESE HUGHS 25 Dec. 1770, who
sold to Rev. JAMES CAMPBELL, dec'd., on 10 Dec. 1771, JAMES & ALEXANDER
CAMPBELL, heirs at law of JAMES CAMPBELL, dec'd. JAMES & ALEXANDER
hath constituted ROBERT JAMESON as their attorney to sell the land.
Wit: GARDNER JAMESON, ARCHEBALD BOYD. Signed: ROBERT JAMESON, seal.

Page 590: Indenture made bet. JOHN CHAMBERS of York Co., yeoman and
           JOHN LATTA of Chester Co., wagonmaker. Dated 29 June 1792.
Sum of 60 pds. sterling for 200 acres on both sides of Fishing Creek
and West side of Catawba River. Orig. granted to WILLIAM NEELY by ARTHUR
DOBBS, Gov. of N. C. on 21 Oct. 1758, then in Anson Co., N. C. now
Chester Co., S. C. WILLIAM NEELY sold to SAMUEL NEELY from him to JOHN
CHAMBERS on 22 Mar. 1789. Adj. ARCHEBALD ELLIOTT & HUGH WHITESIDE.
Wit: HUGH WHITESIDE, JR., SAML. NEELY, HUGH WHITESIDE. Signed: JOHN
CHAMBERS, seal. Attested bef. HUGH WHITESIDE, J.P. by SAML. NEELY,
23 June 1792.

Page 593: Indenture made bet. ROBERT MORRISON and JOHN MC CULLOUGH
           both of Chester Co. Dated 8 June 1792. Sum of 20 pds. for
100 acres on branch of Rockey Creek, adj. on NE by SAML. MC CULLOUGH,
JAMES CRAWFORD, ALEXANDER HENRY, on SE by WILLIAM FERGUSON, on W by
EDWARD HENDERSON, MATHEW GASTON, ALEXANDER ROSEBOROUGH. Wit: ABRAHAM
WRIGHT, AUSBEN CULP. Signed: ROBERT MORRISON, seal.

Page 595: Indenture made bet. SAMUEL NEELY, yeoman and THOMAS NEELY,
           wagon maker, both of Chester Co. Dated 9 Feb. 1792. Sum
of 50 pds. sterling for 150 acres on Fishing Creek. Orig. granted to
SAMUEL NEELY 27 Mar. 1755 by Arthur Dobbs, Gov. of N. C., land thought
to be in Anson Co., N. C. now in Chester Co., S. C. Wit: JOHN MILLS,
JAMES SMITH, DANIEL COOK. Signed: SAMUEL NEELY, seal. Attested bef.
HUGH WHITESIDE, J.P. by JOHN MILLS, 17 May 1792.

Page 597: Indenture made bet. JAMES DILLARD and PERCILLA his wife
           of Fairfield Co. and JOHN FOOTS of Chester Co., 31 Dec.
1791. Sum of 75 pds. sterling for 160 acres on the south side of Sandy
Creek, commonly called river bulling. Wit: NATHAN JAGGERS, WILLIAM
FOOTS. Signed: JAMES DILLARD, PERCILLA (X) DILLARD. Attested bef. RICH.
TALIAFERRO, Clk. Chester Co. by WILLIAM FOOTS. 13 Apr. 1792.

Page 598: Bill of sale from GEORGE FOOTS, JR. unto my well beloved
           son WILLIAM FOOTS one negro girl named Silva and one negro
boy named Hanible for and in consideration of love and good will that
I have for my son. Wit: BENJAMIN SHULTS, SAMUEL DAWSON, JOHN FOOTS.
Signed: GEORGE FOOTS, seal. Attested bef. RICH. TALIAFERRO, Clk. Chester
Co. by BENJAMIN SHULTS & JNO. FOOTS. 2 Mar. 1792.

Page 599: Bill of sale from GEORGE FOOTS, JR. unto my well beloved
           son JOHN FOOTS one negro mulatto girl named Rachel, one
negro boy named Eli for and in consideration of love and good will
that I have for my son. Wit: BENJAMIN SHULTS, SAML. DAWSON, WM. FOOTS.
Signed: GEORGE FOOTS, seal. 2 Mar. 1792. Attested bef. RICHD. TALIA-
FERRO, Clk. Chester Co. by BENJAMIN SHULTS, WILLIAM FOOTS. (Note: GEORGE
FOOTS does not sign his name with the Junior.)

Page 599: Bill of sale from ARCHEBALD ELLIOTT in the sum of 40 pds.
           sterling pd. by ARCHEBALD ELLIOTT, JR. both of Chester Co.
for one dark brown horse, one red cow and heifer. Household items named.
Wit: HUGH DOBBS, WILLIAM ELLIOTT, 10 Mar. 1792. Signed: ARCHEBALD (ae)
ELLIOTT. Bef. RICH. TALIAFERRO by HUGH DOBBS, 26 June 1792.

Page 600: Indenture made bet. JAMES ARTHER & AGNES TURNER formerly
           wife of CHARLES ARTHER, now the wife of JOHN TURNER of Fair-
field Co. and THOMAS FARRIS of Chester Co., 12 Jan. 1787. Sum of 20
pds. sterling for 120 acres being part of the orig. grant to MATTHEW
PATTON on 21 Mar. 1753 by Matthew Rowan, Gov. of N. C. land on a creek
called Terrell Creek on the west side of Catawba River, land was convey-

Cont'd from page 76:
ed to MICHEAL PATTON by JAMES PATTON who was adm. of MATTHEW PATTON
estate. MICHAEL and his wife JEAN sold to CHARLES ARTHER the 120 acres.
Now JAMES ARTHER heir of CHARLES ARTHER with AGNES TURNER sells to
THOMAS FARRIS the land. Wit: WM. BOYD, WILLIAM FARRIS, JOHN TURNER.
Signed: JAMES ARTHER, AGNES (X) TURNER, seals. Attested bef. RICHD.
TALIAFERRO, Clk. Chester Co. by WM. BOYD, 26 June 1792.

Page 602: Indenture made bet. EDWARD WILSON of Burke Co., N. C. and
           WILLIAM WOOD of Chester Co., 15 Sept. 1792. Sum of 100 pds.
sterling for 200 acres on north side of Broad River, adj. JOHN BOSER,
EDWARD WILSON own land. Wit: THOMAS B. FRANKLIN, GENERAL WILSON. Signed:
EDWARD (X) WILSON, MARTHA (X) WILSON, seals. Attested bef. JOHN PRATT,
J.P. by THOMAS B. FRANKLIN, he sd. that MARTHA is the wife of EDW.
WILSON. 1 Aug. 1796.

Page 603: Indenture made bet. WILLIAM HUGHES, SR. of Ninety Six Dist.
           Union Co. and THOMAS HUGHES, JR. of Chester Co. 28 July
1792. Sum og 50 pds. for 144 acres on waters of Terrible Creek on the
Broad River, adj. THOMAS HUGHES own line, THOMAS COSBEY line, and DAVID
HAYES. Wit: WM. EMERY, JOHN HUGHES, ISAAC HUGHES. Signed. WILLIAM HUGHES.

Page 604: Indenture made bet. EPHRAIM MC CULLEY and JOHN JOHNSTONE
           both of Chester Co., 10 Dec. 1789. Sum of 12 pds. sterling
for 100 acres on Rockey Creek. Orig. granted to MARGARET MC CULLEY
17 Mar. 1775. Land conveyed to EPHRAIM MC CULLEY as an heir at law
of MARGARET MC CULLEY. Wit: JAMES YOUNG, THOS. MC CULLEY. Signed: EPH-
RAIM MC CULLEY, seal.

Page 605: Indenture made bet. JOHN HARLOW and JOHN MC KEWN both of
           Chester Co., 22 July 1774. Sum of 100 pds. current money
for 100 acres on waters of Rockey River, adj. ANNA HANNA, JOHN DOWNEY.
Wit: JAMES F. HARLOW, ROBERT (rc) CALDWELL. Signed: JOHN HARLOW, seal.
Attested bef. JOHN GASTON, J.P. by ROBERT (rc) CALDWELL on 9 Sept.
1774.

Page 607: Indenture made bet. JOHN MC COLL and JANE his wife of Chester
           Co. and THOMAS MC DANEL of Union Co. Dated 7 Aug. 1792.
Sum of 275 pds. sterling for 235 acres on the east side of Broad River.
Orig. granted to ADAM MC COOL by Matthew Rowan, Gov. of N. C. in 1753.
Grant for 600 acres. ADAM MC COOL conveyed by deed of gift to JOHN
MC COOL for 235 acres on 10 July 1784. Wit: THOMAS BRANDON, JAS. LOVE,
CHARLES SIMS, ADAM MC COOL, JR., MARGARET GASTON, JOHN GASTON. Signed:
JOHN MC COOL & JEAN MC COOL. Attested bef. WILLIAM GASTON, J.P. by
CHARLES BRANDON on 8 Aug. 1792.

Page 609: Indenture made bet. WILLIAM PAUL and JAMES PAUL and BRAHAM
           FURGUSON all of Chester Co. Dated 15 Sept. 1788. Sum of
7 pds. 2 shillings for 50 acres on a branch called Beaver Dam on the
north fork of Rockey River. Orig. granted to HENRY MC MURDY on 6 Apr.
1770. The 50 acres being one sixth part of the grant. (No reason given
for this division.) Wit: WILLIAM FULLINGTON. Signed: WILLIAM PAUL,
JAMES PAUL. Attested bef. JAMES KNOX, J.P. by WM. GASTON, 8 Sept. 1790.

Page 611: Bond from JOHN MC COOL and THOMAS BRANDON are firmly bound
           unto THOMAS MC DANEL in the full sum of 800 pds. Dated 7
Mar. 1785. The above bond is secured by a deed for 200 acres of land
formerly his fathers ADAM MC COOL. Lying bet. him and JOSEPH MC COOL
land. Wit: WILLIAM GASTON, CHARLES SIMS.

Page 612: Indenture made bet. ROBERT WILSON of York Co. and AARON
           LOCKART of Chester Co. Dated 4 Mar. 1792. Sum of 10 shillings
current money for 50 acres on the north side of Broad River, adj. JOSEPH
ROBERTSON, FRANCIS RAY, ROBERT BLEUK, DRURY GOING. Orig. granted to
HUGH WILSON on 20 Nov. 1771. Wit: JOHN LOCKART, JNO. (X) JOHNSEY.
Signed: ROBT. WILSON, seal. Attested bef. PHILIP WALKER, J.P. by JOHN
LOCKART, 3 Apr. 1792.

Page 613: Indenture made bet. WILLIAM STROUD & SARAH his wife and

Cont'd from page 77:
        THOMAS MORTON both of Chester Co., 5 July 1770. Sum of 200
pds. lawful money for 50 acres on Rockey Creek, adj. JAMES BIGGAM all
other sides vacant. Wit: JOHN BOYD, JOHN KELL. Signed: WILLIAM (X)
STROUD, SARAH (X) STROUD, seals. Attested bef. JOHN GASTON, J.P. by
JOHN KELL, 25 Dec. 1779.

Page 615: Indenture made bet. CHRISTOPHER STRONG & ELIZABETH STRONG
        and JOHN SIMONTON and JOHN LINN all of Chester Co. Dated
9 Aug. 1792. Sum of 26 pds. 5 shillings for 100 acres on (torn) orig.
granted to ELIZABETH STRONG on 14 Oct. 1774. "This deed witnessth that
CHRISTOPHER STRONG & JOHN SIMONTON and their wives are sole heirs of
ELIZABETH STRONG, dec'd. Wit: THOMAS MORTON, ROBERT MILLIN. Signed:
CHRISTOPHER STRONG, ELIZABETH (X) STRONG. JOHN SIMONTON & MARGARET
(X) SIMONTON, seals. Attested bef. JOHN MILLS, J.P. by THOMAS MORTON,
15 Aug. 1792.

Page 618: Indenture made bet. CASPER SLEIGER, SR. and CASPER SLEIGER,
        JR. both of Chester Co., dated 17 Feb. 1792. Sum of 50 pds.
sterling for 150 acres on the waters of Fishing Creek. Wit: THOS. WALK-
ER, JOHN MC CURRY. Signed: CASPER SLEIGER, seal.

Page 619: Indenture made bet. Captain JAMES WALKUP and MARGARET his
        wife of Mecklenburgh Co., N. C. and JAMES BOYD of Camden
Dist. Dated 11 June 1779. Sum of 4000 pds. current money for 360 acres
on West side of Catawba River and Rockey Creek. Orig. granted to WILLIAM
PICKENS and GRIFFITH RUTHERFORD by King George the second, and by a
deed from GRIFFITH RUTHERFORD & ELIZABETH his wife, dated 16 July 1795.
Wit: ROBERT DAVIS, JOHN ROGERS, JAS. DAVIS. Signed: JAMES WALKUP and
MARGARET WALKUP. Attested bef. J. S. DOMMON, J.P. by ROBT. DAVIS, 8
Nov. 1792.

Page 621: Power of attorney from ROBERT BOYD of Chester Co. to Rev.
        JOHN BOYD formerly of Franklin Co., state of Pennsylvania.
To sell, grant or convey all or part of ROBERT BOYD share in his bro.
SAMUEL BOYD, dec'd. estate in the county of Franklin, Penn. Wit: SAMUEL
WILLIAMSON, JAMES BRATTON. Signed: ROBERT BOYD, seal. Dated 10 Dec.
1792. Attested bef. JOE PALMER, J.P. by SAMUEL WILLIAMSON, same date.

Page 622: This lease and release bet. ROBERT DUKE and JOHN LENARD
        both of Chester Co. Dated 6 Jan. 1779, sum of 10 shillings
for one whole year on 300 acres on the waters of Fishing Creek bet.
it and the Catawba River adj. THOMAS STEEL, ARTHUR HICKLIN, JR., ROBERT
SWANN. Wit: JOHN (X) DUKE, ALEXANDER MC NEILL. Signed: ROBERT DUKE.
Attested bef. JOHN EASTON, J.P. by ALEXANDER MC NEILL. Dated 11 Jan.
1779.

Page 623: Indenture made bet. EDMOUND LEA & NANCY his wife and HASEL
        (also HAZEL) HARDWICK, JR. both of Chester Co., 27 July
1792. Sum of 56 pds. 1 shilling, 6 pence sterling for 100 acres on
a branch of Sandy River known as Stump branch. Orig. granted to JOSEPH
BROWN, from BROWN to JOHN MOBERLY, from MOBLEY to ELIZABETH NUNN, from
NUNN to EDMOUND LEA. Wit: EZEKIEL LANDERS, JAS. HARDWICK. Signed: EMOUND
LEA, NANCEY LEA, seal.

Page 624: Indenture made bet. SOLOMON PETERS and WILLIE CARRELL both
        of Chester Co., 23 July 1789. Sum of 60 pds. sterling for
400 acres on the east side of Broad River. One half of the orig. grant
given to SOLOMON PETERS in 1774. Wit: ROBERT COLLINS, JACOB CROCHER,
LESSLEY (X) OBROYAND. Signed: SOLOMON (X) PETERS, seal. Attested bef.
JOHN BELL, J.P. by LESSLEY OBRIANT. 22 Dec. 1790.

Page 626: Indenture made bet. HUGH THOMAS and WILLIAM ARTERBERRY both
        of Chester Co., 5 Aug. 1791. Sum of 100 pds. sterling for
200 acres on waters of Sandy River and Wright Mill Creek, adj. HOLLIS
TIMMS. Wit: JAMES CARR, JANE (X) THOMAS, THOMAS ONEAL. Signed: HUGH
THOMAS, seal. Attested bef. RICHD. TALIAFERRO, Clk. by THOMAS ONEAL,
dated 20 Aug. 1792.

Page 627: Indenture made bet. WILLIAM RODEN and EDMAN MAYFIELD both

Cont'd from page 78:
of Chester Co., dated 4 July 1790. Sum of 50 pds. for 75
acres on Brushey fork of Sandy River on or adj. JOHN RODEN line, JAMES
ATTERBERRY line, ABRAHAM MAYFIELD. Wit: ELIJAH MAYFIELD, ALLEN MAYFIELD.
Signed: WILLIAM RODEN, MARY RODEN, seal. Attested bef. ELIJAH NUNN,
J.P. by ELIJAH MAYFIELD, here he states that MARY is wife of WILLIAM
RODEN. Dated 26 Jan. (torn).

Page 628: Indenture made bet. JOHN WALKER, saddler and WILLIAM MORROW,
shoemaker, both of Chester Co. Dated 18 Apr. 1792. Sum of
180 pds. 15 shillings sterling, 100 acres on a small branch of Rockey
Creek. Orig. granted to SAMUEL WALKER 18 May 1772. After the death
of SAMUEL WALKER, the land descended to JOHN WALKER, his bro.
Wit: HUS. MC CLURE, WM. WALKER. Signed: JOHN WALKER, seal.

Page 628: Bill of sale bet. WILLIAM STROUD and JOHN RATTERY both of
Chester Co. Sum of 5 pds. 10 shillings sterling, for one
negro named London. Wit: JAS. KNOX, ___(?) MC DONALD. Signed: WILLIAM
STROUD, seal, dated 25 Oct. 1791.

Page 629: Indenture made bet. WILLIAM THOMAS and Col. DAVID HOPKINS
both of Chester Co. dated 19 July 1784. Sum of 2000 pds.
sterling for 640 acres in Ninety Six Dist. on Twelve mile creek. Vacant
land on all sides. Wit: THOMAS GREEN, SR., THOMAS PITT. Signed: WM.
THOMAS, seal. Attested bef. CHARLES SIMS, J.P. by THOMAS GREEN, SR.,
seal, dated 16 Dec. 1784.

Page 629: Bill of sale from JONATHAN JONES to JOSEPH JONES for the
sum of 100 pds. sterling, one negro named Cate, two feather
beds, four horses, all cattle I now have. Wit: WILLIAM JONES. Signed:
JONATHAN JONES, seal. Dated 16 Nov. 1792.

Page 630: Indenture made bet. ELIZABETH MILLER and THOMAS MILLER both
of Chester Co. 5 Nov. 1791. Sum of 60 pds. lawful money
for 200 acres on a small branch of Rockey Creek, adj. JOHN MILLS, other
sides vacant. Wit: CHARLES MILLER, JAMES MILLER, JAMES WILLSON. Signed:
ELIZABETH (X) MILLER, seal. Attested bef. JOHN BELL, J.P. by JAMES
MILLER, 3 Dec. 1791.

Page 631: Indenture made bet. THOMAS RODEN and JOHN RODEN both of
Chester Co., 3 Feb. 1786. Sum of 40 pds. sterling for 170
acres on waters of Sandy River. Wit: ENOCH PEARSON, DANIEL HEAD, WIL-
LIAM HEAD, JAMES RODEN, GREENBERRY RODEN. Signed: THOMAS RODEN, MARY
(X) RODEN, seal. Attested bef. RICHD. TALIAFERRO, Clk. by GREENBERRY
RODEN (no date).

Page 632: Indenture made bet. MICHAEL WORNAL (a poor boy) and JOSEPH
SIMMS, overseer of the poor for Chester Co. of the one part
and JOHN TERRY, wheelwright of the other part. MICHAEL WORNAL fifteen
years and six months old, binds himself to JOHN TERRY to the age of
21, he shall serve him well and faithfully in all things, etc. etc.
JOHN TERRY shall teach or cause to be taught, instructed, informed
in the best manner the craft, etc. of the wheelwright, etc. etc. Wit:
JOHN PRATT, J.P. Signed: JOHN TERRY, seal. MICHAEL (X) WORNAL, seal.

Page 633: Indenture made bet. JOHN OWEN and ALEXANDER MC GAUGHEY both
of Chester Co. dated 25 Apr. 1791. Sum of 40 pds. lawful
money for 200 acres on waters of Sandy River. Part of a grant given
to JOHN OWEN in 1790 for 500 acres. Wit: JAMES MC GAUGHEY, EDW. (X)
GRIFFIN, ROBT. OWEN. Signed: JOHN OWEN, seal. Attested bef. HUGH WHITE-
SIDE, J.P. by EDWARD GRIFFIN, dated 25 Jan. 1792.

Page 634: Indenture made bet. WILLIAM RODEN and PRISSEY ARTHURBERRY
both of Chester Co., dated 19 May 1790. Sum of 50 pds. current money for 75 acares on Smith Creek of brush fork on Sandy River,
adj. THOMAS MORRISS line at ROBERT MAYFIELD corner, JAMES ARTHURBERRY
line. Wit: ELIJAH MAYFIELD, ALLEN MAYFIELD. Signed: WILLIAM RODEN,
MARY RODEN, seals. Attested bef. ELIJAH NUNN, J.P. by ELIJAH MAYFIELD
(here the name PRISSEY is PRISCELLA), dated 25 Jan. 1792.

Page 635: Indenture made bet. JAMES GORE and PATRICK MC GIFF both
          of Chester Co., dated 12 June 1784. Sum of 100 pds. sterling
for 100 acres, orig. granted to ZACHARIAH ISBELL on 8 Mar. 1763, adj.
Widow NANTZ's line. Wit: JOHN ASHFORD GORE, ELIJAH GORE. Signed: JAMES
GORE.

Page 636: Indenture made bet. JAMES NICHLES of Lancaster Co. and GEORGE
          MINNIS of Chester Co., dated 2 Jan. 1790. Sum of 30 pds.
sterling for 100 acres on a branch of Rockey and Fishing Creeks, orig.
granted to THOMAS PATTERSON on 28 July 1769. PATTERSON sold to NICHLES.
Wit: JAMES GASTON, THOMAS GASTON. Signed: JAMES (X) NICHLES, seal.
Attested bef. JOSEPH LEE, J.P. by ELIZABETH ALEXANDER, dated 27 May
1790.

Page 638: Indenture made bet. WILLIAM BOYLES and GEORGE ADAMS both
          of Chester Co., dated 27 Feb. 1774. Sum of 10 shillings
for one year. This is a lease and release for 150 acres on Rockey Creek.
Wit: ALEX. TURNER, JEREMIAH (X) MEEKS. Signed: WILLIAM BOYLES. Attested
bef. PHILIP WALKER by JEREMIAH MEEKS, dated 24 Mar. 1792.

Page 639: Indenture made bet. WILLIAM BOYLES and MARTHA his wife and
          GEORGE ADAMS both of Chester Co., dated 28 Feb. 1774. Sum
of 130 pds. lawful money for 150 acres on a branch called Bullskin
branch of Rockey Creek. Orig. granted to WILLIAM BOYLES on 13 May 1768.
Wit: ALEXANDER TURNER, JEREMIAH (X) MEEKS. Signed: WILLIAM BOYLES,
MARTHA (X) BOYLES, seal. Attested bef. PHILIP WALKER, J.P. by JEREMIAH
(X) MEEKS (also spelled MEEK). Dated 14 Mar. 1792.

Page 641: Indenture made bet. GEORGE ADAMS and LYDIA his wife and
          JAMES DOUGLASS both of Chester Co., dated 14 June 1788.
Sum of 40 pds. for 150 acres on a branch called Bullskin branch of
Rockey Creek for one year. This is a lease and release. Wit: JOHN JOHN-
STON, THOS. MC CALLA. Signed: GEORGE ADAMS, LYDIA ADAMS, seals. Attested
bef. PHILIP WALKER, J.P. by JOHN JOHNSTON. Dated 16 Feb. 1792.

Page 642: Indenture made bet. GEORGE ADAMS and LYDIA his wife and
          JAMES DOUGLASS both of Chester Co., dated 14 June 1788.
Sum of 75 pds. sterling for 150 acres on Bullskin branch of Rockey
River. Orig. granted to GEORGE ADAMS on 6 Nov. 1786 with vacant land
on all sides when surveyed. Wit: JOHN JOHNSTON, THOMAS MC CALLA. Signed:
GEORGE ADAMS, LYDIA ADAMS, seals. Attested bef. PHILIP WALKER, J.P.
by JOHN JOHNSTON, 16 Feb. 1792.

Page 644: Indenture made bet. HUGH THOMAS and LEAH his wife and THOMAS
          ARTERBERRY. Dated (day and date not clear) 1792. Sum of
25 pds. sterling for 100 acres on the waters of Sandy River, adj. WILL-
IAM RAINEY, WILSON HENDERSON, JOHN THOMAS lines. Wit: JOHN BENNETT,
JOHN ROBINSON, PREDY WILLIAMS. Signed: HUGH THOMAS, LEAH THOMAS, seals.
Attested bef. RICHD. TALIAFERRO, Clk. by JOHN BENNETT, 9 Aug. 1792.

Page 645: Indenture made bet. SOLOMON PETERS and WILLIS CARRELL both
          of Chester Co. Dated 22 July 1789. Sum of 10 shillings with
the consent of his wife SARAH, for 400 acres on the Broad River. This
is a lease and release for one year. Wit: JOHN COLLINS, JACOB CROCKER,
JESSE (X) OBROYAND. Signed: SOLOMON PETERS, seal. Attested bef. JOHN
BELL, J.P. by JESSE BRIANT (also OBRIANT). Dated 23 Dec. 1790.

Page 647: Bill of sale from ALEXANDER WILSON for the sum of 4 pds.
          10 shillings, 6 pence and 1/2 penny, pd. by JEREMIAH KINGLEY
for one negro girl named Patt. Dated 5 Sept. 1792. Wit: ELYAH NUNN,
STEPHEN CLEMENT. Signed: ALEXANDER (X) WILSON, seal. Attested bef.
JOHN PRALL (PRATT?), J.P. by ELIAH (ELYAH) NUNN, Esq. 5 Dec. 1792.

END OF DEED BOOK B

Page 1:   Bill of sale. THOMAS BRAGG, yeoman, to JOHN GREEN, planter,
            both of Chester Co., S. C. Consideration: 20 pds. sterling
money. 1 negro man named Cato. Signed: THOMAS BRAGG. Dated 19 Sept.
1792. Wit: PHILIP FOX & ROBERT HEMPHILL. Proved by PHILIP FOX bef.
JOHN MILLS, J.P. on 15 Apr. 1793.

Page 2:   Bill of sale. AUSTIN CULP to JOHN CULP, both planters of
            Chester Co. Consideration: 40 pds. sterling money. 1 negro
man named Thomas; also 1 bay mare, 6 years old about 15 hands high.
Signed: AUSTIN CULP, dated 8 Jan. 1793. Wit: WILLIAM WHITESIDES & HENRY
CULP (his mark). Proved by WM. WHITESIDES bef. JOHN MILLS, J.P. on
28 Jan. 1793.

Page 3:   Deed of conveyance. THOMAS BAKER FRANKLIN to JAMES STUART
            both of Chester Co. Consideration: 12 pds. 13 shillings
4 pence sterling. 50 acres being part of 276 acres granted on 3 Jan.
1791 by Gov. Charles Pickney (in Columbia) on the South Fork of Sandy
River, Camden Dist. "Beginning at a white oak on land surveyed for
EDWARD WILSON, now JAMES STUART's. Running N 82 W to a pine eight chains
thence S 63 W to a pot ash oak, 10 chains on land surveyed for EDWARD
WILSON, thence S 23 E to a black jack, 28 chains on THOMAS BAKER FRANK-
LIN's land, thence N 63 E to pot ash oak 18 chains on S. D. FRANKLIN's
land, from thence to the beginning corner, last line on MAJOR GRISOM's
land." Signed: THOS. B. FRANKLIN. Dated 23 May 1791. Wit: HASEL HARWICK,
JOHN FRANKLIN. Proved by HASEL HARWICK bef. JOHN PRATT, J.P. on 23
May 1793. 23 May 1791 Receipt. For money "within mentioned." Signed:
THOMAS B. FRANKLIN. Wit: JOHN FRANKLIN, ALEXANDER JOHNSON & HASEL HAR-
WICK.

Page 4:   Bond of apprenticeship. FRANCES GORE, a poor girl and JOSEPH
            TIMMS, overseer of the poor, to JOHN ASHFORD GORE, planter,
all of Chester Co. FRANCES GORE, until she becomes 18 years old or
until the day of her marriage, shall dwell with JOHN ASHFORD GORE,
serve faithfully and well sd. GORE and his household; JOHN ASHFORD
GORE shall on his part teach FRANCES the art of serving, spinning and
knitting, furnish food, lodging and all other things needed, and also
teach the sd. girl to read the Bible well; this shall be done in such
a way that there shall be no expense at all to the county. Signed:
JOHN ASHFORD GORE, FRANCES GORE (by her mark). Wit: JOHN PRATT, J.P.
Dated 14 June 1792.
            Affidavite - dated 14 June 1792. "JOSEPH TIMMS declares
approbation to the binding of FRANCES GORE, apprentice to sd. JOHN
ASHFORD GORE. The within named JOHN ASHFORD GORE receiveth sd. FRANCES
GORE at the age of 11 years and 8 months." Signed: JOHN PRATT, J.P.

Page 5:   Deed of conveyance. JAMES GREER, jobber to JAMES ADAMS,
            planter, both of St. Mark's parish, S. C. Whereas 100 acres
granted on 13 May 1768 by Gov. Charles Montague to JAMES GREER, lying
on Susa Bowles, "It being by land surveyed for THOMAS RODEN and all
other sides by vacant land, plat attached to grant recorded in secretary's office; now in consideration of 50 pds. S. C. money, JAMES GREER
conveys sd. tract of 100 acres to JAMES ADAMS. Signed: JAMES ADAMS.
Dated 17 Nov. 1768. Wit: WILLIAM HADIN, ABRAHAM ADAMS (by mark) and
HANNA OGLETHORPE (by mark). Proved by WILLIAM HADIN bef. JOHN OGLE-
THORPE, J.P. on 17 Nov. 1768.

Page 8:   Mortgage Deed. HUGH WHITE, miller, York Co. to SAMUEL NEELY
            and THOMAS NEELY, Chester Co., also ROBERT LUSK and JOHN
CHAMBERS, yeomen of York Co., all of S. C. Whereas HUGH WHITE is indebted to above named SAMUEL and THOMAS NEELY, ROBT. LUSK, JOHN CHAMBERS
for several sums of money totaling 200 pds. S. C. money on security
of a bond by sd. WHITE to JOHN WALKER, Chester Co. Consideration: 100
pds. S. C. money to be pd. on 25 Aug.1794, and part by an amount of
money pd. and laid out by SAMUEL & THOS. NEELY for sd. HUGH WHITE;
now for the better securing and more sure payment of the other 100

Cont'd from page 81:
pds. to ROBERT LUSK and JOHN CHAMBERS as also other sums to SAMUEL
& THOMAS NEELY on or bef. 25 Aug. 1794, also that all future indebted-
nesses of sd HUGH WHITE to SAMUEL & THOMAS NEELY, ROBERT LUSK & JOHN
CHAMBERS shall be agreed upon from time to time as such accounts may
arise; due to the fact that HUGH WHITE is moving, JOHN CHAMBERS, ROBERT
LUSK, SAMUEL & THOMAS NEELY accepted a mortgage to 4 tracts of land
viz: one tract of 21 acres on Fishing Creek, Camden Dist.; two tracts
of 50 acres orig. granted to PHILIP WALKER on Fishing Creek including
one grist mill, one saw mill, one flax seed oil mill, the other tract
granted and conveyed to HUGH WHITE by PHILIP & JOHN WALKER, orig. proprietors. Signed: HUGH WHITE. Dated 29 Aug. 1792. Wit: DAVID NEELY,
JAMES NEELY & ANDREW DOWNING. Proved by DAVID NEELY bef. HUGH WHITE-
SIDES, J.P. On 29 Aug. 1792.

Page 11:   Blank

Page 12-13:Omitted or not numbered

Page 14:   Deed of Conveyance. JOEL ANTHONY, Abbeville Co. to JOHN
           QWENS(?), Chester Co., all of S. C. Considerations: 20 pds.
sterling, 200 acres, known as Lewis' Old Place, on Sandy River granted
on 11 Aug. 1774 to WM. LEWIS, conveyed by LEWIS to JOHN ANTHONY. Land
joins the land of THOMAS HANEY and DANIEL MOATS near the land of JOSIAH
KITCHEN's and the land of WM. FURGUSON. Plat is attached. Signed: JOEL
ANTHONY. Dated 25 Mar. 1793. Wit: HYRAM TAYLOR, WILLIAM GRIFFIN & ROBERT
OWENS. (Note - QWENS may be OWENS)

Page 16:   Deed of Conveyance. AUGUSTEEN CULP of North Carolina to
           WILLIAM SHADRICK, Chester Co., S. C. Whereas a certain grant
was made on 2 Jan. 1786 by Gov. Wm. Moultrie to AUGUSTEEN CULP of 95
acres on a small branch of Fishing Creek, waters of Catawba river,
plat attached to grant recorded in Secretary's office; now the sd.
AUGUSTEEN CULP conveys to WILLIAM SHADRICK, all of the above mentioned
tract of 95 acres. Signed: AUGUSTEEN CULP. Dated 10 June 1787. Wit:
WILLIAM MC KINNEY, THOMAS NEELY & DANIEL COOK. Proved by THOMAS NEELY
bef. JOHN MC CREARY, J.P. on 25 Apr. 1793.

Page 21:   Deed of Conveyance. WILLIAM SHADRICK to ROBERT FEE, both
           of Chester Co., S. C. Consideration: 50 pds. S. C. money.
30 acres on Fishing Creek in Chester Co., bounding on E side by WM.
HARPER's line and W by sd. SHADRICK's line "beginning at a pine running
N 50 E 10 to a pine thence N 20 W 35 to a black oak, thence S 58 W
3 to a hickory, thence S 35 E 3 to a black oak, thence S 28 E 33 to
the beginning corner." "Land granted to BENJAMIN RIVERS, trans. by
RIVERS to SHADRICK, now the sd. SHADRICK is conveying sd tract to ROBERT
FEE." Signed: WILLIAM SHADRICK. Dated 14 Mar. 1793. Wit: THOMAS NEELY,
JOHN MC KANON & JOHN FLEMING. Proved by THOMAS NEELY bef. HUGH WHITE-
SIDES, J.P.

Page 24:   Deed of Conveyance. BENJAMIN RIVERS, planter of S. C. to
           WILLIAM SHADRICK, planter. Consideration: 5 pds. 30 acres
lying on west side of sd. RIVER's land bounding on NW by GREEN's land,
E by sd RIVER's land, being part of 396 acres granted to sd. RIVERS,
bounded SE by SWINT's land on all other sides by SHADRICK's land. Signed
by BENJ. RIVERS. Dated 15 Jan. 1791. Wit: WM. HENDERSON, JACOB COOPER
& THOMAS NEELY. Proved by THOS. NEELY on 15 Apr. 1793 bef. J. MC CREARY,
J.P.

Page 26:   Deed of Conveyance. WILLIAM SHADRICK to ROBERT FEE, tinner,
           both of Chester Co., S. C. Consideration: 50 pds. S. C.
money. 95 acres on Fishing Creek, Chester Co. bounding on S by JOHN
MC KANAN's land, on E by WILLIAM CREATH's land, on W by BARNETT's land,
on all other sides by lands unknown, "beginning at a black jack running
S 53 W 30 to a pine S 18 E 175 to a black Jack, thence to a pine S
23 E 22 to a hickory, thence N 29 W 50 to a hickory, thence to the
beginning corner." Being land granted on 2 Jan. 1786 by Gov. Wm. Moultrie to AUSTIN CULP, transferred by CULP to sd SHADRICK. Signed: WILLIAM
SHADRICK. Dated 15 Mar. 1793. Wit: THOMAS NEELY, JOHN MC KANAN & JOHN

Cont'd from page 82:
FLEMING. Proved by THOMAS NEELY bef. HUGH WHITESIDES, J.P. on 15 Mar.
1793.

Page 28:   Deed of Conveyance. JOHN MC FADDIN to ROBERT MC FADDIN both
            of Chester Co. Whereas 331 acres of land were granted on
18 May 1770 by Gov. Wm. Bull to JOHN MC FADDIN on Fishing Creek in
S. C. bounding on NW by MATTHEW's land, the other sides by JACOB BEKLEY
(BLECKLEY), ROBERT MARTIN, ANDREW & THOMAS MARTIN, now in consideration
of 500 pds. sterling JOHN MC FADDIN conveys to ROBERT MC FADDIN 281
acres of the above mentioned tract. Signed: JOHN MC FADDIN. Dated 8
Mar. 1791. Wit: JOSEPH BOOTH, RICHART WYAT & WILLIAM WILLEY. Proved
by WM. WILLEY bef. JOHN MC CREARY, J.P. 7 Feb. 1792.

Page 32:   Sheriff's Deed. HUGH KNOX, sheriff of Chester Co. to WILLIAM
            ROBERTSON, planter, Chester co., both of S. C. Whereas OWEN
EVANS in the county court of Chester, obtained a judgement on action
of a debt of 35 pds. sterling with interest and 7 pds 2 shillings 9
pence costs against JOSHUA REPAULT, and after due and legal notice,
sd. HUGH KNOX, sheriff, sold 6 Oct. ... the first Sat. in October at
public outcry, 200 acres on Reedy Fork of Sandy River. Being part of
600 acres granted 23 Dec. 1771 by Gov. Wm. Bull to RICHARD WARING,
conveyed by WARING to DAVID PRUIT, by PRUIT to OWEN EVANS, by EVANS
to sd JOSHUA REPAULT; now conveyed by HUGH KNOX, sheriff to WM. ROBERT-
SON, the highest and last bidder for the sum of 16 pds sterling money.
Signed: HUGH KNOX. Dated 9 Nov. 1792. Wit: WILLIAM MORROW, HUGH STEWART
& DAVID BOYD.

Page 35:   Deed of Conveyance. JOHN FRANKLIN and MOURNING, his wife
            to JONATHAN DUNGAN, all of Chester Co. Consideration: 50
pds. sterling. Whereas 200 acres on Flimthem Creek, Chester Co. granted
in Dec. 1772 to THOMAS FRANKLIN, dec'd, by Gov. Charles Montague, sd.
part containing 18 acres on NE of sd tract joining lines with WILLIAM
TRUSSEL, ROBERT KENNEDY & THOMAS B. FRANKLIN, now JOHN FRANKLIN and
MOURNING his wife convey sd 18 acres to JONATHAN DUNGAN. Signed: JOHN
FRANKLIN & MOURNING FRANKLIN. Dated 23 Feb. 1793. Wit: WILLIAM BOYD,
JACOB DUNGAN & JAMES KENNEDY. Proved by WM. BOYD bef. JOHN PRATT, J.P.

Page 38:   Deed of Conveyance. THOMAS B. FRANKLIN and ANN his wife
            to JONATHAN DUNGAN, all of Chester Co. Consideration: 30
pds sterling. 77 acres on Filthem Creek, branch of Sandy river. Being
part of two grants: one a part of 100 acres granted by Gov. Wm. Moultrie
on 2 Oct. 1786 to WILLIAM GRISSOM and transferred to THOMAS B. FRANKLIN:
the other part of 363 acres on Flimthem's Creek, branch of Sandy river.
Signed: THOMAS B. FRANKLIN. Dated 23 Feb. 1793. Wit: JOHN FRANKLIN,
JAS. KENNEDY, JACOB DUNGAN (also DUGAN). Also, signed by ANN FRANKLIN.

Page 40:   Deed of Conveyance. ANDREW STEPHENSON and his wife, ELIZABETH
            Chester Co. to JOHN SIMONTON of York co., all of S. C. Con-
sideration: 100 pds sterling. 253 acres in three tracts "by Pattens"
(patents): first tract granted by Gov. Chas. Pinkney on 22 Apr. 1790
to ANDREW STEPHENSON containing 103 acres; second tract was granted
by Gov. Thos. Pinckney to JOHN CARSON containing 50 acres, conveyed
to ANDREW STEPHENSON on 16 Apr. 1788 (recorded in Clerk's Office, Chester Co. Book A pages 534-535); third tract granted by Gov. Chas. Montague
on 13 May 1768 to JOHN CARSON containing 100 acres conveyed to ANDREW
STEPHENSON on 7 Sept. 1787 (recorded in Clerk's Office, Chester Co.
Book A pages 531-532); the sd three tracts on Rocky Creek, "beginning
at a pine and running N 62 E 10:50 to a pine on MARY HARBERSON's line,
N 65 W 8 to a black Jack on MARY HABERSON's line, N 25 W 46.50 to a
stake on DOUOGALE BALENTINE's line, S 65 W 23 to a white oak on JOHN
COOPER's line, N 65 W 31 to a stake on JOHN COOPER's line, S 20 W 12
E 1 to a dogwood on BENJAMIN MITCHELL's line, S 70 E 31.50 to a black
oak on ANN HARBENSON's line, N 2 E 3.50 to a pine on MARY HARBERSON's
line, N 22 E 17 to a hickory on MARY HARBERSON's line, S 70 E 31 to
a pine on MARY HARBERSON's line; "now ANDREW STEPHENSON and ELIZABETH
his wife convey sd 253 acres to JOHN SIMONTON. Signed: ANDREW STEPHEN-
SON, ELIZABETH STEPHENSON. Dated 8 Nov. 1792. Wit: WILLIAM BOYD, ROBERT
HARBERSON & WM. MC CULLOUGH. Proved by WILLIAM MC CULLOUGH bef. RICHARD

Cont'd from page 83:
TALIAFERRO, Clerk, Chester County Court.

Page 44:   Deed of Conveyance. THOMAS B. FRANKLIN to JOHN FRANKLIN
            both of Chester Co. and both planters. Consideration: 40
pds. sterling 265 acres on Flimthem Creek, branch of Sandy River, grant
from Gov. Wm. Moultrie on 6 Mar. 1789 to MINOR WINN, transferred by
WINN to sd THOMAS B. FRANKLIN; now FRANKLIN conveys same to JOHN FRANK-
LIN. Signed: THOMAS B. FRANKLIN, 15 Mar. 1792. Wit: ALLEN DE GRAFFEN-
REID, WILLIAM WOOD & PHILIP KNOWLING. Also JAMES STEWART. Proved by
DE GRAFFENREID bef. RICHD. TALIAFERRO, Clk Chester Co. Crt.

Page 46:   Deed of Conveyance. ESEN FRANKLIN, planter to THOMAS B.
            FRANKLIN, both of Chester Co. Consideration: 10 pds. sterling
for 128 acres on Sandy River in Pinckney dist., surveyed for sd THOMAS
B. FRANKLIN on 3 Jan. 1792. "Bounded by lines running NW and SE by
RICHARD TALIAFERRO's land; NW by THOMAS RODEN's land." Being part of
a tract granted by Gov. Chas. Pinckney in 1792 to ESEN FRANKLIN, rec.
in Book BBB, page 55; now sd ESEN FRANKLIN conveys sd tract to THOMAS
B. FRANKLIN. Signed: ESEN FRANKLIN (by mark). Dated 22 Jan. 1792. Wit:
PATRICK MC GRIFF, WM. ARMOUR (by mark) and DANIEL TRUSSEL. Proved by
PATRICK MC GRIFF bef. RICHD. TALIAFERRO, Clk. Chester Co. Crt.

Page 49:   Deed of Conveyance. THOMAS B. FRANKLIN, planter to JOHN
            FRANKLIN, both of Chester Co. Consideration: 100 pds. ster-
ling. 202 acres on Flimthem Creek, branch of Sandy river. Being part
of four different tracts and one entire tract of 50 acres: one granted
by Gov. Chas. Montague on 24 Nov. 1767 to THOMAS B. FRANKLIN containing 100 acres; part of 100 acres granted by Gov. Wm. Moultrie on 2
Oct. 1786 to THOS. B. FRANKLIN; part of 360 acres granted on 5 Feb.
1787; also a tract of 50 acres granted by Gov. Wm. Moultrie on o7 Aug.
1786 to MAJOR GRISSOM, transferred by GRISSOM to THOS. B. FRANKLIN;
all above grants lying on Sandy river. Signed: THOMAS BAKER FRANKLIN.
Wit: ALLEN DE GRAFFENREID, PHILIP NOWLAND, WM. WOOD & JAMES STEWART.
Dated 30 Mar. 1792. Proved by ALLEN DE GRAFFENREID bef. RICHD. TALIA-
FERRO, Clk. Chester Co. Crt. Proved 22 June 1792.

Page 52:   Deed of Conveyance. JAMES HUGHEY and SARAH his wife to JOHN
            FRANKLIN all of Chester Co. Consideration: 100 pds. ster-
ling 50 acres. "Beginning at a post oak running SW 15.65 to a small
post oak on JOHN HOPKINS' line, S 30 W 32 chains to a small black oak
on JAMES HUGHEY's line, N 60 E 15 to an ash on THOMAS B. FRANKLIN's
line, M(?) 30 W 32 on THOMAS FRANKLIN's line to the beginning corner."
Being part of 100 acres surveyed and laid out 3 June 1766 to EDWARD
FLIMTHEM on north side of Broad river, on a branch called Flimthem's
Creek, "Butting and bounding on all sides by vacant lands" when surveyed. Signed: JAMES HUGHEY, SARAH HUGHEY. Dated 20 Aug. 1792. Wit:
JOHN KENNEDY, THOMAS B. FRANKLIN, JOHN WEIR.
            Renunciation of Dower. SARAH HUGHEY, wife of JAMES HUGHEY
            "appears and swears that of her own free will she joins
her husband, JAMES HUGHEY in the within conveyance and that she re-
linquishes her right to dower in same." Signed: SARAH HUGHEY bef. JOHN
PRATT, J.P.

Page 54:   Sheriff's Deed. HUGH KNOX, sheriff of Chester Co. to JOHN
            FRANKLIN, planter. Chester Co., S. C. Whereas SAMUEL CULWELL
and HUGH MILLING, executors of the estate of ALEXANDER MILLER, dec'd
in county court of Chester Co. on action of debt, obtained a judgement
against THOMAS B. FRANKLIN and NOTLEY COATES for their debts and costs;
and in consequence of sd judgement an execution was issued to the sheriff of sd co. to seize all lands, chattels, goods and tenements of
sd THOS. B. FRANKLIN and NOTLEY COATES for the sum of 42 pds. sterling
for the debts, costs and charges; and after due process of law sd sheriff sold at public outcry at the Chester Co. Court house on the first
Sunday of Dec. 1791, 297 acres on Sandy River. HUGH KNOX, the sheriff
conveyed sd land to JOHN FRANKLIN, who was highest and last bidder
for the sum of 42 pds. Signed: HUGH KNOX, dated 25 Mar. 1793. Wit:
D. SIMS & SAMUEL LACEY.

Page 58:;   Deed of Conveyance. JAMES HUGHEY, planter to JAMES STEWART,

Cont'd from page 84:
                  both of Chester Co. Consideration: 50 pds. sterling for
50 acres "beginning at a post oak and running N 88 W 15.81 to a gum,
thence S 7 W 31.62 to a hickory, thence S 83 E 15.81 to a white oak,
thence N 7 E 31.62 to the beginning corner." Being part of 200 acres
on Stoney Fork of Sandy river, granted to EDWARD WILSON. Signed: JAMES
HUGHEY. Dated 20 Mar. 1790. Wit: THOMAS JINKINS, JAMES GORE & JAMES
HARDWICK. Proved by THOS. JINKINS bef. JOHN PRATT, J.P. on 20 Mar.
1790.

Page 60:   Bill of Sale. ROBERT FULWOOD, Clarendon Co. to THOMAS GATHER,
           Kershaw Co., both of Camden Dist. 1 negro named Peter, form-
erly the property of MOSES BROWN. Signed: ROBERT FULWOOD. Dated 3 Mar.
1792. Wit: THOMAS DINKINS. Proved by THOMAS JINKINS bef. PHILIP WALKER,
J.P. on 29 Apr. 1792.

Page 61:   Bill of Sale. CHARLES FINKLEA, planter of Prince Fredricks
           Parish, Liberty co., to JAMES HEAD, planter both of S. C.
Consideration: 40 pds. sterling. 1 negro girl named Jemimah. Signed:
CHARLES FINKLEA. Dated 24 Dec. 1792. Wit: THOMAS FINKLEA, GEORGE HEAD.
Proved by GEO. HEAD bef. RICHD. TALIAFERRO, Clk. Chester Co. Crt. on
15 Apr. 1793.

Page 62:   Deed of Conveyance. ARCHIBALD ELLIOTT, JR, Chester Co. to
           DAVID DAVIS, planter. Consideration: 14 pds. sterling. 52
acres, 3 rods on Fishing Creek in Chester Co., S. C. "Beginning at
a post oak and running thence S 63 W 27.62 to ROBERT GILL's line, thence
with sd line N 14 W 24 to a black jack, thence N 30 E 16.50 to a stone,
thence S 35 E 27 to a hickory, thence S 70 E 7.50 to the beginning
corner." Being part of a tract conveyed to ARCHIBALD ELLIOTT, JR. from
ARCHIBALD ELLIOTT, SR. in 1792. Signed: ARCHIBALD ELLIOTT, JR. Dated
24 June 1793. Wit: WILLIAM SHAW, JAMES BARRON, ELIJAH DAVIS. ARCHI-
BALD ELLIOTT, JR. used his mark.

Page 63:   Deed of Conveyance. WILLIAM STONE and his wife ELIZABETH,
           to DENNIS CARRELL, all of Chester Co. Consideration: 100
pds. sterling for 100 acres on north side of orig. tract "beginning
at the creek and running N 50 chains to a red oak then W 35 chains
to a stake on the bank of the creek and up the several meanders of
the creek to the beginning corner." Being part of 300 acres granted
by Gov. Thomas Boone on 17 June 1760 to WILLIAM STONE, lying on Sandy
Creek of Broad River, bounding on all sides by vacant land at the time
of survey. Signed: WILLIAM STONE (his mark), ELIZABETH STONE (her mark).
Dated 23 Mar. 1791. Wit: ROBERT LEMONDS, JAMES HEAD, HENRY HEAD.

Page 65:   Deed of Conveyance. JOHN GORE and his wife, MARY, to NATHAN
           COFFEE, all of Chester Co. Consideration: 100 pds. sterling,
126 acres "beginning at a post oak and running S 50 E 42 on DAVID BOYD's
and SAMPSON NOLAND's lines, thence N 50 W 42 to a stake on the aforesd
Plantation, thence S 40 W 30 to the beginning corner." Being part of
a tract granted by Gov. Thos. Boone on 5 Oct. 1762 to ZACHARIAH ISBELL,
bounding on all sides by vacant lands at the time of the survey by
JAMES TIMMS, SIMPSON NOLAND and DAVID BOYD, situated on Sandy River,
conveyed by ZACHARIAH ISBELL to JAMES GORE, dec'd., transferred by
JAMES GORE in his last will and testament to the sd. JOHN GORE. Signed:
JOHN ASHFORD GORE, MARY GORE (by mark). Dated 17 Jan. 1793. Wit: WILLIAM
BOYD, MAJOR GRISSOM (by mark), and PHILIP NOLAND. Proved by PHILIP
NOLAND bef. ELIJAH NUNN, J.P. 25 Apr. 1793.

Page 67:   Deed of Conveyance. THOMAS FLETCHALL to ALLEN DE GRAFFEN-
           RIED, both of Chester Co. Consideration: 65 pds. sterling.
85 acres on Sandy river "beginning at a white oak and running S 28
to the creek on land laid out to SAMUEL WELLS, thence up the various
courses of the creek to the upper line on land sold off the same tract
to JOSEPH DAVIS, thence N 28 to a stake on land claimed by THOMAS JINK-
INS, thence S 62 W 24 to the beginning." Being part of a tract granted
by Gov. Wm. Bull on 5 Oct. 1758 to JAMES FLETCHALL. Signed: THOMAS
FLETCHALL. Dated 17 Apr. 1793. Wit: HOLLIS TIMMS, THOMAS SATES WHITE
& JEREMIAH THOMAS. Also signed by FRANCES ROGERS (by mark). Proved

Cont'd from page 85:
by HOLLIS TIMMS bef. ELIJAH NUNN, J.P. on 25 June 1793.

Page 70:   Deed of Conveyance. DENNIS CARRELL and SARAH his wife, to
           WILLIAM STONE, all of Chester Co. Consideration: 100 pds.
sterling for 77 acres on north side of original tract "beginning at
creek at a stake and running S 26 W 10.50 to a white oak, thence W
35.75 to a White oak, thence N 50 to a red oak on part of DANIEL RICE's
land, thence E 15 to the creek on the aforesd line, thence up several
meanders of the creek to the beginning." Being part of 300 acres granted
by Gov. Thomas Boone on 17 June 1760 to WILLIAM STONE on Sandy Creek
a branch of Broad river, bounding on all sides by vacant lands when
surveyed, sd 77 acres transferred by JOHN STONE, MOSES STONE and JACOB
STONE "to sd DENNIS CARRELL and WILLIAM STONE on 19 Oct. 1783"; now
DENNIS CARRELL conveys sd 77 acres to WILLIAM STONE. Signed: SARAH
STONE & SARAH CARRELL (by mark). Dated: 23 Mar. 1791. Wit: ROBERT LEM-
ONDS, JAMES HEAD & HENRY HEAD.

Page 72:   Deed of Conveyance. JOHN MORRIS , planter and MARY, his
           wife, to JOHN BANKHEAD, planter, all of Craven Co., Camden
Dist., St. Mark's parish, S. C. Whereas 200 acres, granted by Gov.
Wm. Bull on 23 June 1774 to JOHN MORRIS on Rocky Creek in Craven Co.,
bounding on the SE and NE by JOHN COOPER's land, on S by SARAH KNOX's
land and to the W and SE on PATRICK MC GARITY's land, on all other
sides by vacant land; now in consideration of 21 pds 8 shilling and
6 pence sterling money, JOHN MORRIS and wife MARY, convey sd 200 acres
to JAMES BANKHEAD. Signed: JOHN MORRIS and MARY MORRIS (by mark). Dated
18 Feb. 1785. Wit: JAMES MC GARITY, WILLIAM MC GARITY (by mark). Proved
by JAMES MC GARITY bef. ANDREW HEMPHILL, on 23 June 1793.

Page 75:   Deed. WILLIAM FORD, eldest son and heir of THOMAS FORD,
           dec'd. to JAMES CLARK, both of Chester co. Consideration:
26 pds sterling. 50 acres "beginning at the SE corner and the NE corner
and to run across the entire survey." Being part of 100 acres granted
by Gov. Wm. Bull on 4 Oct. 1768 to THOMAS FORD on Hagues Branch of
Rocky Creek on SW side of Catawba River. Signed: WM. FORD (by mark).
Dated 12 Mar. 1793. Wit: WILLIAM HAWKINS, BURRELL SANDIFER. Proved
by WM. HAWKINS bef. ANDREW HEMPHILL, J.P. 22 June 1793.

Page 78:   Deed of Conveyance. HASEL HARDWICK, SR. to JAS. SIMS, both
           of Chester Co. Consideration: 6 pds sterling. 61 acres on
Sandy river in Chester Co. "beginning at a hickory corner and running
thence S 52 1/2 W 70.20 to a black oak, thence S 50 E 18.50 to a hickory
from that place N 30 E 66.30 to the beginning." Being part of 500 acres
orig. granted to the beforenamed HARDWICK, with vacant lands on all
sides. Signed: HASEL HARDWICK. Dated 4 Sept. 1792. Wit: AMOS TIMMS,
JAMES HARDWICK. Proved by AMOS TIMMS bef. JOHN PRATT, J.P. 5 Sept.
1792.

Page 81:   Quit Claim Deed. MARY SIMS and WILLIAM SIMS to FERDINAND
           HOPKINS, all of Chester Co. In consideration of a bond given
by NATHAN SIMS, dec'd. to DAVID HOPKINS for 16,000 pounds merchantable
tobacco, sd MARY & WILLIAM SIMS in consequence of sd bond, delivered
to them by FERDINAND HOPKINS (son of DAVID HOPKINS) do forever quit
claim to sd FERDINAND HOPKINS a tract of 160 1/2 acres conveyed by
DAVID HOPKINS to NATHAN SIMS. Being part of 321 acres granted by Gov.
Wm. Moultrie, 5 Feb. (no year) to DAVID HOPKINS on Sandy River in Chester county known as the place whereon MARY SIMS now lives. Signed: MARY
SIMS, WILLIAM SIMS. Dated 31 Dec. 1792. Wit: ROBERT GLENN, RICHARDSON
MAYO & MARY VAUGHAN (by mark).

Page 82:   Mortgage Bond. JOHN PUGH to Col. EDWARD LACEY both of Chester
           Co. In consideration of 4 pds sterling that sd LACEY stands
security for sd PUGH to HAMBLETON BROWN, payable on demand; also 14
pds 12 shillings 6 pence sterling balance on debt of 1 July 1790, to
sd LACEY; also a settled account of 2 pds 12 shillings 6 pence; a total
debt of 18 pds 12 shillings 6 pence sterling, which sum sd PUGH acknowledges as just and herein bargains and sells to sd LACEY 3 cows
one being red about four or five years old, another red and white bet.

Cont'd from page 86:
six and seven years old with a last spring calf of red and white color,
one other cow red and white on back, three or four years old, one red
heifer about two years old and one heifer one year old, all marked
with a crop in left ear and half crop in right ear; also one roan mare
seven or eight years old branded on (right) mounting shoulder, about
14 hands high, one bay about 13 handss high, branded on mounting (right)
shoulder and buttock that is about eight years old; also a last spring
horse colt with white legs and face; also all sd PUGH's hogs, mark
crop off left ear and half crop off right; all this years crop of corn
about 6 acres; conditions: if PUGH shall pay to HAMBLETON BROWN the
4 pds mentioned above; also PUGH shall pay to sd LACEY 14 pds 12 shillings 6 pence within two years "then everything herein contained shall
cease" otherwise to remain in full force. Signed: JOHN PUGH. Dated
27 July 1791. Wit: SAMUEL PUGH, DAVID PATTERSON. Proved by SAMUEL PUGH
bef. JOHN PRATT, J.P. 6 July 1793.

Page 85:   Deed. JOHN STEELE, planter to THOMAS STEELE, both of Chester
             Co. Whereas 400 acres on Fishing Creek in Craven Co. (now
Chester) granted by Gov. Chas. Montague on 17 Nov. 1771 to CATHERINE
STEEL "beginning at a white oak and running thence N 84 W to a stake
18 chains, thence N 20 to a stake 70 chains and 30 links, bounded by
land formerly belonging to WILLIAM GASTON and vacant land, from thence
N 50 to a stake 60 chains, bounded by land formerly belonging to JOHN
GASTON and vacant land now surveyed for JAMES GASTON, from thence S
15 E to a stake 24 chains bounded by land belonging to JOHN WHITE from
thence S 5 E to a stake 98 chains and 50 links, bounded by land formerly
belonging to JOHN MC FADDEN and CATHERINE STEEL, from thence (?) 65
W to the beginning white oak 27 chains and 50 links, bounded by JOHN
LEONARD's land; sd CATHERINE STEEL died intestate, making JOHN STEEL,
her son, become her heir; now in consideration of 50 pds sterling JOHN
STEEL conveys to sd THOMAS STEEL 200 or one-half above described tract.
Signed: JOHN STEEL, MARGARET STEEL. Dated 1 Aug. 1788. Wit: JOHN MC
CRARY, ANDREW LOCKHART.

Page 90:   Deed of Conveyance. JOHN MC CREARY, Esq. to JOHN BANKHEAD,
             planter, both of Chester Co. Consideration of 25 pds ster-
ling. 125 acres on Fishing Creek "beginning at a pine, thence N 45
29 chains to a stake, thence N 85 E 21 to a pine, thence N 50 E 6 to
a stake, thence to the beginning." Bounded on NE lines by lands belong
to JAMES GASTON on the NW line by land belonging to the sd JOHN BANK-
HEAD and on the SW line by BEESLEY's and JOHN MC DILL's land. Being
land granted by Gov. Thos. Pickney on 5 Mar. 1787 to sd JOHN MC CREARY.
Signed: JOHN MC CREARY. Dated 1 Mar. 1793. Wit: JOSEPH BOOTH, JAMES
CAKIN, THOMAS WOOD.

Page 92:   Deed of Conveyance. ISHAM STRANGE to ANDREW KIDD both of
             Wilkes Co., Ga. Consideration of 80 pds sterling. 200 acres
in Fairfield Co., S. C. on Rockey branch of Rocky Creek, joining lines
with JOHN WINN and WILLIAM MC GOMERY and RANDLE WRIGHT. Signed: ISHAM
STRANGE, ANN WILSON, SAMUEL WILSON, RACHAEL STRANGE & ELIZABETH STRANGE
(by mark), and SARAH LINCECUM (by mark). Dated 21 July 1787. Wit: ISAAC
BELL, JANE BELL & JAMES ROBERTSON. Proved by JAMES ROBERTSON bef. ANDREW
HEMPHILL, J.P. on 26 Jan. 1792.

Page 93:   Deed of Gift. CHARLES WALL to JANE WALL, daughter of JOHN
             WALL, and niece of CHARLES WALL. Consideration of love and
affection. 100 acres on Big Rocky Creek on S side of Catawba river.
Being part of a tract orig. granted to BIRD WALL, dec'd. bounding NW
by BENJAMIN STREET's and WILLIAM NETTLE's land, NE by ABRAHAM STEVEN's
and WILLIAM WILKES' land, all other sides by vacant lands when laid
out, conveyed on 29 Nov. 1786 by JOHN WALL, lawful heir of BIRD WALL,
dec'd to CHARLES & WM. WALL as recorded in Clerks office, Chester Co.,
Book A page 255, conveyed by WILLIAM WALL to sd CHARLES WALL on 4 Aug.
1790; also 3 cows and calves, 3 breeding mares, 2 feather beds with
furniture, a lot of pewter, 2 pots, 1 Dutch oven, and other small articles. Signed: CHARLES WALL. Dated 18 Apr. 1793. Wit: JOHN HEMPHILL,
HAMPTON STROUD & WILLIAM WALL. Proved by HAMPTON STROUD bef. ANDREW
HEMPHILL, J.P. on 21 May 1793. Memorandum: Land, goods and chattles

Cont'd from page 87:
delivered to JANE WALL on 18 Apr. 1793.

Page 95:   Deed of Conveyance. ANDREW KIDD, planter to NATHANIEL DURHAM,
           Chester Co., Consideration of 100 pds sterling. 200 acres
on Rocky Creek, Camden Dist. Being land granted to MICHAEL STRANGE
2 Apr. 1773. Signed: ANDREW KIDD. Dated 16 Aug. 1791. Wit: JOHN POLLEY
& JAMES BROWN (by mark).

Page 96:   Deed of Conveyance. KEMP T. STROTHER, Fairfield Co. to FERDI-
           NAND HOPKINS, Chester Co. Consideration of 1000 pds sterling.
A certain tract of land on Brushy Fork of Sandy Run granted by Gov.
Wm. Bull on 25 Apr. 1775 to DAVID HAYS, "beginning at a hickory and
running N 75 W 70.72 to a post oak and hickory, thence S 75 E 70.72
to a stake on the bank of Brushy Fork thence down the creek to the
beginning." Containing 400 acres conveyed by DAVID HAYS to WILLIAM
STROTHER, dec'd; now KEMP T. STROTHER, heir of WILLIAM STROTHER, conveys
sd tract of 400 acres to FERDINAND HOPKINS. Signed: KEMP T. STROTHER.
Dated 17 Apr. 1788. Wit: MINN WINN, ELISHA HUNTER, & JOHN WINN, JR.
Proved by MINN WINN bef. J. C. PEARSON, J.P. in Fairfield Co. on 12
August 1790.

Page 99:   ROBERT CHAPMAN, Union Co., to WILLIAM GASTON, Chester Co.
           both of S. C. Consideration of 300 pds 15 shillings "lawful
money." 200 acres on Wilson's Branch, Chester Co. "Being part of land
granted to WILLIAM CHAPMAN, dec'd, brother to ROBERT CHAPMAN, bounding
S on land belonging to the estate of ALEXANDER TOMB, dec'd. on all
other sides by vacant land; now ROBERT CHAPMAN conveys sd tract of
land to WILLIAM GASTON. Signed: ROBERT CHAPMAN. Dated 18 June 1793.
Wit: JOSEPH BROWN, JAMES LOVE GASTON & JOHN BROWN. Proved by JOSEPH
BROWN bef. JOHN MC CREARY, J.P. on 25 June 1793.

Page 100: Deed of Conveyance. FRANCIS GREENWOOD to ROBERT WALKER,
           both of Chester Co. Consideration of 50 pds sterling. 100
acres on Sandy river in Chester Co. Being land granted by Gov. Benjamin
Guerard on 15 Oct. 1784 to EPHRIAM MITCHELL; conveyed by MITCHELL on
29 Mar. 1785 to DAVID HOPKINS who conveyed it to FRANCIS GREENWOOD
on 26 Nov. 1792, sd tract bounding by a line running NW on HENRY HARDEN,
by a line running SE on DAVID HUDSON land and by lines running NE and
NW on land claimed by STEPHEN TERRY. Signed: FRANCIS GREENWOOD. Dated
26 Nov. 1792. Wit: JOHN PRATT, LYDIA PRATT (by mark) and JENNET PRATT
(by mark). Proved by JOHN PRATT bef. RICHD. TALIAFERRO, Clk of Chester
Co. Court on 24 Jan. 1793.

Page 102: Deed of Conveyance. DAVID HOPKINS and MARY his wife to FRAN-
           CIS GREENWOOD, all of Chester Co. Consideration of 100 pds
sterling for a certain tract on Sandy River, granted by Gov. Benjamin
Guerard on 15 Oct. 1784 to EPHRIAM MITCHELL, Esq., containing 100 acres
bounding by a line running NW on HENRY HARDEN's land, by a line running
SE on DAVID HUDSON's land and by a line running NE and NW on land claimed by STEPHEN TERRY, conveyed 29 Mar. by EPHRIAM MITCHELL to sd HOPKINS
now HOPKINS conveys sd 100 acres to FRANCIS GREENWOOD. Signed: DAVID
HOPKINS, MARY HOPKINS (by mark). Dated 1 Nov. 1792. Wit: SAMUEL HARRIS,
FREDERICK HOPKINS. Proved by FREDERICK HOPKINS bef. JOHN PRATT, J.P.
on 26 Nov. 1792.

Page 104: Bill of Sale. JAMES GASTON to BENJAMIN MORRIS, both of Chest-
           er Co. Consideration of 32 pds sterling. 1 negro boy named
Jeremiah. Signed: JAMES GASTON. Dated 21 May 1793. Wit: MARK EAVES
& SAMUEL MC CREARY. Proved 22 June 1793.

Page 106: Deed. NATHANIEL PACE, Kershaw Co., Camden Dist. to JOHN
           MORRIS, Chester Co. Consideration of 15 pds sterling. 55
acres on a ridge of Rocky Creek on NW side of Catawba river, bounding
on E lands laid out for THOMAS MORRIS, on SE by vacant land, on SW
by MIDDLETON's land, on NW by JOHN COOPER's land. Being part of land
granted by Gov. Wm. Moultrie on 5 Feb. 1787 to (name not shown). Signed:
NATHANIEL PACE. Dated 2 Mar. 1793. Wit: ELIJAH BANCKSTON & THOMAS BRIT-
TON. Proved by ELIJAH BANCKSTON bef. ANDW. HEMPHILL, J.P. 22 Jun.1793

Page 108:   Deed of Conveyance. JOHN WALKER and AGNES, his wife to JOHN
             WALKER, son of SAMUEL WALKER, all of Chester Co. Consider-
ation: 60 pds sterling. 140 acres on Sandy river in Chester Co. bound-
ing on lands belonging to JONATHAN DUNGAN. Being land granted by Gov.
Wm. Moultrie on 2 Oct. 1786 to JOHN WALKER. Signed: JOHN WALKER, AGNES
WALKER (by mark). Dated May 1793. Wit: HUGH STEWART, JAMES NORTON.
Proved by HUGH STEWART bef. ANDW. HEMPHILL, J.P. 25 June 1793.

Page 110:   Deed of Conveyance. JAMES BURNS, planter to LAIRD BURNS,
             saddler, both of Camden Dist., S. C. Consideration: 6 pds
sterling, S. C. money "together with what property he has already rec'd
from the undernamed estate JAMES BURNS conveys to LAIRD BURNS all rights
titles or claims to the estate of LAIRD BURNS, dec'd. Signed: JAMES
BURNS. Dated 1 Mar. 1784. Wit: ROBERT BOYD, HUGH WEIR. Proved by HUGH
WEIR bef. PHILIP WALKER, J.P. 27 June 1793.

Page 112:   Deed of Conveyance. WILLIAM BOYD and ANN his wife to JAMES
             SLOAN, all of Chester Co., S. C. Whereas 100 acres on Bull-
skin Run in Craven (now Chester) county granted by Gov. Chas. Greville
on 14 Sept. 1771 to WILLIAM HOUSTEN, bounding on two sides by MICAJAH
PICKETT's land, on all other sides by vacant land; conveyed by sd WM.
HOUSTEN and ELINOR, his wife, to sd WM. BOYD; now BOYD conveys sd tract
to JAMES SLOAN. Signed: WILLIAM BOYD & ANN BOYD. Dated 26 June 1793.
Wit: JOHN MC DONALD, JAMES NYLE.

Page 115:   Deed of Conveyance. JAMES BANKHEAD to THOMAS MC DILL both
             of Chester Co. Consideration: 30 pds sterling. 150 acres
on Rocky Creek joining plantations of JAMES BANKHEAD, PATRICK HARBISON,
JOHN MC DILL and EDWARD LOWRANCE. Being part of a tract on Rocky Creek,
bounded NE by MARY BAYELY's land, on all other sides by vacant lands;
granted by Gov. Wm. Bull on 16 June 1768 to SAMUEL FREIZER and wife
ELIZABETH who conveyed it to RICHARD BURKELE on 15 Dec. 1768. Sd tract
was conveyed by BURKELE on 24 Feb. 1774 to JOSEPH MILICAN, conveyed
by MILICAN on 13 Apr. 1775 to ALEXANDER ROGERS, "Doctor of Fisick",
at whose death sd land devolved to his executors and heirs, JOHN &
REBECCA GRAY, conveyed by GRAY on 4 Jan. 1788 to sd JAMES BANKHEAD.
Signed: JAMES BANKHEAD. Dated 22 June 1793. Wit: JOHN MC DILL, PATRICK
MC ALLA & SAMUEL MC DILL.

Page 119:   Deed of Conveyance. JOSIAH HILL to THOMAS WALLACE both of
             Chester Co. Consideration: 90 pds sterling. 339 acres "by
estimation" lying on Rocky Creek, Chester Co. Being a tract laid out
or granted by patent in 1786 to JOSIAH HILL. Signed: JOSIAH HILL. Dated
26 June 1793. Wit: JOHN PRATT & D. SIMS.

Page 120:   Deed of Conveyance. JOHN GRAY and REBECCA, his wife, Fair-
             field co. to JAMES BANKHEAD, Chester Co. all of S. C. Con-
sideration: 73 pds sterling. 150 acres on Rocky Creek in Chester Co.,
bounding at time of survey NE on MARY BAILEY's land and all other sides
vacant. Being land granted by Gov. Wm. Bull on 16 June 1768 to SAMUEL
FREIZER, conveyed by him on 15 Dec. 1768 to RICHARD BURKELE; by him
on 24 Feb. 1774 to JOSEPH MILLIGAN by him on 13 Apr. 1775 to ALEXANDER
ROGERS, "Doctor of Phisic", by whose death sd tract devolved to sd
JOHN GRAY and REBECCA, his wife, as executors and heirs of ALEXANDER
ROGERS. Signed: JOHN GRAY & REBECCA GRAY. Dated 14 Jan. 1788. Wit:
DANIEL COCKRAN & JAMES HANNA. Proved by JAMES HANNA bef. ARCHIBALD
MC QUESTON, J.P. Fairfield Co., 24 June 1793.

Page 124:   SAMUEL ATKINS to HENRY JORDON both of Chester Co., S. C.
             Consideration: 10 pds. 225 acres on Catawba river in Chester
Co. Being land orig. granted to ____ CULP and by him conveyed to JAMES
PATTON, dec'd and by Sheriff's deed conveyed to sd SAMUEL ATKINS, sd
land bounded on one side by Catawba river, on a second side by REBECCA
PATTON's land and on other sides by lands belonging to SAMUEL & RICHARD
ATKINS; now the sd tract of 225 acres is conveyed by SAMUEL ATKINS
on condition that 10 pds shall be pd to him by HENRY JORDON on or bef.
5 Apr. next (1794) and also in case of failure shall be made, each
year thereafter shall be pd one pepper corn and after 500 years sd
land shall be returned to SAMUEL ATKINS. Signed: SAMUEL ATKINS. Dated

Cont'd from page 89:
4 Jan. 1793. Wit: THOMAS BAIRD, THOMAS WOOD & JOHN MC CREARY. Proved
by JOHN MC CREARY bef. HUGH WHITESIDES, J.P. on 25 Jan. 1793.

Page 127: Sheriff's Deed. HUGH KNOX, sheriff of Chester Co. to ROBERT
          WALKER, planter. Whereas RICHARD EVANS obtained a judgement
for debt and cost in Chester Co. court in July 1788 against THOMAS
B. FRANKLIN, JOHN FRANKLIN & SAMSON NOLAND; as a result of sd judgement
HUGH KNOX, Sheriff, was ordered to seize properties of THOMAS BAKER
FRANKLIN, JOHN FRANKLIN & SAMSON NOLAND, for the sum of 9 pds 4 shillings sterling money; after the required legal proceedings HUGH KNOX,
Sheriff, sold at public sale at Chester Co. Court House, Sat. 4 May
past (1793) a certain tract of 128 acres, more or less, on Sandy river,
in Camden Dist., bounded on NW and SE by RICHARD TALIAFERRO's land,
NE by JEREMIAH DAVIS' land and NW by THOMAS RODEN"s land. Being land
granted by Gov. Chas. Pinckney to ISHAM FRANKLIN, conveyed by him to
THOMAS BAKER FRANKLIN by deed; now in consideration of 6 pds 15 shillings sterling HUGH KNOX, sheriff, conveys to ROBERT WALKER, the last
and highest bidder for the above described tract of land. Signed: HUGH
KNOX, Sheriff. Dated 5 June 1793. Wit: JOHN MILLS, JR., & RICHARD EVANS.

Page 129: Deed of Conveyance. WILSON HENDERSON to ROBERT FROST, SR.
          both of Chester Co. Consideration: 100 pds S. C. money.
276 acres on Sealy's Creek of Sandy river in Camden dist., being land
granted by Gov. Thos. Pinckney, 3 Dec. 1787 to sd ROBT. FROST, SR.
Signed: WILSON HENDERSON. Dated 25 June 1793. Wit: HOLLIS TIMMS, WIL-
LIAM ESTES & JOSEPH TIMMS. Proved by WM. ESTES bef. JOHN PRATT, J.P.
on 25 June 1793.

Page 131: Deed of Conveyance. THOMAS BAKER FRANKLIN, planter to DENNIS
          CARREL yeoman, both of Chester Co. Consideration: 30 pds
sterling. 100 acres on Flimthem Creek of Sandy River, Chester Co.,
bounded SE by DENNIS CARREL's land, SE and NE by land laid out to RICH-
ARD HEAD, NW by land laid out to JAMES HUGHEY. Being part of 265 acres
granted 6 Mar. 1786 by Gov. Wm. Moultrie to MINOR WINN, Esq., conveyed
to THOMAS BAKER FRANKLIN on 22 May 1789. Signed: THOMAS BAKER FRANKLIN.
Dated 17 May 1791. Wit: JAMES HUEY, JOHN COCKRELL (by mark) and THOMAS
COCKRELL (by mark).

Page 133: Deed of Conveyance. JOHN MC COMBS and ANN, his wife, to
          PARKER ADKINS, both of Chester Co. Consideration: 50 pds
sterling. 50 acres on Sandy river joining the property of THOMAS CAB-
INESS & JOHN MC COMBS. Being part of 640 acres granted 5 May 1786 by
Gov. Wm. Moultrie to JOHN MC COMBS. Signed: JOHN MC COMBS. (Note:
it does not appear his wife, ANN signed the deed. Also, the names of
witnesses are omitted.)

Page 135: Quit Claim Deed. EDWARD ALLEN, Salem, Mass. to FERDINAND
          HOPKINS, Chester Co., S. C. Consideration: 157 pds 18 shill-
ings 3 pence sterling. For sd sum already paid quit claim is now made
for these lands, parts of 5 tracts: one granted 1 Aug. 1785 to LITTLE-
BURY, bounded by Col. JOHN WINN and THOMAS ADDISON's land; another
granted 1 Aug. 1785 to DANIEL COTVILLE bounded by THOMAS SHANNON's
land, all other sides vacant; another granted to EDWARD COTVILLE on
5 Sept. 1785 bounded by lands of WILLIAM THOMAS, DAVID HOPKINS and
vacant land; another granted to DAVID HOPKINS on 15 Oct. 1785 bounded
by lands of CHARLES COLEMAN, DAVID RICHARDSON and NATHANIEL HARBIN
and vacant land; another granted to JAMES MOORE bounded by lands of
WM. TUCKER, ____ MOBLEY, RICHARD CROSBY and DAVID LINDSAY: the __ tract
total 2,642 acres. Signed: EDWARD ALLEN. Dated 10 Feb. 1793. Wit: ROBERT
GLEEN and JAMES DILLARD.

Page 138: Deed of Gift. LEVY SMITH, Chester Co., S. C. to his daughter
          SALLEY. Consideration: love and affection. 1 negro boy named
Jack about 6 years old. Signed: LEVY SMITH. Dated 20 June 1793. Wit:
JOSEPH BENNETT.

Page 139: Deed of Conveyance. JOHN COLVIN to RICHARD HEAD, both of
          Chester Co. Consideration: 150 pds sterling money. 250 acres

90

Cont'd from page 90:
on Stone's Creek of Sandy river in Camden Dist., bounded by lands of JOHN COCKRELL, JAMES HUGHEY, JAMES DOUGHARTY and JOHN COLVIN, plat attached to orig. grant recorded in secretary's office Grant Book GGGG page 411. Being land granted 6 Feb. 1786 to JOHN COLVIN. Signed: JOHN COLVIN, HANNAH COLVIN. Wit: JOHN PRATT, JAMES HEAD and GEORGE HEAD (by his mark). Proved by GEORGE HEAD bef. RICHD. TALIAFERRO. Clk. of Chester Co. Dated 7 Feb. 1792.

Page 141: Deed of Conveyance. LUCY COLLINS to DENNIS CARRELL of Craven Co., both of S. C. Consideration: 100 pds S. C. money. Whereas 100 acres granted 17 Feb. 1767 "by his letters patents King George, the Third", to LUCY COLLINS on Sandy Creek of Broad river, bounding on all sides by vacant lands, grant recorded in secretary's office of sd Province; now LUCY COLLINS conveys to DENNIS CARRELL sd tract of 100 acres. Signed: LUCY COLLINS (by mark). Dated 9 Mar. 1771. Wit: ANTHONY DUFFIELD, WILLIAM STONE (by mark) and JAMES STONE (by mark).

Page 143: Deed. This indenture made bet. ISAAC TAYLOR and RICHARD HEAD both of Chester Co. The sum of 50 pds sterling for 300 acres, lying and being a part of 640 acres granted unto RICHARD HEAD 5 Feb. 1787 adj. land of MOSES STONE, RICHARD HEAD and ISAAC TAYLOR line. On the waters of Sandy river. Wit: JAMES HEAD, HENRY HEAD, SARAH TAYLOR. Signed: ISAAC TAYLOR and his wife, JANE (X) TAYLOR. Seals.

Page 145: Deed of Conveyance. JOHN COLVIN to RICHARD HEAD, both of Chester Co. Consideration: 60 pds sterling money. 100 acres on Sandy Creek of Broad river in the Province of S. C. bounded on all sides by vacant lands, granted 17 Feb. 1767 by Gov. Chas. G. Montague to LUCY COLLINS conveyed 9 Mar. 1771 by LUCY COLLINS to DENNIS CARRELL, transferred 3 Feb. 1784 by CARRELL to JOHN COLVIN. Signed: JOHN COLVIN, HANNAH COLVIN. Dated 7 Feb. 1792. Wit: JOHN PRATT, JAMES HEAD, GEORGE HEAD (by mark).

Page 147: Bill of Sale. JACOB ROBERTS to JAMES HEAD. Consideration: 30 pds sterling. 1 negro man named Hall, thru disguise called Joseph, about 36 years old. Signed: JACOB ROBERTS. Dated 12 Dec. 1792. Wit: JAMES HUGHEY, WILLIAM WOODWARD, RICHARD HEAD.

Page 148: Deed of Gift. CHARLES BOYD to ANN, JONATHAN, NANCY & WILLIAM DUNGAN, children of JACOB & ANN DUNGAN, all of Chester Co. Consideration: love and affection, also other good causes, one moving. To JONATHAN DUNGAN, 2 sorrel horses; to NANCY & ANN, all household furniture, sheep and cows; to WILLIAM, the drove of hogs, a loom, 2 saddles and all sheep and hogs bought at constable sale which was taken in execution from JACOB DUNGAN. (Note: also spelled DUNGA). Signed: CHARLES BOYD. Dated 11 Mar. 1793. Wit: WM. BOYD, CHARLES BOYD, JOHN CERD(?).
        Memorandum: On the day mentioned CHARLES BOYD delivered to JONATHAN, ANN, NANCY and WILLIAM DUNGAN above named articles and livestock. Signed: CHARLES BOYD. Dated 15 Apr. 1793.

Page 150: Deed of Conveyance. DENNIS CARRELL, planter to JOHN COLVIN, planter, both of Chester Co. Consideration: 500 pds S. C. money. 100 acres on Sandy Creek of Broad river, bounded on all sides by vacant land at the time of running. Being land granted 17 Feb. 1767 to LUCY COLLINS, conveyed by COLLINS to DENNIS CARRELL. Signed: DENNIS CARRELL. Dated 3 Feb. 1784. Wit: JOHN COCKRELL, JOHN PRATT, WILLIAM ARMER (by his mark).

Page 155: Deed. (Release preceded by Lease). ROBERT ROWAND to Miss HARRIETT ROWAND, ELLIOTT ROWAND & CHARLES ELLIOTT ROWAND. Consideration: 5 shillings S. C. money. 5 tracts: 1st tract 1500 acres surveyed 8 Sept. 1772 for JACK SIMMONS, granted 28 Oct. 1774 to sd ROBERT ROWAND in Craven Co. on Brushy Fork, six miles below Love's Ford, bounded S by CLEMENT LEMPRIER, W by WILLIAM ANDERSON, on all other sides by vacant lands; 2nd tract, 1000 acres surveyed for ARCHIBALD SIMPSON granted 28 Oct. 1774, to sd ROBERT ROWAND in Colleton Co. on waters of "Salt Catcher", bound on all sides by vacant lands; also 3rd tract

Cont'd from page 91:
of 500 acres, making 1500 acres, adj. each other in Orangeburg dist.,
being what is called Three Ponds, bounded on all sides by vacant lands;
sd 5 tracts making together 4,000 acres. Signed: ROBERT ROWAND. Dated
27 Aug. 1790. Wit: MARY WELLS, JAMES RIVER MAXWELL, ALEXANDER WALKER.

Page 157:   Deed of Conveyance. BENJAMIN MITCHELL, planter and SUSANNAH,
            his wife of Ninety-Six dist. to ADAM AGERS, tailor of Camden
dist., St. Mark's parish, all of Craven Co., S. C. Consideration: 400
pds S. C. money. Whereas 150 acres on Rocky Creek, Craven Co. granted
4 May 1775 to sd BENJAMIN MITCHELL, bounding SE on BENJ. MITCHELL's
land, on all other sides by vacant lands, plat attached to grant recorded in secretary's office, Book KKK page 345. Signed: BENJAMIN MITCHELL,
SUSANNAH MITCHELL (by her mark). Dated 4 Feb. 1778. Wit: JOHN SAMSON,
MICHAEL BLAIN.

Page 160:   Deed of Conveyance. JAMES WINN, Fairfield Co., to ROBERT
            GASTON, Chester Co. both S. C. Consideration: 50 pds sterling
for 90 acres on N side of Fishing Creek in Camden dist., plat attached
to orig. grant. Signed: JAMES WINN. Dated 10 Aug. 1790. Wit: DAVID
HAMILTON & RICHARD GLADNEY.

Page 162:   Deed of Conveyance. THOMAS MORRISS to PETER JONES, both
            of Chester Co. Consideration: 28 pds sterling. 173 acres
on Catawba river in Chester Co. bounding SE on JONATHAN HEMPHILL, NE
on CHARLES WALL & DONALD MC DONALD, SW on JAMES CLOUD. Being land granted 6 Feb. 1792 "by Patent" to THOMAS MORRISS. Signed: THOMAS MORRISS.
Dated 13 May 1792. Wit: SAMUEL LOWRIE, ROBERT BRADFORD.

Page 164:   Deed of Conveyance. WILLIAM MASSEY, Lancaster Co. to JOHN
            EDWARDS, Chester Co., both of S. C. Consideration: 100 pds
sterling. 183 acres in Chester Co. Being part of 2 grants: 59 acres
on N side of Fishing Creek, bounded NW by LAWRENCE GALAKER, opposite
side by Fishing Creek, on a third side by BRADLEY, on fourth side by
JOHN MC COWN, transferred from ALEXANDER MC COWN to JOHN MC COWN, from
JOHN MC COWN to JOSHUA EDWARDS; sd JOSHUA EDWARDS authorized WILLIAM
ROBERTSON by Power of Attorney who released sd land to above WM. MASSEY;
one other tract of 122 acres granted to WM. MASSEY, recorded in sec.
offie, Book YYYY page 92; now sd WILLIAM MASSEY conveyed the 59 acres
and 122 acre tracts to JOHN EDWARDS.

Page 166:   Bill of Sale. ALEXANDER WILSON to HANSEL HARDWICK, planter,
            Chester Co. 1 negro woman named Patt, about 6 years old;
terms of sale were WILSON shall pay taxes, cloth and "everything else
same as negro of her own" for 6 years, after 6 years sd negro Patt
shall return to WILSON. Signed: ALEXANDER WILSON (by his mark). Dated
1 Mar. 1793. Wit: JOHN SALSE, WILLIAM ESTES.

Page 167:   Deed of Conveyance. WALTER BROWN, planter, to SAMUEL MC
            DILL, blacksmith, both of Chester Co. Consideration: 30
pds sterling money. Whereas 100 acres, granted 20 July 1772 to WALTER
BROWN, on Snail branch of Rocky Creek in Chester Co., plat attached
to grant, recorded in secretary's office. Signed: WALTER BROWN. Dated
23 Jan. 1793.

Page 170:   Deed of Conveyance. JAMES COBB, Union Co. to WILLIAM BOYD,
            Cheser Co. both of S. C. Whereas 400 acres, granted 23 Dec.
1771 to RICHARD WARING in Cainey fork of Sandy river in Craven (now
Chester) county, bounded W by JOHN EVANS, NE and NW by BENJAMIN CERTER,
Sw and SE by EDMOND RUSSEL, other sides on vacant land, plat attached
to grant recorded in secretary's office, conveyed 16 Oct. 1775 by sd
WARING to DAVID PRUIT, recorded 24 Aug. 1776, Book Y No. 4, pages 147
and 148, conveyed 16 Nov. 1776 by DAVID PRUIT to JAMES COBB, now COBB
in consideration of 200 pds sterling conveyed same to WILLIAM BOYD.
Signed: JAMES COBB. Dated 31 Aug. 1791. Wit: JOHN TERRY, ASAM WILLIAMSON
and JONES TAYLOR.

Page 173:   Deed of Conveyance. JOHN CULP, father, son of PETER CULP,
            dec'd. to PHILIP CLINE, both of Camden dist., Chester Co.,

Cont'd from page 92:
S. C. Consideration: 30 pds sterling. 75 acres on Fishing Creek in Chester Co., running agreeable to plat "on the north east side of sd JOHN CULP or sd PHILIP CLINE choice of sd land." Signed: JOHN CULP. Dated 19 Feb. 1793. Wit: HUGH WHITESIDES, AUSTIN CULP, ABRAHAM WHITE-SIDES.

Page 176: Deed of Conveyance. JOHN HITCHCOCK, planter, to HUGH STUART, blacksmith, both of Camden dist., S. C. Consideration: 1 pd sterling. 200 acres. Being part of 400 acres on Sandy Creek of Broad river bounded on all sides by vacant land at the time of running out and lying on the east side of sd 400 acre tract, "granted 7 Nov. 1778 to JOHN HITCHCOCK" plat attached to original grant recorded in secretary's office. Signed: JOHN HITCHCOCK. Dated 12 Mar. 1785. Wit: JAMES GORE, RICHARD EVANS, JOHN PRATT.

Page 178: Sheriff's Deed. HUGH KNOX, Sheriff of Chester Co., S. C. to THOMAS NEELY, wagon maker, Chester Co., S. C. Whereas PHILIP WALKER in Chester Co. Court obtained in June 1792, a judgement against DANIEL COOK for debt and costs; in consequence of sd judgement an execution to levy on the property of DANIEL COOK the sum of 13 pds 15 shillings 10 pence sterling; debt and cost and by nature of the execution HUGH KNOX, Sheriff, after due process of law sold at public sale at Chester Court House 5 Jan. 1793, "past", one tract of about 300 acres, more or less, in Chester Co. on SW with land belonging to NATHANIEL SIMPLE, on NE by JOHN MC KINNEY and on all other sides by vacant land at the time of the orig. survey; also another tract containing 100 acres on Fishing Creek, adj. the above mentioned tract, both tracts making 350 acres; now HUGH KNOX, Sheriff conveyed to THOMAS NEELY, the last and highest bidder, the above mentioned 2 tracts for the sum of 15 pds 5 shillings sterling. Signed: HUGH KNOX, Sheriff. Dated 2 Mar. 1793. Wit: HUGH MC CLURE, HUGH WHITESIDES, WILLIAM WHITE-SIDES.

Page 180: Mortgage. THOMAS MORRISS to ROBERT WALKER, Chester Co., S. C. Consideration: 10 pds sterling money. 1 feather bed, other furniture in house, 4 head wagon horses (1 team). Condition: "that on or bef. 1 Dec. 1793 next" 10 pds sterling shall be pd by THOMAS MORRISS or any of these present to sd ROBERT WALKER then these conditions are void, otherwise remain in full force. Signed: THOMAS MORRISS. Dated 14 Jan. 1793. Wit: JAMES H. WALKER, SAMUEL WALKER.

Page 181: Deed of Conveyance. RICHARD NANCE and MIMA, his wife to JAMES TIMMS, all of Pinckney Dist., Chester Co., S. C. Consideration: 70 pds S. C. money. 112 acres on Sandy creek of Broad river north side of sd river; 50 acres being a part of 250 acres granted to ZACHARIAH BELL, sd 50 acres beginning at the south east corner at a Wawnoo tree running thence with his line NW 50 degrees 29 chains 27 links to a post oak, thence 40 degrees SE 17 chains 15 links to a white oak on the north side Sandy Creek, thence SE 50 degrees 29 chains 72 links to a hickory on the sd ISBELL"s line, thence NE 40 degrees 70. 15 links to the beginning running with an open line thereunto; another 50 acres granted 27 Sept. 1769 to THOMAS RODEN, joining the above described 50 acres, bounded NW by ZACHARIAH ISBELL"s land NE by JEREMIAH POTES, SW by THOMAS RODEN, all other sides on vacant land; the 12 acres is bet. the two 50 acre tracts. Signed: RICHARD NANCE, JEMIMA NANCE. Dated 30 Nov. 1792. Wit: HOLLIS TIMMS, AMOS TIMMS, DANIEL ROGERS (by his mark).

Page 183: Deed of Conveyance. JOHN HAYS, blacksmith, and MARY, his wife, to CHRISTOPHER STRONG, all of Chester Co. Consideration of 20 pds S. C. money. 100 acres on N side of South Fork of Fishing Creek, bounding on E by CHRISTOPHER STRONG's land, S and W by ROBERT HARPER, on N by WILLIAM WIER, JOHN HAYS and CHRISTOPHER STRONG, plat attached. Being part of sundry grants granted 26 Oct. 1767 to JOSEPH MITCHELL, conveyed by MITCHELL to JAMES JACK, by JACK to JOHN HAYS, recorded 26 Jan. 1788 in Clerk's Office, Chester Co.; another part granted 1 Sept. 1785 to ROBERT HARPER by "Patent", conveyed 31 Mar. 1788 by HARPER to HAYS, recorded in clerk's office, Chester Co. Signed:

Cont'd from page 93:
JOHN HAYS. Dated 23 Aug. 1792. Wit: JOHN MILLS and ROBERT COOPER.

Page 187: Deed (Release preceded by Lease). ABNER WILKS and his wife
           MARTHA WILKS to JAMES BLAIR all of Pinckney Dist. Chester
Co. In consideration of 60 pds sterling. 150 acres on S side of HAGUE's
branch, being part of 300 acres granted 15 Feb. 1769 to JOHN RENNOLDS,
plat attached to grant recorded in secretary's office. Book DDD, convey-
ed 9 Sept. 1769 to BENJAMIN STREET and by STREET on 27 Aug. 1787 to
ABNER WILKS, recorded in clerk's office, Book A page 287 in Chester
Co. Signed: ABNER WILKS, MARTHA WILKS. Dated 28 June 1792. Wit: DAVID
RODDEY, WILLIAM SPROWL.

Page 189: Deed of Conveyance. THOMAS NEELY, sadler to HENRY JORDAN,
           yeoman, both of Chester Co. Whereas 220 acres granted 26
July 1774 to JAMES NEELY on Fishing Creek in Craven Co., bounded on
SW and NW by sd NEELY, NW by WILLIAM KING, plat attached to grant,
recorded in secretary's office, a part of sd grant conveyed to THOMAS
NEELY by deed recorded in clerk's office, Chester Co. Book A pages
337 and 338; now in consideration of 10 pds sterling, THOMAS NEELY
conveyed to HENRY JORDAN a part of the sd 220 acres, containing 16
acres, bounding north and east on sd JORDAN's land. Signed: THOMAS
NEELY. Dated 4 Jan. 1793. Wit: DAVID WYATT, CASPER SLEEKER, BRITTON
CORRELL.

Page 192:± Deed of Conveyance. ALEXANDER TENANT to HUGH GASTON, both
           of Chester Co. Consideration: 75 pds sterling money. 147
acres on Wilson's Spring Branch of Bull Run, bounded west by HUGH GASTON
land, north by vacant land, when surveyed, on all other sides by lands
granted to MICHAEL DICKSON and JOHN WALKER of Bull Run. Being part
of lands granted 1 Jan. 1787 "by Patent" to ALEXANDER TENANT, plat
attached to orig. grant. Signed: ALEXANDER TENANT and MARTHA TENANT.
Dated 23 Oct. 1792. Wit: EDWARD MC DANIEL, JOHN CALDWELL.

Page 194: Deed of Conveyance. CATHERINE STEEL to WILLIAM REAVES, plant-
           er, both of Camden dist., S. C. Consideration: 500 pds ster-
ling money. Whereas 200 acres on Fishing Creek, granted 29 Nov. 1771 to
CATHERINE STEEL, bounded on NE by JOHN MC FADEN's land, SW by JOHN
LEONARD and NW by CATHERINE STEEL's land. Signed: CATHERINE STEEL.
Dated 20 Dec. 1784. Wit: WILLIAM WILEY. WILLIAM MC DONALD and BENJAMIN
REAVES.

Page 197: This indenture made bet. ROBERT MORRISON and JEAN his wife,
           tailor and JAMES MONTGOMERY, a weaver, both of Chester Co.
Dated 18 Nov. 1782. In the sum of ten shillings current money of S.
C. for 100 acres lying on Culps Mill Branch, bounded on all sides by
vacant land. Wit: JOEL WYLIE, ALEXR. GASTON. Signed: ROBERT MORRISON,
JANET (X) MORRISON. Seal.

Page 199: Deed of Conveyance. WILLIAM COCKRELL, planter to ROBERT
           NIX, both of Chester Co. Consideration: 40 shillings. 90
acres surveyed for him 14 Nov. 1792, situated in Pickney dist. on Sandy
river, bounded southwest by ARCHIBALD ROBERT, northwest by vacant lands,
northeast and southeast by Captain RICHARD TALIAFERRO, southwest by
JEREMIAH DAVIS. Being a tract granted in 1792 to WILLIAM COCKRELL,
recorded in Book BBBB, page 55 in the secretary's office. Signed: WIL-
LIAM COCKRELL (by his mark). Dated 16 Mar. 1793. Wit: JAMES HUEY, MOSES
COCKRELL (by his mark).

Page 201: Sheriff's Deed. PETER JONES, late sheriff of Chester Co.,
           to HUGH COOPER, blacksmith, both of Chester Co. Whereas
JOHN FERGUSON in an action for a debt of 25 pds sterling against JOHN
GILLAM obtained a judgement for sd debt and cost in the Chester Court
in 1790, to be levied on property of sd JOHN GILLAM and pursuant of
this judgement an execution was issued to PETER JONES, then sheriff
of Chester Co. to seize lands, goods and chattels of sd GILLAM for
the sum of 27 pds 16 s 3 d sterling money, debt and costs; after due
and legal notice did sell at public sale, first Monday in April 1791,
a tract containing 100 acres on Rocky Crk. known as CARROLL's old place.

Cont'd from page 94:
Being land granted 1 Sept. 1768 to MARY BIGHAM; now PETER JONES conveyed
land to HUGH COOPER, the last and highest bidder for 13 pds 18 s sterling money for sd JOHN FERGUSON. Signed: PETER JONES, Sheriff. Dated
16 May 1793. Wit: JOHN RAY, JACOB BREAKFIELD, ROBERT OWENS.

Page 202: Deed of Conveyance. JAMES TIMMS to DANIEL ROGERS, both of
           Chester Co. Consideration: 20 pds sterling money. 85 acres
on the waters of Sandy river, surveyed and granted 15 Mar. 1792 to
JAMES TIMMS "bounding south on HASEL HARDWICK's land; north on JOHN
DONALD's land; northwest on JOHN MOULTRIE's land. Being part of a tract
granted to HASEL HARDWICK." Signed: JAMES TIMMS. Dated 21 Jan. 1793.
Wit: RICHARD TALIAFERRO, JUDITH N. CORDELL.

Page 204: Deed of Conveyance. WILLIAM WYLIE and ISABELLA, his wife
           to JOHN HAYS, all of Chester Co. Consideration: 20 pds sterl-
ing. 100 acres bounded by JOHN MC CLURE and WILLIAM WYLIE on Fishing
Creek, Chester Co. Being part of 898 acres granted 2 Nov. 1789 to WM.
WYLIE. Signed: WILLIAM WYLIE, ISABELLA WYLIE. Dated 24 Jan. 1791. Wit:
SAMUEL KNOX, ROBERT KELSEY, PHILIP WALKER.

Page 206: Bill of Sale. ISAAC PRITCHARD to THOMAS WALLACE both of
           Chester Co. Consideration: 50 pds sterling. 1 bay mare,
2 year old colts, 4 cows, 3 year old calves, 2 two year old heifers,
all the hogs, 1 wagon and gears, all the household furniture, all the
corn, 1 loom; the above mentioned articles are sold to THOMAS WALLACE
by ISAAC PRITCHARD for a debt, the amount being the above mentioned
consideration. Signed: ISAAC PRITCHARD. Dated 10 Feb. 1790. Wit: PETER
STRAINS, MARGARET PORTER.

Page 206: Deed of Conveyance. DAVID PATTERSON to WILLIAM RAINEY, both
           of Chester Co. In consideration for 35 pds S. C. money,
100 acres by estimation orig. granted to DAVID PATTERSON "by Patent"
on 4 Dec. 1771, plat attached to grant. Signed: DAVID PATTERSON. Dated
14 Nov. 1791. Wit: JOSIAH HILL, ARTHUR TRAVERS.

Page 208: Deed of Conveyance. WILLIAM KIRKLAND, Fairfield Co., to
           WILLIAM GOAD, Chester Co. Consideration: 10 pds sterling.
Whereas 150 acres granted 6 Mar. 1786 to sd WM. KIRKLAND on Turkey
Creek in Camden dist., plat attached to grant recorded in secretary's
office. Signed: WILLIAM KIRKLAND. Dated 25 Nov. 1790. Wit: ZACHARIAH
KIRKLAND, EDWARD LACEY.

Page 209: Power of Attorney. ROBERT SMITH, York Co., to PHILIP WALKER,
           Esq., Chester Co. to act for him as if he was present. Signed
by ROBERT SMITH. Dated 8 Jan. 1793. Wit. MICHAEL HOGAN, AGNES VANCE,
WILLIAM GUTHERY.

Page 210: Deed of Conveyance. ANDREW MORROWSON, yeoman to HUGH MORROW-
           SON and ANDREW MORROWSON, JR., sons of sd ANDREW MORROW-
SON. Consideration: love and affection, and also the sum of 5 s money
of America, pd by each of them. 150 acres on which ANDREW MORROWSON
now lives, on Sandy river, Pinckney (formerly Camden) dist., bounding
E on HARDIN's land, N of FERGUSON's land, and on all other sides by
vacant lands. Signed: ANDREW MORROWSON. Dated 29 Oct. 1792. Wit: PHILIP
WALKER, JOHN HEMPHILL.

Page 211: Deed of Conveyance. JAMES SMITH to JAMES HAMBLETON, both
           planters of Camden dist. 150 acres on N side of Fishing
Creek, Chester Co. bounded agreeable to grant with plat attached. Sd
grant recorded in secretary's office. Consideration: 40 pds sterling.
Signed: JAMES SMITH, LILLES SMITH. Dated 23 Jan. 1793. Wit: DANIEL
COOKE, ROBERT SMITH, JOHN MC CROREY.

Page 214: Deed of Conveyance. JAMES SMITH to JAMES HAMBLETON both
           planters of Camden Dist. Whereas a certain grant dated 25
Apr. 1767 to JAMES SMITH for 83 acres on the N side of Fishing Creek,
Chester Co., S. C. bounded agreeable to grant recorded in secretary's
office. Consideration: 35 pds sterling. Signed: JAMES SMITH, LILLES

Cont'd from page 95:
SMITH. Dated 23 Jan. 1793. Wit: DANIEL COOKE, ROBERT SMITH and JOHN
MC CROREY.

Page 217: Deed of Conveyance. ROBERT MORRISON, tailor and JANET, his
           wife, to JAMES MONTGOMERY, all of St. Mark's Parish, S.
C. Whereas 100 acres granted 8 Mar. 1768 to JANET CAMPBELL, now the
wife of ROBERT MORRISON, 100 acres on JACOB CULP's Mill branch, bounded
on all sides by vacant lands plat attached to grant recorded in secretary's office. Consideration: 100 pds S. C. money. Signed: ROBERT MORRI-
SON, JANET MORRISON. Dated 19 Nov. 1782. Wit: JAMES WYLIE, ALEXANDER
GASTON.

Page 220: Deed of Conveyance. AUGUSTINE CULP and AGNES, his wife,
           Camden dist., S. C. to ANDREW JETER, Greenville Co., Va.
Whereas 100 acres granted 2 Mar. 1768 to ELIZABETH CRAIG, on Fishing
Creek, on the Great Road that leads from LYLE's ford, on Broad River
to LAND's ford on Catawba river, bounded SW by TINLER's land, N by
ROBERT BROWN's land, all other sides by vacant lands, plat attached
to grant recorded in secretary's office. Sd land conveyed by ELIZABETH
CRAIG at her death to GEORGE CRAIG, transferred by GEORGE CRAIG on
4 June 1774 to AUGUSTINE CULP. Consideration: 60 pds sterling. Signed:
AUGUSTINE CULP, AGNES CULP (her mark). Dated 28 July 1784. Wit: BENJAMIN
REAVES, JOHN TOMLINSON, JAMES MASSEY.

Page 223: Deed of Conveyance. AUGUSTINE CULP and AGNES, his wife,
           Camden dist. to ANDREW JETER, Greenville Co., Va. Whereas
100 acres granted 2 Mar. 1768 to ELIZABETH CRAIG, on Fishing Creek
on the Great Road that leads from Lyle's ford on Broad river to Land's
ford on Catawba river; bounded SW by Tinler's land, N by ROBERT BROWN's
land, all other sides by vacant lands, plat attached to grant recorded
in secretary's office. Sd land conveyed by ELIZABETH CRAIG at her death
to GEORGE CRAIG, transferred by Geo. on 4 June 1774 to AUGUSTINE CULP.
Consideration: 60 pds sterling. Signed: AUGUSTINE CULP, AGNES CULP.
Dated 28 July 1784. Wit: (same as above p. 220).

Page 223: Deed of Conveyance. AUGUSTINE CULP and AGNES, his wife,
           Camden dist. to ANDREW JETER, Greenville Co., Ga. Whereas
100 acres on W side of Catawba river, Camden dist. granted 4 Oct. 1768
to ROBERT BROWN, bounded SW by MATTHEW's land, on all other sides by
vacant lands, plat attached to orig. grant, conveyed 6 Sept. 1769 by
sd ROBT. BROWN to HENRY CULP, 26 acres being part of sd grant, sold
6 Mar. 1775 by HENRY CULP to AUGUSTINE CULP for the sum of 26 pds sterling; now in consideration of 3 pds sterling money AUGUSTINE CULP conveys
to ANDREW JETER the above mentioned 26 acres that was part of the 100
acres granted orig. to ROBT. BROWN, bounded SW and NW by WILLIAM MC
KINNY's land, on all other sides by HENRY CULP's land, plat certified
by ANDREW MC DOWELL. Signed: AUGUSTINE CULP, AGNES CULP. Dated 28 Jul.
1784. Wit: BENJAMIN REAVES, JOHN TOMLINSON, JAMES MASSEY.

Page 225: Deed of Conveyance. ANDREW JETER, Columbia Co., Ga. to HENRY
           JORDAN, Chester Co., S.C. Whereas 100 acres on Fishing Creek,
on the Great Road that leads from Lyle's Ford on Broad river to Land's
Ford on Catawba river, bounded SW by Tinker's land, NW by Robt. Brown's
land, all other sides vacant land, plat attached or orig. grant rec'd
in sec'y. office, granted on 2 Mar. 1768 to ELIZABETH CRAIG, sd Plantation at the death of ELIZABETH CRAIG became the property of GEORGE
CRAIG, sold 4 June 1774 by GEO. CRAIG to AUGUSTINE CULP, sold by CULP
to ANDREW JETER. Consideration: 100 pds sterling. Signed: ANDREW JETER.
Dated 28 Dec. 1792. Wit: BENJ. REAVES, MARY REAVES (her mark) and WILL-
IAM REAVES.

Page 228: Deed of Conveyance. ANDREW JETER, Columbia Co., Ga. to HENRY
           JORDAN, Chester Co., S.C. Whereas 100 acres on NW side of
Catawba river, Chester Co., S.C. granted 4 Oct. 1768 to ROBERT BROWN,
bounded SW by MATTHEW's land and on all other sides vacant lands, plat
attached to orig. grant; conveyed 6 Sept. 1769 by ROBT. BROWN to HENRY
CULP for sum of 20 pds; HENRY CULP transferred on 6 Mar. 1775 26 acres
of above described 100 acres to AUGUSTINE CULP for 26 pds S.C. money;

Cont'd from page 96:
now in consideration of 10 pds sterling ANDREW JETER conveyed to HENRY
JORDAN the 26 acre tract. Signed: ANDREW JETER. Dated 28 Dec. 1792.
Wit: BENJAMIN REAVES, MARY REAVES (by her mark) and WILLIAM REAVES.

Page 230: Deed of Conveyance. JOHN TERRY to WILLIAM MORRISS, both
of Chester Co. Consideration: 25 pds sterling. 54 3/4 acres
being part of 200 acres on the waters of Sandy river, granted 10 July
1766 to STEPHEN TERRY. Signed: JOHN TERRY. Dated 23 Jan. 1793. Wit:
GEORGE BLISSIT, REASON BLISSIT and STEPHEN BLISSIT.

Page 231: Sheriff'd Deed. HUGH KNOX, Sheriff, Chester Co. to ALEXANDER
ROBINSON, Fairfield Dist., both of S. C. Whereas a judgement
for debt and cost in June court, Chester Co. and an execution from
clerk's office of sd county, obtained by ALEXANDER ROBINSON against
ROBERT MC CLELAND, sheriff HUGH KNOX seized and after due process of
law, sold at public auction a tract of 350 acres on Cassel's Creek
of Little river, bounded at the time of survey on all sides by vacant
lands. Being land granted orig. to JOHN MC CLELAND, at whose death,
it passed to his son and heir, the sd ROBERT MC CLELAND now in con-
sideratin of 15 pds 10 s sterling, Hugh Knox conveyed to ALEXANDER
ROBINSON, the last and highest bidder, sd tract of 350 acres. Signed:
HUGH KNOX, Sheriff. Dated 6 Aug. 1792. Wit: ARCHIBALD BOYD, HANCE HAMIL-
TON.

Page 233: Deed of Conveyance. ROBERT SMITH to JOHN WRIGHT, both of
Chester Co., S. C. Consideration: 70 pds sterling. A tract
of land being part of a grant "laid out" for AMBROSE NIX, bounded by
THOMAS RODEN's land and CHARLES HUMPHRIES' land. Signed: ROBERT SMITH
(by his mark). Dated 22 Sept. 1788. Wit: JOHN FLEETWOOD, ABRAHAM MYERS.

Page 234: Deed of Conveyance. ROBERT SMITH to JOHN WRIGHT, both of
Chester Co. Consideration: 10 pds sterling. 23 acres lying
in the NE corner of a grant laid out for MANNON GORE, conveyed 21 Jan.
1785 by GORE to WILLIAM YOUNG. Signed: ROBERT SMITH (by his mark).
Dated 22 Sept. 1788. Wit: JOHN FLEETWOOD, ABRAHAM MYERS.

Page 235: Deed of Conveyance. JAMES HANNA, planter to SAMUEL CALDWELL,
weaver, both of St. Mark's parish, Craven Co., S. C. Whereas
100 acres on Fishing Creek in Chester Co., granted 8 Dec. 1774 to JAMES
HANNA, bounded by lands of JOHN STEVENSON on the N, SAMUEL CROSS on
the NE, by unknown landss on the SW, plat attached to grant recorded
in secretary's office. Consideration: 300 pds S. C. money. Signed:
JAMES HANNA (by his mark). Dated 24 Feb. 1779. Wit: ALEXANDER GASTON,
SAMUEL WEIR, MATTHEW JOHNSTON.

Page 239: Deed of Conveyance. JAMES GILL, planter, and MARY, his wife,
York Co., to THOMAS NESBETT, planter, Chester Co., all of
S. C. Consideration: 20 pds sterling. 100 acres on Fishing Creek, bound-
ed on two sides by HUGH GASTON, on all other sides by vacant lands.
Being that tract granted 17 Mar. 1775 to MARY GASTON, now wife of sd
JAMES GILL, plat attached to grant in the secretary's office, Book
NNN, page 292. Signed: JAMES GILL & MARY GILL. Dated 4 Aug. 1792. Wit:
ROBERT STEEL, HENRY REA.

Page 243: Deed of Conveyance. JOHN FERGUSON, planter, and ELIZABETH,
his wife, to ROBERT STEEL, planter, all of Camden Dist.,
Craven Co., S. C. Whereas 100 acres on a branch of Fishing Creek in
Craven Co. granted 18 May 1773 to JOHN FERGUSON, bounded on the N by
THOMAS PETERSON, on all other sides by vacant lands, plat attached
to grant recorded in secretary's office. Consideration: (amount not
shown). Signed: JOHN FERGUSON, ELIZABETH FERGUSON. Dated 4 Feb. 1782.
Wit: CONRAD MC FADDIN, SAMUEL FERGUSON.

Page 246: Deed of Conveyance. SAMUEL CALDWELL, planter, Fairfield
Co. to ROBERT STEEL, planter, Chester Co., both of Camden
dist. Consideration: 10 pds sterling. 100 acres on Fishing Creek, Chester Co. bounded N by JOHN STEVENSON, NE by SAMUEL CROSS, SW by unknown
lands. Signed: :SAMUEL CALDWELL. Dated 7 Mar. 1788. Wit: JOSEPH BOOTH

Cont'd from page 97:
and JAMES PEDEN.

Page 248: Deed (Release followed by Lease). JOSEPH TELFORD, Rocky
Creek, to JAMES MC ALONAN, both planters of Chester Co.,
Camden dist., S. C. Whereas by a certain grant dated 9 Sept. 1774 BENJA-
MIN MITCHELL rec'd 150 acres on Rocky Creek, Chester Co., bounding
NE by FRANCES HENDERSON and on all other sides by vacant lands, plat
attached to grant recorded in secretary's office, Book SSS, sold 21
June 1776 by MITCHELL to ROBERT MC CLELAND, sold 16 Nov. 1778 by the
heirs of ROBT. MC CLELAND to JAMES TELFORD; now in consideration of
60 pds sterling, JAMES TELFORD conveyed same to JAMES MC ALONAN. Signed:
JOSEPH TELFORD (by his mark) and RACHAEL TELFORD (by her mark). Dated
10 Sept. 1787. Wit: SAMUEL TELFORD, MATTHEW HARBISON.

Page 256: Deed (Release preceded by Lease). JOHN MC CLELAND, cooper,
to JOSEPH TELFORD, planter, both of Craven Co., Camden dist.,
St. Mark's parish, S. C. Whereas 150 acres on a branch of Rocky Creek
in Craven Co. granted 9 Sept. 1774 to BENJAMIN MITCHELL, bounded NE
by FRANCES HENDERSON, and on all other sides by vacant lands, plat
attached to grant recorded in Book SSS, page 697 in the secretary's
office, sold 21 June 1776 by sd MITCHELL to ROBERT MC CLELAND. Consideration: 10 pds sterling. Signed: JOHN MC CLELAND. Dated 17 Nov. 1778.
Wit: JOHN CARSON, JAMES HARBISON.
17 Nov. 1778. Receipt. For 336 pds 13 shillings 4 pence
the one third due her as widow of the above mentioned ROBERT MC CLELAND.
Signed: REBECCA MC CLELAND.

Page 260: Deed of Conveyance. JOSEPH LYON, yeoman to ROBERT HARPER,
yeoman, both of Chester Co. Whereas 290 acres granted 29
Apr. 1768 to ALEXANDER BROWN, SR. in Mecklenburg Co., N. C. at the
time of survey now in Chester Co., S. C. on both sides of the south
fork of Fishing Creek, joining and between lines of GEORGE CRAIG, HENRY
CULP, WILLIAM MILLER, JOHN BOYD & DAVID LEWIS "including his (BROWN's)
plantation," plat attached to grant recorded in sec'ys office of that
province (N. C.) Part of grant sold to JOSEPH LYON by attorney of ALEX-
ANDER BROWN, recorded in clerk's office in Chester Co.; now in consideration of 100 pds sterling JOSEPH LYON conveyed to ROBERT HARPER 160
acres of sd plantation on south side of the south fork of Fishing Creek.
Signed: JOSEPH LYON. Dated 29 Jan. 1791. Wit: WILLIAM WILSON, WILLIAM
JACK.

Page 263: Deed of Gift. VALENTIN BELL, planter, to SARAH BELL, his
daughter, both of Chester Co., S. C. 1 negro girl, 10 years
old, named Becca. Signed: VALENTIN BELL. Dated 22 June 1793. Wit: WIL-
LIAM BELL.

Page 264: Deed of Conveyance. JAMES HOUSTON to THOMAS CABEEN, both
of Chester Co. Consideration: 10 pds S. C. money. Whereas
125 acres on Sandy river in Chester Co. granted 2 Oct. 1786 to JAMES
HOUSTON. Signed: JAMES HOUSTON. Dated 23 Feb. 1792. Wit: EDWARD LACEY
and JAMES GORDON.

Page 265: Deed of Conveyance. EDWARD WHITE, Camden dist., Chester
Co., S. C. to THOMAS WHITE. Whereas 160 acres sold 2 Jan.
1792 by EDWARD WHITE to THOMAS WHITE, being part of sd EDWARD WHITE's
tract, sd 160 acres "to be out of the NW part of sd tract", plat attached to grant in sec'ys office. Consideration: 5 pds strerling. Signed:
EDWARD WHITE. Dated 7 Feb. 1793. Wit: ROBERT WHITE, ROBERT LINN & JOHN
MC CANNON.

Page 268: Deed of Conveyance. LAIRD BURNS and JANE, his wife, to ALEX-
ANDER ENGLISH. Consideration: 105 pds S. C. money. 270 acres
on Rocky creek in Chester Co. being part of four tracts: one tract
of 100 acres granted by Patent to PETER CULP, conveyed 15 Sept. 1762
by CULP to LAIRD BURNS; one other tract of 100 acres granted 17 Mar.
1775 by Patent to ANDREW GRAHAM; a third tract of 100 acres granted
15 Oct. 1784 by Patent to LAIRD BURNS; a 4th tract of 148 acres granted
3 Sept. 1792 to LAIRD BURNS. Signed: LAIRD BURNS, JANE BURNS (by her

98

Cont'd from page 98:
mark). Dated 3 Aug. 1793. Wit: PHILIP WALKER, GEORGE MORROW.

Page 271:   Sheriff's Deed. HUGH MILLEN, former Sheriff of Camden dist.,
            to JOHN MILLS, Chester Co, both S. C. Whereas JAMES MITCHELL
of York Co. obtained in the Apr. term of Common pleas, Camden dist.,
a judgement for 116 pds debt and also interest from June 1784, and
cost against WILLIAM JONES and JOHN SIMPSON, securities for JAMES LANG-
BEY; and whereas an executioin from the clerk of court's office, order-
ing that the properties of WILLIAM JONES and JOHN SIMPSON be seized
and levied upon, after a due process of law, HUGH MILLEN, then sheriff
of Camden dist., sold 7 Jan. 1793 at public auction 400 acres in 2
tracts on south side of the south fork of Fishing Creek. Being two
grants: one for 150 acres to ALEXANDER BALENTINE with bounderies recorded with orig. grants; now HUGH MILLEN conveyed sd 400 acres to
JOHN MILLS, the last and highest bidder, for the sum of 67 pds 7 s
5 d sterling. Signed: HUGH MILLEN, former sheriff. Dated 7 Jan. 1793.
Wit: T. W. YOUNG, D. EVANS, WILLIAM JONES.

Page 272:   Deed of Conveyance. THOMAS HALSELL, Edgefield Co., to RICHARD
            YARBOROUGH, Chester Co., both of S. C. Consideration: 20
pds. 410 acres situated on Sandy river and Little river, bounded by
the lands of WILLIAM MURRY, JOHN GEVIN, WILLIAM PENIEL and vacant lands.
Being part of 640 acres granted 5 May 1787 to THOMAS HALSELL. Signed:
THOMAS HALSELL. Dated 20 Nov. 1792. Wit: ISAAC WAGGONER, EPHRAIM PADGETT
(by his mark) and BENJAMIN HALSELL.

Page 274:   Deed of Conveyance. THOMAS MACKLER to DAVID HOPKINS, Camden
            dist., S. C. Consideration: 1000 pds S. C. money. 640 acres
according to plat and grant, on north side of South Fork of Saluda
river, granted 16 July 1784. Signed: THOMAS MACKLER. Dated 14 July
1784. Wit: JOHN TERRY, DANIEL LEHALF, EDWARD MC NEAL.

Page 275:   Deed of Conveyance. SAMUEL THOMSON to DAVID HOPKINS, Camden
            dist. Consideration: 1000 pds S. C. money. 286 acres accord-
ing to plat and grant on both sides of South Fork of Saluda river,
granted 15 Oct. 1784. Signed: SAMUEL THOMSON (by his mark). Dated 17
1784. Wit: EDWARD S. COLEMAN, WILLIAM WILCOCKS, ARCHIBALD STEELE.

Page 276:   Deed of Conveyance. WILLIAM LEESLAND, gentleman, to DAVID
            HOPKINS, Camden dist. Consideration: 1000 pds sterling.
640 acres on Great Rocky Creek in Ninety-six dist., S. C. bounded all
sides by vacant lands, plat attached to grant dated 15 Oct. 1784. Signed
by: WILLIAM LEESLAND (by his mark). Dated 23 Oct. 1784. Wit: JOSEPH
HALL and EDMUND S. COLEMAN. (Note: above shows EDWARD not EDMUND).

Page 277:   Deed of Conveyance. THOMAS HALSELL, Edgefield Co., to WILLIAM
            MURREY, Chester Co., both S. C. Consideration: 10 pds ster-
ling. 200 aces being part of 640 acres granted 5 Feb. 1787 by THOMAS
HALSEY. Signed: THOMAS HALSEY and MARY HALSEY. Dated 17 Aug. 1792.
Wit: RICHARD YARBOROUGH, ANDREW PANNELL (by his mark).

Page 279:   Deed of Conveyance. SOLOMON PETERS, Orangeburg Dist., to
            CHARLES COLEMAN, Camden Dist., both S. C. Consideration:
150 pds sterling money. 400 acres in Camden dist. on a branch of Sandy
river, on NE side of Broad river. Being part of 800 acres granted 17
May 1774 to SOLOMON PETERS. Signed: SOLOMON PETERS. Dated 1 July 1786.
Wit: JAMES PARKS, JOHN COLEMAN and GEORGE ALLCORN.

Page 280:   Deed of Conveyance. JAMES ADAMS, Greene Co., Ga. to WILLIAM
            BELL, Chester Co., S. C. Consideration: 30 pds. 100 acres
on Susa Bolen Creek, which is 6 feet wide and 5 inches deep, a branch
of Broad river on north side, being land granted 13 May 1768 to JAMES
GREER by Patent. Signed: JAMES ADAMS. Dated 8 Nov. 1792. Wit: SARAH
BELL, NANCY BELL and VALENTINE BELL (by his mark).

Page 282:   Deed of Conveyance. JAMES TIMMS, and PATTY, his wife, to
            THOMAS FLETCHALL, of Pinckney dist., Chester Co., S. C.
Consideration: 75 pds S. C. money. 112 acres on Sandy river, branch

Cont'd from page 99:
of Broad river being part of 240 acres granted to Capt. ZACHARIAH ISBELL and another grant of 50 acres granted 29 Sept. 1769 to THOMAS RODEN, bounded by lands of ZACHARIAH ISBELL, JEREMIAH POTTS and by vacant lands. Signed: JAMES TIMMS, PATTY TIMMS (by her mark). Dated 17 Apr. 1793. Wit: HOLLIS TIMMS, THOMAS SATERWHITE, JEREMIAH THOMAS.

Page 284: Bill of Sale. CLAUDIUS CHARVIN to EDWARD LACEY, both of Chester Co., S. C. Consideration: 25 pds sterling. 1 blue roan mare about 15 hands high, 8 years old, paces, trots, canters. Signed: CLAUDIUS CHARVIN. Dated 4 Apr. 1789. Wit: JOHN MILES, RICHARD MILES.

Page 286: Deed (Release preceded by Lease). MINOR WINN, Mill Creek, Fairfield Co., to THOMAS BAKER FRANKLIN, Chester Co., both of S. C. Consideration: 54 pds 7 shillings. 265 acres on Sandy river in Camden dist., joining JAMES HUGHEY's land on one side and vacant lands on all other sides. Being a tract granted 6 Mar. 1786 to MINOR WINN, plat attached to grant. Signed: MINOR WINN. Dated 21 May 1789. Wit: K. T. STROTHER and WILLIAM EVANS.

Page 288: Bill of Sale. JOHN MILLS, JR., to GEORGE GILL, silversmith, both of Chester Co., S. C. Consideration: 80 pds sterling money. 1 negro slave named Guy. Signed: JOHN MILLS. Dated 13 June 1789. Wit: ARCHIBALD GILL.

Page 288: This indenture made 5 Jan. 1792, bet. ROBERT JAMESON and GARDINER MILLER both of Chester Co. for the sum of 10 shillings sterling for 150 acres on Bullskin branch of Sandy river. Orig. granted 10 July 1766 to JASPER ROGERS, who deed by lease and release on the 21-22 Dec. 1770 to REESE HUGHES who deed on 10 Dec. 1771 to Rev. JAMES CAMPBELL, dec'd. land conveyed to his sons JAMES and ALEXANER CAMPBELL, heirs, who by power of attorney dated 10 Feb. 1789, transferred to GARDINER MILLER. Wit: GARDINER JAMESON, ARCHD. BOYD. Signed: ROBERT (X) JAMESON and GARDINER MILLER.

Page 290: This indenture made 5 Nov. 1791 bet. ELIZABETH MILLER and THOMAS MILLER, both of Chester Co. for the sum of 10 shillings lawfull money for 200 acres being one half of a grant of 400 acres on a small branch of Rockey Creek. Bounded by land of JOHN and JOSIAH MILLER, vacant land on all other sides. Wit: CHARLES MILLER, JAMES MILLER, JAMES WILSON. Signed: ELIZABETH (X) MILLER. Recorded 3 Dec. 1791.

Page 292: Deed of Conveyance. HUGH WHITESIDES, yeoman, Chester Co. to SAMUEL LUSK, York Co., both of S. C. Whereas 200 acres on a branch of Fishing Creek in Camden dist., bounded SE by JAMES ROBESON, on all other sides by land, owners unknown, being all of a tract granted 7 Nov. 1785 to JANE WALKER; now in consideration of 50 pds sterling money HUGH WHITESIDES, attorney for JANE WALKER, conveys to SAMUEL LUSK all the above tract of 200 acres. Signed: HUGH WHITESIDES. Dated 26 June 1786. Wit: WILLIAM WHITESIDES, THOMAS WHITESIDES, JAMES PATTON.

Page 295: Power of Attorney. JANE WALKER, spinster, to HUGH WHITESIDES both of Chester Co., S. C. For divers consideratioin and reasons me hereunto moving. Especially to recover and sell 200 acres from the Land Office surveyed for sd JANE WALKER, lying on north side of Fishing Creek. Signed: JANE WALKER (by her mark). Dated 27 Aug. 1785. Wit: SAMUEL LUSK, JOHN WALKER, JR.

Page 296: Deed of Conveyance. JAMES GILL, yeoman, formerly of St. Mark's parish, S. C. to JOHN COOPER, yeoman, St. Mark's parish, S. C. Whereas 200 acres granted 22 Sept. 1769 to JAMES GILL situated on South Fork of Fishing Creek in Craven Co., bounded north and east by JOHN MC NITT ALEXANDER on south by GEORGE GLOVER, dec'd and JOHN DAVIS, west by GEORGE GILL, on all other sides by vacant land. Consideration: 200 pds lawful current money of sd province. Signed: JAMES GILL. Dated 14 Aug. 1777. Wit: CHRISTOPHER STRAIGHT, JAMES COOPER

Cont'd from page 100:
and GEORGE GILL.

Page 299: Deed of Conveyance. THOMAS RODEN, planter, to DENNIS CARRELL, planter, both of Chester Co. S. C. Consideration: 90 pds. 238 acres in 4 tracts, situated on Welch's Ford of Sandy River. Being land granted 21 Jan. 1785 to JOHN DOUGHERTY, surveyed 23 Aug. 1784, recorded in Book AAAA, page 405. Sold on 5 Feb. 1787 by sd DOUGHERTY to THOMAS RODEN. Signed: THOMAS RODEN and MARY RODEN. Wit: MARTIN ELAM, MOSES STONE (by his mark) and GEORGE ELAM. 4 Dec. 1793.

Page 302: Deed of Conveyance. 31 Dec. 1791. JAMES BROWN to ALEXANDER BROWN, both of Chester Co., S. C. Consideration: 100 pds. 116 acres of land on Turkey Creek. Being part of a tract granted 23 Jan. 1773 to CATHERINE BROWN, transferred by CATHERINE's will to ALEXANDER BROWN, conveyed by deed from ALEXANDER BROWN to JAMES BROWN. Signed: JAMES BROWN. Wit: HAMBLETON BROWN, JOHN REED and GEORGE CONN (by mark).

Page 304: 8 June 1792. HUGH BOYLES to WILLIAM BOYD, both of Chester Co., S. C. Consideration: 35 pds S. C. money. 100 acres on a branch of Rocky Creek, Chester Co., S. C., bounded NW and NE by WILLIAM ROTTENBERRY's land, SW by SOLOMON HOLMES' land, all other sides vacant. Signed: HUGH BOYLES (by his mark). Wit: ANDREW WALKER, JR., ANDREW WALKER and ANDREW CRAWFORD.

Page 308: This indenture made 19 Jan. 1785 bet. AGNES HANNA, spinster of 96 Dist. and PAUL FERGUSON of Chester Dist. for 10 shillings sterling for 200 acres on a branch of Rockey Creek, bounded on land of JAMES MC CLURE and ELIZABETH WHITE. Wit: WILLIAM STERLING, THOMAS HANNA and JAMES HANNA. Signed: AGNES (X) HANNA. Recorded 27 Apr. 1793.

Page 310: Deed. 28 Feb. 1774. GEORGE ADAMS to WILLIAM BOYLES, both of Chester Co. Consideration: 100 pds S. C. money. 100 acres on a small branch of Rocky Creek, Craven Co. granted 24 Aug. 1770 to GEORGE ADAMS, bounded by lands of WILLIAM ROTTENBERRY on NW and on NE by SOLOMON HOLMES, and on all other sides by vacant land. Signed: GEORGE ADAMS. Wit: SAMUEL CRAIG, ANDREW WALKER, JOHN BELL. Recorded 1 Aug. 1792.

Page 313: Indenture made 29 Feb. 1774 bet. GEORGE ADAMS and WM. BOYLES both of Chester Co. for the sum of 10 shillings current money for 100 acres on a branch of Rockey Creek, bounded by land of WM. ROTTENBERRY and WM. SOLOMON and HOLMAN land. Wit: SAMUEL ADAMS, ANDR. WALKER, JOHN BELL. Signed: GEORGE ADAMS, seal. Recorded 1 Aug. 1792.

Page 315: Deed of Gift. 2 Nov. 1791. ELIZABETH MILLER to JANE KNOX, both of Chester Co. Consideration: love and affection for my loving daughter. All goods and chattles including household furniture beds and bedding, all stoc, horses, cows, sheep, hogs, wagon and all farm tools. Signed: ELIZABETH MILLER (by her mark). Wit: JAMES MILLER, CHARLES MILLER, JAMES WILSON.

Page 315: Deed of Gift. 5 OCt. 1793. SARAH GOLDEN, Chester Co., S. C. to SALLIE GOLDEN. Consideration: (not recorded). SARAH GOLDEN gave to her daughter, SALLIE GOLDEN, 1 bay horse, a gelding, branded R on rear side, saddle, 1 bridle, 8 year mare, 1 feather bed and furniture, a chest, 1 little spinning wheel. Signed: SARAH GOLDEN. Wit: HUGH KNOX, PHILIP NOLAND. RICHARD TALIAFERRO, Clk. of Chester County.

Page 316: Mortgage. ALEXANDER WILSON to HAZEL HARDWICK, both of Chester Co. Consideration: 19 pds 3 shillings 2 pence sterling. 1 negro girl named Patt or Patsy. Condition - that is HAZEL HARDWICK shall pay 20 pds on or bef. 5 OCt. 1794, then this obligation is void, otherwise to remain in full force. Signed: ALEXANDER WILSON (by his mark). Wit: JOHN PRATT.

Page 317: Deed of Conveyance. 27 Oct. 1793. THOMAS CABEEN, tanner,

Cont'd from page 101:
of Chester Co. to FRANCIS NESBIT. Consideration: 30 pds
S. C. money. 125 acres on Sandy river beginning at a stake and running
to a white oak being land granted 2 Oct. 1786 to JAMES HOUSTON, conveyed
by sd HOUSTON on 23 Feb. 1792 to THOMAS CABEEN. Signed: THOMAS CABEEN.
Wit: JAMES MC NEEL, DAVID MORROW. 2 Nov. 1793.

Page 318: Deed of Conveyance. 5 Oct. 1793. JOHN GILL, SR., farmer
of Chester Co. to WILLIAM LEWIS. Consideration: 50 pds sterling. 150 acres on Rocky Creek, Chester Co., S. C. Being part of two
tracts: one granted to GEORGE WEIR on 18 May 1771 and conveyed by him
on 20 Jan. 1777 to JOHN GILL; the other tract granted 20 Oct. 1772
to JOHN GILL. Signed: JOHN GILL. Wit: WILLIAM WHITESIDES and JAMES
GILL. The records show JOHN GILL's wife was named SARAH, but she did
not sign the deed.

Page 320: Deed. 1 Sept. 1789. JOHN BELTON, surveyor, to JOHN MILES
and wife, Chester Co., all of Camden dist. Consideration:
14 pds sterling. 100 acres on Mill Creek on north side of Broad river,
Chester co. bounded on all sides by vacant lands, described by plat.
Dated 14 Feb. 1763. Signed: JOHN BELTON. Wit: BENJAMIN PERKINS and
JOHN HOLZEN.

Page 323: Deed of Conveyance. 10 Oct. 1792. JOHN MILES, Mercer Co.
in Kentucky, State of Virginia (?) to JOSEPH FEEMSTER, York
Co., S. C. Consideration: 30 pds sterling. 100 acres on Mill Creek
on Broad River, called Susey's Creek, bounded by WILLIAM MINTER on
the W, by SAMUEL GIVENS on the N, by JAMES BROWN on the S, by MILES
on the E, known as MAHAFIE's land in Chester Co., S. C. Being a tract
granted on 14 Feb. 1763 to JOHN BELTON, transferred on 31 Aug. 1789
from BELTON to JOHN MILES. Signed: JOHN MILES. Wit: WILLIAM MILES and
JOHN ADAIR. 13 Dec. 1793.

Page 326: 31 Dec. 1791. JOHN CHESNUT and his wife, ESTHER, to SAMUEL
MAPRET(?), all of Chester Co. 150 acres of land granted
to 13 Aug. 1756 to JOHN JACOB CULP on Rocky Creek, on south side of
Catawba river, bounded then by vacant land, now by GEORGE CHERRY's
widow's land, transferred by CULP on 5 Apr. 1787 to JAMES CHESTNUT
and his wife, ESTHER. Consideration: 100 pds sterling. Signed: JAMES
CHESTNUT, ESTHER CHESTNUT (by her mark). Wit: WILLIAM MOFFETT, HUGH
PARK and WILLIAM CHESTNUT.

Page 328: Deed of Conveyance. 18 Sept. 1788. RICE HUGHES, JR. to JOHN
BANKHEAD, both planters of Rocky Creek, Chester Co., S.
C. 100 acres on Fishing Creek in Craven (now Chester) Co. granted 1
Feb. 1768 to ROBERT MARTIN, bounded on all sides by vacant lands, trans-
ferred by sd MARTIN on 13 Dec. 1787 to RICE HUGHES, JR. Consideration:
65 pds S. C. money. Signed: RICE HUGHES. Wit: JOS. H. BOOTH and RICHARD
WYATT.

Page 330: 5 Sept. 1787. JOHN JACOB CULP to JAMES CHESTNUT, both planters of Camden Dist., S. C. A certain grant dated 13 Aug.
1756 to JOHN JACOB CULP. CHESTNUT pd to CULP 50 pds for 150 acres on
both sides of Little Rocky Creek, a west branch of Catawba River, lying
bet. Broad and Catawba rivers, sd tract adj. lands of GEORGE CHERRY's
widow CARR. Signed: JOHN JACOB CULP (by his mark). Wit: ANDREW GRAHAM,
ALEXANDER CHESTNUT and JOHN MC DILL.

Page 334: This indenture made 2 Jan. 1794 bet. JAMES MEEK and HANCE
HAMBLETON both of Chester Co. In the sum of 36 pds sterling
for 140 acres lying on Cobs Creek and Little River. Being part of an
orig. grant dated 16 June 1768 to THOMAS KIRKPATRICK, from him to MEEKS
by lease and release, dated 16-18 Sept. 1776. Wit: WILLIAM MC QUISTON,
JAMES WYLIE, JAMES MEEKS. Signed: JAMES MEEKS, seal.

Page 336: Deed of Conveyance. 10 Aug. 1793. THOMAS MITCHELL and his
wife, HEPSABETH to ELIZABETH MOORE, all of Chester Co. Consideration: 100 pds sterling. 190 acres. Being a tract granted on 7
Aug. 1786 to EDWARD ATTERBERRY, transferred from him to THOMAS MITCHELL.

Cont'd from page 102:
Signed: THOMAS MITCHELL (by his mark) and HEPSABETH MITCHELL (by her mark). Wit: ELIAS MITCHELL, ISIAH MITCHELL, DAVID MITCHELL.

Page 337: Bill of Sale. NICHODEMUS BARNES to CORNELIUS DORCEY, both of Chester Co. Consideration: 10 pds S. C. money. 1 grey mare, 3 head of cattle, 25 hogs, 2 beds and furniture. Signed: NICHODEMUS BARNES. Wit: PHILIP WALKER, CALEB BARNES (by his mark). 24 Jan. 1794.

Page 338: Relinquishing of Title. 30 Sept. 1793. JAMES ELLIOTT of Lancaster Co. to ROBERT ELLIOTT both of S. C. All right and claim to a piece of property on Broad river in Chester Co., formerly owned by JAMES ELLIOTT, dec'd. Signed: JAMES ELLIOTT. Wit: JOSEPH DOUGLAS, ANTHONY COX, JOHN ELLIOTT. The records show there was an exchange of 50 pds.

Page 339: 30 Oct. 1793 personally appeared before me MARY SEEBREE and being duly sworn according to law - deponent saith that whereas a report has prevailed by means of a certain THOMAS HAIL that a certain FIELDER BELL hath been found guilty of fornication with a certain negro man slave named George, property of VALENTINE BELL, the sd FIELDER's father, and gave for this author the sd MARY SEEBREE. Now the sd MARY on her oath doth say that she never knew or heard of sd FIELDER being guilty of any such crime with white or black and further saith that she never did inform the sd THOMAS HAIL or any other person whatsoever anything of or concerning that report. Given under my hand and seal the day and year first written. WES. ALEXANDER, J.P.
    26 Nov. 1793 - This day meet at Mr. VALENTINE BELL and THOMAS HAIL and certain other neighbors on an examination of a slanderous report told on Miss FIELDER BELL which show and how and have been told by the sd THOMAS HAIL which report he the sd HAIL, he had from a certain woman under an infamous character which he never believed and does confess his faults in telling after such another. In the presence of: THOS. (X) ROBIN, WILLIAM BELL, THOMAS HOUSE, JOHN WILLIAMS, GEORGE CORN, JOHN NICESON, JOHN GALLIKER.
    25 Jan. 1794 personally appeared WM. BELL, JOHN WILSON and made oath that they saw the above named THOMAS HAIL acknowledge and deliver the above confession as it states and shows for the use therein contain. Signed: JAMES LACY, Clerk C. C.

Page 340: Deed of Conveyance. 1 Mar. 1793. PETER NANCE and his wife, URSULA, of Fairfield Co. to SAMPSON NOLAND, Chester Co., all of S. C. Consideration: 100 pds sterling. 97 acres on Sandy river granted on 17 Feb. 1767 to THOMAS RODEN, bounded by lands belonging to JAMES GRAHAM and JAMES TIMMS, on other sides by vacant lands. Conveyed by THOMAS RODEN to PETER NANCE. Signed: PETER NANCE. Wit: WILLIAM BOYD, THOMAS WILKES (by his mark) and EDMOND TILLEY (by his mark).

Page 342: Deed of Conveyance. 4 Feb. 1794. SAMPSON NOLAND to NATHAN COFFEE, both of Pinckney Dist., Chester Co., S. C. Consideration: 35 pds sterling. 50 acres on Sandy river, being part of 100 acres granted on 17 Feb. 1767 to THOMAS RODEN, conveyed to PETER NANCE, dec'd. and from PETER NANCE by will to his son, RICHARD NANCE, from him to his brother PETER NANCE, from him to SAMPSON NOLAND. Signed: SAMPSON NOLAND. Wit: NICHOLAS COLVIN, WILLIAM PRICE.

Page 344: Deed of Conveyance. 21 Jan. 1794. GEORGE MORRISS and his wife, AGNES, to BENJAMIN MORRISS, all of Pinckney dist., Chester Co. Consideration: 50 pds sterling. 200 acres being part of a grant dated 6 Oct. 1788 to GEORGE MORRISS; and another tract granted 5 Feb. 1788 to HUGH MONTGOMERY, conveyed from him to MOSES REEVES, from him to CHRISTOPHER MORGAN and wife MARTHA MORGAN, from them to GEORGE MORRISS on 5 Feb. 1788. Signed: GEORGE MORRISS, AGNES MORRISS. Wit: JOSIAH ALLEN, WILLIAM SIBLEY, ANDREW HEMPHILL.

Page 346: 24 Nov. 1789. ALEXANDER MC COWN to THOMAS STROUD, both of Chester Co. Whereas 2 grants, one on 18 May 1773 and the other dated 19 Aug. 1774, 150 acres made to ALEXANDER MC COWN, were

Cont'd from page 103:
conveyed on the above date to THOMAS STROUD. Signed: ALEXANDER MC COWN.
Wit: JAMES MC COWN, MARTIN RUNNOLDS.

Page 349:   Bill of Sale. 11 Dec. 1793. RICHARD SMITH to JONATHAN MC
            KAY, both of Chester Co. Consideration: 65 pds. 1 negro
girl named Bett, 14 years old. Signed: RICHARD SMITH. Wit: THOMAS MOR-
RISS, BURRELL SANDIFER (by his mark) and GEORGE MORRISS.

Page 350:   Personally appeared JAMES WALKER of Chester Co. and on oath
            saith that a certain horse about 14 hands height and about
9 or 10 years old, branded with 3F on shoulder. That the horse was
tolled(?) to WALKER and is now dead, through no fault or neglect of
him. Dated 23 Nov. 1793. Sworn bef. JOHN MC CREARY, J.P. Personally
appeared JOHN WALKER and on oath saith that the horse is dead, and
does not believe the horse died from any cause of JAMES WALKER. Dated
23 Nov. 1793. Signed: JOHN WALKER bef. JOHN MC CREARY, J.P.

Page 351:   Deed of Conveyance. 26 Jan. 1794. JONATHAN JONES and his
            wife, BETHSHEBA, to JOHN THOMPSON, all of Chester Co. Con-
sideration: 20 pds sterling. 55 acres on Fishing Creek, being part
of a tract granted on 2 Oct. 1786 to JONATHAN JONES. Signed: JONATHAN
JONES. Wit: WILLIAM BOYD, JOSEPH TIMMS, JOHN WALKER. (Adj. land of
SAMUEL BROWN on GEORGE CRAIG's line and PETER OWENS line.)

Page 352:   Mortgage. 8 Jan. 1794. FRANCIS HENDERSON to ABRAHAM FERGUSON
            both of Chester Co. Consideration: 25 pds sterling. 1 grey
gelding 13 1/2 hands high, 1 sorrel horse 13 1/2 hands high, with a
blaze face, 1 sorrel horse 14 hands high, 1 black horse colt, 9 head
of cattle marked with a crop off of each ear, also a slit in each ear,
12 head of hogs same mark as cattle, all household furniture, beds,
bedding, pots, pewter. Condition - being that or or bef. 1 Nov. 1794,
25 pds sterling shall be paid to sd ABRAHAM FERGUSON, then this mortgage
is void, otherwise to remain in full force. Signed; FRANCIS HENDERSON.
Wit: PHILIP WALKER, SAMUEL JACK (by his mark).

Page 354:   Deed of Conveyance. 18 Oct. 1793. JOHN HAGANS to ALEXANDER
            CRAWFORD, both of Chester Co. Consideration: 5 pds sterling.
14 acres of land granted to JOHN MC CLEAHAN, on the SW side of Catawba
river in Chester Co. Signed: JOHN HAGANS, ELIZABETH HAGANS. Wit: HUGH
HAGANS, ROBERT KING, WILLIAM HAGANS.

Page 355:   Deed of Conveyance. 13 Nov. 1793. DENNIS CARRELL, planter,
            to JOHN COLVIN, planter, both of Chester Co. Consideration:
50 pds sterling. 100 acres on Hinthems Creek of Sandy river, Chester
Co. bounded by lands of RICHARD HEAD and JAMES HUEY. Being part of
a tract of 265 acres granted 6 Mar. 1786. Granted 25 Nov. 1785 to MINOR
WINN, conveyed by him to THOMAS BAKER FRANKLIN, by him to DENNIS CARRELL.
Signed: DENNIS CARRELL, SARAH CARRELL. Wit: NICHOLAS COLVIN, JOSEPH
PRICE, JESSE SIMPSON.

Page 357:   Deed of Conveyance. 17 Jan. 1789. OWEN EVANS to MARY EVANS,
            both of Chester Co. Consideration: 50 pds sterling. 100
acres of land on South Fork of Sandy river. Being part of a grant dated
1 Jan. 1771 to OWEN EVANS. Signed: OWEN EVANS. Wit: RICHARD EVANS,
ADAM WILLIAMSON.

Page 358:   Deed of Conveyance. 29 July 1793. ABRAHAM MYERS to NATHANIEL
            NORWOOD, both of Chester Co. Consideration: 100 pds. 50
acres granted 4 Sept. 1786 to JAMES ATTERBERRY, being part of 641 acres
situated on Smith's Creek a branch of Bush Fork bounded by lands of
NATHANIEL NORWOOD and WILLIAM NORWOOD. Signed: ABRAHAM MYERS and SARAH
MYERS (by her mark). Wit: ELIJAH NUNN, JOSIAH COOK, ALLEN MAYFIELD.

Page 360:   Deed of Conveyance. 29 July 1793. ABRAHAM MYERS to WILLIAM
            NORWOOD, both of Chester Co. Consideration: 100 pds. 50
acres lying on Smith's creek a branch of Bushey Fork, being part of
64 acres granted 4 Sept. 1786 to JAMES ATTERBERRY. Signed: ABRAHAM
MYERS and SARAH MYERS (by her mark). Wit: (same as above names).

Page 362: Bill of Sale. 16 Nov. 1792. JOHN EDWARDS to ARTHUR SHUFIELD,
both of Chester Co. Consideration: 80 pds sterling. 1 negro
boy named Jacob, 17 years old. Signed: JOHN EDWARDS. Wit: ALEXANDER
CRAWFORD and JAMES PATTON.

Page 362: Deed of Conveyance. 7 Aug. 1793. THOMAS STEVENSON and his
wife, MARY, to JAMES EGGER, all of Pinckney Dist., Chester
Co. Consideration: 30 pds sterling. 100 acres being a tract granted
on 5 Feb. 1787 to JAMES ADAIR, adj. the lands of THOMAS HAIL on the
W, on the S by the lands of JAMES ADAIR and on the E by the lands of
WILLIAM MINTER. Signed: THOMAS STEVENSON, MARY STEVENSON. Wit: WILLIAM
EGGER, JOHN JAMES NORTON, SARAH STEVENSON.

Page 364: Deed of Conveyance. 18 May 1793. DAVID HOPKINS to ELIAS
MITCHELL, both of Chester Co. Consideration: 100 pds sterl-
ing. A parcel of land on the north side of Broad River, being part
of a tract granted on 16 July 1784 to DAVID HOPKINS. Signed: DAVID
HOPKINS, MARY HOPKINS. Wit: THOMAS MITCHELL (by his mark), FERDINAND
HOPKINS and H. ANDERSON.

Page 366: Deed of Conveyance. 16 May 1793. FERDINAND HOPKINS to THOMAS
MITCHELL both of Chester Co. Consideration: 100 pds sterling. A tract of land being part of a grant on 26 Aug. 1774 to JAMES
O'NEAL, conveyed by him to sd HOPKINS lying on north side of Broad
river near WILSON's boat landing on THOMAS HUGHES, SR. line, containing 202 acres. Signed: FERDINAND HOPKINS. Wit: ELIAS MITCHELL, ISAIAH
MITCHELL, bef. ELIJAH NUNN, J.P.

Page 368: Deed of Conveyance. 26 Oct. 1793. JAMES TIMMS, Administrator
of the estate of GEORGE CARTER, dec'd. to SAMUEL CARTER,
both of Chester Co. Consideration: 5 pds. 32 acres on Sandy River.
Signed: JAMES TIMMS. Wit: JOSEPH BENNETT, THOMAS O'NEAL.

Page 369: Bill of Sale. 11 May 1792. JOHN MC GALMERY, yeoman to JAMES
ENGLISH, clothier, both of Chester Co. Consideration: 50
pds S. C. money. 1 negro boy named Sank, aged 19 years. Signed: JOHN
MC GLAMERY. Wit: JOHN MILLS, MARY MILLS.

Page 370: Deed of Conveyance. 26 Oct. 1793. JAMES TIMMS, Adm. of the
estate of GEORGE CARTER, dec'd, to THOMAS O'NEAL, both of
Chester Co. Consideration: 10 pds. 89 acres belonging to the estate
of GEO. CARTER, dec'd. Signed: JAMES TIMMS. Wit: JOSEPH BENNETT, SAMUEL
CARTER.

Page 371: Deed of Conveyance. 30 Sept. 1793. JOHN CARTER and his wife,
ELIZABETH, to HENRY COTTERELL, all of Chester Co. Consider-
ation: 100 pds sterling. 400 acres of land on Sandy river. Signed:
JOHN CARTER, ELIZABETH CARTER. Wit: WILLIAM ATTERBERRY.

Page 373: Deed of Conveyance. 29 Mar. 1793. THOMAS EAKINS and his
wife, ELIZABETH to ROBERT EAKINS, all of Chester Co. Consideration: 20 pds S. C. money. 150 acres being land granted on 8 July
1774 to THOMAS EAKINS. Signed: THOMAS EAKINS, ELIZABETH EAKINS (by
her mark). Wit: ROBERT DAVIS, THOMAS EAKINS, JR., ALEXANDER EAKINS.

Page 374: Deed of Conveyance. 25 Mar. 1793. HUGH MC COWN to JAMES
MC COWN, both of Chester Co. Consideration: 20 pds sterling.
100 acres on a branch of Little River in Chester Co., being part of
a tract granted in 1772 to EDWARD NIXON, conveyed by NIXON to ROBERT
MC COWN, by him to HUGH MC COWN. Signed: HUGH MC COWN. Wit: WILLIAM
MC QUISTON, ISAAC BEAM, SAMUEL MC COWN. (Note: MC COWN may be MC KEOWN.)

Page 376: Deed of Conveyance. 8 Oct. 1793. JOHN HAGANS to ALEXANDER
CRAFFORD(?), both of Chester Co. Consideration: 5 pds sterl-
ing. 163 acres being land orig. granted to JOHN LANCE. Signed: JOHN
HAGANS, ELIZABETH HAGANS. Wit: ROBERT KING, WM. HAGANS, HUGH HAGANS.

Page 377: Deed of Conveyance. 12 Jan. 1791. WILLIAM WORTHY to THOMAS
COWSART, both of Chester Co. Consideration: 100 pds sterling.

Cont'd from page 105:
A tract of 100 acres on Turkey Creek in Chester Co., being part of
2331 acres granted on 15 July 1784 to DAVID HOPKINS. Signed: WILLIAM
WORTHY (by his mark). Wit: JAMES MC CALL, FRANCIS RAY and JOHN COWSART.

END OF DEED BOOK C

FAIRFIELD COUNTY, S. C. WILL BOOK 3

Page 1:   Administration on the estate of GEORGE LEISTER, late of
             Fairfield Dist., dec'd...who died intestate, granted to
SARAH LEISTER. 4 Mar. 1800.

Pages 2-4: 7 Mar. 1800, last will and testament of SAMUEL GLADNEY was
           proved; AGNES GLADNEY and RICHARD GLADNEY, exrs.
Will of SAMUEL GLADEN of Fairfield Co., finding myself weak of Body...to
wife AGNES two cows, the use of the negro wench Sarah, to devolve and
be the property to my two sons RICHARD and HUGH, one bedding of cloaths,
to be found in a house; to my son JOSEPH 10 pds to be pd by my two
sons RICHARD and HUGH; to my son PATRICK 50 pds, to say 50 shillings
to himself and fifty to his son SAMUEL; to my son THOMAS 11 pds likewise 100 acres to his son SAMUEL whereon his Father formerly lived,
called Kerrell's (?) land; to my son JAMES 20 pds sterling; to my daughter MARY, two cows and calves; in case my son JOSEPH does not claim
or find a lawful power to receive his 10 pds in the space of 7 years
from the date, it is my will that sd money to be paid to my grandson
SAMUEL, son of PATRICK; my two tracts of land I now possess to my two
sons RICHARD and HUGH to be equally divided between them, quality and
quantity considered; HUGH to hold the house I now live in with the
land convenient thereto; his mother to have the convenience in sd house
during her widowhood, and RICHARD the other end of sd lands; wife AGNES
and son RICHARD, Exrs. 23 Oct. 1799.
                              SAMUEL GLADNEY (LS)
Wit: DAVID CAMMOCK
     JAMES MC CRORY
     H. MILLING Rec: 7 Mar. 1800

Page 5:   Administration on the estate of HENRY SHROCK, late of Fair-
             field Dist., dec'd, who died intestate, granted to JONATHAN
BELTON. 7 Mar. 1800.

Page 6:   Administration on the estate of WILLIAM RICHARDSON, late
             of Fairfield Dist., dec'd, who died intestate, granted to
ELEANOR RICHARDSON. 26 Apr. 1800.

Page 7:   Inventory and appraisement of the estate of WILLIAM RICHARD-
             SON, dec'd. Total 149 pds 14 shillings 4 pence, 1 May 1800,
by JAMES DAVIDSON, WILLIAM BELE(?), WILLIAM THOMSON.

Page 8:   Administration on the estate of JOHN SHANNON, late of Fair-
             field Dist., who died intestate, granted to CREATION BUCK-
ANNON and SAMUEL CLERK. 20 May 1800.

Page 9:   Inventory and appraisement of the estate of JOHN SHANNON,
             dec'd Appraised 24 May 1800, total 40 pds 13 shillings 9
pence, by DAVID PATTON, SIMEON CAMERON, ROBERT STILE. Rec. 27 May 1800.

             Inventory and appraisement of the estate of SAMUEL GLADNEY
             7 June by DAVID CAMOCK, WM. MC CRORY, ALEXR. ROSEBOROUGH.
Total 241 pds 18 __ . Rec. 9 June 1800.

Page 10:   Inventory and appraisement of the estate of HENRY SHROCK,
             includes cooper tools; total 4 pds 9 s 1 d by JOHN PICKETT,
GARDNER FORD, WILLIAM DUNAVON, July 29. Rec. 29 July 1800.

Pages 10-11: A Bill of Sale of the property of WILLIAM RICHARDSON.
             Purchasers: HILLANDER RICHARDSON, JACOB BONY, JAMES DAVIDSON,

Cont'd from page 106:
SAML. CLAMPET, WM. GIBSON, GEORGE SUMMERS, WM. RICHARDSON, JOS. RICHARD-
SON, THOM. RICHARDSON, BARW. TURNIPSEED, JACOB GIBSON, NIMROD BUSBY,
THOS. GARNER, JOHN PEARSON, WM. KENADY, BURREL COOK, ROBERT MARTIN,
WM. DAVIDSON, WM. WATT, JOHNSN. MC KENY, JAS. LONG, WM. BU___(?), WM.
YARBOROUGH, certified June 2, 1800 by ELEANOR (X) RICHARDSON, admx.
Rec. 31 July 1800.

Page 12:   Administration on the estate of WILLIAM NETTLES, late of
            Fairfield Dist., dec'd, who died intestate, granted to ZACHA-
RIAH NETTLES. 23 Aug. 1800.

Pp 13-17:   Will of JOHN WILSON, late of Fairfield Dist., dec'd, proved
            23 Aug. 1800.
Will of JOHN WILSON of Fairfield County...to wife REBECCAH WILSON,
during her life time my plantation whereon I now live, also one negro
man Tom, and his wife Cloe, a negro boy Jacob and four cows and calves,
and two sows and pigs, one riding horse, feather bed and furniture,
etc.; to my son JAMES WILSON, 237 acres which was formerly the property
of RICHARD TAYLOR, and negro man named Tom Minor; to my son THEOPHILUS
WILSON, 100 acres whereon there is a griss (sic) mill, and about 50
acres, part of a tract called Sawyers Beach on the north side of Bear
Creek adj. my old tract, originally granted to JAMESS FREEMAN, also
100 acres of land formerly granted unto LEWIS PERRY, one negro fellow
named Isaac, and a new waggon I am now possessed of; to my son JESSE
WILSON, five shillings sterling; to my daughter NANCY MITCHEL, 60 pds
sterling, to purchase a young negroe wench; to my daughter SUSANNAH
RUSH, one negroe wench named Cloe, which I purchased from old Capt.
KIRKLAND, and one feather bed and furniture; to my daughter MARTHA
NORRIS, one negroe wench named Cloe; to my son JOEL WILSON, five shillings sterling; to my grandson WILLIAM WILSON, son of JOHN WILSON, tract
named Sawyers tract on the south side of Bear Creek; to my grandson
JAMES WILSON, this my plantation where I am now living, at his grand-
mothers decease, and 221 acres granted unto my own self, on round top
branch, a horse, etc., and he to live with his grandmother her life
time; to my grandson JOHN NORRIS, 100 acres on round top branch formerly
the property of SAMUEL NIPPER; to my daughter MARY LAUGHON, after her
mothers decease, one negro boy Jacob; to my son WILSON (sic), five
shillings sterling; my two plantations on bear creek whereon my son
THEOPHILUS WILSON now lives, to be sold and 60 pds be paid unto NANCY
MITCHELL; and remainder divided among my four heirs JAMES WILSON, THEO-
PHILUS WILSON, SAMUEL LAUGHON and JOHN RUSH; sons JAMES WILSONL, THEO-
PHILUS WILSON and SAML. LAUGHON, exrs. 23 Dec. 1799.
                              JOHN WILSON (LS)
Wit: GEORGE WATTS
     RANDAL SUMMERS
     PATRICK MORRIS (X) Rec. Aug. 23, 1800.

Pp 17-18:   Administration on the estate of JOHN FROST, late of Fair-
            field Dist., dec'd, who died intestate, granted to JUDITH
FROST, 15 Sept. 1800.

Page 18:   Appraisement of the estate of WILLM. NETTLES, dec'd. Total
            $ 146 50 1. (sic) Certified 13 Sept. 1800 by REUBIN HARRISON,
JOSEPH CLOUD, WILLM. DUNAVANT, appraisers.

Pp 18-19:   Administration on the estate of RICHARD DUGGINS late of
            Fairfield Dist., who died intestate, granted to ELIZABETH
DUGGINS, 2 Oct. 1800.

Pp 19-22:   Will of MARY PEARSON, late of Fairfield Dist., proved 7
            Oct. 1800.
Will of MARY PEARSON of Fairfield County, my negro wench Bunk(?) to
my grandson NATHANIEL COOK, my stock of sheep running at NATHANIEL
COOK's and cow and calf marked with JOHN COOK's mark to NATHANIEL COOK;
my two negroe boys Dick and Jesse and one feather bed and furniture
to my son JOHN PEARSON; my negro girl Jude to my son PHILLIP PEARSON,
until my grandson ISAAC COOK comes of age; one feather bed, two sheets,
my riding saddle, etc. to my daughter MARY BOND; my riding mare and

Cont'd from page 107:
fillie to my grandson WILLIAM FRANCIS PEARSON; one cow and calf to
my grand daughter MARY REDDISH(?); to my beloved son JOHN PEARSON and
my daughter in law MARY PEARSON, my wearing apparel...remainder to
son PHILLIP PEARSON; sons JOHN PEARSON and PHILLIP PEARSON, exrs. 13
Mar. 1798.
MARY (M) PEARSON (LS)
her mark
Wit: JON. PEARSON
    WM. PEARSON
    MARY PEARSON

Pp 22-24: 9 Oct. 1800, will of THOMAS GRIGS YARBOROUGH, late of Fair-
           field Dist. was proved, JESSE KIRKLAND, exr.
Will of THOMAS GRIGGS YARBOROUGH of Fairfield County, to wife RACHEL
YARBOROUGH, all my estate consisting of negroes, horses, cattle, with
all my plantation tools and household furniture; JOHN TURNER and JESSE
KIRKLAND, exrs. 15 Nov. 1799.
THOS. GRIGGS (X) YARBOROUGH (LS)
his mark
Wit: MARTHA TURNER
    ELIZABETH TURNER
Rec. 9 Oct. 1800.

Page 24: Bill of Sale, property of WILLM. NETTLES, dec'd. Only pur-
         chaser: ZACHARIAH NETTLES. ZACH. NETTLES, admr. 27 OCt.
1800.

Page 25: Bill of appraisement of estate of JOHN FROST, dec'd. 27
         Sept. 1800. Includes 10 negroes (named), by SAML. DOUHARTY,
ALEXR. CRUMPTON, MOSS WOOTEN, appraisers. Rec. 4 Nov. 1800.

Pp 26-28: 26 Nov. 1800, will of WILLIAM MC QUISTON late of Fairfield
          Dist., was proved; ANDREW MC QUISTON, ABNR. CHESTNUT and
ARCHIBALD MC QUISTON, named exrs. 26 Nov. 1800.
Will of WILLIAM MC QUISTON of Fairfield Disrict, being very sick and
weak in body...to my wife the use and benefit of my plantation we are
now living on during her widowhood; to my son JAMES, the same at her
death or marriage; to my daughter JENNET 50 acres of land which I bought
from JOHN GREEN(?); to each of my children at their marriage such portion of what property they may be possessed of; ANDREW MC QUISTON,
ALEXR. CHESNUT and ARCHD. MC QUISTON, exrs. 12 Aug. 1800.
WILLM. MC QUISTON (LS)
Wit: JAMES MURDOCK
    HUGH MC QUISTON. Rec. 26 Nov. 1800.

END OF BOOK

FAIRFIELD WILL BOOK 4

Page 1: Administration on the estate of EDWARD HUSSEY, who died
       intestate granted to JOHN GLAISHER and ELIZABETH HUSSEY,
13 Mar. 1801.

Pp 2-4: Will of SAMUEL RICHISON, being in a very helpless and weak
       condition...my executors ELISABETH RICHISON, ROBERT RICHISON
& JAMES ELLIOTT; estate real and personal to my dear wife ELISABETH
RICHISON and my oldest son JOHN RICHISON, THOMAS RICHISON & MARGRET
RICHISON share and share alike; to DUDLEY an orphan child 20 pds in
money. 19 Apr. 1800.   SAMUEL RICHISON (LS)
Wit: WILLIAM KENNEDY
    J. MC KAIN. Rec. 13 Mar. 1801. Proved by WILLIAM KENNEDY, 13 Mar.
1801.

Pp 4-5: Administration on the estate of HUGH ELLIOTT, who died in-
       testate, granted to ROBERT RICHISON and JAMES ELLIOTT. 17
Mar. 1801.

Pp 5-6: ELIZABETH BURGE, widow and relict of BURRELL BURGE, dec'd.,
       has applied in behalf of GREEN BURGE, BERRYMAN BURGE, HEZEAH
FOARD BURGE, and BURRELL GUARDNER FOARD BURGE, children of sd BURRELL
BURGE, infants within the age of 14 years, to be guardian. 14 Jan.1801.

Pp 7-8:   Letters of Guardianship on above granted to ELISABETH BURGE,
            14 Jan. 1801; NATHANIEL FORD, security.

Pp 8-9:   ROBERT RICHESON, JAMES ELLIOTT, admrs. of estate of HUGH
            ELLIOTT, dec'd., admn. bond, to JOHN BUCHANAN, Ordy. of
Fairfield Dist., WM. BROWN, THOS. RICHESON, security. 10 Apr. 1801.

Pp 10-11:   JOHN GLAZER and ELIZABETH HUSSEY, admrs. of estate of EDWARD
            HUSSEY, dec'd., to JOHN BUCHANAN, Ordy. of Fairfield Dist.;
HUGH BARKLEY, JAMES BEATTEY, securities, 12 Mar. 1801.

Pp 11-13:   Will of JAMES AUSTON of the Town of Winnsborough...all estate
            to be divided in shares to my beloved wife, son JOSEPH,
my daughter SUSANNAH, save one tract of land which lyes on Bear Creek,
to my son WILLIAM and my daughter AGNES; exrs. DAVID R. EVANS and JESSE
HROIS(?). 12 Sept. 1796.
                              JAMES AUSTON (LS)
Wit: JNO. BUCHANAN
     JAMES BARKLEY
     GUARD DUNOSE(?)
Proved by JAMES BARKLEY, 14 May 1801. Letters testamentary granted
14 May 1801 to JESSE HROIS(?)

Pp 14-16:   ALEXANDER WILSON an orphan within the age of 21 years has
            chosen GREEN THOMPSON to be his guardian, 28 May 1801. Letter
of guardianship issued to GREEN THOMPSON, ALEXANDER JAMISON, security.
28 May 1801. Rec. 2 June 1801.

Page 16:   THOMAS GLADNEY's account with GREEN THOMPSON, gdn. of ALEX-
            ANDER WILSON, a minor. Estate of ALEXANDER WILSON, dec'd.,
1797 to GREEN THOMPSON for boarding A. WILSON 2 years and MARY WILSON.
May 28, 1801. Rec. 17 Aug. 1801.

Pp 17-19:   Will of JAMES ROBISON of Fairfield Dist., being sick and
            weak of body...to my beloved wife MARGRET ROBISON, my plan-
tation during life, two cows and calves, furniture, etc., and at her
death to be equally divided betwixt my daughters AGNES BOYD and SARAH
STERLING; to my beloved grandson JAMES BOYD, my best mare, but not
to enjoy her until she suckle the colt at her feet; and my well beloved
grandson SAMUEL STERLING, shall possess the colt; to aforesd SAMUEL
STERLING a three year old dun heffer; to my granddaughter MARGT. STER-
LING, the no horned heffer; to my granddaughter MARGRET BOYD, the big
heffer; to my grandson JAMES STERLING, the two young bulls and all
my sheep and hoggs; I will that ANDREW BOYD be given up his note of
hand I have against him; JACOB (?) STERLING should receive all the
cash arising from my book accounts; JAMES BOYD shall have my saddle
and all my wearing apparel; to grandson JAMES STERLING $30 cash in
hand...my friend and neighbour STAFFORD CURREY(?), son in law JOHN
STERLING, exrs...(no date)
                              JAMES (X) ROBISON (LS)
Wit: S. CURREY
     GREEN CURREY
Proved by GREEN CURREY, 15 July 1801. Letters testamentery granted
to JOHN STERLING, 15 July 1801.

Pp 20-22:   Administration on the estate of HARRIS FREEMAN, late of
            Fairfield Dist., who died intestate granted to REEVES FREE-
MAN, 13 July 1801. Adm. bond, 13 July 1801, REEVES FREEMAN, admr.,
JOHN CHAPPLE, JACOB BONEY, securities.

Page 23:   Will of ISAAC HUSSEY of Fairfield County, being weak of
            body...to wife NELLY HUSSEY, all property real and personal;
at her decease to be given to NANCY HOGAN a cow and calf, and the remainder to be equally divided bet. my son ISAAC HUSSEY and daughter
BETTEY HUSSEY and daughters LUCY HUSSEY, NELLY HUSSEY; wife NELLY and
son ISAAC HUSSEY, exrs. ...(no date)
                              ISAAC (his mark) HUSSEY
Wit: JOS. MC CREIGHT
     GEORGE (H) HUSSEN(?)
Proved by JAMES MC CREIGHT, 29 July 1801. Rec. 5 Aug. 1801.

Pp 24-25: Letters testamentary to NELLY HUSSEY, 5 Aug. 1801. Warrant of appraisement on estate of ISAAC HUSSEY, dec'd.

Pp 25-26: JOHN ROBISON and ALEXANDER ROBISON, orphans within the age of 21 years, have chosen SIMON CAMRON for their guardian, 4 Sept. 1801.

Pp 26-29: Letters testamentary on the estate of WILLIAM EWING, dec'd., will having been proved 22 Sept. 1801, to WILLIAM EWING, JR. and JAMES BARBER, exrs. 24 Sept. 1801. Warrant of appraisement on estate dated 3 Oct. 1801.
Will of WILLIAM EWING of Fairfield District, planter, being very sick and weak in body...to wife the mare named Cato, cows and calves; to my brother ROBERT, 5 pds to be pd in one year after my decease; to ANDREW MC PETTERS 5 pds; remainder to be divided into 3 equal shares between my wife, my brother ROBERT's two sons WILLIAM and JOHN EWING; and I make my nephew WILLIAM EWING and JAMES BARBER, exrs., 30 Aug. 1802 (sic)

                                    WILLIAM EWING (LS)
Wit: JOHN ARNETT
     HUGH (X) WHITE. Rec. 23 Jan. 1802. Proved by JOHN ARNETT, 20 Sept. 1801.

Pp 29-30: Warrant of appraisement on the estate of WILLIAM MC MORRIS, dec'd, as you will be directed by WILLIAM MC MORRIS and JAMES MC MORRIS, exrs. to W. BELL, ___ HERVY, ___ JOHNSTON, ___ RABB, J. BELL. 25 Sept. 1801.

Pp 30-31: Administration on the estate of SAMUEL NESBETT, late of Fairfield Dist., who died intestate, granted to THOMAS NES-BITT and SAMUEL NESBETT, 8 OCt. 1801.

Page 32: Administration on the estate of JOHN PAUL, late of Fairfield Dist., who died intestate, granted to JEAN PAUL and ARCHIBALD PAUL, 3 Nov. 1801.

Page 33: Will of WILLIAM MC MORRIS of the Dist. of Fairfield...to my beloved wife, $20 to be paid by each of my legatees namely WILLIAM, JOSEPH, ALEXANDER, JOHN and JAMES MC MORRIS, and ALEXANDER KINCAID yearly during the life of my beloved wife, JANE MC MORRIS; to my son JAMES MC MORRIS, the plantation of 150 acres where I now live, and his choice of my negroes; the remaining part of my negroes, cattle, etc., to be sold and that JAMES KINCAID and MARY KINCAID my beloved son and daughter the sum of 10 pds sterling; remainder divided between my children WILLIAM, JOSEPH, ALEXANDER and JOHN MC MORRIS and ALEXR. KINCAID; sons WILLIAM and JAMES, exrs. 15 Sept. 1801.

                                WILLIAM (his mark) MC MORRIS (LS)
Wit: ALEXANDER MC MORRIS
     MARGRET KINCAID
     ELIZABETH RABB.   Rec. 20 Dec. 1801.

Pp 34-35: Warrant of appraisement on the estate of JOHN WRIGHT, dec'd., directed to ANDW. HEMPHILL, ANDW. DUNN, JAMES BLAIR, DAVID RODDEY, JAS. HARPER by MARY WRIGHT, admx., 30 Nov. 1801. Sworn 18 Feb. 1801 bef. JNO. TURNER, J.P.: ANDW. HEMPHILL, JAS. BLAIR, JAMES HARPER. Order of sale dated 18 Nov. 1801. Rec. 8 Aug. 1802.

Pp 35-41: Warrant of appraisement on estate of JAMES KINCAID, dec'd, directed to MARY KINCAID, extx and WILLIAM KINCAID, exr., 11 Jan. 1801 to JAMES BARKLEY, JAMES MC MORRIES, ALEXR. KINCAID, JOSEPH MC MORRIES, CHARLES MONTGOMERY, SR. Sworn bef. EDWARD MARTION, J.P., 26 Jan. 1801: JAMES BARKLEY, JAS. MC MORRIS, ALEXR. KINCAID. Rec. 9 Aug. 1802. Order for sale dated 11 Jan. 1802. Dedimus to JOHN MITCHELL, J.Q., to examine witnesses to the will of JAMES KINCAID, dec'd., 5 Nov. 1801. Will proved by JOHN NOBLE, ALEXANDER HENRY, ROBT. FLEMING, who swore in Charleston, 18 Dec. 1801.
Will of JAMES KINCAID of Fairfield Co., planter and store keeper, being weak of body...to my son WILLIAM KINCAID, all my plantation butting on Mills Creek, and land adj. sd plantation; wife MARY KINCAID shall

Cont'd from page 110:
have a comfortable room in my mansion House of her own and choice,
and sd WILLIAM to pay her 50 pds per annum; negroes and other items
to be sold to the highest bidder; to daughter NANCY HALL, 300 pds sterling; daughter MARY KINCAID, MARGARET KINCAID, ELIZABETH KINCAID and
REBECKAH KINCAID; son WILLIAM and wife MARY, exrs. 20 Oct. 1801.
Wit: JOHN NOBLES   JAMES KINCAID (LS)
     ROBT. FLEMING. Rec. 12 Aug. 1802.

Pp 42-43: SAMUEL OATS late of Fairfield Dist...lately dyed intestante..
           admn. granted to FANNY OATES and JESSE HAVIS, 23 Mar. 1802.
Rec. 12 Aug. 1802.

Page 43:   MARGET MEEK an orphan within the age of 21 years has chosen
           ALEXANDER GALLOWAY for her guardian, 25 Mar. 1802.

Page 44:   JOHN WRIGHT, late of Fairfield Dist., lately died intestate..
           admn. granted to MARY RIGHT (WRIGHT), 10 Dec. 1801. Rec.
15 Aug. 1802.

Page 45:   JAMES MC MEKAN, late of Fairfield, lately died intestate,
           admn. granted to ELIZABETH MC MEKAN, 14 Oct. 1801.

Pp 46-47: JAMES HANAN, late of Fairfield, died intestate, admn. granted
           to AGNES HANAN and ROBERT HANAN, 14 Dec. 1801. Rec. 16 Aug.
1802.

Pp 47-48: MAJOR DILLARD, late of Fairfield, died intestate, admn.
           granted to RICHARD WINN and FRANCIS DILLARD, 14 Dec. 1801.
Rec. 16 Aug. 1802.

Pp 48-49: ELISHA MC FADDEN, late of Fairfield, died intestate, admn.
           granted to MOSES AIRS, 26 Dec. 1802. Rec. 17 Aug. 1802.

Pp 49-50: JAMES HOLLIS, late of Fairfield died intestate, admn. granted
           to SARY HOLLIS and BURWELL HOLLIS, 20 Jan. 1802.

Pp 50-51: WILLIAM LYLES, late of Fairfield, died intestate, admn.
           granted to ELIZABETH LYLES and EPHRAIM LYLES, 13 Feb. 1802.
Rec. 17 Aug. 1802.

Pp 51-52: SARY FALAS an orphan within the age of 21 years, has chosen
           JOHN COLDWELL as her guardian, 4 Feb. 1802. Rec. 17 Aug.
1802.

Pp 52-53: LYTTLETON ISBEL, late of Fairfield, died intestate, admn.
           granted to ANNE ISBEL, 9 Mar. 1802. Rec. 17 Aug. 1802.

Pp 53-54: JAMES HAMILTON lately died intestate, admn. granted to SARAH
           HAMILTON, 10 Aug. 1802. Rec. 18 Aug. 1802.

Pp 54-56: Warrant of appraisement on the estate of SAMUEL OATES, dec'd.
           as directed by FANNY OATES and JESSE HAVIS, admns., to QUIN-
TON HOY, WILLM. BRYANT, CANNON CASON, WILLIAM MILLER, JOHN TIDWELL.
Sworn bef. CHARLES PICKETT, J. P., 24 Mar. 1802: JOHN TIDWELL, CANNON
CASON, QUINTON HOY. Order of sale dated 23 Mar. 1802.

Pp 56-58: Warrant of appraisement on the estate of ELISHA MC FADDEN,
           as directed by MOSES AIRS, JR., admr., to RICHD. CAMPBELL,
ENOCH SEAL, THOS. TRAP, ANTHONY SEAL, ALEXR. CRUMPTON, 12 Jan. 1801.
Sworn bef. N. PEAY, J.P., 28 Jan. 180_: RICHD. CAMPBELL, THOS. TRAP
and ANTHONY SEAL. Rec. 23 Aug. 1802. Order of sale dated 12 Jan. 1802.

Pp 58-60: Warrant of appraisement on the estate of LYTTLETON ISBEL,
           as directed by ANN ISBEL, admx., to JESSE PERRY, LEWIS PERRY,
THEOPHILUS WILSON, HUGH RANDAL, SAML. PERRY, 9 Mar. 1802. Sworn to
1 May 1802, bef. ELIJAH JONES, J.P.: JESSE PERRY, HUGH RANDOLPH, THEO-
PHILUS WILSON. Rec. 25 Aug. 1802.
(Note: spelling varies from page to page).

111

Pp 60-61:   Warrant of Appraisement on the estate of JAMES HAYMAN as
             directed by AGNES HANAN and ROBERT HANAN, admrs., 14 Dec.
1801, to Capt. FORT, WILLM. ARMSTRONG, THOMAS SAINT, WM. ELLISON, JAS.
MUSE. 28 Dec., sworn bef. NICHOLAS PEAY, J.P.: GARDNER FORT, WILLM.
ARMSTRONG, J. MUSE.

Pp 61-63:   Warrrant of Appraisement on the estate of JAMES HOLLIS,
             as directed by SARAH HOLLIS and BURWELL HOLLIS, admrs.,
20 Jan. 1802, to JOHN HALL, JESSE HAVIS, JAS. HARVEY, JNO. HARVEY,
JNO. TIDWELL, SR. Sworn 30 Jan., bef. NICHOLAS PEAY, J.P.: JESSE HAVIS,
JOHN HALL, JAMES HARVEY, JOHN HARVEY. Rec. 30 Aug. 1802. Order of sale
dated 20 Jan. 1802.

Pp 63-64:   Warrant of Appraisement on the estate of MAJOR DILLARD,
             as shown by RICHARD WINN & FRANCIS DILLARD, admrs., direct-
ed to JOHN WINN, JNO. MC DOWALL, NATH. SMITH, CREIGHTON BUCHANAN, HUGH
AKIN. 22 Jan. sworn bef. EDWARD MARTIN, J.P.: JOHN WINN, SR., NATHANIEL
SMITH, HUGH AKIN.

Pp 64-65:   Warrant of Appraisement on estate of JAMES MC MEEKAN, as
             shown by ELIZABETH MC MEEKAN, admx., directed to JAS. DAVI-
SON, WILLM. WATT, JACOB GIPSON, WILLM. CRAIG, WILLM. THOMSON. 21 Jan.
sworn bef. BURWELL COOK: JAMES DAVIDSON, WILLIAM WATT, JACOB GIBSON.
(Note: surnames spelled both ways). Rec. 30 Aug. 1802.

Page 65:   Order of Sale on estate of JAMES HAYNAN; AGNES HAYNAN,
             ROBERT HAYNAN, admrs., 14 Dec. 1801.

Page 66:   Order of Sale on estate of WILLIAM EWING; WILLIAM EWING
             and JAMES BARBER, exrs., 22 Oct. 1801.

Pp 66-67:   Warrant of Appraisement on estate of EDWARD HUSSEY; JOHN
             GLAZIER and ELIZABETH HUSSEY, exrs., 12 Mar. 1801, directed
to JOHN HAVIS, JOHN HARBRY, JAMES MC CAIN, HUGH GORLEY, JAS. BARKLEY.
Sworn 16 Mar. 1801 bef. D. R. EVANS, J.P.Q.U.: JOHN HAVIS, JOHN HAR-
BROUGH, HUGH GOURLEY.

Page 68:   Warrant of Appraisement on estate of JAMES AUSTIN; JESSE
             HAVIS, exr., 14 May 1801, directed to JAS. BEATTY, JAS.
BARKLEY, JAS. WORKMAN, ALEXR. MC HENRY. Sworn 29 May 1801, bef. DAVID
READ EVANS, J.P.: JAMES WORKMAN, JAMES BARKLEY, JAS. BEATTY.

Page 69:   Warrant of Appraisement on estate of HUGH ELLIOTT, as shown
             by ROBERT RICHARDSON & JAMES ELLIOTT, admrs., 17 Mar. 1801,
directed to WILLM. KENNEDA, DAVID ANDREWS, BARTH. TURNIPSEED, WM. CRAIG
& JACOB BONEY. Sworn 27 Mar. 1801: Capt. DAVID ANDREWS, BARTHOLOMEW
TURNIPSEED & WILLIAM KENNEDA, bef. BURWELL COOK, J.P.

Page 70:   Order for sale, dated 18 Mar. 1801 on above estate.

Pp 70-72:   Warrant of Appraisement on estate of JEREMIAH BURGE, as
             shown by REUBEN HARRISON, admr., 16 Nov. 1801, directed
to ZACH. NETTLES, JAMES ROCHELL, DARLING JONES, WILLM. DUNNAVAN & GARD-
NER FORT. Sworn 28 Dec., bef. NICHOLAS PEAY: ZACH. NETTLES, DARLING
JONES & WILLIAM DUNNAVAN. Order of sale, 16 Nov. 1801.

Pp 72-73:   DANIEL SHAW late of Fairfield Dist., died intestate, admn.
             granted to NANCY SHAW, 10 Sept. 1802.

Pp 73-74:   NICHOLAS THOMSON, late of Fairfield, died intestate, admn.
             granted to JESSE HAVIS, 13 Sept. 1802.

Pp 74-76:   Warrant of Appraisement on estate of JAMES HAMILTON, as
             directed by SARAH HAMILTON, admx., to JAS. KENNADA, SR.,
Capt. JNO. SMITH, ALEXR. ROBINSON, JOHN BONER, ROBINSON BRATTON, 10
Sept. 1802; sworn 22 Sept. 1802, bef. ELIJAH JONES, J.P.: JAS. KENNADA,
SR., ALEXR. ROBISON, JNO. SMITH. Order of sale dated 10 Sept. 1802.

Pp 76-79:   Warrant of Appraisement on estate of HARRIS FREEMAN, as
             directed by REEVES FREEMAN, exr., to DAVID ANDREWS, STEPHEN

112

Cont'd from page 112:
GIPSON, JOHN CHAPPLE, JOS. WOODWARD, 13 July 1801. Sworn 16 July: JOSEPH
WOODWARD, JOHN CHAPPEL, STEPHEN GIPSON, by BURWELL COOK, J.P. Order
of sale dated 19 July 1801. Rec. 6 Nov. 1802.

Pp 79-80:   Warrant of Appraisement on estate of SAMUEL NISBET, as
             directed by THOMAS NISBET and SAMUEL NISBET, admrs., 12
Oct. 1801, to JOHN MARSHALL, SAML. ARNET, ROBERT LATHIN, ROBERT GAMBEL,
DAVID PATTON. Sworn bef. JOHN TURNER, J.P.: ROBERT GAMBEL, SAML. ARNET,
JOHN MARSHALL, 4 Nov. 1801. Rec. 12 Nov. 1802.

Pp 80-82:   Warrant of Appraisement on estate of NICHOLAS THOMSON,
             directed by JESSE HAVIS, admr., to JAS. SEAL, JOHN KELLY,
ALEXR. CRUMPTON, JOS. CLOUD, 13 Dec. 1802; sworn 6 Nov. 1802, bef.
ELIJAH JONES, J.P.: JAMES SEALE, JNO. KELLY, ALEXR. CRUMPTON. Order
of sale dated 13 Sept. 1802.

Pp 82-83:   Will of ELIZABETH WOODWARD of dist. of Fairfield, being
             sick and weak of body...all debts which my daughter LUCY
WOODWARD has contracted previous to this date..to my daughter SARAH
RILEY, 1 bay horse, half of my stock of hogs, have of what remains
of my crop, andnegroes is supported; to my son HENRY WOODWARD, remaining half of my stock of hogs; to my daughter ELIZABETH MC MORRIES,
one bed and furniture; to my daughter LUCY WOODWARD one bed and all
the furniture that she now claims; remainder to be equally divided
bet. BENJAMIN MAY, THOMAS MAY, ELIZABETH MC MORRIES, JANE FREEMAN,
LUCY WOODWARD, JOSEPH WOODWARD & HENRY WOODWARD, only $15 to the heirs
of my son THOS. WOODWARD; JOSEPH WOODWARD, exr. 12 Aug. 1802.
Wit: JOHN BELL
     WM. SCOTT   ELIZABETH (X) WOODWARD (LS)
Rec. 24 Nov. 1802.   her mark

Pp 83-84:   Order for sale of the estate of SAMUEL NISBET, dec'd.,
             dated 18 Oct. 1801. Rec. 27 Nov. 1802.

Page 84:   Order for sale of estate of NICHOLAS THOMSON, 13 Sept.
             1802. Rec. 30 Nov. 1802.

Page 85:   Will of PETER ARSKIN being weak of body...executors to
             vendue all my property and plantation to be divided bet.
my wife and children; young child that is yet unborn; JAMES LYNN &
WILLM. ADGER and DAVID HOMES, exrs. 17 June 1801.
Wit: WILLIAM MC CROREY
     JAMES MC MELLENE   PETER ARSHINE (O)
Rec. 30 Nov. 1802.

Pp 85-87:   Will of ARCHIBALD PAUL of S. C. and Fairfield Dist., being
             weak in body...to my daughter SARAH ROBINSON, 7 pds; to
BETTY RUSSEL, 7 pds; to MARTHA ROBINSON, 7 pds; to my son WILLIAM PAUL,
7 pds; and to MOSES PAUL, 7 pds; to my son JOHN PAUL all this planta-
tion with houses, horses, cows, hogs, etc.; to my daughter MARGARET
RUSSEL, 7 pds; to my son JAMES PAUL's two children, the land at the
Catawba; to the covenanted Society in Winnsboro for the use of building
a meeting house $10.; son WILLIAM PAUL & JOHN PAUL, exrs. 3 Sept. 1802.
Wit: JAS. BECKET   ARCHD. (AP) PAUL
     WM. RUSSELL   his mark
     MOSES PAUL
Proved by JAMES BECKET & WILLIAM RUSSELL, 20 Sept. 1802. Rec. 1 Dec.
1802.
Warrant of Appraisement directed to JOHN ROSBOROUGH, JAMES RUSSELL,
JOHN MC VEY, THOS. GLADNEY, JR., SAMUEL CLARK. Sworn 24 Sept. bef.
EDWARD MARTIN, J.P.: JNO. ROSBOROUGH, SAML. CLARK, THOS. GLADNEY.

Page 88:   Warrant of Appraisement on estate of JAMES ROBISON, directed
             by JOHN STERLING & STAFFORD CURRY, exrs., to SAML. COLDWELL,
GAVIN CURRY, DANL. HUFFMAN, ALEXR. DICKEY, ROBT. GIBSON, 15 July 1801.
Sworn 23 July bef. STAFFORD CURRY, J.P.: SAML. COLDWELL, GAVIN CURRY,
DANL. HUFFMAN, ROBT. GIBSON.

Pp 89-90:   Warrant of Appraisement on estate by MARGARET ROCHELL,

Cont'd from page 113:
        admx. of estate of JAMES ROCHELL, to THOS. STARKE, ZACH.
NETTLES, DARLING JONES, DAVID GEORGE, GARDNER FORD, 20 Sept. 1802.
Sworn 14 Dec. 1801 bef. JOHN MICKLE, J.Q.: THOMAS STARKE, JR., DARLING
JONES, ZACH. NETTLES. Order of sale dated 16 Nov. 1802.
(Note: FORD also spelled FORT).

Pp 90-91:   Will of ARCHIBALD PAUL was proved 20 Sept. 1802.

Pp 91-92:   Letters of Adm. on estate of JAMES ROCHELL, granted to
             MARGARET ROCHELL, 20 Sept. 1802. Rec. 23 Dec. 1802.

Page 93:   JOHN COOK, late of Fairfield, died intestate, admn. granted
             to PHILIP COOK, 16 Nov. 1802. Rec. 23 Dec. 1802.

Page 94:   PATRICK LOGAN, late of this dist., died intestate, admn.
             granted to HENRY MC CAULEY, 23 Sept. 1802.

Page 95:   WILLIAM BRYANT, late of the dist...died intestate, admn.
             granted to SIBBA BRYANT & BENONA ROBERTSON, 29 Sept. 1802.
Rec. 23 Dec. 1802.

Page 96:   Letters of Adm. on estate of ELIZABETH WOODWARD, granted
             to JOSEPH WOODWARD. (not completed or dated).

Page 96:   Citation on the estate of WILLIAM NETTLES, by ZACH. NETTLES
             24 June 1800. Rec. 28 Dec. 1802.

Page 97:   Letters testamentary on the estate of ELIZABETH WOODWARD,
             whose will was proved 31 Nov. 1802. Dated 31 Nov. 1802.
Rec. 23 Dec.1802.

Page 98:   Letters of Adm. on the estate of ELIZABETH THOMSON, to
             DAVID THOMSON, 14 Dec. 1802. Rec. 23 Dec. 1802.

Page 99:   Letters Testamentary on the estate of JOHN LIGHTNER, whose
             will was proved 10 Dec. 1802. Rec. 23 Dec. 1802.

Pp 100-101: Warrant of Appraisement on estate of DANIEL SHAW, 10 Sept.
             1802, directed by NANCY SHAW to JAS. CRAIG, ROBT. RABB,
ISAAC BEAN, WILLM. SIMS. Sworn 16 Oct. bef. EDWARD MARTIN, J.P.: JOHN
BELL, WILLM. SIMS, JAMES CRAIG. Order of sale dated 16 Nov. 1802. Rec.
23 Dec. 1802.

Pp 102-103: Warrant of Appraisement on estate of JOHN PAUL, directed
             by ARCHD. PAUL and JANE PAUL, admrs., 3 Nov. 1801 to JAS.
RABB, ALEXR. KINCAID, CHARLES D. BRADFORD, JAS. MC MORRIES, JOHN OGIL-
VIE. Sworn 6 Nov. 1801 bef. JAS. MC MORRIES, J.P.: JAS. RABB, C. D.
BRADFORD, ALEXR. KINCAID. Rec. 23 Dec. 1802. Order of sale dated 3
Nov. 1801.

Pp 103-104: Administration bond on estate of PATRICK LOGAN, penalty
             $2000, 29 Nov. 1802, HENRY MC CAULEY, admr., JAS. MC MORRIES
and JAS. BARKLEY, securities. Rec. 28 Dec. 1802.

Page 105:   Admn. bond on estate of WILLIAM BRYANT; penalty $3000,
             29 Nov. 1802; SIBBA BRYANT and BENONI ROBERTSON, admrs.,
WM. ROBERTSON, security. Rec. 28 Dec. 1802.

Page 106:   Warrant of Appraisement on estate of WILLIAM NETTLES, as
             directed by ZACHARIAH NETTLES, admr., to THOS. MUSE, GARDNER
FORD, JOS. CLOUD, REUBEN HARRISON, WILLM. DUNAVEN, 23 Aug. 1800; sworn
bef. JOHN MICKLE, J.Q.: WILLIAM DUNAVANT, JOS. CLOUD, R. HARRISON.
Rec. 28 Dec. 1802.

Page 107:   Admn. bond on estate of DANIEL SHAW, penalty $4000, 11
             Sept. 1802; NANCY SHAW, admx., JOHN BELL, JAMES BARKLEY,
securities.

Pp 108-109: Admn. bond on estate of JAMES HOLLIS, penalty $2000, 20

                                    114

Cont'd from page 114:
        Jan. 1802; SARAH HOLLIS, BURWELL HOLLIS, admrs., JOHN DUN-
LAP, WILLIAM HOLLIS, securities. Citation dated 28 Dec. 1801. Rec.
29 Dec. 1802.

Pp 110-111: Admn. bond on estate of WILLM. LYLES, penalty 2000 pds.,
        2 Mar. 1802; ELIZABETH LYLES, EPHRAIM LYLES, admrs., ARO-
MANUS LYLES, JNO. MORRIS, securities. Rec. 29 Dec. 1802.

Pp 111-113: Will of JOHN LIGHTNER, being weak in body...to my beloved
        wife MARY LIGHTNER, one horse named Prince, one womans
saddle and bridle, 3 cows and calves; to my son CHRISTIAN LIGHTNER,
tract on Little River, 150 acres, and one cow and calf; to my son
PHILIP LIGHTNER my tract of land on Cannons Creek, 125 acres and one
cow and calf and four head of sheep; to my son JOHN LIGHTNER, tract
on the long meadows 100 acres and one cow and calf; to my daughters
ELIZ. LIGHTNER, CATY LIGHTNER & MARY LIGHTNER, land on twenty five
mile creek 350 acres to be equally divided betwixt them; to my daughter
BARBARA LIGHTNER, my tract of land on Wateree Creek, 100 acres and a
cow and calf; to my wife MARY LIGHTNER equal share with all my children
of what is left...wife MARY and son PHILIP, exrs. 19 Sept. 1794..
Wit: JOHN CHAPPEL
        PETER (X) COGLER   JOHN (Ɪ L) LIGHTNER
        GEORGE (+) LIGHTNER.   his mark
Rec. 29 Dec. 1802.
Will of JOHN LIGHTNER proved by GEORGE LIGHTNER, ____ 1802.

Pp 113-114: Admn. bond on estate of RICHARD DUGANS, penalty 150 pds.
        sterling, ELIZABETH DUGANS, admx., AMBROSE KIRKLAND, CHRIS-
TOPHER ADDISON, securities, dated 2 Oct. 1802. Rec. 30 Dec. 1802.

Pp 114-115: Admn. bond on estate of LYTTLETON ISBELS, penalty $3000,
        9 Mar. 1802, ANNE ISBELS, admx., JESSE PERRY, LEWIS PERRY,
securities. Rec. 31 Dec. 1802.

Pp 116-118: PHILIP COOK applied for letters of admn. on estate of JOHN
        COOK, 29 Dec. 1802; rec. 24 Jan. 1803. Statement of PHILIP
COOK, admr.: no property belonging to the estate of JOHN COOK, dec'd.
have come to my knowledge except a bond given by JOHN HAMPTON and WADE
HAMPTON payable to JOHN COOK, 125 pds, due 1 Jan. 1803 with interest
from 1 Jan. 1792, on which I am informed by JOHN TAYLOR, Esq., judgement
has ben obtained. Rec. 24 Jan. 1803.
Admn. bond, dated 16 Nov. 1802, penalty $5000, PHILIP COOK, admr.,
THOMAS HUTCHESON, security.

Pp 118-120: Warrant of Appraisement on estate of ELIZABETH WOODWARD,
as directed by JOSEPH WOODWARD, 30 Nov. 1802, to JAMES MC MORRIS, WILL-
IAM KINCAID, ALEXR. KINCAID, WILLIAM SCOTT & JOHN BELL. Sworn by JAS.
MC MORRIS, J.P. and SAML. ALSTON, J.P., 4 Dec. 1802: WILLIAM KINCAID,
WILLIAM SCOTT, JAMES MC MORRIS (also MC MORRIES). Order of sale dated
31 Nov. 1802.

Pp 120-122: JUDITH FROST applied for letters of admn. on estate of
        JOHN FROST, 4 July 1801. Warrant of appraisement 15 Sept.
1800, to SAML. LOUGHON, ALEXR. CRUMPTON, JOHN KELLY, SAML. DOUGHARTY,
MOSES WOOTEN. Sworn 27 Sept. 1800 bef. ELIJAH JONES, J.P.: MOSES WOOTEN,
SAM'L DOUGHARTY, ALEXR. CRUMPTON.
Admn. bond: JUDITH FROST, admx., SAMUEL PERRY, SAMUEL DOUGHARTY, secur-
ities, penalty 1000 pds sterling, 15 Sept. 1800.

Page 122:   Estate of JAMES ROBISON, dec'd. Mar. 12, 1802. Received
        this day from JOHN STERLING and STAFFORD CURRY, exrs. of
our Father and Mothers estates, all and every part, either mentioned
in their last wills and testaments, and all our part of that property
which the will did not include, as adjudged by WILLIAM MC CRORY, JAMES
CHESNUT, GAVIN CURRY called as arbitrators for ourselves and families,
and is fully ___ ? having the whole ....
Rec. 3 Feb. 1803.   ANDREW BOYD
                                  AGNES (+) BOYD

115

Pp 122-123: AGNES SHAW applied for letters of admn. on the estate of
DANIEL SHAW, dec'd., 4 Sept. 1802. Rec. 3 Jan. 1803.

Page 123: ELIZABETH DUGGANS applied for letters of admn. on the estate
of RICHARD DUGGANS, 2 Sept. 1800. Rec. 3 Feb. 1803.

EDWARD HUSSEY estate; ELIZABETH HUSSEY and JOHN GLAZIER
applied for letters of admn. 17 Jan. 1801. Rec. 4 Mar.
1803.
Pp 124-125: Admn. bond on the estate of JOHN WRIGHT, dec'd., $4000
penalty 30 Nov. 1801; MARY WRIGHT, admx., ANDW. DUNN, SR.,
HENRY MC BRIDE, securities. Rec. 3 Feb. 1803.
MARY WRIGHT applied for admn. on estate of JOHN WRIGHT,
14 Nov. 1801.

Pp 125-126: Warrant of appraisement on estate of WILLIAM MC QUISTON,
as shown by ANDREW MC QUISTON, ALEXANDER CHESNUTT and ARCHI-
BALD MC QUISTON, exrs., 26 Nov. 1800 to JAMES MURDOCK, JAMES STEEL,
JAMES MILLER, HUGH MC QUISTON. Sworn 11 Dec, 1800 bef. MOSES HILL,
J.P.: JOHN SIMINGTON, JAMES MURDOCK, HUGH MC QUISTON. Rec. 3 Mar. 1803.

Pp 126-127: Admn. bond on estate of WILLIAM NETTELS, penalty 100 pds
sterling, 23 Aug. 1800; ZACHARIAH NETTLES, admr. BENJAMIN
HART, security.

Pp 127-130: Warrant of appraisement on estate of HENRY SHROCK, dated
29 Apr. 1800 to JOHN PICKETT, GARDNER FOARD, WILLIAM DUNI-
VAN, WM. ALDRIDGE, JR., JOHN STONE, JR. Sworn 19 July 1800 bef. JOHN
MICKLE, J.Q.: JOHN PICKETT, G. FOARD, WM. DUNNIVANT.
JONATHAN BELTON applied for admn., 3 Mar. 180_?
Admn. bond: JONATHAN BELTON, admr., JESSE HAVIS, security, penalty
50 pds sterling, dated 11 July 1800.

Pp 130-132: Citation on estate of JOHN SHANNON: CREIGHTON BUCHANAN
and SAMUEL CLARK applied for letters of admn., 16 May 1800.
Admn. bond: penalty 100 pds sterling, 16 May 1800, DAVID PATTON, secur-
ity. Rec. 4 Mar. 1803. Warrant of appraisement directed to DAVID PATTON,
JAMES ROGERS, SIMON CAMERON, WM. YONGUE, ROBT. STILL. Sworn bef. EDWARD
MARTIN, J.P., 24 May 1800: SIMON CAMERON, DAVID PATTON, ROBERT STILL.
Rec. 4 Mar. 1803.

Pp 132-134: ELEANOR RICHARDSON applied for admn. on estate of WILLIAM
RICHARDSON, 18 Apr. 1800. Appraisers sworn 20 Apr. 1800,
bef. BURRELL COOK, J.P.: JAMES DAVIDSON, WILLIAM BELL, WILLIAM THOMPSON.
Rec. 10 Mar. 1803. Admn. bond ELEANOR RICHRDSON, admx., JAMES DAVIDSON
and DAVID KENNEDY, securities, penalty 200 pds sterling, 26 Apr. 1800.

Pp 134-137: Dedimus to JAMES BEATEY, Esq., to qualify admrs. on the
estate of JOHN MASON, dec'd., 23 Mar. 1803. Admn. bond
MARY MASON, admx., JOHN BELL and JAMES CRAIG, securities, 1 Mar. 1803,
penalty $2000. Warrant of appraisement to EDWARD ANDREWS, DAVID ANDREWS,
DAVID MC GRAW , JOHN BELL, JAMES CRAIG. Sworn 2 May 1800 bef. SAMUEL
ALSTON, Esq., JAMES CRAIG, JOHN BELL, DAVID ANDREWS, DAVID MC GRAW.
Rec. 2 Apr. 1803. MARY MASON applied for admn. 7 Mar. 1803. Order of
sale dated 24 Nov. 1803. Rec. 3 Apr. 1803.

Page 138: ANNE ISBELS applied for admn. on estate of LITTLETON ISBALS,
3 Mar. 1803.

Pp 138-139: Guardianship bond: 1 Feb. 1802, JOHN COLDWELL guardian
of ELIZABETH FALIS, penalty 500 pds; GEORGE COLDWELL, security. Rec. 3 Apr. 1803.

Pp 140-141: Guardianship bond: 25 Mar. 1802, ALEXANDER GALLOWAY, guardian of MARGARET MEEK; CREIGHTON BUCHANAN and SMITH PHILIPS,
securities, penalty $500.

Pp 141-142: Guardianship bond: 4 Sept. 1801, SIMEON CAMERON guardian
of JOHN ROBISON and ALEXANDER ROBISON, penalty $2400; JAMES

Cont'd from page 116:
CAMERON, security. Rec. 23 April 1803.

Page 142:   ELIZABETH LYLES and EPHM. LYLES applied for admn. on the
            estate of WILLIAM LYLES, 16 Feb. 1802.

Pp 143-145: Letters testamentary on estate of BARTLETT HENSON, 20 Apr.
            1803.
Will of BARTLET HENSON of Fairfield Dist., being weak of body...to
my son BENJAMIN HENSON, all that plantation in the fork of Wateree
and Fry fork creeks, 75 acres; to my wife ELIZABETH HENSON, all house-
hold furniture, stock, etc., and at her death to my son JOHN HENSON:
ROBERT HENSON & BENJAMIN HENSON, exrs. 19 July 1800.
Wit: ROBERT SHURLEY
     JOHN TIDWELL (T)   BARTLET (X) HENSON (LS)
     NICHOLAS PEAY. Rec. 23 Apr. 1803.   his mark
Proved by ROBERT SHURLEY, 20 Apr. 1803.
Warrant of appraisement to JOHN KING, JR., MOSES KING, AMOS MILDREDGE(?)
CLEMT. AULDREDGE, ISAAC GIBSON. Rec. 23 Apr. 1803.

Pp 145-147: MARGRET ROCHELL applied for admn. on estate of JAMES ROCHELL
            28 Aug. 1802.
Bond: MARGRET ROCHELL, admx., GEORGE EVANS, WILLIAM MC GEE, security,
20 Sept. 1802, penalty $4000.

Pp 147-149: Admn. bond on estate of GEORGE LEESTER: SARAH LEESTER,
            admx., JAMES MOOTY, security, penalty 200 pds, 7 July 1800.
SARAH LEESTER & JAMES MOOTY applied for admn. 23 Nov. 1799. Rec. 3
April 1803.

Pp 149-150: Warrant of appraisement on estate of SAMUEL GLADNEY, as
            directed by AGNESS GLADNEY and RICHARD GLADNEY, exrs.,
7 Apr. 1800 to WM. MC CRORY, JAS. PHILLIPS, HUGH MILLING, ALEX. ROSS-
BOROUGH. 7 June 1800, sworn: EDWARD MARTIN, J.P.: DAVID CAMMACK, SR.,
ALEXANDER ROSSBOROUGH, WM. MC CRORY.

Pp 150-154: SARAH BOWIN applied for admn. on estate of WILLIAM BOWIN,
            6 May 1803. Admn. bond: SARAH BOWIN, admx., AARON DUKES,
SAMUEL DOHERTY, securities, penalty $1000, 7 June 1803. Warrant of
appraisement to SAM PERRY, LEWIS PERRY, SAML. DOHERTY, AARON HUGHS,
THEOPHILAS WILLSON. Sworn 27 June 1803 bef. ELIJAH JONES, J.P.: :SAMUEL
PERRY, SAML. DAUGHERTY, AARON DUKES. Order of sale dated 7 June 1803.

Pp 154-156: Warrant of appraisement on estate of JOHN LIGHTNER, 10
            Dec. 1802, to BARTHOLOMEW TURNIPSEED, BENJN. SCOTT, STEPHEN
LEE, GEORGE LIGHTNER, JAS. ELLIOTT. 4 Jan. 1803: sworn bef. SAMUEL
ALSTON: BENJAMIN SCOTT, BARTHOLOMEW TURNIPSEED, JAMES ELLIOTT. Order
of sale dated 10 Dec. 1803.

Pp 156-157: Will of PETER ARSKIN, dec'd...being weak of body...all
            to be equally divided bet. my wife and children, and for
child yet unborn...exrs: JAMES LINN, WILLIAM EDGER, DAVID HOMES...17
June 1801.
Wit: WILLIAM MC CRORY   PETER (P) ARSKIN (LS)
     JAMES MC MILLENE   his mark
Rec. 7 June 1803. Proved by WILLIAM MC CRORY & JAMES MC MULLIN (no
date).

Pp 158-161: Letters testamentary on estate of SAMUEL MOBLEY, whose
            will ws proved 24 Jan. 1803, dated 27 Jan. 1803. Warrant
of appraisement directed by MARY MOBLEY and SAMUEL MOBLEY, exrs., 24
Jan. 1803, to THOS. SHANNON, EDWARD MOBLEY, DAVID SHANNON, THOS. KILL-
PATRICK, GEORGE HALLSEL. Sworn bef. STAFFORD CURREY, 9 Feb. 1803: THOS.
SHANNON, GEORGE HALLSEL, DAVID SHANNON.
Will of SAMUEL MOBLEY, SR. of the Dist. of Fairfield, being weak of
body...to wife MARY MOBLEY, all my estate for the time of her life,
and after her death to my son EDWARD MOBLEY, one shilling sterling
with what I have already given him; to my daughter ELISABETH MANSELL,
negro boy Bob and then to be left to her daughter SUKEY; to my son

117

Cont'd from page 117:
SAMUEL MOBLEY, one shilling sterling; to my son BIGGERS MOBLEY, one
shilling sterling; to my son JOHN MOBLEY, one negro boy Daniel, with
100 acres I now live on; rest of tract to daughter DARKEY; wife MARY
and son SAMUEL, exrs. 21 Dec. 1802
Wit: JAMES KIRKPATRICK
     RODRICK MC DONELL   SAMUEL (X) MOBLEY (LS)
     JOHN WOODS   his mark
Proved by JAMES KILLpatrick, 24 Jan. 1803 bef. JNO. BUCHANAN.

Pp 162-165: On 14 Jan. 1803, will of NORTHROP MAPLE, late of Fairfield
            Dist., was proved, letters testamentary.
Will of NORTHROP MARPLE of Fairfield Dist., being weak in body...wife
ANN MARPLE sole extx. and to have all estate...9 Aug. 1800.
Wit: GEORGE REDDISH
     AARON A. THORP   NORTHROP MARPLE (LS)
     PHIL PEARSON. Rec. 7 June 1803.
Proved by THORP, 13 Jan. 1802. Warrant of appraisement to JAS. DAVIS,
JOS. DURHAM, ALEXR. KINCAID, JAS. MC MORRIES, JOSEPH MC MORRIES, 14
Jan. 1803.

Pp 165-169: Letters testamentary on estate of HENRY WALKER, will proved
            27 Jan. 1803.
Will of HENRY WALKER, 15 Dec. 1802, being sick of body...to my stepson
WM. DAY, all that tract of land known by BOB NEILs; my stepbrother
JAMES WALKER have $30, and his two sisters NANCY and BETSY have $10
each; to my wife MARY WALKER, all the rest of my personal and real
property; my two daughters have the rest equally divided betwixt them.
Wit: MARY WALKER, extx.
     ELIZABETH (X) HENDRICK   HENRY WALKER (Seal)
     ELIAS HENDRIX
Proved 27 Jan. 1803, by ELIZABETH & ELIAS HENDRIX.
Warrant of appraisement to JAS. ALSTON, JNO. BROWN, NICHOLAS WARICK,
WM. KIRKLAND, JACOB TURNIPSEED. 1 Feb. 1803, sworn bef. S. ALSTON,
J.P.: WM. KIRKLAND, JOHN BROOM, JAMES ALSTON.

Pp 169-174: Letters testamentary on estate of ELIZABETH AUSTIN, whose
            will was proved 5 Feb. 1803, dated 5 Feb. 1803.
Will of ELIZABETH AUSTIN of Fairfield Dist., being weak of body...to
my son JOHN AUSTIN, one half of a plantation originally granted to
WILLIAM NEWMAN, 200 acres on a branch of Little River and Austin Mill
Creek, or should the heirs of sd NEWMAN refuse to make titles, one
half of whatever may be recovered; to ROBERT FERRELL and my grand daughter ELIZABETH FERRELL, the other half of sd plantation; to my daughter
EDY and WILLIAM HATCHER, 150 acres on Mill branch or Mill Creek, being
the plantation I now live on; to my daughter EDY and WILLIAM HATCHER,
one horse I now have, etc.; to my grandson BARTHOLOMEW AUSTIN BUSBY,
one Rifle gun; to the heirs of my son WILLIAM AUSTIN, one shilling;
to the heirs of my son DRURY AUSTIN, one shilling; to the heirs of
my son DAVIS AUSTIN, one shilling; to the heirs of my son BARTHOLOMEW
AUSTIN, one shilling; to my daughter MARY NEWMAN, one shilling; to
my two sons JAMES and JOSEPH AUSTIN, one shilling each; son JOHN AUSTIN
and daughter EDY, exrs. 4 Aug. 1802.
Wit: ALEXANDER HERVEY
     WM. MC MORRIES   ELIZABETH (E) AUSTIN (LS)
     ELIZABETH MC MORRIES
Proved by WM. MC MORRIES and ALEXANDER HARVEY, 5 Feb. 1803. Rec. 7
June 1803.
Warrant of appraisement 7 Feb. 1803, to WM. MC MORRIES, ALEX. HARVEY,
JAS. TABB, JOHN SLOAN, JAS. NEALLEY. 23 Feb. 1803 sworn bef. JAS. MC
MORRIES, J.P.: JOHN SLOAN, JAMES NEILLEY, ALEXANDER HERVEY.

Pp 174-179: Letters testamentary on estate of HENRY WOODWARD, proved
            13 Jana. 1803, dated 13 Jan. 1803.
Will of HENRY WOODWARD of the Dist. of Fairfield, planter...to my wife
ELIZABETH WOODWARD, one tract of land, 250 acres, whereon I now live,
also four negroes, Jack, Milley, Saney and Jesse, and negroe girl Rose,
and after her death to be equally divided bet. my brother THOMAS, dec'd,
three children to wit THOMAS WOODWARD, ELIZABETH WOODWARD and JOSEPH

118

Cont'd from page 118:
H. WOODWARD; to my wife all household furniture and horses, etc. ...my
brother JOSEPH WOODWARD and WILLIAM MC MORRIES, SR, exrs...25 Nov.
1802.
Wit: WM. WOODWARD   HENRY WOODWARD (Seal)
     JOHN MAY
     JOSEPH GIBSON, SR.
Proved by JOHN MAY 13 Jan. 1803. Rec. 7 June 1803.
Warrant of appraisement to AUGUSTIN WILLIAMS, HENRY SIGHTS, STEPHEN
GIBSON, JACOB GIBSON, DAVID ANDREWS, 17 Jan. 1803. Order for sale dated
13 Jan. 1803.

Pp 180-183: DAVID THOMSON of Fairfield Dist., applied for admn. on
            estate of ELIZABETH THOMPSON, 7 Dec. 1802. Admn. bond:
DAVID THOMPSON, admn., JOHN BROWN and THOMAS MC KINSTRY, securities,
penalty $2000, 14 Dec. 1802. Warrant of appraisement to JOHN BROWN,
JAS. BROWN, JAS. ALSTON, THOS. MC KINSTRY and JAS. AULLICH(?). 29 Dec.
1802, sworn bef. SAML. ALSTON, J.P.: JAMES BROWN, SR., THOMAS MC KIN-
STREY and JAMES ALSTON. Order of sale dated 14 Dec. 1802. Rec. 7 June
1803.

Page 184:   SIBE BRYANT and BENONE ROBERTSON applied for admn. on the
             estate of WILLIAM BRYANT, dec'd., 22 Nov. 1802.

Pp 184-185: Order of sale on the estate of JAMES ROCHELL, dec'd., 20
            Sept. 1802.

Pp 185-187: HENRY MC CAULLEY applied for admn. on the estate of PATRICK
            LOGAN, dec'd., 23 Nov. 1802. Warrant of appraisement to
WM. KINCAID, ALEXR. KINCAID, WM. BELL, JR., WM. BELL & JNO. BELL. Sworn
bef. JAS MC MORRIES, J.P., 2 Nov. 1803. Order of sale dated 29 Nov.
1803.

Pp 188-191: DAVID MARPLE applied for admn. on estate of JOHN MARPLE,
            12 Jan. 1803.
            24 Jan. 1803, letters of admn. issued. Admn. bond: DAVID
MARPLE, admr., JAMES DAVIS, JOSHUA DURHAM and EDWARD MARPLE, securities
penalty $6000, 24 Jan. 1803. Warrant of appraisement to JAS. DAVIS,
JOSHUA DURHAM, ALEX. KINCAID, JAS. MC MORRIES, JOSEPH MC MORRIES.

Pp 192-197: MARY WILLINGHAM applied for admn. on estate of JOHN WILLING-
            HAM, 3 Jan. 1803. Letters of admn. issued 30 Jan. 1803.
Bond: MARY WILLINGHAM, admx., RALPH JONES, DAVID MC GRAW, security;
penalty $5000, 30 Jan. 1803. Warrant of appraisement to DAVID ANDREWS,
JNO. BELL, EDW. ANDREWS, ROBT. RABB, JAS. CRAIG, 10 Jan. 1803. Sworn
bef. S. ALSTON, JAS. MC MORRIES, J.P., 5 Mar. 1803: ROBERT RABB, DAVID
ANDREWS, EDWARD ANDREWS, JAMES CRAIG. Order of sale dated 3 Jan. 1803.
Dedimus to JAMES MC MORRIES, Esq., to administer the oath of admn.
to MARY WILLINGHAM, 10 Jan. 1803.

Pp 198-201: Letters of admn. on estate of SAMUEL PARKS who died intes-
            tate, granted to BARBARA PARKS, 9 Mar. 1803. Admn. bond:
BARBARA PARKS, admx., JAMES DAVIS & HUGH MILLING, securities; penalty
$2000 9 Mar. 1803. Warrant of appraisement to ROBT. RABB, JNO. BELL,
JAS. CRAIG, ROBT. BOYD, WM. DELANEY, 26 Jan. 1803. Rec. 14 June 1803.

Pp 201-204: Last will and testament of JOHN THOMPSON of Fairfield Dist.,
            being very weak in body...unto JAMES THOMPSON my oldest
son, 150 acres in Lawrence (sic) Dist. adj. SAML. BISHOP and SYE PRATA;
the other part of the tract of land whereon I lived, to WILLIAM THOMPSON
my youngest son; to ELIZABETH THOMPSON my daughter 15 pds; to ALEXANDER
THOMPSON my son, the bay mare colt valued at $60; to JOHN THOMPSON
my grandson 5 pds sterling; ALEXANDER THOMPSON, SAMUEL CLARK, exrs.
(no date).
Wit: SIMEON CAMERON (X)   JOHN THOMPSON (his mark)
     WM. MC CREARY
     IZABEL CAMERON
Proved by SIMEON CAMERON, 15 Jan. 1803. Rec. 18 June 1803.
Letters testamentary issued.

Pp 204-207: Will of GEORGE BELL of Fairfield County...to my daughter
AGNES FLOYD's child, the lower end of plantation on which
I now live ; to my daughter MARY, his part if he does not live to the
age of 21, and negroes Harey and Fanny, with $100, cattle, etc.; to
my daughter JANE, one negro Jacob and $100; to daughter ELIZABETH my
plantation on S side of Broad River, 100 acres and $100; to my two
grand children SARAH and MARY BELL, $200 each; negro Bob is to remain
on the plantation...to WILLIAM FEEMSTER, $22; SAMUEL FEEMSTER & ADAM
COOPER, and SAMUEL JOHNSON, exrs....30 Sept. 1802.
Wit: DAVID JOHNSON
    BENJN. (X) KNIGHT   GEORGE BELL (LS)
    WM. FEEMSTER. Proved by BENJAMIN KNIGHT, 8 July 1803, bef. JOHN
BUCHANAN, J.C.P. Letters of testamentary issued.

Pp 207-209: MARY POWELL applied for letters of admn. on the estate
of WILLIAM POWELL, 5 July 1803.
Admn. bond: MARY POWELL, admx., JOHN FINLEY, THOMAS POWELL, securities,
penalty $3000, 5 July 1803.

Pp 210-212: REBECCA MARTIN, MARY MARTIN, MARGRET MARTIN & MARTHA MC
CLURE MARTIN, orphans within the age of 21 years, have
chosen EDWARD MARTIN as their guardian, 13 July 1803. Bond for $1000,
DAVID MARTIN and JAMES BECKET, security.

Pp 212-214: MOSES AIRS, JR. applied for letters of admn. on the estate
of ELISHA MC FADDIN, 26 Dec. 1801. Bond: MOSES AIRS, JR.,
admn., JACOB AIRS and JAS. HOWARD, security, penalty $3000, 12 Jan.
1802.

Pp 214-216: SAMUEL NESBETT and THOMAS NESBETT applied for letters of
admn. on estate of SAMUEL NESBETT, dec'd., 3 Oct. 1801.
Bond: SAMUEL NESBETT, THOS. NESBETT, admrs., SAMUEL ARNOT, JOHN MARSHALL
as securities, penalty $3000, 18 Oct. 1801.

Pp 217-219: AGNESS HAYNAN and ROBT. HAYNAN applied for letters of admn.
on estate of JAMES HAYNAN, 5 Dec. 1801. Admn. bond: AGNESS
HAYNAN, ROBERT HAYNAN, admrs., JOHN HARVEY, SAMUEL WELLDON, security,
penalty $2000, 14 Dec. 1801.

Pp 219-221: ARCHIBALD PAUL and JANE PAUL applied for letters of admn.
on estate of JOHN PAUL, dec'd., 20 Oct. 1801. Admn. bond:
ARCHIBALD PAUL, JANE PAUL, admrs., JAMES RABB, DAVID BOYD, security,
penalty $3000, 3 Nov. 1801.

Pp 221-223: FANNY OATES and JESSE HAVIS applied for letters of admn.
on the estate of SAMUEL OATES, 16 Mar. 1802. Admn. bond:
FANNY OATES, JESSE HAVIS, admrs., JAS. BARKLEY & QUINTIN HOY, security,
22 May 1802, penalty $3000.

Pp 223-225: Admn. bond on estate of MAJOR DILLARD: RICHARD WINN, FRANCES
DILLARD, admrs., BENJAMIN HART, sec., penalty $2000, 8
Jan. 1802.

Pp 225-227: ELIZABETH MC MEEKIN applied for letters of admn. on estate
of JAMES MC MEEKIN, 16 Nov. 1801. Admn. bond: ELIZABETH
MC MEEKIN, admx., WILLIAM WATTS, JAMES DAVISON, security, penalty $2000,
14 Dec. 1801.

Pp 227-230: JEREMIAH BURGE, died intestate, letters of admn. granted
to REUBEN HARRISON, 16 Nov. 1801. Bond: REUBEN HARRISON,
admr., BENJAMIN HART and CHARLES PICKETT, security, penalty $4000,
16 Nov. 1801.

Pp 231-232: EDWARD LOWERY applied for letters of admn. on estate of
NICHOLAS THOMPSON, 26 Aug. 1802. Bond: JESSE HAVIS, EDWARD
LOWREY, DIXSY WARD, penalty $1000, 13 Sept. 1802.

Pp 232-234: SARAH HAMILTON applied for letters of admn. on estate of
JAMES HAMILTON, 10 Aug. 1803. Bond: SARAH HAMILTON, admx.,

Cont'd from page 120:
JAMES STEWART and JAMES KENEDY, JR., security, penalty $4000, 10 Sept.
180_2_.

Pp 234-236: Warrant of appraisement on estate of WILLIAM POWELL, dec'd.,
            directed by MARY POWELL, admx., to ISHAM DANSBY, JOHN FINLEY,
JACOB FREE, WM. MC GRAW. Dated 18 July 1803. Sworn 10 Aug. 1803 bef.
JAMES MC MORRIES: JACOB FREE, ISAAC DANSBY, THOMAS POWELL. Order of
sale also.

Pp 236-238: Warrant of appraisement on estate of GEORGE BELL, directed
            by SAMUEL FEEMSTER, ADAM COOPER & SAMUEL JOHNSON, exrs.,
to STEPHEN DUMAS, HUNDLY MC ASHAN, ROBT. MOREMAN, CHARLES SPIVA, WIL-
LIAM CHAPMAN, 8 July 1803. Sworn 27 July 1803 by DANL. MABREY, J.P.:
WILLIAM CHAPMAN, ROBERT MOREMAN, STEPHEN DUMAS, HUNDLY MC ASHAN. Rec.
28 Aug. 1803.

Pp 238-240: Will of JOHN MILLER, 2 Sept. 1802, Fairfield Dist., being
            weak in body...to wife the management and benefit of the
plantation, tolls, etc., for the benefit of her and my children, until
such time as she may marry, or any of the children be of age, and then
to divide the property...wife JINNEY, extx. and ROBERT FOSTER, exr.,
with my son GEORGE as soon as he is of sufficient age...
Wit: MARY (X) FOSTER
     JAMES BARBER   JOHN MILLER (LS)
Proved by JAMES BARBER. Letters testamentary issued 23 Aug. 1803. Rec.
30 Aug. 1803.

Pp 241-244: WILLIAM NETTERVILL applied for admn. on estate of JOHN
            HARRIS, who died intestate, dated 22 Aug. 1803. Bond: WIL-
LIAM NETTERVILL, JESSE NETTERVILL, penalty $1000, 22 Aug. 1803. Rec.
2 Sept. 1803.

Pp 244-247: HANNAH ROBERTSON applied for letters of admn. on estate
            of REBECCA MUSE, 5 Aug. 1803. Admn. bond: HANNAH ROBERT-
SON, admx., BENONI ROBERTSON, security, penalty $2000, 15 Aug. 1803.
Letters of admn. also.

Pp 247-249: JOSEPH DANIEL MUSE an orphan within the age of 21 years
            has chosen HANNAH ROBERTSON for his guardian, 15 Aug. 1803.
Bond with BENONI ROBERTSON, security, penalty $500.

Pp 249-253: MARY LOWHAN applied for letters of admn. on estate of SAM-
            UEL LOWHAN, 1 Aug. 1803. Letters of admn. issued 16 Aug.
1803. Admn. bond: MARY LOWHAN, admx., THEOPHILAS WILSON, MOSES WOOTON,
security, penalty $2000, 16 Aug. 1803. Warrant of appraisement directed
to ALEXR. CRUMPTON, HUGH RANDOLPH, JOHN KELLEY, RICHARD CAMPBELL, CHAS.
MC DONALD, 16 Aug. 1803. Order of sale also.

Pp 253-257: CHARITY BUZBY applied for letters of admn. on estate of
            NATHANIEL BUZBY, dec'd., 20 Aug. 1803. Letters of admn.
issued 4 Oct. 1803. Admn. bond: CHARITY BUZBY, admx., WILLIAM CATO
and JOSHUA DURHAM, security, penalty $1000, 4 Oct. 1803. Warrant of
appraisement directed to WILLIAM WOODWARD, JOSHUA DURHAM, GOSPER BYER-
LY, THOMAS NELSON, WILLIAM CATO, 4 Oct. 1803. Order of sale also. Appraisers sworn bef. JAMES MC MORRIES, J.P.: JOSHUA DURHAM, THOMAS NELSON
& GOSPER BYERLY, 21 Oct. 1803.

Pp 257-259: Warrant of appraisement on estate of JOHN MILLER, dec'd.,
            as directed by JEAN MILLER and ROBERT FOSTER, exrs., to
ALEXR. MC KAIN, JAMES MC KAIN, HUGH WHITE, ALEXANDER MC DOWELL, GEORGE
ARNETT, 23 Aug. 1803. 19 Sept. 1803 sworn bef. JAMES BEATY, J.P.: HUGH
WHITE, GEORGE ARNETT, ALEXANDER MC DOWELL. Order of sale.

Pp 259-263: RICHARD WINN applied for admn. on estate of JOHN CLARK,
            20 Aug. 1803. Admn. bond: RICHARD WINN, admr., DAVID CAMP-
BELL, security, penalty $5000, 24 Sept. 1803. Letters of admn. 24 Sept.
1803. Warrant of appraisement directed to _____(no name here),
24 Sept. 1803.

Pp 262-266: WILLIAM PANNELL applied for letters of admn. on estate
of THOMAS PANNELL, 3 Oct. 1803. Admn. bond: WILLIAM PANNELL,
admr., JOHN WHITEHEAD, BENJAMIN PANNELL, securities, penalty $2000,
17 Oct. 1803. Letters of admn. issued 17 Oct. 1803. Warrant of appraisement to THOMAS GUINN, WILLIAM JOINER, WILLIAM CARTER, JOHN WILLARD,
ANDW. PANNELL. Sworn bef. DAVID COLEMAN, J.P. 3 Nov. 1803: JOHN WHITTED,
THOMAS GWINN, WILLIAM JOINER. Order of sale.

Pp 267-269: Admn. bond on estate of PETER ARSKINS. PETER HAMILTON and
JEAN HAMILTON, admrs., with the will annexed. SAMUEL DODDS,
security, penalty $500, 5 Oct. 1803. Letters of admn. issued 5 Oct.
1801. Warrant of appraisement to JAMES MC MULLIN, GEORGE ARNETT, DANL.
COLLINS, JAMES MERSHALL, JOHN MC DOWELL, 5 Oct. 1803. Rec. 10 Dec.
1803. WILLIAM ADGER, DAVID HOLMES and JAMES LINN, exrs. of the L. W.
& T. of PETER ARKINS, relinquish every power to PETER HAMILTON and
wife JEAN as nighest of kin, 5 Oct. 1803.

Pp 269-273: GARDNER FOARD applied for letters of admn. on estate of
SAMPSON BRUCE, 7 Oct. 1803. Admn. bond: GARDNER FOARD,
admr., THOMAS MUSE, security, penalty $1000, 21 Oct. 1803. Letters
of admn. issued 25 Oct. 1803. Warrant of appraisement to THOS. MUSE,
WM. ARMSTRONG, THOMAS SAINT, JOHN LONG, JR., and JAMES SEAL, SR., 21
Oct. 1803. Sworn 21 Oct. 1803 bef. NICHOLAS PEAY, J.P.: THOS. MUSE,
WM. ARMSTRONG, THOS. SAINT. Order of sale dated 21 Oct. 1803.

Pp 273-277: ANNE FREEMAN applied for admn. on estate of JAMES FREEMAN,
JR., 4 Oct. 1803. Admn. bond: ANNE FREEMAN, admx., JOHN
CHAPPEL, THOMAS REEVES, security, penalty $2000, 27 Oct. 1803. Letters
of admn. issued 7 Oct. 1803. Warrant of appraisement to BENJ. SCOTT,
BARTHW. TURNIPSEED, HENRY SIGHTS, GEORGE LIGHTNER, JOSEPH GIBSON, 27
Oct. 1803. Sworn bef. JAMES ALSTON, J.P.: BARTHOLOMEW TURNIPSEED, GEORGE
LIGHTNER, HENRY SIGHTS & BENJAMIN SCOTT, 10 Nov. 1803. Return from
the appraisers: There are no goods, no chattels of the deceased shown
us by ANNE FREEMAN, but she informed us that he held a right in the
hands of Rev. FREEMAN, admr. of HARRIS FREEMAN, SR., dec'd., to a division of the estate of his father, $556.30 2 mills, 10 Nov. 1803.

END OF FAIRFIELD WILL BOOK 4

GREENVILLE COUNTY, S. C. - DEED BOOK A

Pp 1-3:   23 Dec. 1786 PATTY PRINCE of 96 Dist., Spartanburgh Co.,
S. C. to THOMAS FARRAR of Dist., Co., and State afsd. for
250 pds sterling, 550 acres lying in Dist. 96, W of Road on Waters
of Golden Grove, E of the Road on Waters of Reedy River, butting NW
by MOODY's land, NW by WILLIAM MILLER's land, SW by RICE's land, SE
by vacant land. Orig. survey granted to PATTY PRINCE by Gov. Wm. Moultrie, 1 May 1786 and rec'd in Secretary's office in Grant Book III
page 460. Wit: ROBERT PRINCE, THOMAS P. CARNES. Signed: PATTY PRINCE.
Rec. 21 May 1787.

Pp 3-8:   23 Nov. 1786 HANCE BLACK of Greenville Co., S. C., planter,
to HENRY LINDERMAN, weaver of sd Co. and State for 20 pds
sterling, 200 acres lying in Greenville Co. on the Pigeon Roost Branch
of Waters of Reedy River, above the ancient boundary line NE by MATHEW
ARMSTRONG, his land and all other sides vacant when surveyed and rec'd
in Sec. Office in Book LLLL page 93. Wit: JAMES WEST, JACOB BLACK,
THOMAS JONES. Signed: HANCE BLACK & ANN (X) BLACK. Rec. 22 May 1787.

Pp 8-10:   24 Oct. 1785 JAMES MC WILLIAMS to HENRY LINDERMAN, lease,
planter of Laurence Co., S. C. to HENRY LINDERMAN, Greenville, S. C., weaver, for 50 pds, 140 acres being part of 640 acre
tract granted 21 Jan. 1785 by Gov. Guerard, rec'd in Sec. Office, Book
GGGG page 312, lying on Reedy River above the ancient boundary line,
bounding NE of Reedy River, S by a part of sd tract laid out to MATHEW
ARMSTRONG. Wit: GENJ. RAINEY, BITHIAH RAINEY, SARAH RAINEY. Signed:

Cont'd from page 122:
JAMES (X) MC WILLIAMS & ROSANNA MC WILLIAMS. Rec. 22 May 1787.

Pp 10-12:   25 Oct. 1786 Lease, KENNER HUDSON, planter, Greenville
             Co., S.C. to HANCE BLACK, planter, Greenville Co., S. C.
for 20 pds sterling, 200 acres, granted 15 Oct.1784 by Gov. Benj. Guerard, in Greenville Co., S. C., N of Saluda River situate lying and
being on waters of Reedy River; S side bounding on all sides vacant
land. Wit: JAMES WEST, DAVID BLACK, ROBERT (X) GILLIAND. Signed: KENNER
(X) HUDSON & SARY (X) HUDSON. Rec. 22 May 1787.

Pp 12-15:   Lease & Release, 8 Dec. 1785 JAMES MC WILLIAMS, planter,
             Laurence Co., S.C. to LAZARUS SUMMERLIN, planter of afsd.
Co. and State for 28 pds sterling, 200 acres, being part of tract of
640 acres granted 21 Jan. 1785 by Gov. Benj. Guerard, rec'd in Sec.
Office Book CCCC page 312, lying on Reedy River above ancient boundary
line bounding N on JOHN BROWN's land; SE on HUGH RORK's land; W on
MATHEW ARMSTRONG's land. ROSANAH MC WILLIAMS, wife of sd JAMES MC WIL-
LIAMS, in testimony of her consent to the sale set her hand and seal.
Wit: NATHANIEL AUSTIN, HUGH RORK. Signed: JAMES (X) MC WILLIAMS. Rec.
22 May 1787.

Pp 15-18:   Lease & Release, 20 Dec. 1786 BENJAMIN RICE, planter, Green-
             ville Co., S.C. to EDMUND EDWARDS, planter of sd Co. and
State, for 20 shillings sterling 73 acres being part of tract of 400
acres granted by Gov. Guerard, rec'd in Sec. Office 15 Oct. 1784, lying
in Greenville Co. on waters of Golden Grove Creek a branch of Saluda
River above the ancient boundary line bounding SW by JAMES SEABORN's
land and NATHANIEL PENDLETON's land. Wit: HENRY MACHEN, JOHN EDWARDS,
ROBERT RAMSEY. Signed: BENJAMIN RICE. Rec. 22 May 1787.

Pp 18-21:   Lease & Release, 8 Feb. 1787 ROBERT GILLILAND, planter,
             Greenville Co., S.C. to WILLIAM POKE, planter of afsd Co.
and State for 10 pds sterling, 271 acres lying in Greenville Co. on
S branches of Golden Grove Creek, waters of Saluda River, W of the
ancient boundary, being whole tract 271 acres granted by Gov. Wm. Moultrie 5 Dec. 1785 and rec'd in Sec. Office Grant Book GGGG page 280.
Wit: THOMAS LEWIS, AMBROSA BLACKBURN. Signed: ROBERT (X) (his mark)
GILLILAND. Rec. 20 Aug. 1787.

Pp 22-25:   Lease & Release, 17 Aug. 1787 DRURY SMITH in Laurence Co.,
             96 Dist. to JAMES MC CANE, a Minor for 1 shilling and six
pence, 166 acres lying both sides of the Reedy fork of River bounded
NW on ABNER BISHOP's land, SE by MICHAEL PURTLE's, granted by Gov.
Moultrie, 8 Oct. 1785. Wit: ELLIOTT (E) his mark SMITH, DANIEL FORD.
Signed: DRURY (his mark) SMITH, SARAH (her mark) SMITH. Rec. 20 Aug.
1787.

Pp 25-28:   Lease & Release, 15 Aug. 1787 ABNER BISHOP of 96 Dist.,
             Greenville Co., S.C. to DANIEL FORD of same place for 10
shillings sterling, 165 acres being part of land containing 330 acres,
granted by Gov. Wm. Moultrie 5 June 1785, situate lying and on both
sides Reedy fork of Reedy River, 96 Dist., Greenville Co. bounded by
MARY BURNS' land and Col. WINN's land. Wit: JESSE (B his mark) FORD,
ELLIOTT (E his mark) SMITH. Signed: ABNER (his mark) BISHOP & MARY
(M her mark) BISHOP. Rec. 20 Aug. 1787.

Pp 28-31:   Lease & Release, 17 Aug. 1787 DRURY SMITH, planter, 96
             Dist., S.C. to JESSE FORD of same place, 1 shilling six
pence, 100 acres situate in 96 Dist. on Reedy fork of Reedy River bounded on DRURY SMITH's land on S side, all other sides vacant. Orig. grant
bearing date 5 June 1786. Wit: ELLIOTT (E his mark) SMITH, DANIEL FORD.
Signed: DRURY (his mark) SMITH & SARAH (her mark) SMITH. Rec. 20 Aug.
1787.

Pp 31-34:   Lease & Release, 8 Feb. 1787 JOHN ALEXANDER, planter, Green-
             ville Co., S.C. to JAMES HIETT of same place for 30 pds
sterling, 194 acres lying on Zachariahs fork of Reedy fork of Reedy
River W of ancient boundarys, it being part of tract granted by Gov.

123

Cont'd from page 123:
Moultrie 4 July 1785, rec'd in Sec. Office in Grant Book DDDD page
407. Wit: WILLIAM (W his mark) TISDALE, ABSALOM (X) CREEMER. Signed:
JOHN ALEXANDER. Rec. 20 Aug. 1787.

Pp 35-38:   Lease & Release, 14 Aug. 1787 MARY BURNES of 96 Dist.,
            Greenville Co., S.C. to ELLIOTT SMITH of same place for
10 shillings sterling, 100 acres, situate on Cedar shoal Creek a branch
of Reedy River, 96 Dist., Greenville Co., S.C., bounded NE by DANIEL
FORD's land, SE by RICHARD RICHARDS' land and to SE land (315 acres)
granted to MARY BURNES by Gov. Moultrie 3 Oct. 1785. Wit: DANIEL FORD,
JESSE (B his mark) FORD. Signed: MARY (her mark) BURNES. Rec. 20 Aug.
1787.

Pp 38-41:   Lease & Release, 21 July 1786 REUBEN BARRETT, Greenville
            Co., S.C. to BENJAMIN ELLIS, of same place for 100 pds
sterling, 350 acres lying and being in 96 Dist., Greenville Co., S.C.,
W of ancient boundary lying both sides of Packs Creek, SW by ARCHIBALD
DILLS land, all other vacant. Orig. grant 3 Oct. 1785 by Gov. Benj.
Guerard. Wit: JAMES COPELAND, JOHN BATES. Signed. REUBEN BARRETT &
HANNAH BARRETT. Rec. 20 Aug. 1787.

Pp 41-42:   Deed of Conveyance. 19 Jan. 1787 TIMOTHY TONEY, Greenville
            Co., S.C., 96 Dist. to DANIEL BUSH of same place, for 500
pds, 250 acres orig. granted by Gov. Benj. Guerard 15 Oct. 1784. Wit:
JOSEPH WHITNER, LEMUEL T. ALSTON. Signed: TIMOTHY (T) TONEY. Rec. 20
Aug. 1787.

Pp 42-44:   Deed of Conveyance. 19 Jan. 1787 ISOM CLAYTON, Greenville
            Co., S.C. to DANIEL BUSH of same place for 200 pds, 180
acres. Orig. granted 5 Dec. 1785 by Gov. Moultrie, situate Greenville
Co., on N side of Saluda River. Wit: LEMUEL ALSTON, JOSEPH WHITNER.
Signed: ISHAM (his mark) CLAYTON. Rec. 20 Aug. 1787.

Pp 44-45:   Deed of Conveyance. 1 Feb. 1787 JAMES HENDERSON of S. C.,
            96 Dist. and Spartanburgh Co., to DANIEL BUSH of sd state
and Dist. Greenville Co., for 20 pds, 63 acres being part of 178 acre
tract of land granted to JAMES HENDERSON 21 Jan. 1785 by Gov. Benj.
Guerard, situate on branches of Saluda River, beginning on DANIEL BUSH's
line. Wit: ISOM (C) CLAYTON, WILLIAM BROWN. Signed: JAMES HENDERSON.
Rec. 20 Aug. 1787.

Pp 45-47:   Deed of Conveyance. 8 June 1787 JOHN WATSON, Greenville
            Co., S.C. to GEORGE UNDERWOOD of same place for 30 pds,
300 acres orig. granted by Gov. Wm. Moultrie 3 Apr. 1787, rec'd in
Sec. Office in Grant Book TTTT page 324, land situate in 96 Dist.,
W of the Old Indian line on branch of Maple Crek of Reedy River, bounded
on all sides by vacant land. Wit: THOMAS UNDERWOOD, HENRY CARRON, JOHN
HAMMET. Signed: JOHN WATSON & ELIZABETH WATSON. ELIZABETH WATSON, wife
of JOHN WATSON, relinquished her Right of Dower. Rec. 20 Aug. 1787.

Pp 47-50:   Lease & Release. 29 Mar. 1787 HANNAH YOUNG, 96 Dist., S.C.
            to ABRAHAM BRADLEY, planter of same place for 60 pds sterl-
ing, 400 acres situate in 96 Dist. above ancient boundary line on Armstrongs Creek, branch of Saluda River, bounding SE by MRS. ANN ARM-
STRONG's land and on all other sides vacant land at the time of orig.
survey made and granted by Gov. Benj. Guerard 21 Jan. 1785. Wit: GEORGE
SALMON, GEORGE (H his mark) TUBB, JAMES CONN. Signed: HANNAH YOUNG.
Rec. 20 Aug. 1787.

Pp 50-53:   Lease & Release. 18 Aug. 1787 CHARLES SULLIVANT of 96 Dist.,
            Greenville Co., S.C. to JOSEPH DUNKLIN of same place for
50 pds, 240 acres, situate on Carils Branch of fork of Horse Creek,
waters of Reedy River, 96 Dist., bounded on NE by JESS CHANDLER's land
and vacant on all other sides when surveyed and granted by Gov. Moultrie
1 May 1786. Wit: WILLIAM TISDEL, JOHN HUGHES, JOHN STORY. Signed: CHAR-
LES SULLIVANT. Rec. 20 Aug. 1787.

Pp 53-54:   Deed of Conveyance. 16 July 1787 REUBEN STRINGER, Greenville
            Co., S.C. to RICHARD BRIANT of same place for 100 pds sterl.

Cont'd from page 124:
200 acres lying on N side of Saluda River, bounded on the southward by sd River and all other sides vacant. Granted 21 Jan. 1785 and rec'd in Sec. Office in Book CCCC page 399. Wit: AMBROSE BLACKBURN, THOMPSON DICKERSON, JAMES (X) BRIANT. Signed: REUBEN STRINGER & ELIZABETH (X) STRINGER. Rec. 20 Aug. 1787.

Pp 54-55:   Deed of Conveyance. 18 Nov. 1786 MAJOR PASSONS & ELIZABETH his wife, of 96 Dist., Greenville Co., S.C. to JOHN THOMAS, SR. of same place for 60 pds, 200 acres being part of 640 acres granted by Gov. Benj. Guerard, lying on S fork of Tyger River above the old boundary line in sd Dist. on the lower end of sd tract and on the S side of sd River. Wit: WILLIAM NELSON, DANIEL (D his mark) MC MILLIAN, WILLIAM (X) TWITY. Signed: MAJOR PASSONS & ELIZABETH (*) PASSONS. Rec. 20 Aug. 1787.

Pp 55-56:   Deed of Conveyance. 21 Mar. 1787 HULET SWEVELENT, Greenville Co., S.C. to WILLIAM STORY of same place for 100 pds, 180 acres situate in afsd. Co. on Horse Creek, branch of Reedy River. Orig. granted 1 May 1786, rec'd in Sec. Office Grant Book KKKK page 492. Wit: JOHN STORY, ANDREW JONES, JOSEPH DUNKLIN. Signed: HEWLET SWILLIVANT. Rec. 20 Aug. 1787.

Page 57:   Power of Attorney. 5 Oct. 1785. I, HUGH LEWIS about to remove from S. C. to Cumberland River, N. C. appoint my trusty and well beloved friend BAYLIS EARLE of Spartanburgh Co., S. C. my true and lawful Attorney for me, and in my name to make over, convey and confirm unto ESLY HUNT of State and Co. last mentioned 100 acres situate on Saluda River, Spartanburgh Co., about a mile below the mouth of the N fork of sd River surveyed for me by WILLIAM BENSON, Esq. Wit: JOHN GOWEN, CHARLES LITTLETON. Signed: HUGH LEWIS. Rec. 20 Aug. 1787.

Pp 57-61:   Lease & Release. 23 Feb. 1787 JOHN CHILDRESS, Greenville Co., S. C. to GEORGE SALMON of same place for 50 pds sterl. 200 acres granted by Gov. Moultrie 5 Dec. 1785, rec'd in Sec. Office, lying in afsd. Co. on the N side of Tyger River, bounded S on land laid out for JEREMIAH DUTTON, NW on land laid out for MOSES WOOD, on NE on land unknown; on E land laid out for JOHN RUSSELL. Wit: JEREMIAH (J his mark) DUTTON, JOHN STILES, JOHN CHILDRESS. Signed: JOHN (his mark) CHILDRESS, JR. Rec. 20 Aug. 1787.

Pp 61-64:   Lease & Release. 23 Feb. 1787 JEREMIAH DUTTON & SARAH, his wife, of Grenville Co., S. C. to GEORGE SALMON of same place for 25 pds sterling, 220 acres being part of a 420 acre tract granted 3 Oct. 1785 by Gov. Wm. Moultrie and rec'd in Sec. Office, lying in afsd Co. on both sides of Tyger River; bounded W on part of same tract; S on land laid out to JOHN CHILDRESS, SR., E on land laid out to MAJOR PARSON: N on land laid out to JOHN CHILDRESS, JR. Wit: JOHN STILES, JOHN (his mark) CHILDRESS (Jr. or Sr.?), JOHN CHILDRESS. Signed: JEREMIAH (J his mark) DUTTON, SARAH (X) DUTTON. Rec. 20 Aug. 1787.

Pp 65-68:   Lease & Release. 23 Feb. 1787 JEREMIAH DUTTON & SARAH, his wife, Greenville Co., S. C. to JOHN CHILDRESS, hatter, of same place for 50 pds sterling, 200 acres situated in afsd Co. on S side of Tygar River being part of 420 acres granted to JEREMIAH DUTTON 3 Oct. 1785 beginning on wash on the Beaver dam creek of Tygar River running E with original line; then NE to Tygar River; W land laid out to sd JOHN CHILDRESS: W to JOHN STILES; N to MOSES WOOD. Wit: GEORGE SALMON, JOHN STILES, JOHN CHILDRESS. Signed: JEREMIAH (his mark) DUTTON & SARAH (+ her mark) DUTTON. Rec. 20 Aug. 1787.

Pp 69-70:   Deed of Conveyance. 13 Mar. 1787 CRAWFORD GOODWIN, Greenville Co., S. C. to JOHN BIRDSONG of same place for 100 pds sterling, 150 acres situate and lying onN side of Saluda River; bounded S by sd River and on W land laid out to AMBROSE BLACKBURN; N to ROBERT MAXWELL's land; SE by sd BLACKBURN's land granted 21 Jan. 1785 and rec'd in Sec. Office Grant Book CCCC page 123. Wit: AMB. BLACK-

Cont'd from page 125:
BURN, JOHN MAXWELL, BARTON SCROGIN. Signed: <u>CRAFFORD GOODEN</u>. Rec. 20
Aug. 1787. (In Deed name written GOODWIN, signed GOODEN.)

Pp 70-71:   Deed of Conveyance. 20 Feb. 1787 WILLIAM WOOD & ELIZABETH
             WOOD, his wife, of S. C. to JOHN TYLE of S. C. for 300
pds, 300 acres situate W of Mile Creek Branch of the Golden Grove being
part of 640 acres tract orig. granted to WILLIAM WOOD 16 July 1784
and rec'd Grant Book AAAA page 561. Land joins JAMES SOUTHERN's on
SE. Wit: T. LEWIS, CHARLES SULLEVANT, JAMES SOUTHERN. Signed: WILLIAM
WOOD & ELIZABETH WOOD. Rec. 20 Aug. 1787.

Pp 72-73:   Deed of Conveyance. 20 Aug. 1786 ROBERT PRINCE & JEAN,
             his wife of Greenville Co., S. C. to JOHN NICOLL, SR. of
same place for 50 pds, 210 acres that was granted to ROBERT PR<u>IC</u>E by
Gov. Wm. Moultrie, situate in 96 Dist., above ancient boundary line
on the branches of Tygar River. Wit: JAMES NICOLL, JOHN FORD, AMB.
BLACKBURN. Signed: ROBERT PRINCE. Rec. 20 Aug. 1787.

Pp 73-76:   Lease & Release. 22 Feb. 1787 WILLIAM BARTON & ELIZABETH,
             his wife of Spartanburgh Co., S. C. to THOMAS BARTON of
Greenville Co., S. C. for 50 pds sterling, 338 acres lying and being
in Greenville Co., S. C. on both sides of Bartons Fork of South Tygar
River; SW by EPHRIAM REESE. Wit: THOMAS MGREW (MC GREW?), WILLIAM AND-
ERSON, JOHN CAMPBELL. Signed: WILLIAM BARTON & ELIZABETH (X) BARTON.
Rec. 20 Aug. 1787.

Pp 77-80:   Lease & Release. 5 Mar. 1787 EPHRAIM REESE & NANCY REESE,
             his wife of Spartanburgh Co., S. C. to THOMAS BARTON of
Greenville Co., S. C. for 60 pds sterling, 300 acres lying in Green-
ville Co. on the waters of the N fork of South Tygar River bounding
SW by ROBERT GOODLETT's land. (Land granted to EPHRAIM REESE 15 Oct.
1784 by Gov. Benj. Guerard and rec'd in Sec. Office.) Wit: THOMAS M.
GREW, WILLIAM ANDERSON, ELI SAVAGE. Signed: EPHRAIM REESE & NANCY (X)
REESE. Rec. 20 Aug. 1787.

Pp 80-83:   Lease & Release. 18 July 1786 WILLIAM BENSON of Spartan-
             burgh Co., S. C. to JOSEPH BENSON of same place for 100
pds sterling, 167 acres situate in 96 Dist. above ancient boundary
line on N side of Saluda River & Beaverdam Creek, sd tract of land
granted to WILLIAM BENSON by Gov. Benj. Guerard 21 Jan. 1785. Wit:
THOMAS FARRAR, THOMAS B. WYATT. Signed: WILLIAM BENSON & NELLEY BENSON.
Rec. 20 Aug. 1787.

Pp 83-86:   Lease & Release. 12 June 1786 WILLIAM BENSON of Spartan-
             burgh Co., S. C. to JOHN EVANS of State of Virginia and
Caroline County for 100 pds sterling, 202 acres situate in 96 Dist.
above ancient boundary line on the South fork of the three forks of
Tygar River, bounding SE to ROBERT GOODLETT's land, all other sides
vacant at time of orig. survey 15 Oct. 1784 granted by Gov. Benj. Guerard. Wit: THOMAS FARRAR, THOMAS B. WYATT. Signed: WILLIAM BENSON, NELLEY
BENSON. Rec. 20 Aug. 1787.

Pp 86-89:   Lease & Release. 18 July 1786 JOSEPH BENSON of Saint Marys
             Parish in Caroline County and State of Virginia to WILLIAM
BENSON of Spartanburgh Co., S. C. for 200 pds sterling, 320 acres sit-
uate in 96 Dist. above ancient boundary line on the Golden Grove Crk.
of Saluda River, it being 1/2 the tract of 640 acres granted by Gov.
Guerard 16 July 1784. Wit: THOMAS B. WYATT, THOMAS FARRAR. Signed:
JOSEPH BENSON. rec. 20 Aug. 1787.

Pp 89-92:   Lease & Release. 13 Apr. 1787 JOHN PORTMAN, JR. & MARGARET
             PORTMAN, his wife of 96 Dist., S. C. to PHILIP SHEREL,
Greenville Co., S. C. for 60 pds, 190 acres being part of tract of
490 acres granted by Gov. Moultrie 5 June 1786, being in Co. of Greenville, S. C. on S side of South Tygar River and on both sides of Mush
Creek of sd River, bounded NW on JOHN NICOLL's land, N on HENRY PRINCE's
land, NE on Tygar River and land laid out for TOBIAS PUTTIT, S on part
of same tract. Wit: GEORGE SALMON, WILLIAM GRANT, JOHN NICOLL. Signed:

Cont'd from page 126:
JOHN (P his mark) PORTMAN, JR. and MARGARET (T her mark) PORTMAN. Rec.
20 Aug. 1787.

Pp 93-95:   Lease & Release. 21 Feb. 1787 ELI HUNT & NANCY HUNT, his
             wife, of 96 Dist., S. C., planter, GAYLIE EARLE, planter
of same place for 60 pds sterling, 250 acres, orig. granted by Gov.
Moultrie 4 Apr. 1785, situate 96 Dist. above ancient boundary line
on Mush Creek, bounding on all sides vacant land. Wit: G. SALMON, W.
H. LACY. Signed: ELI HUNT & NANCY HUNT. Rec. 20 Aug. 1787.

Pp 96-98:   Lease & Release 21 Feb. 1787 HUGH LEWIS of 96 Dist., S.
             C., planter to ESLI HUNT of same place for 60 pds sterling,
135 acres 96 Dist., above the ancient boundary line on the N side Saluda River bounding S on Saluda River and all other sides vacant at the
time of orig. survey granted by Gov. Moultrie 7 Nov. 1785. Wit: G.
SALMON, W. H. LACY. Signed: BAYLIS EARLE for HUGH LEWIS & his wife
ELIZABETH LEWIS by virtue of a Power of Attorney herewith recorded.
Rec. 20 Aug. 1787.

Page 99:   Deed of Conveyance. 21 Aug. 1787 ROBERT PRINCE, Greenville
             Co., S. C. to Rev. JOSEPH LOGAN of same place for 50 pds,
206 acres orig. granted by Gov. Moultrie 3 Apr. 1786, situate in Greenville Co., S. C. on the branches of Harpers Creek and branches of Foun-
tains Creek, waters of Saluda River. Wit: RYARS LOGAN, CHARLES BENSON.
Signed: ROBERT PRINCE. Rec. 20 Aug. 1787. (Note conveyance date day
later than that recorded).

Pp 100-101: Deed of Conveyance. 27 Jan. 1787 THOMAS LEWIS, Greenville
             Co., S. C. to THOMAS CAMP of same place for 45 pds sterling,
172 acres orig. granted by Gov. Guerard 21 Jan. 1785 rec'd in Sec.
Office in Grant Book AAAA page 278, situate W side of Reedy River bounded SE by old Indian line, SW on PETER RAGSDAILE's land, W by JOEL CHAND-
LER's. Wit: STEPHEN MARCHBANKS, BRADFORD CAMP. Signed: T. LEWIS. Rec.
20 Aug. 1787. Money receipt of 45 pounds sterling witnessed by JOHN
LEWIS.

Pp 102-103: Deed of Conveyance. 4 Nov. 1786 WILLIAM HEADEN to ANTHONY
             BEVERLY, both of 96 Dist., S. C. for 25 pds sterling, 100
acres being tract granted by Gov. Moultrie 5 Dec. 1785, situate in
96 Dist., Greenville Co., S. C. and Little Fork of Reedy River. Wit:
THOMAS JENKINS, MACAJAH JENKINS. Signed: WILLIAM HEADEN. Rec. 20 Aug.
1787.

Pp 103-107: Lease & Release. 17 July 1787 WILLIAM WOOD, Greenville
             Co., S. C. to JAMES SOUTHERN of same place for 200 pds
sterling, 340 acres (being part of tract granted 13 July 1784 rec'd
in Sec. Office Grant Book AAAA page 561) situate E side of Mile Creek
waters of Golden Grove branch of Saluda River in afsd. Co. Wit: T.
LEWIS, JOHN LEWIS. Signed: WILLIAM WOOD. Rec. 20 Aug. 1787.
THOMAS JENKINS and AMB. BLACKBURN, Justices of Court examined ELIZABETH
WOOD, wife of WILLIAM WOOD, who could not travel to court, and she
relinquished her right of Dower to a certain tract of land which her
sd husband, WILLIAM WOOD conveyed to JAMES SOUTHERN & JOHN TYLE. 26
July 1807. THOMAS LEWIS, Clk. of sd Court.

Pp 108-111: Lease & Release. 20 Apr. 1786 PETER BROOKS, 96 Dist., S.
             C., planter to NATHANIEL PERRY & BENJAMIN PERRY of same
place, merchants, for 45 pds sterling, 289 acres situated in 96 Dist.,
W of ancient boundary line on the branches of Enoree River bounding
SE on JOHN ROSS land and ISAAC MORGAN land; SE on MICHAEL JOHNSTON's
land, SW on land surveyed by THOMAS LEWIS and all other sides vacant.
Orig. survey granted PETER BROOKS by Gov. W. Moultrie 7 Nov. 1785.
Wit: PETER (+ his mark) BROOKS, MARY (X) BROOKS, NATHANIEL & BENJAMIN
PERRY. Rec. 20 Aug. 1787. Memorandum - 15 Apr. 1786 H. M. WOOD, Esq.,
one of the Justices assigned to keep the Peace in the County of Spar-
tanburgh came and appeared bef. EDMUND LEAGUE and gave oath of signing
of sd deed and was so recorded.

Pp 111-112: Deed of Conveyance. 8 Oct. 1786 AARON KEMP, Greenville

Cont'd from page 127:
              Co., S. C. to MOSES KEMP of same place for 50 pds sterling,
100 acres situate in Co. and State afsd on both sides of Bushey Creek
of the waters of the Enoree S side. Land granted AARON KEMP 5 Dec.
1784. Wit: ELI NORMAN, PLEASANT HUDSON. Signed: AARON KEMP. Rec. 21
Aug. 1787.

Pp 111-113: Deed of Conveyance. 29 Oct. 1786 HENRY HAYES of Spartan-
              burgh Co., S. C. to BENJAMIN WHORTON of state aafsd, for
50 pds sterling, 202 acres situate on both sides of Brushey Creek joining ELI NORMAN lands to the W side where sd WHORTON now lives. Wit:
EDWARD BALLANGER, ISAAC MORGAN, MOSES (X) KEMP. Signed: HENRY HAYS.
Rec. 21 Aug. 1787.

Pp 113-114: Deed of Conveyance. 4 Nov. 1786 PAUL ABNER of Greenville
              Co., S. C. to AARON KEMP of same place for 50 pds sterling,
100 acres situate on both sides of Brushey Creek waters of Enoree River.
Wit: :BENJ. WHORTON, ELI NORMAN, JOSEPH DUNAGAN. Signed: PAUL ABNER.
Rec. 21 Aug. 1787.

Pp 114-115: Deed of Conveyance. 8 Jan. 1787 BAYLIS EARLE, Esq.,   96
              Dist., S. C., Spartanburgh Co., to JOSEPH WHITNER of 96
Dist., S. C., Greenville Co., for 35 pds, 32 acres being part of tract
of 500 acres granted BAYLIS EARLE by Gov. Benj. Guerard (no date) lying
on both sides Reedy River above old boundary line in sds Dist. Wit:
EPHRAIM REES, JOHN EARLE, JR., BAYLIS EARLE, JR. Signed: BAYLIS EARLE.
Rec. 21 Aug. 1787.

Pp 116-117: Deed of Conveyance. 27 Nov. 1786 RICHARD GOODE & REBEKAH,
              his wife of Surry Co., N. C. to WILLIAM NELSON, Greenville
Co., S. C., for 45 pds sterling, 100 acres orig. granted by Gov. Guerard
21 Jan. 1785, situate in 96 Dist. on the W side Golden Grove waters
of Saluda River. Wit: ISAAC (E his mark) WILSON, JAMES MOOR. Signed:
RICHARD GOODE & REBEKAH GOODE. Rec. 20 Aug. 1787.

Pp 117-121: Lease & Release. 14 Sept. 1787 WILLIAM SMITH & MOURNING,
              his wife of Spartanburgh Co., S. C., planter, to JOHN FOSTER
of Greenville Co., S. C., planter, for 200 pds sterling, 350 acres
granted to sd SMITH by Gov. Guerard 15 Oct. 1784, situate on main Saluda
River in Greenville Co., S. C. Wit: GEORGE SINGLETON FOSTER, RICHARD
THOMPSON, JOHN CROW FOSTER. Signed: WILLIAM SMITH & MOURNING (X) SMITH.
Rec. 19 Nov. 1787.

Pp 121-125: Lease & Release. 3 Oct. 1787 ISAAC BROWN & MOLLY, his wife,
              Greenville Co., S. C. to ELIAS EARLE of same place for
250 pds sterling, 500 acres orig. granted by Gov. Guerard 21 Jan. 1785,
situate in the fork between Rivers Saluda and Checkaroa in Greenville
Co., S. C. Wit: HENRY M. WOOD, JOHN GRIGSBY. Signed: ISAAC BROWN &
MOLLY BROWN. Rec. 19 Nov. 1787.

Pp 125-128: Lease & Release. 14 Sept. 1786 DENNIS DUFF, Greenville
              Co., S. C., planter to SAMUEL EARLE, planter of same place
for 30 pds sterling, 124 acres orig. a grant by Gov. Moultrie 5 June
1786, situate on N side of South Fork Saluda River, Greenville Co.,
land joining JOSEPH HUGHES' line, JOHN EARLE's line. Wit: JOHN FORD,
JAMES MC ELHENNEY. Signed: DENNIS DUFF. Rec. 19 Nov. 1787.

Pp 128-130: Deed of Conveyance. 17 Aug. 1787 GEORGE SALMON, Greenville
              Co., S. C. to JAMES PATTERSON of same place, for 5 pds
sterling, 115 acres orig. granted GEORGE SALMON by Gov. Wm. Moultrie
4 Sept. 1786, situate in 96 Dist., on S side of Saluda River. Wit:
SAMUEL EARLE, JOHN FRENCH. Signed: G. SALMON. Rec. 19 Nov. 1787.

Pp 130-133: Lease & Release. 14 Nov. 1787 JESSE CHANDLER, 96 Dist.,
              Greenville Co., farmer to SHADRACK CHANDLER of same place
for 20 pds sterling, 229 acres part of a tract of land containing 640
acres granted by Gov. Wm. Moultrie 21 Jan. 1785, situate on Horse Creek
waters of Reedy River, vacant on all sides at time of survey. Wit:
WILLIAM FARISS, SIMON LINDLY. Signed: JESSE (J his mark) CHANDLER.

Pp 133-135: Lease & Release. 20 Sept. 1787 SIMCOCK CANNON, 96 Dist.,
        Greenville Co., S. C. to RUSSELL CANNON of same place for
45 pds sterling, 105 acres being tract of land granted by Gov. Moultrie
4 Sept. 1786, situate in 96 Dist. on both sides of a branch of the
Middle fork of Saluda River butting NE on DENNIS DUFF's land and on
all other sides vacant at time of orig. survey. No witnesses recorded.
Signed: SIMCOCK CANNON. Rec. 19 Nov. 1787.

Pp 135-137: Deed of Conveyance. 14 Nov. 1787 JOHN EARLE, JR. of Spartan-
        burgh Co.,S.C. to SAMUEL EARLE of Greenville Co., S. C.
for 100 pds sterling, 200 acres granted to him by Gov. Guerard beginning on a Buck Eye on the middle fork Saluda River. Wit: JOHN GRIGSBY,
JR., ELIAS EARLE. Signed: JOHN EARLE, JR. Rec. 19 Nov. 1787.

Pp 137-139: Lease & Release. 11 Oct. 1787 ROBERT DUNCAN & JECHONIAS
        LANGSTON, 96 Dist., S. C. to HARDEN CAMP for 45 pds sterling
244 acres, orig. granted 1 Aug. 1785 to sd DUNCAN's patent and sd LANG-
STON's patent bearing date 3 Apr. 1786, situate above ancient boundary
line in 96 Dist. on DUNCAN's branch of Reedy River bounding on sd ROBERT
DUMAS and JAMES MC ROY and JAS. NEALEY's land. Wit: W. H. LACY, JAMES
(E his mark) MC ROY. Signed: ROBERT DUNCAN & JECHONIAS LANGSTON. Rec.
19 Nov. 1787.

Pp 139-141: Deed of Conveyance. 28 Feb. 1787 JOHN WATKINS & JANE his
        wife, Greenville Co., S. C. to DRUERY MORRIS for 100 pds
sterling, 300 acres orig. granted 4 Sept. 1786 by Gov. Moultrie, situate
lying & being in 96 Dist. on Mountain Creek waters of Saluda River.
Wit: CHARLES ESTES, JOHN REID. Signed: JOHN (+ his mark) WATKINS, JANE
(X) WATKINS. Rec. 19 Nov. 1787.

Pp 141-142: Deed of Conveyance. 23 Feb. 1787 MOSES SHELBY & ELIZABETH,
        his wife of 96 Dist., S. C. to JOHN NICOLL of afsd Dist.
& State, Greenville Co., for 100 pds current money of the State, 289
acres, orig. granted 7 Nov. 1785 by Gov. Moultrie, lying on Mush Creek
in 96 Dist., bounded NW on JAMES NICOLL land, SW on JOHN NICOLL land,
all other sides vacant at time of survey. Wit: JAMES NICOLL, ANN NICOLL.
Signed: MOSES SHELBY & ELIZABETH SHELBY. Rec. 20 Nov. 1787.

Pp 142-144: Lease & Release. 17 Oct. 1785 THOMAS DOEG, weaver, 96 Dist.,
        S. C. to WILLIAM ROSS of afsd State & Dist. (late of Scot-
land), merchant, for 13 pds sterling, 100 acres, being part of a tract
of 206 acres granted sd THOMAS DOEG by Patent 21 Jan. 1785, situate
on a small branch of Mush Creek a branch of Tygar River bounded on
NE land surveyed for JOHN NICOLL, JR., SW on the other 106 acres now
sold by sd DOEG to a certain MICHAEL MILLER; the other side on vacant
land. Wit: JOHN NICOLL, JAMES NICOLL. Signed: THOMAS DOEG. Rec. 20
Nov. 1787.

Pp 145-146: Deed of Conveyance. 13 Oct. 1787 JOHN LUCAS & SARAH, his
        wife, Greenville Co., S. C. to JOHN CHILDRESS of same place
for 100 pds sterling, 100 acres being part of a tract containing 200
acres orig. granted 21 Jan. 1785 by Gov. Benj. Guerard, situate in
96 Dist., on both sides Wildcat Branch of S. Tygar River, bounded on
all sides vacant at time of survey. Wit: ROBERT NELSON, JORDON HOLCOM,
JONATHAN HOLCOM. Signed: JOHN LUCAS & SARAH (X) LUCAS. Rec. 20 Nov.
1787.

Pp 146-149: Lease & Release. 21 June 1787 GEORGE JEFFERAS, Craven Co.,
        S. C. to JOHN STANFORD, JR. Greenville Co., S. C. for 100
pds sterling, 200 acres orig. granted 30 Aug. 1784 by Gov. Guerard,
situate in 96 Dist.; W ancient boundary line on Beaverdam of Toogaloo
River. Wit: ABRAHAM SHATEEN, WILLIAM STANFORD, DANIEL DUTTON. Signed:
GEORGE (his mark) JEFFERAS. Rec. 20 Nov. 1787.

Pp 149-151: Deed of Conveyance. 24 Oct. 1787 JOHN CLAYTON to JONAS
        DAWSON, Greenville Co., S. C. for 40 pds sterling, 100
acres orig. granted by letters Patent 6 June 1785, situate Greenville
Co., bounding near Morgansford of Middle Tygar River above the old
Indian line. Wit: JAMES STEVENSON, JOHN MOTLOW, JAMES MC ELHENNEY.

Cont'd from page 129:
Signed: JOHN CLAYTON, SARAY (X) CLAYTON. Rec. 20 Nov. 1787.

Pp 151-152: Deed of Conveyance. 22 Aug. 1787 CHARLES TANKERSLEY, Green-
          ville Co. to ROBERT PRINCE of same place for 30 pds sterling
146 acres, granted 5 June 1786 by Gov. Moultrie, situate Greenville
Co., S. C., 96 Dist. on N fork of Enoree River. Wit: JESSE CARTER,
WILLIAM TUBB. Signed: CHARLES (T his mark) TANKERSLY. Rec. 20 Nov.
1787.

Pp 152-154: Deed of Conveyance. 17 Nov. 1787 ROBERT PRINCE, Greenville
          Co. to WILLIAM TUBB for 50pds sterling, 270 acres orig.
granted 2 Jan. 1786 by Gov. Wm. Moultrie, situate in Greenville Co.,
96 Dist. on Moores Branch of Enoree including Moores improvement; N
of ridge of Mountains surveyed for WILLIAM FRENCH 11 Apr. 1785. Wit:
THOMAS LEWIS, JOHN LEWIS. Signed: ROBERT PRINCE. Rec. 20 Nov. 1787.

Page 154:   Bill of Sale. 29 Mar. 1787 ROBERT MONTGOMERY of Burke Co.,
          N. C., planter to ROBERT PRINCE for 60 guineas, a sorrel
stallion 6 years old neither darked or branded, with a small black
spot on the mountain shoulder. Wit: WILLIAM TUBB, OBADIAH HOOPER, THOMAS
AIKENS. Signed: ROBERT MONTGOMERY. Rec. 20 Nov. 1787.

Pp 154-156: Deed of Conveyance. 17 May 1787 JOHN MOTLOW, Greenville
          Co., S.C. to ROBERT LAUGHRIDGE of same place for 60 pds,
400 acres granted 21 Jan. 1785 by Gov. Guerard, rec'd in Sec. Office
Book CCCC page 479, situate in 96 Dist., West of old Indian Boundary
line on both sides of Reedy River bounding N by THOMAS BRANDON's land,
S and SW vacant land, SE by HEZEKIAH RECE's land, all other sides vacant.
Wit: L. T. ALSTON, _____ BLASINGAME, H. M. WOOD. Signed: JOHN MOTLOW.
Rec. 20 Nov. 1787.

Pp 156-158: Deed of Conveyance. 15 Nov. 1787 ROBERT PRINCE, Greenville
          Co. to MARTIN ADAMS of State of Virginia for 25 pds. sterl-
ing, 144 acres granted 6 Feb. 1786 by Gov. Moultrie, situate in Greenville Co., 96 Dist., on branches of Beaverdam Creek, surveyed for STACY
HOOPER 19 July 1784 and granted to aafsd ROBERT PRINCE. Wit: T. LEWIS,
JOHN LEWIS. Signed: ROBERT PRINCE. Rec. 21 Nov. 1787.

Pp 158-161: Lease & Release. 21 Nov. 1787 THOMAS LEWIS, Greenville
          Co., S.C., Clerk, to WILLIAM FERGERSON of same place,
planter, for 20 pds sterling, 100 acres, being part of a tract orig.
granted to PATRICK LAFFERTY situate in afsd. Co. & State on Mountain
Creek of Saludy River by grant of 5 Sept. 1785, rec'd in Sec. Office
Grant Book FFFF page 41 and conveyed from sd PATRICK LAFFERTY to sd
THOMAS LEWIS by deed of lease & release 20 Nov. (No witnesses recorded).
Signed: THOMAS LEWIS. Rec. 21 Nov. 1787.

Pp 161-164: Lease & Release. 10 Oct. 1787 TOBIAS POTEET of Greenville
          Co., 96 Dist., S.C. to JOHN SANFORD of same place for 125
pds. sterling, 200 acres, orig. grant 25 Jan. 1785 by Gov. Benj. Guer-
arad, situate on both sides of South Tygar River of Greenville Co.,
96 Dist. Wit: ROBERT NELSON, WILLIAM WHITE, JAMES WALES. Signed: TOBIAS
(I his mark) POTEET.

Pp 165-168: Lease & Release. 15 Jan. 1788 JOHN WAKEFIELD, Greenville
          Co., S.C., planter, to THOMAS MAYFIELD of same place, for
50 pds lawful money of S.C., 200 acres, granted 15 Apr. 1785 by Gov.
Wm. Moultrie, situate on Enoree River lying on the old Boundary. Wit:
WILLIAM WILLSON, HENRY WOOD, ROBERT (X) WOOD. Signed: JOHN WAKEFIELD.
Rec. 18 Feb. 1788.

Pp 168-169: Deed of Conveyance. 18 Mar. 1787 JOHN COLLINS, Spartanburgh
          Co., 96 Dist., S.C. to HUGH WARRAN, SR., Greenville Co.,
96 Dist., S.C. for 100 pds current money, 205 acres, orig. granted
21 Jan. 1785 by Gov. Guerard, situate on both sides of South Tygar
River. Wit: HUGH WARRAN, JR., RICHARD COLLINS. Signed: JOHN COLLINS.
Rec. 18 Feb. 1788.

Pp 169-173: Lease & Release. 1 Feb. 1788 JOHN DENNING of 96 Dist.,

Cont'd from page 130:
Greenville Co., S.C. to CLABOURN SWILLIVANT of same place, sum of 30 pds current money of S.C., 100 acres on Horse Creek, waters of Reedy River, joining WILLIAM RAY and ARTHUR MEEKS, where CLABOURN SWILLIVANT now lives. Part of a tract of 640 acres granted to JOHN DENNING 1 Jan. 1787. Wit: HEWLET SWILLIVANT, STEPHEN SWILLIVANT, MOSES SWILLIVANT. Signed: JOHN DINING (Release signed DINNING). Rec. 18 Feb. 1788.

Pp 173-174: Bill of Sale. 16 Feb. 1788. DAVID MOORE of Greenville Co., to JOHN THOMAS, JR. of same. One sorrel gelding, 2 cows, 6 calves, all household stuff and implements in my possession lent by the sd JOHN THOMAS, JR., for 30 pds. Wit: DANIEL MC MILLION, THOMAS BENNETT. Signed: DAVID (X) MOORE. Rec. 18 Feb. 1788.

Pp 174-175: Deed of Conveyance. 27 June 1787 ISAAC MORGAN of Greenville Co. to PAUL ABNER of same, for 60 pds sterling, 400 acres lying on both sides of Brushy Creek. Wit: BENJ. WHORTEN, SOLOMAN KEMP, SAMUEL (X) BANKS. Signed: ISAAC MORGAN. Rec. 18 Feb. 1788.

Pp 175-179: Lease & Release. 2 Jan. 1788. JOSEPH HUGHS of Union Co., S.C., planter, to SAMUEL EARLE of Greenville Co. for 700 pds sterling, 640 acres N side of the South fork of Saluda River, bounded NE by HENRY WOLF's corner. Land granted to JOSEPH HUGHES 15 Oct. 1784. Wit: ELIAS EARLE, BENJAMIN BARTON, JOHN GRIGSBY. Rec. 18 Feb. 1788.

Pp 179-181: 18 Nov. 1787. JOHN CLAYTON & SARAH, his wife to THOMAS SPRIGGS, both of Greenville Co., for 60 pds sterling, 125 acres East side of the North fork of Saluda River, above the old Indian Boundary, beginning where sd SPRIGGS now lives, to JOHN FORD's line, being part of a tract of 250 acres granted to JOHN CLAYTON 15 Oct. 1784. Wit: WILLIAM LYNCH, JAMES STEVENSON. Signed: JOHN CLAYTON, SARAH (X) CLAYTON. Rec. 18 Feb. 1788.

Pp 181-184: Lease & Release. 18 Feb. 1788 JESSE CHANDLER of Greenville Co., farmer, to ANDREW JONES, of same, for 30 pds sterling, 202 acres on Horse Creek, waters of Reedy river, bounded by SHADRACH CHANDLER's corner. Part of a tract of 640 acres granted to sd CHANDLER 25 Jan. 1785. (No witnesses). Signed: JESSE (his mark) CHANDLER. Rec. 18 Feb. 1788.

Pp 184-186: 18 Feb. 1788. JAMES WRIGHT of Spartanburgh Co., planter, to THOMAS BRASURE of Greenville Co., planter, for 110 pds S.C. money, 500 acres on Cripple Creek, waters of Reedy River, orig. granted to JAMES WRIGHT 21 Jan. 1785. Wit: KERNER (X) HUTSON, THOMAS BRASHER. Signed: JAMES WRIGHT, ANN (X) WRIGHT. Rec. 18 Feb. 1788.

Pp 186-187: 14 Dec. 1788. JOHN JUSTICE of Greenville Co., planter, to THOMAS BARTON, gent., of same county for 20 pds sterling, 100 acres, the SE end of a tract of 200 acres granted to JOHN JUSTICE 4 Sept. 1786, bet. the N and middle forks of the Tyger River, beg. at WILLIAM BARTON's corner. Wit: JESSE LARSON, HUGH (H) WARREN, ISAAC (X) CASEY. Signed: JOHN (X) JUSTICE. Rec. 18 Feb. 1788.

Pp 187-191: Lease & Release. 18 Feb. 1788. WILLIAM TISDELL of Greenville Co. to AUSTIN SIMS of same place, for 50 pds sterling current money of S.C., 200 acres on S side of Reedy Fork and Zacharies Creek, waters of Reedy River, bounded by JONATHAN DOWNS, WILLIAM TISDELL and STEPHEN FORD at the time of surveying, where sd SIMS now resides, including the Grist Mill. Part of a tract of 400 acres granted to WILLIAM TISDELL 4 Sept. 1786 by Gov. Moultrie. Wit: HEWLET SWILLIVANT, JOSEPH DUNKLIN, FREDERIC FARMER. Signed: WILLIAM (X) TISDELL. Rec. 18 Feb. 1788.

Pp 191-193: 16 Feb. 1787. JOHN CLAYTON and SARAH, his wife to JOHN FORD, both of Greenville Co. for 60 pds sterling, 125 acres on the North fork of the Saluda River above the Old Indian Boundary, bordering JOHN MC ELLOW's line. Part of a tract of 250 acres granted

Cont'd from page 131:
to JOHN CLAYTON 15 Oct. 1784 by Gov. Guerard. Wit: JOHN (X) DUGLAS, MARY (X) CLAYTON. Signed: JOHN CLAYTON, SARAH (X) CLAYTON. Rec. 18 Feb. 1788.

Pp 193-196: Lease & Release. 17 Aug. 1787. DAVID BROWN of 96 Dist.
to DAVID LOVELL of same, for 25 pds sterling, 208 acres on the branches of Reedy River and Armstrong Creek, bounded SW by Col. JAMES HAWTHORNE, SE by JOSEPH BOX, other sides vacant when granted to DAVID BROWN 4 Dec. 1786 by Gov. Moultrie. Wit: WM. H. LACEY, WILLIAM LOVEL, DAVID (X) NORRIS. Signed: DAVID BROWN, SARAH (X) BROWN, DAVID (X) LOVELL. Rec. 18 Feb. 1788.

Pp 196-197: ___ Jan. 1788, HUGH MOORE of Abbeville Co., S.C. to ROBERT
PRINCE of Greenville Co., for 40 pds sterling, 202 acres bordering PRINCE's line, part of a tract containing 340 acres surveyed by JAMES SEABORN 4 May 1785, and granted to HUGH MOORE 5 June 1786 by Gov. Moultrie. Wit: ENOCH BENSON, JOHN TUBB, WM. TUBB. Signed: H. MOORE. Rec. 18 Feb. 1788.

Pp 197-201: Lease & Release. 17 May 1787. JOHN TUBB of Greenville Co.
to GEORGE TUBB of same, for 20 pds, 200 acres on South side of Enoree River, part of a tract of 385 acres granted to JOHN TUBB 5 June 1786 by Gov. Moultrie. Wit: JAMES TUBB, GEORGE (X) TUBB, WM. KITCHEN. Signed: JOHN TUBB. Rec. 18 Feb. 1788.

Pp 201-205: Lease & Release. 18 Feb. 1788. THOMAS LEWIS of Greenville
Co. (Clerk of sd county), to WILLIAM HIMMELWRIGHT of Philadelphia, Penn., cooper, for 700 pds sterling, 640 acres on Horse Creek a branch of Reedy River, also 149 acres on Horse Creek bounded NW by the above mentioned tract of land, SE by the Old Indian Boundary line, all other sides vacant at time of orig. survey. The 640 acres granted to LEWIS 16 July 1784, recorded Grant Book LLL p 65. The 149 acres granted to LEWIS 21 Jan. 1785, recorded Grant Book AAAA p 279. Wit: JESSE CARTER, VINCENT LEWIS, JOHN LEWIS. Signed: THOMAS LEWIS . Rec. 18 Feb. 1788.

Pp 205-207: Mortgage. 18 Feb. 1788. WILLIAM HIMMELWRIGHT, cooper, of
Philadelphia, Penn., to THOMAS LEWIS, Clerk of County Court, payment of 500 pds on 25 Dec. 1788 for the land in the above deed. Wit: JESSE CARTER, VINCENT LEWIS, JOHN LEWIS. Signed: WILLIAM HIMMELWRIGHT. Rec. 18 Feb. 1788.

Pp 208-211: Lease & Release. 27 Sept. 1786. ROBERT PRINCE of Greenville
Co. to JOHN BATES of same, 50 pds current money of S.C., 200 acres on head branch of Enoree and a branch of Saluda River, bounded SE on BLACKWELL land. Granted to ROBERT PRINCE 4 July 1785. Wit: JOHN TUBB, JAMES DOUGHERTY. Signed: ROBERT PRINCE. Rec. 18 Feb. 1788.

Pp 211-213: 12 Oct. 1787. ROBERT HENDERSON of Spartanburgh Co., S.C.
to JOHN CLAYTON of Greenville Co., 60 pds sterling, 250 acres on a small creek of the north fork of the Saluda River, called Wiers Creek or Patterson's Branch, granted to ROBERT HENDERSON 21 Jan. 1785. Wit: PHILIP (S) SHEREL, LEVI CASEY. Signed: ROBERT HENDERSON. Rec. 18 Feb. 1788.

Pp 213-214: Power of Attorney. 20 Sept. 1787. I, JOHN COMBS of Wash-
ington Co., N. C., appoint my trusty and well beloved friend JOHN MOLIN of Greenville Co., S.C., Gent., my true and lawful attorney, and in my name to sell, etc., a tract of land lying on Beaverdam Creek on the W side of the N fork of Saluda River, joining the lands of WILLIAM GUDLOW, sd land being surveyed by JAMES SEABORN for sd JOHN COMBS, containing 400 acres. Wit: ALLEN GOWEN, JOHN GOWEN. Signed: JOHN COMBS. Rec. 20 Feb. 1788.

Pp 214-215: 1 July 1787. JAMES HENDERSON of Spartanburgh Co., to ISHAM
CLAYTON of Greenville Co., for 30 pds current money, 108 acres granted to JAMES HENDERSON by Gov. Guerard 21 Jan. 1785, on the branches of Saluda River. Wit: DANIEL BUSH, WILLIAM BROWN. Signed:

Cont'd from page 132:
JAMES HENDERSONN. Rec. 20 Feb. 1788.

Pp 215-216: Power of Attorney. 20 Feb. 1788. HUGH LEWIS, being about
to remove from the State of South Carolina, to Cumberland
River of North Carolina, appoint my trusty and well beloved friend
JOHN GOWEN, gent., of Spartanburgh Co. as my attorney to sell, convey,
etc. a tract of land on the Reedy River in Greenville Co., joining
the lands of WILLIAM YOUNG, JOHN GOWEN, FRANCIS CLAYTON, and another
tract surveyed by Capt. WILLIAM BENSON for whom I know not; sd land
being surveyed for me by Capt. WM. BENSON, containing 213 acres. Wit:
BAYLIS EARLE, CHARLES LITTLETON. Signed: HUGH LEWIS. Rec. 20 Feb. 1788.

Pp 216-218: 8 May 1788. JOHN CHILDRESS of Greenville Co., yeoman, to
ROBERT NELSON of same place, DMD, for 50 pds sterling,
100 acres on Wildcat Creek of South Tyger River, part of a grant for
200 acres granted 1 Jan. 1785 to JOHN LUCAS and conveyed from him to
JOHN CHILDRESS. Wit: DANIEL (0) MC MILLIAN, JEREMIAH DUTTON DANIEL
DUTTON. Signed: JOHN CHILDRESS. Rec. 19 May 1788.

Pp 218-219: 14 Feb. 1788. THOMAS DAVIS and MARY his wife of Spartanburgh Co. to GEORGE HAINS of Greenville Co. for 6 pds sterling, 140 acres on both sides of S. Tyger River, bounding on PRITTEET's
land, land surveyed for ABRAHAM CHOSTAIN, and land surveyed for THOMAS
DAVIS. Part of a tract of 240 acres granted to DAVIS by Gov. Moultrie
(no date). Wit: JOHN CHILDRESS, ABRAHAM CHOSTAIN. Signed: THOMAS DAVIS,
MARY DAVIS. Rec. 19 May 1788.

Page 220: Deed of Gift. 28 Feb. 1788. MARTHA PARSONS of Greenville
Co. give to my loving children LUCY & SARAH PARSONS of
same county, all my goods and chattels in my present dwelling house.
Wit: ROBERT NELSON, WILLIAM NELSON. Signed: MARTHA PARSONS. Rec. 19
May 1788.

Pp 220-222: 19 May 1788. JOSEPH BOX of 96 Dist. to JOSEPH WILLIAMS
of same, for 60 pds current money, 100 acres on S side
of Reedy River, part of 400 acres on both sides of Reedy River granted
to JOSEPH BOX 21 Jan. 1785 by Gov. Guerard. Wit: WILLIAM YOUNG, JOHN
YOUNG. Signed: JOSEPH BOX. Rec. 19 May 1788.

Pp 222-223: 19 May 1788. JOSEPH BOX of Greenville Co. to ABNER NORRIS
of same, for 120 pds current money, 200 acres on both sides
of the Reedy River, part of 400 acres granted to sd BOX 21 Jan. 1785
by Gov. Guerard. Wit: WILLIAM YOUNG, JOHN YOUNG. Signed: JOSEPH BOX.
Rec. 19 May 1788.

Pp 223-225: 19 May 1788. JOSEPH BOX of 96 Dist. to WILLIAM WOODY of
the same for 60 pds current money of S.C. 100 acres S side
of Reedy River, part of 400 acres granted to sd BOX 21 Jan. 1785. Wit:
JOHN YOUNG, JR., THOMAS (X) NORRIS. Signed: JOSEPH BOX. Rec. 19 May
1788.

Pp 225-229: Lease & Release. 5 Jan. 1788. WILLIAM FERGUSON of Greenville
Co. to MICHAEL HENDERSON of same, for 40 pds, 100 acres
bordering WILLIAM NEAL. Part of a tract orig. granted to PATRICK LAFFER-
TY on Mountain Creek of Saluda River 5 Sept. 1785, conveyed from sd
LAFFERTY to THOMAS LEWIS, Clerk of Greenville Co. 20 Nov. 1787, from
sd LEWIS to WILLIAM FERGUSON 21 Nov. 1787. Wit: DRURY (M) MORRIS, PEGGY
(X) FERGUSON, JOHN HENDERSON. Signed: WILLIAM (W) FERGUSON, CATY (H)
FERGUSON, MICHAEL HENDERSON. Rec. 19 May 1788.

Pp 229-230: 19 May 1788. BENJAMIN CLARK to BENJAMIN MERIT, both of
96 Dist., for 100 pds sterling, 200 acres including the
old town house, north fork of the Saluda river, a tract granted to
sd CLARK 21 Jan. 1785. Wit: JOHN MALIN, JOHN WILLIAMS. Signed: BENJ.
CLARK. Rec. 19 May 1788.

Pp 230-232: 18 Feb. 1788. JOHN MALIN and ELIZABETH his wife to BENJAMIN
MERIT, both of Greenville Co., for 30 pds sterling, 40

Cont'd from page 133:
acres on a creek of the North Fork of the Saluda River about a half
mile above the old town house near the creek where the mill stands,
part of the tract where MALIN now lives, granted 21 Jan. 1785 by Gov.
Guerard. Wit: JOHN WILLIAMS, ELIKSANDER MC KINEY. Signed: JOHN MALIN,
ELIZABETH (+) MALIN. Rec. 18 May 1788.

Pp 232-234: 20 Oct. 1787. JOHN STANFORD of Greenville Co. to ABRAHAM
HARGISS of the same, for 40 pds sterling, 100 acres on
the waters of Salude River, part of grant to sd STANFORD of 343 acres
granted 5 Feb. 1787 by Gov. Moultrie. Wit: JEREMIAH (D) DUTTON, JOHN
STANFORD, JAMES WALES. Signed: JOHN STANFORD. Rec. 19 May 1788.

Pp 234-235: 7 Sept. 1787. WILLIAM DANIEL, son of NANCY HICKMAN of Greenville Co. by her consent is apprenticed to JOHN WARE of
sd co., blacksmith to learn his trade, keep his secrets. The sd master
shall give him a set of blacksmiths tools and teach him arithmetic
as far as the rule of three. Wit: BENJAMIN TARRANT, THOMAS HAM. Signed:
WILLIAM (+) DANIEL, NANCY (+) HICKMAN. Rec. 19 May 1788.

Pp 235-237: 9 Apr. 1788. JOHN HENDERSON of Abbeville Co. to ISAAC MAY-
field of Greenville Co. for 60 pds sterling, 100 acres
both sides of the North fork of Saluda river, bordering Maj. JOHN FORD's
line, granted to HENDERSON 21 Jan. 1785. Wit: JOHN NELSON, JOHN CLAYTON.
Signed: JOHN HENDERSON. Rec. 19 May 1788.

Pp 237-239: 13 Jan. 1787. JEREMIAH RUSSEL of 96 Dist. to WM. LYNCH
of the same, for 50 pds current money, 190 acres both sides
of Wyers Creek, a branch of the N fork of Saluda River, land granted
to RUSSEL in 1786 by Gov. Moultrie. Wit: THOMAS BARTON, JAMES MC EL-
HENNY, MICHAEL (M) MADDEN. Signed: JEREMIAH RUSSEL. Rec. 19 May 1788.

Pp 239-240: Bill of Sale. 23 Jan. 1788. I, NATHANIEL AUSTIN of Green-
ville Co., for 100 pds lawful money of S. C., pd by WIL-
LIAM AUSTIN, SR., of S. C. planter, deliver unto WM. AUSTIN one horse
named Bobin Jone, cows, heifers, hogs, feather beds, etc. etc. Wit:
NANNA (+) SHELTON, NATHANIEL (his mark) AUSTIN, JR. Signed: NATH'L
AUSTIN. Rec. 19 May 1788.

Pp 241-243: 19 May 1788. CHARLES SWILLIVANT of Greenville Co. to JERE-
MIAH WEBB, JR. of the same, for 20 pds sterling, 240 acres
on the Reedy Fork of the Little Fork of Reedy River, bounded E by ROBERT
GILLIAM's land; orig. granted to JAMES CALDWELL by Gov. Moultrie 7
Aug. 1786 and by CALDWELL to sd CHARLES SWILLIVANT May 1788. Wit: JOHN
LEWIS. Signed: CHARLES SWILLIVANT. Rec. 19 May 1788.

Pp 243-245: 21 Jan. 1788. ISHAM FOSTER of 96 Dist. to THOMAS BRIDGES
of the same, for 50 pds current money, 200 acres on both
sides of Reedy River; land granted to FOSTER 21 Jan. 1785 by Gov. Guerard. Wit: OVERTON (X) GOODMAN, BENJAMIN (X) BRIDGES. Signed: ISHAM
FOSTER. Rec. 19 May 1788.

Pp 245-247: 1 Mar. 1788. MATTHIAS SULSER of Greenville Co. to JOHN
GOWEN of Spartanburg Co. for 200 pds sterling, 400 acres
on both sides of S. Tyger River, granted 15 Oct. 1784 to THOMAS DAVIS,
and from him to sd SULSER 14 Jan. 1786, recorded in clerk's office
in Spartanburg Co. 15 Aug. 1787. Wit: ROBERT MC CREARY, HENRY (his
mark) BATES, GEORGE THOMSON. Signed: MATTHIAS SULSER, EVE (+) SULSER.
Rec. 19 May 1788.

Pp 247-249: (No date) 1786. JAMES CLAYTON of 96 Dist. to JOHN SPENCE
of the same, for 50 pds current money, 262 acres orig.
granted to CLAYTON 21 Jan. 1785, bounded E by HENRY WHITE's land, N
by JOHN JORDAN's land. Wit: JOHN GOWEN, ROBERT HARPER, ALLEN GOWEN.
Signed: JAMES CLAYTON. Rec. 19 May 1788.

Pp 249-252: Lease & Release. 20 Nov. 1787. PATRICK LAFFERTY of Greenville Co., planter to THOMAS LEWIS, clerk, of the same
co., for 100 pds lawful money of S.C., 490 acres on Mountain Creek

134

Cont'd from page 134:
of the Saludy River, granted to LAFFERTY 5 Sept. 1785, rec'd Grant
Book FFFF page 45. Wit: R. MAXWELL. Signed: PATRICK (P) LAFFERTY. Rec.
19 May 1788.

Pp 253-255: 22 Mar. 1788. JAMES NEELEY of 96 Dist. to WILLIAM HUNT
of same, for 30 pds current money, 260 acres on the branches
of Reedy River, granted to JAMES NEELEY 19 Nov. 1786 by Gov. Moultrie.
Wit: WILLIAM ANDERSON, THOMAS MC KEE. Signed: JAMES NEELEY, MARGARET
(X) NEELEY. Rec. 20 May 1788.

Pp 253-255: 3 Jan. 1788. AMBROSE BLACKBURN of Greenville Co. to JOEL
CHARLES of the same, for 25 pds sterling, 110 acres on
the North side of the Saluda River, bounded South by the sd River,
all other sides vacant when surveyed. Granted to sd BLACKBURN 1 May
1786, rec'd in Grant Book IIII page 469. Wit: WILLIAM WILSON, JOHN
WARE. Signed: A. BLACKBURN. Rec. 20 May 1788.

Pp 255-256: 20 May 1788. JOHN YOUNG, JR. of 96 Dist. to JOSHUA HAWKINS
of the same, for 100 pds current money, 200 acres which
was part of a tract of 640 acres granted 17 Feb. 1785 to JOHN YOUNG,
JR. on Reedy River at a place known by LANGSTON's improvement, bounded
NW by WILLIAM YOUNG's land. The sd 200 acres taken off lower end of
tract including JOSEPH LANGSTON's former improvement. Wit: ___ WHITNER,
JOSIAH HAWKINS. Signed: JOHN YOUNG, JR. Rec. 20 May 1788.

Pp 256-258: 14 May 1788. AMBROSE BLACKBURN of Greenville Co. to JOHN
WARE of same, for 20 pds sterling, 150 acres E side of
Golden Grove Creek, bounded SE by Capt. MAXWELL's line, DICKERSON's
Ridge Road, JOHN BOWIE's land; part of a tract granted to sd BLACKBURN
15 Oct. 1784, rec'd Grant Book ZZZ page 154. Wit: SOLOMON STONE. Signed:
A. BLACKBURN. Rec. 20 May 1788.

Pp 258-260: 19 May 1788. REUBEN STRINGER of Greenville Co. to HENRY
LANGFORD of the same, for 60 pds sterling, 300 acres N
side of Saluda River, bounded S by Saluda River, SE by ANDREW WOOD's
lands, E by AMBROSE BLACKBURN's lands, NW by JAMES HARRISON's and BLACK-
BURN's lands. Granted to sd STRINGER 14 Feb. 1786, rec'd in Grant Book
NNNN page 417. Wit: A. BLACKBURN, JOHN LEWIS. Signed: REUBEN STRINGER.
Rec. 21 May 1788.

Page 260: 15 Dec. 1785. DAVID HUGHES of Spartanburg Co. to LEMUEL
JAMES ALSTON, for a valuable consideration, to make bond
for a title, 378 acres (inc. a tract of 150 acres purchased of HUGH
MC MILLIAN) on Reedy River. Signed: DAVID HUGHES. Wit: JOSEPH WHITNER.
Rec. 19 May 1788.

Pp 261-265: Lease & Release. 21 Feb. 1788. SAMUEL EARLE of Greenville
Co. to JOHN GRIGSBY of same, for 16,000 pds of crop tobacco
delivered at the Congaree Inspection, 320 acres on N side of South
fork of Saluda River, half of a tracat of land which SAMUEL EARLE purchased of JOSEPH HUGHES. No witnesses. Signed: SAMUEL EARLE. Rec. 18
Aug. 1788.

Pp 265-266: 31 Mar. 1788. ROBERT MAXWELL of Greenville to GEORGE GOODWIN
blacksmith, of the same, for 50 pds sterling, 200 acres
on the Saludy River granted to MAXWELL 4 Sept. 1786, rec'd Grant Book
NNNN page 583. Wit: AMBROSE BLACKBURN. Signed: R. MAXWELL. Rec. 18
May 1788.

Pp 266-268: 18 Aug. 1788. REUBEN STRINGER of Greenville Co. to JOSEPH
SOWEL for 40 pds sterling, 200 acres at the mouth of Grove
Creek, waters of Saluda River, bounded N by JAMES BLASSINGAME, W by
REUBEN STRINGER. Granted to sd STRINGER 15 Oct. 1787, rec'd in Grant
Book BBB page 421. Wit: A. BLACKBURN, CRAFFORD GOODWIN. Signed: REUBEN
STRINGER. Rec. 18 Aug. 1788.

Pp 268-271: Lease & Release. 10 June 1788. JAMES SAXON of Laurence
Co. to WILLIAM AUSTIN of Greenville, for 50 pds sterling,

Cont'd from page 135:
346 acres both sides of Gilders Creek, granted to JAMES SAXON 1 Jan.
1787. Rec'd Grant Book PPP page 383. Wit: WM. MITCHUSSON, RICHARD COLL-
INS. Signed: JAMES SAXON. Rec. 18 Aug. 1788.

Pp 271-273: 15 Aug. 1788. HENRY LANGFORD of Greenville Co. to GEORGE
            GOODWIN of the same, for 10 pds sterling, 50 acres on Saluda
River, part of a tract granted to REUBEN STRINGER by Gov. Moultrie
7 Aug. 1786. Rec'd Grant Book NNNN page 417. Wit: A. BLACKBURN, CRAF-
FORD GOODWIN. Signed: HENRY (X) LANGFORD. Rec. 18 Aug. 1788.

Pp 273-275: 24 June 1788. ALEXANDER MC ELHANY of Greenville Co. to
            WILLIAM D. THOMAS of same, for 100 pds sterling, 200 acres
North side of the Saluda River, including the mouth of the Checkoroa
River; land granted to MC ELHANY 16 July 1784 by Gov. Guerard. Wit:
ANN JONES, JOHN WATSON, I. THOMAS, JR. Signed: ALEXANDER MC ELHENNY.
Rec. 18 Aug. 1788.

Pp 275-278: Lease & Release. 21 June 1787. WILLIAM HOGANS of Chester
            Co., S.C. to THOMAS JENKINS of Greenville Co. for 100 pds,
237 acres on Reedy River, bounding RICHARD WINN, JANE CAMPBELL. Land
granted 3 Apr. 1786, rec'd Grant Book KKKK page 55. Wit: F. LEWIS,
JOHN PRICHARD, JAS. DILLARD. Signed: WILLIAM HOGANS. Rec. 18 Aug. 1788.

Pp 278-282: Lease & Release. 9 Feb. 1787. JESSE MOODY of Greenville
            Co., planter, to JOSEPH MEACHAM, planter, of the same co.,
for 100 pds sterling, 100 acres on Golden Grove Creek, waters of Saluda
river, south of JAMES SEABORN's and NATHANIEL PENDLETON's land, part
of a tract of 400 acres orig. granted to BENJAMIN RICE by Gov. Guerard
15 Oct. 1784. Wit: THOMAS WEST, JOSEPH (E) RICHARDSON, RICHARD WEST,
JAMES WEST, AMOS WEST. Signed: JESSE (E) MOODY, DINAH (her mark) MOODY.
Rec. 18 Aug. 1788.

Pp 282-283: 18 Aug. 1788. ROBERT PRINCE to HUGH MC VAY for the full
            and just sum of 10 pds sterling, 300 acres on the branches
of the Beaverdam of Enoree river, bordering PERRY's line, MARY PRINCE,
HOOPER, JOHN ANDERSON, BENJAMIN WORTON, JOHN TURNBOUGH. Land orig.
granted to ROBT. PRINCE 7 Mar. 1787, rec'd Book VVVV page 144. No witnesses. Signed: ROBT. PRINCE. Rec. 18 Aug. 1788.

Pp 283-284: 1 Mar. 1788. SAMUEL EARLE of Greenville Co., to HUGH MC
            VAY, JR. of Laurens Co., for 100 pds, 240 acres on the
Beaverdam of Enoree river orig. granted to sd SAML EARLE 8 June 1784.
No witnesses. Signed: SAMUEL EARLE. Rec. 18 Aug. 1788.

Pp 284-285: 19 Nov. 1786. TAPLEY HENSON of Fauquier Co., Va., planter,
            to AQUILA BRAISHER (BRASHER, BREASHER), planter of Green-
ville Co., S.C. for 60 pds, 200 acres on Reedy Fork, a branch of Reedy
River. Wit: CINNER HUDSON, SARAH HUDSON. Signed: TAPLEY HENSON. Rec.
18 Aug. 1788.

Pp 285-287: 5 Aug. 1788. SOLOMON KING of Abbeville Co., to WILLIAM
            TUBB for 40 pds sterling, 176 acres on south side of Tyger
River, granted to SOLOMON KING 5 June 1786. Wit: ROBERT NELSON, REUBEN
BARRETT. Signed: SOLOMON (X) KING. Rec. 18 Aug. 1788.

Pp 287-289: 9 Mar. 1788. LEWIS DEVALL of Greenville Co., to NOAKANA
            HUDSON of the same, for 100 pds, 540 acres orig. granted
to LEWIS DEVALL 4 Sept. 1786, on the Reedy river near the dwelling
house of sd DEVALL. Wit: JOHN BRESHER, DANIEL RICHARDSON. Signed: LEWIS
DUVALL, THERESEY (her mark) DUVALL. Rec. 18 Aug. 1788.

Pp 289-290: 17 Aug. 1788. WILLIAM RUSSELL of Greenville Co. to WILLIAM
            SILVERSIDES & WILLIAM GOODWIN, both of Greenville Co.,
40 pds sterling for 200 acres part of a tract of 640 acres granted
to sd WM. RUSSELL 5 June 1786, on both sides of Enoree River and Mountain Creek, including the land where WM. SILVERSIDES and WM. GOODWIN
now live, beginning at Russels station on his lower line on the bank
of Mountain Creek, head of Shiting Swamp. Wit: ABSALOM CARNER, JOSEPH

Cont'd from page 136:
(his mark) KING. Signed: WILLIAM (X) RUSSELL, SUSANNAH (X) RUSSELL.
Rec. 18 Aug. 1788.

Pp 290-292: 20 May 1788. JOHN PORTMAN of 96 Dist., planter, to ABRAHAM
        CHASTAIN of Greenville Co., planter, 30 pds sterling for
100 acres bounding PRITEET's corner, part of a tract of 490 acre grant
5 June 1786, on the branches of the S fork of Tyger River bounding
WILLIAM GRANT, SR. and TOBIAS PRITTEET. Wit: PETER HOWARD, GEORGE HAYNS.
Signed: JOHN (P) PORTMAN. Rec. 18 Aug. 1788.

Pp 292-293: 21 Apr. 1788. JAMES CLAYTON of Spartanburg Co., S.C. to
        WILLIAM YOUNG of Abbeville Co., S.C. for 170 pds, 170 acres
on the Saludy River opposite the confluence of George's Creek, granted
to sd CLAYTON 21 Jan. 1785. Wit: JAMES YANCY, JR., THOMAS HUNT. Signed:
JAMES CLAYTON. Rec. 18 Aug. 1788.

Pp 293-295: 18 Aug. 1788. WILLIAM YOUNG of Abbeville Co. to MILLINGTON
        EASLEY of Greenville Co., for 190 pds, 170 acres on Saludy
River opposite the confluence of George's Creek, granted to JAMES CLAY-
TON 21 Jan. 1785, conveyed from sd CLAYTON to the above sd WILLIAM
YOUNG 21 Apr. 1788. Wit: JAMES YANCY, JR. Signed: WILLIAM YOUNG. Rec.
18 Aug. 1788.

Pp 295-298: Lease & Release. 6 Mar. 1788. ISABELLA GOTTIER of Charles,
        widow, to JOHN BOWIE of Abbeville Co., Esquire, for 122
pds 13 shillings 8 pence, 640 acres on Golden Grove Creek branch of
the Saludy River, granted to the late FRANCIS GOTTIER by Gov. Benj.
Guerard. Wit: CR. WILLIMAN, J. H. HARRIS. Signed: ISABELLA GOTTIER.
Rec. 18 Aug. 1788.

Pp 298-302: Lease & Release. 25 Jan. 1787. NATHANIEL WEED, planter,
        of Abbeville Co. to JOHN BOWIE, Esq. of the same, for 90
pds, 440 acres granted to NATHANIEL WEED 16 July 1784 on branches of
Golden Grove Creek, a branch of Saludy River, bounded SW on land granted
to FRANCIS GOTTIER. Wit: JOHN MC CARLEY, SAMUEL MC CARLEY, DAVID KENNEDY.
Signed: NATHANIEL WEED. Rec. 18 Aug. 1788. Note: In General Sessions
Court for 96 Dist., ADAMS BURKE, Esq., presiding, held in the town
of Cambridge 27 Apr. 1787, NATHANIEL WEED ack. the written release
and his wife MARGARET renounced her right of dower.

Pp 302-303: 10 July 1788. JAMES MANNEN GORE of Chester Co., S.C. to
        THOMAS LEWIS of Greenville Co. for 100 pds, 200 acres on
Saludy River including the Cedar Islands, granted to sds JAMES MANNEN
GORE 4 July 1785, recorded Book BBBB. Wit: PETER JONES, WILLIAM FILSON.
Signed: JAMES MANNEN GORE. Rec. 19 Aug. 1788.

Pp 303-305: 24 Mar. 1788. JOHN JACKSON of Louisa Co., Va. to REUBEN
        SIMS of Newberry Co., S.C. for 320 pds current money of
S.C., 640 acres on the Cheekoroa River bounded by GEORGE SALMON. Wit:
JOHN SANDERS, HEZEKIAH RICE, PATRICK HENRY SIMS. Signed: JOHN JACKSON.
Rec. 18 Aug. 1788.

Pp 305-306: 30 July 1788. JACOB GARDNER of Abbeville Co. to NICHOLAS
        FISHER of Greenville Co. for 50 pds sterling, 200 acres
both sides of Reedy River bounding DAVID MC COY, WILLIAM HOOPER; granted
to sd GARDNER 1 Jan. 1787. Wit: JAMES DARNOLD, WILLIAM HOOPER, JAMES
FISHER. Signed: JACOB GARDNER. Rec. 18 Aug. 1788.

Pp 306-309: Lease & Release. 17 Aug. 1788. JEREMIAH CHANDLER of Green-
        ville Co. to JOHN GOODWIN of same, for 100 pds current
money (release reads 100 pds sterling), 118 acres on north side of
Reedy River bounded W by DAVID REED EVANS land and JOHN GOODWIN's land.
Granted to sd CHANDLER 7 Aug. 1786. Wit: VINCENT LEWIS, ROBERT MC AFEE.
Signed: JEREMIAH CHANDLER. Rec. 19 Aug. 1788.

Pp 309-311: Lease & Release. 16 June 1788. WILLIAM HOLLEMS of 96 Dist.
        to REUBEN STRINGER of Greenville Co., 5 shillings ster-
ling (lease and release both read 5 shillings), 200 acres on the N

Cont'd from page 137:
side of big Saluda River, bounded NW by EDWIN SMITH, granted to HOLLEMS
2 Oct. 1786, rec'd Grant Book BBBB page 230. Wit: TH. P. CARNES, THOMAS
FARRAR. Signed: WILLIAM (X) HOLLAMS.

Pp 311-313: 19 Aug. 1788. REUBEN STRINGER of 96 Dist. to JOHN MOORE
of S.C. for 60 pds sterling, 200 acres N side of big Saluda
River bounded SW by EDWIN SMITH, land granted to WM. HOLLEMS 2 Oct.
1786. Wit: TH. P. CARNES, A. BLACKBURN. Signed: REUBEN STRINGER. rec.
18 Aug. 1788.

Pp 313-316: Lease & Release. 18 Jan. 1788. JOHN PENNY and ELEANOR his
wife of Spartanburg Co. to JONATHAN STONE, farmer of sd
state and county, 132 acres for 25 pds sterling, on small branches
of the Saluda River, sd land granted to JOHN PENNY 6 Mar. 1786. Wit:
JONATHAN NISBETT, ROBERT NISBETT, NATHAN NISBETT. Signed: JOHN PENNY,
ELLENOR (E) PENNY. Rec. 19 Aug. 1788.

Pp 316-317: 25 Mar. 1788. ROBERT TATE of 96 Dist. to GEORGE PEARCE
for one thousand pds, 1823 acres, N side of Saluda River
bounding RICHARD BROWN and lands of DREWRY MORRIS, SIMON ELLIS, M.
MC NEEL's, orig. granted to MILES JENNINGS in 1786, and from JENNINGS
to ROBERT TATE 2 May 1786. Wit: EDWIN SMITH, JAMES MOORE, AARON BROYLES,
ROBERT MAXWELL, J.P. Signed: ROBERT TATE. Rec. 19 Aug. 1788.

Pp 317-319: 25 Mar. 1788. GEORGE PEARCE of 96 Dist. to JOHN WATKINS
for 25 pds sterling, 275 acres, part of a tract of land
granted to MILES JENNINGS 1786 and conveyed from him to ROBERT TATE
2 May 1786 and from sd TATE to GEORGE PEARCE, land on othe N side of
Saluda River bordering lands of Col. BEELS. Wit: JAMES MOORE, JOHN
MOORE, JOHN MARTIN, ROBERT MAXWELL, J.P. Signed: GEORGE (X) PEARCE.
Rec. 19 Aug. 1788.

Pp 319-320: Power of Attorney. 18 Aug. 1788. I, JOHN HORNADAY of Greenville Co. appoint JOHN PATTERSON of state and co. afsd
my true and lawful attorney to receive from all persons in N. C. any
sums of money, debts, demands, etc. now due me. Wit: J. W. WHITNER,
JAMES PATTERSON. Signed: JOHN (his mark) HORNADAY. Rec. 18 Aug. 1788.

Pp 320-324: Lease & Release. 23 May 1788. THOMAS BRANDON, Esq., of
Union Co., S.C. to LEMUEL JAMES ALSTON, Esq. of Greenville
Co. for 217 pds 10 shillings, 400 acres both sides of Reedy River,
inc. RICHARD PARIS's former plantation, together with his mill seat
on sd river. Wit: ZACHA. BULLOCK, JOHN LINDSEY, SAMUEL EARLE. Signed:
THOMAS BRANDON. Rec. 19 Aug. 1788.

Pp 324-325: 21 Nov. 1787. JAMES BLASINGAME, Esq. of Greenville Co.
to JOHN HUGHS of same for 5 pds, 87 acres on Zachary's
Fork Creek, branch of Reedy River, orig. granted to sd BLASINGAME by
Gov. Moultrie 4 Dec. 1786. Wit: T. LEWIS. Signed: J. BLASINGAME. Rec.
20 Aug. 1788.

Pp 325-327: 14 Aug. 1788. JOHN TUBB of Greenville Co. to JAMES TUBB
for 50 pds sterling, 150 acres on branches of Enoree River
part of a grant cont'g 323 acres dated 20 Oct. 1786 from Gov. Moultrie.
Wit: ABRAHAM HARGISS, GEORGE TUBB. Signed: JOHN TUBB. Rec. 19 Aug.
1788.

Pp 327-330: Lease & Release. 10 Jan. 1787. JAMES CALDWELL of 96 Dist.
planter, to PATRICK RILEY, for 10 pds sterling, 250 acres
on a branch of Reedy Fork of Reedy River bordering JOHN PYLE on one
side, vacant all other sides. Wit: JAMES FORREST, JAMES GOODMAN, CHARLES
SULLIVANT. Signed: JAMES CALDWELL. Rec. 20 Aug. 1788. Note: On 15 Aug.
1788 bef. WM. CALDWELL, J.P. of Newberry Co., JAMES GOODMAN swore that
he saw JAMES CALDWELL sign sd deed.

Pp 330-332: 29 May 1788. DANIEL KELLEY and SARAH his wife of Greenville
Co. to SAMUEL EARLE, SR. of Frederick Co., Va. for 100
pds sterling, two tracts of land cont'g 300 acres. One tract granted

Cont'd from page 138:
to JOSEPH DUNN 21 Jan. 1785 and conveyed from sd DUNN to DANIEL KELLEY, the other tract granted to sd DANIEL KELLEY 5 June 1786, both of which tracts join and are bounded by Col. HENRY M. WOODS, JOHN FOSTER & ELIAS EARLE. Wit: ELIAS EARLE, BENJ. RAGLIN, MATTHEW (X) KELLEY. Signed: DANIEL KELLEY, SARAH (her mark) KELLEY. Rec. 17 Nov. 1788.

Pp 332-333: 12 June 1788. WILLIAM TILLER of Greenville Co. to PLEASANT HUDSON for 25 pds sterling, 50 acres both sides of Rocky Creek of Enoree River which the sd HUDSON now has possession of, bordering sd TILLER and FRANCIS FULLHORN's North line. Wit: HOWARD FINLEY, ABNER SMITH BUTTLER, LUNCEFORD HUDSON. Signed: WILLIAM TILLER. Rec. 17 Nov. 1788.

Pp 333-335: 18 Nov. 1788. ISOM CLAYTON of Greenville Co. to JOHN WEATHERS of same, for 100 pds, 100 acres on branches of Saluda River granted to sd CLAYTON by Gov. Guerard 21 Jan. 1785, bordering Bush's Creek, JOHN WEATHERS' Spring Branch, sd CLAYTON's line. Wit: JAMES YANCEY, JR. Signed: ISOM (his mark) CLAYTON. Rec. 17 Nov. 1788.

Pp 335-336: 18 Feb. 1788. ABRAHAM HUDSON of Greenville Co. to LUNCEFORD HUDSON of same, for 50 pds sterling, 100 acres fork of Rocky Creek of Enoree River, part of the part that sd LUNCEFORD HUDSON is now possessed of. Wit: PLEASANT HUDSON, HOWARD FINLEY. Signed: ABRAHAM HUDSON. Rec. 17 Nov. 1788.

Pp 336-337: 13 June 1788. PLEASANT HUDSON of Greenville Co. to EDWARD TILLER of same, for 25 pds sterling, 100 acres both sides of Rocky Creek of Enoree River, bounded S by JOSEPH WOODALL's land. Wit: LUNCEFORD HUDSON, HOWARD FINLEY, ABNER SMITH BUTLER. Signed: PLEASANT HUDSON. Rec. 17 Nov. 1788.

Pp 337-338: 13 June 1788. WILLIAM TILLER of Greenville Co. to THOMAS FINLEY of same, for 62 pds 10 shillings sterling, 250 acres both sides of Rocky Creek of Enoree River, lying bet. FRANCIS FULCHOR's and JOSEPH WOODALL's land where the sd THOMAS FINLEY now lives. Wit: HOWARD FINLEY, ABNER SMITH BUTLER, LUNCEFORD HUDSON. Signed: WILLIAM TILLER. Rec. 17 Nov. 1788.

Pp 338-339: 10 Oct. 1788. WILLIAM USERY of Greenville Co. to THOMAS USERY of same, for 50 pds, 100 acres part of a tract of 398 acres granted WILLIAM USERY 5 June 1786 by Gov. Moultrie, both sides of Clear Creek of South Tyger River. Wit: JAMES YANCEY, JR. Signed: WILLIAM (X) USERY. Rec. 17 Nov. 1788.

Pp 340-341: 31 Oct. 1788. JOHN CHILDRESS of Greenville Co., hatter, to HENRY PEARSON, planter of the same co., for 100 pds sterling, 200 acres part of a tract of 614 acres granted 6 Feb. 1786 by Gov. Moultrie to sd JOHN CHILDRESS, both sides of Childress's Beavers Creek of South Tyger River, bordering JEREMIAH DUTTON. Wit: REUBEN BARRETT, JESSE SAXON, WILLIAM (his mark) USERY. Signed: JOHN CHILDRESS, OBEDEN (X) CHILDRESS. Rec. 17 Nov. 1788.

Pp 341-343: 15 Nov. 1788. JOHN CHILDRESS, SR. and OBEDIENCE his wife of Greenville Co. to JESSE SAXON, 30 pds current money of S. C. for 100 acres, part of a tract of 420 acres granted to JEREMIAH DUTTON, lying both sides of the south fork of Tyger River, conveyed by sd JEREMIAH DUTTON and SARAH his wife unto sd JOHN CHILDRESS 23 Feb. 1787, bordering SALMON's land, MOSES WOODS and the wagon road. Wit: WILLIAM (his mark) USERY, HENRY PEIRSON, JOHN CHILDRESS (Kentuck). Signed: JOHN CHILDRESS, OBEDIENCE CHILDRESS. Rec. 17 Nov. 1788.

Pp 343-344: 15 Oct. 1788. DUNKLIN CAMPBELL of Greenville Co. to JOSEPH MAXWELL of the same, for 30 pds sterling, 182 acres granted to DUNKLIN CAMPBELL by Gov. Moultrie 5 June 1786, both sides of Green Creek of South Pacolet River. Wit: ROBT. NELSON, WILLIAM NELSON. Signed: DUNKLIN (X) CAMPBELL. Rec. 20 Nov. 1788.

Pp 344-347: 6 Oct. 1788. HUMPHREY SCROGGINS of Greenville Co. to JOHN

Cont'd from page 139:
TARRANT for 95 pds sterling 117 acres on waters of Golden Grove Creek, Saluda River, part of a grant to sd HUMPHREY SCROGGINS by Gov. Guerard 15 Oct. 1784 cont. 117 acres, bord. JUDGE PENDLETON's line, JOSEPH BENSON's land, JEREMIAH SMITH. Wit: JEREMIAH SMITH, BENJAMIN MC KENZIE, BARTON SCROGIN. Note: BENJAMIN MC KENZIE made oath to ROBT. MAXWELL, one of the Justices of Greenville Co. that he saw HUMPHREY SCROGGINS sign sd deed. Signed: HUMPHREY (X) SCROGGINS. Rec. 17 Nov. 1788.

Page 347: Dowery Relinquishment. ELEANOR PENNY, being examined by ROBERT NELSON, Esq., relinquishes her right of dower to a tract of land conveyed by her husband to JONATHAN STONE.

Pp 347-348: 9 Nov. 1787. THOMAS LOWRY of 96 Dist. to WILLIAM WARRAN of same for 20 pds current money, 150 acres, part of a tract of 200 acres granted to THOMAS LOWRY by Gov. Moultrie 4 Dec. 1786, on the waters of the South Tyger River in 96 Dist., bounded SE by ROBERT GOOLEY's land, SW on COLLINS' land. Wit: HENRY PRINCE, HUGH WARRAN, JR, HUGH WARRAN, SR. Signed: THOMAS (X) LOWRY. Rec. 20 Nov. 1788.

Pp 348-350: 13 Oct. 1788. ROBERT PRINCE of Greenville Co. to WILLIAM TUBB of same, for 20 pds sterling, 500 acres on the head of White's Mill Creek of Enoree, part of 4,000 acres granted to ROBERT PRINCE, bordering BLACKWELL's corner, STANFORD's corner. (No witnesses) Signed: ROBERT PRINCE. Rec. 18 Nov. 1788.

Pp 350-352: 13 Nov. 1787. Lease & Release. ROBERT HANNA of Laurence Co., surveyor, to JEREMIAH CHANDLER, planter, of Greenville Co., for 20 pds sterling, 100 acres granted to sd HANNA by Gov. Guerard on Brushy Creek of Reedy River. Wit: ELISHA HUNT, JAMES (his mark) MC WILLIAMS. Signed: ROBERT HANNA. Rec. 18 Nov. 1788.

Pp 352-354: 16 Feb. 1788. JOHN BULL, Esq. of S.C. to BAYLIS EARLE of Spartanburg Co. for 20 shillings, 497 acres on waters of Chicheroah, bordering THOS. MC CARRELL, JACKSON's line, MC ELHENNY's line. Wit: R. HAMPTON, JOHN HAMPTON, ZACHR. BULLOCK. Signed: JOHN BULL. Rec. 18 Nov. 1788. Note: ZACHR. BULLOCK appeared bef. JAMES JORDAN, J.P. of Spartanburg Co. and swore that he saw JOHN BULL sign sd deed.

Pp 354-357: Lease & Release. 20 Jan. 1786. JENNY CAMPBELL to JOHN BUCHANAN both of Fairfield Co. for 5 shillings full purchase money, 350 acres on a branch of Reedy River bounded N by sd. RICHARD WINN's land. Wit: JNO. MILLING, JOHN WINN. Signed: JENNY (X) CAMPBELL. Rec. 18 Nov. 1788. Note: JOHN WINN appeared bef. RICHARD WINN, J.P. of Fairfield Co. and swore that he saw JEAN CAMPBELL sign sd deed.

Pp 357-358: 7 Aug. 1788. JOHN TATE of S.C. to ISAAC GREEN of Greenville Co. for 12 pds 16 shillings 10 pence sterling, 100 acres both sides Mountain Creek, branch of Enoree River, bordering ROBERT MC AFEE, where the sd GREEN now lives, orig. granted to sd TATE by Gov. Moultrie 1 Jan. 1787. Wit: AARON (R) KEMP, MOSES (his mark) KEMP. Signed: JOHN TATE. Rec. 18 Nov. 1788.

Pp 358-360: 18 Nov. 1788. JOSEPH WHITNER of Greenville Co. to JOHN THOMAS, JR., for 30 pds sterling, 144 acres granted to sd WHITNER 7 May 1787 by Gov. Pinckney, situated in Greenville and Spartanburg co.'s, both sides of S fork of Tyger River. Wit: GEORGE SALMON, J. MC COOL. Signed: J. WHITNER. Rec. 18 Nov. 1788.

Pp 360-362: Lease & Release. 15 Feb. 1788. BENJAMIN KILGORE of 96 Dist. to GEORGE BROCK of the same, for 160 pds sterling, 100 acres on the Enoree River, granted to sd KILGORE 5 June 1786. Wit: THOMAS RICE, THOMAS (T) BROCK, GEORGE BROCK. Signed: BENJAMIN KILGORE. Rec. 19 Nov. 1788.

Pp 362-363: 16 Sept. 1788. THOMAS FARRAR of Spartanburg Co. to EDMUND PETERS of Greenville Co. for 50 pds current money, 200

Cont'd from page 140:
acres granted to sd FARRAR 15 Oct. 1784 by Gov. Guerard, on Beaver
Dam Creek of Enoree River. Wit: JAMES YANCEY, JR., MOSES WOOD. Signed:
THOMAS FARRAR. Rec. 19 Nov. 1788.

Pp 363-364: 14 Sept. 1787. ISAAC ROLSTON of 96 Dist. to EDWIN SMITH
of the same, for 60 pds sterling, 166 acres on Saluda River.
Wit: MATTHEW ALEXANDER, ROBT. ROLSTON. Signed: ISAAC ROLSTON. Rec.
19 Nov. 1788. Note: On 13 Nov. 1788 MATTHEW ALEXANDER appeared bef.
WM. HALBERT, J.P. of Abbeville Co. and made oath that he saw ISAAC
ROLSTON sign sd deed.

Pp 364-365: 7 June 1788. ROBERT ANDERSON to JEROMAC WALDROPE, both
of 96 Dist., for 40 pds sterling, 106½ acres, the lower
half of a tract of 213 acres granted to sd ROBERT ANDERSON 21 Jan.
1785, rec'd Grant Book GGGG on both sides of N fork of Saluda River
bordering THOMAS FARRAR's land. Wit: THOMAS MUSICK, WILLIAM (M) MACKEY.
Signed: ROBERT ANDERSON, JEAN ANDERSON. Rec. 19 Nov. 1788.

Pp 365-369: Lease & Release. 29 Oct. 1788. SHADRACH CHANDLER of Greenville Co. to JESSE WEBB for 20 pds sterling, 80 acres,
part of a tract of 640 acres granted to JESSE CHANDLER 21 Jan. 1785,
from sd CHANDLER to SHADRACH CHANDLER in 1788, on Horse Creek, waters
of Reedy River, on NE side of creek bordering ANDREW JONES' corner.
Wit: JOHN BYARS WELL*, JOEL WEBB, JOHN WEBB. Signed: SHADRACH (his mark)
CHANDLER. Rec. 16 Feb. 1789. (*WEBB?)

Pp 369-373: Lease & Release. 29 Oct. 1788. JESSE CHANDLER of Greenville
Co. to JOHN WEBB for 50 pds sterling, 209 acres, part of
a tract of 640 acres described in preceding deed, on the SW side of
Horse Creek, waters of Reedy River, to a line agreed upon by sd JESSE
CHANDLER and ANDREW JONES. Wit: JOEL WEBB, JOHN BYARS WEBB, JESSE WEBB.
Signed: JESSE CHANDLER (his mark). Rec. 16 Feb. 1789.

Pp 373-374: 25 Aug. 1788. WILLIAM STORY of Greenville Co., planter,
to EDWARD BOX of Laurence Co. for 30 pds sterling, 50 acres
part of a tract of 200 acres granted to sd STORY by Gov. Moultrie 10
July 1784. Wit: VINCENT LEWIS, BAUSTON CARPENTER. Signed: WILLIAM (X)
STORY. Rec. 16 Feb. 1789.

END OF BOOK A

GREENVILLE CO. COURTHOUSE DEED BOOK B
1789-1791

Pp 1-2:   Lease & Release. 14 Feb. 1787. JAMES REYNOLDS, farmer
of Spartanburg Co., 96 Dist., to MICHAEL PIRELE of same
place, for 80 pds sterling, 640 acres orig. granted 16 July 1784 by
Gov. Benj. Guerard to sd JAMES REYNOLDS, situate on both sides Reedy
River of Saluda River about two miles above the old Indian boundary,
all other sides being vacant. Wit: JOHN NESBITT, JEREMIAH LUCAS, JOHN
COLLINS. Signed: JAMES REYNOLDS. Rec. 16 Feb. 1789.

Page 3:   Deed of Conveyance. 16 Feb. 1789. JOHN YOUNG, JR., Greenville Co. to EATON HAWKINS of same place, for 50 pds sterling, 84 acres being part of a 640 acre tract granted by Gov. Guerard
7 Feb. 1785, situate lying on both sides of Langston's creek, a branch
of Reedy River adj. lands surveyed for WILLIAM YOUNG & JOSEPH LANGSTON.
Wit: PINK HAWKINS, HARDIN CAMP. Signed: JOHN YOUNG. Rec. 16 Feb. 1789.

Pp 4-5:   Deed of Conveyance. 20 May 1786. ROBERT GILLILAND of Greenville Co. to WILLIAM ARMSTRONG of same place, for 100 pds
sterling, 120 acres situate on the Golden Grove Creek bounding SW land
laid out to HENRY PENDLETON, Esq., on the NW on EDANUS BURKE, Esq.
land, NE sd BURKE & WILLIAM WOODS land and SE on land laid out to JOHN
BOWIE. Land orig. granted to ROBT. GILLILAND 16 July 1784 by Gov. Guerard and rec'd in Sec. Office Grant Book ZZZ page 35. Wit: WILLIAM BRASH-
ER, RICHARD (+) SANDRIDGE. Signed: ROBERT GILLILAND & JEAN (J) GILLI-
LAND. Rec. 16 Feb. 1789. ROBT. MAXWELL, J.P wit. 16 Jan. 1789 to wit.

Pp 5-7:   Lease & Release. 5 Feb. 1789. HEWLET SWILLIVANT of 96 Dist.
            Greenville Co. to PLEASANT SWILLIVANT of same place, for
20 pds sterling, 260 acres, situate on branch of Little Reedy fork
of Reedy River, bounded on N side by lands of Mr. BEALE and all other
sides vacant when surveyed and granted to HEWLET SWILLIVANT by letter
patent by Gov. Wm. Moultrie 1 May 1786. Wit: CHARLES SWILLIVANT, ROBERT
BABER, JOEL WEBB. Signed: HEWLET SULLIVANT. Rec. 16 Feb. 1789.

Pp 7-8:   Deed of Conveyance. 10 Oct. 1788. WILLIAM USERY, Greenville
            Co. to WILLIAM PEARSON of same place for 50 pds sterling,
100 acres being part of 398 acres granted 5 June 1786 by Gov. Moultrie,
situate in afsd county on both sides Clear Creek of S. Tyger River
beg. on lower end of tract on MAJOR PASSON's line. Wit: T. LEWIS. Signed
by WILLIAMA (X) USERY. Rec. 16 Feb. 1789.

Pp 8-9:   Deed of Conveyance. 13 Dec. 1788. OBADIAH HOOPER of Green-
            ville Co. to JOHN CHILDRESS of same place for 20 pds sterl-
ing, 233 acres granted to OBADIAH HOOPER 5 Feb. 1787 by Gov. Moultrie
situate on both sides of Beaverdam Creek of South Tyger River. Wit:
GEORGE SALMON, ROBERT CHILDRESS. Signed: OB. HOOPER. Rec. 16 Feb. 1789.

Pp 9-10:   Deed of Conveyance. 24 Oct. 1787. MICHAEL JOHNSTON, late
            of Greenville Co. for 50 pds sterling, 150 acres orig.
granted 1 Jan. 1787 by Gov. Moultrie, and recorded in Sec. Office in
Grant Book PPPP page 545, situate in Greenville Co. on a branch of
Enoree River. Wit: L. L. ALSTON, ISAAC WEST, ISAAC MORGAN. Signed:
MICHAEL JOHNSTON. Rec. 16 Feb. 1789. (No other name on conveyance)

Page 10:   Deed of Gift. 16 Feb. 1789. ISAAC MORGAN, Greenville Co.
            to GEORGE ROSS of same place, step-son to the sd ISAAC
MORGAN, for love & affection, 40 acres, being part of orig. grant of
640 acres granted to sd MORGAN in 1784 by Gov. Guerard, situate on
S side of Enoree River on S side of a small branch that heads up to
the waggon road. Wit: L. ALSTON, JAMES BLASINGAME. Signed: ISAAC MORGAN.
Rec. 16 Feb. 1789.

Pp 10-11:   Deed of Conveyance. 13 Aug. 1788. MARY PRINCE of Greenville
            Co. to JOHN MC VAY of same place, for 150 pds sterling,
530 acres situate in Greenville Co., 96 Dist. on both forks of Enoree
River, being part of a grant annexed 5 Dec. 1785 for 530 acres by Gov.
Moultrie. Wit: JOHN TUBB, ROBERT PRINCE. Signed: MARY (M) PRINCE. Rec.
16 Feb. 1789.

Pp 11-12:   Deed of Conveyance. 2 Jan. 1789. ROBERT PRINCE of Green-
            ville Co. to JOHN MC VAY of same place, for 50 pds, 146
acres, situate in Greenville Co. on north fork of Enoree River, which
tract was granted to CHARLES TANKERSLEY (also spelled TANKELESLEY,
TANKERLESLY) & conveyed from him to ROBERT PRINCE. Also 200 acres which
bounds MARY PRINCE's line on SW, then NW to WILLIAM WHITE's line. Also
84 acres which bounds MARY PRINCE. Two tracts, one of 200 acres, the
other 84 acres, being part of a tract of 4000 acres granted to ROBT.
PRINCE which more fully appears recorded in Sec. & Surveyors Gen. Office
of the State. Wit: JAMES (0)(his mark) TUBB, JAMES BATES. Signed: ROBERT
PRINCE. Rec. 16 Feb. 1789.

Pp 12-13:   Deed of Conveyance. 14 Feb. 1789. PETER HOWARD, Greenville
            Co., yeoman, to JOHN LUCAS of same place, by a certain
grant 21 Jan. 1785 by Gov. Guerard, did give and grant unto NICHOLAS
JASPER a tract of land containing 200 acres, situate in sd county on
both sides of South Tyger River. Now this indenture witnesseth the
sd NICHOLAS JASPER, did sell & convey to PETER HOWARD, for 10 pds to
JOHN LUCAS, all that land being the North side of sd River above the
50 acres, being part of sd survey. Wit: JONATHAN HOLCOMB, JAMES TUBB.
Signed: PETER HOWARD. Rec. 16 Feb. 1789.

Pp 13-14:   Deed of Conveyance. 13 Nov. 1788. HENRY LANGFORD, Greenville
            Co. to JAMES BLACKSTOCK of same place, for 25 pds sterling,
100 acres situate on North side of Saluda River, bounded by HENRY LANG-
FORD's line, running southward on GEORGE GOODIN's line, orig. granted

Cont'd from page 142:
14 Feb. 1786 and recorded in Sec. Office in Book NNNN page 417. Wit:
SOLOMON STONE, FRANCIS BLACKBURN. Signed: HENRY (X) LANGFORD. Rec.
17 Feb. 1789. Note: FRANCES BLACKBURN subscribes _her_ name as witness.

Pp 14-15:   Deed of Conveyance. 14 Feb. 1789. WILLIAM AUSTIN of Green-
             ville Co. to WILLIAM RICHARDSON of same place for 70 pds,
150 acres granted to JAMES SAXON and surveyed for WILLIAM AUSTIN 28
Dec. 1786 by Gov. Wm. Moultrie, situate on Gilders Creek, Greenville
Co. Wit: W. NICHOLSON, AMOS RICHARDSONN. Signed: WM. AUSTIN & JENNET
(X) AUSTIN. Rec. 17 Feb. 1789. ___ BLACKBURN, J.P. Greenville Co.

Pp 15-16:   Deed of Conveyance. 19 Jan. 1789. JOHN HAVEN of Greenville
             Co. to WILLIAM BROWN of same place, for 60 pds, 232 acres
orig. granted 1 Jan. 1787 by Wm. Moultrie, situate in 96 Dist., on
Enoree River and Brushy Creek of sd river and has such forms and mark-
ings as recorded in Sec. Office Book QQQQ page 354. Wit: JOHN FINLEY,
REUBEN GUNN, GEORGE RUSSEL. Signed: JOHN (X) HAVEN. Rec. 17 Feb. 1789.

Pp 16-17:   Deed of Conveyance. 19 Jan. 1789. JOHN HAVEN of Greenville
             Co. to HENRY WOOD of Spartanburg Co. for 35 pds sterling,
96 acres orig. granted 1 Jan. 1787 by Gov. Moultrie, situate in 96
Dist. on Enoree River and has such forms and marks as recorded in Sec.
Office Book QQQQ page 35. Wit: EDWARD BALLANGER, R. GUNN, WM. (X) BROWN.
Signed: JOHN (+) HAVEN.

Pp 17-18:   Deed of Conveyance. 18 Jan. 1789. JOHN BAKER BENNETT of
             Greenville Co. to JOHN MC ELROY of same place for 40 pds
lawful sterling, 224 acres orig. granted to JOHN BAKER BENNETT by Gov.
Moultrie 6 Nov. 1786, situate in the co. of Greenville, 96 Dist., on
the waters of Reedy River (the name spelled both MC ELROY & MAC ELROY).
Wit: LAURENCE BRASHER, JOHN EVENS. Signed: JOHN BAKER BENNETT, ROSANNAH
(X) BENNETT. Rec. 17 Feb. 1789.

Pp 18-19:   Deed of Conveyance. 13 Feb. 1789. JAMES FORESTER to SOLOMON
             FORESTER, both of Greenville Co. for 50 pds sterling, 200
acres situate in Greenville Co. on the fork of Mush Creek, one of the
head branches of Tygar River, adj. land laid out to BAYLIS EARLE. The
200 acres being part of a tract of 269 acres granted to JAMES FORESTER
by Letters Patent and recorded in Sec. Office Grant Book RRRR page
110, 5 Feb. 1787. Wit: HUGH WARREN, JR., HUGH WARREN, SR. Signed: JAMES
(F) FORESTER. Rec. 17 Feb. 1789.

Pp 19-20:   Deed of Conveyance. 23 Oct. 1788. JOHN PYLE, SR of N. C.
             to JOHN PYLE JR. of Greenville Co., S.C. for 75 pds, 300
acres situate in 96 Dist. Greenville Co. on branch of Reedy River called
the Spring Branch, being orig. granted to JOHN PYLE, SR. by Gov. Moultrie 8 June 1785 and rec'd in Book NNN page 437. Wit: JAMES (ŦG) GILLI-
SON, ROBERT KELLEY. Signed: JOHN PYLE. Rec. 17 Feb. 1789. Memorandum
to the above deed, 23 Oct. 1788, ROBERT MAXWELL, Justice of Peace did
see JAMES GILLISON and ROBERT KELLEY sign the above deed.

Pp 20-23:   Lease & Release. 29 Dec. 1786. JESSIE MOODY, Greenville
             Co., planter, to JEREMIAH SMITH of same place, blacksmith,
for 30 pds sterling, 117 acres lying on waters of Golden Grove Creek,
a branch of Saluda River, Greenville Co., being part of a tract containing 400 acres granted to BENJAMIN RICE 15 Oct. 1784 and sd grant
rec'd in Sec. Office in Grant Book ZZZ page 122. The land is bounded
SW by JAMES SEABOR's land, and NATHANIEL PENDLETON's land. (This deed
does not state how BENJAMIN RICE's land came to JESSIE MOODY). Wit:
JOHN NELSON, MATHEW ARMSTRONG, BENJAMIN RICE. Signed: JESSIE (Ŧ) MOODY.
Memorandum JOHN NELSON swore he saw JESSIE MOODY, NATHANIEL ARMSTRONG
& BENJAMIN RICE sign the above deed 17 Feb. 1789. JAMES BLASSINGAME
signs as J.P.

Pp 23-24:   Deed of Conveyance. 24 Aug. 1788. WILLIAM BRASURE of N.
             C. to JOHN MITCHUM of S. C. for 30 pds sterling, 240 acres
situate in Greenville Co., S.C. on Reedy fork, waters of Reedy River,
orig. granted to WM. BRASURE 4 Dec. 1786 by Gov. Moultrie. Wit: SARAH

143

Cont'd from page 143:
BRASHER, HANNA BRASHER, JAMES HENDERSON, ISAAC HENDERSON, JOHN HENDER-
SON. Signed: WILLIAM BRASHER. (Note - in deed name is written BRASURE
but signed BRASHER) Memorandum: JAMES HARRIS, J.P. saw above wit. sign
16 Dec. 1788. Rec. 17 Feb. 1789.

Pp 24-25:   Deed of Conveyance. 17 Feb. 1789. THOMAS LEWIS, Greenville
             Co. to SOLOMON LITTLETON of same co. for 50 pds sterling,
50 acres of land situate on a branch of Saluda River, the 50 acres
being part of a tract of 200 acres granted to JAMES GARE 4 July 1785
recorded in Sec. Office Grant Book BBBB page 288 and conveyed by JAMES
GARE to THOMAS LEWIS by Deed of Conveyance 10 July 1788. Wit: JOHN
LEWIS. Signed: T. LEWIS. (Name may be GORE).

Pp 25-26:   Deed of Conveyance. This indenture made 22 Aug. 1788 bet.
             OBADIAH HOOPER of Greenville, S.C. to MOSES WOOD of same
place for the just sum of 5 shillings current money 114 acres in afsd
co., situate on a branch of Enoree River bounded on NW
by TURNBOUGH, SE by BENJ. WHORTON, NE by MOSES WOOD, W by vacant land.
Orig. grant rec'd in Sec. Office Grant Book UUU. Wit: JESSIE CARTER,
BOOTH MALONE. Signed: OB. HOOPER. Rec. 17 Feb. 1789.

Pp 26-28:   Lease & Release. 8 Nov. 1787. JOHN MILLING of Fairfield
             Co., S.C. to ALEXANDER PEDDEN of afsd co. and state for
50 pds sterling, 640 acres orig. granted 1 Jan. 1785 by Gov. Guerard
to DAVID MILLING. Rec'd in Sec. Office. The sd land lying in 96 Dist.
on a branch of Reedy River (the deed does not show how JOHN MILLING
obtained land from DAVID MILLING). Wit: JOHN BUCKANAN, WILLIAM BOYD,
JAMES DOUGLAS. Signed: JOHN MILLING. Memorandum: 19 Dec. 1788. JOHN
WINN, J.P. did see the above witnesses sign the deed. Rec. 17 Feb.
1789.

Pp 28-30:   Lease & Release. 5 Feb. 1789. WILLIAM STRIPLAND, Newberry
             Co., S.C. to WILLIAM REED, Greenville Co., S.C. for 50
pds, 200 acres situate on the waters of Rocky Creek of Reedy River
in 96 Dist. the orig. grant rec'd in Sec. Office Grant Book BBB page
403 by Patent 4 Dec. 1786 to sd WM. STRIPLAND. Wit: JOSEPH REED, THOMAS
EASTLAND. Signed: WILLIAM STRIPLIN & CATRON (her mark) STRIPLIN. Memorandum - JAMES HARRISON, J.P. 15 Feb. 1789 did see JOSEPH REED make
oath he was present and WM. STRIPLIN & CATRON STRIPLIN sign and ack.
deed. Rec. 17 Feb. 1789.

Pp 30-31:   Deed of Conveyance. 29 July 1788. JACOB GARDNER of Abbeville
             Co., S.C. to WILLIAM HOOPER, Greenville Co., for 30 pds,
200 acres lying in county of Greenville, S.C. 96 Dist. on waters of
Saluda River bounded SW by GOODLEY's land and MC COY's line and NICHOLAS
FISHER's land. The tract of land orig. granted GARDNER 1 Jan. 1787.
Rec. Grant Book QQQQ. Wit: NICHOLAS FISHER, JAMES DARNALL, JAMES FISHER.
Signed: JACOB GARDNER. Rec. 17 Feb. 1789.

Pp 31-34:   Lease & Release. 2 Oct. 1788. HUMPHREY SCROGIN, Greenville
             Co., planter, to JEREMIAH SMITH of same place, blacksmith,
for 200 pds sterling, 243 acres being part of a grant of 351 acres
granted to sd SCROGIN 1 OCt. 1784, situate in Greenville Co., joining
lines with BENJAMIN RICE, ___ BENSON, GEORGE PENDLETON & JOHN TARRANT.
Wit: R. T. MAXWELL, JOHN TARRANT. Signed: HUMPHREY (X) SCROGGINS. Memorandum - ___ BLACKBURN, J.P. did see ROBT. MAXWELL sign the within
deed 17 Feb. 1789. Rec. 17 Feb. 1789.

Pp 34-36:   Lease & Release. 18 July 1785. WILLIAM MC ELHANNY, Spartan-
             burg Co. 96 Dist. to WILLIAM BENSON of sd Dist. & Co. for
120 pds sterling, 624 acres lying on both sides of Checkaroa River
of Saluda River of the old Indian Boundary bounding SE on land laid
out for JOHN JACKSON, SW land laid out for WILLIAM GOODLETT. Wit: JOHN
COLLINS, ROBERT GOODLETT, HENRY JAMISON. Signed: WILLIAM MC ELHENNY.
Memorandum - Spartanburgh Co.,S.C. 96 Dist. HENRY JAMISON did make
oath that he saw WM. MC ELHANNY sign the above deed and also JOHN COLL-
INS & ROBT. GOODLETT 14 May 1789. JAMES JORDAN, J.P. Rec. 15 May 1789.

Pp 36-37:   Deed of Conveyance. 28 Mar. 1789. JOHN MOLLIN & ELIZABETH

Cont'd from page 144:
MOLLIN, his wife to JOHN WILLIAMS of S. C., 96 Dist. for 100 pds sterling, 100 acres situate in sd state and dist. on the North fork of Saluda River and being a part of a greater tract of 215 acres joining GABRIEL MOFFIT and BENJAMIN MERRIT's Mill Creek, crosses the river at the mouth of sd creek. Wit: JOHN FORD, JOS. GOODWIN. Signed: JOHN MALLIN & ELIZABETH (X) MALLIN. (Note: name is written MALIN, MOLLIN and signed MALLIN in deed.) Rec. 19 May 1789.

Pp 37-38:   Deed of Conveyance. 9 Jan. 1789. RICHARD GOODE of N.C., Surry Co. to JOHN DYCK, Greenville Co., S.C. for 100 pds sterling, 540 acres situate and lying on East side of Golden Grove Creek, orig. granted 21 Jan. 1785 recorded Book GGGG page 69 to sds GOODE. Wit: WILLIAM HALBERT, JNO. GOODE, WILLIAM JEAN. Signed: RICHD. GOODE. Memorandum - 26 Feb. 1789 _____ BLACKBURN, J.P. did see the above wit. sign the conveyance. Rec. 19 May 1789.

Pp 38-39:   Deed of Conveyance. 9 Jan. 1789. DANIEL KELLY, Greenville Co., S.C. to WILLIAM FLIPPS of same place, for 100 acres being that grant to sd KELLY 21 Jan. 1785 by Gov. Guerard, situate 96 Dist. N. side of Saluda River and middle fork of sd river West of the old Indian Boundary, for 60 pds sterling. Wit: VINCENT DAVIS, JESSIE CARTER. Signed: DANIEL KELLEY. Rec. 19 May 1789. (T in Carter was not crossed.)

Pp 39-40:   Deed of Conveyance. 21 Feb. 1789. RICHARD BEARDEN, S.C., 96 Dist. to NATHAN SMITH of Greenville Co.,S.C. for 50 pds, a tract of 458 acres of land situate in 96 Dist., waters of a branch of Reedy River, orig. granted to BEARDEN 7 Aug. 1786 by Gov. Moultrie. Wit: JOHN LEWIS, JOSEPH WHITNER. Signed: RICHARD BEARDEN. Rec. 19 May 1789.

Pp 40-41:   Deed of Conveyance. 19 Nov. 1788. ROBERT PRINCE of Greenville Co., S.C. to DAVID MC VAY of same place for 40 pds, 300 acres lying on branches of Enoree and Saluda in the Dist. of 96 being part of a tract of land granted to sd PRINCE 17 Mar. 1788. Sd grant being 4000 acres and the part sold to DAVID MC VAY lying and beg. at a pine on TERRIS corner along a branch and bounding JEAN MC-JUNKINS' land, bounding SNODDY's land, East by HUGH MC VAY, JOHN MC VAY. Signed: ROBERT PRINCE. Rec. 19 May 1789.

Pp 41-44:   Lease & Release. 13 Dec. 1788. WILLIAM HENDERSON, Greenville Co. to JAMES ALEXANDER of Spartanburgh Co., SC for 50 pds sterling, a tract of 400 acres, orig. granted to sd HENDERSON 21 Jan. 1785 by Gov. Guerard, situate on branches of Rayburns Creek above the Indian Boundary. Wit: JOHN ALEXANDER, JAMES ALEXANDER. Signed: WILLIAM HENDERSON. Rec. 19 May 1789. Memo-18 May 1789 JAMES ALEXANDER made oath he was present and did see WM. HENDERSON sign and ack. within indenture to JAMES ALEXANDER, SR. Proven this day bef. JAMES HARRISON, J.P. Rec. 19 May 1789.

Pp 44-45:   Deed of Conveyance. 3 Jan. 1789. NATHANIEL MILLER, Greenville Co. to JAMES HARRISON for 20 pds sterling, sold 200 acres being a tract orig. granted to sd MILLER 3 Mar. 1788 by Gov. Thos. Pinckney, containing 335 acres, situate in Greenville Co. and waters of Reedy River and Reaborn Creek. Wit: JAMES ALEXANDER, THOMAS (O his mark) BRASURE, NAOMEY (her mark) BRASURE. Signed: NATHANIEL MILLER. Sworn on oath 18 Apr. 1789 bef. ROBERT MAXWELL, J.P. Rec. 19 May 1789.

Pp 46-47:   Deed of Conveyance. __ day of ___ 1789. Bet. JOHN THOMAS, SR. Esq., to DANIEL MC MILLIN, carpenter, for 54 pds 7 shillings 6 pence lawful money of S.C. sold 50 acres, situate in Greenville Co., S.C. on S side of South fork of Tyger river, including part of the plantation whereon the sd DANIEL MC MILLIN now lives, it being part of a tract of 640 acres granted to MAJOR PARSONS and on which sd JOHN THOMAS now lives, orig. granted 21 Jan. 1785 by Benj. Guerard, Gov. unto MAJOR PARSONS, and conveyed from him to THOMAS TODD by Indenture 1 Apr. 1785, from THOMAS TODD to JOHN THOMAS by Indenture 21

Cont'd from page 145:
Mar. 1786. Wit: RICHD. (X) HENSON, JO. THOMAS, JR. Signed: JOHN THOMAS.
Received money 15 May 1789 by JOHN THOMAS. Rec. 19 May 1789. Proved
bef. ROBERT NELSON, Esq.

Pp 47-48:   Deed of Conveyance. 23 Feb. 1787. JAMES BATES of S.C.,
              96 Dist., Greenville Co. to MOSES SPANN, of same place
for 30 pds current money sold 101 acres being part of 150 acre tract
orig. granted 21 Jan. 1785 by Gov. Guerard situate and lying on both
sides of South Pacolate River, all sides vacant when surveyed. Wit:
JOHN SPANN, SAML. (X) EASLEY. Signed: JAMES BATES. 16 May 1789 oath
bef. ROBERT NELSON, Justice for Co. Rec. 19 May 1789.

Pp 48-49:   8 Jan. 1789. JOSIAH CULBERTSON of Spartanburg Co. to JOHN
              THOMAS, JR. of Greenville Co. for 300 pds sterling, 200
acres on North side of S. Fork of Tyger River bordering on the North
lands of JOHN THOMAS; granted to JOSIAH CULBERTSON 16 July 1784 by
Gov. Guerard. Signed: JOSIAH CULBERTSON. Wit: DANIEL (his mark) MC
MILLIN, KEZIAH (her mark) HOLCOM, CELIA (X) CULBERTSON. 19 May 1789
DANIEL MC MILLIN attested to signatures bef. ROBT. NELSON, Esq. and
ordered to be recorded.

Pp 49-50:   19 May 1789. EDWARD BALLINGER of Greenville Co. to HENRY
              MACHIN of same, for 200 pds sterling, 274 acres on both
sides of Enoree River, part of a tract of 587 acres granted sd BALLINGER
7 Nov. 1785 by Gov. Moultrie and rec. in Grant Book EEEE page 534.
Signed: EDWARD BALLINGER. Wit: JOHN LEWIS. 19 May 1789 - deed ack.
by EDW. BALLINGER and ordered recorded.

Pp 50-51:   17 Aug. 1789. JAMES BLASINGAME, Esq., of Greenville Co.
              to ELIAS PHILIPS of same for 100 pds, 217 acres on branches
of Saluda River, bordering PERRY; part of tract of 1800 acres granted
sd BLASINGAME 2 Apr. 1787 by Gov. Thos. Pinckney, rec. in Grant Book
WWWW page 486. Signed: JAMES BLASINGAME. Wit: JOHN LEWIS. 17 Aug. 1789
deed ack. by JAS. BLASINGAME and ordered recorded.

Pp 51-52:   4 July 1789. ALLEN GOWEN of Greenville to RICHARD HENSON
              of same, for 50 pds sterling, 214 acres on the sink hole
fork of Tyger River, bordering NW on THOMAS BENSON, SE on MICHAEL MILLER
and granted to GOWEN 21 Jan. 1785. Signed: ALLEN GOWEN. Wit: THOMAS
(X) PONDER, STEPHEN (X) DILL. 17 Aug. 1789 - deed ack. by GOWEN and
ordered recorded.

Pp 52-53:   4 July 1789. JOSEPH DOUGHTY of Greenville Co., yeoman,
              to REUBEN BARRETT of same, for 40 pds sterling, 100 acres
on Wildcat Creek of South Tyger River, bordering JOHN LUCAS; granted
sd DOUGHTY 5 Feb. 1787 by Gov. Moultrie. Signed: JOSEPH (his mark)
DOWTY. Wit: WILLIAM SILVERSIDES, JEREMIAH DUTTON, RACHEL (R) SILVER-
SIDES. 17 Aug. 1789 - proved by oaths of JEREMIAH DUTTON & WM. SILVER-
SIDES and ordered recorded.

Pp 53-54:   8 Aug. 1789. CHARLES SULLIVANT of 96 Dist. to SAMUEL DEWEAST
              of same, for 500 pds sterling, 170 acres on a branch of
Horse Creek of Reedy River; orig. granted to SULLIVANT 1 May 1785.
Signed: CHARLES SULLIVANT. Wit: HEWLET SULLIVANT, JOSEPH DUNKLIN. 17
Aug. 1789 - ack. by CHAS. SULLIVANT and rec'd.

Pp 54-56:   Lease & Release. 23 Apr. 1789. MICHAEL PURKLE of Greenville,
              planter, to THOMAS SAMFORD of same, for 30 pds sterling,
100 acres on Reedy River bordering HUGH ROARK's line, part of 200 acres
granted sd PURKLE 3 Apr. 1786 by Gov. Moultrie. Signed: MICHAEL (B)
PURKLE, BARBARA PURKLE. Wit: BENJAMIN POLLARD, WILLIAM POLLARD, JAMES
SAMFORD. 17 Aug. 1789 - proved by BENJ. POLLARD & JAMES SAMFORD and
recorded.

Pp 56-58:   Lease & Release. 23 Apr. 1789. MICHAEL PURKLE, Greenville
              Co. to JAMES SAMFORD of same, for 30 pds sterling, 100
acres on Reedy River bordering HUGH ROARK, part of 200 acres grant
to sd PURKLE 3 Apr. 1786. (Same as above lease/release)

Pp 58-61:   Lease & Release. 14 Aug. 1789. JAMES MC WILLIAMS, Greenville
             Co., planter, to BENJAMIN POLLARD of same, planter, for
63 pds sterling, 250 acres, part of 276 acres granted 5 Jan. 1789 to
MC WILLIAMS, on South side of Reedy River bordering sd MC WILLIAMS
and DUNCAN CAMERON. Signed: JAMES (his mark) MC WILLIAMS. Wit: JAMES
SAMFORD, HUGH ROARK, MATTHEW ARMSTRONG. 17 Aug. 1789 - proved by SAMFORD
& ARMSTRONG and recorded.

Pp 61-63:   Lease & Release. 25 Apr. 1789. HENRY DOMENY of Orangeburg
             Dist., planter, to JOHN ALEXANDER, Greenville, planter
for 10 shillings (lease) and 20 shillings (release), 640 acres on waters
of Reedy River bordering THOMAS JENKINS. Signed: HENRY (X) DOMENY.
Wit: JEREMIAH WILLIAMS, MARTIN ARMSTRONG, GEORGE (X) FILLER. 2 June
1789 - proved by ARMSTRONG bef. JAMES HARRISON, J.P. and recorded.

Pp 63-65:   Lease & Release. 17 Aug. 1789. PATRICK RYLEY of Laurens
             Co. to EDWARD SANDERS of same, for 20 pds current money,
250 acres on a small branch of Reedy Fork of Reedy River bordering
JOHN PYLE's, orig. granted JAMES CALDWELL 7 Aug. 1786 and sd CALDWELL
sold to PATRICK RYLEY. Signed: PATRK. RYLEY. Wit: HEWLET SULLIVANT,
JOSEPH DUNKLIN.

Page 65:   Deed of Gift. 8 Apr. 1789. I, ANDREW NELSON of Greenville
             Co., planter, freely give to my two beloved sons ANDREW
NELSON and THOMAS NELSON all my whole estate real and personal. To
ANDREW, horse, cattle and farming utensils. To THOMAS, cattle and a
tract of 200 acres I now live on, on both sides of the Reedy River.
Signed: ANDREW (his mark) NELSON. No witnesses. 17 Aug. 1789- ack.
in open court and recorded.

Pp 65-67:   Lease & Release. 14 Aug. 1789. HENRY LINDERMAN of Greenville
             Co., weaver, to JOHN LINDERMAN of same, planter, for 40
pds sterling, 140 acres part of 640 acres orig. granted to JAMES MC
WILLIAMS 21 Jan. 1785, sold by him to HENRY LINDERMAN, bounded NE by
Reedy River, SE by MATTHEW ARMSTRONG, SW by HANCE BLACK, NW by JAMES
MC WILLIAMS. Signed: HENRY LINDERMAN. No witnesses. 17 Aug. 1789 ack.
by HENRY LINDERMAN and ordered recorded.

Pp 67-68:   12 Aug. 1789. JAMES JORDAN of Spartanburg Co. to SAMUEL
             MILLER for 100 pds sterling, 300 acres granted to JAMES
JORDAN 16 July 1784 on the branches of Reedy River bounded SE by CHARLES
LITTLETON. Signed: JAMES JORDAN. Wit: SAMUEL YOUNG, JOHN TINNEY, LOD
DULIN. 17 Aug. 1789 - ack. by JAMES JORDAN and ordered recorded.

Pp 68-70:   Lease & Release. 14 Aug. 1789. JAMES MC WILLIAMS of Green-
             ville Co., planter, to JOHN LINDERMAN of same, for 5 pds
sterling, 10 acres, part of 276 acres granted to sd MC WILLIAMS 5 Jan.
1789, on south side of Reedy River bounded SE by JAMES MC WILLIAMS,
W by DUNCAN CAMERON. Signed: JAMES (his mark) MC WILLIAMS. No witnesses.
17 Aug. 1789 ack. by JAS. MC WILLIAMS and recorded.

Pp 70-71:   13 June 1789. ANTHONY BEVERLY of Greenville Co. to LEVI
             ROINS of same, for 50 pds, 100 acres orig. granted to WIL-
LIAM HADEN(?) 5 Dec. 1785, bet. the forks of a branch and little fork
of Reedy River. Signed: ANTHONY (A) BEVERLY. Wit: ALBERT ROLINS, THOMAS
BLACK. 17 Aug. 1789 - proved by THOS. BLACK bef. JAS. BLASINGAME, Esq.
and ordered recorded.

Pp 71-72:   17 Aug. 1789. CHARLES SULLEVANT of 96 Dist. to SAMUEL NEIGH-
             BORS of same, for 20 pds, 200 acres orig. granted SULLE-
VANT 3 Mar. 1788, on line creek of Saluda River. Signed: CHARLES SULLE-
VANT. Wit: JOSEPH DUNKLIN, HEWLET SULLEVANT. 17 Aug. 1789 - ack. by
CHAS. SULLEVANT and ordered recorded.

Pp 72-73:   17 Aug. 1789. JOHN CHILDRESS of Greenville Co., hatter,
             to ROBERT CHILDRESS of the same, for 40 pds sterling, 338
acres on the South side of Beaverdame Creek of S. Tyger River, being
part of two tracts, the lower part of a division of 614 acres granted
to sd JOHN CHILDRESS 6 Feb. 1786, and the upper part of a division

147

Cont'd from page 147:
of 233 acres granted OBADIAH HOOPER 5 Feb. 1787 and sold to JOHN CHILD-
RESS. Signed: JOHN CHILDRESS. Wit: GEORGE SALMON, JESSE SAXON. 17 Aug.
1789 - ack. by JOHN CHILDRESS and ordered to be recorded.

Pp 73-74:   17 Aug. 1789. JOHN CHILDRESS of Greenville, hatter, to
            CARTER LANGLEY of same, planter, for 75 pds sterling, 150
acres on south side of Beaverdam Creek of Tyger River bounding HENRY
PEARSON, granted to CHILDRESS 6 Feb. 1786. Signed: JOHN CHILDRESS.
Wit: JOSEPH (his mark) LANGLEY, GEORGE SALMON. 17 Aug. 1789 - ack.
by JNO. CHILDRESS and ordered recorded.

Pp 74-75:   6 June 1789. I, MICHAEL HENDERSON of S. C., having three
            different obligations against the estate of THOMAS HENDERSON,
SR., late of Smith's River in Hennory Co., Va., dec'd, he having a
son MICHAEL which was heir at law and sd MICHAEL it appears that he
has never received any of his sd father's estate, I, MICHAEL HENDERSON
do oblige myself, my heirs, executors, etc. never to apply or call
on sd MICHAEL HENDERSON, heir to THOMAS HENDERSON, SR., dec'd, nor
on his heirs for any part of sd three notes if they are never recovered
out of sd estate otherwise. Signed: MICHAEL HENDERSON. Wit: JAMES HEND-
ERSON, DAVID (D) HENDERSON. 17 Aug. 1789 - proved by JAMES HENDERSON
and ordered recorded.

Pp 75-76:   17 Aug. 1789. JAMES BLASINGAME, Esq. of Greenville Co.
            to REUBIN COUPLAND of same, for 50 pds sterling, 174 acres
bounded by Saluda River and ROBT. HASLIP, part of 1800 acres granted
sd BLASINGAME 2 Apr. 1787, rec'd in Grant Book WWWW page 486. Signed:
JAMES BLASINGAME. Wit: JOHN LEWIS. 17 Aug. 1789 - ack. by JAS BLASINGAME
and ordered recorded.

Pp 76-77:   4 Mar. 1789. WILLIAM GOUGH to WILLIAM STRINGER, both of
            96 Dist. for 40 pds sterling, 110 acres both sides of south
fork of Beaverdame Creek, Checkroe, bordering SMITH, plat certified
22 Jan. 1785. Signed: WILLIAM GOUGH. Wit: REUBEN STRINGER, SAMUEL (X)
MC CONEY. 14 Aug. 1789 - REUBEN STRINGER attested to signatures bef.
JOHN FORD, J.P. Rec. 17 Aug. 1789.

Pp 77-78:   25 Apr. 1789. DUNCAN CAMPBELL of Greenville Co., yeoman,
            to REUBEN BARRETT of same, for 35 pds sterling, 100 acres
on South Tygar River, granted 21 Jan. 1785 to DUNCAN CAMPBELL. Signed:
DUNCAN (X) CAMPBELL. Wit: JORDAN HOLCOM, JOSEPH (X) DAUGHTY. 17 Aug.
1789 - ack. by DUNCAN CAMPBELL bef. ROBT. NELSON, Esq. and recorded.

Pp 78-79:   29 July 1789. JOHN NORWOOD of Abbeville Co., planter, to
            JOSEPH HUGHS of Union Co., planter, for 130 pds sterling,
304 acres on north side of the south fork of Saludy about 1 mile above
the forks, bounded NE by lands of Col. ANDERSON, Esq., granted to JOHN
NORWOOD 16 July 1784. Signed: JOHN NORWOOD. Wit: SAML. HOUSTON, JAMES
MORROW. 28 July 1789 - SAML. HOUSTON attested to signatures bef. ANDREW
HAMILTON, J.P. 17 Aug. 1789 - proved bef. ANDW. HAMILTON, Esq.

Pp 79-80:   30 Mar. 1789. ROBERT HAZLIP of Greenville Co. to MERY HALL
            of same, for 70 pds, 279 acres granted to sd HAZLIP 7 Apr.
1788, on the north side of Saluda. Signed: ROBERT (X) HAZLIP. Wit:
JOHN JETT, ELIAS PHILLIPS. 17 Aug. 1789 - proved by ELIAS PHILLIPS
bef. JAMES BLASINGAME, J.P. and recorded.

Pp 81-82:   24 Sept. 1788. DAVID EVANS of Winnsborough of Fairfield
            Co., S.C., Gentleman, to JOSEPH DUNKLING near Reedy River
in the same state, planter, for 150 pds sterling, 640 acres bounded
SW by Reedy River, NW by CHARLES SULLIVANT. Signed: D. EVANS. Wit:
DAVID READ EVANS, WM. EVANS. Rec. 17 Aug. 1789. 26 Sept. 1788 - proved
by DAVID READ EVANS bef. MINOR WINN, Esq. of Fairfield Co.

Pp 82-85:   Lease & Release. 2 Mar. 1789. THOMAS SCROGIN, planter,
            and HANNAH, his wife of Greenville Co. to JOHN WESTFIELD,
planter of same, for 100 pds sterling, 397 acres on the West branch
of Golden Grove Creek, waters of Saluda. Signed: THOMAS CROGIN, HANNAH

Cont'd from page 148:
(X) CROGIN. Wit: MERRY HALL, REUBEN COPLAND. 5 Mar. 1789 - REUBEN COP-
LAND attested to signatures bef. JAMES BLASINGAME, J.P. Rec. 17 Aug.
1789.

Pp 85-87:   2 Mar. 1789. THOMAS SCROGIN of Greenville Co., planter,
             to oTHOMAS DOGWOOD of same, planter, for 10 pds sterling,
200 acres, granted to THOMAS SCROGIN 2 Oct. 1786, on Brushy Creek of
Saluda River. Signed: THOMAS SCROGIN, HANNAH (X) SCROGIN. Wit: HENRY
MACHEN, BENJAMIN RICE, MERRY HALL, CHATTEN DOGGETT. 7 Aug. 1789 - BENJ.
RICE attested to signatures bef. JAMES BLASINGAME, J.P. Rec. 17 Aug.
1789.

Pp 87-88:   21 May 1789. ZACHARIAH BLACKWELL of Spartanburg Co. to
             JOHN TUBB of Greenville Co. for 15 pds, 200 acres on the
head branches of Enoree, "granted to ZACHARIAH BLACKWELL, heir at law
to DAN'L BLACKWELL, JR., on the bounty", granted by Gov. Moultrie 1
Aug. 1785. Signed: ZACHARIAH (his mark) BLACKWELL. Wit: ROBERT PRINCE,
JACOB (E) DAVIS. 17 Aug. 1789 - proved by ROBT. PRINCE bef. ROBERT
NELSON, Esq. and ordered recorded.

Pp 88-90:   18 Nov. 1788. JOHN MARTIN of York Co. to WILLIAM HOLEBROOK
             of Greenville Co. for 50 pds sterling, 300 acres on the
North side of Saludy, granted to sd MARTIN by Gov. Pinckney 3 Sept.
1787, bounded by DREWRY MORRIS, Widow MANNON, and Saluda River. Signed:
JOHN MARTIN. Wit: MATTHEW ALEXANDER, JAMES MOORE. 20 May 1789, JAMES
MOORE attested to signatures bef. A. BLACKBURN, J.P. Rec. 17 Aug. 1789.

Pp 90-91:   18 Feb. 1789. GEORGE PEARCE of 96 Dist. to EDMUND BLACKWELL
             for valuable consideration (10 pds sterling) 50 acres part
of a tract granted MILES JINNINS in 1786, on the north side of Saludy
River on Holly Springs Branch, bounded on all sides by sd PEARCE's
land, sold by MILES JINNINGS to ROBERT TATE 2 May in the next above
mentioned year, sold by sd TATE to the above mentioned GEORGE PEARCE
25 Mar., year bef. mentioned. Signed: GEORGE (X) PEARCE. Wit: JAMES
MOOR, JAMES ROSS. 17 Feb. 1789, JOHN MARTIN, deputy surveyor, attests
that he laid out the above 50 acres. (Plat accompanies deed.) 1 June
1789, JAMES MOORE attested to signatures bef. R. MAXWELL, J.P. Rec.
17 Aug. 1789.

Pp 91-92:   13 Mar. 1789. AARON KEMP and JOSEPH DUNAGAN of Greenville
             Co. to ISAAC GREEN of same, for 155 pds sterling, 200 acres
on a branch of Enoree River, including the plantation where JOSEPH
DUNIGAN now lives, orig. granted to AARON KEMP by Gov. Moultrie 5 Sept.
1785. Signed: AARON KEMP, JOSEPH DUNNAGAN. Wit: THOMAS DUNNAGAN, JEPHTH-
ER (his mark) DENEY (DENCY?). Rec. 18 Aug. 1789.

Pp 92-93:   18 Aug. 1789. JOSEPH OBANNON of Wilton Co., S.C. (Probably
             Winton) to JOHN THOMAS, JR. of Greenville Co., for 50 pds
sterling, 301 acres on both sides of Hampton's branch of Beaverdam
Creek of South Tygar River, part of 485 acres granted to sd JOSEPH
OBANNON (blank) Oct. 1784. Signed: JOS. OBANNON. Wit: GEORGE SALMON,
J. WHITNER. 18 Aug. 1789, JOSEPH WITNER attested to signatures bef.
ROBERT NELSON, Esq. and ordered recorded.

Pp 93-94:   1 Apr. 1789. EDWIN SMITH and SARAH SMITH his wife of Green-
             ville Co. to BENJAMIN SMITH of same, for 20 pds (25 pds
in another place in deed) for 100 acres on the side of Saluda River,
part of 608 acres orig. granted to EDWIN SMITH by Gov. Moultrie 5 June
1786, bordering EDWIN SMITH and WA (?) BERIS(?). Signed: EDW. SMITH.
Wit: J. HINSON, JOSH N. KENNEDY. 18 Aug. 1789, proved by EDWIN SMITH
bef. AMBROSE BLACKBURN, Esq. and ordered recorded.

Pp 95-96:   29 May 1789. THOMAS JENKINS of Greenville Co. to JAMES
             HARRISON of same, for 10 pds sterling, 20 acres part of
a tract of land orig. granted WILLIAM HOGINS by Gov. Moultrie 3 Apr.
1786, including the sd JAMES HARRISON's dwelling house, bordering JANE
CAMBELL. Signed: THOS. JENKINS. Wit: JOHN MORTON, WILLIAM GILHAM. 29
May 1789, ack. by THOMAS JENKINS, Esq. bef. ROBERT MAXWELL, Esq. Rec.
18 Aug. 1789.

149

Page 96:   19 Aug. 1789. Power of Attorney. I, JOHN BOYD of Greenville
            Co. appoint my trusty and beloved friend JOHN SIZEMORE
of Halifax Co., Va. to be my lawful attorney in fact for me, for the
recovery of a tract of land formerly the property of WILLIAM BIRD,
Esq. and supposed to be conveyed from the sd BIRD to ROBERT BOYD, situate on the South side of Dann River in Halifax Co. opposite PETER TOR-
IANSON, the North side of sd river adj. lands whereon JOHN FAULKNER
and RICHARD WALL now reside. Signed: JOHN BOYD. Wit: THS(?) P. CARNES,
ROBERT NELSON. 19 Aug. 1789 ack. by JOHN BOYD in open court and ordered
recorded.

Pp 96-97:   7 Sept. 1789. HEZEKIAH RICE of Union Co., S.C. to ELISHA
             GREEN of sd county, for 150 pds current money, 300 acres
on both sides of Reedy River bordering land of WILLIAM BRANDON. Signed:
HEZEKIAH RICE, MARY RICE. Wit: JOHN STOKES, JOHN SANDERS. 10 Sept.
1789, proved by JOHN SANDERS bef. THOMAS BLASINGAME, Esq. of Union
Co. Rec. 16 Nov. 1789.

Pp 97-100:   Lease & Release. 3 Sept. 1789. JAMES MC ELHENNY and MARGET MC
              ELHENNY his wife of Greenville Co. to ELIAS EARLE of same,
for 150 pds, 300 acres all that plantation I now live on and part of
my original grant of 400 acres, granted 16 July 1784 by Gov. Guerard,
lying on the north sides of the north Fork of Saluda River. Signed:
JAMES MC ELHENNY, MARGET MC ELHENNY. Wit: GEORGE SALMON, J. GIER(?),
JOHN CLAYTON. 16 Nov. 1789. Proved by GEO. SALMON and ordered recorded.

Pp 100-101:   3 Sept. 1789. WILLIAM BROWN of Greenville Co. to MICHAEL
               WOOD of same, for 60 pds sterling, 232 acres on the south
side of Enoree River bordering EDWARD BALLENGER, FARROW's land, Brushy
Creek. Signed: WILLIAM (M) BROWN. Wit: WILLIAM WILLSON, FENNELL WILSON,
HENRY WOOD. Ack. by WM. BROWN in open court and ordered recorded 16
Aug. 1789.

Pp 101-102:   7 Aug. 1789. HENRY PRINCE of Greenville Co. to JOHN STANFORD
               of the same, for 25 pds sterling, 114 acres on waters of
So. Tygar River bordering SE on HENRY PRINCE and PEETTEAT's land, N
on DAVIS land, granted HENRY PRINCE 4 June 1787 by Gov. Pinckney. Signed
by HENRY PRINCE. Wit: DANIEL DUTTON, JAMES DAUGHERTY, JOHN STANFORD,
Jr. 16 Aug. 1789, ack. by HENRY PRINCE and recorded.

Pp 102-103:   3 Nov. 1789. PATRICK LAFFERTY of Greenville Co. to WILLIAM
               BONDS of same, for 110 pds sterling, 100 acres orig. granted
PATRICK LAFFERTY 5 Sept. 1785 by Gov. Moultrie, on the SW side of Reedy
River. Signed: PATRICK (P) LAFFERTY. Wit: JOHN SMITH, ROBERT RAMSAY,
ANDREW (X) LAFFERTY. 16 Aug. 1789, ack. in court by PATRICK LAFFERTY
and ordered recorded.

Pp 103-104:   13 Oct. 1789. ENOCH BENSON and JEMIMAH his wife of Green-
               ville Co. to DAVID QUARLS of same, for 60 pds current money,
193 acres granted the sd BENSON 2 Oct. 1786 by Gov. Moultrie, on waters
of S Tygar River. Signed: ENOCH BENSON, JEMIMAH (X) BENSON. Wit: WIL-
LIAM (M) BROWN, HENRY PEIRSON, CARTER (I) LONGLEY. 16 Nov. 1789 ack.
by ENOCH BENSON and ordered recorded.

Pp 104-105:   23 Dec. 1788. WILLIAM BRANDON of Union Co. to JEREMIAH
               STOKES of Greenville Co. for 100 pds lawful money of S.C.,
640 acres, granted sd BRANDON 15 Oct. 1784 by Gov. Guerard, west of
the Old Indian Boundary, on both sides of Reedy River, recorded in
Grant Book ZZZ page 160. Signed: WILLIAM (B) BRANDON. Wit: THOMAS BRAN-
DON, ELISHA GREEN. 16 Nov. 1789, proved by oath of ELISHA GREEN and
recorded.

Pp 105-107:   Lease & Release. 12 May 1787. JAMES MC DAVID of Greenville
               Co. to LEWIS WELLS of same, for 2 pds (lease), 3 pds (re-
lease), 100 acres on Rocky Creek of Reedy River, granted sd MC DAVID
3 Apr. 1786, recorded in Grant Book JJJJ page 91. Signed: JAMES MC
DAVID. Wit: DAVID MC DAVID, JOSEPH BOX. 16 Nov. 1789, proved by oath
of DAVID MC DAVID and ordered recorded.

Pp 107-108:   16 Nov. 1789. WILLIAM VERNALL of Greenville Co. to JOHN

Cont'd from page 150:
                    PAUL of Greenville Co., for 30 pds sterling, 20 acres,
part of 345 acres granted to sd VERNAL by Gov. Moultrie, 4 Sept. 1786,
recorded Grant Book MMMM page 587, the sd 20 acres being the north
side of the tract of 345 acres bordering lands of WILLIAM GUNN, and
BEAL. Signed: WILLIAM VARNELL. Wit: JOHN LEWIS. 16 Nov. 1789, ack.
by WM. VARNEL and ordered recorded.

Pp 108-109: 6 May 1789. ROBERT PRINCE of Greenville Co. to THOMAS BENSON
                    of same, for 100 pds sterling, 138 acres near the head
of Enoree River, granted sd PRINCE 1 Aug. 1785 by Gov. Moultrie, recorded Grant Book EEEE page 226, bounded NW on a tract of 200 acres
of land laid out to ROBERT PRINCE. Signed: ROBERT PRINCE. Wit: DAVID
MC NEALY, ALEXANDER GILBERT, BAYLIS EARLE, J. BAYLIS EARLE. 16 Nov.
1789, proved bef. ISAAC MORGAN, Esq. by J. BAYLIS EARLE and ordered
recorded.

Pp 109-110: 6 May 1789. ROBERT PRINCE of Greenville Co. to THOMAS BENSON
                    of same, for 100 pds sterling, 200 acres near head of Enoree
River, granted to sd PRINCE 15 Oct. 1784 by Gov. Guerard, recorded
in Grant Book BBBB page 39. Signed: ROBERT PRINCE. Wit: BAYLIS EARLE,
J. BAYLIS EARLE. 16 Nov. 1789, proved by J. BAYLIS EARLE bef. ISAAC
MORGAN, Esq. and ordered recorded.

Pp 110-111: 1 May 1789. DANIEL BLACKWELL of Rutherford Co., N.C. to
                    THOMAS BENSON of Greenville Co. for 15 pds, 200 acres on
head branches of Enoree, granted to DANIEL BLACKWELL on the bounty
4 July 1785 by Gov. Moultrie. Signed: DANIEL BLACKWELL. Wit: ROBERT
PRINCE, SARAH (X) LYLES. Proved by ROBT. PRINCE 12 Sept. 1789.

Pp 111-112: Power of Attorney. 16 Nov. 1789. I, JOHN THOMAS of Newberry
                    Co. appoint my trusty friend THOMAS LEWIS of Greenville
Co. my true and lawful attorney, to recover two tracts of land in Caswell Co., N.C. on Hogan's Creek, decended to the sd JOHN THOMAS as
the lawful heir to JOHN THOMAS, dec'd, his father, formerly of N. C.
Signed: JOHN THOMAS. Wit: THOMAS CAMP, JOHN CAMP. 16 Nov. 1789, proved
by oath of THOMAS CAMP and ordered recorded.

Pp 112-114: Lease & Release. 1 Jan. 1788. DAVID REID EVANS, Gentleman,
                    to JOHN GOODWYN of Reedy River, Gentleman, for 93 pds 18
shillings current money of S.C., 313 acres on Reedy River, bounded
by sd JOHN GOODWYN, granted to sd EVANS 10 July 1784. Signed: DAVID
READ EVANS. Wit: WM. ROACH, THOMP. WHITEHOUSE. 20 Sept. 1788, proved
by WILLIAM ROACH, Esq. bef. MINOR WINN, Esq., J.P. of Fairfield Co.,
S.C. Recorded 17 Nov. 1789. (Notation in margin: "Copy made for DAVIS
Nov. 1817. Fee 8/3")

Pp 114-116: 24 Sept. 1789. DANIEL JACKSON of Union Co., S.C. to CHRIS-
                    TOPHER BRUNK, SR. of Greenville Co. for 200 pds sterling,
640 acres on Mountain Creek of Saluda River including the fork of sd
creek, granted to WILLIAM NEEL 25 Jan. 1785, recorded Grant Book CCCC
page 337, sold by WM. NEEL to sd JACKSON. Signed: DANIEL JACKSON, CHRIS-
TOPHER (B) BRUNK. (This was a Lease & Release - BRUNK signed Lease
only. No witnesses to Lease.) Release Wit: RT. MAXWELL, THOMAS WHIT-
MAN. 21 Oct. 1789, proved by ROBERT MAXWELL bef. AMBROSE BLACKBURN,
Esq. Rec. 17 Nov. 1789.

Pp 116-119: Lease & Release. 28 Oct. 1785. JOHN WINN of Winnsborough,
                    Fairfield Co., S.C. to GERSHOM KELLY of the Congarees,
planter, for 300 pds sterling, 640 acres on Reedy River near the old
Indian boundary line, commonly called the Poplar Bottom, granted to
sd WINN 16 July 1784. Signed: JOHN WINN. Wit: D. EVANS, ELIAS HUGGINS,
D. R. EVANS. Proved by DAVID R. EVANS bef. RICHARD WINN, Esq. of Fairfield Co., S.C. Rec. 17 Nov. 1789.

Pp 119-120: 14 Aug. 1789. JAMES MC ELHENNEY to DENNIS DUFF, both of
                    Greenville Co., for 40 pds sterling, 30 acres on the North
Fork of Saluda, beginning at the mouth of the first creek above the
Old Indian ford, part of the tract where the sd JAMES MC ELHENNY now

Cont'd from page 151:
lives, part of 400 acres granted to him on 16 July 1784. Signed: JAMES
MC ELHENNY. Wit: JOHN FORD, J. GILL. "I do hereby acknowledge that
within mentioned deed was delivered by twig and turf." Signed: JAMES
MC ELHENNY. 17 Nov. 1789, proved by JOHN FORD, Esq. and ordered recorded.

Pp 120-121: 3 Oct. 1789. JAMES MC ELHENNY and MARGARET his wife to
JOHN MOTLOW, both of Greenville Co. for 100 pds sterling,
"the compliment of acres unknown", all that part of the plantation
where JAMES MC ELHENNY now lives that lies on the South side of the
North Fork of Saluda River, from the lower end of the sd plantation
up to the first small creek and no further, land granted to sd MC EL-
HENNY 16 July 1784. Signed: JAMES MC ELHENNY, MARGET MC ELHENNY. Wit:
ELIAS EARLE, JOHN CLAYTON, HENRY PRINCE. 17 Nov. 1789, proved by oath
of HENRY PRINCE and ordered recorded.

Pp 121-122: 29 Nov. 1788. JOHN CARR of Washington Co., N.C. to WILLIAM
BRIDGES of Rutherford Co., N.C. for 60 pds current money,
97 acres on both sides of Reedy River, granted to sd CARR 21 Jan. 1785
by Gov. Guerard. Signed: JOHN CARR. Wit: JAMES CONN, ROBERT DUNCAN.
17 Nov. 1789, proved by JAMES CONN & ROBT. DUNCAN bef. LEML. J. ALSTON,
Esq. and ordered recorded.

Pp 122-124: Lease & Release. 18 Apr. 1788. NATHL. REED of Greenville
Co. to JOSEPH REED of same, for 50 pds, 350 acres granted
to NATHL. REED 5 June 1786, recorded Grant Book MMMM page 126, on both
sides of Rocky Creek. Signed: NATHANIEL (N) REED. Wit: WILL. NICHOL-
SON, LUVICA (X) WILLIAMS. 17 Nov. 1789, proved by LUVICA WILLIAMS bef.
THOMAS JENKINS, Esq. and ordered recorded.

Pp 124-125: 21 Feb. 1789. THOMAS KEVIL of Laurens Co., planter, to
BEVERLY LYALL of county afsd, for 40 pds sterling, 252
acres bounded by JOSEPH LYNN's line, on Rocky Creek, waters of Enoree
River, granted to THOMAS KEVIL 3 Mar. 1788 by Gov. Pinckney, recorded
Grant Book WWWW page 550. Signed: THOMAS KEVIL. Wit: JOAB LEAGUE, MICA-
JAH COMPTON. 17 Nov. 1789, ack. in open court by THOMAS KEVIL and order-
ed recorded.

Pp 125-126: 9 Nov. 1789. WILLIAM GILHAM of 96 Dist. to THOMAS JENKINS
of same for 50 pds lawful money, 200 acres on Reedy River
granted to WILLIAM GILHAM by Gov. Moultrie 4 Dec. 1786. Signed: WIL-
LIAM GILHAM. Wit: JOHN MC ELROY, WILLIAM (X) TESDELL, JOHN MC ELROY.
(Note: there are evidently two JOHN MC ELROYs) 17 Nov. 1789, proved
by JOHN MC ELROY and ordered recorded.

Pp 126-127: 16 Nov. 1789. EDWARD BALLINGER of Greenville Co. to STEPHEN
CANTRELL of same, for 50 pds sterling, 120 acres on both
sides of the Enoree River bordering sd BALLINGER and MACHEN, part of
587 acres granted sd EDWARD BALLINGER by Gov. Moultrie 7 Nov. 1785,
recorded Grant Book EEEE page 504. Signed: EDWARD BALLENGER. No witnesses. 17 Nov. 1789, ack. by EDW. BALLINGER and recorded.

Pp 127-128: 16 Feb. 1789. LEMUEL JAMES ALSTON, Esq. of Greenville Co.
to ISHAM CLAYTON of same, for 5 shillings sterling, 15
acres on branches of Saludy river, part of 418 acres granted sd ALSTON
3 Oct. 1786 by Gov. Moultrie, recorded Grant Book MMMM page 595. Signed:
L. J. ALSTON. Wit: JAMES YANCY, JR. 17 Nov. 1789, JAMES YANCY, JR.
attested to signatures bef. ROBERT NELSON, J.P. Recorded 11 Jan. 1790.

Pp 128-129: 13 Nov. 1789. JOHN HAM and PHEBE his wife of S. C. to ROW-
LAND TANKERSLY of Henry Co., Va., for 192 pds 10 shillings
sterling, 350 acres on both sides of the North Fork of Golden Grove
Creek of Saluda River, West of the old boundary line, bounded W by
JOSEPH BENSON. Signed: JOHN HAM, PHEBE (X) HAM. Wit: JOHN WESTFIELD,
AMOS MARTIN, GUTRIDGE (GL) LOCKLEEN. 21 Nov. 1789, JOHN WESTFIELD at-
tested to signatures bef. J. BLASINGAME, J.P. Recorded 11 Jan. 1790.

Pp 129-131: Lease & Release. 7 Mar. 1789. PAUL FOUNTAIN of 96 Dist.
to ROBERT CANNON of same for 45 pds sterling, 200 acres

Cont'd from page 152:
above the Antient Boundary Line on Saluda River, granted PAUL FOUNTAIN
4 July 1785 by Gov. Moultrie. Signed: PAUL FOUNTAIN. Wit: STEPHEN (X)
FOUNTAIN, BENJAMIN (C) CORNELIUS. 19 Jan. 1790, BENJ. CORNELIUS attested
to signatures bef. JOHN WILSON, Esq., J.P. of Pendleton Co., S.C. Rec.
9 Feb. 1790.

Pp 131-132: 4 Feb. 1790. ROBERT CANNON of Greenville to ROBERT HARRISON
                of the same, for 100 pds sterling, 200 acres on Saluda
River, granted to PAUL FOUNTAIN 4 July 1785, and sold by FOUNTAIN to
ROBERT CANNON 7 Mar. 1789. Signed: ROBERT CANNON. Wit: REUBEN HARRISON,
GEORGE HARRISON. 8 Feb. 1790, REUBEN HARRISON attested to signatures
bef. JAMES BLASINGAME, J.P. Rec. 9 Feb. 1790.

Pp 132-133: 15 Feb. 1790. GEORGE SALMON of Greenville Co. to SAMUEL
                FRENCH of same, for 2 pds sterling, 10 acres, part of 525
acres granted to GEORGE SALMON 7 May 1787, bet. two branches of Che-
choroa River, waters of Saluda River, bordering sd FRENCH, JOHN JACK-
SON, THOMAS MC CARREL. Signed: GEORGE SALMON. Wit: W. H. LACEY, CHARLES
BENSON. 15 Feb. 1790, ack. by GEO. SALMON and ordered recorded.

Pp 133-134: 16 Jan. 1790. THOMAS FARROW and REBECCA FARROW his wife
                of Spartanburg Co. to PLEASANT SULLIVANT of Greenville
Co., for 100 pds, 320 acres, the upper half of a tract of 640 acres
granted to THOMAS FARROW 16 July 1784, on the East side of the North
Fork of Saluda River, bordering the boundary line of THOMAS FARROW
and JOSEPH TERRY. Signed: THOMAS FARROW, REBECCA FARROW. Wit: HULET
SULLIVANT, STEPHEN SULLIVANT. 15 Feb. 1790, proved by oaths of HULET
& STEPHEN SULLIVANT and recorded.

Page 135: 15 Feb. 1790. PLEASANT SULLIVANT of Greenville Co., to
                STEPHEN SULLIVANT, planter, of same, for 55 pds current
money, 160 acres on North Fork of Saluda River, it being the N.W. and
S.W. part of a 640 acre traact granted THOMAS FARROW 16 July 1784.
Signed: PLEASANT SULLIVANT. Wit: HULET SULLIVANT, JOHN HUGHS, CHARLES
SULLIVANT. 15 Feb. 1790, proved by oath of HULET SULLIVANT and ordered
recorded.

Pp 136-137: 8 Sept. 1789. ROBERT PRINCE of Greenville Co. to JAMES
                TUBB of same, for 40 pds sterling, 230 acres on a branch
of Enoree, granted 22 Apr. 1785 by Gov. Moultrie. Signed: ROBERT PRINCE.
Wit: H. M. WOOD, JOHN TUBB. 15 Feb. 1790, proved by oaths of HENRY
M. WOOD & JOHN TUBB and ordered recorded.

Page 137: 21 Feb. 1790. EDMUND PETERS of Greenville Co. to GIPSON
                SUTHERN(?) of same, for 30 pds sterling, 100 acres on both
sides of Beaverdame Creek of Enoree River, including the farm where
sd EDMUND PETERS now lives bordering MOSES WOOD and SAVAGE's line.
Signed: EDMUND PETERS. Wit: JOHN ANDERSON, WILLIAM RODGERS. 6 Mar.
1790, proved by oath of JOHN ANDERSON bef. LEMUEL J. ALSTON, Esq.

Pp 137-138: 15 Feb. 1790. JESSE LAXON of Greenville, planter, to ROBERT
                CHILDRESS, planter of the same, for 35 pds sterling, 100
acres, part of 420 acres granted JEREMIAH DUTTON 3 Oct. 1785 by Gov.
Moultrie, sold by JEREMIAH DUTTON and SARAH his wife to above mentioned
JESSE LAXON, bordering the waggon road leading from JOHN NICOL to Col.
THOMAS, and SALMON's line. Signed: JESSE LAXON. Wit: GEORGE SALMON,
JOHN YOUNG. 15 Feb. 1790, ack. by JESSE LAXON and ordered recorded.

Pp 138-139: 10 Nov. 1789. THOMAS BRIDGES of Greenville Co. to OVERTON
                GOODMON of same, for 96 pds current money, 200 acres on
both sides of Reedy River near Parises mountain west of the Antient
Boundary line, granted to ISHAM FOSTER 21 Jan. 1785 by Gov. Guerard.
Signed: THOMAS (X) BRIDGES. Wit: HARDIN CEMP, PINKEY HAWKINS. 15 Mar.
1790 proved by oath of HARLEM KEMP bef. LEMUEL ALSON and recorded.

Page 139: 18 Sept. 1789. ROBERT PRINCE of Greenville Co. to JAMES
                YOUNG of same, for 10 pds sterling, part of a certain tract
of land containing 200 acres. Signed: ROBERT PRINCE. Wit: THOMAS (X)

Cont'd from page 153:
NORRIS, JOHN FRENCH. 16 Mar. 1790 proved by oath of THOMAS NORRIS bef.
L. A. ALSTON, Esq. and recorded.

Pp 139-140: 29 Oct. 1789. THOMAS LEWIS of Greenville to CHARLES EASTES
of same, for 10 pds, 26 acres on waters of Mountain Creek,
bounded by WM. WOODS, LEWIS & MATTOCK; being part of a tract of land
orig. granted PATRICK LAFFERTY 6 Sept. 1785, recorded Grant Book FFFF
page 41; LAFFERTY sold to THOMAS LEWIS 20 Nov. 1787. Signed: THOMAS
LEWIS. Wit: VINCENT LEWIS VINCENT DAVIS. 16 Mar. 1790 proved by oath
of VINCENT LEWIS bef. ROBERT NELSON, Esq. and recorded.

Pp 140-141: 29 Oct. 1789. THOMAS LEWIS of Greenville Co. to JESSE
CHANDLER of the same, for 10 pds, 63 acres on waters of
Mountain Creek, bordering MATTOCK's line, WM. WOODS; part of a tract
orig. granted PATRICK LAFFERTY 6 Sept. 1785 and sold to THOMAS LEWIS
25 Nov. 1787. Signed: THOMAS LEWIS. Wit: VINCENT LEWIS, VINCENT DAVIS.
17 Mar. 1790, proved by oath of VINCENT LEWIS bef. ROBERT NELSON, Esq.
and recorded.

Pp 141-142: 3 Feb. 1790. JOSEPH NATIONS, SR. and ELLENDER his wife
to HUGH MC VAY for 40 pds sterling, 251 acres on waters
of Reedy River and Enoree, bordering JAMES CONN, WM. BENSON, granted
sd NATIONS 6 Feb. 1785, recorded Grant Book HHHH page 89. Signed: JOSEPH
(his mark) NATION, ELLENDER (her mark) NATION. Wit: JOHN GOODLETT,
THOS. BENSON. Proved bef. ROBERT NELSON, Esq. by JOHN GOODLETT and
recorded 17 Mar. 1790.

Pp 142-143: 1 Dec. 1789. WILLIAM LINCH and MARY his wife to DAVID HALL,
both of Greenville Co., for 90 pds sterling, 80 acres on
both sides of Greens Creek on South Pacolate River, granted sd LINCH
5 June 1786 by Gov. Moultrie. Signed: WILLIAM LYNCH, MARY LYNCH. Wit:
JAMES STEVENSON, RICHARD BRAZZLE, ELIZABETH STEVENSON. 18 Mar. 1790,
proved by oath of RICHARD BRAZZLE bef. ROBT. NELSON, Esq. and recorded.

Pp 143-144: (blank) Sept. 1789. ROBERT PRINCE of Greenville Co. to
MARSIN COX SMITHSON of the same, for 20 pds, 150 acres
on a branch of the North Fork of Saluda River, bordering ALLEN SMITHSON,
MARSON SMITHSON, JANE MC JUNKEN, part of a tract of 4,000 acres granted
to PRINCE 7 Mar. 1787 by Gov. Pinckney. Signed: ROBERT PRINCE. Wit:
JOHN HOOPER, JOHN GOODLETT. Proved bef. OBADIAH HOOPER, Esq. and rec.
19 Mar. 1790.

Pp 144-145: 15 Jan. 1790. JOHN EVENS, JR. of Caroline Co., Va. to GEORGE
ALLEN of Greenville Co., S.C. for 50 pds sterling, 202
acres on the South Fork of the three forks of the Tyger River bounded
SE on land laid out to ROBERT GOODLETT, the sd 202 acres granted to
WILLIAM BENSON 15 Oct. 1784, conveyed by BENSON to sd JOHN EVENS. Signed
by JOHN EVENS, JR., signed by WILLIAM BENSON by virtue of power of
attorney. Wit: HENRY PRINCE, ELI MC VAY. Proved bef. ROBT. NELSON,
Esq. by oath of HENRY PRINCE. Rec. 19 Mar. 1790.

Pp 145-146: 3 Jan. 1788. JOHN PORTMAN of 96 Dist., planter, to WILLIAM
GRANT, SR. of Greenville Co., planter, for 100 pds sterling,
200 acres granted to sd JOHN PORTMAN 5 June 1786 by Gov. Moultrie,
on the branches of Mush Creek, waters of Tyger River, bounded N by
PHILLIP, E by ABRAHAM CHASTEEN, W by JOHN NICHOLS. Signed: JOHN (X)
PORTMAN. Wit: JOHN STANFORD, JOHN CHILDRESS, JOHN (X) FOSTER. Proved
by oath of JOHN FORREST bef. Robt. Nelson, Esq. Rec. 20 Mar. 1790.

Pp 146-147: 12 Sept. 1789. ROBERT PRINCE of Greenville Co. tc ROBERT
TALKENTON of the same, for divers good causes and considera-
tion and 20 pds sterling money of S.C., 250 acres, part of 4,000 acres
granted to sd PRINCE 7 Mar. 1787 by Gov. Pinckney, bordering WM. PERRY,
TURNBOUGH, SAVAGE, on Enoree River West of the Indian Boundary. Signed:
ROBERT PRINCE. Wit: JEPTHA HOLLINGSWORTH, THOS. BENSON. Proved by JEPTHA
HOLLINGSWORTH bef. ROBT. NELSON, Esq.. Rec. 23 Mar. 1790.

Pp 147-150: Lease & Release. 13 Nov. 1789. JAMES SHIRLEY of Abbeville

154

Cont'd from page 154:
Co., S.C. and MARY his wife to JOHN BOWIE of Abbeville
Co., planter, for 38 pds 17 shillings current money, 340 acres on Golden
Grove Creek of Saluda River, bounded NE by land surveyed for FRANCIS
GOTTIER, sd 340 acres granted to JAMES SHIRLEY 16 July 1784 by Gov.
Guerard, recorded in Grant Book AAAA page 25. Signed: JAMES (X) SHIRLEY
& MARY (X) SHIRLEY. Wit: MARY (X) JONES, JOHN JONES, JOHN ROSAMOND.
Proved bef. ADAM CR. JONES, J.P. of Abbeville Co. by JOHN JONES, 13
Nov. 1789. No recording date.

Pp 150-151: 3 Aug. 1789. OBADIAH HOOPER, JR. of Greenville Co. to SAMUEL
GORDAN of same, for divers good causes and considerations
and the sum of 5 shillings, 600 acres on the South side of the Enoree
River. Signed: OB. HOOPER. Wit: JOSHUA CURTIS, JESSE CARTER, JEPTHA
HOLLINGSWORTH. Proved by HOLLINGSWORTH bef. Robt. Nelson, Esq. Rec.
23 Mar. 1790.

Pp 151-152: 29 Oct. 1789. THOMAS LEWIS of Greenville Co. to JOHN MAT-
LOCK (MATTOCK?) of same, for 100 pds sterling, 350 acres
on Mountain Creek of Saluda River, part of a tract of land orig. granted
to PATRICK LAFFERTY 6 Sept. 1785, recorded in Grant Book FFFF page
45, conveyed from sd LAFFERTY to THOMAS LEWIS 20 Nov. 1787. Signed:
THOMAS LEWIS. Wit: VINCENT LEWIS, VINCENT DAVIS. Proved by VINCENT
LEWIS bef. ROBT. NELSON, Esq. Rec. 24 Mar. 1790.

Pp 152-153: 16 Nov. 1789. JOHN DICKERSON of Greenville Co. to WILLIAM
REED of same, for 10 pds sterling, 100 acres on Reedy Fork
Creek of Reedy River, granted to JOHN DICKERSON by Gov. Pinckney 5
Jan. 1789. Signed: JOHN DICKERSON. Wit: JOHN WARE, GEORGE VAUGHAN.
Proved by JOHN WARE bef. A. BLACKBURN, Esq. Rec. 25 Mar. 1790.

Pp 153-154: 1 Dec. 1789. WILLIAM LYNCH to RICHARD BRAZZLE, both of
Greenville Co., for 50 pds sterling, 50 acres on both sides
of Greens Creek of South Pacolate River, granted to sd LYNCH by Gov.
Moultrie 5 June 1786, bordering RICHARD BRAZZLE and DAVID HALL. Signed:
WILLIAM LYNCH, MARY LYNCH. Wit: JAMES STEVENSON, DAVID HALL, ELIZABETH
STEVENSON. Proved bef. Robt. Nelson, Esq. by oath of DAVID HALL. Rec.
25 Mar. 1790.

Pp 154-155: 15 Feb. 1790. THOMAS KEVIL of Laurence (Laurens) Co., S.C.,
carpenter, to PAGE PUCKET of Greenville Co., planter, for
2 pds 6 shillings 8 pence sterling, 150 acres, part of a tract of 750
acres on Brushy Creek, waters of Enoree, bordering BENJAMIN WHORTON's
line, granted to sd KEVIL 3 Mar. 1788. Signed: THOMAS KEVIL. No witnesses. Proved by THOS. KEVIL Feb. term 1790.

Pp 155-156: 13 Feb. 1790. DANIEL KELLY and SARAH his wife of Greenville
Co. to HENRY M. WOOD of Spartanburg, for 100 pds sterling,
150 acres, part of a tract granted to JOSEPH DUNN 1 Jan. 1785 and trans-
ferred by him to DANIEL KELLY, on the North side of the Chackeroa River.
Signed: D. KELLEY, SARAH (X) KELLEY. Wit: ELIZABETH GILL, B. EARLE.
Deed ack. by DANL. KELLEY Feb. term 1790.

Pp 156-157: 15 Dec. 1789. THOMAS LEWIS of Greenville Co. sells unto
NANCY BIBB TERRY and SALLEY IVY TERRY, both of Greenville
Co., feather bed and furniture, dishes, cows, horse, etc. for 15 pds.
Signed: THOMAS LEWIS. Wit: WILLIAM (X) TERRY, KESIAH C. (X) TERRY.
Feb. term 1790, proved by WM. TERRY and ordered recorded.

Pp 157-158: 13 Feb. 1790. WILLIAM RIGHT of Greenville Co. to HENRY
M. WOOD of Spartanburg Co., for 50 pds sterling, 150 acres,
part of 247 acres orig. granted to WILLIAM RIGHT 1 Jan. 1785, bordering
DAN'L KELLY. Signed. W. RIGHT. Wit: D. KELLEY, ELIZABETH GILL, B. EARLE.
Proved by oath of DAVID KELLEY Feb. term 1790.

Page 159: 9 Feb. 1790. We the subscribers indifferently chosen as
arbitrators to decide a dispute bet. ALEXANDER MC KINNEY
& JONATHAN MUSICK, for MUSICK saying that MC KINEY had acted in a crimi-
nal manner, it was mutually agreed that MC KINEY was innocent and the

155

Cont'd from page 155:
charges groundless. Signed: JOHN FORD, DENNIS DUFF, ABRAHAM DENTON,
BENJA. MERRIT, EDMAN FRANKLIN, JORDAN HOLCOM, JOHN MOTLOW, MARTIN ADAMS,
REUBEN STRINGER, JAMES HENRY ROBERSON, WILLIAM LYNCH, JAMES STEVENSON.
Rec. Feb. term 1790.

Pp 159-160: 17 May 1790, the following papers presented by JOHN GRIGSBY,
        Adm. of the estate of Capt. GERRARD ROBINSON, and ordered
recorded. 21 Nov. 1767, I, GERRARD ROBINSON of King George Co., Va.,
mariner, am firmly bound unto WILLIAM SKYRIN of Whitehaven in Cumberland Co., merchant, for 72 pds 9 shillings ½ penny good and lawful
money of Great Britain. Signed: GERRARD ROBINSON. Wit: WILL'M WITHERALD,
ANT'O WESTRAY. If GERRARD ROBINSON should pay 36 pds 4 shillings and
six pence with interest by 21 Nov. 1770, this obligation will be void.
Signed: GERRARD ROBINSON. Same witnesses. It is agreed that if ISAIAH
ROBINSON of London, mariner, shall pay any part of the above mentioned
sum bef. 21 Nov. 1770, it shall be credited. Signed. WM. SKYRAN. (Same
witnesses). 21 July 1772, rec'd 53 pds 7 shillings 11 pence Virginia
currency in an order on Mr. JAMES ATKINSON for 50 pds sterling and
interest thereon from 2 Oct. 1768, and I oblige myself when I have
advice of the sd order being paid to account with Mr. JOHN GRIGSBY
and wife for what may be due them. Signed: WILLIAM TEMPLEMAN, Attorney
for the Executors of WILLIAM SKYRIN. (The follow three letters to Capt.
GERRARD ROBINSON (ROBERTSON), on board the Snow Aderton, Petapscoe
River, Baltimore, Md 1 Dec. 1769, concerning the delivery of goods
on board his vessel to the merchants of Portabacco and Colechester
and several others. Letters mention Mr. THOMAS BIDWELL of London, RICH-
ARD FULLER, DANIEL OSDILL, Mr. DAVID WALKER, and signed JER. ADERTON.)

Pp 161-163: Mortgage. 8 May 1790. JOHN DYCHE, farmer of Greenville
        Co. stands indebted to JOHN HINSON, merchant of Greenville
Co., in several sums of money amounting to 22 pds sterling, partly
for goods sold and part for cash paid to the sd JOHN DYCHE; for sure
payment of this sum bef. 25 Dec. next, the sd JOHN DYCHE has bargained,
sold, etc. to sd JOHN HENSON a tract of 440 acres on Golden Grove Creek
waters of Saluda River, part of 646 acres granted by Gov. Guerard to
RICHARD GOODE 25 Jan. 1785, recorded in Grant Book CCCC page 169, conveyed to JOHN DYCHE by sd GOODE 9 Jan. 1789. Signed: JOHN (his mark)
DYCHE. Wit: A. BLACKBURNE, JAS. TARRANT. Rec. May term 1790.

Pp 163-164: Power of Attorney. 19 May 1790. I, ROBERT HARRISON of Green-
        ville Co. appoint my trusty friend JOHN LEWIS of the same
county, my true and lawful attorney to recover from a certain JOSHUA
HARPER of Virginia a debt due me by a note dated 25 Mar. 1779, payable
25 Dec. following, for 240 pds Va. currency. Signed: ROBT. HARRISON.
Wit: GEO. SALMON, JAMES JETT. Rec. May term 1790.

Pp 164-165: 19 Sept. 1789. ROBERT PRINCE of Greenville Co. to JOHNSON
        MONROE for 5 shillings sterling, 100 acres, part of a tract
of 4,000 aces granted PRINCE 7 Mar. 1787. Signed: ROBT. PRINCE. Wit:
THOMAS BENSON, J. B. EARLE. Proved bef. GEO. SALMON, Esq. by oath of
JOHN BAYLIS EARLE. No recording date.

Page 165: 15 Sept. 1789. ROBERT PRINCE of Greenville Co. to JOHNSON
        MONROE of same, for 5 shillings, 190 acres on both sides
of Enoree River. Signed: ROBT. PRINCE. Wit: JAMES PERRYMAN, DABNEY
BROOKS. Proved by DABNEY BROOKS. No recording date.

Pp 166-167: 17 May 1790. JEREMIAH CHANDLER of Greenville Co. to JAMES
        MC WILLIAMS of same, for 60 pds sterling, 60 acres, part
of 235 acres granted to sd CHANDLER by Gov. Pinckney 6 Oct. 1788, on
Brush Creek of Reedy River, the sd 60 acres taken from the upper end
of the survey, bordering ROBERT HANNER, HUGH ROARK. Signed: JEREMIAH
CHANDLER. Wit: JESSE CARTER, JOHN LEWIS. Ack. by JEREMIAH CHANDLER
May term 1790.

Pp 167-168: 27 Feb. 1790. WILLIAM WHITE of Greenville Co. to JOHN GORDON
        of same for 5 pds, 300 acres on Mill Creek of Enoree River,
part of a tract granted to ZACHARIAH WHITE, adj. PERRIE's(?) corner.

156

Cont'd from page 156:
Signed: WILLIAM WHITE. Wit: JEPTHA HOLLINGSWORTH, SAMUEL GORDON. Ack.
by WM. WHITE, May term 1790.

Pp 168-171: Lease & Release. 2 Mar. 1790. JOSEPH MC JUNKIN of Union
Co., S.C., planter, to SAMUEL EARLE of Greenville Co.,
for 100 pds 10 shillings sterling, 640 acres on both sides of middle
fork of Saluda River, granted to sd MC JUNKIN by Gov. Benj. Guerard,
adj. land laid out to JOHN EARLE. Signed: JOSEPH MC JUNKIN. Wit: DANIEL
MC JUNKIN, J. B. EARLE, JNO. EARLE. Proven by JOHN BAYLIS EARLE, May
term 1790.

Pp 171-172: 4 Feb. 1790. JOHN LAFFERTY of 96 Dist. to SOLOMON MURPHY
MAGINIS of same, for 20 pds sterling, 100 acres on LAFFER-
TY's branch adj. south on JOHN SMITH's land, N of ROBERT RAMSEY, part
of a tract of 1000 acres granted to JOHN LAFFERTY by Gov. Thos. Pinckney, 6 Oct. 1788. Signed: JOHN LAFFERTY. Wit: JOHN RODGERS, CHARLES
RODGERS. Proven by JOHN & CHARLES RODGERS bef. L. ALSTON, Esq. No rec.
date.

Pp 172-173: 16 Feb. 1790. JONATHAN MUSICK & wife ELIN to SAMUEL MC
KINNEY, both of Greenville Co., for 50 pds sterling, 34
(35?) acres on N fork of Saluda River, part of a tract granted to sd
MUSICK 5 June 1786. Signed: JONATHAN MUSICK, HELLON (+) MUSICK. Wit:
JOHN WILLIAMS, SAML. CLEARY, EDWARD FRANKLIN. Proved by SAMUEL CLEARY
bef. ROBERT NELSON, Esq. Rec. 4 June 1790.

Pp 173-175: 20 Oct. 1789. JOSEPH REID of Greenville Co. to WILLIAM
LACEY of same, for 100 pds sterling, 353 acres orig. granted
to NATHANIEL REED by Gov. Wm. Moultrie 5 June 1786. Signed :JOSEPH
REED. Wit: ISAAC REED, JOHN (his mark) REED, JOHN REED. Proven bef.
JAMES HARRISON, Esq. by ISAAC & JOHN REID. No rec. date.

Pp 175-176: 22 Feb. 1790. WILLIAM STORY to JOHN STORY, both of Green-
ville Co., for 14 pds, 80 acres on Horse Creek Branch of
Reedy River, granted 1 May 1786. Rec. book KKKK page 492. Signed: WIL-
LIAM STORY. Wit: JESSE WEBB, BRYAN WARD NOWLIN, POOL WEBB. Ack. by
WM. STORY, rec. 4 June 1790.

Pp 176-177: 18 May 1790. GERHAM KELLEY of Greenville Co. to JOHN SIMS
of sme, for 80 pds sterling, 228 acres on S side of Ready
River, bounded N by Ready Riv. and NW by Ready Fork of Ready River
inc. 1/2 of the Mill Shoal, orig. granted to JOHN WINN, JR. by Gov.
Benj. Guerard 16 July 1784. Signed: GERSHOM KELLEY. Wit: CLAYBORN SIMS,
JOHN SIMS, MARY SYMS. Ack. by GERSHAM KELLEY, May term 1790.

Pp 177-178: 26 Sept. 1789. JAMES MARTIN of York Co., S.C. to WILLIAM
CLARK of Greenville, for 100 pds sterling, 179 acres on
N side of Saluda River granted to JAMES MARTIN by Gov. Wm. Moultrie
6 Mar. 1786. Signed: JAMES MARTIN. Wit: JAMES MOORE, FINTLEY, JOHN
MARTIN. Proven by JAMES MOORE bef. Robt. Nelson, Esq. Rec. 7 June 1790.

Pp 178-179: 4 Feb. 1790. JOHN LAFFERTY of 96 Dist. to CHARLES ROGERS
of the same, for 40 pds sterling, 200 acres on both sides
of the Quart branch, waters of Ready River, part of a tract of 300
acres granted to JOHN LAFFERTY by Gov. Thos. Pinckney 6 Oct. 1788.
Signed: JOHN LAFFERTY. Wit: JOHN RODGERS, SOLOMON MURPHY (+) MAGINIS.
Full possession made and money received 4 Feb. 1790. Wit: JOHN SMITH,
JOHN RODGERS. Proven bef. L. A. ALSTON, Esq. by JOHN ROGERS and SOLOMON
MURPHY. Rec. 7 June 1790.

Pp 180-181: 20 Oct. 1790. WILLIAM MURPHY, late of Greenville Co., S.C.
to DRURY HODGE of the same, for 34 pds current money, 200
acres on head waters of Horse Creek of Ready River and Mountain Creek
of Saluda River. Signed: by his attorney JOSEPH MURPHY - WILLIAM MURPHY.
Wit: WM. (+) HODGES, POLLY MAXWELL. "Received from DRURY HODGE 35 pds
sterling. 5 Nov. 1789." Signed: JOSEPH MURPHY, Atty for WM. MURPHY.
Proved bef. ROBERT MAXWELL, Esq. by WILLIAM HODGE and rec. 8 June 1790.

Pp 181-182: 29 Apr. 1790. NICHOLAS DARNELL OF Pendleton Co., S.C.,

157

Cont'd from page 157:
        planter, to VALENTINE THACKER of Greenville Co., for 75
pds sterling, 100 acres on Austins Creek of Saluda River, part of a
tract orig. granted to NICHOLAS DARNELL 1 Jan. 1787 by Gov. Wm. Moultrie
and bounded SW by land surveyed by Maj. BOWIE and N by sd DARNELL's
land. Signed: NICHOS. DARNALL. Wit: BENJA. PERRY, WM. DARNELL, W. H.
LACEY, proven bef. OBADIAH HOOPER, Esq. by WM. H. LACEY. Rec. 8 June
1790.

Pp 182-183: 29 Apr. 1790 (also 1789). THOMAS DOEG of Spartanburg Co.
        to JAMES GARRISON of Greenville Co., for 40 pds sterling,
128 acres granted the sd THOAS DOEG 7 May 1787, by Gov. Pinckney, on
both sides of a small branch of Bush Creek, waters of Tyger River.
Signed: THOMAS DOEG. Wit: HU. WARANT, JAMES NICOLL, JOHN NICOLL. Forty
pds received 1789. Rec. 9 June 1790.

Pp 183-184: 1 Apr. 1790. HANES BLACK of Greenville Co. to JAMES SEA-
        BORNE of sme, for 160 pds sterling, 130 acres on Ready
Fork of Ready River, part of a tract granted to HANES BLACK by Gov.
Pinckney 1 Oct. 1787, also including part of a tract of land granted
KENER HUDSON 15 Oct. 1784. Signed: HANES BLACK, AGNES (+) BLACK. Wit:
LAURENCE BRACHER, NATHAN (+) BRYANT, THOMAS BLACK. Proven bef. GEO.
SALMON, Esq. by LAURENCE BRACHER. Rec. 28 June 1790.

Pp 184-185: 28 Apr. 1790. URIAH CONNER late of Wilkes Co., Ga. to ISAAC
        MORGAN of Greenville Co., for 25 pds current money of Ga.,
769 acres, waters of the Golden Grove, granted by Gov. Moultrie, 3
Apr. 1786, rec. grant book HHHH page 46. Signed: URIAH CONNER. Wit:
ELIJAH OLIVER, EDWARD BALLENGER, SOLOMON KEMP. Pr. bef. GEORGE SALMON,
Esq. by EDW. BALLENGER. Rec. 29 June 1790.

Pp 185-186: 1 May 1790. URIAH CONNER of Wilkes Co., Ga. to ISAAC MORGAN
        of Greenville Co., for 20 pds sterling, 980 acres on N
side of Enoree River, granted sd CONNER by Gov. Moultrie 3 Apr. 1786.
Wit: ELIJAH OLIVER, EDWARD BALLENGER, SOLOMON KEMP. Pr. bef. GEO. SAL-
MON, Esq. by oath of EDW. BALLENGER. Rec. 30 June 1790.

Pp 186-187: 15 May 1790. DAN KELLEY of Greenville Co. to WM. FLIPPO
        of same, for 20 pds sterling, 50 acres, part of a grant
by Gov. Pinckney in Apr. 1789, on a branch of the middle fork of Saluda
River, at the mouth of sd river, adj. JOS. RIGHT's land. Signed: D.
KELLEY. Wit: ELIAS EARLE, WM. LAFFOON, WM. RIGHT. Pr. bef. GEO. SALMON,
Esq. by oath of ELIAS EARLE. Rec. 30 June 1790.

Pp 187-188: 7 Feb. 1790. JONATHAN MUSICK to WILSON MC KINNEY both of
        Greenville Co., for 150 pds sterling, 100 acres on N fork
of Saluda River, part of a tract granted to sd MUSICK 5 June 1786,
rec. Grant Book LLLL page 44. Signed: JONATHAN MUSICK, HELLON (X) MUSICK.
Wit: JOHN WILLIAMS, SAML. CLAREY, EDWARD FRANKLIN. Pr. by oath of JOHN
WILLIAMS, bef. ROBT. NELSON. Rec. 30 June 1790.

Pp 188-189: 26 Feb. 1790. JAMES NEALE of Greenville Co., planter, to
        GEORGE KESSEE(?), planter of same, for 100 pds sterling,
200 acres on both sides of Neal's Fork of Tyger River, W of the old
Indian Boundary line, granted to sd NEALE 21 Jan. 1785. Signed: JAMES
NEALE, PRESALONA (X) NEALE. Wit: CHARLES (X) SMITH, EZEKIAL YOUNG.
Pr. bef. ROBT. NELSON, Esq. by oath of CHARLES SMITH. Rec. 2 July 1790.

Pp 190-191: 5 Sept. 1789. ROBERT PRINCE of Greenville Co. to ALLEN
        SMITHSON of same, for 20 pds sterling, 150 acres on a branch
of Bridge Creek of Saluda River, adj. lines of STANFORD, SALMON, ALLEN
& MARSON SMITHSON, part of a tract granted sd PRINCE 7 Mar. 1787, con-
taining 4,000 acres. Signed: ROBT. PRINCE. Wit: JOHN HOOPER, JOHN GOOD-
LETT. Pr. bef. OBADIAH HOOPER, Esq. by oaths of JOHN HOOPER & JOHN
GOODLETT. Rec. 6 July 1790.

Pp 191-192: 15 May 1790. MARSON SMITHSON of Greenville Co. to ALBERT
        (ALLEN in part of deed) SMITHSON of same, for 30 pds ster-
ling, 150 acres which MARSON SMITHSON bought of ROBERT PRINCE, on a

158

Cont'd from page 158:
branch of Bridge Creek of the Saluda River, adj. line of ALBERT SMITH-
SON, part of 4,000 acre tract. Signed: MARSIN SMITHSON. Wit: WILLIAM
WHITE, ZACHARIAH WHITE, THOMAS WHITE. Pr. bef. GEO. SALMON, Esq. by
oath of WM. WHITE. Rec. 6 July 1790.

Pp 192-193: 12 May 1790. DANIEL KELLEY of Greenville Co. to JOSEPH
            WRIGHT of same, for 50 pds sterling, 250 acres on branches
of south and north forks of Saluda River, adj. WILLIAM THOMPSON, FOST-
ER's branch, part of a tract granted Apr. 1789. Signed: D. KELLEY.
Wit: WILM. RIGHT, JOHN JONES, JOHN KELLEY. Pr. bef. HENRY M. WOOD,
Esq. by oath of WM. RIGHT. Rec. 6 July 1790.

Pp 193-194: 18 Mar. 1790. SIMCOCK CANNON of Greenville Co. to DANIEL
            MC JUNKIN of same, for 50 pds lawful money of S.C., 130
acres, part of tract granted CANNON. Signed: SIMCOCK CANNON. Wit: THOMAS
GIBBS, ABNER CHASTIEN, ABSALOM BLYTH. Pr. bef. GEO. SALMON, Esq. by
oath of THOS. GIBBS. Rec. 19 July 1790.

Pp 194-195: 25 Jan. 1790. We, FRANCIS BERMAR and PETER FRENEAU, for
            10 shillings, assign unto JOHN PYLES in trust for the child-
ren of SAMUEL PYLES, dec'd., all our right, title, and interest in
640 acres on both sides of Ready River, including the mouth of Stony
Creek, bounded N by JAMES LESLEY's land. Signed: F. BREMAR, PETER FREN-
EAU. Wit: RT. MAXWELL, JAMES MARTIN. Pr. by oath of ROBT. MAXWELL,
Esq. during Feb. term and rec. 23 July 1790.

Pp 195-197: Lease & Release. 9 Aug. 1786. BENJAMIN RICE of Laurance
            (Laurens) Co., to JESSE MOODY of county afsds, planter,
for 10 pds sterling, 200 acres, part of tract of 400 acres granted
BENJ. RICE 15 Oct. 1784 on waters of Golden Grove Creek, a branch of
the Saluda River, above the ancient boundary line, bounded SW by JAMES
SEABORN's land, and NATHANIEL PENDLETON. (Release gives 400 acres in
one place and 200 in another; consideration in release is also 10 pds
sterling.) Signed: BENJAMIN RICE. Wit: JOHN NELSON, JEREMIAH SMITH,
MATTHEW ARMSTRONG. Pr. bef. GEO. SALMON, Esq. by JEREMIAH SMITH. Rec.
23 July 1790.

Pp 198-200: Lease & Release. 30 Apr. 1788. MINOR WINN, JR. and RICHARD
            WINN, Esq., of town of Winnsboro, Fairfield Co., S. C.
to GERSHOM KELLEY of Greenville, for 200 pds 5 shillings sterling,
640 acres on Reedy River, granted to sd MINOR WINN 21 Jan. 1785. Signed:
MINOR WINN, RICHARD WINN. Wit: D. EVANS, CRISTEN HART. Pr. bef. M.
HARRISON, Esq. by oath of D. EVANS. Rec. 26 July 1790.

Pp 200-203: Lease & Release. 11 Mar. 1790. MICHAEL DILLINGHAM of Green-
            ville to JOSEPH OBANNON, planter, of same, for 5 shillings
and 80 pds sterling, 284 acres part of a tract of 590 acres granted
to DILLINGHAM 4 Sept. 1786, on W side of Chicoroa River, waters of
Saluda, adj. SW and NW land laid out for GEORGE SALMON, and land orig.
surveyed for WILLIAM COLLENS. Signed: MICHAEL DILLINGHAM. Wit: GEO.
SALMON, EZEKIAL YOUNG, ELIZABETH SALMON. Pr. bef. ROBT. NELSON, Esq.
by oath of GEO. SALMON. Rec. 27 July 1790.

Pp 203-206: Lease & Release. 4 Jan. 1790. JOHN MILLER of Greenville,
            planter, to WILLIAM POOLE of Spartanburg Co., iron master,
for 5 shillings 10 pds sterling, 215 acres on both sides of Mush Creek
of Tyger River, adj. SW on ESTHER THOMAS, NE on PHILLIPS SHRRL(?),
NW on JAMES NICOLL, and sd WM. POOLE. Signed: JOHN (X) MILLER. Wit:
GEORGE SALMON, JOHN YOUNG, ELIZABETH SALMON. Pr. bef. OBADIAH HOOPER,
Esq. by oath of GEO. SALMON, Esq. Rec. 29 July 1790.

Pp 206-207: 17 Aug. 1786. JOSEPH STROBEL of Charleston to GEORGE SHULER
            of 96 Dist., for 500 pds sterling, 305 acres granted 16
July 1784, on the South Fork of Saluda River. Signed: JOSEPH (X) STRABEL.
Wit: JOSEPH HALE, GEORGE HOPE. Pr. bef. DAVID HOPKINS, Esq. by oath
of JOSEPH HALE. Rec. 16 Aug. 1790.

Page 207:   20 Dec. 1790. I, OBADIAH HOOPER, of Greenville Co., appoint

Cont'd from page 159:
my trusty friend JAMES HOOPER to be my true and lawful
attorney to make title to a tract of land in Halifax Co., Va. in Pinson's Shole and waters of Hyco River, being the land sold to JOHN GRIF-
FEN which the sd JAMES HOOPER is impowered to make good and sufficient
title to. Signed: OB. HOOPER. Wit: JESSE CARTER, BENJ. PERRY. Pr. by
oath of JESSE CARTER or order to be rec. Rec. 17 Aug. 1790.

Pp 207-208: 31 Mar. 1790. I, WILLIAM HAMMONDS of Greenville Co. appointed AMBROSE FITZGARRALD of the co. afsd, my lawful
attorney to recover the amount of a bond given to PETER HAMMOND by
JOHN WINGO and now in the hands of WILLIAM BUMPASS and now my right
in virtue of my father, PETER HAMMOND's will at his death. Signed:
WILLIAM HAMMONDS. Wit: SAMUEL EARLE, JAMES BYNUM. Pr. by oath of SAML.
EARLE. Rec. 18 Aug. 1790.

Pp 208-209: (n.d.) 1790. JAMES JORDAN of Spartanburg Co., to JOHN MC
ELROY of Greenville, for 150 pds sterling, 300 acres on
the ridge bet. Reedy River and the Little Fork of sd river, granted
to JAMES JORDAN 1 Aug. 1785. Signed: JAMES JORDON. No wit. Ack. in
open court by JAMES JORDAN. Rec. 3 Nov. 1790.

Pp 209-210: 14 Aug. 1790. ISAM CLAYTON of Greenville Co. to WILLIAM
TOWNS of Halifax Co., Va. for 200 pds sterling, 400 acres
on a branch of Saluda River, adj. CLAYTON's old line, MEATHER's spring,
including 15 acres granted to LEMUEL JAMES ALSTON to sd ISAM CLAYTON,
also adj. HENDERSON's line and the line bet. sd CLAYTON & BUSH; it
being two tracts of land or parts of tracts, one for 300 acres granted
to sd CLAYTON, the other 187 acres granted to JAMES HENDERSON and ISAM
CLAYTON 21 Jan. 1785 and rec. in Book CCCC page 229. Signed: ISAM (L)
CLAYTON. Wit: JOHN EASLEY, DANIEL BUSH. Ack. by ISAM CLAYTON Aug. term
1790. Rec. 5 Nov. 1790.

Page 211:   25 July 1790. JACOB CASEY to WILLIAM BACKER both of 96
Dist. for 50 pds sterling, 200 acres both sides of Fall
Creek, one-half mile above the Great Falls of Fall Creek, surv. for
RANDOLPH CASEY and granted 4 Sept. 1787 to JACOB CASEY. Rec. Grant
Book ZZZZ page 236. Signed: JACOB CASEY. Wit: JOHN GOODLETT, PETER
(X) BACKER, JOS. GOODWIN. Pr. by oath of JOHN GOODLETT and ordered
recorded. Rec. 5 Nov. 1790.

Pp 212-213: 29 Dec. 1789. JAMES BLASINGAME, Esq. of Greenville Co.,
to JOHN JONES of the same, for 50 pds sterling, 100 acres,
part of a tract of 818 acres granted sd JAMES BLASINGAME by Gov. Moultrie 7 Aug. 1786, rec. Book MMMM page 182, adj. JOHN HUGGINS, WORKLAW,
on waters of Saluda River. Signed: J. BLASINGAME. Wit: JOHN BLASINGAME,
BENJAMIN TARRANT. Pr. bef. ROBERT MAXWELL, Esq. by BENJAMIN TARRANT,
JR. Rec. 6 Nov. 1790.

Pp 213-214: 6 July 1790. ROBERT RAMSEY of 96 Dist. to ANDREW LAFERTY
of same, for 30 pds, 133 acres orig. granted to ROBERT
RAMSEY by Gov. Moultrie 4 Dec. 1786, on a branch of Ready River. Signed:
ROBERT RAMSEY, ELIZABETH (X) RAMSEY. Wit: HUGH ROARK, WILLIAM (X) BANDS.
Pr. by the oath of HUGH ROARK and WILLIAM BANDS. Rec. 8 Nov. 1790.

Pp 214-216: 8 Feb. 1790. JOHN LAFFERTY of 96 Dist. to CHARLES RODGERS
of same, for 25 pds sterling, 100 acres, part of a tract
of 300 acres orig. granted to JOHN LAFFERTY by Gov. Thos. Pinckney,
6 Oct. 1788, near LAFFERTY's Creek, waters of Reedy River. Signed:
JOHN LAFFERTY. Wit: JOHN SIMS, ANDREW (X) LAFFERTY. Pr. by ANDREW LAF-
FERTY. Rec. 8 Nov. 1790.

Pp 216-217: 9 Aug. 1787. THOMAS WOOD of Camden Dist., to SOLOMON WEST
of 96 Dist., for 200 pds current money, 300 acres granted
to THOMAS WOOD by Gov. Moultrie 2 May 1785, on Muckles Branch a branch
of Ready River. Signed: THOMAS WOOD. Wit: HEZEKIAH (H) COLLINS, ISAAC
WEST, JR. Proved by oath of ISAAC WEST, JR. Rec. 9 Nov. 1790.

Pp 217-218: 16 Aug. 1790. JOHN MOLIN to NATHANIEL BOMUN both of Greenville Co., for 100 pds sterling, 100 acres, being part

Cont'd from page 160:
of a tract of land granted to sd JOHN MOLIN 21 Jan. 1785, adj. mouth
of Mill Creek o the N fork of Saluda Chicoroa River. Signed: JOHN MOLIN.
Wit: JOHN MOTLOW(?), JOHN WILLIAMS. Ack. by JOHN MOLIN, Aug. term.
Rec. 9 Nov. 1790.

Pp 218-220: 8 Oct. 1787. WILLIAM GRANT of Greenville Co., to WILLIAM
TURNBOUGH of same, for 40 pds sterling current money of
the state, 200 acres granted WM. GRANT 5 June 1786 by Gov. Moultrie,
on Beaverdam of the S. fork of Tyger River bounded on all sides by
land laid out to DANIEL BROWN. Signed: WILLIAM (W) GRANT, MARY (M)
GRANT. Wit: JAMES TUBB, GEORGE (blank) TUBB. Proved bef. GEORGE SALMON,
Esq. Rec. 10 Nov. 1790.

Pp 220-222: 29 May 1789. JOHN CLAYTON & SARAH CLAYTON his wife to JOHN
FORD both of Greenville Co., for 60 pds, 40 acres, part
of a tract of 250 acres granted to ROBERT HENDERSON 21 Jan. 1785, rec.
in Grant Book CCCC (no page no.) on the N fork of Saluda River, adj.
JAMES STEVENSON, including the mill seat. Signed: JOHN CLAYTON, SARAH
(X) CLAYTON. Wit: JAS. MC ELHENNY, MARY (blank) CLAYTON. Ack. by JOHN
CLAYTON. Rec. 10 Nov. 1790.

Pp 222-223: 28 Dec. 1789. JOSEPH MC GLAUCHLIN of Greenville Co. to
THOMAS BELL of same, for 19 pds, 100 acres, part of 340
acres granted to sd MC CLAUGHLIN 30 Aug. 1786, on Princes Creek of
Enoree River. Signed: JOSEPH MC GLAUGHLIN. Wit: JOHN ROSS, GEO. (X)
SANDERS, ELY(?) OLIVER. Rec. 10 Nov. 1790. (Spelled both McG and McC)

Page 223: 26 July 1790. I, JOHN WATKINS, give to JEAN PENNINGTON
the plantation whereon I now live and 50 acres adj. the
plantation, and 100 acres I give to her daughter FEEBY, it being part
of the tract of land where I now live, all my cattle, horses, hogs
and sheep and household furniture to be divided between them it being
for value received of them. Signed: JOHN (X) WATKINS. Wit: JOHN COOK,
JOHN (his mark) REID. Rec. 15 Nov. 1790.

Pp 224-225: Title Bond. 1 Nov. 1790. I, JOHN CHILDRESS of Greenville
Co., am firmly bound unto CHARLES BRUCE, carpenter, of
same, for 100 pds sterling. I convey to sd CHARLES BRUCE, on or before,
1 Feb. next, 100 acres on Childress Beaverdam, a branch of S. Tyger
River, including the place where the sd CHILDRESS now lives and to
be divided from the other land as follows - Beaverdam Creek on SALMON's
line to the waggon road leaving from Millford to Mr. NICHOLS. Signed:
JOHN CHILDRESS. Wit: JOHN THOMAS, JEREMIAH BRUCE. Proved bef. ROBT.
NELSON, Esq. by oath of JOHN THOMAS, SR. Rec. 22 Nov. 1790.

Pp 225-226: 16 Nov. 1790. DANIEL BUSH of Greenville Co. to JACOB LIGHT
of same, for 20 pds, 198 acres granted sd DANIEL BUSH 6
Feb. 1786, on Mill Creek of Saluda River. Signed: DANIEL BUSH. Wit:
J. WHITNER, JOHN JETT. Ack. by DANL BUSH Nov. 1791. Rec. 9 Dec. 1790.

Pp 226-227: 13 Nov. 1790. DANIEL BUSH of Greenville to ISAM CLAYTON
of same, for 300 pds current money, 700 acres, part of
the following tracts: 180 acres granted to sd CLAYTON 5 Dec. 1785;;
250 acres granted TIMOTHY TONEY 15 Oct. 1784; 225 acres granted DANIEL
BUSH 6 Feb. 1786; 178 acres granted JAMES HENDERSON, on N side of Saluda
River below Parises Fork on DARNELL's line, sd HENDERSON , WILLIAM
TOWNS, JAMES CLAYTON. Signed: DANIEL BUSH. Wit: J. WHITNER, JOHN JETT.
Ack. by DANIEL BUSH, Nov. court 1790. Rec. 9 Dec. 1790.

Pp 227-229: 30 Jan. 1788. MICHAEL JOHNSTON of Newberry Co., S.C. to
AARON KEMP of Greenville Co. for 27 pds current money,
150 acres granted sd MICHAEL JOHNSTON 1 Oct. 1787, on Brush Creek of
Enoree River, rec. Grant Book UUUU page 342. Signed: MICHAEL JOHNSTON.
Wit: ISAAC MORGAN, ISAAC WEST, JOHN ROSS. Proved by ISAAC MORGAN, Esq.
Nov. Court 1790. Rec. 9 Dec. 1790.

Pp 229-230: 9 Apr. 1790. DAVID MC VAY of Greenville to ISAAC WILKENS
for 60 pds sterling, 250 acres, part of 4,000 acres granted

161

Cont'd from page 161:
to ROBERT PRINCE 7 Mar. 1788, and sold to DAVID MC VAY by sd PRINCE,
adj. JANE MC JUNKIN, sd MC VAY and WILKEN's, SNODDY's corner. Signed:
DAVID MC VAY (his mark) Wit: ANGUS MC ALESTER, JAMES WHITE. Ack. by
DAVID MC VAY Nov. Court 1790. Rec. 10 Dec. 1790.

Pp 230-231: 29 Sept. 1790. MICHAEL MILLER of Spartanburg Co. to WILLIAM
            ANDERSON of Greenville, for 100 pds sterling, 388 acress
granted to sd MILLER 21 Jan. 1785, by Gov. Guerard, on both sides Middle
Tyger River. Signed: MICHAEL MILLER. Wit: JAMES VERNON, JOHN CLAYTON,
JOSEPH THOMPSON. Proved bef. ROBT. NELSON, Esq. by JOHN CLAYTON Nov.
Court 1790. Rec. 10 Dec. 1790.

Pp 231-232: 15 Nov. 1790. WILLIAM BENSON of 96 Dist. to ABRAHAM BRADLEY
            of same, for 30 pds current money, 69 acres granted to
sd BENSON 1787, surveyed for the afsd ABRAHAM BRADLEY 23 Jan. 1786,
on Armstrong Creek of Saluda River adj. ANN ARMSTRONG, HANNER YOUNG,
NICK. DERNAL. Signed: WM. BENSON. Wit: NOBLELO JOHNSTON, JOHN JOHNSTON.
Ack. by WM. BENSON, Nov. Court 1790. Rec. 21 Dec. 1790.

Pp 232-233: 9 Mar. 1790. THOMAS LEWIS of Greenville to CHARLES HUDLES-
            LEY, blacksmith, of same, for 30 pds sterling, 100 acres
on Mountain Creek of Saluda River adj. JOHN MATLOCK, CHARLES EASTES,
BEALS, MICHAEL HENDERSON; part of a tract orig. granted to PATRICK
LAFFERTY 5 Sept. 1785, rec. in Book FFFF page 41. Signed: THOMAS LEWIS.
Wit: VINCENT LEWIS, VINCENT DAVIS, JOHN LEWIS. Proved bef. AMBROSE
BLACKBURN 9 Mar. 1790. Rec. 21 Dec. 1790.

Pp 234-235: 5 June 1790. JECHONIAS WALDROP & MARGARET his wife of Ruth-
            erford Co., N.C. to BENJAMIN MERIT of Greenville, for 100
pds sterling, 106½ acres, being the lower half of 213 acres granted
ROBERT ANDERSON 21 Jan. 1785, rec. in Grant Book GGGG, on both sides
of the North Fork of Saluda River, adj. THOMAS FARROW's line. Signed:
JECHONIAS WALDROP, MARGARET WALDROP. Wit: JOHN GOODWYN, JOHN YOUNG,
WILLIAM GOODWYN. Rec. 21 Dec. 1790.

Pp 235-236: 15 July 1790. THOMAS FARRAR, Esq., Sheriff of 96 Dist.
            to WILLIAM EASLEY: whereas JOHN MC ELHENY was lately seized
in fee simple in a tract of land containing 200 acres, both sides of
the Middle Fork of Tyger River, adj. lands laid out to MICHAEL MILLER
on the wst; whereas ROBERT CARTER in April Court 1784, commenced an
action of damage in the Court of Common Pleas at Charleston against
the sd JOHN MC ELHENY. ROBERT CARTER obtained judgement in May 1785
against JOHN MC ELHENY for 150 pds sterling. The sd. FARRAR, sheriff
did seize the plantation of JOHN MC ELHENY for public auction and sold
to WILLIAM EASLEY for 17 pds sterling, he being the highest bidder.
Signed: THOMAS FARRAR, Sheriff. Wit: JNO. GOWEN, MILLINGTON EASLEY.
Proved by GOWEN. Rec. 22 Dec. 1790.

Pp 236-237: 1 Mar. 1790. WILLIAM RIGHT of Greenville to WILLIAM LAF-
            FOON of Pendleton Co., S.C. for 50 pds sterling, 100 acres
on the N fork of Saluda River, adj. ELIAS EARLE, HENRY MICHAM WOOD,
SAMUEL EARLE; granted by Gov. Moultrie Apr. 1787. Signed: WILLM. RIGHT.
Wit: D. KELLEY, CHARLES DOUGHERTY, DAVID NORRESS. Proved bef. H. M.
WOOD, Esq. Rec. 22 Dec. 1790.

Pp 237-238: 24 Mar. 1790. JOHN MC VAY of Greenville to ABRAHAM NELSON
            of same, for 5 shillings, 230 acres on Enoree River, being
part of a 4000 acre tract granted ROBERT PRINCE and part of a tract
of MARY PRINCE; adj. MARY PRINCE, PERRY's line...Signed: JOHN MC VAY.
Wit: WM. WHITE, JAMES MC CLOUD. Proved bef. GEO. SALMON, Esq. Rec.
22 Dec. 1790.

Pp 238-239: 29 Mar. 1790. REUBEN STRINGER of Greenville to THOMAS MC
            CARRIL of same, for 150 pds sterling, 300 acres on Beaverdam
Cree, a branch of Saluda River, granted to RALPH SMITH, Esq. 15 Oct.
1784. Rec. Grant Book ZZZ page 321. Signed: REUBEN STRINGER. Wit: JOS.
GOODWYN, JESSE CORNELAS, EDWARD STRINGER. Proved bef. ROBT. NELSON,
Esq. Rec. 22 Dec. 1790.

Pp 239-240: 19 June 1790. MARY BURNS to MARTIN GOLORSHEEN, planter, both of Greenville Co., for 50 pds sterling, 200 acres, part of a 325 acre tract granted to MARY BURNS by Gov. Moultrie, 3 Oct. 1785, on Horse Creek, a branch of Reedy River, adj. JOHN DENNY's corner. Signed: MARY (her mark) BURNS. Wit: DANIEL FORD, REUBEN BROWN. Ack. by MARY BURNS. Rec. 22 Dec. 1790.

Pp 240-241: 29 Oct. 1780. JOHN FORD, Esq. and NANCY his wife to WILLIAM CORNELAS, both of Greenville, for 20 pds, 85 acres on N fork of Saluda River, granted to JOHN FORD 6 Apr. 1789, but since some of this 85 acres contains land granted to WM. CORNELAS and THOMAS FARRAR by letters patent of an older date, that land is excepted, and this deed is by estimation 60 acres. Signed: JOHN FORD. Wit: JOHN MOLIN, JOHN MOTLOW, THOMAS (X) BRUMIL. Ack. by JOHN FORD. Rec. 23 Dec. 1790.

Pp 241-243: Lease & Release. 8 Jan. 1790. JAMES WINN of Camden Dist. and Fairfield Co., to WILLIAM CHOICE of Greenville Co., for 1 shilling 6 pence and 75 pds sterling, 294 acres part of 640 acres a tract on Martins Creek, waters of Reedy River, adj. E on the Old Indian Line, N on DAVID MELING, W on JOHN BUCKAN, granted to JAMES WINN by Gov. Guerard 16 July 1784. The 294 acres is the southern part of sd tract, adj. the Old Indian Line, MAHAFY's corner, THOMAS GREGORY's line. Signed: J. WINN. Wit: CH. SENTS(?), JNO. WINN, JR. Proved bef. JOHN WINN, Esq. Rec. 23 Dec. 1790.

Pp 243-244: 29 July 1790. WILLIAM STRINGER to THOMAS MC CARREL, both of 96 Dist., for 40 pds sterling, 110 acres on both sides of the South Fork of Beaverdam, Chicoroa, adj. SMITH, certified 22 Jan. 1785. Signed: WILLIAM (X) STRINGER. Wit: BENJAMIN (X) CORNELAS, JESSE CORNELAS, JOS. GOODWYN. Proved bef. ROBT. NELSON, Esq. Rec. 27 Dec. 1790.
Pp 244-245: 1 May 1790. JOHN DYCHE of Greenville Co. to DAVID RICE of same, for 25 pds sterling, 50 acres on waters of Rocky Fork of Golden Grove Creek, part of a tract granted to RICHARD GOOD by Gov. Guerard 21 Jan. 1785. Signed: JOHN DYCHE. Wit: J. HINSON, JAS. TURLEY, J. KENNEDY. Proved bef. A. BLACKBURN, Esq. Rec. 27 Dec. 1790.

Page 245: 10 Jan. 1789. ROBERT PRINCE of Greenville to BAYLIS EARLE of Spartenburg Co. for 100 pds sterling, 202 acres surveyed by JAMES SEABORN for HUGH MOORE 5 June 1786, and conveyed from him to ROBERT PRINCE 4 Jan. 1788. Signed: ROBERT PRINCE. Wit: A. DILLINGHAM, SAMUEL EARLE, DAMARIS EARLE, ENOCH BENSON. Proved bef. L. ALSTON, Esq. by SAMUEL EARLE. Rec. 27 Dec. 1790.

Pp 245-246: 31 Dec. 1789. JOHN DENING of Greenville Co. to JAMES ANDER-SON of the same, for 15 pds sterling, 120 acres, part of 640 acres on Horse Creek orig. granted to JOHN DENING by Gov. Moultrie 1 Jan. 1787, on SE side of Horse Creek, adj. CLAYBURN SULLIVANT. Signed: JOHN DENNING. Wit: GEORGE GEILLOTT, GEDRICK KEEL. Ack. bef. JAMES HARRI-SON, Esq. Rec. 27 Dec. 1790.

Page 247: 18 Mar. 1790. SIMCOCK CANNON of Greenville to DANIEL MC JUNKIN of same, for 50 pds lawful money, 130 acres part of 230 acres granted to SIMCOCK CANNON. Signed: SIMCOCK CANNON. Wit: THOMAS GIBBS, ABNER CHASTEEN, ABSOLAM BLYTH. Proved bef. GEORGE SALMON, Esq. Rec. 29 Dec. 1790.

Page 248: 10 May 1790. DENNIS DUFF and wife ELIZABETH to JEPTHA COR-NELAS, both of Greenville Co., for 25 pds sterling, 30 acres, Chocoroa Fork on N fork of Saluda River, adj. WILLIAM CORNELAS, and where the Beaverdam empties into the river, being the upper part of a tract containing 158 acres granted DENNIS DUFF 5 June 1786. Signed: DENNIS DUFF, ELIZABETH DUFF. Wit: WILLIAM CORNELAS, REUBEN STRINGER, GEORGE REED. Proved bef. GEO. SALMON, Esq. Rec. 29 Dec. 1790.

Pp 248-249: 1 May 1790. JOHN DYCHE of Greenville Co., to JACOB COOLEY of same, for 75 pds sterling, 50 acres on waters of Rocky Fork of Golden Grove Creek, part of a grant to RICHARD GOODE 21 Jan. 1785, adj. DAVID REECE. Signed: JOHN (his mark) DYCHE. Wit: J. HINSON,

Cont'd from page 163:
JAS. TURLEY, __ KENNEDY. Proved bef. A. BLACKBURN, Esq. Rec. 29 Dec. 1790.

Pp 249-250: 8 Jan. 1790. JOHN CLAYTON to MARY SPRIGS, both of Greenville Co., for 60 pds, 85 acres on Wiers Creek, a branch of the N fork of Saluda, part of a tract granted to ROBERT HENDERSON 21 Jan. 1785, rec. Grant Book CCCC; ROBERT HENDERSON conveyed to JOHN CLAYTON; adj. JOHN FORD, THOMAS SPRIGS, JAMES STEVENSON. Signed: JOHN CLAYTON. Wit: JOHN FORD, JAMES LEATHS(?). Proved by oath of JOHN FORD, Esq. Rec. 29 Dec. 1790.

Pp 250-251: 3 May 1790. WILLIAM DAVIS THOMAS of Greenville Co. to JOHN MOTLOW of same, for 150 pds sterling, 200 acres on N side of Saluda River including the mouth of the Chickaroa River; land granted to ALEX. MC ELHENEY by Gov. Guerard 18 July 1784, rec. in Grant Book ZZZ, the sd ALEXANDER MC ELHENEY conveyed to sd WILLIAM DAVIS THOMAS. Rec. in Deed Bk A, pp 273-274. Signed: :WILLIAM D. THOMAS. Wit: D. LEECH, JAMES RUNALDS, BENJA. JONES. Ack. by WM. D. THOMAS in open court. Rec. 30 Dec. 1790.

Pp 251-252: 31 July 1790. ISAAC REED of Greenville Co. to LEWIS WELLS, planter, of same, for 50 pds lawful sterling, 200 acres on the head of Rocky Creek of Reedy River, granted to sd REED by Gov. Pinckney 2 July 1787. Signed: ISAAC REED. Wit: JOHN GAMBLIN, WILLIAM LACEY. Ack. by ISAAC REED in open court. Rec. 30 Dec. 1790.

Pp 252-253: 9 July 1790. ANDREW JOHNSON, surveyor, and JEAN THOMPSON, his wife, of Spartanburg Co., to ROBERT MARROW, planter, of the county afsd., for 50 pds lawful money of S.C. 500 acres bet. Reedy and Enoree Rivers and on a small branch of Rockey Creek, on the N side of Reedy, adj. N on ISHAM FRANKLIN; granted 2 Feb. 1789 by Gov. Pinckney. Signed: ANDREW THOMPSON, JEAN THOMPSON. Wit: JASON MOORE, JASON MOORE, JR., THOMAS MOORE. Proved bef. ANDREW BARRY, Esq. Rec. 1 Jan. 1791.

Pp 253-254: 16 July 1790. ANNE EASLY of Greenville Co. to EDMUND BEARDEN of same, for 50 pds sterling, 200 acres on S side of Reedy River, part of 287 acre tract granted to ANNE EASLEY 1 Jan. 1785 by Gov. Guerard, adj. ISHAM CLAYTON's branch. Signed: ANN EASLEY. Wit: JNO. GOWEN, ABS. THOMPSON. Proved by oath of ABSOLAM THOMPSON. Rec. 1 Jan. 1791.

Pp 254-255: 17 Apr. 1790. JEREMIAH WEBB, JR. of Greenville Co. to DAVID BLACK of same, for 60 pds sterling, 250 acres on Reedy Fork of Reedy River, orig. granted to JAMES CADWELL by Gov. Moultrie Aug. 1786, adj E on ROBERT GILLIAM. Signed: JEREMIAH WEBB, JR. Wit: JOHN WARE, BENJAMIN TARRANT, JOSIAH KENNEDY. Proved bef. A. BLACKBURN, Esq. Rec. 1 Jan. 1790.

Page 255: 12 May 1790. Whereas CATHERINE ODEAR, widow, now of Greenville Co., did formerly bind or have bound by the worshipful court of Fairfield Co., two children, BENJAMIN & JAMES, ____ ALEXANDER PEADAN, and that sd CATHERINE having made sufficient provision for support of herself and family, releases the sd ALEXANDER PEADEN from his obligation to them. Signed: ALEX. PEDEN, CATHERINE (X) ODEAR. Wit: JOHN PEDEN, JAMES ALEXANDER.

Pp 255-256: 29 Jan. 1791. JOSEPH LANGSTON of Greenville to JOHN LANGSTON of same, for 5 shillings, 100 acres being part of my land grant for 640 acres, taken off the upper part including JOHN LANGSTON's improvements. Signed: JOSEPH LANGSTON. Wit: JESSE CARTER, RAGLAND LANGSTON. Proved by JESSE CARTER Feb. term 1791. Rec. 2 Mar. 1791.

Pp 256-257: 10 Jan. 1790. JOHN STANFORD of Greenville Co. to DAVID MC VAY for 50 pds, 243 acres on the waters of Saluda River, part of a 343 acre tract granted to JOHN STANFORD 5 Feb. 1787, adj. line bet. sd STANFORD and ABRAHAM AHRGUS. Signed: JOHN STANFORD. Wit:

Cont'd from page 164:
JAMES DOUGHERTY, HUGH MC VAY. Proved by HUGH MC VAY. Rec. 4 Mar. 1791.

Pp 257-258: 8 Jan. 1790. RANDOLPH CASEY & wife CHARITY, of Greenville
        Co., planter, to JOHN STANFORD, JR. of same, planter, for
200 pds sterling, 200 acres on S fork of Tyger River, adj. WILLIAM
BENSON's land, granted sd CASEY 5 Dec. 1785. Signed: RANDOLPH CASEY,
CHARITY CASEY. Wit: JAMES DOUGHERTY, RICHARD FOREST. Rec. 5 Mar. 1791.

Pp 258-259: 7 June 1790. LEVI CASEY & wife MARY of Greenville Co.,
        planter, to JOHN STANFORD, JR. of same, planter, for 30
pds sterling, 112 acres, land on N side of Tyger River, adj. the Mountain, granted to sd CASEY 5 Feb. 1787. Signed: LEVI CASEY, MARY (M)
CASEY. Wit: JOHN PRINCE, JAMES DOUGHERTY, WILLIAM STANFORD. Rec. 5
Mar. 1791.

Pp 259-260: 9 June 1788. DAVID HUMPHRYS of Surry Co., N.C. to THOMAS
        WHITMAN of Greenville Co. for 25 pds sterling, 100 acres
adj. XPHER (CHRISTOPHER) BRUNKS' land, being the lower part of a tract
granted sd HUMPHRYS 15 Oct. 1784, on both sides of Beaverdam Creek,
a branch of Mountain Creek of Saluda, adj. NW on land laid out for
WILLIAM NEELE. Signed: DAVID HUMPHREYS. Wit: WM. D. THOMAS, CANDACE
THOMAS, J. THOMAS, JR. Proved by JOHN THOMAS, JR. Rec. 10 Mar. 1791.
Plat follows deed.

Page 261:   21 Feb. 1791. JOSEPH DUNKLIN of Greenville Co. to WILLIAM
        MULLICAN, JR. of S.C., planter, for 100 pds current money
of S.C. 240 acres on waters of Horse Creek adj. E on JESSE CHANDLER's
land, granted to CHARLES SULLIVANT 1 May 1786. Signed: JOSEPH DUNKLIN.
Wit: NATHANIEL SULLIVANT, HEWLET SULLIVANT. Ack. by JOSEPH DUNKLIN
and rec. 10 Mar. 1791.

Pp 261-262: 21 Feb. 1791. AMBROSE BLACKBURN and JAMES HARRISON of Green-
        ville Co., to JOHN BIRDSONG of same, for 7 pds lawful ster-
ling, 150 acres, part of a tract of 467 acres on waters of Saluda River
and Golden Grove Creek, granted to sd BLACKBURN & HARRISON 5 Mar. 1787,
adj. W on MEREDITH BLACKBURN, JOHN BIRDSONG; S & E by MAXWELL & GOOD.
Signed: AMB. BLACKBURN, JAMES HARRISON. No witnesses. Ack. by BLACKBURN
& HARRISON. Rec. 14 Mar. 1791.

Pp 262-263: 12 May 1790. DANL. KELLEY of Greenville to JOHN JONES of
        same, for 50 pds sterling, 200 acres lying on the dividing
ridge bet. the North and South Fork of the Saluda River, adj. EARLE,
FOSTER, H. M. WOOD; part of two tracts, one granted June 1785, the
other Apr. 1789. Signed: D. KELLEY. Wit: WM. RIGHT, JOSEPH WRIGHT,
JOHN KELLEY. Prove by oath of WM. WHITE. Rec. 14 Mar. 1791.

Page 263:   17 July 1789. JOHN CONNER of Franklin Co.,Ga. to JOSEPH
        SHIP of Greenville Co., S.C. for 150 pds sterling, 300
acres on Reedy River adj. NW on land laid out to CHARLES SULLIVANT,
SE to JOEL CHANDLER, NE by Reedy River. Signed: JOHN CONNER. Wit: WM.
WOOD, JAS. FREEMAN, SAML. PORTER. Rec. 16 Mar. 1791.

Page 264:   10 Feb. 1791. AMBROSE BLACKBURN & JAMES HARRISON of Green-
        ville Co. to CRAFFORD GOODWIN of same, for 10 pds sterling,
50 acres part of a tract granted to sd BLACKBURN & HARRISON 5 Mar.
1787, rec. in Grant Book TTTT page 1061, on the waters of Golden Grove
Creek, bounded S by MEREDITH BLACKBURN, SE by JOHN BOWIE, NW by JOHN
MAXWELL, W by land laid out to ANDREW WOOD and the Saluda River. Signed:
AMBS. BLACKBURN, JAMES HARRISON. Wit: JAMES BLACKSTOCK. Rec. 17 Mar.
1791.

Pp 264-265: 21 Dec. 1790. JOSEPH REED of Greenville Co. to WILLIAM
        NICHOLSON of same, for 25 pds sterling, 100 acres, part
of 330 acres orig. granted to sd REED 5 June 1786, on both sides of
Rockey Creek of Reedy River. Signed: JOSEPH REED. Wit: SAML. COBB,
JR., WILLIAM TOWERS, ABEL RICHARDSON. Rec. 17 Mar. 1791.

Pp 265-266: 1 Mar. 1790. HENRY WOOD of Greenville Co. to WILLIAM BROWN

Cont'd from page 165:
    of same, for 45 pds sterling, 90 acres on S side of Enoree
River. Signed: HENRY WOOD. Wit: CHARLES (X) SOWEL, SILAS BROCK, R.
GUNN. Rec. 19 Mar. 1791.

Pp 266-267: 10 Feb. 1791. ATHI MEEKS of Greenville to WILLIAM RAY of
    same, for 12 pds lawful current money, 100 acres, part
of 440 acres on waters of Horse Creek of Reedy River, orig. granted
sd MEEKS 1 May 1786. Signed: ATHI MEEKS. Wit: JAMES HARRISON, JOHN
MC ELROY, REUBEN BROWN. Rec. 19 Mar. 1791.

Pp 267-268: 19 Feb. 1791. MARTIN GOLLIFIN of Greenville to BRYAN WARD
    NOWLIN of same, for 2 pds 7 shillings, 20 acres on branch
of Reedy River. Signed: MARTIN GOLLOTHAN. Wit: LIGHT TOWNSEN, BENJAMIN
BARKER. Rec. 19 Mar. 1791.

Pp 268-269: 7 Sept. 1790. WILLIAM REA of Greenville Co. to JAMES EWIN
    of same, for 30 pds lawful money sterling, 60 acres, part
of a tract orig. granted to JOHN DENING 1 Jan. 1787. Signed: WM. REA.
Wit: JOHN DICKERSON, ELIZABETH HARRISON, JAMES HARRISON. Rec. 21 Mar.
1791.

Pp 269-270: 10 Feb. 1790. ATHE MEEKS of Greenville Co. to REUBEN BROWN
    of same, for 30 pds lawful sterling, 190 acres, part of
a tract on Horse Creek of Reedy River, orig. granted to sd MEEKS 1
May 1786, containing 440 acres. Signed: ATHE MEEKS. Wit: JAMES HARRISON,
WM. REA, JOHN MC ELROY. Rec. 21 Mar. 1791.

Page 271:   18 Feb. 1791. ANDREW JONES of Greenville to THOMAS TOWNSEN
    late of Va., for 100 pds sterling, 150 acres bordering
SW on Horse Creek, including the Mill Shoal, orig. granted to JESSE
CHANDLER 21 Jan. 1785, rec. Grant Bk CCCC page 37, conveyed by sd CHAND-
LER to ANDREW JONES 18 Feb. 1788. Signed: ANDREW JONES, ELIZABETH (X)
JONES. Wit: JESSE WEBB, BRYAN WARD NOWLIN, LIGHT TOWNSEN. Rec. 22 Mar.
1791. (Also shown as Bryan West Nowlin)

Pp 271-272: 17 Jan. 1791. JOHN DICKERSON of Greenville to ROBERT SMITH
    of same, for 20 pds sterling, 100 acres, part of a tract
of 1340 acres on the Grove Creek granted to sd DICKERSON by Gov. Pinckney, rec. in Grant Bk RRRR page 284, adj. BAUGHN's, BOWIE's lines,
CLARK's Trail. Signed: JOHN DICKERSON. Wit: AMB. BLACKBURN, REUBEN
DANIEL, MICAJAH CLARK. Rec. 22 Mar. 1791.

Pp 272-273: 14 Feb. 1791. GEORGE HAINE & MARGET HAINE his wife of Green-
    ville Co. to DUNCAN MC WILKENS for 40 pds sterling, 140
acres, part of 240 acres on both sides of Tyger River adj. ELY PUT-
TETS(?) and ABRAHAM SHATEEN(?), granted 5 Dec. 1785, to THOMAS DAVES,
conveyed from DAVES to HAINE. Signed: GEORGE (H) HAINE, MARGET (her
mark) HAINE. Wit: VINSON ANDERS, JAMES NICOLL, JOHN NICOLL. Rec. 24
Mar. 1791.

Pp 273-274: 1 Mar. 1790. WILLIAM STOREY of Greenville to BRYAN WARD
    NOWLIN of same, for 60 pds, 100 acres on a branch of Reedy
River, granted 1 May 1786, rec. in Grant Bk KKKK page 492. Signed:
WILLIAM STOREY. Wit: JOHN STOREY, JESSE WEBB, WILLIAM BRISTER. Rec.
28 Mar. 1791.

Pp 274-275: 21 Feb. 1791. WILLIAM LYNCH to BRIGHT PREWET, both of Green-
    ville, for 100 pds sterling, 89 acres on the Sink Hole
Fork of Tyger River adj. land laid out to EDMUND BEARDEN and WILLIAM
DAVIS, granted to sd LYNCH 21 Jan. 1785, rec. in Grant Bk CCCC page
304. Signed: WILLIAM (W) LYNCH. Wit: J. CARTER, J. THOMAS, JR., JONAS
DAWSON.

Pp 275-276: 27 Nov. 1790. ISAAC MORGAN, Esq. of Greenville to JOHN
    DANIEL CARNS of Laurance Co., for 100 pds sterling, 769
acres granted to URIAH CONNER, conveyed from CONNER to MORGAN, on a
branch of Golden Grove Creek of Saluda, and a branch of Reedy Fork
of Reedy River, granted 3 Apr. 1786. Signed: ISAAC MORGAN. Wit: WM.

Cont'd from page 166:
GUNN, WILLIAM GRANT, JOHN EVINS. Rec. 29 Mar. 1791.

Page 276:   19 Feb. 1791. MARTIN GOLLITHAN & wife NANCEY of Greenville
             Co. to ANDREW JONES of same, for 60 pds, 123 acres on Horse
Creek, a poplar bottom branch, waters of Reedy River, granted 3 Oct.
(year not given), rec. Grant Bk KKKK. Signed: MARTIN GOLLOTHAN, NANCEY
GOLLOTHAN (her mark). Wit: LIGHT TOWNSEN, JESSE WEBB, BRYAN W. NOWLIN.
Rec. 29 Mar. 1791.

Pp 276-278: 14 Aug. 1790. SAMUEL BRUMMETT and wife ANN of Greenville
            Co. to WILLIAM BILLINGSLEY of same, for 30 pds sterling,
200 acres, part of a 379 acre tract granted 7 May 1787, both sides
of the main fork of Beens Creek of Saluda River, bounding SE on HENRY
WOOFF. Signed: SAMUEL (X) BRUMMETT. Wit: JOHN ROBINSON, JOHN GRIGSBY.
Rec. 1 Apr. 1791.

Pp 278-279: 27 Dec. 1790. RANDOLPH CASEY and wife CHARITY of Greenville,
            planter, to JOHN STANFORD, SR of same, planter, for 100
pds sterling, 161 acres granted sd CASEY 5 Feb. 1786, on the S fork
of the S Tyger River, adj. CASEY's and BARTON's lines. Signed: RANDOLPH
CASEY, CHARITY (X) CASEY. Wit: JAMES HENDERSON, JAMES DOUGHERTY. Rec.
4 May 1791.

Pp 279-280: 7 Feb. 1791. JESSE CHANDLER of Greenville to THOMAS MULLI-
            CAN of same, for 20 pds, 35 acres on waters of Horse Creek,
bounded on two sides by JESSE CHANDLER and WILLIAM MULLICAN and the
other by a branch of Horse Creek, it being the dividing line between
sd THOMAS MULLICAN and BENJAMIN CLEARWATERS, part of a tract orig.
granted to sd JESSE CHANDLER 5 Jan. 1789, rec. in Book YYYY page 319.
Signed: JESSE (his mark) CHANDLER. Wit: DRURY HODGES, SHADRAC CHANDLER.
Rec. 4 May 1791.

Pp 280-281: 19 July 1790. ESTHER THOMAS of Greenville to BENJAMIN PERRY
            of Pendleton Co., for 20 pds sterling, 400 acres on the
long branch of Reedy River, granted sd ESTHER THOMAS 7 Nov. 1785. Signed
by ESTHER THOMAS. Wit: JOHN THOMAS, CHARLES BRUCE, NATHANIEL PERRY.
Rec. 9 May 1791.

Pp 281-282: 18 Feb. 1791. JESSE CHANDLER of Greenville Co. to SHADRACK
            CHANDLER of same, for 20 pds sterling money of S.C., 50
acres on the waters of Horse Creek, adj. CHARLES SULLIVANT & JESSE
CHANDLER, part of a tract orig. granted sd CHANDLER 5 Jan. 1789, rec.
in Grant Bk YYYY page 319. Signed: JESSE (his mark) CHANDLER. Wit:
DRURY HODGES, THOMAS MULLICAN. Rec. 9 May 1791.

Page 282:   15 Feb. 1791. JOHN SIMS of Greenville to JOHN SMITH of
             same, for 20 pds lawful sterling, 100 acres, part of 300
acres orig. granted to JOHN WINN, JR. on Reedy Fork of Reedy River.
Signed: JOHN SIMS. No witnesses. Ack. by JOHN SIMS May term Court.
Rec. 10 May 1791.

Pp 282-283: 26 Oct. 1790. EDMUND PETERS of Greenville, bricklayer,
            to WILLIAM SAVAGE of same, blacksmith, for 30 pds sterling,
1/2 of a survey of 200 acres granted to THOMAS FARRAR 15 Oct. 1784,
on Beaverdam Creek of Enoree River adj. GIBSON SUTHERON. Signed: EDMUND
(X) PEETERS. Wit: ROBT. NELSON, REBECKAL NELSON. Probed by Robt. Nelson
May Term Court. Rec. 10 May 1791.

Pp 283-284: 14 Jan. 1790. JOHN BUCKANAN of Camden Dist. to JAMES HARRI-
            SON of Greenville Co., for 85 pds lawful sterling, 350
acres on Cripple Creek of Reedy River orig. surveyed and granted to
JANE CAMPBELL 21 Jan. 1785, adj. W on land orig. granted to Gen. RICHARD
WINN. Signed: JNO. BUCKANAN. Wit. CREIGHTON BUCKANAN, JOHN CRAIG, WILLI-
AM CHANDLER. Rec. 14 May 1791.

Pp 284-285: 20 Dec. 1788. GEORGE HAYS of Greenville Co. to WILLIAM
            TAYLOR of same, for 40 pds sterling, 200 acres on a branch
of Enoree River, granted sd HAYS 3 Apr. 1786, rec. Grant Bk HHHH paage
481. Signed: GEORGE HAYS. Wit: GEORGE ROSS, JOHN ROSS. Rec. 17 May

Cont'd from page 167:
1791. Proved by oath of JOHN ROSS.

Pp 285-286: 28 Nov. 1790. HENRY LANGFORD of Greenville Co. to BENJ.
SMITH of same, for 50 pds sterling, 130 acres, part of
a grant to REUBEN STRINGER 7 Aug. 1786, rec. Grant Bk NNNN page 417,
bounded SE by Saluda River, S by WILLIAM KELLEY and BLACKSTOCK, E by
JOHN HINSON, AMBROSE BLACKBURN. Signed: HENRY (E) LANGFORD. Wit: AMBS.
BLACKBURN, EDWIN SMITH, JOHN DYCHE (his mark). Proved by oath of JOHN
DYCHE. Rec. 18 May 1791.

Pp 286-287: 12 Mar. 1791. GEORGE RUSSELL of Greenville to SUZANAH JACOBS
of same, for 20 pds sterling, 100 acres, part of 217 acres
granted 3 May 1790, to sd RUSSELL, both sides of Kemp's branch of Enoree
River, the upper part adj. WM. RUSSELL's land. Signed: GEORGE RUSSELL,
JEAN (X) RUSSELL. Wit: ABSALOM CARNEY, JAMES (X) HOLLEMS, EMANUEL HOL-
LEMS. Proved by ABSALOM CARNEY. Rec. 18 May 1791.

END OF DEED BOOK B

GREENVILLE CO., S. C. DEED BOOK C
1791-1794

Pp 1-2:   18 Feb. 1791. ABSALOM CARNEY to JOSEPH KING, both of Greenville Co., for 40 pds, sold 40 acres, being part of orig.
grant in 1785 to sd ABSALOM CARNEY on both sides of Enoree River, adj.
CARNEY. Signed: ABSALOM CARNEY, SARAH (X) CARNEY. Wit: SOLOMON KEMP,
WM. SILVERSIDES.

Pp 2-4:   26 Feb. 1791. WILLIAM TURNBOUGH, planter, to GEORGE MITCHEL,
planter, both of 96 Dist. S. C. for 50 pds, sold 200 acres
orig. granted 5 June 1786 to sd TURNBOUGH, being on Beaver Dam of South
fork of Tygar River. Signed: WILLIAM (X) TURNBOUGH. Wit: THOMAS BENSON,
ARCHEYBEL DILL. Proven bef. HENRY PRINCE, Esq. and rec. 19 May 1791.

Pp 4-6:   13 Dec. 1790. JOHN CHILDRESS to GEORGE GOUGH, both of Greenville Co. for 4 pds, sold 70 acres, being part of 233 acres
granted 5 Feb. 1787 to OBADIAH HOOPER on the Ridge bet. Tygar River
and CHILDRESS's Beaver Dam Creek, adj. WOODS and RAY's line to waggon
road leading from JOHN NICOL's to Col. THOMAS's...to a conditional
line bet. sd JOHN CHILDRESS and ROBERT CHILDRESS. Signed: JOHN CHILD-
RESS. Wit: GEORGE SALMON, JOHN STANFORD. Ack. by JOHN CHILDRESS in
open Court. Rec. 26 May 1791.

Page 6:   Bill of Sale. 6 May 1791. THOMAS LEWIS to VINCENT DAVIS
both of Greenville Co., for 114 pds, sold 3 negroes now
in his possession to wit: negro man Peter, one named Tom, one woman
named Esther. Signed: THOMAS LEWIS. Wit: JOSEPH MAHON, GERSHAM KELLY,
who swore by oath bef. JOHN ALEXANDER, Esq. Rec. 16 July 1791.

(Note: Bill of Sale. THOMAS LEWIS to VINCENT DAVIS struck through.
Note in margin "Carried to Page 43 through mistake").

Pp 7-9:   May 1791. JOHN THOMAS to VINCENT DAVIS, both of Greenville
Co. for 100 pds, sold 160 acres being part of 640 acres
granted 16 July 1784 to THOMAS LEWIS, who conveyed 6 Mar. 1790 to JOHN
THOMAS on Horse Creek of Reedy River. Signed: JOHN THOMAS. Wit: JAMES
KELLY, DAVID (X) FORTNER, GERSHAM KELLY, who swore in open court July
term. Proven bef. JOHN ALEXANDER, Esq. and rec. 16 July 1791.

Pp 9-12:   Mortgage. 10 Nov. 1790. JOHN GOODWYN of Greenville Co.
to JOHN CUNNINGHAM of Charleston, S.C., merchant, for 100
pds, sold two plantations: (1) 118 acres orig. granted 7 Aug. 1785
to JEREMIAH CHANDLER on N side of Reedy River, adj. DAVID REED EVANS
and JOHN GOODWYN; (2) 313 acres on Reedy River of Saluda River...should
JOHN GOODWYN pay 50 pds to JOHN CUNNINGHAM bef. 1st Mar. next, this
be null and void. Signed: JOHN GOODWYN. Wit: DAVID LAMB, LITTLEBERRY
WILSON, ANDREW NORRIS, who swore oath bef. JOHN ROBERTSON, Esq. in
July Court. Rec. 1 Aug. 1791.

168

Pp 13-14:   4 Feb. 1790. SAMUEL ADAMS, considering moving, to JOSEPH
             REED, both of Greenville Co., for 80 pds, sold 300 acres
orig. granted 1 Aug. 1785 to ROBERT PRINCE, being the land where sd
JOSEPH REED now lives. Signed: SAML. ADAMS. Wit: NICHOLAS (X) GARRETT,
TERRY (X) CUMMINS. Proven bef. JAMES HARRISON, Esq. Rec. 1 Aug. 1791.

Pp 14-15:   18 June 1791. GEORGE ROSS to THOMAS BELL, both of Greenville
             Co., for 50 pds, sold 100 acres, being part of 200 acre
tract granted 3 Apr. 1786 to sd ROSS, being on both sides of Morgans
Creek of Enoree River, adj. land where sd BELL now lives. Signed: GEORGE
ROSS. Wit: ISAAC MORGAN, JOHN ROSS, GEORGE (X) SANDERS. Sworn oath
of GEO. SANDERS in open court bef. ROBERT MC AFEE, Esq. Rec. 1 Aug.
1791.

Pp 16-17:   16 May 1791. MAJOR PASSONS, yeoman of Pendleton Co., S.C.
             to ROBERT NELSON, Doctor of Greenville Co., for 5 pds,
sold 65 acres being part of 1542 acres granted 2 June 1788 sd PASSONS
on both sides of Beaver Dam of Middle Tigar and br. of south Tigar,
adj. MOSES WOODS and sd ROBERT NELSON. Signed: MAJOR PASSONS. Wit:
JARRED NELSON, JESSE (X) ASHLOCK. Sworn oath of JARRED NELSON in open
court. Rec. 1 Aug. 1791.

Pp 17-19:   26 Feb. 1791. ZACHARIAH WHITE to JOHN GORDAN, both of Green-
             ville Co., for 100 pds, sold 300 acres being part of a
grant to sd WHITE on Mill Shoal Creek of Enoree River. Signed: ZACHARIAH
WHITE. Wit: ABRAHAM NELSON, JOHN (X) MC VAY, SAMUEL GORDAN. Proved
bef. GEORGE SALMONS, Esq. in open July Court. Rec. 2 Aug. 1791.

Pp 19-20:   4 May 1791. JAMES MC ELROY to EZEKIAH COLLINS, both of
             Greenville Co., for 150 pds, sold 331 acres orig. granted
15 Oct. 1784 to sd MC ELROY on the north side of Reedy River onboth
sides of Saunders branch, adj. WILLIAM YOUNG. Signed: JAMES (X) MC
ELROY, FANNEY MC ELROY. Wit: THOS. MUSICH, ISAAC WEST, JR. Sworn oath
of ISAAC WEST, JR. in open court. Rec. 2 Aug. 1791.

Pp 20-21:   26 Oct. 1791. ROBERT BEAN of Franklin Co., Ga. to JOHN
             OWEN of 96 Dist., S.C. for 20 pds, sold 50 acres, granted
1 June 1787, being one mile below the mouth of Mathers's Creek, adj.
ROBERT BEAN, Col. DAVID HOPKINS and Saluda River. Signed: ROBT. BEAN.
Wit: JAMES DOUTHIT, JOHN DOUTHIT, JR. Proved bef. GEO. SALMON, Esq.
in open July Court 1791. Rec. 3 Aug. 1791.

Pp 22-23:   6 Mar. 1790. THOMAS LEWIS to JOHN THOMAS, both of Greenville
             Co., for 100 pds, sold 300 acres, being part of 640 acres
orig. granted 16 July 1784 to sd LEWIS on Horse Creek of Reedy River,
adj. CHANDLER. Signed: THOMAS LEWIS. Wit: THOS. CAMP, HOSEA CAMP, MARY
(X) CAMP. Proven in open July Ct. bef. JOHN ALEXANDER, Esq. Rec. 3
Aug. 1791.

Pp 23-25:   2 Apr. 1791. JOHN WARE, hereunto moving, to REUBEN TARRANT,
             both of Grenville Co. for 100 pds, sold 200 acres being
part of 300 acres orig. granted 16 July 1784 to sd WARE on Golden Grove
Creek. Signed: JOHN WARE. Wit: REUBEN BARRETT, ROBERT MAXWELL who swore
oath in open Ct. Rec. 10 Aug. 1791.

Pp 25-26:   20 Apr. 1790. DENNIS DUFF, planter, to RUSSEL CANNON, both
             of Greenville Co., for 100 pds, sold 140 acres orig. granted
4 Sept. 1786 to sd DUFF on North side of the South fork of Saluda River
under the Table Mountain. Signed: DENNIS DUFF. Wit: JAMES RUSSELL,
JOHN (X) BARNS, JOHN EVANS, who swore oath of in open court bef. JOHN
GRIGSBY. Rec. 9 Aug. 1791.

Pp 26-28:   13 Jan. 1791. JOSHUA SAXON of Laurence Co., S.C. to JOHN
             CHANDLER of Greenville Co., for 40 pds, sold 250 acres
orig. granted 21 Jan. 1785 to sd SAXON on branch of Horse Creek, adj.
HAMELTON. Signed: JOSHUA SAXON. Wit: JON. MC KINNEY, THOS. CAMP, VINCENT
DAVIS who swore oath bef. JOHN ALEXANDER, Esq. in open ct. Rec. 12
Aug. 1791.

Pp 28-31:   21 Dec. 1789. JAMES FRAZIER of Edgefield Co., S.C. to JOHN

Cont'd from page 169:
REED OF Greenville Co., for 50 pds, sold 215 acres being part of 336 acres orig. granted 5 June 1786 to JOSEPH REED on Rocky Creek of Rocky River, crossing Parris's wagon road. Signed: JAMES FRAZIER. Wit: W. NICHOLSON, JOSIAH COBB, ISAAC REED who swore oath bef. JAMES HARRISON, Esq. Rec. 12 Aug. 1791.

Pp 32-35:   27 Oct. 1789. THOMAS CALLOWAY, yeoman, of Burke Co., N.C. to ROBERT MAXWELL, Esq. of Greenville Co., for 100 pds, sold 400 acres orig. granted 21 Jan. 1785 to sd CALLOWAY on Golden Grove Creek and Saluda River, adj. JOSEPH REED, JOHN WYER & ROBERT MAXWELL. Signed: THOMAS CALLOWAY. Wit: JOSEPH (X) CALLOWAY, NANCY (X) CALLOWAY, BENJAMIN CLEVELAND, who swore oath bef. ROBT. ANDERSON, Esq. Rec. 15 Aug. 1791.

Page 36:   Bill of Sale. 20 Apr. 1791. JOHN CAPEHART to ROBERT MAXWELL, both of Greenville Co., for 25 pds..sold 6 cows and calves, 1 heiffer and yearling, 3 feather beds and pillows and bolster, 1 pair of fire dogs, 7 chairs and 1 pine table, bedstead and mattress, 8 pds of steel and 27 pds of iron, 2 bed cotts and lasy board and small table, 1 grind stone, 3 indigo vatts and 33 poplar planks, 1 marble slab, 63 head of hogs, 30 which are grown. Signed: JOHN CAPEHART. Wit: LARKIN TARRANT, JOHN PYLE.

Pp 37-39:   2 Apr. 1789. JOHN WARE of Greenville Co. but hereunto moving, to SARAH CHARLES, of same place, for 50 pds, sold 100 acres being part of 300 acres orig. granted 16 July 1784 to sd WARE on Golden Grove Creek. Signed: JOHN WARE. Wit: ROBERT MAXWELL, REUBEN BARRETTE. Sworn oath of ROBT. MAXWELl, Esq. in open court. Rec. 16 Aug. 1791.

Pp 39-40:   10 June 1788. DAVID HUMPHREYS of Surry Co., N.C. to ISAAC JAMES of Greenville Co., for 83 pds, sold 640 acres orig. granted 15 Oct. 1784 to sd HUMPHREYS on both sides of Beaverdam Creek a fork of Mountain Creek of Saluda River, adj. WILLIAM NEELE. Signed: DAVID HUMPHREYS. Wit: ?L.T.D.? THOMAS, JOHN THOMAS, JR., CANDACE THOMAS. Sworn oath of JOHN THOMAS, JR. in open court bef. ROBERT MC AFEE, Esq. Rec. 16 Aug. 1791.
(Note: Clerk wrote 640 acres sold, but in repeating acreage, he states 540 acres.)

Pp 40-42:   15 Oct. 1790. EDMUND EDWARDS to ISAIAH PAYNE, both of Greenville Co., for 200 pds, sold 73 acres being part of 400 acres orig. granted 15 Oct. 1784 to sd EDWARDS on waters of the Golden Grove Creek of Saluda River, adj. JAMES SEABORN, NATHANIEL PENDLETON. Signed: EDMUND EDWARDS, ELIZABETH (X) EDWARDS. Wit: AARON PAYNE, HENRY MACHEN, who swore oath in open court July term 1791. Rec. 18 Aug. 1791.

Page 43:   Bill of Sale. 6 May 1791. THOMAS LEWIS to VINCENT DAVIS both of Greenville Co., for 15 pds, sold 2 feather beds and furniture, 1 chest and the books etc. contained. Signed: THOMAS LEWIS. Wit: JOSEPH MAHON, GERSHAM KELLEY, who swore oath bef. JOHN ALEXANDER, Esq. in open court July term 1791. Rec. 18 Aug. 1791.

Pp 43-44:   1790. JOHN FORD to WILLIAM SMITH, both of Greenville Co., for 25 pds, sold 116 acres orig. granted 6 Oct. 1788 to BENJAMIN RANEY on Beverleys branch of Reedy River. Signed: JOHN FORD. Wit: DANIEL FORD, JESSE (X) FORD. Sworn oath of DANIEL FORD in open court bef. JOHN ALEXANDER, Esq. Rec. 22 Aug. 1791.

Pp 45-46:   6 May 1791. THOMAS LEWIS to SOLOMON LITTLETON, both of Greenville Co., for 40 pds, sold 150 acres being part of 200 acres orig. granted on the Bounty 4 July 1785 to JAMES GORE on Saluda River, including the Cedar Island. Signed: THOMAS LEWIS. Wit: JOSEPH MAHON, VINCENT DAVIS, who swore oath in open court 9 July bef. ROBERT MC AFEE, Esq. Rec. 23 Aug. 1791.

Pp 46-47:   6 May 1791. THOMAS LEWIS to THOMAS CAMP both of Greenville Co., for 100 pds, sold 300 acres being part of 640 acres

Cont'd from page 170:
orig. granted 16 July 1784 to sd LEWIS on south side of Horse Creek,
adj. JOHN THOMAS and RAGSDALE. Signed: THOMAS LEWIS. Wit: JOSEPH MAHON,
WILLIAM CHISM, VINCENT DAVIS, who swore oath in open court July term
bef. JOHN ALEXANDER, Esq. Rec. 23 Aug. 1791.

Pp 48-49:   26 Feb. 1791. ROBERT HARRISON to MARTIN WEBB both of Green-
             ville Co., for 75 pds, sold 100 acres being part of 200
acres orig. granted 4 July 1785 to PAUL FOUNTAIN, adj. bank of Saluda
River and sd HARRISON. Signed: ROBT HARRISON. Wit: JOHN JETT, JOHN
(X) WEBB. Ack. bef. ROBERT MC AFEE, Esq. Rec. 29 Sept. 1791.

Pp 50-51:   14 Apr. 1791. OBADIAH HOOPER to JAMES WOODY, both of Green-
             ville Co., for 5 pds, sold 100 acres being part of 422
acres orig. granted 1 Aug. 1785 to sd HOOPER on Armstrong's Creek,
adj. MARY WHITE on Kelleys Branch and sd JAMES WOODY. Signed. OBADIAH
HOOPER. Wit: RICHARD HOOPER, BETY HOOPER, JONATHAN (X) WOODDE, who
swore oath bef. GEORGE SALMON, Esq. Rec. 29 Sept. 1791.

Pp 51-53:   3 Oct. 1791. GIPSON SOUTHERON to ENOCH BENSON, both of
             Greenville Co., for 50 pds, sold 100 acres being part of
200 acres orig. granted 15 Oct. 1784 on Beaver Dam Creek of Enoree
River to THOMAS FARRAR, who conveyed 16 Sept. 1788 to EDMUND PETERS,
who conveyed 21 Jan. 1790 to sd GIPSON SOUTHERON. Signed: GIPSON SOUTH-
ERN. Wit: WILLIAM SAVAGE, THOMAS (X) USREY, ROBERT CHILDRESS, who swore
oath bef. JAMES BLASINGAME, Esq.

Pp 53-55:   3 Oct. 1791. WILLIAM SAVAGE to ENOCH BENSON both of Green-
             ville Co., for 40 pds, sold 100 acres being part of 200
acres orig. granted 15 Oct. 1785 to THOMAS FARRAR, who conveyed 16
Sept. 1788 to EDMUND PETERS, who conveyed 6 Oct. 1790 to sd WM. SAVAGE,
being on Beaver Dam Creek of Enoree River. Signed: WILLIAM SAVAGE.
Wit: GIPSON SOUTHERON, THOMAS (X) USREY, ROBERT CHILDRESS, who swore
oath in open court bef. JAMES BLASINGAME, Esq. Rec. 24 Oct. 1791.

Pp 55-58:   4 May 1791. THOMAS FARRAR to ROBERT GILLILAND, JR., both
             of Greenville Co., for 25 pds, sold 149 acres orig. granted
24 Sept. 1784 to sd FARRAR bet. the Golden Grove Creek and Saluda River
adj. Judge PENDLETON and JOHN BOWIE. Signed: THOMAS FARRAR. Wit: ISAAC
BOGAN, ?R? BROWN, JAMES BLASINGAME, Esq., who swore oath in open court.
Rec. 16 Oct. 1791.

Pp 58-60:   21 Feb. 1791. JAMES MC ELROY to FREDERICK BROCK, both of
             Greenville Co., for 5 shillings, sold 309 acres orig. grant-
ed 5 June 1786 to sd MC ELROY on Sanders Branch of Reedy River, including the west side of Paris's Mountain. Signed: JAMES (X) MC ELROY.
Wit: JOHN LANGSTON, JAMES BROCK, JESSE CARTER, who swore oath in open
court. Rec. 27 Oct. 1791.

Pp 60-63:   Sheriffs Title. 3 Oct. 1791. HUGH MC VAY, Esq., Sheriff
             of Greenville Co., to LEMUEL JAMES ALSTON of same place
for 6 pds...sold 900 acres orig. granted 5 June 1786 on Reedy River,
adj. JESSE GOODWYN, ISAAC CRUIES(?), GEORGE UNDERWOOD. Whereas ROBERT
MAXWELL obtained a Judgement 5 July 1791 against JOHN GOODWYN for his
debt and damage...HUGH MC VAY on 1 Oct. 1791 toward satisfaction seized
and sold land to last and highest bidder. Signed: HUGH MC VAY, DSGC.
Wit: J. CARTER, JOHN PYLE. Proven in open court Oct. Term. Rec. 4 Nov.
1791.

Pp 63-65:   1788. MICHAEL JOHNSTON of Newberry Co., S.C. to ISAAC WEST
             of Greenville Co., for 40 pds, sold 160 acres orig. granted
21 Jan. 1785 to sd JOHNSTON on Richland Creek of Reedy River. Signed:
MICHAEL JOHNSTON. Wit: ISAAC MORGAN, JOHN ROSS, AARON KEMP, who swore
oath in open court Oct. term 1791. Rec. 10 Nov. 1791.

Pp 65-67:   11 May 1791. WILLIAM VARNELL to SAMUEL MOSELY, both of
             Greenville Co., for 150 pds, sold 325 acres being part
of 345 acres orig. granted 4 Sept. 1786 to sd VARNELL on Brushey Creek
of Reedy River, adj. JOHN PAUL. Signed: WILLIAM VARNELL. Wit: JESSE

Cont'd from page 171:
CARTER, WILLIAM GUNN, who swore oath in open court. Rec. 14 Nov. 1791.

Pp 67-70:   10 Jan. 1791. BENJAMIN RICE, hereunto moving, to JEREMIAH
              SMITH, both of Greenville Co., for 100 pds, sold 400 acres
orig. granted 15 Oct. 1784 to sd RICE on Golden Grove Creek of Saluda
River, adj. JEREMIAH SMITH, NATHANIEL PENDLETON & ISAIAH PAYNE. Signed:
BENJAMIN RICE. Wit: AARON PAYNE, WILLIAM FARISS, ARCHIBALD (X) MAHAN,
who swore oath in open court bef. J. BLASINGAME, Esq. Rec. 14 Nov.
1791.
(Note: Clerk wrote 104 acres, also in deed. Uncertain if this is the
actual amount of land sold from Grant).

Pp 71-75:   24 May 1788. RICHARD COLLINS of Spartanburgh Co., S.C.
              to JOSEPH BAUX of Greenville Co., for 90 pds, sold 469
acres orig. granted 5 Mar. 1787 to sd COLLINS on both sides of Gilders
Creek, including the place known as "The Three Forks" of sd creek.
Signed: RICHD. COLLINS. Wit: ASA ESTES, JAMES (X) PEEK, who swore oath
bef. JAMES HARRISON, Esq. Rec. 17 Nov. 1791.

Pp 75-79:   4 Oct. 1788. JOHN BROWN, planter, to HARMON SHUMAKER, plant-
              er, both of Greenville Co., for 60 pds, sold 150 acres
being part of 640 acres orig. granted 21 Jan. 1785 to JAMES MC WILLIAMS
on Reedy River, adj. JOHN SMITH, DANIEL CHANDLER, DAVID MC DAVID. Signed
by JOHN BROWN, MARY BROWN. Wit: JOHN GILLILAND, JAMES SAMFORD who swore
oath in open court. Rec. 18 Nov. 1791.

Pp 79-81:   5 Sept. 1791. WILLIAM HAMBY, hereunto moving, to JOHN HAMBY
              both of Greenville Co., for 75 pds, sold 100 acres orig.
granted 21 Jan. 1785 to sd. JOHN HAMBY on Lawrill Creek. Signed: WILL-
IAM (X) HAMBY. Wit: ABEDNEGO CHANDLER, SAMUEL UNDERWOODS, JNO. GOODWYN.
Ack. in open court Oct. term 1791 by WM. HAMBY. Rec. 9 Dec. 1791.

Pp 81-84:   17 Feb. 1791. CHARLES ROGERS, hereunto moving, to JAMES
              HIDE, both of Greenville Co., for 40 pds, sold 200 acres
being part of 300 acres orig. granted 6 Oct. 1788 to JOHN LAFFERTY
on both sides of Quarl Branch of Reedy River. Signed: CHARLES (X) ROGERS
& AMELIA (X) ROGERS. Wit: JACOB BLACK, JAMES SAMFORD, who swore oath
in open court Oct. Term. Rec. 12 Dec. 1791.

Pp 84-87:   6 Jan. 1791. DANIEL MC MILLIN to JOHN THOMAS, Sr., both
              of Greenville Co., for 54 pds, sold 50 acres being part
of 640 acres orig. granted 21 Jan. 1785 to MAJOR PASSONS, who conveyed
1 Apr. 1785 to THOMAS TOD, who conveyed 21 Mar. 1786 to JOHN THOMAS,
who conveyed 15 Mar. 1789 to DANIEL MC MILLIN and being the land whereon
the sd DANIEL MC MILLIN now lives on the south side of South Fork of
Tygar River, adj. THOMAS. Signed: DANIEL (O) MC MILLIN. Wit: WM. THOMAS,
JANE THOMAS, JOHN THOMAS, JR. who swore oath in open court bef. HENRY
PRINCE, Esq. Rec. 12 Dec. 1791.

Pp 87-89:   1 Sept. 1791. EDWARD BALINGER, planter, of Greenville Co.,
              to ISAAC GRAY, planter, of Laurence Co., SC for 100 pds,
sold 195 acres being part of 587 acres orig. granted 17 Nov. 1785 to
sd BALLINGER on Enoree River, adj. HENRY MITCHEN, STEPHEN CANTREL,
BALLINGER and MORGAN. Signed: EDWARD BALLINGER. Wit: ISAAC MORGAN,
ELIJAH OLIVER, JAMES (X) WHEELER, who swore oath bef. ROBERT MC AFEE,
Esq. Rec. 17 Dec. 1791.
(Note: On the margin of this deed was written, "This conveyance from
BALLENGER to GRAY was the last memorial sent to the Secretary").

Pp 89-90:   Power of Attorney. (No date). THOMAS HOOPER of Greenville
              Co., to JAMES HOOPER of Lunenburg Co., Va. my true and
lawful attorney to convey 150 acres in Lunenburg Co., Va. Signed: THOMAS
HOOPER. Wit: JOHN BLACKWELL, JOHNSON MONROE. Ack. by THOMAS HOOPER
in open court Feb. term 1792. Rec. 15 Feb. 1792.

Pp 90-91:   7 Feb. 1792. JAMES BLASINGAME to JOHN BLASINGAME both of
              Greenville Co., for 60 pds, sold 1127 acres orig. granted on
7 Aug. 1786 to sd JAMES BLASINGAME on branch of Saluda River. Signed:

Cont'd from page 172:
J. BLASINGAME. Wit: WM. PRIDE, JOHN WESTFIELD, who swore oath in open
court Feb. 1792 bef. GEORGE SALMON, Esq. Rec. 16 Feb. 1792.

Pp 92-94:   Sheriff's Title. 4 Feb. 1792. HUGH MC VAY, Sheriff of Green-
              ville Co., to JESSE CARTER of same place for 2 pds, sold
275 acres on waters of Tygar River, whereas DANIEL MC MILLIN in July
term did commence action against JESSE MORTON & JEREMIAH DUTTON, Sheriff McVay did seize and take into execution herein described. Signed:
HUGH MC VAY, DSG County. Wit: H. M. WOOD, ROBERT MAXWELL. Ack. by Hugh
McVay in open court Feb. 1792. Rec. 17 Feb. 1792.

Pp 94-96:   3 May 1791. JOHN PEDEN, planter, of Greenville Co., to
              JAMES COGBURN of Laurence Co., S.C. for 25 pds, sold 51
acres being part of 1759 acres orig. granted 6 Nov. 1786 to sd PEDEN
on Raburn Creek, adj. DAVID MORTON and sd JOHN PEDEN, including the
house and improvement which sd JAMES COGBURN has formerly occupied.
Signed: JOHN PEDEN. Wit: JEREMIAH H. SHEPARD, SAMUEL NISBIETT, JOHN
MORTON, who swore oath in open court Feb. Term 1792 bef. JOHN ALEXANDER,
Esq. Rec. 18 Feb. 1792.

Pp 97-98:   13 May 1791. NICHOLAS DARNALL of Pendleton Co., S.C. to
              FOLTON WOODY of Greenville Co., for 60 pds, sold 204 acres
being part of 304 acres orig. granted 4 July 1785 to sd DARNALL on
branch of Saluda River adj. JOSEPH BRIDGES & JOSEPH DUNCAN. Signed:
NICHO'S DARNALL. Wit: CHARLES BENSON, ABRAHAM BRADLEY, JOHN SLAYTON.
Proven bef. JAMES BLASINGAME, Esq. in open court Feb. Term 1792. Rec.
20 Feb. 1792.

Pp 98-101:   1 Nov. 1791. JOHN BEYTHEIVA GRIGSBY to JOHN MONTIETH ROBIN-
              SON, both of Greenville Co., for 300 pds, sold 370 acres
being of two tracts: (1) 320 acres on the north side of the south fork
of Saluda River, being that valuable tract of land sd JOHN BETHEVIA
GRIGSBY now lives on and was purchased from SAMUEL EARLE; (2) 50 acres
which adj. above sd tract and HENRY WOOLF, being tract purchased frm
Capt. JOSEPH HUGHES of Union Co., S.C. The true intent and meaning
of this indenture shall not claim..any part..during the life of JOHN
B. GRIGSBY or the joint lives of the sd JOHN B. GRIGSBY and ELIZABETH
GRIGSBY his wife or the life of the longest liver of either of them.....
Should JOHN M. ROBINSON die before the sd JOHN B. GRIGSBY and wife
without lawful heirs, in that case the sd JOHN M. ROBINSON shall will
and bequeath the sd lands to any person whom he may think proper after
the decease of sd GRIGSBY and wife. Signed: JOHN BEYTHEIVA GRIGSBY.
Wit: JOSEPH (X) WILLIAMS, SAMUEL EARLE, who swore oath in open court
Feb. Term 1792. Rec. 20 Feb. 1792.

Pp 102-104:   13 Sept. 1791. JOHN CHILDRESS to CHARLES BRUCE, carpenter,
              both of Greenville Co., for 20 pds, sold 100 acres being
part of 400 acres orig. granted 3 OCt. 1785 to JEREMIAH DUTTON and
conveyed 23 Feb. 1787 to sd CHILDRESS, including the plantation sd
CHILDRESS now lives on branch of the south Fork of Tygar River known
by the name of Childress's Beaver Dam, adj. the waggon road leading
from Col. THOMAS's to JOHN NICHOL's and JEREMIAH DUTTON. Signed: JOHN
CHILDRESS. Wit: ENOCH BENSON, REUBEN BARRETT, GEORGE BENSON. Proven
bef. JOHN THOMAS, JR. in open court Feb. Term 1792. Rec. 22 Feb. 1792.

Pp 104-106:   2 Nov. 1791. WILLIAM FLIPPO and ANNE FLIPPO his wife, to
              JOHN M. ROBINSON all of Greenville Co., for 50 pds, sold
246 acres orig. granted 6 Dec. 1790 to sd FLIPPO, adj. SAMUEL BRUMMETT,
SIMCOCK CANNON, DENIS DUFF. Signed: WILLIAM FLIPPO. Wit: JOSEPH (X)
WILLIAMS, SAMUEL EARLE, who swore oath in open court Feb. Term 1792.
Rec. 24 Feb. 1792.

Pp 106-108:   9 Nov. 1791. NICHOLAS DARNALL of Pendleton Co. to JOHN
              SLATEN of Greenville Co. for 50 pds, sold 200 acres being
part of 304 acres orig. granted 4 July 1785 to sd DARNALL on Armstrongs
Creek of Saluda River, adj. WILLIAM MASTON, CHARLES BENSON, ABRAHAM
BRADLEY, ADAM CATWELL, FOLTON WOOD & VALENTINE THACKER. Signed: NICH'S
DARNALL. Wit: ABRAHAM BRADLEY, CHARLES BENSON, JOHN SLAYTON. Proven

Cont'd from page 173:±
before J. BLASINGAME, Esq. in open court Feb. term 1792. Rec. 24 Feb.
1792.

Pp 108-109: 23 Oct. 1790. WILLIAM YOUNG of Greenville Co. to JOHN YOUNG,
            JR. of Spartanburgh Co. for one Spanish Milled Dollar,
sold 600 acres orig. granted 15 Oct. 1784 to sd WM. YOUNG on both sides
of Reedy River, adj. JOHN YOUNG, WILLIAM YOUNG & MAJOR GOWEN. Signed:
WM. YOUNG. Wit: H. M. WOOD, WM. WOOD. Proven bef. GEO. SALMON, Esq.
in open court Feb. term 1792. Rec. 24 Feb. 1792.

Pp 109-110: 23 Oct. 1790. WILLIAM YOUNG of Greenville Co., to JOHN
            YOUNG, JR. of Spartanburgh Co. for one Spanish Milled Dollar
sold 220 acres orig. granted 15 Jan. 1789 to sd WM. YOUNG on south
side of Reedy River, adj. JOHN LANGSTON, JAMES MC ELROY, ROBERT DUNCAN
and sd WM. YOUNG. Signed: WM. YOUNG. Wit: H. M. WOOD, WM. WOOD. Proven
bef. GEO. SALMON, Esq. in open court Feb. term 1792. Rec. 24 Feb. 1792.

Pp 111-113: 2 Dec. 1791. BENJAMIN SMITH and HANARITHER SMITH, his wife
            to ROBERT LANGFORD, all of Greenville Co. for 60 pds, sold
100 acres being part of 608 acres orig. granted 5 June 1786 to EDWIN
SMITH on north side of Saluda River and adj. a conditional line bet.
EDWIN SMITH & WALDROP. Signed: BENJ. SMITH. Wit: W. TOWNS, RICHARD
(X) PAIN. Proven bef. ROBT. MAXWELL, Esq. in open court Feb. term 1792.
Rec. 25 Feb. 1792.

Pp 113-115: 13 Sept. 1791. WILLIAM WHORTON to WILLIAM CHANDLER, both
            of Greenville Co. for 10 pds, sold 100 acres being part
of 300 acres orig. granted 1 Jan. 1787 to WADSWORTH & TURPIN on both
sides of Mountain Creek of Enoree River, adj. WM. WHORTON. Signed:
WILLIAM (X) WHORTON, JEAN (X) WHORTON. Wit: MARK THOMPSON, ELISHA SIM-
MONS, NICHOLAS DARBY, who swore oath bef. ROBT. MC AFEE, Esq. Rec.
1 Mar. 1792.

(Note: DEED BOOK C continues for 400 additional pages, not included
here.)

GREENVILLE CO., S. C. ESTATE RECORDS

REFERNCE: Greenville County Courthouse, Probate Judge Office, Greenville, S. C. Abstracted from BOOK A ESTATE RECORDS & LOOSE PAPERS found
in designated Apartment and File numbers.

Pp 1-5:   PYLE, SAMEUL. Adm. MARY PYLE the 20th Dec. 1787.
Apt. 6-File 369:   Adm. Bond signed by MARY A. PYLE, HANS BLACK, JACOB
1788   BLACK the 21st Nov. 1787. Appraisors, 20th Dec. 1787,
                    HENRY MACHEN, AQUILA BRASHER, JOHN BRASHER, MICHAEL
                    ROBINS.

Pp 6-11   SHIP, WILLIAM. Will proven in Court Feb. Term 1788.
Apt. 7-File 427:   WILLIAM SHIP, Farmer of Greenville Co., S.C. Wife:
1788   ANN SHIP, Ex'trix with JOHN & JOSEPH DUNKLIN, Ex'ors.
                    Son, WILLIAM - land known as WILLIAM WOODS land.
Son, JOSEPH - land where he now lives. Dau. - land known as EVAN's
survey. Others mentioned, but relation not given: ELIZABETH DUNKLIN,
JOSEPH DUNKLIN, JOHN DUNKLIN. Signed: WILLIAM SHIP, the 7th Dec. 1787.
Wit: HULET SWILLIVANT, BRIDGET KELLY. Other data from loose papers:
WILLIAM SHIP in Aug. 1779 borrowed money from FIELD FARRAR (called
Captain FIELD FARRAR in the account). This note was taken from FIELD
FARRAR with other articles by the British when at Captain HALE's. Claim
Filed 9th Apr. 1789. Also a Claim Filed from Estate by WILLIAM WOOD,
State of Georgia, Franklin Co., the 23rd Feb.1790 for a note made 6
Oct. 1784. Another Claim states WILLIAM SHIP of Looningburg Co. was
held bound unto JOHN LAIN of Charlotte Co. for sum of 18 pounds Va.
money. This note was signed the 9th July 1773 by WILLIAM SHIP, and
this claim was filed the 15th Oct. 1790 by the authority of JOHN LAIN.
A Petition (no date) to appear in Court for JOHN DUNKLIN & JOSEPH DUNK-
LIN, Executors and NATHANIEL SULLIVANT & ANN his wife, Executrix of
LW & T of WILLIAM SHIP. (A later Petition of same content as above
has the date of 25 Mar. 1798.)

174

Pp 11-15   MOODY, JESSE. JESSE MOODY died Intestate, was a Plant-
Apt. 5-File 338: er of Greenville Co., S.C. Adm. DINAH MOODY, 10 Feb.
1780   1788. Appraisors: WILLIAM ARMSTRONG, WILLIAM COX,
                  EDMUND EDWARDS, JOHN PYLE, the 18th Feb. 178_. Bond:
DINAH MOODY, AMBROSE BLACKBURN, Esq. & JACOB BLACK the 18th Feb.‾1788.

Pp 16-21   FOSTER, JOHN. Will of JOHN FOSTER, Carpenter of Green-
Apt. 3-File 159: ville Co., 96 Dist., S.C. Wife, unnamed. Dau., MARY
1788   HENDLEY, a negro now in her possession named Silva.
                  Dau., FRANCES, a negro named Sabina. Son, JOHN CROW
FOSTER. Son, GEORGE SINGLETON FOSTER. Son, JOSIAH FOSTER. Son, JAMES
HOCKET FOSTER. Dau., NANCY. Son, ROBERT SINGLETON FOSTER. To my 3 sons
JOSIAH, JAMES HOCKET, ROBERT SINGLETON & daughter, NANCY, the planta-
tion I now live on. Signed: JOHN FOSTER the 9th Oct. 1787. Wit: RICHARD
THOMPSON, DAVE SHIDDEN, JOHN RABUN. Exec.'s JOHN CROW FOSTER & GEORGE
SINGLETON FOSTER. From the loose papers: "Union Co., S.C. the 17th
Jan. 1789. Paid to MARY DAVIS balance due her settlement 1/8/0. Signed
MARY DAVIS & WILLIAM HENDLEY (J.P.?) account in Full 17th Jan. 1789."
"Estate Paid for cost of two Courts at Camden & 3 Courts at Pinkney."
"Received share the 10th July 1795, GEORGE FOSTER, JAMES H. FOSTER,
NANCY FOSTER, ROBERT S. C. FOSTER, BENJAMIN PERRY for NANCY FOSTER."
"22 Dec. 1797 WILLIAM GRANT signed for his wife, FRANCES, Legatee."
"24 Feb. 1798 BENJAMIN PERRY signed for his wife, NANCY, Legatee."
"20 Apr. 1797 GEORGE S. FOSTER, Legatee." One paper with no date signed
by Legatee's WILLIAM GRANT, JAMES H. FOSTER, NANCY FOSTER, GEORGE S.
FOSTER, JOHN C. FOSTER.

Pp 21-24   BROWN, RICHARD. Adm. of estate, ANN BROWN. Appraisors:
Apt. 1-File 34:   ARTHE MEEKS, ISAAC JAMES, DREWRY MORRIS, DAVID ROSS
1788   the 20th Aug. 1788. "Report of Calculations & Reckon-
                  ing of Estate of RICHARD BROWN, dec'd. Filed 7 July
1806" has on one acc't. in 1792 that ANN BROWN received money for support of myselfand seven children.

Pp 24-28   ROBERTS, HARDY. Wife, PATIENCE, Executrix. ROBERT
Apt. 6-File 387: MC AFEE, Executor. Son, JAMES, Son, SHEROD. Son-
1789   in-law, JAMES BARNHILL. Two youngest sons, JOSIAH
                  & HARDEN. Written the 6th Mar. 1789 and signed HARDY
(+) ROBERTS. Wit: ISAAC WEST, WILLIAM (A) CHANDLER, ALEXANDER GLENN.
Appraisors: ISAAC WEST, JOSEPH LANGSTON, JAMES MC ELROY the 19th May
1789.

Pp 28-29   BRASHER, THOMAS (spelled BREASUR on Will). Will proven
Apt. 8-File 577: in open Court Feb. term 1790 by JOHN STEEL & AQUILA
1789   BRASHER & recorded the 6th Apr. 1790. "THOMAS BRASHER
                  of Greenville Co., S.C. the 27th Sept. 1789. Wife,
SARAH. Son, THOMAS - 120 acres. Son, QUELLA - 120 acres. Son, HENRY
- 120 acres. Son, JOHN - 120 acres. Son, SAMUEL - the house and plantation including 100 acres. Signed: THOMAS BRASHER. Wit: JOHN STEEL &
AQUILA BRASHER.

Pp 29-34   LANGSTON, JOHN. Will recorded 11 Nov. 1790. Wife,
Apt. 5-File 288: mentined. Son, JAMES. Son, SOLOMON. Grandson, ASA.
1800   Grandson, WILLIAM. JECHONIAS - land he lives on (JE-
                  CHONIAH LANGSTON in the content of Will). Dau., BECKKA
WILLIAMS. Dau., FANNY LANGSTON. Dau., SALLY SMITH. Son, SAMUEL. Dau.,
ELIZABETH SPANN. Son, JOSEPH. Son, JESSE. Dau., PATTA MC VAY. JOHN,
son of JESSE, my grandson. Son-in-law, THOMAS WILLIAMS. Executors,
my son, JECHONIAS & son-in-law THOMAS WILLIAMS. "I forgot LUSIA THOMSON
to give her to dollars silver". Written 1 Mar. 1782 and signed JOHN
LANGSTON. Wit: JOSHUA SMITH, JOHN WHITE, ELINER (X) WHITE. Inventory
& Appraisement signed by EDMUND BEARDEN, EATON HAWKINS, JAMES BROOKS,
16 Nov. 1790. Appraisors: EATON HAWKINS, PINCK HAWKINS & SOLOMON WEST
took oath 12 Mar. 1800. BENJAMIN BRIDGES named as appraisor the 9th
Mar. 1800 with the above. Expenditures dated 21 Mar. 1801. Paid: JAMES
MC ELROY acct. proved. Paid: LEVI LANGSTON acct. proved. Paid: ALEX
WEST, funeral expenses. Paid: MARTHA MC VAY, her legacy in full. Paid:
JAMES LANGSTON, for hire of negro.

Pp 35-40   (See next page)

Pp 35-40   GILL, JOSEPH. Died Intestate in Greenville Co., S.C.
Apt. 3-File 205:   Application for letters of Adm. by MRS. ELIZABETH
1790   GILL & MR. SAMUEL EARLE 19 July 1790. "17 Aug. 1790
                        Letter of Adm. given to ELIZABETH GILL & SAMUEL EARLE".
"To Mess'ses ELIAS EARLE, JOHN FORD, SAMUEL EARL, SR., HENRY M. WOOD
& JOHN BETHIWAY GRIGSBY any three appraisors. 17 Aug. 1790". "Pursuant
to Appraisors - have qualified HENRY MACHEN WOOD, ELIAS EARLE, SAMUEL
EARLE & JOHN BETHEWAY GRIGSBY. Certified 5 Oct. 1790". At the end of
Inventory list - states "appraised the Estate of Capt. JOS. GILL, dec'd.
17 Aug. 1790". "Acct. of Settlement of Estate the 30th Sept. 1797".
Other names mentioned in settlement of estate: JAMES CONN, ROBERT CHILD-
RESS, RICHARD LEWIS, JEPTHA HOLLINGSWORTH, THOMAS GOODE, WILLIAM BROWN,
JOHN WILLIAMS, JOHN GOODE, JOSEPH THOMPSON, WILLIAM HAWKINS, JOHN STYLES
and WILLIAM HOPSON.

Pp 40-41   FORRESTER, JAMES. (There are no original papers or
Apt. 114-File 31:   Will in the Apartment File) Court held May term 1791,
1791   proved by oath of WILLIAM BRADLEY & EDE JOHNSON,
                        26 May 1791. Will written the 4th July 1790 by JAMES
FORRISTER of Greenville Co., S.C. Wife, ELIZABETH - plantation whereon
I now live etc. during her life. Son, HARDY FORRISTER. Son, RICHARD
FORRISTER - 169 acres. Son, JOHN FORRISTER - plantation of 200 acres
on Buck Creek. Executors: JOSEPH O BANNON & HARDY FORRISTER. Signed:
JAMES (X) FORRESTER. Wit: MARY (X) HOLDER, EDE (X) JOHNSON, WILLIAM
(X) BRADLEY.

Pp 41-47   TARRANT, LEONARD, SR. Will written 23 Feb. 1791.
Apt. 7-File 464:   LEONARD TARRANT of S.C., 96 District to sons (sic)
Year Filed 1834:   BENJAMIN & LEONARD & SAMUEL TARRANTS & NELLY DANIEL,
                        I have given all that I ever meant, or intended,
they should have from me or my Estate, I mean my Children above mentioned is to have no more from my estate. Wife, MARY. Dau., ELIZABETH
KIRBY. Son, REUBEN TARRANT. Granddaughter, ELIZABETH TARRANT, dau.
of SAMUEL TARRANT of which Executors to keep for her until marriage
or become of age. Money from Estate Sale - 1/4 to wife, MARY after
paying my debts, the ballance to be equally divided between my two
sons, JOHN & JAMES TARRANTS. Signed: LEONARD (X) TARRANT. Wit: L. TAR-
RANT, SAMUEL TARRANT, ROWLAND TARRANT. End of Will. "Open Court July
Term 1791 & proven by oath of LARKIN TARRANT & Recorded 24 Aug. 1791".
"MARY TARRANT, Widow, appeared in open Court 14 Jan. 1791, having been
fully satisfied for her part of said estate". The Clerk recorded above
statement, dated 14 Jan. 1791 and MARY (her mark) TARRANT signed 14
JulY 1791. (In Probate Index was written the final return made in 1835).

Pp 47-48   CRAIN, JUDETH. The Will of JUDETH CRANE in open court
Pp 51-52   Feb. term 1792, proven by oaths of WILLIAM USREY
Apt. 2-File 106:   & WILLIAM NELSON and recorded 9 Mar. 1792. JUDETH
1792   CRANE appoints ENOCH BENSON & DOCTOR NELSON, guard-
                        ians for "my five small children". To my three boys
- land. Dau., SUANA. Dau., NANSEY. Son, CHARLES. To POLEY EVANS one
cow. To SAMUEL CRAIN, one shilling. To WILLIAM CRAIN, one shilling.
To JOHN CRAIN, one shilling. Rest of Estate be equally divided amongst
my five small children. Will written 19 Jan. 1791 and signed JUDETH
(X) CRAIN. Wit: WILLIAM NELSON, WILLIAM (X) USREY. End of Will. "Citation for letters of Adm. by ENOCH BENSON for 5 Feb. next. 8 July 1791."
"A Just & True Inventory & Appraisement of CHARLES & JUDETH CRANES,
dec'd., as done on 24 Apr. 1792. Total 88:13:8 by W. D. THOMAS, HUGH
MC VAY, JEPTHA HOLLINGSWORTH, Appraisors." A list of debts due the
Estate of CHARLES & JUDITH CRANE, dec'd. "WILLIAM SHARP the 9th July
1795 for joining in a survey and sold my part." "11 May 1787 WILLIAM
JILES to keeping horses." "11 May 1787 WILLIAM SHARP to keeping horses?"
"THOS. BRANDON to one cow and settlement of a bond the 11th May 1787."
"JOHN ROBERTSON to 5 qts. Rum the 20th Mar. 1785." "5th Aug. 1785 MOSES
WOOD 3 gal. 2 qts. 1 pint Rum." "20th Mar. 1785 SAMUEL HUGHS to a bal-
ance. ROBERT USREY to 5 half pints. WILLIAM USREY to 6 half pints.
NATHL. CLARK 4 half pints. GIDEON CLARK 1 pint. JERRY RUSSEL to balance
due." "5th Aug. 1785 JOHN RUSSELL to balance due. RANDOLPH CASEY to
balance due." "20th Aug. 1785 JOHN CAMPBELL 1 quart." "15th Aug. 1785
WILLIAM PEARSON to balance due." "20th Aug. 1785 JOHN PORTMAN 1 gal.

Cont'd from page 176:
2 qts. 3 half pints." "Sept. 1785 JOSEPH MC COOL 8 days work of JOHN
CRANE." "1785 HENRY PEARSON to one bun, cow & calf." "14th May 1791
JOHN SLONE hire of negro." "A list of debts due Estate of CHARLES &
JUDITH CRANES, dec'd. Not Recovered returned into Office the 22nd Aug.
1801." "An Acc't calculation & reckoning upon the Estate of CHARLES
& JUDITH CRANES, dec'd. done the 16 Nov. 1801." Sales & Assetts 117:
2:2. Paid out of said sales and assetts as follows - Debts & expenses
46:7:8. Each Legacy (17:13:4). Signed: ENOCH BENSON, JR., Adm. Also
"Apr. 1792 BONMON SHUMATE to work of Negroe." "May 1792 ENOCH BENSON
two weeks work."

Page 49   YOUNG, JOHN, SR. The Will of JOHN YOUNG, SR. in open
Apt. 9-File 608: court May term 1792, proven by oath of ANNA STEVENSON
1792   & MARY STEVENSON and recorded 31 Aug. 1792. "Grandson
                 JOHN YOUNG, son of my eldest son JOHN, one guinea.
Dau., MARY STEVENSON. Son, SAMUEL YOUNG. Executor, son, SAMUEL YOUNG.
Written 19 Jan. 1792. Signed: JOHN (X) YOUNG. Wit: ANNA STEVENSON,
JOHN (X) PHILLIPS, MARY (X) STEVENSON. (There were no papers in File).

Pp 49-51:   The following Inventory of part of the Estate of
                 JOSEPH GILL sold on the 18th July 1792, agreeable
                 to the Court of Greenville 7th July 1792, was present-
ed in open court Oct. term 1792 and ordered recorded, which was done
15 Jan. 1793(sale list of personal property, but had no names).

Pp 51-53:   Estate sale of JUDITH & CHARLES CRAIN. (Already in-
                 cluded in JUDITH CRAIN Estate of Pp 47-48)

Page 53   COOPER, WILLIAM. A citation being returned by WILLIAM
Apt. 2-File 102: WELCH and recorded the 15th Jan. 1793. Letters of
1792   Adm. application made by WILLIAM WELCH for Estate
                 of WILLIAM COOPER, dec'd., made 9 Feb. 1792.

Page 54   COLLINS, JOHN. Will presented in open court Oct.
Apt. 8-File 581: term 1792 and recorded 15 Jan. 1793. Will written
1793   8 June 1792 states JOHN COLLINS of Greenville Co.,
                 S.C. Wife, unnamed. Oldest dau., CATHARINE GILBERT
-one shilling. Son, WILLIAM COLLINS - ten dollars. Dau., ELIZABETH
COLLINS - ten dollars. Son, JOHN COLLINS - mare called Phenis and fold
(sic) she had this spring. Rest of Estate to wife and raising of my
children and at my wife's death, what remains "equally divided among
my children, that is small and not mentioned by name but my son ABNER
is to have the land." Signed: JOHN COLLINS. Wit: LEWIS WELLS, ELISHA
(C) NELSON. (No original papers in File).

Pp 54-56   MACHEN, HENRY. Will presented in open court Feb.
Apt. 5-File 337: term 1793 and admitted to record, recorded 22 Apr.
1792   1793. Will - I, HENRY MACHEN of County of Prince
                 William and Colony of Virginia...Wife, GRACE MACHEN
and child she goes with either boy or girl...Children: HENRY MACHEN,
JOHN MACHEN, THOMAS MACHEN & dau., MARY MACHEN (to have negro girl
named Betty when MARY attains age or marriage). Brother, THOMAS MACHEN.
Executors of Estate my loving wife, GRACE MACHEN and loving brother,
THOMAS MACHEN. Written 3 Apr. 1752. Signed: HENRY MACHEN (Seal). Wit:
GEORGE NEVILL, HUM. POPE, THOMAS ATHORPE. At a court held for the County
of Prince William the 24th Aug. 1752 this Will was presented by GRACE
MACHEN and THOMAS MACHEN, Executors and proved by oaths of witnesses
and was admitted to record. Test: JO WAGENOR Cl Cur. A Copy Test: ROBERT
GRAHAM Cl Cur. "I, ROBERT GRAHAM, Clerk of the Court of Prince William
Co. Va certify Will is a true copy this 3rd of Aug. 1790. Signed: ROBERT
GRAHAM." Loose papers in File - An account given upon the estate of
HENRY MACHEN, dec'd., returned into office 28 Oct. 1802. The only name
given was: "Nov. 1794 By Judgement obtained against GEO. SEABORN for
50 pds Va currency with 9 years interest thereon at 5% amounting to
72.10 pds - which expressed in sterling is 56/7/91/4th.

Page 57   GOODWIN, JOSEPH. Inventory of the Estate of JOSEPH
Apt. 3-File 190: GOODWIN, dec'd., presented in open court Feb. term
1792

Cont'd from page 177:
1793, admitted to Record, 30 Apr. 1793. S.C. Green-
ville Co., WILLIAM CORNELAS, MARTIN ADAMS & JOHN WILLIAMS are to make
inventory & appraisement & place in 90 days into hands of FRANCES GOOD-
WYN, Adm. of the Estate of JOSEPH GOODWYN, late of this county 7 May
1792. Aside from the listing of personal estate also list of one Bond
upon JOSEPH THOMAS of the State of Georgia and one note upon THOMAS
MC CARRELL. Appraisement made and given into court 6 Oct. 1792.

Pp 58-59:   The following is an account of the sold part of the
                   Estate of CHARLES & JUDITH CRANE, presented in court
May term 1793 and recorded 21 June 1793. "An acct. of sale of goods
and chattels sold 26 May 1792 by ENOCH BENSON, Adm." Buyers: ENOCH
BENSON, ISAAC GREEN, HUGH MC VAY, DAVID QUALS, JOHN CRANE, JOHN NICOLL,
WILLIAM SILVERSIDES, EPH. REECE, WILLIAM SAVAGE, NANCY CRANE, CHARLES
GILLY, WILLIAM CRANE
                   A list of Buyers of sale of 27 Oct. 1792:
CHARLES CRANE, ENOCH BENSON, DANIEL EVANS.

Page 60:   A Return of the sale of the Estate of JOSEPH GOODWYN
                   presented in open court Oct. term 1793 and recorded
23 Dec.1793. Buyers: FRANCES GOODWYN, URIAH GOODWIN, MRS. GOODWIN.

Page 61:   (First entry of this estate on page 57). Warrant
                   of appraisement of the Estate of WILLIAM COOPER with
WILLIAM WELCH, Adm. presented open court Oct. term 1793 and recorded
23 Dec. 1793. Appraisers: JAMES ALEXANDER, SR., JAMES ALEXANDER, JR.,
SAMUEL PADEN this 7th May 1792. Loose papers in file - "Certify that
valued property in hands of WILLIAM WELCH belonging to the Estate of
WILLIAM COOPER, dec'd., one negro woman appraised at 35 pds sterling.
One negro child at 15 pds this 3 Oct. 1793. Signed: JAMES ALEXANDER,
JAMES ALEXANDER, JR., SAMUEL PEDEN." "Return made 6 Oct. 1806 with
no expenditures by WILLIAM WELCH." "A yearly return of the receipts
and expenditures of the Estate of WILLIAM COOPER, dec'd. by WILLIAM
WELCH. Received nothing in year past...Expended nothing in the year
past 6 Apr. 1807."

Page 62   FISHER, NICHOLAS. Will presented and proven in open
Apt. 8-File 587:   court May term 1794 and ordeded recorded the 25th
1794   June 1794. Will - I, NICHOLAS FISHER, SR, of S.C.
                   Greenville Co....loving wife, ELIZABETH FISHER one-
third of my lands, goods and chattels during her life and after her
death the land be equally divided between my two sons, THOMAS FISHER
& NICHOLAS FISHER. After debts paid unto my youngest son, NICHOLAS
FISHER, I give a certain yearling horse Colt and my saddle and the
rest of my stock be equally divided between THOMAS FISHER and PEGGY
FISHER and ANICE FISHER and NICHOLAS FISHER. To son JOHN FISHER - five
shillings. To son JAMES FISHER - one shilling. To dau., MARY TUBB-
one shilling. To dau., SALLY COOKSEY - one shilling. To dau., ELIZABETH
MC VAY - one shilling. Executors to be JOHN FISHER & THOMAS FISHER.
Written 2 Apr. 1794. Signed: NICHOLAS FISHER. Wit: ELIJAH HUTCHINSON,
ELIZABETH (X) HUTCHINSON.
N.B. I do make JAMES TUBB my Executor with ELIZABETH FISHER & JOHN
FISHER & THOMAS FISHER. (No other papers in apartment file).

Pp 63-64   DUNCAN, JESSE (Loose Papers) "Appraisors & Inventory
Apt. 2-File 125:   Judges of Greenville Co., S.C. Court to WILLIAM ARM-
1794   STRONG, SAMUEL TARRANT, & PHILIP EVANS of the Estate
                   of JESSE DUNCAN, dec'd., & returned to MARY DUNCAN
on or before 5 Feb. next. Wit: JESSE CARTER C C 7 Oct. 1794. LARKIN
TARRANT, Esq., impowered to qualify the above appraisors." "Inventory
and Appraisement made 24 Dec. 1794." "An acct of money rec'd by MARY
DUNCAN, Adm. of Estate of her deceased husband, the money due from
the purchasers of sd Estate 10 Nov. 1796: SILAS WILLIAMS, JOHN BRAZIER,
JOHN PAGE, JAMES BLACKSTOCK, FREDERICK PARMER, HEZEKIAH COCKRAN, WILLIAM
FARIS, JOHN JONES, DAVID CRAWFORD, THOMAS ESLEY, SAMUEL JOHNS, WILLIAM
PAGE." "Accompt of Cash rec'd in favor of the Estate of JESSE DUNKIN,
dec'd - 1793 cash paid to MARTIN ADAMS - 1794 cash paid to CARTER HARI-
SON - 1795 cash paid to JOHN MC BETH - 1797 cash paid to JOHN WHITE

Cont'd from page 178:
-1799 cash paid to JOHN DUNCAN - MARY DUNCAN made above Return May
term 1799." "MARY DUNCAN, Extr'x of JESSE DUNKIN - payment made to
Legatees exhibited 3 Nov. 1806 - 1802 paid JAMES DUNKIN 11:13:4 - June
1804 paid ELISH MOORE 14:9:4 - 9 Jan. 1804 paid ALLEN MOORE 11:13:4
It appears the amount of appraisement was 997.9 pounds taking the widows
third out - leaves each legatee part to be 10:10:6½ (sic) The has over
paid three of the Legatees more than ther dew ther is three on hand
not of age. Signed: MARY (X) DUNCAN." "Yearly return of Estate of JESSE
DUNCAN by MARY DUNCAN, Adm. - Dec. 7, 1807 - Received nothing since
last return - payd nothing since last return." "Whereas, JOHN JONES
complaint to Ordinary of Court states he fears he will be injured by
being surity for MARY DUNCAN for as Adm. of Estate of JESSE DUNCAN,
she is not transacting the business legally. Cited that MARY DUNCAN
appear before court 9 Jan. 1809, Greenville Co. Court. Signed: DAVID
GOODLETT OGD 2 Jan. 1809." "A return of Estate of JESSE DUNCAN, dec'd.,
exhibited 9 Jan. 1809 - 6 Dec. 1080 paid GEORGE DUNCAN $49, 6 Dec.
1808 paid JESSE DUNCAN $49, 6 Dec. 1080 paid MARY DUNCAN $49 making
a total of $147.00. Received nothing since last return. Signed: MARY
(X) DUNCAN, Adm.

Pp 64,65,66   MORGAN, ISAAC. LW & T presented in open court Feb.
Apt. 6-File 347:   Term 1795, proven by oath of JOHN COCKS, JOHN COCKS,
1794   JR. and recorded 3 Feb. 1796. "Will" ISAAC MORGAN
                   of Greenville Co., SC to wife, NANCEY MORGAN one
half plantation and tract I now live on North side of Enoree river
and all my negroes until my son JESSE and dau. JEAN come of age - then
wife is to retain one third part. Son, JESSE the other half of plantation and an equal third of stock of horses, etc...to dau. JEAN, tract
of land on south side of Enoree river where JOHN COXOE now lives immediately after the term is expired that JOHN COX has leased it for, also
an equal third of horses, hogs etc...to my wifes dau., ELIZABETH ELLI-
SON, one fourth part of stock, etc....my wife, NANCY MORGAN and my
friend ROBERT MC AFEE be Executors...this 12th day of Oct. 1794. Signed:
ISAAC MORGAN. L.S. Wit: JOHN COX, JR., JOHN COX, JOHN ROSS.

Pp 67,68,69:   Listing of Inventory made by ISAAC GREEN, HENRY BENSON
                   and MOSES KEMP. Amounted to 421:5:10 of ISAAC MORGAN
estate.

Pp 69,70:   (First entry of this estate on page 63). MARY DUNCAN,
                   JOHN JONES & JOSEPH LANGSTON bound unto Judges of
County Court of Greenville for sum of 100 pds, 5 Oct. 1794. The above
obligation bound MARY DUNCAN, Adm. of goods & chattels of JESSE DUNCAN,
deceased. Signed: MARY (X) DUNCAN, JOHN JONES, JOSEPH LANGSTON. Wit:
JESSE CARTER, R. MAXWELL.

Pp 70,71,73,74   HUDSON, FORREST. "THOMAS EDWARDS, ROBERT MC AFEE,
Apt. 4-File 232:   DAVID GOODLETT bound Judges Court of Greenville Co.
1795   500 pds Oct. 5, 1795 - the above obligation of THOMAS
                   EDWARDS & ROBERT MC AFEE, Adm. of goods & chattels
of FORREST HUDSON, deceased. Signed: T. EDWARDS, R. MC AFEE, ISAAC
GREEN, D. GOODLETT. Wit: JESSE CARTER, THOMAS P. EARLE." "Inventory
and appraisement to DAVID GOODLETT, ISAAC GREEN, ISAAC WICKLETT & ELIAS
EARLE, bef. 5 Feb. next - the 8 Oct. 1794. Signed: JESSE CARTER CGC."
"ROBERT MC AFEE qualified appraisor also." (Loose Papers) "A settlement
of the Estate of FOREST HUDSON, dec'd., between THOS. EDWARDS and the
County Court of Greenville at May term 1799. Debts due the Estate (names
listed only) THOS. GOWEN & BAYLES EARLE, ISAAC WICKLIFF & PETER SORTOR,
ISAAC GREEN & RICHARD SORVEL, BENJAMIN WALKER & JOHN WALKER, WILLIAM
SILVERSIDES & WILLIAM GOODWIN, MARY LANGSTON & HUGH MVEY, MOSES KEMP
& SAMUEL NORTHERN, AARON KEMP, BURREL HUDSON, LEWIS RECTOR, THOS. BENSON
& ROBERT MC AFEE, Esq., Rent for the year 86 (sic) in the hands of
MC AFEE, PETER SORTOR due for rent 98...Amt of debt due 88:8:11, cash
in hand 8:3:4, making a total of 96:12:3, amount of money paid 21:18:8
and 1/2 making a total of 118:10:11 and 1/2, add interest omitted 00:12:
2 and 1/4 making a total of 119:3:1 3/4.."A final settlement of estate
of FORREST HUDSON with the County Court (this last quote was title
of document). "Cash paid different people - SOLOMON MURPHEY, ALEXANDER
GLENN, ALEXANDER WADDLE, 1796 Feb. 5 paid tax & Clarks (sic) fees,

179

Cont'd from page 179:
1797 Mar. 1 paid Tax & RAGLAND LANGSTON, 1797 Poor Tax, THOS. FAUGOUR-
SON, JOHN FORBUSH on acct of a Judgement, PAWL ABNER, Clark (sic) for
recording Dead (sic). Amount of debts paid 21:18:8 1/2". "Cash paid
different people at different times in all amounting to 21:18:8 1/2
A P Statement now in office...1942 acres of land belonging to the Estate signed T. EDWARDS, Adm....and acct. calculation and rechoning
of estate of FOREST HUDSON, deceased, 10 July 1799." "An Accompt of
the Estate of FOREST HUDSON, dec'd., Sale the 22 of Oct. 1795 twelve
months credit." (this is a three column account. The first column is
headed Purchasers at Sale, the second column is titled Securities,
and the third column is amount bought. I will list only the Purchaser
and use a dash for Securities when listed). EDMOND CLAYTON -JAMES BELL,
NATHAN WADDLE - ISAAC WEST, THOMAS GOWEN - BAYLES EARLE, CHARLES SOWEL
- JAMES ROBERTS, THOMAS STAGS - WILLIAM SAVAGE, CHARLES ALLEN - ISAAC
WICKLIFF, ROBERT MASON - JNO. MC CORMACK, ANTHONY GRIFFIN - YOUNG GRIF-
FEN, ROBERT WILLIAMS - THOMAS STAGS, GEORGE LEWIS - GEORGE RUSSEL,
ABNER HOWEL - FRANCIS HOWEL, DAVID GOODLETT - BAYLES EARLE, WILLIAM
STEWART - HENRY PIERSON, PETER SORTER - ISAAC WICKLIFF, HENRY PIERSON
- WILLIAM SAVAGE, JOHN WATSON - ELIAS EARLE, ISAAC WICKLIFF - PETER
SORTER, ELI NORMAN..., FRANCISS HOWEL - JAMES FAUGOURSON, RUBEN BARNET
- JONATHAN STOKES, ISAAC GREEN - RICHARD SOWEL, EDWARD WOLDRIGE - RAG-
LAND LANGSTON, WILLIAM SAVAGE - THOMAS STAGS, RAGLAND LANGSTON - JOHN
LANGSTON, ELIAS EARLE - JOHN ROBINSON, BAYLES EARLE ..., JOHN ROBINSON
- ELIAS EARLE, BENJAMIN WALKER - JOHN WALKER, WILLIAM SILVERSIDES -
WILLIAM GOODDEN, EDWARD WOLDRIGE - THOS. GOWEN, MARY LANGSTON - HUGH
MC VEY, HENRY PIERSON - WILLIAM SILVERSIDES, NATHAN WADDLE - ISAAC
WEST, MOSES KEMP..., RICHARD SOWEL - ISAAC GREEN, CHARLES SOWEL - JAMES
ROBERTS, SOLOMON KEMP - CHARLES SOWEL, SAMUEL NORTHERN - GEORGE RUSSEL,
THOMAS GREEN - BAYLES EARLE. Brought forward 102 pds 12 shillings 2
pence. Clames (sic) against the Estate - RAGLAND LANGSTON, PAUL ABNER
proven accompt. JESSE CARTER for Clerks fees and 3/6 proven (Loose
papers) "Return 1 June 1807 - 1 June 1808. 3 Nov. 1807 paid ELIZABETH
HUDSON 10/0/0. 14 Nov. 1807 paid ELIZABETH HUDSON 5/0/0. 9 Jan. 1808
paid ELIZABETH HUDSON 15/39/7..being the full amount of her part. 10
Apr. 1808 Tax for JOSEPH & JOHN HUDSON 0/43/2//Ordinary fee 1/7/0 total
31/89/9/" "July Term 1799 July 10, Cap. THO. EDWARDS final settlement
as Adm. of FORREST HUDSON, dec'd., and resigned his pretentions as
Adm. to sd estate and the Court then appointed the sd EDWARDS, Guardian
of FRANKY HUDSON." "Cap. ISAAC GREEN applied for Letters of Adm. to
Estate of FORREST HUDSON, dec'd." " JOHN HUDSON, one of the heirs of
FORREST HUDSON, dec'd. came into Court and sd THOMAS EDWARDS, his guardian had not fully paid him - 24 Sept. 1814. by DAVID GOODLETT, Ordinary.
Return Apr. 1806...6 Dec. 1805, Jan. 5, cash paid by ISAAC GREEN $410.
31 Jan., 3 Feb....6 Dec. 1805 Cash paid HENRY HUDSON $60, THOMAS HUDSON
$60, ELIZABETH HUDSON $10, Chain Carriers $2, Surveyor $21.84, Atty.
$36.576, Exp. for Com. $1, Paper for use of Estate 375 cents, expenses
when on business of estate $5. Total $196.791...Bond on ROBERT DUNCAN
$21...Bond on CHARLES ALLEN & D. GOODLETT $70, cash on hand $43.174.
Total $330.965. Signed: THOMAS EDWARDS, Guardian." "JOHN HUDSON vs
THOMAS EDWARDS. In Court of Ordinary Greenville Co., S.C. THOMAS EDWARDS
Guardian of JOHN HUDSON failed to pay $8.22 in addition to $51.25.
JOHN HUDSON demanded that interest be paid on sd sum from the time
EDWARDS received it until he came of age (to wit) $59.475 from the
4th Nov. 1806 until 30 Dec. 1813. Court ruled THOMAS EDWARDS pay inter-
est 20 Oct. 1814. Interest was for 7 years and 56 days." "Return -
Interest of CHARLES ALLEN. Interest had in hand for FRANKEY HUDSON.
The sum to be divided between six children - each childs share $62.45
20 Oct. 1814 D. GOODLETT OGC" "Return - 4 Nov. 1806 rec'd of ISAAC
GREEN $90, CHARLES ALLEN $73, 10 Mar. 1807 rec'd of ROBERT DUNCAN $24.
Cash in hand at last settlement $43. Total $230. 1 Apr. 1806 paid ELIZA-
BETH HUDSON $10, HENRY HUDSON $375, THOMAS $375." "Return made 1 June
1808 - 1 June 1809 return made 1 June 1809 - 1 June 1810 no expenditures
except Ordinary fee." "Return 1 June 1808 - 1811 Ordinary fee $1. Paid
JOHN HUDSON $5. Filed 7 Sept. 1811." "Return 1 June 1811-1 June 1812
Ord. fee $1." Return 1 June 1812-1813 Ord. fee $100. Filed 17 July
1813.

Pp 74,75,76 and 77 (next page)

Apt. 3-File 158:   FORD, JOHN. LW & T presented in open Court Feb. term
1796   1796, proven by oath of JOHN MOLLOW & ELIZABETH SALMON
                    & ordered recorded 29 Apr. 1796. "Will" JOHN FORD
of Greenville Co., SC to wife, ANN FORD, plantation where I now live,
negro man named Tony, negro woman named Beth, negro man named Tony
his service for 11 years after which he is to be set free to act for
himself, tools, bay horse called Cragger, sorrel horse called Chunky,
young bay mare called Young Pups, bay horse called Hackney, stock of
cattle, hogs & sheep, 7 furniture and after her death to descend to
my son ISAAC FORD. After public sale money arising from estate be equally divided between my son, ISAAC FORD, son, WILLIAM FORD, dau., LEAH
FORD & dau., LINNA FORD. To dau., POLLEY FORD a negro woman named Hannah, a tract of land joining THOMAS ROWLAND's land alapsed from WIL-
LIAM FLIPPE. To dau., TRESSIA FORD, a negro woman named Suke, a black
mare called Robinson Black, a tract of land lying in Spartan County
on the waters of Fair Forrest containing 70 acres purchased by me at
sheriff's sale, late property of JAMES WHITE adj. JAMES LUSK's land.
To dau. LEAH FORD a negro girl named Dine, to dau. LINNA FORD, a negro
girl named Fillis. To son ARASMUS FORD & son LEVI FORD, a tract of
land on both sides of Terry's Creek, waters of Green River containing
150 acres granted to JOSEPH TERRY, also a tract of land containing
979 acres lying on both sides of Terry's Creek. To son, WILLIAM FORD,
a tract of land lying in Union County on the north side of Enoree river
and on both sides of Lishas Creek a branch of the Enoree, containing
150 acres, also, a tract of land containing 120 acres in Union County
nearly joining the other, the tract of 150 acres surveyed for & granted
to myself, also a tract of 189 acres in Greenville County on both sides
of Hensons creek, waters of Terrys Creek. To wife, ANN FORD, my still,
and at her death to be sold and the money derived be divided equally
between my four sons. A tract of land lying on the waggon road leading
from MERRITS Mill to BUTLARS on Green River that I alapsed from JAMES
LEAK together with tract joining the last mentioned that I elapsed
from SOUTHERLAND with other personal property be sold to pay debts
and divided equally between all my children. To STACY SIBLEY, for com-
pensation for ten years past services, a sorrel mare called Adams young
mare, also the uninterrupted use of the house and garden where she
now lives, together with provisions for herself and child etc. ANN
FORD, my Executrix & GEORGE SALMON, Executor this 15 Oct. 1795. Signed:
JOHN FORD (L.S.) Wit: JOHN MOTLOW, ELIZABETH SALMON, ARMAND GIPSON.
(Loose Papers) Citation for Kindred of JOHN FORD, deceased. - DAVID
BLYTH, Esq. applied for Letters of Adm. of JOHN FORD, dec'd. as both
of Executors of Estate now deceased. 23 Sept. 1839. Granted 10 June
1839 by JNO. WATSON, Ordinary. Above Citation published in public meeting 22 Sept. 1839 by JAS. GOODLETT. Memorandum of Return of Amount
of Sale of Estate of Major JOHN FORD, dec'd. Sold 25 Aug. 1796. (written
in different hand & ink "After the marriage of the widow sold one still
and vessells for $107.67). Signed: ANN FORD, GEORGE SALMON, Exor's.
Returned into office in 1806. Petition of THOMAS EDWARDS, JR. shows
on 22 Nov. 1804, he married LEAH FORD, daughter of JOHN FORD, Esq.,
dec'd. States no returns have been made and prays the Executors be
compelled to do so. 1 June 1807. Signed: THOS. EDWARDS, JR. Return
1809 on Estate of JOHN FORD, dec'd. 2 Apr. 1810. Signed: ANN GOODLETT,
Ex., GEORGE SALMON, Ex. 27 Mar. 1809 by cash paid ISAAC FORD $44/35/5
as per receipt. Bill of Sale of Major JOHN FORD, dec'd. 26 Nov. 1839.
Filed 6 Jan. 1840 by DAVID BLYTH, Adm. Buyers: DAVID BLYTH, RICHARD
GOODLETT, WILLIAM WOOTON, MATT CAPPS, JAMES MULLIN, D. DICKEY, JOHN
SPRIGGS, JOHN COX, ABSOLAM BLYTH, LEVI GRAMIEL(?), ASBAL BATSON. Inven-
tory appraised 25 Aug. 1796. Signed: JOHN MOLTON, WILLIAM LYNCH, THOMAS
SPRIGS, JOSEPH TERRY. Final settlement of Estate Maj. JOHN FORD, dec'd.
Filed 25 Jan. 1841 by DAVID BLYTH, Adm. Return filed 1 Aug. 1808 by
GEORGE SALMON, Ex. and ANN GOODLETT, Ex. Paid JOHN GEAN (DEAN?) 25
Mar. 1798 $17. Paid JOHN WOOD $2.50. Paid JAMES JONES $10.70. 8 Feb.
1808 delivered to GENNY or VERLINDA FORD, ELIAS MC ELLERY 1 negro girl
named Phillis, with her child Hary, which was willed to her by her
dec'd. father. Citation, GEO. SALMON, Esq. & ANN GOODLETT, Ex'r & Ex'tx
of Estate JOHN FORD, dec'd., appear before Court 12 June 1807 and answer
why no returns have been made as stated by THOMAS EDWARDS 2 June 1807.
Signed: D. GOODLETT. Appraisors JOHN MATLOW, WILLIAM LYNCH, THOMAS
SPRIGGS, & JOSEPH TERRY, ROBERT COOK, 3 May 1796. Signed: JESSE CARTER,

Cont'd from page 181:
C.G.C. A return of 15 June 1807 - 1796 Feb. 22 cash paid YOUNG & FAUST
for enserting and avertisement in papers...April 6 cash paid JEMISON
in Granby...April 12 cash paid CUNNINGHAM in Charleston. 1798 July
17 cash paid W. THOMPSON, Esq....Nov. 13 cash paid WADY THOMPSON, Esq...
Dec. 18 cash paid JOHN CUNNINGHAM (omitted) Sept. 7 cash paid to S.
LUNSFORD. 1797 cash paid R. BARROTT, Esq. Omitted 1796. The above was
paid by myself G. SALMON. 1796 June 12 cash paid DENNES DUFF, cash
paid WILLIAM HODGES, cash paid STACY SIBLEY. 1797 March 10 cash paid
JESSE FORD, THOS. COVENDER for teaching Children...April 11 cash paid
WM. SHAW, Esq. 1796 July 6 cash paid JOHN WRIGHT duty on a Still for
the year 1795, cash paid (?) BEN___?, cash paid WM. GILLIHAM, L. GOOD-
WIN, JOAB HAIL, FRANCIS GOODWIN, JOHN ELLAGE. 1798 Dec. 10 cash paid
JOSIAH FOSTER for M. DILLINGHAM. 1800 Oct. 27 paid THOS. FARROW, Esq.
Signed: ANN (X) GOODLETT, Executrix, GEO. SALMON, Ex'or. 1807 Jan.
3 paid EMSMUS(?) FORD (his part), paid LEVI FORD, paid WILLIAM FORD.

Pp 77,78,79   WICKLIFF, ISAAC. LW & T of ISAAC WICKLIFF, dec'd.
Apt. 8-File 510:   presented in open Court Oct. Term 1797, proven by
1822   oath of CHARLES ALIN, ordered recorded 10 Dec. 1797.
                   "Will" ISAAC WICKLIFF of Greenville Co., SC give
my whole estate to wife, FRANKY WICKLIFF. Executrix wife, FRANKY WICK-
LIFF. 14 July 1797. Signed: ISAAC WICKLIFF (L.S.) Wit: NATHL. MANNING,
GEORGE UNDERWOOD, CHARLES ALLEN. (Loose Papers) Appraised 26 Oct. 1797.
Inventory by NATHANIEL STOKES, THOS. HEARD, CHARLES ALLEN. *(on back
of original Will) Note - this Will has been filed in the Ordinaries
office for many years, but does not appear to have been proven in due
form of law - by SPARTAN GOODLETT O.G.C. Proved 15 Dec. 1822 by oath
of GEORGE UNDERWOOD.

Page 79   WELLS, SAMUEL. LW & T of SAMUEL WELLS, dec'd pre-
Apt. 9-File 525:   sented in open court July term 1797, proven by oath
                   of HENRY MACHEN & ELIZABETH WELLS. Recorded 11 Dec.
1797. Will - SAMUEL WELLS of Greenville Co., SC to his wife, ELIZABETH
WELLS, & son, SAMUEL, Executors of the Estate. Estate to remain in
hands of wife, ELIZABETH WELLS. Son, SAMUEL WELLS to receive 3 cows
and calves and the rest of the Estate be equally divided between my
wife and the rest of my children which are named: ELHANAH, ELKANAH,
PHILLIP, SUSANAH, CARTA, JOHN, ELIZABETH & SARAH. Written 8 Oct. 1796.
Wit: HENRY MACHEN, ELIZABETH (X) WELLS. Signed: SAMUEL WELLS (L.S.)
(Loose Papers) ELHANAH WELLS made suit for letters of Adm. be granted
him of the estate and effects of SAMUEL & ELIZABETH WELLS, dec'd. the
6 Nov. 1804 by JOHN THOMAS, JR. Ordinary G.C. Buyers of the Estate
Sale of SAMUEL WELLS (no date) -

PRINCIPAL	SECURITY	PRINCIPAL	SECURITY
SUSANNA WELLS	---	JOHN WHORTON	NOEL SLIDE
JOSEPH ROACH	JAMES SLIDE? (HIDE?)	ALBERT ROBINS	WILLIAM BLITHE
WILLIAM BLITHE	ALBERT ROBINS	JAMES WILSON	CHRISTOPHER ROBINS
JAMES SLIDE	ALBERT ROBINS	SOLOMON MURPHEY	WILLIAM BLYTHE
ISAIAH SLIDE	NOEL SLIDE	RUBEN DANIEL	BEVERLY DANIEL
BEVERLY DANIEL	REUBEN DANIEL	HENRY LENDERMAN	ANDREW MC DAVID
JOHN PITMAN	MATTHEW ARMSTRONG	DAVID ARMSTRONG	ANDREW MC DAVID
SUSANNA ROGERS	BEVERLY DANIEL	FATHA SAMFORD	DAVID ARMSTRONG
JOHN WHORTON	NOEL SLIDE	JEREMIAH (?) HIDE	NOEL (?) HIDE
NOEL HIDE	BENJ. POLLARD, JR.	ELHANA WELLS	---
AVERY MASSES	JOB MASSEY	TOBIAS PHILLIPS	NEEL HIDE
JOB MASSEY	JAMES HIDE	ANDREW MC DAVID	ALBERT ROBBINS
BENJ. POLLARD, JR.	NOEL HIDE		

(these last names are listed under
PRINCIPAL with no SECURITY) DAVID MASSEY, NATHAN ARMSTRONG, ISIAH LEWIS,
PHILIP WELLS, JAMES ARMSTRONG, SAMUEL SMITH, THOMAS NELSON, ABSOLUM
CARNEY. (Note - written in the old english the name could be SLIDE
or HIDE). Inventory of Estate filed 2 Feby 1805. Estate of SAMUEL WELLS
- Inventory made 4 Dec. 1804 by JAMES THACKSON, SOLOMON (his mark)
MURPHY, WILLIAM (W) BLITH. (Listed 89 acres of land with the inventory).
Appraisors: WILLIAM BLUTHE, SOLOMAN MURPHEY, MC GINES, JAMES THACKSTON
the 12 Nov. 1804. J. THOMAS Jurn. O.B.D. An account calculation & recon-
ing of estate of SAMUEL WELLS made 4 Aug. 1806. Paid to BENJAMIN GRIF-
FITH 50¢, J. THAXSTON 25¢, BENJAMIN POLLARD 50¢, Mr. GOODRICH $1.75,

Cont'd from page 182:
GEORGE OWIN $5.25, JESSE BISHOP 95¢, HORATIO GRIFFIN $7.25, B. POLLARD,
SR. $2.00, Ordinary fee $8.75, ANDREW MC DADE 37 1/2¢.

Pp 79-90   MAXWELL, ROBERT. Intestate. Account of Sale and other
Apt. 5-File 297: papers presented in open Court at sundry times &
1798   ordered recorded 20 Feb. 1799. (Loose Papers in no
                  particular order). Supreme Court of the United States
Dec. term 1849 #42. #12 JOHN MAXWELL, Adm. vs WM. E. KENNEDY & Heirs.
Rec'd of JHON (sic) MAXWELL, Adm. of ROBERT MAXWELL, dec'd. $38.73
on acct of money advanced by Col. J. L. ORR to his concil in the above
dated case 2 Aug. 1850. Signed. B. J. CA___YTON for J. L. ORR. #2 Mobile,
Ala. 24 July 1843 - $150.00 At sight please pay to B. J. EARLE on order
$150 & charge the same to acct of To/R. MAXWELL, Esq. Pendleton SC
Signed JOS M LESENE. 7 Feb. 1798 Mrs. MARY MAXWELL & Genl. ROBERT ANDER-
SON applied for letters of Adm. of ROBERT MAXWELL, deceased. SAMUEL
EARLE & JOHN BLASINGAME, Securities. Signed: J. THOMAS, THOMAS EDWARDS.
JOHN MAXWELL (R. F. SIMPSON Surety) to WILLIAM THOS. CARROLL, Cl of
Sup Ct U.S. Dr. For balance of your cost on appeal from the Circuit
Court U. S. for the district of Alabama taken by you against JOSEPH
S. KENNEDY et al $18.94. Test: WM. THOS. CARROLL, Clk. Sup. Ct. U.
S. 22 Dec. 1849 (on same page) Rec'd 22 Apr. 1850 of JOHN MAXWELL,
Adm. $18.94 in full of the balance of cost in the case of JOHN MAXWELL,
Adm. vs JOHN S. KENNEDY et al. #1 Return JOHN MAXWELL, Adm. of Estte
of ROBERT MAXWELL, Rec'd & Filed 31 Jan. 1845. Recorded in annual Return Book B page 135. 13 June 1842 paid JOHN WATSON, Ordinary of Greenville SC $6.50. 24 July 1843 paid J. W. LESESNE of Mobile, AL draft
for council $150.00. 1 Jan. 1844 paid Cl. of Greenville SC $2.50. Made
on oath 31 Jan. 1845 JOHN MAXWELL, GEO. WATSON O.G.D. Return Filed
9 Jan. 1851. #5 J. MAXWELL Note $50.00 due 2 Dec. 1846. Return 10 Feb.
1854. #3 Annual Return Filed 5 Apr. 1847. #7 Judge BIBB $150.00 - a
fee paid to Judge BIBB of Tennessee in case of MAXWELL vs KENNEDY 25
Mar. 1815. #4 Return Filed 1848. #2 Return Filed 24 Jan. 1846. 23 Sept.
1845 JOS W. LESESNE for extra servesess $50.00. 25 July Tax Cost U.
S. Court $65.00 10 Jan. 1846 Clk of U. S. Court for writing out pro-
ceedings $25.00. Post Office account for 1845 $3.50. Signed: JOHN MAX-
WELL. JNO. WATSON O.G.D. Pendleton 31 Jan. 1845 - JNO. WATSON, Ordinary
Greenville Dist. - as law requires herewith make out & send my returns
as Adm. of my father's estate - I return nothing received - by postage
50¢ Signed: JOHN MAXWELL, Adm. of R. MAXWELL. Warrant of Appr. - Estate
of ROBERT MAXWELL, dec'd. has been shown to us by Mrs. MARY MAXWELL,
Adm. of ROBERT MAXWELL, dec'd and Inventory of which we have certified
under our hands 4 July 1798. Signed: L. TARRANT, WILLIAM ARMSTONG,
DAVID (X) GARRISON. (all genealogical data was listed in loose papers).

Page 90:   (cont. of FORREST HUDSON Estate of pages 70-74).
                  A settlement of Estate of FOREST HUDSON, dec'd. bet.
THOMAS EDWARDS of County of Greenville SC at May Term 1799. Debts due
estate - THOMAS GOWEN & BAYLES EARLE...

Pp 92-95   TOWNSEND, THOMAS. (Loose Papers) An Inventory of
Apt. 7-File 472: the Estate of THOMAS TOWNSEND 19 Aug. 1796. Three
1796   negroes viz Pegg, Doll & a wench Sall mortgaged to
                  sd deceased. One note on PEYTON NOWLIN, one note
on GERSHAM & JAMES KELLEY...list of animals, furniture & tools etc.
amounting to 366 pds 3 shillings 2 pence. Notes not collected: JACOB
WEBB & JOEL CHANDLER for eleven hundred weight of tobacco delivered
at Granby clear of expense. DANIEL CRIDER for twelve hundred & fifty
weight tobacco delivered at sd CRIDER's house. NATHN. SULLIVANT for
125 weight of tobacco. MOSES CRAWFORD for 300 weight of tobacco delivered at sd deceased house. ROBERT FILPOTT & ELIOTT SMITH for 300 weight
of tobacco. JOSEPH COOCK (sic) for 125 weight of tobacco. Signed by
HEWLET SULLIVANT, JOSEPH DUNKLIN, JOHN MC ELROY. An Account of the
Sale: AMPLILADA TOWNSEN, BRYAN WARD, BENJAMIN TOWNSEN, LIGHT TOWNSEN,
STEPHEN STEPHEN, JOHN DOLTON, JEAMS PORTER, THOMAS MULLICAN, BRYAN
NOWLIN, FLEET NEIGHBORS, JEAMS RIDIN, WILLIAM DEPENPORT (sic), WILLIAM
COOK, STEPHEN BENNET, MICIGH JENKINS, JOEL WEBB, JEAMS CAMP, THOMAS
MATLOCK, GEORGE BROWN, NATHANIEL REED, JOHN CAMP, JR., CHARLES ESTES,
WILLIAM DEVENPORT, STEPHEN JEAMS, JEAMS WEBB, WILLIAM COOK, JACOB WEBB,

Cont'd from page 183:
ABEL PENNINGTON, JEAMS DUNKLIN, REUBIN PILES, BETSY THOMASON, HULET
SULLIVANT, CLABORN SULLIVANT, SAMUEL RIDGWAY, MICHAGER JENKINS, ASEY
MICHEL, SAML RIDGEWAY, JOHN CHAPMAN. Amounting to 268 pds 17 shillings
1 pence. Certified from under my hand this 3rd of May 1797. THOS. CAMP,
J.P. CITATION: Letters of Administration applied for by BENJAMIN TOWN-
SEND for the Estate of THOMAS TOWNSEN, late of Greenville Co., SC 20
May 1796. Test.JESSE CARTER CGS. Warrant of Appraisement: To HEWLET
SULLIVANT, JOSEPH DUNKLIN, JOHN MC ELROY & WILLIAM MULLICAN 12 July
1796. Qualified 19 Aug. 1796 HEWLET SULLIVANT, JOSEPH DUNKLINN, JOHN
MC ELROY. Greenville Disrict: To BENJAMIN TOWNSEND, Admr. of THOMAS
TOWNSEND. You are hereby cited and required to be and appear before
me in the court of the Ordinary at the Courthouse of sd Dist. on the
1st Monday in July next then & there render a just & true account of
sd deceased estate herein fail not on pain of having the Adm. taken
from you & you deprived of your commission & expense thereon. 4th June
1800 or 1806. Signed: J. THOMAS JARR, OGD.

Pp 95-96   HUDSON, FOREST. (Estate Book A) A final settlement
Cont. of   of the Estate of FOREST HUDSON, dec'd. between the
Apt. 4-File 232: county of Greenville, SC & THOMAS EDWARDS & ROBERT
1795   MC AFEE, Adm. July Term 1799. Debts & Interest: BURREL
                HUDSON & LEWIS RECTOR, BAYLIS EARLE, BENJAMIN & JOHN
WALKER, ISAAC WICKLIFF, THOMAS GOWEN, THOMAS BENSON, ISAAC GREEN &
RICHARD SOWEL, SAMAUEL NORTHERN, MARY LANGSTON & HUGH MC VEY, AARON
KEMP. PETER SORTON for rent. Balance of judgements, purchases at sale,
years rent in hands of ROBT. MC AFEE. Balance of SILVERSIDES bond in
hands of McAfee. Interest. THOMAS EDWARDS, cash in hand & letting of
Interest. Amount of Debts 85:15:5/2. Cash paid different people at
different times 21:18:8 1/2. As per statement now in office 1942 acres
of land belong to the Estate. Signed: T. EDWARDS, Adm.

Pp 96-97   CHANDLER, JOEL. LW & T (Loose Papers) JOEL CHANDLER
Apt. 12-File 1: of Greenville Co., SC to my three sons, JOHN, SHAD-
1799   RACK & TIMOTHY CHANDLER...to my daughters (not named).
                Executors my wife (not named) and son JOHN...this
16th of Mar. 1798. Signed: JOEL CHANDLER. Wit: HEWLET SULLIVANT, MARY
SULLIVANT. (Loose Papers) Greenville Co., SC Oct. Term 1799. Ordered
the Executor of Estate of JOEL CHANDLER, dec'd. do at his discression,
sell such part of the perishable property, etc. upon a credit of 6
months...Wit: JESSE CARTER, CGC. Date on back of document 7 June 1800.
Recd. of Mr. JOHN CHANDLER. Warrant of Appraisement: HEWLET SULLIVANT,
CHARLES SULLIVANT, JOHN CHANDLER. 7 Oct. 1799. JOSEPH DUNKLIN is appoin-
ted to qualify as appraisor. On back of document named HEWLET SULLIVANT,
JOHN CAMP, SR. & THOMAS BENNETT qualified appraisors, certified 11
Nov. 1799. Signed: JOS. DUNKLIN, J.P. A Return of the Proceedings of
JOHN CHANDLER, Exr. of JOEL CHANDLER, dec'd. Aug. 1799 Funeral rights,
18 Nov. 1799 paid JESSE CARTER, 24 Mar. 1800 pd THOMAS EDWARDS, 10
May 1800 pd JOSEPH DUNKLIN, 7 Jan. 1800 pd THOS. EDWARDS, 20 Dec. 1800
pd HULET SULLIVANT, 14 Jan. 1801 pd JAMES MC CAW, 23 Jan. 1801 pd HUDSON
BERRY, 17 Jan. 1801 pd DUNEAN CAMRON, 24 Jan. 1801 pd MOSES SULLIVANT,
27 Jan. 1801 pd JOHN CHANDLER, 14 Mar. 1801 pd MOSES SULLIVANT, Feb.
1800 rec'd of JOHN CHANDLER, JR., 25 Dec. 1800 rec'd of WILLIAM RILEY,
24 Jan. 1801 rec'd of JOHN CHANDLER, JR., 15 Nov. 1800 sold one mare
& colt & rented one field. An Inventoryof Goods of Estate of JOEL CHAND-
LER, dec'd, sold by JOHN CHANDLER, Exr. 15 Nov. 1799..cattle, waggons,
2 guns, rent on part of the tract of land 13 months. Inventory of the
Estate. 15 Nov. 1799. Wit: HEWLET SULLIVANT, JOHN CAMP & THOMAS BENNETT.
Two negroes, Toney and Chaney, list of farm animals, Notes of HENRY
MICKELS, LITTLE JOHN CHANDLER, JAMES WEBB, balance of note of JEREMIAH
CHANDLER, note of TIMOTHY CHANDLER, BIG JOHN CHANDLER, JACOB & JOHN
WEBB, PETER RAGSDALE acct., accts of OWEN SULLIVANT, JOHN THOMAS, WILIAM
COAL, HENRY MORGAN, WILLIAM FITZ, LITTLE SHADRICK CHANDLER, MOSES SUL-
LIVANT, DAVID TRAINUM, PATRICK RILEY, EDMUND RAGSDALE, PHILLIP MULKEY,
WILLIAM SHIP and continuing list of furniture, farm equipment etc.
amounting to $2085.18. (Loose Papers) Settlement Memo 6 Jan. 1804.
Legatees WILLIAM FITS, REUBEN FITS, WILLIAM SHIP, JOHN CHANDLER, MOSES
SULLIVANT, HENRY MITCHELL (all legatees rec'd an equal share). Signed
by JOHN CHANDLER, Adm., AGNES CHANDLER, Admx. (Loose Papers) Return
of a sale of part of estate 8 Nov. 1808 (also has date 16 Nov. 1808)

Cont'd from page 184:
Sold to JOSEPH CORDAL, ABSALOM CORDAL, JOHN F. CHANDLER, HILLERY THOMAS, JAMES CLEMENTS, JESSE CHANDLER. Total of $71.25. Certified by me JNO. CHANDLER, Exr. Yearly Return of estate 8 Nov. 1808. 25 Dec. 1807 rec'd of JNO. F. CHANDLER on note, WILLIAM GUNNELL part of a note - 2 Jan. 1808 pd to MILLEY SULLIVANT. Signed: JNO. CHANDLER, Exr. Memo of the sale of the last property of Estate sold 2 & 3 Dec. 1808 to: JAMES RYLEY, REUBEN FITTS, WILLIAM DUNKLIN, MARTHA SMALLMAN, JOHN HAMELTON, ELIJAH SHIELLESWORTH, DAVID CHANDLER, WILLIAM CAMP, JOEL SULLIVANT, HENRY MITCHELL, JOHN REAGWAY, VALANTINE BRASWELL, EZEKIAL MATHEWS, ARMSTED AAKELY, SAMUEL NEIGHBOURS, JOHN RIDGEWAY, JOHN F. CHANDLER, MARGARETT THOMAS, GEORGE PEAK, MILEY SULLIVANT, JOHN CHANDLER, WILLIAM GUNELS, THOS. MATLOCK, JOHN OWENS, WILLIAM DOWNS, HILERY THOMAS, TULLEY BOLING, ABSOLON NIXON, WILLIAM ABERCROMBRE, JAMES TAYLOR, LEWIS HAMELTON, JOSEPH CAMP, WILLIAM TRANUM, THOMAS OWENS, JOSEPH MC COLLOUGH, JOHN MORRISON, BIG ANDREW MC KNIGHT, FRANCES POSEY, WILLIAM ADKINS, ROBERT SCOTT, JOHN BAGWELL, DAVID CHANDLER, BENJ. ARNOLD, WILLIAM DEVINPORT, MARGT DEVINPORT, HUGH NIXON, MOSES KELLY, ABNER NIXON, TULLY BOLLING, JAMES THOMPSON, CHARLES FORGUSON, JOHN NABORS. Total sale $1614.76. Exhibited into office 11 Feb. 1811. Yearly Return 1 Nov. 1808 to 1 Nov. 1809. 4 Sept. 1809 rec'd of EZEKIEL MATHEWS, WILLIAM TRANUM & HILLORY THOMAS. 18 Apr. 1809 pd to JOHN NABORS. Signed: JNO. CHANDLER, Exr. Yearly Return made up to 17 Jan. 1811. 17 Jan. 1810 pd JOHN CHANDLER, MILLEY SULLIVAN, REUBIN FITTS, WM. SHIP, to WM. FITTS for JAMES WEBB, WM. FITTS, HENRY MITCHEL credit on his note, JAMES WEBB. Total amount $1108.92 1/2. Signed: JNO. CHANDLER, Exr.

Pp 97-104   WHITE, JOHN. Greenville Co., SC Warrant of Appraise-
Apt. 8-File 512: ment by JOSEPH BENSON, JAMES SEABORN, WILLIAM TEAS-
1797   DALE & DAVID GARRISON directed unto by WM. & HENRY
                  WHITE, Admrs. of the goods and chattels of JOHN WHITE,
dec'd. 22 Nov. 1797. Signed: JESSE CARTER, CGC. AMBROSE BLACKBURN also qualified. (on back of document) JOSEPH BENSON, JAMES SEABORN & DAVID GARRISON qualified & signed 11 Dec. 1797 by AMB. BLACKBURN, J.P. Inventory 11 Dec. 1797 - 400 acres of land; JAMES FARRISEs bond for the titles of 200 acres of land. Negro wench, Grace, tobacco, corn, farm animals & tools, furniture, etc...amounting to $1993.74 1/2. Signed: JO. BENSON, JAS. SEABORN, DAVID GARRISON. A note added "Omitted at appraisement 1 Horsemans Sword & 1 Red pocket book". Inventory of Notes: AMBROSE BLACKBURN to MOORE & WHITE, AUGUSTIN BLACKBURN to MOORE & WHITE, MASON BENNETT, FREDRICK BOWIN, NEDOM BRYANT to JOHN WHITE, ISHAM BOBBET, MASON BENNETT, DAVID CRAFFORD, JOHN DICKERSON, THOMAS DICKERSON, PHILLIP EVANS, LEVI FARIS, DICKERSON & MOSES BARRET, JOHN KELAM, THOMAS LIVINGSTON, MASON MITCHELL, DAVIS MOORE, LEWIS NELSON, THOMAS PERRY, JOSHUA STEVANS & JAMES DALEY, JOHN SCOTT, WILLIAM SMITH, LEVI SALYER, LARKIN TARRANT, SAMUEL TARRANT, REUBIN TARRANT, WILLIAM WILSON, LEWIS WILLIAMS & DRURY MORRICE, WILLIAM BRYANT, BENJAMIN DUVALL, WILLIAM GREEN, SR., JAMES GLIDE, WILLIAM TERRY, THOMAS WALKER, HENRY WHITE, MEDLOCK & STONES note for 1200 pds tobacco. Inventory of cash $900.00. Inventory of Accoumps: AMBROSE BLACKBURN, MAYSON BENNETT, ISAAC BOWEN, MARY BLACKBURN, MERIDETH BLACKBURN, PETER BRYMBERY, FREDRICK BOWEN, JESSE BALLARD, ABSOLAM BRYANT, WILLIAM ASHMORE, SARAH BRAZIER, NANCY BRYANT, JOHN BRYANT son of RICHARD, THOMAS BRAZIER, JAMES BRYANT, WILLIAM BLYTHE, ABNER BROWN - JOEL NORTON sponser, JOSEPH BURNS, STEPHEN BURDINE, HARDY BRYANT, OLIVER CHARLES, JONATHEN CLARK, JESSE COBB, CHARLES CRAFFORD, DENNIS CARPENTER, ELISHA COOPLAND, MICAGER CLARK, JOHN DYKES, THOMAS DICKERSON, JAMES DICKERSON, WILLIAM DICKS, JOHN DOUGLAS, THOMAS DOGGETTE, CHARLES DELANEY, JAMES EASEN, ELIAS ERLS, HECTOR FARIS, JOHN HINSON, JOHN HAMBLETON, DICKERSON GARRET, JOHN GWIN, FRANKEY GORDAN, CORNELIUS GREEN, STURDY GARNER, Capt. DAVID GRIMES, WILLIAM GUNTER, JOHN HILLIAN - JOHN BOOTH sponser, JOHN HORTON, WILLIAM HEMBREE, JOHN HONEYCUTT, JAMES HAYETT, JOHN HUNT, MOSES & JAMES HIDE, JOHN HARRISON, ELIJAH HUTCHINSON, BENJAMIN JONES, THOMAS JENKINS, JOHN JONES, JAMES JONES, ISIAH KERBY, JESSE KERBY, DAVID KERBY, SAMUEL KERBY, JOHN KILLAM, JOHN KERBY, LEONARD KERBY, JAMES KELLEY, JOHN LANDERS, JOHN LINLEY, JAMES LEE, JOHN LINSEY, THOMAS LARKFORD, JOHN LANGFORD, JOHN MC BATH, WILLIAM MARTIN, DAVIS MOORE, JOHN MC ELBRAY, DIDNER MOODY, JOHN NEVILE, JOHN NICHOLSON, WILLIAM NICHOLSON, JOHN OLIVER, BENJAMIN OTWELL, JOHN PYLE, SR., FRANCIS PARKER, WILLIAM PYLE, WILLIAM POLLARD,

THOMAS PERRY, ROBERT PARKER, WILLIAM PERSONS, WILLIAM POPLIN, THOMAS
PHILPOT, ABEL PENNINGTON, NICHOLAS PYLE, WILLIAM PERSONS, SR., JOHN
PAINE, ROBERT PHILPOT, CHARLES POPE, JAMES RICHEE, JOSEPH REED, SUSANNAH
ROY, JOHN RUSSELL, THOMAS ROY, JOHN RICE, JACOB ROBERTS, MARY REED,
JOHN REED, SAMUEL SOUTHERN, JAMES SCOTT, JOHN SCOTT, JAMES SEABORN,
WILLIAM SMITH, LEVI SALLYERS, WILLIAM SIZEMORE, LEANARD D. SHAW, MAJOR
SLATTON, WILLIAM SMITH, Reedy River, JAMES SMITH Greenville, JOHN SMITH
- ROLAND TANKERSLEY sponser. BUCKER SMITH - JOHN PAINE sponser, EDWARD
SCOTT, ISAIAH STEPHENS, RICHARD SLADRIDGE, REUBIN TARRANT, BENJAMIN
TARRANT, SAMUEL TARRANT, ROLAND TANKSLEY, TERRY TARRANT, GEORGE TANKS-
LEY, RICHARD TANKSLEY, WYATT TARRANT, Capt. JAMES WILBORN, JOHN WALDROP
& C. COCKRON, JOHN WILEY, WILLIAM WILSON - J. DARRET sponser, JOHN
YOUNG, WALTER AUSTIN, JAMES ASHWORTH, STEPHEN CROWDER, ROBERT LANKFORD,
JR., JAMES BRAZER, GEORGE SLATTON, JAMES SWILLIVANT, AARON WILLIAMS,
GEORGE WHITE.

Pp 104-105   GOODWIN, JOSEPH (First entry of this estate on page
Cont. of   57. Second entry on page 60). A Return of money paid
Apt. 3-File 190: at different creditors by FRANCES GOODWIN, Adm. of
1792   the Est. of JOSEPH GOODWIN, dec'd. THOMAS M. CARREL
                  for a Bond given JOSEPH TERRY 2700 hundred weight
inspected tobacco. To BENJAMIN MERIT, to JOHN PAUL, to ELIAS EARLE,
to MARTIN ADAMS, to EDMONSON & FARR, to THOMAS SPRIGS, to WILLIAM GRANT,
to WILLIAM CORNELIUS, to JAMES STEVENSON, to WILLIAM GOODWIN, to WIL-
LIAM LYNCH, to THOMAS STEPHENS, to WILLIAM SHAW, to LANGLEY. Written
on back of document a return of accts pd by Mrs. ANN GOODWIN to creditors JOS. GOODWIN, dec'd.

Pp 105-108   ARNOLD, BENJAMIN. LW & T of BENJAMIN ARNOLD presented
Apt. 1-File 7:   in open court Oct. term 1796, proven by oath of HUMPH-
1794   REY COBB, GEORGE GRAN, JAMES CHASTAIN, ordered record-
                  ed 8 Dec. 1799. LW & T: I, BENJAMIN ARNOLD, Greenville
Co., SC, farmer, give to my wife, ANN ARNOLD, negroes Jim, Sam, Sook,
Doll, Kissy and other property...to eldest son, WILLIAM ARNOLD, de-
ceased, negroes James and Nanna, etc....and to his sons (grandsons)
ANDERSON & WILLIAM a tract of land in Bedford Co., Va. where my son
WILLIAM lived at his decease..to son, EDWARD ARNOLD, two negroes Charles
and Betsy etc....to my youngest son, BENJAMIN ARNOLD, negroes Polly,
Frances, Daniel, Balaam, Esther, George and Susey, etc...to son, HEN-
DRICK ARNOLD, deceased, one negro, Phebe and her increase which is
Humphrey, Sarah and Philip, etc...and to his son (grandson) WILLIAM,
etc...to my son JOHN ARNOLD, two negroes Lucy and Jack and a tract
of 199 acres of land where he now lives, etc...to son, THOMAS ARNOLD,
negroes Milly, Amy, Joseph Young and Dick, and a tract of land where
he now lives, etc....to daughter, CHARITY MARTIN, one negro Gill and
her increase, Will, Amy and Cupet, etc...to daughter, TEMPERANCE HAMIL-
TON, one negro, Betsy and her increase, Jim, Samuel and Polly, etc...Exr
THOMAS ARNOLD & BENJAMIN ARNOLD. Signed 13 Jan. 1796 by BENJAMIN (X)
ARNOLD. Wit: HUR'M COBB, GEORGE GRACE, JAMES CHASTIN. Inventory of
Estate: 5 negroes viz James, Sam, Loock, Doll, child Kissey, old still,
farm animals, tools, furniture, etc. amounting to 437:0:7 15 Oct. 1796..
signed by JOHN MC ELROY, HULET SULLIVANT, JOSEPH DUNKLIN. Warrant of
Appraisement, Greenville Co., SC, JOHN MC ELROY, HEWLETT SULLIVANT,
JOSEPH DUNKLIN directed by BENJ. ARNOLD, Exr. of goods and chattels
of BENJ. ARNOLD, dec'd. 10 Oct. 1794 signed, JESSE CARTER, C.G.C. HUMP-
HREY COBB impowered to qualify the above appraisors.

Pp 108-109   PAYNE, THOMAS   LW & T presented in open Greenville
Apt. 9-File 643   Co., SC court Oct. Term 1797, proven by oath of JAMES
1797   & THOMAS PAYNE, recorded 8 Dec. 1799. (Loose Papers)
                  THOS. PEYN of Greenville, SC to daughters PRUDENCE,
RACAHEL, LURANY, to son THOMAS, to wife ANN PAYN etc...4 July 1797.
Signed: THOS. (P his mark) PEYN. Wit: JAMES PAYNE, THOMAS PAYNE. (no
other records).

Pp 109-111   TARRANT, JOHN. LW& T presented in Open Court Green-
Apt. 7-File 476: ville Co., SC May Term 1799, proven by oath of the
1806   Red'd JAMES TARRANT, recorded 9 Dec. 1799. (Loose
                  papers) I, JOHN TARRANT, Greenville Co., SC of Washing-

Cont'd from page 186:
ton District, given to SALLEY MC KINZIE, bed, furniture, mare colt, have given unto SAMUEL TARRANT bed, furniture and mare, being all of my estate I intend for him, to ROWLAND TARRANT, to RICHARD TARRANT, to my three youngest children viz NANCY, JOHN & GEORGE TARRANT...when they come of age or marry..to son, EDWARD HAMPTON TARRANT, son of SAMUEL TARRANT, dec'd., one saddle and briddle when he comes of age. To wife, TABITHA my estate until youngest child becomes of age then to be equal-ly divided between my six children viz: SALLY MC KINZIE, ROWLAND TARRANT, RICHARD TARRANT, NANCY TARRANT, JOHN TARRANT & GEORGE TARRANT, Ex'rs wife, TABITHA TARRANT & sons, ROWLAND & RICHARD TARRANT. 8 Apr. 1799. Wit: JAMES TARRANT, BENJ. TARRANT, DAVID (X) CROFFORD. Signed: JOHN TARRANT. Inventory & Appraisement: farm animals & tools, 7 vols. of Wessley & Fletchers works, 8 other books, furniture, one negro man, Jack, one negro man, Stephen, one negroe man Dick, 1 negroe woman Silva & child. 11 June 1799. Certified 16 June 1799. Signed: L. TARRANT, E. WALKER, JAS. SEABORN. Return 4 Aug. 1806 full amount of estate - $2353.12 1/2. Ex'rs: TABITHA, ROWD. & RICHD. TARRANT. Return 5 Aug. 1807 ibid. Return from 5 Aug. 1807 to 1 Aug. 1808. Rec'd of RICHARD TARRANT 1808 - $57.32. Pd CLEVELAND $41.00, taxes $7.25, blacksmith $14, JOHN & R. TARRANT $31, JAS. WEST $25, WILLIS BENSON $11.12.1/2, WILLIAM COX $1.50, JONAH THOMPSON $12.00, JAMES TARRANT $5.00, Mr. GOODLETT $1.25, JAMES DICKERSON $1.00. Amounting to $150.12 1/2. Signed by TABITHA, ROWLAND & RICHD. TARRANT. Return 25 Dec. 1808 rec'd of RICHARD TARRANT $39, pd Ordinary $1, 10 Apr. 1809 pd to WM. SMITH $8, 15th pd to GEO. TARRANT $20, 16th pd to GUNDIFF $15, pd to JOHN MACHEN $2(?.), 9th May pd tax $4. Signed: ROLAND TARRANT. Return 7 Aug. 1810. Rec'd of RICHARD TARRANT 21 Feb. 1810, $59.27. 4 Aug. 1809 pd $1 to Ordinary. 11 Mar. 1810 pd RICHD. TARRANT $7.40. 16 Apr. pd $25.50 to JOHN HUNTER. 8 May pd tax $4.50. 11 May pd ISAAC WEST $4. 20 July pd JAMES LAWSIN $3.37 1/2. Return 2 Sept. 1811. 15 Dec. 1810 rec'd of LEWIS CANTELEW $56.47. Rec'd of ROLAND TARRANT $4. 1 Dec. 1810 pd $4.50 to WM. SMITH. Pd $4 JAMES WEST, pd $13.60 to BOWIN, pd $9 to JAMES DICKERSON, pd $13 to ISAAC WEST, SR., pd tax $5, pd to CARRUTH $8, pd $4 GEO. TARRANT. Return 2 Dec. 1811 Inventory to be sold seven neg-roes, one wagin, 5 head horses & other stock & household furniture. 2 Dec. 1811 Mr. DAVID GOODLEY, Ord., I give my concent fairly to the sale of this property above mentioned. Signed TABITHA (X) TARRANT. Test. GEORGE TARRANT.

Pp 112-114   SOWEL, JOSEPH (Loose Papers) An Inventory- farm ani-
Apt. 6-File 419: mals, 1 negro woman, 1 negroe boy, negroe gairle,
                  1 negroe child, 1 negroe boy, 200 acres of land, furniture, tools. 13 May 1795. Signed: MERRY HALL, WILLIAM ARMSTRONG, JESE (+) HOLLAND, JOHN JONES. Greenville Co., SC July Term 1796 ordered the personal estate of JOSEPH SOWELL, deceased to be sold at public sale, by order of the court. Test. JESSE CARTER, C.G.C. Inventory & Appraisement: JOHN JONES, WILLIAM ARMSTRONG, MERRY HALL & JESSE HOLLAND. 3 May 1796. Signed: JESSE CARTER, CGC. JOHN BLASINGAME, Esq. is impower-ed to qualify. Account of the sold part of Estate (no date) MARY SOWEL one negroe wench; MARY SOWEL one boy, George; REUBEN MC KENZEY, one girl Milley - note; MARY SOWEL, one child; SARAH SOWEL, one boy - note; REUBIN DANIEL, one shar (sic) 2 pds 8; REWBIN DANIEL, one shar 2 pds-note; MARY SOWEL, one shar 1 pd 3; ROBERT MC AFEE, one shar - 1 pd-3.6 note; WILLIAM SMITH one shar-note 1 pd 5; JOHN BLASSINGAME, one shar - note 1 pd 1; other buyers ROLAN TANKERSLEY, ROBERT MAXWELL, JEREMIAH SMITH, GEORGE TANKESLEY, DAVID CRAFFORD, ELIZABETH DICKERSON, BENJ. MC KENZEN, JOHN PAYNE, WILLIE BENSON, ELISHA LAKE, PATSY WILEY, LARKIN TARRANT. Signed : MARY (+) SUMMERLIN, formerly MARY SOWELL, Adm'x. Return May Term 1799 Money pd by MARY SOWELL as adm'x to JOSEPH SOWELL, dec'd. in behalf of his Estate 20 Mar. 1797, JOHN WOODE 0/6/3, 2 Nov. 1797 ISAAC WEST 0/11/0. 31 Aug. 1798 REUBEN MC KINZEY 22/0/0. 15 Nov. 1797 ELIZABETH DICKERSON 18/14/0. 20 Mar. 1797 ELIJAH WALKER 7 Apr. 1798 JAMES MACEPHE 0/15/0. Money rec'd in behalf of Estate 3 Mar. 1797 WILLICE BENSON 0/16/0. 4 Mar. 1797 DAVID CRAFFORD 2/10/8. Mar. 1797 JEREMIAH SMITH 0.8.8. 22 Oct. 1794 (sic) WILLIAM WOODE 1.15.0. 20 Dec. 1797 JOHN PAYNE 1.9.11. 1797 REUBEN MC KINZEY 18.0.0. 28 Dec. 1798 MRS. MAXWELL & LARKIN TARRENT 1.18.9. 30 Apr. 1799 GEORGE TANKERS-LEY 1.1.0. 2 May 1799 WILLIAM 1.9.2. (numbers are pds, shillings, pence)

Cont'd from page 187:
SMITH, JOEL HUNT O.3.6. Signed: MARY SOWEL. Division of JOS. SOWELL,
deceased, Estate (no date) The amount of property sale 234 pds 9 sh.
O p. Pd REUBEN MC KENZEY his part in full 22 pds 6 sh 7 p. Pd JOEL
HUNT ditto amount. Pd ALBERT ROBINS ditto amount. Pd JOHN SOWEL ditto
amount. Pd ROBERT DICKERSON ditto amount. Total 111 pds 12 sh (?) p.
TREPHENEY & PATSEY SOWEL parts drew which is 44 pds 13 sh (?) p. Total
156 pds 61 sh (?) p. MARY SOWELs third is 79 pds 3 sh (?) p. Total
234 pds 9 sh (?) p. Signed MARY SUMMERLIN, formerly MARY SOWEL. Further
return files 4 June 1803. Written 15 Oct. 1802 A drew(?) return of
money paid to the Legatees of JOSEPH SOWEL, dec'd. by MARY SUMMERLAND,
Adm'x since last return made at Ordinary office pd JOHN SOWEL 22.6.7.
in full for his part. Pd POLLY DICKERSON 22.6.7. in full of her part.
Signed MARY SUMMERLAND, formerly MARY SOWELL. Return exhibited 4 Nov.
1806 MARY SOWEL Adm'x returns to Court of Ord. from 1794 to 1806 by
widows third 78.3.0. Par six Legatees 134 pds. Money pd for the Estate
6 pds 19 sh 1 p. Total 219 pds 2 sh 1 p. Total amount of sales 234
pds 9 sh 1 p. "Ther is seven Legatees of which I have paid six ther
parte in full one on hand" Signed MARY SOWELL. Test. JOHN BLASSINGAME.
Yearly Return exhibited C O office 7 Dec. 1807. Total amount in hand
as per last return 15 pds 7 sh O p. Rec'd & paid 00 last return. Signed
MARY SOWEL, Adm'x.

Pp 114-115   KERBY, FRANCIS. LW & T presented in open Court Green-
Apt. 4-File 260:   ville Co., SC Feb. Term 1799, proven by oath of AMOS
1805   JUSTICE, recorded 9 Dec. 1799. I, FRANCIS CURBY of
                   Grinville 16 Apr. 1798...to wife (not named) all...&
after her death to son, JOHN CURBEY a negro woman Sine; to daughter
ELISABETH HODGES the first living child of sd negro Sine; to son, JESSE
CURBEY my land & plantation by his paying JUDEY HONE & ANN SIMSON 5
pds a peace (sic); to daughter MARY TUCKER my horse & stoke; to daughter
SUSANAH CURBEY a negroe boy, David...Executors - my worthy friends
ALESEBETH CURBY & JOHN CURBEY. Wit: ? JUSTICE, MARY (C) JUSTICE.
Signed: FRANCES CURBY. Inventory exhibited 1 Sept. 1806. Dated 27 Apr.
1805..one negroe wench Sine, 1 negroe boy David, 1 negroe girl Peggy,
furniture. Total $861.43 3/4. Appraisors JAMES WEST, BENJ. TARRANT,
THOMAS PAYN. Letters of Adm. Greenville Dist. SC JOHN THOMAS, JR.,
Ordinary. SAMUEL TUCKER applied for Letters of Adm. to Estate of FRANCIS
KIRBY, dec'd. 19 Mar. 1805. Application 1 Apr. 1805 by SAMUEL TUCKER,
Adm. of FRANCIS KIRBY Estate to authorize sell of personal estate in
order to pay debts & legacies giving 21 days notice of sd sale & credit
until the 25 Dec. next ensuing...Signed 1 Apr. 1805 J. THOMAS, JR.
OGD. Letter of Adm. granted to SAML. TUCKER 1 Apr. 1805. Signed: J.
THOMAS, JR. Warrant of App. JAMES TARRANT, JAMES WEST, BENJAMIN TARRANT
& THOMAS PAIN be directed by SAML. TUCKER, Adm. of FRANCIS KIRBY, dec'd.
Estate for appraisement. 1 Apr. 1804. Signed J. THOMAS, JR. LEONARD
TARRANT authorized to Adm. the usual oath to above appraisors & certify
the same on back of Warrant. Signed: J. THOMAS, JR. OGD. The Adm. of
oath 6 Apr. 1805. Signed: L. TARRANT, J.P. Advice of Mr. TALLIVARRO
to Mrs. KERBY is for her to go to Col. JOHN THOMAS Ordinary & demand
the Will of FRANCIS KERBY. Then to offer to be qualified as Executrix
& he will not admit of that demand, an appeal to court as it can be
proven that Mr. TUCKER has not acted according to law in Reading the
Citation or having it read in such places as the law requires & so
that she did not have legal notice that she might come forward and
administer & she considers herself the proper one to have the prefer-
ence of adm'g, she also wants Mr. THOMAS to call in the Letters of
Administration he has issued. Complaint Greenville Dist. SC To Mr.
SAMUEL TUCKER 12 Apr. 1805. Complaint lodged in Ordinarys office by
the widow of FRANCIS KIRBY, dec'd. setting forth that you have not
published the Citation which you obtained from this office according
to law. She also informs that LW & T of sd FRANCIS KIRBY hath been
duly proved. These are therefore to cite & admonish you the sd SAMUEL
TUCKER to be & appear in Court of Ordinary on Friday next etc...Herein
fail not at your peril. Signed: J. THOMAS, JR. OGC. Papers. We the
subscribers whose names are under written have never heard any letters
of Citation read at any meeting house near to us as near to where FRAN-
CIS KIRBY dec'd. the 12th Apr. 1805. We the Subscribers one & all living
near where Mr. KERBY, dec'd. & has lived there ever since. Signed:

Cont'd:
WHEATON MERITT, JOHN HODGESS, JOSEPH TERRY, BARKSDILL TERRY, JAMES
WALKER, MARTAIN ADAMS. Papers. These are to shew that there is a meeting house about one mile from ELIZABETH KIRBY, widow of FRANCIS KIRBY,
dec'd & also we the members of the church at this meeting house & neigh-
bors of this place do certify that there was no Citation from the Ordi-
narys office been read at this meeting house or any other place in
this neighborhood publicly by SAML. TUCKER etc. 16 Apr. 1805. Signed:
JAMES TARRANT, JR., BENJ. TARRANT, ROBERT TARRANT, LE'D TARRANT, MOSES
BARRISON, JAMES WEST. Warrant of Appraisement 19 Apr. 1805 JAMES WEST,
BENJAMIN TARRANT & THOMAS PAIN, Appraisors with ELIZABETH & JOHN KIRBY,
Executors. Signed J. THOMAS, JR. Certified 27 Apr. 1805 by L. TARRANT
J.P.

Apt. 4-File 260:   KELLY, JAMES. (the data given is from a loose paper
1805   misfiled and placed in the Estate of FRANCIS KIRBY.
                    I do not find a JAMES KELLY indexed in the Probate
Records). Letters of Adm. to KESIAH KELLY of her husband JAMES KELLY,
dec'd. and appear before me in Court of Ordinary for to be holden the
11 Apr. next for the sd district (at Milford) to shew cause if any...31
Mar. 1804. Signed JOHN THOMAS, JR. Ordinary. "I certify that I publicly read the within Citation 4 Mar. ___?. Apr. 1804. Signed: HUDSON
BERRY". "I hereby certify that I have publicly read the within Citation
on the 5 & 6 days of March (sic) April 1804. Signed JOHN HARRISON.
Also has signature of JONATHAN DEWEESE. Citation granted to the widow.

Pp 115-120   FLOYD, JAMES. (To date the Estate File has not been
Apt. 3-File 174:   located, however the Estate Book A gives a detailed
1794   recording of the Estate of JAMES FLOYD. The present
                   copying machine in the Probate Office will not accom-
adate the page size of this book, therefore I will give as complete
a record as the old faded script will permit.) An appraisement of the
articles belonging to the Estate of JAMES FLOYD, dec'd. as follows:
drawing knife, iron wedge, flat iron, 1 pd 0 sh 2 p, six shoats & 1
hogshead 1 pd 2 sh 0 p, 3 pots & 1 Ditch (sic) oven 1 pd 5 sh 0 p,
bed & what belongs to it, 1 meal sifter & trey 1 pd 1 sh 0 p, Glass
& earthenware 6 sh, 2 pocket books & 2 pr shoes 2 pds, dish bason &
spoon moulds & things belong 2 pds, 2 cleavses, 1 ax, 1 bridle, 1
p_? compasses, 1 hand saw 6 sh, 1 chest & a number of small articles
1 pd, 1 pewter dish 2 plates 1 ? slay & looking glass 11 sh, 1 hand
bellows & 2 belts 12 sh, 1 plow hoe & 3 small hoes 3 sh, 1 hat & 2
silk handerchiefs 7 sh, all the body clothes of sd dec'd. 2 pds 17
sh 6 p, 1 saddle & saddle bags 7 sh, 1 pan handle, 1 chair, 1 side
leather 1 sh 6 p, 1 mare & bridle 5 pds, five head of cattle 5 pds
3 sh = 10 pds 3 sh 0 p, 136 acres of land 15 pds, 1 hide 1 plate moute
1 pd 1 sh = 16 pds 1 sh 0 p, note on demand on THOMAS TERRY 2 pds 13
sh 3 p, 1 sow & 6 pigs 1 iron wedge 16 sh. Signed: WM. GASTON, JOHN
SIMS & JOHN MC ELREY (MC ELROY). A Memorandum of the sale of the Estate
of JAMES FLOYD, dec'd. 4 Feb. 1795: SARAH DOWDLE to iron wedg 1 drawing
knife 1 flat iron 1 sh 6 p, 1 pr hand bellowes 1 sh 6 p, 1 hat & 2
handerchiefs 9 sh 6 p, 1 bay mare 6 pds, 1 suit of mens clothes 7/2-
6 pds 7 sh 2 p; MARTIN MEHAFY 1 pot 10 sh 6 p, 1 as 1 clevis handsaw
6 sh; NANCY ELLIOTT to 1 suit clothes 1 pd 6 p, hoes 1 plowhow 4/9
1 pot 6 p = 10 sh 9 p, 1 sifter 1 bread tray 2 sh 1 p, 1 saddle & saddle
bags 9 sh 5 p, 1 iron wedge 1 panhandle 1/10 1 cow & calf 2 pds 1 sh
7 p = 2 pds 3 sh 5 p; ABSOLUM C. CREEMER 1 pot 3 sh 1 p, 1 chest &
spoon molds & sundry articles 1 pd 12 sh ? p, 1 laddle 3?.1.2; MILLEY
FORD 1 bed 16 p 1 looking glass 7/1 = 1 pd 3 sh 1 p; JOHN HARRISON
to earthen ware & glasses 0.12.0; JOHN MACKNIT 2 pr shoes 2 pocket
books 0.5.0, 1 cow & calf 1.10.0; ISHAM YEARBY 1 dish mote 1 plate
1 bason 3.7.6; JOHN SIMS 2 beals 0.11.6; LEE FLOYD 1 great coat 1.6.11,
1 pr stockings 1 pr leggens 150 acres of land 11.3.2; JOHN ALEXANDER
a parcel of hogs 1.14.0; JENET KITTET? 1 cow & calf 1.17.0 1 oven 0.17.0
An Account of the amount of the Vandue money & other notes on act.
due the estate of JAMES FLOID, dec'd. (date of Feb. 4 given in a column)
To ABSOLEM CREAMER note Vandue money 1 pd 15 sh 1 p - note on SARAH
DOWDLE Vandue money 7.4?.10 - an acct. due the Estate from JOHN GOLDEN
0.9.0 - To JENET KITIOT note vandue money 2.11.0 - Acct. due the Estate
from RUBIN GOLDEN 0.11.0 - note on MILLEY FLOYD vandue money 1.5.1

Cont'd:
note due Estate from GEORGE ELLIOTT 2.13.6 - 1 note from ISHAM YEARBY
vandue money 3.7.6 - note on JNO. MC NIGHT vandue money 1.??.0 - 1
ditto 1.10.6 - note on MARTIN MEHAFFY vandue money 0.10.6 - ditto MARY
BURNS ve. money 0.12.4 - ditto MARTIN MEHAFFY ditto 0.6.0 - ditto JOHN
ALEXANDER vandue money 1.11.0 - ditto LEE FLOYD vandue money 12.10.0
- to JOHN SIMS v'ue ditto 0.11.0 - ditto JOHN HARRISON ditto 0.12.0
- ditto THOMAS TERRY due the Estate 1.3.2? - ditto 1.0.0 - to an acct
due the estate from ANN? BROWN 0.16.4 - note on WILLIAM FLOYD due to
CLABURN SULLIVANT & sd JAS. FLOYD Surity & pd same 1.15.0 - by cash
pd by ABSOLEM CREEMER, Exr. & other expenses & C Dec. 13, 1795. - by
cash pd MOOR & WHITE p_ vandue 1.14.6 - by cash to JONATHAN DOWNS ditto
1.3.11 - by cash to JOSEPH DOWNS Justice 0.1.0 - by cash to Justice
ALEXANDER for fees 0.11.6 - by cash to Justice DOWNS for feess 0.4.0
- by cash to THOMAS TERRY for making coffin 0.6.8 - by cash to JAS.
HARRISON for surveying land to estate _.14.0 - cash to JOHN MC ELROY,
Esq. appraiser 0.6.0 - cash to JESSE CARTER CC 0.14.0 - cash to JAS.
GASTIN appraiser 0.6.0 - by cash to JNO. SIMS appraiser 0.7.0 - cash
to L. TARRANT, Sheriff 0.14.0 - cash to JAS. COOPER, constable 0.5.10
- cash to GEORGE ELLIOTT for feeding cattle to the estate 2.2.6 - cash
to JAS. GRIFFIN 0.1.2 - cash to Justice GRIFFIN 0.0.9 1/2 - cash to
RAGLAND LANGSTON p. voucher 0.16.6 - July __ 1796 cash to Justice DOWNS
for fees 0.9.0 - cash to JAMES MC CAW for fees 0.10.2 - cash 1 day
attendance at court for the estate 0.2.6 - by cash ___ing surveyor
and carry chains 0.7.0 - cash bring to JOSEPH LANGSTON on business
on estate 0.4.4 - An acct. of amt. of the vandue money & other accts
due the estate of JAMES FLOYD, dec'd., Jan. 7, 1797. To 1 note RICHARD
FLOYD to ELIZABETH TATE & sd JAMES FLOYD surity & had the same to pay
6.0.0 - Raised of MARTIN KELLET? 0.14.0 - balance 2 pds vs? WILLIAM
KELLIT? for JUNE KELLET? vandue money 2.0.0 - to 1 note vs LEE FLOYD
& interest 13.2.11-ABSOLEM CREAMER by cash & other acct. on acct JAMES
FLOYD, dec'd., by 1 day hunting a mare belonging to estate 0.4.2 -
1 day showing property to appraisors 0.4.2 - by hunting horse for
estate 0.2.0 - by wintering a mare 3 months & 3 wks 1.16.0 - by s days
attending Court 0.5.0 - by 1 days attendance on the sale 0.4.6 - by
riding to the Clerks office 0.3.0 - by attendance 1 day 0.2.6 - by
cash pd Justice BLASSINGAME 0.1.6 - by attendance at Court 1 day 0.2.6-
6th July 1796. By clearing Debts in Newberry County 0.2.0 - by on Quin
of paper 0.2.4 - cash pd LEE FLOYD for feeding hogs 1.0.0 - Jan. 1797
by 1 days attending Court 0.2.6 - ABSOLEM CREAMER, Adm. to the Estate
of JAMES FLOYD, dec'd. Settled with the different Legatees of sd Estate
as follows: WILLIAM FLOYD 3.9.6 - SARAH DOWDLE 3.9.6 = 6.19.4 - MARY
LEE 3.10.0 - JAMES FLOYD 3.9.6 = 6.19.6 - NANCY ELLOT 3.9.6 - LEE FLOYD
3.9.6 = 6.19.5 - RICHD FLOYD 3.9.6 - MILLY HAYS 3.9.6 = 6.19.4 - JASPER
FLOYD 3.9.8? Total = 31.9.0. JOHN FLOYD part not settled. The above
as it stands stated is just as further Reference may be had to the
other "pepirs" if Required. Signed: ABSOLEM (his mark) CREAMER 26 Apr.
1797. (a line is drawn indicating another acct.) A total amt of the
Debts & Cd of JAMES FLOYD, dec'd. brought forward for a final settle-
ment with the court of Greenville setting for the Legatees part by
ABSOLEM CREAMER, Exr. Total amt of Debts & acct due the Estate 66 pds
17 sh 16 p - Cr. ABSOLEM CREAMER 19.16.6 = 47.1.2. Legatees: WILLIAM
FLOYD (1) ELIZ'T CREAMER (2) SARAH DOWDLE (3) NANCY ELIOTT (4) JAMES
FLOYD, JR. (5) JOHN FLOYD (6) RICHARD FLOYD (7) JASPER FLOYD (8) MARY
LEE (9) LEE FLOYD (10) MILLY HAISE (11) Errers Excepted Signed: ABSOLEM
CREAMER Admr for the Estate of JAMES FLOYD dec'd. 28 Apr. (no year)
Cr. ABSOLEM CREAMER by his trouble expended & cash paid up & C 6.9.6
1/2 - cash due from the estate & paid up 13.7.1 1/2 = 19 pds 16 sh
8 p. errers excepted ABSO'M CREAMER, Admr. for the estate of JAS. FLOYD,
deceased.

Page 120   FORD, JOHN. (continuing from pages 74-77) Inventory
cont. of   of Articles of the Estate of JOHN FORD, dec'd. ap-
Apt. 3-File 158: praised the 25 Aug. 1796. 1 mare $40 1 rifle gun
1796 $15 = $55 - 1 case of pistols & 7 wagon boxes $7.92.6-
                  1 cow & calf & 1 barren cow $17 - 1 herfer 1 peded
herfer & 1 red ___ $18.50 - peded steers 1 cow & calf 6 yr olds $37.
- 1 gun barrell & lock $8. Signed JOHN MA(T?L?) LOW, WM. LYNCH, THOMAS
SPRIGS, JOSEPH TERRY.

Pp 120-121:   LANGSTON, HENRY. (not indexed in Probate Records
                     of Estates, but recorded in Estate Book A) We the
sd appraisors repaired to the place appointed by sd MARY LANGSTON and
has made a just inventory and appraisement of the Estate of HENRY LANG-
STON, dec'd. according to the directions given us by Honorable Judges
of the County Court 4 Nov. 1794. Signed: JOEL CHARLES, FREDERICK FARMER,
JAMES SMITH. 10 acres of land at $25 followed by a list of farm animals
and tools and household articles, etc.

                    LAURENS COUNTY, S. C. DEED BOOK A
                              1785-1786

At a Court began and held for the County of Laurens in the State of
South Carolina on Monday the 12th day Sept. 1785 and of the Sovereignty
and Independence of the United States of North America, Present were
JONATHAN DOWNS, JAMES MONTGOMERY, SILVANUS WALKER, WILLIAM MITCHERSON
& CHARLES SAXON, Gentlemen Justices.

Ordered by the sd Court that the following leases and releases be admitted to record, to wit:
Page: (torn not numbered but possibly page 4) Lease & Release
                  for the conveyance of 100 acres of land from ROBERT MC
NEESE to ANDREW ENDSLEY. Ack. in open Court and ordered to be bound,
to wit: 21 Aug. 1785 (lease date) 23 Aug. 1785 (release date) ROBERT
MC NEES, planter of Laurens SC sold to ANDREW ENDSLEY, planter of same
dist., for 300 pds 10 shillings current money 100 acres lying on waters
of Duncan Creek bounded NW by lands laid out on bounty and owner unknown.
Orig. grant to WILLIAM TAYLOR bearing date 13 Aug. 1768 and rec. in
Auditor's Office in Bk. F.N.G. page 195 on 30 Dec. 1763, rec'd in Sec.
State Off. Bk. D.D.D page 39. Sworn to in open Court bef. LEWIS SAXON,
C.C.

Page: (possibly page 6) 12 Sept. 1785-20 Sept. 1785 ROBERT SIMS
                  of 96 Dist., Laurens Co., miller, sold to DRURY BOYCE
of same place for 24 pds sterling 100 acres including gristmill on the
fork of Reyburn's Creek, 96 Dist., Laurens Co. bounded all sides on
vacant land at time of survey. . Orig. granted to JAMES SMITH by patent
by Gov. Chas. Montague bearing date 13 May 1768. In open Court.

Page: (possibly pages 10-16) 10 January 1755-22 Sept. 1785 HENRY
                  NEELY of SC, farmer, and his wife, ELIZABETH, sold to
CABEL JONES of SC for 100 pds 150 acres on S. Branch of Bush Creek,
a branch of Santee, otherwise Grate Salludy, whereon CABEL JONES now
lives. Orig. grant to HENRY NEELY 20 Apr. 1763. Wit: REPENTANCE TOWN-
SEND, WILLIAM NEELY, JOHN JONES. JOSEPH BROWN, J.P. (Name also written
as NEILY).

Pp 17-21:   7 Mar. 1775-22 Sept. 1785 CABEL JONES of 96 Dist., Province
                  of SC, sold to JONATHAN DOWNS, Esq. of sd Province, for
250 pds current money of the Province 150 acres lying on a branch of
Santee (otherwise called Grate Salludy) called Bush Creek. Orig. grant
to HENRY NEILY 1763. Wit: JOHN GOODWIN, MOSES TOMLINSON, ROBERT DUKINSON.

Page: (possibly pages 21-28) 2 Sept. 1785-24 Sept. 1785 PETER
                  EDWARDS of Spartanburg Co., 96 Dist., sold to ZACHARIAH
SIMS for 100 pds old currency 100 acres lying on northside of Saluda
River. Orig. grant 24 Feb. 1770 to ANDREW CUNNINGHAM and conveyed to
PETER EDWARDS on 28 and 29 June 1771. Bounded on the SE by Saluda River,
on NE by WILLIAM CUNNINGHAM's grant but now ZACHARIAH SIMS land, all
other sides vacant when laid out. OPAH EDWARDS signed dower. Wit: NIMROD
WILLIAMS, LEWIS GRAVES.

Pp 29-32:   12 May 1784-26 Sept. 1785 RICHARD ROBINSON, planter, lease
                  to ROBERT ROSS, hatter, for one whole year for 150 pds,
land in Craven County on waters of Little River called Beaverdam and
bounded NW by land of RICHARD ROBINSON; W by land of CHARLES ALLEN;
S by land of ABRAHAM NEIGHBORS and SE vacant land. Granted to RICHARD
ROBINSON 26 Sept. 1772 and rec. in Sec. State Office Bk MMM page 243,
also in Auditor's Office Bk M #12 dated 27 Nov. 1772. Wit: JOHN MC

Cont'd:
ELROY, FRANCIS ROSS and LEWIS DUVALL.

Pp 33-37:   13 May 1780-25 Sept. 1785 RICHARD ROBINSON, planter to
               ROBERT ROSS, hatter, 200 acres lying on waters of Little
River. Wit: FRANCIS ROSS, LEWIS DUVALL, JOHN MC ELROY.

Pp 37-41:   14 May 1784-26 Sept. 1785 RICHARD ROBINSON, planter, to
               ROBERT ROSS, hatter, 100 acres lying in Craven County
on Little River bounded by lands of RICHARD ROBERTSON, NEHEMIAH FRANKS
and CHARLES ALLEN. All other sides vacant. Being conveyed to RICHARD
ROBERTSON, SR. by JAMES BEARD in 1775 and now from RICHARD ROBERTSON,
JR., heir to RICHARD ROBERTSON, SR., deceased, to ROBERT ROSS. Wit:
JOHN MC ELROY, FRANCIS ROSS, LEWIS DUVALL.

Pp 42-45:   28 Jan. 1785-26 May 1785 RATCLIFF JEWELL of 96 District
               to MARK MOORE for 250 pds 150 acres lying in Berkely County
on Beaverdam Creek (4 ft wide and 4 inches deep) waters of Little River.
Bound on all sides by vacant land at time of survey. Wit: PETER RAGS-
DALE, JOEL BURGESS.

Page 46:   28 Jan. 1785-26 Sept. 1785 EDMOND LEARWOOD of 96 District
               sold to MARK MOORE for 250 pds 100 acres lying in 96 Dist.
Bounded on SE by JAMES RYAN, ACQUILLA HALL and vacant land. Wit: PETER
RAGSDALE, JOEL BURGESS.

Pp 49-52:   14 Mar. 1785-26 Sept. 1785 ROBERT DENNIS of 96 District
               sold to WILLIAM NORRIS of same place for 300 pds old cur-
rency 100 acres lying on Beaverdam Branch of Reedy River. Orig. grant
to ROBERT DENNIS bearing date 13 May 1768. Bounded by lands of PETER
ALLEN, HUGH TRIMBLE & HUGH BEARD. CONSTANT DENISON signed dower. Wit:
DAVID DUNLAP, THOMAS CUNINGHAM, JOSEPH DORSET. (He signed as DENNISON
but signed lease as DENNIS).

Pp 53-57:   13 July 1785-27 Sept. 1785 ANDREW RODGERS, SR. and ANN,
               his wife, of 96 Dist. sold to AMBROSE HUDGENS, JR. for
32 pds current money 100 acres lying at the head of North's Creek.
Orig. grant to JEANNE RODGERS, mother to ANDREW RODGERS, SR., bearing date 8 July 1774 by patent. Wit: JAMES MC NEESE, WILLIAM RODGERS,
JOHN RODGERS.

Pp 58-62:   27 Jan. 1780-27 Sept. 1785 THOMAS MC CLERKIN, merchant
               of 96 Dist. sold to THOMAS CUNINGHAM, sadler, of 96 Dist.,
for 100 pds current money 600 acres lying on branches of Reedy River
and Rayburn's Creek and bounded on N and W by lands of DANIEL ALLEN
and all other sides vacant land. Orig. grant to DAVID WEBB bearing
date 18 May 1771 and rec. in Sec. State Office Grant Bk HHH page
               Conveyed by WEBB to JAMES RYAN and from RYAN to THOMAS MC CLERKIN.
Wit: THOMAS RICHARDSON, JAMES CUNNINGHAM, JAMES MC CLERKIN.

Pp   27 Jan. 1780-29 Sept. 1785 THOMAS MC CLERKIN, merchant,
               sold to JOHN CUNNINGHAM, planter, for 5000 pds 200 acres
lying on Reyburn's Creek. Orig. indenture to JOSEPH WAITS bearing date
19 Nov. 1772. WAITS conveyed to RATCLIFF JEWELL and from JEWELL to
THOMAS MC CLERKIN. Wit: THOMAS RICHARDSON, JAMES CUNINGHAM, JAMES MC
CLERKIN.

Pp 65-70:   5 Jan. 1773-4 Oct. 1785 HENRY NEELY of Craven County and
               his wife, ELIZABETH, sold to JAMES YOUNG of sd Province
for 150 pds 200 acres lying on South Branch of Bush Creek of the Grate
Saludy River of the Santee. Orig. grant to HENRY NEELY bearing date
25 Sept. 1766. Bounded by lands of AUGUSTINE WARNER and vacant land.
ELIZABETH NEELY signed dower. Wit: REPENTANCE TOWNSEND, JOHN JONES,
CABEL JONES.

Pp 70-75:   27 Dec. 1773-5 Oct. 1785 JAMES YOUNG and ANN, his wife,
               of 96 Dist. Province of SC, sold to CHARLES SAXON of same
dist. for 200 pds 200 acres lying on Bush Creek bounded by lands of
AUGUSTINE WARNER. Orig. granted to HENRY NEILY bearing date 25 Sept.
1766. Wit: ANDREW ANDERSON, HUGH SAXON, WILLIAM YOUNG.

Pp 76-83:   12 Sept. 1785-10 Oct. 1785 CHARLES SAXON and JUDITH, his
             wife, of Laurens Co., sold to BENJAMIN JONES of same place
for 102 pds sterling 200 acres lying on Bush River, a branch of Grate
Saludy River. Bounded by lands of AUGUSTINE WARNER. Orig. granted to
HENRY NEILY bearing date 25 Sept. 1766 and by HENRY NEELY and ELIZABETH,
his wife, 25 Jan. 1773 to JAMES YOUNG and by JAMES YOUNG and ANN, his
wife, 27 Dec. 1773 to CHARLES SAXON and now to JONES. Wit: WILLIAM
CATE, SAMUEL SAXON. LEWIS SAXON, J.P.

Pp 84-86:   28 Jan. 1785-17 Oct. 1785 JAMES GIBSON, wheelwright, of
             Roan, N. C., sold to ALEXANDER HARPER, planter of 96 Dist.
for 15 pds 3 shillings 100 acres lying on North Fork of Dirbin's Creek,
waters of Enoree River, adj. sd HARPER's land. Wit: JACOB ROBERTS,
JOSEPH BARTON.

Pp 86-89:   28 Jan. 1785-18 Oct. 1785 JAMES GIBSON, wheelwright of
             Roan, NC sold to JACOB ROBERTS, planter of 96 Dist., for
15 pds 3 shillings 100 acres lying on North Fork of Dirbin's Creek,
waters of Enoree River. Land lying between land of ALEXANDER HARPER
and EZEKIEL GRIFFITH. Wit: ALEXANDER HARPER, JOSEPH BARTON.

Pp 89-90:   28 Jan. 1785-18 Oct. 1785 JAMES GIBSON, wheelwright, of
             Roan, NC sold to JACOB ROBERTS, planter of 96 Dist. for
15 pds 3 shillings 100 acres lying on Main Fork of Dirbin's Creek.
Land lying bet. lands of MORDICA MOORE and JOSEPH HOLCOMBE. Wit: ALEXAN-
DER HARPER, JOSEPH BARTON.

Page 93:   23 Aug. 1785-20 Oct. 1785 Indenture of JAMES PARKER, son
             of CATHERINE ALLISON, doth put himself apprentice to THOMAS
CUNINGHAM, sadler, to learn his art or mistry and to serve for a term
of 7 years and 10 months next. He shall faithfully serve his Master,
his secrets keep, lawful commands everywhere gladly do, shall do no
damage to his Master nor see it done by others without giving notice
thereof to sd Master, shall not waste his Master's goods nor lend them
unlawfully to any. He shall not commit fornication nor contract matrimony during sd term, he shall not play at cards nor dice or any other
unlawful game. He shall not absent himself day nor night from his sd
Master's service unlawfully nor haunt ale houses, taverns or play houses
but behave himself as a faithful apprentice in the trade or mistry
he now follows. His Master shall provide for him sufficient meat, drink,
apparel, lodging, washing and all other necessaries during sd term
and to give him a suit of good homespun or broad cloth at the term
of his freedom and also 12 months schooling. Wit: CATHERINE ALLISON,
JONATHAN DOWNS, J.P. (JAMES PARKER was old enough to sign with his
name and seal).

Pp 94-97:   24 May 1774-13 Nov. 1785 WILLIAM HARRIS and FRANCES, his
             wife, planter, of Craven County formerly called Berkely
County (96 Dist.) sold to MICHAEL WALDROUP, blacksmith and planter
of same dist., for 100 pds 150 acres lying on North's Creek, waters
of Little River, bounded by lands of ANDREW ROGERS. Orig. granted HARRIS
7 Jan. 1772 and rec. Sec. State Office Grant Bk KKK page 303. Wit:
SHADRACH MARTIN, ROBERT COOPER, JOHN MINARY, JOHN RODGERS, J.P.

Pp 98-101:   26 Oct. 1783-24 Nov. 1785 SAMUEL COB, planter of 96 Dist.
             sold to WILLIAM MITCHUSON for 100 pds sterling 300 acres
lying on Gilder's creek waters of Enoree River. Orig. granted to JOAB
MITCHELL and conveyed by MITCHELL to SAMUEL COBB and now to MITCHUSON.
Wit: BENJAMIN RAINEY, RAINEY PHILLIPS, BENJAMIN KILLGORE, J.P.

Pp 102-104: 14 Dec. 1785-9 Jan. 1786 WILLIAM IRBY and HENRIETTA, wife,
             of Laurens Co. sold to AMBROSE HUDGINS, SR. of same place,
for 100 pds sterling 150 acres lying on Simmon's Creek, branch of Little
River. Bounded by lands of WILLIAM DENDY, DAVID BURNS and Capt. JAMES
HENDERSON. Being part of 300 acres orig. granted to EDWARD OZBURN bear-
ing date 6 July 1774 and bounded then by lands laid out to MARY CALD-
WELL and vacant land. Wit: ALEXANDER MC DOWEL, ANDREW RODGERS, BENJAMIN
RAINEY.

Pp 104-108: 10 Dec. 1785-13 Jan. 1786 THOMAS DENDY and MARY, his wife,

Cont'd:
of Laurens Co. sold to ROBERT HALL, of the same place, for 50 pds sterling 300 acres lying on North's Creek in the Fork of Broad and Saludy Rivers. Bounded by lands of CORNELIUS TINSLEY and WILLIAM TOLBERT. Wit: SILVANUS WALKER, JOHN DENDY, WILLIAM BAILEY.

Pp 109-112: 18 Nov. 1785 - 13 Jan. 1786 DAVID and FRANCES WELCH, plant-er of Laurens Co., sold to MICHAEL WALLACE, planter, for 42 pds sterling 60 acres lying on Southside of South Fork of Dirbin's Creek. Being part of orig. grant to DAVID WELCH 2 Apr. 1773 and rec. in Sec. State Office Grant Bk M No. 12, page 373. Bounded by lands of MC WILLIAMS, JOHN BARNET & ROBERT SHELTON. Wit: JOHN BARNET, WILLIAM JACKSON, GEORGE BROOKS.

Pp 112-114: 2 Sept. 1785 - 17 Jan. 1786 DAVID and FRANCES WELCH sold to ROBERT SHELTON, planter, for 30 pds 100 acres lying on South Fork of Dirbin's Creek. Being part of 200 acres orig. granted to DAVID WELCH 1773. Wit: ALEXANDER HARPER, JOHN WELLS.

Pp 115-117: 27 Oct. 1785 - 16 Jan. 1786 DAVID WELCH and FRANCES WELCH sold to JOHN BARNET, planter of Laurens Co., for 20 pds sterling 40 acres lying on southside of South Fork of Dirbin's Creek being part of tract granted 1773 to DAVID WELCH. Wit: ROBERT SHELTON, GEORGE BROOKS.

Pp 118-121: 17 Jan. 1785 - 18 Jan. 1786 THOMAS JEFFERIES and his mother ELIZABETH GREEN, widow of JAMES JEFFERIES, of Craven Co., sold to WILLIAM FOWLER for 500 pds old currency 300 acres lying on a branch of Warrior's Creek, waters of Enoree River. Being part of a tract granted 1768 to JAMES JEFFERIES and bounded at that time by vacant land on all sides. "Estate of Inheritance"...Wit: JOHN POWER, JOHN MC CLINTOCK, SILVANUS WALKER, J.P.

Pp 122-123: 26 Sept. 1785 - 18 Jan. 1786 SAMUEL POWEL swore that in March 1772 he bought 200 acres of land from JOHN BAILEY and that he had leases but never recorded them and in time of contest (Rev. War) he lost them. Land located in the Fork of Little River and North's Creek bet. lands of WILLIAM BAILEY and WILLIAM DENDY. Sworn bef. SILVANUS WALKER, J.P. Wit: WITTENHALL WARNER swore bef. S. FELDER, J.P.

Pp 123-127: 20 June 1785 - 18 Jan. 1786 PATRICK CUNINGHAM, planter of 96 Dist. and his wife, ANN, sold to DAVID GREEN, Minis-ter, for 30 pds sterling 100 acres lying on the north side of Reedy River below the old Indian Boundary Line and bounded on the S by sd river. Orig. granted to PATRICK CUNINGHAM 21 Jan. 1785. Wit: WILLIAM HARRIS, EDWARD KEMP, BENJAMIN TURNER.

Pp 127-133: 24 Mar. 1770 - 19 Jan. 1786 JOHN CARGILL, JR. and KEZIAH CARGILL of Berkely County sold to THOMAS DENDY, planter, for 200 pds lawful S.C. money 300 acres lying in the Fork of Broad and Salluda Rivers. Orig. granted to JOHN CARGILL by patent 1769 and bound on all sides by vacant land. Wit: SAMUEL POWELL, SARAH TINSLEY, ELIZABETH TINSLEY. Sworn to bef. JOHN CALDWELL, J.P., one of His Majes-ty's Justices to keep the peace for Craven Co. 7 July 1770.

Pp 134-135: 7 Apr. 1785 - 19 Jan. 1786 Deed of Gift. ALEXANDER DEALE unto his sons, CLEMENT DEALE and ALEXANDER DEALE of 96 Dist., tracts located on Banks Creek "where he now lives". Also slaves. "For natural love and affection, free deed of gift of all my property after my decease." Wit: JOHN ROEN, JOHN MEEK, THOMAS FAKES, J.P.

Pp 135-138: 14 Dec. 1785 - 20 Jan. 1786 ELENOR RICHEY of 96 Dist. to SAMUEL DUNLAP, planter of 96 Dist., for 20 pds sterling 100 acres lying on O'Daniels Branch of Reyburn's Creek. Bounded by lands of BENJAMIN JONES, WILLIAM DANIELS. Orig. grant by patent to ELENOR RICHEY bearing date 4 May 1775 and rec. in Sec. State Office Grant Bk M No. 12, page 114. Sworn to in open Court bef. LEWIS SAXON, C. C.

Page 139:   7 Aug. 1785 - 20 Jan. 1786 CHARLES SAXON sold to LEWIS
              SAXON for 100 pds a negro man named "Prince" who was 18
or 19 years old. JOSHUA SAXON, J.P.

Pp 140-143:   9 Apr. 1777 - 27 Feb. 1786 JOHN MC NEESE, planter of 96
              Dist. in Province of SC, sold to SAMUEL WHARTON, planter
of same dist., for 250 pds 150 acres lying on Cane Creek in Craven
County. Orig. granted by patent to JOHN MC NEESE bearing date 5 May
1773. Wit: ALEXANDER RODGERS, DANIEL OSBORNE, WITTENHALL WARNER.

Pp 144-147:   13 Nov. 1785 - 28 Feb. 1786 JAMES KILGORE of Laurens Co.,
              sold to ALLIAS (ELLIS) CHEEK for 30 pds sterling 100 acres
lying on southside of Beaverdam Creek of Enoree River. Being part of
600 acres granted by patent to JAMES KILGORE 21 Jan. 1785 and bounded
by lands of Widow DUNLAP. Wit: BENJAMIN KILGORE, JOHN MC ELROY, JANE
KILGORE.

Pp 148-152:   18 Apr. 1783 - 2 Mar. 1786 HAMILTON MURDOCK and JEAN,
              his wife, planter of 96 Dist. sold to SAMUEL EAKINS (AKINS)
blacksmith, for 600 pds current money 250 acres and 89 acres which
HAMILTON MURDOCK bought from THOMAS CLARK. Both tracts located on Little
River, a branch of Saluda River. Bounded by lands of THOMAS EDGEHILL
and MATTIAS COOK. Orig. grant of 250 acres 6 Apr. 1778 and grant of
89 acres 13 Oct. 1772 to THOMAS CLARK. Wit: GEORGE GOGGINS, JAMES LITTLE
& JAMES JOHNSON. JOHN HUNTER, J.P.

Pp 153-156:   9 July 1775 - 2 Mar. 1786 ADAM GRENAKER, planter, sold
              to PATRICK CUNINGHAM, Esq. for 50 pds current money 50
acres lying in Craven Co. on north side of Reedy River. Bounded by
lands of HANS HENDRICK and JOHN FOSTER. Orig. granted by patent 4 May
1775 to ADAM GRENAKER. Wit: JOHN BROWN, JANE EDWARDS.

Pp 157-160:   29 Jan. 1785 - 3 Mar. 1786 PATRICK CUNINGHAM and ANN,
              his wife, sold to GEORGE ANDERSON for 20 pds sterling
50 acres lying in Craven Co. on the north side of Reedy River. Orig.
granted 4 May 1775 to ADAM GRENAKER by patent. Wit: JONATHAN JOHNSON,
JOSHUA SAXON.

Pp 161-166:   10 Nov. 1785 - 2 Mar. 1786 DAVID DICKSON, planter of Tyger
              River Settlement, sold to PATRICK CUNINGHAM of 96 Dist.
for 530 pds sterling of Grate Britian 150 acres lying on southside
of Reedy River, thence to W on Reedy River E to PATRICK CUNINGHAM's
N to JOHN WILLARD's and NE to HANS HENDRICK. Formerly the property
of HUGH BROWN, which tracts were sold, in fee simple, and conveyed
by JOHN BERWICK, THOMAS WARING, SR. and JOHN EWING CALHOUN, Commissioners of Forfeited Estates to DAVID DICKSON 8 July 1783. Wit: ISAAC MITCH-
ELL, JOHN ELMORE, ROBERT BROWN & SARAH CUNINGHAM.

Pp 167-170:   14 July 1784 - 23 Mar. 1786 WILLIAM CALDWELL, planter
              of 96 Dist., sold to ROGER MURPHEY of same dist. for 200
pds current money 300 acres located on a branch called Long Lick Creek,
waters of Saluda River. Orig. granted 31 Aug. 1774 to WM. CALDWELL,
bounded at the time of orig. survey by lands of ROBERT WOODS, ROBERT
GILL, EBENEZER STARNES, & PATRICK CUNINGHAM. Wit: SAMUEL SCOTT, JOHN
RICHEY, ROBERT RICHEY.

Pp 171-174:   20 Dec. 1773 - 23 Mar. 1786 BENJAMIN POWEL and MARTHA,
              his wife, planter of 96 Dist. sold to THOMAS DENDY, planter
of same, for 150 pds current money 250 acres located in Berkely Co.
on North's Creek of Little River, waters of Saluda River. Bounded by
lands of WILLIAM DENDY, JAMES HENDERSON & ROBERT SIMS. Orig. grant,
annexed to plat, to sd BENJAMIN POWEL. Wit: WILLIAM DENDY, JAMES HENDER-
SON, ROBERT SIMS.

Pp 175-176:   14 Feb. 1786 - 23 Mar. 1786 NATHANIEL NORWOOD of Camden
              Dist., SC, sold to WILLIAM HALL of Laurens Co. for 35
pds current money of Virginia 100 acres lying on a branch of North's
Creek bounded by lands of THOMAS GAFFORD, JOHN OWINS, deceased, and
GEORGE ANDERSON, Esq. being part of 500 acre tract orig. granted 11

Cont'd:
Feb. 1773 to GEORGE NORWOOD, dec'd. Wit: THOMAS ELLIOT, THOMAS ELLIOT, JR., WILLIAM DARGAN.

Pp 177-180: 21 Nov. 1785 - 24 Mar. 1786 MICHAEL WALDROUP of Spartan-
             burg Co., SC sold to JOHN FARROW, of same, for 40 pds
sterling, 150 acres being part of 300 acre tract orig. granted to ROLLEY
BOWEN. Located on southside Enoree River in Laurens Co., S. C. Wit:
NICHOLAS BROWN, SPENCER BROWN.

Pp 181-184: 3 Aug. 1774 - 25 Mar. 1786 JOHN BROTHERTON and ESTHER,
             his wife, of Berkely Co., Province of S. C., sold to JAMES
CRAGE, of same, for 250 pds lawful money 139 acres lying on a spring
branch of Duncan's Creek in Berkely County, bounded by lands of SAMUEL
AVERY and WILLIAM EWING. Being part of 199 1/2 acres orig. granted,
10 Aug. 1766 to JOHN BROTHERTON sixty acres of which to be reserved
out of sd tract by virtue of bargain bet. JOHN BROTHERTON and JAMES
ADAIR, both of the county. JAMES ADAIR, cooper by trade (son of JOSEPH
ADAIR, SR.) Wit: WILLIAM EWING, THOMAS LOGAN, JOHN OWINS, JOHN CRAIGE.

Pp 185-188: 3 Aug. 1774 - 27 Mar. 1786 JOHN BROTHERTON and ESTHER,
             his wife, of Berkely Co., SC sold to JAMES ADAIR of the
same place, for 100 pds current money 60 acres on a spring branch of
Duncan's Creek. Bounded by lands of SAMUEL AVERY & WILLIAM EWING. Orig.
grant 12 Aug. 1766 to JOHN BROTHERTON. Wit: JOHN JONES, THOMAS EWING,
WILLIAM EWING.

Pp 189-192: 8 Dec. 1778 - 28 Mar. 1786 JOSEPH ADAIR, SR. of Duncan's
             Creek, 96 Dist., sold to BENJAMIN ADAIR of Duncan's Creek,
for 300 pds current money 250 acres lying on Duncan's Creek in Craven
Co. Bounded on N by lands of BENJAMIN KILGORE, on W by lands of JOHN
BROTHERTON and WILLIAM EWING, on E by lands of one MILLER and vacant
land. Orig. grant to JOSEPH ADAIR, SR. 27 Nov. 1770. Wit: JAMES ADAIR,
BENJAMIN KILGORE, WILLIAM ROSS. Signed: JOSEPH ADAIR and JOSEPH ADAIR
(this must have been both Jr. and Sr. JOSEPH ADAIR had sons BENJAMIN,
JAMES, SR., JOSEPH, JR.) (Note by comp. Mrs. Pulley)

Pp 193-196: 22 Oct. 1779 - 29 Mar. 1786 SAMUEL NEIGHBORS, planter
             of 96 Dist. sold to JOEL BURGESS, planter of Laurens Dist.
for 250 pds 75 acres lying on Beaverdam Creek, waters of Saluda River.
Orig. grant 1770 to ACQUILLA HALL and conveyed by him 7 Feb. 1774 to
CHARLES PARROT and from PARROT to SAMUEL NEIGHBORS. By lands of JAMES
RYAN, MAC NEESE GOODE, JOHN BOX & ACQUILLA HALL. Wit: RATCLIFF JOEL,
JOEL HARVEY, CHARLES HARVEY.

Pp 197-200: 13 Mar. 1786 - 29 Mar. 1786 LEWIS SAXON of Laurens Co.
             sold to JOEL BURGESS of Laurens Co. for 43 pds 11 shill-
ings and one penny 150 acres on South Fork of Rayburn's Creek. Bounded
by lands of ALEXANDER MAZZICK, THOMAS CAHOON, JOHN MC CLANNAHAN, MOSES
KIRKLAND, dec'd. Orig. grant to LEWIS SAXON 23 Jan. 1785. In open Court.

Pp 201-205: 12 Mar. 1786 - 30 Mar. 1786 CHARLES SIMMONS and ELIZABETH
             his wife, planter of Laurens Dist. sold to SAMUEL BOLING
of 96 Dist., planter, for 60 pds 168 acres lying on Reedy River, a
branch of Saluda River. By lands of GEORGE MARTIN, JOHN MILLING. Orig.
grant to CHARLES SIMMONS. In open Court, LEWIS SAXON, C.C.
(Note from Mrs. Pulley, comp., my ancestor Capt. CHARLES SIMMONS married
ELIZABETH TWEEDY.)

Page 206:   18 Jan. 1786 - 31 Mar. 1786 WILLIAM STUART and ALSE, his
             wife, adm. of JOSEPH HAYS, dec'd. of Newberry Co. sold
to SAMUEL AKIN for 70 pds "one negro man named Tunis". Wit: JOHN RAINEY,
WILLIAM RAINEY.

Page 207:   4 Mar. 1786 - 31 Mar. 1786 HESTER WILLIAMS swore bef.
             JOSEPH DOWNS, J.P. in presence of JOHN GOODWIN and saith
"her husband, JAMES WILLIAMS, in March 1782, being on his deathbed
devised that his son-in-law ROBERT BOX should inherit the land whereon
sd JAMES WILLIAMS liveth". HESTER WILLIAMS also swore that her first
born son, GEORGE WILLIAMS, was born bef. she married JAMES WILLIAMS.

Cont'd:
Wit: JOSEPH DOWNS, J.P., JOHN GOODWIN.

Page 208:   16 Mar. 1786 - 31 Mar. 1786 DANIEL OZBURN swore bef. WIL-
LIAM MITCHUSON, J.P. that he saw DAVID CRADDOCK sign,
seal and deliver unto WILLIAM DREW a lease and release for 150 acres
adj. upper end of DREW's old survey, which lease and release, with
plat and grant for same, were taken out of deponent's house during
his absence in latter part of 1780 or beginning of 1781. Wit: WILLIAM
MITCHUSON, J.P.

Pp 208-212:   6 Nov. 1784 - 1 Apr. 1786 JOHN RIPLEY and ELIZABETH, his
wife, of 96 Dist., sold to JAMES SULLIVANT, planter of
same place, for 175 pds Virginia money 250 acres lying on Little River,
waters of Saluda River, in Craven Co. Orig. grant to JACOB SCHUMPER
and conveyed to JAMES RYAN 11 Dec. 1771 and from RYAN to JOHN RIPLEY.
Wit: NEHEMIAH FRANKS, SAMUEL WHARTON, ANDREW RODGERS, JR.

Pp 213-217:   13 Sept. 1785 - 3 Apr. 1786 LEWIS DUVAL and TERISSA ,
his wife, to JOHN CRUMPTON for 400 pds old currency 200
acres lying on Duncan's Creek, waters of Enoree River. Orig. grant
to LEWIS DUVAL 13 July 1770 and rec. in Auditor's Office Memorial Bk
K No. 10 page 193, 28 Aug. 1770. Wit: THOMAS WORD, JOHN WORD, JOHN
POWER.

Pp 217-221:   1 Dec. 1785 - 4 Apr. 1786 JAMES KILGORE of Laurens Co.,
Gentleman, sold to JOHN MC ELROY of same place, for 100
pds sterling 500 acres lying on southside of Enoree River from JAMES
WALDROUP's line to Widow HANNAH"s line, thence to JAMES OLIPHANT's
to Beaverdam Creek, thence down the creek to a small branch called
Widow DUNLAP's Spring Branch, thence to orig. line. Granted 21 Jan.
1785 to KILGORE. Mentioned ROBERT HANNAH's line. Wit: BENJAMIN KILGORE,
SAMUEL COBB, HUMPHREY COBB.

Pp 222-224:   27 Feb. 1786 - 5 Apr. 1786 VARDRY MC BEE of Spartanburg
Co. sold to BENJAMIN KILGORE of Laurens Co. for 10 pds
sterling 400 acres on Enoree River at mouth of Gilder's Creek. Orig.
grant to MC BEE by patent rec. in Sec. State Office Grant Bk FFFF page
76. Former survey by warrant for MATIN MATIN (MARTIN MARTIN?) 24 Oct.
1774. Wit: BENJAMIN RAINEY, BENJAMIN KEVEL, LEWIS EAKIN.

Pp 224-227:   6 Jan. 1786 - 6 Apr. 1786 BENJAMIN RAINEY, planter of
Laurens Co. sold to BENJAMIN KILGORE, planter of Laurens
Co. for 60 pds sterling 100 acres lying on Gilder's Creek, a branch
of Enoree River. Being part of 600 acre tract granted 15 Oct. 1784
to a certain WILLIAM MARCHBANK. Bounded by lands of JOHN MARTIN. Wit:
JOHN BROWN, WILLIAM LITTLE, SARAH RAINEY.

Pp 228-231:   12 Dec. 1785 - 7 Apr. 1786 BENJAMIN RAINEY sold to BENJAMIN
KILGORE 100 acres lying on Gilder's Creek waters of Enoree
River. Surveyed for JOHN MARTIN and part of a tract granted to JOHN
CORMIKLE 8 Mar. 1768 and conveyed to BENJAMIN RAINEY 8 Jan. 1778. Wit:
JOHN BROWN, WILLIAM LITTLE, SARAY RAINEY.

Pp 232-236:   12 June 1786 - 3 July 1786 JOHN RODGERS, Esq. and MARGARET
his wife, of Laurens Co., sold to LEWIS SAXON for 10 pds
17 shillings 1 sixpence sterling 10 acres located near the courthouse
of the Co. of Laurens. Being part of 600 acres granted by patent to
JOHN RODGERS on 31 Aug. 1774. In open Court bef. JOHN HUNTER, J.P.
and LEWIS SAXON, C.C.

Pp 237-241:   10 June 1785 - 3 July 1786 DAVID ANDERSON of Spartanburg
Co., planter, sold to CHARLES SIMMONS, planter of Laurens
Co., for 10 pds sterling 150 acres lying on both sides of Little River
and bounded on SE by lands laid out for WILLIAM ANDERSON. Orig. granted
19 Oct. 1770 by patent to DAVID ANDERSON and rec. in Sec. State Grant
Bk FFF page 230. Wit: LEWIS DUVAL, ABRAHAM ANDREWS, J. C. RICE, WILLIAM
MITCHISON.

Pp 242-246:   2 Mar. 1786 - 4 July 1786 NATHANIEL HENDERSON of Enoree

Cont'd:
River Settlement sold to THOMAS TODD of Spartanburg Co.
for 60 pds English crown pieces 432 acres on south side of Enoree River.
Bounded by lands of WILLIAM MARCHBANKS, JOHN HAKKUMS. Orig. granted
to NATHANIEL HENDERSON. Wit: STEPHEN WILSON, WILLIAM HUNT, JAMES CLAYTON

Pp 246-250: 9 Dec. 1772 - 7 July 1786 NATHAN HAMPTON and SARAH, his
wife, of Granville Co. sold to JOSEPH PINSON of Berkely
Co. for 100 pds 200 acres lying on waters of Reedy River, bounded N
on land of LEWIS BANTON, S on land of JOSEPH PINSON, SE by WILLIAM
HENDERSON and E by lands of JOHN CALDWELL and vacant land. Wit: JOHN
HUGHES, ROBERT MIDDLETON, JOSEPH DOOLITTLE.

Pp 251-255: 5 June 1786 - 5 July 1786 JOSEPH PINSON and MARY his wife
lease to STEPHEN WOOD of Laurens Dist. for 28 pds 200
acres on Reedy River by lands of LEWIS BANTON, JOSEPH PINSON, WILLIAM
ANDERSON & CALDWELL land. Orig. grant to NATHAN HAMPTON (same land
as above). Wit: JONATHAN DOWNS, GEORGE ANDERSON, JOSEPH DOWNS.

Pp 256-264: 30 May 1786 - 5 July 1786 WILLIAM MARTIN, planter, Laurens
Co. sold to ALEXANDER HAMILTON for 40 pds 100 acres on
Beaverdam or Mill Creek, waters of Little River, a small fork of Saludy
River. (Note from comp. Mrs. Pulley...there are three Beaverdam Creeks
in Laurens Co...this is the one near Horse Creek toward present day
Ware Shoals). Granted 2 Mar. 1786 to WM. MARTIN. Wit: JOHN RODGERS,
JESSE WEEKS, EDMUND LEARWOOD.

Page 265: 20 Dec. 1785 - 6 July 1786 WILLIAM FREEMAN and MARY his
wife, of 96 Dist. sold to JAMES LITTLE of same place,
for 100 pds old currency 100 acres "where sd JAMES LITTLE now liveth"
on a small branch of Little River. Being part of tract orig. granted
6 Feb. 1773 to WILLIAM FREEMAN. Wit: JOHN HUNTER, RICHARD GOLDING,
ROBERT FREEMAN.

Pp 265-269: 6 July 1786 - 13 June 1786 ROBERT GOODWIN of Laurens Co.
sold to DAVID MC DAVID, planter of Greenville Co. of SC
100 acres. Being part of 250 acre tract orig. granted 6 Feb. 1773 to
WILLIAM FREEMAN and sold by Commissioners of Forfeited Estates to WIL-
LIAM COVINGTON who transferred to ROBERT GOODWIN. Whereas in persuance
of an act of disposing certain estates and banishing certain persons
therein mentioned, the same commissioners did give and grant, by authority invested in them by Legislative Body of sd State, did put up at
Public Auction, after due notice, and on 8 June 1783, part of the real
estate mentioned and WM. COVINGTON was highest bidder. Sworn to in
open Court bef. LEWIS SAXON, C.C.

Pp 270-275: 6 July 1786 - 22 July 1786 LITTLE BERRY HARVEY of Richmond Co., Ga. sold to ROBERT GOODWIN, planter of Laurens
Co., for 100 pds lawful money 100 acres lying on Durbin's Creek, waters
of Enoree River. It being the forfeited estates of WILLIAM GUST (GIST?)
and bought by WILLIAM COVINGTON, then sold by him to LITTLE BERRY HARVEY.
Wit: JOSEPH DOWNS, JOHN GOODWIN, JANE DOWNS.

Pp 276-280: 25 Jan. 1786 - 7 July 1786 JOHN CRADDOCK, planter, Laurens
Co. sold to RICHARD HICKS, planter of Laurens Co. for
40 pds 100 acres lying on southside of Little River bounded by lands
of JAMES HARVEY and JAMES RYAN. Orig. laid out to DAVID CRADDOCK by
patent 7 Jan. 1773. Wit: WILLIAM MARTIN, MARTIN MARTIN, JR., JOHN MARTIN,
JR.

Page 285: 18 Feb. 1786 - 10 July 1786 JAMES TINKER of New York,
Master of the Sloop "Maria", delivered a negro wench named
Hannah, about 16 years old, to LEWIS SAXON from HANE & BERK, Merchants
of Charleston. Wit: JOHN HUNTER, SILVANUS WALKER.

Pp 286-289: 17 Feb. 1786 - 10 July 1786. JOHN CRADDOCK of Orangeburg
Dist., SC sold to SARAH CRADDOCK of 96 Dist. for 5 pds
200 acres lying on Little River. Bounded by lands of JAMES HARVEY,
JAMES RYAN, CORNELIUS CARGIL, MACKNEESE GOODE. Orig. grant 17 Jan.

Cont'd:
1773 to DAVID CRADDOCK, the father of JOHN CRADDOCK, in Berkely Co. now 96 Dist. Wit: JOHN OSBORN, TANDY WALKER, THOMAS CARGIL.

Pp 290-293: 28 Nov. 1786 - 11 July 1786 ALEXANDER MENARY of 96 Dist. now called Oxford, SC sold to MARGARET RICHEY, widow of JOHN RICHEY, dec'd., for 17 pds sterling 125 acres on Duncan Creek, a branch called Lams Reed Ford, bet. Broad and Saluda. Being half a tract JOHN WILLIAMS sold 31 July 1785 to ALEXANDER MENARY. Orig. grant to JOHN WILLIAMS 31 Aug. 1774. Bounded by lands of JAMES YOUNG, ROWLAND MC CURLEY. Wit: ANDREW RODGERS, CISY CURRANCE.

Pp 294-297: 6 Dec. 1774 - 12 July 1786 JAMES STEEN and his wife, ELE-NOR, of Berkely Co. sold to JOHN LINDSAY, son of ABRAHAM LINDSAY of Enoree River Settlement, for 300 pds current money 300 acres on southside of Enoree River by lands of WILLIAM CANNON and vacant land. Orig. grant 19 Aug. 1768 and rec. in Sec. State Office Grant Bk CCC page 365 and in Auditor's Book A-N5 page 145 on 14 Oct. 1768 to JAMES STEEN. Wit: PETER BROOKS, WILLIAM MOORE, JOHN STEEN.

Pp 298-299: 14 Oct. 1785 - 13 July 1786 BENJAMIN BROWN, legal heir to BARLETT BROWN, dec'd. of Berk Co., Ga., sold to ABRAHAM GRAY of Laurens Co., for 60 pds sterling 40 acres lying on southside Enoree River, formerly called King's River. Being part of a 600 acre tract orig. granted to BARTLETT BROWN by Hon. Mathew Rowan, Gov. of N. C., bearing date 11 May 1753 and rec. in Grant Bk. (N.R.) 11 May 1753. Bounded on W by lands of JOHN LINDSAY who bought from sd BROWN and on E by lands of ANDREW CUNINGHAM, also part of sd tract bought from BROWN. Wit: ANDREW CUNINGHAM, JOHN LINDSAY, HENRY HAMILTON.

Pp 300-301: 14 Oct. 1785 - 13 July 1786 BENJAMIN BROWN sold to JOHN LINDSAY for 20 pds sterling 40 acres of same grant as above. Wit: ANDREW CUNINGHAM, ABRAHAM GRAY, HENRY HAMILTON.

Pp 302-304: 10 Aug. 1785 - 14 July 1786 BENJAMIN RAINEY, planter of 96 Dist., sold to NICHOLAS WHITE of same place, for 80 pds sterling 200 acres lying on both sides of Durbin Creek by lands of JOHN YORK and lands laid out for JOHN JONES. Wit: SAMUEL P. JONES, DANIEL WRIGHT.

Pp 304-308: 8 Sept. 1784 - 14 July 1786 NATHANIEL NORWOOD of N. C., laborour, sold to THOMAS GAFFORD, planter of 96 Dist., for 135 pds Virginia money 135 acres lying on North Creek and bounded by lands of GEORGE ANDERSON, JAMES BURNSIDES, JOHN OWINGS, dec'd., JOSHUA ROBERTS & CHRISTOPHER HARDY, dec'd. 100 acres of which was tract orig. granted to MARGARET WISEMAN on 12 Aug. 1774 and 35 acres being part of tract of GEORGE NORWOOD's headrights. Wit: ROBERT YOUNG, WILLIAM BAILEY, MARY ANDERSON.

Pp 308-311: 21 Dec. 1784 - 14 July 1786 MARY HILLAN and JOHN HILLEN, her son and heir to NATHANIEL HILLEN of 96 Dist., sold to JAMES ADAIR of 96 Dist., sadler, for 18 pds sterling 110 acres formerly occupied by ELIJAH BENTON. Being part of 250 acre tract orig. granted 8 July 1774 to NATHANIEL HILLEN and rec. in Sec. State Office Grant Bk M No. 13 page 194. Lying on southside of Enoree River in Craven County. Wit: JOHN HEAD, JOHN CANNON, JOHN CAMPBELL, GEORGE ROSS.

Pp 312-315: 24 Jan. 1785 - 15 July 1786 MARY HILLEN and JOHN HILLEN, her son and heir to NATHANIEL HILLEN, dec'd. of 96 Dist., sold to JOHN CAMPBELL for 20 pds sterling 140 acres being part of 250 acre tract orig. granted to NATHANIEL HILLEN. Bounded by tract sold to JAMES ADAIR and lands of ZACHARIAH THOMAS. Wit: JAMES ADAIR, JOHN HEAD, JOHN CANNON, GEORGE ROSS.

Page 315: 15 July 1786 To determine a dispute bet. CHARITY PARKER, Executrix, and ANDREW RODGERS, JR., of one part and JAMES ABERCROMBIE of the other part, viz, "it is our opinion and award that the Parties De Quit all accounts on even footing - the sd PARKER and RODGERS giving the sd ABERCROMBIE a bond of Indemity against a certain

199

Cont'd:
bond given to Dr. JOHN PARKER for 200 pds old money." Signed: JOHN
RICHEY, MARMADUKE PINSON, JONATHAN DOWNS.

Page 316:   6 Nov. 1785 - 17 July 1786 ISABELLA ROBINSON binds her
             daughter, JENNET WHITE who was born 3 Dec. 1781, to JENNET
TAYLOR, wife of WILLIAM TAYLOR. The sd JENNET WHITE to be brought up
in a decent Christian manner, to be taught the art of spinning and
sewing and to read the Holy Scriptures. She should be faithful to serve
her mistress until she attain the age of 18 years, her commands gladly
obey, her secrets keep, she shall do no damage to her sd mistress nor
see it done by others without letting her know thereof. She shall not
waste her goods nor lend them unlawfully to others. She shall not absent herself day nor night without leave and she shall be given sufficient meat, drink, apparel, washing and lodging. Wit: DAVID ROSS, ANDREW
SPEAR.

Page 317:   10 Jan. 1785 - 17 July 1786 RICHARD DAVIS, son of FREDER-
             ICK DAVIS of 96 Dist., hath of his own free will and con-
sent to his father, bound himself to JAMES MILWEE, farmer of 96 Dist.
The sd RICHARD will gladly obey, faithfully serve - secrets keep. He
shall not embezel nor waste. His master shall teach him, instruct him
and furnish him meat, drink, washing, lodging and wearing apparel,
both linen and woolen. At expiration of 8 years service, he will be
given 2 full suits of cloathes and a horse and one complete year of
schooling. Wit: REUBEN PYLES, J.P., AYRES GOUDY.

Page 318:   10 Mar. 1785 - 17 July 1786 URIAH DAVIS, son of FREDERICK
             DAVIS of 96 Dist., bound himself to JAMES MILWEE, farmer
of 96 Dist. To serve for 8 years under same terms as above. Wit: :REUBEN
PYLES, J.P., ISAAC WILLIAMS.

Page 319:   24 Mar. 1785 - 25 Sept. 1786 Affidavit sworn by WILLIAM
             BARKSDALE. "Previous to my marriage with ANN ADAMS, widow
of CHARLES ADAMS, dec'd., the sd ANN possessed a negro wench named
Sary who later birthed two children, named Jesse and Bunch and whereas
the sd ANN and CHARLES ADAMS had two children, namely ELIZABETH ADAMS
and SILVANUS ADAMS, and whereas I desire to give and secure the sd
Jesse and Bunch unto ELIZABETH ADAMS, dau. of CHAS. ADAMS, dec'd. and
ANN BARKSDALE, my present wife, now know all men that I, WILLIAM BARKS-
DALE of Laurens Co., 96 Dist. do give the sd ELIZABETH ADAMS the two
negro boys named Jesse and Bunch. Wit: THOMAS JONES, JOHN WILLIAMS.

Page 320:   26 Sept. 1786 Affidavit sworn by WM. BARKSDALE that he
             gives to SILVANUS ADAMS, son of CHARLES ADAMS, dec'd.
and ANN BARKSDALE, present wife of WM. BARKSDALE, the negro wench Sary
(see above). Wit: THOMAS JONES, JOHN WILLIAMS.

Pp 321-323: 17 May 1785 - 26 Sept. 1786 WILLIAM HUGGINS, Joint Executor
             with his wife, MARY, Executrix of estate of BENJAMIN DUR-
BOROW, dec'd., sold to WILLIAM SALMON for 107 pds 350 acres lying on
Saluda River. Bounded by lands of ROBERT CUNINGHAM. 150 acres being
part of a tract granted 9 Sept. 1774 to THOMAS YATES, dec'd. 200 acres
being part of a 400 acre tract conveyed 29 Nov. 1769 to THOMAS YATES,
dec'd., by JOHN HAND, dec'd. Wit: JOHN SILLS, SR., JOHN SILLS, JR.,
R. WATTS, GEORGE WATTS, JOHN PERRY.

Pp 323-324: 1 Nov. 1785 - 26 Sept. 1786 Affidavit by WILLIAM CALDWELL
             who swore he and WILLIAM ANDERSON saw WILLIAM THOMAS CALD-
WELL, dec'd., draw the lease and release bet. HANS HENDRICK and ANGUS
CAMPBELL for a tract whereon ANGUS CAMPBELL now lives on Mudlick Creek.

Pp 324-326: 6 Sept. 1786 - 26 Sept. 1786 JOHN PHENDLY (FINLEY), son
             and heir to JOHN PHENDLY, dec'd., sold to PAUL PHENDLY
for 75 pds sterling 150 acres lying on Cain Creek, a branch of Saluda
...all sides vacant. Wit: JOHN MARTIN, SHADRACH MARTIN.

Pp 326-330: 1 Sept. 1786 - 27 Sept. 1786 WILLIAM O'NEAL, planter of
             Newberry Co. and his wife, MARY, sold to JOSEPH ARMSTRONG,

Cont'd:
blacksmith of Laurens Co., for 200 pds sterling 150 acres lying on
Mudlick Creek. Orig. granted 4 Dec. 1771 to ANN HAGAN, the mother of
WILLIAM O'NEAL, and on 1 May 1772 to WILLIAM O'NEAL. By lands of RICHARD
NORTH (for whom North's Creek was named..note from comp.), HENRY COATES,
JOHN RAY & ANTHONY GRIFFIN. Wit: BENJAMIN BUTLER, ELISHA FORD, ROBERT
DUNLAP.

Pp 335-340: 2 Sept. 1786 - 28 Sept. 1786 ABIJAH O'NEAL of Newberry
             Co. and his wife, ANNE, sold to JOSEPH ARMSTRONG, black-
smith of Laurens Co., 75 acres lying on Mudlick Creek. Orig. granted
to ABIJAH O'NEAL 15 Dec. 1784 by lands of RICHARD GRIFFIN, JOHN CALD-
WELL, & JAMES BURNSIDES. Wit: WILLIAM O'NEAL, BENJAMIN BUTLER, ROBERT
DUNLAP.

Page 340:   17 Aug. 1786 - 22 Sept. 1786 JOHN GOODWIN to ELIZABETH
             JONES 70 acres for 5 shillings sterling "love and indebt-
ness". Granted 1 Aug. 1786 to GOODWIN. Wit: ROBERT BOX, SAMUEL NEIGHBORS
& ROBERT BOX, JR.

Pp 341-345: 9 July 1785 - 28 Sept. 1786 GABRIEL SMITHERS, planter
             and MARY, his wife, sold to SAMUEL HARRIS, bricklayer
of Newberry Co. for 100 pds sterling 350 acres on Mudlick Creek. By
lands of MARY HARRIS, WILLIAM CALDWELL & NATHANIEL FOCHEE. 150 acres
being orig. grant to OLIVER TOWLES 12 Apr. 1771 and conveyed by TOWLES
to GEORGE NEELY. 200 acres granted to JOHN ROBERTSON 15 May 1771 and
conveyed 1772 by ROBERTSON to GEORGE NEELY. Wit: WILLIAM MOORE, LITTLE
BERRY HARRIS, ELISHA WILLIS.

Pp 346-348: 29 Mar. 1786 - 28 Sept. 1786 EBENEZER STARNES, planter
             of Laurens Co., sold to AARON STARNES, laborer of same
place, 300 acres lying on Long Lick Creek. Orig. granted to STARNES
7 May 1772 and bounded then by lands of LEWIS BANTON and vacant land.
Rec. in Sec. State Bk KKK (no page given). Wit: THOMAS SUCREY(?), ROGER
MURPHEY, WILLIAM LOWE.

Pp 348-352: 14 May 1785 - 29 Sept. 1786 THOMAS LINDLEY, the eldest
             son of JAMES LINDLEY of Raborn Creek Settlement and his
wife, ELIZABETH, sold to MARMADUKE PINSON for 20 shillings 100 acres
lying in Craven Co., now called 96 Dist., on a small branch of Reighburn's Creek (note from comp. - I find several spellings for Reyburn,
Raybourne, Reighburn and Rabun Creek) and bounded on SW by lands of
GEORGE HOLLINGSWORTH, on SE by lands of JOHN WILLIAMS, W by JAMES LIND-
LEY and all other sides vacant. Orig. grant to CHARLES QUAIL bearing
date 15 July 1768 and conveyed by him to RALPH HUMPHREYS who conveyed
to JAMES LINDLEY, father of THOMAS LINDLEY 12 Dec. 1768. Wit: RICHARD
PUGH, JOHN MITCHELL, JOSEPH PINSON.

Pp 352-356: 10 June 1786 - 29 Sept. 1786 WILLIAM PRICE, planter of
             96 Dist. sold to WILLIAM TAYLOR, planter, for 50 pds ster-
ling 100 acres lying on Todd's Creek, waters of Little River, by lands
of WILLIAM TWEEDY, ROBERT TAYLOR, ELEANOR NELSON and vacant land. Wit:
HUGH O'NEAL, DANIEL MC GIN, WILLIAM MC DONALD.

Pp 356-358: 18 Mar. 1786 - 29 Sept. 1786 WILLIAM CALDWELL, planter
             of Newberry Co., sold to JANE THOMSON of Laurens Co.,
200 acres lying on Little River. Orig. grant 21 Jan. 1785 to WM. CALD-
WELL. By lands of HUGH O'NEAL, JOHN CHESTNUT, HENRY O'NEAL, HASTINGS
DIAL & THOMAS EDGEHILL. Wit: HUGH O'NEL, DANIEL MEGIN, WILLIAM MC DANIEL.

Pp 359-360: 8 Aug. 1786 - 30 Sept. 1786 JOSHUA OWENS, planter of Laur-
             ens Co. sold to DANIEL MARTIN, planter for 5 pds sterling
100 acres lying on North Fork of Durbins Creek bounded by lands of
JAMES BURCHFIELD & ISAAC BARTON. Being part of 400 acre tract orig.
granted 3 Apr. 1788 to JOSHUA OWENS. Wit: JAMES BURCHFIELD, BENJAMIN
KILLGORE, ISAAC BARTON.

Pp 361-363: 7 June 1786 - 30 Sept. 1786 JOSHUA OWENS, planter of Laur-
             ens Co. sold to JAMES BURCHFIELD, planter of same, for

Cont'd:
5 pds sterling 100 acres lying on North Fork of Durbins Creek. Being part of 400 acre tract orig. granted to JOSHUA OWENS 3 Apr. 1788. Wit: BENJAMIN KILLGORE, ISAAC BARTON, DANIEL MARTIN.

Pp 364-366: 5 June 1786 - 30 Sept. 1786 JOSHUA OWENS sold to ISAAC BARTON for 10 pds sterling 200 acres lying on North Fork of Durbins Creek. Being part of 400 acres orig. granted to JOSHUA OWENS. Wit: BENJ. KILLGORE, JAMES BURCHFIELD, DANL. MARTIN.

Pp 366-369: 12 Oct. 1784 - 1 Oct. 1786 JOSEPH KELLET, planter of 96 Dist. sold to HARRIS GILLIAM, planter of same, for 100 pds current money 200 acres lying in Craven Co. on Mudlick Creek by lands of JOHN DONAHUE, JAMES BURGESS, JOSEPH BABB, ALLEN BROWN. Orig. granted 23 Jan. 1773 to JAMES BURGESS and conveyed by him to ROBERT SIMS, then to JAMES HALL 1774 and from HALL to JOSEPH KELLETT 5 Nov. 1776. Wit: JOHN RICHEY, ESTHER KELLETT, CLOUGH HARRIS.

Pp 370-378: 12 Mar. 1786 - 2 Oct. 1786 CHARLES ALLEN, planter of Laurens Co. and SUSAN, his wife, sold to ROBERT MC NEESE, planter of same, for 300 pds 107 acres with dwelling house, lying on Little River, waters of Saluda River, it being part of 200 acre grant to CHAS. ALLEN 31 Aug. 1774. Bounded by lands of CHAS. ALLEN & NEHEMIAH FRANKS. Rec. in Sec. State Grant Bk M No. 13, page 314 with plat annexed. Sworn to in open Court bef. LEWIS SAXON, C.C. (Note from comp.- this grant was made to CHAS. ALLEN, SR. who married LUCY BACON of Va. and inherited by the above CHAS. ALLEN, JR. who married SUSAN GARNER. CHAS. ALLEN, JR. was a Judge in Laurens.)

(Deed Book A material was contributed by Mrs. Charles B. Pulley)

END OF DEED BOOK A

DEED BOOK B

Deed Book A and B have been rebound and pages laminated. On the first two pages of Deed Book B are small fragments of writings but nothing complete enough to learn of grantor, grantee nor date. The first 22 pages are missing entirely and the first feed is not complete. Mrs. Laura M. Pulley)

Page ? No date. PATRICK CUNINGHAM and ANN, his wife, sold to JAMES SAXON and SAMUEL SAXON for 160 pds lawful money (no description of land).

Page ? 31 Mar. 1777 - 1 Jan. 1787 JOHN RODGERS of 96 Dist., planter, sold to WILLIAM DENDY, planter of same, for 163 pds current money 100 acres lying on northside of Little River of the Saluda on a branch called North's Creek. Orig. granted to THOMAS NORTH 31 Nov. 1757 and rec. in Sec. of State Grant Bk SS page 84 and bounded on all sides on vacant land at time of orig. grant. Wit: A. (ANDREW) RODGERS, THOMAS DENDY, CORNELIUS CARGIL.

Pp 23-27: 2 July 1786 - 2 Jan. 1787 JONATHON REED and his wife, JANE, of Laurens Co., 96 Dist., planter, sold to JAMES STRAIN of same, planter, for 20 pds sterling 98 acres lying on Cain Creek in Laurens Co., Dist. of 96, bounded on N by land of JOHN CARTER, S by sd JONATHON REED and all other sides vacant. It being part of 128 acres orig. granted to sd REED by Gov. Wm. Moultrie 6 Feb. 1786. Wit: ROBERT CARTER, WILLIAM BROWN.

Pp 27-29: 3 Nov. 1784 - 2 Jan. 1787 TOBIAS MEYERS of Colleton Co., planter, and ANN, his wife, sold to WILLIAM DENDY, planter for 200 pds current money 150 acres located on a branch of Saluda River called Little River. Wit: CHARLES SULLIVANT, JOHN DUNKLIN, HULET SULLIVANT. JONATHON DOWNS, J.P.

Pp 29-33: 12 Nov. 1786 - 3 Jan. 1787 ROBERT ROSS of 96 Dist. and MARGARET, his wife, sold to HUGH MC VAY of same, for 60

Cont'd:
pds sterling 100 acres lying in Laurens Co. on waters of Little River.
Bounded on E by lands of RICHARD ROBISON, N by NEHEMIAH FRANKS, S by
CHARLES ALLEN, ...(blank)............and all other sides vacant.
Conveyed by JAMES BIRD to RICHARD ROBISON, SR. 1775 and from RICHARD
ROBISON, JR. the proper heir of R. ROBISON, dec'd. to sd ROBT. ROSS
and now from ROSS and wife MARGARET to MC VAY. Orig. grant to JAMES
BAIRD 7 May 1774 rec. in Sec. State Grant Bk MM 12, page 559 dated
14 Sept. 1774. Wit: JOHN RODGERS, JOHN MARTIN.

Pp 33-35:   9 July 1786 - 3 Jan. 1787 CHARLES FINDLEY of Laurens Co.,
             sold to BENJAMIN RAINEY of same, for 50 pds st erling
440 acres located on Dirbin Creek, waters of Enoree River, bounded
by lands of WILLIAM YOUNG, WILLIAM NETHERWELL, JOHN OWINS, JOHN WILLIAMS
& JOSIAH BARTON. Orig. grant of 440 acres to CHARLES FINDLEY 5 June
1786 and rec. in Sec. State Office Grant Bk LLLL page 105 with plat
annexed. Wit: WILLIAM JACKSON, ELIJAH FINDLEY, SARAH RAINEY.

Pp 35-37:   5 Oct. 1786 - 3 Jan. 1787 ALEXANDER HARPER, planter of
             Laurens Dist. sold to BENJAMIN RAINEY, planter, for 10
shillings sterling 85 acres it being part of 640 acre tract orig. granted to sd ALEXANDER HARPER by patent bearing date of 15 Oct. 1784 and
rec. in Sec. State Grant Bk AAAA page 174. Bounded E by lands of THOMAS
SANDERS, S by lands of JOSEPH HOLCUM, N by lands of WILLIAM NETHERWELL.
Wit: WILLIAM JACKSON, SAMUEL COBB.

Pp 37-40:   7 Dec. 1785 - 4 Jan. 1787 BENJAMIN RAINEY of Laurens Co.
             sold to JOSEPH BARTON of same, for 20 pds sterling 220
acres located on the Northside of North Fork of Dirbin Creek being
part of orig. grant of 440 acres by patent to CHARLES FINDLEY 5 June
1786. Rec. in S. S. Office Grant Bk LLLL page 105. Wit: WM. JACKSON,
SAML. COBB.

Pp 40-42:   13 Dec. 1786 - 4 Jan. 1787 BENJAMIN RAINEY, planter, to
             WILLIAM JACKSON, schoolmaster, to teach a grammar school
for three years term, 150 acres being part of 440 acres orig. granted
to CHARLES FINDLEY being on a line bet. BENJAMIN RAINEY and JOHN WIL-
LIAMS until it meets the Great Road leading from BENJ. RAINEY's to
the Indian Line, then along a road until it meets JOSEPH BURTON's line.
Sworn to in open court. LEWIS SAXON, C.C.

Pp 42-44:   27 July 1786 - 5 Jan. 1787 BENJAMIN KEVIL, planter of
             Laurens Co., sold to THOMAS KEVIL, carpenter and mill-
wright of Laurens Co. for 10 pds sterling one half of 200 acres in
sd county orig. granted to ROBERT GOODWIN by Gov. Wm. Moultrie 3 Oct.
1785 rec. in Sec. State Office Grant Bk FFFF page 192 together with
350 acres more or less being part of tract granted BENJAMIN KEVIL containing 640 acres and rec. Sec. State Office Grant Bk FFFF page 118
with plat annexed. Located on Enoree River. Wit: MARTIN WILLIAMS, SAM-
UEL P. JONES.

Pp 44-46:   9 Dec. 1786 - 5 Jan. 1787 SAMUEL BISHOP of Laurens Co.
             and his wife, MARY, sold to JACOB DUCKETT of same for
50 pds sterling 50 acres lying on southside of Enoree River being orig.
granted to CHARLES KING bearing date 5 Nov. 1755 and conveyed by sd
KING and CHARITY his wife, to SAMUEL BISHOP 20 Nov. 1769. Wit: SAMUEL
BISHOP, (JR.), JOEL WHITTEN, JOHN ODELL. (Note from comp. - one SAMUEL
BISHOP died ca 1831 and his wife, VERLINDA (PRATHER) removed to Meri-
wether Co., Ga.)

Pp 46-48:   9 Dec. 1778 - 3 Jan. 1787 Major THOMAS GORDON of 96 Dist.
             and ELIZABETH, his wife, sold to THOMAS DUCKET of same,
for 200 pds S. C. current money 184 acres being part of 300 acres orig.
granted to WILLIAM RAGAN 20 Apr. 1763 and conveyed by sd RAGAN and
LUCY, his wife, to sd GORDON 22 Feb. 1775. Land lying on both sides
of Enoree River. Wit: JOHN ODEL, BENJAMIN GORDON, THOMAS BISHOP.

Pp 48-51:   14 Mar. 1774 - 6 Jan. 1787 SAMUEL BISHOP, planter, and
             wife, MARY of Berkley Co., sold to THOMAS DUCKET for 200

Cont'd:
pds current S. C. money 100 acres lying on southside of Enoree River
bounded by lands laid out to THOMAS FLEWELLING and laid out to ANDREW
OWINS and laid out to WILLIAM RAGAN. Orig. grant to SAMUEL BISHOP 19
Mar. 1773 and rec. in Sec. State Office Grant Bk OOOO page 172. Wit:
WILLIAM HENDRIX, NEELY (HILL), JOHN ODEL.

Pp 51-52:   7 Dec. 1786 - 7 Jan. 1787 ISAAC EDWARDS and JUDITH, his
                wife, of Union Co., of sd State (S.C.) to THOMAS DUCKETT
of Laurens Co. for 50 pds 50 acres lying on southside of Enoree River
orig. granted to sd EDWARDS 6 Feb. 1786. Wit: JACOB DUCKET, HENRY DAVIS,
MARTHA EDWARDS.

Pp 52-55:   21 May 1786 - 9 Jan. 1787 CLEMENT DEAL of Laurens Co.,
                planter, and his wife, JEAN, sold to WILLIAM WATSON, plan-
ter, for 100 pds sterling 150 acres on a spring branch of Mudlick Creek
(waters of Little River). Orig. granted to RICHARD NEILY. Wit: THOMAS
EDGEHILL, JR., ELIJAH WATSON.

Pp 55-57:   19 June 1786 - 9 Jan. 1787 ANDREW RODGERS, JR. of Laurens
                Co., planter, sold to NICHOLAS EVELEIGH of Edgefield Co.,
planter, for 380 pds sterling two tracts commonly known by the name
"Horse Shoe". One tract of 200 acres surveyed 3 May 1763 for JOHN &
JAMES ABERNATHY on northside of Saluda River rec. Sec. State Off. Grant
Bk BBB page 88 and Auditor's Bk H #8 page 240 the 11th Aug. 1767 and
one tract of 150 acres surveyed 4 May 1763 for MICHAEL HUNT lying on
northside Saluda River rec. in S. C. Off. Grant Bk BBB page 148 and
Auditor's Bk K #8 page 252 the 12th Aug. 1767. Wit: GEORGE ANDERSON,
DAVID WEBSTER, ABSOLUM BOBO.

Page 57-58:   11 Dec. 1786 - 10 Jan. 1787 PHILEMON HARVEY of Laurens
                Co. and SARAH, his wife, sold to ANDREW HODGES, SR., for
40 pds sterling 100 acres on Beard's Fork of Duncan's Creek bounded
by lands laid out to WILLIAM HANNA and WILLIAM TAYLOR but now the property of ANDREW ENDSLEY. Orig. granted 16 Sept. 1774 and rec. in S.
S. Grant Bk FFF page 132. Wit: AMBROSE HUDGINS, JR., SAMUEL FLEMING,
JOHN RODGERS.

Page 58:   13 Dec. 1786 - 10 Jan. 1787 THOMAS ELLIOT of Laurens Co.
                and LUCY, his wife, sold to DAVID BURNS, SR., for 75 pds
sterling 150 acres located on Simmon's Creek (waters of Little River)
being part of orig. grant of 300 acres to EDWARD OSBORN, dec'd., and
bounded by lands of WILLIAMSON's Big Survey of DAVID BURNS, JR.,(?)
___ TEAGUE, AMBROSE HUDGINS, JAMES HENDERSON. Wit: ALEXANDER MC DOWELL,
THOMAS WADSWORTH.

Page 59:   11 Dec. 1786 - 10 Jan. 1787 ELIZABETH COKER, daughter
                and heir of JOSEPH COKER, dec'd. and his wife, NELLY COKER,
dec'd., sold to JOHN NORRIS and JOHN BURNS for 100 pds sterling, 200
acres lying on North's Creek bounded by lands of ROBERT HALL, CHARLES
DENDY, dec'd., and WILLIAMSON land orig. granted to MENOAH TINDSLEY, deceased, and by him to JOSEPH COKER, deceased. Wit: SAMUEL SAXON, SIL-
VAANUS WALKER, JOHN A. CARGIL.

Pp 59-62:   11 Sept. 1786 - 12 Jan. 1787 LEWIS BANTON of Laurens Co.,
                and JEDIDA his wife, sold to WILLIAM GOODMAN for 47 pds
sterling 200 acres located on Long Lick Creek, waters of Reedy River
and bounded on E by lands of ENOS STIMPSON, N by lands of EBENEZER
STARNES, S by WILLIAM CALDWELL. Being part of orig. grant of 300 acres
to LEWIS BENTON dated 22 Nov. 1771. Wit: JOSHUA ARNALL, THOMAS BOYCE.

Pp 62-65:   14 Nov. 1770 - 11 Jan. 1787 WILLIAM LINN of Province of
                North Carolina sold to JOHN RODGERS of S. C. for 100 pds
current money 100 acres located in Craven Co. on Reedy Fork of Little
River, waters of Saluda River. "Plat in the Certificate Office". Wit:
WILLIAM GILLISPIE, JOSEPH CRAWFORD, HENRY WHITE.

Page 65:   23 Nov. 1786 - 12 Jan. 1787 THOMAS CARGIL of Laurens Co.
                and his wife ELIZABETH, sold to WILLIAM HILL for 75 pds

Cont'd:
Virginia money 180 acres lying on Little River being part of 200 acres
granted to JOHN CARGIL, dec'd., and by him willed to sd THOMAS CARGIL.
Land bounded by WILLIAM DENDY, SAMUEL POWELL, SILVANUS WALKER & THOMAS
DENDY. Wit: WILLIAM DENDY, JOHN CLARDY, JOHN POWELL.

Page 66:   13 Dec. 1786 - 12 Jan. 1787 THOMAS DENDY, and his wife,
                MARY, sold to DAVID BURNS, JR. for 50 pds sterling 130
acres located on Simmon's Creek, waters of Little River, beg. at Williamson's Big Survey by lands of TEAGUE, lands of GEORGE ANDERSON and
DAVID BURNS, SR. orig. granted to THOMAS DENDY. Wit: SILVANUS WALKER,
THOMAS LEWIS.

Pp 67-68:   28 Oct. 1771 - 13 Jan. 1787 JOHN LEWIS and his wife, PRIS-
                CILLA of Guilford Co., N. C. sold to JOSHUA TEAGUE of
Craven Co., S. C. for 300 pds, 200 acres orig. granted to sd LEWIS
date of 14 Nov. 1754 and located on Bush River. Wit: ELIJAH TEAGUE,
JAMES WILBORN, JAMES KELLY.

Page 69:   13 Jan. 1787 JONATHAN DOWNS, Esq., and DAVID ALLISON swore
                in open court that on the 3rd Mar. 1769 pursuant to a
warrant 200 acres were laid out to WILLIAM BURROWS on Reabon Creek,
Craven Co. and bounded then by lands of JOSEPH BABB and vacant land.
Orig. grant 5 Dec. 1774 and that the sd BURROWS has had peaceful possession of sd land for the last 18 or 20 years uninterupted by any
person or grant of any person. (Note from comp.- this must be the man
for whom Burris Creek, sometimes found as Burrows Creek, was named).

Pp 70-72:   1 Mar. 1787 - 14 Jan. 1787 SOLOMON NIBLET and his wife,
                MARY, sold to JOSHUA SAXON for 200 pds sterling 400 acres
located on Rabon Creek waters of Saluda River orig. granted to NIBLET
dated 12 Mar. 1739 (1759?) Wit: ROBERT COOPER, JOSHUA DOWNS, JOSEPH
DOWNS.

Pp 72-74:   10 Dec. 1773 - 15 Jan. 1787 GEORGE NORWOOD, planter of
                Craven Co., S. C. and his wife, ANN, sold to JOSHUA TEAGUE
for 200 pds current money 350 acres in Berkley Co. on waters of Little
River and bounded by lands of JOHN YOUNG, JAMES STEVENSON, EDWARD OS-
BORN & AMBROSE HUDGINS, being part of 500 acres granted to sd NORWOOD
11 Feb. 1773. Wit: ROBERT SIMS, JOHN MILLER, WILLIAM SIMS.

Pp 74-76:   21 Sept. 1779 - 15 Jan. 1787 GEORGE WIER (WINN?) and his
                wife, MARY, sold to WILLIAM CASON, JR. of S. C. for 700
pds current money 300 acres on northside of Saluda River on a branch
called Bush River bounded by lands of GEORGE DALRYMPLE being part of
orig. grant to ANDREW RODGERS 22 Feb. 1771, conveyed to sd GEORGE WIER
(WINN?) 6 May 1775. Wit: WILLIAM CASON, JOHN ROWE, THOMAS CASON.

Pp 76-78:   18 Jan. 1779 - 16 Jan. 1787 JOSEPH PARSONS, planter, and
                ALCEY, his wife, of Craven Co., sold to JAMES MC CLINTOCK,
planter of S. C. 100 acres being part of orig. grant of 550 acres to
JAMES GOOLSBY 7 May 1767 on Warrior's Creek, branch of Enoree River,
conveyed to JOSEPH PARSONS 3 Oct. 1768. Rec. in Auditor's Office Bk
H N #8 page 210. Wit: WILLIAM FOWLER, JOHN MC CLINTOCK, JOSEPH HALL,
COLEMAN BROWN.

Pp 78-80:   14 Feb. 1786 - 16 Jan. 1787 JOHN MC CRARY and his wife,
                JANE of Laurens Dist. sold to CHARLES HUTCHINGS of same
for 257 pds sterling 300 acres on northside of Duncan's Creek, bounded
all sides by vacant land when orig. granted to DANIEL MOTE and rec.
in Sec. State Off. Book 3 BBB page 370 and from DANIEL MOTE to JOHN
MC CRARY 2 Aug. 1770. Wit: JAMES MONTGOMERY, GEORGE ROSS, ROBERT MC
CRARY.

Pp 80-82:   Same date. Same to same...150 acres on northside Duncan's
                Creek bounded lands of JAMES KILGORE and all other sides
vacant. Orig. grant to WILLIAM COULTER, rec. in Sec. State Office Grant
Bk 3 LLL page 169, sd WM. COULTER deeded to JOHN COULTER 16 Mar. 1773,
from sd JOHN to sd JOHN MC CRARY, 17 July 1774.

Pp 82-84:   3 Sept. 1786 - 16 Jan. 1787 JOHN HALL, planter, sold to
              JOSEPH SOUTH, planter, for 10 pds Virginia money 100 acres
on northside of Saluda River orig. granted to JOHN HALL, rec'd in Sec.
State Off. Grant Book CCCC page 156. Examined by JOHN VANDERHORST,
Sec'y. Wit: WILLIAM DORSEY, JOSEPH REDING, LUKE HANKS, ARTHUR DURROM.

Page 84:   12 Mar. 1787 - 27 Mar. 1787 WILLIAM PRATER, planter, and
              MARY, his wife of Laurens Dist. sold to JOHN POWELL, plant-
er of same, for 40 pds sterling 100 acres on Saluda River bounded by
lands of JOSEPH SOUTH. JOSEPH CHAPMAN and sd River. Wit: THOMAS WIL-
LIAM FAKES, THOMAS DENDY.

Page 85:   21 Jan. 1787 - 27 Mar. 1787 JAMES WALDRUP, SR. of Laurens
              Co. sold to JOHN FARROW for 10 pds sterling 110 acres
on southside Enoree River across Buckhead Creek orig. granted to sd
WALDRUP. Wit: THOMAS FARROW, VENSON BROWN.

Pp 86-88:   26 Sept. 1786 - 27 Mar. 1787 THOMAS MC CLURKEN, planter
              of S. C., Camden Dist., sold to ANDREW ENDSLEY, planter
of 96 Dist. 250 acres orig. granted to JOHN CUNINGHAM 23 Feb. 1771,
on Beard's Fork of Duncan's Creek. Rec'd Sec. State Off. Grant Bk GGG
page 2173. Wit: JOHN GLENN, REUBEN PYLES, AYRES GOULY.

Pp 88-90:   10 Jan. 1787 - 28 Mar. 1787 ROBERT PLUNKETT of Newberry
              Co. sold to ABAJAH O'NEAL of same 150 acres on Beaverdam
Creek waters of Little River. Being part of 350 acre tract orig. granted
to HENRY STONE PARISH by patent 1 Feb. 1768, conveyed by sd STONE PARISH
to WILLIAM PITTS 6 Jan. 1775 and then by sd PITS to PLUNKETT 21 Sept.
1777. Wit: ELISHA FORD, HUGH O'NEL, MARMADUKE JONES.

Pp 90-92:   18 July 1783 - 29 Mar. 1787 SAMUEL PEARSON and MERCER
              BABB, farmers of Newberry Co., SC and as executors of
estate of SAMUEL WORTHINGTON, dec'd., sold to ELISHA FORD, planter,
for 10 pds 200 acres orig. granted to sd WORTHINGTON 21 May 1773, in
Berkley County now Laurens County on waters of Indian Creek bounded
NE by lands of REUBEN PATTERSON, SW by THOMAS GREEN and all other sides
vacant. Wit: SAMUEL KELLY, ABIJAH O'NEAL.

Page 92:   30 May 1785 - 30 Mar. 1787 WILLIAM ANDERSON, Esq. and
              his wife, RACHEL, sold to SAMUEL KELLY, farmer, 200 acres
orig. granted to WILLIAM SAVAGE & JAMES SIMPSON, Esq. dated 5 May 1773
on waters of Reaburn's Creek and bounded by lands of SAVAGE & SIMPSON,
on W by Indian Boundary Line, lands of HENRY POWELL and conveyed by
SAVAGE & SIMPSON to sd ANDERSON 1 Mar. 1778. Wit: SAMUEL KELLY, SR.,
JAMES DAUGHTERY.

Page 92:   10 Aug. 1783 - 31 Mar. 1787 CHARLES SAXON, planter, sold
              to ROBERT YOUNG, labourer, 87 acres being part of orig.
grant to SAXON 6 Feb. 1783, on Beaverdam Creek, bounded by lands of
MC NEESE GOODE & ROBERT YOUNG. Wit: HUGH O'NEAL, NEHEMIAH FRANKS, CLEM-
ENT DEAL.

Pp 93-96:   16 Dec. 1786 - 31 Mar. 1787 GEORGE ANDERSON and his wife,
              MARY, to MARIAH GOODWIN for 100 pds 240 acres on both
sides of North Creek bounded by lands of JAMES BURNSIDES, ROBERT YOUNG,
JAMES COOK, JOHN MILAM & SILVANUS WALKER. Wit: SAMUEL WHARTON, CHARLES
SULLIVANT.

Pp 97-98:   6 Sept. 1773 - 2 Apr. 1787 ROBERT MC CRARY and MARY, his
              wife, sold to JOHN PRUDE 150 acres in Berkley Co. on Enoree
River, bounded by lands laid out to ISAAC PENNINGTON, JAMES BRIGHT.
Orig. grant dated 17 Feb. 1787. Wit: SAMUEL BISHOP, JOHN PEARSON, WIL-
LIAM HENDRICKS. (Note from comp.- WILLIAM HENDRICKS, who owned Hendricks
Mill and Hendricks Inn on Enoree River in Newberry Co. He was son of
HENRY HENDRICKSON whose 1754 plat shows five paths or roads sd to be
the first paths shown on a plat in this area. This land devolved to
WM. HENDRICKS who gave it to his son, JOHN HENDRICKS. WILLIAM died
1797 in East Florida (now Duval Co.) where he owned land on Amelia
Island and also the Cowford.)

Pp 99-100:   1 Sept. 1786 - 2 Apr. 1787 ROBERT HENRY MAGEE of Wake
               Co., N. C. sold to JOHN NEWMAN for 300 pds 370 acres and
a grinding mill on southside of Enoree River. Wit: JOHN BRIGGS, JOHN
ROBINSON, RICHARD BURGESS.

Page 101:   2 Feb. 1787 - 2 Apr. 1787 JAMES ROSAMOND, adm. of Abbeville
               Co., S. C. sold to LEWIS GRAVES of the co. of Laurens,
for 17 pds lawful money 100 acres on Reedy River formerly property
of HENRY PARKER but now the property of sd ROSAMOND. Plat annexed.
Wit: GEORGE ANDERSON, DAVID ANDERSON, DAVID MC CAA.

Page 102:   28 Oct. 1786 - 3 Apr. 1787 JAMES REDMON of Spartanburg
               Co. sold to JAMES BARTON of Greenville Co. for 10 pds
100 acres being part of 640 acre tract orig. granted 21 Jan. 1785 to
sd REDMON by patent, on Dirbin Creek, 96 Dist., now called Greenville
County. Rec. in Office of Sec. State Book CCCC page 495. Wit: SAMUEL
COBB, JESSE GOODWIN, HUMPHREY COBB.

Page 104:   16 July 1786 - 3 Apr. 1787 JOHN REDMON of Spartanburg
               Co. sold to JESSE GOODWIN of Laurens Co. for 20 pds sterl-
ing 220 acres orig. granted to sd REDMON 21 Jan. 1785, located above
the Ancient Boundary Line (Greenville Co.) Wit: SAMUEL COBB, JAMES
BARTON (BURTON?), HUMPHREY COBB.

Pp 106-107:   11 Mar. 1787 - 4 Apr. 1787 ROBERT YOUNG of Laurens Co.
               sold to JAMES COOK for 25 pds sterling 30 acres on north-
side of North Creek and joins JOSEPH YOUNG's land and lands of sd COOK.
In open court, LEWIS SAXON, C.C.

Page 108:   11 Mar. 1787 - 6 Apr. 1787 JOHN DENNING of S.C. and 96
               Dist. sold to WILLIAM RAY, planter of same, for 30 pds
sterling, 320 acres being part of 640 acres granted to sd DENNING by
patent 1 Jan. 1787, on Horse Creek a branch of Saluda River above the
Ancient Boundary Line. Rec'd. in SS Bk OOOO page 578. Wit: BENJAMIN
RAINEY, SAMUEL PERSONS (Note from comp. - WILLIAM REA's will is rec.
in Greenville Co.)

Pp 108-110:   15 Mar. 1775 - 5 Apr. 1787 JOHN CALDWELL, Esq., of 96
               Dist. sold to GILBERT TURNER of same, for 200 pds current
SC money, 63 acres being part of 1250 acres granted to sd CALDWELL
8 July 1774, on Little River by lands of WILLIAM TURNER both NW and
SW, other sides vacant. Wit: THOMAS EDGEHILL, HUGH O'NEAL, HAISTEN
DOYALL (HASTINGS DIAL). No dower.

Pp 110-112:   16 Sept. 1786 - 5 Apr. 1787 THOMAS EDGEHILL, JR., Att'y
               for THOMAS EDGEHILL, SR., of Laurens Co. sold to THOMAS
MC DONALD, planter of same, for 75 pds sterling 150 acres on waters
of Little River being part of grant to sd EDGEHILL dated 17 May 1774.
Bounded by lands laid out to JOHN SIMMONS. Plat annexed. Wit: HUGH
O'NEAL, EDMOND DRAKE, PATIENCE O'NEAL.

Pp 113-114:   6 Apr. 1787 - 12 Oct. 1787 JOHN WIER, planter of Laurens
               Co. sold to HAISTINGS DOYAL (HASTINGS DIAL), planter of
sd state, for 100 pds sterling 100 acres on Saluda River bounded N
by lands laid out to JOHN HELLAMS, W by PATRICK CUNINGHAM. Orig. grant
4 May 1775. Wit: WILLIAM BOYD, SAMUEL MC CLURKEN, CATHERINE BOYD.

Pp 115-116:   6 Mar. 1787 - 7 Apr. 1787 FERRIL RILEY, planter, late
               of 96 Dist., but now of the state of Georgia, sold to
WILLIAM CASON of Laurens Co., SC for 200 pds 200 acres located on Little
River orig. granted to JOHN PURCELL, dec'd. bearing date of 25 June
1765 rec'd SS Office Bk 2XS page 80. Wit: PETER HITT, HUGH O'NEAL,
WILLIAM CASON, JR.

Pp 117-119:   7 Nov. 1785 - 9 Apr. 1787 SAMUEL EAKINS, blacksmith of
               Laurens Co., sold to PETER HITT, planter of same, for
85 pds Va. money 180 acres located on waters of Little River orig.
granted to sd EAKINS and known by name of "Mathais Cook's Old Survey"
dated 1 Aug. 1785. JANE EAKINS signed dower. Wit: THOS. WM. FAKES,

Cont'd:
WILLIAM CASON.

Pp 120-121: 29 Dec. 1786 - 8 Apr. 1787 SAMUEL DILLARD of Laurens Co.
and his wife, ANN, sold to JAMES DILLARD for 50 pds sterling SC money 440 acres on south side of Enoree River below Ancient Boundary Line and bounded by lands laid out to JAMES BRIGHT, JOHN WHITMORE, BRICE PRATHER & JOSEPH WHITMORE and granted to sd SAMUEL DILLARD 4 July 1785. Rec. SS Office Bk DDDD page 453. Wit: THOMAS EWING, JOHN GARRETT, SILAS GARRETT.

Page 122: 1 Mar. 1787 - 9 Apr. 1787 JOHN YOUNG and MARY, his wife,
of Rutherford Co., N. C. sold to GEORGE ANDERSON of Laurens Co. for 50 pds sterling 200 acres on Little River of Saluda being the orig. grant to JOHN YOUNG dated 12 July 1771. Wit: ARCHIBALD YOUNG, JAMES YOUNG, THOMAS WADLINGTON, JR., Rutherford Co., N.C.

Pp 123-125: 12 Mar. 1787 - 9 Apr. 1787 SUSANNAH DEAN, relict of the
late JOB DEAN, dec'd. of Laurens Co., sold to JOHN EDWARDS of same, for 20 pds 52 acres part of 252 acres on Indian Creek waters of Enoree River, formerly belonging to JOHN ENTREKIN who was granted land 4 Dec. 1770 and conveyed to DEAN on 5 Feb. 1785, bounded by lands of JOB DEAN, dec'd., CRAWFER LEWIS & ALLIN WILLSON. Surveyed by JOHN HUNTER, Esq. 3 Jan. 1787. Rec. SS Office Bk KKK page 142. In open court bef. LEWIS SAXON, C.C.

Pp 126-127: 5 Feb. 1785 - 10 Apr. 1787 JOHN ENTREKIN, planter of 96
Dist. and ELIZABETH, his wife, sold to SUSANNAH DEAN, widow, for 35 pds lawful SC money 250 acres on Indian Creek orig. grant to JOHN ENTREKIN 7 May 1771 rec'd SS Office Bk KKK page 142, 9 Mar. 1772. Bounded by lands laid out to JOB DEAN & CRAWFORD LEWIS.

Page 128: 10 Jan. 1787 - 11 Apr. 1787 Whereas ALEXANDER IRWIN, late
of township of West Pennsborough, Cumberland Co., Commanwealth of Penn., dec'd., died intestate without issue, leaving ANN BREWSTER his only sister and heir at law and being possessed with several tracts of land located in Berkley Co., S.C., I, ANNE BREWSTER do appoint JAMES IRWIN of Cumberland Co., Penn. my true and lawful att'y. Signed: ANN BREWSTER. Wit: THOMAS LEE, JOHN LEE. Aff. by SAMUEL IRWIN, J.P. of Cumberland Co. and WILLIAM LYON of Cumberland Co.

Pp 129-130: 11 Apr. 1787 Whereas AGNES IRWIN, widow of ALEXANDER IRWIN
late of Cumberland Co., Penn., appointed friend JAMES IRWIN of Cumberland Co., Penn. her lawful att'y. Wit: WILLIAM BREWSTER, SAMUEL WEEKLEY. Aff. by JOHN GORDON (JORDON?) & WILLIAM LYON. Personally came JOHN LUSK & DAVID RALSTON who being sworn did depose and say that they were acquainted with ALEXANDER IRWIN, now deceased and ANNE IRWIN, now ANNE BREWSTER, widow, (who are) children of WM. IRWIN of West Pennsborough Township from their youth and always understood that the sd ALEXANDER and sd ANNE were full brother and sister and the sd ALEXANDER had not any full brother or sister, only the sd ANNE. Sworn to bef. JOHN JORDON, J.P.

Pp 131-133: 28 Dec. 1773 - 12 Apr. 1787 THOMAS HAIRSTON, freeholder
of Colleton Co., S.C. sold to ALEXANDER IRWIN of same co. and state for 200 pds current money 200 acres orig. granted to HAIRSTON 23 Jan. 1773 in Berkley Co. on Reaburn's Creek and bounded by land laid out to ZEBULON GAUNT. Wit: JOHN SMITH, ALEXANDER MOORE.

Page 134: 1 Oct. 1785 - 12 Apr. 1787 CLEMENT DAVIS, farmer, and
his wife, ELIZABETH of Indian Creek, Laurens Co., sold to THOMAS EAST of same for 71 pds 150 acres being part of 200 acres orig. granted to DAVIS bearing date 3 Dec. 1771, located in Craven Co. now Laurens Co. on Headley's Branch, waters of Indian Creek. Wit: JAMES LINDSEY, JOHN CHAPMAN, ALEXANDER MOORE.

Pp 135-137: 26 Dec. 1786 - 12 Apr. 1787 SUSANNAH DEAN, relict of JOB
DEAN, dec'd. sold to JOSIAH EAST of Laurens Co. for 8 pds sterling 49 acres, part of 250 acres granted to JOHN ENTREKIN,

Cont'd:
and surveyed by WILLIAM HUNTER, deputy surveyor 13 July 1786 and conveyed to SUSANNAH DEAN. Rec. SS Office Bk KKK, page 142. Wit: WILLIAM
MILWEE, JAMES SAXON.

Pp 138-139: 19 Oct. 1786 - 13 Apr. 1787 DAVID WIER, planter of Laurens
             Co. and his wife, JANE, sold to HAISTING DOYEL (DIAL),
planter for 50 pds 100 acres on waters of Saluda River, bounded by
lands laid out to WILLIAM HELLAMS. Orig. grant 20 Oct. 1786. Wit: WIL-
LIAM BOYD, SAMUEL MC CLURKIN, CATHERINE BOYD.

Page 140:   25 Oct. 1786 - 14 Apr. 1787 SAMUEL HENDERSON, planter
             of Laurens Co. and his wife, MARY ANN, sold to LUKE WALD-
ROUP, planter of sd county, for 30 pds sterling 130 acres being part
of a tract of 510 acres orig. granted to SAML HENDERSON 3 Oct. 1785
on a branch of Little River and bounded by lands of WILLIAM EAST, SAMUEL
HENDERSON & MOSES SWITLAND. Wit: WILLIAM OSBORNE, RICHD HENDERSON.

Page 141:   18 Mar. 1787 - 15 Apr. 1787 THOMAS SHIP of Laurens Co.
             sold to MARK MOORE of same place for 100 pds sterling
the following items: six feather beds and furniture, two chests, one
pot, one dutch oven with all my pewter and earthenware, one dark bay
horse, eight head cattle and thirty head hogs. Wit: JAMES YOUNG.

Pp 142-143: 25 Jan. 1779 - 15 Apr. 1787 THOMAS CLARK, planter of 96
             Dist. and his wife, MARY, sold to HAMBLETON MURDOCK, weaver
of same, for 2400 pds current money 250 acres and another certain 89
acres located in Craven Co. on Little River and bounded by lands of
THOMAS EDGEHILL, MATTIAS COOK and orig. granted to THOS. CLARK 1768
and 3 Oct. 1772. Wit: JAMES ABERNATHY, WILLIAM SIMPSON, JAMES DOUGLAS.

Pp 144-146: 15 Mar. 1787 - 18 Apr. 1787 MARTHA BOYD of Chester Co.,
             and SAMUEL BOYD of same, Exr. & Ex'trix of JAMES BOYD,
deceased planter of 96 Dist., sold to VINCENT GLASS, the elder, of
Campbell Co., Virginia, planter, for 200 pds sterling 250 acres on
Little River in two tracts bounded on E by lands of MARTIN MARTIN,
N by JAMES MC NEESE, W by lands of the late ___? YARBOROUGH, and NW
by sd JOHN BOYD. Land orig. granted to JAMES HARVEY in 1772 and by
conveyed to JAMES BOYD, dec'd., in presence of CHARLES GOODWIN and
CHARLES SIMMONS. MARTHA BOYD, widow of JAMES BOYD, dec'd. and SAMUEL
BOYD, one of his sons, and JOHN BOYD, who being the eldest son of JAMES
BOYD, dec'd., inherited the land under JAMES BOYD's will dated 18 Aug.
1781. Deed signed MARTHA BOYD by her att'y SAML. BOYD, & JOHN BOYD.
Wit: CHARLES GOODWIN, CHARLES SIMMONS. (Note from comp. - I believe
MARTIN MARTIN & VINCENT GLASS removed to Madison Co., Ala.)

Pp 147-149: 11 Jan. 1787 - 2 July 1787 JAMES ABERCROMBIE of Laurens
             and his wife, ELIZABETH, sold to ELIAS BROCK for 100 pds
sterling, 170 acres on the mill branch west of Reabon Creek being part
of 230 acres orig. granted 1 May 1786 to sd ABERCROMBIE and now where
"the sd ELIAS BROCK now lives". Wit: HAISTEN DOYALL, JOHN PINSON.

Page 150:   11 June 1787 - 2 July 1787 SILVANUS and SARAH WALKER and
             JAMES BURNSIDES sold to FRANCIS LESTER & THOMAS WILKES
for 135 pds sterling 110 acres on North Creek bounded by lands of JOHN
MILAM, ___ HARDY, THOMAS GAFFORD, sd BURNSIDES & MARIAH GOODMAN, being
part of two tracts granted to GEORGE ANDERSON & ARTHUR SPENCE. Wit:
SAMUEL SAXON, JOHN WILLIAMS, JR.

Page 151:   11 Jan. 1787 - 3 July 1787 GEORGE ANDERSON sold to JAMES
             BURNSIDES 10 acres on Little River bounded by lands of
GEO. BURNSIDES, MARIAH GOODMAN & ROBERT YOUNG. In open court bef. LEWIS
SAXON, C.C.

Pp 151-152: 11 Jan. 1787 - 4 July 1787 ROBERT DUNLAP and his wife,
             ELIZABETH, sold to ABSOLUM BOBO for 20 pds sterling money
200 acres on northside of Saludy River. In open court bef. LEWIS SAXON.

Page 153:   12 Jan. 1787 - 4 July 1787 CHARLES SAXON and his wife,

Cont'd:
JUDITH, sold to JAMES HALSEY, 150 acres on Line Creek, waters of Saluda River. In open court bef. LEWIS SAXON, C.C.

Pp 154-155: 4 Mar. 1777 - 5 July 1787 JOHN HARVEY sold to THOMAS BLAKE-LEY for 150 pds, 150 acres on North Creek, waters of Little River orig. granted 26 July 1774 to sd HARVEY. Wit: RATCLIFF JOWELL (JOEL), PHILEMON HARVEY, WILLIAM HARRIS.

Pp 156-157: 9 Mar. 1787 - 5 July 1787 PATRICK WILEY, farmer, sold to ROBERT SIMS, miller, for 20 pds, 50 acres on north fork of Reaburn's Creek, bounded by lands laid out to THOMAS MC DANIEL, ROBERT SIMS & JAMES MC CLANNAHAN, orig. granted 5 June 1786 to PATRICK WILEY. Wit: WILLIAM FARRIS, ANDREW MC NIGHT, DRURY BOYCE, ABRAHAM RILEY.

Page 158: 24 Oct. 1783 - 7 July 1787 JOSEPH KELLET, planter and wife, JANE to ROBERT SIMS, SR. for 100 pds, 100 acres on South Fork of Reaburns Creek, orig. grant to JAMES SMITH, conveyed to MARTIN MAHAFFEY then to sd KELLET. Wit: MARTIN MAHAFFEY, WM. BURTON, DRURY BOYCE.

Page 160: 1 Jan. 1787 - 9 July 1787 JOHN POLLOCK, planter of Abbeville Co. and his wife, ELIZABETH, to ROBERT SCOTT, planter for 100 pds, 374 acres on South Fork of Duncans Creek, part of 390 acres orig. granted in 1786. Wit: JOHN HUNTER, SAMUEL EWING.

Page 163: 15 Jan. 1787 - 9 July 1787 JOHN O'NEAL, planter, to CHARLES WILSON, planter of Newberry Co., for 80 pds sterling, 350 acres bounded on HASTEN DIAL. Wit: JOHN SAXON, JOHN HUNTER.

Page 164: 4 Dec. 1786 - 9 July 1787 ISAAC WILLIAMS, carpenter & joiner, of Wilkes Co., Ga., to MARY GRIFFIN, widow, and ex'trix of ANTHONY GRIFFIN, dec'd., planter, for 100 pds sterling, 100 acres on Little River, orig. grant to MOSES GREGORY 10 Jan. 1771, conveyed to sd WILLIAMS 14 Oct. 1771. Wit: JOHN HUNTER, JOSIAH EAST.

Page 166: 28 Dec. 1786 - 10 July 1787 HASTEN DOYAL & REBECCA, his wife, to JOHN TODD for 30 pds, 100 acres orig. grant to JOHN WEIR 4 May 1775, bounded SW by JOHN HELLAMS, conveyed to DIAL 1786. Wit: ROBERT TODD, DAVID HELLAMS, WILLIAM HOBES (HOBBS).

Page 167: 23 Oct. 1783 - 11 July 1787 DAVID HUGGANS and wife SUSANNA of Craven Co., to THOMAS CASON for 750 pds, 150 acres on north side of Saluda River, orig. grant 5 Nov. 1755 to CHARLES BANKS, conveyed to PATRICK HUGGINS, falling to sd DAVID by heirship. Wit: RICHARD POLLARD, WILLIAM DAY, JOHN COOK.

Page 169: (blank) - 11 July 1787 DANIEL MC LEAN of 96 Dist., "but now called Oxford Dist." to my loving daughter MARY MC LEAN, "by marriage MARY HUTSON, 100 acres whereon I now dwell, surveyed by a bounty warrant 29 July 1768...4 cows, 1 big pot, 1 little pot ..." Wit: DAVID SPEIRS, JAMES MC CLANAHAN.

Page 170: 11 June 1787 - 12 July 1787 NEHEMIAH FRANKS to CHARLES SMITH for 20 pds, 110 acres granted in 1786, bounded on ROBERT FRANKS. Wit: MARSHALL FRANKS, SAMUEL FRANKS, JOHN WILLIAMS.

Page 171: 15 Apr. 1787 - 13 July 1787 LEWIS DEVALL, hatter, and wife, TERESY to JOHN SIMPSON, merchant, for 90 pds, 250 acres on Dunkans Creek of Enoree River, part of 350 acres orig. granted to JOHN HOWARD 22 Feb. 1771, conveyed to DECALL 25 Mar. 1772. Wit: JOHN HUNTER, MICHAEL WALDROP.

Page 174: 1 May 1787 - 13 July 1787 JOHN KELLET and wife HANNAH, to WILLIAM KELLET for 20 pds sterling, 250 acres on Beaverdam Creek of Reedy River. Wit: WILLIAM FARRIS, ANDREW MC NIGHT.

Page 175: 10 Feb. 1787 - 14 July 1787 JOHN BRYANT, yeoman and FRANCES his wife, to WILLIAM ARNOLD for 100 pds Virginia currency,

Cont'd:
200 acres, part of 450 acres orig. granted in Berkley Co., now Laurens
Co., 13 May 1768 to JAMES WHITE, father of MICHAEL WHITE on branches
of Cain Creek. Wit: SILVANUS WALKER, RICHARD HANCOCK.

Page 178:   11 June 1787 - 16 July 1787 Capt. JAMES DILLARD and wife,
             MARY, to SILAS GARRETT, planter, for 14 pds 311 acres
on a branch of Enoree River, granted 21 Jan. 1785 bounding on JOHN
GARRETT, SILAS GARRETT, JOHN WHITMORE. Wit: JOHN ROBINSON, THOMAS HARRIS
& ENOCH GARRETT.

Page 180:   30 Mar. 1787 - 17 July 1787 SILAS GARRETT, yeoman and
             ANNA his wife to JOHN GARRETT, SR., planter, for 5 pds,
75 acres "at south of the lake up to the Indian Grave upon the Hill",
bounding Enoree River on Hurles(?) Creek, part of 150 acres granted
6 Apr. 1753 to ADAM BENTSLEY, conveyed to ISAAC PENNINGTON, then to
NOLAND, then to JOSEPH GARRETT and after his decease, his eldest son,
SILAS GARRETT fell heir. Wit: THOMAS HARRIS, JOSEPH THOMPSON, MARY
THOMPSON.

Page 183:   27 Jan. 1787 - 18 July 1787 JAMES WALDROP, SR., late of
             Laurens Co., to JOHN WALDROP for 40 pds, 100 acres on
south side of Enoree River, granted by patent 19 June 1772, bounded
by LUKE WALDROP. Wit: JAMES WALDROP, DAVID MC ELROY.

Page 185:   9 Aug. 1772 - 17 Sept. 1787 JOHN WILLIAMS, planter of
             Berkley Co. and wife, ELIZABETH, to JOHN OWINS, black-
smith and planter, for 400 pds currency 150 acres on Reaburns Creek
of Saluda, granted by patent 10 Sept. 1765. Wit: HENRY BOX, JOHN HELLAMS

Page 189:   16 July 1787 - 18 Sept. 1787 SAMUEL WEATHERS and wife,
             MARTHA, to MARY & MARGARET DURRUM for 17 pds, 100 acres
on Cane Creek bounded on ALLMON BROWN, HARRIS GILLAM, ARTHUR DURRAM,
sd SAML. WEATHERS. Wit: JOHN CARTER, DAVID MC GLADERY.

Page 190:   7 Sept. 1787 - 17 Sept. 1787 WILLIAM HELLAMS, SR., and
             wife, CONSTANT to JOHN HELLAMS, planter, for 30 pds ster-
ling, 103 acres on both sides of Reaburns Creek, part of orig. grant
by letters of patent, bounded on RICHD. OWINGS, sd creek, HASTEN DIAL,
across creek, ISAAC HUGER. Wit: JOHN COKER, SAML. WILLIAMS.

Page 193:   10 Sept. 1787 - 20 Sept. 1787 DAVID SPENCE, planter, to
             ROBERT SPENCE for 10 pds, 200 acres on Spence's branch,
of Little River, part of 400 acres granted 12 Aug. 1778. Wit: JOHN
RODGERS, WM. TAYLOR.

Page 196:   6 Sept. 1787 - 21 Sept. 1787 JOHN NEWMAN and wife, FRANCES
             to ROBERT HENRY HUGHES, late of Wake Co., N. C., for 200
pds sterling, 270 acres on Enoree River below the Anshent (Ancient)
Boundary Line. Orig. granted 4 July 1785. Wit: JOHN BRIGGS, JOHN ROBIN-
SON, RICHD. BURGESS. (Release of this is incomplete).

Pages missing to #216.

Page 216:   (Lease and part of release missing) JOHN BAILEY to SAMUEL
             POWEL land adj. WM. DENDY, WM. HALL. Wit: SILVANUS WALKER,
JAMES BAILEY.

Page 217:   6 Apr. 1787 - 6 Oct. 1787 JOHN GRAY and wife ALSI (AILSIE)
             to CHARLES JONES for 150 pds sterling, 65 acres part of
325 acres granted 1 May 1786, on Duncans Creek of Enoree River. Wit:
GEORGE WHITMORE, JOHN GRAY, JR.

Page 218:   10 Sept. 1787 - 9 Oct. 1787 ROBERT MC NEES, planter and
             wife MARY to JOSHUA SAXON for 100 pds sterling, 107 acres
on Little River, bounded on CHARLES ALLEN, NEHEMIAH FRANKS, NATHAN
BARKSDALE, part of orig. grant 31 Aug. 1774 to CHAS. ALLEN, conveyed
to sd MC NEES 1786. Wit: JAMES SAXON, BEN JONES.

Page 220:   16 June 1787 - 9 Oct. 1787 WM. MILWEE, Esq., Sheriff,

Cont'd:
to JAMES MONTGOMERY, Gentleman, for 75 pds sterling, 300
acres on Herills Branch of Enoree River, former property of THOMAS
PEARSON sold for judgement at suit of JOSEPH & JAMES ADAIR. Bounding
on REUBEN FLANAGAN & JAMES MACHAN (MAHAN?) Orig. grant to WM. LACEY,
conveyed to sd THOS. PEARSON. Surveyed by JAMES WOFFORD, Deputy Surv.
Wit: ALEX. MC DOWELL, JAMES SAXON, JOHN DENDY.

Page 222:   5 June 1787 - 10 Oct. 1787 ANDREW RODGERS, son of THOMAS
             RODGERS of Laurens Co., and wife LETTY, to JAMES CLARDY,
son of MICHAEL CLARDY for 180 pds Virginia currency, 240 acres on south
side of Little River, part of 400 acres granted to WM. BAILEY, bounding
on MACKNEES GOOD & WM. DREW, dec'd. Wit: JOHN RODGERS, GEORGE ANDERSON.

Page 223:   10 Sept. 1784 - 10 Oct. 1787 MACAJAH HENDRIX, planter
            of County of Pittsylvania and Parish of Camden, to my
mother, MARGARET, widow of HANS HENDRIX, planter of 96 Dist., deed
of gift of 450 acres in two tracts on north side of Reedy River, bounding on PATRICK CUNINGHAM, THOS. CARTER, RICHD. LANYARD, HENRY PARKER,
MARY ADKINS, SARAH BOWMAN, adj. the river at a branch below the shoals..
for and during her natural life and to whom she pleaseth forever. Wit:
LEWIS BANTON, EDWARD (EDMOND) WARE, MICHAEL LAWLESS. GEO. ANDERSON,
J.P.

Page 223:   8 Mar. 1787 - 12 Oct. 1787 ROBERT TAYLOR, planter and
             wife AGNESS to JOHN MC CELVEY, planter, for 28 pds, 100
acres on Little River, orig. patent by DAVID SPENCE 12 Aug. 1760, conveyed 9 Jan. 1774 to WM. NORRIS, then by sd NORRIS and wife MARTHA
to sd TAYLOR 12 Mar. 1784. Wit: ROBT. ROSS, WM. TAYLOR, ISAAC RODGERS.

Page 226:   11 July 1787 - 13 Oct. 1787 ROBT. TAYLOR and wife AGNES
            to ROBT. ROSS for 13 pds, 43 acres orig. granted to DAVID
SPENCE, bounded on JOHN MC CELVEY, Beaverdam Creek. Wit: WM. & SAML.
TAYLOR, ISAAC RODGERS.

Page 226:   1 May 1787 - 15 Nov. 1787 JOHN GREER, SR., to RUTH ADAIR
             for 150 pds sterling, bond on 150 acres, that part of
300 acre tract whereon sd GREER now lives bounded on land laid out
to JOSEPH GREER & BAZZEL PRATOR. Wit: JAMES MONTGOMERY, JAMES GREER.

Page 227:   23 Oct. 1786 - 16 Nov. 1787 ROBERT GOODWIN, SR. and ROBERT
            GOODWIN, JR., planters, to DANIEL WRIGHT, planter, for
50 pds 152 acres on both sides of Durbins Creek, bounded SE by land
laid out for BENJAMIN RAINEY. Wit: THOS. NICKS, MOLLY MAGULLOU(?),
JOSIAH PRATOR, WM. GILBERT.

Page 229:   14 Aug. 1787 - 17 Nov. 1787 WM. WILSON, planter to LEWIS
            SAXON, planter for 50 pds, 100 acres on Wilsons Branch
of Little River granted by patent to WM. WILSON 14 Oct. 1774, bounding on sd Maj. WM. WILSON & JAMES WILSON. Wit: DAVID MC CAA, JOHN HUGHES
& ALEX. GRANT.

Page 230:   30 July 1787 - 19 Nov. 1787 JOHN KELLET (son and heir
            of JOSEPH KELLET, dec'd.) and wife HANNAH to MARTIN MAHAF-
FEY, planter for 10 pds, 80 acres on the ancient boundary line, bounded
on small branch of Reedy River, on MARY MC DANIEL, PATRICK RILEY. Part
of grant to JOSEPH KELLET 5 Dec. 1785. Plat shown. Wit: WM. KELLET,
ANDREW MC NIGHT.

Page 233:   11 Sept. 1787 - 20 Nov. 1787 JOSHUA ARNALL, planter to
            MARSHALL FRANKS for 50 pds 130 acres part of 640 acres
granted on Connucky Branch of Little River in 1786, bounded on sd FRANKS
& ARNALL, and on NEHEMIAH FRANKS. Wit: JAS. MC LAUGHLIN, WM. TURNER.

Page 234:   12 Sept. 1787 - 22 Nov. 1787 NEHEMIAH FRANKS, planter
            to MARSHALL FRANKS, planter, for 50 pds, 20 acres part
of 200 acres orig. granted to CHARLES ALLEN 2 Apr. 1773, conveyed to
sd NEHEMIAH FRANKS (?) July 1774. Wit: JAMES MC LAUGHLIN, WM. TURNER.

Page 235:   25 July 1787 - 23 Nov. 1787 JOHN BOURLAND and wife MARY

Cont'd:
                to JOSIAH PRATHER for 20 pds sterling, 94 acres on Hendrix
branch of Dunkins Creek, orig. grant 7 Aug. 1786.

Page 236:   10 Dec. 1775 - 26 Nov. 1787 REBECCA BROWN of Berkley Co.,
              Province of S. C. to ROGER BROWN of same place for 100
pds 100 acres orig. granted to sd REBECCA BROWN 29 Aug. 1768, on Dunkins
Creek of Enoree River, bounded on WM. HANNA, JAMES DORROH, JOHN BROWN.
Wit: JOHN BROWN, SR., JOHN BROWN, JR.

Page 239:   11 Sept. 1787 - 27 Nov. 1787 ROBERT SIMS, miller, to MICA-
              JAH SIMS for 40 pds 100 acres on South fork of Reaburns
Creek on south side orig. granted to JAMES SMITH by his majesty's letter
of patent 13 May 1768; also adj. 50 acres granted to PATRICK RILEY
5 June 1768, bounded SW by JAMES MC CLANAHAN, W by THOMAS MC DANIEL,
N by ROBERT SIMS. Wit: LEWIS SAXON, C.C.

Page 241:   20 July 1787 - 28 Nov. 1787 WILLIAM DENDY and wife CLARY
              to THOMAS DENDY for 10 pds 278 acres on Little River bound-
ed on widow TINSLEY, JOHN CARGILL, JAMES YOUNG, THOMAS CARGILL, THOMAS
DENDY. Wit: SILVANUS WALKER, SILVANUS WALKER, JR.

Page 243:   30 Aug. 1787 - 3 Jan. 1788 JOHN MANLEY, JR., planter to
              WILLIAM WILSON for 65 pds sterling 100 acres orig. granted
2 Oct. 1786 on Ryans Branch of Little River bounded on ADAM TAYLOR,
JAMES BACKLEY. Wit: WM. T. RODGERS, JOHN MARTIN.

Page 244:   1 Nov. 1787 - 4 Jan. 1788 ROBERT ALLISON and wife MARY
              to BEVESTER BARTON for 50 pds, 50 acres on SE side of
Warrior Creek of Enoree River, part of 400 acres orig. grant 22 Sept.
1769 to JAMES ALLISON. Wit: PETER BROOKS, SARAH BROOKS.

Page 246:   31 Aug. 1787 - 5 Jan. 1788 JOHN & ELIZABETH COX to CHARLES
              HENDERSON for 42 pds 150 acres on Warriors Creek, bounded
on WM. VAUGHN, orig. grant to sd COX in Berkley Co. 4 Dec. 1771. Wit:
THOMAS HENDERSON, WILLIAM DODD.

Page 250:   12 June 1786 - 6 Jan. 1788 LEWIS SAXON and his wife SARAH,
              to JOHN RODGERS, Esq., and his wife MARGRET, for 65 pds
10 acres on Little River near the court house of Laurens, part of an
orig. grant of 600 acres to JOHN RODGERS 31 Aug. 1774. Wit: WILLIAM
RODGERS, DAVID MC CAA, JOHN GARNER.

Page 254:   9 Dec. 1787 - 7 Jan. 1788 JONATHAN DOWNS to DAVID RIDGE-
              WAY for 50 pds, 100 acres SW side of Reedy River, orig.
grant 22 Mar. 1769. Wit: LEWIS SAXON, C.C.

Page 256:   ? Sept. 1784 - 8 Jan. 1788 WILLIAM PITTS of Province of
              S. C. to ROBERT YOUNG for 300 pds old currency, 100 acres
on Beaverdam branch of Little River, orig. grant to HENRY STONEPARISH
1 Feb. 1768, bounded on sd YOUNG, JOHN ONEAL, dec'd. Wit: JACOB NEAL,
ARON PITTS, JOHN WATSON.

Page 259:   10 Dec. 1786 - 9 Jan. 1788 GEORGE ANDERSON and wife MOLLY
              to ROBERT YOUNG for (?), 100 acres on North Creek of Little
River, part of 400 acres orig. granted 23 June 1774, bounded on JAMES
BURNSIDE. Wit: LEWIS SAXON, C.C.

Page 262:   22 Aug. 1787 - 10 Jan. 1788 JOHN WIDOWMAN of Newberry
              Co., planter to WILLIAM HEAD, planter for 200 pds, 200
acres on south side of Enoree River, orig. grant 30 Oct. 1772 in Craven
Co. Wit: DAVID CHILDERS, JOHN HEAD, ALL(?) GLAZIER.

Page 265:   16 Dec. 1787 - 11 Jan. 1788 CHARLES HUTCHINGS and wife
              ELIZABETH to JOHN ARCHER ELMORE for 200 pds, 300 acres
on north side of Duncans Creek, orig. grant to DANIEL MATE(?) and conveyed 20 Aug. 1770 to JOHN MC CRARY. Wit: SAMUEL SAXON, EDMOND CRADDOCK,
ROBERT H. HUGHES.

Page 267:   19 Nov. 1787 - 12 Jan. 1788 JACOB BOWMAN, son and heir

Cont'd:
to JACOB BOWMAN, deceased, to JOHN BOWMAN for 10 pds, 150 acres on both sides of Reedy River, orig. grant to RICHARD BALLARD in 1778 and conveyed by him to JACOB BOWMAN, dec'd. bounded on ROBERT BOX, DAVID ALEXANDER, JACOB WRIGHT. Wit: GEORGE ANDERSON, SAMUEL WHARTON & SARAH WRIGHT.

Page 268:   21 Oct. 1787 - 14 Jan. 1788 CHARLES HUTCHINGS and wife ELIZABETH to ROBERT HENRY HUGHES for 30 pds, 164 acres on Harrold(?) Creek of Enoree River below the Ancient Boundary, bounded on WILLIAM LAYSON, JAMES MONTGOMERY, JOHN COULTER, ROBERT H. HUGHES. Orig. grant to MATTHEW MC CREARY 6 Mar. 1786. Wit: JOHN TROTTER, JOHN GOWLEY, ISAAC MC CRARY.

Page 271:   10 Dec. 1787 - 15 Ja.n 1788 JOSHUA ARNALL to SAMUEL FRANKS for 20 pds 132 acres granted 6 Mar. 1786 on Little River, bounded on NEHEMIAH FRANKS, J. WILLIAMS, ROBERT ROSS. Wit: CHARLES SMITH, WILLIAM RODGERS, JOHN WILLIAMS.

Page 272:   10 Dec. 1787 - 16 Jan. 1788 JOSHUA ARNALL to NEHEMIAH FRANKS for 20 pds sterling 228 acres granted 1786 on Little River bounded on MARSHALL FRANKS, NEHEMIAH FRANKS, NATHAN BARKSDALE, SAMUEL FRANKS. Wit: CHAS. SMITH, WM. RODGERS, JOHN WILLIAMS.

Page 273:   10 Sept. 1787 - 17 Jan. 1788 WILLIAM HUDDLESTON, black-smith and wife, JEAN to MATTHEW HUNTER for 30 pds, 100 acres on Millers Fork of Duncans Creek, part of orig. 476 acre grant 11 Aug. 1774. Wit: JAMES HUDDLESTON, GEORGE LEVISTON.

Page 275:   5 Nov. 1787 - 7 Apr. 1788 JOHN FALKONER to my well beloved friend NATHANIEL HALL, SR., after my decease and that of my now living wife, ELIZABETH, all my negroes, to wit Priscilla, George, Juda, Ephraim, Milly and all their increase, likewise my stock of every king and household furniture and everything else I possess in the world. Wit: ROBERT HALL, HANNAH CLARDY, JOHN HALL. Affidavit of JOHN HALL & HANNAH CLARDY bef. JAMES MAYSON, J.P., also a lease of 100 acres of land from sd NATHL. HALL to sd JOHN FALCONER as a happy exchange of brotherly love.

Page 276:   1 Dec. 1787 - 18 Jan. 1788 FREDERICK LITTLE to WILLIAMA HUBBS(?) for 30 pds, 100 acres orig. granted to MARGARET TODD by letters patent 17 Mar. 1775, conveyed to F. LITTLE 17 June 1779 on small branch of Reaburns Creek, bounded by JOHN RICHEY. Wit: ALEXANDER HAMILTON, ROBERT TODD, CHARLES GAFFY.

Page 277:   3 Aug. 1787 - 19 Jan. 1788 THOMAS & ELENOR BOYCE to JOHN ADAMS for 40 pds, 250 acres on both sides of Raborns Creek orig. grant 1785 to JAMES TWEDE. Wit: CHARLES WILLSON, JOHN JOHNSTON, ELIZABETH DONAL.

Page 280:   25 June 1787 - 12 Jan. 1788 WILLIAM YOUNG, planter to ALEXANDER HARPER, planter for 30 pds 50 acres part of 173 acre grant 6 Feb. 1786 on Durbins Creek. Wit: BENJAMIN RAINEY, WILLIAM JACKSON.

Page 282:   10 Dec. 1787 - 23 Jan. 1788 ALEXANDER MC DOWELL to JOHN MILWEE of N. C. for 93 pds, 400 acres above the line on Washington Creek of Saluda River, surveyed and certified 25 Sept. 1784 by EPHRAIM MITCHELL, Surv. Gen'l., JOHN MARTIN, Deputy Surv. Wit: WM. DUNLAP, WM. MILWEE.

Page 283:   5 Aug. 1786 - 23 Jan. 1788 JOHN HARVEY and wife MARY of Georgia to WILLIAM RODGERS for 40 pds 100 acres on Beards Fork of Duncans Creek, orig. granted 28 Feb. 1777 bounded by ANDREW RODGERS, SR. Wit: ROBERT CULBERTSON, ANDREW RODGERS, JOHN GARNER.

Page 284:   13 Dec. 1787 - 24 Jan. 1788 ADAM GORDON to SAMUEL DUNLAP for 80 pds 100 acres on Jones Branch of Reaburns Creek, orig. granted 17 Mar. 1775 to MARY RICHEY, the sd GORDON's wife. Wit: LEWIS SAXON, C.C.

Page 287:   13 July 1787 - 25 Jan. 1788 ROBERT SHELTON, planter, to
               DANIEL WRIGHT, for (?) 100 acres on South fork of Durbins
Creek, part of 200 acres orig. granted to DAVID WELCH 1773. Wit: LUTHER
SMITH, MICHAEL WALLACE.

Page 288:   18 Sept. 1787 - 26 Jan. 1788 WILLIAM PRICE, planter and
               his wife MARGRET to JOHN SAXON for 25 pds, 100 acres on
Duncans Creek of Enoree River, part of 150 acres orig. granted to JAMES
YOUNG 31 Aug. 1774. Wit: JOHN HUNTER, ROBERT BLACK, JAMES SAXON.

Page 290:   13 Dec. 1787 - 28 Jan. 1788 JOHN SAXON, planter to ROBERT
               BLACK for 25 pds, 100 acres on Dunkins Creek of Enoree
River above grant to JAS. YOUNG, conveyed to WM. PRICE, then to sd
SAXON. Wit: JAS. FLOYD.

Page 293:   2 Oct. 1787 - 29 Jan. 1788 RICHARD ROBISON, planter of
               Abbeville Co., to WM. DONNAHOE, planter, for 55 pds, 150
acres on Beaverdame Creek of Little River, orig. grant 7 Oct. 1755
to CHRISTOPHER PLYNAS, conveyed (?) Mar. 1756 to JACOB PENNINGTON,
then by sd PENNINGTON's last will and testament to RANDOLPH CASEY and
on 27 Sept. 1787 to sd R. ROBISON. Wit: PATRICK CUNINGHAM, JOEL BURGESS
& CATHERINE HARRIS.

Page 296:   9 Aug. 1787 - 30 Jan. 1788 WILLIAM PRICE to MARY, RUTH,
               SARAH & JENNY, his daughters lawfully begotten with his
wife MARGARET PRICE, one bay mare, two cows, 20 hogs, furniture...Wit:
THOMAS EWING, JOHN HUNTER.

Page 297:   18 Feb. 1788 - 1 Apr. 1788 JOHN WILLIAMS, SR. and wife
               ANN MARIAH to SAMUEL GOODMAN for 53 pds, 100 acres on
Mudlick Creek, orig. grant 9 Sept. 1774 to JOHN ONEAL, conveyed (?)
Jan. 1778 to J. WILLIAMS. Wit: WM. CALDWELL, JOHN RODGERS, HARRIS GILLAM

Page 300:   2 Sept. 1786 - 2 Apr. 1788 I, RICHARD OWINS, freeholder
               on Reedy River, to my loving son BUTLER OWINS for love
and affection my 100 acre plantatioin on Reedy River near the fish
dam ford, which I bought of JAMES HENDERSON, also one feather bed and
furniture, one pewter dish and six plates, two pewter basins, one large
kettle or iron pot, tools .... Wit: WM. BAUGH, SAML. MC CLURKIN, JOHN
BAUGH.

Page 300:   11 Aug. 1787 - 2 Apr. 1788 I, DANIEL MC LAIN, freeholder
               of Reedy River, to my loving daughter ELIZABETH OWINGS
100 acres of land on Reedy River. Wit: WM. OBANNON, JOHN HUTSON.

Page 301:   10 Mar. 1788 - 3 Apr. 1788 JOEL BURGESS and wife ELENOR
               to RICHARD SHIP for 200 pds, 95 acres on Beaverdame Creek
of Little River, 75 acres part of orig. grant to ACQUILLA HALL 1770,
20 acres granted to sd BURGESS 1786; bounded on MC NEES GOOD, MARK
MOORE, ACQUILLA HALL, CHARLES PARROTT, WIDOW HARVEY. Wit: LEWIS SAXON,
C.C.

Page 302:   10 May 1786 - 4 Apr. 1788 I, WILLIAM CLINTON, to my son
               ROBERT CLINTON gift of 188 acres on Flat Shoals Branch
of Enoree River....to my two daughters, MARY CLINTON and PERMELIA CLIN-
TON, my goods and chattels, property except the land. Wit: THOS. GARRI-
SON, JOHN CAMPBELL.

Page 302:   3 Oct. 1787 - 4 Apr. 1788 I, HUGH ONEALL, miller, to my
               son HUGH ONEALL gift of 150 acres on Little River above
the mill; to my son CHARLES a gift of 150 acres on Little River; to
my son THOMAS ONEALL 270 acres on Reaburns Creek, bounded on PATRICK
RILEY, MARY MC DONALD, ROBT. SIMS;; to my daughter ELIZABETH MC DANIEL
and her husband THOMAS MC DANIEL a cow and calf; my four young children
to be well schooled; my moveable effects to be divided among my four
daughters PATIENCE, ANN, RUTH, & RACHEL. Ex'rs: MERCER BABB, WM. PIN-
SON, ELISHA FORD. Wit: JOHN HUNTER, THOS. WADSWORTH, PATK. MC DOWELL.

Page 304:   18 Aug. 1785 - 5 Apr. 1788 GEORGE WHITMORE to REUBEN FLANA-
GAN for 3 pds, 100 acres on Duncans Creek, part of 577 acre tract sur-

Cont'd:
veyed 13 Aug. 1784. Wit: JAMES DUNCAN, NICHOLAS WELCH, ROBERT OLIPHANT.

Page 308:   12 Nov. 1787 - 8 Apr. 1788 ENOCH BRAMBLET the real heir
             of WILLIAM BRAMBLET, dec'd. to THOMAS HIGGINS for 20 pds,
100 acres on Long branch, part of a larger survey granted to sd WM.
BRAMBLET 25 Apr. 1774. Wit: JOHN MC ELROY, SANDFORD BRAMBLET, DAVID
MC ELROY.

Page 309:   25 Oct. 1787 - 9 Apr. 1788 ROBERT ROSS and wife MARGARET
             to ROBERT HANNA for 30 pds, 150 acres on the Dividing
Ridge bet. Enoree River and Duncans Creek, bounded by MARY HANNA and
THOMAS LOGAN. Wit: WM. CHEEK, THOS. WORD, JOHN HANNA.

Page 311:   8 Sept. 1787 - 10 Apr. 1788 JOHN BURNS and JOHN NORRIS
             to FRANCIS CUNNINGHAM for 25 pds, 50 acres on Norths Creek
part of 250 acre grant to MANOAH TINSLEY. Wit: JOHN BLEAKLY, WM. TEAGUE.

Page 312:   15 Nov. 1787 - 12 Apr. 1788 WILLIAM NEILL, planter to
             SAMUEL NEILL, planter, for 20 pds 135 acres orig. grant
3 Apr. 1786. Wit: WM. DUNLAP, WM. EAST.

Page 314:   7 May 1787 - 14 Apr. 1788 THOMAS GORDON, gentleman, and
             wife ELIZABETH of Newberry, to ARON HARLIN, planter for
71 pds 300 acres on Duncans Creek, formerly supposed to be in the Province of North Carolina and granted by Matthew Roan, Esq., Gov. of
N. C. by patent 23 Feb. 1754. Wit: JAMES HANNA, WM. HANNA, THOS. GORDON.

Page 316:   5 Mar. 1788 - 15 Apr. 1788 HUGH MC VAY and his wife MARTHA
             to DANIEL MARTIN for 150 pds, 280 acres on Little River
of the Saludy near Court House of Laurens, granted 21 Jan. 1785, bounded
by JOHN RODGERS, NATHAN BARKSDALE, NEHEMIAH FRANKS, ROBERT CULBERTSON,
ABRAHAM NEIGHBOURS. Wit: MANCIL CRISP, ROBT. CULBERTSON, JAMES CULBERT-
SON.

Page 318:   31 Jan. 1788 - 16 Apr. 1788 JOHN SHIRLEY and his wife
             REBECCA to WM. MITCHELL for 70 pds, 200 acres on Raborns
Creek, orig. granted 28 Aug. 1767. Bounded by GEORGE WRIGHT. Wit: AARON
STARNES, WM. GOODMAN, STEPHEN WOOD.

Page 321:   30 Dec. 1787 - 17 Apr. 1788 PATRICK BRYAN and his wife
             ELIZABETH to JAMES UNDERWOOD for 60 pds, 184 acres on
a branch of Bush River, orig. granted 3 Apr. 1786. Wit: JOHN HUNTER,
WILLIAM DUNLAP.

Page 323:   23 Feb. 1786 - 18 Apr. 1788 ANDREW CUNINGHAM to ABRAHAM
             GRAY for 60 pds 100 acres on south side of Enoree River,
formerly called Kings River, part of 600 acres orig. granted to BARTLETT
BROWN, dec'd., by Gov. Roan of N. C. 4 May 1753. Wit: JOHN LINDSEY,
GEORGE VAUGHN, HENRY HAMILTON.

Page 324:   10 Dec. 1787 - 18 Apr. 1788 ISAAC & SUSANNA HOLLINGSWORTH
             to NATHANIEL ROOK for 10 pds 150 acres part of a grant
dated 8 July 1774 to JOHN THORNTOWN, other part 8 July 1774 to sd ISAAC
HOLLINGSWORTH, bounded by JOHN CALDWELL, WM. LITHGOW, ABRAHAM HOLLINGS-
WORTH. Wit: JOHN COOK, JONATHAN HOLLINGSWORTH, ANGUS CAMPBELL.

Page 327:   18 Jan. 1785 - 20 Apr. 1788 JOSEPH REDDING, minister of
             the gospel, appoints SAMUEL SAXON his attorney to ask,
demand, recover and receive a bay mare from WILLIAM FERCUAHARD(?) CAMP-
BELL of Cumberland Co., N. C. Wit: CHRISTOPHER MATTHEWS, JOHN MITCHELL,
DAVID MC GLADERY.

Page 328:   11 Mar. 1788 - 21 Apr. 1788 THOMAS ALLISON, blacksmith,
             and his wife CATHERINE to JAMES ADAIR, planter, for 57
pds 100 acres on Allisons Creek orig. granted 22 Jan. 1759 to HANS
JORGMAN, conveyed (?) Nov. 1759 to sd ALLISON. Wit: ROBERT HANNA, ROBERT
MC CRAREY, JOHN JONES.

Page 330:   20 Sept. 1787 - 22 Apr. 1788 JOHN GOODWIN and wife RACHEL

Cont'd:
                to REUBIN PYLES for 52 pds 200 acres on Reedy River below
the Old Indian Boundary where sd JOHN GOODWIN now lives on Beaverdam
Creek, orig. grant 9 Sept. 1774. Wit: ABNER PYLES, GEORGE BARNES.

Page 332:   19 Feb. 1787 - 23 Apr. 1788 GEORGE ADAMS, planter of New-
                berry and his wife SARAH to RICHARD TURNER for 60 pds
100 acres part of a grant to JOHN ANSBURY 15 July 1765. Wit: RICHARD
WATTS, JOHN CALDWELL, JOHN TURNER.

Page 335:   28 Feb. 1788 - 24 Apr. 1788 NEBO GAUNT of Dist. of Camden
                son and heir of ZEBULON GAUNT, dec'd., to JONATHAN DOWNS
for 42 pds, 400 acres on Raborns Creek of Saluda, granted 7 Oct. 1762.
Wit: ROBERT COOPER, JOHN CALHOUN.

Page 337:   1 July 1787 - 25 Apr. 1788 GEORGE DALRYMPLE and wife ANN
                to BAILEY MAHON for 50 pds 100 acres orig. granted 13
May 1768 to JOHN READY in Berkley Co. on a branch of Saluday called
Ready Creek, conveyed to sd GEO. DALRYMPLE. Wit: JOSHUA TEAGUE, ALEX-
ANDER MORRISON, JOHN THOMAS.

Page 340:   9 Feb. 1788 - 25 Apr. 1788 JAMES MC NEES to ROBERT MC
                NEES for 100 pds (bond on 160 acres where I now live)
for a likely negro 14-21 (years?) on or bef. Dec. 25 next. Wit: WM.
JONES, ANDREW RODGERS, JOHN RODGERS, J.P.

Page 341:   6 Nov. 1787 - 16 June 1788 I, MARY EDWARDS to my loving
                grandsons JAMES & JOHN EDWARDS my tract of 150 acres on
Cain Creek, to be equally divided; to my loving granddaughter MARY
EDWARDS one featherbed, bedstead and furniture, one cow and calf,
one iron pot, 3 pewter dishes, 8 plates, 2 basons, one box iron, 1
pair fire tongs. Until grandchildren are of age unto my loving daughter
-in-law, now MARY CRAIG, who now lives with her husband WILLIAM CRAIG.
Wit: CHARLES WILSON, JOHN NEILEY, JOSEPH NEILEY.

Page 343:   2 June 1788 - 17 June 1788 ANDREW CUNINGHAM as attorney
                for JAMES HAMILTON to SPENCER BOBO for (?) 100 acres on
Beverlys branch of Warrior Creek of Enoree River, bounded on lands
laid out for WM. HUTCHINSON, JOHN HALL, surveyed by ROBT. HANNA and
JAMES HAMBLETON. Wit: JAMES CUNINGHAM, ELIZABETH CUNINGHAM.

Page 344:   9 June 1788 - 18 June 1788 JAMES MILLER, yeoman of Lancast-
                er Co., S.C. to WILLIAM DEAN for 25 pds 100 acres on War-
riors Creek, orig. granted to MARTHA RUSSEL 5 Aug. 1768, now MARTHA
MILLER. Wit: FRANCIS SPENCER, WARRINGTON __?__, JOSEPH DEAN.

Page 346:   9 Feb. 1788 - 19 June 1788 JOHN SOUTH of Bluford(?) Dist.,
                S. C. to JOSIAH CHILES for 80 pds 100 acres on north side
of Saluday River part of grant to JOHN OXBERRY conveyed to PATRICK
HIGGINS then to sd J. SOUTH on GEORGE ADAMS, WM. THOMAS, _____ WATTS,
dec'd. Wit: NIMROD CHILES, WILLIAM SMITH.

Page 350:   6 June 1788 - 20 June 1788 WILLIAM COKER and wife MARY
                to JAMES BROWN for 100 pds 150 acres part of 300 acres
granted 23 Dec. 1771 to ROLLY BOWEN on south side of Enoree River.
Wit: JOHN FARROW, JOHN BROWN.

Page 352:   Ninety Six (Dist.) 25 Jan. 1778. Sir, I desire you if
                suitable to make titles to 250 acres, being part of 1250
acres, to Mr. ANGUS CAMPBELL. The land lyes on Warriours Creek adj.
Capt. BERRY's and MC CRERY's, also to 450 acres on Enoree River, joining lands of WALDROP & PETERSON and Capt. BERRY. Capt. CALDWELL prom-
ises to receive titles by whom I have sent your obligations...I am
Sir, your H. Serv't...WILLIAM SIMS. To WM. WILLIAMSON, Esq. (Enclosed
a note asking conveyance of 1250 acres granted 5 May 1772, from THOMAS
WOODWARD to WILLIAM SIMS).

Page 353:   WILLIAM SIMS bound to ANGUS CAMPBELL for 1000 pds. Dec.
                1776. Wit: JAS. BURNSIDE, SAMPSON MUNGER. SILV. WALKER,
J.P. 9 June 1788.

Page 353:	11 June 1788 - 20 June 1788 CHARLES SMITH, GEORGE ANDERSON, SILVANUS WALKER, Esqs., bound unto LEWIS SAXON, Guardian of LYDALL ALLEN in sum of 222 pds. Wit: JOHN HUNTER, ROBT. ROSS, D. ANDERSON, MANSILL CRISP.

Page 354:	4 Apr. 1788 - 20 June 1788 REUBIN PYLES and his wife S. E. to LEWIS SAXON, for 75 pds, negro woman and child. Wit: LYDALL ALLEN, JOHN PILES.

Page 355:	10 June 1788 - 23 June 1788 HASTING DIAL and his wife REBECCA to JOHN SWEARINGS for 47 pds 247 acres on Williams Creek below the Line, orig. grant 3 Oct. 1785 bounded on sd H. DOYAL (DIAL) and THOMAS ALLISON. Wit: MANSIL CRISP, JOHN RITCHEY, JOSEPH PINSON.

Page 357:	1 Jan. 1787 - 24 June 1788 MARY WILLIAMS, Executrix of the late Col. JAMES WILLIAMS, to my beloved daughter ELIZA-BETH TINDSLEY, (slaves named). Also 150 acres of land, orig. granted to JOSEPH HUTCHERSON 6 Mar. 1770 on Mudlick Creek. Wit: JOHN WILLIAMS, JR., ROBERT SAYER, ANTHONY GOLDEN, JAMES CRESWELL, PRESTINGS TINDSLEY.

Page 358:	14 May 1788 - 24 June 1788 JOSEPH GRIFFIN and his wife MARY to JAMES WILLIAMS and WASHINGTON WILLIAMS for love and affection as well as 434 pds, ten negroes...two feather beds...to be equally divided when JAMES comes of age. If either of them should die before then, his quota shall be equally divided among the sons and daughters of the late Col. JAMES WILLIAMS, deceased.

Page 359:	1 Apr. 1788 - 25 June 1788 JOSEPH GRIFFIN and his wife MARY to SARAH GRIFFIN for love and affection and 207 pds, (5 slaves named), one feather bed and furniture. Wit: ARCHIE SIERS, JOHN NEILEY. (Receipt 5/13/1788 SARAH GRIFFIN by the hand of her husband JOHN GRIFFIN 207 pds, signed by JOS. GRIFFIN.)

Page 360:	26 Jan. 1787 - 26 June 1788 MARY WILLIAMS to JOHN WILLIAMS JR., five negroes. Wit: SILVANUS WALKER, JOSEPH GRIFFIN, WILLIAM CALDWELL.

Page 360:	12 Feb. 1788 - 27 June 1788 JOSHUA CATES to JOSEPH PARSONS for 20 pds 640 acres granted 6 Feb. 1786 except 50 acres laid out for MIDDLETON COUCH on side side of Enoree River including mouth of Cox's Branch E of the Indian Boundary. Wit: SAMUEL PARSONS, JOSEPH DEAN.

Page 363:	6 Feb. 1788 - 28 Oct. 1788 JOHN ENTREKIN to WILLIAM DUNLAP for 6 pds sterling, 2 cows, 1 heifer...Wit: THOMAS GREEN(?) & JOHN HUNTER, J.P.

Page 363:	9 Sept. 1788 - 28 Oct. 1788 GEORGE HOLLINGSWORTH, eldest son of ABRAHAM HOLLINGSWORTH, dec'd., late of Laurens, formerly of Virginia, to BENJAMIN GRUBB, power of attorney to ask, demand, etc. bequests left unto me by my grandfather and father in the state of Virginia. Wit: LEWIS SAXON, C.C.

Page 364:	9 Sept. 1788 - 17 Sept. 1788 MARY BABB, Executrix of the last will and testament of JOSEPH BABB, dec'd, appoints friend PETER TUBB(?) (BABB?) her atty. to settle the accounts of her late husband with JOHN HARRIS, Exr. of JOHN MC COOL, dec'd. of the state of Pennsylvania, also with JOHN ANTRUN & for others.

Page 364:	11 Sept. 1788 - 15 Sept. 1788 SARAH RIGHT (WRIGHT) appoints JACOB BOWMAN her atty relative to her part of her deceased father, GEORGE BOWMAN's esate in Virginia. Wit: LEWIS SAXON, C.C.

Page 365:	5 Sept. 1788 - 15 Sept. 1788 EBENEZER STARNES appoints JACOB BOWMAN his attorney to recover or receive payment for a good mare lost in 1782, supposed to be carried from here by a certain DANIEL WILLIAMS. Wit: LEWIS SAXON, C.C.

Page 365:	11 Sept. 1788 - 15 Sept. 1788 SARAH BOWMAN, Admr. of JACOB

Cont'd:
                  BOWMAN, deceased, appoints her son JACOB BOWMAN her atty
relative to her part of her father, LAURENS (LAWRENCE) STEPHENS' Estate.
Wit: LEWIS SAXON, C.C.

Page 366:   27 Dec. 1787 - 23 Oct. 1788 JOEL BURGESS to LEWIS SAXON,
                  for 60 pds 150 acres on south fork of Reaburn Creek, bound-
ing on lands of ALEXANDER MAZICK, THOMAS CAHOON, JOHN MC CLANAHAN,
MOSES KIRTLAND, granted to sd LEWIS SAXON 1 Jan. 1785, conveyed to
sd JOEL BURGESS and now back to LEWIS SAXON. Wit: JOSHUA DOWNS, WM.
RODGERS.

Page 367:   11 Mar. 1788 - 27 June 1788 WILLIAM GUNTER and his wife
                  ANN to ROBERT HAND for 20 pds sterling 100 acres on south
side of Enoree River, bounding on ROLLY BOWEN, ENOCH PEARSON, WILLIAM
HUMPHREYS. Wit: ENOCH PEARSON, DAVID CHILDRESS, JAS. MONTGOMERY, J.P.

Page 369:   10 Mar. 1788 - 1 Nov. 1788 EDMOND LEARWOOD and JESSE MEEKS
                  to THOMAS JONES for 17 pds 100 acres on Beaverdam Creek
and Little River, part of orig. 600 acre grant adj. the Big Survey.
Wit: ALEXANDER HAMILTON, STEPHEN PLANT, DAVID BURRISS. JOHN RODGERS,
J.P.

Page 370:   17 July 1788 - 3 Nov. 1788 ROGER BROOKS, blacksmith of
                  Edgefield Co. to LEWIS SAXON, farmer for 50 pds, 200 acres
on Reedy River orig. granted 3 Sept. 1787, bounding on HUGH BEARD,
WM. NORRIS. Wit: JOHN H. HUGHES, CHAS. SMITH. JOHN RODGERS, J.P.

Page 372:   3 Mar. 1788 - 28 June 1788 WILLIAM GUNTER and his wife
                  ANN to WILLIAM HEAD for 20 pds, 52 acres part of a 445
acre grant 2 May 1785, on south side of Enoree River, bounded by WM.
HUMPHREYS, ENOCH PEARSON, ROBT. HAND. Wit: ENOCH PEARSON, ROBT. HAND.
JAMES MONTGOMERY, J.P.

Page 375:   19 Jan. 1787 - 30 June 1788 MARY WILLIAMS to JAMES ATWOOD
                  WILLIAMS, (slaves - Indian man named Thom, negro woman
named Flora, 3 others). Wit: SILVANUS WALKER, JOSEPH GRIFFIN, WM. CALD-
WELL. Affidavit of S. WALKER 9 June 1788; MARY WILLIAMS now MARY GRIFFIN
& ANGUS CAMPBELL, J.P.

Page 375:   29 Jan. 1787 - 30 June 1788 MARY WILLIAMS to JAMES ATWOOD
                  WILLIAMS, 150 acres of land. (Same wit. etc. as above).

Page 376:   11 Apr. 1787 - 30 June 1788 CHARLES SAXON and his wife
                  JUDITH to their son SAMUEL SAXON for 40 pds, 200 acres
on Three and Twenty Mile Creek in Abbeville Co., granted 6 June 1786.
Wit: JAMES YOUNG, JAMES MERONEY.

Page 381:   7 Sept. 1787 - 1 July 1788 RANDOLPH CASEY and his wife
                  CHARITY of Greenville Co. to RICHARD ROBISON of Abbeville
Co., for 50 pds sterling, 150 acres on Beaverdam Creek of Little River,
orig. granted to CHRISTOPHER PLINES 23 July 1755; conveyed to JACOB
PENNINGTON, then by will to CASEY and wife. Wit: LEVI CASEY, WM. DONAHOE.

Page 382:   ......- 15 Sept. 1788 JOHN BOWLES to THOMAS RODGERS and
                  JANE his wife, relinquishes (at their suit) 100 acres
on Little River, orig. surveyed for SAMUEL FULLERTON, bounded on T.
CARTER, HENRY ONEAL, JAS. HUNTER. Wit: WM. MC DONALD, CURTIS MOORE.

Page 383:   14 Oct. 1775 - 15 Sept. 1788 RALPH HUMPHREYS, Surveyor
                  of Crven Co., Province of S. C., to JOHN WILLIAMS, planter,
for 300 pds, 100 acres on Durbins Creek, orig. granted 15 July 1768
to JOHN HUMPHREYS and conveyed to RALPH HUMPHREYS bounded on JOHN BOYD's
land. Wit: LEWIS DUTARGUE, JOHN BOYD. JAMES LINDLEY, Esq., J.P. (17
Oct. 1775).

Page 385:   19 Mar. 1788 - 5 July 1788 JOSEPH CHAPMEN, planter, and
                  his wife MARY to WILLIAM POWELL, planter, for 156 pds,
250 acres on northeast side of Saluda River, orig. granted to ARON
PINSON 2 June 1769, conveyed by him to sd CHAPMAN 18 Nov. 1784, bounded

Cont'd:
on JOSHUA MOORE. Wit: BARNETT COMBS, ABSALOM BOBO, ELLENDER HOOD. GEO.
ANDERSON, J.P.

Page 388:   14 June 1785 - 7 July 1788 GEORGE BERRY, planter, to SETH
               PETTY POOL, planter, for 100 pds, 100 acres part of 450
acres granted 17 Apr. 1767 to WILLIAM BERRY, deceased, on north side
of Warriors Creek of Enoree River. Wit: PETER BROOKS, ANDREW CUNINGHAM,
JOHN HALL.

Page 390:   10 June 1788 - 8 July 1788 SAMUEL NEIGHBOURS to ABRAHAM
               BOX for 100 pds sterling, 114 acres on Reedy River, part
of 640 acres granted 5 Sept. 1785, bounding on JOHN BOX, S. NEIGHBOURS.
Wit: LEWIS SAXON, C.C.

Page 393:   3 Jan. 1788 - 9 July 1788 GEORGE BERRY, planter and his
               wife MARY to WM. BERRY for 50 pds, 80 acres part of orig.
grant of 24 Nov. 1767 to WM. BERRY, deceased, on Warrior Creek bounding on SUSANNA BROOKS. Wit: PETER BROOKS, SPENCER BOBO, JR.

Page 395:   13 Aug. 1788 - 15 Sept. 1788 JOHN HENDERSON to MARY HENDER-
               SON for 20 pds, 150 acres on Rabourns Creek below the
Ancient Boundary Line, granted 4 July 1785 bounding on NICHOLAS HILL.
Wit: JOHN BAUGH, JOHN BRODEY.

Page 396:   ...... - 13 Mar. 1789 JOHN THOMAS to RICHARD GRIFFEN for
               11 pds sterling, one brown bay horse ten years old by
gates & trotter named Pardoner branded on the near shoulder, one certain
bay mare named Diamond 3 years old Gaits and pacer branded on near
shoulder, red and white cow named Lilly...heifers...two feather beds....
chest with lock and kee....Wit: JOHN COMMINS.

Page 397:   13 Jan. 1789 - 18 Mar. 1789 CURTIS MOORE to LEVY MOORE
               for 100 pds, horses, cows, feather beds, furniture...Wit:
JAS. MC NEES, JOHN BOYD...JOHN RODGERS, J.P.

Page 398:   19 Mar. 1789 - 24 Mar. 1789 ROBERT BOX appoints three
               trusty friends, ADONIJAH MORGAN, Col. GEORGE DOHERTIE
& ROBERT CAMBLE all of Green Co., N.C. his attorneys to execute deed
to THOMAS DAVIS for 100 acres of land in sd co. entered in Washington
Co. on Camp Creek on LEWIS MORGAN's line. Wit: JAS. CUNINGHAM, JOHN
JONES, JOHN ABERCROMBY. JOHN RODGERS, J.P.

Page 399:   18 July 1788 - 16 Sept. 1788 JOHN WALDROP, planter and
               his wife ELIZABETH to SETH PETTY POOL for 100 pds, 100
acres on Enoree River granted 1772 to JAMES WALDROP, conveyed by lease
and release. Wit: PETER BROOKS, WM. BERRY.

Page 401:   1 Feb. 1789 - 7 Apr. 1789 JOHN DONNAHOW, planter to COR-
               NELIUS DONNAHOW, planter for 225 pds sterling, 450 acres
on Mudlick Creek, orig. grant 1 Oct. 1767 and 5 Nov. 1771, on which
he now lives. Wit: WM. DONNAHOE, MARY KELLEY.

Page 403:   10 June 1788 - 7 Apr. 1789 WILLIAM DONNAHOW to CORNELIUS
               DONNAHOW for 54 pds, 150 acres on Beaverdam Creek bounded
S & W on JOSEPH BABB, N & E on WM. DREW, granted 3 June 1755 to CHR.
PLINES, var. conveyed to JACOB PENNINGTON, RANDOLPH CASEY, RICHARD
ROBINSON, sd WM. DONNAHOW. Wit: JOHN WILLIAMSON, JOHN BARNET WILLIAMSON.

Page 406:   29 Mar. 1786 - 17 Sept. 1788 ABIJAH ONEAL of Bush River
               to JONATHAN JOHNSON for 50 pds, 75 acres on Mudlick Creek
bounding on RICHARD GRIFFIN, ANGUS CAMPBELL, JAMES BURNSIDE. Wit:
WM. ONEALL, JAMES BROOKS, JOSEPH ARMSTRONG.

Page 408:   24 Apr. 1788 - 17 Sept. 1788 WM. RUCKS to JONATHAN JOHN-
               SON, merchant, for 13 pds, mortgage on negro. Wit: THOMAS,
WM. & MARGARET FAKES.

Page 409:   4 Apr. 1788 - 18 Sept. 1788 LUKE WALDROP, planter and

Cont'd:
                his wife MARY to WILLIAM EAST, JR. for 36 pds, 130 acres
on Little River, orig. grant 3 Oct. 1785. Wit: SHADRACH EAST, WILLIAM
EAST.

Page 411:   9 Mar. 1789 - 23 Apr. 1789 CLAYBOURN SIMS and his wife
                MARTHA to JAMES BURNSIDE for 20 pds, 100 acres south side
of Little River.

Page 412:   3 May 1788 - 19 Sept. 1788 JOHN ONEALL to son-in-law WM.
                SHANLEY, a negro girl Milley. Wit: ANGUS CAMPBELL, MAR-
GRET SCOTT, JOHN COOK.

Page 412:   4 Aug. 1786 - 3 May 1789 HENRY PEARSON and his wife FRANCES
                of Newberry Co. to DAVID MC GLADERY for 28 pds, 90 acres
on northeast side of Reedy River below the Ancient Boundary, granted
4 Apr. 1785. Wit: JONATHAN DOWNS, CHARLES GARY.

Page 414:   27 Apr. 1789 - 30 May 1789 MICAJAH SIMS, farmer, to ROBERT
                FILPOT for 20 pds, 100 acres on South Fork of Raburns
Creek, granted 13 May 1768 to JAMES SMITH. Wit: SAMUEL BARTON, ELIAS
WASHER.

Page 416:   22 Aug. 1788 - 30 June 1789 JOHN GREER, SR. to RUTH ADAIR
                for 50 pds, 150 acres on Duncans Creek, part of 300 acre
tract where sd JNO. GREER now lives, bounded on BASIL PRATHER. Wit:
JOHN OWINS, JOSIAH GREER, JOHN ROBINSON.

Page 419:   8 June 1789 - 30 June 1789 THOMAS ELLIOTT, SR., freeholder
                and planter, of Reaburns Creek settlement, to my loving
son THOMAS ELLIOTT, JR. bachelor, all my lands and tenements, all my
estate real and personal. Wit: JONATHAN DOWNS, J.P., WM. SIMMONS.

Page 419:   16 July 1788 - 8 July 1789 THOMAS DENDY and his wife MARY
                to WILLIAM DENDY for 50 pds, 125 acres on both sides of
Little River, bounded by MC KINZE, WM. HALL, JAMES YOUNG, JOHN OSBURN,
MC NEES GOOD.

Page 420:   16 July 1788 - 10 July 1789 WILLIAM DENDY and his wife
                CLARY, to JOHN MILAM for 146 pds, 225 acres on both sides
of Little River, part of orig. grant to JOHN MC KINZY, conveyed to
TOBIAS MYERS, to WM. DENDY, part to THOMAS DENDY, SR., conveyed to
WM. DENDY.

Page 421:   22 Mar. 1788 - 15 July 1789 JAMES DILLARD and his wife
                MARY, to JOSEPH WHITMORE for 4 pds, 17 acres low ground
on Enoree River, orig. grant to SAMUEL DILLARD 4 July 1785, conveyed
to sd JAMES DILLARD, bounded on BAZEL PRATHER & JOHN SANDERS. Wit:
NICHOLAS WELCH, GEORGE WHITMORE.

Page 423:   27 Dec. 1785 - 21 July 1789 JAMES BRIGHT and his wife
                SARAH, of Spartanburg Co. to MARGARET HENDRIX for 150
pds, 100 acres on branch of Enoree River, granted 29 Apr. 1768. Wit:
GEO. WHITMORE, SAML. BISHOP, CHARITY BRIGHT.

Page 425:   1 Nov. 1788 - 27 July 1789 REUBIN FLANAGIN and his wife
                AVERILLA to BRICE PRATHER for 20 pds, 100 acres on south
fork of Dunkins Creek. Wit: GEO. WHITMORE, NICHOLAS WELCH, JOSEPH WHIT-
MORE.

Page 426:   1 June 1788 - 3 Aug. 1789 THOMAS JONES, planter of Mill
                Creek, to JOHN SADLER, planter, for 65 pds, 100 acres
on (?) side of Cason's road. Wit: SAMUEL WHARTON.

Page 428:   12 Sept. 1788 - 13 Aug. 1789 BAZELL PRATHER and his wife
                PRISCILLA to WILLIAM PRUDE for 60 pds, 150 acres on south
side of Enoree River, surveyed 1 Aug. 1762 and granted 25 Aug. 1768.
Wit: JOSEPH WHITMORE, JOSEPH ADAIR, JOHN ROBINSON.

Page 431:;   12 Sept. 1788 - 14 Aug. 1789 JOSEPH WHITMORE and his wife

Cont'd:
MARGARET to WILLIAM PRUDE, 17 acres low ground, part of
440 acres orig. granted to SAMUEL DILLARD 4 July 1785, conveyed to
JAMES DILLARD then to JOS. WHITMORE, bounded on BAZZEL PRATHER & JOHN
SANDERS. Wit: JNO. ROBINSON, EDMOND SIMPSON, JOHN PROUD.

Page 435:   10 June 1788 - 23 Aug. 1789 JOHN PRUDE, SR. to JOHN PRUDE,
              JR. 250 acres whereon the Senior now lives. Wit: JOHN
& MARGARET ROBINSON, JOHN GARRET, JAMES FINDLEY.

Page 435:   6 Feb. 1789 - 26 Aug. 1789 LEWIS DUVALL, hatter and his
              wife TERRESA to JOHN SIMPSON, merchant, for 150 pds 1475
acres on Duncans Creek of Enoree River granted 4 Dec. 1786. Wit: JOHN
MC COSH, ANDREW SMITH, CHARLES SAXON, J.P.

Page 435:   15 Jan. 1789 - 1 Sept. 1789 THOMAS DAVIDSON, planter and
              his wife SARAH to ANDREW SMITH, surgeon, for 95 pds 100
acres on Little River part of 350 acres orig. granted to CHARLES HARVEY
(?) May 1771, conveyed to JACOB JONES, then to JAMES LEFFAN, then to
sd DAVIDSON 29 Dec. 1785. Wit: ROBERT MC CLINTOCK, JOHN SIMPSON, JAMES
DAVIDSON. CHARLES SAXON, J.P.

Page 437:   14 Aug. 1788 - 1 Sept. 1789 WILLIAM CASON and his wife
              ANN to HENRY HARDING for 75 pds 100 acres on Banks Branch
of Saluda, part of 300 acres orig. granted to WM. WATSON 7 June 1774.
200 acres conveyed to sd CASON 22 Sept. 1785 of which 100 acres was
conveyed to his brother and now remainder to the sd HARDING. Wit: JOHN
MILAM, BENJAMIN CASON.

Page 439:   20 Nov. 1788 - 1 Sept. 1789 JOHN STEPHENS, blacksmith
              and his wife MARY to ROBERT HAMBLETON, planter for 40
pds 100 acres on Cain Creek, part of 250 acres orig. granted to JOHN
OWINS 14 Sept. 1771, then in Berkley Co., then conveyed to WM. ONEAL
(?) Apr. 1775, then to JOHN WILLS 1785, then to sd STEPHENS 1788. Wit:
BENJAMIN CARTER, ELISHA CARTER.

Page 441:   27 Jan. 1789 - 8 Sept. 1789 WILLIAM THOMASON and wife
              MOURNING to JOHN FRANCIS WOLFF for 10 pds 300 acres on
Raburns Creek, part of an orig. grant to SOLOMON NIBLET 22 Mar. 1769,
bounded by EZEKIEL MATHEWS, WM. THOMASON. Wit: JONATHAN DOWNS, JOHN
RODGERS. JONATHAN DOWNS, J.P.

(Torn and missing pages)

Page 458:   25 June 1789 - 20 Sept. 1789 WILLIAM MILWEE, JAMES MILWEE
              and wife MARGARET to THOMAS WADSWORTH and WILLIAM TURPIN,
merchants for 50 pds 100 acres on Bush River orig. granted to sd WM.
MILWEE 9 Sept. 1774. Wit: JOHN TROTTER, JOHN GENT, THOMAS GARVIN, AMB-
ROSE HUDGINS.

Page 460:   31 June 1789 - 28 Sept. 1789 WILLIAM DENDY and wife CLARY
              to THOMAS WADSWORTH and WM. TURPIN, merchants for 10 pds
100 acres on Simmons Creek.

Page 463:   4 Aug. 1789 - 24 Nov. 1789 WM. THOMASON mortgage to NATHAN
              (NATHANIEL) AUSTIN on two negroes. Wit: CHARLES SULLIVANT,
BENJ. CAMP, JONATHAN DOWNS, J.P.

Page 463:   9 Feb. 1789 - 20 Sept. 1789 HUGH MC VAY and wife MARTHA
              of Greenville Co. to ROBERT CULBERTSON for 60 pds 100
acres on Little River orig. granted 7 May 1774 to JAMES BEARD(?). Wit:
JAS. CULBERTSON, JNO. ANDERSON.

Page 464:   11 Nov. 1788 - 21 Sept. 1789 DUNKIN CAMPBELL and wife
              MARY of Greenvile Co. to JAMES GAMBLE, SR. for 12 pds
70 acres on Enoree River part of 250 acres orig. granted to REUBEN
PAXON 27 Nov. 1770, then in Craven Co., conveyed to WM. THOMAS, then
to sd CAMPBELL. Wit: JAMES GAMBLE, JR., WM. NEEL, JOHN ROBINSON.

Page 466:   7 Aug. 1789 - 7 Dec. 1789 MACAJAH SIMS to JOHN F. WOLFF

222

Cont'd:
for 10 pds mortgage on present crop of tobacco now growing,
1 featherbed, cattle, mares, hogs....

Page 467:   9 Oct. 1789 - 24 Dec. 1789 ROBERT HENRY HUGHES, planter
              to WILLIAM SHAW, attorney of Edgefield Co., for 22 pds
270 acres with mill on Enoree River orig. granted to JOHN NEWMAN, conveyed to sd HUGHES. Wit: P. CUNINGHAM, ELANOR WEITZELL. WM. MOORE,
J.P.

Page 468:   8 Mar. 17(?) - (....) LEWIS AKINS appoints BENJAMIN KIVELL
              his attorney to receive from PAGE MAN a certain legacy
in Charlotte Co., Va., from FRANCIS MAN, deceased, for whose estate
PAGE MAN became administrator.

Page 469:   3 Oct. 1789 - 24 Dec. 1789 RICHARD CARROL to JAMES PARKS
              for 5 pds, a cow, a sorrel mare...

Page 469:   10 May 1790 - 16 July 1790 JOHN WELLS and wife REBECCA
              to MOSES WELLS & CLEMENT WELLS for 30 pds 100 acres on
Cain Creek granted to BENJAMIN MOORE, by var. conveyed to ISAAC GUIL-
LARD, then to PETER CASITY, then to sd WELLS. Wit: WM. RUCKS, JESSE
MOBS(MOTES?), MOURNING MOBS(MOTES?). GEO. ANDERSON, J.P.

END OF DEED BOOK B

LAURENS COUNTY, S. C. DEED BOOK C

Contributed by Bernice A. George

Pg 1-3:   Deed dated 28 June 1772 - recorded 15 Mar. 1789 JACOB
              JONES of St. .... Parish, Province of S. C. to JAMES LAFFEN
weaver of the same place, for 100 pds current money 100 acres being
part of a 350 acre tract in Craven Co., SC on waters of Little River,
granted 18 May 1771 by Wm. Bull, Lt. Gov. to CHARLES HARVEY, who deeded
250 acres of this to JACOB JONES 22 June 1772. This 100 acres bounded
by MOSES CALDWELL, ELIZABETH CALDWELL. No renunciation of dower. Wit:
CHRISTOPHER NEILLY, JAMES JOHNSON, JEAN CALDWELL. CHRISTOPHER NEELY
signed probate bef. JOHN CALDWELL, J.P. 29 July ....

Pp 3-5:   29 Dec. 1785 - rec. 16 Mar. 1789 JAMES LAFFEN, weaver
              and RHODA LAFFEN, his wife, of 96 Dist., SC to THOMAS
DAVISON of the same, 100 acres (same as acreage in above deed) for
100 pds on branches of Little River, waters of Saludy. Wit: WM. GALLEG-
LY, ROBERT FREEMAN, MARK FREEMAN.

Pp 5-6:   2 Feb. 1786 - rec. 20 May 1789 GEORGE ANDERSON and MARY
              his wife, SC, Laurens Co., to JAMES COOK of same, laborer,
for 10 shillings, 150 acres in Laurens Co. on North Creek bounded by
ROBERT YOUNG, JOHN YOUNG & SILVANUS WALKER being part of two surveys,
one granted to ____YOUNG by Wm. Bull, Lt. Gov. 12 July 1771 containing 200 acres, the other granted to GEO. ANDERSON by Wm. Bull (date
missing). Wit: LEWIS BANTON, CLABORN GOODMAN. Probate made by BANTON
& GOODMAN bef. SILVANUS WALKER, J.P.

Pp 6-7:   1 June 1789 - rec. 15 June 1789 JOHN HUNTER, Esq. and
              SARAH his wife, 96 Dist., SC, to JOHN BLACK, JR. of same,
for 15 pds, 74 acres in 96 Dist. on branch of Little River called Carson's Creek orig. granted to JOHN HUNTER, Esq. by Gov. Wm. Moultrie
6 Mar. 1786. No witnesses, CLABURN GOODMAN swore to deed bef. SILVANUS
WALKER, J.P.

Pp 7-8:   Deed dated 2 Feb. 1786 GEORGE ANDERSON and MARY his wife
              of Laurens Co., SC to JAMES COOK of same, for 10 pds 150
acres on North Creek, waters of Little River, being part of two tracts
orig. granted to JOHN YOUNG & GEORGE ANDERSON. Adj. ROBERT YOUNG &
SILVANUS WALKER. Wit: CLABOURN GOODMAN, LEWIS BANTON.

Pp 9-10:   16 Apr. 1788 - rec. 15 June 1789 JONATHAN SARAGIN, Charles-
              ton, SC to WM. JOHNSON, plantation of land (no acreage)

Cont'd:
for 40 pds 10 shillings, land being in Craven Co. on waters of Raeburns
Creek, adj. JAMES LINLEY, DAVID RIGGS & PHILLIP ____?. Wit: MATTHEW
(X) MC DANIEL, THOMAS (X) JOHNSON. The two witnesses made probate bef.
JONATHAN DOWNS, J.P. 9 Mar. 1789.

Pp 10-12:   30 Dec. (or Nov.) 1788 - rec. 16 June 1789 ROBERT GILLIAM,
               Esq. of S.C. Newberry Co. for 10 shillings to DANIEL WOOD
of Laurens Co. 91 acres on Saluda River adj. FREDERICK WARD & JOHN SILLS,
JR. Wit: ____ MAYSON, GEORGE TAYLOR, JOHN SILLS, JR.

Pp 12-15:   2 Sept. 1785 - rec. 17 June 1789 JAMES SIMPSON of 96 Dist.
               in Craven Co. to THOMAS CLARK, of same, 100 acres on War-
riors Creek for 50 pds 10 shillings. Wit: JOHN THOMAS, JOHN ABERNATHY
& ____ MC CRACHIN. JOHN THOMAS made probate bef. WM. CALDWELL.

Pp 15-17:   5 Apr. 1789 - rec. 18 June 1789 THOMAS DENDY and MARY
               wife wife, of S.C., planter to JAMES KIRK, planter of
same, for 52 pds 10 shillings 300 acres on North Creek adj. WILLIAM
BRYSON, being granted to THOS. DENDY by Wm. Bull, Esq. Lt. Gov. of S.C.
8 July 1774. Wit: WILLIAM BRYSON, JOHN KIRK & WILLIAM BAILEY. JOHN KIRK
made probate bef. JOHN RODGERS, J.P. 10 Mar. 1789.

Pp 17-18:   9 Mar. 1789 WILLIAM DENDY & CLARY (X) DENDY his wife
               of S.C. Laurens Co. to THOMAS DENDY, SR. of same, for
35 shillings 100 acres. No witnesses but WM. & CLARY ack. deed bef.
JOHN RODGERS, J.P. 10 Mar. 1789.

Pp 18-20:   27 Jan. 1774 - rec. 19 June 1789 WILLIAM ARTHER, of e-
               the Congarees in Province of S.C. to GEORGE COPELAND of
Craven Co. in same Province, 200 acres for 200 pds 10 sh. in Craven
Co. on Beaverdam, branch of Little River, the same being orig. grant
to WM. ARTHER 13 Oct. 1772. Wit: ROBERT TWEEDY & WM. PULLIAM on 9 June
1789 Capt. CHARLES SIMMONS, WM. TWEEDY & ROBERT SPENCE made a sworn
statement that the name of ROBERT TWEEDY subscribed to the deed was
the signature of ROBERT TWEEDY, deceased, to best of their knowledge.
Bef. SILVANUS WALKER, J.P. JONATHAN DOWNS made sworn statement that
the name of WM. ARTHER subscribed to the deed is signature of WILLIAM
ARTHUR, deceased, bef. SILV. WALKER, J.P.

Page 20:   (Personal) 3 May 1788 - rec. 19 June 1789 JOHN O'NEAL
               of S.C. Laurens Co. deeds for love and affection 1 negro
girl Milley to his son-in-law WILLIAM SHANLEY. Wit: ____ CAMPBELL, J.P.,
MARGARET SCOTT & ____ COOK.

Pp 21-22:   17 June 1779 - rec. 20 June 1789 MARGARET (X) TODD , of
               96 Dist. SC to FREDERICK LITTLE, of same, laborer, for
400 pds 10 sh., 100 acres in Craven Co. on a small branch on the NE
side of Raeburns Creek, adj. JOHN RITCHIE, SR. Wit: WETTENHALL WARNER,
TANDY WALKER, ELIZABETH WARNER. This land granted to MARGARET TODD 17
Mar. 1775 by Wm. Bull, Lt. Gov. of SC. TANDY WALKER signed probate bef.
JOHN HUNTER, J.P. 14 Mar. 1789.

Page 22:   7 Mar. 1789 - rec. 21 June 1789 THOMAS DENDY, SR. and
               MARY (X) DENDY his wife of Laurens Co., SC to THOMAS DENDY,
JR. of same, for 20 sh. 200 acres on North Creek in Laurens Co. includ-
ing 150 acres granted to THOS. DENDY, SR. 7 Aug. 1786. Bounded by ____
TINDSLEY and head of Double Branches. Wit: JOHN WATTS, CORNELIUS DENDY.
CORNELIUS DENDY made probate bef. JNO. RODGERS, J.P.

Pp 23-25:   96 Dist., SC 12 Sept. 1787 ROBERT GILLIAM & MARY (X) GIL-
               LIAM his wife of Newberry Co., SC and Dist. above, to
ISAAC RODGERS for 25 pds 5 sh, 145 acres on Beaverdame Creek, orig.
granted to ROBT. GILLIAM 2 Oct. 1786. Wit: WILLIAM STONE, URIAH STONE,
JOSHUA GILLIAM. WM. & URIAH made probate bef. ANGUS CAMPBELL, J.P. 22
Aug. 1789.

Pp 25-26:   9 Dec. 1788 (no rec. date) JOHN BARNET of Laurens Co.,
               SC to HENRY FAGAN of same for 30 pds, 40 acres on Durbins
Creek, waters of Enoree River, bounded by COALMAN BROWN. Wit: DANIEL

Cont'd:
WRIGHT & SELETER (X) BARNET. SELETER BARNET made probate bef. DANIEL
WRIGHT, J.P. same date.

Page 26:   Deed of Gift. Rec. 15 Sept. 1789 Laurens Co., SC Cambridge
                 Dist. ELIZABETH JONES of afsd st. and co. to REUBIN PYLES
a plantation of 200 acres which was deeded to her by JOHN GOODWIN. Wit:
ABNER PYLES, JOHN PYLES. ABNER PYLES made probate bef. JONATHAN DOWNS,
J.P. 24 Aug. 1789.

Page 29:   10 Mar. 1788 - rec. 22 June 1789 WILLIAM DENDY & CLARY
                 (X) DENDY, his wife of Laurens Co. to HARDY CONANT of
same place for 40 pds, 75 acres in Laurens Co. on north side of North
Creek, being part of 150 acres granted to WM. DENDY in 1771, bounded
by BETTY TINDSLEY & ROBERT HALL. No wit. WM. & CLARY ack. the deed bef.
JOHN RODGERS, J.P. same day.

Page 30:   29 Oct. 1788 - rec. 23 June 1789 Deed of Slave. JOHN ED-
                 WARDS & MARY (X) EDWARDS, his wife, to JOHN BRISON, one
negro named Clary. Wit: MIKLE ABNEY, JAMES BRISON. JAS. BRISON made
probate 1 Nov. 1789.

Pp 30-32:   10 Nov. 1788 WM. DENDY & CLARY (X) DENDY his wife of Laur-
                 ens Co. to BETTY TINDSLEY of same place, for 40 pds, 75
acres lying on N side of Norths Creek, of Little River, being part of
a grant to WM. DENDY in 1771, adj. THOMAS DENDY, SILVANUS WALKER. No
wit. WM. & CLARY ack. deed bef. JOHN RODGERS, J.P.

Page 32:   17 Dec. 1788 - rec. 24 June 1789 DALLEY WALKER & HANNAH
                 (X) WALKER, his wife of Burk Co., N.C. to MORGAN HOOD
of Laurens Co., S.C. for 20 pds, 100 acres on a branch that empties
into N side of Saluda River. Plat and grant laid off 24 Oct. 1788 (no
name) Wit: JAMES SMITH, JOHN HALL. HALL made probate bef. JOHN RODGERS
10 Mar. 1789. (Walker signed his name "DALY" WALKER).

Pp 33-36:   23 Aug. 1788 - rec. 24 June 1789 JOHN CHESTNUT of Camden
                 Dist., planter, to SAMUEL EAKIN, planter of 96 Dist. for
80 pds, 150 acres on Simmons Creek in Barkley (Berkley) bet. Saluda
and Broad Rivers, bounded by THOMAS EDGEHILL & HUGH O'NEAL. Wit: HENRY
RUGELY, ROBERT HENRY, ZACHARIAH CANTY. Land orig. granted to JOHN HOPE
2 Aug. 1775. Rec. in Sec. Office Book SSS page 672. ZACHARIAH CANTY
made probate bef. ISAAC ALEXANDER, J.P. 23 Aug. 1788.

Page 37:   16 July 1788 - rec. 25 June 1789 WILLIAM- DENDY & CLARY
                 (X) DENDY his wife, for 100 pds, 100 acres on both sides
of Little River to MANSFIELD WALKER, of same. Land bounded by WILLIAM
HALL, SAMUEL POWELL, WILLIAM BAILEY, MC NEESE GOOD. Land orig. granted
to WM. DENDY & JOHN MC KENZIE and by sd MC KENZIE conveyed to TOBIAS
MYERS and by MYERS to WM. DENDY. No wit. WM. & CLARY ack. deed bef.
SILV. WALKER, J.P. on same day.

Pp 37-38:   (Personal) Agreement - Certain disputes and controver-
                 sies have arisen bet. WILLIAM BARKSDALE of Bush River
and ANN BARKSDALE, his wife, in consequence of which she has eloped
his bed and board. They enter into an agreement whereby he delivers
to her all the goods she had before their marriage; she renounces dower
in his estate and claimed no support. 16 May 1789. Wit: JOHN HUNTER,
ANTHONY WATSON.

Page 38:   (Personal) 26 Nov. 1788 - rec. 25 June 1789 SAMUEL CRAB-
                 TREE, SR. of Laurens Co. sold to JOHN CRABTREE of same
place, horses, hogs, furniture, corn, tobacco, fodder and plantation
tools.

Pp 38-40:   17 Mar. 1789 - rec. 25 June 1789 Deed of Trust. EDMOND
                 CRADDOCK of Laurens Co. for love and affection which he
has for his children, to wit: MARY CRADDOCK, ANN CRADDOCK, EDMOND CRAD-
DOCK, JR., THOMAS CRADDOCK, JOHN CRADDOCK & JUDITH CRADDOCK and "my
friend" _____ YANCEY, Esq. of same place, deeds to YANCEY several negros,

Cont'd:
horses one of which is now in possession of JOHN A. ELMORE, cattle
hogs household furniture, in trust, for the purpose of maintaining,
educating, and clothing his children until they become of age – then
to be divided among them. Wit: AMBROSE YANCEY, WILLIAM DUNLAP.

Pp 40-43:   21 June 1784 – rec. 26 June 1789 AMBROSE HUDGENS & JOANNA
                 (X) HUDGENS his wife, planer of Craven Co., SC to JOSEPH
BLACKERBY, planter of same place, for 5 shillings and one slave and
one child, 100 acres on Little River of Saluda, orig. granted to HUGH
YOUNG in 1771, conveyed to LUKE WALDRUP 22 Aug. 1772 and by sd WALDRUP,
SR., willed to his son JECHONIAS WALDROP and he conveyed to AMBROSE
HUDGENS 28 June 1780. Wit: JOSEPH YOUNG, SARAH BLACKERBY, CHARLES MET-
CALFE. JOS. YOUNG made probate 29 June 1784 bef. GEO. ANDERSON, J.P.

Pp 43-44:   19 June 1789 DAVID SPENCE of Laurens Co., SC sold to
                 WILLIAM NORRIS, mare, cows, calves. Wit: JOHN DORROH,
ROBERT (X) MC CURLEY.

Page 44:   28 Feb. 1789 – rec. 27 June 1789 WILLIAM (X) WILLSON
                 and MARGARET (X) WILLSON his wife, of Laurens Co. to
JESSE MEEKS of same place, for 65 pds, 100 acres lying on a branch
of Little River called Ryan's Creek, orig. granted to JOHN MANLEY,
JR. in 1786 by Gov. Moultrie. Wit: JOHN RODGERS, JOSHUA DOWNS. DOWNS
made probate bef. RODGERS on same day.

Pp 45-46:   3 Dec. 1788 – rec. 27 June 1789 WILLIAM KELLET of 96
                 Dist. to ABRAHAM RILEY, PATRICK RILEY & SAMUEL RILEY,
minors, of same place, for 100 pds, 250 acres lying on Beaverdame Creek
waters of Reedy River, 96 Dist. (formerly Craven co. now Laurens Co.)
orig. granted to JEFFERY SCRUGGS 2 Mar. 1769. Wit: WILLIAM FARIS, JOHN
KELLET & NATHAN KEMP.

Pp 47-48:   28 June 1788 – (....) JOHN COX & SARAH COX, his wife
                 of Indian Creek land, planter, Co. & State of S.C. (sic)
to SANDFORD BERRY, 100 acres being part of an orig. grant of 400 acres
to JAMES ALLISON, on south side of Enoree River. Wit: JOHN CANNON,
JOHN HALL.

Pp 48-50:   17 Jan. 1789 – (.....) THOMAS JONES, JR. of Laurens Co.,
                 to JOHN SADLER, of same, for 10 sh. 100 acres in Laurens
Co., 96 Dist. on waters of Mill Creek, orig. granted to THOMAS JONES,
JR. on 27 Nov. 1770.

Pp 50-52:   9 June 1788 – (.....) PATRICK RILEY of 96 Dist., Laurens
                 Co., to MARTIN HUGHEY, of same, for 20 pds, 106 acres
on NE side of South Fork of Reaburn's Creek, 96 Dist., Laurens Co.,
SC bounded by ROBERT SIMS, THOMAS MC DANIEL & JAMES DOWNING, orig.
granted to PATRICK RILEY 5 June 1786. Wit: WM. KELLET, WM. SIMS.

Pp 53-54:   17 Dec. 1788 – (....) DALLY WALKER of Burk Co., N.C.,
                 planter, to ARCHIBALD SHIRLEY of Laurens Co., SC, planter,
for 5 pds, 200 acres being part of a 300 acre tract granted to WALKER
5 June 1784, or 1786 (not clear) on Walnur Creek. Deed signed by DALY
WALKER, HANNAH (X) WALKER. Wit: JAMES SMITH, MORGAN WOOD.

Page 55:   20 Oct. 1788 – (....) JOHN FIELDS & BETTY ANN FIELDS,
                 his wife of Laurens Co. to ROGER MURPHY of same, for
29 pds 16 sh. sterling, 125 acres in 96 Dist. on a branch of Reaburn's
Creek called Ritchey's Branch, orig. granted to JOHN FIELDS 5 June
1786. Wit: EBENEZER MURPHY, GEORGE MADDEN.

Pp 55-57:   2 June 1788 – (....) WILLIAM BAUGH, Exex. of WILLIAM
                 ELLISON, deceased, of Laurens Co., to THOMAS CUNNINGHAM,
of same, for 80 pds sterling, 150 acres in Berkeley Co. now 96 Dist.
or Oxford Dist. on Reaburn's Creek, bounded by ROBT. BOX, land granted
to ELLISON 4 Nov. 1762. ELLISON's will dated 23 Dec. 1780. Deed wit.
by JNO. CUNNINGHAM & WILLIAM MC DAVID.

Page 58:   (no date) – rec. 30 June 1789 EDWARD GARRET of Laurens

Cont'd:
                    Co. to DOUGLAS PUCKET of same, for 40 pds, 100 acres
on south side of Enoree River in Laurens Co., the same being granted
to EDW. GARRET 21 Jan. 1770. No wit.

Pp 59-61:   5 June 1789 - (....) THOMAS WADSWORTH and WILLIAM TURPIN
                mechants of S. C. to BENJAMIN CLARDY of sd state, planter,
for 45 pds, 217 acres on Saluda River bounded by lands laid out to
Capt. ROSAMOND & ROBERT MAXWELL, orig. granted to WADSWORTH & TURPIN
4 Jan. 1787. Wit: JOHN TROTTER, PATRICK MC DOWELL.

Pp 61-63:   10 Mar. 1789 - rec. 25 Aug. 1789 PETER FAYSSAUX & ANN
                FAYSSAUX, his wife of the City of Charleston, S.C. to
LEWIS SAXON of Laurens Co., for 75 pds, 150 acres on a branch of Little
River in Laurens Co., being part of a tract of 1400 acres granted to
BENJAMIN WILLIAMSON 23 Jan. 1773, conveyed by WILLIAM WILLIAMSON to
afsd FAYSSAUX. A plat of land surveyed by JONATHAN DOWNS 24 Jan. 1789
is included. Deed witnessed by SILVANUS WALKER, WILLIAM MILWEE & JOSHUA
SAXON.

Page 64:   30 Jan. 1789 - rec. 25 Aug. 1789 JOHN (X) WILLIAMS, plant-
                er of Laurens Co. to ELISHA HOLCOMB, of same, for 3 pds,
43 acres being part of a tract of 640 acres granted to ALEXANDER HARPER
15 Oct. 1784 on N fork of Dirbin's Creek below the Indian Boundary
in Laurens Co. Wit: JAMES RUSSELL & CALEB HUGHES. RUSSELL signed probate bef. DANIEL WRIGHT, J.P. 7 Feb. 1789.

Pp 65-67:   3 Apr. 1789 - rec. 26 Aug. 1789 PETER CASSITY of Clear-
                mont Co., SC to JOHN WELLS of Laurens Co. for 20 pds
sterling, 100 acres in Laurens Co. on E side of branch known by name
of JENNY GRIMES's branch, waters of Cain Creek on the N side of Saluda
River, being part of a tract of 250 acres orig. granted to BENJAMIN
MOORE 3 Nov. 1770; bounded by WILLIAM PURSE & MARY EDWARDS. This land
sold by MOORE to TACITUS GAILLARD 20 Nov. 1775, and by him to ISAAC
GAILLARD and by him, the son and heir of TACITUS GAILLARD, to PETER
CASSITY. CASSITY was attorney for ISAAC GAILLARD. Wit: PATRICK CUNNING-
HAM, ELIJAH BURGESS & RICHARD DUTY. CUNNINGHAM signed probate bef.
GEO. ANDERSON 1789 (sic).

Pp 67-69:   17 July 1789 - (....) CORNELIUS (X) DONOHOE and ELIZABETH
                (X) DONOHOE, his wife, to CHARLES PARKS, both of Laurens
Co., 96 Dist., SC 100 acres being part of 300 acres on waterss of Mudlick Creek in Laurens Co., orig. granted to JOHN DONOHOE 25 May 1772
and conveyed by him to CORNELIUS DONOHOE. No witnesses. Both granters
signed probate bef. SILV. WALKER, 25 July 1789.

Pp 70-71:   5 Aug. 1789 - rec. 16 Sept. 1789 MARGARET RICHEY, widow
                of Laurens Co., to ELLENER (X) RICHEY of same, 125 acres
on Duncan's Creek, being part of a 250 acre tract granted to JOHN WIL-
LIAMS 31 Aug. 1774 bet. Broad and Saluda Rivers on a branch called
Leonard's Fork, waters of Duncan's Creek, adj. JAMES YOUNG, ROLAND
MC CURLEY. JOHN WILLIAMS conveyed to ALEXANER MC NARY 31 July 1785;
MC NARY conveyed to MARGARET RICHEY, widow, 29 Nov. 1785. Wit: JAMES
FINDLEY, REBECCA ADAIR & ISABELLA ROSS. FINDLEY signed 6 Aug. 1789
bef. JAMES MONTGOMERY, J.P.

Pp 71-72:   8 Sept. 1787 - rec. 16 Sept. 1789 EDMOND MARTIN, Esq.,
                Sheriff of 96 Dist. to AARON STEEL, planter, 200 acres
at the suit of AARON STEEL vs THOMAS RICHARDSON, late of same district,
the land being in Laurens Co. on Reedy Fork of Reedy River, adj. PATRICK
CUNINGHAM, JOHN BAUGH, THOMAS CUNINGHAM, DAVID DUNLAP & ROBERT HOOD.
Wit: JONATHAN DOWNS & SAMUEL TAYLOR. DOWNS made probate bef. JOS. DOWNS,
J.P. 20 Aug. 1789.

Pp 72-74:   8 Sept. 1787 - rec. 17 Sept. 1789 EDMOND MARTIN, Esq.,
                Sheriff of 96 Dist. to AARON STEELE, planter, 50 acres
in 96 Dist. on Reedy River, adj. river on north, DANIEL MC LAIN & MC-
ANULTY......Wit: JONATHAN DOWNS & SAMUEL TAYLOR. DOWNS signed probate
bef. JOSEPH DOWNS.
20 Aug. 1789.

Pp 74-76:   8 June 1789 - rec. 18 Sept. 1789 MICAJAH SIMS of Laurens
             Co., 96 Dist., farmer, to EDMOND NASH (should have been
EDWARD) of same place, 100 acres on south fork of Reaburn's Creek in
Laurens Co., 96 Dist. orig. granted to JAMES SMITH 13 May 1768; and
also part of a tract of land containing 50 acres bounded by the following: THOMAS MC DONALD, ROBERT SIMS, JAMES MC CLANAHAN. The 50 acres
was granted to PATRICK RILEY by Gov. Moultrie 5 June 1786. Wit: ANDREW
(X) MC KNIGHT & DRURY BOYCE. MC KNIGHT made probate 15 Sept. 1789.

Pp 76-79:   1 Jan. 1789 - 18 Sept. 1789 BENJAMIN RAINEY & BETHIAH
             RAINEY, his wife of Laurens Co. to HUDSON BERRY, of same,
85 acres for 52 pds sterling, being part of a tract of 640 acres granted to ALEXANDER HARPER 15 Oct. 1784. Land lay on Durbin's Creek of
Enoree River. Wit: RICHARD JONES & JOHN REDMAN. JONES signed probate
5 Sept. 1789 bef. WM. MITCHERSON, J.P.

Pp 79-80:   13 Dec. 1788 (no recorded date) BENJAMIN RAINEY of Laurens
             Co., planter to HUDSON BERRY of same, 150 acres on Durbins
Creek of Enoree River, orig. granted to THOMAS SANDERS 28 Aug. 1772.
Wit: ALEXANDER HARPER & RICHARD JONES. JONES signed probate 5 Sept.
1789 bef. WM. MITCHERSON.

Page 81:   Deed of Gift. 27 Nov. 1789 Recorded same day. SHADRACK
             MARTIN of Laurens Co., Little River settlement, freeholder
and planter, for love and affection to his daughter JEAN (JANE) MARTIN
of same place, 1 horse and bed and furniture; to his daughter MARGARET
MARTIN, negroes and all his goods and chattels. Wit: EZEKIEL ROLAND
& JOSHUA DOWNS. Roland signed probate bef. Wm. Mitcherson, J.P. same
day.

Pp 81-82:   Deed of Gift. 27 Nov. 1789. SHADRACK MARTIN of Little
             River settlement, freeholder and planter, to his son
WM. MARTIN, freeholder of same place, all his lands, 180 acres, it
being part of a tract granted to "me Shadrack Martin", being on a branch
of Little River. Wit: EZEKIEL ROLAND & JOSHUA DOWNS. Roland signed
probate same day.

Pp 82-84:   29 May 1789 - rec. 21 Sept. 1789 ABIJAH O'NEAL and HUGH
             O'NEAL, both of Newberry Co., 96 Dist., S.C., exec'rs
of the Last Will and Testament of WILLIAM O'NEAL, deceased, to JONATHAN
HOLLINGSWORTH, of 96 Dist., 300 acres for 100 pds 10 shillings; being
part of a tract of 350 acres granted to JOHN THORNTON on Saluda River
in S. C. 8 July 1774. Wit: DAVID HOLLINGSWORTH, JAMES HENDERSON & THOS.
MC FARNOS. Hollingsworth signed probate 6 June 1789 bef. ANGUS CAMPBELL
J.P.

Pp 84-85:   16 Dec. 1788 - rec. 21 Dec. 1789 JOHN (X) WILLIAMS of
             Laurens Co., SC to JACOB MANOR, of same, for 6 pds sterl-
ing, 100 acres on waters of Durbin's Creek in Laurens Co., being part
of 640 acres granted to JOHN WILLIAMS. Line runs up the branch to a
ford of the branch where a path crosses sd branch, that goes to a cabin
that MOSES MURPHY lived in. Wit: DANIEL WRIGHT, MARTHA (X) MULKEY.
Martha Mulkey made probate 16 Dec. 1788 bef. DANL. WRIGHT, J.P.

Pp 85-86:   8 June 1789 - rec. 22 Dec. 1789 DANIEL WRIGHT of Laurens
             Co. to LEWIS EAKINS of same place, for 50 pds sterling,
100 acres on north side of South Fork of Durbin's Creek in Laurens
Co., being part of 200 acres granted to DAVID WELCH in 1773. No wit.

Pp 86-87:   14 Jan. 1789 - rec. 22 Dec. 1789 JOHN HUNTER & MARGARET
             (X) HUNTER, his wife of 96 Dist., to JOHN BLACK, carpen-
ter, of same place, 22 acres for 5 pds 10 sh., on waters of Carson's
Creek, on a branch called Quaker Branch, being part of 250 acres granted
to JOHN HUNTER 6 Feb. 1773. Wit: ROBERT BLACK & SARAH WOFFORD. Black
made probate 1 June 1789 bef. JNO. HUNTER, J.P.

Page 88:   13 Mar. 1789 - rec. 22 Dec. 1789 BENJAMIN SOUTH to JAMES
             CUNINGHAM of 96 Dist. for 70 pds 1 sh, 200 acres in fork
bet. Broad and Saluda Rivers, lying on a long branch of Reaburn's Crk.

228

Cont'd:
Wit: JOHN PRINGLE and CHARLES GAREY. PRINGLE signed probate before
JONATHAN DOWNS, 18 Mar. 1789.

Pp 89-92:   6 Mar. 1789 - rec. 23 Dec. 1789 RICHARD GRIFFIN, planter
               of Laurens Co. to JONATHAN JOHNSON for 25 pds 10 sh ster-
ling, 55 acres in Laurens Co. on waters of Mudlick Creek, bounded by
JOHN COOK, EDWARD JONES, JONATHAN JOHNSON. Wit: WILLIAM POLLARD & JOHN
COOK. POLLARD & COOK made probate 23 Apr. 1789 bef. ANGUS CAMPBELL,
J.P.

Pp 92-93:   22 Nov. 2788 - rec. 24 Dec. 1789 WILLIAM HUMPHRIES of
               Spartanburg Co., SC and LUCY (X) HUMPHRIES his wife,
to ENOCH PEARSON of Laurens Co. for 50 pds sterling, 150 acres in Laur-
ens Co. on south side of Enoree River, bounded by WM. GUNTER, WM. HEAD.
Land granted to WM. HUMPHRIES 3 Sept. 1787. Wit: WM. HEAD, JOHN PEAR-
SON. Probate signed by WM. HEAD, JR., 8 Dec. 1788 bef. JOHN RODGERS,
J.P.

Pp 93-95:   2 Apr. 1789 - rec. 24 Dec. 1789 PETER CASSITY of Clare-
               mont Co., Camden Dist., SC to PATRICK CUNINGHAM, of Laur-
ens Co., 96 Dist. for 17 pds 10 sh sterling, 150 acres being in Craven
Co. formerly but now in Laurens Co. 96 Dist., being part of 200 acres
orig. granted to BENJAMIN MOORE 3 Nov. 1770, on waters of Cain Creek
on north side of Saluda River, bounded by WM. PURSE's land and MARY
EDWARDS. Sold by BENJ. MOORE to TACITUS GAILLARD 20 Nov. 1772, then
conveyed by GAILLARD to his son, ISAAC GAILLARD, all of Laurens Co.
On 28 Dec. 1785 it was conveyed to PETER CASSITY by ISAAC GAILLARD.
Wit: RICHARD DUTY, ELIJAH BURGESS, JOHN WATTS. BURGESS signed probate
8 June 1789 bef. GEO. ANDERSON, J.P.

Pp 95-98:   2 Sept. 1788 - rec. 24 Dec. 1789 JOHN WELLS & REBECCA
               (X) WELLS, his wife, of Laurens Co., 96 Dist., planter,
to MARGARET CUNINGHAM, of same place, planter, for 100 pds sterling,
150 acres on Cain Creek in Laurens Co., bounded on NE on Reaburn's
Creek, SARAH HODGES' land, RICHARD PINSON, JACOB BOWMAN, JOHN RITCHEY.
Wit: JOHN HEMPHENS, MOSES WELLS, CLEMENT WELLS. Both Moses and Clement
signed probate bef. GEO. ANDERSON.

Pp 98-199:   10 June 1788 - rec. 1 Jan. 1790 JACOB LEWIS of Georgia
               to DAVID MAYSON of Laurens Co., 96 Dist., planter, 150
acres JACOB LEWIS acting for his father JOHN LEWIS by power of attorney. This land located in Laurens Co. on waters of Indian Creek, which
sd tract of land on the demise of BENJAMIN LEWIS, devolved to the sd
JOHN LEWIS his brother by heirship. Wit: LEWIS SAXON, CHARLES SAXON
& SAMUEL WHARTON. This land orig. granted to BENJ. LEWIS. Samuel Wharton
made probate bef. JOHN HUNTER, J.P. 12 June 1788.

Pp 100-103:   10 June 1788 - rec. 3 Jan. 1790 JACOB LEWIS, of Georgia
               to DAVID MASON, planter of Laurens Co. by the power vested
in me by "my father JOHN LEWIS" deeded 100 acres on a small branch
of Indian Creek 2 inches wife and 1 inch deep. Sd land was granted
to and conveyed by THOMAS DALRYMPLE, dec'd. to BENJ. LEWIS 28 July
1771 and devolved on the demise of sd BENJ. to JOHN LEWIS, his brother.
Wit: LEWIS SAXON, CHARLES SAXON, SAMUEL WHARTON.

Pp 103-104:   26 Apr. 1789 - rec. 2 Jan. 1790 JOSHUA (X) ROBERTS and
               SARAH (X) ROBERTS his wife were indebted to JOHN SIMP-
SON, merchant of Laurens Co. for 27 pds for goods. They gave mortgage
on one negro girl. Wit: ANDREW SMITH, JAMES SIMPSON.

Pp 105-106:   13 Mar. 1789 - rec. 4 Jan. 1790 NIMROD MITCHELL to BENJA-
               MIN SMITH of 96 Dist., Laurens Co. for 60 pds 1 sh for
200 acres on a long branch of Reaburn's Creek, granted 20 Aug. 1769
by Hon. Chas. Montague of the Province of S.C. rec. in Book 1 #9 page
369 (does not say to whom). Wit: WILLIAM MORTIMER & AM. ARTHER, J.P.
ARTHER made probate 24 Mar. 1789.

Pp 107-109:   23 Dec. 1788 - rec. 5 Jan. 1790 PATRICK RILEY & ANN RILEY
               his wife of 96 Dist., Laurens Co. for 100 pds 1 sh 6

Cont'd:
pence to WILLIAM KELLET, of same, 100 acres lying on South Fork of
Reaburn's Creek in Laurens Co., orig. granted to JOHN RILEY 27 Mr.
1775; likewise all that part of a tract containing 106 acres lying
on South Fork of Reaburn's Creek on SW side, bounded by THOMAS MC DANIEL,
ROBERT SIMS, JAMES DOWNING; orig. granted to PATRICK RILEY 5 June 1786
excepting 6 acres adj. ROBERT SIMS' mill as was sold to SIMS by RILEY,
together with a tract of 10 acres being on SW side of sd creek. Wit:
WILLIAM FARRIS, JOHN KELLET, NATHAN (X) CAMP. Signed: PATRICK RYLEY
& ANN RYLEY. JOHN KELLET made probate bef. JOHN RODGERS, J.P.

Pp 109-111:   22 Feb. 1789 - rec. 5 Jan. 1790 CHARLES SIMMONS & ELIZA-
               BETH SIMMONS, his wife of Laurens Co. to JAMES TEMPLETON
of same place, for 50 pds sterling, 225 acres on waters of Little River
called Beaverdam, bounded by ROBERT SPENCE, ABRAHAM NEIGHBORS, JAMES
MC NEESE, WILLIAM TWEEDY. Wit: WM. TAYLOR, WILLIAM TAYLOR (one Jr.
and one Sr.?)

Pp 112-113:   31 Oct. 1788 - rec. 6 Jan. 1790 WILLIAM (X) COOPER of
               Laurens Co., planter to AGNESS COUCH, 200 acres for 10
pds sterling, land located on south side of Enoree River, bounded by
JOHN BLACKSTOCK & WM. COOPER, JR. Wit: JOHN D. (X) COUCH, & SOLOMON
LANGSTON.

Page 114:   28 July 1788 - rec. 6 Jan. 1790 RICHARD JOWEL of Laurens
               Co., freeholder, to ROBERT TODD of same, for 30 pds ster-
ling, 150 acres on the south or southwest end or part of 250 acres
granted to RATTLIFT JOWEL 4 Apr. 1785; bounded by young MC NEESE GOOD,
DANIEL OZBURN & old MC NEESE GOOD. RICHARD JOWEL, oldest son and heir
to the afsd RATTLIFT JOWEL, now deceased. Wit: JOHN (X) TODD, WM. (X)
HUBBS. HUBBS made probate bef. JNO. RODGERS, 9 Dec. 1788.

Pp 115-117:   24 & 25 Apr. 1789 - rec. 7 Jan. 1790 WILLIAM COOPER of
               Laurens Co., planter, to SOLOMON LANGSTON, of same, plan-
ter, for 10 pds 6 sh sterling, 200 acres in Laurens Co. on waters of
Enoree River, bounded by ANTHONY MILLER, THOMAS MURPHY, JOHN BLACKSTOCK
& WM. COOPER, SR. Wit: JOHN (X) CAMMILL & AGNESS (X) COUCH & JOHN MATHE-
SON.

Pp 117-118:   10 Dec. 1788 - rec. 7 Jan. 1790 WILLIAM PRICE & MARGARET
               (X) PRICE his wife, of 96 Dist., to ROBERT BLACK, of
same, for 25 pds, 42 acres on branches of Duncan's Creek, waters of
Enoree River; adj. ISHAM EAST & JOHN HUNTER, being part of a tract
of 150 acres orig. granted to JAMES YOUNG 31 Aug. 1774. Wit: JOHN ADAIR
& JAMES BROWN. Brown made probate 10 June 1789 bef. JNO. HUNTER, J.P.

Pp 118-120:   12 June 1785 - rec. 8 Jan. 1790 ABEL THOMAS of 96 Dist.,
               to GEORGE HOLLINGSWORTH of same, for 17 pds, 150 acres
in Craven Co. in sd dist. on a branch of Saluda River called Reaburn's
Creek, adj. JOHN TURK. This land granted to ABEL THOMAS 7 Oct. 1762.
Wit: JOHN HOLLINGSWORTH, ELIAS (X) BROCK, ISAAC HOLLINGSWORTH. John
Hollingsworth made probate bef. John Rodgers, J.P. 8 June 1789.

Pp 121-122:   Bill of Sale. JOHN SHIRLEY, of Laurens Co., to his son,
               AARON SHIRLEY, 3 horse kind of creatures, 4 cows, 3 sheep,
30 hogs, and all his household furniture for 60 pds sterling on 20
Feb. 1788. Wit: GEORGE HOLLINGSWORTH & MARMADUKE PINSON. Pinson made
probate 28 Dec. 1789.

Pp 122-124:   26 Aug. 1774 - rec. 2 Mar. 1790 JAMES (X) DICKERSON &
               BETTY (X) DICKERSON his wife, of Berkley Co. to JOHN
DUNLAP of Co. and Province of SC for 125 pds 10 shillings sterling,
150 acres being part of 250 acres granted to JAMES DICKERSON (no date)
lying on Bush Creek, adj. JOSEPH ADKINS, JAMES ANDERSON & lands laid
off to LAR(?) HAMMOND. Wit: JOHN JONES, CHARITY (X) JONES, LEWIS JONES.

Pp 124-126:   10 Nov. 1779 - rec. 3 Mar. 1790 JOHN DUNLAP & MARGARET
               DUNLAP his wife of 96 Dist., for 2000(?) pds 10 sh, for
150 acres on Bush River pd by ROBERT MC NAIR; land bounded by JOSEPH
ADKINS, JAMES ANDERSON, JOHN GOODWIN, LEROY HAMMOND, orig. granted

Cont'd:
to JAMES DICKERSON 18 May 1771. Wit: JAMES BRYSON & WILLIAM BRYSON.
WILLIAM DUNLAP made probate bef. GEORGE ROSS 6 Aug. 1782(?).

Page 126:   Mortgage. 12 Dec. 1789 JOHN SAXON, of Laurens Co. gave
               mortgage to MICHAEL SWINDLE, of Abbeville Co. and JOHN
STEPHENS of Laurens Co. Wit: JAMES THOMPSON & JAMES STEPHENS.

Pp 126-128:   7 Sept. 1789 - rec. 15 Mar. 1790 JAMES ROSAMOND of Abbe-
               ville Co. to HUGH THOMPSON of Laurens Co. for 12 pds
5 shillings sterling, 120 acres being in Laurens Co. on Saluda River
and joining DANIEL SOUTH, the same being granted to JAMES ROSAMOND
by Gov. Thos. Pinckney, Esq., rec'd in Sec. Off. in Book UUUU page
454. No date given. Wit: JOHN STEPHENS & JOHN JONES.

Pp 128-129:   4 Feb. 1789 - rec. 16 Mar. 1790 WILLIAM HEAD, SR. & MARY
               (X) HEAD his wife of Laurens Co. to THOMAS HOLDEN of
same, for 121 pds sterling, 175 acres in Laurens Co. on E side of Enoree
River, being part of 200 acres assigned to JOHN WIDOWMAN 13 Oct. 1772
by Chas. Montague, Esq., and assigned to WM. HEAD, SR. by WIDOWMAN
23 Aug. 1787. Wit: WM. (X) BOND, MOSES WHITE. Bond made probate 22
Feb. 1790 bef. DANL. WRIGHT, J.P.

Page 130:   26 Dec. 1789 - rec. 16 Mar. 1790 MARTIN (X) MARTIN of
               Laurens Co. to JOHN WALDROP of same, for 10 pds sterling,
150 acres on Ted's Creek of Little River. Wit: JOHN FIELDS, ROBERT
MC NEES.

Pp 130-131:   18 Aug. 1789 - rec. 16 Mar. 1790 JAMES THOMSON to DANIEL
               SOUTH, SR., both of Laurens Co. for 3 pds 7 sh 8 p, 30
acres on N side of Saluda River, being part of a tract purchased of
JAMES ROSAMOND of Abbeville Co. and rec. in the year 1787 at Charleston.
Signed: JAMES THOMSON. Wit: JOHN DANIEL, SR. & WILLIAM SOUTH.

Pp 131-132:   8 Nov. 1789 - rec. 16 Mar. 1790 RICHARD FOWLER & DEBBY
               (X) FOWLER his wife of Laurens Co. to NATHAN BRAMLETT
of same, for 45 pds sterling, 225 aacres on which BRAMLETT now lives,
being on Zeak's Branch of Enoree River and granted to RICHD. FOWLER
1 June 1789 by Hon. Chas. Pinckney, Gov., rec'd in Sec's office Book
ZZZZ page 372. Qit: REUBEN BRAMLETT & FREDERICK (X) BURDETT; also WM.
(X) STONE. Burdett made probate 27 Feb. 1790 bef. DANL. WRIGHT. J.P.

Pp 133-134:   Deed dated .....1789 - rec. 16 Mar. 1790 DAVID ANDERSON,
               Sheriff of Laurens Co. of 96 Dist. to WILLIAM SHAW of
Edgefield Co., Att'y at law - the sheriff sold 100 acres belonging
to WILLIAM PUGH, late of Laurens Co., planter, to SHAW, highest bidder,
to satisfy a debt. Sold for 3 pds 5 sh sterling. Wit: GEORGE ANDERSON
& WILLIAM DALRYMPLE.

Pp 134-136:   14 OCt. 1789 - rec. 16 Mar. 1790 DAVID ANDERSON, Sheriff
               of Laurens Co. to WM. SHAW, Att'y of Edgefield Co., SC
150 acres owned by ROBERT HENRY HUGHES, planter of Laurens Co., to
satisfy HUGHES' indebtedness to Col. ROBERT RUTHERFORD of Newberry
Co., SC. This land orig. granted to WILLIAM COULTER and was bounded
by JAMES KILGORE and located on Duncan's Creek. Land sold for 22 pds
10 sh 8 p.

Pp 136-137:   11 May 1789 - rec. 17 Mar. 1790 HENRY MEREDITH of Spartan-
               burg Co., SC to TRAVIS MORRIS of Laurens Co. for 30 pds
10 shillings, 150 acres being part of a tract of 640 acres granted
to THOMAS EWIN and conveyed to BARTLETT BROWN in 1755. Land situated
on south side of Enoree River, adj. GEORGE ROSE. Wit: JOHN FARROW &
HAMMOND MORRIS. Both these made probate bef. THOMAS FARROW 4 June 1789.

Pp 137-139:   5 Mar. 1790 - 17 Mar. 1790 DAVID (X) CHILDERS, planter
               of Laurens Co. to JACOB ROBERTS, of same, minister, for
85 pds, 200 acres granted to JOHN WIDOWMAN in 1772. Wit: HUDSON BERRY,
ALEXANDER HARPER. Harper made probate 9 Mar. 1790 before DANIEL WRIGHT,
J.P.

Pp 139-140:   5 Mar. 1790 - rec. 17 Mar. 1790 DAVID CHILDERS, planter
                of Laurens Co. to JACOB ROBERTS, minister, for 15 pds
sterling, 100 acres on Enoree River granted to DAVID CHILDERS 1 Jan.
1787 by Wm. Moultrie, Gov. Wit: HUDSON BERRY & ALEXANDER HARPER. Berry
made probate bef. DANIEL WRIGHT, J.P. 9 Mar. 1790.

Pp 140-141:   No date on deed recorded 18 Mar. 1790 SUSANNA (X) MAN
                and JOHN (X) MAN, of Duncan's Creek in Laurens Co., yeoman
for 20 pds to JOHN DANIEL KERN, of Charleston, merchant & gentleman,
a tract of land (no acreage) adj. ROBERT MAN, JAMES MAN, JOHN ELMORE.

Pp 141-143:   5 Mar. 1790 - rec. 18 Mar. 1790 JAMES POLLOCK & ANN (X)
                POLLOCK, his wife, planter, of 96 Dist., Laurens Co.,
to ANN WILLSON, single woman of same place, for 100 pds 10 sh, 100
acres on Duncan's Creek, bounded by ROBERT PROCTER, BENJAMIN WILLSON,
being part of a tract of 350 acres granted BENJ. WILLSON by Wm. Moultrie
1 May 1786, which 100 acres was conveyed to JAMES POLLOCK by BENJ.
WILLSON & ELIZABETH, his wife, 26 Feb. 1790. Wit: JOHN EDWARDS & JOHN
RYAN.

Pp 143-144:   26 Feb. 1790 - rec. 18 Mar. 1790 BENJAMIN WILLSON & ELIZA-
                BETH (X) WILLSON his wife, of Duncan's Creek in Laurens
Co., for 100 pds, 100 acres to JAMES POLLOCK. Wit: ROBERT LONG & RICHARD
BELL. Long made probate bef. JAMES MONTGOMERY 9 Mar. 1790.

Pp 144-146:   26 Feb. 1790 - rec. 19 Mr. 1790 ANDREW OWENS & JANE (X)
                OWENS, his wife, of Duncan's Creek Settlement of Laurens
Co., for 200 pds 10 sh, 100 acres on a small branch on south side of
Enoree River, bounded by THOMAS ALLEN. Wit: JAMES WRIGHT, ADAM BELL.
This land was a part of a grant to ANDREW OWENSON 12 Jan. 1768. (300
acres).

Pp 146-148:   14 Dec. 1778 - rec. 19 Mar. 1790 ROBERT (X) PROCTOR of
                Duncan's Creek, 96 Dist. to BENJAMIN WILLSON of same,
for 630 pds sterling, 100 acres being part of a tract of 200 acres
in Berkley Co. in fork of Broad and Saluda Rivers on south fork of
Duncan's Creek of Enoree River, bounded by JAMES PAGE. Wit: JAMES ADAIR,
DAVID MC CLUR, WILLIAM ROSS. McClur made probate 25 Dec. 1778 bef.
GEORGE ROSS, J.P.

Pp 148-150:   27 Oct. 1789 - 24 Apr. 1790 Hon. NICHOLAS EVELEIGH &
                MARY EVELEIGH his wife to Rev. ROBERT SMITH, EDWARD RUT-
LEDGE & JOHN BEE HOLMES for 5 shillings, 2886 ½ acres consisting of
several tracts as follows: 50 acres in 96 Dist. on south side of Saluda
River granted to JAMES MAYSON 1 Aug. 1785, by him conveyed to EVELEIGH
on 17 and 18 Nov. same year; also 450 acres in sd Dist. adj. lands
purchased of Capt. WILLIAM ANDERSON, surveyed in name of JOHN CAMP-
FIELD 20 Apr. 1784; 229 acres on north side of Saluda River bought
of JOSEPH WHITE 27 and 28 Mar. 1786; 640 acres in 96 Dist. above the
Ancient Boundary on Savannah River, called the Coves, surveyed for
EVELEIGH by JOHN PURVIS in 1784; 640 acres bought by EVELEIGH from
JOHN HARLSTON on west side of Cape Fear River in Brunswick Co. 13 Oct.
1779; 700 acres in 96 Dist., 350 acres of which were bought of JAMES
& JOHN MARTIN 15 Aug. 1775 on Ninety Six Creek; 379 acres on Drey Creek
branch of Horn's Creek in 96 Dist. granted to JOHN RUTLEDGE 21 July
1775, conveyed by JOHN PURVIS to NICHOLAS EVELEIGH about month of Dec.
1779; 200 acres on Crooked Run, branch of Turkey Creek, conveyed by
PURVIS to EVELEIGH about Dec. 1779, granted to DONALD SIMPSON ab. Feb.
1773; 100 acres on Black Rocky Creek sold by RICHARD ANDREWS RAPLEY
to EVELEIGH; 350 acres called Horse Shoe on north side of Saluda River,
bought of ANDREW RODGERS and conveyed by him to EVELEIGH; 450 acres
on Reedy River bought of DANIEL WILLIAMS and his son, NIMROD WILLIAMS
9 Mar. 1780; 450 acres bought of WILLIAM FURLOU in Berkley Co. on north
side of Saluda River; 600 acres bought of ALEXANDER FRASER, JR. 4 Jan.
1780, orig. granted to EDWARD EDWARDS on west side of Edisto River;
350 acres bought of ALEX. FRASER situated within 3 miles of the former
tract in Colleton Co.; orig. granted to JAMES WALKER; 550 acres bought
of RICHARD ANDREWS RAPLEY, as att'y for JOSEPH SALVADORE, situated
on Black Rocky Creek above Ninety Six and is part of a tract granted

Cont'd:
to WILLIAM LIVINGSTON, Esq.; 5689(?) acres bought of RAPLEY 18 Mar.
1780, being part of the lands granted to WM. LIVINGSTON on Saluda River
in 96 Dist. 3900 acres conveyed by RICHARD ANDREWS RAPLEY by deeds
of lease and release 29 and 30 Apr. 1778; 1450 acres on Black Rocky
Creek in 96 Dist., 3022 acres being part of land granted to WM. LIV-
INGSTON and purchased by RICHD. ANDREWS RAPLEY 10 Dec. 1777; 1048 acres
being part of lands granted to LIVINGSTON and conveyed by RICHARD AND-
REWS RAPLEY EVELEIGH 29 and 30 Apr. 1778; all that plantation situated
in Craven Co. on or near the High Hills of Santee containing 1107 acres
adj. BENJAMIN WARING & GEORGE JOOR(?); one undivided moiety of a tract
of 1000 acres in the North Britain tract, situated on the High Hills
of Santee; 213½ acres situated on the south side of Santee in St. John's
Parish, adj. lands of RALPH IZARD, Esq. and W. SAMUEL IRVING; 274 acres
on south side of Santee in St. James Parish adj. lands of ANTHONY SIM-
MONS & CHARLES PINCKNEY, Esq.; also an undivided moiety in 1-75 acres
in Craven Co. bounded on the Berkley Co. line and HENRY MOWSON; also
1000 acres on Pee Dee River adj. JOHN STONE & ELIZABETH RAVEN; also
500 acres in 96 Dist. on a branch of Little Stephen's Creek; also 500
acres bet. Saluda and Savannah Rivers on Turkey Creek; also 1000 acres
on Lower Bridge Creek, a branch of Horn Creek; also 640 acres in 96
Dist. on a branch of Twenty Six Mile Creek. Wit: THOMAS BEE & THOMAS
EVELEIGH. Probate made bef. DANIEL MAY MASYCK, J.P.

Pp 151-154:   6 June 1789 - 26 Apr. 1790 JOHN RAMAGE & JANE RAMAGE,
               his wife of Laurens Co. to ROBERT BELL of same, for 20
pds 5 sh, 90 acres being part of a tract of 500 acres granted to JOHN
RAMAGE on Duncan's Creek. Wit: JAMES FINDLEY, THOMAS MURDOUGH & RICHARD
BELL. Murdough made probate 26 Feb. 1790. JANE signed her name as JEAN.

Pp 154-156:   24 & 25 Mar. 1783 - rec. 26 Apr. 1790 ELIZABETH (X) BOWLS,
               widow of Duncan's Creek to ROBERT BELL of same, 200 pds
for 150 acres on South Fork of Duncan's Creek, orig. granted to ELIZA-
BETH BOWLS 10 Aug. 1768. Wit: ADAM BELL, DAVID MC CLUER & BENJAMIN
WILLSON. Willson made probate 7 July 1783.

Pp 156-157:   28 Sept. 1789 - 26 Apr. 1790 JACOB NEAL & ANN (X) NEAL
               his wife of Laurens Co. to THOMAS GAFFORD of same, 30
pds for 140 acres on branches of Walnut Creek, being part of a grant
of 170 acres to sd NEAL in 1788, bounded by THOMAS MOORE, CHRISTOPHER
MATHEWS, ARTHUR DURROW. Wit: JAMES CLARDY, MICHAEL GAFFORD.

Page 157:   21 Dec. 1789 - 27 Apr. 1790 DUNCAN O'BRIAN & JANE O'BRIAN
               his wife of Laurens Co. to WILLIAM O'BRIAN of same, for
150 pds sterling, 250 acres in Laurens Co. on Beaverdam Creek, waters
of Little River, bounded by JOHN PHILPOT, JOHN DONNAHOW, JAMES WHITE
& THOMAS BOYCE. Signed: DUNCAN O'BRYANT (X). O'BRYANT ack. deed on
9 Mar. 1790.

(No page notation; also incomplete)...borrowed a set of leases from
SAMUEL HENDERSON given to him by MICHAEL WILLSON & ELIZABETH his wife
and that he believes it was the sd WILLSON's handwriting and to best
of his knowledge for 200 acres, the plantation whereon the sd HENDERSON
now lives and that the leases had proven bef. JOHN CALDWELL, Esq.,
dec'd., and by best of his knowledge by THOMAS EDGEHILL, HUGH O'NEAL,
& LUKE WALDROP, SR., dec'd.

Page 158:   An affidavit to the same effect as the above made by
               ISAAC WILLIAMS on 8 Oct. 1788 bef. CHAS. SAXON, J.P.
Also an affadavit by JEREMIAH SEARCY saying that sometime in 1769 he
was present at a plantation formerly called MICHAEL WILLSON's on Simmons Creek and saw SAML. HENDERSON pay MICHAEL WILLSON, SR. a negro
man in consideration for sd land and plantation which HENDERSON had
purchased of WILLSON and then resided on. Says he is positive of every
statement except the time; bef. JOHN HUNTER.

Pp 158-159:   2 Sept. 1789 - 27 Apr. 1790 JOHN MICKLE of Camden Dist.,
               to JOHN JONES of Laurens Co. for 100 pds sterling, 100
acres on Horse Creek of Reedy River. Wit: JOHN DORAH, DARLING JONES,

Cont'd:
HENDERSON FERGUSON. Ferguson made probate bef. ISAAC LOVE, J.P. 2 Sept. 1789.

Pp 159-161:   10 Dec. 1775 - rec. 27 Apr. 1790 WILLIAM (X) VAUGHAN
                & BARBARA (X) VAUGHAN, his wife, planter of Craven Co.
to JOHN STONE of same, planter, for 300 pds 10 shillings sterling,
200 acres on Beaverdam Creek of Enoree River, being part of a 500 acre
tract granted to sd VAUGHAN 16 Jan. 1772. Wit: WM. BRAMLETT, FREDERICK
(X) BURDIET & WILLIAM THOMPSON. Bramlet made probate 30 Mar. 1778.

Pp 161-162:   1 Mar. 1790 - rec. 28 Apr. 1790 JOHN BAUGH, JR., son
                of WILLIAM BAUGH, deceased, freeholder, of Laurens Co.,
to JOSEPH PINSON of same, for 25 pds sterling, 50 acres on Raborn's
Creek, land granted to WILLIAM ALLISON 26 Aug. 1767, bounded by EDWARD
BOX & CHARLES BRADY. Wit: JOHN PINSON, MOSES PINSON.

Page 162:   1 Mar. 1790 - rec. 28 Apr. 1790 JOHN BAUGH, JR., son
                of WM. BAUGH, dec'd., of Laurens Co. to JOSEPH PINSON
of same, for 7 pds 10 shillings sterling, 20 acres on east side of
Rabourns Creek, being part of 150 acres granted to WM. ALLISON 4 Nov.
1762. Wit: JOHN PINSON, MOSES PINSON. Jos. Pinson made probate 3 Mar.
1790.

Pp 162-163:   28 Mar. 1789 - rec. 29 Apr. 1790 JAMES PUCKETT & MARTHA
                PUCKETT, his wife of Laurens Co. to JOHN SMITH, JR. of
same place, for 20 pds sterling, 25 acres on Cain Creek and Saluda
River, being part of a tract granted to ALEXANDER HAMILTON in 1768
and sold by HAMILTON to PUCKETT. Located near COLE's spring. Wit: JOHN
COLE, JOHN SMITH & WM. CRAIG. Cole made probate 11 Apr. 1789 bef. GEORGE
ANDERSON.

Page 163:   8 Dec. 1789 - rec. 29 Apr. 1790 RICHARD (X) NORTH & SARAH
                (X) NORTH his wife of Orange Co., SC to BENJAMIN DRUMMON
of Laurens Co. for 150 pds sterling, 400 acres on Mudlick Creek, land
granted to JOSHUA INMAN & RICHARD FOUNTAIN and part of a tract granted
to WM. MARSH in 1769. JOSHUA INMAN's grant was in 1772. RICHARD FOUN-
TAIN's in 1770. North ack. deed 8 Dec. 1789.

Pp 164-165:   8 Aug. 1789 - rec. 29 Apr. 1790 JOSHUA GILLIAM of Newberry
                Co., SC to DANIEL WRIGHT of Laurens Co. for 20 pds sterl.
200 acres on a fork of Gilder's Creek known as Bridge Fork of Enoree
River in Greenville Co. adj. NATHANIEL AUSTIN. Wit: JOSEPH REED, JACOB
(X) CRO(W?). Reed signed probate bef. JAMES MONTGOMERY, J.P. on 12
Sept. 1789.

Pp 165-166:   9 Nov. 1789 - rec. 29 Apr. 1790 CORNELIUS CARGILE, son
                and heir of CORNELIUS CARGILE, dec'd. and SAMUEL CLARY
& SARAH (X) CLARY his wife, widow of sd dec'd CARGILE of Laurens Co.,
to SILVANUS WALKER, SR. of same, for 100 pds sterling, 420 acres on
south side of Little River and on both sides of Beaverdame Creek being
lands granted to sd CARGILE, dec'd., by two grants: one for 400 acres
the other for 200 acres and bounded as follows: JOHN CARGILE, dec'd.
and BOYD's line. Wit: SAMUEL WHARTON, SILVANUS WALKER, JR., Capt. SAMUEL
WHARTON made probate 14 Dec. 1789 bef. GEO. ANDERSON, J.P.

Pp 166-167:   Bill of Sale. 14 Dec. 1789 - rec. 29 Apr. 1790 DUNCAN
                O'BRYANT of Laurens Co. sold to WADSWORTH & TURPIN, mer-
chants of same place, horses, cattle, hogs, sheep, feather beds and
all his household furniture. Wit: WILLIAM O'BRYANT & JOHN TROTTER.
John Trotter made probate 11 Mar. 1790.

Page 167:   Bill of Sale. 24 Dec. 1789 - rec. 29 Apr. 1790 DAVID
                BAILY of Laurens Co., blacksmith, to THOMAS WADSWORTH
& WILLIAM TURPIN, merchants, 1 negro, two horses, 10 head of cattle.
Wit: JOHN TROTTER & JOHN CARGILL, JR. Probate by Trotter 11 Mar. 1790.

Pp 167-168:   ___ Mar. 1790 - rec. 20 Apr. 1790 JOHN RAINEY (signed
                RANY) to WADSWORTH & TURPIN, merchants of Laurens Co.

Cont'd:
several horses, cows, hogs, 3 feather beds and furniture, 2 iron pots and one Dutch oven and "all my pewter". Wit: PATRICK MC DOWALL & JOSHUA SYMMES. McDowall made probate 11 Mar. 1790.

Pp 168-169:   Lease & Release. 11 & 12 Dec. 1789 - rec. 30 Apr. 1790.
               CLABURN SIMS of Laurens Co. to CLEMENT DEAL, of same, for 21 pds 10 shillings, 168 acres being part of a tract of 535 acres granted to THOMAS FARR 8 July 1774, lying in Laurens Co. on Lynches Branch of Enoree River. Wit: ANDREW RODGERS, JR. & WILLIAM H. RODGERS. Andw. Rodgers made probate 14 Dec. 1789 bef. ANGUS CAMPBELL, J.P.

Pp 169-170:   4 & 5 Sept. 1789 - rec. 30 Apr. 1790 WILLIAM MOORE, son
               and heir of FRANCES MOORE, dec'd. of Edgefield Co., 96 Dist. to JOSEPH COX, planter of Laurens Co., for 300 pds sterling, 150 acres on south branch of the Beaverdam, orig. granted to JOHN BOX 3 Aug. 1765, conveyed by him to FRANCES MOORE, dec'd. by lease 1 Aug. 1769. It fell by heirship from FRANCES MOORE to his son WILLIAM MOORE. Wit: JAMES YOUNG & NATHANIEL DRUMMOND; also BENJAMIN (X) COX. Young & Drummond made probate 31 Oct. 1789 bef. SILV. WALKER. (Note: Frances should be spelled Francis).

Page 171:   16 Jan. 1790 - rec. 1 May 1790 DANIEL WRIGHT, Esq. of
               Laurens Co. to JOHN WILLSON of same, for 60 pds sterling, 152 acres on both sides of Dirbins Creek of Enoree River; land orig. granted to ROBERT GOODWIN 5 June 1786, including the plantation whereon JOHN WILLSON now lives. No witnesses.

Pp 172-175:   21 Aug. 1769 - rec. 1 May 1790 JOHN BOX, planter of Berk-
               ley Co., SC to FRANCES MOORE, of same, for 200 pds sterl. for 150 acres in Berkley Co. in fork bet. Broad and Saluda Rivers, bounded on all sides by vacant land. Wit: M. GOODE, JOHN GOODWIN & JESSE SCRUGGS. Probate made by MAGNEESE GOOD 30 Apr. 1769 bef. JAMES LINDLEY, one of his Majesty's justices to keep the peace.

Pp 175-177:   Lease & Release. 15 & 16 Sept. 1789 - rec. 1 May 1790.
               BENJAMIN WARING of Camden Dist., SC to EDMOND MARTIN, Esq. for 135 pds 5 shillings 300 acres in Berkley Co. on Little River adj. THOMAS EDGEHILL, JOHN SIMMONS & WILLIAM TURNERN and being a tract orig. granted to RICHARD WARING in 1771 and by his widow, ANN WARING conveyed to BENJAMIN WARING. Wit: ROBERT MAXWELL, Esq., and THOMAS WARING, SR. and ROBERT WARING. Maxwell made probate bef. JOHN HUNTER, 19 Jan. 1790.

Page 177:   8 Jan. 1789 - rec. 1 May 1790 ROBERT CARTER & BETTY (X)
               CARTER his wife of Laurens Co. to JOHN WEATHERS of same, for 20 pds sterling, 75 acres on Cane Creek, adj. RICHARD CARTER & WILLIAM PURSE, which sd land was granted to RICHD. CARTER and by him deeded to ROBT. CARTER & BETTY, his wife. Wit: JOHN CARTER, WM. BROWN & JOHN CARTER, JR. John Carter, Jr. made probate 9 Jan. 1789 bef. GEO. ANDERSON.

Pp 178-179:   Lease & Release. 10 & 11 July 1788 - 3 May 1790 JOHN
               CARTER & RACHEL (X) CARTER his wife to ROBERT CARTER both of Laurens Co., planters, for 30 pds 10 shillings sterling, 104 acres on Cane Creek of Saluda River being part of 200 acres granted to RICHD. CARTER, dec'd., father of sd JOHN CARTER, 25 Aug. 1769, this land joined JAMES CARTER, CROJIAH(?) FOSTER, WM. BROWN & JONATHAN REED. Wit: WM. BROWN & JAMES (X) STRAIN. Signed: JOHN CARTER & RACHEL (X) CARTER. Both wit. made probate 1 Nov. 1788 bef. GEO. ANDERSON, J.P.

Page 180:   Deed of Gift. 27 Oct. 1789 - rec. 3 May 1790 THOMAS EL-
               LIOTT, JR. of Laurens Co., Reaburn's Creek Settlement, freeholder and planter, for love and affection for his father, THOMAS ELLIOTT, SR., of same place, "all my lands, tenements and estate, real and personal, in sd state and co." Wit: WILLIAM SIMMONS & DAVID MC CAA who made probate bef. ANGUS CAMPBELL the same day.

Page 180:   Deed of Gift. 14 Dec. 1789 - rec. 3 May 1790 WILLIAM
               (X) DAVIS, planter unto his two children SARAH & ABRAHAM

235

Cont'd:
DAVIS the following: to ABRAHAM 100 acres on waters of Duncan's Creek, Miller's Fork, cow and calf, and 1/2 my sheep, 1/2 of my household furniuture; to SARAH, cow and calf, 1/2 my sheep and hogs and 1/2 the furniture; "and if God be pleased to call me from time to eternity before I return again, I do commit to my wife CASIAH the care of my whole estate that she may receive her support and the children while she remains unmarried. Wit: JOHN CALDWELL & BENJAMIN ADAIR. N.B. If I should not return and my wife marry, I appoint JOSEPH ADAIR my executor. ADAIR made probate bef. JAMES MONTGOMERY 8 Mar. 1790.

Page 181:   22 Feb. 1790 - rec. 4 May 1790 GEORGE BROOKS of Laurens
               Co. to JOHN WALLACE of same, for 50 pds, 170 acres on
a branch of Durbin's Creek, adj. VANDERHOST & JOHN BARNET. Wit: HENRY FAGIN, PATTY (X) AHIN. Fagan made probate bef. DANL. WRIGHT, 22 Feb. 1790.

Pp 181-182:   13 Jan. 1790 - rec. 4 May 1790 CORNELIUS DANNAHOO of
               Laurens Co. to MOSES SULLIIVANT of SC, planter, for 115
pds sterling, 150 acres in Laurens Co. on Beaverdam Creek adj. JOSEPH BABB, DAVID CRADDOCK & WILLIAM DAVIS(?). Land orig. granted to CHRISTOPHER PLINES 3 Jan. 1755. Wit: SAMUEL WHARTON & STEPHEN MULLINGS.

Pp 182-184:   Lease & Release. 13 & 14 Mar. 1780 - 5 May 1790 WILLIAM
               (X) CASEY, JR. and MARY (her mark) CASON, his wife of
96 Dist. to JOHN MILLER, shoemaker, for 20 pds 10 shillings, 10 acres being part of that plantation of 300 acres where CASON, JR. now lives on Bush River, adj. GEORGE DALRYMPLE, orig. granted to ANDREW RODGERS 22 Feb. 1771, conveyed by GEORGE WIER to WILLIAM CASON, JR. 21 & 22 Sept. 1779. Wit: JOSHUA TEAGUE, PHILIP TINSLEY & THOMAS CASON. Teague made probate 15 Dec. 1789 bef. JONATHAN DOWNS.(CASEY & CASON in text)

Pp 184-185:   8 Mar. 1790 - rec. 5 May 1790 DANIEL MARTIN, tailor of
               Laurens Co. to GEORGE MARCHBANKS for 50 pds sterling,
100 acres being land granted to JOSHUA OWINS on 3 Apr. 1784 which was a tract of 400 acres; OWINS deeded this 100 acres to DANIEL MARTIN 9 June 1786. Land situate on North Fork of Duncan's Creek, adj. JAMES BARCHFIELD & ISAAC BARTON. No witnesses given.

Page 185:   1 Aug. 1780 - rec. 5 May 1790 JOHN GRAY & AILSEY (X)
               GRAY, his wife of Laurens Co. to THOMAS MC CREARY for
25 shillings 4 pence, 34 acres on Duncan's Creek, adj. THOMAS MC CREARY & JAMES KELLY. Wit: THOMAS MC CREARY, JR. & ROBERT MC CREARY. Robt. McCreary made oath bef. JAMES MONTGOMERY, 11 Jan. 1790.

Pp 186-188:   Lease & Release. 16 & 17 Nov. 1789 - rec. 5 May 1790
               JAMES (X) DICKINSON, planter, and BETTY (her mark) his
wife of Camden Dist. for 40 pds 10 shillings, 50 acres to JOSEPH GALAGLY wheelwright of 96 Dist., land adj. JAMES ANDERSON and was part of a 200 acre tract orig. granted to JAMES DICKINSON 18 May 1771. Wit: BENJAMIN MC KINNEY, JOHN MC KINNEY & JON. BARNES. The probate was made in Fairfield Co., SC by Benj. McKinney bef. ISAAC LOVE, J.P. 10 Nov. 1789.

Pp 188-189:   20 Oct. 1789 - rec. 6 May 1790 KITT SMITH of 96 Dist.,
               planter and ANN (X) SMITH, his wife, to JOSEPH GALAGLY,
wheelwright of same place, for 10 shillings sterling, 50 acres in Laurens Co. on waters of Bush River, being part of a tract orig. granted to KITT SMITH 22 Aug. 1771. Wit: JAMES CUMMINGS, JAMES JOHNSTON & GEORGE BROCK. Cummings made probate.

Pp 189 - 192: 23 Jan. 1790 - rec. 6 May 1790 JOHN CUNNINGHAM of the
               City of Charleston, SC, merchant, to CHARTER NICKLES
of 96 Dist., planter, for 51 pds sterling, 100 acres on Cain Creek on north side of Saluda River. Wit: WM. ANDERSON, MATTHEW HUNTER, & WM. NICKLES. Hunter and Nickles made probate bef. ANGUS CAMPBELL 13 Feb. 1790.

Pp 192-193:   Lease & Release. 8 & 9 June 1789 - rec. 17 June 1790
               MACKERNUSS GOODE, gentleman of Edgefield Co., SC to RICHD.

Cont'd:
SHACKELFORD, pastor of the Baptist Church, Laurens Co., for 500 pds
sterling and 10 shillings, 500 acres situated on the Beaverdams and
bounded by CORNELIUS CARGILE, DAVID CRADDOCK, JOHN BOX, WILLIAM ARTHER
& granted to sd GOODE 30 Oct. 1767. Wit: SAMUEL GOODE, JOSEPH BOX &
FRANCES BROOKS. Cox made probate 12 Dec. 1789.

Page 193:   Lease & Release. 8 & 9 June 1789 - rec. 17 June 1790
             SAMUEL GOOD, gentleman of Edgefield Co., SC to RICHARD
SHACKELFORD, pastor of the Baptist Church Laurens Co. for 100 pds 10
sh. sterling, 100 acres on Little River in Laurens Co., adj. DANIEL
OZBURN, MACKERNESS GOOD, deceased, who dying intestate, the land fell
to SAMUEL GOOD, heir at law. Wit: JOSEPH COX, FRANCES BROOKS & ALEXANDER
STUART.

Pp 196-197:   Lease & Release. 11 & 12 Dec. 1789 - rec. 17 June 1790
              WILLIAM (X) HUBBS, planter and ELIZABETH (X) HUBBS, his
wife of Laurens Co., to GEORGE FULLER of same, planter, for 20 pds
10 sh. sterling, 100 acres on a small branch of Raburn's Creek, orig.
granted to MARGARET TODD 17 Mar. 1775. Sd MARGARET TODD conveyed to
FREDERICK LITTLE 17 June 1779 and sd LITTLE conveyed to WM. HUBBS 1
Dec. 1787. Wit: MANSIL CRISP, JAMES (X) WILLSON & GEORGE McVAY. Willson
made probate 15 Dec. 1789 bef. Jonathan Downs.

Page 197:   9 Feb. 1789 - rec. 18 June 1790 JOHN OZBURN, SR. of Laur-
             ens Co., to CHRISTOPHER ROLAND of same, for 50 pds stg.,
83½ acres being part of a tract orig. granted to JOHN OZBURN. Wit:
TANDY WALKER & ANDREW RODGERS, JR. Rodgers made probate 8 June 1789
bef. Silvanus Walker.

Pp 198-199:   23 Feb. 1790 - rec. 18 June 1790 BENJAMIN KILLGORE of
              Laurens Co. to JAMES KILLGORE of same, for 50 pds stg.,
100 acres in Laurens Co. bet. Gilder's and Peter's Creeks, being part
of tract granted to JAMES WHITE (no date) and conveyed to BENJ. KILL-
GORE 24 Dec. 1789. Wit: MOSES WHITE, JOHN MESSER, ROBERT GREER. Messer
made probate 11 June 1790 bef. WM. MITCHERSON, J.P.

Page 199:   22 Feb. 1790 - rec. 18 June 1790 MOSES WHITE of Laurens
             Co. to JAMES KILLGORE for 50 pds stg., 110 acres in Laur-
ens Co. on Gilder's Creek, bounded by ZACHARIAH HOLCOMB & JAMES WHITE.
This land was granted 5 Oct. 1788 to MOSES WHITE. Wit: BENJ. KILLGORE,
JOHN MESSER & ROBT. GREER. Messer made probate 11 June 1790 bef. Wm.
Mitcherson.

Pp 200-201:   9 Feb. 1789 - rec. 18 June 1790 JOHN OSBURN, SR. of Laur-
              ens Co. to JOHN WALKER of same, for 40 pds stg., 83½
acres being part of tract orig. granted to JOHN OSBURN, SR. (no description). Wit: TANDY WALKER & ANDREW RODGERS. Walker made probate
10 June 1789 bef. JOSEPH DOWNS. JERIAH (X) OSBURN, the wife of JOHN
OSBURN renounced dower bef. SILVANUS WALKER 4 July 1789.

Pp 200-201:   13 Mar. 1789 - rec. 18 June 1790 BENJAMIN RAINEY of Laur-
              ens Co. to WILLIAM MANLEY of same, for 40 pds, 129 acres
on Durbin's Creek, waters of Enoree River, being part of tract of 440
acres granted to CHARLES FINDLEY 5 June 1786. This 129 acres was sold
by BENJ. RAINEY to WILLIAM JACKSON of Laurens Co. and then sold by
execution at the instance of WILLIAM SHAVE 10 Apr. 1788, then struck
off to BENJ. RAINEY as highest bidder. Land bounded by WILLIAM YOUNG,
JOHN WILLIAMS, JOSEPH BURTON. Wit: ALEXANDER HARPER & HUDSON BERRY.
Berry made probate bef. DANIEL WRIGHT 15 June 1790.

Pp 202-203:   25 Feb. 1790 - rec. 19 June 1790 TIMOTHY GOODMAN, con-
              stable of Laurens Co. and NANCY (X) GOODMAN, his wife,
to THOMAS RILEY of same, for 15 pds stg. 100 acres in Laurens Co. on
waters of Saluda River, bounded at time of orig. survey by ALEXANDER
DEAL, GEORGE HOLLINGSWORTH, WILLIAM O'NEL & JOHN COOK. The same was
granted to TIMOTHY GOODMAN 6 Nov. 1786. Wit: JAMES TINSLEY, JOSEPH
GRIFFIN, HENRY PEARSON. Pearson made probate 12 June 1790 before ANGUS
CAMPBELL.

Pp 203-205:   Lease & Release. 3 & 4 Mar. 1790 - rec. 19 June 1790
                 JOHN COLE of Laurens Co. to JONATHAN JOHNSON for 50 pds
sterling 10 shillings, 115 acres on Cain Creek in Laurens Co., bounded
by PETER SMITH & DRAPER. Land granted to JOHN COLE 4 Dec. 1786. Wit:
WILLIAM P. JOHNSON, WM. JONES, JOHN (X) JONES. Johnson made probate
14 June 1790 bef. Angus Campbell.

Pp 205-207:   Lease & Release. 14 & 15 June 1790 - rec. 19 June 1790
                 JAMES PUCKET of Laurens Co., planter, to JOHN PINSON,
of same, planter, for 75 pds 10 sh., 150 acres on Cain Creek of Saluda
River. Same granted to JAMES PUCKET 2 May 1785. Wit: EDWARD GIDDENS
& PETER (X) GRIFFIN; also JESSE MEEKS.

Page 207:   Bill of Sale. 7 Jan. 1790 - rec. 25 June 1790 SARAH (X)
                 CLARY and CORNELIUS CARGILE to PATRICK CUNINGHAM for
70 pds, 1 negro woman and child. Wit: MIMURANT(?) WALKER, RICHARD DUTY.
An affidavit was made by HARDY (X) CONANT saying that SAMUEL CLARY
sold this negro woman and child unto CORNELIUS CARGILE about 6 weeks
or 1 month before date of the within bill of sale. Bef. JONATHAN DOWNS.

Pp 207-209:   29 Jan. 1789 - rec. 21 June 1790 WILLIAM THOMASON of
                 Laurens Co. to BENJAMIN CAMP of Rutherford Co., N.C.
for 250 pds sterling, 200 acres on Rayburn's Creek on north fork of
sd creek and on both sides of same, including Thomason's mill; adj.
WOLFF, MORGAN, NIBLET's old line to the Mountain Creek; granted to
SOLOMON NIBLET 27 Mar. 1769 and conveyed from him to BISHOP and from
him to NATHAN AUSTIN and from him to THOMASON. Deed signed by WM. THOMA-
SON and MOURNING THOMASON. Wit: CHARLES SULLIVANT, NATHAN CAMP & JOHN
THOMASON. Camp made probate 4 Feb. 1790.

Pp 209-210:   Mortgage. 10 June 1790 - rec. 27 July 1790 MICAJAH SIMS
                 of Laurens Co., gave mortgage to JOHN FRANCIS WOLFF of
same, on his crop of corn and tobacco "now growing", 1 feather bed
and house hold furniture, 3 cows, 10 hogs, 2 mares. Wit: MARTIN DIEL
& JOHN W. CAMBRIDGE. Cambridge made probate 29 June 1790.

Pp 210-211:   21 Mar. 1790 - rec. 2 Aug. 1790 BENJAMIN KILGORE & JANE
                 KILGORE, his wife, of Laurens Co. to BENJAMIN BYRD of
same, for $700, 400 acres lying on both sides of Dunkin's Creek, a
branch of Enoree River (the same granted to KILGORE 21 Jan. 1785) adj.
lands of JOHN MC DAVID, THOMAS WOODS & LEWIS DUVALL. Wit: JAMES MC
DAVID & JOHN KILGORE. McDavid made probate bef. JAMES MONTGOMERY, 6
Apr. 1790.

Pp 211-212:   31 Mar. 1790 - rec. 2 Aug. 1790 BENJAMIN KILGORE and
                 JEAN, his wife of Laurens Co. to BENJAMIN BYRD of same,
100 pds sterling for 50 acres on a branch of Duncan's Creek of Enoree
River, adj. JOHN MC DAVID. Wit: JAMES MC DAVID, JOHN KILGORE. McDavid
made probate 6 Apr. 1790 bef. James Montgomery, J.P.

Pp 212-214:   6 Apr. 1790 - rec. 3 Aug. 1790 LEWIS SAXON, Laurens Co.
                 to JOSEPH DORSET, planter of same, for 35 pds 10 shill-
ings, 150 acres on north side of Reedy Rier, bounded by JAMES DORROUGH,
Maj. PIERCE BUTLER, granted to LEWIS SAXON 14 Aug. 1786. Wit: JOHN
A. ELMORE, JOSHUA DOWNS. Downs made probate 10 Apr. 1790.

Page 214:   Mortgage. 5 Oct. 1789 - rec. 3 Aug. 1790 WILLIAM (X)
                 THOMASON gave mortgage to THOMAS CUNINGHAM. Wit: ISAAC
JAMES & JOHN W. CAMBRIDGE.

Page 215:   21 Jan. 1790 - rec. 4 Aug. 1790 DANIEL CLARY of Newberry
                 Co. planter to NATHANIEL NICHOLS of Laurens Co. planter,
for 100 pds stg., 300 acres in Greenville Co., 96 Dist., below the
ancient boundary line, orig. graned to JACOB MORRIS 1 Aug. 1785. Signed
D. CLARY & FANEY CLARY. Wit: JOHN NICKELLS & SAMUEL CALDWELL. Caldwell
made probate bef. Angus Campbell 1 May 1790. AMBROSE HUDGINS, JR. wit.
CLARY's receipt of the consideration money.

Pp 216-217:   25 Feb. 1790 - rec. 5 Aug. 1790 JOHN ATKINS & MARGARET
                 (X) ADKINS his wife of Moore Co., N.C. to GEORGE MORGAN,

238

Cont'd:
of Laurens Co., SC for 100 pds, 179 acres in Laurens Co. on both sides
of Reedy River, adj. JOHN BROWN, JOHN CARGILE, HANCE HENDRICK, orig.
granted to JOHN WILLARD, being part of a tract of 250 acres. Wit: LEWIS
GRAVES, MIDDLETON PRATER, JAMES MORGAN. Prater made probate bef. GEO.
ANDERSON, 25 May 1790.

Page 217:   6 Feb. 1790 - rec. 5 Aug. 1790 RICHARD (X) FOWLER of
               Laurens Co. and DEBBY (X) FOWLER, his wife, to ISAAC
FOWLER for 30 pds, 100 acres bet. Enoree River and Zeak's Branch, adj.
THOMAS MOORE, NATHAN BRAMLETT, orig. granted to RICH. FOWLER 1 June
1789. Wit: THOMAS (X) MOORE, NATHAN BRAMLETT, ROSEANNAR MOORE. Thos.
Moore made probate bef. DANL. WRIGHT 10 June 1790.

Pp 221-223:   (No dates shown) BENJAMIN POWEL of Craven Co., SC & MARTHA
               (X) POWEL to WILLIAM SIMS of same, for 150 pds sterling
current money of Great Britain, 150 acres on North's Creek waters of
Little River, bounded by WM. DENDY, ROBT. SIMS, GEORGE NORWOOD, JAMES
BURNSIDES, ROBERT SIMS, JR. & JOHN BAILEY. Wit: WM. DENDY, TANDY WALKER
& THOMAS CARGILL. Dendy made probate 9 Mar. 1790 bef. SILVANUS WALKER.

Pp 223-225:   23 Dec. 1776 - rec. 7 Aug. 1790 WILLIAM SIMS of 96 Dist.,
               SC, planter to SAMPSON MUNGER of same, hatter, for 150
pds 10 shillings stg., being the same land described in the above deed.
Land orig. granted to BENJAMIN POWELL 21 May 1772. ANDREW RODGERS,
WETTENHALL WARNER, CLABOURN SIMS. Andrew Rodgers, Jr. made probate
3 Jan. 1778 bef. Jonathan Downs.

Pp 225-227:   18 Nov. 1782 - rec. 7 Aug. 1790 SAMPSON MUNGER, hatter
               of 96 Dist. to JOHN CLARDY, planter of same, for 250
pds 10 sh., 150 acres having same description as the two above deeds.
Wit: ISAAC WILLIAMS, WILLIAM (X) ELLIOTT & SARAH (X) WILLIAMS. Elliott
made probate bef. Geo. Anderson 10 May 1784.

Pp 227-228:   14 Nov. 1789 - rec. 7 Aug. 1790 JOHN CLARDY, SR. & SUSANNA
               (X) CLARDY his wife of Laurens Co. to TYRA GLENN for
100 pds stg. for 150 acres (same description as three deeds above).
JOHN & SUSANNA ack. deed 15 Nov. 1789 bef. Silvanus Walker.

Pp 228-231:   28 Apr. 1790 - rec. 9 Aug. 1790 WILLIAM PANTON of the
               Kingdom of Great Britain, by EDWARD PENMAN, Esq. of Charl-
eston, S.C., merchant, attorney for WM. PANTON, to PETER GRIFFIN of
96 Dist. for 110 pds sterling, 200 acres on north side of Saluda River,
granted to MICHAEL SWARTZ, who conveyed it to ROBERT GOWDY, who conveyed to WM. PANTON. Wit: CHARLES COLCOCK & HENRY W. DESAUSSURE. Desaussure made probate 29 Apr. 1790 be. Angus Campbell. The following
is an extract from a letter from WM. PANTON, Esq. to EDW. PENMAN, Esq.:
"As Mr. MC GILLERAY is now on the way to meet the Commissioners of
Congress, I expect (and with some degree of confidence) that peace
will take place between this nation and the Georgians, in which case
I shall have frequent opportunities to write you by that route. Ands
soon as I can lay my hands on a proper form, I shall forward to you
a power of attorney for sale of my land in Carolina." WILLIAM PANTON,
Pensacola, 24 Aug. 1789.

Pp 231-233:   Lease & Release. 15 & 16 Aug. 1790 - rec. 17 Aug. 1790
               BENJAMIN (X) CAMP, planter, and ELIZABETH (X) CAMP, his
wife, to JOHN WOLFF, merchant both of Laurens Co., for 50 pds 5 shillings, 98½ acres on Reaburn's Creek, bounded by EZEKIEL MATHEWS, SARAH
MORGAN & WILLIAM THOMASON, orig. granted to SOLOMON NIBLET 27 Mar.
1769, conveyed to ABNER BISHOP, then to NATHAN AUSTIN, then to WILLIAM
THOMASON, then to BENJ. CAMP. Plat included, showing land to be on
both Reaburn's and Mountain Creeks. Wit: LEWIS SAXON, ROBERT ATKINS
& JOSEPH CAMP.

Pp 233-235:   22 July 1790 - rec. 17 Aug. 1790 JOHN KELLET & JENNET
               (X) KELLET of Laurens Co., farmer, to WILLIAM THOMASON,
carpenter of same, for 10 pds 5 sh., 200 acres on Raborn's Creek, waters
of Saluda, being part of a tract orig. granted to SOLOMON NIBLET 22

Cont'd:
Mar. 1769. Wit: JOHN F. WOLFF & ELISHA HUNT. Wolff made probate 16 Aug. 1790.

Pp 235-236: 8 Apr. 1790 - rec. 21 Sept. 1790 RICHARD SHACKELFORD & MARY SHACKELFORD, his wife, of Laurens Co. to JOSEPH COX for 25 pds, 23 acres on Little River. Wit: SILVANUS WALKER, JR. & JOHN COX & RICHARD BATTEN. Plat included, survey made by JOHN RODGERS.

Pp 236-237: 8 Apr. 1790 - rec. 25 Sept. 1790 RICHARD SHACKELFORD & MARY ANN (X) SHACKELFORD his wife of Laurens Co. to JOSEPH COX of Laurens Co. for 10 pds 33 acres on Little River. Wit: SILV. WALKER, JOHN, RICHD. BATTEN. Cox made probate 13 Sept. 1790.

Pp 237-238: Bond. 16 Feb. 1790 - rec. 25 Sept. 1790 THOMAS SHIP, MARK MOORE, JEDIDIAH SHIP & ELSE MOORE gave bond to JOHN COX, all of Laurens Co., for 150 pds, for 70 acres on Beaverdam Creek of Little River. Title to land to be made by 25 Dec. 1805. Wit: SILVANUS WALKER & JOSEPH COX. Walker made probate 13 Sept. 1790 bef. GEO. ANDERSON, J.P.

Pp 238-240: 8 Sept. 1790 - rec. 22 Sept. 1790 JAMES FINNEY, planter to ALEXANDER DEALE, planter, both of Laurens Co. for 50 pds stg., 133 acres in Laurens Co. on Saluda River, orig. granted to JAMES FINNEY 2 Oct. 1786, bounded at time of orig. survey by MATHEW LOVE, one JONES and WILLIAM RUCK.

Pp 240-242: 2 July 1790 - rec. 22 Sept. 1790 LEWIS DUVALL, hatter, to ANDREW PARKS, planter, both of Laurens Co., for 54 pds stg., 300 acres on a branch of Duncan's Creek in 96 Dist. below the Indian Boundary, bounded by WILLIAM TAYLOR, JOHN MC NEES, JOHN HOWARD, land orig. granted to LEWIS DUVALL. Wit: JOHN SIMPSON & DAVID SPEARS.

Pp 242-245: 22 Apr. 1784 - rec. 22 Sept. 1790 JOHN COPELAND, son and heir of GEORGE COPELAND, deceased, and MARGARET (X) COPELAND, his wife, to JOSHUA ARNALL, both of SC, for 200 pds 10 sh., 200 acres on Beaverdam of Little River. Wit: ROBERT SPEARS & ELIZABETH (X) SPEARS.

Pp 245-247: 6 Oct. 1785 - rec. 23 Sept. 1790 JAMES RABB of Fairfield Co., SC, planter, to JOSEPH WOOLBANKS, of Laurens Co., for 10 shillings, 250 acres on Gilder's Creek of Enoree River, orig. granted to sd RABB 31 Aug. 1774. Wit: RICHARD (X) WOOLBANKS & HENRY (X) WOOLBANKS. Richd. Woolbanks made probate 10 Sept. 1790 bef. WM. MITCHERSON.

Pp 247-249: 10 Sept. 1790 - rec. 23 Sept. 1790 JOSEPH (X) SOUTH, planter, and MARY SOUTH, his wife of Laurens Co., to EDWARD HUNTER, tailor for 80 pds stg., 250 acres on Pinson's branch on North side of Saluda River, being part of a grant of 300 acres to sd SOUTH 14 June 1788. Wit: JOHN DANIEL, SR. & JOHN DANIEL, JR. John Daniel, Sr. made probate 11 Sept. 1790 bef. Daniel Wright.

Pp 249-250: 13 Dec. 1789 - rec. 23 Sept. 1790 WILLIAM (X) THOMAS to BENJAMIN FOUSHEE, planter, both of Laurens Co., for 56 pds stg, 100 acres in 96 Dist. on waters of Saluda River, orig. granted to THOMAS CAHUNE 25 Feb. 1773. Wit: RICHARD (X) HOGANS, JOHN NEWMAN. Deed signed by WILLIAM THOMAS & ANKEY (X) THOMAS. Newman made probate 10 Sept. (no year).

Pp 250-251: 15 Aug. 1789 - rec. 24 Sept. 1790 GEORGE (X) MORGAN to MIDDLETON PRAYTOR, both of Laurens Co. for 32 pds stg, 61 acres adj. Reedy River, JACOB BOWMAN & HANCE HENDRICKS. Signed GEORGE (X) MORGIN & ELIZABETH (X) MORGIN. Wit: LEWIS GRAVES, ZACARIAH SIMS & ANN (X) JONES. Lewis Graves made probate 26 Dec. 1789 bef. Geo. Anderson, J.P.

Pp 251-252: 12 Mar. 1790 - rec. 24 Sept. 1790 NATHANIEL NEWMAN planter

Cont'd:
                    to HENRY BROCKMAN, planter, both of Laurens Co. for 75
pds sterling, 150 acres on Enoree River. Wit: JOSEPH LYONS & BENJAMIN
KILGORE. Kilgore made probate 6 Mar. 1790 bef. DANL. WRIGHT, J.P.

Page 253:   6 Jan. 1790 - rec. 24 Sept. 1790 JAMES WHITE of Laurens
                 Co. to NATHANIEL NEWMAN of same, for 50 pds stg., 150
acres in Laurens Co. on south side of Enoree River, being part of an
800 acre tract granted to JAMES WHITE, SR. 26 Aug. 1774. Wit: BENJAMIN
KILGORE, MOSES WHITE & ROBERT GREEN. Kilgore made probate 6 Mar. 1790
bef. Daniel Wright, J.P.

Pp 253-254:   8 Dec. 1789 - rec. 25 Sept. 1790 CORNELIUS CARGILL to
                 JOSEPH GROVES, both of Laurens Co. for 30 pds, 100 acres
on waters of Cain Creek being part of a tract of 350 acres granted
to CARGILL, now deceased, bounded on the Bee Branch, GEORGE CARTER,
JOHN FINDLEY & DEDGINS. Cargill ack. the deed 8 Dec. 1789 bef. Silvanus Walker, J.P.

Pp 254-256:   8 Aug. 1777 - rec. 25 Sept. 1790 RICHARD (X) CARTER of
                 96 Dist., planter, and MARGARET CARTER, his wife, to
GEORGE CARTER, their son, for 10 shillings, 100 acres in Berkeley Co.,
waters of Cain Creek, being part of 300 acres granted to sd RICHD.
CARTER 6 Feb. 1773. Wit: JOSEPH CARTER, JAMES CARTER, ROBERT CARTER.

Pp 256-259:   Lease & Release. 6 & 7 Aug. 1771 - rec. 26 Sept. 1790
                 WILLIAM TURK and RACHEL (X) TURK his wife, planer, to
GEORGE CARTER, planter both of Berkeley Co. for 60 pds 10 sh., 100
acres on Cain Creek orig. granted to WM. TURK 22 Feb. 1771. Wit: PA.
CUNINGHAM, HUGH BROWN, ROBERT CARTER. Brown made probate bef. Robt.
Cuningham, J.P. 24 Aug. 1771.

Pp 259-261:   3 June 1777 - rec. 26 Sept. 1790 CORNELIUS CARGILL of
                 Little River, 96 Dist., planter, to GEORGE CARTER of
Cain Creek, 96 Dist., for 100 pds 10 sh, 91 acres being part of a grant
to CORNELIUS CARGILL 8 July 1774. Wit: STEPHEN DURRAM, AURTHOR DURRAM,
ROBERT SIMS. Stephen Durram made probate 9 Jan. 1789. Deed signed by
CORNELIUS CARGILL & SARAH CARGILL.

Pp 261-263:   6 Aug. 1771 - rec. 28 Sept. 1790 ROBERT CARTER, planter
                 to GEORE CARTER, planter, both of Berkeley Co., SC for
60pds 10 sh., 100 acres on waters of Cain Creek. Wit: PA. CUNINGHAM,
HUGH BROWN & WM. TURK. Brown made probate 24 Aug. 1771 bef. Robt. Cuningham.

Pp 263-265:   5 & 6 Aug. 1777 - rec. 28 Sept. 1790 RICHARD CARTER,
                 planter and MARGARET CARTER, his wife, to JOSEPH CARTER,
their son, all of Cain Creek, 96 Dist., for 5 pds 10 shillings, 125
acres in Berkeley Co., waters of Cain Creek, orig. granted to RICHARD
CARTER 11 Feb. 1773. Wit: GEORGE CARTER, JAMES CARTER, ROBERT CARTER.
Robert Carter made probate 9 Jan. 1789 bef. Geo. Anderson, J.P.

Pp 265-268:   Lease & Release. 22 & 23 Apr. 1784 - rec. 28 Sept. 1790
                 Province of East Florida - JOSEPH CARTER to JOHN CARTER,
both of the Province of East Florida, for 50 pds 5 shillings, 125 acres
being on waters of Cain Creek in S. C. in Berkeley Co., bounded by
PATRICK CUNINGHAM, RICHARD CARTER, WILLIAM PURSE. Wit: NICHOLAS WELSH,
RICHARD KING. King made probate bef. GEORGE FARDO, one of his Majesty's
justices to keep the peace for Prov. of East Florida, 11 May 1784.

Pp 268-269:   24 Apr. 1784 East Florida. JOSEPH CARTER to JOHN CARTER
                 both of Province of East Florida, for 100 pds stg., 200
acres on Cain Creek in Berkeley Co., Province of S. C., land granted
to sd JOS. CARTER 15 May 1772. Wit: NICHOLAS WELSH, RICHARD KING. Probate made by King in East Florida bef. Geo. Fardo, J.P. In Laurens
Co., THOMAS CARTER made oath bef. Geo. Anderson that he was personally
present and saw the within deed legally probated 9 Jan. 1789.

Pp 269-270:   8 Aug. 1790 - rec. 30 Sept. 1790 ROBERT (S) SMART & ELIZA-
                 (X) SMART his wife of 96 Dist., Newberry Co. to JOHN

241

Cont'd:
PRATHER of Laurens Co. for 10 pds, 50 acres in Laurens Co. on waters
of Enoree River, adj. JOHN WHITMORE, JOHN MACHON. Land orig. granted
to ROBERT SMART 6 Feb. 1773. Wit: REUBEN FLANAGIN, AMOS PRATHER & MARTHA
PRATHER. Flanagin made probate 11 Sept. 1790 bef. DANL. WRIGHT, J.P.

Pp 270-271:   (No date) - rec. 30 Sept. 1790 JOSIAH GREER & MARGARET
               GREER, his wife to JOHN HANNA both of Laurens Co., for
100 pds, 181 acres on a branch of Duncan's Creek called Allison's Branch.
Wit: WILLIAM CRAIG, WILLIAM HANNA. Hanna made probate bef. JOHN HUNTER,
5 Aug. 1790.

Pp 271-272:   28 Mar. 1790 - rec. 30 Sept. 1790 SHEARWOOD ALLEN & MARY
               ALLEN, his wife of Richmond Co., Georgia to THOMAS JONES
of Laurens Co., SC for 50 pds stg., 100 acres on waters of Little River
being part of a grant of 300 acres to JOHN CARGILL, dec'd., conveyed
to sd ALLEN & wife by will of JOHN CARGILL, dec'd.; adj. lands surveyed
for DAVID TIGER, CORNELIUS CARGILL, dec'd., and DAVID BAILEY; also
NATHAN CRENSHAW. Wit: JAMES TUTT & TANDY WALKER. Walker made probate
14 Sept. 1790.

Page 272:   Personal. 13 Mar. 1789 - rec. 30 Sept. 1790 DUKE WILLIAMS
               sold to his father, JOHN WILLIAMS, 1 negro girl aged
10-12 years, for 25 pds sterling. Wit: JONATHAN JOHNSTON & WILLIAM
P. JOHNSON.

Pp 272-273:   15 Sept. 1790 - rec. 30 Sept. 1790 WILLIAM (X) WILLSON,
               son and heir of JAMES WILLSON, dec'd. of Laurens Co.,
to JAMES WHITE of same, planter, for 50 pds sterling, 200 acres on
a small branch of Enoree River in Laurens Co., same was granted to
JAMES WILLSON, dec'd., 1 Sept. 1788. Wit: LEWIS SAXON, JONATHAN JOHN-
SON, WILLIAM HUNTER. Saxon made probate 15 Sept. 1790 bef. JOSHUA SAXON.

Pp 274-275:   Lease & Release. 13 & 14 July 1790 - rec. 13 Oct. 1790
               JAMES HANNA, blacksmith and MARGARET HANNA, his wife
of Laurens Co. to JOHN HUNTER, yeoman of same, for 120 pds 10 shillings
for 200 acres on Warrior Creek, orig. granted to JAMES MASON 31 Oct.
1769 and by him conveyed to WILLIAM ANDERSON 13 & 14 Oct. 1770; by
Anderson conveyed to ABNER BISHOP 8 & 9 July 1777 and by Bishop conveyed on 24 & 25 Mar. 1785 to JAMES HANNA. Wit: JOHN MC CLINTOCK &
JAMES MC CLINTOCK.

Page 275:   An affadivit by THOMAS YORKE on 25 Feb. 1790. YORKE made
               oath that on 20 Feb. he and WILLIAM PUGH had a dispute
and agreed to fight, and that after engaging in battle, the deponent
(YORKE) "did git sd PUGH's ear in his mouth and bit a piece out of
the left ear of sd PUGH." Sworn bef. DANIEL WRIGHT, J.P.

Page 276:   Personal. 2 Feb. 1790 - rec. 13 Oct. 1790 PATRICK RILEY
               of Laurens Co. sold to WILLIAM KELLET several cows, 2
old horses, 3 feather beds and furniture, kitchen utensils, 1 woman's
saddle, farm implements, chairs, pigs and all other moveable property
he was possessed with. Wit: JOHN RYLEY & MARTIN MAHAFFEY. Signed: PAT-
RICK RYLEY. Probated signed by MARTIN MAHAFFEY, JR. 4 Apr. 1790.

Pp 277-278:   6 Mar. 1790 - rec. 14 OCt. 1790 JOHN ADAIR and JEAN (X)
               ADAIR his wife, to WILLIAM DAVIS, all of Laurens Co.,
for 40 pds, 100 acres on Duncan's Creek of Enoree River in Laurens
Co., orig. granted to sd JOHN ADAIR 5 June 1786, bounded by JOSEPH
ADAIR, JAMES MILLER, JOSEPH GLENN, JOHN JONES. Wit: AYRES GORELY &
SALLY JONES. Gorely made probate 21 Sept. 1790 bef. JOHN HUNTER, J.P.

Pp 278-279:   12 ___ 1790 - rec. 14 Oct. 1790 DAVID SPEARS of Laurens
               Co. to ANDREW SPEARS for 20 pds, 100 acres in Laurens
Co. on waters of Little River, adj. AGNES SPENCE, WILLIAM TAYLOR, DAVID
SPENCE, orig. granted to ROBT. SPEARS, dec'd., and conveyed by will
to sd DAVID SPEARS. Wit: JAMES KILLGORE, JOHN MESSER. Killgore made
probate 13 Oct. 1790 bef. John Hunter, J.P.

Pp 279-281:   Lease & Release. 27 Dec. 1788 WILLIAM (X) DUNLAP to WIL-

Cont'd:

LIAM BRAMLET, both of 96 Dist., for 60 pds 10 shillings 125 acres on small branch of Beaverdam Creek of Enoree River, bounded by ISAAC GRAY, NEWTON HIGGINS, JAMES MC DAVID, BURGESS GOOLSBY at time of survey. Wit: MC ELROY & NEWTON (X) BRAMLET.

Pp 281-283:   19 Aug. 1790 - rec. 15 Oct. 1790 HENRY HARDEN and CLARY (X) HARDEN, his wife to JOHN MEEK, all of Laurens Co., for 50 pds stg., 100 acres on Banks' Branch of Saluda River, adj. ALEX-ANDER DEALE. This tract was a part of 300 acres orig. granted to WILLIAM HUTSON (or WATSON?) on 7 June 1774, then conveyed by HUTSON (WATSON) to WILLIAM CASON 22 Sept. 1775, and now a part of it is sold to his brother BENJAMIN CASON. Wit: SAMUEL STEDMAN & BENJAMIN ROWE. Rowe made probate 11 Oct.1790.

Pp 283-285:   Lease & Release. 24 July 1790 - rec. 15 OCt. 1790 PATRICK (X) MITCHELL, planter, to DAVID COWIN, planter, both of Laurens Co., for 100 pds stg, 160 acres in Laurens Co. on a branch of Warrior Creek, adj. THOMAS JONES & EDWARD GARRET, orig. granted to sd MITCHELL 7 May 1787. Wit: FRANCIS ROSS & FRANCIS GLEN. Ross made probate 12 Oct. 1790 bef. John Hunter, J.P.

Pp 285-286:   20 Aug. 1789 - rec. 16 Oct. 1790 GEORGE MADDEN & ANN MADDEN, his mother, planter, to DAVID RAGSDAIL, planter, all of Laurens Co., for 25 pds, 100 acres in Laurens Co. on waters of Reedy River, bounded by JACOB WRIGHT. Wit: DAVID MADDEN & THOMAS RAGSDALE. In the probate ANN is called NANCY MADDEN.

Pp 286-289:   Lease & Release. 5 Aug. 1790 - rec. 11 Nov. 1790 WILLIAM CASON & ANN CASON, his wife, to JOSEPH BLACKERBY, planter, all of Laurens Co. for 100 pds 5 shillings, 200 acres on Little River of Saluda. Land was orig. granted by bounty to JOHN PURSELL 25 June 1765. CASON bought this land from TERREL RILEY and RILEY, at the demise of the afsd JOHN PURSELL adminiistered on the estate. This land was sold at public auction to the highest bidder and TERREL RILEY, in his own right, purchased it. Wit: DANIEL SYMMES & THOMAS WADSWORTH. Wads-worth made probate 23 Aug. 1790 bef. John Hunter.

Page 289:   Personal. 7 Apr. 1789 - rec. 11 Nov. 1790 JOSEPH DORSETT of Laurens Co., to his sons JAMES & THOMAS DORSETT for love and affection and for the better maintenance and livelihood of my self and family, the plantation that I now live on, with all my goods and chattels. Wit: ISAAC TOWERS & PETER RAGSDALE. Towers made probate 16 Apr. 1790 bef. JOSEPH DOWNS.

Pp 289-290:   8 Apr. 1790 - 12 Nov. 1790 WILLIAM WHITEHEAD to WILLIAM BOYD, of Laurens Co., for 60 pds sterling, 100 acres on Cain Creek of Saluda River, bounded by GEORGE CARTER, DUDGENS, THOMAS BOYD, JAMES WHITE, Bee Branch. Wit: JOHN FINLEY & ROBERT (X) SHAW. Shaw made probate 10 Nov. 1790.

Page 290:   30 Jan. 1790 - 12 Nov. 1790 JOHN WILLIAMS of Edgefield Co., SC to JAMES THURSTON of Laurens Co., for 5 pds stg., 100 acres on a branch of Mudlick, called Thurston's branch, being part of a tract of 650 acres, bounded by JAMES MC GILL, NATHANIEL NICKLES. Wit: JAMES CALDWELL & JOHN GATES. Caldwell made probate 9 July 1790, bef WM. CALDWELL.

Page 291:   Personal. 17 Dec. 1790 - 27 Dec. 1790 WILLIAM RUCKS of S. C., planter, sold to JONATHAN JOHNSON, collector of Laurens Co., for 50 pds sterling, negroes(no number shown). Wit: SAMUEL STEDEMAN, DANIEL (X) MYIN & ALEXANDER DEALE. Deale made probate bef. Angus Campbell 27 Dec. 1790.

Pp 292-294:   11 Sept. 1789 - rec. 22 Jan 1791 THOMAS CUNINGHAM to JAMES MC DAVID, both of Laurens Co, for 39 pds 10 sh., 200 acres in Laurens Co. on a branch of Reedy River and Reaburn's Creek bounded by land surveyed for DANIEL ALLEN, being part of a tract of 600 acres granted to DAVID WEBB 18 May 1771, conveyed to JAMES RYAN 9 & 10 Oct. 1771, then conveyed to THOMAS MC CLURKEN 15 Apr. 1778 &

Cont'd:
conveyed to THOMAS CUNINGHAM 7 Jan. 1780. Deed signed by THOMAS CUN-
INGHAM & MARY (X) CUNINGHAM. Wit: RICHARD PUGH & GEORGE (X) CUNINGHAM.
Plat included.

Pp 294-297:   26 July 1790 - rec. 22 Jan. 1791 JAMES MC DAVID, free-
               holder of Laurens Co. to JONATHAN COX, of Abbeville Co.,
SC, 96 Dist., for 10 shillings, 100 acres in Laurens Co. on Reedy River
being part of the land described in the above deed. Last part of deed
refers to PENELLABB MC DAVID, as the wife of JAMES MC DAVID; she also
signed the deed. Wit: RICHRD BATTEN, BENJAMIN (X) COX, THOMAS (X) COX.
Batten made probate 15 Dec. 1790 bef. Jonathan Downs, J.P.

Pp 297-298:   31 Dec. 1890 - rec. 15 Feb. 1791 BENJAMIN TOWNSAN of
               Laurens Co., to JAMES & THOMAS DORSETT of same, for 100
pds sterling, 4 horses. Wit: ISAAC TOWERS & WILLIAM DORROH.

(Skips to page 305)

Pp 305-307:   7 Dec. 1790 - rec. 5 Mar. 1791 DAVID TAGGART of the North-
               ern Liberties, of the City of Philadelphia, in the state
of Pennsylvania, hatter, only son and heir at law of DAVID TAGGART,
late of 96 Dist., Laurens Co., SC, killed by the Indians, appointed
JAMES IRWIN, of West Pennsborough Township, county of Cumberland and
state of Penn., miller, his attorney to demand possession of his tract
of land on Little River, Dist. of 96, Laurens Co., SC, 150 acres adj.
SILVANUS WALKER et al. Wit: DEBORAH SHOEMAKER, WILLIAMS AURENCE & ABRA-
HAM SHOWMAKER. Abraham Showmaker certified this document as Nortary
Public.

Page 307:   24 Apr. 1790 - rec. 5 Mar. 1791 ELIZABETH SHOTE of Laurens
               Co., to BRADFORD CAMP, Greenville Co., SC for 100 pds,
296 acres on a branch of Raburn's Creek, being part of a tract of 300
acres granted to sd SHOTE 6 Apr. 1789. Wit: ABRAHAM BOLT & JOSEPH HOLMS,
both signed by mark.

Page 308:   10 Dec. 1788 - rec. 7 Mar. 1791 JOHN MILAM & NANCY (X)
               MILAM his wife, to THOMAS WILKS & FRANCES LESTER, all
of Laurens Co., for 125 pds, 160 acres on North Creek, orig. granted
to JOHN YOUNG, bounded by Widow GOODMAN, JAMES COOK, THOMAS WOODWARD
& WILLIAM RAINEY. Wit: AMBROSE HALL & JAMES CLARDY. Clardy made probate
9 Mar. 1789.

Pp 309-310:   THOMAS DORSETT, JAMES DORSETT & JOSEPH DORSETT of Laurens
               Co. to BENJAMIN TOWERS, later of the State of North Caro-
lina, for 100 pds stg., 150 acres in Laurens Co. on north side of Reedy
River bounded by JAMES DOROUGH and PIERCE BUTLER, Esq., orig. granted
to LEWIS SAXON, 7 Aug. 1786, being the same land deeded by JOSEPH DOR-
SETT, by deed of gift to his sons THOMAS & JAMES DORSETT on 7 Apr.
1790. Wit: ISAAC TOWERS, WM. DOROUGH, JAMES DOROUGH. Wm. Dorough made
probate 14 Feb. 1791 bef. Joseph Downs.

Pp 310-312:   15 & 16 July 1788 - rec. 8 Mar. 1791 JOHN MC GEE of the
               State of Virginia, mill carpenter, to Col. GEORGE REID
of Abbeville Co., 96 Dist., for 5 pds 8 shillings, 300 acres in Laurens
Co. on a branch of Reedy River called Horse Creek, bounded on SW on
lands laid out to the Cherokee Indians. Land was orig. granted to JAMES
REID (no date) and conveyed by him on 10 & 11 Oct. 1774 to JOHN MC
GEE. JOSEPH REID made probate bef. ADAM CRAIN JONES, J.P. Abbeville
Co., S.C. 5 July 1789.

Page 312:   Personal. 15 Mar. 1790 - 9 Mar. 1791 JOSEPH GRIFFIN of
               Laurens Co. to JAMES GOODWIN of Newberry Co., SC, 1 negro
man 35 years, native African, for 35 pds. Wit: JOHN TROTTER & THOMAS
WADSWORTH.

Pp 312-313:   Personal. 13 Aug. 1790 - rec. 17 Mar. 1791 ELIZABETH
               BERRY to WILLIAM BERRY both of Laurens Co. for 14 pds,
1 negro girl about 4 years old. Wit: SPENCER BOBO & JOSEPH HALL. Hall
made probate bef. Angus Campbell, 15 Mar. 1791.

Page 313:   17 Feb. 1789 - rec. 9 Mar. 1791 JOHN YOUNG & MARY YOUNG,
             his wife of Rutherford Co., N. C. to GALANUS WINN of
Laurens Co., for 100 pds Virginia currency, 200 acres in Laurens Co.
on both sides of Simmons Creek, being land granted to sd JOHN YOUNG
(no date), bounded by JOSEPH BLACKERBY, JOSEPH YOUNG & JAMES COOK.
Wit: FRANCES LESTER & ROBERT YOUNG. Both made probate bef. WILLIAM
NEVILL, J.P. of Rutherford Co., NC 17 Feb. 1789.

Page 314:   7 Nov. 1789 - rec. 15 Dec. 1790 MARTIN (X) MARTIN to
             JAMES COOK both of Laurens Co., for 20 pds, 25 acres
in Laurens Co. on waters of Saluda River being granted to MARTIN in
1787, bounded by JOHN YOUNG, Widow HANCOCK. Wit: JOSUAH ARNALL & JAMES
MC NEES. Arnall made probate 7 Nov. 1789 bef. JOSEPH DOWNS.

Pp 315-317: Lease & Release. 2 & 3 Jan. 1789 - rec. 9 Mar. 1791 DUNCAN
             O'BRYANT of Laurens Co., planter, to ROBERT MC FADDEN
of Abbeville Co., planter, for 10 pds 10 sh., 100 acres being part
of a tract of 350 acres belonging to sd O'BRYANT and granted to him
2 Sept. 1773. Land situated on a branch of Beaverdam Creek. Wit: JAMES
RODGERS, MARGRET CRISP, PATTY RODGERS. James Rodgers made probate 6
Apr. 1789 bef. John Rodgers.

Pp 317-318: 5 & 6 Nov. 1790 - rec. 9 Mar. 1791 THOMAS NORRIS, black-
             smith of Laurens Co. to SAMUEL PUTT, planter of same,
for 25 pds 5 sh., 73 acres on north side of Reedy River bounded by
ELIJAH TAYLOR, JONATHAN DOWNS. Land orig. granted to DOWNS on 3 Mar.
1788. Wit: ELISHA HUNT & JAMES DOWNIN. Hunt made probate 10 Dec. 1790
bef. Joseph Downs.

Pp 318-320: 18 Apr. 1788 - rec. 9 Mar. 1791 BENJAMIN WILLSON & ELIZA-
             BETH (X) WILLSON, his wife, planter to JAMES MC CLUER,
planter, both of Laurens Co. for 42 pds, 100 acres on south fork of
Duncan's Creek being part of a tract of 350 acres laid out to sd WILL-
SON 3 Dec. 1784, bounded by JAMES POLLOCK, ALEXANDER ADAIR (bounty
survey). Wit: ADAM (X) BELL, JAMES BELL, JOHN ROBINSON. Adam Bell made
probate 3 Nov. 1790.

Page 320:   An affadavit by BENJAMIN (X) STONE on 18 Feb. that he
             had received 9 pds 18 shillings 9 pence for all blacksmith
work done for PATRICK CUNINGHAM in 1790. Wit: JAMES PINSON.

Page 321:   22 Jan. 1791 - rec. 9 Mar. 1790 ELLINOR MC CLUER made
             an affadavit that she bought of ELLICK MENARY two sows
and pigs which increased to 14 head and as her brother ROBERT RITCHEY
was often disputing with her concerning the increase, they being marked
with the same mark they formerly gave on the plantation, she is of
necessity making oath. Bef. CHARLES SAXON, J.P. She made another affa-
daavit concerning a cow willed to her by her deceased father JOHN RITCH-
EY on the same day.

Pp 321-322: 5 Apr. 1783 - rec. 9 Mar. 1791 DAVID LEVESTON of state
             of Virginia and county of Aring (Oring?), weaver, to
BENJAMIN RAINEY, planter of 96 Dist., for 8 pds 40 sh., 100 acres on
Reaburn's Creek, a branch of Saluda River. This land was granted to
JOSEPH LEVESTON 6 Apr. 1768. DAVID LEVESTON was the eldest brother
and heir at law to the estate of JOSEPH LEVESTON, dec'd. Wit: THOMAS
(X) CAVE & SARAH (X) CAVE. Probate made at Camden Dist., SC by THOS.
CAVE bef. PHILLIP WALKER.

Pp 323-325: JACOB LEWIS, planter of State of Georgia, to DAVID MAYSON
             of Laurens Co., SC, planter, for 20 pds 5 sh., 200 acres
on Indian Creek, bounded by JOHN MAYSON. Land orig. granted to DAVID
LEWIS 17 Apr. 1764, and conveyed by him to BENJAMIN LEWIS and conveyed
to JOHN LEWIS by heirship and conveyed by him to JACOB LEWIS by power
of attorney. Wit: JAMES MILLWEE, DAVID COLLIOR & MONEY SHERELL. Probate
was made at Pendleton Co., SC by David Collior bef. WILLIAM HALBERT.

Pp 325-327: 25 & 26 Sept. 1773 - rec. 9 Mar. 1791 BENJAMIN BROWN,
             planter to WILLIAM MARTIN, merchant, both of Craven Co.,

Cont'd:
Province of S. C., for 150 pds 10 shillings, 100 acres on Reaburn's
Creek, being part of 150 acres granted to BENJAMIN BROWN 19 Nov. 1772.
Deed signed by BENJAMIN BROWN & SARAH (X) BROWN. Wit: JONATHAN DOWNS
& ACQUILA (X) HALL.

Pp 327-329:   25 & 26 June 1771 - rec. 9 Mar. 1791 RICHARD OWINGS &
               ANN (X) OWINGS, his wife of Craven Co., Province of SC,
planter, to SILVANUS WALKER, of same, for 325 pds, 150 acres on both
sides of Reaburn's Creek, orig. granted to OWINGS 25 June 1770. Wit:
WILLIAM DOWNS & ZACHERI PHILLIPS. Downs made probate bef. JAMES LIND-
LEY 4 Sept. 1771.

Pp 329-331:   5 & 6 Aug. 1777 - rec. 14 Mar. 1791 RICHARD CARTER &
               MARGARET CARTER, his wife, planter of Cain Creek, 96
Dist. to ROBERT CARTER, their son of same place, for 5 pds 10 shillings,
75 acres in Berkeley Co. on waters of Cain Creek. Deed signed by BETY
CARTER instead of MARGARET. Wit: GEORGE CARTER, JOSEPH CARTER, JAMES
CARTER & ANDREW (X) STRAIN. THOMAS CARTER, SR. made probate as well
as did JOHN CARTER, JR. on 9 Jan. 1789 bef. GEORGE ANDERSON.

Page 331:   Power of Attorney. 28 Feb. 1791 WILLIAM BROWN of Camden
               Dist., SC, appointed his friend JOHN M. CAMBRIDGE, of
same place, his attorney to make titles to a tract of 156 acres of
land in 96 Dist. the same having been granted to JOHN BOYKIN, of Camden
Dist., and by him conveyed to WM. BROWN. Wit: JOHN YARBROUGH & MOSES
KING. Proven bef. JOHN KING, J.P. Mar. 1, 1791.

Pp 331-332:   Personal. 31 Jan. 1791 - 14 Mar. 1791 WILLIAM (X) WALLACE,
               aged 13 years of Laurens Co., was indentured to serve
as an apprentice and to be taught by FRANCIS ROSS, hatter, the art
of hat making; also to learn to read and write the English language;
the term of apprenticeship was 6 years and at the end of that time
ROSS was to give WALLACE a horse, valued at 7 pds sterling, saddle
and bridle and a suit of clothes. Wit: ROBERT MC CLINTOCK & GEORGE
ROSE.

Page 332:   Personal. 31 Jan. 1791 - rec. 14 Mar. 1791 JOHN RUTLEDGE,
               JR., Esq. of Charleston, SC, appointed JOHN HUNTER, Esq.,
a member of the present House of Representatives of the State for Laurens Co., his attorney to sell certain parcels of land. Wit: FREDERICK
RUTLEDGE, CHARLES RUTLEDGE, J. RUTLEDGE. Probate made 18 Ja. 1791 by
JOHN RUTLEDGE, SR. who stated that he saw his son JOHN RUTLEDGE, the
younger, sign the power of attorney bef. ANDREW PERKINS.

Pp 332-333:   JOHN DENDY & SALLY DENDY, his wife of Laurens Co., to
               JAMES CLARDY of same place, for 10 pds, 187 acres on
South side of Little River, adj. HENRY ISBELL & CORNELIUS CARGILL.
Wit: THOMAS DENDY & JAMES CLARDY.

Pp 333-335:   Mortgage. BENJAMIN STONE & JOSEPH COBBS gave mortgage
               ot LEWIS BANTON & JACOB BURGESS, 25 June 1790.

Page 335:   Deed of Gift. 10 Jan. 1791 - rec. 14 Mar. 1791 CHARLES
               (X) PUCKETT of Laurens Co., to his eldest daughter MARY
PUCKETT, one bay mare, one cow and calf, two sheep, one feather bed
and furniture; to his second daughter ELY, one cow, 2 sheep, 30 geese,
one feather bed and furniture; to his second son, CHEATIAM, similar
things; to his third son JOHN, similar things; to his fourth son DOUGLAS
his present tract of land. Wit: ALEXANDER MORRISON & GEORGE GORDON.

Pp 335-336:   Deed of Trust. 9 Feb. 1791 - 17 Mar. 1791 WILLIAM HUDDLE-
               STON of Laurens Co., blacksmith, to PATRICK BRYAN, in
trust for the heirs of JOHN JONES, dec'd., 250 acres on branch of Duncan's Creek, being part of 476 acres granted to HUDDLESTON; adj. JOHN
ADAIR and is now in possession of PATRICK BRYAN in his wife's right
of dower and as administrator of the estate and guardian to the heirs
of JOHN JONES, dec'd. Signed by both WILLIAM & JANE (X) HUDDLESTON.
Wit: ROBERT HANNA, THOMAS EWING, JOHN ADAIR. Ewing made probate 17
Mar. 1791 bef. Joseph Downs.

Pp 336-337:   Personal. 21 Aug. 1790 - rec. 15 Mar. 1791 STEPHEN (X)
                HUTSON to his daughter AGNES MC MEHAN, 1 heifer; to his
daughter TABITHA BROWN, the rest of his goods and chattels. Wit: CHARLES
SMITH & LUCY SMITH. Chas. Smith made probate 15 Mar. 1791 bef. JOS.
DOWNS.

Pp 337-338:   ___ Sept. 1789 - rec. 15 Mar. 1791 DAVID (X) BURNS & MARY
                BURNS, his wife to JOHN CHANDLER, both of Laurens Co.,
for 125 pds sterling, 183 acres on Simmons Creek, being part of two
grants, one to EDWARD OZBURN and one to THOMAS DENDY. Land bounded
by WILLIAMSON & JAMES HENDERSON. Wit: JAMES CLARDY & TANDY WALKER.

Pp 339-340:   28 & 29 July 1790 - 14 Mar. 1791 ANDREW SMITH, surgeon
                to JOHN SIMPSON, JR., merchant, Laurens Co., for 95 pds
10 sh., 100 acres on branch of Little River, orig. granted to CHARLES
HARVEY May 1771 and conveyed by him to JACOB JONES 21 & 22 June 1772,
from him to JAMES LEFFAN 29 June 1772, and by him to THOMAS DAVIDSON
& wife, SARAH, 29 Jan. 1785, and by him to ANDW. SMITH 15 Jan. 1789.
Wit: ALEXANDER SIMPSON & DAVID SPEARS.

Pp 341-342:   8 July 1790 - 14 Mar. 1791 WILLIAM RUCKS, planter, to
                DRURY SIMS, planter, both of Laurens Co., for 40 pds,
50 acres on Cane Creek, NE side of Saluda River, bounded by THOMAS
CHAPPELL, JOHN SAVAGE, Esq., JOHN CHESTNUT and ROBERT FINNEY. Land
was granted to BARBARY NALE (MALE?) (Note - most likely NEAL) 14 Oct.
1774. She conveyed it to DAVID CUNINGHAM in 1774, by him conveyed to
ROBERT PAGE, and after death of sd PAGE, ELIZABETH PAGE, widow of ROBERT
PAGE, married WILLIAM TAYLOR; then ELIZABETH TAYLOR conveyed it to
WM. RUCKS 9 Jan. 1786. Wit: WILLIAM BALL, WILLIAM BALL (JR.?) & GEORGE
BALL.

Page 342:   Bill of Sale. 10 Mar. 1791 - 15 Mar. 1791 LITTLE BERRY
                HARVEY of Laurens Co., to THOMAS DENDY, 1 horse and all
his household furniture and plantation tools. Wit: SAMUEL HARRIS &
THOMAS DENDY, JR.

Pp 342-345:   10 & 11 Mar. 1791 - rec. 15 Mar. 1791 CLEMENT DEAL to
                THOMAS WM. FAKES, both of Laurens Co., for 21 pds 10
shillings, 168 acres being part of a tract of 535 acres granted to
THOMAS FAKES 8 July 1774 on Enoree River. Wit: JOHN COLE & WM. PRICE.

Page 346:   4 & 5 Oct. 1790 - rec. 15 Mar. 1791 PETER (X) GRIFFIN
                & ELIZABETH (X) GRIFFIN his wife, to MESHAK OVERBY, plant-
er, both of Laurens Co., for 55 pds 5 sh., 105 acres on north side
of Saluda River. Wit: JAMES PUCKETT, JOHN LAND & RICHARD PUCKETT.

Pp 346-347:   14 Sept. 1790 - 15 Mar. 1791 JOSEPH (X) ALLISON & ELIZA-
                BETH (X) ALLISON, his wife of Laurens Co., to HENRY HIG-
GINS for 45 pds, 107 acres on a branch of Beaverdam, of Enoree River,
adj. MARTIN WILLIAMSON, BENJAMIN GRIFFITH, WILLIAM HIGGINS. Wit: RAUGH-
LEY (ROLLEY also) (X) STONE, & NATHAN BRAMLETT. Bramlett made probate
8 Mar. 1791 bef. DANL. WRIGHT, J.P.

Pp 347-349:   16 June 1790 - 15 Mar. 1791 CALEB HUGHES of Laurens Co.,
                to GEORGE WALTON of the state of Virginia, Cumberland
Co., for 50 pds, 55 acres on Durbin's Creek, orig. granted in a tract
of 100 acres to JOHN HUMPHREYS. Wit: THOMAS KIVELL, AGA KIVELL, EDWARD
(X) DIAL (also DYAL).

Pp 349-350:   ..... 1790 - 15 Mar. 1791 CORNELIUS CARGILL to JAMES
                CLARDY for 25 pds sterling, 100 acres on Little River.
Rest of deed illegible.

Pp 351-352:   10 Jan. 1790 - rec. 15 Mar. 1791 LUCY PEARSONS to MARY
                PUCKETT for 10 pds sterling, 100 acres on Cain Creek.
Wit: WILLIAM ANDERSON & JOHN SAMPLE. Rest of deed illegible.

Page 353:   14 Mar. 1791 - 16 Mar. 1791 JESSE MEEKS to JAMES MC DOAL
                both of Laurens Co., for 80 pds, 100 acres on branch

Cont'd:
of Little River, called Ryan's Creek, bounded by ADAM TAYLOR, JAMES
BLAKELY & THOMAS JONES. Wit: ROBERT MC NEES & SILVANUS WALKER, JR.

Pp 353-354:   24 Nov. 1790 - rec. 16 Mar. 1791 DAVID ANDERSON, sheriff
                of Laurens Co. to GEORGE (X) MORGAN, of same place, for
15 pds 10 sh., paid as highest bidder in the case of MARY WILLIAMS
vs ROBERT TOOMBS, of Laurens Co., for a tract of 100 acres on Little
River. Land was orig. granted to HENRY SEYMORE 21 Mar. 1768. SEYMORE
conveyed it to JAMES WILLIAMS 2 Nov. 1774. Wit: LEWIS GRAVES & MIDDLE-
TON (X) PRATHER.

Pp 354-355:   19 Feb. 1791 - 16 Mar. 1791 AYERS GORELY of Laurens Co.
                to PATRICK BRYANT for 50 pds, 90 acres on Duncan's Creek.
Wit: EDWARD GIDDEN & WILLIAM UNDERWOOD.

Pp 355-356:   14 Mar. 1791 - rec. 17 Mar. 1791 JOSHUA ARNALL to THOMAS
                SHIP, both of Laurens Co., for 200 pds, 200 acres on
Beaverdam Creek of Little River, orig. granted to WILLIAM ARTHER, con-
veyed by him to GEORGE COPELAND, by JOHN COPELAND, son and heir of
GEO. COPELAND, dec'd. to JOSHUA ARNOLD. Wit: MARSHALL FRANKS & ABRHAM
(X) NEIGHBOURS. Deed signed by JOSHUA ARNALL & LEANNA (X) ARNALL. Neigh-
bours made probate bef. Joshua Saxon, J.P. 17 Mar. 1791.

Pp 357-359:   5 Feb. 1791 - rec. 17 Mar. 1791 RICHARD JOWELL, planter
                of Laurens Co., to JOEL BURGESS for 100 pds 5 shillings,
200 acres on Beaverdam Creek of Little River, being part of 210 acres
granted to RICH. JOWELL, 4 Apr. 1785. Wit: THOMAS SHIP & THOMAS BABB.
Ship made probate 17 Mar. 1791 bef. Joshua Saxon.

Page 359:   Personal. 17 Oct. 1787 - rec. 23 Mar. 1791 Bond. SILVANUS
                WALKER is bound to JOHN FALCONER for 2000 pds sterling.
Wit: CORNELIUS DENDY, JOHN DENDY & ARMISTED STOKES. John Dendy made
probate 22 Mar. 1791 bef. Charles Saxon.

Pp 359-361:   17 Mar. 1791 - rec. 23 Mar. 1791 NEHEMIAH FRANKS of Laur-
                ens Co. to MORGAN MORGAN for 33 pds 2 sh, 140 acres in
Laurens Co. on a small branch of Reaburn's Creek called McHarg's Creek
being part of a tract orig. granted to FRANKSZ 5 June 1786. Wit: JAMES
CUNINGHAM, JOSHUA DOWNS, ABRAHAM (X) NEIGHBOURS. Cuningham made probate
17 Mar. 1791.

Page 361:   Gift. 14 Feb. 1791 - rec. 24 Mar. 1791 BENJAMIN (X) WIL-
                LIAMS of Laurens Co., Reaburn's Creek Settlement, free-
holder and planter, for love and affection to his son JONATHAN WILLIAMS,
of same place, bachelor, a tract of land (no acreage given) on Reedy
Fork od Dirty Creek. Wit: JAMES PARKER & THOMAS ELLIOTT. Probate made
by THOMAS ELLIOTT, JR.

Pp 361-363:   24 ... 1791 - rec. 24 Mar. 1791 JOHN RODGERS to MANSIL
                CRISP, both of Laurens Co., 50 pds for 165 acres being
on waters of Dirty Creek, waters of Reaburn's Creek. Land was part
of 640 acres granted to JOHN RODGERS (no date). Wit: ROBERT CULBERT-
SON, EZEKIEL ROLAND, JOSHUA DOWNS. Downs made probate bef. Joshua Saxon.
(1791, no other date).

Page 362:   Gift. 26 Feb. 1791 - 24 Mar. 1791 THOMAS PARKER of Laur-
                ens Co., carpenter, to his brother, JAMES PARKER, of
same place, bachelor, all his estate, real and personal. Wit: ROBERT
COOPER & SAMUEL COOPER. Robt. Cooper made probate 26 Feb.1791 bef.
JONATHAN DOWNS.

Page 363:   30 Mar. 1791 - rec. 29 Apr. 1791 JESSE MEEKS of Laurens
                Co. to LARKIN SULLIVANT for 15 pds, 67 acres on Beaver-
dam, of Little River, bounded by ALEXANDER HAMILTON, PATRICK CUNINGHAM,
JAMES SULLIVAN. Wit: JOHN RODGERS, EZEKIEL ROLAND & JAMES RODGERS.
John Rodgers made probate 31 Mar. 1791 bef. Joshua Saxon. Plat included.

Page 364:   Gift. 9 Oct. 1790 - rec. 12 Apr. 1791 WILLIAM CRAIG,
                planter, to JAMES EDWARDS, step-son of sd CRAIG, both of

248

Cont'd:
Laurens Co., 25 acres for love and affection. Land situated on Cain Creek. Deed signed WM. CRAIG. Wit: P. CUNINGHAM, MEMUSAN (?) WALKER & JOHN CUNINGHAM.

Pp 364-366:   14 Mar. 1785 - rec. 17 Apr. 1791 WILLIAM (X) GRAY & CATH-
              ERINE (X) GRAY, his wife of Berkeley Co., to JOHN CASON
of Halifax Co., state of Virginia, for 92 pds 17 shillings, 100 acres
on Bush Creek, branch of Saluda River, bounded by lands laid out to
HEDLY SMITH. Wit: WILLIAM CASON, WM. CASON (JR.?) & THOMAS CASON.

Pp 366-367:   30 Mar. 1787 - rec. 17 Apr. 1791 SAMUEL EAKINS & JANE
              EAKINS, his wife to JOHN CASON, JR. of Laurens Co., for
5 pds 5 sh., 89 acres on Little River, bounded by PETER HITT, THOMAS
MC DANIEL, being granted to THOMAS CLARK 13 OCt. 1772. Wit: PETER HITT,
MICHAEL WALDROUP & JOHN CASON.

END OF DEED BOOK C

LAURENS CO., S. C. PLAT BOOK A

Some years ago I found in Laurens Courthouse these plats and index
in a linen-covered narrow ledger, which book has since been laminated.
However, many plats were repeated, dates omitted, surveyers omitted
and writing hard to read. I may have made some mistakes in the names
but in the main, I think most are correct, and will be helpful in de-
termining just where land lay. I will begin with the names from the
index and pick up where the plats begin:

Plat #:	Name	Acres	Plat #:	Name	Acres
1	JOEL FOWLER	32	20	JOHN HILL	86
2	ISAAC DIAL	64	20	THOMAS CARGIL	78
3	ISAAC DIAL	205	21	JOHN DIXON, JR.	62
4	WILLIAM SIMS	45	21	WILLIAM FOWLER	124
5	SOLOMON NIBLET	178	22	THOMAS CHILDRES	44
6	ROBERT HUTCHERSON	58	22	WILLIAM SIMS	16
7	JAMES ATAWAY	57	23	WILLIAM BRYSON	18
8	ISAAC DIAL	52	23	HUGH CRUKS	73
9	ARCHIBALD MC HARGE	196	24	BENJAMIN PITTS	230
10	LEWIS GRAVES	26	24	WILLIAM FOWLER	124
11	WILLIAM CALDWELL	23	25	MARY ANN WALDROP	19
12	ROBERT CUNNINGHAM	288	25	LAZRIUS HITT	34
13	RICHARD EDWARDS	288	26	ROBERT YOUNG, JR.	30
14	CORNELIUS CARGIL	261	26	SAMUEL NEIGHBORS	163
15	CHARLES RUSELL	56	27	SOLOMON COLE	197
16	JOSEPH PERSON	65	27	JOHN BOYS	163
17	HENERY STRANGE	45	28	JOHN A. ELMORE	10
18	GEORGE MADDEN	45	29	JOHN A. ELMORE	76
19	ARCHIBALD MC HARGE	229	30	.... ASHLEY	50
31	(torn out)		47	COLVIN ABERCRUMBY	135
32	JESSE CHILDRES	(torn)	48	WM. ABERCRUMBY	777
33	WILLIAM COLINGS	(torn)	49	ALEXANDER ABERCRUMBY	200
33	THOMAS W.....	(torn)	50	JOHN KELLY	40
34	GEORGE FLINN	(torn)	51	JOHN MAXWELL	26
35	ENOCH GARETT	(torn)	52	JOHN MAXWELL	91
36	GEORGE DILLARD	26	53	BOLING BUSHOP	600
36	AARON HOLLING	104	54	ALEX. ABERCRUMBY	500
37	JOHN PRATER	55	55	JOEL BURGESS	37
37	ISERAL CHANDLER	84	56	BENJAMIN HITT	92
38	THOMAS O'NEAL	63	57	DAVID REEDER	39
39	WILLIAM MADDOX	100	58	DANIEL REEDER	15½
40	JOHN A. ELMORE & ROSS	314	59	WM. NEIGHBORS	100
41	(ditto)	333	60	SOLOMON COLE	349
43	HENRY RAY	61	61	THOS. MATHIS, JR.	30
43	HENRY RAY	14	62	SAML. C. STIDMAN	37
44	JAMES CRAIG	322	62	JOS. BROWN & WM	
45	DAVID VANCE	180		COLINGS	200
46	WILLIAM MOOR	119	63	WILLIAM MARTIN	450

Cont'd:

Plat #:	Name	Acres	Plat #:	Name	Acres
64	HASTINGS DIAL	112	75	GEORGE (?) BROWN	57
65	ROBT. WORD (Capt)	100	76	JAMES ap WILLIAMS	31
66	JOHN NICKLES	92	77	EZEKIAL S. ROLAND	64
67	AGNES MC CLINTOCK	64	77	CHAS. PORTERFIELD	224
68	JOHN PUCKET	(torn)	78	JONATHON YORK	%$
69	SAMUEL TAYLOR	(torn)	79	ALLAMAN GANTT	152
70	.... MC KNIGHT	402	80	JOHN WAIT	44
71	STEPHEN GAINS	25	81	CHARLES WATKINS	24½
72	(torn)		82	GEORGE FEGAN	13
73	(torn)		83	JOHN PUCKET	63
74	WILLIAM DOWNS	30	84	JACOB NISEMONGER	74

(The first 84 pages missing, see above index):
Plat 85: 8 July 1806 ANDREW ANDERSON, 97 acres lying on Saluda River
by lands of WILLIAM Z. RUTLEDGE, ABSOLUM BOBO; SAMUEL ANDERSON
and sd ANDREW ANDERSON land. ROBERT YOUNG, D.S.

Plat 86: 24 July 1806 ELIJAH WHITEFIELD, 489 acres lying on Durbin
Creek by lands of JOSEPH BROWN, JACOB MINARD, FULLER land,
JAMES HOLCOMB, JOSEPH HOLCOMB, SOLOMAN NIBLET, MC CLURKIN land and
GORDON land. KILGORE, D.S.

Plat 87: 8 Nov. 1806 MARY ROBERTS, 35 acres lying on Durbin Creek
of Enoree River by lands of JOHN GILBERT, EZEKIAL GRIFFIN,
JACOB ROBERTS & JOSEPH BROWN. JAMES KILGORE, D.S.

Plat 88: 22 Apr. 1806 SAMUEL BELL, 50 acres lying on Beaverdam Creek
waters of Enoree River by lands of WILLIAM ROUNDTREE, sd
SAMUEL BELL and lands laid out to GILLIS KILLET but now for SAMUEL
BELL & MAJOR PUCKET. (No surveyor named)

Plat 89: 19 Nov. 1806 MICHEL WALDROUP, JR., 31 acres lying on Tweedy's
Creek by lands of WILLIAM TAYLOR, JOHN WORKMAN & JOHN WALDROP.
JOHN RODGERS, D.S.

Plat 90: 22 Dec. 1806 BRADDOCK HARRIS, 392 acres lying on Beaverdam
Creek waters of Warrior Creek of Enoree River, by lands of
SAMUEL DUNLAP, JOHN SPELCH, NATHAN CURRY, MARY ROBERTS & sd BRADDOCK
HARRIS. (no surveyor named).

Plat 91: 6 Jan. 1807 RICHARD MILLNOR, 492 acres lying on Little River
and Raburn Creek by lands of ARCHER WARIN, JESSE BARKER,
DRUE COKER, sd RICHARD MILLNER and unknown land. JONATHON DOWNS, D.S.

Plat 92: 30 Dec. 1806 WILLIAM ABERCRUMBY, 46 acres lying on Raburn
Creek by lands of THOMAS BURTON, MATTHEW JOHNSON, LEWIS LAY-
SON, WILLIAM MC DANIEL. JONATHON DOWNS, D.S.

Plat 93: .... WILLIAM JOHNSON, 411 acres

Plat 94: .... JOHN COCHRAN, 512 acres

Plat 95: 27 Jan. 1807 LEANARD BEZLEE (BEASLEY), 105 acres lying on
Duncan's Creek by lands of JAMES MC CLURE, WILLIAM HANNA,
ISAAC RODGERS, and sd LENARD BEZLEE. JOHN RODGERS, D.S.

Plat 96: 29 Jan. 1807 JAMES HANNA, 52 acres lying on south fork of
Duncan's Creek by lands of LENARD BEZLEE, ISAAC RODGERS,
JAMES HANNA, WILLIAM HANNA, WILLIAM MC CLURE. J. A. ELMORE, D.S.

Plat 97: 11 Feb. 1807 JOHN HARRIS, 78 acres lying on Reburn Creek
on a brnch there of called Joneses Branch by lands of sd
JOHN HARRIS, & DAVID DOROUGH (DORRAH). JONATHON DOWNS, D.S.

Plat 98: 1 Aug. 1807 BENJAMIN NEBORS, 664 acres lying on Reedy River
by lands of JOHN RIDGEWAY, JOHN CHILDRESS, SAMUEL DUNKLIN,
THOMAS GORDON, HENERY MORGAN and MATHIS land. JOHN COCKRAN, D.S.

Plat 99: 11 Aug. 1807 GEORGE MARTIN, 554 acres lying on Reburn Creek
          and Peachland Creek, waters of Reedy River by lands of WILL-
IAM THOMASON, all other sides unknown land. BENJAMIN ARNOLD, D.S.

Plat 100: 20 Oct. 1807 ELIJAH CARSEY, 537 acres lying on branches of
          Pitchland's Creek and Rock House Branch waters of Reburn
Creek and Reedy River by lands of BENJAMIN NEIGHBORS, JOHN RIDGEWAY,
MACKLIN MITCHEL, ABRAM BOLT and other side unknown. JOHN RODGERS, D.S.

Plat 101: 4 July 1807 JOHN PITTS, 525 acres lying on Reburn Creek waters
          of Reedy River by lands of sd JOHN PITTS, all other sides
unknown land. (No surveyor named).

Plat 102: NATHAN HENDERSON, 250 acres (torn out of book) from index.

Plat 103: JOSHUA HOLCOMB, 580 acres (torn out)

Plat 104: SAMUEL PERSONS, 80 acres (torn out)

Plat 105: JOHN D. KERN, 80 acres (torn out)

Plat 106: JOHN ADAMS, 100 acres (torn out)

Plat 107: 23 Dec. 1807 ASA LANGSTON, 236 acres lying on Duncan's Creek
          of Enoree River by lands of LENARD BEAZLIE, WILLIAM HANNA,
deceased, RODGER BROWN, WILLIAM MC CLUER, ROBERT TEMPLETON, DAVID TEMP-
LETON, ROBERT TEMPLETON, ROBERT HANNA, C.C. JOHN PUCKET, D.S.

Plat 108: 25 Dec. 1807 WILLIAM RODGERS, JR., 340 acres lying on Little
          River on a branch called Metheses Branch by lands of JAMES
HAMILTON, WILLIAM BRYSON, JACOB MILLER, HAMON MILLER C.C.: THOMAS
RODGERS, HAMON MILLER. JOHN RODGERS, D.S.(this WILLIAM BRYSON died
1807 ..note from comp.)

Plat 109: (date?) JONATHON OWENS, 65 acres lying on Reburn Creek by
          lands of JACOB MINARD, THOMAS CHILDRES, GEORGE FULLER, JOHN
MEDEY. C.C.: CHARLES SMITH, JOHN MEDDY. JOHN RODGERS, D.S.

Plat 110: 5 Jan. 1808 JACOB MILLER, 61 acres lying on Dunkin (Duncan's
          Creek) by lands of sd JACOB MILLER, WILLIAM TAYLOR, other
sides unknown land. C.C. RICHARD HOLEN (HOLLAND), GEORGE MC CREARY.
JOHN RODGERS, D.S.

Plat 111: 6 Jan. 1808 JACOB MILLER, 31 acres lying on Miller's Fork
          of Duncan's Creek by lands of JOHN ADAIR, JAMES ADAIR and
sd MILLER. JOHN RODGERS, D.S.

Plat 112: (no date) REUBEN POWELL, 400 acres lying on Walnut Creek,
          waters of Saluda River by lands of ALLMOND SIMONS, CHARTES
SIMMONS, JAMES POWEL, JOHN STEPHENS, GAINS land, GEORGE SWINDLE, and
other side unknown land. JOHN RODGERS, D.S.

Plat 113: 8 Feb. 1808 RICHARD CHILDRES (CHILDRESS), 340 acres lying
          on Reburn Creek by lands of JESSE CHILDRES, JOHN JONES, MC
KNIGHT land, other side unknown. JOHN RODGERS, D.S.

Plat 114: 2 Feb. 1808 JESSE CHILDRES, 216 acres lying on Reburn Creek
          by lands of RICHARD CHILDRES, all other sides unknown land.
C.C.: RICHARD CHILDRES, JESSE CHILDRES. JOHN RODGERS, D.S.

Plat 115: 8 Jan. 1808 JONATHON OWENS, 121 acres lying on Reburn Creek
          by lands of JACOB MINER, THOMAS CHILDRES, GEORGE FULLER.
JOHN RODGERS, D.S.

Plat 116: 1 Jan. 1808 HENRY FEIGAN, SR., 344 acres lying on Walons
          Creek a branch of Beaverdam of Enoree River by lands of MICHEL
WALLER, HENRY FEIGEN & other sides unknown. C.C.: HENRY FOWLER, HENRY
FEIGEN. JOHN RODGERS, D.S.

Plat 117: 1 Jan. 1808 JOHN PITTS, 900 acres lying on Reburn Creek of

Cont'd:
Reedy River by lands of JOHN SPELTZ, WILLIAM OWENS, NATHAN
CURRY, BENJAMIN HARRIS and unknown land. JAMES KILGORE, D.S.

Plat 118: 1 Jan. 1808 DAVID MASON, 167 acres lying on Indian Creek
of Enoree River by lands of DAVID MASON and other boundaries
unknown. JOHN RODGERS, D.S.

Plat 119: 1 Jan. 1808 ROBERT YOUNG, 170 acres lying on Indian Creek
joining FRANCIS BRADDOCK's land, DUCH bounty and ROBERT SCOT.
C.C.: JAMES BRADOCK, ...ADAIR. JOHN RODGERS, D.S.

Plat 120: (date?) HENRY MORGAN, 325 acres lying on branches of West
Fork of Reburn Creek by lands of sd MORGAN, THOMAS MATHERS,
ALEXANDER ABERCRUMBY, HUGH MAHAFY, other sides unknown. JOHN RODGERS,
D.S.

Plat 121: 1 Jan. 1808 JACOB NISWANGER, 30 acres lying on Reedy River
including the island in sd river by lands of sd NISWANGER,
JOHN SHIRLEY, plat shows Turkey Creek running into Reedy River. C.C.:
RICHARD DAVENPORT, JOHN ROBERTSON. JOHN RODGERS, D.S. (Note from comp.:
the name is found as NUSCHANGER, NISSWANDER, NISWANGER in Winchester,
Va., connected with HITE, BOWMAN, WRIGHT families. JACOB died in 1835
in Tenn., but many descendants live in Laurens Co., S.C. re: WARDLAW,
WATSON, GOLDING, SIMS, CROCKER, CARGIL).

Plat 122: 11 May 1808 WILLIAM GAREY, 74 acres lying on Rebon Creek
waters of Reedy River by lands of MARTIN DIAL, WILLIAM HALLUMS
and sd GAREY. C.C.: JACOB GAREY, WILLIAM HILL. JOHN COCHRAN, D.S.

Plat 123: 20 May 1808 WILLIAM BOWEN, SR., 24 acres lying on both sides
of Beaverdam Creek, waters of Enoree River by lands of SAMUEL
VAUGHN, DAVID COWEN, WILLIAM HIGGINS, WILIE TILLER. C.C.: SAMUEL BAUGH-
MAN, WILLIAM BASCOM, JR. JAMES KILGORE, D.S.

Plat 124: 10 June 1808 WILLIAM ARNOLD, 4 acres lying on Reedy River
by lands of BENJAMIN ARNOLD, WILLIAM ARNOLD, & JAMES TRENO-
MEN. C.C.: JOSEPH MAHORN (MAHON?), THOMAS KELLY. BENJAMIN ARNOLD, D.S.

Plat 125: 15 July 1808 WILLIAM MADDEN, 410 acres lying on northside
of Saluda River bounded on east by lands of ANDREW ANDERSON,
JR.; north by WILLIAM BOBO; west by ANDREW ANDERSON, SR., and sd Saluda
River. C.C.: JOHN MADDEN, GEORGE MADDEN. JOHN RODGERS, D.S.

Plat 126: 1 Nov. 1808 JAMES RODGERS, 474 acres lying on Thomases Creek
of Lick Creek bounded north by lands of JOHN FRANCIS WOLF,
NORMAN GANTT, south by RICHARD MILLNOR, east by NATHAN HENDERSON and
other sides unknown land. JOHN RODGERS, D.S.

END OF PLAT BOOK A

LAURENS CO., S. C. PLAT BOOK B

Plat 1:   5 July 1808 JACOB GAREY, 336 acres located on branches of
Rabon Creek, waters of Reedy River, bounded by lands of JONA-
THON DOWNS & WILLIAM J. GAREY. Chain Carriers were N. HILL & WM. HILL.

Plat 2:   18 June 1808 OBIDIAH ROBERTS, 159 acres located on Indian
Creek, branch of Enoree River, bounded by lands of OBIDIAH
ROBERTS, JOHN CANNON, WILLIAM DAVIS, THOMAS LOFTON & JOHN JOHNSON.
WILLIAM WILLSON, D.S. Chain Carriers: JOHN BONDS, JOHN NORIS.

Plat 3:   29 Aug. 1808 JAMES TODD, 30 acres located on Reburn's Creek,
bounded by lands of SOLEMAN COLE, ROBERT TODD, JAMES TODD,
PAUL FINLEY and Mr. HOOD. C.C. ROBERT BRYSON, WILLIAM MC CLANNAHAN.

Plat 4:   20 Sept. 1808 For JAMES MILLS, 144 acres located on McDoul's
Branch, waters of Warrior Creek, bounded by lands of ALEXAN-
DER TAYLOR, JOHN MC CLINTOCK, SR. & sd MILLS. C.C.: JAMES MILLS, JAMES
RODGERS.

Plat 5:   12 Nov. 1808 For JOHN FARROW, 139 acres lying on Rabun's
           Creek, bounded by lands of JOHN MC KNIGHT, ... BABB, JESSE
CHILDRES, RICHARD CHILDRESS and unknown land. C.C.: CHARLES SMITH,
.... FARROW.

Plat 6:   4 Nov. 1808 For WILLIAM ANDERSON, 180 acres located on north-
           side of Saluda River, bounded by lands of SOLOMON BOBO, JOHN
ABERNATHY & ANDREW ANDERSON. C.C.: JAMES ANDERSON, JOSIA ANDERSON.

Plat 7:   12 Oct. 1808 For JOHN HOWARD, JR., 24 acres located both
           sides of Bibb Branch, waters of Enoree River, bounded by
lands of JOHN HOWARD, JR., WILLIAM GILBERT, WILLIAM JOHNSON & JACOB
LEAGUE. J. L. KILGORE, D.S.

Plat 8:   16 Feb. 1809 EZEKIEL YAGER, 12 acres located on Reedy River.
           JOHN COCHRAN, D.S. Bounded by lands of JOSEPH WHITE, JOHN
YAGER, SAM. MC GLADERY & JAMES BOYD. C.C.: JESSE YAGER, LEWIS YAGER.

Plat 9:   5 Mar. 1809 For JOHN BLAKELY, 36 acres located on Rabon Creek,
           bounded by lands of JAMES BOYD on east, Widow CUNINGHAM on
north, CHARLES MILLER on west and lands of JOHN BLAKELY on south.

Plat 10:   26 Mar. 1809 For DAVID MC CAA, 37 acres located on Beaver-
           dam Creek, waters of Little River, bounded by lands of JOEL
BURGESS, deceased, JOHN BROWNLEE, deceased and sd MC CAA.

Plat 11:   19 Sept. 1809 For DAVID MASON, 282 acres located on Indian
           Creek, bounded by lands of DAVID MASON, JOHN CANNON & SUSANNAH
DEEN. C.C.: ABNER YOUNG & SAM YOUNG.

Plat 12:   30 Sept. 1809 Recorded some minutes after 5 o'clock at night
           for THOMAS DALRYMPLE, JR., 47 acres located on Bush River
waters of Saluda River, bounded by lands of ELIJAH TEAGUE on NE, ANN
DALRYMPLE on SE, DAVID MASON on SW and ANN DALRYMPLE on NW. WM. WILLSON,
D.S. C.C.: MICAJAH GRESHAM, WILLIAM DALRYMPLE.

Plat 13:   30 Sept. 1809 Recorded some minutes after 11 o'clock at night
           for DAVID MASON, 265 acres located on Indian Creek of Bush
River of Saluda River, bounded by lands of JACOB MASON, THOMAS DALRYMPLE
ELIJAH TEAGUE, JOHN CANNON, ABRAM JONES & EZECIL TEAGUE. ROBT. YOUNG,
D.S.

Plat 14:   19 Oct. 1809 For ROBERT BOLING, 227 acres located on Beaver-
           dam Creek, waters of Little River, bounded by lands of JOHN
HUSE, deceased, JOHN WALKER, CHARLES WHITE & DANIEL FULLER. JOHN RODGERS,
D.S. DANIEL FULLER, JOHN ABERNATHY, C.C.

Plat 15:   18 Nov. 1809 For CHARLES NEIGHBORS, 90 acres located on Dun-
           can's Creek, bounded by lands of WILLIAM RODGERS on north,
GILBERT MC NAIRY on west, WILLIAM LITTLE on south, other not known.
JOHN RODGERS, D.S. F. NABORS, Mr. CRADDOCK, C.C.

Plat 16:   19 Nov. 1809 For THOMAS DALRYMPLE, 39 acres located on Bush
           River bounded by lands of CHARLES HUETT, WILLIAM DEAL, WILLIAM
BARKSDALE, JOHN SINKLER, THOMAS ENTRICAN. C.C.: JOSEPH WILLSON, JOHN
HUETT.

Plat 17:   25 Dec. 1809 For JOHN CLARK COCHRAN, 28½ acres located on
           Sandy Branch, waters of Rabon Creek, bounded by lands of
SOLEMAN COLE, WILLIAM LLOYD, JAMES TODD, WILLIAM WILSON. C.C.: W. WILSON
SR., W. WILSON, JR. JOHN COCHRAN, D.S.

Plat 18:   26 Jan. 1810 For HARDIMAN DUKES, 28 acres located on Duncan's
           Creek, waters of Enore River, bounded by lands of Widow CUN-
INGHAM, J. DUVALL. C.C.: ROGER BROWN, HARDIMAN DUKES.

Plat 19:   23 Feb. 1810 For JOHN DILLARD, son of JAMES DILLARD, 74 acres
           located on Enoree River, bounded by lands of ELENOR ROSS,
MRS. BARBARY BURK, HENRY RAY & HINDMAN land. J. A. (JOHN ARCHER) ELMORE,
D.S.

Plat 20: 26 Feb. 1810 For JOHN DILLARD, 110 acres located on Enoree
        River, bounded by lands of ALEXANDER PHILSON & _____ LEASON.
JOHN RODGERS, D.S.

Plat 21: 26 Feb. 1810 For ASES BURELS, 13 acres located on Little
        River, bounded by lands of ROBERT SPENCE, ABRAHAM NEIGHBORS.
JOHN RODGERS, D.S. C.C.: Mr. BURELS, Mr. NICKELL.

Plat 22: 14 Apr. 1810 For DANIEL WRIGHT, Esq., 596 acres located on
        Little Beaverdam and Boggy Branch, waters of Enoree River,
bounded by lands of YOUNG & GRAY on north, TULLY & VAUGHN on west,
VAUGHN & DOWNEY on south, BOWEN land on east. JAMES KILGORE, D.S.

Plat 23: 6 June 1810 For JOSIAH WILLIAMS, 56 acres located on Duncan's
        Creek, waters of Enoree River, bounded by lands of JOSEPH
ADAIR on west, ROBERT LONG on east, THOMAS EWING on south.

Plat 24: 9 June 1810 For ALEXANDER WILKENSON, 73 acres located on
        Duncan's Creek, a branch of Enoree River, bounded by lands
of ALEXANDER WILKENSON, JOSIAH WILLIAMS, MENASAH FINNIE. ALEXANDER
WILKISON, D.S. GEORGE MC CLEARY, JOSEPH MC CLEARY, C.C.

Plat 25: 25 June 1810 For ALEXANDER WILKISON, 72 acres located on
        Miller's Fork of Duncan's Creek, a branch of Enoree River,
bounded by lands of MANASAH FINNEY, ALEXANDER WILKENSON, ALEXANDER
LUKE, JOSIAH WILLIAMS. THOMAS MC CRAY, D.S. JOHN LUKE, JOS. MC CREARY,
C.C.

Plat 26: 26 June 1810 For BENJAMIN BIRD (BYRD), 51 acres located on
        Duncan's Creek, bounded by lands of ROBERT WORD, ROBERT HUT-
ISON, JOHN MC LAUGHLIN and sd BENJAMIN BIRD.

Plat 27: 19 July 1810 For ELIJAH ADAIR, 375 acres located on O'Neal's
        Fork of Duncan's Creek, bounded by lands of ALEXANDER LUKE
on NW, GEORGE MC CREARY on SW, JACOB MILLER on NW & SW, RICHARD HOLLAND
on SE, ROBERT FRYER on SE & SW, JOSEPH ADAIR & ALEXANDER WILKISON on
NE. J. A. ELMORE, D.S.

Plat 28: ROBERT POOLE (350 acres listed in index but plat lost out
        of book)

Plat 29: EDMOND CRADDOCK (80 acres listed in index but plat lost out
        of book)

Plat 30: 1 Sept. 1810 For JAMES SMITH, 1000 acres lying in Laurens
        and Greenville Co. on Allison Creek bounded NE by lands of
JOSEPH HOLCUM, NW by lands of REUBEN BRAMLING (BRAMLETTE), NW by lands
of PHILIP HENSWORTH, S by lands of JOHN HOWARD, JR. and NE by lands
of JAMES SMITH. JAMES KILGORE, D.S.

Plat 31: 1 Sept. 1810 For JAMES SMITH, 1000 acres lying on Durbin
        Creek, waters of Enoree River by lands of WILLIAM GIST, JAMES
HOLCUM, ELIJAH WHITEFIELD, JOHN HARRIS & JAMES SMITH. (On plat is wagon
road leading from Laurens Courthouse to Greenville Courthouse.)

Plat 32: 9 Oct. 1810 EDMOND CRADDOCK, 80 acress (same as #29; mis-
        numbered?) lying on Enoree River by lands of JOSEPH LINCH,
SAMUEL STILES, MRS. MILLER & FRANCES GLENN. (Does not show chain carriers nor surveyor.)

Plat 32: 10 Nov. 1810 For REUBEN POWELL, 595 acres lying on Walnut
        Creek, waters of Saluda River by lands of ALMOND SIMONS,
CHARLES SIMONS, JAMES POWELL, JOHN STEPHENS, __(?_ GAINS, GEORGE
SWINDLE. JOHN RODGERS, D.S.

Plat 33: 17 Nov. 1810 For SAMUEL YOUNG, 57 acres lying on Buck Head
        Creek, waters of Enoree River by lands on N of GEORGE MOSLEE
(MOSELEY), NW by LITTLE PERSONS, S by SAMUEL PERSONS (PARSON), and
SW by SAMUEL YOUNG. C.C.: WILLIAM YOUNG, JOHN MOSLEE. J. A. ELMORE,
D.S.

Plat 34: 1 Feb. 1810 THOMAS EVANS, 20½ acres lying on Hartlies Branch,
        waters of Enoree River by lands of sd THOMAS EVANS, JOHN
JOHNSON, BENJAMIN WILLSON, & SAMUEL MC CRICH. C.C.: JOHN WILSON, JAMES
WILSON. WILLIAM WILLSON, D.S.

Plat 35: 6 Feb. 1810 For JOHN DILLARD, son of SAMUEL DILLARD, 47 acres
        lying on South fork of Duncan's Creek on the southside of
creek by lands of JULES WESON & MRS. PEARSON, (could be WILLIAM PEAR-
SON). C.C.: ISAAC JACKS, ROBERT BURNS. J. A. ELMORE, D.S. Index says
JAMES DILLARD.

Plat 36: 6 Feb. 1810 For JOHN DILLARD, son of SAMUEL, 70 acres lying
        on water of south fork of Duncan's Creek by lands of JOSEPH
JONES, WILLIAM ABRIAM, HENRY WESON & JOHN DILLARD. C.C.: ISAAC JACKS,
JOSEPH JONES. J. A. ELMORE, D.S. Index says JAMES DILLARD.

Plat 37: 14 Feb. 1810 WILLIAM LIGON, 17 acres lying on Little River
        by lands of WILLIAM FLEMING, WILLIAM HUGHES and heirs of
____? THOMPSON. WILLIAM DUNLAP, D.S.

Plat 38: 11 May 1810 LECIL BOBO, 63 acres lying on Smith's Creek,
        waters of Saluda River by TODD land, STONE's land, MC CALLE
land, PROCTOR land and WILLIAM SMITH land. C.C.: THOMAS TODD, JACOB
WHITWORTH. LECIL BOBO, D.S.

Plat 39: 13 May 1810 JOHN CLARK, 89 acres lying on Smith's Creek,
        waters of Saluda River by lands of THOMAS TODD, NATHAN TODD,
WILLIAM SMITH, EPHRAIM KING. C.C.: JACOB WHITWORTH, THOMAS TODD. LECIL
BOBO, D.S.

Plat 40: 15 May 1810 JACOB WHITWORTH, 9 acres lying on Smith's Creek,
        waters of Saluda River by lands of JAMES WATTS, WILLIAM SMITH,
unknown land. C.C.: JACOB WHITWORTH, THOMAS TODD, LECIL BOBO, D.S.

Plat 41: 11 May 1810 ANDREW MC CALL, 87½ acres lying on Smith's Creek,
        waters of Saluda River by lands of DANIEL DENDY, WILLIAM
SMITH, NATHAN TODD, JOHN BOYD, E. NIGHTS. C.C.: WILLIAM SMITH, URIAH
STONE. THOMAS ANDERSON, D.S.

Plat 42: 17 May 1810 EPHRAIM KNIGHT, 245 acres lying on Smith's Creek,
        waters of Saluda River by lands of JAMES DAY, JOHN WATTS,
DANIEL DENDY, JOHN BOYD, JAMES WATTS, BENJAMIN FORSHEE, FRANCIS DAY.
C.C.: JAMES WATTS, WILLIAM SMITH. THOMAS ANDERSON, D.S.

Plat 43: 20 June 1811 ROBERT STUART, 14 acres lying on Doches(?) Creek,
        waters of Saluda River by lands of RICHARD WATTS, and sd
ROBT. STUART. C.C.: JOHN CHAPMAN, NATHANIEL CHAPMAN. LECIL BOBO, D.S.

Plat 44: 19 June 1811 SAMUEL SMITH, 174 acres lying on Duncan's Creek
        by lands of MRS. HARLINGS (HARLAN), CHARLES FERGUSON, and
sd SMITH. C.C.: JOHN STUART, SOLOMAN SMITH. J. A. ELMORE, D.S.

Plat 45: 20 June 1805-28 Oct. 1811 EZIKIAL S. ROLAND, 103 acres lying
        on Beaverdam Creek, waters of Little River by lands of DANIEL
OZBON (OSBORN), BOLING BUSHOP (BISHOP) and STROMAR land.

Plat 46: 8 Nov. 1811 JOHN BOYCE, 22 acres lying on Duncan's Creek
        by lands of JOSEPH JONES, GEORGE DILLARD, JOHN MC CRARY,
JOSEPH LIGON. C.C.: ALEXANDER BOYCE, ALEXANDER MC CLUER. J. A. ELMORE,
D.S.

Plat 46: (misnumbered again) 23 Nov. 1811 ALFRED D. CLEARY, 37 acres
        lying on Duncan's Creek by lands of WILLIAM NUGENT, NATHANIEL
GORDON, ADAM GORDON. JOHN RODGERS, D.S.

Plat 47: 18 Nov. 1811 JOHN WILLIAMS, 42 acres by Little River by lands
        of MARSHALL FRANKS, sd JOHN WILLIAMS, CHARLES ALLEN, Esq.,
CHARLES LLOYD. C.C.: LEMUEL WILLIAMS, LYDALL WILLIAMS. WILLIAM COWEN,
D.S. (Note from comp.: Squire CHARLES ALLEN, Rev. Patriot, one of first

Cont'd:
Judges in Laurens County; son of CHARLES & LUCY (BACON) ALLEN, who married SUSAN GARNER. The above JOHN WILLIAMS was brother-in-law to CHARLES ALLEN, having married CYNTHIA CATHERINE ALLEN and LYDALL WILL-IAMS was their son. Squire CHARLES ALLEN was father of JOEL ALLEN, SOPHIA ALLEN, wife of Rev. SAMUEL B. LEWERS who went to DeSoto, Miss.; MATILDA HOOKER who went to Hinds Co., Miss.; MANIMA DAVIS; and SARAH, wife of JOHN RODGERS CRISP of Laurens Co., SC).

Plat 48: 26 Nov. 1811 For JOHN CUMMINGS, 133 acres lying on Mudlick Creek, waters of Little River, by lands of JOHN PORTERFIELD, COKER, ARMSTRONG & JOHN BOYS (BOYCE) JOHN CALDWELL, D.S.

Plat 49: 27 Dec. 1811 EDWARD GARRETT, 31 acres lying on Beaverdam Creek, waters of Enoree River (this Beaverdam Creek is a near Warrior Creek, where the GARRETT's are buried...comp.) by lands of BERRY MARTIN, JOHN PATTERSON. C.C.: DAVID HAGEN, JAMES HAGEN (HOGAN?) WILLIAM COWAN, D.S.

Plat 50: 8 Feb. 1812 HUGH CROOKS, 270 acres lying on Duncan's Creek, waters of Enoree River by lands of sd CROOKS and PARKER's land. C.C.: THOMAS GARRETT, ALEXANDER MILLS. WM. COWAN, D.S.

Plat 51: 27 Feb. 1812 JOSEPH THOMPSON, 14 acres lying on East side of Reedy River, waters of Saluda River by lands of DAVID ROSS, CHARLES COLEY. C.C.: WILLIAM MC DAVIT, WILLIAM MILLER. BENJAMIN ARNOLD, D.S.

Plat 52: 21 Jan. 1812 JOSEPH GARRETT, 20 acres located on Haril's (known today as Harold's) Creek, waters of Enoree River by lands of JOSEPH THOMPSON, LINDSAY WHITTEN, GEORGE DILLARD, JOHN GARRETT and sd JOS. GARRETT. C.C.: JOHN DILLARD, JOS. WILLIAMS. ALEX. WILKIN-SON, D.S.

Plat 53: 20 Jan. 1812 JOSEPH GARRETT, 41 acres lying on Haril's Creek, waters of Enoree River by lands of JOHN GARRETT, ENOCH GARRETT & ANNA DILLARD. C.C.: JAMES BURK, LEVI GARRETT. ALEX. WILKERSON, D.S.

Plat 54: 11 Feb. 1812 JOHN BOYCE, 26 acres lying on Duncan's Creek, waters of Enoree River by lands of sd BOYCE, HUGH SKILLINS, J. A. ELMORE, J. D. KERN & CANNING land. C.C.: TURNER RITCHERSON (RICH-ARDSON), BENJAMIN FILMORE, D.S.

Plat 54: (misnumbered again) 14 Mar. 1812 WILLIAM DOWNS, 215 acres lying on Reabon's Creek by lands of JACOB GARY, JOHN F. WOLF, ALEXANDER BELL, Heirs of KERSHAW, DRURY COKER, ROBERT COKER & ISAAC DIAL. WILLIAM F. DOWNS, D.S.

Plat 55: 6 Apr. 1812 JAMES HANNA, 85 acres lying on Enoree River by lands of SAMUEL LUKE, JOHN HANNA, NISBET land, JOHN RITCHEY & JOHN WHITEN. C.C.: JAMES TEMPLETON, JAMES CEKOWN (COWAN?). ELMORE, D.S.

Plat 56: 4 July 1812 ABNER RODGERS, 37 acres lying on Dunkin Creek, waters of Enoree River by lands of ... NUGENT & NATHAN GORDON, deceased. (No chain carriers nor surveyor).

Plat 57: 14 Apr. 1812 BENJAMIN LEWIS, 34 acres lying on Indian Creek by lands of JOHN HUSTIN, THOMAS GREEN, JOHN ENTREIKEN & PRATER land. (no C.C. nor D.S.)

Plat 58: 22 Sept. 1812 REUBEN MARTIN, 142 acres lying on both sides of small Beaverdam of Enoree River by lands of DAVID HIGGINS, BENJAMIN MARTIN, EDWARD GARRETT & PATTERSON land. JAMES KILGORE, D.S.

Plat 59: 7 Sept. 1812 JOSEPH WILLSON, 45 acres lying on Bush River by lands of CHARLES HUSETS, JOHN SINKLER, WILLIAM BARKSDALE. C.C.: WILLIAM NAIL (NEAL), WILLIAM YARBEY (IRBY).

Plat 59: (misnumbered again) 5 Mar. 1812 SAMUEL HANNA, 8 acres lying

Cont'd:
        southside of Duncan's Creek by lands of JAMES HANNA, the
sd SAMUEL HANNA & JAMES FAIRBURN. C.C.: WM. HANNA and his son (no name).
J. A. ELMORE, D.S.

Plat 60:   8 Oct. 1812 SAMUEL NABORS, 216 acres on Line Creek, waters
           of Saluda River by lands of ROBERT CRESWELL, sd SAMUEL NABORS,
Old Indian Boundary Line, NATHANIEL MATCOCKS (MADDOX), THOMAS KINMAN,
CORNELIUS CARGIL & BENJAMIN MADOKS (MADDOX).

Plat 61:   21 Dec. 1812 WILLIAM OWINGS, 214 acres lying on Durbin Creek
           and Rabon Creek, waters of Enoree River by lands of JOSEPH
ALISON, WILLIAM CARNES, JANET MC CLURKIN & BATES land. C.C.: ARCHIBALD
OWINS, JOHN OWINGS. WILLIAM COWAN, D.S.

Plat 62:   4 Jan. 1813 LECIL BOBO, 905 acres lying on Enoree River by
           lands of S. SMITH, CHARLES FERGUSON, J. GILLILAND, SOLOMAN
LANKSTON (LANGSTON), JAMES COWAN, J. HANNA, PARSON land and LUKE land.
C.C.: TILLMAN BOBO, THOMAS BERRY. LECIL BOBO, D.S.

Plat 63:   27 Feb. 1812 JOSEPH THOMPSON, 14 acres lying on Eastside
           of Reedy River by lands of CHARLES COKER, lands of DAVID
ROSS and sd River. JONATHON MC DAVID, D.S.

Plat 64:   4 June 1813 THOMAS TODD, 36 1/4 acres by lands of JOHN CUM-
           INGS, JOHN PORTERFIELD & ANGUS CAMPBELL. WILLIAM SIMPSON,D.S.

Plat 65:   2 Aug. 1813 JOHN COWN & JAMES GLENN, 130 acres lying on War-
           rior Creek, waters of Enoree River by lands of NICHOLAS GAR-
RETT, WILLIAM HIGGINS, RANDEL COOK, JOHN RIDDLE, WILLIAM FOWLER. C.C.:
NICULES GARRETT, JOHN RIDLE. WM. COWAN, D.S.

Plat 66:   2 Oct. 1813 WILLIAM SANDERS, 19 acres lying on Saludy River
           by lands of DAVID COX, DANIEL COX & JAMES ATWOOD. C.C.: WIL-
LIAM POLLARD, JAMES ATWOOD. WM. WILSON, D.S.

Plat 66:   (misnumbered again) 2 Oct. 1813 WILLIAM SANDERS, 18 1/4 ac.
           lying on Saludy River by lands of JOHN COOK on east and north,
and sd WM. SANDERS. C.C.: DANIEL DAY, WM. SANDERS. WM. WILSON, D.S.

Plat 67:   2 Oct. 1813 JOHN RODGERS, JR., 20 acres lying on Mudlick
           Creek, waters of Saluda River by lands of MRS. WILLIAMS,
LIGON land and BLEDIAS(?) land. WM. DUNLAP, D.S.

Plat 67:   (misnumbered) 10 Dec. 1813 THOMAS LIGON, 21 acres located
           on Rabon Creek by lands of sd THOMAS LIGON and lands of JAMES
H...(?).... WM. DOWNS, D.S.

Plat 68:   10 Jan. 1814 BENJAMIN LEWIS, 7 acres lying on Indian Creek
           by lands of ENOCH BROWN, ..., THOMAS GREEN, WILLIAM
HUNTER and sd BENJ. LEWIS. (D.S. not named).

Plat 69:   28 Jan. 1814 SAMUEL SMITH, 12 1/4 acres lying on Duncan's
           Creek, Enoree River, by lands of CHARLES FERGUSON, SAMUEL
SMITH. C.C.: SOLOMAN SMITH, JOSEPH HARLING (HARLAN). THOMAS MC CREARY,
D.S.

Plat 70:   16 Feb. 1814 THOMAS SADLER, 43 1/4 acres lying on Mill Creek
           by lands of ELIZABETH THOMASON, GEORGE GRANT, SWIFT's land
and WILLSON land. C.C.: WM. THOMASON, RANSOM WORTH. ELIHU CRESWELL,
D.S.

Plat 71:   13 Feb. 1814 ALEXANDER WILKISON, 223 acres lying on McCool's
           Fork of Duncan's Creek by lands of J. ADAIR, ELISHA ADAIR,
FINNEY land and fields owned by ALEXANDER WILKISON. C.C.:   JOHN HEWIT,
ALEXANDER LUKE. WM. WILSON, D.S.

Plat 72:   9 Mar. 1814 JOSEPH THOMPSON, 14 1/4 acres lying on Reedy
           River by lands of DAVID ROSS & CHARLES COLIE. (Surveyor not
named).

Plat 73: 25 Feb. 1814 JOSEPH GRIFFIN, 110 acres lying on Rabon Creek by lands of MOSES PINSON, HASTEN DIAL, WILLIAM SUBER & unknown land. (Surveyor not named).

Plat 73: (misnumbered) 13 Apr. 1814 JAMES A. WILLIAMS, 147 acres lying on Mudlick Creek by lands of sd WILLIAMS and WILLIAM BURNSIDE. (Chiles Ferry Road drawn on plat). C.C.: JOHN W. WILLIAMS, JAMES A. WILLIAMS. WILLIAM WILLSON, D.S.

Plat 74: 26 Apr. 1814 JESSE COATS, 40 acres lying on Rabon Creek by lands of WILLIAM JOHNSON, sd COATS and Rabon Creek. WILLIAM F. DOWNS, D.S.

Plat 75: 16 May 1814 WILLIAM POLLARD, 279 acres lying on Banks Creek waters of Saluda River by lands of JOHN SMITH, JOSEPH RUNNELLS, JAMES NEELEY, DANIEL JONES, ROBERT WORD, JAMES ATWOOD. ELIHU CRESWELL, D.S.

Plat 76: 19 Nov. 1814 ANA SMITH, 109 acres lying on North Rabon Creek by lands of ARON JONES, NANCY OWENS, GEORGE FULLER, JOHN HARRIS, TULLY CHOICE, D.S.

Plat 77: 1 Nov. 1814 ROBERT CAMPBELL, 12 acres lying on Mudlick Creek waters of Saluda River by lands of sd CAMPBELL, JOHN COOK & WIDOW RAIBRES. (No surveyor named).

Plat 78: 6 Feb. 1815 ELIZABETH HARLEN, 61 acres lying on Duncan's Creek, waters of Enoree River by lands of ARCHIBALD SMITH, ROBERT TAYLOR, & WILLIAM CLARK. C.C.: JOHN STEWART, ARCHIBALD CRADDOCK. THOMAS MC CRARY, D.S.

Plat 79: 31 Jan. 1815 ADAM GARMON, 105 acres lying on Rabon Creek on a branch called Bursses Branch by lands of JOHN MADIN (MADDEN), PAUL FINDLEY, sd ADAM GARMON, JAMES TODD and unknown land. JOHN RODGERS, D.S.

Plat 80: 20 Mar. 1815 JAMES A. WILLIAMS, 450 acres lying on Mudlick of Saluda by lands of WILLIAM LIGON, JOHN STURGESS, ELIJAH WATSON, JOHN GOLDING & ANTHONY GOLDING. C.C.: J. W. WILLIAMS, A. WILLIAMS. WILLIAM WILLSON, D.S.

Plat 81: 18 Jan. 1815 JOHN BLACK, Esq., 7 acres lying on Little River of Saluda by lands of WASHINGTON WILLIAMS, JOHN SIMMONS and by Simmons Creek. WILLIAM DUNLAP, D.S.

Plat 81: (misnumbered) 4 May 1815 PLEASANT SHADEA, 56 acres lying on Boggy Branch, waters of Enoree River by lands of THOMAS MOORE, DAVID HOGAN, JOHN WINN. C.C.: HENRY BURDIT (BURDETTE), WILLIAM HARRIS. WILLIAM COWAN, D.S.

Plat 81: 15 Sept. 1815 JOHN PELCE, 109 acres lying on North Rabon Creek by lands of ARON JONES, JOHN HARRIS, & GEORGE FULLER. (Note from comp.: same as #76 ANA SMITH).

Plat 82: 7 Nov. 1815 GEORGE POOL, 20 acres lying on Rabon Creek by lands of BOYD, DIAL, CUNINGHAM & CUNINGHAM. S. MOOR, D.S.

Plat 84: (no date) JOHN JOHNSON, 13 acres lying on Rabon Creek by lands of MATTHEW CUNINGHAM, BOYD, DIAL, TULLY CHOICE, D.S.

Plat 85: 15 Nov. 1815 JONATHON JOHNSON, Esq., 118 acres lying on Cain Creek waters of Saluda, lands of WILLIAM CALDWELL, deceased, DAVID WHITEFIELD, deceased, WILLIAM POWER & sd JOHNSON, Esq. JAMES YOUNG, D.S.

Plat 86: 16 Dec. 1815 DAVID MASON, 1000 acres lying on Indian Creek, waters of Enoree River by lands of sd MASON, JOHN CANNON, LEVERAL land, FEAGAN land, Widow DEEN's land and lands of Big Survey. C.C.: JAMES MASON, JOHN MASON. THOMAS MC CREARY, D.S.

Plat 87:   12 Dec. 1815 DAVID MASON, 900 acres lying on Indian Creek
            waters of Enoree River by lands of ABRAHAM GRAY, WILLIAM
GRAY, MURPHY land, and JOHN RAGAN's land. C.C.: JOHN MASON, JAMES MASON.
THOMAS MC CREARY, D.S.

Plat 88:   (no date) DAVID TEMPLETON, 35 acres (from index, lost out
            of plat book).

Plat 89:   8 Apr. 1816 GEORGE YOUNG, 16 acres lying on Duncan's Creek
            waters of Enoree River by lands of sd YOUNG, SALLY DUCKET,
WILLIAM ABRAMS. C.C.: GEORGE YOUNG, JOHN WHITMORE. THOS. MC CREARY,
D.S.

Plat 89:   26 Mar. 1816 BENJAMIN WILLIAMS, 304 acres lying on Rabon
            Creek by lands of THOMAS B. WILLIAMS, JOHN FOWLER, NICHOLL's
land, HILL's land, HENDERSON's land, CHARLY BRUSHE(?), MARGARET BOX's
land and JAMES HENDERSON's land. WM. F. DOWNS, D.S.

Plat 90:   15 Apr. 1816 CHARLES C. COLCOCK, 1100 acres lying on Reedy
            Fork, waters of Little River, WM. D. DOWNS, D.S. (no other
description, no C.C.)

Plat 91:   16 Apr. 1816 GEORGE MC CREARY, 477 acres lying on Miller's
            Creek, waters of Enoree River by lands of BADALE HOLLAND,
JOHN LUKE, ALEXANDER LUKE, ELISHA ADAIR, JAMES MILLER, JOHN MILLER,
JACOB MILLER, SR. C.C.: WILLIAM CRADDOCK, ALEX. LUKE. THOS. MC CRARY,
D.S.

Plat 92:   17 June 1816 WILLIAM ATKINS, 152 acres lying on Rabon creek
            by lands of JAMES JOHNSON, JONATHON DOWNS and heirs of THOMAS
LINDLEY, deceased. WM. F. DOWNS, D.S.

Plat 93:   5 July 1816 THOMAS MC CREARY, SR., 183 acres lying on Miller's
            Fork branch waters of Enoree River by lands of MANASSA FINNEY,
deceased, ALEXANDER WILKISON, JAMES ADAIR, JAMES HOWERTON, WILLIAM
GAMBLE, DAVID GAMBLE. C.C.: THOMAS HOLLAND, JAMES ADAIR. THOMAS MC
CRARY, D.S.

Plat 94:   5 Nov. 1816 WILLIAM GAMBLE, 22 acres lying on Duncan's Creek
            by lands of JAMES GAMBLE, GEORGE GAMBLE, DAVID GRAHAM & WIL-
LIAM GAMBLE. ISAAC UNDERWOOD, D.S.

Plat 95:   9 Oct. 1816 SAMUEL FARROW, 109 acres lying on Enoree River
            by lands of GEORGE GORDON. ....(nothing more).

Plat 96:   9 Oct. 1816 JOHN SAXON, 31 acres lying on Duncan's Creek
            by lands of Capt. JESSE JOHNSON, JOHN COPELAND. J. A. ELMORE,
D.S.

Plat 97:   18 Dec. 1816 WAYMON HOLLAND, 275 acres lying on Enoree River
            by lands of JAMES DILLARD, sd HOLLAND, JOHN COULTER, General
JOHN A. ELMORE, JOHN F. KERN (also spelled CARNES). ISAAC UNDERWOOD,
D.S.

Plat 98:   6 Dec. 1816 WILLIAM FULTON, Esq., 286 acres lying on Duncan's
            Creek by lands of SAMUEL BOYD, Capt. ABNER RODGERS, SAMUEL
SOUTHERLAND, JOHN MC KELVIE, SAMUEL NEILL. ISAAC UNDERWOOD, D.S.

Plat 99:   22 Oct. 1816 ELISHA ADAIR, 14 1/2 acres lying on Brown's
            Creek of Duncan's Creek of Enoree River by lands of JOHN
COPELAND, WILLIAM GAMBLE, JOHN HARDEN, WILLIAM LOVELESS. C.C.: JAMES
COPELAND, JAMES ADAIR. THOMAS MC CREARY, D.S.

END OF PLAT BOOK B

LAURENS CO., S.C . GUARDIANS RETURNS

FIRST ANNUAL RETURNS of JOHN S. JAMES, Commissioner in Equity, Laurens,

South Carolina on the SUBJECT OF GUARDIANS...Filed June 9, 1825:
In compliance with the requisitions of an Act of the General
Assembly passed on 17 December 1824, requiring the Master and Commissioners in Equity to report annually to the Court what guardians and
trustees have not made annual returns of all monies received and expended and which of them have so made their returns, the Commissioner
of Equity for Laurens District begs leave to submit the following report on that subject, viz:

SAMUEL NABORS - That he has been unable to find any record of appointment by the court further back than the year 1804. That in March term
of that year, SAMUEL NABORS was appointed guardian for WILLIAM MYERS
and it does not appear that he has ever made any returns.

URSULA BROOK - That at March term 1807, URSULA BROOK was appointed
guardian for ELIZABETH BARTLETT; and MARIAH BROOKS and who filed a
return on the 2nd of Oct. 1809 charging herself with $171.40, two neg-
roes and four head of cattle. She made several returns from that time
up to the 22nd of July 1826 when she filed a return by which it appeared
that her three children had come of age or married and she had come
to a final settlement with them and that she holds their receipts in
full of all demand against her as their guardian.

GEORGE LAWING - That at the same time, GEORGE LAWING was appointed
guardian for JAMES, SARAH & JOHN KIRK. It does not appear that he ever
made any returns. (GEORGE LAWING was step-father of the above children).

JOHN MILAM, JR. - That at the same term, JOHN MILAM, JR. was appointed
guardian for JONES, ISREAL, MARYANN, PETER & ARCHIBALD FULLER. He filed
a return on the 19th June 1815 by which it appeared that some of the
minors had attained full age and others had chosen another guardian.
It further appears that he has fully settled with those who were of
age and with the new guardians of those that were not. (The above named
minors were the children of ISHAM FULLER, who died 1805 and JOHN MILAM,
JR. was their brother-in-law, who married their sister, SARAH).

EDMUND GATES - That at March term 1808, EDMUND GAINES was appointed
guardian for MARGARET, CATHERINE & SARAH GAINES. It does not appear
that he has ever made any returns.

DANIEL COX - That at Feb. term 1809, DANIEL COX was appointed guardian
for WILLIS, WILEY & ALLEN ROBERTSON. He has filed returns as follows:
One return filed on the 10th Feb. 1810; one on 19th June 1815; and
one on 10th Feb. 1820. None since.

EDITH BERRY - That at the same term, EDITH BERRY was appointed guardian
for POLLY M. & ROBERT G. H. BERRY (ROBERT GOODLEE HARPER BERRY). She
filed a return on April 25, 1812 and one on the 15th June 1815. None
since.

MARTHA CHAMBERS - That at the June term 1809, MARTHA CHAMBERS was appointed guardian for JANE, MARGARET, POLLY, WILLIAM, RACHEL & MANS-
FIELD CHAMBERS. She filed a return on the 1st June 1815...none before
and none since.

REUBEN GRIFFIN - That at the June term 1809, REUBEN GRIFFIN was appointed guardian for JAMES, BENJAMIN & JESSE GRIFFIN. He filed a return on 6 June 1815; one on 6 Oct. 1816. By the first return, it appeared that he had settled in full with JAMES & BENJAMIN and by the last
that he had settled in full with JESSE, the amounts that had come into
his hands.

ARCHIBALD SAWYER - That at the June term 1809, ARCHIBALD SAWYER and
POLLY, his wife, were appointed guardian for SALLY & WILLIAM MC DANIEL.
It does not appear that they have ever made any returns.

REBECCA BROWN - That at the Fe. term 1811, REBECCA BROWN was appointed
guardian for LARKIN, LETTA, JAMES, POLLY & CLAIRBORN BROWN. It does
not appear that she has ever made any return.

HANNAH GARRETT - That at the June term 1811, HANNAH GARRETT was appointed guardian for REBECCA & CHARLES GARRETT. She made a return on 25 Mar. 1815 by which it appeared that she had settled in full with JOHN C. MURRELL who had married REBECCA. She filed another return on 2 Aug. 1816 and one on 1 Sept. 1817. None since.

BENJAMIN JOHNSON - That at the June term 1812, BENJAMIN JOHNSON was appointed guardian for LEWIS FEATHERSON. It does not appear that he has ever made any return.

DR. JOEY FINCH - That at the same term, DR. JOEY FINCH was appointed guardian for LEWIS GRANT. He filed a return on 19 June 1815. None since.

JOHN CALDWELL - That at the same term, JOHN CALDWELL was appointed guardian for DAVID DE WATT. He filed a return on 19 June 1815. None since.

HANNAH SWINDLE - That at Feb. term 1814, HANNAH SWINDLE was appointed guardian for WILLIAM, GEORGE W. & REBECCA SWINDLE. It does not appear that she has ever made any returns.

WILLIAM F. DOWNES - That at the same time, WM. F. DOWNES was appointed guardian for ROBERT PAULDING. He filed a return on the 1st day of May 1815 and another sometime in 1819 and one on the 2nd day of June 1825 by which it appears that having arrived at full age a final settlement has taken place between them.

JAMES HUNTER - That at June term 1814, JAMES HUNTER was appointed guardian for MARY & NANCY MILLS. That he has made a return for MARY MILLS for the year 1816 and for NANCY MILLS for the years 1816, 1819, 1820 and up to the 17th July 1823 and none since.

STARLING L. WESTMORELAND - That at the June term 1814, STERLING L. WESTMORELAND was appointed guardian for WILLIS W. DICKIE & MORNING DICKIE. He filed a return for 1816 and one for 1818 and on the 1st July 1822 made a return by which it appeared he had settled in full with WILLIS W. DICKIE and he has made no return since.

JOHN GARLINGTON - That at June term 1814, JOHN GARLINGTON was appointed guardian for MARY R., PARTHENA E. & PATSY DICKIE. He filed a return on the 3rd day of June 1825 by which it appeared that he had fully settled with EDWARD HIX who had married MARY R. DICKIE and with ROBERT W. SAUNDERS who had married PARTHENA E. DICKIE.

CRADDOCK DICKIE - That at June term 1814, CRADDOCK DICKIE was appointed guardian for MELINDA DICKIE. He has filed no return since 12 Apr. 1819.

ELIZABETH ANDERSON - That at June term 1814, ELIZABETH ANDERSON was appointed guardian for POLLY, SALLY & PATSEY WESSON. She has filed no return since 3 Nov. 1817. (These are children of JOHN WESSON who died 1805..comp.)

ALEXANDER MILLS - That at the same term, ALEXANDER MILLS was appointed guardian for WILLIAM MILLS and that he made something that resembled a return in Feb. 1818 and none since.

DAVID SPEERS - That at the Feb. term 1815, DAVID SPEERS was appointed guardian for ROBERT & ELIZABETH BLAKELY. It does not appear that he ever made a return.. He has long since been dead. (These are the children of JONATHON BLAKELY and the step-children of HENRY MC KELVEY..comp.)

JOHN COPELAND - That at the same term, JOHN COPELAND was appointed guardian for MARGARET BLAKELY. He made a return on 1 Sept. 1817 and one on 29 Oct. 1821 and one since.

HENRY MC KELVEY - That at the same term, HENRY MC KELVEY and wife were appointed guardians for MARTHA & AGNES BLAKELEY. He has made no return since 1821.

JAMES WILLIAMS - That at the same term, JAMES WILLIAMS was appointed

Cont'd:
guardian for FRANCES & MATILDA TINSLEY. He made return as follows:
one on 12 Apr. 1816; one on 14 Apr. 1817; one on 21 June 1819 and one
on 19 Feb. 1820 which from the remarks made there on by the late Commissioner appears to have been intended for a final settlement.

JAMES WILLIAMS - At the same term, JAMES WILLIAMS was appointed guardian
for SARAH, JAMES, DUKE & BEAUFORTE GOODMAN. He made no return since
1820 nor does it appear that any final settlement has taken place between them.

JOHN CALDWELL - That at the Feb. term 1815, JOHN CALDWELL was appointed
guardian for JAMES, PATRICK C. & ELIZABETH A. CALDWELL. It does not
appear that he has made any return whatever. All parties however have
long since been of age.

WILLIAM FULLER - At the same term, WILLIAM FULLER was appointed guardian for ARCHIBALD FULLER and wife. (She was LUCY YOUNG, daughter of
JAMES YOUNG, SR. and his wife, ELIZABETH. LUCY's sister, KITTURAH YOUNG
married JONES J. FULLER, brother of ARCHIBALD FULLER & WILLIAM FULLER.
The above appointment of guardianship was made because of settlement
of ARCHIBALD FULLER's share of his grandfather, Capt. JONES FULLER's
estate settlement in Randolph Co., North Carolina..comp.) It does not
appear that any return has ever been made.

ROBERT ROBERTSON - At the same time, ROBT. ROBERTSON was appointed
guardian for his heirs and children. He has made no return since 3
Apr. 1815.

WILLIAM HUDGENS - That at the June term 1816, WM. HUDGENS was appointed
guardian for JANE CUNNINGHAM. His last return was filed on May 12,
1819 and contains a final settlement.

JAMES CLARDY & WIFE - At the same term JAMES CLARDY and wife were appointed guardian for JOSEPH, SALLY, ELIHU, JACOB, MARGARET & POLLY
CUNNINGHAM. They have made no returns since 20 July 1821.

BENJAMIN HITT - That at the Feb. term BENJAMIN HITT was appointed guardian for KEZIAH RUSHING. He made a return on 7 Dec. 1819 which appears
to have been intended for a final settlement.

TIMOTHY SWANN - At the same term, TIMOTHY SWANN was appointed guardian
for MATTHEW HENRY. It does not appear that he has ever made any returns.

NANCY DORAW - At the same term, NANCY DORAW was appointed guardian
for MARY DORAW. (I am not sure if this name is DORRAH, DORAW or DORAN...
more likely to be DORRAH...comp.) Sometime afterwards JOSHUA TEAGUE
intermarried with the said NANCY and has made his return regularly
up to the 1st Jan. last.

JAMES YOUNG - At the same term 1816, JAMES YOUNG was appointed guardian for ALBERT WALLER. He made a return in 1822 by which it appears
he had settled with his ward in full. (See Rev. JOHN WALLER and Rev.
RICHARD SHACKELFORD, Baptist Ministers of Laurens, SC..comp.)

ANDREW SPEERS - That at the June term 1816, ANDREW SPEERS was appointed
guardian for ROBERT, JANE, ANDREW, JOHN & DAVID SPEERS. He has been
very regular in making his returns. His last was made 16 Mar. 1825
by which it appears that he has come to a final settlement with THOMAS
ARCHIBALD who has since been chosen guardian for JANE, JOHN, ANDREW
& DAVID SPEERS and paid to him their full share. He still continues
the guardian of ROBERT SPEERS.

VOLUNTINE HARLAN - At the same term, VOLUNTINE HARLAN was appointed
guardian for THOMAS KILPATRICK. He filed a return on 1 Jan. 1823 by
which it appears that a final settlement has been made. (These two
were half-brothers...comp.)

WILLIAM GILLIAM - At the same term, WILLIAM GILLIAM was appointed guardian for WILLIAM C. GILLIAM. He has made no returns to this office.

Cont'd:
At the Feb. term 1820, an order was made permitting him to make his returns to the Commissioners in Equity for Newberry District.

JOSHUA & RACHEL GAREY - At the same term, JOSHUA GAREY was appointed guardian for DORATHY GAREY & RACHEL GAREY for BENJAMIN & WILLIAM GAREY. Neither of them appears to have made any return.

JESSE MABRY - At the same term, JESSE MABRY was appointed guardian for JEMINA MABRY. He has never made any return.

BARBARA MOORE - At the Feb. term 1817, BARBARA W. MOORE was appointed guardian for ROBERT B., ELIZA, HARRIET, LOUISA, WILLIAM & SARAH MOORE. She has made no return since 1818.

ROBERT GRAY - At the same term 1817, ROBERT GRAY and JANE, his wife, were appointed guardian for JANE, DAVID & PEGGY BLAKE. They have made no return. (JANE ROSS BLAKE married 2nd to ROBERT GRAY and had GRAY children...comp.)

PATSY HUDGINS - At the same time, PATSEY HUDGINS was appointed guardian for NANCY HUDGINS. She has made no return.

THOMAS HILL - That at the June term 1817, THOMAS HILL was appointed guardian for WILLIAM ATWOOD. He has made no return. (WILLIAM ATWOOD was step-son to THOMAS HILL...comp.)

CHARLES C. MAYSON - That at the Feb. term 1818, CHARLES C. MAYSON - was appointed guardian for GEORGE C. & HENRIETTA MAYSON. He has made no return since 1822.

ELIZABETH & SAMUEL S. KERNS - At the same term, ELIZABETH & SAMUEL S. KERNS was appointed guardian for JOHN KIRK. It does not appear that they have made any return whatever. (ELIZABETH was widow of JOHN KIRK, SR. and moved to Mississippi...comp.)

EPHRAIM PITTS - At the same term, EPHRAIM PITTS was appointed guardian for MADISON MOTES. He has made no return since 1822, however, JESSE MOTES has since been appointed guardian for the sd MADISON and has made his regular annual returns.

NANCY MOTES - At the same term, NANCY MOTES was appointed guardian for DAVID, MARY, REBECCA & LYNDIA MOTES. Her last returns come up to 1 Jan. 1825.

JAMES HENRY - At the same term, JAMES HENRY was appointed guardian for MATTHEW HENRY. He filed a return on 17 Jan. 1825 by which it appeared that he had fully settled with his ward who has arrived of age.

BEAUFORTE T. WATTS - At the same term, BEAUFORTE T. WATTS was appointed guardian for JOHN P. WATTS. He made only one return in Oct. 1823.

JAMES TAYLOR - At the same term, JAMES TAYLOR was appointed guardian for MARGARET & NANCY MC CLINTOCK. He has made no return to this office. (See HAMILTON, LAW & TURNER family...comp.)

CHARLES DENDY - At the same term, CHARLES DENDY was appointed guardian for NANCY T. DENDY. He has made no return since 1820.

ANTHONY SAVAGE - At the Feb. 1819 term, ANTHONY SAVAGE was appointed guardian for WILLIAM & JOHN M. HARRISON. He has filed a receipt for his wards dated 18 Jan. 1822 which appears to have given final settlement.

JAMES YOUNG - At the same term, JAMES YOUNG was appointed guardian for WILLIAM & AGNES YOUNG. He has made no return since 1823. He died last summer.

JOHN BLACK - At the June term 1819, JOHN BLACK was appointed guardian for HENRY & WILLIAM O'NEALL. He made a return of guardianship for sd

Cont'd:

WILLIAM O'NEALL on 26 June 1824. On 8 Feb. 1825, he made return as guardian for HENRY O'NEALL by which it appears that he has fully settled with him.

CHARLES FOWLER - That at Feb. term 1820, CHARLES FOWLER was appointed guardian for ANDREW FOWLER. He filed a return on 16 Feb. 1825 by which it appears that ANDREW FOWLER being dead, he has come to a settlement with JOHN STUART, the administrator of ANDREW FOWLER, deceased and settled with him in full.

JOSEPH BABB - At the same term, JOSEPH BABB and wife were appointed guardian for JAMES COOK. He has made no return since 26 Apr. 1821. His guardianship has since been surrendered to ROBERT MC NEES, Esq. (JAMES CLAYTON COOK was son of CLAYTON COOK and his wife, MARGARET MC NEES. She married 2nd to Rev. JOSEPH BABB...comp.)

JAMES BATES - At the same term, JAMES BATES was appointed guardian for ELENOR, ABNER, JOHN & MAHALA BELTON. He has made no return. (These are children of WILLIAM BELTON...comp.)

EDWARD OSBORN - At the same term, EDW. OSBORN was appointed guardian for RUTHY OSBORN. He has made no return since 9 June 1821.

CHARLES PITTS - At the same term, CHAS. PITTS was appointed guardian for FRANCES BELL. And I am told that a bill for an account is now pending in Abbeville Court.

TURNER RICHARDSON - That at the Feb. term 1821, TURNER RICHARDSON was appointed guardian for WILLIAM, SALLY S. & FANNY HILL. His last return was made 7 Mar. 1825.

MARY HILL - At the same term, MARY HILL was appointed guardian for ROBERT & JAMES HILL. She made return on 1 Jan. 1825. She was appointed at the same term as guardian for WILLIAM ATWOOD. She has made no return for WILLIAM since 20 Feb. 1823. (See THOMAS HILL, COOK family, MITCHELL family...comp.)

JOSHUA GORE - At the same term 1820, JOSHUA GORE was appointed guardian for GILES & MARY ANN GOODWIN. He has made no return since 18 Jan. 1824.

AMBROSE HUDGINS - That at the June term 1821, AMBROSE HUDGINS, JR. was appointed guardian for ALLEN DUNN. He has not given security nor made any return.

ELIZABETH WORD - At the same term, ELIZABETH WORD was appointed guardian for WILLIAM, SARAH, THOMAS, JAMES, CHARLES, ROBERT & ELIZABETH WORD. She made return on 8 June 1825.

JOHN WALKER - At the same term, JOHN WALKER was appointed guardian for WILLIAM & CHARLES WALKER. He has made no return since 31 Jan. 1824.

JEREMIAH TRIBLE - At the same term, JEREMIAH TRIBLE and wife were appointed guardian for JANE TEMPLETON. They have made return on 8 June 1825.

ROBERT MC NEES - At the same term, ROBT. MC NEES was appointed guardian for JAMES C. COOK. He has made no return since 30 May 1823. (ROBT. MC NEES was grandfather of JAMES CLAYTON COOK...comp.)

WILLIAM WRIGHT - At the same term, WILLIAM WRIGHT was appointed guardian for JAMES T., MARY W., NANCY R., ELIZABETH A., & LUCINDA B. WRIGHT. No return.

MARY HILL - At the same term, MARY HILL was appointed guardian for TRISLENA A. BALL. Her last return was made on 20 Dec. 1824.

JACOB NISWANGER - At the same term, JACOB NISWANGER was appointed guardian for WILLIAM LINDLEY. He has made no return. (See Winchester Co., Va.; Tipton Co., TN; CROCKER, WATSON, WRIGHT, WARDLOW, SIMS, CARGIL

Cont'd:
and CROCKETT families...comp.)

SAMUEL FIFER - At the same term, SAMUEL FIFER was appointed guardian for ALSEY WALKER. His last return was made on 31 May 1825 by which it appears that he has come to a final settlement with his ward and settled with him in full.

DANIEL COOK - That at the Feb. term 1822, DANIEL COOK was appointed guardian for FRANCES COOK. His last return is made on 14 Feb. 1825. (Widow married PAISLEY; see PAISLEY family, Dr. DANIEL COOK family; MITCHELL family; COLEMAN family....comp.)

JAMES PEADON - At the same term, JAMES PEADON was appointed guardian for WILLIAM WELCH. His last return was made 14 May 1825.

RICHARD C. PLUNCKET - That at the June term 1822, RICHD. G. PLUNCKET (PUCKETT?) was appointed guardian for GEORGE C. MAYSON. He has made no return nor given security.

WILLIAM GREEN - At the same time, WILLIAM GREEN was appointed guardian for SARAH G. HUNTER. He made return on 21 Feb. 1825. (See FULLER & COLEMAN family....comp.)

WILLIAM BRADEN - At the same term, WM. BRADEN was appointed guardian for SAUNDERS, THOMAS & POLLY WILLIAMSON. He has made no return nor given security for guardianship.

JAMES MC KITRICK - At the same term, JAMES MC KITRICK was appointed guardian for ROBERT & LUCRETIA K. MC KITRICK. He made return on 21 Feb. 1825.

ALEXANDER SIMPSON - At the same term, ALEX. SIMPSON was appointed guardian for NANCY & JOHN MC CAREY. He has made no return.

DANIEL WILLIAMS - That at the Feb. 1823 term, DANL. WILLIAMS was appointed guardian for WILLIAM THOMPSON WILLIAMS. He has made no return.

SARAH MC CRADY - At the same term, SARAH MC CRADY was appointed guardian for JANE, MARY & CAROLINE MC CRADY. She has made no return since 28 Jan. 1824.

PATSEY DENDY - At the same term, PATSEY DENDY was appointed guardian for ELIZA, WILLIAM G. & DANIEL DENDY. This appointment was afterwards recalled and JOSHUA TEAGUE became their guardian.

JOHN JONES - At the same term, JOHN JONES was appointed guardian for ELIHU & ELIAS F. CRAIG. He died afterwards and before he had made any returns.

REBECCA SOUTH - At the same term, REBECCA SOUTH was appointed guardian for LUCY, HUDLY, FRANCES, ELISHA, FRANKLIN, REBECCA & NEWBERN SOUTH. She made return on 6 June 1825.

HENRY MORGAN - At the same term, HENRY MORGAN was appointed guardian for FANNY & HENRIETTA JOHNSON. He died shortly afterwards and before he had made any returns.

THOMAS LOCKHART - That at the same June term 1823, THOMAS LOCKHART was appointed guardian for MATHEW J. LOCKHART. He has made no returns.

NANCY COOPER - At the same term, NANCY COOPER was appointed guardian for POLLY & LETTICIA COOPER. She made return on 3 Nov. 1824.

WILLIAM W. SIMPSON - At the same term, WM. WISTER SIMPSON was made guardian for NANCY FOWLER. He made return on 6 June 1825.

ANNA JOHNSON - At the same term, ANNA JOHNSON was appointed guardian for LEWIS, ALLEN & WILLIAM JOHNSON. She made return 14 Mar. 1825.

WILLIAM HUTCHINSON - At the same term, WM. HUTCHINSON was appointed guardian for WILLIAM FOWLER. He has lately died without making any return.

ESTHER HUNTER - At the same term, ESTHER HUNTER was appointed guardian for POLLY ANN, ROBERT, ISABELLA, CATHERINE, MARGARET & JANE HUNTER. She has made no return.

WILLIAM GREEN - At the same term, WM. GREEN was appointed guardian for ELIZABETH HUNTER. He made return on 21 Feb. 1825.

JAMES E.HUTCHINSON - At the same term JAMES E. HUTCHINSON was appointed guardian for ELENOR HUNTER. He made return on 22 Oct. 1824.

SYLVANIUS WALKER - At the same term SYSLVANIUS WALKER was appointed guardian for ELIZA DENDY. This appointment has since been recalled and JOSHUA TEAGUE has become guardian.

STARLING K. SMITH - At the same time, STARLING K. SMITH was appointed guardian for LOUISA, POLLY, JOHN & DIANNA SMITH. He has made no return.

WILLIAM PUCKETT - At the same term WM. PUCKETT was appointed guardian for JOHN, WILLIAM, ANDREW & ALEXANDER PUCKETT. He has made no return.

WINNEFRED KINMAN - At the same term, WINNEFRED KINMAN was appointed guardian for ABNER, MELTON & SARAH KINMAN. She has made no return.

BENJAMIN ARNOLD - At the same term, BENJ. ARNOLD was appointed guardian for QUITON KINMAN. He has made no return.

JOHN DUNLAP - At the same term, JOHN DUNLAP was appointed guardian for POLLY, NEHEMIAH, DAVID, MATILDA, NANCY & EMELINE DUMAS. He made a return on 30 May 1825.

JOHN WILLSON - At the same term, JOHN WILLSON was appointed guardian for BERRY, JOHN & SARAH WILLSON. He made return on 14 Feb. 1825.

JOHN OWENS - That at Feb. term 1824 JOHN OWENS was appointed guardian for SARAH OWENS. He has made no return.

ROBERT COKER - At the same term, ROBERT COKER was appointed guardian for BETSY SIMPSON. He has made no return.

REUBEN THOMAS - At the same term, REUBEN THOMAS was appointed guardian for SALLY SIMPSON. He made return 4 Apr. 1825.

HOSEA HOLCOMB - At the same term, HOSEA HOLCOMB was appointed guardian for PETER, PEGGY, WILLIAM & JAMES SIMPSON. He made return 7 Mar. 1825.

HICKS WESSON - At the same term, HICKS WESSON was appointed guardian for REUBEN, ELIZABETH & LEWIS ANDERSON. He made return 20 Dec. 1824.

JESSE MOTES - At the same term, JESSE MOTES was appointed guardian for MADISON MOTES. He made return 4 Apr. 1825.

CATHERINE MC CLANAHAN - At the same term, CATHERINE MC CLANAHAN was appointed guardian for JOHN, ROBERT, MARY, SARAH, WILLIAM & MARGARET MC CLANAHAN. She made return 6 June 1825.

JASON MEADORS - At the same term, JASON MEADORS was appointed guardian for PATSEY & CATHERINE REEDER. He died shortly afterwards and before making any return.

THOMAS ARCHIBALD - That at the June term 1824, THOS. ARCHIBALD was appointed guardian for JANE, JOHN, ANDREW & DAVID SPEERS. He made return on 1 Aug. 1824. And has since that time removed with his wards to the State of Alabama. (He was their step-father...comp.)

JOHN DUNLAP - At the same term, JOHN DUNLAP was appointed guardian for WILLIAM D. UNDERWOOD. He made return 30 May 1825.

JOHN ODELL - At the same term, JOHN ODELL was appointed guardian for PATSEY FOWLER & NEWTON FOWLER. He made return on 1 May 1825. (Children of JOSIAH & SARAH DUCKETT FOWLER. JOHN ODELL was brother-in-law to minors...comp.)

JOSHUA TEAGUE - At the same term, JOSHUA TEAGUE was appointed guardian for THOMAS, MARTHA, MENETTA, WILLIAM G., DANIEL & ELIZ. DENDY. He made return on 18 Feb. 1825.

JOHN GARLINGTON - The commissioners further report that JOHN GARLING-TON, who has been appointed trustee by this court for MRS. JANE FRANKS, made a return the 6th June 1825 showing that MRS. JANE FRANKS lately died and he is trustee for her children. (JANE SIMMONS FRANKS was a daughter of Capt. CHARLES & ELIZABETH (TWEEDY) SIMMONS...comp.)

NANCY MAHERG - It seems that NANCY MAHERG who is guardian for JOHN MAHERG has made no return since 1818.

ANDREW SPEERS - SPEERS, who is guardian for ELIZABETH BLAKELY, made return on 21 Jan. 1822. It appears that ELIZABETH had married JAMES PARMER with whom he has made final settlement.

HENRY MC COY - Guardian for PATSEY, POLLY & SALLY WESSON made return on 15 Apr. 1822 by which it appears that he has fully settled with POLLY & SALLY. Nothing said as to PATSEY. He has made no return since. (Step-father of the above minors whose father was JOHN WESSON..comp.)

JAMES HUNTER - Guardian for WILLIAM MILLS and who has made no return since 17 July 1823.

NANCY RHODES - Appointed guardian for DAVID, PRISCILLA, ALEXANDER & NANCY MILLS. She has made no return since 18 Feb. 1821.

NANCY BRADLEY - Guardian for POLLY BRADLEY and has made no return since 15 Feb. 1819.

THOMAS GAREY - Guardian for DORATHA GAREY and has made no return since 1 June 1818.

HOWELL MOSELY - Appointed guardian for ELIZABETH COLEMAN and has made no return since 22 June 1819.

GEORGE YOUNG - Appointed guardian for THOMAS, GEORGE & JACOB YOUNG. He has made no return since 5 Aug. 1822.

JOSHUA TEAGUE. We further report that at Feb. term 1824, JOSHUA TEAGUE who is the administrator of WILLIAM DENDY, deceased, requested to make reports for minors of DENDY for guardianship, instead of both administration and guardianship. The commissioners would recommend that the necessity in the future of his making returns to this office as adm. be dispensed with inasmuch as the whole may properly be included in his returns as guardian.

June Term 1825: Exparte of the Commissioners of Laurens District in Equity: It is ordered that the commissioners do forthwith institute actions at law against all guardians and their securities who have entered into bond and failed in the performance of their duty. It is further ordered that if any guardians shall have been appointed by this court who have removed from this State or have not entered into bonds awarding to such appointment, that such order be recinded and other guardian or guardians be appointed in their stead. In the case of JOHN GARLINGTON who was appointed trustee for MRS. JANE FRANKS, a former court has directed the course to be pursued and it is not competent for me to rescind it. In the case of JOSHUA TEAGUE, his making his returns as adm. may be dispensed with upon his regularly making his return as guardian. Signed: W. THOMPSON C.E.L.D. (Comm. in Equity Laurens Dist.)

END OF GUARDIANS RETURNS

NAMES AND PLACES OF RESIDENCE
JAMES McCAA & COMPANY, LAURENS, S.C.
Abstracted from a statement of the balances due James McCaa
on 1 Sept. 1804, as recorded by James McCaa.

NAME	PLACE OF RESIDENCE
WALTER ASHMORE	40 mi. from Charleston on Wateree or Santee
WILLIAM ARTHUR	n. Rutherford Court House, N. C.
MICHAEL ALLEN	Saluda n. "the grove" (Spring Grove)
JOHN ARNOLD	Horse Creek
MOSES ALLISON	Tennessee
JOHN ALEXANDER	Greenville
WILLIAM ATKINS	Greenville
JOHN ADAIR	Wateree
DAVID ALLEN	Georgia
SAMUEL AUSTIN	Grove Creek
JAMES ABERNATH	Bush River
ELIJAH BENNETT	Kentucky
JOHN BRATCHER	Kentucky
BENJAMIN BREWER	Georgia
JOHN BURNS	Reedy River T. S. (Tumbling Shoals)
SAMUEL BRAZIER	Reedy River
JOHN CHAPMAN	Kentucky
ZECHARIAH CHANDLER	Kentucky
SOLOMON K. CHANDLER	Kentucky
WILLIAM CRAWFORD	Georgia
DUNCAN CAMMERON	Georgia
WILLIAM CAMP	Georgia
STERLING CAMP	West Point
NATHAN CAMP	Georgia
THOMAS CAMP, JR.	Georgia
JAMES CAMP	Reedy River
JOSIAH CHANDLER	Kentucky
JOHN CROWDER	Knoxville
PHILIP COKER	Georgia
BENJAMIN CAMP	Georgia
ROBERT COKER, SR.	Georgia
JOHN COLLEY	Pendleton
SALLY DOWDLE	S. Reedy River (South side?)
JOEL CHANDLER, dead	Wife lives Reedy River
BURRELL CAMP	Georgia
MOSES CRAFFORD	Pendleton
SALLY DURHAM	Edgefield District, Stephens Creek
WILLIAM DIXON	Pendleton
WILLIAM DIXON, SR.	Pendleton
BAILEY DEVALL	Knoxville
ALEXANDER DEVALL	Knoxville
THOMAS ELLIOTT	S. Reedy River (South side?)
WILLIAM FOWLER	Warrior Creek
CHARLES FERGUSON	Pearcy's Ford, Saluda (River)
JOHN P. FRENCH	Mountain Creek, n. Pearcy's Ford
DELPHY GREEN	S. Reedy Creek
CHARLES GUNTER	Georgia
ANDERSON GREEN	n. Hewlett's Sullivant's
JAMES GILLELAND	Pendleton
WILLIAM GARY	above Wolff's (Rabun Creek)
JOHN GUTTERY	n. Allen's
THOMAS HATCHER	Bunkham Co., N. C.
ELISHA HALCOMB	Durbin Creek
NANCY HATCHER	S. F. (South Fork) Rabun Creek
FELT & FLEMING HATCHER	N. F. (North Fork) Rabun Creek
JOHN HUGHES	Rabun Creek
ISHAM HISTERLOW	Pendleton
ELISHA HUNT	Tyger at Bobo's Mills (Tyger River)
JOHN HENDERSON	Chatham Co., N. C.
THOMAS JENKINS	Georgia
MICAJAH JENKINS	Reedy River
STEPHEN JAMES	Mountain Creek, Saluda (River)
JESSE KERBY	Horse Creek
JAMES KELLY, dead	Wife lives at MICAJAH JENKINS
JACOB LEAR	Georgia

MC CAA's cont'd:
<pre>
          NAME   PLACE OF RESIDENCE
SPENCER LAWS   Georgia
JOHN LEWIS   Clinch River
JOHN & THOMAS LEWIS   Clinch River
STEPHEN LACY   Clinch River
JOHN LYNCH   Pendleton
MARTIN MAHAFFEY, dead
JOHN MC DONALD   South Reedy River
WARREN MERCER   Mountain Creek
ABIGAIL MC KNIGHT, dead
ASA MITCHELL   Reedy River
PHILLIP MULKEY   Georgia
JOHN OWENS   Kentucky
RICHARD OWENS   North Fork of Rabun Creek
THOMAS OWENS   North Fork of Rabun Creek
HENRY O'DANIEL   n. Col. COCHRAN's
JOHN PHILPOT   Kentucky
PETER PRO   Pendleton
ABEL PARKER   Mountain Creek
ANDREW REID   Georgia
SAMUEL RIDGEWAY   Miamma
JOHN ROBINSON   Reedy River
ROBERT ROSS   Kentucky
HENRY REID   South Reedy River
JOSEPH REID   Kentucky
MC NEESE RODGERS   Tennessee
NELLY SIMS, dead
WILLIAM SULLIVANT   Mountain Creek
CLAYBOURN SIMS   Reedy River
JAMES TERRELL   Rutherford, North Carolina
HUGH WOOD, dead
BARNETT WHARTON   n. SHELTON's
JOHN YOUNG, dead   Wife lives at A. OWENS'
SAMUEL SWAN   Rutherford, North Carolina
JOHN SCRIMSHAW   Pendleton 7 mi. from Courthouse
WILLIAM TOMESON, SR.   Georgia
L. D. TOMESON   Reedy River
WILLIAM TOMESON, JR.   Georgia
WILLIAM TOLBERT   Georgia
WILLIAM TERRY   R. R. (Reedy River) Tumbling Shoals
JOHN TOMESON, SR   1 mi. from WOLFF's
JOHN TWEEDY   Bush River
</pre>

PETITIONS FOR PENSIONS BY REVOLUTIONARY SOLDIERS

Copied from originals

Ex Parte   )   Petition for pension   Filed 18 Oct. 1830
BENJAMIN GRIST)
          Recorded in Journals of Court, Laurens, S. C. Bk 4, p. 44

....Enlisted for a term of three years during the war - about two year
and nine months before peace was declared, in the State of North Carolina in the company commanded by Captain PETER HEDRICK, in regiment
commanded first by Col. DUDLEY, afterwards by Cols. MAIBEN, BELFORD
and LETTRELL who were killed in the service, the last at Lindley's
Mill and lastly by Col. COLYAR. Continued to serve in sd corps until
shortly after the surrender of Cornwallis when the regiment was allowed
to go home, but ordered to keep themselves in readiness to assemble
at three hours warning, but in consequence of peace, was never called
on and was never regularly discharged. The discharge, however, which
was received was in Randolph County, N. C.

Has not made application earlier for a pension for the following reasons: Made application while living in Greenville Dist., and has not
yet received his pension certificate and so far as his feeble means
have allowed him, he has been incessant in collecting the necessary
evidence to entitle him to a pension; and in pursuance of the Act of

Cont'd:
1 May 1820, "I do solemnly swear that I was a resident citizen of the
U. S. on the 18th day of March 1818, and I have not since that time
by gift, sale, or in any manner disposed of my property or any part
thereof, with interest thereby to diminish it as to bringing myself
within the provisions of an act of Congress entitled 'An Act to provide for certain persons engaged in the land and naval services of
the U. S. in The Revolutionary War', passed on 18 Mar. 1818, that I
have not nor has any person in trust for me any property or securities,
contracts, or debts due me; nor have I any income or property whatsoever.

"I was a farmer, but from age and infirmity, I am now unable to pursue
it. I have no family and reside occasionally with my children, who
are in indigent circumstances."   his
                        (signed) BENJAMIN   X   GRIST
                                                  mark
Sworn to in open court
JOSIAH J. EVANS, Circuit Judge

South Carolina   )
Laurens District) 4 Oct. 1829 BENJAMIN PUCKETT, aged 72 years, resi-
Ex Parte   ) dent of Laurens District, appeared in open court
BENJAMIN PUCKETT) and declared on oath that he was 72 years old
                     "on the 15th of this inst"; that he enlisted in
the month of July 1776 for a term of three years in the company of
Capt. THOMAS SCOTT and Col. JAMES SCRIVEN's regiment in Prince Edward
County, Virginia; that he faithfully served that term and in one month
afterwards enlisted again in Capt. HUSE WOODSON's company which belonged
to the regiment commanded by Cols. HEATH and BEAUFORT in Cleveland
County, State of Virginia for the term of two years; stated that he
received a regular discharge at the close of his first tour from Col.
Scriven in the State of Georgia, but he has since lost it; that he
also received a regular discharge at the close of his second tour from
Col. Beaufort which he has also lost, but he subsequently obtained
a certificate from Capt. MORTON who commanded the company to which
he belonged when discharged, signed likewise by Col. HOPKINS certifying
that this deponent had rendered the service herein alleged.

    He stated also that he was a farmer as long as he was able and
that he has no house nor home but lives with one of his children who
is in indigent circumstances.
Sworn to before
ALEXANDER JEANS
WM. A. TEMPLETON   BENJAMIN PUCKETT
Recorded in Journals of the Court of Common Pleas, Bk 4, page 30

                    PETITIONS FOR NATURALIZATION
    Copied from the original applications on file with Clerk of Court
Label 1
Roll #1: JAMES KYLE, a native of Ireland, petitioned for naturalization
          on Apr. 15, 1806 and stated that he had resided in the U.
S. about twelve years and in S. C. for eight years. Certifying as to
his character were: GEORGE BOWIE, THOS. LEWERS, BENJ. TANKERSLEY, SAML.
LAW, JR., JNO. SIMPSON, M. HUNTER.

Roll #2: ALEXANDER STUART petitioned for naturalization Apr. 16, 1806,
          stating that he was a native of County Antrim, Ireland and
that he has resided in the U. S. for 10 years and upwards and in this
state for this space of time. Certifying as to his character were:
WM. CALDWELL, JNO. SIMPSON, WM. DUNLAP, GEORGE BOWIE, WM. NIBBS, J.
W. MC KEBBIN.

Roll #3: JOHN BLACK petitioned to be admitted a citizen of U. S. 18
          Nov. 1806, stating that he was a native of Scotland and that
he had resided in this state 7 years. Certifying concerning his character were: ROBT. CRESWELL, JOHN SIMPSON, CHAS. GRIFFIN, JNO. GARLINGTON,
JNO. WATTS, JAS. CALDWELL, ABNER PYLES.

Roll #4: SAMUEL TODD and ROBERT ALEXANDER petitioned the court for

Cont'd:
citizenship on 17 Apr. 1807, stating that they were subjects of Great Britain, but had resided in the U. S. and in this state since the year 1800. Character testimonials by B. H. SAXON and SILVANUS WALKER, JR.

Roll #5: CHARLES LITTLE petitioned the court for citizenship on 16 Apr. 1807, stating that he was a native of Ireland and had resided in this state for 13 years. Citizens certifying as to his character were: ROBT. HUTCHESON, JNO. SIMPSON, JAS. SIMPSON, A. RODGERS, JR., WM. HUTCHINSON, W. BURNSIDE, WM. DUNLAP, DAVID SPEERS.

Roll #6: WILLIAM COWAN, a native of Ireland, stated that he had resided in the U. S. and in this state for 10 years and wished to become a citizen. Certifying were: R. CRESWELL, WM. HUTCHINSON, THOS. PARKS, THOS. WRIGHT, STARLING TUCKER, ROBT. HUTCHESON, CHARLES ALLEN, W. BURNSIDE. Petition filed 14 Apr. 1807.

Roll #7: DAVID WHITEFORD, a native of County Antrim, Ireland, petitioned the court for citizenship and stated that he had resided in S. C. upwards of 17 years. Certifying as to character were: W. BURNSIDE, Justice of the Quorum, MATTHEW HUNTER, JNO. WISEMAN, JAS. YOUNG, WM. MC CREDY, JNO. WATTS, RICH'D WATTS. Filed 14 Apr. 1807.

Roll #8: The petition of JAMES MC CAREY stated that he was a native of Ireland and that he sailed from Ireland 14 Apr. 1792 and arrived in Charleston, S. C. 26 July 1792; also that he had resided in the U. S. and this state for 15 years. Petition filed 17 Apr. 1807. Character witnesses: JNO. SIMPSON, STARLING TUCKER, THOS. LEWERS, JNO. RITCHEY, JOSHUA HITCH, ROBT. HUTCHESON, SAM'L TODD.

Roll #9: The petition of ALEXANDER HENRY showed that he was a native of Ireland and that he had resided in the U. S. and this state for 15 years. Character witnesses: BENJ. LEWIS, W. BURNSIDE, WM. CRAIG, J. PUCKETT, ROBT. HUTCHESON, JAMES PARK, ABNER RODGERS, JNO. DAVIS, JNO. SIMPSON, Z. BAILEY, CHARLES ALLEN. Filed 15 Apr. 1807.

Roll #10: The petition of JOSEPH LYONS stated that he was a subject of the King of Great Britain and that he had resided in the U. S. and particularly in this state since the year 1781. Character witnesses: DAN'L WRIGHT, ANDREW B. MOORE, JNO. MEADOR, WM. BOWEN, THOS. PARKS, JONATHAN DOWNS. Petition filed 13 Apr. 1807.

Roll #11: JAMES HUNTER, a native of Ireland, filed petition for naturalization 17 Apr. 1807 in which he stated he embarked from there 15 or 16 years before and that he arrived at the harbor in Charleston, S. C. some short time thereafter; also that he had resided in this state 14 years. Testifying that they have known HUNTER for 10-12 years were: JAS. H. LAWING, CHAS. SMITH, THOS. WRIGHT, GEORGE ROSS, W. FOWLER, WM. BARKSDALE, THOS. PORTER, ROBT. HUTCHESON, W. D. DOWNS, J. RODGERS, JR.

Roll #12: The petition of MATTHEW HUNTER showed that he was a native of Ireland and had resided in this state 14 years. Character witnesses: WM. DUNLAP, JNO. GARLINGTON, JNO. SIMPSON, ELIHU CRESWELL. Filed 17 Apr. 1807.

Roll #13: The petition of DAVID GREER showed that he was a native of Ireland and had resided in the U. S. and this state for 10 years. Character witnesses: JNO. SIMPSON, WM. DUNLAP, JNO. BLACK, JAMES NICKELS. Filed 20 Apr. 1808.

Roll #14: Petition of DAVID LITTLE showed that he was a native of Ireland and that he had resided in this state for 14 years. Character witnesses: CHAS. ALLEN, ROBT. LONG, ROBT. HUTCHESON, JNO. BOYD. Filed 18 Apr. 1808.

Roll #15: ANDREW TODD, a native of Ireland, stated in his petition that he had resided in the U. S. since Jan. 1794 and in this state. Character witnesses: M. HUNTER, THOS. LEWERS, SAMUEL TODD, JNO.

Cont'd:
COOK. Filed 19 Apr. 1808.

Roll #16: WILLIAM MC GOWAN, a native of Ireland, petitioned for naturalization and stated that he had resided in the U. S. since May 1801 and for seven years past in this state. Testifying as to character were: JOSIAH EVANS, SAMUEL LEMON, MESHAC OVABY, JNO. BEASLEY. Filed 18 Apr. 1808.

Roll #17: MAXWELL MC CORMACK, a native of Ireland petitioned the court for naturalization and stated that he had resided in the U. S. since October 1790 and for 18 years in this state. Testifying to character were: CHAS. SIMMONS, THOS. PORTER, THOS. LEWERS, SAMUEL TODD, B. NABERS, CHAS. ALLEN, P. BRANNON, M. HUNTER. Filed 19 Apr. 1808.

Roll #18: DAVID GLEN made petition for naturalization and stated that he was a native or Ireland and that he had resided in the U. S. and in this state for 20 years. Testifying as to character were: WM. COWAN, STARLING TUCKER, DAVID SPEERS, JNO. SIMPSON, ROBT. HUTCHESON. Filed 19 Apr. 1808.

Roll #19: JAMES LAUGHRIDGE, a native of Ireland, petitioned for citizenship and stated he had resided in the U. S. since July 1801 and for 3 years past he resided in this state. Certifying to character were: THOS. PORTER, THOS. WRIGHT, JONATHAN DOWNS, JOHN SIMPSON. Filed 19 Apr. 1808.

Roll #20: JOHN CRAWFORD, a native of Ireland petitioned for naturalization and stated that he was a native of Ireland and that he had rsided in the U. S. and this state for 18 years. Testifying were: JNO. SIMPSON, WM. DUNLAP, JAS. NICKELS, JNO. BLACK. Filed 20 Apr. 1808.

Roll #21: JAMES BOYD, JR., petitioned for naturalization, stating that he had resided in the U. S. and this state for 6 years. Certifying as to character were: WM. KINGSBOROUGH, JNO. SIMPSON, JAS. NICKELS, ROBT. HUTCHESON, JOHN BLACK, WM. DUNLAP. Filed 20 Apr. 1808.

Roll #22: JOHN TODD, a native of Ireland, petitioned for naturalization and stated that he had resided in the U. S. and this state since December 1790. Testifying: THOS. LEWERS, DAVID GLEN, WM. COWAN, DAVID CONOR, SAMUEL TODD. Filed 21 Apr. 1808.

Roll #23: WILLIAM BLACK, a native of Scotland, petitioned for naturalization and stated that he arrived in Charleston about 1 Nov. 1803 and has since resided in Laurens District. Citizens and freeholders testifying as to character were: R. WORD, JNO. CLARK, WM. DENDY, W. BURNSIDE, JNO. SIMPSON, DAVID ANDERSON, ROBT. CRESWELL, JNO. GARLINGTON. Filed 16 Nov. 1808.

Roll #24: WILLIAM HOLIDAY petitioned for naturalization and stated that he was a native of Ireland and that he had resided in this state 18 years. Testifying as to character were: ROBT. HUTCHESON, J.P.; W. BURNSIDE, J.Q.; SAMUEL CUNNINGHAM, J.P.; THOS. LEWERS, JOS. DOWNS, J.P.; DAVID ANDERSON. Filed Nov. 16, 1808.

Roll #25: JAMES BOYD, a native of Ireland, petitioned for naturalization and stated that he had resided in the U. S. between 1795 and 1796 and for the last 13 years in this state. Testifying to character: JNO. SIMPSON, ROBT.HUTCHESON, JAS. HOLLEY, W. BURNSIDE, R. CAMPBELL, JONATHAN DOWNS, J.Q.; JAS. ABERCROMBIE. Filed 15 Nov. 1808.

Roll #26: SAMUEL WIER, a native of Ireland, petitioned for naturalization and stated that he had resided in the U. S. between 25 Dec. 1792 - 1793 and for the last 10 years had resided constantly in this state. Testifying were: CHAS. ALLEN, DAVID SPEERS, JNO. SIMPSON, CAPTORS HUGENS, ROBT. HUTCHESON, W. BURNSIDE. Filed 15 Nov. 1808.

Roll #27: WILLIAM FULTON, a native of Ireland, petitioned for naturalization stating that he had resided in the U. S. between
4 Sept. 1787 - 1788 and for the last 20 years in this state. Testifying were: B. H. SAXON, CHAS. ALLEN. Filed 16 Nov. 1808.

Rol #28: WALTER STEWART, a native of Ireland, petitioned for naturalization and made oath of allegiance to the U. S.; also stated
that he had resided in this state 20 years. Filed Nov. 1808. Among
those testifying were: JAMES FLEMING, ROGER BROWN, J. A. ELMORE, JAS.
MILLS.

Roll #29: THOMAS FULTON asked for naturalization and made oath; he
stated that he was a native of Ireland and had resided in
the U. S. since the 15th June 1795 and for the last 17 years in this
state. Testifying to character were: JOSEPH DOWNS, THOS. LEWERS, CHAS.
ALLEN, J.Q. Filed 16 Nov. 1808.

Roll #30: ROBERT FLEMING petitioned and made oath, stating that he
was a native of Ireland and had resided in this state 11
years. Testifying were: ROBT. WORD, A. LAWRENCE, THOS. PARKS, JOHN
WILLIAMS. Filed Nov. 16, 1808.

Roll #31: ROBERT GILLILAND, a native of Ireland, petitioned and made
oath; also stated he had resided in this state 22 years.
Testifying were: ANDREW RODGERS, SR., BENJ. BYRD, ROBT. WORD, JNO.
PUCKETT. Filed 17 Apr. 1809.

Roll #32: JOHN LUKE, a native of Ireland, petitioned for naturalization and made oath; also stated he had resided in this state
15 years. Among those testifying were: GEORGE MC NARY, JAMES HOLLEY,
GEORGE ROSS. Filed 18 Apr. 1809.

Roll #33: ALEXANDER LUKE, a native of Ireland petitioned for naturalization and made oath; also stated he had resided in this
state 15 years. Testifying were: ALEXANDER FILLSON, ALEXANDER HENRY,
JAMES PARK. Filed 14 Nov. 1809.

Roll #34: JOHN WILKERSON, a native of Scotland, petitioned and made
oath; also stated he had resided in this state 24 years.
Testifying were: H. T. MARTIN, J. UNDERWOOD, WM. DENDY. Filed 14 Nov.
1809.

Roll #35: ALEXANDER WILKINSON, a native of Scotland, petitioned and
made oath; also stated he had resided in this state 25 years.
Filed 17 Apr. 1810.

Roll #36: JOHN STEWART, a native of Ireland, petitioned and made oath;
also stated he had resided in this state 21 years. Testifying were: GEORGE ADAIR, W. H. ALEXANDER, JOHN COCHRAN, SAMUEL TAYLOR.
Filed 17 Apr. 1810.

Roll #37: Petition and oath of SAMUEL STEWART, native of Ireland stated
he had resided in this state 21 years. Filed 17 Apr. 1810.
Wit.: JNO. MC LAUGHLIN, J. A. ELMORE and others.

Roll #38: WM. BOYD, JR., a native of Ireland, petitioned and gave oath;
also stated he had resided in this state 6 years. Filed 12
Nov. 1810.

Roll #39: SAMUEL BOYD, native of Ireland, petitioned and gave oath;
stated he had resided in this state 6 years. Filed 12 Nov.
1810.

Roll #40: ROBERT SINKLER, being native of Ireland, petitioned and gave
oath; stated he had resided in this state 6 years. Filed
12 Nov. 1810.

Roll #41: PATRICK TODD, native of Ireland, petitioned and gave oath;
stated he had resided in this state 7 years. Wit: JAMES STRAIN

Cont'd:
and JONATHAN JOHNSON. Filed 13 Nov. 1810.

Roll #42: FRANCIS STEWART, petitioned for naturalization and gave
oath; also stated that he was a native of Ireland and had
resided in this state 15 years...Testifying were JAS. FAIRBAIRN, GEORGE
JONES, ISAAC UNDERWOOD. Filed 13 Nov. 1810.

Roll #43: JOHN BOYD, a native of Ireland, petitioned and gave oath;
stated that he had resided in this state 5 years. Filed
2 Nov. 1810.

Roll #44: WILLIAM BOYD, SR., a native of Ireland petitioned and made
oath and stated that he had resided in this state 6 years.
Filed 12 Nov. 1810.

Roll #45: JON MC GOWAN, a native of Ireland, petitioned and gave oath;
stating that he had resided in the U. S. since Dec. 1791
and in this state. Filed 15 Apr. 1811.

Roll #46: WILLIAM BLACK, a native of Scotland petitioned and gave
oath; stating that he arrived in the City of Charleston
in the spring of 1803 and immediately removed to Laurens District.
At the Nov. term of court in 1808 he gave notice of his intention of
becoming a citizen. Among those test. was WILLIAM NIBBS. Filed 19 Nov.
1811.

Roll #47: WILLIAM MC CULLOUGH, a native of Ireland petitioned for
citizenship and stated that he had resided in S. C. since
1796. Filed 19 Nov. 1811.

Roll #48: SAMUEL THOMB, a native of County Antrim, Ireland, petitioned
and gave notice of his intention of becoming a citizen.
He stated that he arrived in Charleston in June 1811 and immediately
removed to Laurens District where he has resided ever since. Filed
14 Apr. 1812.

Roll #49: JOHN PATTERSON, a native of Ireland, petitioned and gave
oath; stating that he had resided in the U. S. since 1793
and in this state for same time. Filed 16 Apr. 1812.

Roll #50: JOSEPH MC CULLOUGH gave notice of becoming a citizen-native
of Ireland. Lived in U. S. and S. C. since Feb. 1808. Filed
16 Apr. 1812.

Roll #51: Filed 21 Sept. 1812. JOHN JOHNSON, born in Kingdom of Prussia
and about 32 years of age; arrived in the U. S. at Port
of New Orleans in 1807; is a preacher of the Gospel; had no family.

Roll #52: Missing

Roll #53: JOHN DRENNON, a native of Ireland filed petition for naturalization and took oath Nov. 16, 1813; stated that he had
resided in the U. S. and in state of S. C. since Feb. 1787. Among those
test. as to his character were: N. DURKEE, JAS. LONGRIDGE & WILLIS
FARR.

Roll #54: ROBERT SLOAN, a native of County Antrim, Ireland filed his
petition and took oath in open court 10 Nov. 1813. He stated
that he arrived in Charleston 7 Jan. 1800. In May he left there and
resided in Newberry where he spent seven years; then he came to Laurens
Dist.where he since resided. JOHN SLOAN made a sworn statement that
this was true.

Roll #55: JAMES GAGE, native of Ireland took oath 19 Apr. 1814; he
was of Union District.

Roll #56: HENRY FEARNES, native of Warwickshire, England petitioned
for naturalization and took oath 26 Sept. 1814. He arrived
in Charleston 25 Jan. 1811.

Roll #57: JOHN MC WILLIAMS, a native of Ireland petitioned for naturalization and stated that he had resided in state of S. C.
since November 1805.

Roll #58: DAVID GRAHAM, a native of County Antrim, Ireland, petitioned
the Court 16 Nov. 1815. He arrived in Dec. 1788 and had
ever since resided in S. C.

Roll #59: Ex parte - ALEXANDER AUSTIN, SR., JAMES AUSTIN, SR., JAMES
AUSTIN, JR., J. ALEXANDER AUSTIN, JR. Petition for naturalization filed Nov. 14, 1815. Natives of County Antrim, Ireland, arrived
in Charleston 13 Nov. 1804 and immediately removed to Laurens Dist.
where they ever since resided.

Roll #60: Petition and oath of GEORGE CRUICKSHANKS filed 14 Apr. 1819.
A native of the north of Scotland, aged 23, born in Province
of Rhynie, Aberdeenshire; left Scotland 1 June 1817; landed in Quebec,
lower Canada the end of July; left lower Canada Jan. 18, 1818; had
been in Laurens Dist. 12 months on 20 Apr. 1819; aged 23 years in May
1819.

Roll #61: Petition of FRANCIS GLENN filed 14 Apr. 1819; native of
Ireland; resided in S. C. since month of Feb. 1788.

Roll #62: THOMAS MC CARLEY, a native of Ireland, filed petition for
naturalization 16 Apr. 1819. Landed in the U. S. Aug. 1800
in state of Delaware; removed to S. C. in 1802 and resided there ever
since. Among those test.: C. SAXON, THOMAS F. JONES.

Roll #63: WILLIAM HAMILTON filed his intention to become a citizen
16 Nov. 1819. He was upwards of 50 years of age; migrated
from County of Trine in Ireland; arrived in U. S. Dec. 1803 and settled
in S. C., Laurens Dist.

Roll #64: JAMES GARNER, a native of Ireland, arrived in Georgetown,
S. C. July 1796 and has ever since resided in this state.
Sworn in Court 19 Nov. 1819. JOHN GARLINGTON, Clk. of Court.

Roll #65: Reverend ALEXANDER KIRKPATRICK, a native of County Antrim,
Ireland, appeared in open court 18 Nov. 1817; arrived in
Charleston 26 Nov. 1816 and immediately removed to Laurens Dist. where
he has ever since resided.

Roll #66: ANDREW TODD, native of County of Monaghan, Ireland, filed
notice of intention to become a citizen and took oath 19
Nov. 1817; arrived at Charleston 26 Nov. 1816; immediately removed
to Laurens Dist. where he has resided since.

Roll #67: JOHN PEARSON, native of England, aged about 32 years, made
petition and took oath 20 Apr. 1820. A free white person.

Roll #68: JOHN HENDERSON, native or Ireland made petition and took
oath 15 Nov. 1820; resided in U. S. since June 1818. Character test.: JASON MEADORS, JAMES TOLLAND & ELISHA ADAIR.

Roll #69: JOHN MC WILLIAMS, native of Ireland, petitioned and took
oath 15 Nov. 1820. Resided in Laurens Dist. for 15 years.

Roll #70: ROBERT ROSS, native of Ireland, resided in U. S. since 18
May 1818; in Laurens Dist. since December last. Filed and
took oath 16 Nov. 1820.

Roll #71: ALEXANDER AUSTIN, JR., native of Ireland, filed petition
and took oath 15 Nov. 1820. Arrived in Charleston Nov. 1805
and came to this district where he has since resided.

Roll #72: THOMAS QUINN, native of County of Sligo in Ireland, and
Parish of St. John's, arrived at Port of Charleston, S.
C. in 1817 from which place he removed to Chester Dist. and from thence
to Dist. of Laurens where he intended finally to settle himself; aged

Cont'd:
28 years. Filed notice of becoming a citizen on 16 December 1820.

Roll #73: SAMUEL AUSTIN petitioned for citizenship and gave notice
of his intention to become a citizen 18 Apr. 1821; a native
of County Antrim, Ireland, aged 60 years, a free white man.

Roll #74: FRANCIS TOURELL, a native of the City of Versailles in France
aged 51 years, born under the allegiance of Louis 18th,
filed 18 Apr. 1821 petition for denizeship and also notice of intention
to become a citizen of the U. S.

Roll #75: ALEXANDER AUSTIN, SR. petitioned for naturalization and
took oath 18 Apr. 1821. A native of Co. Antrim, Ireland.
Arrived in Charleston about 17 years ago. Immediately removed to this
district where he has ever since resided. Filed notice 14 Nov. 1815
of his intention and obtained from the Clerk of Court of Laurens Dist.
a certificate of same. Took oath 18 Apr. 1821.

Roll #76: ARCHIBALD CRAIG petitioned for denizenship 15 Apr. 1822;
a native of Scotland; arrived in Charleston, S. C. 15 June
1821, had family of wife and two children, viz: (1) JANE, aged 3 years
and 1 month; (2) JAMES 1 year and 11 months, born in Scotland; oath
taken 15 April 1822.

Roll #77: JOHN KENNEDY, a native of Ireland, petitioned to become
a denizen of the state of S. C. 17 Apr. 1822; had resided
in the U. S. since 10 Nov. 1819; oath taken 17 Apr. 1822.

Roll #78: ANDREW TODD, a native of Ireland, filed petition for naturalization 20 Nov. 1822; certificate drawn; resided in U. S.
and S. C. since Nov. 1816, certificate dated 19 Nov. 1817; sworn Nov.
21, 1822. Test.: WM. RANSON, AMBROSE HUDGENS, JR. & HENRY C. YOUNG.

Roll #79: ROBERTSON HAMILTON, born in County Tyrone, Ireland; age
26; free white man; petitioned to become a denizen and gave
notice for naturalization. Filed 19 Nov. 1822.

Roll #80: SAMUEL HAMILTON, a native of County Monaghan, Ireland, filed
petition and took oath 20 Nov. 1822; arrived in Charleston
about 26 Nov. 1816 and ever since resided in this state.

Roll #81: WILLIAM BAXTER, a native of County Antrim, Ireland; aged
26; free white man; petitioned and took oath 18 Nov. 1822.

Roll #82: ALEXANDER KIRKPATRICK, a native of Ireland, filed application 19 Nov. 1822. Took oath 12 Nov. 1822. Emigrated to
the U. S. in 1816 and has lived in the state and district nearly 6
years.

Roll #83: ROBERT BELL, a native of County of Londonderry, Ireland;
aged 28 years; had been a resident of this dist. about four
years and intended to continue a resident of this state. Oath taken
19 Nov. 1823; filed same date.

Roll #84: HUGH WILSON, a native of County Aire (Eire) in North Britain, born in 1778, about 45 years old (under King George
3rd); arrived in S. C. the month of October 1822 and intends settling
in Laurens Dist.; has wife JANNET, about 42 years of age; three children, viz: (1) WILLIAM, about 20 years; (2) JOHN, about 11; (3) HUGH
about 3 years; the whole of them were born in County of Air (Eire)
under the allegiance of the late King of Great Britain; except HUGH
who was born under allegiance of George IV and his wife JANNET who
was born in County of East Lothan in North Britain; arrived in S. C.
at the same time with the petitioner in Dist. of Laurens and has resided
in same state about a year. Oath 20 Nov. 1823. Filed 15 Nov. 1827.
Renunciation of allegiance to George IV, 15 Nov. 1827.

Roll #85: ANTHONY MC FAUL (MC FALL), a native of County Antrim, Ireland, aged about 26 years, arrived in U. S. the month of

Cont'd:
November 1811 and has ever since resided in this state. Certificate
od denizenship of this state dated Nov. 20, 1824. Oath taken 21 Nov.
1823.

Roll #86: JOHN CANNON, a native of County Dengal, Ireland, aged 21,
free white man, has been a resident of Laurens District
about 6 months, oath taken 19 Nov. 1823.

Roll #87: ANDREW MATTHEWS, a native of the City of Londonderry, Ireland; arrived in the City of Baltimore, Maryland Sept. 1818
and has since resided in the U. S.; in Nov. 1819 he removed to Columbia in this state and on 1 Apr. 1820, filed his petition in the Court
of Common Pleas for Richland District. Renunciation in Columbia 1 Apr.
1820. JAMES L. GUIGNARD, Clerk. Oath taken in Laurens Dist. 13 Nov.
1823.

Roll #88: ROBERT MONRO, 30 years of age, born in County of Rophair,
Scotland; has been a resident of this state about 5 years.
Took oath 19 Nov. 1823; filed his petition for denizenship and natural-
ization the same day.

Roll #89: WILLIAM MILLIGAN, a native of County Antrim, Ireland, a
free white man, aged 60 years; has been a resident of this
state near 20 years; oath taken 19 Nov. 1823; filed same day.

Roll #90: JOHN RANSON, a native of County of Monaghan, Ireland, resided in State of S. C. since 1 Dec. 1818; sworn in open
court, 14 Apr. 1824; filed petition same day.

Roll #91: PATRICK SYNNOTT, a native of Waxford, Ireland, aged 30,
a free white man, has been a resident of this state since
1821 and of this district since 1822. Oath and renunciation of allegiance 14 Apr. 1824. Filed petition same day.

Roll #92: WILLIAM RANSON, a native of County Monaghan, Ireland, aged
36, a free white man, a resident of this district since
1812. Oath and renunciation made 14 Apr. 1824.

Roll #93: JOHN ROSS, a native of County Monaghan, Ireland, has resided in the U. S. in S. C. since 20 Apr. 1823. Oath and
renunciation 15 Apr. 1824.

Roll #94: THOMAS KIRKPATRICK, a native of Londonderry, Ireland, aged
28; sailed from Belfast and arrived in S. C. in 1818 where
he has lived since that time and still intends to reside. Oath 19 Nov.
1824.

Roll #95: ANDREW KENNEDY and family - ANDREW KENNEDY, a native of
County Antrim, Ireland, aged 41, free white man; wife MRS.
ANN KENNEDY, aged 40 and born in same county. Three children: (1) CUN-
NINGHAM MOORE KENNEDY, born in Antrim, aged 17; (2) ISABELLA, aged
14, born in County of Meath, Ireland; (3) JOHN, aged 13, born in County
of Meath; arrived in Charleston from Belfast in October 1823 and has
resided in this district about 12 months. RICHARD GANTT, one of the
associate Judges stated that KENNEDY took oath 18 Nov. 1824.

Roll #96: PETER GALAHER, a native of County Leitrim, Ireland, aged
about 35 years; left Ireland June 1822 and arrived in Charleston 11 Sept. the following; filed petition 16 Nov. 1824.

Roll #97: WILLIAM GILCHRIST, a native of Scotland, about 23 years
old; arrived in Charleston 5 June 1821. Petition filed 19
Apr. 1825.

Roll #98: JOHN CAMPBELL, a native of County Antrim, Ireland, aged
35 years; embarked from Port Rush in North Ireland; had
been a resident of this district since 1820. Filed 20 Apr. 1825.

END OF PETITIONS

(Located at Society Hill,Darlington County, South Carolina)
In the year 1737, a party of immigrants from the Welch Tract in
the State of Delaware removed to Pee Dee River, South Carolina which
place they designated the Welch-Neck in rememberance of their former
residence. The following are the names of the individuals who composed
this party which was embodied into a church, viz:

PHILIP JAMES and his wife
ABEL JAMES and his wife
DANIEL JAMES and his wife
DANIEL DEVONALD and his wife
THOMAS EVANS and his wife
THOMAS EVANS, JR. and his wife
JOHN JONES and his wife
THOMAS HARRY and his wife

DAVID HARRY and his wife
JOHN HARRY and his wife
SAMUEL WILDS and his wife
SAMUEL EVANS and his wife
GRIFFITH JONES and his wife
DAVID JONES and his wife
THOMAS JONES and his wife

In January 1738, the above named persons was constituted a Church
under the style and title of the "Baptist Church of Christ at the Welch-
Neck." The following pages will disclose so much of the proceedings
of sd Church as have escaped the ravages of time. It is a subject of
regret that so much valuable information has been lost but as the de-
ficiency can be supplied by no human effort, the remainder should be
treasured with more care.

PHILIP JAMES, son of JAMES JAMES, Esq., was the first Pastor of this
Church. He was ordained 1742 and died 1753. Rev'd JOHN BROWN succeeded
Mr. JAMES but continued for a short time when Rev'd JOSHUA EDWARDS
was called to the pastoral office. He had the care of the Church six
years. Mr. EDWARDS was succeeded by the Rev'd ROBERT WILLIAMS, with
this we have some account of the transactions of the Church. The records previously have been lost. (end of page 1).

In 1759 March 12th a list of the Members was taken which is as follows:
PHILIP DOUGLASS (died Oct. 17, 1766)
ELIZABETH JAMES
HANNAH EVANS
MARTHA ROGERS
WM. FERREL &)
ANNE his wife) Apr. 2, 1743
BARBARAY MONOCHON (died June 19, 1761)
SAMUEL WILDS
JOHN EVANS
THOMAS EVANS (died Jn. 28, 1785)

DANIEL MONOCHON(died Apr. 30, 1785)
SARAH JAMES
SARAH BOWDRY (BOWDY?)
ELIZABETH WILDS
WILLIAM JAMES
GRIFFITH JOHN (died Aug. 1, 1765)
ABEL EVANS (died June ??)
PHILIP EVANS (died 5 Dec. 1771)
JAMES HARRY (Dismissed to Cashaway)
HANNAH HOWEL (died Oct. 1751)
SAMUEL REREDON
EDWARD JONES
JENKYN DAVID
ELEANOR EVANS (died Feb. 16, 1765)
MARGARET EVANS
ANNE JONES (now DOUGLASS)
    (died Apr. 12, 1766)
SARAH JAMES
MARY HOLLINGSWORTH
HOWEL JAMES
JOHN SUTTON
MARY PLATHRO (died Feb. 21, 1766)
JACOB D'SURRENCY

MARGARET JOHN
JAMES JAMES (died 21 Nov. 1769)
WILLIAM JONES (died July 2nd)
JOHN PERKINS (Dismissed 1778)
DAVID EVANS
VALENTINE HOLLINGSWORTH (died
    Aug. 6th)
ELIZABETH POWERS (died Oct. 1st)
SARAH MC DANIEL (died May 12,
    1744)
ELEANOR HARRY (Now JONES)
    (Died Apr. 20, 1745)
ABEL WILDS (died May 1781)
SAMUEL EVANS
MARY JONES (died Dec. 1751)
SARAH JAMES
___ JONES (now MC INTOSH) (died
    (Dec. 30th, 1764)
MARTHA ROACH (now EVANS)
SARAH JAMES
THOMAS JAMES
WALTER DOWNES
RACHEL DOWNES
SARAH BOOTH (now WILDS)
JANE POLAND (died Nov. 30, 1766)
NAOMI HARRY (now UNDERWOOD)
MARY EDWARDS
MARY WILDS
ELIZABETH EVANS
JAMES ROGERS
JOSHUA EDWARDS
CHARITY EDWARDS
THOMAS EDWARDS
SARAH EDWARDS

cont'd:

MARY CLEARY   ANN ROBLYRS?
     There were several other names to this list but so entirely de-
faced, that they could not be decyphered (end of page 2)
1759 April 5 Rev. Mr. NICHOLAS BEDGEGOOD of Charleston called. SAMUEL
REREDON suspended for obscene conversation. The Rev. Mr. JOHN BROWN
& SARAH his wife dismissed to Cashaway Church.

July 1 WILLIAM JAMES baptized & received into full communin. JACOB
D'SURRENCY suspended - absenting himself from worship. WALTER DOWNES
suspended - letter of admonition, etc.

Aug. 9 DAVID HARRY, SENR. died. Rev. Mr. WILLIAMS applied to absent
himself, etc.

Sept. 2 Letter sent to JOHN PERKINS "living at a distance from us"

Sept. 19 Departed the Life JOHN JONES (end of page 3)
1759 Oct. 6 ROBERT LLOYD & JOHN BOOTH baptized & admitted. Letter to
Rev. Mr. WILLIAMS. Three messengers were appointed (not named) to go
to Association to meet in Charleston Nov. 12th.

Dec. 14 SARAH KILLINGSWORTH died

Dec. 15 NICHOLAS ROGERS died
1760 Jan. 4th JAMES FINLEY died
Jan. 5th Messengers sent to Mr. WILLIAMS. Letter of admonition to JACOB
DE SURRENCY...

Feb. 2nd Mr. WILLIAMS refusing to receive the Letter a second time.
JOHN BOOTH publicly suspended.

March 8th RACHEL DAVID, wife of JENKYN DAVID, was baptized. Called
Mr. BEDGEGOOD as pastor, he accepted. Admitted a Member from Charleston
Church.

Mar. 26th VALENTINE HOLLINGSWORTH departed this life.

Apr. 15th JAMES JAMES suspended for beating his neighbor. Messengers
to ANNE WILLIAMS for absenting herself from church (end of page 4)

1760 June 1st Messengers sent to ANNE WILLIAMS and Mr. WILLIAMS. PHILIP
DOUGLASS ordered publicly suspended for drinking to excess and to the
public reproach of Religion. WILLIAM JAMES, JUNR. ordered to be publicly
suspended for the same crime.

July 5th Messengers failed to see Mr. WILLIAMS (to try again). Inquiry
directed to be made why ELEANOR the wife of ABEL EVANS doth not live
with her husband. Let Friday to be kept as a day of public prayer during the present public calamities and war. Ordered that every quarterly
meeting Deacons shall receive such donations as God shall be pleased
to influence the hearts of the Members to give. Letter to be sent to
Mr. WM. ROWEL and his wife living at the Congarees directing them to
apply for a Letter of dismission.

Aug. 2nd Church covenant adopted (end of page 5)
Aug. 2nd Church covenant continued. (Note in margin) "This covenant
was signed by the Pastor and the Church. We deem it unnecessary to
copy the names as they can be seen by referring to the original." (end
of page 6)

1760 Aug. 2nd THOMAS JONES was baptized and received full communion.
JOHN BOOTH asked to be restored.

Sept. 6th PHILIP DOUGLASS appeared before the Church and acknowledged
his sin.

Nov. 1st WILLIAM KILLINGSWORTH died.

Dec. 7th Messenger sent to Mr. and Mrs. WILLIAMS.

<u>1761</u> Jan. 4th Mr. WILLIAMS and his wife ejected Jan. 5th.

Jan. 9th HANNAH EVANS died.

Jan. 26 WILLIAM JAMES, Esq. and MARTHA ROGERS died.

Jan. 28 SARAH JAMES wife of WM. JAMES, Esq. died.

Jan. 30 DANIEL MONAHON died.

Jan. 31 JAMES JAMES who was suspended Apr. 5, 1760 was this day restored to his place. Messenger sent to JANE POLAND (absenting and selling liguor).

Feb. 11 ELIZABETH WILDS died (end of page 7).

<u>1761</u> Apr. 4 JANE POLAND suspended. JOHN BOOTH — repentence — to take his place tomorrow. MARTHA MARTIN received upon examination and recommendation. ELISHA JAMES baptized and received full communion. Messenger sent to JACOB D'SURRENCY.

May 2 ALEXANDER MC INTOSH and RODERICK MC IVER Members of the Church of Scotland received on confession of faith etc. (end of page 8).

<u>1761</u> May 2 PHILIP HOWEL publicly suspended on Sabbath May 3rd

June 6 Messenger again to JACOB DE SURRENCY. JAMES HARRY suspended (drinking).

June 19 BARBARA MONAGHON died.

July 4 JACOB DE SURRENCY made confession — but remained under suspension.

Aug. 1 ELIZABETH SIMONSON (formerly JAMES) was suspended under suspicion of her having been guilty of very abusive language.

Sept. 6 ELIZABETH SIMONSON's case found not so bad as represented — suspension taken off. JAMS HARRY again received. JOSHUA EDWARDS publicly suspended. ROBERT EDWARDS residing at Cape Fear made application for a letter of dismission, which was granted him. JAMES HARRY, MARY HARRY and ELIZABETH WILDS (the wife of GEORGE) residing near the Church at Cashaway, requested a letter of dismission; which was granted. ABEL EDWARDS received from Cashaway by letter. (end of page 9).

<u>1761</u> Oct. 3 WILLIAM THOMAS and wife and JOHN BOWEN received by Letters from Church at Cashaway.

Dec. 24 HANNAH HOWEL died.

<u>1762</u> Jan. 2 Mr. WILLIAMS (under excommunication) made application to the Association in Charleston, etc. DAVID & MARTHA EVANS guilty of criminal conversation before marriage — suspended. Messenger to JACOB DE SURRENCY.

Feb. 6 Mr. WILLIAMS refuses to comply etc. Messenger to JACOB DE SURRENCY. Messenger to PHILIP HOWEL, and one to WALTER DOWNES. SARAH HICKS received by letter from Cashaway Church.

Mar. 6 PHILIP HOWEL admonished for his faults.

Apr. 3 A messenger of care sent to WILLIAM JAMES under suspension. Another sent to JACOB DE SURRENCY. Same to DAVID EVANS and to MARTHA EVANS. (end of page 10).

<u>1762</u> May 1 GEORGE HICKS and MARY WHITE were baptized. MARTHA EVANS repented, admitted to communion. JACOB DE SURRENCY was again sent to.

June 5 WILLIAM JAMES professing repentance was restored. GEORGE HICKS & MARY WHITE baptized May 1st received the right hand of fellowship. Aug. 1 MARY HICKS was baptized 31st July.

Sept. 4 TABITHA JAMES was baptized. Complaint against WILLIAM JONES for drinking excess. Messenger to JANE POLAND and to GRIFFITH JOHN for non-attendance.

Oct. 2 LYDIA EUSTICE was baptized. ELIZABETH COUNSEL examined (was formerly baptized in No. Carolina) and received. MARTHA FAOX(?) received by letter from Catfish.

1763 Feb. DAVID EVANS restored to Communion. WILLIAM JONES publicly suspended.

Mar. 5 SUSANNAH YOUNG was baptized.

June 4 ELIZABETH SIMONSON suspended (lives in wilful separation from her husband).

JulY 2 ROBERT HICKS baptized.

1764 Sept. 1 Mr. WILLIAM JAMES suspended (drunkenness). Mr. WILLIAM JONES restored. ELIZABETH SIMONSON restored.

1764 Nov. 15 Mrs. MARY WHITE died.

Dec. 30 Mrs. JANE MC INTOSH died. (end of page 11).

1765 Feb. 16 Concluded public suspension not to be practiced in this Church. ROBERT HICKS died Feb. 12th. Mrs. ELEANOR EVANS died Feb. 16th.

Mar. 2 Mr. WILLIAM THOMAS suspended (drunkeness). Mrs. POLAND restored. Rev. Mr. BEDGEGOOD Letter of Dismission to Church in Charleston.

May 4 Miss HANNAH SUTTON baptized by Rev. Mr. OLIVER HART. Mr. PUGH appointed to write a letter to Mr. PHILIP HOWEL to come to the Church. Also to go to Mr. JOSHUA EDWARDS and to Mr. WILLIAM THOMAS to admonish them. Mr. JOHN BOOTH died Mar. 9th.

June 1 Mr. JOSHUA EDWARDS restored to his place.

July 6 Mr. WILLIAM THOMAS restored to his place.

Aug. 3 Call to Rev'd Mr. HART in Charleston come and be minister. GRIF-FITH JOHN died.

Oct. 5 ABEL WILDS messenger to JACOB DE SURRENCY & WILLIAM JAMES. SAMUEL WILDS messenger to Mrs. COX. Other names - PHILIP HOWEL, Mr. PUGH, THOMAS EVANS, SAMUEL EVANS, Mrs. MARTIN, DAVID EVANS. Mr. PUGH messenger to the Association.

Dec. 17 Rev'd Mr. HART declined to accept the call of the Church. Mrs. COX appeared and was acquited.

1766 Jan. 4 Rev'd Mr. PUGH became the Church's Pastor.

Feb. 21 Mrs. MARY PRETHRO died.

Apr. 12 Mrs. ANNE DOUGLASS died. (end of page 12).

1766 July 5 DAVID BALDY & SARAH his wife received from Catfish. WILLIAM & MARY THOMAS dismissed by Letter.

Oct. 4 PHILIP HOWEL & WILLIAM JAMES excommunicated. Rev'd PUGH apapoint-ed messenger. Rev. BEDGEGOOD dismissed by Letter. His dismission began "The Church of Christ" in the Welch-Neck on Pee-Dee. (Rev'd Mr. NICHOLAS BEDGOOD).

Oct. 17 PHILIP DOUGLASS died.

1767 Dec. 6 Letter of Dismission (another for Rev. BEDGGOOD). Mr. PUGH asked to leave.

Mar. 7 Mr. BEDGGOOD recalled and accepted.

Apr. 12 Mr. BEDGGOOD returned to Church.

(Nothing of genealogical note until)

Oct. 3 AGNES MC LEMORE presented Letter from Catfish.

Oct. 4 AGNES MC LEMORE admitted.

Oct. 17 JAMES ROGERS complaint aagainst MARTHA MARTIN. WALTER DOWNS a messenger. JOHN ABRAM received from Catfish.

1768 Jan. 2 Mrs. MARTIN's case postponed.

Apr. 16 WALTER DOWNS & DAVID EVANS suspended. (end of page 15).

Apr. 16 JAMES JAMES & THOMAS JONES have a difference, arbitrators appointed were THOMAS JAMES, HOWEL JAMES & THOMAS EVANS. Mr. DANIEL DEVONALD gave deed of Fit (gift?) of 2 acres of land whereon the Church is situated. JHN SUTTON & ABEL EDWARDS were appointed Trustees.

May 1 ____ BROWN received by Letter from North Carolina. ANNE ROLLYN died.

June 4 WALTER DOWNES still suspended. Messengers to Mrs. CLAY and Mrs. CHARITY EDWARDS.

Sept. MARTHA MARTIN suspended.

Oct. Messengers to THOMAS EDWARDS & DAVID BALDY.

1769 May 6 THOMAS EDWARDS reply. Examined D. BALDY. Messengers to ABEL EDWARDS & THOMAS EDWARDS.

1770 Oct. 13 THOMAS EDWARDS & SARAH his wife dismissed to Catfish. Messengers to SARAH BALDY & WALTER DOWNES. (end of page 15)

Nov. 3 S. BALDY appeared.

1774 Feb. 1 Rev. Mr. BEDGOOD died. 15 years after first coming to Church and 7 years after 2nd call.

Sept. 3 THOMAS SHIRLEY & wife MARTHA and JANE HEWSTESS received by Church and baptized by Mr. PUGH Minister at Cashaway.

Oct. 1 WILLIAM EDWARDS, JR. & his wife CATHERINE & ELIZABETH EVANS received and baptized by Mr. PUGH. JOHN DAVID, JOHN PLEDGER, THOMAS HARRY, SARAH EDWARDS same as above. DAVID ROACH & JOHN EVANS, JR. same as above. The above account of members added after death of Rev. BEDGGOOD until successor Rev. ELKANON WINCHESTER came. (end of page 16).

A list of the Members of the Church 1775 - 1778

1.	ELHANAN WINCHESTER, Pastor	16.	GRESSEBE? JOHNSON
2.	JOHN EDWARDS	17.	ABEL EVANS
3.	ABEL EDWARDS	18.	BENJAMIN JAMES
4.	AARON PEARSON	19.	WALTER DOWNES
5.	MAGNIS CARGILL	20.	CHARLES LOWTHER
6.	MOSES PEARSON	21.	JOSIAH PEARCE
7.	JOSEPH LUKE	22.	SAMPSON THOMAS
8.	WILLIAM LANG	23.	DANIEL MC DANIEL
9.	JOHN WILLIAMS	24.	ROBERT WHITE
10.	WILLIAM JONES	25.	JOHN STINSON
11.	JOHN HUGHES	26.	WELCOME HODGES
12.	OBEDIAH HEDSON	27.	GIDEON PARISH
13.	AMOS PILGRIM	28.	JOHN DOWNS
14.	WILLIAM MASON	29.	WILLIAM HEWSON
15.	DANIEL SPARKS	30.	JOHN STEVENS

Members List cont'd:

31.	JOSEPH MASON	92.	WINIFORD PEARSON
32.	WILLIAM JAMES	93.	ANNE HARGROVE
33.	MATTHEW GRIFFITH	94.	MAHETABEL IRBY
34.	ENOCH EVANS, JUNR.	95.	ANNE CLEARY
35.	WILLIAM CHERRY	96.	EDDY JOHNSON
36.	ALEXANDER WALDEN	97.	SARAH FOSTER
37.	JOSEPH PLEDGER	98.	MARY HUDSON
38.	JOHN CHAMBLISS	99.	PEGGY DARBY
39.	HALL HUDSON	100.	TABITHA WILLIAMSON
40.	ABEL KALB	101.	(no name)
41.	JEREMIAH BROWN	102.	ELIZABETH LUKE
42.	MATTHEW HEWSTESS	103.	MARTHA MC NATT
43.	JOHN HEWSTESS	104.	CHARITY HURD
44.	WILLIAM HEWSTESS	105.	ELIZABETH HODGES
45.	JAMES HEWSTESS	106.	SARAH PLEDGER
46.	THOMAS AYER	107.	SARAH DOWNS
47.	HEWRY SPARKS	108.	ANN PEGGY AYER
48.	BURREL HUGGINS	109.	FERIBE LANG
49.	CHARLES MASON	110.	ELIZABETH LIDE
50.	OWEN DARBY	111.	DEBORAH GEER
51.	ARNOLD COLVIN	112.	ELIZABETH HICKS
52.	MICHAEL FITZGERALD	113.	MARTHA PEARCE now SPARKS
53.	SHADRACK FULLER	114.	ELIZABETH SUTTON
54.	GEORGE TRAWELKS?	115.	ELIZABETH THOMAS
55.	PAUL BALDY	116.	ANNE LOWTHA
56.	EVANDER MC IVER	117.	MARTHA LAMPLEY
57.	ROBERT HODGES	118.	HANNAH KIMBROUGH
58.	JOHN HODGES	119.	SARAH STEWARD
59.	THOMAS EVANS, JUNR.	120.	SARAH EVANS
60.	JOEL MC NAT	121.	CATHARINE ROSS
61.	TRISTAN THOMAS	122.	SARAH STUBBS
62.	WILLIAM LUKE	123.	SARAH WALDON
63.	JOSIAH JAMES	124.	SARAH JAMES
64.	ABEL GOODWIN	125.	ELIZABETH COUNSEL
65.	JOHN EDMUNSON	126.	AGNES CREELE?
66.	ENOCH EVANS, SENR.	127.	ELIZABETH PLEDGER
67.	RUTH ASKEW	128.	MARY COOPER
68.	ELIZABETH PILGRIM	129.	MARY WALSH
69.	MARTHA EVANS	130.	ELIZABETH WALSH
70.	ALICE LUCAS	131.	ANNE STEVENS
71.	RACHAEL PEARSON	132.	MARY EVANS
72.	MARY WILDS	133.	ZILPHAH WALSH
73.	MARY HOLLINGSWORTH	134.	LYDIA HOWEL
74.	MARY ANDREWS	135.	MARTHA WILSON
75.	SARAH HICKS	136.	MARY WILDS
76.	SARAH JAMES	137.	SARAH FEARSON
77.	MARGARET JAMES	138.	SARAH LOCK
78.	ANNE TERREL	139.	RHODA BOOTH
79.	SARAH WILDS	140.	MARY COX
80.	RACHEL DAVID	141.	MARY PEARCE now THOMAS
81.	RUTH WRIGHT	142.	NANCY WILLIAMSON
82.	MARY JONES	143.	SUSANNAH BINGHAM
83.	MARY TERREL	144.	ELIZABETH HEWSON
84.	SARAH LANG	145.	PHEBE PLEDGER
85.	SARAH POUNCEY	146.	REBECCA SCOTT
86.	MARY CHAMBLESS	147.	SEDONA UNTHEGREVE?
87.	REBECCA JAMES	148.	CELIA JAMES
88.	MARY EVANS	149.	CELETE MORGAN
89.	SARAH HEWSTESS	150.	MARY EVANS
90.	ELIZABETH FLENEGALD	151.	MARY GRIFFITHS
91.	SARAH WINCHESTER	152.	ELIZABETH MASON
153.	MARY VANN	154.	MARY ANNE FITZGERALD
155.	EDDY STINSON	156.	RACHEL GROVES
157.	ELIZABETH LUKE	158.	LYDIA EVANS
159.	SARAH KOLB	160.	CELETE LUKE
161.	ISABEL DAVID	162.	ELEANOR HEWSTESS
163.	ANNE LAMPLEY	164.	HONOR DARBY

Members List cont'd:
165. COMFORT PEARSON
166. ELEANOR HUDSON
167. LYDIA TREWEEKS?
168. ELIZABETH MEDFORD
169. ANNE ROACH
170. SUSANNAH LAMPLEY
171. MARY LIDE
172. AGNES HEWSTESS
173. ELIZABETH RABURN
174. SARAH CHERRY
175. BIBBE BRUCE
176. MARY HUGGINS
177. CATY MC IVER
178. GRACE BROWN
179. ANNE BALDY
180. NANCY BROWN

181. ELIZABETH AYER
182. SARAH HORRY (HARRY?)
183. SARAH RABURN
184. REBEKAH HODGES
185. ELIZABETH EVANS
186. MARTHA MC NATT
187. ANNE POLAND
188. BETSEY HICKS
189. ANNE EVANS
190. ELIZABETH JAMES
191. SARAH MUMFORD
192. MARY HARPER
193. FERIBE LANG
194. MARY IVY
195. ANNE BROWN
196. SARAH MC IVER
197. JAMIMAH BRUCE

(end of page 18)

1775 Mar. 12 Call to Mr. ELHANAN WINCHESTER to be Minister. He came from Bellingham - Letter signed by NOAH ALDEN, Pastor Aug. 14, 1775.

1776 Nov. 2 JOHN GEER received and baptized.

Dec. 1 Baptized the widow REBECCA JAMES having been examined and received the day before.

1777 Apr. 6 TABITHA JAMES wife of WILLIAM JAMES died.

May 3 1. JAMES CROCKER received. 2. Mrs. ANNE LIDE received. 3. JOSHUA TERREL admitted a member. 4. ELIZABETH TERREL also received. 5. Minister accepts call for another year. 6. Minister to go to the Hill (Cheraws) once in 3 Sundays. (end of page 20).

1777 May 3 WILLIAM JAMES guilty of drunkeness.

May 4 SARAH WINCHESTER and 1-4 above baptized.

May 18 1. JOHN PLEDGER received (baptized before). 2. JOHN BOWEN excluded for drinking. 3. WALTER DOWNS excluded for drinking.

May 31 Mr. ABEL EDWARDS & Mr. WILLIAM TERREL, JUNR. chosen deacons. ELIZABETH MASSY received. SARAH SPARKS & MARTHA EDWARDS received.

June 1 (Baptized 3 ladies above).

June 8 Baptized JOHN HUGHES & OBADIAH HUDSON.

June 15 Baptized DANIEL SPARKS, MOSES PEARSON, AMOS PILGRIM, MARY TERREL & ELIZABETH PILGRIM.

June 22 Baptized MAGNUS CARGILL, JOSEPH LUKE, WILLIAM MASON, JAMES BROWN, MARY JONES & RUTH WRIGHT.

June 29 AARON PEARSON & WINIFORD his wife and RACHEL the wife of MOSES PEARSON were baptized.

1777 July 3 Died much lamented, Mrs. SARAH WINCHESTER.

July 5 (Those lately baptized received to Communion).

July 6 JOHN EDWARDS, RUTH ASKEW & SARAH LANG examined and baptized.

Oct. 10 JAMES BROWN going home to New England - received letter of recommendation and dismissed.

Oct. 18 WILLIAM LANG examined - baptized on 19th by the Rev'd Mr. FURMAN.

Nov. 1 JOHN EDWARDS, JOHN WILLIAMS, ELIZABETH PILGRIME & RUTH ASKEW

Cont'd:
received to full communion. Call to Rev. Mr. FURMAN at the High Hills
of Santee. Letter written by Mr. JENKYN DAVID & Mr. ABEL WILDS. Mr.
WILDS & Mr. WINCHESTER (to ill to remain pastor) to be messengers to
carry letter and to "entreat in our favor."

Dec. 6 Letter withdrawn. WILLIAM MASON received into full communion
(already baptized).

1778 Jan. 3 GRESSET JOHNSON & SARAH POUNCEY examined. Call to Mr. GANO.

Jan. 5 GRESSET JOHNSON, SARAH POUNCEY & MARY CHAMBLESS baptized and
received with MARY TERREL & SARAH LANG. (end of page 22).

Feb. 5 Died Mrs. MARY EDWARDS.

Feb. 28 AMOS PILGRIM & ELIZABETH his wife moving - dismissed.

Mar. 15 SARAH WINCHESTER baptized (he must have married another SARAH).

Mar. 20 Col. HICKS Moderator, Mr. WINCHESTER called for another year.

List of Members, April 5, 1778

1.	ELHANAN WINCHESTER, Pastor	43.	SARAH WINCHESTER
2.	Col. GEORGE HICKS, Deacon	44.	SARAH HICKS
3.	ABEL WILDS, Deacon	45.	MARY WILDS
4.	ABEL EDWARDS, Deacon	46.	SARAH EDWARDS
5.	WILLIAM TERREL, JUNR., Deacon	47.	ELIZABETH TERREL
6.	JENKYN DAVID	48.	RACHEL DAVID
7.	WILLIAM TERREL, SENR.	49.	ANNE TERREL
8.	THOMAS JAMES	50.	SARAH JAMES
9.	THOMAS EVANS	51.	MARGARET EVANS
10.	JOHN EVANS	52.	ELIZABETH EVANS
11.	JOSIAH EVANS	53.	MARY EVANS
12.	THOMAS SHIRLEY	54.	MARTHA SHIRLEY
13.	EDWARD JONES	55.	MARY JONES
14.	WILLIAM EDWARDS	56.	CATHARINE EDWARDS
15.	MAC KEY MC NATT	57.	DINAH MC NATT
16.	JOSHUA TERREL	58.	MARY TERREL
17.	DANIEL SPARKS	59.	SARAH SPARKS
18.	AARON PEARSON	60.	WINIFRED PEARSON
19.	MOSES PEARSON	61.	RACHEL PEARSON
20.	JOHN EDWARDS	62.	MARTHA EDWARDS
21.	MAGNUS CARGILL	63.	SARAH CARGILL
22.	JOHN HUGHES	64.	ANNE HUGHES
23.	JOHN PLEDGER	65.	MARY ANDREWS
24.	JOSEPH LUKE	66.	SARAH HEWSTESS
25.	JOHN GEER	67.	ANNE HEWSTESS
26.	JOHN WILDS	68.	ANNE CLEARY
27.	DAVID ROACH	69.	ANNE LIDE
28.	JAMES CROCKER	70.	ELIZABETH MASSEY
29.	JOHN WILLIAMS	71.	SARAH LANG
30.	JOHN EVANS, JR.	72.	MARY HOLLINGSWORTH
31.	JOHN DAVID	73.	ELIZABETH SIMONSON
32.	WILLIAM LANG	74.	ELIZABETH COUNSEL
33.	ABEL EVANS	75.	ELIZABETH FLENEGAL
34.	WILLIAM JONES	76.	MARTHA EVANS
35.	GRESSET JOHNSON	77.	SARAH WILDS
36.	CHARLES LOWTHER	78.	ALICE LUCAS
37.	JAMES ROGERS	79.	AGNES CREELE
38.	EDWARD GILLMAN	80.	REBECCA JAMES
39.	JOHN ABRAM, Esq.	81.	RUTH ASKEW
40.	WILLIAM MASON	82.	RUTH WRIGHT
41.	THOMAS HARRY	83.	MARY EVANS
42.	OBADIAH HUDSON	84.	MARY CHAMBLESS

1778 Apr. 20 Died Mrs. ELIZABETH SIMONSON. She was formerly the wife
of the Rev. Mr. JAMES, first Minister of this Church. (end of p 23)

1778 May ANNE HARGROVE, baptized and received.

June 7 MAHITABLE IRBY recieved by Letter from Cashaway Church. SARAH PLEDGER (wife of JOHN) and EDDY JOHNSON (wife of GRESSET JOHNSON) baptized.

Sept. 26 Mrs. SARAH WILDS died.

Oct. 31 Brother THOMAS SHIRLEY & wife MARTHA dismissed.

Dec. 5 BENJAMIN JAMES and JANE his wife brought Letter from Cashaway Church. Received as members.

(Compiled by Virginia Terry, from microfilm at the Historical Commission Southern Baptist Convention, Nashville, TN. Pub. No. 305)

The act of incorporation, passed March 17, 1785, names the "Baptist Church at the Welsh-Neck on Peedee River," with no hint, of course, of how far its influence ranged beyond the Welsh Neck. Its ministers preached or assisted weak congregrations up and down the river; its people left it to aid in forming other Baptist groups; its descendants covered the Peedee section with such churches as Catfish, Mars Bluff, Cashaway, Beauty Spot, Lynches Creek, Cheraw Hill and many others. These were separated from Welsh Neck to form new organizations which in turn developed branches in different directions; other churches of the Peedee were connected with it only by the slender bonds of tradition or of pastoral aid; while still others were sporadic growths with no apparent relation to any of the Welsh Neck group. ("South Carolina Baptists 1670 - 1805")

END OF WELCH(WELSH) NECK RECORDS

1811, 1814 & 1824 MARION DISTRICT, S.C., TAX LISTS

AYERS, DERIOUS	$ .58	BURCH, EDWARD	$9.82
ADAMS, ELIAS	.18	BROWN, JEREMIAH	5.73
ANDREW, BENNET	.23	BARTELL, MARY	.90
ALLEN, ELIAS	.17	BLACKWELL, JACOB	.80
ABBOT, HOLLOWAY Est.	.60	BASS, BRYAN	.35
ADAMS, ABNER	1.21	BRASSWELL, RICHARD	.10
ALLIN, MATTHEW	.32	BASS, JETHRO	.35
ALLIN, JOHN	.30	BRASSWELL, TOBIAS	.90
ALSOBROOK, WILLIAM	2.10	BRASSWELL, HENRY	.18
AVANT, THOMAS	3.91	BETHEA, PHILIP	6.21
ALKIESON, JESSE	.15	GEORGE FEAWELLS Est.	.41
ANDREWS, JOEL	.30	BRICE, WILLIAM	.57
AVANT, LEVY	.14	Ditto for DL. MC NEILL	.15
AMMONS, JOSHUA	.80	BLACKMAN, SOLOMON	.80
ALTMAN, JOHN	.20	BLACKMAN, DAVID	.80
AVANT, FRANCIS	1.10	BAILEY, WILLIAM	.80
ALTMAN, WILLIAM	.60	BAILEY, JAMES	.90
AVANT, JOSHUA	3.75	BRADY, JOHN	2.60
AVANT, ABRAHAM	6.70	BERRY, HENRY	3.10
AVANT, WILLIAM	1.50	BAILEY, JONAS	.40
ABBOT, CALEB	.70	BETHEA, JESSE	2.42
ALLIN, WILLIAM	3.41	BETHEA, GOODMAN Est.	2.51
ALLIN, SAMUEL	.12	BETHEA, ELISHA	.76
ALLIN, BENNET	.12	BETHEA, JOHN P(?)	11.89
ALLEN, RICHARD	2.21	BASS, JOSEPH	.60
AMMONS, THOMAS	.13	BASS, JOSEPH Est.	4.93
ALLIN, DRURY	.90	BARFIELD, ELISHA	.19
ANDERSON, CLAIBORN	.23	BUTLER, WILLIAM	.80
ALISON, H. JAMES	5.68	BERRY, ANDREW, JR.	.30
BETHEA, JOHN Estate	4.54	BERRY, ANDREW, SR.	.35
BOLDWRIGHT, DANIEL	3.39	BARFIELD, BARROT	.20
BRYAN, TURNER	.77	BURNS, JAMES	.14
BURCH, JOSEPH	9.21	BERRY, STEPHEN	.09
BENNET, JOHN Jr.	.87	BARFOOT, NOAH	.50
BIGHAM, JAMES	.69	BARNES, CHARLES	.24

BECKWORTH, HENRY	$ .15	CRAWFORD, HARDY Est.	$1.75
BIGHAM, WILLIAM	.77	CLARK, GEORGE	.90
BURNET, JOHN SR.	3.12	CARMICHAEL, DUNCAN	1.56
BLACKMAN, JOHN	.80	CARMICHAEL, DUGAL JR.	1.21
BETHUNE, FARQUHARD	.12	CUSACK, JOSEPH	4.80
BIGHAM, DAVID	.14	CUSACK, ADAM	1.35
Ditto for Est. SETH STAFFORD	.70	COOPER, LEVI	.37
Ditto for Est. DL. BARE	1.75	CAMPBELL, JAMES	5.40
Ditto Ditto Ditto	.12	Ditto Ditto	.17
BIGHAM, JOHN	1.56	Ditto for TABITHA A. M. STEWART	.35
Ditto Ditto	.50	Ditto for Ditto Ditto	.30
BIGHAM, SAMUEL	.70	CAMPBELL, ANN	.12
BRUCE, BENJAMIN	1.60	CRIBB, ELIZABETH	.10
BROWN, D. JAMES	1.50	COLEMAN, JOHN	.33
BIRD, ELIZABETH	.60	COX, JUDITH	1.63
BIRD, MALICHI	.38	CALCOT, SAMUEL C.	.35
BEVERLY, DAVID	.50	COX, WILLIAM	5.83
BAKER, WILLIAM JR.	7.65	CRAWFORD, JAMES SR.	10.38
BARNES, CHRISTIAN	.40	COLEMAN, GRIFFIN	.38
BAXLEY, THOMAS	.13	COOK, MATTHEW	.20
BATH, DANIEL	.18	COLLINS, JONAH	.13
BOLDRIGHT, THOMAS Est.	1.70	CARMICHAEL, DANIEL SR.	.12
BAXLEY, BARNABAS	.50	CAMPBELL, PETER	3.00
BROWN, EDWARD	1.10	CARMICHAEL, JOHN	.70
BRYAN, JAMES	.17	CARMICHAEL, B. JOHN	.45
BARTELL, JESSE	1.52	CAMPBELL, EDWARD	1.50
BOLDRIGHT, WILLIAM	1.49	CAMPBELL, ARCHIBALD	.17
BROWN, THOMAS	.50	COWARD, BURRELL	.41
BUTLER, NATHAN	.80	CARMICHAEL, NEILL	.38
BROWN, WILLIAM	.30	CARMICHAEL, DOUGALD C.	.26
BROWN, STEPHEN	.25	CARMICHAEL, DUNCAN, JR.	.98
BAKER, WILLIAM SR.	7.26	CARMICHAEL, DUGAL SR.	1.91
BROWN, JOSHUA	.10	COOPER, THOMAS	.47
BLANCHARD, HENRY	.60	CARMICHAEL, ARCHIBALD	.27
BAKER, JOHN	2.45	CARMICHAEL, NEILL Est.	3.22
Ditto for Est. JOHN JACKSON	2.92	COLEMAN, ROBERT	1.69
BUTLER, WILLIAM	.40	COCKFIELD, JOSIAH	1.75
BARFIELD, ROGER	.30	Ditto Ditto	.11
BARFIELD, WILLIAM	.30	COOPER, JOHN	2.62
BREWER, ASA	.11	COOPER, JEHU W.	.35
BUTLER, JOHN	.60	CARTER, JOSIAH Est.	1.63
BUTLER, STEPHEN	.40	Ditto for WM. KEITH	.60
BAFIELD, ARCHIBALD	.30	CUMMINGS, DAVID	.11
BREWER, NEEDHAM	.50	COWARD, EPHRAIM	.41
BENNET, MARY	.90	CALCOT, JAMES	.79
BREWER, DAVID	.14	CHANCE, ELIZABETH	.90
BRITTON, THOMAS G.	4.55	COX, GEORGE	2.86
BELLUNE, JAMES C.	3.85	CAMPBELL, DUNCAN	1.42
BELLUNE, WILLIAM	4.38	DAVIS, JOSEPH	12.48
BELLUNE, WILLIAM G.	12.70	DAVIS, HENRY SR.	10.54
BUTLER, LUCRETIA	.90	DAVIS, DANIEL	.93
BRADLEY, JOHN	2.18	DEW, CHRISTOPHER	3.90
BAILEY, CHRISTOPHER	.40	Ditto Est. LEVI GIBSON	1.20
BULLARD, ROBERT	.90	DEW, JOHN	.34
BETHEA, WILLIAM	.35	DAVIS, HENRY JR.	11.50
BULLARD, WILLIAM	.90	DAVIS, NIMROD	7.70
BRYAN, WILLIAM	.16	DOZER, BENJAMIN	.70
BETHEA, WILLIAM SR.	3.77	DOZER, WILLIAM	.20
BASS, JOHN	.35	DAVIS, JOHN	1.28
BIRD, ARTHUR	3.86	DAVIS, HENRY M.	1.26
CLARK, JOSEPH	.20	DOZER, JAMES	.32
COWARD, LEWIS	1.17	DUE, JOHN	.20
CLARK, MALCOLM	1.54	DONNELLY, ANN W.	1.87
CROSBY, THOMAS	.65	DOZER, ELIAS	1.52
COLLINS, THOMAS	.70	Ditto for WM. PALMER	.60
CRAWFORD, STEPHEN	1.55	DAVIS, WM. JR.	2.67
CRAWFORD, GADI	2.17	DAVIS, FRANCIS	4.48
COWARD, WILSON	.52	DAVIS, MARY	3.89
CASE, JOHN Est.	.70	DAVIS, DAVID	1.90
CRAWFORD, JAMES G.	1.40	Ditto Ditto	1.24

DAVIS, PHILIP	$1.31	FINKLEA, JOHN SR.	$ .24
DAVIS, JOHN C.	14.34	FLINT, THOMAS	.67
DILLON, JOSHUA	.60	GRICE, WILLIAM	.51
DRIGGINS, ISAAC	.50	GALE, JAMES	.80
DRIGGINS, EPHRAIM	.10	GOODYEAR, WILLIAM	.76
DUKES, KEITON	.80	GRICE, THOMAS	2.49
DAVIS, ZABON	.50	GODBOLD, THOMAS JR.	13.53
DEES, MALICHI	.18	GODBOLD, ABRAHAM	3.15
DANIEL, EZEKEL	.12	GARRAWAY, ROBERT	.28
DEWIT, CHARLES	.57	GALE, SOLOMON	.15
DAVIS, WM. SR.	11.45	GRAVES, JOHN	.21
ditto ditto	.80	GREGG, ROBERT	3.42
DRIGGERS, THOMAS	2.30	Est. WM. ORR	11.41
DEES, MALICHI	.30	GREGG, WILLIAM	5.65
DRIGGERS, ELIZABETH	2.00	GREGG, ROBERT	4.66
DILLIN, WILLIAM	.60	GREGG, JAMES	.40
DAVIS, SAMUEL	.80	GREGG, ALEXR. JR.	4.37
DEWIT, JAMES	.13	GASQUE, JOHN	1.50
DEES, ARTHUR	1.12	GASQUE, ARCHIBALD	.35
DANIEL, JOHN	.40	GODBOLD, THOMAS SR.	2.97
DAVIS, BENJAMIN SR.	11.39	GRICE, WILLIAM B.	.47
DEALE, JAMES	.30	GASQUE, ABSOLEM	.60
DAVIS, DANIEL	.70	GASQUE, HENRY	1.23
DAVIS, BENJAMIN JR.	1.75	GASQUE, SAMUEL	.50
DOZER, ANN	3.15	GODBOLD, DAVID	1.58
EAGERTON, WM. JR.	1.80	GODBOLD, THOS. son of THOS.	.97
EDWARDS, RICHARD	4.60	GODBOLD, STEPHEN	5.68
EVANS, THOMAS	.40	GREEN, UNITY	.60
EDWARDS, SAMUEL	2.99	GADDY, ITHAMER	.30
EAGERTON, GEORGE	.23	GREAVES, BENNET	7.21
EAGERTON, WILLIAM	.63	ditto Est. FRANCES ALISON	5.71
EAGERTON, DOROTHY	.35	GREAVES, WILLIAM H.	5.62
EXUM, ROBERT	1.40	GREAVES, JOSEPH	4.50
EWIN, HUGH	11.83	GREGG, ALEXANDER JR.	3.50
EADDY, HENRY	3.83	GREGG, JOHN	5.69
ditto ditto	.82	ditto Est. IS. HUDSON	4.35
EADDY, SAMUEL	.40	GARDENER, JOHN	.35
EXUM, WILLIAM	1.43	GARDENER, STEPHEN	1.20
ERVIN, JAMES R.	2.83	GRICE, JACOB	1.96
ERVIN, JOHN Est.	.66	GLAWN, ELIZABETH	.37
EXUM, DELILAH	.35	GRAVES, HARDY	.24
EXUM, BENJAMIN	2.19	GREGG, WILLIAM JR.	1.90
FINKLEA, THOMAS	.90	GREAVES, SARAH	1.46
FORD, JESSE	.44	GREAVES, FRANCES	5.57
FORD, PRESERVED	4.76	GREGG, JOSEPH	6.52
FORD, JOHN	1.80	GIBSON, JOHN	16.49
FORD, JOSEPH	2.34	ditto ditto	8.44
FORE, RICHARD	.80	ANN ROE & CAROLINE BALLARD	6.80
FINKLEA, JOHN	2.62	JOHN MIDDLETON	.73
FORE, MARY for Est. of WM.		GODFREY, RICHARD	10.75
HAZELDEN	1.54	ditto for WM. GODFREY	1.47
FOXWORTH, HENRY	2.34	HOOKS, DORCAS	.26
FLOWERS, RACHEL	.70	HAYS, JAMES	.30
FLOWERS, BENNET	.93	HAYS, WILLIAM	1.46
FOWLER, WILLIAM	.70	HAYS, NEWTON	.60
FOXWORTH, ABEL	.57	HODGES, WILLIAM	.30
FOXWORTH, JOHN	.50	HAYS, DRURY	.90
ditto Est. THO. TURBEVILLE		HUGGINS, JOHN	.33
FLOWERS, ANN	.57	HULAN, THOMAS	.23
FOXWORTH, STEPHEN	.48	HARELSON, RUTH	.41
FOXWORTH, ABSOLEM	1.52	HAYS, JOSEPH	.76
FORD, GEORGE	2.98	HERRON, ANTHONY	.21
FOXWORTH, JOB	3.91	HILL, WILLIAM	.53
FORD, MARY	.23	ditto ditto	.30
FORD, STEPHEN SR.	1.50	HODGES, FRANCES	.70
Est. JEREMIAH PAINE	1.39	HERRIN, DANIEL	.21
Est. THOMAS ARD	.30	HERRIN, FREDERICK	.20
FLADGER, HENRY	1.50	HERRIN, WILLIAM	.90
FOXWORTH, JESSE	1.40	HORN, NATHAN	.13
FOXWORTH, STEPHEN JR.	.77	HAMILTON, JOHN	.14

HAMILTON, FRANCES	$ .12	JOLLY, JOSEPH Est. ditto ditto	$ .18
HENDERSON, RICE	.90	JONES, REUBEN	.12
HOWARD, RICHARD	3.85	JACKSON, JAMES	.30
HUDSON, JOHN	.12	JONES, BRYAN	.63
HENDERSON, HOPKINS	.30	JONES, FREDERICK	2.87
HARRELL, DAVID	.80	KING, CHARNEY	1.50
HYMAN, EDMUND	.90	KEIFFE, SARAH	1.40
HARRELL, EPHRAIM	.38	KERTON, PHILLIP	.82
HARMAN, SHOECRAFT	2.32	KERTON, THOMAS	.15
HARMAN, THOMAS Est.	3.96	KERBY, ARCHIBALD	1.26
HERRIN, EDMUND	.30	KEITH, STEPHEN	4.35
HERRIN, FRANCES	.35	ditto for W. H. PERKINS	.35
HARRELLEE, THOMAS	6.30	LEE, JOHN JR.	.36
ditto for STEPHEN GIBSON	.18	LANE, JAMES	.82
HODGES, JAMES	.31	LANE, THOMAS	.70
HOLDEN, JOHN	.90	LEE, LAZARUS JR.	.18
HERRIN, ARTHUR	.60	LEEPER, WILLIAM	.22
HARRELSON, JESSE	.47	LANE, OSBORNE	2.29
HUGGINS, LEWIS	.20	LACEY, MARY	1.75
HAGIN, THOMAS	1.50	LEGGETT, ELIAS	.30
HAYS, BENJAMIN	1.20	LEGGETT, ABNER	2.90
HARTSFIELD, FREDERICK	.20	LEGGETT, JESSE	1.12
HAYS, JAMES	.60	LEGGETT, JAMES	1.58
HUGGINS, LEVI	.40	LEWIS, JOEL	.44
HUGGINS, WILLIAM	.30	ditto ditto	.34
HANNAH, RICHARD	.30	LEWIS, JAMES	.56
ditto SARAH ALLEN	.90	LEWIS, ELISHA	.49
HANKS, JAMES	.20	LAMBERT, HENRY	.12
HALL, WILLIAM	.30	LEWIS, JONATHAN	.59
HAIRGROVE, JOHN	.80	ditto ditto	.59
HAIRGROVE, GEORGE	.15	LEE, LAZARUS SR.	.50
HENRY, JOHN	3.47	LOWRIMORE, JOHN	.41
HODGES, ROBERT	10.98	LONG, JOHN	.44
ditto ditto	.80	LEACH, JOHN	.20
HOYT, WILLIAM	.20	ditto ditto	.31
HAILE, JOHN	1.90	LEWIS, BENJAMIN	.33
HINDS, DAWSON	.70	ditto ditto	.45
HUSSAY, MILDRED	.12	LEE, JAMES	.25
HINDS, ROBERT	3.20	LEE, THOMAS Est.	.50
HOLLAND, JAMES	1.45	LAMBERT, HUGH	.70
HURCHESON, ARTHUR	.80	LEWIS, RUTH	.60
HAMILTON, WILLIAM	.25	LEWIS, ISAAC	.43
HARRELL, JACOB	3.40	MC LELLON, NEILL	.27
HARRELL, LEWIS	27.43	MANNING, JOHN	2.18
ditto ditto	4.27	MC ARTHUR, JAMES	.17
HAMILTON, FRANCES D.	.70	MC CUAIGUE, JOHN	.90
HORN, HARDY	.20	MC KENZIE, ROBERT	.41
JACKSON, OWEN	.15	MC ARTHUR, JOHN	1.22
JACKSON, EDWARD JR.	.10	MACE, JOHN	.60
JACKSON, WILLIAM	.27	MC INNIS, DANIEL JR.	.18
JACKSON, PHEBE	.70	MC INNNIS, DANIEL SR.	.12
JARRELL, MARGARET	2.30	MATHEWSON, JAMES	2.30
JOLLY, WILLIAM	.30	MC LAURIN, JOHN	.60
JACKSON, EWIN	.50	MILES, JESSE	.22
JOHNSTON, FRANCES	2.80	MC LAURIN, DANIEL	.38
JONES, JESSE	.44	MC CARMAIG, JOHN	.30
JONES, JOHN	2.60	MILES, JESSE	2.37
JONES, DAVID	2.40	MILES, DAVID	.40
JOHNSTON, JAMES	2.72	MARTIN, JOHN	1.45
ditto for DAVID & ARON HERRIN		MC KELLER, PETER	.11
	.70	ditto for PETER MC ARTHUR	1.61
JONES, NATHAN	.30	MC DONALD, FLORA	.11
JONES, JAMES	.15	MC CAIN, NEILL	.20
JOHNSTON, SAMUEL	.25	MC INTIRE, JOHN	.78
JOHNSTON, BENJAMIN	.14	MC LELLON, ALEXANDER	.44
JOHNSTON, LEWIS	1.33	MC QUEEN, NEILL	.27
JOHNSTON, LEWIS C.	2.54	MC NEILL, HECTOR SR.	1.75
JAMES, JAMES	.50	MC INTIRE, MALCOM	.30
JOLLY, JOSEPH Est.	5.10	MC LAURIN, NEILL	.30

MC LAURIN, NEILL	$ .12	MURFEE, NATHANIEL	$ .35
MOREE, JOHN	.70	MC DANIEL, JAMES	2.81
MOREE, ISAAC	.70	MC NEILL, SARAH	1.92
MUIM(?), CHARITY	.90	MC NEILL, HECTOR	.26
MC KISSACK, ARCHD.	3.45	MITCHELL, JAMES	.44
MC PHERSON, JAMES	2.51	MANNING, SARAH	.70
MARTIN, THOMAS	.60	MC SWAIN, FLORA	2.55
MUSSELWHITE, JOSHUA	.75	MC DANIEL, SARAH	.20
MUNNERLYN, LOFTIS R.	1.75	MC RAE, CHRISTOPHER	2.36
MUNNERLYN, BENJAMIN	1.75	MC LEAN, DUNCAN	.60
MILLER, NATHANIEL	.15	ditto ditto	.11
MORRIS, JOSEPH	.30	MC INNIS, DANIEL	.24
MILLER, ELIAS	.40	MIDDLETON, DELILAH	.30
MARTIN, JOHN SR.	.60	MUCKERSON, MURDOCK	.90
MARTIN, MATTHEW	2.80	MUCKERSON, PHILIP	.11
ditto for HUGH HARRALSON	.44	MUCKERSON, RHODRICK	1.10
MARTIN, AARON	.60	MC NEILL, TURQUILL	.81
MARTIN, ELIAS	.20	MARTIN, SARAH	.50
MOODY, THOMAS	1.19	NAPPER, ROBERT	.23
MOODY, JESSE	.57	NORTON, JAMES	.29
MOODY, CHARLES SR.	3.65	ditto ditto	.23
MOREE, DAVID	.27	NEWTON, JOHN	9.90
MOODY, ROBERT	.30	NORMAN, JEREMIAH	2.20
MOODY, ROBERT JR.	5.47	ditto for NICHS. PUNCH	.35
MC LEAN, JOHN	6.15	OWENS, PHILLIP	4.78
MC DANIEL, SARAH	.20	OLLIVER, RHESA	.57
MC RAINEY, JOHN	.68	OLLIVER, AARON	.60
MC ECHAIN, GILBERT	.36	ODOM, LEVI	.17
MURFEE, JOHN	.42	OWEN, WILLIAM	.82
MEDLIN, TURNER	.80	OWINS, SOLOMON	3.29
MC DUFFEE, ALEXANDER	.72	ditto ditto	.33
MC DANIEL, RANDAL	.80	OWENS, LUCY	.80
MC CALL, DONOLD	.23	OWINS, JOHN	3.44
MOODY, TAPLEY	.10	ditto ditto	.90
MOODY, CHARLES JR.	.76	OWINS, SHADRACH	.42
MOODY, ROBERT Est.	.26	OWEN, JOHN	2.29
MILLER, WILLIAM	.60	PRICE, WILLIAM	1.46
MEDLIN, NICHOLAS	.60	PRICE, JONATHAN	.60
MOODY, JAMES	.86	PLATT, DANIEL	4.33
MARES, LEWIS	.30	PROCTOR, JESSE	.40
ditto for GIDEON GIBSON	.30	PRICE, BENJAMIN	.60
MUNNERLYN, JOHN	6.10	PRICE, NATHAN	.30
ditto Est. IS. KEEN	1.10	PAGE, THOMAS	.17
MYERS, JOHN	.80	PAGE, JOHN	.60
MULDROW, SAMUEL	9.16	PAGE, SOLOMON	2.56
ditto ditto	1.33	PRICE, EDMUND SR.	.42
MYERS, JAMES	6.61	PAGE, JOSEPH	2.39
MYERS, GEORGE	7.26	PRICE, EDMUND JR.	.70
ditto ditto	.90	PRITCHARD, SIMON	3.15
MC NEILL, HECTOR	.60	PILKINTON, DURA	3.32
MC RAE, JOHN T.	.52	ditto ditto	.27
ditto for BENJ. COVINGTON	.90	PIGOT, NATHANIEL	2.19
MC LEAN, MALCOM	3.83	PHILLIPS, THOMAS	1.00
MC RAE, ISABEL	.60	PHILLIPS, WM. Est.	3.63
MULDROW, JAMES	4.76	PAISLEY, THOMAS	2.15
MC DUGAL, JOHN	.14	PAUL, ANDREW	23.26
MATTHEWSON, JOHN	.12	PHILLIPS, PHILIP Est.	2.59
MILLER, RICHARD	.21	PHILLIPS, JOHN J.	1.78
ditto ditto	.15	PHILLIPS, JOHN Estate	.80
MC CALL, JOHN	.27	POWERS, JOHN	.11
MC LEOD, RODICK	.10	PERRETT, DAVID	.17
MC CRIMMON, ARCHD.	.82	PERRETT, SARAH	1.70
MC INNIS, NEILL	.90	PAGE, WILLIAM	.82
MC CUARIGUE, JOHN JR.	.60	PASSMORE, JOSEPH	.60
MC RAE, JOHN	.12	PERRETT, JAMES	.30
MC DUGAL, JOHN	.12	POWELL, JORDON	.11
MUNNERLYN, ANN	.16	PITMAN, HARDY	1.63
MC KAY, DANIEL	5.33	PITMAN, SAMUEL	.15
MC DANIEL, JOHN	2.00	PALMER, DAVID	3.14

PITMAN, ABNER	$5.50	SMITH, JAMES	$ .30
POWELL, ROBERT	.30	SMITH, ANN	1.50
POSTON, ELI	.31	SMITH, SAMUEL JR.	1.43
POSTON, JOHN	.40	SMITH, SAMUEL SR.	3.30
POSTON, THOMAS	.12	SHACKELFORD, FRANCIS	2.10
POSTON, FRANCIS	.60	SCOTT, ELI	.57
POSTON, HUGH	.30	SCOTT, PHAROAH	.75
POSTON, WILLIAM	.30	STEWART, ALLEN	.20
POSSER, WILLIAM	.41	SHACKELFORD, JOHN	5.59
PALMER, WILLIAM	.14	SMITH, WILLIAM	.18
POWELL, NICHOLAS	.40	STONE, AUSTIN	1.64
PEPPIN, MICAJAH	1.48	ditto ditto	.80
PROCTOR, JESSE	.40	STONEY, HENRY	.12
PROCTOR, FREDERICK	.30	SMITH, JOHN L.	.30
PARKER, ICHABALD SR.	.56	POSTON, DANIEL	.30
ROGERS, ROBERT	.50	SMITH, JOHN SR.	3.99
ROWELL, DAVID	.20	SWEET, GOSPERO	9.12
ROWELL, VALENTINE	.14	SMITH, JOHN WARD	3.42
ROGERS, TIMOTHY	1.90	SHELLY, PHILIP	1.63
ROGERS, LOT	.13	SHACKELFORD, STEPHEN SR.	8.42
ROWELL, JACOB	.24	SHACKELFORD, STEPHEN JR.	.31
ROWELL, DAVID JR.	.42	SUMMERFORD, ANN	.11
RUNNELS, DAVID	.47	SWENNEY, JOHN	1.53
RICE, CHARLES	2.19	SANDERS, JOHN	.60
REAVES, CHARLES	1.50	SHANKS, GEORGE	.43
ROWELL, VALENTINE, JR.	3.36	SMITH, JOHN L. P.	.21
ROZER, WILLIAM	.21	SHOEMAKE, SAMPSON	.57
ROGERS, JOSEPH	.50	SCOTT, LEWIS	.200
ROGERS, SAMUEL	.30	SHACKELFORD, STEPHEN J.	3.63
ROGERS, DEW	.12	THOMAS, WILLIAM	1.30
ROZERS, ELIS	.30	THOMAS, JOSEPH	.30
ROZER, JIMIMA	.47	TURNER, REUBIN	.50
ROGERS, ROBERT JR.	.15	TURNER, WILLIAM	.17
ROBERTS, ROGER	2.10	THOMPSON, NEILL	.90
ROBERTS, READING	1.52	THOMPSON, JOHN	.60
RICHARDSON, JOHN	5.73	THOMPSON, LEWIS	2.70
ditto ditto	1.80	TREAWEEK, WILLIAM	.47
RICHARDSON, HARDY	.90	TIMMON, SIMMEON	.65
ditto ditto	.36	TURBEVILLE, SOLOMON	.30
ROGERS, SILAS	.73	TART, ENOS	4.11
RICE, SHADRACH	1.23	ELIAS FINKLEA	.15
Est. of JACOB WOODWARD	.17	ALEXR. FINKLEA	.35
ROGERS, JOHN	.27	TAYLOR, NOWELL	.40
ROPER, JOHN	.82	TURBEVILLE, WILLIAM	.60
ditto ditto	.60	TURBEVILLE, JOHN	.20
ROWELL, DAVID SR.	1.66	TAYLOR JANE	.50
ditto ditto	.15	THOMPSON, STEPHEN	2.72
RICE, JOHN	.88	THOMPSON, SAMUEL	1.57
ROGERS, R. JOSEPH	.35	Est. of CHARLES FINKLEA	1.00
ROGERS, G. THOS. & D. JOSEPH	.20	TIMMONS, JOHN SR.	4.37
RAWLS, WILLIAM	2.98	TIMMONS, WM. Est.	2.31
ROGERS, ELI	2.23	TIMMONS, SAMUEL	1.40
RIDGELL, JOEL	5.67	TURNER, AMOS	.19
STACKHOUSE, JOHN	1.36	THOMPSON, JAMES	.31
STAFFORD, NEILL	.90	TART, SARAH	.35
SWEAT, GEORGE	.30	TIMMONS, JOHN JR.	1.57
STEWART, JAMES	.14	THOMAS, ROAN	.50
SHOOTER, MARY	.82	TOWNSEND, THOMAS	.20
SANDERS, THOMAS	.38	TART, JOHN	2.10
STEPHINSON, THOMAS	8.51	TART, ENOS Estate	1.11
SMITH, HUGH	.22	TAYLER, ROBERT	.30
SHELLY, NOAH	.30	THOMPSON, JOHN W.	.70
SMITH, JOHN G.	.23	WATERS, MOSES	.30
SMITH, MOSES	.21	WATERS, WILLIAM	.70
SHELLY, STEPHEN	.18	WATSON, MARK	.12
SHELLY, WILLIAM	.60	WIGGINS, MICAJAH	.41
SWEET, ANTHONY	7.34	WATERS, DAWSON	.12
SAWYER, WILLIS	.54	WATSON, BOOKSCASE	6.34
SMITH, ABRAHAM G.	.21	WARD, WILLIAM	.15

291

WHITE, DANIEL	$5.10	ALTMAN, WM.	$ .61
WIGGINS, JESSE	.39	AVANT, FRANCIS	6.46
WILSON, ROBERT W.	4.90	ABBOT, CALEB	.28
WOODROW, MALCOM	.90	ALTMAN, JOHN	.70
WHITE, JAMES	.38	ALLIN, ELIAS	.70
WHITE, JOSEPH	.18	ANDREW, BENNIT	.34
WALL, THOMAS	.47	ALLIN, JOHN	.14
WOOD, JESSE	1.10	AYRES, DERIUS	2.66
WOOD, SARAH	.35	AMMONS, THOS.	.27
WHITE, DARLING	.30	AMMONS, WM.	.81
WAYNE, FRANCIS A.	.70	ALLIN, RICHD.	11.30
Est. of NATHAN EVANS	2.21	ADAMS, ELIAS	1.00?
WATSON, BARNABAS	.19	ABBOT, HOLOWAY Estate	.27
WHITE, WILLIAM	.48	BOSTICK, JAS.	8.42
WOODBERRY, COLLINS	5.23	BUTLER, LUCRETIA	.34
Est. of ANDREW F. JOHNSON	.45	BRYAN, SAML.	12.24
WELSH, WILLIAM	.79	ditto Estate WM. WEST	.48
WILLIAMSON, JOHN	3.93	BOND, JAS.	.54
WATSON, NEEDHAM	.90	BUTLER, WM. SR.	.34
WIGGINS, WILLIAM	.30	BURRIL, MARY	.73
WOODDARD, HEARTWELL	.30	BELLUNE, WM. G.	57.44
WATSON, GHAM(?)	.45	BREWER, Dd.	.62
WINSLOW, WILLIAM	.90	BRADLEY, JOHN	8.40
WISE, AMBROSE	.22	BRASWELL, HENRY	.80
WOODBERRY, RICHARD	8.90	BOGLE, JAS.	14.17
WOODBERRY, RICHARD Estate	5.23	BARNES, JAS. JR.	.14
WOODBERRY, ELIZABETH	3.00	BRASWELL, TOBIAS	.41
WOODBERRY, MARGARET	2.46	BARFOOT, WM.	.91
WOODBERRY, WILLIAM	9.53	BARFOOT, NOAH	.25
WILSON, JOSEPH	1.78	BELLUNE, WM.	19.13
WIGGINS, BAKER	13.29	BREWER, ASA	.47
ditto ditto	2.45	BARFIELD, BARROT	.81
WIGGINS, CHARITY	.60	BROWN, THOS.	.18
WHITTINGTON, NATHAN	.50	BASS, JETHRO	1.57½
WALL, WRIGHT	1.86	BETHEA, JOHN SR.	53.48
WATERS, JEREMIAH	.47	BETHEA, ELISHA	3.41
WILLIAMS, RICHARD G. Est.	.90	BARNES, JOEL	.18
YELVERTON, ZADOCK	.18	BAXLEY, THOS.	.59
YELVERTON, JESSE	.14	BAKER, JOHN	13.45
YELVERTON, JOHN	.53	" Est. JNO. JACKSON	14.70
YELVERTON, ZADOCK JR.	.18	BROWN, WM.	.14
JESSE SCOTT	2.00	BATH, DANL.	.79
PATIENCE SCOTT	2.00	BRYAN, JAS.	.33
JAMES BOGLE	1.75	BOLDWRIGHT, DL.	14.45
SAMUEL BRYANT	3.50	BRYAN, JESSE	7.15
Est. of WM. WEST	.11	BAKER, WM. JR.	41.53
CHESLEY, DANIEL	6.22	BAKER, WM. SR.	16.27
		BREWER, NEEDHAM	.32
1814 MARION DISTRICT TAX LIST		BEVERLY, Dd.	.20
		BROWN, JOSHUA	.14
ALSOBROOK, BARTHW.	1.65½	BARNES, THOS.	.17
AULD, ALEX. M.	15.75	BROWN, STEPH.	.36
ANDERSON, CLABOURN	1.40	" for JESSE FOWLER	.55
ALSOBROOK, WM.	8.35	BROWN, EDWD.	4.95½
AVANT, JOSHUA	23.35	BARFIELD, ELISHA	.71
ALLIN, SARAH	.27	BLANCHARD, HENRY	.27
ALLIN, WM.	18.55	BUTLER, JNO.	.27
ALLIN, SAML.	.54	BRADDEY, JNO.	13.68
ALLIN, BURRIL	.54	BETHEA, JESSE	18.13
ALLISON, H. JAMES	23.98	BETHEA, HUGH	.27
ALLIN, MATHW.	1.43	BLACKMAN, JNO.	.14
ADAMS, ABNER	6.35	BETHEA, MARY	3.69
AVANT, LEVI	.66	BETHEA, CADE	6.72
AMMONS, JOSA.	.20	BRIDGES, FRANCIS	4.95
AVANT, ABRAM	28.73	BAILEY, WM.	.35
AVANT, WM.	4.73	BETHUNE, FARQUEHARD	.95
ANDREWS, JOEL	.11	BETHEA, JNO. JR.	3.62
AVANT, THOS.	20.67	BARFIELD, WM.	.14
ATKEISON, JESSE	.68	BARNES, JAS.	.49

BRUCE, BENJ.	$7.10	CRISSEY, JAS.	$ .87
BARNES, CHAS.	.27	COX, GEO.	12.90
BROWN, JAS. D.	4.73	CARMICHAEL, JNO. SR.	.30
BIGHAM, SAML.	6.30	CAMPBELL, CATHE.	.50
BIGHAM, JAS.	3.11	CAMPBELL, LIDIA	.50
BIGHAM, WM.	3.46	CARMICHAEL, Dl.	.34
BRYAN, TURNER	3.48	CARMICHAEL, DOUGAL C.	1.90
" Est. JNO. LONG	2.10½	CARMICHAEL, DUNCAN SR.	4.10
BARFIELD, JAS.	.14	COLEMAN, ROBT.	6.46½
BURCH, JOS.	38.80	CARTER, JOSIAH Estate	7.33½
BECKWORTH, HENRY	2.25	COX, ARCHD.	.21
BETHEA, WM. JR.	3.63	Estate of AMOS TURNER	.81
BASS, BRYAN	1.57½	CROSBY, THOS.	2.87½
BLUE, WM.	9.77	CARMICHAEL, Dl.	.47
BASS, MARTHA	26.64	COOPER, THOS.	.54
BASS, JOS.	2.41½	CAMRON, LAVENDER	3.44
BERRY, STEPH.	.41	CAMPBELL, JAS.	27.72
BERRY, ELI	.61	CAMPBELL, JAS.	.74
BERRY, ANDW.	.43	TABITHA M. STEWART	1.57½
BERRY, ANN	1.57½	" " "	.13
BETHEA, WM.	18.59	CAMPBELL, JNO.	.16
BELLUNE, JAS. C.	19.73	CAMPBELL, ANN	.61
BAILEY, JONAS	.29	CRIB, ELIZ.	.45
BUTLER, ELIAS	.14	CRIB, THOS.	.70
BUTLER, STEPH.	.17	CAPS, WM.	.10
BUTLER, NATHAN	.34	COLLINS, JONAH	.48
BUTLER, WM. JR.	.17	CASE, JNO. Estate	4.73
BLACKMAN, SOL.	.34	CHINNERS, HARDY H.	.38
BETHEA, ANN	27.47	COLEMAN, JOHN	1.79
BIRD, ARTHUR	18.34	CARMICHAEL, DOUGAL JR.	5.41
BLACKWELL, JACOB	.34	CARMICHAEL, NEILL	1.52
BAILEY, CHRISTR.	.16	COLLINS, THOS.	4.12
BAGGET, DELILAH	.70	CAMPBELL, PETER	14.95
BASS, JNO.	1.71½	COLEMAN, GRIFFEN	3.43½
BROACH, ABNER	.16	CARMICHAEL, DUNCAN SR.	6.58
BERRY, HENRY	14.52	CARMICHAEL, NEIL Estate	16.60
BERRY, DENNIS	1.35	CARMICHAEL, ARCHD. M.	1.22
BURCH, EDWD.	47.35	CAMRON, NEPSEY	.14
BROWN, JER. SR.	21.60	COOK, MATHW.	.70
BLACKMAN, Dd.	.34	COWARD, BURWELL	1.84½
BIGHAM, JNO.	5.44	COWARD, WILLSON	2.31½
BIGHAM, JNO.	.22	CAMPBELL, ARCHD.	.75
BIGHAM, Dd.	3.44	COWARD, EPHRAIM	1.84½
BARR, DL. Estate	7.88	CALCOTE, JAMES	3.29
BARR, Dl.	.54	CUSACK, ADAM	7.93
Est. of SETH STAFFORD	3.15	CHANCE, ELIZ.	.16
BRASWELL, RICHD.	.61	COLE, HOZIER	.27
BURNIT, JNO.	2.46	COOK, ANN	.14
BOLDRIGHT, THOS. Estate	2.35	CUMMINGS, Dd.	.47
BROWN, JER. JR.	2.13½	DEWIT, JAS.	3.60
BIRD, ELIZ.	.27	DAVIS, SAML.	4.73
BARNES, VINEY	.18	DAVIS, PHILIP	4.10
BRYANT, WM.	.75	DAVIS, JAS.	25.20
BARTELL, MARY	.26	DAVIS, ZABON	3.82½
CLARK, GEO.	5.20	DAVIS, NIMROD	35.50
CARMICHAEL, DOUGALD SR.	7.07½	DAVIS, BENJ. JR.	9.45
CAMPBELL, DUNCAN	8.60	DAVIS, JOSEPH	40.38
CLARK, MALCOM	6.86	DAVIS, HENRY JR.	54.86
CRAWFORD, JAS.	49.83	KESSIAH ROBERTS	6.60
COX, JUDITH	6.37	DAVIS, FRANCIS	23.32
CALCOT, CHRISTR. Estate	3.15	DOZIER, ELIAS	6.70
COX, WM.	24.48	ditto for WM. PALMER	.21
CAMPBELL, EDWARD	8.35	DAVIS, JOHN C.	66.80
CRAWFORD, JAMES G.	17.33	DAVIS, MARY	19.80
CRAWFORD, HARDY Estate	9.46	DOZER, JAS.	1.55
CUSACK, JOS.	18.37	DOZER, WM.	.80
COWARD, LEWIS	5.34	DAVIS, HENRY M.	7.23
COOPER, JNO.	11.30	DAVIS, JOHN	7.73
CARMICHAEL, JNO.	1.40	DANNELLY, ANN W.(?)	8.42

DEER, JOHN	$ .76	Ditto Est. of THOS. TURBEVILLE	
DANIEL, CHESLEY	30.50		$ .14
DREW, ANN	.70	FORD, JOHN	11.16
DILLEN, WM.	.34	FORD, PRESERVED	20.36
DEW, CHRISTR.	14.40	FORD, STEPH. SR.	4.64
DRIGGERS, THOS.	3.14	FLADGER, HENRY	4.73
DAVIS, MICHL.	.79	FORD, MARY	1.40
DANIEL, JOHN	.20	FERRELL, REBECCA O.	.13
DEWIT, CHAS.	3.39½	FINKLEA, CHAS.	1.30
DREGGERS, ISAAC	.14	FLINT, THOS.	1.23
DAVIS, SAML.	.41	GREGG, ROBERT H.	22.54
DEES, MALAKIAH	.14	GIBSON, JORDAN	16.32
DENNIS, JOSHUA	.22	GREAVES, FRANCIS	24.85
DEES, ARTHUR	3.45	GADDY, ITHAMAR	1.34
DEW, JNO.	1.51	GREAVES, BENNIT	34.39
DREGGERS, EPHRAIM	.41	ditto Est. FRANCIS ALISON	19.39
DAVIS, BENJ. SR.	42.94	GREEN, UNITY	.24
DAVIS, THOS. P.	9.46	GANEY, THOS.	2.56
DAVIS, DANIEL	4.16	GREAVES, JOS.	19.31
DAVIS, HENRY SR.	48.70	GREGG, JOS.	24.59
DAVIS, WM. SR.	52.11	GREGG, ALEX. SR.	21.61
DAVIS, WM. SR.	.35	GREAVES, WM. H.	28.89
DUNNAM, ROBT. Estate	3.15	GREGG, JAS.	1.57½
DAVIS, WM. JR.	13.57	GRICE, WM.	2.45½
DRIGGERS, ELIZ.	3.00	GRANTHAM, RICHD.	.59
DOZIER, ANN	14.18	GODBOLD, STEPH.	31.39
EAGERLIN, HENRY	3.15	GRICE, JACOB	10.29
EAGERLIN, DOROTHY	1.57½	GASQUE, ABSALOM	.31
ERVIN, HUGH	53.75	GODBOLD, THOS. son of THOS.	4.47
EDWARDS, CULLIN	.62	GASQUE, JOHN	7.20
EDWARDS, RICHD.	16.72	GODBOLD, THOS. SR.	12.96
EDWARDS, SAML. Estate	16.40	GODBOLD, Dd.	7.88
ERVIN, JAMES R.	27.46	GRICE, WM.	.54
ERVIN, JAMES	.26	GRICE, WM.	1.75
ERVIN, JOHN Estate	2.29	GASQUE, ARCHD.	1.57½
ERVIN & GIBSON	2.70	GOODYEAR, WM.	3.84
EDDY, SAML.	.67	GREAVES, HARDY	1.00
EVANS, THOMAS	.10	GREAVES, HARDY	.70
EXUM, ROBT.	6.30	GOODYEAR, JOHN	.27
EAGERTON, WM. SR.	3.54	GALE, LEURANEY	.19
EAGERTON, GEO.	.95	GRICE, ALEX.	1.10
EAGERTON, WM. JR.	8.80	GRICE, THOS.	10.60
EADDY, HENRY	20.24	GREGG, ALEX. JR.	21.24
EADDY, HENRY	3.68	GASQUE, HENRY	5.51
EXUM, BENJ.	8.86	GASQUE, SAML. Estate	.23
EXUM, WM.	6.43	GARRAWAY, ROBT.	1.24
FORE, JOEL	.25	GREGG, WM. JR.	12.20
FORD, GEORGE	5.59	GRAVES, JOHN	.95
FORD, JOS.	8.72	GARDNER, STEPH.	4.86
FOXWORTH, HENRY	11.30	GREGG, WM. SR.	31.71
FINKLEA, JNO.	6.90	GREGG, ROBT. Estate	15.33
FORD, JESSE	3.56	Estate of WM. ORR	56.40
FINKLEA, THOS.	.38	GREGG, JNO.	31.30
FORE, RICHD.	3.51	Estate JAS. HUDSON	22.81
FUTRILL, JOS.	.14	GERRAL, MARGT.	10.53
FORD, JAS.	.14	GRAVES, SARAH	8.15
FROST, WM.	.14	GALE, MIRIAM	.34
FOXWORTH, ABSALOM	7.57	GODBOLD, THOS. JR.	74.90
FLOWERS, ANN	3.27	GODBOLD, THOS. JR.	.75
FLOWERS, RACHEL	.30	Estate ELIZ. FOXWORTH	4.73
FOXWORTH, STEPH.	6.53	GIBSON, JOHN	78.68
FLOWERS, BENNIT	2.68½	GIBSON, JOHN	37.80
FOXWORTH, JESSE	4.62	Ditto for ANN RAE & C. BALLARD	
FOXWORTH, STEPH.	1.89½		30.58
FOXWORTH, ABEL	1.08½	Ditto for JNO. MIDDLETON	3.25
FINKLEA, WILLIS	1.95½	GODFREY, RICHD.	48.36
FINKLEA, ALEX	.39	HARLEE, THOS.	28.69
FOXWORTH, JOB	16.12	Ditto STEPH. GIBSON	.81
FOXWORTH, JNO.	2.07½	HAMILTON, JNO.	.54

HAMILTON, LIDIA	$ .41	JAMES, THOS.	$ .14
HALE, WM.	.13	JOHNSON, SAML.	1.21
HERRIN, EDMUND	.60	JOHNSON, BENJ.	.63
HERRIN, FRANCES	1.57½	JONES, DAVID	8.93
HOWARD, RICHARD	43.99	JOHNSON, BENJ. JR.	.14
HUDSON, JNO.	.67	JOHNSON, SHEROD	.14
HARRELL, EPHRAIM	1.71½	JONES, JOHN D.	1.82½
HALE, JNO.	3.65	JONES, JOHN	11.40
HERRIN, JAS.	.67½	JONES, ROBT.	5.22
HARRELL, Dd.	.67½	Est. PETER HICKSON	.49
HAYS, JAS.	.39	JACKSON, JAS.	.31
HOLLAND, JAS.	6.29	JONES, JESSE	2.40½
HUDSON, RICHD.	.67½	JACKSON, OWEN	.67½
HYMAN, DELILAH	.27	JACKSON, ERVIN	.20
HUDSON, ALEX.	.54	JACKSON, WM.	1.22
HAYS, JAS.	.27	JACKSON, EDWD. JR.	.36
HENDERSON, HOPKIN	.14	JOHNSON, JAS.	15.40
HERRIN, ANTHONY	.95	Ditto & AARON HERRIN	3.15
HIOT, WM.	.20	JAMES, JAS.	.19
HERRIN, FREDK.	.12	JOLLY, A. JOS.	24.13
HAIRGROVE, GEO.	.65	" "	.81
" "	.14	JACKSON, JAS.	.14
HILL, WM.	2.52	JONES, JOHN G.	7.31
" "	1.35	JONES, JOHN	.19
HIOT, ISAAC	3.84	KERTON, PHILIP	4.98
HUGGINS, JOHN	1.47	KING, CHARNEY	4.23
HULON, THOMAS	.45	KERBY, ARCHD.	5.67
HASLEDEN, WM. Estate	6.80	KEEFE, SARAH	7.88
HODGES, ROBT.	48.93	KERTON, THOS.	.66
" "	.34	KEITH, STEPH.	10.50
HUGGINS, LEWIS	.70	KEITH, ANN SAR. Estate	9.45
HAIRGROVE, JNO.	.37	KILLPATRICK, GEO.	.90
HENRY, JNO.	15.75	LEWIS, RUTH	.27
HUPSEY(?), MILLEY	.49	LEGGIT, ABNER	23.55
HOLDEN, JNO.	.34	LEACH, JOHN	.87
HERRIN, ARTHUR	.14	" "	1.32
HARRELL, JESSE	.11	LOURIMORE, JOHN	1.83½
HARELSON, JOSIAH	.20	LEGETT, ABSALOM	9.72
HODGES, JAS.	1.38	LEGETT, HENRY C. Estate	6.22
HAYS, BENJ.	9.31	LEWIS, JAS.	.81
HARWELL, AMBROSE	4.89	LEGETT, JESSE	9.42
HARMAN, SHOECRAFT	4.43	LEWIS, BENJ.	6.19
HARMAN, THOS. Estate	17.17	" "	2.30
HODGES, FRANCIS	.17	LEWIS, ELISHA	2.13½
HAYS, DRURY	.41	LEWIS, JON.	2.62½
HUGGINS, LEVI	.16	" "	2.61
HUGGINS, WM.	.11	LEWIS, JOEL	2.13½
HARRELSON, JESSE	2.11½	" "	1.16
HAYS, JOS.	2.36	LAMBERT, HENRY	.40
HOOKS, DORCAS	1.13	LUPO, WM.	.95
HARTSFIELD, FREDK.	.89	LEE, LAZARUS JR.	.95
HARRELL, JACOB	15.84	LANE, THOS.	.30
" "	1.49	LEGETT, JAS.	9.00
HAMMELLTON, WM.	2.68½	LEE, JAS.	2.69½
HARRELL, LEWIS SR.	33.38	LEWIS, ISAAC	2.69½
HARRELL, LEWIS	19.20	LEWIS, MILLS	11.30
HAGINS, THOS.	13.80	LANE, JAS.	3.69
HARRELL, JAS.	19.30	LANE, OSBORNE	12.81
HINDS, ROBT.	14.74	LEE, JOHN	2.64½
HINDS, DAWSON	6.73	LACEY, MARY	9.46
HUTCHINSON, ARTHUR	.34	LEGETT, Dd.	5.10
HATCHELL, JOHN	.78	MC CUAGE, JOHN	.37
JOHNSON, FRANCIS	14.18	MC KAY, JOHN	.47
JOHNSON, LEWIS	5.11	MC SWAIN, FLORA	.47
JORDAN, JOHN	10.33	MC INNIS, MALCOM	14.52
JOLLY, WM.	.14	MC RAE, JOHN T.	1.23½
JONES, BRYAN	2.83	Ditto for BENJ. COVINGTON	.38
JONES, NATHAN	.81	MC KAY, Dl.	25.60
JONES, JAS.	.65	MOODY, TAPLEY	1.17

MC QUEEN, ALEX.	$7.88	MUNNERLYN, BENJ.	10.81
MILES, JESSE	.14	MOODY, ROBT.	.16
MURKERSON, MURDOCK	4.54½	MORRIS, JOS.	.13
MURKERSON, RODERICK	.41	MARTIN, SARAH	.20
MURKERSON, PHILIP	.47	MARTIN, ELIAS	.20
MC LELLAND, ALEX.	3.48	MEDLIN, TURNER	.33
MC NEILL, SARAH	9.95	MILLER, RICHD.	.94
MC NEILL, HECTOR	2.60½	MC DANIEL, WM.	.60
MC INAGARD, ALEX.	.54	MUNNERLYN, JOHN	31.22
MYERS, GEO.	38.34½	ditto Est. JAS. KEEN	3.95
" "	1.10	MC CALL, JOHN	1.20
MUNN, Dl.	.49	MILLER, WM.	.27
MC INNIS, NEILL, JR.	.14	MOREE, Dd. Estate	1.17
MC INNIS, Dl.	.28	MUSSELWHITE, JOSHUA	.27
MC INNIS, HECTOR, SR.	1.18	MOREE, JOHN	.51
MC RAE, JOHN	2.11½	MOREE, ISAAC	.31
MC INNIS, NEILL	.41	MOODY, THEOPHILUS	3.90
MC CALL, Dl.	5.14	MOODY, THOS.	5.34
MC LELLAN, MALCOM	18.86	MARTIN, AARON	.27
MC LEGLAN, NEILL	1.22	MC CLEAN, JOHN	14.13
MATHEWSON, JAS.	.54	MEDLIN, ROBT.	.14
MC RAE, CUTHE.	12.35	MC LEAN, DUNCAN	.48
MC KILLAR, PETER	8.17	MC DANIEL, RANDAL	3.66½
MC ARTHUR, PETER	.48	MC NEILL, HECTOR JR.	.27
MC LAURIN, Dl.	.95	MC CUAGE, JOHN JR.	.27
MC INNIS, Dl.	1.28	MAJORS, Dl.	.14
MACE, JNO.	8.67	MOODY, ESTHER	.18
ditto Est. WM. OWEN	2.40½	MC EACHIN, GILBERT	1.43
MC RAE, ISABEL	.27	MC NEILL, TURQUILL	3.90
MOODY, JAS.	3.87	MYERS, JAS.	35.55
MILLER, NATHL.	.44	MC DUFFIE, ALEX.	1.36
MC ARTHUR, JAS.	.67	MC DUFFIE, DUNCAN	.37
MC DUGALD, JNO.	.41	MURPHY, JOHN	1.87½
MC DUGALD, Dl.	.20	MC DUFFIE, ANN	.67½
MANNING, JNO.	8.36	MC ARTHUR, JOHN	1.83
MC QUEEN, NEAL	1.93½	MARTIN, JOHN	.18
MC CALL, DUNCAN	.14	MURPHY, NATHL.	1.57½
MC PHERSON, JAS.	7.14	NAPPER, ROBT.	.90
MC PHERSON, JNO. Estate	11.30	NEWSOM, JAS.	3.15
MULDROW, SAML.	44.62	NORTON, WM.	1.50
MULDROW, JAS.	19.79	NEWSOM, JOHN	47.67
MIDDLETON, DELILAH	.18	NORMAN, JER.	11.50
MC PHERSON, DUGALD	3.57	NORMAN, JER.	.70
MILES, JESSE	.24	NORTON, JAS.	1.26
MUNN, CATHE.	.29	" "	.96
MILES, Dd.	15.40	OATS, ZACHARIAH	.14
MC KINSEY, ROBT.	1.24	ODOM, LEVI	.54
MC RAINEY, JOHN	3.16	OWINS, PHILLIP	16.79
MANNING, SARAH	3.15	OWINS, SHADRACK	3.46
MC LAURIN, NEILL	1.50	OWINS, SOL.	23.92
" "	.51	" "	2.49
ditto for LAUCHLAN CUERY	.14	OWINS, WM.	15.46
MATHEWSON, JOHN	.53	" "	.41
MC LAURIN, JOHN	14.90	OWINS, WM. JR.	.27
MC CREMAN, ARCHD.	5.27	OWEN, JOHN	10.31
MOODY, CHAS. JR.	3.42	ODOM, ARCHD.	2.25
MILLER, SAML.	.10	OLIVER, AARON	.17
MC DANIEL, SARAH	.50	OLIVER, RHISA	2.56½
MOODY, CHAS. SR.	11.69½	PILKINGTON, DURA	15.88
MAIRS, LEWIS	.38	" "	1.18
MARTIN, MARY	6.30	POSTON, JNO. SR.	.17
MARTIN, THOS. Estate	1.85	POSTON, JNO. JR.	.27
MUNNERLYN, ANN	.76	PROSSER, WM.	1.82½
MOODY, JESSE	2.41½	POSTON, HUGH	.27
MARTIN, MATHW.	8.26	POSTON, THOS.	.59
ditto for HUGH HARRILL	1.95	POSTON, FRANCIS	.27
MC DONALD, FLORA	5.68	PITMAN, HARDY	7.34
MARTIN, JNO.	.27	POWELL, ROBT.	.14
MILLER, ELIAS	.90	PITMAN, SAML.	.67½
MUNNERLYN, THOS.	3.15	POSTON, ELI	1.80

POSTON, JAS.	$ .70	ROGERS, JOS.	$ .20
PRICE, HENRY	.24	ROZIER, JEMIMA	2.80½
PRICE, EDMD.	.77	ROGERS, TIMOTHY	8.50
PRICE, WM. S.	.34	ROBERTS, ROGER	7.31
PHILLIPS, JOHN D.	4.40	ROGERS, ETHELRED	.27
PHILLIPS, ISAAC	9.52	ROSS, THOS.	.80
PHILLIPS, JOHN J.	8.00	RAY, GILBERT	1.84½
PHILLIPS, JNO. Estate	.23	RIDGELL, JOEL	22.37
PHILLIPS, PHILIP Estate	11.13	RODGERS, ROBT.	.22
PAUL, ANDW.	109.39	ROPER, JOHN	.54
PAGE, JOHN	.24	ROWELL, VALENTINE SR.	.77
PAGE, THOS.	11.85	ROGERS, LOT	.55
PHILLIPS, WM. L.	2.45½	RAWLS, WM.	7.32½
PHILLIPS, Dd.	1.97½	ROWELL, VALENTINE JR.	18.20
PHILLIPS, ANN	8.37	ditto Est. Dd. MOREE	.39
PERRIT, JAS.	.11	ditto Est. WM. BOLDRIGHT	6.70
PAISLEY, THOS.	11.69½	STACKHOUSE, JOHN	5.93
PALMER, Dd. SR.	13.84	STAFFORD, NEILL	.41
POWERS, JOHN	.20	DITTO FOR LAUCHLIN MC NEILL	.88
PERRIT, SARAH	6.38	SHACKELFORD, FRANCIS	11.30
PALMER, Dd. JR.	1.20	SANDERS, THOS.	9.72½
PALMER, WM. SR.	3.82½	STONE, WM.	53.52
PASMORE, JOS.	2.72½	STONE, Dl.	8.20
PERRIT, DAVID	.73	SHOOLER, MARY	5.27
PITTMAN, NOAH	3.38	SMITH, JOHN M.	1.10
PAGE, JOS.	10.73	SMITH, JAS.	.14
ditto for WM. HERRIN	.41	SMITH, ANN	3.29
POWELL, JORDAN	.45	SMITH, SAML. JR.	6.42
POWERS, JOHN JR.	.22	SMITH, SAML. SR.	16.40
PRICE, WM. SR.	3.63½	SHELLY, NOAH	.10
PAGE, WM.	3.69	SMITH, HUGH G.	.73
PEGOT, NATHL.	9.79	SINGLETARY, WM. G.	35.78
PARKER, JOS.	1.57½	Est. of JAS. & JNO. MC REE	31.50
PEPPEN, MICAJAH	8.27	SIMKINS, THOS.	.63
PLATT, Dl.	22.63	SHELLY, PHILLIP	7.32
PARKER, ICHABOD	3.47½	SHELLY, STEPH.	.67½
PROCTOR, JESSE	.17	SHELLY, WM.	2.67
PRICE, JON.	.14	SANDERS, JOHN	.70
PRICE, NATHL.	.14	SWEET, GOSPERO	47.63
PROCTOR, FREDK.	.14	SWEET, ANTHY. Estate	57.77
PRICE, BENJAMIN	.22	Est. of JOHN AVANT	.14
PRICE, EDMUND	.70	SMITH, ABRAM G.	.95
PAGE, SOLOMON	5.00	SMITH, MOSES	.92
PRITCHARD, SIMON	14.90	SMITH, JOHN SR.	25.30
ROGERS, JOHN	2.75½	SCOTT, PHAROAH	3.37
ROGERS, JOHN SR.	1.96	SMITH, JOHN WARD	15.39
ROGERS, SILAS	3.27½	" "	3.57
RICHARDSON, JOHN	30.47	SHACKELFORD, SEPT. JR.	16.33
" "	5.57	SHACKELFORD, JOHN	23.59
" "	1.75	STONE, HENRY	.52
RICHARDSON, HARDY	6.30	STONE, AUSTIN	7.34
RICE, SHADRACH	4.77	" "	.37
RICE, CHAS.	11.77	SMITH, WM.	.79
RICE, JOHN	4.55	SMITH, JNO. (Lynches Creek)	1.35
ROWELL, Dd. SR.	9.20	ditto for Dl. POSTON	.14
ROWELL, Dd.	.67½	STEVENSON, THOS.	48.38
ROZER, WM.	.92	SHACKELFORD, STEPH. SR.	39.20
RICE, HENRY	.67½	" "	1.37
ROWELL, JACOB	1.80	SWETT, GEO.	.14
REAVES, CHAS.	6.29	SHOEMAKE, SAMPSON	2.38½
ROWELL, Dd. JR.	1.89	SHANKS, GEO.	1.94½
ROBINS, THOS.	2.70	SMITH, MALCOM Estate	.27
RUNNILS, Dd.	.27	SCOTT, ELI	2.16
ROGERS, ROBT.	.74	SCOTT, LEWIS	3.00
ROGERS, JOHN	.34	SAWYER, WILLIS	3.99
ROGERS, DEW	.18	THOMPSON, STEPH.	13.81
ROWELL, DAVID C.	.88	THOMPSON, JOHN W.	.67
ROBERTS, REDIN	6.97½	TIMMONS, SAML.	4.64
ROGERS, SAML.	.17	TIMMONS, WM. Estate	10.40
ROGERS, ELI	13.58	THOMPSON, JAS.	4.16

TIMMONS, JOHN SR.	$14.00	WILLIAMS, RICHD. G. Estate	$3.64
TIMMONS, ISAAC	5.68	WATSON, BOOK SEACE	28.54
THOMAS, WM.	10.99	WINSLOW, WM.	.41
THOMPSON, NEILL	.41	WILSON, THOS.	6.30
TRAWICK, WM.	2.11½	WILSON, ROBT. W.	20.30
TAYLOR, ROBERT	.14	WATERS, MOSES	.40
TEES, WM.	15.76	WIGGINS, WILLIS	.50
TIMMONS, SIMEON	6.80	WHITTINGTON, FRANCIS	.34
ditto Est. JNO. BURNELL	13.95	YELVERTON, JESSE	.64
TURNER, JOHN	1.57½	YELVERTON, ZADOCK, JR.	.82
THOMPSON, LEWIS	9.33	YELVERTON, JOHN	2.89
TART, JOHN	9.65	YELVERTON, ZADOCK	.68
TART, ENOS Estate	4.49	HAYS, WM.	6.54
TART, SARAH	1.57½	HALE, ROBT.	3.00
THOMAS, JOS.	2.84	HORN, HARDY	.70
THOMAS, ROAN	.22	HAYS, NEWTON	.25
TART, ENOS	23.50		
TAYLOR, NOEL	.17	1824 MARION DISTRICT TAX LIST	
TURBEVILLE, SOL.	.14		
TAYLOR, JANE	.20	AVANT, ASA	9.15
TURBEVILLE, JOHN	.15	AVANT, MARY	3.75
THOMPSON, JOHN	.24	ALSTON, JOHN	.11
TIMMONS, JOHN JR.	6.84	ASKINS, WILLIAM T.	6.73
THOMPSON, SAML.	5.49½	ADKISON, JESSE	1.80
Est. CHAS. FINKLEA	1.56	ANDERSON, SILSA S.	12.82
TOWNSEND, THOS.	.70	ADAMS, ELIAS	.69
TREAWICK, GEO. Estate	.14	ALTMON, JOHN	.13
TURNER, WM.	.48	ALLEN, RICHARD	8.55
WHITE, Dl.	22.52	ALLEN, JOEL	.75
WILLIAMSON, SAR.	.14	AMMONS, THOMAS	.15
WOODROW, MALCOM	.90	ARNETT, BENJN.	.10
WIGGINS, BAKER	95.97	ALLEN, SHADRACH	1.05
" "	18.90	AYRES, DARIAS	.58
WARD, WM.	.58	AYRES, WM.	.19
WATERS, DAWSON	.48	ALL, MC DANIEL	1.00
WIGGINS, MICAJAH	2.10½	ABBOT, CALEB	.58
WHITE, WM.	2.12½	ALLEN, JOHN	1.05
WATSON, ISHAM	1.55	ALLEN, WILLIAM SR.	4.41
WATERS, JER.	5.40½	ALLEN, BURNETT	1.88
WRIGHT, JNO. M.	9.11	ALLEN, MATTHEW Est. of	2.47
WISE, AMBROSE	1.60	ALLEN, SELAH	1.14
WHITE, JOS.	.15	AVANT, THOMAS	20.30
WILLIAMSON, JOHN	20.87	ALLISON, JAS. H children	3.75
WAYNE, A. FRANCIS	6.96	ALTMON, WILLIAM	.50
Est. NATHAN EVANS	7.84	AMMONS, JOSHUA	.28
WHITE, DARLING	1.23	BIGHAM, SAML.	5.44
WHITE, SILAS	.23	BERKET, LEVI	.22
WOODBERRY, COLLINS	31.12	BELLUNE, WM. SR.	6.00
JOHN P. DUNNAM	1.57½	BRADLEY, JOHN	7.03
WOOD, JESSE	3.66	BERRY, ANDREW	.12
WOOD, SARAH	1.57½	BETHUNE, PHILIP	10.58
WOODARD, HARTWELL	.13	BETHUNE, ELISHA	10.38
WATSON, BARNABAS	.84	BASS, JOHN	.94
WATSON, NEEDOM	.36	BASS, ROBERT	2.47
WIGENS, JESSE	1.73½	BASS, BRYANT	1.99
WIGENS, WM.	.13	BASS, MARTHA	7.92
WALL, WRIGHT	9.92	BRYAN, BROWN	5.02
WOODBERRY, RICHD.	38.90	Guardian of Est. of HARREL	
" " Estate	7.88	BRYAN, LEMUEL	7.97
" " Estate	.70	BASS, JOSEPH	2.97
" " Estate	.95	BERRY, HENRY JR.	1.97
WOODBERRY, FRANCIS	7.88	BERRY, DENNIS	.19
WISE, MOSES	.12	BERRY, HENRY	10.40
WATSON, MARK	.50	BARTELL, PETER	.70
WIGGINS, CHARITY	.57	BARTELL, PHILIP	.51
WOODBERRY, WM.	44.40	BARTELL, MARY	.20
WOODBERRY, MARGT.	11.13	BARTELL, WILLIAM	1.65
WOODBERRY, ELIZABETH	14.50	BURNET, JOHN	3.00
WALL, THOMAS	2.80	BAILEY, CHRISTOPHER	.10
WHITE, JAS.	1.71½	BAILEY, MATTHEW	.90

BIGHAM, WM.	$ 3.20	CLARK, WINNEY	2.25
BIGHAM, MARTHA	.84	CUSAAC, ADAM	6.87
BIGHAM, DAVID	.10	CHARMICHAEL, DANL.	1.22
MC BRIDE, MARY	.15	MC CRAY, JOHN	5.73
BETHUNE, FARQUARD	.82	CAMPBELL, LEVI	.07
BENJAMIN, BRIDGES	2.20	CAMPBELL, JEREMIAH	.22
BLACKMAN, JOHN	.03	CAMPBELL, PETER	4.43
BARFIELD, BARROT JR.	.15	CARMICHAEL, ARCHD.	.67
BARNES, DAVID	.04	ditto Est. of NEALE CARMICHAEL	
BUTLER, WM.	.18		6.62
BUTLER, LEURESE	.21	MC CLEAN, JOHN	2.63
BARFIELD, ELIZABETH	.26	CAMPBELL, CATHARINE	.09
BARFIELD, HENRY	1.18	CARMICHAEL, ARCHD.	.42
BUTLER, SAML.	.03	CAMPBELL, DUNCAN	.24
BUTLER, ELIAS	.07	COWARD, BURRIL	.15
BUTLER, JOHN	.03	CAMPBELL, ARCHD.	.42
BARFIELD, WINNEY	.09	CAMPBELL, DAVID	2.31
BLANCHET, JAS.	.10	CAMPBELL, JAS.	2.55
BETHEA, TRISTRAM	14.56	CAMPBELL, HUGH	1.50
ditto for Est. M. MC LELLAN		CHARMICHAEL, MALCOLM	.41
	13.59	" , MICHAEL	1.03
BECKWORTH, MORNING	1.87	" , NEAL	.27
BRADDY, JOHN	8.92	" , DUGAL	.28
BETHEA, WILLM.	4.48	CLARK, GEORGE	3.48
ditto for Est. CALCUT	1.72	CALL, MC HUGH	4.65
BETHEA, JOHN	10.42	(HUGH MC CALL?)	
BLEW, WILLIAM	8.55	CARTER, JAS. MC.	.86
BAYLEIGH, WM.	.19	CAMPBELL, DANL.	1.57
BETHEA, CADE	5.11	CAMPBELL, DUNCAN	8.79
BAYLEIGH, JONAS	.15	COWARD, WILSON	2.81
BETHEA, JAMES	8.43	CALL, ROBERT MC (MC CALL?)	.22
BARNES, CHARLES	.15	CARTER, CHARLES MC (MC CARTER?)	1.06
BLACKMAN, DAVID	.03	" , MARGARET	.42
BARFIELD, FURNEY	.19	CHARMICHAEL, DUGAL JR.	3.50
BARFIELD, ELIZABETH	.07	CRIB, DEMPSEY	.07
BARFIELD, WM.	.08	CRIB, ELIZABETH	.25
BARFIELD, CHARLES	.30	CHARMICHAEL, DUGAL	1.79
BARFIELD, BARROT	.38	CRIB, JOHN	.10
BREWER, DAVID	.37	CHARMICHAEL, MALCOM	.80
BAKER, JOSEPH	.14	CHARMICHAEL, JOHN	.20
BREWER, ACRY	.26	COWARD, LEWIS	2.58
BARFIELD, JAS.	.07	COGNOUN, ALEXR.	.49
BROWN, THOMAS	.11	COLLINS, JOHN	.26
BROWN, WILLIAM	.15	COLLINS, JONAH	.75
BROWN, STEPHEN	.19	COOK, WILLIAM	7.45
BIRD, PETER	10.05	COLLINS, THOMAS	.17
BLEW, ARCHIBALD	5.32	ditto Est. of CRIB	29.21
BROWN, CHRISTOPHER B.	.75	CRAWFORD, JAS.	2.48
Est. of MARGT. BOATRITE	.39	COLMAN, JOHN	.03
BOATRITE, DANIEL	12.40	CAIN, ARRINGTON	.07
BROWN, JULIA	2.25	COOK, NANCY	.15
BRIANT, SMITHY	1.57	MC CRAE, ELIZTH.	1.53
BANLEY, THOMAS	.33	COLMAN, GRIFFIN	1.95
BEVERLY, SARAH	.09	CHARMICHAEL, NEALE	.03
BOATRITE, MARTHA	.75	" , DUNCAN	1.65
BROWN, RICHARD	.31	CAMPBELL, WM.	.42
BAKER, JOHN	13.28	MC CLOUD, JAS.	.32
BAKER, WILLIAM	24.66	MC CARTER, PETER	.26
BIGHAM, JOHN	4.01	MC CLOUD, JOHN	5.48
BAXLEY, BARNABAS	.11	CLARK, MALCOLM SR.	1.61
COLMON, ROBERT	1.53	CLARK, MALCOLM	3.62
CRAWFORD, M.	.40	COOPER, JOHN	5.20
CULPEPPER, HENRY	1.66	COX, ARCHD.	.10
CREEL, JAMES	.30	CARTER, STEPHEN	2.10
CAMPBELL, ARCHD.	.25	CURRY, DAVID	.07
CUNNINGHAM, JOSEPH S.	8.80	CAIN, BAT.	1.50
COLLINS, JOHN	3.23	COX, GEORGE	15.21
CHARMICHAEL, DUNCAN	2.79	CAIN, WILLIAM	.19
CORMIC, MC NEAL	1.03	CARTER, GEORGE	.28
CLARK, ARCHD.	.07	CALCOTE, JOHN	.07

CAIN, LARRY	$ 1.18	FLOWERS, NATHAN	$ .11
ditto Est. EXUM	3.14	FORD, MARY	.28
BRIGMAN, THOS.	1.16	FREEMAN, STARKEY	.68
BERRY, STEPHEN	1.12	FERRIL, JAMES	.07
BETHEA, PARKER	6.62	FOLKS, WILLIAM	.07
BRYANT, JAS.	.56	FOLKS, JOEL	.07
BROWN, EDWARD	4.28	FINKLEY, WILLIS	.53
BARFIELD, BARROT JR.	.15	FINKLEY, CHARLES	.38
BIRD, MARTIN	.15	FINKLEY, ABNER	.75
BUTLER, ROBERT	.09	FORES, JOEL	.64
BETHEA, WM.	15.64	FINKLEA, WILLIS	.15
BOSTIC, JAMES	6.07	FLINT, THOMAS	.86
ditto Est. of SARAH BURKET	1.60	FRYER, WILLIAM	9.81
DAVIS, THOMAS	3.72	FERREL, JAMES	5.36
DAVIS, ANN G.	9.00	FINKLEA, JOHN	.30
DAVIS, JOHN C.	47.09	FINKLEA, CHARLES	.16
DRIGERS, ISAAC	.07	FINKLEA, JOHN	1.33
DANIEL, WILLIAM	.07	FORD, WILLIAM	2.77
DANIEL, JOHN	.10	FORD, JESSE	8.50
DRIGGERS, THOMAS	.07	FORD, CHARLES	.22
DEW, JOHN	1.50	FORD, PRESERVED	6.30
DEW, CHRISTOPHER SR.	3.00	FORD, JOHN	5.70
DAVIS, JOSEPH SR.	5.76	FLOYD, NEAL	1.84
DRIGGERS, TILLEY	2.22	FLOYD, FRANCIS	2.16
DEES, MALACHI	.08	FORD, JOHN	.45
DENNIS, JOSHUA	.19	FOWLER, WM.	.11
DENNIS, THOMAS	.10	FOXWORTH, JOHN	3.00
DAVIS, SAMUEL	.34	FOXWORTH, JOB	8.83
DEWETT, JAS.	1.98	FOXWORTH, JOHN	4.08
MC DANIEL, RANDAL	4.72	FOXWORTH, JOSEPH	.54
DAVIS, HENRY	35.62	FOXWORTH, ABEL	1.18
MC DUFFIE, DANL.	.37	FLOWERS, BENNETT	.07
MC DANIEL, INTYRE (DANIEL MC INTYRE)	FOXWORTH, HENRY	3.86
	2.76	FORES, WM.	.63
MC DUFFEE, DUNCAN	4.37	FORES, JOHN	.10
DRIGGERS, AVIS	.22	ditto Est. of HASSELTON	7.07
DAVIS, MICHAEL	.40	FORE, JAMES	.85
DEW, CHRISTOPHER	12.44	FLOWERS, ANN	1.62
DAVIS, SARAH	6.72	GILLIS, ANGUS	.22
DAVIS, JOHN	10.12	GRICE, THOS.	.69
ditto Est. of JAMES DAVIS	12.00	GADDES, JAS.	.75
DAVIS, ELIZABETH	3.75	GADDES, WILLIAM	.99
MC DANIEL, SARAH	.03	Estate of HUDSON	3.27
DAVIS, HENRY	14.42	Estate of GREGG, WM.	12.88
DEW, ABSALOM	.60	Estate of STAFFORD, SETH	1.50
DAVIS, HENRY	5.59	Estate of BROWN, JAS.	.45
DOZIER, JAMES	.68	GREGG, JOHN	34.09
DAVIS, SARAH	.18	GREGG, ALEXANDER	16.63
DEER, JAMES	.37	ditto Est. of MAJ. GREGG	9.96
MC DUFFEE, ALEXR.	1.81	ditto Est. of GREGG, ROBERT	.10
MC DOUGALD, DANL.	.49	GIBS, CANNON	.06
DEAN, NANCY	.70	GOUD, WM.	.52
EVANS, THOMAS	24.88	GRAVES, WM. C.(?)	18.30
ditto Est. CALCOTE	3.00	ditto Estate of GRAVES, JOHN	3.00
EDWARDS, RICHARD	7.85	GRAVES, ARCHD.	.03
ELMORE, WM.	.11	GROVES, JOHN HAIR	.31
EAGERTON, MARY	1.50	GIBSON, DAVID	.83
EAGERTON, DOROTHY	1.50	GODBOLD, HUGH G.	2.46
EAGERTON, CHARLOTTE	3.00	GASQUE, ABSALOM	.62
EAGERTON, WILLIAM	7.50	GODBOLD, THOS.	6.36
Est. of JOSEPH CUSAAC	10.27	ditto Estate of GODBOLD	1.62
MC EACHERN, GILBERT	1.45	GASQUE, HENRY	3.03
MC EACHERN, CHRISTOPHER	6.64	ditto Est. of SAML. GASQUE	.13
EASTERLING, JAS.	1.15	GODBOLD, STEPHEN	28.95
EDWARDS, RICHARD	.39	ditto Est. of CALCOTE	.75
EDWARDS, DAVID	.75	GASQUE, JOHN	5.81
EXUM, MARY	5.25	GASQUE, ELLY	2.93
FREEMAN, WILLIAM	.03	GOODYEAR, WM.	3.99
FLETCHER, HUGH	10.50	GOODYEAR, JOHN	.13
FOXWORTH, STEPHEN	5.27	GADDY, ITHAMER	2.24

GRAVES, JOHN	$ .55	HODGES, JOHN	$ .07
GRAVES, HARDY	.38	HAYS, JOSEPH SR.	1.39
GOODYEAR, LOVET	.10	HARREL, JESSE	.20
MC GILVERY, JOHN	.09	HARRILSON, HUGH	.15
GROVES, ISA HAIN	.27	HALL, ALLEN	.70
GREGG, ROBERT	.94	HOLDEN, JOHN	.10
GREGG, WM. G.	2.25	HILLIN, MARY	.18
GREGG, WM.	12.34	JOHNSON, SARAH	3.75
GREGG, JOSEPH	1.50	JACKSON, JAMES	10.71
ditto Est. of K. BAR, ELIZTH.?		JACKSON, EDWARD	.08
	3.00	JONES, THOMAS H.	.33
ditto Est. of GREGG, JOSEPH		JACKSON, WM.	1.16
	10.80	JACKSON, LABAN	.22
GRAVES, ELIZABETH	.*@	JACKSON, WILLIAM	.19
GRAVES, SARAH	3.15	JONES, SUSANNAH	.41
GRAVES, BENNET	29.43	JONES, JOHN	.07
ditto Est. GRAVES, ALEXR.	11.25	JONES, WILEY	.13
GRAVES, JOSEPH	15.18	MC INNIS, MILES	.22
GRAVES, FRANCIS	16.56	MC INNIS, NEILL	.11
GRAVES, JOHN J.	6.75	JACKSON, REUBEN	.44
GIBSON, GURDIN	8.00	JOHNSON, LEWIS	.41
ditto Est. GUIRLEY, JOSEPH	10.50	JOHNSON, SAML.	1.14
HIGGINS, JOSEPH	.07	JOHNSON, BENJAMIN	3.76
HUGGINS, WILLIAM	.15	JOHNSON, RICHARD	.08
HODGES, HUGH	.30	JARNAGAN, WILLIS	.75
HODGES, SAMUEL	14.58	JACKSON, OWEN	.46
HAMBLETON, JOHN	5.41	JOHNSON, GARDNER	.72
HARREL, MATTHEY T.	12.30	JOHNSON, ALLEN	.17
HULON, WILEY	.08	MC INTYRE, DANL.	.63
HULON, WILLIAM	.07	JONES, DAVID	.28
HULON, NATHAN	.05	JONES, THOMAS	1.36
HAYS, HESTER	4.00	JOHNSON, JAMES	.23
HANNA, WILLIAM	.70	JAMES, ADDIN	29.05
HAGINS, THOMAS	4.50	JAMES, MALACHI	.33
HARREL, DAVID	.32	IKNER, JESSE	.23
HARMAN, ALRAM	.22	JONES, JOHN	.30
HINES, ASA	3.02	JONES, JOHN	6.19
HATCHELL, JOHN	3.43	JAMES, MC DANL.(JAS. MC DANIEL?)	
HUSTON, MARY	3.37		2.39
HUSTON, ROBERT	3.38	MC INNIS, MURDOCH	3.22
HARMON, CRAFTS SHOE	3.60	JOHN AYRES	2.70
HUTCHERSON, ARTHUR	.19	MC INNIS, MALCOLM	6.82
HARMON, DANIEL	.17	MC IVER, EVANDER	24.15
HAIL, ROBERT	3.76	ditto Est. HARREL, JAS.	2.09
HINES, DEMPSEY	2.01	MC INNIS, MURDOCH	1.00
HAMBLETON, WM.	.75	Est. of HODGES, ROBT.	1.87
HAMBLETON, JOHN	2.02	HILL, MOSES	6.16
HAYS, FARMER	.75	HARREL, STEPHEN	.03
HENDERSON, HOPKIN	.82	HILL, WILLIAM	.21
HUGGINS, JOHN	.99	HILL, DAVID	.26
HUGGINS, WILLIS	.16	HUDSON, JANNETT	5.43
HAYS, DRURY	.30	HOLDEN, JOSEPH	.07
HAYS, JOSEPH B.	.93	HAIL, JOHN	4.74
HAIRGROVES, NEWEL	.38	Est. of HINSONS, EDOM	.14
HARLLEE, DAVID S.	4.50	HINSON, LARY	.52
HARLLEE, THOMAS & SON	2.25	HARREL, LEVI	.31
HARLLEE, THOMAS	22.23	HARREL, JOSIAH T.	21.88
ditto Est. BETHEA, PHILIP	.60	HENRY, EADY	19.70
ditto Est. of CHISOLM	.33	HANNERS, RILHARD (RICHARD?)	.19
HIOTT, ISAAC	1.50	KIRTON, HENRY	.75
HERRIN, MICHAEL	.22	KIRTON, PHILIP	.19
HAYS, JAMES	.31	KELLY, JOHN	.15
HUGGINS, LEWIS	.13	KELLER, MC. JOHN (MC KELLER?)	1.80
HERRIN, RHODA	.25	MC KAY, JOHN	.25
HIOT, LEWIS	.15	MC KAY, DANIEL	17.60
HAYS, BENJAMIN	7.45	MC KELLER, PETER	3.82
HARREL, ZEPHANIAH	.63	MC KINLEY, JOHN	.17
HAYS, JOSEPH	.18	MC KINLEY, DANIEL	.07
HORN, HARDY	.33	MC KENZIL, ROBERT	.54
HAYS, JESSE	.10	MC KENZIL, JOHN	.18

KEIFFER, LEWIS	$ .75	MC NEILL, LACHLIN	$1.23
KEIFFER, SARAH	7.10	NORTON, JOHN	.21
KIRTON, PHILIP	3.14	NORTON, WILLIAM	.17
ditto Est. of SWEETS, ANTHONY		MC NAB, JOHN	.30
	2.59	NORMAN, JEREMIAH	.33
MC LELLAN, ARCHD.	.13	NAPPER, ROBERTS	.21
LEWIS, CADER	4.69	OWENS, SOLOMON	23.09
LEWIS, PRIOR	.75	ODAM, LEVI	.27
LEGGETT, JESSE	6.09	ODAM, ARCHIBALD	1.78
LELLAN, MC DANIEL	.23	OLIVER, LEVINA	.14
(DANIEL MC LELLAN)		OLIVER, REACY	2.52
MC LUCRES, DANIEL	1.87	OLIVER, ALFRED	.27
MC LAURIN, DANL.	1.29	OWENS, PENELOPE	3.90
LEACH, JOHN	.91	OWENS, SHADE	2.91
LAIN, JAMES	1.80	OWENS, ESTHER	.07
LAIN, THOMAS	.99	PLAT, DANIEL	14.12
LEE, JOHN	1.68	PROSSER, JOHN	.15
LAIN, AUSBURN	5.11	POWEL, JAS. G.	.07
LEE, JAMES	.62	PROSSER, WILLIAM	.55
LAIN, JAMES	33.45	PILKINTON, DRURY	10.38
MC LAURIN, NEILL	3.88	MC PHERSON, JAS.	9.87
LOOPO, WILLIAM	2.12	ditto for MCPHERSON, JAS.	5.25
MC LELLAN, ANGUS	.67	ditto for MC PHERSON, SARAH	.75
MC LELLAN, ALEXANDER	3.18	ditto for MC PHERSON, SELAH	.75
LEGGETT, REBECCA	.56	ditto for Est. PRITCHET, SIMON	
LAMBERT, ELIZABETH	.34	PIGOT, NATHANIEL	3.68
LAMBERT, WILLIAM	.13	PATE, SAML. R.	1.62
LEGGETT, EBBY	.75	PARKER, ICHABOD	7.83
LEGGETT, ABNER	5.48	PROCTOR, JESSE	.30
MARTIN, MATTHEW	4.46	PAGE, ABRAHAM	1.01
MAREE, PENELOPE	.19	PAUL, CHERRY	2.00
MARTIN, WILLIAM	.07	PAGE, WM.	4.80
MOODY, TAPLEIGH	.09	POWEL, JORDAN	.25
MANNING, JOHN	6.76	POWEL, DEMPSEY	.15
MC MILLAN, DUGALD	3.74	MC PHERSON, GEAN	.75
MUNN, ARCHIBALD	.18	PRIEST, ALEXR.	.30
MOTT, STEPHEN	1.83	PAGE, THOMAS	7.96
MOORE, JOHN L.	.14	PRICE, WILLIAM	3.49
MOODY, BARFIELD	14.08	PASSMORE, JOSEPH	4.53
MEGGS, JOHN	.02	PETHNAN, HARDY	5.00
MOODY, ROBERT	.03	PETHNAN, SAML.	.37
MOODY, ISAM	.86	PHILIPS, WILLIAM	.15
MOODY, THOMAS	.10	PHILIPS, ANN	5.40
MACE, JOHN	5.55	PAIN, ELIZABETH	1.50
MURRY, PETER G.	.75	PHILIPS, ALICE	3.03
MUNLIN, ANN	.30	PERRITT, DAVID	.59
MIRES, JOHN	.93	PAGE, JOSEPH	.22
MELTON, THOMAS	.12	PAGE, JOHN F.	.27
MOODY, JAMES	3.00	PAGE, JOHN D.	1.51
MURPHY MARGARET	1.76	PAGE, SOLOMON	3.82
MILLER, WILLIAM	.15	PHAIL, ALLEN	.11
MILLS, DAVID	15.67	POWERS, JOHN W.	.70
MANNING, SARAH	3.00	PILKINTON, DRURY	2.55
MOODY, ROGER	1.57	POSTON, SAML.	.12
MOODY, JAMES	3.34	POSTON, FRANCIS	.22
MURCHASON, A.	1.12	POSTON, THOMAS	.32
ditto for Est. of MURCHISON	.25	POWEL, ROBT.	.14
ditto MURCHISON, ANN	.75	PRICE, JOHN	.14
ditto Est. MURCHISON, R.	.22	MC QUEEN, DANIEL	1.78
MOODY, THOMAS	4.12	MC QUAGE, JOHN	.75
MUSSLEWHITE, JOSEPH	.11	MC QUEEN, JOHN SR.	.20
MEMLIN, BENJAMIN	9.15	RICE, JOHN	7.75
MARTIN, AARON	.37	ROWEL, MARTHA	3.78
ditto Est. of BRIANT, JESSE	4.19	REASONOVER, JOSEPH M.	.26
MORRIS, PHILIPS	.24	ROSIER, WM. K.	.10
MOODY, IRVIN	.62	ROSIER, CHLOE	.22
MC NEILL, HECTOR	2.51	REAVES, CHARLES	14.52
MC NEILL, HURKWELL	3.75	RICHARDSON, JOHN SR.	.11
MC NEILL, HECTOR	1.06	RICHARDSON, JOHN	19.75

302

ROGERS, SILAS	$6.71	SMITH, JOHN M.	$ .53
ROGERS, JOHN	3.72	SMITH, ELIZABETH	.97
ROGERS, ELI	6.30	STAFFORD, NEILL	.96
ROSS, THOMAS	.04	STACKHOUSE, TRISTRAM	1.33
RAY, GILBERT	1.20	STONE, ELIZABETH	15.36
ROPER, JOHN	5.36	SHANKS, GEORGE	1.50
ROGERS, LOT	3.31	SUMMERFORD, NANCY	.26
RIGEL, JOEL	10.91	SANDERS, THOMAS	.03
ROGERS, DUE	.61	SWEAT, GEORGE	.25
MC RIMMON, ARCHD.	4.84	SHERWOOD, JOHN	.14
ROPER, FREDERIC	.38	STONE, DOTSON	2.63
ROWEL, WM.	.41	ditto Est. of PARSONS	8.23
ROGERS, TIMOTHY	5.81	STONE, WILLIAM	.41
ROGERS, PHILIP	2.25	SWEETS, GOSPRO	28.15
ROGERS, HENRY	.23	ditto Est. SWEETS, ANTHY.	24.86
ROBERTS, RIDDIN	6.01	TIMMONS, ISAAC	11.80
ROWEL, ELIZABETH	.04	ditto Est. of TIMMONS, JUD.	3.00
ROWEL, DAVID C.	1.02	ditto Est. of MILLER, GEORGE	7.50
ROBBINS, THOMAS	1.05	Ditto Est. of BURTON, JOSEPH	3.75
ROWELL, DAVID	.32	THOMPSON, SAML.	9.49
ROWELL, VOLUNTINE	2.28	TURNER, WM.	.28
RICE, SHADRACH	.17	TART, ENOS	23.84
ROWELL, DAVID	3.30	TURNER, DANIEL	.03
ROGERS, NOAH	.10	TURBILLEE, WM.	.11
ROWELL, WM. B.	3.68	TART, JOHN	8.73
RICE, HENRY	1.54	TIMMONS, JOHN	1.69
ROBERTS, NORTON	4.32	TIMMONS, WILLIAM J.	3.52
SMITH, THOMAS	.14	TIMMONS, ALEXR.	.03
SMITH, SAMUEL	11.76	TAYLOR, ROBERT	.07
SINGLETARY, WM.	26.04	THOMPSON, LEWIS	9.60
SHELBY, JOSEPH	.22	THOMPSON, JOHN	.27
SHELBY, WILLIAM	1.36	TIRBELLEE, JOHN	.38
SHAW, THOMAS	.03	TIRBELLEE, SOLOMON	.07
SHELLEY, WILLIAM	.44	TART, JAMES	.26
SHELLEY, STEPHEN	.37	THOMAS, JOSEPH	3.70
SMITH, DANIEL	2.47	TAYLOR, WILLIAM	1.83
SCOTT, ELI	1.31	TAYLOR, NOEL	.10
SWINNEY, JOHN	2.92	TANNER, NATHAN	.04
SINCLAIR, DANIEL	.33	TURBIEVILLE, WM.	.06
STEWART, PETER	.18	TAYLOR, JONATHAN	.10
STEEL, THOMAS	.33	TAYLOR, SILAS	.07
STONE, HENRY	3.09	THOMPSON, JOHN	2.07
SHAW, WILLIAM	.07	THOMPSON, ELIZABETH	.22
SANDERS, NATHANIEL	.22	TIMMONS, SIMEON	7.42
SMITH, JAMES	.09	ditto Est. of BOSTIC	3.63
SMITH, JOHN G.	3.10	TIMMONS, SAML.	7.51
SMITH, CHARLES	.75	THOMPSON, JAMES	1.17
SMITH, LEONARD	5.86	WALL, STEPHEN	.63
SMITH, NANCY	.07	WALL, THOMAS K.	.70
SMITH, SAMUEL	.41	WALL, THOMAS	2.92
SMITH, WILLIAM	1.39	WIGGINS, BAKER	76.43
STACKHOUSE, SELAH	3.05	WATSON, BARNABAS	1.19
STACKHOUSE, ISAAC	1.48	UNDERWOOD, HARTWELL	.16
SMITH, SAMUEL	5.10	WISE, MOSES	.90
SHOOTER, BENJ.	1.02	WILSON, ROBERT W.	7.16
SHELLY, NOAH	2.77	ditto Est. of CAMPBELL	16.87
SMITH, HUGH	.49	WOODROW, JOHN	.50
SNIPES, WM.	.10	WOODBERRY, ELIZABETH	9.10
SMITH, MOSES	.53	WOODBERRY, WILLIAM	24.10
SMITH, ABRAHAM G.	1.07	WOODBERRY, MARGARET	8.95
SHOEMAKE, SAMPSON	.45	WOODBERRY, RICHARD	39.00
STONE, SAMUEL E.	.32	VAUSS, WILLIAM	7.28
SMITH, JOHN	.45	WALL, PATIENCE	.23
SWET, SAML. S.	1.12	WILLIAMS, HENRY L.	4.60
SMITH, SAML. W.	2.25	WALL, KITT	10.94
STEPHERSON, ELIZABETH	6.00	WHITTINGTON, NAT	7.16
STACKHOUSE, JOHN	.75	WHITTINGTON, BARRIL	.07
STACKHOUSE, HEROD	.43	WATSON, ISAM	6.63
SHAW, DANIEL	.07	WHITE, RICHARD	2.40

WHITE, ESTHER	$1.62	GRICE, JAMES	$7.82
WATSON, NEDOM	.18	GRICE, WILLIAM H.	25.52
WILSON, HUGH	2.00	GODBOLD, THOMAS	39.28
WATSON, MARK	.27	ditto Est. ABRM. GODBOLD	4.78
WOODWARD, WILLIAM	.33	KIRBY, ARCHIBALD	.53
WARSON, SCAREEBOOK	17.11	Williamsburg:	
ditto Est. NEDOM BREWER	.15	EADY, HENRY	2.87
WALTERS, JEREMIAH	6.37	RICHERSON, JOHN	2.51
WARD, JOHN	.07		
WATSON, GILBERT	.07	Darlington:	
WISE, AMBROSE	.49	MC DANNEL, CHARLES H.	.75
WILLIAMSON, JOHN	2.25	Est. of LEWIS HARRELL	1.20
WILLIAMSON, MARTHA	9.58	LANE, JAMES	.07
WILLIAMSON, JOSEPH	2.38	ROSS, MICHAEL	....
WHITE, DARLING	1.02		
WIGGINS, JESSE	.08	Horry Dist.:	
WIGGINS, CHARITY	.25	RICHERSON, JOHN	.55
WANE, FRANCIS A.	4.87	RICHERSON, JOHN	1.86
ditto Est. of EVANS	1.50	WOODBERRY, RICHD.	.22
WHITE, STEPHEN	2.33	ROGERS, SILAS	.30
WIGGINS, CAGE	1.19	GRICE, WM.	1.12
WHITE, BENJAMIN	3.00	OWENS, SOLOMON	1.38
YELVERTON, ZADOC	.29	HILL, WILLIAM	.41
YELVERTON, JESSE	.52	HILL, MOSES	1.12
YELVERTON, JOHN	1.80		
YELVERTON, NATHN	.38	Georgetown:	
		WOODBERRY, WM.	.37

END OF MARION DISTRICT TAX LIST

NEWBERRY COUNTY, S. C. WILL BOOK A

Newberry County was formed in 1785 out of the old Ninety-Six District. The county seat is Newberry and the records now (1972) in the courthouse are very complete. The first settlement of the city was two miles below the present site, near the old village cemetary, near what was then known as "Cedar Spring", which was the home of JOHN COATE. He gave two acres of land providing the two acres be used for a courthouse or other public buildings. This offer was accepted when court convened in March 1789 and a deed made in September 1789. In 1790, the first courthouse was built on the two acres (now the public square). Before then, in 1785 through 1787, the first sessions of court were held at the home of Col. ROBERT RUTHERFORD, one of the first County Judges. In 1799, this first small frame courthouse was torn down and work began on the new courthouse which was not completed until (1801). To the rear of the courthouse was built a two-storied stone gaol and the present stone terraces on the sides of the Confederate monument contains the stone blocks that were part of the foundation of the old jail. The present brick courthouse was built in 1850, the architect was JACOB GRAVES. It was during the reconstruction days, just after the Civil War, when repairs were being made to the courthouse by the contractor, OSBORNE WELLS, who added the symbols on the front gable. The explanation of the design is that the palmetto tree (this tree is a part of the South Carolina Court of Arms) signifies an uprooted State government which is being held in the beak of the Americn Eagle, as the Federal government, who weighs in the "scales of justice" the people of the State, represented by the crowing cock which stands on the base end in an attitude of being not conquered even though down, and on the other end, among the branches and leaves, is the dove of peace, with the olive branch in it's mouth, an emblem ever significant among an enlightened people.

****

According to the late LEONARDO ANDREA, well known genealogist, "Cambridge was the county seat of old Ninety-Six District but most of the old records are lost or scattered. Some are at the University of Wisconsin and some are at the Newberry Library in Chicago, having been sold to collectors who have donated them to the above repositories. A few are at the Leland Stanford Library in California. These libraries do not have complete collections, some have mere fragments and some possess full books. Charleston County Courthouse has alal records of deeds, wills, and administrations, or they are in the Books of Miscellany at the S. C. Historical Commission for the period up to 1782. Abbeville has some records 1782-1785, mostly wills and administrations. Other records are scattered in York, Camden, Chester and Winnsboro. A few years ago, an old Surrogate Court Book, 1781-1783, was found in the North in private hands but the S. C. Archives has a microfilm copy. Some of the border counties of North Carolina and Georgia have a few early S. C. wills and deeds, notably Richmond County, Ga. which has some old Edgefield records and Rutherford, Lincoln, Mecklenburg, Anson, Robeson and Bladen in North Carolina which have a few records from the border counties.

In researching a county, it is wise to see what church records exist and Furman University, seven miles north of Greenville, S. C. has all the Baptist church records which are still in existence for old Ninety-Six. In Wofford College Archives are found many of the early Methodist records."

WILL BOOK A - 1787 - 1796

P 1:   WILL of JAMES MURPHEY, deceased, dated 27 Mar. 1787, proven 5 June 1787. Wife SARAH - to have homeplace and all moveable property during life; children: (1) eldest son, JOHN - to have 30 acres out of the 330 acre tract on Dry Creek; (2) son, DOWDELL - to have 150 acres out of the 330 acre Dry Creek Tract; (3) JEMINA ROLAND; (4) ANN MAYBIN; (5) REBECCA MURPHEY. Exors.: wife SARAH and son DOWDELL. Wit: THOMAS GARDON, WILLIAM CHANDLER, WILLIAM HAMPTON CHANDLER.

P. 2:   WILL of JAMES HODGES, deceased, dated 19 May 1787, proven 5 June 1787, wife MARTHA; children: (1) JOSEPH, (2) CHRISTINA, (3) JESSE, (4) REBECCA SHAW, (5) PATTY SHAW. Other legatees: (1) SARAH GLASS (2) TOBY GLASS. Wit: REUBEN GOLDING, GEORGE ELLIOT, HALEY SHAW, JOSEPH HODGES.

P 3:   WILL of THOMAS GREEN, deceased, dated 30 Apr. 1787, proven 6 June 1787. Brother, JOHN GREEN - to have 250 acres with homeplace and slaves. Wit: EDWARD KELLY, EDMOND KELLEY, MARY ANN SMITH.

P 4:   WILL of RICHARD BONDS, deceased, dated 24 Sept. 1786, proven 6 June 1787. Wife JOICE - to have residue of estate during her lifetime then to children: (1) MENOAH BONDS - to have 157 acres on both sides Beaverdam Creek; (2) RICHARD - to have land he lives on and the 50 acre tract bought from JOHN ANDERSON; (3) WILLIAM - to have 1,000 wt. tobacco and the hogs on Reedy River; (4) SALLY - cattle and other property; (5) RETTER - 2 cows; (6) BETTY - other property. Wit: EDWARD KELLY, THOMAS LAKE, ANN JOHNSON. Exors.: MENOAH BONDS and his mother, JOICE.

P 5:   WILL of JOHN GLENN (who lived near the Saluda River), deceased, dated 20 Sept. 1784, proven 3 Sept. 1787, wife mentioned but not named. Children: (1) JAMES (2) JOHN (3) WILLIAM, these to have all of my 300 acres - 200 of which is where I live and 100 acres bought from my brother, WILLIAM HERBISON and not yet released by his widow, ANN HERBISON, (4) JEAN, (5) MARY, (6) MARGARET (7) ANN. Wit: ROBERT SPEER, JAMES DOUGLAS, JAMES MC LONER. Exors.: JOHN DOUGLAS, THOMAS BROWN.

P 6:   WILL of PETER GALLOWAY, deceased, dated 26 Oct. 1774, proven 3 Sept. 1787. Wife, MARGARET - to have 100 acres whereon we now live during her life and then to my son PETER. Children: (1) PETER - 50 acres and 150 acres granted to GEE HAYWORTH; (2) JOHN - 100 acres granted to GEORGE HAYWORTH with 50 acres adj. it; (3) MARY DOUGLAS and her husband, JOHN DOUGLAS; (4) ELIZABETH; (5) JEAN; (6) ANNA; (7) MARTHA. All 5 to share the 200 acres surveyed for JAMES BROOKS. Wit: ROBERT SPEER, JOHN DOUGLAS, WILLIAM HERBISON. Ex'rs: WILLIAM HERBISON, ROBT. SPEER.

P 7:   WILL of JOHN NEWMAN, deceased, dated 16 Aug. 1780, proven 3 Sept. 1787. Wife - NIMA. Children: (1) JAMES - 150 acres

Cont'd:
adj. JOSEPH JOHNSON, with its Patent, when he reaches 18 years; (2)
SAMUEL - 225 acres next to the river, part of the old survey, when
he reaches 18 years; (3) JOHN, my youngest son, 150 acres with its
Patent, being the place whereon I live, when he reaches 18 years -
also my silver watch; to my brother, SAMUEL NEWMAN, my square barrel
gun and a smooth bore. Wit: PHILLIP PHEAGIN, SARAH INMAN & THOMAS BUR-
TON. Exr's: NIMA NEWMAN, JOSEPH JOHNSON.

P 8:   WILL of JOHN LINDSAY, SR., deceased, dated 9 Aug. 1783, prov-
           en 6 Sept. 1787. Wife - ELCE - all estate during her life;
children: (1) JAMES, my oldest son, (2) JOHN, (3) SARAH SPEAKES, (4)
ABIGAIL WELLS, (5) THOMAS, (6) SAMUEL, (7) Son-in-law, JERRORD SMITH.
Wit: THOMAS DUGAN, ISAAC MORGAN, MOSES LINDSAY, WILLIAM HAMILTON. Exrs:
wife ELCE and SAMUEL LINDSAY.

P 9:   WILL of ROBERT MANN, deceased, dated 27 Mar. 1782, proven
           6 Sept. 1787. Wife - SUSANNAH - plantatioin where (he) lives,
and all moveable property during her life. Children: (1) JAMES - 100
acres adj. Farr Springs, (2) JOHN - 100 acres adj. above tract, (3)
ROBERT - 100 acres whereon he lives, (4) JEAN NIX, (5) SUSANNAH, (6)
Grandson, MANASSE MANN - 50 acres next to JOSEPH GREEN's. Wit: SOLOMAN
REESE, ELIZABETH REESE, GEORGE GAGGAN. Exr's: JAMES MANN, SUSANNAH
MANN.

Pp 10-12: WILL of JAMES FORD of King's Creek, deceased, dated 13 May
          1787, proven 6 Sept. 1787. Wife mentioned but not named -
to have my old horse, called 'Shoemaker'. Children: (1) oldest dau.,
RAACHEL, to have feather bed and furniture but no more of my estate,
(2) REBECCA ANDERSON, now a widow, (3) ELIZABETH LINDSAY, the wife
of SAMUEL LINDSAY, (4) JOHN FORD, son of my deceased son JAMES. Wit:
ROBERT BROWN, GEORGE GRAY, JAMES LINDSAY. Exr's: REBECCA ANDERSON,
SAMUEL LINDSAY.

Pp 13-14: WILL of JOHN JOHNSTON, deceased, dated 7 Sept. 1787, at a
          court held in Newberry, letters of adm. were granted to JOHN
BARLOW in right of his wife, ELIZABETH, on the estate of JNO. JOHNSTON,
dec'd. Bondsmen were JOHN BARLOW, JEREMIAH WILLIAMS & WILLIAM YOUNG.
Appraisers were JOSEPH CALDWELL, WILLIAM CALDWELL & WILLIAM YOUNG.

P 15:   WILL of JOHN VAUN (VAUGHN?), deceased, dated 2 Jan. 1779,
           proven 2 June 1788. Wife ELIZABETH - to have all lands and
other property to be willed as she wishes. Wit: JOHN WALDROP, JOHN
MOTES, WILLIAM MURDOCK. Exr's: ELIZABETH VAUN, GEORGE GOGGANS.

P 16:   WILL of NATHANIEL HARRIS, deceased, dated 30 Dec. 1787, proven
           2 June 1788. Wife MARY - to enjoy all estate, both real and
personal, during her lifetime, then divided among my children and grandson. Children: (1) MOSEBY, (2) REBECCA, (3) RICHARD, (4) JEMINA GILLIAM,
(5) SAMUEL, (6) LITTLEBERRY, (7) CLOUGH - grandson, DAVID GILLIAM.
Wit: LEWIS MITCHELL, MOSEBY HARRIS, GEORGE ELLIOTT. Exr's.

Pp 17-18: Estate of ROBERT MANN, deceased, dated 3 June 1788, SUSANNAH
          MANN, Admx. JAMES MONTGOMERY, empowered to qualify appraisers.
EDWARD MUSGROVE, ROBERT HANNAH, Esq., JAMES CRAIG, BRASWELL PRATHER
Inventory dated 10 July 1788. Note: all the above named appraisers
lived on Enoree River in Laurens Co.

P 19:   WILL of ENOS ELLIMAN, deceased, dated 21 Apr. 1787, proven
           2 June 1788. Wife CATHERINE. Children: (1) JOHN, (2) WILLIAM,
(3) ELIZABETH, (4) AMEY, (5) HANNAH, (6) MARY BONDS. Wit: ROBERT SPEER,
ISAAC BALLENGER & SAMUEL BROWN. Exr's: JOHN ELLIMAN & CATHERINE ELLIMAN.

P 20:   WILL of ISAAC PARMER, deceasede, dated 31 Mar. 1787, proven
           2 June 1788. Wife SARAITH - 100 acres. Children: (1) WILLIAM
100 acres (2) my four daughters (not named) to have 51 pds 7 sh 7 p
current SC money. Wit: WILLIAM HERRING, ROBERT BROWN & CATREN RYLEY.
Exr's: SARAITH & WILLIAM PARMER.

P 21:   WILL of MATHIAS WICKER, JR., deceased, dated 5 June 1778,

Cont'd:
        proven 2 June 1788. Wife - SIBLA. My four children: (1) JOHN
ADAM (died ca 1827), (2) SIMON (died ca 1845), (3) MARY, (4) CATHERINE.
Exr's: JOHN ADAM YOUNG, MICHAEL DICKERT.

P 22:   WILL of GEORGE DAWKINS, deceased, (no date), proven 4 June
           1788. On oath of WILLIAM BALENTINE, a subscribing witness
to the will of GEORGE DAWKINS, dec'd. and ELIZABETH BEARD who had sd
will in her custody at the time of the death of the deceased but swore
the will was destroyed. Legatees: (1) MRS. JENINA HERBERT - to have
2 slaves and at her death to go to her children except NANCY BARRAT
to have one slave, (2) MRS. MARY ANN LANE - 2 slaves and at her death
to go to her children, (3) daughter, SUSANNAH POPE - 2 slaves, (4)
daughter, Widow GRIGABY - 2 slaves to go to her children at her death,
(5) ELLEN HAMPTON - granddaughter - 2 slaves, (6) son, GEORGE, JR.
- slaves, (7) grandson, THOMAS BARRETT - 1 slave, (8) grandson, WILLIAM
DAWKINS LANE - 1 slave. Exr's: son, GEORGE DAWKINS, JR. and nephew,
THOMAS DAWKINS.

P 25:   WILL of BENJAMIN PEARSON of Bush River, dated 10 Dec. 1784,
           proven 6 June 1788. Wife - MARGARET - to have 400 acre plan-
tation whereon I live during natural life or widowhood. Children: (1)
WILLIAM, (2) ABEL, (3) SAMUEL, (4) ROBERT, (5) JOSEPH, (6) JOHN, (7)
ENOCH. "Whereas I sold a tract of 200 acres to my brother, WILLIAM
PEARSON, now deceased, which if my sons pay the balance due, comes
to them.", (8) my daughter, ROSANNAH RUSSELL, (9) my daughter, MAJORY
BUFFINGTON. Wit: ZEBULAN GAUNTT, JOHN WILKERSON & JAMES KELLY. Exr's:
my wife MARGARET, my cousin, WILLIAM PEARSON, my son, ENOCH PEARSON.

Pp 26-27: WILL of GERALD SMITH, deceased, dated 3 June 1788. Admn.
          granted to widow ESTHER SMITH. Appraisers: JOHN LINDSAY,
Esq. and ROBERT RUTHERFORD.

Pp 30-32: WILL of JOHN GALLMAN, deceased, dated 3 Sept. 1788. Admn.
          granted to GASPER PIESTER. Appraisers: FREDERICK GRAY, JERE-
MIAH WILLIAMS, GEORGE RUFF, Esq. and JAMES SHEPPARD.

Pp 33-34: WILL of JACOB ANDERSON, deceased, dated 8 Sept. 1788. Admn.
          granted to JAMES STROTHER. Appraisers: LEVI ANDERSON, JOHN
BLALOCK, ABEL ANDERSON, SR. & ABRAHAM ANDERSON, JR.

Pp 35-37: WILL of JAMES WILLSON, deceased, dated 3 Sept. 1788. Admn.
          granted to JAMES WILLSON. Appraisers: DUDLEY BONDS, SAMUEL
CONNON, JESSE BROOKS, WILLIAM BLACKBURN.

Pp 38-40: WILL of WILLIAM O'NEALL, deceased, dated 15 July 1786, proven
          3 Sept. 1788. Wife - MARY - land whereon we live on west
side of Bush River. Children: (1) ABIJAH - land he lives on, (2) HUGH
- land with Grist Mill, (3) WILLIAM - land on North side Bush River
and saw mill, (4) JOHN - land on south side of Bush River, (5) HENRY
- land bet. JOHN's land and land of JAMES BROOKS, (6) THOMAS, (7) SARAH
FOARD. Trustees for children: WILLIAM PEARSON & HENRY STEDDOM. Wit:
ELISHA FORD, DAVID HOLLINGSWORTH & JOHN SANDERS.

Pp 42-45: WILL of DANIEL DE WALT, deceased, dated 17 Oct. 1776, proven
          2 Sept. 1788. Wife - SUSANNAH. Children: (1) MARY MAGDELINE,
(2) CATHERINE, (3) DANIEL, (4) PETER, (5) SUSANNAH. Ex'r: wife. Wit:
JOHN GALLMAN, MARTIN LEVISTON & MICHAEL DICKERT. Appraisers: JAMES
SHEPPARD, THOMAS SPEARMAN, WILLIAM SHEPPARD & JAMES SHEPPARD, JR.

Pp 46-48: WILL of RANDOLPH ROBINSON, deceased, dated 2 Mar. 1789. Admn.
          granted to widow, SUFFIAS ROBINSON and THOMAS GORDON, SR.
Appraisers: EDWARD KELLEY, JOHN LILES, SR., WILLIAMSON LYLES & THOMAS
LAKE.

P 49:   WILL of JACOB SHEARLY, dated 2 Mar. 1789. Admn. granted to
           widow, URSLEY SHEARLY.

P 51:   WILL of CHARLES KING, deceased, dated 21 Jan. 1789, proven
           2 Mar. 1789. Wife mentioned but not named. Children: (1)
)

Cont'd:
JACOB, (2) PENNINGTON KING, (3) LYDIA LINDSAY, (4) MARY STARKE, (5) CHARITY GORDON, (6) REBECCA KING, (7) KIZEAH KING. Wit: MICAJAH BEN-NETT, WILLIAM RAGLAND & SAMUEL RAGLAND. Ex'rs: son JACOB KING, son-in-law, JEREMIAH STARKE and friend, SAMUEL CANNON.

Pp 55-56: WILL of PETER DE WALT, deceased, dated 2 Feb. 1789, proven 2 Mar. 1789. Legatees: (1) brother-in-law, GEORGE GRAY, to have 100 acres that was willed to my father, (2) Mother, (3) Sisters: (1) CATHERINE, (2) MARY, (3) SUSANNAH, (4) RUTH. Wit: JOHN RILEY, WILLIAM MOORE & FREDERICK GRAY. Exr's: GEORGE GRAY & JAMES BOYLE.

Pp 57-60: WILL of JOHN GARY, JR. dated 29 Aug. 1785, proven 2 March 1789. Wife and children "to have all" - no names given. Wit: JOHN CALL & DANIEL WILLIAMS. Exr's: PROVIDENCE WILLIAMS.

Pp 61-62: WILL of HUGH CALDWELL, deceased, dated 2 Mar. 1789. JACOB ROBERTS BROWN to qualify the following appraisers: REUBEN GOLDING, GOLDING TINSLEY, JOHN TINSLEY, JAMES TINSLEY. Admr. granted to SAMUEL CALDWELL.

Pp 63-64: WILL of STEPHEN LEWIS, deceased, dated 11 Aug. 1788, proven 3 Mar. 1789. Wife MARY - 1/3 of land where she chooses, for her use during her life. Son, JAMES - rest of land and all moveable property and wife's 1/3 after her death (when he is 21 years old). Wit: DANIEL JOHNSON & SARAH JOHNSON. Exr's: GEORGE GOGGANS, MICHAEL SANDERS.

Pp 66-69: WILL of WILLIAM GILLIAM, dated 27 Feb. 1789, proven 3 March 1789. Wife, (not named). Children: JOHN, ANN, WILLIAM, HANNAH & MARY. WILLIAM to have all tenaments on Bush River and 165 acres where-on I now live and all of my carpenter tools. My daughter ANN to have one-half rent of tenaments for the maintences of my son, JOHN. Ex'r: HARMON DAVIS, JR. & DANIEL PERKINS. Wit: SAMUEL PEARSON, SR., THOMAS RIED, SR. & WILLIAM MC DARVELL.

P 70: WILL of WILLIAM TAYLOR, deceased, dated 10 Oct. 1781, proven 4 Mar. 1789. Wife, MARY. Children: (1) SAMUEL to have 250 acres whereon I now live, (2) JONATHAN - 200 acres, (3) MARTHA - 200 pounds lawful money, (4) PRUDENCE - youngest daughter - 200 pounds lawful money. Wit: SAMUEL KELLY, SAMUEL RIDGELL, JOSHUA REEDER. Exr's: MERCER BABB, SAMUEL PEARSON.

Pp 72-73: WILL of JOSEPH HOGG, deceased, dated 4 June 1789, Admnd. (granted) by GABRIEL ANDERSON. Appraisers: SAMUEL LINDSEY, JAMES STROTHER, ABRAHAM ANDERSON, LEVI ANDERSON.

P 74: WILL of CORNELIUS COX, deceased, dated 2 Nov. 1784, proven 8 Jan. 1790. Wife, ANN. Children: (1) WILLIAM, (2) GEORGE, (3) JAMES - to have 250 acres, (4) MARGARET, (5) SARAH, (6) ELIZABETH STEWART, (7) MARY STEWART, (8) JOHN. Wit: ROBERT SPEER, JAMES COX, MARGARET COX. Exr's: sons, GEORGE COX & WILLIAM COX.

P 75: WILL of THOMAS GRASTY, deceased, dated 1 Sept. 1789, proven 9 Dec. 1789. Sister, MARTHA GRASTY to have 150 acres and a slave. Brother, JOHN GRASTY to have a slave. Wit: EDWARD KELLY, JOHN LILES & ANN CHANDLER.

Pp 76-77: WILL of GEORGE COX, deceased, dated 10 Dec. 1789. Admr. grant-ed to JAMES COX. Appraisers: WILLIAM WEEKS, JOSHUA STEWART, THOMAS SPRAGGINS, JAMES WELLS.

Pp 78-79: WILL of GILES CHAPMAN, deceased, dated 18 Dec. 1789. Admr. granted to the widow, SARAH CHAPMAN. Appraisers: ELIAS HOL-LINGSWORTH, DAVID PUGH, DANIEL SMITH & MATHIAS ELMORE.

Pp 80-81: WILL of SAMUEL PEARSON, deceased, dated 16 Jan. 1788, proven 2 Mar. 1790. Wife, MARY to have 300 acres where I live, during her life. Children: (1) BENJAMIN, (2) SAMUEL, (3) ENOCH, (4) WILLIAM, (5) MARY TAYLOR, (6) MARTHA STEDDOM, (7) HANNAH, (8) EUNICE, (9) SARAH.

308

Cont'd:
My share of the mill, which is one-half to be sold and the price converted to the children above named. My step-father to be properly cared for during his life. Wit: WILLIAM HAWKINS, HUGH O'NEALL & WILLIAM O'-NEALL. Trustees: ZINURI GAUNTT, WILLIAM JENKINS.

Pp 82-84: WILL of WILLIAMS TURNER, deceased, dated 30 Dec. 1789, proven 3 Mar. 1790. Wife MARY to have the plantation we live on during her life or widow hood. Children: WILLIAM, DAVID, REBECCA, RHODA, EDWARDS, ABSALOM, SUSANNAH and ANN. Wit: JOSHUA INMAN, REBECCA TURNER, MICHAEL BURTZ. Exr's: wife MARY TURNER & friend, MERCER BABB.

Pp 85-86: WILL of JACOB HUFFMAN, deceased, dated 3 Mar. 1790. Admn. granted RACHEL DUNCAN. Appraisers: SAMUEL CANNON, JOSHUA REEDER, JAMES CASSELLS, JOHN CANNON.

P 87:   WILL of HANNAH RILEY, deceased, dated 10 Nov. 1788, proven 7 June 1790. Legatees: JESSE GRAHAM (or RILEY), JAMES GRAHAM, JOHN GRAHAM, JOEL GRAHAM. Beloved son, THOMAS RILEY, to have all personal property, etc. Exr's: THOMAS RILEY & JEREMIAH WILLIAMS. Wit: GEORGE NALLY, MARY ANN SMITH, CHRIS. HARDGROVES.

Pp 88-89: WILL of ENOCH PEARSON, deceased, dated 19 Jan. 1790, proven 7 June 1790. Wife PHEBE - to have plantation where we live during her life or widowhood. Children: SAMUEL - to have one-half of land we live on, also 290 acres I bought from JOHN RILEY; WILLIAM - to have other half of land I live on. Exr's: wife PHEBE PEARSON, bro., WILLIAM PEARSON, ABEL THOMAS & HENRY STEDDOM.

Pp 90-91: WILL of JOHN WRIGHT, SR. dated 17 Sept. 1789, proven 8 June 1790. Wife mentioned (no name). Children: (1) my deceased son JOSEPH - to his son, JOHN, (2) My deceased son JOHN - to his son JESSE, (3) my deceased son Nathan - to his son WILLIAM, (4) my son-in-law ISAAC HOLLINGSWORTH to have my shoe-makers tools and one certain cow and calf, (5) My son-in-law ISAAC COOK to have the price of a cow he never paid for. Other legatees: (1) JOAB BROOKS, son JAMES BROOKS, (2) JOSEPH COOK (my grandson) son of ISAAC COOK, (3) WILLIAM HOLLINGS-WORTH (my grandson), son of ISAAC HOLLINGSWORTH, (4) ISAAC COOK (my son-in-law) to have the price of a cow he never paid for, (5) RACHEL COOK, daughter of ISAAC COOK. Wit: ISAAC HOLLINGSWORTH, JOHN COATE, CHARITY COOK. Exr.: My son, JOSEPH WRIGHT.

Pp 92-93: WILL of THOMAS WILSON, dated 31 Mar. 1790. Admr. THOMAS GOR-DAN, SR. Admx.: SUFFIAS ROBINSON. Appraisers: JOHN LILES, SR., EDWARD KELLY, THOMAS LAKE, WILLIAMSON LILES.

Pp 94-96: WILL of CATHERINE HART, dated 7 June 1790. Admr. JAMES MAYSON & ISAAC CROWTHER. Appraisers: JAMES MAYSON, JR., JAMES CRES-WELL, BENJAMIN GLOVER, JR. & RICHARD GROOMS.

P 97:   WILL of WILLIAM SPEAKMAN, dated 15 Feb. 1786, proven 6 Sept. 1790. Wife MARY. Children: JOHN, ROBERT, MARGARET KELLY, ELIZABETH WELCH, CHRISTINA SPEAKMAN, WILLIAM SPEAKMAN, THOMAS SPEAK-MAN (William and Thomas to have the care of their mother) MARY SPEAK-MAN. Wit: JOHN LOFTON, JAMES KENNEDY, JOHN GARRIOT.

P 98:   WILL of JOHN BLALOCK, SR. (carpenter), dated 5 Aug. 1790, proven 16 May 1791. Wife (not named). Son: LEWIS, other lega-tees: (1) MICIJAH BENNETT, (2) REUBEN ROLAND, (3) JOHN BLALOCK BENNETT, (4) JOHN BLALOCK ROLAND, (5) LABARD OGLESBY, SR. and his seven child-ren. Wit: GEORGE BUSH, JOHN HOUSEN BUSH, JOHN BLALOCK ROLAND & LEWIS BLALOCK.

P 99:   WILL of JOSEPH CAMPBELL, dated 1 Sept. 1790, proven 16 May 1791. Wife SARAH - to have remainder of land located on Spring Branch. Children: (1) WILLIAM CAMPBELL, (2) JARIAT CAMPBELL - to have all land on Spring Branch and the orchard, (3) granddaughter, BETTY ANDERSON, other legatee, WILLIAM COATE. Wit: JOHN WALDROP, JAMES JOHN-SON & BENJAMIN JOHNSON. Exr's: SARAH CAMPBELL, JARIAT CAMPBELL.

Pp 100-102: WILL of PETER RUBLE, dated 24 Oct. 1789, proven 18 June
1791. (1) Son, SAMUEL - to have 150 acres, the southwest
part of land on branch of Bush River, (2) dau., SUSANNAH, the wife
of WILLIAM MC DOWELL, to have the northeast corner of tract to line
adj. WILLIAM GILLIAM's land, ZIMRI GAUNTT's and WALTER HARBOUR's land,
(3) MARY and her husband, WILLIAM MURDOCK to have 50 acres adj. WALTER
HARBOUR's, JOSEPH FREEMAN's and SAMUEL DUNKINS', (6) JANE LESTER to
have 25 pds sterling money. "This estate left to me by my father in
Frederick County, Virginia, near Winchester and to be equally divided
as aforesaid". Exr's: SAMUEL RUBLE, WILLIAM MC DOWELL, PETER LESTER,
WILLIAM MURDOCK. Wit: JOHN JOY & BETTY JOY.

P 103:   WILL of JOHN KELLY, dated 26 Aug. 1775, proven (no date).
Affidavit dated at Camden, S. C., 1 Nov. 1775, wife MARY
to have plantation whereon I live and one third of all personal property
during her life and then to my children. Children: (1) ISAAC, (2) SAM-
UEL, (3) Others whose names are not given. Exr's: wife and sons ISAAC
and SAMUEL. Wit: BENJAMIN PIDGEON, SARAH MAJOR. Wit to codicil: BENJAMIN
PIDGEON, JOHN MILHOUSE & Z. GAUNTT.

P 105:   WILL of BENJAMIN HEATON, dated 25 June 1790, proven 29
June 1791. Granddaughter HANNAH WEEKS; grandsons: WILLIAM
WEEKS, JOHN WEEKS, BENJAMIN WEEKS - these to have tract on Beaverdam
Creek, branch of Little River, in Laurens Co. JOHN to have the part
where house is located. JAMES WEEKS - 100 acres on King's Creek which
was bought from JOHN ATKINS. Great granddaughter, CHARITY WEEKS. Wit:
RHODAH BABB, SARAH HASKET, JUDE STIDMAN. Exr.: MERCER BABB.

P 107:   WILL of JOSEPH FISH, dated 16 May 1791. Admr. granted
to widow, ANN FISH.

Pp 109-111: WILL of SAMUEL CANNON, (no date), proven 16 May 1791.
Wife, LYDA - to have 100 acres - original grant in CLEMENT
DAVIS name. Children: (1) JOHN CANNON, (2) ISAAC CANNON, (3) JAMES
CANNON (my three eldest sons), (4) MARY CANNON (my eldest daughter),
(5) WILLIAM, (6) KIZIAH, (7) LYDA, (8) ELIZABETH (my youngest daughter).
Exr's: JOHN & ISAAC CANNON, my sons. Wit: THOMAS CLARK, KIZIA CANNON
& ELIZABETH C. CANNON.

Pp 112-114: WILL of JOSEPH DAVENPORT, dated 5 Aug. 1788, proven 16
May 1791. Wife (not named). Children: (1) REBECCA SATTER-
WHITE to have 200 acres where she now lives, (2) AMY PHILLIPS to have
certain slaves and personal property, (3) DAVID DAVENPORT. Granddaughters: (1) JEMINA SATTERWHITE, dau. of BARTLETT and REBECCA, (2) EDNA
and (3) JEMINA GOODE, daus. of SAMUEL and JEMINA GOODE. Grandsons:
(1) JOSEPH PHILLIPS, son of JOHN and AMY, (2) JOSEPH DAVENPORT, son
of DAVID and HANNAH. Other legatees: NILOT WELCH to have 3 pds sterling
during her life and a small room and fireplace in east end of my dwelling house and provisions. Exr's: WILMA MOORE & JAMES CALDWELL. Wit:
JOHN THOMAS SATTERWHITE, STARLING DIXON & ALEXANDER MC MULLEN.

Pp 115-119: WILL of NICHOLAS SLIKE, dated 27 Sept. 1790, proven 16
May 1791. Wife CATRINA SLIKE - 1/3 of my estate. Children:
(1) JOHN UVEY, (2) JACOB (all land) "oldest children to have certain
slaves". Exr's: JOHN LIVINGSTON, JR., PHILLIP SLIKE & JACOB BUZZARD.
Wit: JOHN LIVINGSTON, FREDERICK BOOZER & JACOB LIPPELMAN.

Pp 120-121: WILL of CHRISTIAN HOUPTE, dated 10 Mar. 1790. Admr. granted
to widow, MARY HOUPTE. Appraisers: WILLIAM HOUSEAL, ADAM
LAGRANNE, JOHN LIVINGSTON, JOHN EICHLEBERGER.

Pp 122-124: WILL of JOHN GREEN, dated 16 Nov. 1790, proven 16 May
1791. Neice: GREEN GREEN. Nephew: WILLIAM GREEN (children
of my deceased brother, WILLIAM GREEN "all lands and property". Wit:
LEWIS HUNT, EDMUND KELLY, AGNES KELLY. Exr's: JAMES KELLY & WILLIAM
WADLINGTON. Named by court, 25 May 1791.

Pp 125-127: WILL of SAMUEL CHAPMAN, dated 16 May 1791. Admr. granted
to JOSEPH & WILLIAM CHAPMAN. Appraisers: THOMAS SMITH,
ISREAL GAUNTT, WILLIAM ASPERNELL, FRANCIS ATKINS.

310

Pp 129-131: WILL of EDWARD WADLINGTON, dated 24 Dec. 1790, proven
16 May 1791. Wife, FRANCES. Children: JOHN, SARAH ANN,
JESSE, BAILEY, SPENCER, NANCY. Exr's: wife, FRANCES and brother, WIL-
LIAM WADLINGTON, WILLIAM MALONE, SR. Wit: GEORGE WADLINGTON, JOHN WALSH
& ANN HAMPTON.

Pp 132-133: WILL of JAMES SPROUL, dated 28 July 1791. Admr. granted
JEAN SPROUL and JOHN BOYER (BOYCE?). Appraisers: JOHN
BOYER, GEORGE ATKINS, EDWARD GOREE, THOMAS DUCKETT.

P 134: WILL of ANNA MARY BUZHARDT, dated 13 Nov. 1790, proven
27 July 1791. Husband, JOHN BUZHARDT. Children: BARBARA
MOFFETT, ANNA MARY HAIR, MATTHAIS HAIR, JOHN HAIR (to have 100 acres
willed me by my first husband, PETER HAIR), CATHERINE VEITS, RACHEL
CHARLES, AGNES STOCKMAN, MARGARET MC CALLIE and MOLLY THOMAS. Wit:
LORENTZ RIGART, JOHN RIGART (RICKART?) and MICHAEL DICKERT, SR. Exr's:
sons, JOHN & MATTHAIS HAIR.

P 135: WILL of PETER HAIR, dated 24 Aug. 1772, proven 25 Nov.
1790. HETTIE HAIR, JR. "to have 100 acres on Cannon's
Creek. Sons: JOHN - 100 acres on Cowpen Creek; MATTHAIS - 100 acres
on Cowpen Creek; wife, MARY - 1/3 personal estate and 100 acres on
Cannon's Creek then to the two children as she seep proper". My nine
children: (1) MARY, (2) JOHN, (3) CATHERINE, (4) RACHEL, (5) AGNES,
(6) MARGARET, (7) MOLLY, (8) MATTHAIS, (9) BARBARA. Wit: SAMUEL CANNON,
LYDIA CANNON & SAMUEL LONUM.

P 136: WILL of ELIZABETH VAUGHN, dated 2 Feb. 1791, proven 18
Oct. 1791. Children: (1) WILLIAM DODGEN, (2) ELIZABETH
COLE, (3) OLLEMAN DODGEN. Grand children: (1) ANN TOLAND, (2) JAMES
DODGEN. Exr's: GEORGE GOGGANS, DANIEL PITTS, SR. Wit: WILLIAM SMITH,
CHRISTIAN PITTS.

P 137: WILL of SHADRACK CARTER, dated 17 Oct. 1791. Admr. granted
to ELIZABETH CARTER. Appraisers: LEVI MANING, CHARLES
BANKS, ETHELRED KING & DAVID LINDSEY. PETER JULIEN, J.P.

Pp 138-139: WILL of JAMES SHEPPARD, dated 11 Oct. 1791. Admr. granted
to JANNET SHEPPARD. Appraisers: GEORGE GRAY, FREDERICK
GRAY, DANIEL DE WALT.

Pp 141-142: WILL of ELISHA BROOKS, SR., dated 29 July 1791. Admr.
granted to ELISHA BROOKS, JR.

Pp 142-143: WILL of JOHN DOYLE, dated 17 Oct. 1791. Admr. granted
to MARY DOYLE. Appraisers: ADAM CHAMBERS, JAMES MC CRACKEN,
GEORGE AUBREY, ARTHUR MC CRACKEN.

Pp 144-145: WILL of THEODORES FELTMAN, dated 29 July 1791. Admr. grant-
ed to JACOB BUZHARDT, who was guardian of son, FREDERICK
FELTMAN and other children. Appraisers: WILLIAM ELMORE, GEORGE SUBER,
RUDOLPH BUZARD.

Pp 146-147: WILL of AMBROSE WHITTEN, dated 18 Oct. 1791. Admr. granted
to ELIJAH WHITTEN. Appraisers: ABNER CASEY, ROBERT WILSON,
JOSIAH DUCKETT, JOHN DUNCAN.

P 149: WILL of JOHN DOYLE, dated 10 Jan. 1792. Admr. granted
to MARY DIAL (DOYLE). Buyers at sale were JEREMIAH DIAL,
MARY DIAL and others.

P 150: WILL of RICHARD BARTWISLE, dated 25 June 1789, proven
2 Mar. 1791. MILLY LAYTON - 1/3 part of my estate as wages
for her constant care and service done to me with 1/3 part of remainder
to her use for life. Balance of estate to MARY BARTWISLE LAYTON, daughter of MILLY LAYTON, plus 5 pds. sterling to help having her schooled.
Exr's: HENRY STEDDOM, WILLIAM PEARSON. Wit: ROBERT SPEER, AMOS DUNKIN
(DUNCAN), & JUDITH PEMBERTON.

(above must include pp 151-152; following starts p. 153)

Pp 153-154:   WILL of GEORGE GRAYHAM, dated 9 Feb. 1792. Admr. to JESSE
              GRAYHAM. Buyers were: JESSE GRAYHAM, JAMES GRAYHAM, MARY
GRAYHAM, WILLIAM RIDDLE & DAVID CANNON.

P 155:   WILL of JACOB GRAY, dated 16 Jan. 1792, proven 22 May
              1792. Exrt'x: (3) daughters, ANN PITTS, AGNES BUTLER &
ELIZABETH GRAY. Wit: DAVID MOTES, AARON BUTLER & WILLIAM DODGEN.

P 156:   WILL of SHADRACK CARTER (Estate Sale). Dated 12 June 1792.
              Widow - ELIZABETH.

P 157:   WILL of JOHN HELLER, dated 17 Oct. 1792. Admr. granted
              to CATHERINE HELLER. Appraisers: CHRISTIAN RUFF, CONRAD
ZUBER, LEONARD ZUBER, SANFORD COCKRELL.

Pp 159-160:   WILL of HENRY OXNER, deceased, dated 21 May 1792. Admr.
              granted to JACOB OXNER. Appraisers: ADAM KELLER, MICHAEL
SUBER, DAVID COLLINS.

Pp 161-162:   WILL of ROBERT JOHNSON, deceased, dated 28 July 1792.
              Admr. granted to JOHN GATES. Appraisers: WILLIAM FARROW,
SR., JOHN MOORE & THOMAS FARROW.

Pp 163-164:   WILL of MARTIN SINGLEY, deceased, dated 15 Mar. 1780,
              proved 1 Mar. 1793. Wife - (German letters) (also-FANNY
ROSIER) (also ZR. FOURINGRISER) to have all my estate, both real and
personal as long as she remains single and to pay my debts. Children:
(1) JACOB, my son - 150 acres (at mother's death), (2) my son, FREDER-
ICK - 25 pds gold or silver, (3) my youngest daughter, to be maintained
and schooled, (4) other children not named. Wit: RUDOLPH LE GRONNE,
ROBERT LE GRONNE, THOMAS HUGHES. Appraisers: JAMES MC MASTERS, FRED-
ERICK BOOZER, PHILLIP SLIGH, JOHN LIVINGSTON.

P 165:   WILL of JOHN BUCHANAN, deceased, dated 14 June 1785, proven
              28 Feb. 1793. Wife ELIZABETH - to have use of 2/3 land
on northside of Heller's Creek adj. Broad River. Children: (1) NANCY
TURLEY - to have 1/3 part of my land whereon I now live on southside
of Heller's Creek, (2) JESSE, (3) JOHN, (4) MICAJAH, (5) WILLIAM, (6)
MARCY HUTCHINSON, (7) ANNA FORD, (8) SUSANNAH. Exr's: son-in-law JAMES
FORD and son, WILLIAM BUCHANAN. Wit: NIMROD MORRIS, THOMAS THOMLEY,
JACOB GIBSON, SR.

P 166:   WILL of SAMUEL LONAM, deceased, dated 12 July 1777, proven
              20 May 1793. Wife OLIVE LONAM - 100 acres during her life,
which was granted to GEORGE HARTLEY; son - SQUIRE LONAM - to have all
land after death of my wife. "Every sister of SQUIRE to have 5 shillings sterling to be paid by OLIVE LONAM, Extr'x. Wit: BERNARD MOUNTZ,
JOHN GEORGE MOUNTZ & BARBARY MOUNTZ.

(Note: another copy of pp 163-164: on Will of MARTIN SINGLEY, shows
daughter, ROSANNAH, who married HENRY WERTZ.)

P 167:   WILL of DR. DANIEL HANING, deceased, dated 28 July 1793.
              Admr. granted to PETER BRAZZELMAN. Appraisers: ROBERT
POWELL, CHARLES CRENSHAW, WILLIAM WILSON & JOHN C. ROYSTON.

P 171:   WILL of WILLIAM TAYLOR, deceased, dated 28 Feb. 1793.
              Admr. granted to MERCER BABB.

P 176:   WILL of JOHN KELLY, SR., deceased, dated 2 Mar. 1793.
              Admr. granted to SAMUEL KELLY, JR. & ABIJAH O'NEAL.

P 181:   WILL of JANNETT WALKER, deceased, dated 26 June 1775,
              proven 20 May 1793. Legatees: JOHN KINARD and his heirs
- 100 acres on Indian Creek. Wit: GEORGE ANDERSON, WILLIAM GARY.

P 182:   WILL of JAMES JOHNSTON, deceased, dated 28 Feb. 1793.
              Admr. granted to ELLENDER JOHNSTON. Appraisers: ISAAC
EVANS, HUGH MARSHALL, JACOB KING & MICHAEL JOHNSTON.

Pp 184-187: WILL of WILLIAM FARROW, deceased, dated 28 May 1792, proven
26 July 1793. Wife LEONY FARROW - to have use of all property as long as she lives. Children: (1) THOMAS, (2) WILLIAM, (3) SARAH,
(4) JEAN D., (5) SAMUEL JACKSON, (6) ELI. Grand-daughter, SYDNEY FARROW,
eldest dau. of my son THOMAS. Wit: THOMAS FARROW, J. R. BROWN, WILLIAM
MALONE (C.C.N.D.) Clerk of Court, Newberry District. Appraisers: JACOB
ROBERTS BROWN, JAMES CALDWELL, WILLIAM CALDWELL & JOHN MOORE.

Pp 188-189: WILL of WILLIAM WILSON, deceased, dated 20 May 1793. Admr.
granted to JAMES WILSON. Appraisers: JAMES BARNS, THOMAS
DAVIS & DUDLEY BARNES.

Pp 190-191: WILL of WILLIAM JOHNSTON, deceased, dated 20 May 1793.
Admr. granted to NELLY JOHNSTON. Appraisers: EPHRAIM CAN-
NON, RICHARD GAINS, ROBERT STEEL, ALEXANDER JOHNSTON.

Pp 192-193: WILL of WILLIAM ELMORE, deceased, dated 31 Jan. 1780,
proven 20 May 1793. Wife ABIGAIL ELMORE - to have 300
acares on Bush River during her lifetime. Children: (1) JOHN, (2) RIDGE-
WAY, (3) JOSEPH, (4) STEVEN, (5) MARY, (7) RACHEL. Exr's: wife ABIGAIL
ELMORE and son, JOHN ELMORE. Wit: TERRANCE RILEY, JOHN KINARD, THOMAS
SMITH.

Pp 194-195: WILL of JAMES GLASGO, deceased, dated 17 Oct. 1775, proven
30 July 1793. Wife MARY - to have 1/3 of all personal
property, house and 50 acres, formerly belonging to JAMES CANNON. Children: (1) ROBERT - to have 100 acres with house in which I now live
in Gilder's Creek, (2) MARGARET, (3) JOHN - to have 50 acres, (4) RACHEL,
(5) ARCHIBALD WILSON GLASGO. Wit: JAMES FINLEY, ANN FINLEY, THOMAS
DUGAN.

Pp 196-198: WILL of WILLIAM MILES, deceased, dated 30 July 1793. Admr.
granted to SAMUEL MILES, DAVID MILES & WILLIAM MILES,
JR. Sale dated 28 Dec. 1793.

Pp 199-200: WILL of ALLEN ROBINSON, deceased, dated 28 July 1793.
Admr. granted to the widow, SARAH ROBINSON. Appraisers:
LEVI MANNING, DANIEL PARKINS, MARK SMITH.

Pp 202-203: WILL of PETER GALLOWAY, deceased, dated 28 July 1793.
Admr. granted to the widow, MARY GALLOWAY. Appraisers:
ROBERT SPEAR, JAMES PLUNCKETT, THOMAS BROWN, JOHN DOUGLAS.

Pp 204-205: WILL of JOHN CARLE, deceased, dated 21 Oct. 1793. Admr.
granted to THOMAS HASKETT. Appraisers: JAMES WADLINGTON,
BENJAMIN EVANS, ABIJAH O'NEAL.

Pp 206-208: WILL of THOMAS CLARK, deceased, dated 21 Dec. 1790, proven
21 Oct. 1793. Wife MARY (mother of my children) to have
250 acres plantation during her life or until her youngest son is 21
years old. Children: (1) eldest son, JOHN, (2) second son, THOMAS,
(3) third son, GEORGE, (4) JAMES, (5) ROBERT, (6) MARY, wife of JOHN
LEWIS, (7) JEAN, wife of JOHN REES, (8) ELIZABETH, (9) ANN, (10) PRIS-
CILLA. Exr.: wife MARY and son, JOHN CLARK. Wit: JOB CALVIN, CHARLES
GARY, JR. & JAMES LINDSEY.

P 209: WILL of ALEXANDER BUOYS (BOYCE), deceased, dated 31 July
1793. Admr. granted to JOHN BUOYS (BOYCE).

P 210: WILL of HENRY ANDERSON, deceased, dated 28 Feb. 1794.
Admr. granted to JESSE ANDERSON. Appraisers: THOMAS GORDAN,
MICAJAH HARRIS, LEVI ANDERSON.

Pp 211-213: WILL of SOLOMON NICHOLS, deceased, dated 6 Apr. 1791,
proven 28 Feb.1794. Wife ELIZABETH and her children by
a former marriage (previous transfers of land confirmed). Wit: WILLIAM
WILSON, SIMS BROWN, ROBERT BROWN.

Pp 214-215: WILL of ROBERT KENNEDY, deceased, dated 28 Feb. 1794.
Admr. granted to LUCRETIA KENNEDY and GEORGE HERBERT.

Cont'd:
Appraisers: CHARLES CRENSHAW, THOMAS HARDY & JOHN MAXFIELD.

Pp 216-217: WILL of ADAM CLAY, deceased, dated 28 Feb. 1794. Admr.
granted to JAMES CLAY and JAMES MC MASTER. Appraisers:
JOHN H. RUFF, JOHN KINARD, EPHRAIM CANNON.

Pp 218-219: WILL of WILLIAM CAMPBELL, deceased, dated 2 Mar. 1793.
Admr. granted to JOHN BOYCE. Appraisers: PATRICK LOWREY,
JAMES MC MAHAN, EDWARD GOREE, WILLIAM SCOTT.

Pp 220-221: WILL of JAMES COX, deceased, dated 20 May 1794. Admr.
granted to WILLIAM COX. Appraisers: ROBERT SPEAR, DANIEL
RICHARDSON, GEORGE ARNOLD.

Pp 222-224: WILL of HENRY DUNN, deceased, dated 19 May 1794. Admr.
granted to DANIEL PARKINS. Appraisers: DANIEL RICHARDSON,
WILLIAM CARWELL, WILLIAM GOULD.

Pp 225-226: WILL of JOHN WALDROP, deceased, dated 27 June 1794, proven
20 Oct. 1794. Wife TABE (TABITHA?) to have all moveable
property and 200 acres during widowhood. Children: (1) EZEKIEL - if
he dies before his children marry and before ROBERT WALDROP comes of
age - money to be kept by the Executors until children come of age
or marry, (2) HEZEKIAH, (3) STEPHEN, (4) DAVID, (5) WILLIAM, (6) ISAAC,
(7) JOHN, (8) ANN ELIZABETH, (9) TABBY, (10) JUDEY, (11) CHRISTINA
PITTS, (12) SARAH CAMPBELL. Exrs: CHARLES GRIFFIN, STEPHEN WALDROP.
Wit: BARTLETT SATTERWHITE, SR., DAVID DAVENPORT, WILLIAM WALLACE.

Pp 227-229: WILL of JOHN HARMON, deceased, dated 20 July 1789, proven
19 May 1794. Wife MARY - 150 acres whereon I now live.
Children: (1) GODFREY - 250 acres on northside of Saluda River called
Beaverdam Creek, (2) JOHN - 100 acres on Buffalo Creek adj. JOHN RUFF,
(3) THOMAS - 200 acres on Buffalo Creek adj. JAMES WILLIAMS, (4) WILLIAM
- 139 acres adj. LIGHTNER's land. Exrs: THOMAS SMITH, JACOB HARMON.
Wit: CHARLES THOMPSON, ABRAHAM THOMPSON, SAMUEL MC QUERNS.

Pp 230-232: WILL of JOHN ODELL, deceased, dated 19 May 1794. Admr.
granted to ELLENOR ODELL. Appraisers: RIGNAL ODELL, GASSA-
WAY ROGERS, HENRY DAVIS. (Note: JOHN ODELL is said to have been a son
of THOMAS ODELL of Maryland. Some of his land holdings lay in Laurens
Co. and devolved to his children (1) RUTH who married MOSES HENDRICKS,
(2) JOHN, JR. who married REBECCA HENDRICKS, (3) MARTHA who married
THOMAS HENDRICKS, (4) others.)

Pp 233-235: WILL of JOHN WILSON, deceased, dated 7 Apr. 1794, proven
19 May 1794. Wife ELIZABETH - 1/3 of land during her life
or widowhood; daughters: (1) SARAH, (2) MARY (2/3 of all property).
Exrs: (Brothers) JAMES WILSON, THOMAS WILSON. Wit: H. W. WILSON, CHARLES
WILSON, MARY WILSON. (Actually, Sarah and Mary to get the 2/3's, Ed.)

Pp 237-239: WILL of DAVID MARTIN (Minister of Gospel), deceased, date
4 May 1794, proven 29 July 1794. Wife MARTHA - to have
1/3 part of money from estate. Children: (1) my daughter, CATRON BLACK,
(2) my daughter, HESTER COLLEY, (3) my daughter, DEBOROUGH MARTIN,
(4) my daughter, RUTH MARTIN, (5) my son, DAVID, (6) my son, GEORGE,
(7) my son, SOLOMON, (8) my son, SAMUEL. Exrs: wife MARTHA and son
DAVID MARTIN and WILLIAM SUMMER. Wit: D. CLARY, JOSHUA MARTIN, PETER
HAWKINS.

P 240: WILL of AZARIAH PUGH, deceased, dated 9 Apr. 1794, proven
20 Oct. 1794. Wife (not named). Children: (1) THOMAS -
plantation whereon I now live, (2) WILLIAM - 143 acres, (3) my other
children - all moveable property, (4) one share to PETER JULIEN's children. Exrs: ELLIS PUGH, JESSE PUGH. Wit: ISAAC JENKINS, JESSE JENKINS,
DAVID JENKINS.

P 241: WILL of JOHN CRUMLEY, deceased, dated 19 June 1794, proven
20 Oct. 1794. Wife HANNAH - land whereon I now live during

Cont'd:
her life. Children: (1) eldest son, THOMAS - to have 5 shillings sterling money, (2) CHARLES - 250 acres whereon he now lives originally
surveyed for WILLIAM CALDWELL, (3) SAMUEL - 251 acres being part of
two surveys laid out for DAVID PUGH, (4) JAMES - 251 acres being part
of tract laid out to JAMES COATES, (5) BENJAMIN - 200 acres on Beaverdam Creek surveyed for JOSEPH BUCKAM, or the homeplace if he chooses,
after the death of my wife, (6) daughter, RACHEL, (7) daughter, CATHER-
INE, (8) JEMINA, (9) daughter, SARAH - "There being 300 pds sterling
in Virginia in the hands of ROBERT BULL and JOSEPH LUPTON due next
May and which is to be sent for and all debts paid, then remainder
to be divided equally amongst all my children and their mother. Exrs:
Wife, HANNAH CRUMLEY, JOSHUA INMAN, ROBERT RICHARDSON. Wit: THOMAS
COATS, RACHEL BURTS, JEMINA CRUMLEY.

Pp 242-243: WILL of ISAAC PUGH, deceased, dated 19 May 1794. Admr.
             granted to WILLIAM RICHARDS. Appraisers: GEORGE JOHNSON,
JAMES HARDIMAN, BENJAMIN HAMPTON, WILLIAM CALMES.

P 244:   WILL of JOSEPH WRIGHT, deceased, dated 1 June 1794. Admr.
             granted to CHARITY WRIGHT. Appraiser: JAMES BEATTY.

P 245:   WILL of ALLEN COX, deceased, dated 19 May 1794. Admr.
             granted to JAMES COX. Appraisers: JOHN ATKINSON, DANIEL
DYSON, JAMES HILL, BARTLETT SATTERWHITE, SR.

Pp 248-249: WILL of JOHN WALLER, deceased, dated 19 May 1794. Admr.
             granted to WILLIAM HILL. Appraisers: THOMAS GORDAN, SR.,
DAVID FERGUSON, JOHN CLARK, JOHN MAXEDUN.

Pp 250-251: WILL of SAMUEL CHAPMAN, deceased, dated 20 May 1794. Admr.
             granted to JOSEPH CHAPMAN. Appraisers: JOHN COATE, FRANCIS
ATKINS, BENJAMIN ATKINS, JOHN WILSON.

P 252:   WILL of JOHN MANGUM, deceased, dated 20 May 1794. Admr.
             granted to WILLIAM MANGUM. Appraisers: JAMES WALDROP,
JOHN FLOYD, DANIEL MC KIE.

Pp 254-256: WILL of HUGH CREIGHTON, deceased, dated 5 Aug. 1793, proven
             21 Oct. 1794. Wife (not named) - 100 acre plantation where-
on I now live and personal property. (1) Grand-daughter, MARY DENNIS
to have a riding saddle and the bed we lie on, after my wife's death,
(2) my two grandchildren, JOEL DENNIS and CREIGHTON WARD, when they
arrive at age, all monies equally divided between them, (3) my daughters, MARY WARD and ANNE DENNIS. Exr: DANIEL PARKINS. Wit: :SAMUEL
KELLY, SR., SAMUEL KELLY, JR., JOHN KELLY, SR.

Pp 257-260: WILL of ROBERT SPENCER, deceased, dated 20 Oct. 1794.
             Admr. granted to RACHEL SPENCER. Appraisers: JOSHUA INMAN,
WALTER BARBOUR, JOSEPH COOK.

P 261:   WILL of WILLIAM GIBREATH, deceased, dated 2 Oct. 1794,
             proven 3 Mar. 1795. Wife MARY. Children: (1) JESSE - 1/3
price of land in Wilkes Co., N. C., (2) MARY, (3) JOHN, (4) WILLIAM,
(5) ALEXANDER, (6) GEORGE - 1/3 price of land in Wilkes Co., N. C.,
(7) SARAH THOMPSON and her heirs, (8) NANCY TURNER - 1/3 price of land
in Wilkes Co., N. C. Exrs: wife, MARY, son GEORGE, and son, JESSE GIB-
REATH. Wit: CHARLES CRENSHAW, STEPHEN PEARSON, ELIZABETH CAMPBELL.

Pp 262-267: WILL of ANDREW MC LEASE, SR., deceased, dated 11 Sept.
             1794, proven 28 Feb. 1795. Wife, JEAN - to have 100 acres
adj. JOHN WILSON's line. Children: (1) ANDREW - 100 acres after death
of my wife, (2) ROBERT - 100 acres after death of my wife, (3) MARTHA
- 50 acres after death of my wife, (4) JENNET - 50 acres after death
of my wife. Exrs: wife JEAN and son ROBERT. Wit: PATRICK SCURRY, WILLIAM
WILSON, JAMES HAYS.

Pp 268-271: WILL of JOHN CLARKE, deceased, dated 7 Jan. 1795, proven
             28 Feb. 1795. (1) my brother3, J. THOMAS CLARKE - 270
acres on west fork of Tyger River, (2) GEORGE CLARKE, (3) my brother,

Cont'd:
JAMES CLARKE, (4) my brother, ROBERT CLARKE, (5) my sister, PRISCILLA
CLARKE. Exrs: THOMAS CLARKE, brother, and PATRICK LOWERY. Wit: REUBEN
FLANNEGAN, JOHN WILLIAMS, ROBERT CALDWELL.

Pp 272-273:   WILL of SAMUEL PROCTOR, deceased, dated 24 Oct. 1794,
               proven 19 May 1795. "Late of Newberry County but now of
Laurens County, S. C." Wife (not named). Children: (1) SAMUEL - 50
acres, (2) PHILLIP - 50 acres being part of 350 acres adj. Dr. JOHN
CALDWELL and his wife, MARGARET, deceased. Then after PHILLIP's death,
to be property of my grandson, HENRY PROCTOR, (3) EDWARD - 50 acres
adj. DANIEL CLARKE, (4) JEAN MC CALL - 15 pds sterling, (5) SARAH ADAMS
- 10 pds sterling, (6) son-in-law, JOSEPH WHITE remainder of the above
mentioned 350 acres except 50 acres to my grandson, SAMUEL ADAMS, (7)
my other daughter, MARY WININGHAM - 15 pds sterling. Exrs: JOSEPH WHITE
& THOMAS FRAKES. Wit: JOHN DENDY, EPHRAIM NIGHT, STEPHEN KESSOLO(?).

P 274:   WILL of JONATHAN TAYLOR, deceased, dated 9 Oct. 1793,
               proven 18 May 1795. Wife MARY - 1/3 land during widowhood.
Children: (1) WILLIAM, deceased - his heirs to have land whereon his
widow, MARY, now lives, (2) RICHARD, deceased _his widow, MARY, to
have 5 shillings sterling, (3) JONATHAN - land whereon I now live,
(4) ISAAC - land on Indian Creek, (5) son-in-law, JOHN THOMAS and his
son, WILLIAM THOMAS - 50 acres on Indian Creek, (6) ANN CHANDLER -
land, then to her sons, ISREAL CHANDLER & JONATHAN CHANDLER. Exrs:
sons-in-law, RICHARD LEAVELL, JOSHUA REEDER and son, JONATHAN TAYLOR.
Wit: ABRAHAM (...?...), RHODA TAYLOR, WILLIAM BELTON.

Pp 276-279:   WILL of RICHARD STRAWTHER, deceased, dated 28 Feb. 1795.
               Admr. granted to GABRIEL GERRALD. Appraisers: NIMROD HARRIS,
JAMES BAIRD, LANGFORD COCKRELL.

Pp 280-286:   WILL of HENRY WILSON, deceased, dated 6 Apr. 1795, proven
               18 May 1795. Children: (1) NANCY, (2) MARY, (3) TAPPHENAS,
(4) EDNA (my four daughters), (5) my son, JAMES, (6) my son HENRY.
Exrs: JAMES CALDWELL & ROBERT GILLIAM, JR. Wit: PHILLIP PROCTOR, and
MARGARET PROCTOR.

P 287:   WILL of JOHN WILKINSON, SR., deceased, dated 13 May 1795,
               proven 28 July 1795. Children: (1) son, JOHN WILKINSON,
(2) daughter, SARAH WILKINSON - 100 acres whereon I now live. Exr.:
EDWARD BENBOW. Wit: EDWARD BENBOW & THOMAS REID.

Pp 288-290:   WILL of JOHN GAREY (GOREE), SR., deceased, dated 19 May
               1795, proven 28 July 1795. Wife SARAH - all my estate
during her life. Children: (1) JOHN, (2) JOSEPH, (3) CLAUDIUS, (4)
JOICE LYLES, (5) MOLLY FERGUSON. Exrs: sons, JOHN GOREE & JOSEPH GOREE.
Wit: RICHARD BONDS, JOHNSON FERGUSON, JAMES WATERS.

P 290:   WILL of ALEXANDER CHALMERS, deceased, dated 7 July 1795,
               proven 27 July 1795. Wife JANE - plantation for life.
Children: (1) DAVID, (2) WILLIAM, (3) MATTHEW and his son, ALEXANDER
- 1/3 land, (4) JANE HOPPER, (5) ALEXANDER (JR.) - 2/3 of sd plantation after death of my wife. Exrs: wife JANE CHALMERS and WILLIAM WIL-
SON. Wit: URIAH HARDIMAN, ROBERT POWELL, WILLIAM LEAVELL.

Pp 291-194:   WILL of MARY ANN LANE, deceased, dated 10 Nov. 1792, proven
               19 May 1795, "widow of Lexington District, S. C.". Child-
ren: (1) THOMAS, (2) WILLIAM, (3) JAMES (minor), (4) MARY TAYLOR. Whereas under the will of my father, GEORGE DAWKINS, deceased, certain negroes were lent to me during my life are to be divided amongst my heirs.
Exrs.: JAMES BAIRD & WILLIAM DAWKINS. Wit: BARBARA BAIRD, HANEY DAW-
KINS, BETTY BAIRD.

Pp 295-299:   WILL of MRS. MARY DAVIS, deceased, dated 19 Mar. 1791,
               proven 18 May 1795. (1) my son, CHESLEY DAVIS, (2) My
son, SAMUEL DAVIS (to have all land). Exrs: sons, CHESLEY & SAMUEL.
Wit: E. WORTHINGTON, JAMES BLACK, DAVID BERRY. (Note: actually both
sons to have land. Ed.)

Pp 299-306: WILL of MATTHEW SIMS, SR., deceased, dated 14 Apr. 1795,
proven 18 May 1795. Wife JEMINA - all lands during life.
Children: (1) son, CHARLES, (2) son, MATTHEW, deceased - to his wife,
MARY, (3) son, JAMES, deceased - to his heirs, (4) son, NATHAN, deceased
-to his heirs, (5) son, REUBEN, (6) son, DAVID, (7) daughter, HANNAH
HENDERSON, (8) dau. DRUCILLA BACKLEY, (9) dau. MARY SANDERS, (10) dau.
ANN HENDERSON. Grandchildren: WILLIAMS SIMS and SARAH SHELTON, the
children of my son, CHARLES. "If MATTHEW's wife, MARY, should take
her third part or right of dower of a certain tract of land in Hanover
County, Va., which I did purchase from my son, MATTHEW, and did give
to my son, NATHAN, I direct my executors to detain out of my son, MATT-
HEW's estate as much as will fully satisfy my son NATHAN's estate and
pay to admrs. of estate of sd NATHAN. And in case my widow does not
claim dower, my executors are not to detain any part of my son MATTHEW,s
deceased, estate. Exrs: son, REUBEN SIMS and kinsman, BERNARD GLENN.
Wit: JOHN STEWART, FANNY STEWART, GEORGE WILSON.

Pp 304-305: WILL of HENRY LYLES, deceased, dated 18 May 1795. Admr.
granted to the widow, NANCY LYLES. Appraisers: JOHN GOREE,
THOROUGHGOOD CHAMBERS, JAMES KELLY.

P 306: WILL of ARCHIBALD MC QUERNS, deceased, dated 8 July 1795.
Admr. granted to JAMES MC QUERNS.

Pp 305-310: WILL of JAMES FINLEY, deceased, dated 1 Sept. 1787, proven
9 July 1795, of Indian Creek. Wife ANN - all property.
My brother, ROBERT's heirs - one shilling, my brother HUGH's heirs
- one shilling, my sister, MARGARET - one shilling, my sister MARY
- one shilling, my sister ELENOR - one shilling. Extrx: wife, ANN.
Wit: ROBERT GLASGOW, JOHN GLASGOW, ARCHIBALD GLASGOW.

Pp 311-313: WILL of JAMES PATTY, deceased, dated 8 July 1795. Admr.
granted to RICHARD THOMSON. Appraisers: JACOB BEILLER,
DANIEL PARKINS, GABRIEL MC COOL.

Pp 314-315: WILL of JOSEPH THOMSON, deceased, dated 28 July 1795.
Admr. granted to RICHARD THOMSON. Appraisers: EDWARD BEN-
BOW, WILLIAM JENKINS, DAVID JENKINS.

Pp 316-317: WILL of FREDERICK LA GRONNE, deceased, dated 28 July 1795.
Admr. granted to widow, SUSANNAH, who signed sale bill
on 6 Nov. 1795 as SUSANNAH COUNTS (indicating her remarriage). Appraisers: FREDERICK BOOZER, MARTIN TAYLOR, JOHN LIVINGSTON.

P 318: WILL of JOHN WEDAMON, deceased, dated 28 July 1795. Admr.
granted to "Little" JOHN KINARD. Appraisers: LAURENCE
RICKART, HENRY BOOZER, WILLIAM STONE.

Pp 320-321: WILL of DAVID COX, deceased, dated 7 June 1795, proven
19 Oct. 1795. My brother, JAMES COX to have all of my
estate. Exrs: JAMES COX, brother, and JAMES DYSON, friend. Wit: JOSEPH
TOWLES, JOHN HILL, DARAIS SARGENT.

Pp 322-330: WILL of JOHN RILEY, deceased, dated 24 June 1794, proven
19 Oct. 1795. Beloved wife, RACHEL RILEY - to have 144
acres whereon I now live and all moveable property for life. At her
death, land to go to my two grandsons, (1) JOHN RILEY, (2) WILLIAM
RILEY (sons of my son JEREMIAH), (1) son JEREMIAH, (2) son ZACHARIAH,
(3) son HEZEKIAH, (4) dau., KEZIAH THOMPSON. Exr.: MERCER BABB. Wit:
JAMES WADLINGTON, MERCER WADLINGTON, CATHERINE UTZ.

P 331: WILL of MARY WILSON, deceased, dated 4 Oct. 1795, proven
19 Oct. 1795. (1) dau. MARY WILSON, (2) dau. HESTER WILSON,
(3) dau. MARGARET MC CLELLAND, (4) dau. ELIZABETH WILSON, (5) son ANDREW
WILSON, (6) son HUGH WILSON. Exrs: JOHN BARLOW, JOHN STEWART, JOHN
B. MITCHELL. Wit: SAMUEL MC CONNELL, JOHN SLOAN, HUGH WILSON.

Pp 332-333: WILL of JAMES DAUGHERTY, SR., deceased, dated 15 Nov.
1794, proven 19 Nov. 1795. My wife, MARY - property. (1)

Cont'd:
my oldest son, JAMES - to his son, JAMES, I give a large Bible, (2)
my second son, JOHN - I give a horse to be purchased from money due
me by JAMES HUTCHINSON, (3) my third son, GEORGE - to have 180 acres
being part of the tract whereon I now live. Also, 28 acres adj. JACOB
SLIGH's and SETZLER's land, (4) my son CHARLES - homeplace after death
of my wife and 75 acres adj. GEORGE RUFF, URIAH ZUBER & ASHEFORD's
land - after CHARLES' death, land to go to my grandson, GEORGE - the
son of my son JAMES. Exrs: my son, GEORGE DAUGHERTY and friend DAVID
CANNON. Wit: A. GLAZIER, MARGARET GLAZIER, JOHN BOYD.

Pp 334-339: WILL of JACOB HALFACRE, deceased, dated 1 Sept. 1795,
             proven 19 Oct. 1795. Wife (not named). Children: (1) JACOB
to have 20 pds sterling money, (2) ELIZABETH to have 20 pds sterling
money, (3) BARBARA to have 20 pds sterling money, (4) HENRY to have
plantation whereon I now live with wagon, the distillery, and one half
present year's crop, the other half to go to BARBARA. Exrs: son, HENRY
HALFACRE and son, GEORGE GRAY, JR. Wit: JOHN PEASTER, JACOB BOSSART
(BUZHARDT) and LAURENCE RIKART.

Pp 340-342: WILL of WILLIAM GILLIAM, deceased, dated 19 Oct. 1795.
             Admr. granted to JOHN JUSTICE. Appraisers: SAMUEL BROWN,
JOSEPH FURNAS, WILLIAM MURDOCK.

Pp 343-346: Estate of RICHARD STROWTHER, deceased, dated 7 Apr. 1796.
             Sale Bill. (see page 276).

Pp 347-348: WILL of LINEY FARROW, deceased, dated 19 Oct. 1795. Admr.
             granted to THOMAS FARROW. Appraisers: WILLIAM CALDWELL,
JOHN MOORE, JOHN SATTERWHITE, SR.

Pp 348-349: WILL of JACOB REPLOGLE, deceased, dated 28 Nov. 1795,
             proven 28 Feb. 1796. Beloved wife JUDITH - estate during
her life. Stepchildren: (1) GEORGE LONG, (2) JACOB LONG, (3) MICHAEL
LONG, (4) CATHERINE MILLER, (5) ANN MARY READER. After death of my
wife, all stepchildren to share alike. ANN MARY is to have my plantation cart in consideration of her love and affection by nursing me
in this my illness. Exr.: MICHAEL KINARD. Wit: MARTIN HAUGH, FRED-
ERICK JAMES WALLERN, JOHN QUADDELBUM, JR.

Pp 350-354: WILL of GEORGE GRAY, SR., deceased, dated 9 Nov. 1795,
             proven 28 Feb. 1796. Wife EVA MARGARET to have slave and
$200.00 cash. Also, furniture, books, livestock, and to live on the
plantation during natural life. Children: (1) GEORGE, JR., (2) FRED-
ERICK, (3) PETER, (4) CHRISTINA GALLMAN - 150 acres adj. JOHN GALL-
MAN's land, (5) BARBARA, wife of FREDERICK BOOZER, (6) ELIZABETH, wife
of DAVID RUFF, Esq. Remainder of estate divided among my six children
above named. Exrs: GEORGE RUFF & JACOB BUZHARDT. Wit: MICHAEL DICKERT,
SR., FREDERICK BOOZER, MICHAEL LONG.

Pp 355-356: WILL of GEORGE SPARKS, deceased, dated 20 Oct. 1795, proven
             2 Mar. 1796. Sister, RACHEL BICKNELL of North Carolina
to receive estate and use it until my son, REUBEN SPARKS, is 21 years
old. Exr: GEORGE POWELL. Wit: VALENTINE BRASWELL, REASON DAVIS.

Pp 359-361: WILL of JOHN CALDWELL, SR., deceased, dated 5 Feb. 1796,
             proven 29 Feb. 1796. Wife SUSANNAH to have use of dwelling,
stock and plantation during life. Children: (1) JOHN CALDWELL, JR.
168 acres where he now lives, (2) WILLIAM 100 acres where he now lives,
(3) MARGARET DYSON 150 acres being part of tract called Halfway Branch,
(4) JAMES dwelling plantation after death of my wife, also $200.00
and all estate his mother leaves, (5) ROBERT five acres on Saluda River,
(6) ELEANOR CALDWELL, (7) DAVID balance of Halfway Branch tract. Exrs:
son, JOHN CALDWELL and son-in-law, DANIEL DYSON. Wit: WILLIAM ALLEN,
PHILLIP PROCTOR, HENRY PROCTOR.

Pp 362-364: WILL of ROBERT GILLIAM, SR., deceased, dated 22 Jan. 1796,
             proven 29 Feb. 1796. Wife MARY lend her during life two
slave-women and remainder of EDMOND ELLISON's land on northside of

Cont'd:
Page's Creek. Children: (1) JOSHUA - land whereon he now lives including a small tract Col. MAYSON is to make right to, (2) ROBERT, JR.,
(3) SUSANNAH MARTIN, (4) MARTHA SMITH, (5) FRANCES GILLIAM. Grandchildren: (1) JAMES FINLEY, (2) CALEY MARTIN. Exrs.: son, ROBERT GILLIAM,
JR., JOHN WALLACE, ISAAC MITCHELL, SR. Wit: FIELDS RED, SUSANNAH RED,
HARRIS GILLIAM.

Pp 365-367: WILL of NATHAN WILLIAMS, deceased, dated 31 Mar. 1795,
            proven 29 Feb. 1796. Wife SARAH - estate during life.
Children: (1) PATIENCE, (2) JOHN, (3) the infant expected. Exrs.: THOMAS
GARY and STEPHEN WILLIAMS. Wit: MICHAEL SANDERS, JOHN GARY and STEPHEN
HILL.

Pp 368-370: WILL of DR. JOHN WILSON, deceased, dated 16 Oct. 1795,
            proven 29 Feb. 1796. "All my lands and tenements in Ire-
land, County of Antrim, Barrentre of Tome, Townland of Cloughan, to
be sold and debts paid." (1) my brother, JAMES WILSON - one shilling
sterling and no mare (more?), (2) my sister, JANETT ALEXANDER - one
shilling and no mare, (3) my sister, ELIZABETH WILSON - one shilling
sterling and no mare, (4) my sister, SARAH WALKER - 50 pds sterling
in fee simple, (5) my sister, SARAH WALKER's children - 100 pds sterl-
ling in fee simple equally divided amongst them, (6) my sister, MARTHA
FIGS - 100 pds in fee simple, (7) my sister, MARTHA FIG's children
- 40 pds equally divided amongst them, (8) my cousin, JOHN MOORE -
5 pds sterling. Exr's: DANIEL CLARY, WILLIAM SUMMERS & JOHN SUMMERS.
Wit: GILES CHAPMAN, JESSE SUMMERS, SAMUEL SUMMERS.

P 371:   WILL of JAMES WINNINGHAM, deceased, dated 19 Oct. 1795.
            Admn. granted to GEORGE ADAMS. Appraisers: SAMUEL PROCTOR,
JOHN CALDWELL, WILLIAM ALLEN, ELISHA BROOKS.

Pp 372-374: WILL of EDWARD KELLY, deceased, dated 20 Oct. 1795. Admr.
            granted to the widow, MARY KELLY. Appraisers: JOHN GOREE,
THOROGOOD CHAMBERS, JOHN STEWART.

Pp 375-376: WILL of JOHN GOREE, deceased, dated 29 July 1795. Admr.
            granted to JOHN GOREE & JOSIAH GOREE. Appraisers: DAVID
SIMS, THOMAS LAKE, JOHN STEWART.

Pp 377-378: WILL of SAMUEL JONES, deceased, dated 28 Feb. 1796. Admn.
            granted to REBECCA JONES. Appraisers: JAMES GRIFFIN, THOMAS
GARY, ISAAC TAYLOR.

Pp 379-380: WILL of ABNER ELLIMON, deceased, dated 29 Feb. 1796. Admr.
            granted to JOHN ELLIMAN and WILLIAM ELLIMAN. Appraisers:
AARON HILL, ALEXANDER CATHRON, DANIEL RICHARDSON.

P 381:   WILL of JOHN PORTERFIELD, deceased, dated 21 Oct. 1796.
            Admn. granted to SARAH PORTERFIELD. Appraisers: JOHN MOORE,
RICHARD GRIFFIN, JOHN FIFER.

Pp 382-383: WILL of JOHN LANGFORD, deceased, dated 16 June 1791, proven
            29 Feb. 1796. Wife WINNEFRED - balance of estate after
shares to children. Children: (1) WILLIAM - to have one-half of land
whereon I now live on west side of Buffalo Creek and stock, (2) JACOB
to have one-half of land whereon I now live - his share lying on east
side of Buffalo Creek, (3) ANNE - to have certain property and 200
acres adj. CARTER's land, (4) my grandson, ASA LANGFORD - one shilling
sterling. Exrs.: wife WINNIFRED and son, WILLIAM. Wit: JACOB FREE,
JOSEPH COTTON, JACOB LANGFORD.

END OF WILL BOOK A

NEWBERRY DISTRICT, S. C. EQUITY RECORDS

Box #1, pkg. #6: Bill for Partition of Slaves. 29 Jan. 1818. THOMAS
               SATTERWHITE, NARCISSA SATTERWHITE, FRANCIS SATTER-
WHITE, THERESA CAROLINE SATTERWHITE, by their next friends and gdns.
J ON K. GRIFFIN & JAMES GILLIAM, Ad litem vs JAMES DYSON, surviving
exr. of DRURY SATTERWHITE, dec'd.
     Instrument shows that DRURY SATTWHITE, late of Newberry Dist.,
on 30 Oct. 1812 made and executed his L.W. & T. and died shortly after,
survived by widow SUSANNA and five children, viz. THOMAS, NARCISSA,
ELIZABETH, who has died since her father, FRANCIS, THERESA CAROLINE.
SUSANNAH, widow of DRURY SATTERWHITE, died 1816 intestate. BARTLETT
SATTERWHITE, brother of DRURY, was Exr. of DRURY's will and has died
in 1818.. JAMES DYSON is surviving Exr.

Box #1, pkg. #7: Bill for partition of land. JESSE SPARKS, ISAAC SPARKS,
     PHOEBE LEWIS, ELIZABETH SPARKS, vs ZACHARIAH SPARKS, JOSEPH K.
SPARKS, SARAH ANN SPARKS (minor), MARY SPARKS (minor).
     Instrument shows that STEPHEN SPARKS, late of Newberry Dist.,
died 1816 intestate, survived by the following children: ZACHARIAH,
JESSE, JOSEPH K., ISAAC PHOEBY LEWIS, ELIZABETH, SARAH ANN & MARY SPARKS.
STEPHEN died possessed of 300 acres on Indian Creek, adj. lands of
DANIEL LOFTON, Lt. Col. JOHN GLEEN, CHESLEY DAVIS, DUDLEY BONDS, Dr.
HILERY HERBERT, and a tract of 227 acres lying in Laurens Dist., S.
C. on south fork of Duncan's Creek adj. lands of JAMES BELL, PETER
BRAZELMAN, DAVID MC CLURE, dec'd., MANASAH WILSON and others. On 20
Oct. 1820, JESSE SPARKS, JOSEPH K. SPARKS, & WILLIAM POOL, who inter-
married with ELIZABETH SPARKS, all of Shelby Co., Alabama, appoint
ISAAC E. SPARKS, of same county, our lawful attorney, WILLIAM CAMERON,
J.P. of Shelby Co., Ala. THOMAS A. ROGERS, Sec. State Ala. "in town
of Cahaba(?), Ala." Appraisers of land were ISAAC GARY, ISAAC EVANS,
JOHN CANNON, LEWIS LINVALL & WILLIAM BLACKBURN.

Box #1, pkg. #8: Bill for alimony injunction, etc. Filed 18 Feb. 1817,
     with Exhibit A, CALDWELL, Sol.
     MARGARET SUMMER by her next friend GASPER PEASTER vs ELIJAH SUMMER.
MARGARET SUMMER and ELIJAH SUMMER married Dec. 1807. Lived together
about 10 years...had 4 children, a son who is dead, and 3 daughters
now living to wit SUSANAH about 9 years old, MARY ANN about 5 years,
and REBECCA quite an infant.

Box #1, pkg. #9: Bill for Discovery. 28 Nov. 1818. HUGH O'NEALL vs
     JESSE DOBBINS, TIMRI PALMER. CALDWELL, Sol.
     To Hon. HENRY W. DESAUSURE, THEODORE GAILLARD, THOMAS WATERS,
WADDY THOMPSON & WILLIAM D. JAMES, Judges of the Court of Equity in
sd state: that JOHN PALMER, dec'd., was indebted in 1810 to HUGH O'NEAL.
Sd JOHN PALMER died possessed with a tract of 100 acres lying on Bush
River adj. lands of GEORGE HUNTER, MATTHEW ALBRITAN, WILLIAM DOBBINS,
and others, which tract was sold to JESSE DOBBINS who later sold to
TIMRI PALMER, son of sd JOHN PALMER. Further shews that the sd JESSE
DOBBINS and sd TIMRI PALMER intend removing from the limits of this
state.

Box #1, pkg. #10: Bill of Injunction and Relief. 27 Feb. 1818. DANIEL
     MC MAHAN vs JOHN O'NEAL, Exr. of WRIGHT COATE, dec'd., estate,
JESSE COATE, a man of colour by his gdn. SAMUEL COTHREN.
     Instrument shows that Captain WRIGHT COATS died 1809 testate.
Wife MARY COATE and JOHN O'NEAL, Exrs. Dr. MOON was attending WRIGHT
COATE in last illness. JAMES COATES, brother to WRIGHT COATES, has
disappeared from this area. DANIEL MC MAHAN of Pinckneyville, Union
Dist., S. C. shows that on 24 Feb. 1808, he petitioned in Equity Court
against sd WRIGHT & JAMES COATE, showing that on 13 Aug. 1804, he fur-
nished sd COATES with a load of cotton, weighing 2187 lbs. which Capt.
WRIGHT COATES delivered in Charleston, the carriage of which amounted
to $43.74. Sd COATES brought from Charleston and delivered at Pinckney-
ville merchandise weighing 2606 lbs. and carriage was $50.12. PENDLETON
PAGE was clerk and agent for MC MAHAN. WILLIAM LASHLEY and his wife,
SARAH of Newberry Dist. were witnesses.

320

Box #1, pkg. #11: Bill for Partition of land. 9 Feb. 1818. THOMAS MORGAN & REBECCA his wife, ROBERT RAMAGE & MARY his wife vs MARY COATS, BENJAMIN LAKE & ANN, his wife. CALDWELL, Sol. JOHN COAT, late of Newberry Dist., died (no date) intestate being possessed with 102 acres of land adj. JOHN MORGAN, CHRISTOPHER WHITMON, THEUBEN MORGAN, WILLIAM WATSON & others, survived by widow, MARY and three daughters, viz. MARY who intermarried with ROBERT RAMAGE, REBECCA who intermarried with THOS. MORGAN, and ANN who intermarried with BENJAMIN LAKE. Appraisers of land were HUGH O'NEAL, CLEMNT. NANCE, JOHN RAMAGE & SAMUEL MC CALLA (MC CULLOUGH).

Box #1, pkg. #12: (missing)

Box #1, pkg. #13: Bill of Complaint. Filed 26 Aug. 1816. STARK, Sol. FREDERICK HOGELL vs JOHN SMILEY & wife REBECCA, CHRISTOPHER STEPHEN HOGELL & DANIEL DEWALT.
Orator, FREDERICK HOGELL of Newberry Dist. Bill states that JOHN FREDERICK HOGELL, the grandfather of the orator FREDERICK HOGELL in the year 1776 owned a tract of land in the District of Newberry 300 acres on Cannon's Creek between Broad and Saluda Rivers bounded on E by vacant land laid out to ZIMMERMAN and on all other sides vacant.... was indebted to CURB and offered to contract with the above named STEPHEN HOGELL, he being the elder son and heir at law of the sd JOHN FREDERICK HOGELL to become the purchaser. STEPHEN refused to become purchaser of land and therefore preserve the patrimony in the family. Then the grandfather offered same tract to GEORGE HOGELL (the orator's father) and he became the purchaser and paid amount of the debt to CURB and delivered plat and grant to the orator's father in 1776. The Rev. War having "broke" out, the orator's father unfortunately for himself and his property took part vs his country and proceeded with a party of Royalists to Fort Augusta where he continued till his death in 1783. Shortly after GEO. HOGELL purchased the land, JNO. FREDERICK HOGELL died intestate, the land descended to STEPHEN HOGELL who also went off with a party of Royalists about the same time to St. Augustine from whence at close of war he removed to Nova Scotia where he has resided ever since. Orator is only child and heir of GEO. HOGELL and of right intitled to the land. DANIEL DEWALT, now dec'd., being in Halifax in sd province of Nova Scotia, and knowing of the orator's claim to the land, proposed to STEPHEN HOGELL to buy the same. STEPHEN then sold same to DANIEL DEWALT....shows that JOHN SMILEY & REBECCA his wife by virtue of a title by DANIEL DEWALT entered upon same land in Jan. 1812. REBECCA is daughter of DANIEL DEWALT.
GEO. GRAY, SR., as att'y. sold to Capt. JOHN SMYLEY, as a rep. and legatee of DANIEL DEWALT, dec'd., 200 acres of the land originally granted to JNO. FREDERICK HOGLE, 13 Sept. 1815. Wit: SIMON P. GRAY & BENJ. H. GRAY.
Power of att'y. from CHRISTOPHER HOGELL, late of 96 Dist., S. C. now of Halifax, Prov. of N. S., yeoman, appointed GEO. GRAY and WM. DAWKINS LANE (now or late of Newberry Dist.) to sell 6 Nov. 1787.

Box #1, pkg. #14: 28 May 1818. CALDWELL & O'NEAL, Sol. NANCY CHAPMAN and others vs JOSEPH CHAPMAN and others.
Instrument shows that JOHN WEST GRESAM & ISAAC CANNON bound to JOSHUA GRIFFITH on 21 _____ 1797. Obligation is that JOHN WEST GRESAM, together with the lawful heirs of WILLIAM CHAPMAN, dec'd., have sold to JOSHUA GRIFFITH a tract of land lying on Timmerman's Creek in Newberry County, originally granted to WILLIAM CHAPMAN, dec'd., and whereas the widow of sd CHAPMAN, dec'd. has not conveyed away her dower to same and is now MARY RIDGEDELL, former widow aforesaid. Wit. by JOSHUA TEAGUE & JAMES TEAGUE who are both now (1818) dead but ISAAC TEAGUE, son of JOSHUA, made affadavit.
That SAMUEL CHAPMAN, brother to sd WILLIAM CHAPMAN, died 1790, survived by widow NANCY, and her children: MARMADUKE JACKSON CHAPMAN, b. 30 Jan. 1776; ROBERT HANNAH CHAPMAN, b. 28 Nov. 1777, JOSEPH CHAPMAN, b. 16 Mar. 1779; ELIJAH CHAPMAN, b. 7 Sept. 1780; JANE CHAPMAN, b. 30 Sept. 1782; ARCHIBALD CHAPMAN, b. 21 Sept. 1784; MARY CHAPMAN, b. 31 Nov. 1786; NANCY CHAPMAN, b. 29 Sept. 1788.
21 Jan. 1797, JOHN WEST GRISAM & wife MARY, JOHN DOUGLAS & wife LYDA, and DELILAH D. CHAPMAN, all of Pendleton County, S. C. sold to

Cont'd:
JOSHUA GRIFFITH of Newberry County, 100 acres on Timmon's Creek, waters
of Cannon's Creek, originally granted 19 June 1772 to sd WILLIAM CHAP-
MAN, dec'd., adj. land of SAMUEL CHAPMAN, JAMES ODLES & WILSON land
and vacant land. Power of atty. from DELILAH CHAPMAN, to JOHN WEST
GRISAM, dated 14 Jan. 1797.
    13 Nov. 1795. JAMES MC NEAL, SR. & JAMES MC NIELL, JR. of New-
berry Dist., bought from CHAPMAN, for 25 pds sterling, 100 acres on
south branch of Cannon's Creek, orig. granted to TARODY NEILL, who
conveyed same to WM. CHAPMAN, adj. lands of SAML. CHAPMAN, CHARLES
BARTAM, ABRAHAM THOMPSON, ROBERT HANNAH. Wit: WILLIAM TWEED, DAVID
TWEEDY, FRED. NANCY, J.P. Rec. in Deed Book C, p. 550, dated 13 Nov.
1795.

Box #1, pkg. #15: Bill for Discovery & Relief & Partition. Filed 28
    Apr. 1818. SARAH DOWNS, (widow of DAVID DOWNS, dec'd.), SAMUEL
HALL & ABIGAIL his wife, JOHN DOWNS, MARY DOWNS and minors SARAH, NANCY,
BETSEY, JAMES & DAVID DOWNS by their next friend JOHN DOWNS vs AARON
BURTON, HUGH O'NEAL. CRENSHAW, Sol.
    DAVID DOWNS was about to remove to State of Ohio 5 Sept. 1801,
being indebted to HUGH O'NEALL & JOSEPH FURNACE, conveyed to HUGH O'-
NEALL, 150 acres on Beaverdam Creek, in fork bet. Broad and Saluda
Rivers. JOSEPH FURNACE believed dead. DAVID DOWNS died intestate some-
time in forepart of 1814 and left above complainants as heirs.

Box #1, pkg. #16: Bill for Partition. Filed 7 May 1818. MICHAEL DICKERT,
    REUBEN REID & wife ELIZABETH & minors, ADAM DICKERT, under 21,
HENRY DICKERT, under 1(?) ad litem GEORGE METZ vs SIMON WICKER & CHRIS-
TINA his wife. P. B. HIGGINS, C. I. Equity, O'NEALL, Sol.
    CHRISTOPHER DICKERT died intestate (no date) left widow CHRISTINA
who since his death married SIMON WICKER and following children: MICHAEL
DICKERT, ELIZABETH who married REUBEN REID, ADAM DICKERT & HENRY DICKERT
had 200 acres in Newberry Dist., adj. SIMON WICKER, GEO. CLYNE, MARTIN
KINARD, JAMES HUGHEY & ADAM WICKER. Land could not be equally divided,
therefore assigned to WICKER and wife as they are ordered to pay certain amount to ADAM & HENRY DICKERT.

Box #1, pkg. #17: Bill for Discovery & Relief..a contested will. Filed
    20 June 1816. RICHARDSON, C. J. Equity, Washington Dist. O'NEALL,
Sol.
    WILLIAM CARMICHAEL and wife MARY vs JAMES MC MORRIS, JOHN MARS,
ROBERT MARS, JOHN HALL & wife BETSEY. ROBT. MARS died, left will dated
16 Oct. 1812, leaving 3 children: JOHN MARS, BETSEY married JNO. HALL,
MARY, your oratrix, married WILLIAM CARMICHAEL.
    JOHN HALL and wife were living in the State of Ohio. JAMES MC
MORRIES, Exr. of will of ROBT. MARS....weak in body...to grandson,
ROBT. MARS, a tract of land whereon I now live...to dau. MARY MARS,
the residue of land not before willed. Son JOHN MARS, excluded as he
had already received considerable property...son-in-law of State of
Ohio...Exrs. JNO. MARS, JAMES MC MORRIES. Wit: JAMES MC MORRIES, JNO.
MARS, ROBT. MARS.

Box #1, pkg. #18: Washington Dist. Bill for Discovery & Relief & In-
    junction. Filed 18 Jan. 1818. THOMAS BUSBY vs JOHN BOYD, SR. and
wife ANN, and minors, JOHN, JAMES, BETSEY & WILLIAM BOYD.
    THOMAS BOYD of Newberry Dist. shows that sometime in the fall
or winter of 1812, JOHN BOYD, SR. of same, gave him a deed for 26 acres
on branch of King's Creek, waters of Enoree River, to which MARGARET
BOYD his wife signed dower. On 28 Dec. 1816, JOHN BOYD made a deed
of the same land to ANN BOYD, JOHN, JANE BETSEY, & WILLIAM BOYD jointly.
JOHN BOYD had been residing in Kentucky but returned to Newberry.

Box #1, pkg. #19: Bill for Partition. Filed 9 Apr. 1818. Ord. pro.
    confesso 1 June 1818. JOHN JAMISON and minors FRANCES W. JAMISON
by gdn. ad litem JOHN JAMISON vs JAMES WALLACE, MARGARET WALLACE, ROBERT
G. WALLACE, MARY M. WALLACE, infants by their gdn. HUGH WALLACE.
    Orators JOHN JAMISON, FRANCES WALLACE, JAMISON infants under 21
show that WM. WALLACE, late of Newberry Dist., died intestate in 1816,
left widow FRANCES WALLACE and the following children: JAMES WALLACE,
MARGARET WALLACE, ROBT. GILLAM WALLACE & MARY MOSS WALLACE, all of

Cont'd:
whom are infants under 12 years. WM. WALLACE died possessed of 300
acres in Newberry Dist., adj. WM. WALLACE, dec'd., JOHN GRIGSBY, EDMUND
PAYNE, & THOMAS DYSON, Esq. Widow FRANCES WALLACE married JAMES JAMISON
and she died 1818 intestate, leaving oratrix FRANCES W. JAMIESON, the
only child of her marriage with orator JOHN JAMIESON, and the other
named children of the first marriage...asks for division.

Box #1, pkg. #20: State of S. C., Washington Dist. Bill for Discovery
& Relief. Filed 19 June 1817. ALLEN LESTER, Admn. of SAMUEL LESTER,
dec'd. vs. ABNER LESTER. SAMUEL LESTER, dec'd., died latter part of
Feb. 1817. ABNER LESTER had in his possession notes given to him by
SAMUEL LESTER shortly before his death for safekeeping. ABNER LESTER,
a brother of SAMUEL LESTER, dec'd. ALLEN LESTER is a nephew of SAMUEL.
SAMUEL was sick at the house of WILLIAM BRAZIL (now dec'd.) ABNER claims
that SAMUEL made a gift of the notes to him as his brother, believing
that he would shortly die. One note was on WILLIAM R. LESTER (now dec'd)
ABNER is the youngest of all the brothers.

Box #1, pkg. #21: Bill for Partition. Exhibits A & B, Filed 26 Mar.
1818, ord. pro. confesso. JAMES LINDSEY vs JOHN LINDSEY (son of
CALEB), ELIZABETH LINDSEY, JOSEPH C. LINDSEY, JAMES M. LINDSEY, FAMA
LINDSEY, ALSEA LINDSEY & CALEB LINDSEY.
On 6 Dec. 1804, JAMES LINDSEY and his brothers, CALEB & JOHN,
bought from Maj. WM. DUNLAP of Laurens Dist. as agent for CHARLES GRAVES
of City of Charleston, Exr. of ANTHONY TOOMER, dec'd., 400 acres in
Dist. of Newberry, granted to JAMES MIRACLE, adj. Saluda River, JNO.
ATKINSON, THOS. HILL, HOWELL COBB, now dec'd. This tract was late the
property of Col. JOHN LINDSEY, dec'd. DUNLAP gave orator JAMES LINDSEY
and sd CALEB a bond for the execution of titles. Orator says he and
his brothers CALEB & JOHN paid the money. On 1 Feb. 1816, CALEB died
intestate leaving a widow TABITHA LINDSEY, and the following children
of CALEB LINDSEY, dec'd.: JOHN, ELIZABETH, JOSEPH G., JAMES M., FAMA,
ALSEA, ANN TOOMER, Execx. and CHARLES GRAVES, the Exr. of ANTHONY TOOMER,
dec'd., executed titles to orator JAMES and his brother JNO. LINDSEY,
and the widow and children of CALEB, dec'd. TABITHA LINDSEY died 1
Feb. 1818 intestate, leaving children of CALEB LINDSEY. THOMAS GOODMAN
was appointed guardian for the children of JOHN LINDSEY. ABRAHAM ANDER-
SON was the guardian of JOSEPH G. LINDSEY, JAMES M. LINDSEY, ALSEA
LINDSEY and CALEB LINDSEY, infants under 21 years.

Box #1, pkg. #22: Bill for Sale & Partition. Filed 7 Feb. 1818. DANIEL
KELLER & wife ELIZABETH & MARY WICKER (minor) by her next friend,
LEWIS HALTON vs JOHN OWEN.
They also show that (JOHN) HENRY WICKER died and left will Sept.
1805. Will shows: daughters ELIZABETH & POLLY, DAVID OWENS (moved to
Tennessee) and THOMAS OWENS, Exrs...23 Aug. 1805. Wit: CHARLES SINGLEY,
NASBROD WICKER, GEORGE MANN. Complaint shows ELIZABETH, one daughter
of WICKER married DANIEL KELLER. After 1819 MARY WICKER married ANDREW
CROMER and died being still a minor without issue.

Box #1, pkg. #23: 1818. JOHN LEGROON (LEGRONE) & wife MARGARET, FRED-
ERICK PRISOCK, JOHN PRISOCK, & ADAM PRISOCK, SALLY PRISOCK, MOLLY
PRISOCK, ROSANNAH PRISOCK, DAVID PRISOCK, minors under 21 by their
gdn. ad litem JOHN PRISOCK vs. CATY PRISOCK. Bill for partition filed
6 May 1818. ROSANNAH & DAVID PRISOCK are grandchildren, children of
GEO. PRISOCK, dec'd., who was the son of FREDERICK PRISOCK, dec'd.
Instrument shows that FREDERICK PRISOCK, late of Newberry Dist.,
25 Mar. 1817, died intestate...left widow CATY PRISOCK and the following children: MARGARET LEGRONE, FREDERICK & JOHN PRISOCK...left 69
acres Newberry Dist. adj. MICHAEL KIBLER, JR., MATTHIAS KINARD, GEORGIA
KINARD, PETER RICHARDSON & JONADAB RICHARDSON.

Box #1, pkg. #24: 1818. THOS. HILL vs JOHN HILL. Bill for specific
performance, acct. & writ of ne exeat.
THOS. HILL purchased of his brother JOHN HILL, 31 Dec. 1807, land
on north side of Saluda River, 300 acres.

Box #1, pkg. #25: 1818. Bill for Discovery & Relief. Filed 21 Feb.
1818. WILLIAM HAWKINS vs GEORGE D. LESTER, administrator of WILLIAM

Cont'd:
BRASWELL, dec'd., SUSAN BRASWELL, RUTHERFORD BRASWELL, ALLEN BRASWELL;
and minors DAVID, ARTHUR, POLLY, BETSEY, JAMES, WILLIAMS, AARON, NANCY
BRASWELL by their guardian, RUTHERFORD BRASWELL.
    16 May 1814 orator sold to THOS. RIDDLESPURGER for $1480.62 1/2
a tract of land in Newberry Dist., called Stoney Battery containing
31 acres adj. orator, FRANCIS HATTON, JACOB HAWKINS & WM. BRASWELL,
dec'd. THOMAS, after paying only a small part of the money, sold it
to WM. BRASWELL, now dec'd. THOS. RIDDLESPURGER, in 1817, before his
note came due left the state and resides in parts unknown to orator.
WM. BRASWELL died in 1816 intestate, left widow SUSAN and the following
children: RUTHERFORD & ALLEN of full age, DAVID, ARTHUR, POLLY, BETSEY,
JAMES, WILLIAM, AARON & NANCY infants under 21.

                        END OF EQUITY RECORDS

              PICKENS COUNTY, S. C. REAL ESTATE SALES

        Pickens Co., S. C. was created in 1826 out of Old Pendleton Dis-
trict, S. C. which originally was a part of Old Ninety-Six District,
S. C. Geographically it is situated on the line of Western N. C., to
its East is Greenville Co., and on its Western boundary is Oconee County
and due South is Anderson Co. Pendleton was the most western of the
S. C. Districts and served as a gateway following the Revolutionary
War as a gateway to Georgia, Alabama, and later to the West. Most of
its settlers from North Carolina and Virginia later moved southward
and westward.
        The chief road from the North into western S. C. was the great
Indian Warpath or Great Road from Philadelphia which ran through the
Shenandoah Valley of Virginia. Old Lunenburg Co., Virginia and the
Yadkin country of North Carolina, connecting with the lower Cherokee
Traders Path. east of Spartanburg Dist., South Carolina. A few hardy
souls lived in Pendleton District before the opening of land for sale
in the 1780's - deeds for Pendleton land are found as early as 1781
in Abbeville County. Ninety-Six District was formed in 1769 and was
discarded in 1798; and from this judicial district, Pendleton was set
off in 1789.

Bk A, p. 1:   WILLIAM NORTON's real estate valued by EDWARD NORTON
        on oath 650 acres at $1000 on 2 Nov. 1829. EDWARD NORTON appli-
cant viz JEPHTHA NORTON, BARAK NORTON, ALBERT ROBBINS and wife SUSANNAH,
DAVID MC COY and wife ELIZABETH, WILLIAM BEVERT and wife KATHARINE,
LYDIA NORTON, Heirs of HENRY NORTON, dec'd., LATHE NORTON in right
of her husband GIDEON, Heirs of SAMPSON NORTON, dec'd. Owned 650 acres
on waters of Little River, bounded by lands of JOHN LEWIS, JAMES GUTH-
RIE and others. Originally granted to RICHARD POLLARD.

Bk A, p. 2:   HARDY GILSTRAP owned 300 acres lying on waters of
        Twelve Mile Creek. Dated Jan. 18, 1830. JOHN GILSTRAP, Admr. viz
ANNE GILSTRAP, Heirs of CYNTHIA ROE, JAMES HAMBLETON, HAMPTON CHUMBLY,
JAMES GILSTRAP & PETER GILSTRAP a minor over 14 years.

Bk A, p. 3:   JOHN FREEMAN owned 175 acres of land. Dated 19 Apr.
        1830. JOHN & FRANCIS FREEMAN, legal heirs viz FANNY FREEMAN widow,
WESTLY FREEMAN, WILLIAM FREEMAN, ALEXANDER FREEMAN, JOHN FINDLEY and
wife, JANE FREEMAN, SALLY FREEMAN, WILEY FREEMAN, JOHN FOWLER and wife
BIDY, MARSHALL HOLLEY and wife PARTHMIA, MARY FREEMAN.

Bk A, p. 4:   ABEL HILL owned 75 acres in Pickens District. Dated
        5 July 1830. JAMES FINDLEY, Admn. ABEL HILL applicant viz KEZIAH
HILL, widow, ASHWORTH HILL, HULDY HILL, LEWIS HILL, ELIZABETH HILL,
KETURAH HILL, KEZIAH HILL guardian of sd minors under 14 years.

Bk A, p. 6:   RICHARD SMITH owned land on Doudies Creek, waters
        of Saluda River. Dated 26 Oct. 1830. SAMUEL SMITH states that
he having come to the age of 21 years that the land belonging to his
father RICHARD SMITH be sold. Be sold on a credit of 3 years pursuant
to an agreement made with his brother and sister MOSES SMITH & ELIZABETH
SMITH.

Bk A, p. 7:   MARSON SMITHSON owned 115 acres on waters of Choestoe
        bounded by lands of ELI DAVIS and BENJAMIN PERRY. Sept. 6, 1830.
NIMROD LEATHERS, Admn. applicant vizt. WILLIAM SMITHSON, SELAH SMITHSON,
SARAH SMITHSON, ANSON SMITHSON & JAMES JOLLY.

Bk A, p. 8:   JOSHUA THOMPSON owned 212 acres on waters of Twelve
        Mile River bounded by DANIEL DURHAM, LEVI MURPHY, B. BARTON &
HUNTER. Dated 6 Dec. 1830. JAMES THOMPSON applicant vizt. MARY THOMP-
SON now EVATT, SAMUEL SMITH & wife WINNY..Heirs of JOHN THOMPSON, dec'd.
JONATHAN GREGORY & wife JANE, ELIJAH THOMPSON, CHARLOTTE THOMPSON,
MARY THOMPSON, LOUISA THOMPSON, ETHALIND THOMPSON, WILLIAM THOMPSON.

Bk A, p. 9:   JAMES BRUCE owned 201 acres on Wolf Creek. Dated
        3 June 1833. STEPHEN ADAMS applicant and wife PATIENCE vizt. NANCY
BRUCE and heirs in right of WILLIAM BRUCE, dec'd., Heirs of BURT MOORE
and wife, Heirs of JAMES BRUCE and wife PRISCILLA, HENRY Wolf and wife
REBECCA, JOHN BRUCE, GEORGE BRUCE, DANIEL BRUCE, SARAH BRUCE, JAMES
BRUCE owned land on 12 Mile River bounded by land of ARCHABALD MILLER,
JOSEPH A. FIELD, ELISHA LEAGUE & SAMUEL HALL.

Bk A, p. 10:   JOSHUA FOWLER owned 662 acres on waters of Georges
        Creek bounded by lands of EDMOND SINGLETON, SAMUEL HALL & others.
Dated 7 Oct. 1833. WILLIAM JAMISON applicant to MARK FREEMAN and wife
ELIZABETH, Heirs of JOSHUA FOWLER, JR., dec'd., Heirs of THOMAS FOWLER,
dec'd., Heirs of JOHN LEONARD, MOSES CANTREL and wife RUTH, WILLIAM
FOWLER, JOHN FOWLER, JOSIAH FOWLER.

Bk A, p. 11:   THOMAS MASTERS, JR. owned 250 acres lying in Pickens
        on the Saluda River. Dated 4 Nov. 1833. CATHARINE MASTERS widow
applicant vizt. ROSEY CATHARINE MASTERS. AUSTIN EDWARDS MASTERS. AMANDA
M. MASTERS minors under 14 years. JAMES H. DENDY, guardian.

Bk A, p. 12:   THOMAS BLACKBURN owned 195 acres of land on Little
        River and known by the name of White Oak Cove. Dated 27 Jan. 1834.
LYDIA HUGHEY states that she has no interest in the real estate of
her son THOMAS BLACKBURN, dec'd. LYDIA HUGHEY applicant vizt. AMBROSE
REID, WILLIAM H. ADAIR, Heirs of SILVY WILLIAM BLACKBURN, BARTLEY W.
F. CAPEHART, MATILDA, MALINDA & GEORGE W. BLACKBURN minors.

Bk A, p. 13:   DAVID POER owned 400 acres on the North fork of Toza-
        way Creek, waters of Tugaloo River bounded by lands of HUGER,
BLAIR & CHAMBERS. Dated 15 Nov. 1834. FRANCES POER widow applicant
vizt. JAMES M. POER, MARTIN DICKSON, WILLIAM ROTHEL (ROTHER?), JAMES
M. POER assignee for ISAAC HOLDEN, GREEN B. GILASPIE, EMILA POER, FRAN-
CES POER minors daughter of your petitioner.

Bk A, p. 14:   WILLIAM WILSON owned 552 acres on waters of Brushy
        Creek bounded by lands of JOHN AIRAIL, JAMES OSBORN, JOHN WILLIAMS.
Dated 2 Mar. 1835. ROBERT WILSON applicant vizt. EDLEY HAMBLETON, ANDREW
WILSON, DANIEL WILSON, CUNNINGHAM WILSON defendants residing out of
this state.

Bk A, p. 15:   DAVID SLOAN owned land called Fairplay in Pickens
        District bounded by lands of LARKEN BROWN & JACOB R. COX containing
2 acres. Dated 10 Mar. 1835. The two acres should not be divided or
sold, allotting to BENJAMIN F. SLOAN surviving copartner of DAVID SLOAN
& Company. BENJAMIN F. SLOAN applicant vizt. NANCY SLOAN widow, WILLIAM
D. SLOAN, JOHN T. SLOAN, JOHN W. BLASINGAME, GEORGE W. BOMER, SUSAN
SLOAN, LUCY SLOAN, THOMAS SLOAN, BENJAMIN F. SLOAN, JR.

Bk A, p. 16:   THOMAS ALLEN owned 150 acres opposite Paris's Ford
        on Saluda River. That was sold by the Sheriff as the property
of NATHANIEL DACUS and purchased by THOMAS BRACKENRIDGE and sold by
sd BRACKENRIDGE to THOMAS ALLEN. Dated 27 Apr. 1835. ELIZABETH ALLEN
applicant vizt. WILLIAM H. ALLEN & JANE T. ALLEN minors. R. LOVELAND
was guardian.

Bk A, p. 18:   WILLIAM ALLEN owned 250 acres on waters of Olenoy
        Creek. Dated 31 Aug. 1835. ABNER RUSSELL applicant vizt. ABNER
CHASTAIN, JAMES ALLEN, JOHN ALLEN, Heirs of AMBROSE REID and his wife,

Cont'd:
ELIZABETH A. REID, guardian. Heirs of ABRAM POWELL and wife SARAH A.
CHASTAIN, WILLIAM S. ROBERTSON, HUGH ALLEN, CORNELIUS KEITH, Heirs
of JOHN CASTLE and wife MILLEY, ABIGAIL ALLEN widow.

Bk A, p. 20:   JOSEPH UNDERWOOD owned 500 acres on waters of Cane
     Creek, part of which was originally granted to JOHN C. KILPATRICK
and the other part to JESSE NEVILL. Dated 7 Oct. 1835. BENJAMIN KING
applicant vizt JOHN DAVENPORT, ELIZABETH LEWIS widow of CHARLES LEWIS,
dec'd., Heirs of JOHN WHITESIDES, dec'd. GEORGE RUSSELL, MARY KELLEY,
JOSEPH KING, SAMUEL KING, JONATHAN KING. LETTY GUFFEE.

Bk A, p. 21:   JAMES BLACKSTOCK owned land on waters of Tugaloo
     River bounded by WILLIAM BARTON, Esq., THOMAS COLLINS and others.
Dated Jan. 1836. LEVINA BLACKSTOCK applicant vizt. SARAH BLACKSTOCK,
JOHN EVANS and wife MILLY, NEHEMIAH BLACKSTOCK, JOHN BLACKSTOCK, RICHARD
BLACKSTOCK defendants. Advertised 8 weeks for absent legatees.

Bk A, p. 22:   JAMES HENSON owned 100 acres on waters of Conneross
     Creek. Dated 17 May 1836. THOMAS VISSAGE plaintiff vizt. CLAY-
BORN ROTHEL and wife DELILAH. ELIJAH LEATHERS & wife MELINDER. WALTER
BILLINGSBY & wife SUSANNAH. JOHN GRINDAL and wife RACHEL. JOSEPH HENSON,
CHARLES HENSON, Heirs of JAMES HENSON, dec'd. ROBERT TAYLOR & wife
NANCY.

Bk A, p. 23:   BENJAMIN MORGAN owned 240 acres lying on Keowee River
     near the village of Pickens. Dated 6 June 1836. MAHLON MORGAN
applicant vizt. FRANCES MORGAN widow. SARAH TEAGUE (or RABKIN), THOMAS
MORGAN, NANCY TENCH, WILLIAM MORGAN, MANOS MORGAN, JOHN O'BRYANT &
wife ELIZABETH, JOHN MORGAN, BENJAMIN MORGAN, CHARLES C. MORGAN, ISEBEL-
LA MORGAN, BENSON STEPHENS & wife ELEANOR.

Bk A, p. 24:   ELI DAVIS owned 250 acres on Tugaloo River. Dated
     6 June 1836. BIRDWELL HILL applicant vizt. JOHN L. DAVIS, ELI
SOUTH, JOHN L. M. THOMPSON, SARAH CLANAHAN, MEAD DAVIS minor, T. W.
HARBIN guardian, DEMSEY YOW. Advertised for absent legatees.

Bk A, p. 25:   MORGAN MORGAN owned 200 acres on Cane Creek bounded
     by lands of JOHN RUSK and others on which is a grist mill. Dated
6 June 1836. BENJAMIN SEGO applicant vizt. ELIZABETH MORGAN widow.
JOSEPH MORGAN, DAVID MORGAN, HENRY HEAD & wife MARY, BENJAMIN HEAD
& wife KATHARINE, JOSHUA STEPHENS & wife ELIZABETH....POOL & wife MIR-
IAM. JOSEPH STEPHENS & wife ANNA.

Bk A, p. 26:   BURWELL GREEN owned 200 acres on Conneross Creek
     joining lands of JOHN ADAIR. Tract of 257 acres on Chauga River
joining lands of ALMOND POWELL, 93 acres joining ABNER HONEA and SAMUEL
HUNT on waters of Choestoe. Dated 9 June 1836. ASA A. GREEN & JOHN
O. GREEN applicants vizt. PHOEBE GREEN widow, ARCHBALD WALKER & wife
MARGARET, GARLAND HARDWICK & wife LUCY, JEREMIAH GIBSON & wife ELIZA-
BETH, JANE CALDWELL, WILLIAM GREEN, BURWELL GREEN & LEWIS T. GREEN
defendants. Notice was given to absent legatees.

Bk A, p. 27:   HENRY H. ANDERSON owned 164 acres on waters of Cane
     Creek bounded by lands of WILLIAM HALL & PHOEBE PITMON. Dated
24 July 1836. SUSAN ANDERSON widow applicant vizt. ELIZABETH ANDER-
SON mother of deceased. HIRAM BENNET & wife. DENNY ANDERSON, WILLIAM
LEONARD, JAMES ANDERSON, JR., THOMAS LEONARD & wife. Heirs of SAMUEL
ANDERSON, dec'd. JOHN ANDERSON defendants. MARY ANDERSON a minor.

Bk A, p. 28:   LAZARUS MOORE owned 636 acres on Snow Creek joining
     lands of JOHN C. KILPATRICK & JONATHAN REEDER. Dated November
1836. AGNES MOORE defendant vizt. THOMAS MOORE, defendant.

Bk A, p. 29:   MOSES HENDRICKS owned 1 tract called the School House
     tract 100 acres more or less bounded by lands of DANIEL LOOPER,
MOSES HENDRIX and others. On other tract 100 acres bounded by JEREMIAH
LOOPER & DANIEL LOOPER. Dated January 1837. DUNCAN HENDRIX saith that
the Real Estate of his Grandfather MOSES HENDRIX, dec'd. is not worth
one thousand dollars. MOSES HENDRIX applicant vizt. SUSAN HENDRIX,

Cont'd:
widow. DAVID HENDRIX, ALEXANDER CLARK & wife ELIZABETH, Heirs of JOHN
CHAPMAN and wife, DAVID HAYS and wife BARBARA, WILLIAM LASLAY and wife
ROSANNA...LARKIN HENDRIX defendants.

Bk A, p. 30:   NICHOLAS HUNT owned 400 acres on Peters Creek waters
        of Saluda River joining lands of MARTIN WHITMIRE & others. Dated
17 Mar. 1837. MARTIN HUNT applicant vizt. SARAH HUNT, widow. DUDLY
PATTERSON and wife CYNTHIA, NANCY HUNT and WILLIAM HUNT minors.

Bk A, p. 31:   WILLIAM BAKER owned 200 acres on waters of Cheostoe
        joining lands of RICHARD DEAN, JOHN VERNER and others. Another
tract of 100 acres joining lands of JOHN O. GREEN and others known
by the name of Cains old field. Dated 2 Oct. 1837. GARRET FITZGERALD
and wife MARGARET applicant vizt. the heirs of SAMUEL PATTERSON, WEBB,
and BEN BAILEY in right of their wives. ELISHA LAWLEY and wife FRANCES,
WILLIAM BAKER. GILBERT BAKER. SAMUEL SEATON and wife. Heirs of JONATHAN
BAKER. REASON BAKER. ISAAC BAKER. Advertising for the legatees all
of whom are absent without the limits of this state.

Bk A, p. 32:   LANGSWORTH CLARDY owned 436 acres on Buck Creek waters
        of Saluda River. GEORGE DILWORTH the Uncle of the Legatees. Dated
27 Aug. 1837. GEORGE D. CLARDY applicant vizt. JOHN B. CLARDY and ANDREW
N. CLARDY defendants.

Bk A, p. 34:   TATE ALEXANDER owned 500 acres lying on Longnose
        Creek, waters of Tugaloo River joining lands of CHRISTOPHER WHISE-
NANT, Major DAVID HUMPHREYS and others. Dated August 1837. JOHN PULLIAM
applicant in right of his wife..vizt. ROBERT ALEXANDER, WILLIAM ALEX-
ANDER, ROBERT BALLEW, JOHN ALEXANDER, JOSEPH RUSK, JONATHAN WILLIAMS,
JOSEPH ALEXANDER, SAMUEL ALEXANDER defendants.

Bk A, p. 35:   JAMES STANDRIDGE, SR. owned 310 acres lying on waters
        of Chauga Creek, joining lands of EDWARD HUGHS, WILLIAM SHEAD,
SR. and others. Also 143 acres on Toxaway Creek bounded by lands of
JOHN RIDER, NATHANIEL PERRY..ISAAC STANDRIDGE applicant vizt. POLLY
STANDRIDGE, widow..JOHN STANDRIDGE, JAMES STANDRIDGE, SAMUEL STANDRIDGE
..JOSEPH STANDRIDGE..Heirs of WILLIAM ROPER and wife..SAMUEL MAGBY
and wife NELLY...JOHN RIDER and wife NANCY ...WILLIAM SWEATMAN and
(or) ELIZABETH STANDRIDGE..CHARLES PITTS and wife MAGY..ALLEN DOWNS
and wife ALSE.

Bk A, p. 36:   ELISHA HEDDEN owned 244 acres on waters of Little
        River, now occupied by SOLOMON WOODS, joining lands of JAMES LAY,
MOSES CANTRELL and DANIEL ALEXANDER. Dated 2 Oct. 1837. ELISHA HEDDEN
and JEFFREY HEDDEN applicants vizt. WILLIAM VISSAGE and wife ELIZABETH..
GEORGE HEDDEN..JOSEPH HEDDEN..JACOB HEDDEN..ELIZABETH HEDDEN..KATHARINE
HEDDEN..MARIA HEDDEN defendants.

Bk A, p. 37:   DAVID HAMILTON, SR. owned 108 acres willed to his
        grandson ALEXANDER HAMILTON, dec'd. having died previously to
his grandfather. Dated 1839. ANDREW W. KIRKPATRICK and wife MARY applicants vizt. EDMUND PARSONS and wife ELIZABETH. JOHN PRATER and MARGARET
his wife. DAVID HAMILTON. Heirs of JANE HAMILTON. SAMUEL FRASUER and
wife BETHSHEBA.

Bk A, p. 38:   CALEB MAY owned 600 acres on Waltons Ford Road leading
        from Pickens Court House to Clarksville in Georgia known by the
name of the Double Cabins...281 acres lying on Battle Creek granted
to CALEB MAY by his Excellency RICHARD J. MANNING..81 acres lying on
waters of Brass Town Creek waters of Tugaloo River all in Pickens Dist.
MARTHA M. MAY applicant vizt. HORACE NAREMORE and CALEB BABBITT defendants. Dated 1839.

Bk A, p. 39:   AARON or HUMPHREY LINDSEY owned 100 acres on Chauga
        Creek. Dated 11 Oct. 1841. JEMIMA WRIGHT a first cousin to sd
LINDSEY aforesaid and who died about 10 years ago having neither wife
or child...JEMIMA WRIGHT applicant vizt. JOHN LINDSEY and heirs defendants. Having advertised for absent legatees there being none in
the state on whom summons in partition could be served.

327

Bk A, p. 43:   JAMES MC KINNEY owned 800 acres one tract lying on
     Boons Creek, the other lying on both sides of White Water River
containing 133 acres, and one other tract lying on the waters of Devils
Fork containing 110 acres. Dated 17 Jan. 1842. To CHARLES MC KINNEY.....
JAMES LAY..DAVID MC KINNEY..JESSE MC KINNEY, PRESTON MC KINNEY..WILSON
MC KINNEY..JAMES ROBERTSON..Heirs of JAMES MC KINNEY.

Bk A, p. 45:   DAVID WADE owned 140 acres lying on Saluda River.
     Dated 23 Jan. 1843. SIMEON WADE applicant vizt. HENRY WADE heirs
out of the state..NOAH WADE heirs out of state..SOLOMON WADE heirs
in the state..ELIJAH WADE heirs out of the state...TABITHA WADE out
of the state...SARAH WADE out of the state.

Bk A, p. 46:   HANNAH NICHOLSON owned 100 acres on waters of Little
     River joining lands of JOHN HOLDEN and others. Dated 2 June 1843.
BENJAMIN NICHOLSON applicant vizt. ISAAC NICHOLSON of Missouri..JACOB
NICHOLSON of Arkansas...WILLIAM NICHOLSON. JOEL HEDDEN and wife ELIZA-
BETH of Georgia. WILLIAM QUEEN and wife MARY of North Carolina. MARTIN
MOODY and wife LUCINDA..BENNET MOODY and wife HANNAH..DREAD MASSINGALE
and wife DEBORAH.

Bk A, p. 47:   WILLIAM JOLLY, SR. owned 200 acres on Choestoe Creek,
     waters of Tugaloo River. Dated 3 Apr. 1843. Heirs MARTIN HARRISON,
MARGARET JOLLY.

Bk A, p. 50:   JAMES KELLY owned 120 acres lying on Little River
     joining lands of JOSEPH BENNETT, M. M. NORTON, & JOHN J. HOWARD.
Dated 1 May 1843. JOHN O. GRISHAM applicant vizt. in behalf of SARRA
KELLY, REBECCA KELLY, EZEKIEL KELLY, TALTON KELLY, HIRAM KELLY, ANN
CALHOUN widow..ANDREW JACKSON and wife...RICHARD JACKSON and wife...LU-
CINDA KELLY minor over 14 years.

Bk A, p. 53:   JAMES RUSSELL owned 98 acres on waters of Twelve
     Mile River, joining lands of ABNER RUSSELL & HENRY RUSSELL & HUND-
LEY EVATT. Dated 25 Mar. 1843. ZACHARIAH POWER applicant vizt. MALINDA
RUSSELL et al.

Bk A, p. 56:   ABSALOM MARTIN owned 95 acres lying on Golden Creek
     bounded by WILLIAM BOGGS, HENRY SERGEANT & MARY HOLLAND. Dated
20 May 1844. JOHN M. HENDRIX and wife RUTHA were heirs.

Bk A, p. 57:   DAVID HAMILTON owned 250 acres. Dated 3 Apr. 1844.
     BENJAMIN NICHOLSON vizt. JANE HAMILTON..SHILVY BATES applicants
vizt. MARGARET PRATER and MARY KIRKPATRICK.

Bk A, p. 56 or   ABSALOM MARTIN..JOHN M. HENDRIX and wife RUTHA vizt.
     EDY MARTIN widow. DUDLY WOOTON and wife ELIZABETH..CLABORN WILKER-
SON and wife MARGARET..RACHEL MARTIN..JUDE MARTIN a minor..LYDIA MARTIN
a minor...MARY MARTIN a minor.

Bk A, p. 59:   PETER CORBIN owned 273 acres of the north fork of
     Georges Creek on which his widow ELIZABETH lived and died. Dated
1 July 1844. JAMES MANSELL applicant vizt. SAMUEL CORBIN..JOHN CORBIN..
JUDY CORBIN..WILLIAM CORBIN heirs..SARAH CORBIN..ELIJAH CORBIN..DAVID
CORBIN..ELIZABETH CORBIN..JESPER (JESSE?) CORBIN. Land bounded by RICH-
ARD BURDINE, SIMEON WADE, JOHN BOWEN and others.

Bk A, p. 59:   WILLIAM CANNON owned 207 acres on Rices Creek bounded
     by land of JOHN ARIAL and others. Dated 5 Nov. 1844. ELIZAH CANNON
applicant vs ABRAHAM DUKE and wife..JUDY KENDRICK..JAMES CANNON..JOSIAH
MARCHBANKS and wife..CARTER CANNON and heirs of WILLIAM CANNON defendants. The last five legatees reside without the limits of this state.

Bk A, p. 60:   JONATHAN WHITTEN owned 200 acres lying on Cane Creek
     whereon DAVID CALDWELL now lives. Dated 10 Jan. 1845. DAVID CALD-
WELL entitled to one third of the estate as assignee of ELIZABETH WHIT-
TEN widow and one fourth of the other two thirds as assignee of WIL-
LIAM ROCHESTER and wife and to one childs part of the fourth of two
thirds in right of his wife and to one childs part as assignee of JON.

Cont'd:
W. ROCHESTER and wife MARGARET WHITTEN, JACKSON WHITTEN & AUSTEN M.
WHITTEN children of AARON WHITTEN whose wife was a daughter of intestate. And allowing one fourth of two thirds to WILLIAM PHILLIPS and
wife PEGGY and one fourth of two thirds to FRANCIS WHITTEN and a childs
part to the young children of AARON WHITTEN. RACHEL F. CARSON and JOHN
C. WHITTEN heirs of JONATHAN WHITTEN. GREENBERRY WHITTEN also an heir.
SARAH AYRES or SARAH BARRETT owned 50 acres lying on Carpenters Creek
joining lands of JAMES BURDINE and others. SARAH AYRES was married
to ARTHUR B. BARRETT in her first husbands life time and was after
wards known as SARAH BARRETT. Her husband is dead and ARTHUR BARRETT
is also dead. REDEN RACKLEY states that his Father was a brother to
sd SARAH. Dated 24 Apr. 1845.

Bk A, p. 71:   JOHN J. BARNETT owned 149 acres of one half. The
        other half is owned by MOSES HENDRICKS on waters of Georges Creek.
MELINDA BARNETT the widow..MELINDA BARNETT vs JUDY C. & ROSANNAH J.
BARNETT minors. Dated 15 Nov. 1845.

Bk A, p. 72:   POWELL RIGGINS owned 150 acres lying on Twelve Mile
        River joining lands of SION RIGGINS, ALLEN RIGGINS and others.
SARAH RIGGINS..HARMON COX..ISIAH WOOD and wife, applicants vs the Heirs
of ELI RIGGINS..WILLIAM RIGGINS..ANDREW RIGGINS..JAMES RIGGINS..WILLIAM
WOOD and wife NANCY..SAMUEL COX and wife JINCY..JOHN HARBIN and wife
POLLY, defendants. Dated 31 Jan. 1846.

Bk A, p. 74:   ELIJAH BARNETT owned two small tracts lying on waters
        of Georges Creek, one containing 50 acres joining lands of WILLIAM
JAMISON and others..17 acres joining lands of MOSES HENDRICKS and others
..Applicants petition. NATHANIEL DUNCAN..DAVID HARRIS and wife LURANY...
RILEY CORBIN and wife MELISSA..THOMAS BARNETT..RIAL BARNETT..ANN BARNETT
..MARY BARNETT widow. Dated 30 July 1846.

Bk A, p. 77:   GEORGE DILWORTH owned 173 acres on Jones Fork of
        Dodeys Creek waters of Saluda River joining lands of LEWIS HILL,
HENSON HUNT, & JAMES LATHEM..REBECCA DILWORTH applicant vs WILLIAM
BOWEN guardian for MARY DILWORTH, BENJAMIN DILWORTH, ELIZABETH DILWORTH,
FRANCES DILWORTH, ROBERT DILWORTH, CATHARINE DILWORTH minors, defen-
dants. Dated 2 Nov. 1846.

Bk A, p. 78:   BENJAMIN DAY, JR. owned 160 acres on waters of Golden
        Creek joining lands of JOHN AIRIAL, WILLIAM ODELL, ELIHU GRIFFIN
and others. JANE E. DAY widow applicant vs JOHN GEARIN guardian for
JACOB L. DAY a minor. Dated 4 Jan. 1847.

Bk A, p. 79:   DUKE W. GLENN owned real estate..ANNA GLENN and JAMES
        GLENN applicants vs NOBLE GLENN guardian for ROBERT GLENN, WARREN
GLENN, WILLIAM GLENN minors. WILLIAM GLENN is out of the state. Dated
1 Mar. 1847.

Bk A, p. 82:   LEVI TANNERY owned 380 acres lying on Choestoe Creek
        joining lands of MAJOR COLE, COLEMAN FOWLER, JOHN ANDERSON and
others. B. B. MOOR (or MOON?) and wife NARCISSA applicants vs PARTHENIA
TANNERY, ALFRED TANNERY, S. W. NORRIS, JR. guardian for WILLIAM TANNERY,
JOHN TANNERY, EVELINE TANNERY, SAMUEL TANNERY minors. Dated 1 Mar.
1847.

Bk A, p. 87:   JOHN YOUNG owned 115 acres lying on Mile Creek. CLAR-
        INDA YOUNG the widow...CLARINDA YOUNG vs ROBERT STEWART guardian
for GEORGE YOUNG and RICHARD YOUNG minors under 14 years. Dated 6 Sept.
1847.

Bk A, p. 96:   ELIZABETH HENDERSON owned land on Georges Creek join-
        ing Col. HOLCOMBE and others. Heirs JOHN HENDERSON, NATHANIEL
HENDERSON, JOHN CANSLER ..ABIGAIL GEARIN..Heirs of WILLIAM CANSLER
reside out of the state. Dated 1 May 1848.

Bk A, p. 97:   DAVID H. BOGGS owned 165 acres of land on branches
        of Rices Creek and Goldens Creek..joining lands ROBERT MC WHORTER,

Cont'd:
ELIHU GRIFFIN and others..JOSEPH G. BOGGS applicant vs MARTHA BOGGS
widow..WILLIAM BOGGS..AARON BOGGS..Heirs of J. N. BOGGS..JOHN R. BOGGS
and wife JANE..MARTIN BOGGS..Heirs of THOMAS BOGGS..Heirs of ELIZABETH
NALLY, defendants. Part of the heirs reside out of the state. Dated
1 May 1848.

Bk A, p. 98:   HENRY GRIFFIN owned land in Pickens District. BENJAMIN
      HAGOOD states that he has four ninths of two thirds and one sixth
of one ninth of sd estate. BENJAMIN HAGOOD assignee vs ELIZABETH GRIF-
FIN, ALVAH GRIFFIN, JOSEPH LEAGE and wife..Heirs of WILLIAM GRIFFIN.
Heirs of ROBERT GRIFFIN, defendants. Part of the heirs reside out of
the state. Dated 1 May 1848.

Bk A, p. 99:   STARLING GARNER owned 155 acres lying on waters of
      Conneross Creek joining lands of JOHN C. GORDON, B. W. BURNES,
HENRY MC DANIEL and others..Heirs SARAH GARNER, H. M. GARNER..R. T.
GARNER..MARY GARNER..JOHN GARNER..STARLING GARNER..H. M. GARNER guardian
for C. C. GARNER..HARRIET GARNER..JAMES M. GARNER..SARAH J. GARNER..WIL-
LIAM R. GARNER minors under 21 years. Dated 27 July 1848.

Bk A, p. 100:   ADAM RICHARDS owned 273 acres lying near Fair Play
      joining lands of A. P. REEDER, LILBURN WRIGHT and others. Heirs
WATSON COLLINGS..MARY COLLINGS..T. P. RICHARDS, F. M. JONS, S. T. RICH-
ARDS. Dated 25 Sept. 1849.

Bk A, p. 100:   WILLIAM ADDIS owned 100 acres on waters of Beaver-
      dam Creek joining lands of C. HUNT, WILLIAM GRANT and others.
SAMUEL ADDIS, PINCKNEY MASON and wife ELIZABETH, JOHN ADDIS, JOHN THOMAS
and SARAH his wife, THOMAS SMITH and wife NANCY C., WILLIAM ADDIS applicants vs MARY ADDIS..GEORGE W. FULLER and wife JANE, and the children
of JAMES ADDIS, dec'd. defendants. Dated 2 Apr. 1849.

Bk A, p. 113:   JOHN CLAYTON owned 2 lots of land, one town lot in
      the Village of Pickens, one tract called the Collings tract con-
taining 120 acres more or less, on waters of Little River, Corn House
Creek..HANNAH CLAYTON the widow..left 7 children..SARAH ANN, wife of
CHARLES ALLEN, JR., THOMAS of Mississippi..MARY ELIZABETH, wife of
JAMES YOUNG..ROBERT CARTER a minor..STEPHEN GARRISON a minor..MARGARET
a minor..JESSE MADISON a minor. Dated 22 May 1849.

Bk A, p. 118:   THOMAS BRYCE owned 230 acres lying on Conneross Creek.
      One third to JONATHAN R. CLEVELAND and wife ELIZABETH..WILLIAM
HAYS and wife JANE..JAMES R. G. BRYCE. Dated 9 Nov. 1849.

Bk A, p. 122:   WILLIAM VANZANT owned 400 acres lying on Ramsays
      and Chauga Creeks, where on W. SIMPSON, Esq. formerly lived, join-
ing lands of JOSEPH GRISHAM, JAMES FERGUSON, CLAYTON JENKINS & JOHN
HUGHS..Heirs..AMANDA JANE VANZANT, JEPTHA NORTON VANZANT, ROBERT WILLIAM
VANZANT, LAVINA ELIZABETH VANZANT, GEORGE THOMAS VANZANT. All children.
Dated 1 Apr. 1850.

Bk A, p. 123:   SAMUEL EDENS owned 200 acres lying on waters of Oole-
      noy Creek joining lands of JACOB CHASTAIN, JAMES KEITH and others.
Heirs ..TYRE L. ROPER and wife MALINDA..WILLIAM EDENS..ALEXANDER EDENS..
PASCAL SOUTHERLAND and wife ESTHER..JESSE ADAMS and wife POLLY. Dated
2 Feb. 1850.

Bk A, p. 125:   ROBERT KYLE owned land on both sides of Little River.
      DAVID LESLY states that some years since ROBERT KYLE died..Dated
9 Aug. 1850. Had no children..left a widow, CATHERINE KYLE since deceased and her heirs and the children or heirs of the following deceased
brothers viz JAMES KYLE, LAUGHLIN KYLE, JOHN KYLE, WILLIAM KYLE..MATHEW
& HENRY KYLE who may yet be living. All out of the state except WILLIAM
MC WHORTER and wife MARGARET and ELIZA KYLE who were children of the
sd JAMES KYLE, dec'd.

Bk A, p. 129:   JOSEPH TAYLOR owned 187 acres lying on Goldens Creek
      joining lands of RANSOM BANKS, B. F. HOLLAND..G. W. TAYLOR and
others. Heirs ..LUCINDA TAYLOR widow, G. W. TAYLOR, A. R. TAYLOR, JOSE-

Cont'd:
PHINE TAYLOR, EVELINE TAYLOR, EMILINE TAYLOR, LAURENCE TAYLOR, ELAM
TAYLOR, CATHARINE TAYLOR. Dated 16 Sept. 1850.

Bk A, p. 130?:   WILLIAM P. MC DOW owned 60 acres on 18 Mile Creek.
     Left widow MARGARET who later married G. W. MITCHELL. Children:
ELIZABETH MC DOW, WILLIAM H. MC DOW. Dated 6 Dec. 1850.

Bk A, p. 133:   HENRY MYERS owned 100 acres on Beaverdam Creek. Heirs
     JOHN MYERS, BALUS GREEN and wife CHARLOTTE, Heirs of ROBERT JONES
7 children part out of the state. HENRY MYERS. Dated 24 Feb. 1851.

Bk A, p. 136:   ADAM THOMPSON owned 260 acres on Uttys Creek. Left
     one daughter SUSANNAH SANDERS (wife of PATRICK SANDERS) now de-
ceased, having her husband and four children. Dated 11 Aug. 1851.

Bk A, p. 137:   SUSANNAH HAMMOND owned 101 acres on waters of 18
     Mile Creek joining lands of JOHN MC WHORTER, SAMUEL MAVERICK and
others. Heirs..THOMAS PRATER, PHILIP PRATER..AARON PRATER..JOSIAH PRATER
..JOSEPH PRATER. The heirs of JOHN PRATER and of SALLY WALLACE and
the heirs of POLLY HUBBARD all the heirs absent from the state except
JEREMIAH PRATER. Dated 6 Oct. 1851.

Bk A, p. 138:   RICHARD POE owned 250 acres in Pickens District lying
     on Town Creek. He bequeathed this land to LUCINDA HARRIS during
her lifetime and at her death to her children. The sd LUCINDA HARRIS
has (since) deceased. Children: JOHN HARRIS, DORCAS HARRIS, JAMES HARRIS,
SARAH HARRIS, CARTER B. HARRIS, NATHANIEL HARRIS. Dated 1 Mar. 1852.

Bk A, p. 141:   JOHN DORSEY owned 100 acres lying on Cane Creek join-
     ing lands of ALEX NEVILL, JOSEPH KELLY and others. Heirs: MARY
DORSEY widow...POLLY DORSEY and the heirs of WILLIAM DORSEY are in
this state and the following heirs are absent from the state viz ELISHA
DORSEY, DAVID DORSEY, JOHN DORSEY, JR., HARDIN PERKINS and CATHARINE
his wife, HENRY MEDFORD and wife RACHEL and the heirs of ELIZABETH
SHIELD, dec'd. Dated 4 Oct. 1852.

Bk A, p. 143:   JOHN JONES, deceased, owned 120 acres lying on Long
     Nose Creek..JOHN JONES applicant vs ELIAS JONES and others. Dated
4 Jan. 1853.

Bk A, p. 146:   DANIEL MERK (written also MARK) owned 409 acres on
     Twelve Mile River joining lands of JOSHUA CHAPMAN, CARTER CLAYTON
and others. Heirs: EMILIA MERK widow...JOSEPH MERK, BLOOMER MERK, DANIEL
L. MERK, JACOB CHAPMAN and wife RACHEL, VINCENT JAMES and wife MARTHA,
JANE MERK. The heirs of MARY BANKS. Dated 15 Apr. 1853.

Bk A, p. 152:   DREWERY POWER owned 184 acres lying on 18 Mile Creek.
     Heirs: MARIAH POWER widow..R. P. LANDRETH and wife EMILY C., WILLIS
G. GRANT and wife DELLA E., MARY L. POWER, HARRIET O. POWER, W. L.
POWER, JAMES G. POWER. Dated 23 July 1855.

Bk A, p. 153:   L. D. DICKERSON owned 100 acres on waters of Gingrus?
     Creek joining lands of JOEL ELLISON, WILLIAM BENSON and others.
Heirs: RUTH DICKERSON. Dated 4 Sept. 1853.

Bk A, p. 157:   JOHN MC ADAMS owned 230 acres on Doddys Creek, waters
     of Saluda River joining lands of JAMES M. PONDER, JAMES MC ADAMS
and others. Heirs: JAMES MC ADAMS, SR., JAMES MC ADAMS, JR., JAMES
H. CLEMMONS and wife SUSAN, MASON BURDINE and wife MALINDA, GEORGE
W. FARR and wife JEMIMA, THOMAS TUMBLING and wife SARAH, JAMES W. HUNT
and wife AMELIA, GEORGE MC ADAMS, MARY JANE MC ADAMS. Dated 7 Dec.
1855.

Bk A, p. 159:   DANIEL LOOPER owned 198 acres on Carpenters Creek,
     waters of Saluda River joining lands of L. HENDRICKS, Esq., SOLOMON
LOOPER, SR. and others. Heirs: JOYCE LOOPER, ARMINDA A. LOOPER, DANIEL
LOOPER, SOLOMON LOOPER, JR., JEREMIAH TRAINUM guardian for minors viz
ELENDER P. LOOPER, ELIZABETH LOOPER, SAMUEL LOOPER, ARMINDA LOOPER,

Cont'd:
RACHEL LOOPER, MARY LOOPER. Dated 23 July 1855.

Bk A, p. 163:   EDWARD CLANIHAN owned 210 acres on Crooked Creek
        joining lands of JOSEPH BREWER and others. Heirs: SARAH L. CLAN-
AHAN, WILLIS CARVER and wife HARRIET. Dated 15 Dec. 1855.

Bk A, p. 164:   FRANCIS JENKINS owned 240 acres on Choestoe Creek,
        waters of Tugaloo River, bounded by lands of RICHARD DEAN, SAMUEL
VERNER and others. Heirs: RICAHRD DEAN and wife SYNTHA, ANDREW JENKINS,
WILLIAM JENKINS, THOMAS JENKINS, JESSE JENKINS, J. M. JENKINS and wife
ELIZA. The heirs of JOHN M. JENKINS, ARCHIBALD E. JENKINS, LOVICY(?)
C. JENKINS, ALVIN JENKINS, NANCY JENKINS. Dated 3 Aug. 1855.

Bk A, p. 169:   HEZEKIAH FINDLY owned 92 acres on Shoal Creek, waters
        of Saluda River joining lands of ROSWELL HILL, RACHEL HORTON and
others. Heirs: ELIZABETH CRAIN, widow of HEZEKIAH FINDLEY, MARTHA FIND-
LEY, JOSEPH FINDLEY, JOHN M. FINDLEY. Dated 20 Feb. 1857.

Bk A, p. 172:   WINNY NIMMONS owned 26½ acres on Conney Ross Creek
        joining lands of ABNER SHUTTLES and JOHN HARDIN and others. Heirs:
ABNER SHUTTLE and wife MARGARET, ELEANOR NIMMONS, EBENEZER THOMAS and
wife MARTHA, ELIJAH EMERY and wife SARAH. Dated 7 Mar. 1856.

Bk A, p. 179:   JOHN M. KLINBECK was administrator of MRS. GESINA
        KLENBECK sheweth that MMRS. GESINA KLEINBECK was administratrix
of J. D. KLENBECK estate. J. D. KLEINBECK owned 118 acres of a Mill
Tract, also one small farm near Walhalla containing 50 acres, also
two town lots in Walhalla. Children..JULIANA KLENBECK, ELIZA KLENBECK,
JOHN H. KLEINBECK all minors. Dated 28 Feb. 1857.

Bk A, p. 183:   JEREMIAH FIELDS owned the following lands...No. 1-
        One tract on Big Laurel Creek containing 1000 acres..No. 2- One
tract on Nine Times Creek containing 664 acres..No. 3- One tract on
Big Eastatoe containing 791 acres..No. 4- One tract on Nixes Branch
containing 502 acres..No. 5- One tract bounded on one side by Jocasse
River containing 640 acres..No. 6- One tract on Devils Fork containing
265 acres..No. 7- One tract on Big Eastatoe containing 602 acres..Heirs
are JOHN D. FIELDS, B. W. FIELD, JAMES M. FIELD, JOSEPH DOLHRON and
wife MALINDA A. The heirs of JOSEPH A. FIELD. Dated 23 ___ 1857.

Bk A, p. 187:   GEORGE W. KING owned land lying on Martins Creek,
        waters of Seneca River joining lands of BAYLIS EARLE, DEMPSEY
YOW and others, containing 290 acres. Heirs..LUCINDA PHILIPS late his
widow..one child, GEORGE W. KING. Dated 25 Dec. 1853.

Bk A, p. 190:   ABSALOM GIBSON owned 460 acres on both sides of Little
        River joining lands of Col. JEPHTHAH NORTON, JOHN CAPEHART and
others..Heirs: ABNER LEWIS and wife MARY, SOBRINA GROGAN, HIRAM GIBSON,
VILANTY COBB. The heirs of SELA BOON, deceased. SALINNA GROGAN, HIRAM
GIBSON, the heirs of of SELA BOON are out of this state. Dated 13 Jan.
1857.

Bk A, p. 192:   SION COOPER owned 132 acres lying on Cain Creek join-
        ing lands of JACOB SCHROEDER and others. Heirs..NANCY SMITH, Heirs
of ANSEL COOPER, Heirs of VINCENT COOPER, dec'd. JAMES KELLY and wife
MARY, RAHAB FIELDS, CELIA NIX, LEWIS COOPER, JOHN FERGUSON.

Bk A, p. 194:   RHODA BERRY owned 100 acres on waters of Choestoe
        joining lands of E. P. VERNER, JANE ANDERSON and others. Heirs
MARY JANE BERRY, DAVID BERRY, EMALINE BERRY. Dated 5 Jan. 1857.

Bk A, p. 196:   NIMROD LEATHERS owned 173 acres on waters of Chohee
        waters of Tugaloo River, joining lands of JAMES DAVIS, F. N. GAR-
VIN and others. Tract No. 2 on waters of Devils Fork containing 150
acres joining lands of F. N. GARVIN, STEPHEN NICHOLSON and others.
RUTH B. LEATHERS heir. Dated 20 June 1853.

Bk A, p. 198:   CLARISSA D. ELLIOTT owned 110 acres on waters of

Cont'd:
    Choestoe waters of Tugaloo River joining lands of L. TOWERS, Capt.
JAMES JOHNS and others. Heirs: W. T. HOLLAND, SUSAN DOYLE, ELIZABETH
BREWER, D. T. HOLLAND, ELIZABETH HOLLAND. Also mentioned JAMES BREWER.
Dated 4 Oct. 1855.

Bk A, p. 200:   ASA CARVER owned 215 acres on Conneross Creek, waters
    of Tugaloo River joining lands of JOHN ADAIR, Esq., WILLIAM ADAIR
and others. ARA CARVER the widow..AMANDA JANE CARVER a minor. Dated
8 Jan. 1858.

Bk A, p. 203:   CLAYTON JENKINS owned 100 acres on waters of Toxaway
    Creek, waters of Tugaloo River joining lands of R. A. GILMER,
ISAAC STANDRIDGE and others. No. 2 tract on waters of Colonels Fork,
on the road leading from Jarretts Bridge to Pickens Court House, joining lands of Doctor EARLE, THOMAS JONES and others, containing 75 acres.
Heirs..ELIZABETH JENKINS the widow, JOHN M. JENKINS, MARY JANE JENKINS,
GEORGE M. JENKINS, JAMES G. JENKINS, ARA A. JENKINS, URIAH JENKINS
all minors..Dated 19 Dec. 1857.

Bk A, p. 206:   HENRY GASSAWAY owned 213 acres on Long Creek waters
    of Chattaga River joining lands of JONAS PHILLIPS, JOHN MAXWELL
and others. Heirs ..JOHN GASSAWAY, JAMES GASSAWAY, RACHEL GASSAWAY,
WILLIAM GASSAWAY, JEREMIAH SUTTON and wife SARAH, Heirs of ELIZABETH
BUTT, WESLEY GASSAWAY, IRA GASSAWAY, BRYANT BANDY(?) and wife PHEBE,
HENRY LEUREY(?) and wife SARAH, JAMES C. LEE and wife HARRIET, HENRY
GASSAWAY, NATHAN PHILLIPS and wife MAHALA, EDWARD WILLIAMS and wife
MARY. Dated 16 Jan. 1858.

Bk A, p. 211:   ALLEN BLACK owned 148 acres on Long Nose Creek, waters
    of Tugaloo River. No. 2 on Long Nose Creek containing 183 acres.
No. 3 on Little Toxaway Creek, waters of Tugaloo River containing 271
acres. Heirs: JANE BLACK, widow...T. JOHNS and wife NANCY out of this
state. ROBERT POWELL and wife POLLY ANN, J. G. BROWN out of this state.
SARAH A. BLACK, WILLIAM BLACK, JOHN BLACK, D. W. BLACK, MARTHA J. BLACK.
Dated 21 Dec. 1857.

Bk A, p. 214:   JAMES GILLILAND owned 100 acres on waters of Oolenoy.
    Heirs : MARY ANN GILLILAND widow. MELINDA ROPER, ELIZABETH TROTTER.
Heirs of JESSE SIMMONS and wife MATILDA. Heirs of ELIZA TROTTER, dec'd.
ANDREW SIMMONS and wife REBECCA. EMILY C. GILLILAND. JAMES A. GILLILAND.
ELIJAH H. GILLILAND. DAVID GILLILAND. Dated 24 Aug. 1858. ISAM SIMMONS
and NANCY SIMMONS.

Bk A, p. 218:   JOSHUA CHAPMAN owned 192 acres on Shoal Creek. Heirs
    J. MERCK and wife SUSANNAH, THOMAS MC KINNEY and wife MARY, JACOB
CHAPMAN, RACHEL CHAPMAN, ISAAC A. CHAPMAN, MARGARET CHAPMAN, ISREAL
CHAPMAN, O. J. WIGINGTON and wife RUTH, Widow ELIZABETH CHAPMAN..Out
of state are: THOMAS MC KINNEY and wife MARY, JOEL CHAPMAN, O. J. WIG-
INGTON and wife RUTH, ISREAL CHAPMAN.

Bk A, p. 221:   ANDREW KELLY owned 228 acres on Keowee River joining
    MILES M. NORTON, MRS. ALEXANDER and others. No. 2 to be 75 or
100 acres on waters of Little River joining lands of L. N. ROBINS and
others. Heirs..ELIZABETH KELLY widow..JAMES J. KELLY, THOMAS JACKSON
and wife LUCY, JOSEPH W. KELLY, SAMUEL C. KELLY, JOHN CHASTAIN and
wife FEEBY, ADELINE KELLY. Dated 5 July 1858.

Bk A, p. 222:   THOMAS ALEXANDER owned tract No. 1 of 345 acres on
    waters of 12 Mile River joining lands of WESLEY GRANTT, JENKINS
ADAMS and others. No 2 on Keowee River of 50 acres joining lands of
WILLIAM ALEXANDER, JOHN OWENS...Heirs: GEORGE GIBSON and wife NANCY,
ELIJAH GIBSON and wife POLLY, JORDAN RICE and wife EMILA, JOSHUA HOLDEN
and wife KEZIAH, CARTER DURHAM and wife HANNAH, JOSEFH DURHAM and wife
ELIZABETH, GEORGE JAMES and wife DIANAH, WILLIAM HERD and wife LETTY.
Heirs out of the state are, JAMES ALEXANDER, WILLIAM DURHAM and wife
MALINDA, SALLY BOATNER formerly SALLY ALEXANDER. Dated 21 June 1858.

Bk A, p. 226:   JOSHUA COX owned 479 acres on Long Nose Creek, waters

333

Cont'd:
of Tugaloo River bounding land of Z. HALL, J. R. HUNNICUTT and others. Heirs: Z. B. COX, EDWARD COX, JOHN E. LODEN and wife ELIZA...... Heirs out of the state are JOHN COX..MARINDA COX..GABRIEL COX..GEORGE NAVES and wife JANE..LITTLE EDGE and wife MANERVA..GEORGE GLOW and wife RHODA and NANCY COX widow. Dated 15 Mar. 1858.

Bk A, p. 228:   WILLIAM ABBOTT owned tract No. 1 of 150 acres on Conneross Creek joining lands of FOSTER PERRY, NATHANIEL HULL and others...Heirs: JULIA ABBOTT the widow..JOHN MASON and wife ELIZA-BETH..BIRD ABBOTT..NOAH ABBOTT..JOHN DOWIS and wife SARAH..LEWIS EATON and wife MARY..JACOB ABBOTT, deceased, son a minor JACOB ABBOTT, JR. ALEXANDER GRAHAM and wife TEMPERANCE..The heirs of SIMPSON L. FOUNTAIN viz MARY M. FOUNTAIN..JAMES FOUNTAIN & WILDEY FOUNTAIN all minors..JAMES M. ABBOTT..WILLIS W. ABBOTT..JEPHTHAH G. ABBOTT..L. M. CRENSHAW and wife MARTHA. Dated 5 July 1858.

Bk A, p. 230:   DANIEL J. CHAPMAN owned 70 acres on 12 Mile River joining lands of ANDREW NEAL, JAMES CHAPMAN and others. Heirs: JAMES CHAPMAN..MILES & CAROLINE. Dated 26 Feb. 1858.

Bk A, p. 236:   NATHANIEL DUNCAN owned 196 acres on the head waters of Georges Creek of Saluda River joining lands of MOSES HENDRICKS, J. R. TROTTER and others. Heirs: DAVID DUNCAN, JAMES HIT and wife ELEN-DER, NATHANIEL DUNCAN, JOHN C. DUNCAN, SAMUEL P. BRAZEALE and wife SARAH ANN. Dated 4 Oct. 1858.

Bk A, p. 239:   J. E. SOUTHERLAND owned 300 acres on Weavers Creek joining lands of JAMES KEITH, WILLIAM SOUTHERLAND and others. Heirs all minors viz WILLIAM F. SOUTHERLAND, THOMAS SOUTHERLAND, MARY JANE SOUTHERLAND, JOHN SOUTHERLAND. Dated 20 Sept. 1858.

Bk A, p. 243:   ROBERT STEWART owned 700 acres on Little Eastatoe waters of Keowee River joining lands of WILLIAM GILSTRAP, ENOCH CHAPMAN and others. Heirs: ISABELL STEWART, widow..7 children all minors viz JAMES MADISON STEWART, MARIAH MALINDA STEWART, NANCY JANE STEWART, NAOMI STEWART, JOSEPHINE STEWART, JOHN RUFUS STEWART, MARY STEWART, ROBERT STEWART. Dated 8 Sept. 1858.

Bk A, p. 247:   JAMES W. COUCH owned 223 acres on Little Georges Creek waters of Saluda River joining lands of WILLIAM BENSON, deceased, JOEL ELLISON and others. Heirs: CYNTHA J. HENDRICKS the widow. MATILDA F. COUCH. Dated 6 June 1859.

Bk A, p. 252:   ANDREW H. ARCHER owned 110 acres on Little Georges Creek waters of Saluda River joining lands of MRS. MALINDA ARCHER, WILLIAM JAMESON and others. Heirs: PERMELIA T. ARCHER the widow. .. EUGENIA ARCHER..OLIATHA ARCHER. Dated 3 Oct. 1859.

Bk B, p. 27:   JACOB B. PERRY owned 200 acres on Mile Creek waters of Keowee River joining lands of JOHN DODSON, W. J. PARSONS and others. Heirs: MARY A. PERRY widow..J. A. MC KEE and wife ELIVIRA E., WILLIAM J. HUNNICUTT and wife ELMINA M. Dated 14 Dec. 1859.

Bk B, p. 29:   JOHN C. KALMBACK owned one lot in the town of Walhalla on Main Street and known in the place of sd town as No. 77 join-ing lots of MEUKE BULLWICKEL containing one half acre whereon a com-fortable house and work shop stands. Dated 19 Dec. 1859.

Bk B, p. 30:   JOHN A. CHILDRESS owned 150 acres on waters of Saluda River and 12 Mile River joining lands of JOHN FINDLEY, WINCHESTER CARY, LEVI WIMPEY and others. Heirs: SARAH CHILDRESS..JOHN H. CHILDRESS, ABRAHAM C. CHILDRESS, MARY M. CHILDRESS, ANDERSON M. CHILDRESS, LAURISSA J. CHILDRESS, BETHANY C. CHILDRESS,..Heirs of NICEY GANTT viz CAROLINE GANTT, JOHN GANTT, WILLIAM GANTT, ALEXANDER GANTT. Dated 9 Aug. 1858.

Bk B, p. 32:   THOMAS GARVIN owned 1030 acres on Laurel Fork waters of Keowee River joining lands of HENRY MORTON and others. Owned 350 acres on Mile Creek waters of Keowee River, joining lands of B.

Cont'd:
HAGOOD, F. N. GARVIN and others. Heirs: F. N. GARVIN, SAMUEL SMITH
and wife BETSY, E. W. MERRETT and wife ANN out of the state...THOMAS
D. GARVIN, SAMUEL PARSONS and wife MATILDA, ROBERT JOHNSTON and wife
FERDELIA, GREEN S. GARVIN, JAMES H. EVATT and wife MARILDA out of the
state. Dated 5 Dec. 1859.

Bk B, p. 34:   JOEL MASON owned 280 acres on waters of Choestoe
      Creek joining lands of THOMAS W. H. HARBIN, THOMAS JENKINS, JOHN
MASON and others. Heirs: FRANCES MASON widow..B. C. WHISENANT and wife
MILLY..SAMUEL LYLES and wife MARY..D. L. LYLES and wife MARTHA ANN.
CHARLES W. MASON a minor. Dated 19 Oct. 1859.

Bk B, p. 35:   HENRY WHITMIRE owned two tracts - No. 1 containing
      566 acres or the home place joining lands of DANIEL WHITMIRE,
ISAAC CROW and others; No. 2 on Toxaway River joining No. 1 and lands
of ISAAC ANDERSON and others, containing 134 acres. Heirs: WILLIAM
WHITMIRE..Heirs of MARY HINKLE, dec'd. viz HENRY HINKLE..JOHN HINKLE.
PETER BUTLER and wife ELIZABETH. WILLIAM HUNTER and wife MARY. ELIJAH
HINKLE, JR. CARR HINKLE. ELIAS HINKLE. A. J. STEWART and wife LUCINDA.
SILAS HINKLE. MARTHA HINKLE. JEREMIAH MORTON and wife LUCINDA. DANIEL
WHITMIRE. JOHN WHITMIRE. JONATHAN KING and wife NANCY. HENRY WHITMIRE.
Dated 13 Jan. 1860.

Bk B, p. 38:   ELIZABETH SMITH owned 400 acres on Chauga Creek join-
      ing lands of MESIAH LONG and others. Heirs: WILLIAM B. LONG and
wife JEMIMA..JAMES SMITH..TONEY SMITH..MARY SMITH..F. W. L. SMITH..PEGGY
SMITH..WILLIAM SMITH..ELIZABETH SMITH. Dated 10 Jan. 1860.

Bk B, p. 40:   WASHINGTON SMITH owned 550 acres on waters of Whet-
      stone Creek joining lands of GAMBRELL BREAZEAL, JORDON MOORE and
others. Heirs: WILLIAM B. LONG and wife JEMIMA..JAMES SMITH..TONEY
SMITH..MARY SMITH..F. W. L. SMITH..PEGGY SMITH..WILLIAM SMITH..ELIZABETH
SMITH. Dated 10 Jan. 1860.

Bk B, p. 42:   FRANCIS JENKINS owned 122 acres on waters of Cane
      Creek joining lands of W. H. STRIBLING, T. J. HALL and others.
Heirs: Heirs of ABNER JENKINS, dec'd. number and names unknown. One
of the heirs of ANDERSON JENKINS, dec'd. viz THOMAS JENKINS and STEWART
and wife ELIZA out of this state. ZACHARIAH HALL and wife RUTH.. WILLIAM
HALL and wife SARAH..RUFUS WARD and wife BELINDA..HENRY MYER and wife
NANCY..Heirs of ANDERSON JENKINS viz DANIEL HALL and wife CAROLINE
and MARY JENKINS in this state. Dated 28 Nov. 1859.

Bk B, p. 44:   BAILEY A. BARTON owned 80 acres joining lands of
      J. W. WILSON, J. W. WALKER and others. Heirs: CAROLINE J. CLYDE
formerly widow of the deceased..AUGUSTA BARTON. Dated 12 Jan. 1860.

Bk B, p. 46:   JOSEPH WOOD owned 200 acres on waters of 12 Mile
      River joining lands of JACOB LEWIS, WILEY REEVES and others. Heirs
WILLIAM MORGAN and wife SARAH..CHARLES WOOD..ALEXANER WOOD..MARY WOOD...
ROBERT WOOD..TILMAN HOWARD and wife ANNA. Dated 10 Feb. 1860.

Bk B, p. 48:   JESSE STRIBLING owned 178 acres on waters of Richland
      Creek joining lands of MRS. MC ELROY, MRS. STEELE and others.
Heirs - WILLIAM H. STRIBLING..DAVID S. STRIBLING..W. W. STRIBLING..THOS.
R. SHELER and wife SUSAN..H. N. WHITE and wife NANCY..THOMAS S. STRIB-
LING & M. S. STRIBLING in this state. ROBERT STRIBLING..B. F. KILPATRICK
and wife REBECCA..JOSIAH HARKEY and wife CATHARINE..The heirs at law
of MARY JONES, deceased. Dated 6 July 1860.

Bk B, p. 50:   WILLIAM GRANT owned 134 acres lying on Little Beaver-
      dam Creek, joining lands of ROBERT C. TRIBBLE, WILLIAM HUNT and
others. Heirs: NANCY GRANT widow..WILLIAM GRANT..TULLY SIMMONS and
wife MARY..GEORGE GRANT..JORDAN SIMMONS and wife MARTHA C., BIRD C.
GRANT..NOAH W. GRANT..PRESSLY A. GRANT..NANCY E. GRANT. The last 3
are minors. Dated 11 Oct. 1860.

Bk B, p. 53:   ROBERT L. MILLER owned 130 acres on waters of Chauga

Cont'd:
Creek joining lands of WILLIAM LAND, ROBERT MAXWELL and others.
Heirs: MARTHA JAUDEN MILLER..LAURA EMALINE MILLER.

Bk B, p. 55:   DAVID GILLILAND owned 150 acres on waters of Oolenoy
Creek joining lands of JESSE SIMMONS, RILEY LAWSON and others.
Left 7 children viz JOHN R. T. GILLILAND, LEMUEL J. GILLILAND, ABSALOM
ROPER and wife MALINDA, HENRIETTA J. GILLILAND, HARRISON ROPER and
wife SUSAN, RICHARD T. GILLILAND, NANCY E. GILLILAND, NANCY A. E. GIL-
LILAND, widow. LEMUEL J. GILLILAND out of the state. Dated 18 May 1861.

Bk B, p. 58:   ELISHA ALEXANDER owned 142 acres on Big Crow Creek
joining lands of WILLIAM ALEXANDER, WATSON COLLINS and others.
Heirs: MARY A. ALEXANDER widow. Heirs: WILLIAM J. ALEXANDER, SELA A.
ALEXANDER, GEORGE W. ALEXANDER, NANCY ANN ALEXANDER, ELISHA MARION
ALEXANDER. Dated 1 Oct. 1861.

Bk B, p. 60:   JOHN CASSELL owned 1000 acres on Davises Creek, waters
of Oolenoy joining lands of EDWARD CHASTAIN, NATHANIEL LYNCH and
others. Heirs: FANNEY CASSELL widow, THOMAS MASTERS and wife NANCY,
WILLIAM MASTERS and wife TEMPY, LEMUEL A. HOWARD and wife CATHERINE,
ROBERT MC JUNKIN and wife ROSE, SAMUEL HAMILTON CASSELL, ZELIA A. CASS-
ELL, NATHANIEL CASSELL, MARION CASSELL, SAMUEL E. ROPER and wife LOUISA,
EPHRAIM CASSELL, MARY CASSELL, JOHN CASSELL, RANSOM HENDERSON and wife
SARAH...Of whom the following are out of the state viz JOHN CASSELL,
RANSOM HENDERSON and wife SARAH, SIMEON YOUNGBLOOD and wife MEELY and
heirs of WILLIAM CASSELL. Dated 23 Nov. 1861.

Bk B, p. 64:   Z. B. COX owned 30 acres on a branch of the north
fork of Cane Creek joining lands of SOLOMON IVESTER, G. F. COX
and others. Heirs: AMANDA COX widow..3 minor children viz JOHN P. COX,
FRANCES E. COX, Z. F. COX. Dated 12 Sept. 1862.

Bk B, p. 66:   QUINCEY D. ELROD owned 50 acres on waters of Snow
Creek joining lands of J. A. ELROD, MOSES CAIN and others. Heirs:
6 children viz JOHN C. A. ELROD, FRANCES E. ELROD, GEORGE C. ELROD,
FRANKLIN W. ELROD, ELIJAH J. ELROD, ANNE Q. D. ELROD, MARY N. ELROD
the widow. Dated 12 Jan. 1863.

Bk B, p. 70:   MILTON M. HENDRICKS owned 59 acres on Shoal Creek
waters of Saluda River, joining lands of ABEL HENDRICKS, J. C.
HENDRICKS and others. Died leaving neither wife or child. Heirs: J.
C. HENDRICKS, MARCUS ROPER and wife SUSAN, JESSE CRENSHAW and wife
JINCY, DAVID HENDRICKS, JAMES B. HENDRICKS, THOMAS P. LOOPER and wife
MATILDA..The heirs of TEMPERANCE LOOPER, deceased, viz JAMES PERRY
LOOPER, WILLIAM ANDERSON LOOPER, TEMPERANCE LOOPER. Dated 5 Jan. 1863.

Bk B, p. 72:   HAMILTON BURDINE owned 129 acres on Little Georges
Creek waters of Saluda River joining lands of JOHN T. GOSSET,
RICHARD BURDINE's estate and others. Left 6 children viz JOHN W. BUR-
DINE, HENRIETTA ROBINSON, JAMES BURDINE, SARAH JANE BURDINE, THOMAS
BURDINE, WILLIAM M. BURDINE..Of whom three are minors. All in this
state except JAMES & SARAH JANE BURDINE. Dated 19 Oct. 1863.

Bk B, p. 74:   THOMAS HOLLINGSWORTH owned 100 acres on Waters of
Georges Creek, waters of Saluda River, joining lands of R. LEND-
HART, WILLIAM JAMISON and others. Heirs: Widow EVELINE who married
IBSAN VANDIVER. Heirs 6 children viz ANN HOLLINGSWORTH, ELIAS HOLLINGS-
WORTH, THOMAS HOLLINGSWORTH, WILLIAM HOLLINGSWORTH, SAURAH? HOLLINGS-
WORTH, WARREN HOLLINGSWORTH. Dated 18 Mar. 1864.

Bk B, p. 76:   WILLIAM M. FENNEL owned 70 acres joining on Hamby
Branch of Three and Twenty Creek joining lands of H. J. FENNEL,
L. J. HAMBLETON and others. Heirs: Widow MARY A. E. who married HARRY?
JONES. His father, HARDY H. FENNEL. Brothers and sisters to wit - EVA-
LINE HOLLINGSWORTH, W. J. FENNEL, F. G. FENNEL, THOMAS HINTON and wife
ELIZABETH, MARY KING, MARTHA FENNEL. Dated 27 Nov. 1865.

Bk B, p. 78:   THOMAS A. WHITE owned 50 acres, joining the lands

Cont'd:
of GIDEON ELLIS, JACOB BOROUGHS and others. Widow, ELIZABETH WHITE the only heir. Dated 30 Dec. 1865.

Bk B, p. 80:   THOMAS THOMPKINS owned 3 tracts of land. No. 1 - the home place on Buck Creek, Saluda River joining lands of LEVI WIMPEY, JOHN FINLEY and others, containing 109 acres. No. 2 - of 30 acres on head waters of Buck Creek joining lands of MARY E. BURDINE, WILLIAM BURDINE and tract No. 1; No. 3 on waters of Wolf Creek joining lands of HARRIET DUKE, the Estate of GIDEON ROPER and others, containing 140 acres. Heirs: DAVID C. THOMPKINS, MARY E. TOMPKINS, SARAH A. TOMPKINS, JOHN B. TOMPKINS... JOSEPH J. TOMPKINS..JEPTHA FREEMAN their grandfather. Dated 25 Dec. 1865.

Bk B, p. 83:   JOHN H. BLACK owned 350 acres on head waters of Wolf Creek joining lands of NANCY BLACK, ELIZABETH FIELDS and others. Heirs are his mother and ten brothers viz JAMES G. BLACK, WYATT HUDSON and wife MARGARET, ISAAC RICE and wife ANNA, JAMES BRAZEAL and wife AMANDA, MATTIE BLACK, AMOTHE? BLACK, JOHN ERVIN and wife JENNIE, MALINDA ALEXANDER in this state, out of the state in Georgia the heirs at law of ELIZA CRANE, deceased. Dated 1 Nov. 1865.

Bk B, p. 86:   CHRISTOPHER WHISENANT owned 142 acres on Beaverdam Branch waters of Toxaway Creek joining lands of S. E. MAXWELL, JOSEPH LILES and others. Heirs: JANE WHISENANT his widow with whom he lived several years and had no children...Following children are by his former wives. The heirs of NICHOLAS WHISENANT, deceased. Heirs of ROBERT WHISENANT, deceased. GEORGE WHISENANT, FLEMMING BATES and wife POLLY, ____(?) DICKEY and wife SARAH, SALINA LILES, JEREMIAH H. JOHNS and wife REBECCA. Heirs of ELIZA NORRIS, deceased, viz J. J. HUNNICUTT and wife NANCY, BARBARY ALBERSON, T. R. NORRIS and wife REBECCA, LEVI PHILLIPS and wife RACHAEL. Heirs of LETTY A. LYLES, deceased JONAH ARENA, FANNY DEBBS(?), ANN RACHEL, NANCY J., JOHN BELL. Heirs of BARTHOLOMEW WHISENANT, deceased viz SARAH F., WILLIAM L., MARY ANN...JEFFERSON DAVIS WHISENANT. Dated 20 Nov. 1865.

Bk B, p. 89:   HAYNES ABERCOMBIE owned 72 acres on waters of Saluda River joining lands of JOHN S. LATHAM, O. ARMSTRONG and others. Left a widow CLARINDA who married ROBERT E. CLARK. Left a minor, LOU E. ABERCROMBIE. Dated 2 Apr. 1866.

Bk B, p. 91:   GEORGE F. ROSS owned 137 acres on Stamp Creek joining lands of JOHN ROSS, THOMAS R. DAVID and others. Left neither wife or child. Heirs: JOHN ROSS. Heirs of WILEY ROSS, deceased viz THOMAS MORGAN, RICHARD, MARY, MELISSA ROSS...ALEXANDER WHITE and wife MILLY, ELIZABETH BARKER, REUBEN LEE and wife GILLA. MILES MOSS and wife MANERVA. HARRIET ROSS. JESSE R. ROSS. Heirs of JOHN ROSS, JR. deceased viz MELISSA, SARAH M., WILLIAM L. and JESSE A. ROSS and LUNSFORD M. ROSS and heirs of MELISSA VAUGHN, deceased viz HARRIET VAUGHN all in this state except LUNSFORD M. ROSS. Dated 23 Jan. 1866.

Bk B, p. 94:   SARAH CHAPMAN owned 118 acres on 18 Mile Creek joining lands of WILLIAM S. WILLIAMS, GEORGE CHAPMAN and others. Children: SARAH widow of W. A. CHAPMAN and her 6 children viz NANCY S., MARTHA E., SARAH C. widow of THOMAS H. CHAPMAN, dec'd. who has married EBEN SMITH and his child, by a former marriage. CYNTHA J. CHAPMAN a minor. REBECCA SWORDS. W. J. FENNEL and wife MARTHA. JOHN W. CHAPMAN. GEORGE J. CHAPMAN. BENJAMIN P. CHAPMAN. HARVEY JONES and wife MARY A. E.; ANDREW MAULDEN and wife JOSEPHINE A.; ELIZA A. CHAPMAN a minor..all of Pickens Districts, except REBECCA SWORDS and BENJAMIN J. CHAPMAN who reside out of the state. Dated 27 Nov. 1865.

Bk B, p. 97:   E. H. HUDSON owned an undivided half of two acre lot lying on the south side of the road leading from West Union to Walhalla known as lot No. 9, three quarters of one acre is fronting on the road, that his father, W. M. HUDSON and his brothers and sisters viz JOHN M. HUDSON, MALINDA MC DOWELL, F. J. HUDSON, AMANDA L. HUDSON..are the legal heirs. Dated 27 Aug. 1866.

Bk B, p. 99:   SAMUEL ALBERTSON owned two tracts of land. No. 1

Cont'd:
the home place on both sides of Little River joining lands of
WILLIAM WHITMIRE, PHILLIP SNEED and others, containing 160 acres. No.
2 on Fidlers Creek, waters of Little River joining lands of A. B. GRANT,
WILLIAM WHITMIRE and others, containing 120 acres. Heirs: CYNTHA AL-
BERTSON, widow, Heirs of ELIZA COX, dec'd. viz J. C. ALBERTSON & SAMUEL
COX. JULIA A. STEPHENS. ELIAS F. ALBERTSON. FELL DURHAM and wife SARAH
C.; ELIZABETH E. ALBERTSON. Heirs of J. D. ALBERTSON, dec'd. viz his
widow CATHERINE and 4 children viz LUCINDA J., RACHEL M., SARAH E.,
and MARY M. ALBERTSON. JOEL R. BUCKHUSTER? and wife NANCY M.; MALINDA
B. and J. B. SMITH.

Bk B, p. 103:   JOHN W. MC KINNEY owned 120 acres - No. 1 known as
the home place on Indian branch waters of Three and Twenty creek
joining lands of LEVI HENDRICKS, JANE MC WHORTER and others. No. 2
on waters of 18 Mile Creek joining lands of JOHN HINTON, LEVI HENDRICKS
and others, containing 39-1/4 acres. M. A. E. MC KINNEY the widow and
4 minor children viz SARAH G., ALICE T.?, VESTA K. and JOHN C. W. MC
KINNEY. Dated 10 Aug. 1866.

Bk B, p. 105:   GEORGE W. ABBETT owned 140 acres on waters of Coneross
Creek joining N. J. F. PERRY, the estate of JOHN ABBETT and others.
Heirs: S. C. ABBETT the widow. Children: J. B. ABBETT, W. T. ABBETT,
J. W. ABBETT, M. M. ABBETT, E. P. ABBETT and WILLIAM T. ABBETT all
of age except the last 3 who are minors. Dated 5 Sept. 1866.

Bk B, p. 107:   WILLIAM G. BLACK owned 148 acres on Long Nose Creek,
waters of Tugaloe River, joining lands of J. J. NORTON, JOHN
R. BLACK and others. Heirs: MARY JANE BLACK, JESSE R. BLACK, NANCY
E. BLACK all minor children. Widow SARAH BLACK married WILLIAM MC CRACK-
IN who is a minor. Dated 23 Aug. 1866.

Bk B, p. 110:   TOLIVER ARMSTRONG owned 64 acres on Fowlers Creek,
waters of Saluda River joining lands of R. E. CLARK, E. W. ABER-
CROMBIE and others. Heirs: widow HANNAH ARMSTRONG. FANNIE JANE ARM-
STRONG. N. W. E. ARMSTRONG. Dated 3 Sept. 1866.

Bk B, p. 113:   JOHN ADAIR owned 150 acres on Big Conneross Creek
joining lands of ALFRED ADAIR, J. O. LEWIS and others. Owned 150
acres on Ramsey Creek joining lands of MEMORY ALEXANDER, THOMAS WAT-
KINS and others. Heirs: WILLIAM ADAIR, MEMORY ALEXANDER and wife MARY,
M. H. D. COBB and wife REBECCA; E. F. P. MC ALISTER and wife SARAH
A.; ALFRED A. ADAIR. JOHN C. COBB and wife ARY. GRAFTON ADAIR. THOMAS
M. ADAIR. S. ABBETT and NARCISSA ABBETT. Dated 13 Aug. 1868.

Bk B, p. 115:   JOHN MC WHORTER owned 116 acres one mile below Pick-
ensville joining lands of FIELDS WELBORN, W. A. LESLEY and others.
Heirs: widow HARRIET E. MC WHORTER. 5 children viz MARCUS L. MC WHORTER,
FRANCIS C. MC WHORTER, MARY T. MC WHORTER, ALLEN D. MC WHORTER, ANDREW
F. MC WHORTER. Dated 15 Feb. 1867.

Bk B, p. 117:   GODFREY MAULDIN owned 164 acres joining lands of
JOEL ELLISON and others. No. 2 of 104 acres joining STERLING TURN-
ER, JOEL ELLISON and tract No. 1. Heirs: JOHN MC CLAHAN and wife; JAMES
MAULDEN and the heirs of JOEL ELLISON, dec'd. number and names unknown
who resides out of the state. The heirs of JANE WOOD, dec'd. viz ISAAC
N. WOOD, GODFREY WOOD, JANE WOOD, FANNIE WOOD, SARAH HUGHS. Dated 31
Oct. 1866.

Bk B, p. 120:   JOHN E. ARCHER owned 112 acres on branches of Brushy
Creek joining lands of WILLIAM COUCH, A. A. H. MOON and others.
Heirs: mother MALINDA ARCHER. Brothers and sisters viz S. N. WILLIAMS
and wife ANN, E. H. BARTON and wife MARY, FANNIE ARCHER all in this
state. Heirs of ANDREW H. ARCHER, dec'd. number and names unknown who
resides out of the state. Dated 19 Nov. 1866.

Bk B, p. 122:   BENJAMIN W. MARET owned one acre lot in the town
of Fair Play joining D. S. STRIBLING, BENJAMIN HOLLAND and others.
There is a good store house on the lot. Heirs: LUCINDA W. MARET the

Cont'd:
widow..6 children viz ELIAS J. MARET, FREDERICK S. MARET, LUCY E. BLAS-
SINGAME and her husband JOHN BLASSINGAME, JOHN W. MERET and JOANNA
C. MARET in the state of Mississippi. NANCY E. BRANNON and JAMES W.
BRANNON in this state. Dated 14 July 1866.

Bk B, p. 124:   STEPHEN GARRETT owned 50 acres on the west side of
          Crooked Creek joining lands of JOHN R. M. CANNON and others. Heirs
are widow MARTHA GARRETT and 7 children viz VILANTA wife of FRASIER
M. CARTEE(CARTER?), MILTON GARRETT, FRANKLIN GARRETT, BLUFORD GARRETT,
HARRISON GARRETT, ELIZABETH GARRETT and WARREN GARRETT all of whom
are minors except FRASIER MC CARTER (Note: also looked like FRASIER
M. CARTEE (CARTER) Dated 15 Feb. 1867.

Bk B, p. 128:   JOHN SMITH owned 40 acres on Saluda River joining
          lands of H. G. SMITH, MATHEW MANSELL and others. Heirs: widow
SUSANNAH SMITH who later married T. or G. W. SMITH. Minor child A.
SMITH. Dated 28 Feb. 1868.

Bk B, p. 131:   WILLIAM HESTER owned 160 acres on waters of Saluda
          River joining lands of ESLI HUNT, A. J. ANDERSON and others. Also
another tract of 90 acres. Widow LOUISA HESTER..5 children viz MICHAEL
HESTER, MARY JANE HESTER, LOUVINA J. HESTER, WILLIAM ANDERSON HESTER
and JOHN BUTLER HESTER all minors. Dated 22 Dec. 1868.

Bk B, p. 138:   WILLIAM BARRETT owned 100 acres joining lands of
          MRS. MALINDA ARCHER, W. F. KING, MARY JANE BARTON and others.
Heirs: JOSEPH KING and wife MALINDA, JESSE MC MAHAN and wife MARY,
JOHN BARRETT, SARAH J. HAMILTON. The heirs of JAMES MC COY and wife
EMALINE?, ALLIS MC COY, LAURENCE MC COY, ANNICE MC COY. Heirs of BEN-
JAMIN BARRETT, dec'd. viz WILLIAM BARRETT, MILTON BARRETT, DAVID BAR-
RETT, BENJAMIN BARRETT. Dated 24 Nov. 1868.

Bk B, p. 146:   JOHN ERWIN died 4 Nov. 1864. Owned land of 300 acres
          on Town Creek waters of 12 Mile River. Widow, NANCY ERWIN. Heirs:
WILLIAM ERWIN of Tennessee, THOMAS ERWIN of North Carolina, JOHN B.
ERWIN and RACHEL HENDRICKS of Pickens County and the heirs of a predeceased son GEORGE ERWIN who are all minors and reside in North Carolina. Heirs of ISAAC ERWIN a predeceased son - six in number who are
all minors and reside in North Carolina. Dated 10 Feb. 1869.

Bk B, p. 152:   MICAJAH ALEXANDER, JR. owned 300 acres on waters
          of Little Eastatoe Creek and joining J. J. PARROTT, MRS. WINCHESTER
and others. Heirs: father, MICAJAH ALEXANDER, ..left brothers and sisters and their heirs viz ELISHA ALEXANDER, JOHN ALEXANDER, ELIZABETH
MURPHEE, JERRY J. PARROTT and wife MILLY, EPHRAIM GILLSTRAP and wife
LOUISA. The heirs of MARY CANTRELL, dec'd. viz JOHN CANTRELL, STATIN
CANTRELL, BAILUS STEPHENS and wife LOUISA, MICAJAH CANTRELL. Heirs
of WILLIAM CANTRELL, dec'd. Heirs of ANNA ROBERTS, dec'd. names and
numbers unknown. Heirs of MELVIAN ROBERTS, dec'd. viz JEREMIAH ROBERTS,
LOUISA ROBERTS and husband PINCKNEY ROBERTS, MILLA ANN who married
(not given) and WALLIS ROBERTS who reside in Greenville County, S.
C. The other 3 out of the state, names unknown. Heirs of DAVID ALEX-
ANDER, dec'd. names unknown, out of the state. Heirs of DANIEL ALEX-
ANDER, dec'd. viz heirs of MICAJAH ALEXANDER, dec'd. out of the state.
DAVID ALEXANDER, dec'd. children of ISAAC ALEXANDER dec'd. in Oconee
County, S. C. JACOB ALEXANDER, JORDAN? ALEXANDER, ELIAS ALEXANDER in
Oconee County. NANCY J. MADDEN wife of THOMAS E. MADDEN. Heirs of ELIZA-
BETH WATSON viz DANAL A. JAMES and ELIZABETH MATISON in Oconee County
and heirs of MELISSA PARROTT, dec'd. viz DANIEL, ELIZABETH & LEVINA
PARROTT. Dated 13 July 1869.

Bk B, p. 154:   LABAN MAULDIN owned 90 acres on waters of Brushy
          Creek lying in Pickens and Anderson Counties joining lands of
WILLIAM PHILLIPS, ELIZABETH WILLIAMS and others. Heirs: widow MARY
MAULDIN. OSBAN NALLEY and wife ELIZABETH. WILLIAM JONES and wife MALIN-
DA. THOMAS M. HAMBY and wife MALISSA. MARY MAULDIN. NANCY MAULDIN.
JOHN MAULDIN. JOHN NORRIS and wife CANDIS. All in this state except
BIRD MARTIN and wife CAROLINE who reside in Florida. VARDY MAULDIN
and HARVY SMITH and wife ADALINE who reside in Georgia. 2 Aug. 1869.

Bk B, p. 157:   JOSHUA CHAPMAN owned 800 acres lying on Shoal Creek
    joining lands of SAMUEL CHAPMAN, BLOOMER MERCK and others. Heirs:
SAMUEL CHAPMAN, SUSANNAH MERCK, ELIZABETH GARRETT, JACOB CHAPMAN. Heirs
of GILES CHAPMAN, dec'd. viz TOLIVER ROPER and wife MARY E. Heirs of
ISAAC CHAPMAN, dec'd. viz DAVID THOMPKINS and wife MARY, CLINTON HOL-
LINGSWORTH and wife ELIZABETH R. who reside in this state and JOEL
CHAPMAN who resides in Tennessee. MARY MC KINNEY who resides in Georgia.
Heirs of RUTHA WIGINGTON number and names and whereabouts unknown and
the heirs of ISRAEL CHAPMAN, dec'd. number and names and whereabouts
unknown. Dated 2 Aug. 1869.

Bk B, p. 163:   THOMAS MONTGOMERY owned 200 acres in Pickens District
    joining lands of Z. A. COUCH, ANNA COUCH and others. Heirs: widow
MARY A. now the wife of WILLIAM M. STEGALL. Heirs: JOHN T. MONTGOMERY.
MARY E. MONTGOMERY. Dated 23 Aug. 1869.

Bk B, p. 166:   PRIOR ALEXANDER owned 125 acres on Keowee River join-
    ing lands of MRS. POWERS, PRIOR ALEXANDER, SR. and others. Heirs
are widow VICTORIA ALEXANDER. RICHARD ALEXANDER. JOSEPHINE ALEXANDER
minor children. Dated 1 Dec. 1869.

Bk B, p. 168:   WILLIAM BENSON RACKLEY died on or about the 12th
    May 1870. Owned 150 acres on Shoal Creek waters of Saluda River.
Heirs: JOHN L. RACKLEY, REDDEN RACKLEY, MAHALEY C. RACKLEY, LUCRETIA
DARCUS all of Pickens Dist., R. T. RICHARDS and wife ELIZA of Georgia.
Heirs of WARREN B. RACKLEY, a deceased brother. WILLIAM BENSON RACKLEY
of Illinois. MALISSA RACKLEY of Georgia. THOMAS HORTON and wife MANURVA
of Laurens County. ADALINE RACKLEY. JOHN RACKLEY. JAMES RACKLEY. MARY
RACKLEY. THOMAS RACKLEY. Dated 19 July 1870.

Bk B, p. 172:   JOHN PRINCE died 1862. Owned 174 acres lying on 12
    Mile River joining lands of CHARLES PRINCE, JOHN P. PERRETT, MARY
BAKER and estate of R. Y. H. GRIFFIN and others. Heirs: widow RUTHA
PRINCE. Children: MARGARET PRINCE, SARAH PRINCE, NARCISSA PRINCE all
of who reside in Jackson County, North Carolina. WILLIAM PRINCE. Dated
30 May 1870.

Bk B, p. 175:   ARTHUR BRASWELL owned 100 acres on Shoal Creek. Widow
    RUTHA BRASWELL and 8 children viz JOSEPH MASSINGAIL and wife PER-
UINA?, WILLIAM, CLEVELAND, MARION & THOMAS BRASWELL sons, all of whom
are dead two of whom WILLIAM & CLEVELAND sold to their sister SUSAN
TURNER their shares and the other two MARION & THOMAS died without
wife or child and four daughters viz SUSAN TURNER, ADALINE wife of
JOHN BOYD, ELIZABETH wife of DAVID LESLEY and PERUNIA? who married
JOSEPH MASSINGILL. Dated 29 June 1870.

Bk B, p. 178:   NANCY WADE owned 150 acres on waters of South Saluda
    River, joining lands of the estate of REUBEN TALLY, dec'd., JOHN
RIDGEN, TURNER and others. Heirs: RICHARD HOLDEN and wife CATHARINE,
STEPHEN RAINES and wife PHALBA, JOSEPH HARDIN (also written HARBIN)
and wife ELIZA who live in Greenville County. Grandchildren of NANCY
WADE, dec'd. BURRELL PACE and wife HANNAH, HENRY NORMAN and wife HARRIET
and SAMUEL WADE grandchildren of the sd NANCY WADE, who reside in Alabama. HAMPTON WADE of Greenville Co. Dated 8 Aug. 1870.

Bk B, p. 178:   WILLIAM D. STEELE owned land in Pickens District.
    Heirs: widow MARGARET STEELE. Children: JANE DENDY, AGNES ELLISON.
Dated 8 Aug. 1870.

Bk B, p. 180:   J. I. WASHINGTON MAVRICK owned 215 acres on Plung-
    ing Branch waters of 18 Mile Creek joining lands of ROBERT JOHN-
STON, G. BROCK and others. Widow, HARRIET BLACK formerly HARRIET MAV-
RICK. 3 children: MARGARET age 21 years, SAMUEL & RHODA MAVERICK. Dated
6 Jan. 1871.

Bk B, p. 184:   PRIOR ALEXANDER died in 1870. Owned 131 acres on
    Four Mile Creek waters of Keowee River joining lands of JN. HOOPER,
JOHN O'BRYANT and others. Heirs: E. B. ALEXANDER, MINERVA wife of M.
A. BILLINGSLY of Alabama. THOMAS P. ALEXANDER, ELIZABETH wife of _____

Cont'd:
BILLINGSLY of Georgia..EUNICE wife of JOHN H. BELL. AMANDA wife of
WILLIAM H. BILLINGSLEY. CAROLINE wife of IRVIN ALEXANDER. RICHARD P.
ALEXANDER. JOSEPHINE ALEXANDER. Dated 3 Apr. 1871.

Bk B, p. 187:   A. JACKSON KELLEY owned 52 acres on branches of Town
     Creek joining lands of J. G. FERGUSON, J. E. HAGOOD and others.
Widow MARY KELLEY(KELLY) HUNT. Children: SARAH ANN KELLEY, JOHN A.
KELLEY. Dated 15 Mar. 1871.

Bk B, p. 190:   BRADWELL DAY owned land in Pickens District. Widow
     ELIZABETH DAY. Heirs: ELIAS DAY, JOHN DAY, LUCRETIA A. COOPER,
ANDREW J. H. DAY, ELIZABETH DAY, ALONZO DAY, FRANCES M. DAY, LAURA
C. DAY, MARTHA P. KELLY. Dated 2 Oct. 1871.

Bk B, p. 194:   WILLIAM EDENS owned 125 acres - the home place join-
     ing lands of JAMES KEITH, PEGGY EDENS and others. No. 2 known
as the CHASTAIN place containing 75 acres joining lands of TYRE ROPER
and others. Heirs: widow MARY EDENS..children: JOHN M. C. EDENS of
Texas, ALEXANDER EDENS, SARAH A. EDENS, WARREN D. EDENS, SAMUEL S.
EDENS, REBECCA wife of NATHANIEL LYNCH, ADLINE wife of JAMES JONES,
EVELINA B. wife of BARRING GALLAWAY resident of North Carolina. Heirs
of the wife of WILSON JONES viz MARY J. JONES, heirs of WILLIAM J.
EDENS number and names unknown. Dated 22 Feb. 1871.

Bk B, p. 204:   TEMPERANCE CHASTAIN died 25 March 1871. Heirs: LUCINDA
     CHASTAIN. NANCY EVALINE BURGESS wife of D. M. BURGESS. Heirs of
WILLIAM CHASTAIN, a deceased son, to wit: ABNER D. CHASTAIN, JOHN B.
CHASTAIN, MARY M. CHASTAIN, WASHINGTON PERCE CHASTAIN, SUSAN CHASTAIN,
MARTHA L. CHASTAIN & WILLIAM CHASTAIN. The heirs of TILMAN CHASTAIN,
deceased, to wit: ABNER CHASTAIN, NELSON CHASTAIN, ROWLAND CHASTAIN,
JOHN CHASTAIN & JOSEPH TILMON CHASTAIN. The heirs of A. M. CLEVELAND
CHASTAIN, deceased, - NANCY R. CHASTAIN, & RACHEL L. CHASTAIN who reside
in Transylvania County, North Carolina. Dated 18 Apr. 1871.

Bk B, p. 209:   GIDEON E. MC WHORTER owned 130 acres on Wolf Creek.
     Widow, L. H. MC WHORTER. Dated 2 Feb. 1873.

Bk B, p. 209:   ELIZABETH WILSON owned 130 acres in Pickens District.
     Heirs: JOHN W. WILSON, NANCY HENDERS (must have been meant for
HENDERSON) Heirs of JANE FORISTER viz WILLIAM FORISTER. Heirs of ROBERT
WILSON viz SAMUEL M. WILSON. Heirs of SARAH JONES viz ANNE JONENS.
Heirs of MARGRET NALLY viz JAMES A. NALLY, JOSEPH NALLY, SAMUEL NALLY,
ELIZABETH BENSON, SARAH BENSON, WILLIAM NALLY of Pickens County, J.
W. NALLY of Texas, CUNNINGHAM NALLY & NANCY NALLY of Georgia and JEFFER-
SON NALLY of Mississippi. Heirs of ISABELLA WILLIAMS viz SARAH ELLIS,
ELIZABETH BROCK, ADLINE GRANT & JEREMIAH WILLIAMS of Georgia. Heirs
of DAMUEL WILSON viz GEORGE WILSON & SUSAN GRIFFIN of Texas. Dated
2 Sept. 1873.

Bk B, p. 212:   ALEXANDER EDENS, widow was MARGARET EDENS. Heirs:
     SAMUEL EDENS, ALLEN R. EDENS, JAMES M. EDENS, REBECCA WILLIAMS,
PINKNEY N. B. EDENS, MARY JANE ROPER, WILLIAMA E. EDENS, CRAFTON ALEX
EDENS, ELIJAH C. EDENS, WARREN D. EDENS, JAMES W. SOUTHERLAND..."That
when her husband died in the troublesome and distressing times of 1864
she found herself left with a large family of little helpless children,
one an infant of 3 months." Dated 23 Oct. 1873.

Bk B, p. 223:   WILLIS TRAINNUM owned 100 acres in Pickens District
     joining lands of the estate of ROBERT LATHAM, dec'd., JAMES MC
ADAMS, SR, dec'd., HARVEY C. HUNT, dec'd. and others. Children: JERE-
MIAH TRAINNUM, ANNIE wife of WILLIAM BRADLEY of North Carolina, MARY
NORRIS wife of ABSALUM NORRIS, dec'd., GEORGE W. TRAINNUM, JOHN W.
TRAINNUM and CATHERINE TRAINNUM. Dated 9 Dec. 1873.

Bk B, p. 226:   JOHN BOWEN owned several tracts of land viz No. 1
     one half interest in the Mill tract containing 26 acres joining
BENNETT FREEMAN, L. T. ADDINGTON and others. No. 2 known as the Powder
Mill tract, joining lands of F. N. GARVIN, GREEN STEPHENS and others,

341

Cont'd:
containing 215 acres. No. 3 known as the MAJOR and MORGAN tract join-
ing lands of L. HUGHES, A. T. CLAYTON and others, containing 259 acres.
No. 4 known as part fo the CORBAN tract joining lands of W. MANNING
JONES and others, containing 77½ acres. Heirs: R. E. BOWEN, T. J. BOWEN,
W. R. BOWEN, JOHN H. BOWEN, SAMUEL H. BOWEN, M. D. L. BOWEN. The heirs
of MALINDA TAYLOR viz FLORA TAYLOR, JOHN TAYLOR, ELLA TAYLOR, IDA TAY-
LOR, ELVIRA wife of R. E. HOLCOMBE, DORCAS J. wife of L. R. DALTON,
M. E. BERRY wife of LAWRENCE BERRY and M. T. BOWEN..W. R. BOWEN resides
in Missouri. JOHN H. BOWEN of Georgia. S. H. BOWEN of Texas. The heirs
of MELINDA TAYLOR are all minors. JOHN BOWEN died 4 June 1871.

Bk B, p. 230:   CALVIN O'DELL owned 150 acres the home place known
      as the Pickensville Tract joining lands of BENAJAH WILLIAMS, SAMUEL
CHAPMAN and others. Heirs: widow, MARY A. O'DELL. M. MARGARET wife
of J. PERRY LOOPER. JAMES A. O'DELL. FREDRICK E. O'DELL. NANCY L. O'-
DELL. JULIUS P. O'DELL. LAUVINA B. O'DELL. Dated 4 Sept. 1874.

Bk B, p. 241:   ABRAHAM BURDINE owned 130 acres on the north side
      of Little Georges Creek waters of Saluda River. Heirs: CHARLOTTE
ANTHONY, MARY BURDINE, MARY A. SHOCKLEY, MARY J. FREEMAN, JAMES FREEMAN.
Dated 10 Aug. 1874.

Bk B, p. 243:   CHARITY WILLIAMS owned 475 acres on Twenty Three
      Mile Creek joining lands of LEMUEL G. HAMILTON, CHARLOTTE BARKER?,
...CHERRY?, ...MC WHORTER and others. Heirs: W. S. WILLIAMS, TONY?
WILLIAMS, NANCY WILLIAMS, BENAJAH WILLIAMS, R. WILLIAMS. The heirs
of T. P. WILLIAMS, dec'd. viz IDA wife of R. R. CHILD, WALTER WILL-
IAMS, JOLLY WILLIAMS, ERNEST WILLIAMS, ELIZABETH WILLIAMS. Dated 21
Aug. 1874.

Bk B, p. 250:   SYLUS STONE owned 140 acres joining lands of the
      estate of GARNER BOGGS, THOMAS CRAIG and others. Heirs: JOHN STEW-
ART & AARON STONE. Petitions against WILLIAM STONE..JOHN STONE..RUFUS
MERCK, SUSAN STEWART, RACHEL DURHAM..SARAH NIGHBERS? The heirs of MARG-
RET MERECK (MERCK) viz RUFUS MERCK, PARTHENIA MERCK, MACK MERCK, HENRY
MERCK, JAMES MERCK & DELONEY? MERCK all of Pickens Dist. WILLIAM STONE
of Oconee Co. The heirs of THOMAS STONE viz MARGRET MARY STONE, LUCINDA
STONE & ISAAC STONE who resides out of the state. Dated 4 May 1875.

Bk B, p. 259:   ABRAHAM HESTER owned 379 acres on both sides of Rices
      Creek near Central Station. Widow, E. C. HESTER. Heirs: SAMUEL
J. HESTER, ELIZABETH HESTER, LULA HESTER, & LUCY HESTER are minors
of whom RICHARD A. HESTER was their guardian. W. W. HESTER. Dated 4
May 1875.

Bk B, p. 264:   WILLIAM O. DURHAM owned land on Mile Creek joining
      lands of JOHN DURHAM, THOMAS KNIGHT and others. Heirs: widow,
LUCINDA DURHAM..Heirs: brothers and sisters viz JOHN DURHAM, ISAAC
DURHAM, MARY ANN DURHAM..MARY ANN DURHAM who married CHARLES DURHAM
and lives in Anderson County..REBECCA wife of WILLIAM SMITH..NARCISSA
the widow of _____ KELLY..ELLIS DURHAM a minor and DAVID JAMES the father
of LUCINDA DURHAM the widow of sd interstate. Dated 29 June 1875.

Bk B, p. 273:   WILLIAM W. WALKER, Plaintiff against and REBECCA
      L. (S.?) CORBIN, WILY T. WALKER, ROBERT M. WALKER, ANDREW B. WALKER,
CHARLOTTE WALKER, DANIEL WALKER, JAMES R. A. WALKER of Pickens District.
ANDREW J. WALKER, MARY ANN STANCIL of Georgia. SUSAN WALKER & MAXWELL
WALKER of Mississippi. "Parent not given." Dated 14 Aug. 1875.

END OF REAL ESTATE RECORDS

PICKENS DISTRICT, S. C. NATURALIZATIONS

Taken from records now on file in South Carolina State Archives.

H. FAGEN, a native of Hanover, about the age of 31 years, appeared
in open court and declared his intention to become a citizen of the
U. S. A. and renounced all allegiance to Frederick Augustus, King of
Hanover, of whom he was a subject. 29 Mar. 1852. H. FAGEN, W. L. KEITH,
C.C.

Pickens Dist., S. C.: The petition of CHRISTIAN CRANFROST aged
28 years, Shoemaker, born in Prussia, arrived in the U. S. at the city
of New York in 1851...on __ Oct. 1855 appeared before WILLIAM L. KEITH,
Clerk of Court for Pickens Dist...he renounces allegiance to Frederick
William, King of Prussia of whom he was a citizen...CHRISTIAN CRAN-
FROST (signed in German). Bef. J. H. WHITNER.
We, the subscribers, certify that we have known CHRISTIAN CRAN-
FROST, for five years during which time he has resided at Walhalla.
H. GISSEL, G. CRAMER. J. E. HAGOON, CCP.

At a Court of General Sessions at Pickens, 15 Oct. 1855, CHRISTIAN
CRANFROST, born in Cologne, Germany, aged 25, declared his intention
to become a citizen..W. L. KEITH, C.C.P. & G.S.

Pickens Dist., S. C.: The petition of H. FAGIN, aged 24, Taylor,
born in Hanover, Germany, arrived in the U. S. in 1854 at Charleston,
appeared on 1 Mar. 1852 before W. L. KEITH...H. FAGEN. Before W. L.
WARDLAW.
We, the subscribers, do certify that we have known H. FAGIN for
five years, during which time he has resided in Charleston...19 Mar.
1855, D. B_____, W. S. GRISHAM, MARK(?) BULLWINKEL.

Petition of C. FAGEN, aged 22, following the occupation of a Smith,
born in Hanover, Germany, arrived in Charleston, 27 Apr. 1850, before
he was of 18 years, and he has since resided in the U. S., it has been
his intention to become a citizen for three years...C. H. FAGEN. Before
J. H. WHITNER.
We do certify that we have been acquainted with C. FAGEN for three
years last, during which time he resided in Pickens Dist...2 Nov. 1853,
WM. C. JEE(?), C. F. SEEBER. Before E. M. KEITH.

Before me, W. L. KEITH, appeared CHARLES H. NIEBURH, a native
of Hamburg, Germany, age about 24 years, who declares that it is his
intention to become a citizen of the U. S..C. H. NIEBUHR. 1 Nov. 1853.
Petition of C. HENRY NIEBURH, aged 25, a Butcher, born in Hamburg,
Germany, arrived in Charleston, 28 July 1851, renounces all allegiance
to Frederick Augustus...C. H. NIEBUHR. J. E. HAGOOD, C.C.P. 26 Oct.
1856.

Before me, W. L. KEITH, appeared JOHN WM. F. STRUKS, a native
of Hanover, about 23, declares his intention to become a citizen of
the U. S., renounces allegiance to Frederick Augustus...1 Nov. 1853,
J. W. F. STRUKS.

Petition of H. STUCK, aged 23, a Baker, born in Hanover, arrived
at Charleston in 1851..F. STUCK, 17 Oct. 1854. W. L. KEITH, C.C.

Before me, W. L. KEITH, appeared HENRY HOOPS, a native of Hanover,
Germany, about 26, declares his intention to become a citizen of the
U. S...HINNERICH HOOPS, 21 Oct. 1853, W. L. KEITH, C.C.

Before me, JAMES E. HAGOOD, C.C., appeared JACOB HEINR BESENFELDER
a native of Bavaria in Germany, about the age of 53, declares his intention to become a citizen of the U. S., renounces allegiances to
Maximillian the Second of whom he is a subject, 2 July 1857, JACOB
HEINR BESEMFELDER. J. E. Hagood, C.C.P. & G.S.

Petition of FREDERICK BISCHOFF, aged 21, occupation of a Miner, born in the free city of Bremen, arrived at Baltimore in June 1854. F. BISCHOFF, 15 Feb. 1859. J. E. HAGOOD, C.C.P.

Petition of JOHN GLAUSS, aged 29, farmer, born in Prussia in Germany, arrived at the City of New York, 8 Jan. 1855, renounces allegiance to Frederick William the 4th, JOHANNES GLAUS (signed in German), 5 Mar. 1860. J. E. HAGOOD, C.C.P.

Petition of LUDWICK SCHAFFERT, aged 33, Cabinet maker, born in Prussia, arrived in New York in November 1850, then moved to South Carolina, declared his oath 17 Oct. 1856 before W. L. KEITH, renounces allegiance to Frederick the fourth, King of Prussia. LUDWIG SCHAFFROTT, before J. N. WHITNER.
We the subscribers have known the petitioner for three years. 26 Oct. 1856, C. F. LEILA, H. LEGIA, W. LADEY.
Before W. L. KEITH, appeared LUDWIG SCHAFFROTT, aged 31, declares that he arrived in 1851...17 Oct. 1854. LUDWIG SCHAFFROTT.

Petition of E. D. C. BRANDT, aged 46, a farmer, born in Hanover Germany, arrived in Charleston December 1850, declared his oath on 17 Oct. 1856 before W. L. KEITH, renounces allegiance to Frederick Augustus...E. D. C. BRANDT, before J. N. WHITNER.
We, the subscribers, have known the petitioner for three years, and he has resided in Pickens District..21 Oct. 1856 C. F. LEILA, H. FAGEN, W. FADEY.
Be it remembered that on 17 Oct. 1854, E. D. C. BRANDT, aged 44 years, declared his intention to become a citizen..W. L. KEITH, Clerk.
Received of C. BRANDT by hand of H. D. BRIGGMAN $3.00 for administering the oath 8 Dec. 1854. W. L. Keith.

Petition of F. AFFHUPPER, a farmer, born in Prussia, arrived in the U. S. at Charleston, 1840, declared his oath before W. L. Keith, 2 Nov. 1852, renounces allegiance to Frederick William the fourth of whom he was a subject..F. AFFHUPPER bef. D. L. WARDLAW.
We, the subscribers, have known the petitioner for five years, and he has resided in S. C....20 Mar. 1855 MINK BULLWINKLE, L. BUNNAU?, C. F. SEEBA.
In open court, S(?) AFFHUPPER, a native of Prussia about the age of 32, who declares his intention to become a U. S. citizen...29 Nov. 1852 W. L. Keith, CCP.

Before me, W. L. Keith, appeared CHRISTIAN HENRY ISSERTEL, a native of Hefajeismar in Germany, about the age of 54 years, who declares his intention to become a citizen of the U. S., renounces his allegiance to Kuykh-Hessen...7 Nov. 1854, CHRISTIAN HENRY ISERTEL...W. L. Keith, CCP.
Petition of CHRISTIAN HENRY ISSERTEL, about the age of 58, a merchant, arrived at Charleston, 8 Jan. 1854...C. H. ISSERTEL, J. N. Whitner.
We, the subscribers, have known the petitioner at which time he has resided at Walhalla..25 Mar. 1859, L. C. CRAIG, H. GISSEL..J. E. HAGOOD, CCP.

JOHN HUSCAMP, a native of the Kingdom of Hanover, about the age of 27 years, appeared before W. L. Keith, declares his intention to become a citizen of the U. S. 31 Mar. 1851.
Petition of JOHN HUSCAMP, aged 30 years, a farmer, born in Hanover, Germany, arrived in Charleston, S. C. 1849..JOHN HUSKAMP before J. N. Whitner.
We, the subscribers, have known the petitioner for five years, during which time he has resided in Pickens District..16 Oct. 1855, FREDERICK WALD, JOHN CAPEHART, WM. H. STRIBLING.

The petition of JOSEPH DAWSON, aged 51 years, sheweth that he is a native of Lyme Regis, Dorsetshire, England, that he arrived at Charleston about the 2nd of Feb. 1846, and that he is a resident of Pickens District, declares his intention to become a citizen and renounces allegiance to the Queen of England. JOSEPH DAWSON, 4 Apr. 1848.

Petition of GEORGE LEOFFEL, aged 41 years, born in Weinhem, Grand Dukedom, Baden, Germany, arrived at New York City...GEORG LOEFFEL, 15 Feb. 1859, J. E. HAGOOD, CCP.

Petition of RICHARD ISERTELL, aged 23 years, born in Hassen Cassell, Germany, arrived in New York, 3 Oct. 1853, renounces allegiance to Frederick William...19 Jan. 1856, RICH'D ISSERTEL.

Before W. L. Keith, appeared HENRY CHRISTIAN L. MAX, a native of Clouthal in the Kingdom of Hanover, about the age of 29 years, declares his intention to become a citizen, renouncing allegiance to King George of whom he is a subject..20 Mar. 1855, H. CH. L. MAX, W. L. Keith, CCP & GS.

The petition of CHRISTIAN SLATER, aged 31 years, of the occupation of a miner, arrived in the City of Baltimore, 1 June 1857..C. SLUTER, 15 Oct. 1860. J. E. Hagood, CCP.

Petition of SAMUEL B. DAWSON, aged 28 years, a native of Maidstone, Kent, England, arrived at Charleston about 2 Feb. 1846, now residing in Pickens Dist., S. C., declares his intention to become a citizen. Renounces fidelity to the Queen of England. SAMUEL B. DAWSON, 4 Apr. 1848.
We, the subscribers, have known the petitioner SAMUEL BAKER DAWSON, for five years...E. J. HUNNICUTT, W. L. KEITH, ANDERSON BURNS, JOSEPH BREMER, J. B. CARRADINE, C. H. P. FANT, E. E. ALEXANDER, ALLEN R. ELLIOTT, JAMES YOUNG, P. ALEXANDER, JAMES LAWRENCE, T. C. MEGEE.

I, DANIEL HORLBECK, Clerk of Court for Charleston Dist., do certify that MARTIN C. WENDELKEN, aged 30 years, a grocer, appeared and declared that he arrived in Charleston, December 1839, where he has ever since resided, renounces all allegiance to Earnest Augustus, King of Hanover..18 Aug. 1849, MARTIN C. WENDELKEN.
Pickens Dist.: to the Hon. EDWARD FROST, one of the law Judges, the petition of MARTIN C. WENDELKEN, aged 32 years, a grocer, a native of Hanover, Germany, arrived at Charleston and was a resident there until last year when he removed to Pickens District. Nov. 1851.
We, the subscribers, have known the petitioner for three years. D. BIEMANN, E. CAPPELMANN, WILLIAM ROBINSON.

The petition of G. H. CRAMER, aged 51 years, a teacher, born in Hanover, Germany, arrived in Charleston in December 1849, appeared before W. L. Keith, 2 Nov. 1852, renounces allegiance to Frederick Augustus, King of Hanover...G. H. D. CRAMER, before J. N. Whitner.
We, the subscribers, have known the petitioner for five years, during which time he has resided in South Carolina. 15 Oct. 1855. W. LADER, _____, MARTIN C. WENDELKEN, D. BIEMANN.

The petition of MARTIN KNECHT, aged 28, born in Hessen, Damstardt in Germany, arrived in the City of New York, 7 May 1852, renounces allegiance to the Grand Duke Louis the Second..A. M. KNECHT, 15 Oct. 1860.

The petition of HENRY HARTMAN, aged 28 years, occupation of a miner, born in Wintenburg, Germany, on the 17th day of March 1830, arrived in the City of New York 1 May 1849..renounces allegiance to King William of Wurtenburg..H. HARTMANN. Petition of HENRY HARTMANN, dated 6 Nov. 1858. J. E. Hagood, CCP.

State of S. C.: I, JOHN GOTLIEG HOFER, do swear that I was born in Saxony, on 9 March 1828, and resided there until the year 1853, when I removed to the U. S., to wit, to Charleston, 20 Nov. 1853..23 Nov. 1853 at Charleston, before me EDWARD FROST, JOHANN GOTTLIEB HOFAR.
Pickens Dist.: The petition of JOHN G. HOFER, aged 32 years, a house Carpenter, has resided in Walhalla...J. G. HOFER, bef. J. N. Whitner.
We, the subscribers, do certify that we have known the petitioner for six years, during which time he has resided in Walhalla. 19 Mar. 1860. JACOB STRODER, H. P. STRODE.

Pickens County, S. C.: The petition of FRANCIS HEWER, aged 50 years, a farmer, sheweth that he was born in Gloucestershire County, England, arrived in New York about 1 March 1852, renounces allegiance to Queen Victoria..15 Mar. 1871.

Before W. L. KEITH, appeared JOHN E. FREDRICK MYER, a native of Hanover, about the age of 30 years, who declared his intention to become a citizen..4 Apr. 1853. J. E. FRIDICH MAYR (signed in German).

The petition of J. W. F. STRUHS, aged 27 years, a carpenter, born in Hanover, Germany, arrived in the U. S. in 1851, appeared before WILLIAM L. KEITH, 3 Nov. 1853, renounces allegiance to Frederick Wm. Augustus..J. W. F. STRUKS, before J. N. WHITNER.
We, the subscribers, have known the petitioner for 3 years, during which time he has resided in Pickens Dist...MARTIN C. WENDELKEN, H. MEYER, T. HOFER. 20 Oct. 1856.
Certificate has J. W. F. STRAUSS.

END OF NATURALIZATION RECORDS

PICKENS COUNTY, S. C. ESTATE RECORDS

THOMPSON, JOSHUA Box 1 No. 1
Estate Admr. 5 Oct. 1829 by JAMES THOMPSON, DANIEL DURHAM, JOEL MORTON, bound to JAMES H. DENDY, ord'y. in the sume of $300...ELIJAH THOMPSON, rec'd $15.27. On 7 Feb. 1831, ELIJAH THOMPSON a minor over 14 years. Left widow and ten children..Sale made 13 Jan. 1829. Buyers: MARY THOMPSON, GEORGE MILLER, SARAH THOMPSON, ABSALOM REID, JAMES THOMPSON, DANIEL DURHAM, ISAAC MURPHEA, WILSON VERMILON, JERRY DURHAM, REUBEN BAKER, JOEL DURHAM. Power of Attorney viz JONATHAN GREGORY & SAMUEL SMITH of Blount Co., Ala. appointed MARSHALL MORTON of sd County their att'y. in right of their wives, JANE THOMPSON GREGORY, WINNY THOMPSON SMITH. Dated 24 Sept. 1835...JONATHAN M. GREGORY, SAMUEL D. SMITH.

BOYD, ROBERT, JR. Box 1 No. 2
Estate Admr. 23 Jan. 1829 by ELIJAH CANNON, ROBERT BOYD bound to JAMES H. DENDY, Ordy. for $2000..Sealed in presence of THOMAS & WILLIAM BOYD. MOSES SMITH, JR. state that he is the husband of the late widow of ROBERT BOYD, JR. Inventory of Estate made 29 Jan. 1829 by ARCHIBLE MILLER, MARK FREEMAN, JOHN T. BLACK. Sale made 19 Feb. 1829. Buyers: MARY BOYD, BENJAMIN HAGEWOOD, ROBERT BLASSINGAME, WILLIAM TATUM, ABRAHAM LESLEY, ABSOLUM HOWARD, HENRY GRIFFIN, JOSEPH YOUNG, JOHN BOWEN, ELIJAH CANNON, JOHN PRINCE. 2 May 1829 Notes owing to the estate: JAMES CARY, SAMUEL MC CULLUM, JOHN CHAPMAN, BENTON FREEMAN, WILLIAM L. KEITH, JOHN S. EDWARDS, REDEN FREEMAN, DAVID DONOL, JOHN H. ROE, JOHN JONES, RILEY SMITH, REASON JULIN, WILLIAM LESLEY, MORGAN DANOL, ABEL HILL, WILLIAM BRAY, WILLIAM PHILLIPS, JOHN WRIGHT, JOSEPH B. READ, LEWIS BARRET, ESLEY HUNT, ALEXANDER CLARK, PETER CORBIN, ENOCH HOOD, RASHA BRUSE..State of Tennessee, Wayne County: 2 Nov. 1835, JOSIAH FOWLER appointed Guardian of GETER LEWIS BOYD, orphan and minor heir of ROBERT BOYD.

BUTT, JOHN, SR. Box 1 No. 3
Estate admr. 15 Oct. 1829 by JAMES COAL, MOSES SWAFFORD, JOHN COAL, bound to JAMES H. DENDY, Ordy., for $400. Inventory made 26 Oct. 1829 by CHARLES MC CLURE, MACKEY BROWN, MOSES SWAFFORD.

TRIMMIER, COL. OBEDIAH Box 1 No. 4
Estate admr. 9 Feb. 1829 by DAVID SLOAN, NATHAN BOON, THOMAS B. REID bound unto JAMES H. DENDY, Ordy. for $10,000. 5 Dec. 1831 Paid SELINA TRIMMIER $291. Pd. LUCY TRIMMIER $359.66. Inventory made 10 Feb. 1829 by JABEZ JONES, JOHN ROBINSON, EDWARD HUGHEY, CALEB BABBITT, NIMROD LEATHERS.

GRIFFIN, ELIZABETH Box 1 No. 5
Estate admr. 20 Apr. 1829 by SARGEANT GRIFFIN & BAILEY BARTON bound unto Ordy. for $500. Sale bill made 30 Apr. 1829. Buyers: SARGENT GRIFFIN, HENRY GRIFFIN, SARAH BRAZEAL, ISIAH TROTTER, WILLIAM MERONEY,

Cont'd:
CORNELIUS KEITH, JAMES TROTTER, JOHN KEITH, ARCHIBALD MILLER, CANNON STEPHENS, JAMES GILLILAND, JOEL THACKER, WILLIAM GRIFFIN, NOBLE GLENN, WILLIAM BAKER, ROBERT TROTTER, SHERIFF HAYNES, REBECCA TROTTER, ABSALOM HOWARD, B. HAGOOD, JAMES SOUTHERLAND, WILLIAM SOUTHERLAND, RICHARD POE, ELIHU GRIFFIN, STEPHEN C. REID, BAILEY BARTON. HENRY & SARGEANT GRIFFIN, WILLIAM MERONEY, JAMES TROTTER. Rec'd. from Estate $106.65 each.

YOUNG,   Box 1 No. 6
        Dated 27 July 1829. Recorded 7 Sept. 1829. Will names REBECCA YOUNG..."Will to GIBSON PORTER"...Children (not named). Exrs.: REBECCA YOUNG, BAILEY BARTON. Wit: AMBROSE PETTY, WILEY PETTY, JAMES PORTER. Inventory made 21 Sept. 1829 by JACOB LEWIS, JOAB LEWIS, AMBROSE PETTY.

ISBELL, PENDLETON, SR. Box 1 No. 7
        Estate admr. 25 May 1829 by THOMAS W. HARBIN & PENDLETON ISBELL bound to JAS. H. DENDY, Ordy. for $400. Sale made 3 July 1829. Buyers: JOHN HUGHES, DRURY HUTCHINS, PENDLETON ISBELL, FOSTER BAILEY, ADAM RICHARDS, JOHN MILLER, MARY ISBELL, VINCENT BROWN, JONATHAN REEDER, WILLIAM B. HONEYCUT, CHARLES WHITWORTH, PETER L. BARTON, OSBURN CLEVELAND, STEPHEN HOWARD, FREDERICK MOSS, THOMAS GUEST, HENRY BROWN, THOMAS W. HARBIN, MORGAN HARBIN, OBADIAH BROWN, JOHN MILLER, ALLEN GUEST.

WOOD, JOSEPH Box 1 No. 8
        Will dated 6 Jan. 1829. Rec. 2 Feb. 1829. "Allow all the children I had by my first wife LAVISA, $1 each viz NANCY, CHARITY, WILLIAM, SOLOMON, WINNY, ISAIAH, CATHARINE, LAVISA WOOD. "What is left I want my present wife MARY to have to raise her children on." Wit: PHILIP SNEAD, JACOB LEWIS, DANIEL G. NIX. Inventory made 6 Mar. 1829 by JACOB GUYTON, JACOB LEWIS, THOMAS ALEXANDER.

DICKSON, WILLIAM Box 1 No. 9
        Will dated 26 June 1827. Rec. 3 Aug. 1829. Children: JAMES DICKSON, SIMPSON DICKSON, JOHN DICKSON, JOSEPH DICKSON, ANDREW DICKSON, ROBERT DICKSON, ABBY COBB, MARY HUGHS, LINEY DICKSON, DAVID DICKSON. Wife (not named). "Tract that lies above the Old trail leading from what was formerly called Butts Ford on Chauga to the ford on Ramseys, just above my plantation." Wit: WILLIAM SIMPSON, REBECCA SIMPSON, CANDAS CAIN. Wife POLLY DICKSON.

MAY, CALEB Box 1 No. 10
        Estate admr. 3 Mar. 1829 by WILLIAM SIMPSON, JABEZ JONES bound to JAMES H. DENDY, Ordy. for $1000...Inventory made 5 Mar. 1829 by JABEZ JONES, JOHN ROBERTSON, THOMAS COLLINS, NIMROD LEATHERS, EDWARD HUGHS. Citation published at Chawgy. By cash pd GEORGE B. REID, husband of ELIZABETH RICHARDS, $79.68 3/4. On 14 Nov. 1839 WM. SIMPSON states that HORACE NARAMORE of New York gave him power of atty. executed by Dr. CALVIN MAY and another executed by his mother, MARY NARAMORE, heirs of CALEB MAY. Signed: MARTIN MAY. Sale made 30-31 Mar. 1829. Buyers: LEONARD TOWERS, CALEB BABBITT, THOS. HARBIN, WIDOW ERASTUS, WM. CLARK, JOHN DICKSON, WM. BARTON, REV. G. VANDIVER, JAS. C. GRIFFIN, JAMES GREENWOOD, SIMEON BRADLEY, JESSE STAPP, ALMON POWELL, THOS. COLLINS, DEBUX JARROTT, OBADIAH TRIMMIER, NIMROD LEATHERS, EDWARD HUGHS, JAMES DRUMMONS, DAVID CLINTON, JOHN HUMPHRIES, DAVID BARTON, JOHN RIDER, JOHN ADAIR, JOHN ROBERTSON, JOHN VERNER, LEMUEL DOWDY, JOHN CALHOUN, SAMUEL KING, HUGH HALL, ELI FITZGERALD, WIDOW MAY, JAS. BLACKSTOCK, GEORGE BLAIR, GEO. PHILIPS, JAS. FERGUSON. On 7 Oct. 1839 MARTHA M. MAY & WM. SIMPSON promised to pay J. H. DENDY, Ordy., $172. value rec'd.

LAY, CHARLES Box 2 No. 11
        Will dated 20 Feb. 1829. Rec. 14 Sept. 1829. Wife NANCY LAY, children: DAVID LAY, JOHN JAMES LAY, WILLIAM LAY. Exr.: WILLIAM LAY. Wit: ELIHU CRESWELL, ROBERT H. CRESWELL, JOHN KNOX.

GILSTRAP, HARDY Box 2 No. 12
        Estate admr. 7 Dec. 1829 by JOHN GILSTRAP, LEVI MURPHREE, DANIEL DURHAM bound to J. H. DENDY, Ordy. for $400. On 19 Feb. 1831 ANN GILSTRAP states she is not able to act as Admr. and wants JOHN GILSTRAP to act for her. Sale made 18 Feb. 1829. Buyers: JAS. FERGUSON, JOHN

Cont'd:
GILSTRAP, GIDEON ELLIS, CHAS. DURHAM, GEO. MILLER, DANIEL DURHAM, GEO.
HENDRIX, WM. ELLENBURG, REUBEN BAKER, JOHN CLAYTON, SHERIFF HAYNES,
JOHN KARR, JACOB GUERIN, JAMES GILSTRAP, JOHN HOOD, WM. BAKER, JAS.
THOMPSON, WASHINGTON YOUNG, MARSHAL MARTIN, JOHN BLACK, HENRY SARGANT,
JAMES LANGSTON. ANNE GILSTRAP, Widow.

CROSBY, ABNER Box 2 No. 13
     Estate admr. 4 Jan. 1836 by BENJAMIN D. DUPRE, WM. L. KEITH, ALEXR.
HARRIS, bound to J. H. DENDY, Ordy. for $6000. Estate admr. again 2
Feb. 1829 by ROBERT ANDERSON, RICHARD HARRIS bound for $3000. Inven-
tory made 6 Feb. 1829 by JAMES ALLEN, JAS. SANDERS, OWEN MOORE, SAMUEL
THOMAS. Return of notes taken for property sold by the admr. viz JOHN
DAVIS, JAS. O. LEWIS, JAMES BROWNLOW, THOS. DAWSON, FRANCIS CROSBY,
GEO. FREDRICK, RICHD. HARRIS, DAVID HALL, WM. HALL, R. ANDERSON, REUBEN
HIX, JAMES ALLEN, THOS. PATTERSON, WM. SANDERS, JOHN FERGUSON, CHARLES
HUNT, JOHN ROBINSON, JOHN EVANS, CHARLES PITTS, RANDOLPH LEE, JONATHAN
GILLISON, WM. FRASHER, ALEXR. BRYCE, SAML. THOMAS, GEO. WRIGHT, WM.
ALLEN, ANANIS TILLISON, THOS. B. LOVE, JOHN COLLINS, E. B. BENSON,
NATHL. SHIRLEY, CALEB ROTHEL, NANCY MC DONALD, ELIZA. MC DONALD, SHAD-
RACK HARRIS, SIDNEY COLE, ROBT. COBB, WM. HAYES, SAML. KING, SARAH
SKELTON, JOSIAH WRIGHT, ELIZA. WRIGHT, JOHN P. GREENWOOD, THOS. MC
DANIEL, JOHN SMITH, WM. MILLS, JAMES GREENWOOD, WM. BECK, MOSES MC
DOUGAL, JOHN WELCH, JOSEPH STAFF, ELISHA C. HAYES, WM. CARSON, JOHN
LATTA, BARTIN LOVELESS, JOHN MC CARLY, JAS. DICKSON, DAVID NIMMONS,
FARRELL MC GAHA, DANIEL BRYSON, REBECA MORGAN, JOSEPH WRIGHT, JOHN
BROWN, HENRY HEAD, ANDW. FERGUSON, WM. BEAVERT, AMOS ROBINSON, WM.
WILLIS, ROBT. BEATY, WM. DOYLE, THOS. JENKINS, JAS. W. DRENNON, JOHN
BLACKSTOCK, ISRAEL GILLISON. Mrs. FRANCES CROSBY (widow?). 5 Sept.
1838 pd. for Georgia land, $200. Citation published at Rock Spring
Church, Jan. 1836. Owned 5 slaves...Paper mentioned ANNANIAS TILLOT-
SON deed now belonging to ABNER CROSBY estate, 202½ acres in Carroll
County, Georgia.
     Letter: 1 Jan. 1836 to JAMES H. DENDY, Esq.
Very Dear Sir,
     I have just received your note containing the request for MRS.
CROSBY. Although aware of the trouble and responsibility of an admin-
istrator I do not feel at liberty to decline it The destitute Orphan
has a strong claim to the sympathies and services of the intelligent
and prudent, on account of the children and only on their account can
I get my consent to accept the office. I will see you Monday morning
at Pickens, when the requisite arrangements will be made.
               Yours truly, BENJ. D. DUPRE.

MC ELVANY, ANDREW K. Box 2 No. 16
     Estate admr. 1 Feb. 1830 by WILLIAM OLIVER, ROBERT GAINES, JAMES
GAINES bound to JAS. H. DENDY, Ordy. for $200. Inventory made 20 Feb.
1830 by ROBT. GAINES, JAMES POWERS, WM. D. ARNOLD. Citation published
at Mt. Zion Meeting House. 10 Jan. 1830 ANDRW. K. MC ELVY, dec'd. debtor
to WM. OLIVER for 15 months boarding and nursing in sickness, $150.

MC CLURE, JAMES Box 2 No. 17
     Estate admr. 7 June 1830 by EASTER MC CLURE, ROBT. ANDERSON, ALEX-
ANDER RAMSEY, RICHD. HARRIS for $15,000. Inventory made 11 June 1830
by JONATHAN REEDER, JOHN HARRIS, NATHL. HARRIS. Owned 13 slaves. ESTHER
MC CLURE, widow. JAMES YOUNG in right of wife ANNA who was a sister
to said deceased. Citation published at Beaverdam Meeting House 23
May 1830.

HILL, ABEL Box 2 No. 18
     Estate admr. 3 May 1830 by JAMES FINDLEY, JR. & BENJAMIN HAGOOD
bound to J. H. DENDY, Ordy. for $300. Heirs: CASEY HILL, ASHWORTH HILL,
HULDY HILL, LEWIS HILL, ELIZABETH HILL, KETURAH HILL. Inventory made
by JOEL JONES, ABEL HENDRICKS, DAVID HENDRIX. KEZIAH HILL, the widow.

SMITHSON, MARION Box 2 No. 19
     Estate admr. 8 Feb. 1830 by NIMROD LEATHERS, FOSTER PERRY & WILLIAM
JEANS bound to J. H. Dendy, Ordy. for $400. On or before 1 Feb. 1831,

Cont'd:
SELAH & SARAH SMITHSON promise to pay J. H. Dendy, Ordy. $200 rec'd.
Power of attorney on 6 Apr. 1833 ANSON SMITHSON of Jefferson Co., Ala.
appointed BIRDWELL HILL of Pickens Dist., his atty. to collect his
part of estate of MARION C. SMITHSON, dec'd. On 6 Sept. 1830 NIMROD
LEATHERS, JR. states that he has an interest in the estate of MARION
SMITHSON, dec'd., that he claims his claim from the right of his de-
ceased mother, MARY LEATHERS, formerly the wife of his father BENJAMIN
LEATHERS...Heirs: WILLIAM SMITHSON, SELAH SMITHSON, SARAH SMITHSON,
JAMES JOLLY. Real estate on waters of Choestoe adj. lands of ELI DAVIS,
BENJAMIN PERRY, 115 acres. Sale made 18 Feb. 1830. Buyers: WIDOW SMITH-
SON, JOHN JOLLY, NIMROD LEATHERS, CHARLES VERNER, ABNER HONEA, GREEN
HARDEN, SELAH SMITHSON, PHILIP JONES, BIRDWELL HILL, SARAH SMITHSON,
FOSTER PERRY, JOHN HARRISON, ROBERT HACKETT. 18 Feb. 1830 FEBY SMITH-
SON, SELAH & SARAH SMITHSON value.

CANNON, RANSOM Box 2 No. 20
     Estate admr. 1 Mar. 1830 by ELIJAH CANNON, MALINDA A. CANNON,
ABSALOM REECE, JEREMIAH FIELDS, bound to James H. Dendy, Ordy. for
$3000. Sale made 18 Mar. 1830. Buyers: HUGH TATUM, JAMES LANGSTON, JESSE
RACKLEY, JOEL BURHAM, GIDEON ELLIS, DAVID H. BOGGS, ELLIS MURPHREE,
ABSALOM REECE, MALINDA A. CANNON, CHARLES DURHAM, JAS. THOMPSON, JANE
CANNON, SAML. HALL, ELIZABETH BAKER, ROBT. BOYD, LEVI MURPHREE, DANIEL
MURPHREE, WILLIAM ELLIS, WILLIAM BAKER. Inventory made 5-6 Mar. 1830
by ABSOLEM REECE, DANIEL DURHAM, ARCHIBALD MILLER. Paid MARTHA CANNON
$8.00. 7 Aug. 1835 ordered that $3.83 be paid to the widow, now MRS.
SMITH and the balance to MOSES SMITH, guardian of JOHN H. BOYD, a minor.

MC CLANAHAN, ROBERT Box 3 No. 21
     Estate admr. 1 Feb. 1830 by JOSEPH GRISHAM, JAMES GAINS, WILLIAM
OLIVER bound to J. H. Dendy, Ordy. for $80. SARAH L. CLANAHAN rec'd
$40 from real estate of EDWARD CLANAHAN, rec'd 22 Feb. 1858.

GASSAWAY, THOMAS JR. Box 3 No. 22
     Estate admr. 7 Nov. 1831 by ROBERT KIRKSEY, WILLIAM KIRKSEY, CHRIS-
TOPHER KIRSEY bound to J. H. Dendy, Ordy. for $400. Sale made 19 Nov.
1831. Buyers: HANNAH GASAWAY, DAVID CHERRY, CHARLES THOMPSON, DANIEL
GASAWAY, WILLIAM GARNER, THOMAS EVATT, JOHN RUSSELL, JAMES MARTIN,
FREDERICK GARVEN, WAYMON HOLLAND, C. P. DU PRE, JOHN RUSSELL, HUNDLEY
EVATT, COLEMAN GASAWAY, JAMES POWER. Inventory made 18 Nov. 1831 by
JAMES POWERS, SAMUEL MC WHORTER, JAMES HENDRIX.

PATTERSON, THOMAS Box 3 No. 23
     Estate admr. 13 Dec. 1830 by JOHN DAVIS, CLARY PATTERSON, ALEX-
ANDER RAMSEY bound to J. H. Dendy, Ordy. for $500. Power of Att'y DUDLEY
R. & SYNTHIA PATTERSON of Franklin Co., Ga., appointed WM. ROBINSON
of Pickens Dist. their att'y and do convey to WM. ROBINSON 1/6 part
of tract of land whereon NICHOLAS HUNT lived and died, on waters of
Peters Creek adj. MARTIN WHITMIRE, THOS. SINGLETON, JOSEPH ROBINSON.
Signed in presence of EDWARD H. EDGAR, CHESLEY CAWTHON.

PRATER, JOHN Box 3 No. 24
     Estate admr. 7 Nov. 1831 by JOHN COUCH, REUBEN BAKER, WILLIAM
NIMMONS bound to J. H. Dendy, Ordy. for $1800. JOHN PRATER was late
of the state of Alabama.

MASTERS, THOMAS JR. Box 3 No. 25
     Estate admr. 3 Jan. 1831 by AARON ROPER, D. W. GLENN, SARGENT
GRIFFIN bound to J. H. Dendy, Ordy. for $1500. Inventory made 30 Sept.
1831 by JOSEPH B. REID, ABSALOM BLYTHE, WILLIAM SOUTHERLAND. Had notes
on WM. R. BURGESS, JOHN PHILLIPS, JOHN WITSEL, DAVID JOHNSTON, ANDREW
THACKER, JAMES & WM. SOUTHERLAND, WM. STAFFORD, BENJ. ROPER, JAMES
CLARK, WALTER NICKELSON, WM. CARR, JAS. BLACKLEY, F. B. DARNOLD, WM.
F. GALLOWAY. Open Accounts viz RICHARD MASTERS, MICAJAH TURNER, JOHN
TURNER, HENRY COOPER, DAVID CORBIN, JOHN ELLIOTT, J. M. KEITH, D. W.
GLENN. CATHARINE MASTERS, the widow. Sale made 26 Jan. 1831. Buyers:
D. W. GLENN, J. M. KEITH, NATHANIEL COLLINS, NOBLE GLENN, TILMON ROPER,
REUBEN ROPER, WILLIAM ELLIOTT, NATHL. REID, JAMES FORKNER, YEAERBY
CORBIN, SIMEON BURGESS, AARON ROPER, WILLIAM SOUTHERLAND, WM. CHASTAIN,

349

Cont'd:
SILAS DOWTHIT, HEZEKIAH ANDERSON, WM. G. FIELDS, JACOB ROPER, DAVIS
DOUTHIT, WM. W. WARD, CHAS. ROPER. 1831 pd. RICHARD MASTERS $79.07.
Pd MARADITH BARNET for plantation expenses, $8.

ROPER, BENJAMIN Box 3 No. 26
     Estate admr. 8 Aug. 1831 by WILLIAM SOUTHERLAND, WILLIAM L. KEITH
bound to J. H. Dendy, Ordy. for $400. Inventory made 23 Aug. 1831 by
JOSEPH B. REID, STEPHEN C. REID, ABSALOM BLYTH, JOHN KEITH. 1832 pd.
KEZIAH ROPER legacy, $12. Pd the widow for NANCY, $13.15. Estate div.
bet. Widow and 12 children. SUSANNAH ROPER, widow. Heirs: MEREDITH
ROPER, JOHN H. ROPER, JACOB ROPER, AARON ROPER, J. M. KEITH, RACHEL?
WARD, SARAH ROPER. 18 Oct. 1836 Mr. Dendy, Sr. you will please pay
to Mr. BENJAMIN ROPER $60 the part dew(sic) JOHN BIRUS the husband
of CAZZY ROPER as I hold the recpt for the same. WM. SOUTHERLAND.

LEWIS,LINDAMIRA Box 3 No. 28
     Will dated 30 May 1834. Rec. 16 Nov. 1836. Brothers: JOHN E. LEWIS,
JAMES OVERTON LEWIS; to nephew JOSEPH MC DOWELL, to MIRA ELIZABETH
MC DOWELL, to EDWARD HENRY SHANKLIN. Exrs.: JOHN E. & JAS. OVERTON
LEWIS. Wit: J. L. LORTON, SUSAN M. LEWIS, JESSE P. LEWIS.

COOPER, SION Box 3 No. 29
     Will dated 23 Feb. 1831. Proven 7 Nov. 1831. Children: ANCEL,
NANCY, POLLY, LEWIS, ALEXANDER, RAHAB, VINCON, DELILE, SALE COOPER.
Wife, POLLY COOPER. Exr. wife POLLY COOPER. Wit: MICAJAH HUGHES, JOHN
FIELD, SR., JOHN FERGUSON. 27 Apr. 1856 FRANCIS & NANCY SMITH rec'd.
share. Heirs: BASEL S. PORTER, grandson DAVIS COOPER. RAHAB FIELDS,
WARREN COOPER, NANCY COOPER, HANNAH COOPER, MATILDA COOPER, ELIZABETH
STACKY, ROBERT F. MORGAN, J. L. KILBY?. Owned 132 acres on waters of
Cane Creek adj. lands of JACOB SCHRODER and others, perhaps JAMES KELLY?
Inventory made 4 Jan. 1832 by JOHN FIELD, SR., JOSHUA MANSELL, WILLIAM
MAYFIELD.

CLEVELAND, BENJAMIN Box 3 No. 30
     Will dated 1830. Heirs: wife, PEGGY CLEVELAND, children (not named)
Exrs.: ROBERT & JACOB HOLLAND. Wit: KENNETH MC KENZIE, WILLIAM MILES,
JAMES JONES. Estate also admr. 12 Oct. 1857 by JEREMIAH CLEVELAND,
A. J. LOONEY, MARTIN L. LOONEY bound to W. J. PARSONS, Ordy. for $15,000.
Heirs out of this state are THOMAS CLEVELAND, GIBSON HIX & wife NANCY,
MARTIN L. LOONEY & wife MARIAM. Heirs in this state are A. J. LOONEY
& wife MARGARET, SARAH C. ABBOTT, WILLIAM B. DICKSON & wife ELIZABETH,
and the heirs of B. MILTON CLEVELAND, deceased, viz ADAALINE KEESE,
formerly ADALINE CLEVELAND, and widow of deceased and her two children
LEWIS & MARGRET CLEVELAND both minors. Dated 15 Dec. 1859. 25 Dec.
1858, amount of sale in Georgia, $20.51. Owned 8 slaves. Inventory
made 13 Oct. 1831 by JONATHAN REEDER, KENNETH MC KENZIE, WILLIAM MILLS.
Inventory mentioned 4 slaves. (The above could be of two different
persons by the name of BENJAMIN CLEVELAND, since the dates are for
1831 and 1857..Ed.)

ALEXANDER, ELISHA SR. Box 3 No. 31
     Will dated 8 Aug. 1832. Rec. 10 Sept. 1832. Wife NANCY ALEXANDER.
Children: ELIJAH, THOMAS, DANIEL, GEORGE WASHINGTON, ELISHA ALEXANDER.
Son-in-law HENRY GROGAN. Wit: CHARLES M. REESE, ELIJAH ALEXANDER, JOHN
F. HERD. "Land on Crow Creek". Estate also admn. 15 Oct. 1832 by PRIER
ALEXANDER, WM. ALEXANDER, GEORGE W. ALEXANDER, ELIJAH ALEXANDER, PLEAS-
ANT ALEXANDER, HENRY GROGAN. Owned 4 slaves..left 7 heirs. Also men-
tioned JOHN FERGUSON, JUDGE G. FERGUSON, JAS. FERGUSON, NANCY BARNET
(BARRET?), BENTON FREEMAN, MARY STEPHENS.

DAVIS, ELI Box 3 No. 32
     Will dated 30 Oct. 1832. Rec. 16 Nov. 1832. Heirs: wife, SARAH
DAVIS, children: KIZZIAH SOUTH, JOHN L. DAVIS, JANE YOW, FRANCES HILL,
SARAH L. CLANAHAN, CATHARINE JEANS, son-in-law FLEMING THOMPSON. Grand-
sons ELI SOUTH, JOHN L. M. THOMPSON, MEAD DAVIS. Exrs.: BIRWELL HILL,
THOMAS W. HARBIN. Wit: SQUIRE HUGHES, WILLIAM JOLLY, THOMAS W. PRICE.
Estate appraised 14 Dec. 1832 by THOMAS W. HARBIN, WILLIAM JOLLY, MARTIN
HARRISON.

STEWART, CYRUS Box 3 No. 33
     Estate admr. 2 July 1832 by ALLEN POWELL, JACOB GUERIN, bound
to J. H. Dendy, Ordy. for $60. Was late of the state of Georgia.

PALMER, BENJAMIN Box 3 No. 34
     Estate admr. 2 Apr. 1832 by LEWIS BARKER, FRANCIS BURT bound to
J. H. Dendy, Ordy. for $70. BENJAMIN PALMOUR was late of Tuscaloosa,
Alabama.

ARMSTRONG, BENJAMIN Box 3 No. 35
     Will dated 19 Oct. 1832. Proven 13 Dec. 1832. Children: ABNER
CROSBY ARMSTRONG, CHARLES ARMSTRONG, NANCY GAINS, REBECKAH MC WHORTER,
ZILLAH WOOTEN, SYNTHA ARMSTRONG. "BENJ. CORNELIUS WOOTON son of ZILLAH
WOOTON..." Wit: BENJAMIN D. DUPRE, JAMES H. DENDY, WILLIAM PERKINSON.
Letter from Tunnel Hill, Georgia, 7 June 1875 to Ordy. of Pickens Co.,
of S. C. .."Mrs. CHARLOTTE WOOTEN has got me to write to you. She says
her husbands name was BENJAMIN C. WOOTEN, and that BENJAMIN ARMSTRONG
was B. C. WOOTEN's grandfather, and B. ARMSTRONG maid(sic) a will and
willed to B. C. WOOTEN some five or six hundred dollars. She has never
got the money nor made any power of attorney. She says B. C. WOOTEN
died in the ware(sic) and she does not know who the admr. was. Mrs.
WOOTEN is poor and in need of the money. L. B. HAMBRIGHT.

FOWLER, JOSHUA SR. Box 4 No. 38
     Estate adm. 4 Feb. 1833 by WILLIAM JAMESON, ABRAHAM BURDINE, MARK
FREEMAN, CHARLES DURHAM bound to J. H. Dendy, Ord. for $2000. Power
of atty. on 17 Sept. 1836 JOHN LENARD of Madison Co., Ala. and husband
of HANNAH LENARD, a daughter of sd deceased appointed JOSIAH FOWLER
of Wayne Co., Tenn. his attorney. Power of atty. 11 Sept. 1834, WILLIAM
FOWLER of Lauderdale Co., Ala. appoints brother JOSIAH FOWLER my att'y.
Power of att'y 18 Apr. 1837 SALLY FOWLER, ROBERT & POLLY PEEK, THOMAS
& JONATHAN FOWLER, PAUL S. & SALLY MOORE appointed RUSSEL MARCHBANKS
of Jackson Co., their att'y. Power of att'y ELIZABETH FOWLER of Wayne
Co., Tenn. appointed JOSIAH FOWLER her att'y. JOHN FOWLER of Wayne
Co., Tenn. appointed JOSIAH FOWLER his atty. 11 Sept. 1836 NANCY FOWLER
& DENNIS HOUSE, admrs. of estate of THOMAS FOWLER of Lauderdale Co.,
Ala. who was son and heir of JOSHUA FOWLER appointed JOSIAH FOWLER
their atty. Inventory made 9 Feb. 1833 by LEVI (LEWIS?) BURTZ, JOHN
FINLEY, JOSHUA BURTZ. Citation published at Cross Road Meeting House,
27 Jan. 1833.

SOUTHERLAND, AMOS Box 4 No. 39
     Estate admr. 28 Oct. 1833 by WILLIAM SOUTHERLAND, WILLIAM L. KEITH
& FRANCES BURT, bound to J. H. Dendy, Ordy. for $5000. Citation was
published at Oolenoy Church, 27 Oct. 1833.

HUMPHRIES, CATHARINE Box 4 No. 40
     Will dated 6 Oct. 1832. Rec. 9 Dec. 1833. Heirs: WILLIAM, JOHN
HUMPHRIES, daughters ELIZABETH & RICHARD JONES, REBECKY & WILEY THOMAS,
CATHARINE PAYNE, ISAAC HUMPHRIES. Exrs.: REBECKY THOMAS, ROBERT H.
BRIGGS. Wit: EDWARD NORTON, JAMES MC COLLUM, JOSEPH TAYLOR, ROBERT
EMMERSON. Inventory made 26 Dec. 1833 by JAMES MC COLLUM, JOHN FERGU-
SON, ANDERSON SMITH.

STEPHENS, DANIEL Box 4 No. 41
     Will dated 12 Apr. 1830. Rec. 11 Nov. 1833. Wife, MORNING STEPHENS.
Children: SAMUEL, WILLIAM, PATSY, LINNY STEPHENS. Exrs.: BAILEY BARTON,
SAMUEL STEPHENS. Wit: GIDEON ELLIS, JAMES THOMPSON, JOHN STEPHENS.

CRESWELL, ELIHU Box 4 No. 42
     Estate admr. 30 Aug. 1833 by JAMES, ROBERT CRESWELL, ALBERT WALLER
bound to J. H. Dendy, Ordy. in sum of $30,000. Also SARAH CRESWELL.
Inventory made 11 Oct. 1833 by JAMES KNOX, SR., JAMES MC KINNEY, JOHN
WADDILL..owned 32 slaves. Buyers at sale: DAVID MC KINNEY, JAMES MC
KINNEY, SARAH & HENRY H. CRESWELL, JOHN SHARP, JAMES LAURENCE, JOHN
WADDILL, WM. COBB, JOHN QUARLES, MAGNUS TEAGUE, JOHN KNOX, ALEXANDER
ZAGHRA, BENJ. GRIST, JOHN CARTER, ADAM HILL, JAMES ALY, WILEY MOODY,
CUNNINGHAM ORR, JAMES LEEMAN.

GAINES, SIMEON Box 4 No. 43 (cont'd next page)

SIMEON GAINES cont'd:
    Estate admr. 20 Aug. 1833 by JAMES OVERTON LEWIS, BENJAMIN D.
DU PRE bound to J. H. Dendy, Ordy. for sum of $200. Citation published
at Rock Spring Meeting House, 21 July 1833. Sale made 21 Sept. 1833.
Buyers: NANCY GAINES, ROBERT GAINES, RICHARD HARRIS, J. O. LEWIS, CAPT.
JOHN ABBET, JOHN ABBETT, JR., J. H. DENDY, ELI CLEVELAND, ANDERSON
BLALOCK, ABNER ARMSTRONG, JOSEPH BEATY, JOHN MC WHORTER. Inventory
made 3 Sept. 1833 by JOHN MC WHORTER, ROBERT BEATY, WILLIAM PERKINSON.

WRIGHT, THOMAS Box 4 No. 44
    Estate admr. 13 Nov. 1833 by MARTHA WRIGHT, JAMES WRIGHT, GEORGE
C. CLEVELAND, ROBERT H. CLEVELAND bound to J. H. Dendy, Ordy. in sum
of $6000. MARTHA WRIGHT, widow. Inventory made 3 Nov. 1829 by JONATHAN
REEDER, JAMES MC CLURE, BENJAMIN MC GEE. Owned 13 slaves. Sale made
27 Nov. 1829. Buyers: MARTHA WRIGHT, WILLIAM WRIGHT, MORGAN HARBIN.

PETTY, AMBROSE Box 4 No. 45
    Will dated 14 Mar. 1834. Rec. March 1834. Wife, POLLY PETTY, child-
ren (not named). Exrs.: POLLY PETTY, BAILEY BARTON. Wit: DAVID MOSLY,
HIRAM HAYNES, ELIZABETH CANTRELL.

WILSON, WILLIAM Box 4 No. 46
    Power of Atty. 17 Oct. 1837 MARTHA WILSON of Talladega, Ala. and
WALKER REYNOLDS, exr's. of WILLIAM WILSON of sd Co., was one of the
sons of WILLIAM WILSON of Pickens Dist. S. C. appoint WM. WILSON of
Talladega Co., Ala. our attorney. Owned 2 slaves. Inventory made 23
Jan. 1835 by ANDREW HAMILTON, JOHN COUCH, SAMUEL JONES. Buyers: ROBT.
WILSON, JR., ANDREW HAMILTON, BENJAMIN DILWORTH, THOMAS MONTGOMERY,
JOHN W. WILSON, ABEL WILLIAMS, BRADWELL DAY, WM. M. HAMBY, JOHN WILL-
IAMS, MIDDLETON NALLEY, EPHRAIM SMITH, BARKSDALE NALLEY, RUCKER MAULDIN,
JACKSON HOLLINGSWORTH, ROBERT WILSON of Anderson Dist. applied for
letters of admn. 25 Dec. 1826. CUNNINGHAM WILSON of Talladega Co.,
Ala., a son appointed his brother ROBERT WILSON his atty. To Waggon
advance by admn. to DANIEL WILSON, $40. ANDREW WILSON, a son.

FITZGERALD, AMBROSE Box 4 No. 47
    Will dated 8 Apr. 1834. Rec. 5 May 1834. Children: GARRET FITZ-
GERALD, ELIZABETH ANDERSON, ANNA ROWEL, THOMAS, AMBROSE, DUDLEY & ELI
FITZGERALD. Granddaughter JULITY ROWEL. "Owned land on Tugaloo River."
Exrs.: CAPT.DAVID SLOAN, ELI FITZGERALD. Wit: THOMAS LAMAR, JAMES ADAIR,
ELIZABETH LAMAR. Inventory made 30 May 1834 by ASA SANFORD, AARON &
MOSES TERRELL, A. SMITHSON.

BLACKSTOCK, JAMES Box 4 No. 48
    Estate admr. 10 Mar. 1834 by THOMAS W. HARBIN, WILLIAM BARTON,
Esq., MARCUS T. TRIMMIER bound to J. H. Dendy, Ord. for $700. Citation
published at Chauga Meeting House, 2 Mar. 1834 by WILLIAM BARTON, Clerk.
Amount rec'd of LEVINA BLACKSTOCK on account of the land, $69.90. Inven-
tory made 26 Mar. 1834 by JOHN ROBERTSON, EDWARD HUGHS, MARCUS T. TRIM-
MIER. Buyers at sale: MRS. BLACKSTOCK, JOHN T. HUMPHRIES, JONATHAN
WILLIAMS, HUGH HALL, JAMES BLACKSTOCK, WILLIAM CLARK, DAVID PANNEL,
EDWARD HUGHES, JOHN R. BOGGS, EDMUND THORN, NEEDOM GEORGE, BENJAMIN
PADGET, THOMAS W. HARBIN.

HILL, GEORGE Box 4 No. 49
    Will dated 13 May 1834. Proven 23 July 1838. Children: LEWIS HILL,
MELINDA HENDRIX, RACHEL HILL, ASAPH HILL, son-in-law MOSES HENDRIX.
"Bequeath the tract orig. granted to DOMINICO HOLLAND, the other half
which I have deed to ISAAC WILLIAMS." Wit: SUSAN HUGG, WILSON LESLEY,
ROSWELL HILL, C. PACKARD. Citation published at Oollenoy Meeting House,
15 July 1838. Left 10 heirs viz JOHN & JAMES VANCE, NATHANIEL REID,
ISAAC HOWARD, Heirs of ABEL HILL, RACHEL & JOHN HILL, MOSES HENDRICKS.
Pd ASHWORTH B. HILL, heir of ABEL HILL, $9.80. Pd ELIZABETH HILL, heir
of ABEL HILL, $11.80. 1846 pd. MARGARET REID, wife of NATHANIEL REID,
$51.00 Cash pd. HULDAH HILL, $9.80. On 10 May 1855, SUSAN HILL WILLIAMS
of Lumpkin Co., Ga., aged 45 years, heir of GEORGE HILL who was a private soldier in the Company commanded by Capt. BUTLER in the Regiment
commanded by JOHN EARL, in the Revolutionary War.

UNDERWOOD, JOSEPH Box 4 No. 50 (cont'd next page)

JOSEPH UNDERWOOD cont'd:
Estate admr. 7 Feb. 1834 by JOHN QUARLES, JR., THOMAS FITZGERALD,
WILLIAM GABLE, DAVID QUARLES bound to J. H. Dendy, Ordy. sum of $3000.
Citation published at Long Creek Meeting House, 3 Nov. 1833. Owned
4 slaves. Buyers: WASHINGTON SMITH, HENRY GASSAWAY, ISAIAH STARKEY,
ISAAC BARRON, ROBERT QUARLES, JAMES COAL, COONROD WEAVER, JOSEPH WIL-
LIAMS, CHARLES MC CLURE, JOSEPH JONES, WILLIAM CROW, JAMES HERON, JOSHUA
DARNELL, JAMES REID, HIRAM ROACH, JAMES GEORGE, ELI WIGGINS, JACOB
BUTT, STOKES PYNIAN, ROBERT QUARLES, HENRY WATKINS, GRIEF WILLIAMS,
THOMPSON M. HANSON, HUBBARD QUARLES, ZACKARIAH KELLY, RICHARD EDMONDSON.

ALLEN, WILLIAM Box 5 No. 52
Estate admr. 21 July 1834 by JOHN ALLEN, CORNELIUS KEITH, WILLIAM
L. KEITH bound to J. H. Dendy, Ordy. for $1000. Citation published
5 July 1834 at Oolenoy Church Meeting House. Inventory made 31 July
1834 by PETER ROBINSON, SAMUEL EADENS, JOHN KEITH, JOSEPH B. REID.
JOHN ALLEN, a son. F. M. REID received a share. ABRAHAM & SALLY POWELL
received a share. ANDREW CORBIN & wife NANCY CASTLE received a share.
SIMEON YOUNGBLOOD and wife received a share. ABAGAIL ALLEN, the widow.
CLAYTON N. REID received a share. On 7 Dec. 1839, SIMEON YOUNGBLOOD
of Benton Co., Ala. states "You will please send by BARTON GRIFFIN
my wifes part of estate of WILLIAM ALLEN. My wife is a daughter of
JOHN CASTLE WYLEY, ANN..we were married by JOSEPH REID, Esq." SIMEON
YOUNGBLOOD. WILLIAM H. & JANE T. ALLEN were the two minor children
of THOMAS ALLEN. His widow was ELIZABETH C. ALLEN.

SMITH, BENJAMIN Box 5 No. 53
Will dated 18 Apr. 1834. Rec. 2 June 1834. Heirs: children REBECCA
CHAPMAN, MARY AGNEW, HANNAH ADAMS, ELIZABETH MC KINNEY, JAMES SMITH,
JONATHAN SMITH, WILLIAM SMITH, DAVID SMITH, SIDNEY SMITH. Exrs.: JAMES
SMITH, WILLIAM SMITH, ELIJAH DAVIS. Wit: WILLIAM MURRY, BENJAMIN &
ELIZABETH CHAPMAN. Inventory made by THOMAS H. MC CANN, WILLIAM MULLI-
KEN, ROBERT PICKENS.

POOR, DAVID Box 5 No. 54
Estate admr. 4 Nov. 1834 by JAMES M. POER, WILLIAM SIMPSON, FRANCES
POER bound to J. H. Dendy, Ordy. sum of $1600. DAVID POER was a hatter.
JAMES MADISON POER. Citation published at Holly Spring Meeting House
on 1 Nov. 1834. Owned 3 slaves. FRANCES POER, widow.

SMITH, ANDREW Box 5 No. 55
Estate admr. 10 Nov. 1834 by BENJAMIN SMITH, JEREMIAH WILLIAM
bound to J. H. Dendy, Ordy. for $6000. Citation published at Sharon
on 5 Nov. 1834. Inventory made by ROBERT RUSSEL, JR., HARDY FENNELL,
JEREMIAH WILLIAMS, ANDREW HAMILTON. Sale made 4 Dec. 1834. Buyers:
ELIZABETH SMITH, WILLIAM HAMBY, HAMBLETON HAMBY, LAWSON MULLINIX, JOBE
SMITH, JOHN BELL, ADAM HILL, AMOS VOILS, SAMUEL MC DOW, JAMES OLIVER,
ABLE WINTERS, HARRY WILSON, ROBERT JOHNSON, BENJAMIN SMITH, JEREMIAH
WILLIAMS, JOHN GUNTER, WILLIAM GARNER, JAMES BARROT, JAMES SMITH. Left
widow and 3 children, one child having died. Pd. JESSE SMITH, $12.25.

DURHAM, CHARLES Box 5 No. 56
Will dated 4 Jan. 1834. Rec. 13 Jan. 1834. Wife MARY DURHAM. Child-
ren: POLLY DURHAM, JEREMIAH DURHAM, JOSEPH DURHAM, LUCY MORTON, ELIZA-
BETH MORTON, PATSEY GILLSTRAP, DELILAH GILLSTRAP, NANCY CANTRELL, RHODAH
HENDRICKS. Exrs.: brother, DANIEL DURHAM, GIDEON ELLIS, BARNETT H.
ALLGOOD. Wit: THOMAS MOORE, READIN FREEMAN, JAMES LANGSTON. Sons: BEN-
JAMIN DURHAM, CHARLES DURHAM, JR. Inventory made 13 Jan. 1834 by JAMES
LANGSTON, JOHN STEPHENS, ISAAC MILLER.

SLOAN, CAPT. DAVID Box 5 No. 57
Estate admr. 3 Nov. 1834 by BENJAMIN F. SLOAN, THOMAS M. SLOAN,
NANCY SLOAN, JESSE STRIBLING, JOHN T. SLOAN bound to J. H. Dendy, Ordy.
for $50,000. 12 Feb. 1837 cash of BENJ. F. SLOAN on account of Fair-
play, $1000. Citation published at Richland Church, 2 Nov. 1834. In-
ventory made 16 Dec. 1834 by M. P. EARLE, ELIAS EARLE, SAMUEL REEDER.

SMITH, JOHN Box 5 No. 58
Estate admr. 3 Mar. 1834 by WILLIAM SMITH, FREDERICK N. GARVIN,

Cont'd:
CARTER CLAYTON bound to J. H. Dendy, Ordy. in sum of $300. Citation
published at Liberty Meeting House 23 Feb. 1834. Inventory made 22
Mar. 1834 by F. N. GARVIN, JOSEPH TAYLOR, BARNETT H. ALLGOOD, WILLIAM
ODELL. Buyers: MELINDA SMITH, ZIPHANIAH SMITH, JAMES MC WHORTER, B.
H. ALLGOOD, WM. SMITH, WM. BOGGS, THOMAS GIBSON, WM. ODELL, LOT KENNE-
MORE, EDWARD NORTON, RIAL KENNEMORE, BILLY STEPHENS.

ANDERSON, COL. ROBERT Box 5 No. 59
    Estate admr. by MARIA ANDERSON, the widow, GEORGE T. ANDERSON,
F. W. SYMMES, JOHN MAXWELL, T. J. PICKENS bound to J. H. Dendy, Ordy.
sum of $30,000. Citation published at Hopewell Church. Owned 25 slaves.
Cash advanced to JOSEPH D. SHANKLIN, Trustee of Pendleton Male Academy,
$1118.87.

HOLLAND, WEYMON Box 5 No. 60
    Estate admr. 21 May 1838 by COL. FREDERICK N. GARVIN, JOSEPH TAYLOR
& THOMAS GARVIN, bound to J. H. Dendy, Ordy. for $10,000. HOLLAND was
late of Abbeville District. Citation published at Mt. Zion Meeting
House, 21 May 1838. Inventory made 29 May 1838 by JOSEPH TAYLOR, THOMAS
G. BOGGS, JOHN TEMPLETON. Owned 5 slaves. MARY & SARAH HOLLAND were
minor children. Buyers: MARY HOLLAND, STEPHEN SMITH, JOSEPH TAYLOR,
GREENBERY GARVIN, WM. SMITH, NATHANIEL MERRIT, EZEKIEL MADDEN, RICHARD
DENTON, JOHN MAJOR, WM. BOGGS, JAMES J. HOLLINGSWORTH, CARTER CLAYTON,
JOHN DOWIS, AARON BOGGS.

BLACKBURN, THOMAS Box 5 No. 61
    Estate admr. 21 Oct. 1833 by WILLIAM L. KEITH, SAMUEL REID, bound
to J. H. Dendy, Odry. for $3000. Citation published at Keowee Meeting
House. WASHINGTON BLACKWELL, his brother. Legatees: LYDIA HUGHEY, WIL-
LIAM BLACKBURN, B. W. F. CAPEHART, AMBROSE REID, MALINDA BLACKBURN,
MATILDA BOWMAN. GEORGE W. BLACKBURN states that the estate is indebted
to him. Inventory made 29 Oct. 1833 by FRANCIS BURT, SILAS KIRKSEY,
WM. R. DUFF, WM. D. SLOAN.

BOGGS, AARON Box 5 No. 62
    Estate admr. 1 Jan. 1835 by MARTIN BOGGS, PLEASANT ALEXANDER,
CARTER CLAYTON bound to J. H. Dendy, Ordy. for $2000. Inventory made
25 Jan. 1833 by T. G. BOGGS, W. HOLLAND, HENRY SARGEANT. Sale made
26 Jan. 1835. Buyers: A. M. BOGGS, JOSEPH G. BOGGS, WM. BOGGS, ABSALOM
MULLINIX, WM. ODELL, THOMAS BOGGS, DAVID H. BOGGS, JONATHAN LEE, HENRY
SARGENT.

LANDRITH, THOMAS Box 5 No. 62
    Estate admr. 7 Dec. 1835 by FREDERICK N. GARVIN, JOHN DOWIS, BEN-
JAMIN CHAPMAN bound to J. H. Dendy, Ordy. for $200. THOMAS LANDRITH
died in the U. S. Service.

SMITH, JOEL Box 5 No. 63
    Estate admr. 7 Dec. 1835 by DAVID SMITH, JOHN SMITH, JONATHAN
L. BOLDING bound to J. H. Dendy, Ordy. for $300. Citation published
at New Liberty Church. Inventory made 23 Dec. 1835 by STEPHEN CLAYTON,
BARNETT H. ALLGOOD, GIDEON ELLIS. Cash pd. MARY SMITH note $5.50. Buyers
at sale: JOHN CLAYTON, JOHN SMITH, JOEL DURHAM, JONATHAN BOLDING, WIL-
LIAM POWELL, DAVID SMITH.

NEEL, JOHN Box 5 No. 64
    Will dated 16 July 1835. Proven 8 Mar. 1836. Children: SARAH COPE-
LAND, MARGARET HILLIAN, MARY HILLIAN, MARTHA WEEMS, JAMES NEEL, JOHN
NEEL, ANDREW NEEL, son-in-law ANDREW WEEMS. Wit: WM. L. KEITH, JAMES
A. EVATT, HUNDLEY EVATT. Inventory made 7 Apr. 1836 by JAMES LAWRENCE,
ELISHA LAWRENCE, WILLIAM OLIVER.

HALL, JESSE Box 6 No. 66
    Will dated 2 Apr. 1833. Rec. 4 Nov. 1833. Wife (not named). Child-
ren: MARY HALL, NANCY HALL, RUTH HALL, HENRY HALL, THOMAS HALL, GEORGE
HALL. Exrs.: THOMAS HALL, ZACHARIAH HALL. Wit: RICHARD HARRIS, D. SLOAN,
WILLIAM HALL.

OLIVER, JILSON Box 6 No. 67 (cont'd next page)

JILSON OLIVER cont'd:
    Estate admr. 9 Mar. 1835 by EDWARD HUGHS, THOS. HARBIN, THOMAS
W. HARBIN bound to J. H. Dendy, Ordy. for $1000. Inventory made 20
Mar. 1835 by JOHN ROBERTSON, THOMAS VISAGE, MARCUS T. TRIMMIER. SARAH
OLIVER, the widow. Letter from WILLIAM MORRIS to J. H. Dendy.."Please
pay EDW. HUGHS what money due me from the estate of JILSON OLIVER,
deceased." 14 Nov. 1840.

ROBERTSON, THOS. Box 6 No. 68
    Estate admr. 17 Aug. 1835 by JAMES ROBERTSON, JOHN MC KINNEY,
JESSE MC KINNEY bound to J. H. Dendy, Ordy. for $1000. Citation publish-
ed at Antioch Meeting House.

GRISHAM, JOHN SR. Box 6 No. 69
    Will dated 1 May 1826. Rec. 6 July 1835. Wife: ELIZABETH GRISHAM.
"Bequeath to my wife's grand daughter SARAH HIX, the orphan child of
AIRY WATSON, as admr. of THOMAS WATSON." Children: JOSEPH GRISHAM,
ELIZABETH MC DANIEL, LUCINDA CRAIG, FRANCES HAMMOND, JOHN GRISHAM,
WILLIAM GRISHAM, MELINDA GRISHAM, REUBEN GRISHAM. Wit: JAMES DOUTHET,
BENJAMIN HAGOOD, MILES M. NORTON. In 1835, REUBEN GRISHAM was living
in Louisiana. Inventory made 9 Oct. 1835 by ELIJAH ALEXANDER, WILLIAM
ALEXANDER, JEPHTHA NORTON, TARLETON LEWIS. Owned 8 slaves. 10 Nov.
1826 Pd. ELISHA ALEXANDER legacy left his wife by deceased, $67.68.

MOORE, LAZARUS Box 6 No. 70
    Estate admr. 8 Nov. 1836 by AGNES MOORE, JOHN A. MOORE, SHIELDS
MARTIN, LEONARD TOWERS bound to J. H. Dendy, Ordy. for $600. SAMUEL
HAMBY of Anderson Dist., married ELIZABETH O'BRYANT who was a half-
sister of LAZARUS MOORE...Power of Atty. on 30 Mar. 1843 ELIZABETH
MOORE, WILLIAM P. MOORE, JAMES MOORE, SOLOMON FLOYD, the husband of
RUTH MOORE & CURTIS GREEN, the husband of REBECKAH MOORE, all of Floyd
Co., Georgia, appointed NATHAN MOORE of Floyd Co., Ga. their attorney
....which is due to us as the lawful heirs of JAMES MOORE, dec'd. In-
ventory made 24 Nov. 1836 by JOHN MC WHORTER, JAMES SANDERS, R., ALEX-
ANDER BRYCE. Citation published at Richland Church.

STEGALL, RICHMOND Box 6 No. 71
    Estate admr. 4 Jan. 1836 by WILLIAM HOLCOMBE, JOHN BOWEN, JOHN
COUCH, bound to J. H. Dendy, Ordy. for $4000. Citation published at
Zion Church. 1 Jan. 1838 rec'd. of BLACKWELL STEGALL for rent, $15.

LATHEM, JOHN Box 6 No. 72
    Estate admr. 2 Sept. 1836 by JAMES LATHAM, JOHN BOWEN, ABRAHAM
BURDINE, bound to J. H. Dendy, Ordy. for $18,000. Citation published
at Peters Creek Church. Left 8 legatees. Owned 13 slaves. Inventory
made by JOHN BOWEN, WILLIAM HUNT, JOSHUA BURTZ. Buyers at sale: SINKLER
LATHAM, JOHN LATHEM, ANTHONY LATHAM, GEORGE LATHAM, etc.

COBB, JOHN S. Box 6 No. 73
    Estate admr. 28 Mar. 1836 by ROWLAND COBB, JOHN FERGUSON, LITTLETON
FOUNTAIN bound to J. H. Dendy, Ordy. for sum of $300. JOHN S. COBB
was the son of Rev. JOHN COBB. Citation published at New Hope Church.
Buyers: VILANTY COBB, ROWLAND COBB, A. A. COBB, JOHN COBB, JOHN COBB,
SR., JESSE CARNE, STEPHEN WHITMIRE, WM. J. PARSONS, WILLIAM NIMMONS,
GRIFFIN GREGORY, ISAAC MURPHREE, RICHARD BAKER. One paper states that
LUCINDA COBB was born 27 July 1818. ROWLAND COBB was born 20 May 1796.
LEWIS BALLARD was born 25 June 1798. JAMES COBB was born 12 Nov. 1777?.
Inventory made by RICHARD BAKER, WILLIAM NIMMONS, WILLIAM CRANE.

DICKSON, SAMUEL H. Box 6 No. 74
    Estate admr. 7 Mar. 1836 by GEORGE REESE, JAMES LAURENS, WILLIAM
D. SLOAN bound to J. H. Dendy, Ordy. for $500. Inventory made 3 May
1836 by MILES M. NORTON, SAMUEL REID, JAMES LAWRENCE, JAMES ROGERS.

CHAPMAN, JOSEPH Box 6 No. 75
    Estate admr. 1 Feb. 1836 by BENJAMIN HAGOOD, WILLIAM L. KEITH,
JOHN BURDINE bound to J. H. Dendy, Ordy. in sum of $25,000. JOSEPH
CHAPMAN, SR...Hall Co., Ga., JOSEPH CHAPMAN of Pickens Dist., S.C.
states at the intermarriage of his daughter POLLY to WILLIAM LADD he

Cont'd:
gave up $800 in property and part negroes...Dated 5 Mar. 1827. Owned
18 slaves...left 12 legatees..viz NANCY PATTERSON, ELIZABETH MC GEE,
JOHN THOMAS, ELIZABETH CHAPMAN, SOLOMON MC GEE, JEREMIAH CHAPMAN, ARCH-
IBALD CHAPMAN, JOSEPH CHAPMAN, JAMES CHAPMAN, JOHN HENSON, SAMUEL SULLI-
VAN, JOHN GARNER, ENOCH CHAPMAN, GEORGE CHAPMAN.

MORGAN, BENJAMIN Box 6 No. 76
     Estate admr. 1 Feb. 1826 by JOHN O'BRIANT, EPHRAIM PERRY, WILLIAM
L. KEITH, bound to J. H. Dendy, Ordy. for sum of $400. Inventory made
16 Feb. 1826 by WM. L. KEITH, EPHRAIM PERRY, JOHN ODELL. Heirs: BENJAMIN
MORGAN, NANCY BYRAM, CHARLES MORGAN, JOHN O'BRIANT, MAHLON MORGAN,
THOMAS MORGAN, JOHN MORGAN, BENSON STEPHENS, WILLIAM MORGAN, NANCY
TINCH, SARAH RANKIN, ISABELLA MORGAN. Left 12 children...FRANCES MORGAN,
etc. bought at the sale. MANOS MORGAN was of Marion Co., N. C. NANCY
& JESSE BYRAM were of Monroe Co., Tenn.

LOW, JESSE Box 6 No. 77
     Estate admr. 16 May 1836 by HENRY WHITMIRE, WM. L. KEITH, PLEASANT
ALEXANDER bound to J. H. Dendy, Ordy. for $1000. Inventory made July
1836 by NATHAN LUSK, JAMES LAY, JOHN HOLDEN. Heirs: JESSE LOW, VINEY
CROSS, ELIZABETH MILLSAP, NANCY DODGEN, NATHANIEL LOW, PHILIP LOW.

MOORE, BURT Box 6 No. 78
     Will dated 3 Apr. 1836. Wife: MARY MOORE. Sons: HUGHEY MOORE,
DAVID MOORE. Exr.: BAILEY BARTON. Wit: PHILIP YOUNG, ISAAC ANDERSON,
WILEY REAVES. Inventory made 6 May 1836 by BRIGHT GILSTRAP, WILEY REAVES,
ISAAC ANDERSON, ABRAHAM STUART. Buyers: MARY MOORE, JOSEPH MOORE, etc.

BOWEN, JOHN Box 6 No. 79
     Will dated 13 Aug. 1820. Proven 3 Dec. 1832. Wife: PATSEY BOWEN.
Son: JOHN BOWEN. Other children (not named). Wit: ABRAHAM BURDINE,
JAMES LATHEM, BIRD STEGALL. Widow mentioned as MARTHA BOWEN. Owned
15 slaves. Inventory made 24 Dec. 1832 by ABRAHAM BURDINE, RICHARD
BURDINE, JOSEPH G. EVATT. RICE BOWEN & JOHN BOWEN bought at the sale.

HARRISON, JOHN Box 6 No. 80
     Estate admr. 2 Feb. 1826 by THOMAS HARRISON, JOHN T. HARRISON,
WILLIAM JOLLY, THOMAS W. HARBIN bound to J. H. Dendy, Ordy. for $6,000.
Citation published at the Block Meeting House. Owned 11 slaves. Settle-
ment made 5 Jan. 1839. Cash pd. H. HARRISON his share in full $164.96.
Cash pd. H. HARRISON, Atty. for ROBERT HARRISON and W. W. SHORT and
MARY SHORT. Pd. JOHN ROBERTSON his share $389.34. Descendant of STACY
ROBERTSON, dec'd., $549.34. 5 Feb. 1839 pd. SQUIRE HUGHES in full of
$364.35. Pd. MATILDA HARRISON in full $429.35. Pd. NAOMI HARRISON in
full, $1890.88. Pd. E. ALEXANDER, Atty. for POSEY MADDOX, $501.61.
Pd. SOLOMON O'KELLY and wife, $352.86. THOMAS HARRISON has retained
his share of $366.86. JOHN T. HARRISON has retained his share $372.36.

MORGAN, MORGAN Box 7 No. 81
     Will dated 27 Aug. 1827. Proven 12 Feb. 1836. Wife: ELIZABETH
MORGAN. Son: DAVID MORGAN. "Money left us by our friend BARKER of Eng-
land." Wit: NIMROD LEATHERS, JAMES CANNON, HENRY COBB. Heirs: BENJAMIN
SEAGO and wife, HENRY HEAD and wife. Inventory made 24 Feb. 1836 by
JOHN G. MAULDIN, ZACHARIAH HALL, EZEKIEL MC WHORTER.

HUNT, LACY Box 7 No. 82
     Estate admr. 19 Sept. 1836 by KEZIAH HUNT, JOHN BOWEN, SOLOMON
WADE bound to J. H. Dendy, Ordy. for $1600. Citation published at Peters
Creek Church. KEZIAH HUNT, widow. On 4 Jan. 1837 KEZIAH HUNT states
that she will start to the Mississippi. KEZIAH HUNT states that her
husband died on 21st. Dated 4 Sept. 1836.

ANDERSON, HENRY H. and DENNY, SR. Box 7 No. 83
     Will dated 27 Nov. 1832. Wife: ELIZABETH ANDERSON. Children: HENRY,
JOHN, JAMES ANDERSON. "Give to son-in-law THOMAS LEONARD, son-in-law
JOHN L. BENNETT, WILLIAM O. BENNETT, son of my daughter MARTHA, dec'd."
MARY ANDERSON, dtr.-in-law, widow of SAMUEL ANDERSON, dec'd. Wit: Z.
F. WESTMORELAND, STEPHEN MARCHBANKS, WILLIAM HENDERSON..was of Spartan-

Cont'd:
burg District...Citation published at Rock Springs Church. Estate of
HENRY H. ANDERSON, admr. 1 Mar. 1836 by SUSAN ANDERSON, FRANCES KNOX
bound to J. H. Dendy, Ordy. for $3000. HENRY H. ANDERSON left a widow,
SUSAN and 8 legatees. Estate of H. H. ANDERSON inventory made 18 Mar.
1836 by FRANCIS JENKINS, WILLIAM H. STRIBLING, ISRAEL GILLISON.

ARIAL, JOHN SR. Box 7 No. 84
    Estate admr. 5 Sept. 1836 by JOHN ARIAL, LUKE J. ARIAL. WM. HUNTER,
Esq. and WM. L. KEITH bound to J. H. Dendy, Ordy. for $6000. Inventory
made 17 Nov. 1836 by JOHN LESLY, JAMES HENDERSON, JAS. OSBORN.

THOMBS, SAMUEL Box 7 No. 85
    Estate admr. 27 Feb. 1836 by ALEXANDER BRYCE, WILLIAM PERKINSON,
STARLING GARNER, bound to J. H. Dendy, Odry. for $300. Pd. WILLIAM
THOMBS $18.55. Citation published at Perkins Creek Meeting House. In-
ventory made by SMITH WHITE, JOHN A. MOORE, JAMES BIDY.

ANDERSON, MARIA Box 7 No. 86
    Estate admr. 12 Dec. 1836 by ROBERT ANDERSON, GEORGE T. ANDERSON,
JACOB WARLEY, J. P. HARRIS bound to J. H. Dendy, Ordy. in sum of $30,000.
Had 15 slaves. Citation published at Hopewell Church.

BRIGGS, ROBERT H. Box 7 No. 87
    Estate admr. 2 May 1836 by JANE L. BRIGGS, WILLIAM HOLCOMBE, BAILEY
BARTON, BENJAMIN HAGOOD, ELIJAH WATSON, JR. bound to J. H. Dendy, for
$30,000. Left 4 legatees. A. S. BOGGS rec'd $2700.68 from sd estate
due him. JOHN O. GRISHAM rec'd from MRS. JANE L. ARNOLD, formerly one
of the admrs. $114.00. For the benefit of my wife. Due to his wife
HARRIET GRISHAM...Citation published at New Hope Church. Inventory
made 12 May 1836 by R. B. DUNCAN, JOHN BOWEN, WM. BOWEN, JAMES OSBORN,
JOHN ROBINSON. Owned 14 slaves. MYRA L. BRIGGS, a legatee. 1 Jan. 1841
pd. JANE L. ARNOLD for HENRY, $17.75.

HAMILTON, DAVID SR. Box 7 No. 89
    Will dated 20 Feb. 1830. Proven 7 Nov. 1837. Wife, JANE HAMILTON.
Granddaughters: MARGARET & JANE HAMILTON. Children: MARGARET PEATEE,
MARGARET PRATER, ELIZABETH PERRONS, ANDREW HAMILTON, DAVID L. HAMILTON,
MARY HILLPATRICK?, BETHSHABA FRASER. Stepson: THOMAS G. BOGGS. Exrs.:
son, ANDREW HAMILTON, MAJOR ANDREW HAMILTON, COL. DAVID K. HAMILTON.
Wit: J. L. MC CANN, FIELDING FENNELL, ROBERT MC CANN, D. CHAMBLIN.
MARGARET & SHELBY BATES & JOHN E. ODELL rec'd $32.58½ from sd estate.

MULLINIX, MATTHEW SR. Box 7 No. 90
    Estate admr. 20 Mar. 1837 by WILLIAM SMITH, ELIAS MULLINIX, FIELDS
MULLINIX bound to J. H. Dendy, ORdy. for $2000. Citation published
at Providence Church. Left a widow and 9 children. To 1 mare taken
by ABNER MULLINIX, at appraisement of $100. Bed, cow, side board taken
by KETURAH MULLINIX, $67.00. Inventory made by EDWARD NORTON, BARNETT
H. ALLGOOD, JOSEPH TAYLOR, Legacy coming from estate of JOHN MULLINIX,
late of Spartanburg Dist., $266.86. Pd. ABNER MULLINIX for proven acct.
$229.

HENDRICKS, MOSES SR. Box 7 No. 91
    Estate admr. 30 Jan. 1837 by MOSES HENDRICKS, DUNCAN HENDRICKS,
WILLIAM L. KEITH bound to J. H. Dendy, Ord. for $800. DAVID HAYES had
money coming from lands of MOSES HENDRICKS. Citation published at Oolenoy Church. Heirs: MOSES HENDRICKS, SUSANNA HENDRICKS. Rec'd of LARKIN
HENDRICKS, $52.00. Rec'd of MOSES HENDRICKS, JR. $55.

MC DOW, WILLIAM PINKNEY Box 7 No. 92
    Estate admr. 4 Dec. 1837 by WILLIAM MC DOW, ROBERT GAINES bound
to J. H. Dendy, Ord. for $900. WILLIAM H. MC DOW & ELIZABETH M. MC-
DOW of Monroe Co., Miss. were minor heirs. On 6 Dec. 1850, G. W. MITCH-
ELL states that WM. P. MC DOW died some 10 or 15 years since, leaving
a widow MARGARET A MC DOW and two children, since that time I have
married the widow. Owned land on 18 Mile Creek.

STANDRIDGE, JAMES SR. Box 7 No. 94
    Estate admr. 5 Sept. 1837 by ISAAC STANDRIDGE, WILLIAM SIMPSON,

Cont'd:
JOHN RIDER bound to J. H. Dendy, Ord. for $4000. Inventory made by
JOHN HUGS, LAMECH CHAMBERS, JOHN CHAMBERS. On 20 Apr. 1842, JAMES CHAMB-
ERS of Lauderdale Co., Ala. appointed JOSEPH W. MC BEE of Dade Co.,
Ga. his attorney to receive his portion of his fathers estate of Pickens
Dist., S. C. Pd. JOHN STANDRIDGE $150.44. Pd. SAMUEL STANDRIDGE $150.55.
Pd. JOHN RIDER $150.44. Pd. SINTHY WIGINGTON $11.43. Pd. MARY STAND-
RIDGE $828.57. Pd. JOHN CARVER $11.43. Pd. THOS. VISAGE $11.43. JOSEPH
STANDRIDGE bought one plough and stock.

MURPHREE, LEVI Box 7 No. 95
    Will dated 22 Oct. 1836. Proven 20 Feb. 1837. Wife:THURSEY MUR-
PHREE. Children: JEMIMA LOOPER, ELISHA MURPHREE, HUDGINS MURPHREE,
ELIAS MURPHREE, RUTH HAINS, MARGARET DILLARD, DELILA ROPER, RODA HEN-
DRIX, ENOCH MURPHREE. "Leave one mare colt to JOHN BARIN provided he
stays out his time until he become 21." Wit: JOHN STEPHENS, READIN
FREEMAN, J. M. BARTON. Son: ENOCK MURPHREE.

THOMAS, ISAAC Box 8 No. 97
    Estate admr. 26 Feb. 1838 by MARTHA THOMAS, LEMUEL THOMAS,WILLIAM
K. ALEXANDER, W. L. KEITH bound to J. H. Dendy, Ord. in sum of $6000.
Inventory made 24 Mar. 1838 by WILLIAM K. ALEXANDER, ELIJAH ALEXANDER,
WILLIAM W. GASSAWAY.

HANES, JOHN Box 8 No. 98
    Will dated 11 Apr. 1838. Proven 18 June 1838. Wife: SUSANNAH HANES.
Children: LIDIAN ANN & (rest is missing from notes..Ed.)

BRUCE, CHARLES Box 8 No. 99
    Estate admr. by ROBERT BRUCE, JAMES M. BRUCE of Georgia, GEORGE
C. CLEVELAND bound to J. H. Dendy, Ord. sum of $1600. Dated 8 Mar.
1838. CHARLES BRUCE, late of the state of Georgia. ROBERT BRUCE, the
father of sd deceased. Pd. BENJAMIN F. BRUCE, $30.70. 12 Mar. 1838
to cash rec'd in settlement with the admrs. of DAVID SLOAN, dec'd.
as pr. enclosed statement. $544.61.

CARNE, THOMAS WILLIAM Box 8 No. 100
    Will dated 8 Sept. 1838. Proven 8 Oct. 1838. Wife: ELIZABETH CARNE.
Children (not named). Owned land on Cane Creek. Wit: FRANCIS JENKINS,
ANDERSON JENKINS, CORNELIUS P. DUPRE. 3 slaves.

YOUNG, ANNA Box 8 No. 101
    Estate admr. 31 July 1838 by JAMES YOUNG, JAMES FANT, JESSE BRAD-
BERRY bound to J. H. Dendy, Ord. for $3000.

SMITHSON, ASA Box 8 No. 102
    Estate admr. 23 Nov. 1838 by LEONARD TOWERS, BIRDWELL HILL, JOSHUA
PERKINS bound to J. H. Dendy, Ord. sum of $8000. Pd. C. A. SMITHSON
legatee, $592.87. Citation published at Bachelors Retreat. VIOLET BOW-
MAN, rec'd $103.50. Pd. DAVID E. SMITHSON, legatee, $542.60½. Owned
8 slaves. Pd. NANCY SMITHSON, legatee, $582.37.

SMITH, JOE Box 8 No. 103
    Will dated 22 Apr. 1835. Proven 15 Jan. 1838. Wife: ELIZABETH
SMITH. Children: HANNAH BLAIR, JOHN O. SMITH, PERMERLY SMITH, REBECCA
MULLINAX, SARAH NORRIS, BENJAMIN SMITH, JOBE SMITH, EZEKIEL SMITH,
ANDREW SMITH, dec'd. children. Wit: JEREMIAH WILLIAMS, DAVID WILLIAMS,
JOSIAH FARMER. Rec'd of LEURANA SMITH, $31.25. Citation published at
Merritts Meeting House.

YOWELL, JAMES Box 8 No. 104
    Owned 3 slaves. Sale bill made 2 Mar. 1839.

SIMS, JOHN Box 8 No. 105
    Estate admr. 9 Oct. 1838 by WILLIAM SIMS, JAMES A. DOYLE, BARTON
ABBETT, CUNNINGHAM ORR bound to J. H. Dendy Ord. for $1200. 3 Feb.
1845. JAMES A. DOYLE, ANDREW F. LEWIS Guardians of JOHN SIMS, a minor
under 21 years..a son..Advanced to JACOB SIMS $59.00. Advanced to JAMES
NICHOLS $67.25. To WILLIAM SIMS $54.50. To GEORGE SIMS $30.00. Advanced

Cont'd:
$40.00 to PATTERSON ORR(?). Left a widow and 7 children.

CANNON(?), RICHARD L. Box 8 No. 107
Estate admr. 29 July 1839 by WILLIAM HOLCOMBE, ELIJAH WATSON bound to J. H. Dendy, Ord. for $900. Citation published at Poplar Springs Meeting House. RICHARD L. CANNON(?) was a young man who died near Pendleton, had several brothers and sisters living in different states.

MC WHORTER, JOHN Box 8 No. 108
Will - 23 Jan. 1839. Wife, MARY MC WHORTER. Children: SARAH L. MC WHORTER, MARY M. MC WHORTER, BELINDA A. MC WHORTER, ELIZA ANN MC WHORTER, DAVID W. MC WHORTER, MOSES E. MC WHORTER, JOHN N. MC WHORTER, ISAAC A. MC WHORTER, ANDREW P. MC WHORTER. Wit: JAMES H. DENDY, PENDLETON ISBELL, RANSOM FRACHURE.

CROW, FRANCIS Box 8 No. 109
Estate admr. 11 Feb. 1839 by RICHARD BRYAN, MILES M. NORTON bound to J. H. Dendy, for the sum of $260.

LIVELY, THOMAS SR. Box 8 No. 110
Will dated 8 May 1836. Proven 10 June 1839. Wife, RACHEL LIVELY. Children: JANE LIVELY, JOHN LIVELY. Grandson, MARK LIVELY. "Give JOHN LIVELY land near Stewart Creek." Wit: BAILEY BARTON, THOMAS GARVIN, VINCENT JAMES.

CLEVELAND, ABSALOM Box 9 No. 112
Estate admr. 5 Mar. 1839 by THOMAS HARBIN, LEONARD TOWERS, bound to J. H. Dendy, Ord. for $700. Was late of Franklin Co., Georgia. Citation published at Bethel Meeting House 17 Feb. 1839. Inventory made 10 May 1839 by JABEZ JONES, JOSEPH RUST, WM. BARTON..."Mr. BENSON states he has heard CLEVELAND say his wife had left him, did not appear to think she was dead, would not speak to some persons. Not long before his death, seemed to think his wife was dead." Mr. BOGGS arrested him for shooting HARBIN, his son-in-law.

COLLINS, JOHN Box 9 No. 113
Estate admr. 3 June 1839 by JOHN CLAYTON, WILLIAM W. GASSAWAY, bound to J. H. Dendy, Ord. for $200. Inventory made 16 Mar. 1840 by WM. GASSAWAY, HIRAM GIBSON. Buyers: JOHN REED, HIRAM GIBSON, JOHN CALHOUN, FOUNTAIN MC KINNEY, NAMAN CURTIS, JAMES AKIND, WM. W. GASSAWAY, DAVID ALEXANDER, JOHN OWENS, JAMES M. LEACH.

STEGALL, SPENCER Box 9 No. 114
Estate admr. 18 Mar. 1839 by WILLIAM HOLCOMBE, JOSEPH B. REID, bound to J. H. Dendy, Ord. for $300. Citation published at Watsons Meeting House, 21 Apr. 1839. Late of Georgia.

MILLER, ELISHA Box 9 No. 116
Will proven 24 Oct. 1839. Children: CATHARINE, wife of JAMES BEATY, SALLY, wife of REUBEN BARRATT, ELIZABETH, wife of JOSEPH ROBERSON, MARGARET, wife of PINGUE HAWKINS FRASER, JANE, wife of JOHN DOYAL, FANNY, wife of RICHARD DENNINGTON, POLLY MILLER, ELISHA MILLER, PARKER C. MILLER. Wife: JANE MILLER. Wit: N. HULL, PARKER C. MILLER, ELISHA MILLER, JR.

REEDER, THOMAS MILTON Box 9 No. 117
Will dated 27 Feb. 1840. Proven 11 Apr. 1840. Heirs: brothers BENJAMIN F. REEDER, LEWIS W. REEDER, SAMUEL C. REEDER, ANDREW P. REEDER; sisters MATILDA HARBIN, MARY CLEVELAND. Half-sister SARAH WARD. Half-brother JOEL REEDER. AMANDA F. REEDER, an heir.

CHAPMAN, JOHN Box 9 No. 118
Estate admr. 6 Apr. 1840 by SAMUEL CHAPMAN, MOSES HENDRICKS, JOSHUA CHAPMAN, bound to J. H. Dendy, Ord. for $1000. SAMUEL CHAPMAN, a son. Left a widow and 4 children. Inventory made 21 Apr. 1840 by J. B. REID, MOSES HENDRICKS, STEPHEN C. REID, JAMES TROTTER.

ANDERSON, JOHN Box 9 No. 119 (cont'd next page)

Cont'd:
Estate admr. 17 Feb. 1840 by WILLIAM NIMMONS, WILLIAM L. KEITH, ELIJAH ALEXANDER, bound to J. H. Dendy, Ordy. in sum of $600. 18 Nov. 1841, RACHEL REESE rec'd $32.00 from estate..was an heir. ANDREW J. ANDERSON note $30. ANDREW DAVIS & MARY ANDERSON bought goods at sale $9.62½. Heirs: RHODA BERRY, JANE ANDERSON, MOSES ANDERSON..Pd. to THOMAS & MARY TURNER pr their Power of Attorney $82.27. Citation published at Mountain Spring 16 Feb. 1840.

HALLUMS, WILLIAM Box 9 No. 120?
(This package was too dirty to copy..Ed.)
SANDFORD, WILLIAM Box 9 No. 120
Will dated 9 Aug. 1838. Proven 18 Oct. 1839. Son, BARACK J. SAND-FORD..Wife (not named) "remaining part of estate to be divided between JOHN & ROBERT DICKSON." Wit: JOHN HUGHS, SPENCER CHAMBERS, JOHN CHAMBERS.

ADAMS, JACOB Box 9 No. 121
Estate admr. 17 May 1841 by MARY ADAMS, THOMAS GASSAWAY, LEWIS OWEN bound to J. H. Dendy, Ordy. for $1600. MARY ADAMS, the widow. Left widow and 4 heirs. 1841 cash pd to JOHN ADAMS, $1.50. JOHN ADAMS, a son. MARY ANN ADAMS, a daughter. NANCY C. STRICKLIN, a daughter and MARSHALL STRICKLIN rec'd share. Citation published at Mt. Zion. S. J. ADAMS, a son.

HARRISON, THOMAS Box 9 No. 122
Estate admr. 24 Nov. 1841 by MARTIN HARRISON, J. N. F. PERRY, ARON TERRELL bound to J. H. Dendy, Ordy. for $16,000. Citation published at Bethel Church 14 Nov. 1841. 1 Jan. 1841 pd. taxes for Georgia land two years $12.64. 3 Jan. 1841 rec'd of CATHARINE BLAIR, $25.00 on a lease of land. 13 Mar. rec'd of OLIVER HARRISON $4.18 3/4. Owned 9 slaves. Inventory made by M. J. F. PERRY, GEORGE C. CLEVELAND, E. P. VERNER. Widow, NANCY HARRISON, $2887.00. Settlement, pd. MARY STO-VALL in full $1251. Pd. S. D. DORTCH in full $624.59. Pd. ELIM FARMER in full $632. Pd. AARON TERRELL in full $579.93. Pd. SHADRACK HARRISON in full $1036.93 3/4. Pd. JOHN LEGRAND in full $888. Pd. CATHARINE BLAIR in full $617.60. Left widow and 8? legatees.

BARTON, DAVID Box 9 No. 123
Will dated 11 Feb. 1842. Proven 9 Mar. 1842. Wife, WINNA BARTON "Give place along sd road to Jenkin's line, and Tugaloos River: Children ELEANOR, DAVID, WILLIAM E. BARTON." "Give WILLIAM land deeded to me by WILLIAM BLAIR in Franklin Co., Ga." Sons: CLOUD T. BARTON, ELIAS BARTON, DANIEL BARTON, PETER BARTON, DAVID O. BARTON. Daus.: SALLY BAKER, RUTHY CALHOUN, FANNY CALHOUN. Owned land leading from Cleveland's Ferry to Fair Play, S.C. Owned 16 slaves. Wit: JOHN VERNER, LEONARD TOWERS, EBENEZER VERNER.

WALKER, WILLIAM Box 9 No. 124
Estate admr. 22 Feb. 1841 by JOHN S. WALKER, THOMAS H. MC CANN, W. L. KEITH, WILLIAM BOGGS, F. N. GARVIN bound to J. H. Dendy, Ordy. for $50,000. Citation published at Carmel Church. Pd. A. FULLER for sale of rail road stock, $350. Left a widow and 7 children. Advanced to D. K. HAMILTON, T. W. ALEXANDER, T. H. MC CANN, JAMES WALKER, MATILDA WALKER, ELIZA WALKER. Advanced to J. S. WALKER. Cash pd J. S. LORTON on 4 shares in Louisville, Cincinatti & Charles Rail Road $20. Pd. ALFRED FULLER in full $225.74 1/4. Pd. JANE WALKER in full $790.09 1/2. Pd. T. W. ALEXANDER share in full $223.68 1/4. Owned 29 slaves.

BOYD, RACHEL Box 9 No. 125
Estate admr. 6 Sept. 1841 by JOSIAH W. COBB, AZARIAH P. COBB, FREDERICK N. GARVIN bound to J. H. Dendy, Ordy. in sum of $2000. Pd. expenses from Washington to Baltimore $5.00. From Philadelphia to Baltimore $21.50. RACHEL CANNON (alias BOYD) rec'd. $135.62 as her proportion of the estate of JAMES BOYD, dec'd. Pd. expenses of admr. to and from Lancaster, Penn. $191.75. Letters: Pickens Dist.: 18 Aug. 1841, "This is to certify that I am the brother of RACHEL BOYD, dec'd., who was a transient person having no permanent place of residence. She resided the greater portion of her time with her friends in Pickens Dist., S. C., Habersham Co., Ga., was not her home. She deceased there

Cont'd:
while on a visit." RT.(?) BOYD before JOSEPH POWELL, Notary Public, JOHN MASINGIL.

HENDERSON, MAJOR THOMAS Box 10 No. 126
Estate admr. 14 June 1841 by JAMES HENDERSON, JOHN ARIAIL, STEPHEN WATSON, STEPHEN REID bound to J. H. Dendy, Ordy. for $20,000. Citation published at Carmel Church. 3 Apr. 1845 pd. NATHANIEL HENDERSON his share in full $1362.53. Pd. JACOB GEARIN & ABIGAIL GEARIN as Pr. their rec't. $1062.53. Pd. JOHN M. CANSLER in full his share $262.58. Pd. THOMAS M. CANSLER his share $264.48. Pd. F. H. CANSLER his share legatee $100. Pd. JOHN CANSLER, SR. legatee, $10. Owned 11 slaves. Inventory made by WILLIS ROBINSON, STEPHEN C. REID, WILLIAM S. BIRGE. Advances were made to JOHN HENDERSON, JOHN CANSLER and wife ANN, WILLIAM CANSLER and wife ELIZABETH, NATHANIEL HENDERSON, JACOB GUERIN and wife ABIGAIL.

RICHARDS, THOMAS Box 10 No. 127
Estate admr. 3 May 1841 by WILLIAM TODD, JAMES DOYLE, JOHN RANKINS, P. ALEXANDER bound to J. H. Dendy, Ordy. for $1000. 1842 pd. ELIZABETH RICHARDS $146.25. Citation published at Bethel Church. JAMES TODD, the bro.-in-law of JANE, wife of HUGH ERSKINE now residing in Tenn. Entitled to a share from her father's estate, she has a large family to support.

RACKLEY, WILLIAM Box 10 No. 128
Estate admr. 7 Sept. 1841 by REDEN RACKLEY, LARKIN HENDRICKS, HENSON HUNT bound to J. H. Dendy, Ordy. in sum of $1200. Left widow and 9 children. Pd. WINNEY E. RACKLEY, ELIZA C. RACKLEY, ADALINE RACKLEY, REDEN RACKLEY a son..B. RACKLEY, a son, MARY RACKLEY, widow. Citation published at Cross Roads Church. WARREN B. RACKLEY, a son, MAHALA C. RACKLEY, a dau. THOMAS & LEWIS RACKLEY state "if the heirs of SARAH AYRES never apply for amount due them, the note be void otherwise."

MARTIN, GIDEON Box 10 No. 129
Estate admr. 21 Dec. 1840 by MARGARET MARTIN, GARNER EVANS, JAMES MAULDIN of Georgia, bound to J. H. Dendy, Ordy. for $6000. One note on E. MERITT and E. MADDEN for $400(?) due 1 Oct. 1840 given 12 Oct. 1838 interest 1/2 on date. Put in suit in Georgia, Admr. granted to D. MARTIN. Inventory made 27 Feb. 1841 by T. G. BOGGS, C. H. BROCK, JOHN TEMPLETON. Citation published at Carmel Church. MARY HAMILTON saw GARNER EVANS deliver papers to GIDEON MARTIN..EDY MARTIN also an admr.

END OF RECORDS

PICKENS CO., S. C. MISCELLANEOUS RECORDS

JOHN MILLER. Attempt to Ravish. Pack. 539-14
ELIZABETH PRATHER the proscr. sworn says, On the 9th June 1886 she had been to MR. KENNEMORE's after some honey and came back by Mr. KIRK MAULDIN's mill in Pickens Co. for her meal...it was near sundown when she left the mill and JOHN MILLER was going home and went along with her from Mr. SMITH's the miller..he went with her about 1/4 of a mile to where the path left the public road but did not say anything disrespectful up to that time. Mrs. SMITH asked to carry the meal for her, the sd proscr. and he did so, to where the path left road that after she started along the path thru the woods home, JOHN followed her a short distance from the public road and said he wanted to have to do with her and she said she had quit all such as that and would not, that she was trying to live right, he said he would have to do with her..she told him no that if he did she would hollow and cry, but he took hold of her around the waist and throwed her down in the road and tryed to pull up her clothes and did prevent him from getting them up much, she told him she would tell it if he did not let her alone and he quit and told her if she would not tell it he would get her some coffee, she told him she did not want the coffee, she told it to her daughter as soon as she got home and to Mrs. JOHN SMITH the next morning. ELIZABETH PRATHER.

JAMES AIKEN. Disturbing Religious Meeting. Pack. 539-16, Pickens, S.C.
Clerk of Court
          T. P. LOOPER one of the proscr. says, I know JAMES AIKEN. I saw
him at Cross Roads Church on the 5th Sunday in May 1886. I saw him
coming down by the grave yard in a lope hollowing at persons whom he
knew as if he had been at muster ground. What acquaintance I had with
him I knew he was under the influence of spirits. Some time after he
came I was assisting the congregation in getting seated so as to make
as much room as possible and was getting some boys to come out to make
room for some ladies. AIKEN was standing in front of the door and he
commenced saying come out of there seat. The last time I saw him during
the service he was at a window talking to a girl which attracted the
attention of many. Cross Examined. How do you know that I was under
the influence of spirits because you was acting the fool and talking
so much and having so much to attend to and using almost any expression
that anybody could think of. I heard you use the word hell more than
once...J. B. HOWARD sworn says. The first time I saw AIKEN was early
in the day coming up by the school house walking, then I did not see
him for some time after about ten oclock I saw him coming down by the
grave yard and he met some one and he hollowed out. Ha I wish every
other day was sunday and the other a wet day and buckries? was bis-
cuits and Jesus Christ was down here on earth would we not have a time.
Some time after this I saw him in the church yard and he had a piece
of bread in his hand and I heard him say to DANIEL BOYD dont you want
a piece of bread and DAN said no and AIKEN said take it take it and
go off in the woods and eat it like a dog.....

SAM CANNON. Escape. Pack 539-17, Clerks Office, Pickens, S.C.
          NERO HALLUMS says, I live in Pickens Co. I know the defendants
A. T. BAKER and PATRICK RUSSELL. They live in Pickens County. They
had a man in a wagon unknown to me, they were in my yard. I live on
the road from Central to Pickens, 4 miles from Central. Mr. BAKER said
his horse had given out and they had a prisoner going to jail and wanted
to get a horse. I had only one mule at home and it had never been worked
we put the harness on it and it kicked the harness off and they were
afraid to work it, they then sent up to my brothers for a horse or
mule and they failed to get one. They started down to ELIAS ANDERSON
and BAKER asked me to go with them to get a horse and left his horse
at my house. The prisoner was in the wagon. RUSSELL pulling the wagon.
BAKER told RUSSELL to stay there and mind the prisoner until he came
back, and as they were getting back into the prisoner escaped. It was
dark and about 7 or 8 oclock, heard them running. RUSSELL ordered the
prisoner to stop and shot 5 or 6 times. BAKER turned back, he was in
the road between my house and ELIAS ANDERSON's and went to RUSSELL
who was in pursuit of the prisoner, they followed about a quarter of
a mile, until they got in the woods. I went up to the woods. They came
back to my house and stayed a while about 1/2 an hour then went back
towards Central. The prisoner went that direction to. They put the
horse to wagon and both got in wagon, they had brought the wagon in
the yard after the escape..they drove out the yard. The first I knew
he was trying to escape was when AARON GARVIN told RUSSELL his man
was out the wagon and RUSSELL immediately ordered him to stop. AARON
GARVIN has gone to Arkansas. The escape was on sat. night.

ALLEN GILLAM & ARMINDA FORTNER. Rape. Pack. 544 No. 2 Clerks Office.
Pickens, S. C.
          ARMINDA FORTNER sworn says, that on thursday evening the 29th
April 1875 in Pickens County one ALLEN GILHAM the prisoner in court
was in a gully, as she passed along a path way up the creek lying or
squatted down, at a distance 10 steps, he said Stop right there dam
you or I will kill you, at which time I started to run and he ran to
me and took hold of me in the road, and said to me go up the gully
and let him.....or he would kill me. I said let me go home to my children and don't kill me, to which he replied hush or he would kill me
right there. He then caught me by the right arm, and forced me to follow
him into the gully, about 10 steps and forced me by strength and against
my will, and when he had done as he desired, he said to me to get up
from there and run home and not stop until you get there, that if I
did, he would kill me and said he was one of these robbers and had

362

Cont'd:
killed 2 or 3 already and that he was going to my house that night
and that he was going to kill me. He had red mud rubbed on both sides
of his face. When I first saw him, and had his pants down as he came
up, with his nakedness visible and also had a rock in each hand, one
of them wider than my hand, and held these rocks in his hands all the
time and had them in his hand when I left him...Cross Examined. Says
she is 41 yrs old, is a widow, her husband died in the war, has 6 children, youngest 3 yrs old in July. The rape occured between 1 and 2 oclock
P.M. did not eat any dinner that day at SAM GILHAM's house. I stopped
a few minutes, went in the house, ALLEN was in the yard when I got
to the house and was gone when I came out, did not see him any more
until I saw him in the gully. He had on a pale dirty looking pants,
did not leave the house before ALLEN. I was on the direct road from
ALLEN's house to my house when I was abused. I did not stay at ALLENs
house more than 1/4 hour do not think. After the act I went by JASPER
FORTNER's and by JAMES FORTNER's and from there home. I saw CHARLOTTE
FORTNER, JASPER's wife at J. F. house and did not stay very long, had
the head ache and was sick, and did not say anything to them about
ALLEN, then went to old lady FORTNER's, stayed there some time and
did not say any thing there about ALLEN and from there went home and
found my children late in the evening. Stayed there with my three children until about dark and went to GEORGE FORTNER and found his wife
and did not say anything about (end of page - no continuation).

Murder of FRENCH P. WILLARD. Pack. 545 No. 2 Clerks Office, Pickens,
S.C.
    On July 28, 1869, THOMAS E. WILLARD made oath that he is the father
of FRENCH P. WILLARD with whose murder T. EDWARD BOGGS and MARCUS BOGGS
are charged with. That the warrant against them was issued upon the
affidavit of JOHN B. HUBBARD Chief Constable of the State of S. C.
and that this deponent supposed and believed that sd HUBBARD was the
Proscr. against sd defendants and would take all the steps which were
necessary to collect testimony and secure the attendance of all the
witnesses at this term of the court, that this deponent relying upon
the sd HUBBARD taking these steps did not begin to make any preparation
for the trial of the above case until some 10 days ago, when he did
have a number of witnesses recognized to attend court, but that the
shortness of the time has prevented him from procuring the attendance
of several important witnesses. This deponent therefore prays for a
continuance of the case and believes that if sd continuance is granted
he will be able to procure important testimony which he will be unable
to present at this time. That there is a freed woman whose name and
exact residence this deponent is at present was acquainted with, but
which he can procure who testimony he believes to be important, and
will go to show that these defendants were guilty of the crime with
which they are charged. That MISS AMY YOUNG is an important witness
for the prosecution but is at present too sick to attend and consequently has not been recognized to this court, that she had a conversation with one of the defendants which showed that he had some knowledge of the sd murder. That S. F. TEMPLETON lives in Anderson as this
deponent believes and believes the sd TEMPLETON to be an important
witness, but has not had time to procure his attendance. Sworn to this
July 28, 1869.

A drawing of the killing in this package.

JAMES LADD, Disturbing Religious Meeting. Pack. 546 No. 1 Clerks Court.
Pickens, S. C.
    A complaint was made by WESLEY GRIFFIN that at the Negroes Church
in Pickens County on June 19, 1881 one JAMES LADD did disturb a religious meeting, by selling candy...that he sold candy about 100 yards
distant. Saw a large crowd around him...That several parties carried
candy into the church, there was continually some one going from the
church to where LADD was selling the candy...that the meeting was dis=-
turbed by the raising from church to where LADD was selling the candy.

JEFF HAGOOD. Burglary. Pack. 546-2. Clerks Office. Pickens, SC.
    WILLIAM WATKINS states at his house in Pickens County on or about
the 20th day April 1881 JEFF HAGOOD did break open his corn crib after

Cont'd:
night and steal about 1 bushel of corn. The corn crib was about 10 yards from his dwelling house and that he did remove the stick that fastened the door...JOSEPH WERNER sworn says on the night of April 21, 1881 as he was going from Central he met JEFF HAGOOD about 200 yards from WATKINS house in a pine thicket with about 4 pecks of corn on his back. Said that he had got it from WATKINS. After talking with him a while he confessed to entering the crib and taking the corn.

MACK GOWAN. Murder of ANDY ANDERSON. Pack. 546 No. 3 Clerks Office, Pickens, S. C.
An inquest was held in Pickens County Jan. 5, 1881 before THOMAS PARKINS Coroner to view the body of ANDREW ANDERSON of Pickens Co. where and by what means the sd ANDERSON came to his death and upon the jurys oath do say, That the blow given by MACK GOWAN alias MACK BLYTHE upon the head of the dec'd. in the kitchen of Major JAMES H. AMBLER on last sunday night 3 weeks was the cause of his death...JACOB LAY sworn says, I know the dec'd. On sunday Dec. 1880 I was in Major Ambler's kitchen. Mr. Anderson went in and called for me and when he got to me caught me by the hair of the head, says where is that God dam nigger and struck MACK GOWAN on the shoulder. Mack moved his chair but said nothing, reached over and got a piece of pine and struck Mr. Anderson who fell on the floor. Struck him on the forepart of his head. Mr. Anderson lay about a second or more and trying to get up caught the door and it gave way so he fell out at door backward on his head. Door about 3 ft. high. Was a rock and block at door but do not know if he struck either. Have seen him several times at his house since that. About 3 weeks since he was struck...ALFRED PRICE sworn says, I live in Pickens County with Mr. Ambler...Have known the dec'd. for 6 or 7 years. I was in Mr. Ambler's kitchen on sunday night about 3 weeks ago and Mr. Anderson came in and got after Mack Gowan for some money he owed him. Mack told him he did not have it. He came into the kitchen the 2nd time and after taking hold of Jake and me he asked for that damned nigger and says here he is and struck Mack on shoulder.. Mrs. ROSA ANDERSON sworn says the dec'd. is my husband.

On Jan. 12, 1881 THOMAS A. MC MAHAN made oath that he is informed that MILLY BOWEN did on Jan. 11, 1881 go into his cornfield and steal thereof run and carry away one fourth bushel of corn...PERRY MANSELL sworn says he lives upon THOS. A. MC MAHAN land...I know MILLY BOWEN. On Tues., Jan. 10th I saw her at FED BLASSINGAMES house. She had some corn at Feds. I asked her where she got it, she first denied having got it out of Mr. McMahans field. Afterwards she owned that she did, said it was not stealing, that she took it in broad open daylight. Clerks Office, Pickens, S.C. Pack. 546-4.

BETSEY LEWIS a single woman of Pickens Dist. that on Jan. the 14th last she was delivered of a femal bastard child and that HUGH CRAFFORD is the father of said child. JOHN LEWIS made oath that BETSEY LEWIS was delivered of a child. Dated Sept. 14, 1843. Clerks Office, Pickens Co. Pack. 547-1.

On Sept. 23, 1842 THOMAS LEGRAND made oath that JAMES PARTAIN is now living in adultry with MARY HONEA a widow. That JAS. PARTAIN has a wife and seven children now living in Anderson Dist. Clerks Office, Pickens, S. C. Pack. 547 No. 2.

POLLY ANN MILLER. Vagrancy. Pack. 547-3. Clerks Office, Pickens, SC.
The charge made against POLLY ANN MILLER for Vagrancy is for being to great with a negro boy belonging to Mrs. MC CLURE...ABNER HUTCHINS sworn says that on last saturday on his way to church about half a mile from home he saw Polly Ann Miller and Mrs. McClure's negro man Jeff together in the very act, he stopped and they appeared very loving as much as any two he had ever seen...Mrs. ESTHER MC CLURE sworn says that Polly Ann Miller has lived about her house about 2 years, the first part of her time (that is the defendants). She further states that the def't. is a smart and industrious girl as regarding work. She had a mind of turning her off some time before the above took place. She also stated that Jeff wished Polly to stay if she was turned off,

Cont'd:
he Jeff would not stay any longer with his mistress. JAMES YOUNG states
that all he knows is mostly from report, mostly he saw the negro Jeff
and defendant conversing very friendly together...THOMAS HUTCHINS he
has understood her character heretofore had been bad, that she was
drove from Georgia for taking up with a mulatto, also reports says
that def't. stayed all night in Mrs. McClure's negro house...JOHN MYERS
says all he knows is that she was caught in a negro house in the neighborhood of Bachalors Retreat...The court found her not guilty....

On Dec. 10, 1838 CATHARINE ROTHEL made oath that on May 5th last
at the house of her father CLAYBORN ROTHEL in Pickens Dist. she was
delivered of a male bastard child and that WILLIAM D. DEATON is the
father of said child. Clerks Office, Pickens, S.C. Pack. 549-3.

On March 11, 1836 MARY NIX of Greenville Dist., single woman made
oath that on Sept. 2 last past in Pickens Dist. she was delivered of
a femal bastard child and that FRANCIS HOLDEN, farmer, is charged with
being the father of sd child. Clerks Office, Pickens. Pack. 549-4.

PICKENS CO., S. C. VARIOUS PROBATE LETTERS

Addressed to M. M. NORTON, Esq., Pickens CH, S.C. Postmarked Greenville
CH March 12...Greenville Mar. 12, 1843. Dear Sir, I recd yours of this
morning and should ___? very glad to have seen you...I spoke to Mr.
JOS. JAMES and it will suit him well for me to get the note he gave
to Mr. GRISHAM. I hope Genl. GARVIN can pay the note at Court. I send
below a copy of a note which I request you to issue on for MAY? PERRY
as he told me you acted for him. I will send the original over by him.
Yrs. respect'y, JOSIAH KILGORE. (Copy) $168.59 One day after date I
promised to pay LESTER KILGORE & BATES on order One hundred & sixty
eight dollars 89/100 for value rec'd this 8 Feb. 1841. JOHN A. GUNTER.
1842 March 18 by 298 poor cotton at 5 $14.90

Post card: Postmarked Pickens; addressed to JAYNES & SHELON?, Walhalla,
S. C.
ALLEGHEIN RICE   ) In Common pleas
     vz   ) State of South Carolina
RUTH ALEXANDER et al)County of Pickens

Due legal services in this case acknowledged at Pickens, SC Feby. 9th
1899
                    MINYARD(?) BLASSINGAME
                    Plaintiffs attorney

Post card: Postmarked Liberty, S. C.; addressed to JOAB MAULDIN, Pickens
CH, SC. Dear Sir, Theris an Bale of Cotton on the Platform marked JLM
#3 sold by W. A. HUNTER, ther is a remnent put in this bale if you
can find it did go in this go far it the old man HUNTER sead that it
was put in it No. 22 J. L. CRENSHAW.

Letter postmarked Pickens, return address CHAS. E. ROBINSON, Attorney
at Law, Pickens, S. C. Letter dated Apr. 21, 1896, to Maj. WHITNER
SYMMES, Greenville, S.C...mortgage against the land of Mrs. S. E. WIL-
LIAMS...Very Respectfully, C. E. ROBINSON.

Letter addressed to Mr. WILLIAM A. YOUNG, Pendleton CH, S.C. Dated
25 Feb. 1839. Sir, I have just rec'd youg ___? of the inclosure Col.
ROBT. ANDERSONs acct...receipt dated 17 Dec. 1834...Yrs. respectfully,
ROBERT ANDERSON.

Letter postmarked Greenville CH, S.C. Sept. 8; addressed to WM. L.
KEITH, Esq., Clerk of the Court, Pickens Court House, SC. Headed: Greenville 7th Sept. 1841. Dr. Sir: I enclosed a writ to you to sign and
deliver to your Sheriff you will please observe that the original and
copy are not cut apart, please separate them, and fold them up properly
...my relation to the case of HUFF vs HOLCOMB was complied with, for
which you and Mr. HARRISON will please receive my thanks and I am much
obliged to you for your Kind assurance of a readiness to attend to

Cont'd:
any business for me...G. F. TOWNS.

Letter addressed to Mr. HENRY VICKERS, Greenville, S.C.
    Augusta, 12th Dec. 1835...
Mr. HENRY VICKERS   Bot of Beard and Pitts
5 gals. Cognac Brand (Reg 1.25...............$ 9.69
1 Bbl Rum   43 gals   48............... 20.64
1 Keg Cracker   26   2.86
Paid Drayage & ferriage to Hamburg   .75
                                             33.94
Friend Henry

Your favor covering forty dollars dated the 3rd inst. came to hand
last Saturday and above you have a bill of such articles as I could
purchase...

I recd your letter to WALKER, COVINGTON & FAIR, Hamburg...Oysters and
Oranges there are none in town, but there are some expected in a day
or two...Yours truly, B. GRANGER.

Letter postmarked Decatur, Jan. 22: addressed to HENRY VICKERS, Esq.
Greenville C.H., S.C. Headed: Decatur, Ga., Jan. 22nd 1836. Dear Uncle,
I received your favor of the 10th inst. which I perused with pleasure
until I reached the intelligence of the death of A. DULOE(?), you stated
in your last that you thought I had an heir in that village which belongs to Mr. CAUBLE. Since you have put into my head, I think altogether
yours and you wished to let me know it and did not want to come out
and say it was yours. You as well as I know its not mine for I have
been long enough from home from there to have one in this village and
consequently if it had have been mine it would have disclosed ___?
before this time to confirm my word with Regard to it being yours.
I will give you a Province the first to accuse is generally the actor
of the crime, give my compliments to all inquiring friends. Yrs., H.
O. HORTON.

Letters addressed to MRS. JAMES DEEN(?) in Care of MRS. NOME(?) CRUPTON,
Anderson Co., S.C., Belton(?) P. O...Headed Greenville County, March
6, 1880. Dear Cousent Nancey...(personal letter) (signed) JANE CARR.

Letter addressed to Maj. WHITNER SYMMES, Greenville, S. C. return address W. H. HESTER, Central, S. C. Dated 4/4/1887. Headed: Office of
W. H. HESTER Merchandise and Guanos...Signed, W. H. HESTER.

Letter addressed to A. BLYTHE, Esq., Greenville, S. C.
Dear BLYTHE: Enclose you P. C. from ROBINSON-MOONEY is paid and has
furnised(?) so often to attend to the case...I cannot get a thing except what I can mortgage on HESTER is absolutely insolvent...have ROB-
INSON fix day positively and no continuances. Apr. 18, 1900. WHITNER
SYMMES.
Post card enclosed: Addressed to Major WHITNER SYMMES, dated April
17, 1900. Dear Major: See your attorney and any day that will suit
you all I can hold the reference in your case against HESTER...Yours
truly, C. E. ROBINSON.

Letter postmarked Apr. 21, 1891. Mize, Ga. Addressed to J. B. NEWBERY,
Pickens New Pickens Co. Dated Apr. 20, 1891, Franklin Co.(?), Ga.
Mr. NEWBERY: I received your letter wer glad to hear from you you wanted
gran mas Name her Name wer MARY all ways went by the Name of POLLEY
the Widdow of TOMEY ALEXANDER Mr. GURDEN BISE wer the DARIUS(?) STRATER.
Yours truley, MARTHA G. GIBSON.

Letter addressed to Mr. T. H. NEWTON, Attorney, Pickens C. H., S.C.
Headed: Sedalis Texas, May the 22, 1891. Mr. J. H. NEWTON, I receive
them summons and don as you sed I want my part of granfathers ALEXANDER
estate give to MILLY RICE and DIANER   JAMES & HANNAH DURHAM and LETTIE
HERD & MALINDA DURHAM & SARAH OAKLEY*BOATNER. HIZZEY LEWIS
(* stricken through)

Letter postmarked Menardville, Texas June 17, 1891; addressed to Mr.

J. H. NEWTON, Pickens C. H., S.C. Dated: June 13, 1891; Dear Sir: I received your summons re regard to the division of the estate of THOMAS ALEXANDER and MARY ALEXANDER. I am one of the heirs of JAMES ALEXANDER. Very resptly, B. O. ALEXANDER, Menardville, Meanrd Co., Texas

Letter postmarked: Shellmound, Tenn. Addressed to J. H. NEWTON, Esq. Pickens, S.C. Dated: May 12, 1891. Dear Sir: The notis came to hand this day. I want the estate to be setled up as the law directs for I am olde and kneed my part. I thought from letters received from JORDAN RICE that you was to wind up the business for us and pay each one what wood be coming to them. Now you have placed me as a defendant and sine your name as Aty for plaintiff. I have never got anything from my father estate at any time. I have understood there was about $300.00 in the office for me and again I heard it was gone and could not be found. I wish you wood investigate the matter and let me know what thear is of it. I dont think I showd loos it for I am in __? life and kneed it. Hoping to hear from you soon. Yours trowley, SARAH BOATNER.

Letter postmarked: Menardville, Texas, May 30, 1891; addressed to J. H. NEWTON, Pickens C. H. Dated: May 12, 1891, Franklin Co., Ga. Mr. Newton. I received your note requesten me to send the names of NANSEY GIBSON children SARY BOYERS is Deed. I will Give you the names of her childring NANSEY MULKEY, FRANK BOYERS, HIZZEY DROGERS(?), MARGIT WHITE dirrect thair letters to Walhalla, S. C. W. H. GIBSON was my husband an is Deed. HIZZEY CRANE her postofs Oakway, S. C. I JOSEPH GIBSON Oakway, S. C. MARY SLONE Mize, Ga. if it is nessery that should send my childrings names le me know when you wright to MARY SLONE. Yours truley, MARTHA J. GIBSON.

Letter postmarked Oakway, S. C. May 26, 1891. Addressed to Mr. J. H. Newton, Pickens. (two letters inside) (1) dated: 5/28/91 Dear Sir: We have received the summons. Respectfully, J. L. ALEXANDER, ALCY CHAS-TAIN. (2) MILLY RICE et al)
        vs   )   In common Pleas Court
    SARAH BOATNER et al)
We hereby accept due and legal service of a copy of the summons in this action May 13, 1891. JOSEPH GIBSON, HEZZIA CRAIN.

Post card postmarked: Mize, Ga., May 21, 1891. Addressed to Mr. Newton, New Pickens P. O., S.C. Mr. Newton: I received you notes with plesure. It wer all wright. I am the youngest child of NANSEY GIBSON. Please let me no when the money will be redy for me..MARY SLONE.

Letter addressed to Mrs. SARAH OKLEY, Toccoa, Ga., marked Return to sender. Summons enclosed: Pickens Co., Court of Common Pleas. MILLY RICE..HANNAH DURHAM..DIANNA JAMES, Plaintiffs Against
SARAH BOATNER, MALINDA DURHAM, LETTIE HERD, SARAH OAKLEY, THOMAS GIBSON, BENJAMIN GIBSON, JANE RICE, SARAH ANN STEWART, ADALINE MARTIN, NEWTON FOSTER, JANE FOSTER, MARY FOSTER, MARTHA FOSTER, MILLIE FOSTER, JAMES MC DUFFIE FOSTER, JAMES L. ALEXANDER, DANIEL C. ALEXANDER, ANNIE M. ALEXANDER, MARY E. ALEXANDER, MARTHA A. ALEXANDER, LILLIE M. ALEXANDER, the heirs of NANCY GIBSON deceased, names and number unknown, the heirs of JAMES ALEXANDER, deceased, names and number unknown, KIZZIE LEWIS, MARTHA J. GIBSON, JN. MURPHREE, T. F.NELSON and HENRY FOSTER, Defendants. To partition the Real Estate of THOMAS ALEXANDER and MARY ALEX-ANDER, deceased, situated in the county and state aforesaid, on waters of Twelve Mile River, 207 acres. May 5, 1891, J. H. Newton, Plaintiff's Attorney. J. M. STEWART, C.C.P.

Letter postmarked: Menardville, Texas, May 29, 1891, addressed to J. H. Newton, Pickens Co., SC. Return address: BALLOU & Co., Dealers in General Merchandise, Menardville, Texas. Dated: May 30, 1891. I received the summons in the case of MILLY RICE, HANNAH DURHAM, and others vs SARAH BOATNER, MALINDA DURHAM and others. I as an heir of JAMES ALEXANDER have no objection to the partition of the real estate of THOMAS & MARY ALEXANDER, dec'd. Yours, JAMES W. ALEXANDER.

Letter addressed to Mr. JORDAN RICE, Nine Times, Pickens Co., S.C. Headed: Shellmound, Apr. 24, /91 Dear Brother: Your note to hand found

Cont'd:
all tolerable well. As to writing the Business in ___? to winde up.
I am willing to do what you think best. I supos Judge Newton will do
right and pay the money over without any troble. Yours, etc. SARAH
BOATNER.
We hereby accept due and legal service of a copy of the summons. May
7, 1891. THOMAS GIBSON, BENJAMIN (X) GIBSON.

Letter addressed to J. H. G. MC DANIAL, Pickens, S.C. Headed: Autun,
S.C. Mch. 17, 1898. Enclosed you will find check for $.46 to pay tax
of WM. WATKINS this was a clear oversight in us & we never once thought
of it until this week. Yours, H. B. DOUTHIT.

Letter postmarked: Mize, Ga., addressed to J. H. Newton, Atty. New
Pickens, S.C. Headed: Ardmore, Ind. Ter., May 23, 1891. Dear Sir: W.
F. BOWEN of Elmont has sent to JNO. T. ALEXANDER of this place your
letter to MRS. KIZZIE LEWIS and printed citation for partition of est.
of THOMAS & MARY ALEXANDER. THOMAS ALEXANDER is the great-grandfather
of JNO. T. ALEXANDER and J. T. A.'s mother and father are both dead.
He has no brothers and sisters living. His father was named J. T. ALEX-
ANDER and we think he is doubtless interested in the estate. He requests
us to write to you, and tell you the facts and ask you to advise him
what interest he has in the estate. Its probably value..and what information if any you desire at his hands? ALEXANDER is engaged in the
Drug Business here and is a good citizen.
                    Yours, HERBERT & LEDBETTER, Atty.
          (above appears to have been in wrong envelope)

Letter postmarked: Liberty, S.C. Feb. 23, 1898. Dated: Feb. 21, 1898.
Dear Mr. MC DANIEL: Your letter recd. contents noted. I am not able
to go to Pickens today will please write me how much the cost is and
cant I attend to it through the mail as money is very limited with
me...Mr. BOGGS has allready caused it to cost me so much unnecessary
trouble and expense. I went to see Mr. STEWART when.....I was up there.
Respt. MRS. JANE SMITH.

Envelope postmarked: Elmont, Tex., May 21, 1891: Five letters inside,
ack. receipt of notice of THOMAS & MARY ALEXANDER Estate...signed by
(1) B. F. ALEXANDER, Elm View P. O., Grayson Co., Texas, son of JAMES
ALEXANDER, dec'd., (2) D. L. ALEXANDER, Elm View P. O., Grayson Co.,
Texas, son of JAMES ALEXANDER, dec'd., (3) D. H. ALEXANDER, Elm View
P. O., Grayson Co., Texas, son of JAMES ALEXANDER, dec'd., (4) M. C.
BURK, Elmont, Grayson Co., Texas, daughter of JAMES ALEXANDER, dec'd.,
(5) J. B. BOWEN, Elmont, Grayson Co., Texas, son-in-law of JAMES ALEX-
ANDER, dec'd. All dated 5/21/91 and addressed to J. H. Newton, Pickens,
So. Carolina.

Letter from Z.(?) S. Pension Agency, Knoxville, Tenn.
Letterhead: J. M. STEWART, Clerk of Court, Pickens Co., SC. Dated:
Jany. 24, 1891. WM. RULE, U. S. Pension Agt., Sir: I write to inform
you of the death of MRS. FRANCIS LIGON. She died 19th of this month.
I am a son-in-law of hers and she made my house her home and died there.
Will you please be so Kind as to furnish me blanks sufficient to draw
the Balance on this quarter. Also blanks to be filled defraying burial
expences, nursing and etc. I bought up all claims in said estate. Very
truly, J. H. G. MC DANIEL. Another page: I, J. M. STEWART, Clerk of
Court for Pickens Co., SC hereby certify that I am personally acquainted
with J. H. G. MC DANIEL and know the statements contained in his letter
to be true. J. M. Stewart, C.C.P. Form letter from Pension Agency.
Apparently, pensioner was a widow of a soldier of War of 1812.

                    END OF RECORDS

Pp 1-2:   8 July 1801. JOHN WEBB of Sumter District, to ROBERT MC
               FADDIN of same, tract on which I now live, 100 acres in
the fork of Black river on both sides of Tear Coat Swamp, and pen branch
adj. ARTHUR GRAHAM, granted to ARTHUR GRAHAM, rec. in Sec. office Book
GGG, p. 116...transferred by JAMES GRAHAM heir to ARTHUR GRAHAM, to
JAMES DICKEY, from DICKEY to JOHN WEBB, for $300...JOHN WEBB (Seal).
Wit: ROBERT MALONE, BURWELL EVANS, HOWELL MOSS. Proved by ROBERT MALONE
bef. WM. TAYLOR, J.Q., 1 Dec. 1801. Dower signed by SUSANNA WEBB bef.
Wm. Taylor, J.Q., 1 Dec. 1801. Rec. 2 Jan. 1802.

Pp 2-3:   8 July 1801. JOHN WEBB of Sumter District, to ROBERT MC
               FADDIN of same, all that tract (a part of which I occupy
at this time), 406 acres in the fork of Black River on pen branch,
part of 640 acres granted to DAVID BRUNSON, SR., rec. in Grant Book
OOOO, p. 335...Wit: ROBERT MALONE, BURWELL EVANS, HOWELL MOSS. Proved
by ROBT. MALONE. Dower signed by SUSANNA WEBB. Rec. 2 Jan. 1802.

Pp 4-5:   20 Jan. 1797. THOMAS LILLY of Claremont Co., Camden Dist.,
               planter, to JOHN CATER, blacksmith, of same, 10 acres more
or less, on S. side Maine's branch, waters of the Wateree, part of
300 acres granted to MOSES FERGUSON, rec. in Book AAAA, p. 464, which
fell to THOMAS LILLY by lawful heirship from MOSES LILLY who had the
same from MOSES FERGUSON by a deed of conveyance, for 10 pds..THOMAS
LILLY. Wit: BENJAMIN FERGUSON, SAMUEL HOUZE. Proved by BENJAMIN FERGU-
SON bef. WM. WHITAKER, J.P., 18 Sept. 1797.

Pp 5-6:   18 Sept. 1797. JOHN CATER of Claremont Co., to GEORGE PY-
               LAND, of same, 10 acres (same as in preceding deed) for
5 pds sterling..JOHN CATER (Seal). Wit: BENJAMIN FERGUSON, WM. WHITAKER.
Proved by FERGUSON bef. DEVEREAUX BALLARD, J.P. Rec. 4 Jan. 1802.

Page 6:   _____ 1800. BENJAMIN FERGUSON, SR., of Claremont Co.,
               to GEORGE PYLAND, 17 acres on N. side of the South prong
of Mains's branch, part of 100 acres granted to sd BENJ. FERGUSON and
part of 150 acres granted to ANN HIGH, for 5 pds sterling..BENJ. FERGU-
SON. Wit: EDWARD PYLANT, JAS. SHARPLIN. Proved by PYLANT bef. DEVER-
EAUX BALLARD, J.P. 14 Nov. 1800. Rec. 4 Jan. 1802.

Page 7:   18 Sept. 1797. BENJ. FERGUSON, of Claremont Co. to GEORGE
               PYLAND of same, 100 acres on S. side of Maines branch,
part of 150 acres granted to ANN HIE..for 46 pds sterling...BENJ. FER-
GUSON (Seal). Wit: JOHN CATER, WM. WHITAKER. Proved by CATER bef. DEV.
BALLARD, J.P., 2 May 1800. Rec. 4 Jan. 1802.

Pp 7-8:   9 Dec. 1799. JESSE COOK of Claremont Co., to GEORGE PYLAND,
               of same, 115 acres granted to JOSEPH FERGUSON, 12 Aug.
1772 bet. Raftin and Swift Creeks on the east side of Wateree river,
adj. ELIAS FORT, MARGARET FERGUSON, JOHN SMITH, part of grant to JOHN
SMITH, adj. 100 acres, for 50 pds sterling..JESSE COOK (Seal). Wit:
WM. WHITAKER, EDWARD PYLANT. Proved by PYLANT bef. DEV. BALLARD, J.P.
Rec. 4 Jan. 1802.

Pp 8-9:   24 Feb. 1798. HENRY DURANT, planter, of State of S. C.,
               County of Salem, to JOSIAH BRADLEY the following described
tract of land: "A plantation or tract of land containing 300 acres,
situate in the District of Camden on both sides of the back Swamp,
bounded on othe south West by lands of JAMES RATCLIFF, on all other
sides by vacant lands, the same being orig. granted to GEORGE WHITE,
in the year of our Lord one thousand seven hundred and sixty five,
having such shape and form as a plat thereunto will more fully and
clearly appear." Consideration: 50 pds good and lawful money. Signed:
HENRY DURANT (Seal). Wit: THOMAS ROSE, JAMES BRADLEY & SHEPARD ROUSE.
Proved by THOS. ROSE bef. JNO. CASSELS, J.P. Feb. 24, 1798. Dower:
Signed by SARAH DURANT, wife of HENRY DURANT bef. JNO. CASSELS, J.P.
13 Dec. 1801. Rec. 5 Jan. 1802. Rec. in clerks office of Salem County,
11 May 1798.

369

Page 10: 14 Dec. 1801. WILLIAM MURPHEY of State of S. C., Sumter District, to JOSIAH WM. BRADLEY, of the afsd. Dist., the following described tract of land: "All that tract of land containing forty acres, binding on the NW by BARTLY's land, NE by JOSIAH WM. BRADLEY's land, SE by ASHE's land, and a line running SW 30 degrees from the SE corner of BARTLY's land to ASHE's land, which sd forty acres of land being orig. granted to WILLIAM MURPHEY in the year of our Lord one thousand seven hundred and ninety nine." Consideration: 14 shillings. Signed: WILLIAM MURPHEY (Seal). Wit: RICHARD MURPHEY, WILLIS MURPHEY, MATTHEW BRADLEY. Proved by MATTHEW BRADLEY bef. JNO. CASSELS, J.P., 14 Dec. 1801.

Pp 10-11: 13 June 1801. WILLIAM BROWN to JEREMIAH BROWN, five slaves: Milly, 34 years, her children, Teller, boy of 12, Lively, a boy of 8, Menda, girl of 5, Lydia, girl of 2. Bill of Sale. Consideration: 1500 dollars. Signed: WILLIAM BROWN. Wit: ROBERT BROWN, JR., CHAS. MC COY. Proved by CHARLES MC COY bef. JOHN MC DONNELL, J.P., 6 July 1801. Rec. 7 July 1801.

Pp 11-12: 2 June 1797. RICHARD RATCLIFF, planter, State of S. C., Dist. of Camden, County of Salem, to his loving cousins, JOHN, SAMUEL and SARAH COMMANDER of the State, District and County afsd. the two sons and daughter of SAMUEL COMMANDER and SARAH his wife, the following personal property: (Deed of Gift) "One negro wench named Celah, one sorrel horse branded F on the mounting buttock 14 hands high, one year old filly, brown bay branded on the mounting shoulder thus S C, one cow and calf, two dry cows, two yearling heiffers fiften head of hogs, marked with a crop and half crop in one ear, and split in the other ear, which mark is to be continued, two beds and furniture and household and kitchen furniture." Consideration: Love, good will and affection. Signed: RICHARD RATCLIFF (LS). Wit: JOHN RATCLIFF and MICHAEL OWENS. Proved by MICHAEL OWENS bef. JO. DOUGLASS, J.P. Rec. 3 Nov. 1802.

Pp 12-13: 3 May 1794. JAMES SCOTT, planter of State of S. C., Claremont County and CHARITY, his wife, to EPHRAIM ADAMS of sd county and state, planter, the following described tract of land: (Lease and Release) "All that plantation or tract of land containing one hundred and fifty acres, situate in the County and State afsd., beginning at a red oak and running SE 20 to a post oak, from thence NE 78 to a line dividing MESHACK MATHCOCK's land from sd tract, and along sd line to the line running SW 70 from the corner of sd MESHACK HATHCOCK's land to sd red oak at beginning, the sd tract of one hundred and fifty acres of land is part of a tract of three hundred and fifty acres granted to sd JAMES SCOTT the 3rd day of April 1786, and recorded in Grant Book KKKK, page 108." Consideration: 60 pds current money. Signed: JAMES SCOTT (Seal) (by mark) and CHARITY SCOTT (LS) (by mark). Wit: JOHN CAIN and JOHN BRADFORD. Proved by JOHN CAIN bef. JOHN HORAN, J.P., 24 June 1794. Receipt signed by JAMES SCOTT to EPHRAIM ADAMS. Rec. 8 Jan. 1802. (Orig. rec. 5 July 1794).

Page 14: 9 Dec. 1800. EPHRAIM ADAMS, planter, and wife, ELIZABETH, of Sumter District, State of S. C., to JAMES SCOTT, of state and district afsd., the following described tract of land: (Deed of Conveyance).. "All that tract or parcel of land containing 200 acres situate in the Dist. and State afsd., beginning at a red oak, and running SE to a post oak from thence NE 78-60 Ch. 50 links to a Station in WILLIAM GRIMES' land thence NE 45 to the branch, thence up sd branch to a dividing line thence sd branch to MESHACK HATHCOCK's line, thence along sd line SW to the beginning." Consideration: 365 dollars and 25 cents. Signed: EPHRAIM ADAMS (Seal) and ELIZABETH ADAMS (Seal), (by mark). Wit: GEORGE BRASINGTON and JOHN MC CAULEY. Proved by JOHN MC CAULEY bef. JOHN HORAN, J.P. 28 Feb. 1801. Rec. 8 Jan. 1802. (Rec. orig. 3 Mar. 1801.)

Pp 14-15: 8 July 1802. (Deed) JOHN MOORE, of Claremont County, State of S. C., planter, to MRS. MARY E. HUGER, of sd county and state, the following described tract of land: "All that plantation, parcel, or tract of land containing 537 acres, situate lying and being in Clare-

Cont'd:
mont County on Raften Creek, waters of the Wateree River, comprehending
part of three original surveys, to wit, part of 300 acres, orig. granted
to JOHN WHELER on or about the 26th day of June 1765, duly recorded
in the Secretarys Office, Grant Book YY, page 548. Also part of one
other tract of 250 acres, orig. granted to sd JOHN WHELER on or about
the 10th day of January Anno Domini 1771, recorded in Sec. Office,
Grant Book GGG, page 36 and also part of one tract containing one half
of 400 acres, orig. granted to ELEANOR RICHARDSON on or about the 25th
day of Nov. 1771 and by the sd ELEANOR RICHARDSON sold and conveyed
to the above named JOHN WHELER by deed of lease and release, bearing
date of 22nd and 23rd days of December 1772, which sd tract or tracts
of land were bequeathed by the sd JOHN WHELER to his daughter, CATHER-
INE WHELER, as may appear by a reference to the record of his last
will and testament, and descended to the sd JOHN MOORE, party to these
presents, being the husband and heir at law of the sd CATHERINE, now
deceased; and hath shape, form and marks, as may appear by a plat of
the whole hereunto annexed. Consideration: 500 pds sterling. Signed:
JOHN MOORE (Seal). Wit: REUBEN LONG and JOHN HORAN. Proved by JOHN
HORAN bef. WM. MURRELL, Q.U. Dower: SARAH MOORE, wife of the within
named JOHN MOORE, not signed by SARAH MOORE; given under hand and seal
of WM. MURRELL, 8 July 1801.

Page 16:   27 June 1802. Map showing copy of part of three tracts
          of land, one orig. granted to JOHN WHELER for 250 acres, another
granted to JOHN WHELER for 300 acres, and the other granted to ELEANOR
RICHARDSON for 400 acres, and adj. lands of THOS. SUMTER, WILLIAM WRIGHT
and PETER MC INTOSH. RICHD. MOORE, surv. Orig. rec. 9 July 1801. Now
15 Jan. 1802.

Pp 17-18:   2 Nov. 1801. HUBERD REES, Sheriff of Sumter Dist., to CLE-
          LAND KINLOCH, of state of S. C., Dist. of Georgetown, the follow-
ing described tract of land: (Deed) "All the afsd. plantation or tract
of land containing 200 acres more or less, situate on the high hills
of Santee, about two miles to the Northward of Statesburg whereon the
sd THOMAS SUMTER now resides bounded Northward by WILLIAM HAMPTON's
lands, and on all other sides by lands belonging to sd THOMAS SUMTER
as appears by a plat of the sd plantation, or tract of land hereunto
annexed." Consideration: 3000 dollars. Signed: H. REES, Shff. S.D.(seal)
Wit: SAMUEL FLEY and W. G. RICHARDSON. Proved by SAMUEL FLEY bef. JOHN
HORAN, J.P. 14 Jan. 1802. (Suit of THOMAS SUMTER and ASA & WILLIAM
DINKINS.)

Page 19:   Plat. Representing 200 acres of land, situate in State
          and District afsd., on South side of Dry Swamp the waters of
the Wateree River, sd land belonging to GENERAL SUMTER, bounded North-
wardly by WILLIAM HAMPTON lands and on all other sides by lands belonging to sd THOMAS SUMTER. Certified 23 Sept. 1801. JOHN J. BRADFORD,
D.S.

Page 19:   14 Jan. 1802. Affidavit by JOHN HORAN, who deposeth and
          saith that JOHN MAYRANT, Esquire, deposited in his office as
Clerk of Sumter Dist., a deed in trust from ANN BAY and WILLIAM BAY
to WADE HAMPTON and sd JOHN MAYRANT for 12 negro slaves, for the use,
benefit and behoof of the children of WILLIAM R. DAVIS, deceased, sd
deed being consumed by fire in his office on 27th Nov. 1801. Sworn
14 Jan. 1802, signed: JOHN HORAN, 16 Jan. 1802.

Pp 20-21:   6 Apr. 1801. (Deed) HUBERD REES, Esquire, Sheriff of Sumter
          Dist., State of S. C., to JOSEPH WILLIAMS, of sd state and dist.,
the following described tract of land: "All that afsd plantation or
tract of land containing 295 acres, situate in Sumter District on the
main road leading from Camden to Stateburg, the plantation whereon
the sd HENRY CLARK now resides, which was granted to THOMAS SUMTER
and by him conveyed to sd HENRY CLARK, bounded by lands belonging to
WILLIAM MOORE, HUDSON, the Estate of ROGERS & CHARLES SPEARS, a plat
of which and the titles from THOMAS SUMTER to HENRY CLARK are hereunto
annexed." Consideration: 72 pds 6 s. and 8 p. sterling money. Signed:
H. REES, Shff., Sumter Dist. (Seal). Wit: JOHN HORAN and BILLUPS GAYLE.

Cont'd:
Proved by JOHN HORAN bef. WM. MURRELL, J.P. 19 Jan. 1802. (HENRY CLARK
indebted to WILLIAM MURRELL).

Page 22:   18 Jan. 1802. Affidavit of WILLIAM MURRELL certifying that
          CHARITY CLARK of the state and district, afsd. did appear before
him and relinquished unto JOSEPH WILLIAMS all her interest, right and
claim of Dower in and to the plantation or tract of land containing
295 acres, as above described.

Pp 22-23:   2 Apr. 1800. (Deed) CHARLES CASSITY and HUGH CASSITY of
          the county of Claremont, State of S. C., to JOSEPH WILLIAMS,
of county of Claremont, State of S.C., the following described tract
of land: "All that plantation or tract of land containing 50 acres,
situated, lying and being between Swift Creek and the Wateree River,
orig. granted to THOMAS CASSITY, deceased, and now in the possession
of the sd CHARLES CASSITY and HUGH CASSITY, butting and bounding to
the North upon lands of the sd HUGH CASSITY, E on lands of the sd HUGH
CASSITY, and S on lands in possession of JOHN CHESNUT and W upon the
sd Wateree River." Consideration: 800 dollars. Signed: CHARLES CASSITY
(seal), HUGH CASSITY (seal). Wit: JAS. BATES & WM. MOORE. Proved by
JAS. BATES bef. JOHN HORAN, J.P. Sworn 28 Feb. 1801. (Orig. rec. 28
Feb. 1801, now 20 Jan. 1802).

Pp 23-24:   11 Nov. 1796. JOHN JAMES and JAMES CASSITY, of the County
          of Clarendon, State of S. C., to JOSEPH WILLIAMS, of the county
of Claremont, State of S. C., the following described tract of land:
"All that plantation or tract of land containing 100 acres more or
less, situate lying and being between Rafting Creek and Swift Creeks,
on the Wateree River, orig. granted to THOS. CASSITY, deceased, and
now in the possession of the sd JOHN JAMES, butting and bounding to
the N on lands of CHARLES SPEARS, deceased, E by lands now in possession
of THOMAS SUMTER, S on lands now in the possession of JAMES BARNES,
and W on lands in the possession of JOHN CHESNUT." Consideration: 70
pds sterling. Signed: JNO. JAMES (seal) and JAMES CASISY (seal). Wit:
DANIEL MC GIRTT & THOS. CASSITY. Proved by THOS. CASITY bef. JOHN HORAN,
J.P. 7 Feb. 1797. Rec. 20 Jan. 1802.

Pp 24-25:   10 Jan. 1802. (Deed) JOSEPH WILLIAMS of Sumter District,
          State of S. C., to THOMAS HALL of Edgefield Dist., sd State,
the following described tract of land: "All those two plantations,
parcels or tracts of land, hereinafter particularly mentioned and described, that is to say, all that plantation or tract of land containing 100 acres more or less on which I now live, situate lying and being
in the District and State afsd. between Raften Creek and Swift Creek
near the Wateree River Swamp orig. granted to THOMAS CASITY, dec'd.,
bounding Eastwardly on WILLIAM SANDERS, JR. land, S by JAMES BARNES
land, W by ASBERY SYLVESTER's land, N by land belonging to the Estate
of CHARLES SPEARS, dec'd. and was sold and conveyed to JOHN JAMES &
JAMES CASIDY to the above named JOSEPH WILLIAMS, party to these presents
by deed of release bearing date 11 Nov. 1796. Also all that other plantation or tract of land containing 50 acres more or less, situate lying
and being in the sd Dist. and State, bet. Swift Creek and the Wateree
River, bounding Westwardly by the sd river to the N and Eastwardly
on HUGH CASSITY's land, to the S on ASBERY SYLVESTER's land, and was
sold and conveyed by CHAS. CASITY and HUGH CASITY to the above named
JOS. WILLIAMS, part to these presents by deed of release bearing date
of 7 Apr. 1800." Consideration: 600 dollars. Signed: JOS. WILLIAMS
(seal). Wit: ISAAC LENOIR & JOHN HORAN. Proved by JOHN HORAN bef. WM.
MURRELL, J.P. 19 Jan. 1802. Rec. 20 Jan. 1802. (See page 324 for dower).

Pp 25-26:   25 Nov. 1801. (Deed) THOMAS LILLEY of State of S. C., County
          of Claremont, to THOMAS CASSITY of sd state and county, the follow-
ing described tract of land: "All that tract or parcel of land containing 142 acres more or less lying and being in South Carolina in Claremont County and is bound N by JONATHAN BUNCKLEY's land and RICHARD
GARNER, E by vacant land, S by the remainder of the sd tract; W by
land granted DANIEL GAROTT, and hath such shape and form as appears
by a plat of the same, the afsd 142 acres being part of the afsd tract
of land which was granted to MOSES FERGUSON now the afsd 142 acres

Cont'd:
of land may be known and understood the course and corners hereafter
expressed, begins at the N end of the orig. tract, running S to a pine
on the W line, and also to a pine on the E line and marked a cross
on a black oak station and post oak station, and post oak d.p. post
oak to pine on W line." Consideration: 300 dollars. Signed. THOMAS
LILLEY (seal) (by mark). Proved by JOSEPH WILLIAMS bef. JOHN HORAN,
J.P. 21 Jan. 1802. Wit: RICHD. WILSON & JOS. WILLIAMS, 25 Nov. 1801.

Pp 26-27:   8 Feb. 1800. HENRY VAUGHAN, SR. of Claremont Co., State
            of S. C., to JOHN VAUGHAN, JR., of the sd co. and state,
the following described land: "All that plantation or tract of land
containing 178 acres, situate in Claremont County, Camden (now Sumter)
District, on the N side of the Wateree River, bounding to the NE on
lands of NATHANIEL BRADFORD and WILLIAM VAUGHAN, to the SE on lands
of WM. VAUGHAN and General SUMTER, to the SW on lands laid out to NATH-
ANIEL PACE and JOHN MITCHELL, and comprehends part of two orig. surveys
to wit, one of 640 acres granted to DAVID NEILSON, the other 150 acres
granted to JOHN FLIN and passed by divers conveyances to the above
name HENRY VAUGHAN, SR. party to these presents, which sd tract or
parcel of land hereby conveyed hath such shape form and marks buttings
and boundings, as may appear by a plat thereof hereunto annexed certified by EZEKIEL EVANS, Surveyor the 14th day of Jan. 1800." Consideration: 40 pds sterling money 8 Feb. 1800. Signed: HENRY VAUGHAN (seal).
Wit: HENRY ABBOTT & JOHN HORAN. Proved by JOHN HORAN bef. ISAAC LENOIR,
J.P. 22 Mar. 1800. (Plat orig. rec. 9 Apr. 1800, now 25 Jan. 1802.)

Pp 28-29:   5 Aug. 1778. (Deed) SILAS PERRY, Carpenter of the parish
            of St. Marks in the province of S. C., to JOB PERRY, planter
of the parish and province afsd., the following described tract of
land by grant dated 10 Apr. 1771 to SILAS PERRY: "All the sd plantation
or tract of land of 100 acres together lying in the parish of St. Marks
with all and singular the houses, out houses, edifices, buildings,
barns, stables, yards, gardens, orchards, woods, under woods, timber
and timber trees, meadows, ponds, pastures, lakes, fishing ways, water
courses, paths, passages, liberties, privileges, profits, hereditaments,
rights, members and appurtenances whatsoever thereunto belonging or
in any wise appertaining." On N side of S fork of Blade River joining
land laid out to NATHL. PACE. Consideration: 1000 pds currency. Signed:
SILAS PERRY (seal) and ESTHER PERRY (by mark). Wit: ROGER ROBERTS,
ELIZABETH ROBERTS (by mark) and ANN ROBERTS (by mark). Proved by ELIZA-
BETH ROBERTS bef. JOHN MC DONNELL, J.P., 9 Mar. 1778. Rec. 2 Feb. 1802.

Page 30:   31 July 1801. (Deed) JOB PERRY of the Dist. of Sumter,
            State of S. C., to JOHN BRINSON, SR. of the dist. and state
afsd., the following described tract of land: "A plantation or tract
of land containing 190 acres, granted to JOB PERRY by his Excellency
CHARLES PINCKNEY the 7th day of Aug. 1797, situate in the Dist. afsd.
on big branch waters of Black river, bound N by WILLIAM RICHBOURG,
S by MC INTOSH, SE by vacant land." Consideration: 90 dollars. Signed:
JOB PERRY (seal). Wit: WM. RICHBOURG & GEO. L. PEEBLES. The above instrument of writing wa signed, sealed and delivered bef. JNO. RIDGILL,
J.P. 31 July 1801. Release of claim of dower signed by JEMIMA PERRY,
wife of JOB PERRY, bef. WM. RICHBOURG, J.P., 1 Feb. 1802. Rec. 2 Feb.
1802.

Pp 30-31:   31 Oct. 1801. (Deed). WILLIAM MURPHREY, planter of the
            State of S. C., Sumter Dist., to JAMES BRADLEY, planter,
of afsd dist. and state, the following described tract of land: "A
plantation or tract of land containing 125 acres, situate in the dist.
of Sumter on S side of Lynches Creek, bounded SE by Bartley's land,
NE by MRS. BRADLEY's land, and NW by lands granted to EPHRAIM PRESCOT
and SW by EPHRAIM PRESCOT's lands, the same being a part of a tract
of land orig. granted to PRESCOT in the year of our Lord 1787." Consideration: 12 pds. Signed: WILLIAM MURPHY (seal). Wit: SAMUEL SHADDOCK,
GEORGE CHANDLER & JOSIAH WM. BRADLEY. Proved by SAML. SHADDOCK bef.
JNO. CASSELS, J.P., 31 Oct. 1801. Rec. 2 Feb. 1802.

Page 32:   ELIJAH PRICE. Stock mark of cattle. ELISHA HODGE. Stock
            mark of cattle. Rec. 2 Feb. 1802.

Pp 32-33:   9 Dec. 1800. JOHN WEBB, of Sumter Dist. State of S.C.,
             to WILLIAM MALONE of the dist. and state afsd, the follow-
ing described tract of land: "All that parcel or part of land containing 234 acres on pen branch on the fork of black river, it being part
of a tract of 640 acres orig. granted to DAVID BRUNSON, SR., and hath
such shape, form, buttings and boundings as is fully represented in
the plat hereunto annexed." Consideration: 300 dollars 9 Dec. 1800.
Signed: JOHN WEBB (seal). Wit: R. MC FADDIN, ROBERT MALONE. Proved
by ROBERT MALONE bef. WM. TAYLOR, J.Q., 2 Feb. 1802. Release of claim
of dower, signed by SUSANNAH WEBB (by mark) bef. WM. TAYLOR, J.P. 2
Feb. 1802. Rec. 5 Feb. 1802.

Page 34:   2 Feb. 1802. (Deed) WILLIAM MALONE, State of S. C., Dist.
             of Sumter, to ROBERT MC FADDIN of the Dist. and State afsd.,
the following described tract of land: "All that parcel or part of
land containing 234 acres, on pen branch in the fork of black river,
it being part of a tract of 640 acres orig. granted to DAVID BRUNSON,
SR. and hath such shape, form, buttings and binding as fully represented in the plat hereunto annexed. Consideration: 300 dollars. Signed:
WILLIAM MALONE (seal). Wit: WM. POTTS, JOHN CONYERS. Certified by WM.
TAYLOR, J.P. Plat 5 Feb. 1802.

Page 34:   1 Feb. 1802. (Bill of Sale). From WILLIAM MALONE of Sumter
             Dist., S. C. to MOSES GORDON FRIERSON, one negro boy, Limas.
Consideration: $472.00, 1 Feb. 1802. Signed: WM. MALONE (seal). Wit:
R. MC FADDIN. Proved by MC FADDIN bef. JNO. DICKEY, J.P., 2 Feb. 1802.
Rec. 5 Feb. 1802.

Pp 35-36:   4 Jan. 1802. HUGH CASSITY of Claremont Co., S. C. to WILLIAM
             BRACEY of state and county afsd., the following described
tract of land: "260 1/2 acres, it being part of four tracts of land
granted to THOMAS CASSITY, one in 1759, one in 1763, and one in 1771
and the other 1772 and willed to HUGH CASSITY by his father, THOMAS
CASSITY, agreeable to the plat annexed, and hath such marks and boundaries as will more fully appear by the plat annexed." (Plat shown on
page 35 of this book.) 4 Feb. 1802. Consideration: $1000. Signed: HUGH
CASSITY (seal). Wit: WILLIAM FOLKS & MERRY BRACEY. Proved by MERRY
BRACEY bef. JOHN HORAN, J.P., 4 Feb. 1802. Rec. 5 Feb. 1802.

Pp 36-37:   4 Feb. 1802. HUGH CASSITY to WILLIAM BRACEY, two negroes,
             Brister and sister Jenny. Bill of Sale. Consideration:
$1000.00. Signed: HUGH CASSITY. Wit: MERRY BRACEY. Proved by BRACEY
bef. JOHN HORAN, J.P. 4 Feb. 1802.

Page 37:   6 May 1802. (Deed) REBECCA JAMES of Claremont County, S.
             C., to SAMUEL JAMES of sd county and state, the following
described tract of land: "All that plantation, parcel or tract of land
containing by the orig. survey, 354 acres, situate lying and being
in the county and state afsd. on Mush Swamp, waters of Black river,
which sd tract of land was orig. granted to JOHN JAMES, deceased, and
by him bequeathed to his daughter, the above named REBECCA JAMES, party
to these presents as may appear by a reference to the last Will and
testament of the sd JOHN JAMES, dec'd. and the record thereof." May
1801. Consideration: 50 pds sterling. Signed: REBEKAH JAMES (seal).
Wit: JNO. LONG & REUBEN LONG. Proved by REUBEN LONG bef. JOHN HORAN,
J.P. Rec. 8 Feb. 1802.

Pp 38-39:   30 July 1801. (Deed). THOMAS SUMTER, SR. of Claremont Co.,
             State of S.C., to HENRY VAUGHAN, JR. of the state and co.
afsd., the following described tract of land: "All those three plantations parcels or tracts of land herein mentioned and described, that
is to say all that plantation or tract of land to the SE end of the
Plat granted to JAMES & JOHN COOK and also the other end granted to
THOMAS SUMTER, JR. containing 500 acres situate lying and being in
Claremont Co. on the N side of Mush Swamp and also on both sides of
Bluff head Swamp and hath such shape form and marks as the Plat hereunto annexed represents." (Plat shown on page 39). Consideration: 150
pds sterling money. Signed: THOMAS SUMTER (seal). Wit: SAMUEL FLEY,
MIDDLETON BELK. Proved by FLEY bef. JNO. HORAN, J.P. 30 July 1801.

Cont'd:
(Plat shows land of A. N. LEWIS, FRANCIS RICHARDSON, JACOB BOATNERS, WILLIAM BRACEY, R. LONG, ... DUGGAW, Gen. SUMTER.)

Page 39:   5 May 1801. (Bill of Sale). FRANCIS RICHARDSON of Claremont
             Co., S. C. to HENRY VAUGHAN, JR., two negroes, woman Suckey
and child Clabin. Consideration: $400.00. Signed: FRANCIS RICHARDSON
(by mark). Wit: JNO. VAUGHAN. Proved by JOHN B. VAUGHAN bef. JNO. HORAN,
J.P. 5 May 1801. Rec. 17 Feb. 1802. (Orig. rec. 5 May 1801.)

Page 40:   14 Dec. 1803. (Bill of Sale). WILLIAM WALLIS of North Caro-
             lina, Pitt County, to HENRY VAUGHAN, of S. C., Claremont
Co., four negro slaves: Nan, 55 yrs, Hannah, 20 yrs., Pzt, 6 yrs.,
Dimpsey, 2 yrs. Consideration: $700.00. Signed: WILLIAM WALLIS (seal).
Wit: JOHN ANDERSON. Proved by ANDERSON bef. JNO. HORAN, J.P. 6 Feb.
1802. Rec. 17 Feb. 1802.

Pp 40-41:   15 Nov. 1801. (Bill of Sale). JAMES COBB to HENRY VAUGHAN,
             JR., a negro boy, Nat, 17 yrs. Consideration: $450.00.
Signed: JAMES COBB. Wit: J. B. VAUGHAN. Proved by VAUGHAN bef. Jno.
Horan, J.P. 8 Feb. 1802. Rec. 17 Feb. 1802.

Page 41:   15 Jan. 1802. HENRY VAUGHAN, SR., planter, of S. C., Sumter
             county, to WILLIAM VAUGHAN, SR., of sd dist. and state,
the following described tract of land: "All that plantation, parcel
or tract of land containing 200 acres, situate in Camden, now Sumter
Dist., orig. granted to sd HENRY VAUGHAN on 21 Jan. 1785, and hath
such shape, etc. as may appear by a plat annexed to sd grant duly recorded in Sec. Office, Grant Bk AAAA, p. 413. Also all that other plantation adj. to the above survey, being part of a tract of 150 acres,
orig. granted to JOHN FLIN on 2 June 1769, recorded in Grant Bk DDD,
p. 198." Consideration: $300.00. Signed: HENRY VAUGHAN (seal). Wit:
JOHN JS. BRADFORD & SAMUEL HATFIELD. Proved by JOHN JS. BRADFORD bef.
JNO. HORAN, J.P. 30 Jan. 1802. Rec. 18 Feb. 1802.

Page 42:   10 Feb. 1802. (Deed). JAMES RICHBOURG, SR. of Clarendon
             County, S. C., Sumter Dist., to CLAUDIUS RICHBOURG of state
and dist. afsd., the following described tract of land: "A plantation
or tract of land containing 400 acres, situate in Sumter Dist. on Sam-
ey's Swamp, waters of Black River, bounding on E by land granted to
HENRY RICHBOURG and on all other sides vacant lands and hath such shapes
(etc.) as appear by an orig. plat thereof ...annexed reference thereunto being had will more fully and at large appear." Consideration:
60 pds sterling. Signed: JAMES RICHBOURG (seal). Wit: HENRY RICHBOURG
(Min.r.), JAMES RIDGWAY. Proved by HENRY RICHBOURG, Min.r bef. WM.
RICHBOURG, J. g.m 12 Feb. 1802. Rec. 18 Feb. 1802.

Pp 42-43:   10 Nov. 1801. (Deed) HESTER RICHBOURG of Clarendon Co.,
             S. C., Dist. of Sumter, to SUSANNA GILLEY, of sd state
and county, the following described tract of land: " A plantation or
tract of land containing 107 acres 33 perches situate in Sumter Dist.
on Cypress branch bounded on N by land belonging to SUSANNA GILLEY,
westwardly and southwardly by lands belonging to NARCISSUS GRAHAM being
part of a tract of land containing 200 acres granted to me by his Exc.
WILLIAM MONTRU, Esq., 6 Feb. 1786, reference being had to the annexed
plat will more fully appear." Consideration: 50 pds sterling. Signed:
HESTER RICHBOURG (seal). Wit: NATHANIEL RICHBOURG and CLAUDIUS RICH-
BOURG. Proved by CLAUDIUS RICHBOURG bef. WM. RICHBOURG, J.P., 9 Jan.
1802. (See copy of Plat p. 46.) Rec. 18 Feb. 1802.

Pp 44-46:   4 Apr. 1794. (Deed) From THOMAS DEARINGTON of Claremont
             Co., S. C. to HENRY VAUGHAN of sd co. and state, planter,
of the following described tract of land: "All that plantation or tract
containing 100 acres lying and being in sd county and state afsd. near
Mush Swamp one of the branches of Black river bounding SE by lands
laid out to JOHN JAMES and on the SW by sd lands and on the NW side
by lands belonging to WM. REES & THOMAS SUMTER and on all other sides
by lands belonging to JOHN JAMES together with all and singular the
houses and outhouses edifices and hath such shapes and marks as the

Cont'd:
plat represents by a plat thereof to the sd grant as in and by the
sd plat and grant reference being thereunto had may more fully appear
now this indenture witnesseth that the sd THOMAS DERRINGTON for and
in consideration of the sum of 100 pds current money of the state afsd
in hand pd by HENRY VAUGHAN at or bef. the sealing and delivering of
these presents the right whereof he doth ack. have granted bargained
and sold aliened demised conveyed and confirmed unto the said HENRY
VAUGHAN in his actual possession now being by virtue of a bargain and
sail(sic) to him thereof made for one whole year by force of the statute
putting of use into possession and to his heirs and assigns forever
all the plantation or tract of land of 100 acres together with all
and singular the houses, etc." Consideration: 5 shillings lawful money.
Signed: THOMAS DEARINGTON (seal). Wit: ROBT. JOHNSTON & REUBEN LONG.
Proved by LONG bef. JNO. HORAN, J.P. 1 Aug. 1794. Rec. 19 Feb. 1802.
(Plat of land granted to HESTOR RICHBOURG surveyed 18 Aug. 1801.)

Pp 46-47:   4 Apr. 1794. (Deed) THOMAS DEARINGTON of Claremont Co.,
             S. C., planter, to WILLIAM MURRELL, Merchant, of sd state
the following tract of land: "100 acres situate lying and being in
Claremont Co. and state afsd. being on N side of Wateree River and
granted to MOSES FERGUSON and bounding on all sides by vacant land
at the time of the surveying and hath such shapes and marks as the
Plat represents by a Plat thereof to sd grant as in and by the sd Plat
and grant reference being...may more fully appear, now this indenture
witnesseth that the sd THOMAS DEARINGTON for and in consideration of
the sum of 100 pds current money of S. C. in hand paid by WM. MURRELL
at on or bef. the sealing and delivery of these presents the receipt
whereof he doth hereby ack. have granted bargained and sold...etc.
unto sd WM. MURRELL in his actual possession now being by virtue of
a bargain and sale to him...made for one whole year by force of statute
for uses ...possession and to his heirs and assigns forever all the
plantation or tract of 100 acres together with all the houses, edifices
buildings yards gardens orchards woods underwoods timber and timber
trees pastures ponds lakes fishing ways waters and water courses etc."
Consideration: 100 pds current money. Signed: THOS. DEARINGTON (seal).
Wit: ROBT. JOHNSTON & REUBEN LONG. Proved by Long bef. Jno. Horan,
J.P. 24 June 1794. Rec. 20 Feb. 1802.

Pp 47-48:   13 June 1801. (Bill of Sale) MARTHA RIDGWAY of Clarendon
             Co., S. C. to JAMES TIMOTHY STRANGE, of same place, one
negro boy named Kent, age 14 yrs. Consideration: 50 pds. Signed: MARTHA
RIDGWAY (seal). Wit: JESSE LOWDEN & WILLIAM RAFFIELD. Proved by Raffield bef. JNO. RIDGILL, J.P. Sworn 24 Nov. 1801. Rec. 20 Feb. 1802.

Pp 49-51:   13 Dec. 1786. (Deed) THOMAS SUMTER of Claremont Co., S.
             C. to WILLIAM MURRELL of same, the following described
tract of land: "All that lot or piece of land containing 1 acre 3 rods
and 9 perches situate in the High Hills of Santee at a place called
Stateburg, and being the place whereon the dwelling house and other
improvements of sd WM. MURRELL now stands..and also all that other
lot or piece of land containing one quarter or fourth part of an acre,
situate on the High Hills of Santee at same place, called Stateburg
and being the place whereon sd WM. MURRELL's store house now stands
having 105 ft front (or nearly) on the main public road and the like
front on a street laid out from the sd public road to the present race
course, the sd two lots of land having such shape...etc....general
plat hereunto annexed...together with all and singular houses, etc.
Consideration: 500 pds sterling. Signed: THOS. SUMTER. Wit: THOMAS
ANDREWS & JOHN BENNETT. Proved by Andrews bef. Jno. Horan, J.P. (Plat
on page 51).

Page 51:   14 Dec. 1799. (Bill of Sale) JESSE LEE & WILLIAM WELLSBY
            of No. Carolina, to GEORGE JOOR of So. Carolina, 8 negroes:
Tom, Dick, Hardy, Betty, Tisby, Amy, Sally, and Beck. Consideration:
$2,700.00. Signed: JESSE LEE (seal), WM. WELLSBY. Wit: W. G. RICHARD-
SON. Proved by Richardson bef. Jno. Horan, J.P. 13 Feb. 1802. Rec.
20 Feb. 1802.

Pp 52-53:   28 May 1801. (Deed) TIMOTHY DARGAN of S. C., Darlington

Cont'd:

District, to HENRY VAUGHAN, JR., Sumter Dist., S. C., the following tract of land: "A certain plantation or tract of land containing 300 acres be the same more or less as does appear by a plat annexed to the orig. grant to JAMES SMITH in the year 1772, the 26 Sept. and recorded in Grant Bk. M, No. 12, p. (24) and conveyed from sd JAMES SMITH to the Rev'd. TIMOTHY DARGAN, deceased, as will appear on record. I the sd TIMOTHY DARGAN, JR. became legally seized and possessed of the above described landed property, by the last Will and testament of sd TIMOTHY DARGAN, my Father, dec'd., the sd tract of land situate lying and being in Sumter Dist. on Bluff-head one of the branches of Black river bounded NW on lands orig. granted to ____ PINCK-NEY, S by Capt. LONG's land, W by SAMUEL FLEY's land, E by Genl. SUM-TER's lands." Consideration: $500.00. Signed: TIMOTHY DARGAN (seal). Wit: ROBERT ELLISON, THOMAS JONES. Certified by ROBT. ELLISON. Release of all rights and claim of dower signed by LYDIA DARGAN, wife of within named TIMONTY DARGAN. Rec. 3 Mar. 1802. (Orig. rec. 24 June 1801, now 3 Mar. 1802).

Page 53:   18 Nov. 1801. (Bill of Sale) ELIZABETH WORNUCK of S. C., Sumter Co., to her son JOSEPH WORNUCK of sd state, one negro man, Peter, and sorrel mare, all household and kitchen furniture. Consideration: $500.00. Signed: ELIZABETH WORNUCK (by mark) (seal). Witnesses not named. Proved by JOHN TAYLOR & ELIZABETH GORDON (by mark) bef. CHARLES F. GORDON, J.P. Rec. 3 Mar. 1802.

Pp 54-55:   2 Sept. 1778. (Deed) WILLIAM RICHARDSON of the Parish of St. Mark, State of S. C., planter, to GABRIEL GERALD, of sd parish and state, planter, the following described tract of land: "A certain plantation or tract containing 300 acres situate lying on Sammy Swamp a branch of Black River in Craven Co., bounding N on land granted to RICHARD KATTON, NE on RICHARD WELLS and vacant land, SE on land granted & NW on JOSEPH CORBET and hath such shape...etc. plat thereof annexed to orig. grant of same to WM. RICHARDSON party hereto together with all and singular gardens, etc." Consideration: 10 shillings current money. Signed. WILLIAM RICHARDSON (seal). Wit: THOMAS ALLISON & ROBERT WHITE (by his mark). Proved by ROBT. WHITE bef. WILLIAM MARTIN, J.P. of Camden Dist. Rec. 3 Mar. 1802.

Pp 55-57:   3 Sept. 1778. (Deed) WILLIAM RICHARDSON of Parish of St. Mark, S. C., planter, to GABRIEL GERALD, of same, planter, the following described tract of land: "All that plantation or tract of 500 acres situate....on Sammy Swamp, branch of Black river in Craven Co., bounding N on land granted to RICHD. KATTON, NE on RICHARD WELLS and vacant land, SE on land granted and NW on JOSEPH CORBET and hath such shape...etc. plat annexed to orig. grant to WM. RICHARDSON....with all gardens, etc." Consideration: 1,400 pds current money. Signed. WM. RICHARDSON (seal). Wit: THOS. ALLISON & ROBT. WHITE (by his mark). Proved by WHITE bef. WM. MARTIN, J.P. Rec. 3 Mar. 1802.

Pp 57-60:   21 Oct. 1792. (Deed) GABRIEL GERALD & ELIZABETH, his wife of Clarendon Co., S. C., Dist. of Camden, to THOMAS NIGHT-INGALE JOHNSTON of afsd co. and state, the following described tract of land: "A certain tract of land of 600 acres more or less situate on Sammey Swamp and Hungry Hold branches of Black river in Clarendon Co., bounding N on lands granted to WM. RICHARDSON, RICHARD WELLS and vacant land, W on lands granted to THOMAS WILLIAM JENKINS, S on lands granted to JOHN SMITH, WILLIAM MC CONNICO & WILLIAM ____ and E on vacant land and hath such shape...etc....plat annexed to orig. grant to sd GABRIEL GERALD dated 7 Nov. 1785..together with all gardens, etc." Consideration: 5 shillings current money. Signed: GABRIEL GERALD & ELIZABETH GERALD (seal). Wit: BENJAMIN GERALD & WM. TERRY. Proved by TERRY bef. SAML. REILY, Esq., J.P. Rec. 3 Mar. 1802.

Pp 60-65:   22 Oct. 1792. (Deed) GABRIEL GERALD & ELIZABETH GERALD, his wife, to THOMAS N. JOHNSTON, Esq. of the afsd co. and dist. the following described tract of land: "All that plantation of 384 acres lying on Sammy Swamp a branch of Black river in Clarendon Co...being part of a grant to WM. RICHARDSON on 9 June 1775 bounded

Cont'd:
N on land granted to RICHARD KATTON, NE on RICHARD WELLS and vacant
land, SE on land granted and NW on JOSEPH CORBETT and hath such shape...
etc....plat annexed to orig. grant, together with all singular gardens,
orchards, etc....to sd Plantation or tract of 384 acres (excepting
such privileges and rights which have been conveyed in writing by sd
GABRIEL GERALD to JAMES RICHBOURG, WILLIAM RICHBOURG and concerns a
Mill built on a stream, ..etc." Consideration: 230 pds sterling. Signed:
GABRIEL & ELIZABETH GERALD (seal). Wit: BENJAMIN GERALD & WILLIAM GERALD.
Proved by JAMES RICHBOURG, J.P. of Clarendon Co., bef. JAMES RICHBOURG,
J.P. Rec. 4 Mar. 1802. (Orig. rec. 2 Feb. 1794.)

Pp 63-64:   13 Dec. 1800. (Deed) From ZACHARIAH CANTEY of the town
             of Camden, S. C., merchant, to THOMAS NIGHTINGALE JOHNSTON
of sd state, Sumter Dist., planter, the following described tract of
land: "All that plantation or tract containing 50 acres more or less
situate...in Sumter Dist. on N side of Santee river, Rights Bluff bounded SW by Santee River, W by land granted to THOMAS BROWN, NW and NE
by THOMAS JOHNSTON's land, SE by land granted to THOMAS MAPLES and
land granted to WILLIAM CANTEY." Consideration: 30 pds sterling money.
Signed: ZACH. CANTEY (seal). Wit: ALEX. MATHISON & ROB. KELLY. Proved
by ROB. KELLY bef. ISAAC ALEXANDER, J.P. 19 Feb. 1801 (J.P. quorum
unus.) Release of Interest and claim of Dower by SARAH CANTEY, wife
of sd ZACHARIAH CANTEY, bef. ISAAC ALEXANDER, J.P. of Kershaw Co.,
S. C. (Orig. rec. 3 Mar. 1801, now 4 Mar. 1802.)

Pp 64-66:   13 Dec. 1800. (Deed) JAMES CANTEY of state of Georgia,
             planter, to THOMAS NIGHTINGALE JOHNSTON, of S. C., Sumter
Dist., planter, the following tracts of land: "A certain tract or plantation containing 250 acres more or less situate on N side of Santee
River in Sumter Dist. at time of orig. grant in Craven Co. rec'd. in
Sec. Office, Bk DDD, p. 604, granted to JOHN CANTEY 1 Dec. 1769 as
by reference will appear bounded at the time of orig. grant on SE side
of lands granted to JOHN HORSKINS and on all other sides by vacant
land ..etc....descended to me, sd JAMES CANTEY from my Father, sd JOHN
CANTEY, deceased, in right of Inheritance. Also a certain other tract
or plantation situate as afsd adj. the other tract containing 100 acres
more or less orig. granted to JOHN HORSKINS rec. in Bk LL, folio 13,
sold and conveyed by him to sd JOHN CANTEY, deceased, and descended
as afsd by right of Inheritance to me, sd JAS. CANTEY..bounded at time
of orig. grant on all sides by vacant land..also another tract of 300
acres more or less situate...adj. first mentioned tract, granted to
THOMAS MAPLES rec. in Sec. Office, Bk PP, p. 305, and sold and conveyed
by him to JOHN CANTEY, dec'd., and descended as afsd to me, JAMES CANTEY
bounded at time of orig. grant on all sides by vacant land...etc."
Consideration: 370 pds sterling money. Signed: JAS. CANTEY (seal).
Wit: WM. BRUNSON & S. BROWN. Proved by SAMUEL BROWN bef. ISAAC ALEXAN-
DER, J.P. of Kershaw Dist., 19 Feb. 1801. Release of all right and
claim of Dower signed by MARTHA CANTEY, wife of sd JAMES CANTEY, bef.
I. ALEXANDER, J.P. 13 Dec. 1800. Rec. 4 Mar. 1802. (Orig. rec. 3 Mar.
1801).

Page 66:   Rec'd 25 Jan. 1794 of JOHN DARGAN sum of 79 pds 6 shillings
             8 pence for a negro wench named Jeney and her son, Dan'l.
Signed: JNO. GAYLE. Wit: ROBT. H. WARING. Above instrument of writing
ack. by JOHN GAYLE as his act and deed on 6 Oct. 1800, rec. in Rec.
Bk. L, p. 35. JOHN HORAN, Clerk, 4 Mar. 1802.

Pp 66-67:   29 Jan. 1800. (Bill of Sale) from SOLOMON THOMSON of Camden
             Dist., S. C., planter, to JOHN DARGAN of state and dist.
afsd., one negro man named Jack. Consideration: 30 pds sterling. Signed:
SOLOMON THOMSON (seal). Wit: ABRAHAM POOL (by mark) and NATHAN THOMSON.
Proved by POOL bef. JNO. HORAN, J.P. 13 Oct. 1800. (orig. rec. 15 Oct.
1800, now 5 Mar. 1802.)

Pp 67-68:   25 Sept. 1801. (Deed) JOHN MC CANTS, planter, of S. C.,
             Sumter Dist., Salem Co., to THOMAS GORDON, planter, sd
state and co., the following tracts of land: "One of sd tracts containing 200 acres situate in co. afsd. in fork of Black river on Long

Cont'd:
Branch bound on S by MARY ARNET all other sides vacant at time of survey
..the other tract containing 100 acres bounded on above mentioned tract
by a line running SE and NW and SW by DAVID MC CLOUD's land NE by JOHN
MC CAY's land all other sides vacant at time of survey running together.
Consideration: $400.00. Signed: JOHN MC CANTS (seal). Wit: WM. DICKSON
& THOS. WELLS. Proved by DICKSON bef. THOS. NELSON, J.P. 25 Sept. 1801.
Release of all right in property and claim of Dower signed by JANE
MC CANTS wife of sd JOHN MC CANTS, bef. G. COOPER of the county afsd,
25 Sept. 1801. Rec. 6 Mar. 1802.

Pp 68-69:   11 Sept. 1801. (Bill of Sale) JOHN BURGESS, JR., planter,
             to THOMAS GORDON, planter, both of Salem Co., S. C., two
negroes, wench named Doll and a boy, Prince. Consideration: $200. Signed
by JOHN BURGESS, JR. (seal). Wit: JOSEPH BURGESS & THOMAS MC CANTS.
Proved by BURGESS bef. THOS. WILSON, J.P. 27 Jan. 1802.

Pp 69-71:   2 Mar. 1781. (Deed) HUBERD REES, Sheriff of Sumter Dist.,
             in S.C., to JOHN DARGAN of same: "Witnesseth: Whereas THOMAS
COULLIETTE of state and dist. afsd. was seized in his demesne as of
fee and some other good estate and inheritance to him and his heirs
forever of and in all that tract of land hereinafter mentioned and
described of 400 acres situate on Cane savanah Creek, branch of Black
River, in dist. and state afsd granted to THOMAS COULIETTE on 5 June
1786 bounded NW by ANN CLARK's land, NE by land laid out for JOHN SING-
LETON, and on all other sides vacant lands, ref. being had to sd plat
which accompanies this deed ... more fully explain boundaries, etc.
..the sd THOS. COULLIETTE by his bond or obligation became holder and
firmly bound unto THOMAS N. JOHNSTON in the penal sum of 20 pds sterling
money of state afsd, conditioned to pay 35 pds like money, and whereas
JOHNSTON did for the recovery of sd debt commence an action in Court
of Common Pleas in dist. afsd. against sd THOMAS COULLIETTE which action
such proceedings were had that sd JOHNSTON did in Nov. Term 1800 at
the house of JOHN GAYLE recover against sd COULLIETTE the afsd. debt
of 70 pds and also 4 pds 8 shillings 9 pence sterling for his costs
in and about his prosecuting sd suit in that behalf ..... prodeedings
remaining in Office of Clerk of sd Court relatioin being had may better
appear." Consideration: $340.00. Signed: H. REES, Sheriff Sumter Dist.
(seal). Wit: ULYSSES ROGERS & RICHARD SINGLETON. Proved by ROGERS bef.
JOHN HORAN, J.P. 15 Apr. 1801. Rec. 9 May 1802. (Orig. rec. 20 Apr.
1802.)

Page 71:   3 Feb. 1802. (Deed) JOHN HATHCOCK, SR. of Kershaw Dist.,
             S. C., to FREDERICK MATHIS, Dist. of Sumter, S.C., the
following described tract of land: "All that tract or parcel containing
4900 acres granted to DAVID REYNOLDS on 6 Nov. 1786 and transferred
to JOSEPH PAYNE 30 Apr. 1793 by REUBEN LONG, State Sheriff of Dist.
afsd. and from PAYNE conveyed to JOHN HATHCOCK, SR., sd land containing
300 acres more or less situate in Sumter Dist. in state afsd. on head
of Big Raften Creek, waters of Wateree River bounded NE and NW by MILES
POTTER, SW by JAMES & JOHN COOK's land." Consideration: 10 pds sterling money. Signed: JOHN HATHCOCK (by mark). Wit: EZEKIAH MATHIS &
RICHARD WILLIAMS. Proved by MATHIS bef. JNO. HORAN, J.P. 6 Mar. 1802.
Rec. 9 Mar. 1802.

Page 72:   JOHN HATHCOCK, SR. of Kershaw Dist. sells to RICHARD WIL-
             LIAMS of Sumter Dist. a tract containing 240 acres situate
in Sumter Dist. on Big Radfen Creek, waters of Wateree River being
part of tract containing 340 acres granted to JOHN COLUNS by grant
dated 3 Apr. 1786; was conveyed by _____? COLUNS to SOLOMON BOLTON
and conveyed by him to HATHCOCK, now conveyed from him to WILLIAMS.
Consideration: 40 pds sterling. Signed: JOHN HATHCOCK (by mark). Wit:
EZEKIAH MATHIS & FREDERICK MATHIS (by mark). Proved by EZEKIAH MATHIS
bef. JNO. HORAN, J.P. Sworn 6 Mar. 1802. Rec. 9 Mar. 1802.

Pp 73-74:   9 Feb. 1802. (Bill of Sale). HENRY SONES of Sumter Dist.,
             S. C. to ELIZABETH MACNAIR of same, "A certain family of
five negroes." (family - DICK MOORE, 38 yrs., SUDEY his wife, under
35 yrs.; son DANIEL 13 yrs.; DOLLY, dau. 9 yrs.; JOSHUA son 4 yrs.).

Cont'd:
Consideration: $2,200.00. Signed: HENRY SONES (L.S.) Wit: WILLIAM MUR-
RELL & MARTHA MILLER. Proved by WM. MURRELL bef. JOHN HORAN, J.P. 13
Mar. 1802. Rec. 13 Mar. 1802.

Pp 74-75:   21 Sept. 1801. (Deed) HENRY DUNN of S. C., Dist. of Sumter,
             Co. of Salem, planter, to WILLIAM WILSON of same, planter,
the following described tract of land: "460 acres situate on SW side
of Black River, being parts of survey, and E on viz 100 acres of land
granted to SYLVESTER DUNN, SR., 16 July 1765, 100 acres granted SYLVES-
TER DUNN, SR., 20 Dec. 1762, and part of 1,000 acres granted to DUNN
4 Nov. 1793 as may more fully appear by having recourse to orig. Plat,
and also a plat of the above bargained premises ... annexed..containing
460 acres more or less." Consideration: $500.00. Signed: HENRY DUNN
(seal) Wit: JOSEPH BURGESS & THOS. WILSON. Proved by BURGESS bef. THOS.
WILSON, J.P. 23 Sept. 1801. Release of all right and claim of dower
in or to the above premises, signed by ELIZA DUNN bef. G. COOPER, Q.U.
25 Sept. 1801.

Page 75:   Plat of land owned by HENRY DUNN on the SW side of Black
             River Swamp, certified by DANL. DUBOSE, D.S., adj. lands
of WILLIAM WILSON, WM. NEILSON, ELIZABETH FLEMING, THOS. WILSON & ...
CARTER. 17 Mar. 1802.

Page 76:   9 Jan. 1802. (Deed) WILLIS ROBISON, of Sumter Dist., Salem
             Co., S. C. to WILLIAM DANIEL of same, the following describ-
ed tract of land: "40 acres more or less situate on W side of North
Prong of Black River, bounded on N side by EZEKIEL GASKIN on W by WM.
DANIEL and S also by WM. DANIEL, on E by JAAC (JACOB?) HURST being
part of a survey of 100 acres, granted to GEORGE RENNERSON 3 Feb. 1775
as may appear by having recourse to orig. plat of same and deeded in
sundry deeds and conveyance as may also appear." Consideration: $11.00.
Wit: WILLIAM SINGLETON, DAVID JOHNSTON & HENRY PARISH (by their marks).
Proved by JOHNSTON bef. JO. DOUGLASS, J.P. 9 Jan. 1802. Rec. 17 Mar.
1802. Signed: WILLIS ROBINSON (L.S.)

Page 77:   15 Nov. 1799. (Deed) DAVID PETTIPOOL of S.C., Co. of Clare-
             mont, planter, to WILLIAM DANIELS, of S.C., Co. of Salem,
planter, the following described tract of land: "All that tract/parcel
of land containing 380 acres more or less, as appears by plat of same
annexed..part of a tract of 1000 acres granted to SYLVESTER DUNN 4
July 1791 situate in co. of Salem on Black River, bounding NW on STEPHEN
DANIEL's and WILLIS ROBINSON's land, and EZEKIEL GASKIN's land, SE
on JOHN DOUGLAS, Esq. land, NE on SIMON STUKEY's land sd land was deeded
to sd PETTIPOOL by SYLVESTER DUNN, JR. bef. JNO. CASSELS, J.P. 28 Feb.
1800. Rec. 17 Mar. 1802. (copy of Plat p. 79).

Pp 77-79:   7 Sept. 1801. (Deed) HUBERD REES, Sheriff of Sumter Dist.
             S.C. to JAMES DAVIS of Clarendon Co., sd dist and state,
planter, "Witnesseth whereas JOHN SKRINE & THOMAS SKRINE were seized
in their demesne as of fee, or some other good estate and inheritance
to them and their heirs forever, of and in all that plantatioin or
tract of land containing 800 acres, situate in Clarendon Co. in dist.
afsd., on N side of Santee River, bounded by lands of Doctor JAMES
LYNAH, General MARION and JOHN MC KELVIN, and hath such shape form
and marks as may appear by a plat thereof deposited in the Treasurers
office of this state at Charleston, whereas also the sd JOHN SKRINE
and THOMAS SKRINE mortgaged the above described tract of land to the
state, in pursuance of an Act of Legislature passed on 12 Oct. 1785,
and the sd JOHN SKRINE and THOMAS SKRINE having failed to make payment
of the principal and interest of sd debt, as required by law, the sd
tract of land was sold, purchased by the Treasurer in behalf of the
State, whereas it was directed by an Act of Legislature passed on 20
Dec. 1800, that all such lands should be sold by the Sheriffs of the
dist. where they were severally situate on a public sale day in pursuance of which sd Act and directions from DANIEL DOYLEY, Esq., Treas.
at Charleston, the sd HUBERD REES, Sheriff as afsd. after giving due
and legal Notice, exposing same at Sale at public outcry, did for/in
satisfaction of afsd debt/mortgage, at Court House for Dist. afsd.,

Cont'd:
on 7 Sept. 1801, openly, publicly and fairly according to custom of
Venders sell and dispose of sd tract of land, above mentioned and des-
cribed." Consideration: $200.00. Signed: H. REES, (seal) (Shff. Sumter
Dist.) Wit: JOHN R. SPANN & WM. WHITEHEAD. Proved by WHITEHEAD bef.
JOHN HORAN, J.P. 5 Mar. 1802. Rec. 17 Mar. 1802. (Plat on page 79).

Page 80:   ROBERT JOHNSTON, Stock Mark and a swallow fork in one ear,
             a cinder bit in the other and brand RJ. Rec. 27 Mar. 1802...
SAMUEL HIGH's mark and brand - marke a swallow fork and under bit in
the right ear, and a crop and split in the other - Brand S. FI. Rec.
27 Mar. 1802.

Pp 80-81:   14 Sept. 1801. (Deed) GEORGE REESE of Pendleton Dist.,
             S. C. to THOMAS MC FADDIN of Sumter Dist., S.C. the follow-
ing described tract of land: "All that plantation or tract of land
containing 200 acres situate in Sumpter Dist. on N.o.E.t. side of Black
River Swamp, bounding (at time of grant) S.o.E.t. on ROBT. HUME's land,
N.o.E.t. on EDWARD DICKEY and S.o.W.t. on WM. PARKER and hath such
shape, form and marks as will appear by a plat annexed to orig. grant
which was granted to CHARLES STORY on or about 13 July 1770." Consideration: $420.00. Signed: GEORGE REESE (seal). Wit: MARY STOREY and ROBT.
MC CANN. Proved by MARY STOREY bef. G. COOPER, J.Q., 29 Dec. 1801.
Release of all her interest and estate, also right and claim of dower,
signed by ANNA REESE, wife of GEORGE REESE, bef. JOHN WILSON, J.Q.
14 Oct. 1801. Rec. 31 Mar. 1802.

Pp 81-82:   1 Oct. 1801. (Deed) JONATHAN MC KINNEY, Sumter Dist., SC,
             planter, to THOMAS MC FADDIN, of same, planter, the follow-
ing described tract of land: "All that plantation and tract containing
168 acres situate in Sumpter Dist. on home branch on the NE side of
Black River Swamp, bounded on the one side on lands of RICHARD KARLINE,
on three sides on lands of the sd THOMAS MC FADDIN, and hath such shape,
etc....as is represented in a plat which sd tract of land was granted
to sd JONATHAN MC KINNEY 7 Jan. 1788." Consideration: $172.00. Signed:
JONATHAN MC KINNEY (seal). Wit: WILLIAM BEARD & PATRICK BYRD. Proved
by BEARD bef. G. COOPER, J.Q. 24 Oct. 1801. Release of right and interest and claim of Dower, signed by MARY MC KINNEY bef. G. Cooper, J.P.
24 Oct. 1801. Rec. 31 Mar. 1802.

Pp 83-84:   17 Apr. 1793. (Deed) ROBERT LAWS and ROSE LAWS, his wife,
             Claremont Co., Camden Dist., S. C., planter, to SAMUEL
CHRISMAS, a Minor, the following described tract of land: "A plantation
or part of a tract which sd part contains 75 acres, to be taken off
the SE part of a tract of 375 acres, beg. on a corner stake joining
lands of JAMES CLARKE and running N 10° W the corner of the other lines
are S 70° W and S 20° E for complement, the orig. grant of 375 acres
to DANIEL CLARKE 5 Nov. 1787, under hand of his Excellency THOMAS PINCK-
NEY, situate in dist. of Camden on NE side of Cowpen Swamp, waters
of Black River, bound NW on JAMES MC COY's and vacant land, NE on vacant
land SE on JAMES & DANL. CLARK's. Rec. in Sec. Office Grant Bk. TTTT,
p. 59, reference being had to the orig. grant will more fully appear."
Consideration: 3 pds lawful sterling money. Signed: ROBERT LAWS (seal)
and ROSE LAWS (seal) (by her mark). Wit: AARON CHRISTMAS, JOHN CHRIST-
MAS (by mark) and ROBERT CROSSON. Proved by AARON CHRISTMAS bef. JOHN
HORAN, J.P. 11 Mar. 1794. (Now rec. 1 Apr. 1802.)

Page 85:   20 Oct. 1797. (Deed) JOHN CHRISMAS of S. C., of Black River,
             planter, to NATHAN CHRISTMAS of Black River, S.C. the fol-
lowing tract of land: "All that plantation/tract of land containing
150 acres more or less situate in Camden Dist. and state afsd. and
bounded by lines running SE-RUTLEDGE's land; SW WM. BROWN's land; NW
on AARON CHRISTMAS land, NE on MOSES CHRISTMAS land being part of tract
of 427 acres granted 2 June 1794 to JOHN REMBERT by his Excellency
WILLIAM MOULTRIE, Esq., Gov. in Chief." Consideration: 20 pds. Signed:
JOHN CHRISTMAS (seal-by mark) and NANCY CHRISTMAS (by mark) (Note:
also spelled CHRISMUS). Wit: WILLIAM BROWN, MOSES CHRISTMUS (by mark),
AARON CHRISTMUS. Proved by AARON CHRISTMAS bef. JNO. HORAN, J.P. Rec.
1 Apr. 1802. (Orig. rec. 17 Nov. 1797.)

Page 86:   22 Mar. 1796. (Deed) JOHN REMBERT of Camden Dist., Clare-
             mont Co., S. C., planter, to JOHN CHRISTMAS of Camden Dist.,
S.C., planter, the following tract of land: "All that plantation/tract
containing 427 acres, being the NW part of a tract of land containing
1000 acres granted to above JNO. REMBERT 2 June 1794...by WM. MOULTRIE..
above sd parcel hereby designed to be conveyed is at present bounded
SE on lands belonging to WILLIAM POWEL BROWN, SWbounds land to the N. W.
on WILLIAM CARTER and WILLIAM LOCOOK, on N by JOHN CHRISTMAS and to
NE lands laid out to JOHN RUTLEDGE, Esq...reference being had to orig.
grant...more fully appear..." Consideration: 49 pds 16/4. Signed: JOHN
REMBERT (Seal) Wit: JAMES REMBERT & SAML. REMBERT. Proved by James
Rembert bef. John Horan, J.P. 15 June 1796. Rec. 2 Apr. 1802. (Orig.
rec. 1 July 1796.)

Page 87:   8 Nov. 1797. (Deed) JOHN CHRISTMAS of Black River, S.C.,
             planter, to AARON CHRISTMAS of Black River, S.C., the fol-
lowing tract of land: "All that plantation/tract of land containing
150 acres more or less situate in Dist. of Camden and State afsd.,
bounded by lines running and binding now on LOWNES's land, NE on land
of CARTER, SE on land of LOCOCK and land of NATHAN & MOSES CHRISTMAS,
SW on WM. BROWN's land..being part of a tract of land of 427 acres
granted to JOHN REMBERT 2 June 1794 by WM. MOULTRIE, Esq. Gov. in Chief.
Consideration: 20 pds. Signed: JOHN CHRISTMUS (seal) (by mark). Wit:
JAMES REMBERT, JR., & NATHAN CHRISTMUS (by mark). Proved by CHRISTMUS
bef. JNO. HORAN, J.P. 17 Nov. 1797. Rec. 2 Apr. 1802.

Page 88:   15 Dec. 1797. (Deed) SAMUEL DWYER of Black River, S.C.,
             planter, to JOHN CHRISTMAS of Black River, the following
tract of land: All that plantation/tract of land containing 90 acres,
situate in Camden Dist. S.C. bounded by lines running NE 78° on sd
JOHN CHRISTMAS's land; NW 38° on JOHN RUTLEDGE's lands; SE 12° on lands
supposed to be granted to CHS. GORDIN being part of a tract surveyed
17 Aug. 1784 - and granted by Wm. Moultrie, Esq., Gov. on 3 Apr. 1786
- to the sd SAMUEL DWYER. Consideration: 21 pds. Signed: SAMUEL DWYER
(seal). Wit: HENRY BROWN and JAMES REMBERT, JR. Proved by REMBERT bef.
Jno. Horan, J.P. 21 July 1798. Rec. 2 Apr. 1802. (Orig. rec. 23 July
1798).

Pp 88-90:   7 Sept. 1801. (Deed) HUBERD REES, Esq., Sheriff of Sumter
             Dist., S.C. to JAMES BURCHILL RICHARDSON of dist. and state
afsd., "Witnesseth SAMUEL LITTLE, deceased, in his life time, was seized
in his demesne, as of fee, or some other good estate and inheritance
to him and his heirs forever, of and in all those three tracts of land
...particularly mentioned..described ...one tract of 400 acres, orig.
granted to JOHN MOORE 5 Sept. 1735, also one other tract of 100 acres,
orig. granted to WILLIAM SWINDLE 25 Sept. 1766; and also one tract
of 500 acres, orig. granted to EDWARD RICHARDSON 12 July 1771...which
sd three tracts containing in the whole 1,000 adj. each other and are
situate.....in Clarendon Co., Dist. of Sumter, on E side of Santee
River .....general plat of same deposited in Treasurers office of this
state at Charleston...whereas sd SAMUEL LITTLE by his act and deed,
mortgaged the above premises to the state, in pursuance of an act of
Legislation, passed 12 Oct. 1785. Consideration: $3,100. Signed: H.
REES (seal) Shff. of Sumter Dist. Wit: JOHN R. SPANN & WM. WHITEHEAD.
Proved by Whitehead bef. Jno. Horan, J.P. Sworn 5 Mar. 1802. Rec. 3
Apr. 1802.

Pp 90-91:   3 Oct. 1801. (Deed) CHARLES RICHARDSON and his wife, ELIZA-
             BETH, both of Sumter Dist., S.C., to JAMES BURCHILL RICHARD-
SON, of same, planter, the following tracts of land: All that plantation
etc...containing 50 acres more or less, granted to JOHN DOWLING 15
Mar. 1756, situate on N side of Santee River on Halfway Swamp Creek
bounded on all sides by vacant land....copy of orig. Plat annexed...also
one other plantation of 100 acres more or less, granted to THOMAS DAVIS
1 Aug. 1769 situate in Craven Co. on Halfway Swamp waters of Santee,
bounded NE on GEORGE SANDERS, SW on WILLIAM KERBY, other sides vacant
land....reference to a copy of orig. plat annexed. Consideration: 150
pds. Signed: CHAS. RICHARDSON and ELIZABETH RICHARDSON (seal). Signed
in presence of MARGARET SINKLES and ANN JAMES. Proved by ANN JAMES
bef. W. R. J. STUKES, Clarendon Co., 14 Jan. 1802.

Page 92:   Plat or tract of land granted to THOMAS DAVIS 1 Aug. 1769,
             containing 100 acres, situate in Craven Co. on Halfway
Swamp, waters of Santee, bounded NE on GEORGE SANDERS, SW on WILLIAM
KERBY, the other sides by vacant land. Rec. 3 Apr. 1802.

Pp 92-93:   4 Mar. 1802. (Deed) MARY ESTHER HUGER of Claremont Co.,
             S.C. to Rev'd. JOHN MITCHELL ROBERTS of sd co. and state,
the following tract of land: All that plantation/parcel/tract of land
containing 32 acres situate...etc...in county and state afsd. on a
branch of Dry Swamp, waters of Wateree River, part of a tract of ___?
acres orig. granted to DAVID NELSON and passed by divers conveyances
to above named MARY ESTHER HUGER....hath such shape, form, etc...appear
by plat thereof annexed, certified by JOHN MC DONNELL deputy surveyor
on 28 Oct. 1801. Consideration: $100.00. Signed: MARY E. HUGER (seal).
Wit: JOHN S. RICHARDSON & WM. WHITEHEAD. Proved by WHITEHEAD bef. Jno.
Horan, J.P. 25 Mar. 1802. Rec. 3 Apr. 1802. (Plat shows land of WILLIAM
HAMPTON, JOHN MURRAY & MARY E. HUGER. Rec. 3 Apr. 1802. Surveyed 28
Oct. 1801.)

Page 94:   15 Jan. 1798. Will of MARGARET DAY, requesting that a negro
             wench be freed from slavery, at her death. Signed: MARGARET
DAY (by mark). Wit: HANNAH HUDSON & MRS. MARSH (by their mark). JOHN
MARK and JOS. SPROTT. Proved by HANNAH HUDSON bef. ROBT. GREGG, J.P.,
Marion Dist. 8 Apr. 1802. Rec. 19 Apr. 1802.

Pp 94-95:   4 Feb. 1802. (Bill of Sale). STEPHEN MITCHELL, of S.C.,
             Sumter Dist. to JAMES GAMBELL of same, one negro woman
named Dinah, 19 yrs. Consideration: $235.00. Signed: STEPHEN MITCHELL.
Wit: ROBERT WITHERSPOON, JR. Proved by WITHERSPOON bef. SHAD ATKINS,
J.P., 11 Apr. 1802. Rec. 19 Apr. 1802.

Pp 95-96:   11 Dec. 1801. (Deed) JACOB STOKES of Salem Co., S.C., plant-
             er, to JAMES KELLEY of same, following tract of land: 200
acres more or less being part of the tract whereon sd JACOB STOKES
now lives beginning at a stake on JOHN WARD's line running 75° SE 39
chains, 35 links on FREDERICK BELL's line to a hickory thence 70° SE
22 chains, 50 links on JOHN MARTHION's line to a stake, hickory thence
10° NE 26 chains to MILES BONFIELD's line to a long pine thence ___?
N 66 chains to JOEL STOKES line thence NW 70° 62 chains it being the
dividing to a stake on JOHN WARD's line passing by a marked hickory
to a pine thence SW 10° 32 chains to beginning stake. Consideration:
$100. Signed: JACOB STOKES (L.S.) Wit: WILLIAM KELLEY and MOORE DAVIS
and WILLIAM HICKS (by mark). Proved by KELLEY bef. Jno. Horan, J.P.
12 Apr. 1802. Rec. 19 Apr. 1802.

Pp 96-97:   3 Mar. 1800. (Deed) WILLIAM BATEMAN of Sumter Dist., S.C.
             to UNDERHILL ELLIS of same, the following tract of land:
All that tract/parcel containing 200 acres more or less, situate in
Dist. of Sumter on NE side of Scape whore Swamp bounded SE by ISAAC
ROBERTS' land, NE by JESSE MC KAY land, NW vacant, SW by main stream
of Scape whore at the time of running sd land for WILLIAM ROBSON in
1794 and has such shape...etc...plat annexed. Consideration: 80 Spanish
Milled Dollars. Signed: WILLIAM BATEMAN (seal) (by mark). Wit: SHADRACH
ELLIS & GEORGE BALDWIN. Proved by ELLIS bef. THOS. WILSON, J.P. 28
Mar. 1800. Rec. 19 Apr. 1802.

Page 97:   1 Mar. 1802. (Deed) CATHARINE WOODS of Sumter Dist., S.C.
             to ARTHUR WHITE of same, the following tract of land: A
plantation/tract containing 100 acres, situate in Sumter Dist. on Black
River bounding on W by ROBT. GAMBEL's land and on all other sides by
sd ARTHUR WHITE's land, orig. granted to HANNAH STONE by his Excel-
lancy CHAS. E. MONTAGUE, dated 13 May 1768, being a mortgage of a tract
of 200 acres granted as afsd. Consideration: $100. Signed: CATHARINE
WOODS (seal). Wit: JAMES WHITE & JAMES CONYERS. Proved by JOHN RIDGILL,
J.P. Sworn 1 Mar. 1802. Rec. 16 Apr. 1802.

Page 98:   14 May 1790. "This is to certify that I have sold and de-
             livered to JOHN JAMES a negro girl named Hannah, a negro
lad named Quibass, also a tract of land binding by WILLIAM SANDERS

Cont'd:
on one side, CHARLES SPEARS and JOHN BATES. Also part of a tract of
Swamp land that is between JAMES CASSITY and HUGH CASSITY for value
received. Signed: JAMES CASSIDY. Wit: THOS. CASSITY. Proved by THOS.
CASSITY bef. John Horan, J.P. 21 Mar. 1795. Rec. 27 Apr. 1802.

Pp 98-99:   (no date or month) 1802. (Deed) ISAAC JACKSON of Claremont
             Co., S.C. to ABRAHAM GIDDINS of same, following tract of
land: A tract containing 123 acres ..being part of a tract containing
640 acres orig. granted to USEBROUS STONE by his Excellency WM. MOULTRIE
Gov. and rec. in Grant Bk. MMMM page 173 and hath such shape, etc...as
may more fully appear by a plat annexed. Consideration: $200.00. Signed:
ISAAC JACKSON (seal) and ELIZABETH JACKSON, his wife (by her mark)
(seal). Wit: ASA PIPKIN & JOHN P. POOL (by mark). Proved by PIPKIN
bef. Jno. Horan, J.P. (Plat on page 99 records land on Nasty Branch
in Sumter Co. 22 Apr. 1802.)

Pp 99-100:   27 Feb. 1802. (Deed) SIMON STUCKEY of S.C., Co. of Salem,
             Dist. of Sumter, planter, to GILBERT CROSWELL, of same,
planter, the following tract of land: 100 acres on lower part with
swamp of Scape-hore being part of a survey of 200 acres granted to
JOHN MC COY, 6 Nov. 1786, sd 100 acres more or less situate next the
bridge on sd Scape-hore. Ref. of boundaries, etc. of whole survey may
be more fully had by having recourse to orig. plat of same. Consideration: $200.00. Signed: SIMON STUCKEY (L.S.) and AMERICA STUCKEY, his
wife (L.S.) (by her mark). Wit: UNDERHILL ELLIS, JOSHUA HICKMAN. Sworn
27 Feb. 1802. Proved by JOSHUA HICKMAN bef. JO. DOUGLASS, J.P., 22
Apr. 1802.

Pp 100-101: 7 Mar. 1801. (Deed) WILLIAM BROWN of Salem Co., S.C. to
            STEPHEN EVANS of sd state, the following tract of land:
A certain parcel/tract containing 106 acres being 1/6th part of a tract
of land containing 638 acres bought from WILLIAM HASEL GIBBS, Master
in Chancery by GEORGE WRIGHT, SR., deceased, which appears by a deed
of conveyance for same bearing date of 1 Dec. 1787, lying in Salem
Co. on Bull Savannah, butting and bounding N on WILLIAM GAMBLE, dec'd.
land, NE on WITHERSPOON's land, SE on sd STEPHEN EVANS land and SW
on Black River and hath such shape...etc. as plat of the same. Consideration: 32 pds 10 shillings. Signed: WM. BROWN (seal). Wit: JAMES
MC KNIGHT & WM. MOOR. Proved by JAS. MC KNIGHT bef. G. COOPER, J.P.
25 Jan. 1802. Release of all interest, also right and claim of Dower
signed by ELIZABETH BROWN, wife of sd WILLIAM BROWN, bef. G. COOPER,
J.P. Rec. 23 Apr. 1802.

Pp 101-102: 25 Mar. 1800. (Deed) JAMES KELLEY of Salem Co., S.C., a
            planter, to WILLIAM KELLEY of same, planter, the following
tract of land: All that piece or tract which is represented by the
above plat as it is represented containing 100 acres more or less,
being part of 440 acres orig. granted to MC KENETH MC CULLUM 11 June
1785 and transferred from him to JACOB CHAMBERS, from him to sd THOMAS
DAVIS and from him to JAMES KELLEY and from him to WILLIAM KELLEY.
Consideration: 250 Spanish Milled Dollars. Signed: JAMES KELLEY (L.S.)
(by mark). Wit: SAMUEL MAYO & THOMAS MAYO. Proved by Thomas Mayo bef.
THOS. WILSON, J.P. 27 Mar. 1802. Rec. 23 Apr. 1802.

Pp 102-103: JAMES KELLEY of Salem Co., planter, sell to WILLIAM KELLEY,
            of same, planter, 100 acres, being part of a tract granted
to JOEL STOKES 17 May 1787 and from him to ABEL DIXON and from him
to JAMES KELLEY and from him to WM. KELLEY. Consideration: 150 Spanish
Milled Dollars, 25 Mar. 1780. Signed: JAMES KELLY (by mark). Wit: SAMUEL
& THOMAS MAYO bef. THOS. WILSON, J.P. Sworn 27 Mar. 1802. Rec. 23 Apr.
1802.

Pp 103-105: 2 June 1790. (Deed) ROBERT FULLWOOD, Salem Co., S.C., to
            DAVID DAVIS, carpenter, of same, following tract of land:
All that parcel/tract containing 400 acres being part of 14,900 acres
orig. granted to ROBERT FULLWOOD 1 Oct. 1792 situate in Camden Dist.
on waters of Newmans Branch bounding NE & SW on WILLIAM MC ELVEEN &
JOHN BURGESS land, SW & NW on HICK's land, SW on ZACHARIAH BIRD's land,

Cont'd:
NW on DAVID DAVIS' land, having such shape, form etc. as is laid down
in a Delienated plat of sd land hereunto annexed, reference being...had
will more fully appear. Consideration: 3 pds sterling. Signed: ROBERT
FULLWOOD. Wit: THOMAS FULLWOOD, JESSE HICKS, ZACHARIAH BIRD. Proved
by BIRD bef. WM. KENNEDY, J.P. 6 July 1801. Rec. 24 Apr. 1802. (Page
105 shows plat.)

Pp 105-106: 9 Mar. 1801. (Deed) DAVID DAVIS of Orangeburg Dist., S.C.
            to JOHN PATRICK of Sumpter Dist., S.C. "Whereas in and
by a certain Deed of Feoffment dated 2 June 1793 ROBT. FULLWOOD (also
FULWOOD) did transfer unto DAVID DAVIS of Orangeburg Dist., a plantation
of 400 acres on waters of Newmans Branch, in Salem Co., having such
shape...etc....as are represented by a plat thereof to sd Deed annexed
and being part of a tract of 14,900 acres orig. granted to sd FULLWOOD
and whereas the sd DAVID DAVIS hath since the execution of afsd Deed
transferred to ZACHARIAH BYRD OF Sumter Dist., 100 acres of the afsd.
400 acres, and separated from the remaining 300 acres by a line agreeed
on, now know all men by these presents, that I the sd DAVID DAVIS for
and in consideration of $60 to me pd by JOHN PATRICK of Sumter Dist.,
state afsd, all the remaining part of afsd 400 acres, being 300 acres
more or less beg. on DAVIS's line at a blazed pine, thence along the
forementioned agreed line through the Gallden pond to the back line
and down the back line; JESSE PATRICK's land to the corner; thence
across to WILLIAM MC ELVEEN's line to sd DAVIS's corner thence up DAVIS'
line to sd agreed line; sd land situate bet. Newman's branch and Cain
branch as may better appear by ref. to plat to the afsd Deed of Feoffment, have granted, ..etc... sell and release to sd JOHN PATRICK ..etc.
Consideration: $60. Signed: DAVID DAVIS (L.S.) (by mark). Wit: WILLIAM
KENNEDY & JESSE PATRICK. Proved by PATRICK bef. WM. KENNEDY, J.P. 9
Mar. 1801. Rec. 24 Apr. 1802.

Pp 106-107: (no date or month) 1801. (Deed) DAVID DAVIS of Orangeburg
            Dist., S.C. to JOHN PATRICK of Sumter Dist., S.C. the fol-
lowing tract of land: A plantation or tract of 300 acres (surveyed
for BENJAMIN CASSELS 4 Oct. 1785) granted to sd DAVIS 2 Feb. 1801 situate in Camden now Sumter Dist. on Newman Branch bounded on all sides
(at time of orig. survey) by vacant land and of such shape, etc. as
appear by a plat thereof...grant annexed duly rec. in Sec. Office in
Columbia in Grant Bk TTT no. 5 reference being had may more fully appear.
Consideration: 61 pds. Signed: DAVID DAVIS (L.S.) (by mark). Wit: WM.
KENNEDY & JESSE PATRICK. Proved by Patrick bef. Wm. Kennedy, J.P. Rec.
24 Apr. 1802.

Pp 107-108: 25 Nov. 1801. (Deed) SHADRACK MC CORMACK, of Salem Co.,
            S.C. to WILLIAM RATLIFF, sd co. and state, planter, the
following tract of land: Tract containing 450 acres, part of four tracts
of land, two tracts granted to NATHANIEL PIGGOT, one tract granted
23 Mar. 1762 and one granted 19 Nov. 1772, one granted to HENRY MOTTE
20 Oct. 1785, one granted to ROBERT FULLWOOD situate in Co. of Salem
on S side of Linches Creek, bounded on upper line by GEORGE CHANDLER's
land and lower line by HENRY MOTTE's land as part of 4 tracts of 450
acres as above mentioned. Consideration: $400. Signed: SHADRACK MC
CORMACK (seal) and DREWSELLA, his wife (by her mark). Wit: CHARLES
PIGGOT & JOHN MC CORMACK. Proved by PIGGOT bef. JNO. CASSELS, J.P.
10 Apr. 1802. Rec. 24 Apr. 1802.

Pp 108-111: 6 Jan. 1801. (Deed) HUBERD REES, Sheriff of Sumter Dist.,
            S.C. to ROBERT DINGLE of same, Wit: whereas MOSES GREEN
in his lifetime of state and dist. afsd. was seized in his demesne
as of fee, or some other estate and inheritance to him and his heirs
and in all the several tracts of land hereinafter mentioned and described to wit: five several tracts, one containing 50 acres surveyed
for HENRY SPRY 23 Mar. 1767, one tract of 100 acres surveyed for HENRY
SPRY 20 Nov. 1769, one containing 40 acres surved for SPRY 20 Jan.
1777, one other of 100 acres surveyed for SPRY 20 July 1758, one of
150 acres, surveyed for SPRY 7 Feb. 1765, in all five tracts containing on the whole 440 acres, situate in Clarendon Co., S.C. dist. afsd.
on Santee River Swamp adj. each other, reference to orig. plats which

Cont'd:
accompanies this deed will more fully explain the buttings and boundings and situation of sd tracts of land...whereas sd MOSES GREEN in
his life time by his bond or obligation became held and firmly bound
to HENRY SPRY of state and dist. afsd. in the sum of 1,326 pds 7 shillings and 6 pence sterling money as above mentioned, mortgage to HENRY
SPRY, JR. the above named five tracts of land, etc. Consideration:
$446.00. Signed: H. REES, Shff. Sumter Dist. (seal). Wit: ULYSSES ROGERS
& AD. THOMAS, JR. Proved by ROGERS bef. Jno. Horan, J.P. Rec. 25 Apr.
1802. Orig. rec. 15 Apr. 1801.

Pp 111-112: 11 Feb. 1795. (Deed) JOHN NELSON and MARGARET, his wife,
              of Clarendon Co., S.C. to JAMES RICHBOURG of afsd co. and
state, the following tract of land: A certain plantation containing
100 acres more or less, being the third lot of a certain tract containing 400 acres granted to EASTER SULLIVAN and her two daughters,
MARGARET & EASTER SULLIVAN on 13 Feb. 1753 under the hand of JAMES
GLEN, Esq. then Gov. of province and state afsd, lying on a swamp called
Taw-Caw bounding on all sides by vacant land as appears by plat of
same, drawn by MARGARET NELSON, ref. to a division of same will more
fully appear...etc. Consideration: 5 pds sterling. Signed: JOHN NELSON,
(seal), MARGARET NELSON (seal). Proved by CLAUDIUS RICHBOURG bef. CHAS.
F. LESESNE, J.P. Wit: CLAUDIUS RICHBOURG & DAVID WHITE. Rec. 25 Apr.
1802.

Pp 112-114: 11 Feb. 1795. (Deed) JAMES NELSON and ISABELLA, his wife,
              of Clarendon Co., S.C. to JAMES RICHBOURG of afsd co. and
state, the following tract of land: A certain plantation of 100 acres
more or less being the 4th lot (a certain tract of 400 acres granted
to EASTER SULLIVAN and her two daus. MARGARET & EASTER SULLIVAN 13
Feb. 1753 under hand of James Glen, Esq., then Gov.) on a swamp called
Taw-Caw bounding on all sides by vacant land as appears by plat of
same, drawn by ISABELLA NELSON ref. to a division of same...etc. Consideration: 5 pds sterling. Signed: JAMES NELSON (seal) and ISABELLA
L. NELSON (seal). Wit: CLAUDIUS RICHBOURG & D. WHITE. 19 Feb. 1795.
Proved by RICHBOURG bef. Chas. F. Lesesne, J.P. 19 Feb. 1795. Rec.
26 Apr. 1802. (Orig. rec. 15 Apr. 1795.)

Pp 114-115: 19 Feb. 1795. (Deed) SUSANNA RICHBOURG of Clarendon Co.,
              S.C., the following tract of land: A certain plantation/or
tract of 100 acres more or less, being the 2nd lot(of a certain tract
of 400 acres granted to EASTER SULLIVAN and her two daus. MARGARET
& EASTER SULLIVAN 13 Feb. 1753 (same as above)....plat drawn by SUSANNA
RICHBOURG...(same as above) ...Consideration: 5 pds sterling. Signed:
SUSANNA RICHBOURG (seal). Wit: HENRY RICHBOURG & WILLIAM BRUNSON. Proved
by RICHBOURG bef. Chas. F. Lesesne, J.P. 19 Feb. 1795. Rec. 26 Apr.
1802. (Orig. rec. 15 Apr. 1795.)

Pp 115-117: 20 Feb. 1795. (Deed) JAMES RICHBOURG, SR. and LOVICI, his
              wife, of Clarendon Co., S.C. to ROBERT DINGLE of same,
a tract of land: A certain plantation/tract of 300 acres more or less,
being part of a tract of 400 acres orig. granted to EASTER SULLIVAN
and her two daughters, MARGARET & ESTHER SULLIVAN (the rest is same
as above deeds).....duly registered in the Sec. Office..sd 300 acres
being the 2nd, 3rd and 4th lots drawn by MARGARET NELSON, ISABELLA
NELSON & SUSANNA RICHBOURG as appears by a Lease and Release givenn
by each of the afsd..MARGARET NELSON's husband, JOHN· NELSON, ISABELLA
NELSON's husband, JAMES NELSON and SUSANNA RICHBOURG to the sd JAMES
RICHBOURG for the sd 300 acres situate on north side of Santee River
on branch of sd river called Taw-Caw bounded on all sides by vacant
land when surveyed....etc. Consideration: 105 pds sterling current
money. Signed: JAMES RICHBOURG (seal) and LOVEY RICHBOURG (seal) (by
her mark). Wit: WILLIAM BUDDIN & SOLOMON BUDDIN. Proved by Wm. Buddin
bef. THOS. N. JOHNSTON, J.P. of Clarendon Co., S.C. 20 Feb. 1795. (Plat
mentions land of MARGARET BOCHER.)

Page 118:   22 Oct. 1790. (Bill of Sale & Deed) SAMUEL BENNETT of St.
              Marks Parish, S.C., planter, to ROBERT DINGLE, the follow-
ing: Nineteen negro slaves, by name: Betty, Tenah, Nelly, Big Peter,

Cont'd:
Succy, Joe, Stephen, Jack, Baccus, Arch, Dafney, Little Peter, Minny,
Setirah, Charley, Billy, Caesar, Philis, Bella, them and their increase
forever and the plantation whereon I now live, together with the crop
that is now on the plantation, and all the best of my goods and chattels, property, properties claimed by me in any wise whatever. Consideration: 400 pds. Signed: SAMUEL BENNETT (seal). Wit: BENJAMIN DAVIS
& PHILIP BENORST. Proved by Davis bef. ISAAC CONNOR, J.P. Rec. 27 Apr.
1802.

Page 119:   13 Dec. 1794. (Bill of Sale) JOSEPH BARR, S.C., Co. of
             Clarendon, Camden Dist., to ROBERT DINGLE, one negro woman
named Nancy. Consideration: 60 pds sterling money. Signed: JOSEPH BASS
(seal). Wit: LAWRENCE FRANKLIN & WM. BUDDIN. Proved by Buddin bef.
JNO. RIDGILL, J.P. 17 Jan. 1795. Rec. 27 Apr. 1802. (Orig. rec. 19
Jan. 1795).

Pp 119-120: 26 Oct. 1796. (Deed) JANE GIBSON, Clarendon Co., S.C.,
            to ROBERT DINGLE, of same, the following tract of land:
All that tract lying on Pen Branch North side of Santee, bounding to
SW on SULLIVAN & NELSON's lands, and all other sides on vacant land,
at time of orig. survey, which tract was orig. granted to ROBERT GIBSON
by a grant dated 4 Oct. 1768, rec. in Sec. Off. in Book E N 9 page
(203). Consideration: 52 pds sterling. Signed: JANE GIBSON (seal).
Wit: LAWRENCE FRANKLIN and THOMAS BOSHER. Proved by Franklin bef. WM.
HUMPHREY, Clerk of Court, 29 Oct. 1796. Rec. 27 Apr. 1802.

Pp 120-121: 23 Apr. 1793. (Bill of Sale) PETER MORLAND to ROBERT DINGLE
            one negro wench by name of Sarey, formerly the property
of WILLIAM BENNETT, deceased. Consideration: 130 pds sterling. Signed:
PETER MORLAND (seal). Wit: ISAAC CONNOR, DAVID DAVIS & JAMES GOUDY.
Proved by Goudy bef. CHAS. F. LESESNE, J.P. C.C. 17 June 1793. Rec.
28 Apr. 1802. (Orig. rec. 20 June 1794.)

Page 121:   10 Sept. 1791. (Bill of Sale). ALEXANDER COLCLOUGH to ROB-
             ERT DINGLE, six negroes, by name: Wench Saray and child,
Darey Betty & Molly, Victor & Sharlot. Consideration: 100 pds sterling.
Signed: ALEXANDER COLCLOUGH (seal). Wit: JOHN MC GINNEY & THOMAS BOSHER.
Proved by Bosher bef. JAMES RICHBOURG, J.P. 11 June 1792. Rec. 28 Apr.
1802. (Orig. rec. 20 July 1792.)

Page 122:   9 Dec. 1800. (Deed) WILLIAM DREGGARS & MARY DREGGARS, his
             wife of Clarendon Co., S.C. to DAVID SHORTER (in trust
as guardian of BLACK JAMEY PEARSON, freeman of color) of the co. and
state afsd., the following tract of land: All that plantation/tract
containing 200 acres 20 yards square at the Grave yard excepted out
of the sd 200 acres, situate in Camden Dist., when surveyed, now in
Sumter Dist. on Cudjo Branch and waters of Black River bounding on
all sides by vacant land when surveyed, and hath such shape..etc..marked
trees as a plat to the orig. grant annexed and accompanying these presents doth represent...recorded in Sec. Off. Grant Bk. GGGG, page 208,
....etc. Consideration: 60 pds sterling money. Signed: WILLIAM DRIGGARS
(seal) by his mark) and MARY DRIGGARS, (seal) by her mark). Wit: WM.
HUMPHREY, ROBERT DINGLE, WM. SAVAGE (by his mark). Proved by Dingle
bef. Jno. Horan, J.P. 12 Dec. 1800. Rec. 28 Apr. 1802. (Orig. rec.
12 Dec. 1800).

Pp 122-123: 1 Jan. 1790. (Bill of Sale). ISAAC CONNOR & BENJAMIN DAVIS,
            of S.C., Camden Dist., Clarendon Co., to a Negro man known
by the name of Jamey, formerly the property of WM. PEARSON, dec'd.
of province and co. afsd., one negro wench named Judy and one child
named Phoebe. Consideration: 138 pds sterling money. Signed: ISAAC
CONNOR (seal), BENJAMIN DAVIS (seal). Wit: PHILIP BENORIT & JOS. CANTEY.
Proved by JOSEPH CANTEY bef. ISAAC CONNOR, 14 June 1791. (Orig. rec.
13 July 1791, now 20 Apr. 1802.)

Pp 123-124: "Know all men by these presents that I, a Negro known by
            the name of BLACK JAMEY PEARSON, a freeman, have purchased
a Negro woman named Judy and child named Phoeby of ISAAC CONNOR, Esq.
& BENJAMIN DAVIS, both of Camden Dist., and that I do of my own free

Cont'd:
will do give to the sd woman and her two children that is Phoebe and
Jane there (sic) freedom from this day and that I do warrant and defend
the same to each and every one of them from my heirs. Executors Administrators and Assigns forever as witness whereof I have interchange-
ably set my hand and seal this third day of June 1791 and in the sixteenth year of American Independence. Signed: BLACK JAMEY PEARSON (seal)
(by his mark). Wit: ROBERT DINGLE, MARY DINGLE & FREDERICK CARTER (by
his mark). Proved by Robt. Dingle bef. Isaac Connor, J.P. 25 Aug. 1791.
Rec. 29 Apr. 1802. (Orig. rec. 13 July 1791.)

Pp 124-125: 7 Sept. 1799. (Bill of Sale) AMOS THAMES, Sheriff of Claren-
            don Co., S.C. to JOHN JAMES of same: Two negroes named
January and Ben being late the property of the Estate of JOHN JAMES,
deceased, and the sd JOHN JAMES & REUBEN LONG, Exrs. of all and singu-
lar the Goods and Chattels, Rights, Credits and effects of the sd JOHN
JAMES, dec'd., being arrested at the suit of HENRY SHOOLBRED & BENJAMIN
MOODY and judgement obtained in the Co. Court for Clarendon afsd. where-
on an execution was issued under the hand and seal of WILLIAM HUMPHREY,
Clerk of sd County, etc. Consideration: 100 pds 5 shillings Sterling
Money. Signed: A. THAMES, Shff. S.D. (seal). Wit: JOHN BOYD, JR. &
GEORGE D. SLATER. Proved by Boyd bef. W. L. STUKES, J.P., Clarendon
Co. 8 Jan. 1801. Rec. 29 Apr. 1802. (Orig. rec. 21 Mar. 1801.)

Pp 125-126: 20 Dec. 1800. (Bill of Sale) HENRY WHITE of Sumter Dist.,
            S.C. to JOHN JAMES of same, the following negroes: Lucy,
Elam, Philis and Betty. Consideration: $1000. Signed: HENRY WHITE (seal)
Wit: JAMES BRUNSON and J. E. BRUNSON. Proved by J. E. BRUNSON bef.
JESSE NETTLES, J.P. Rec. 30 Apr. 1802. (Orig. rec. 18 Apr. 1801.)

Pp 126-127: 16 Feb. 1802. (Deed) NELSON GRAHAM of Sumter Dist., S.C.
            to JAMES FULWOOD of same, the following tract of land:
One plantation or tract containing 100 acres in Craven Co. in the fork
of Pudding Swamp the N side of Black River, orig. granted to WILLIAM
FULWOOD on or about 13 May 1768..ref. being had will more fully appear
by orig. grant that is bounded E on Mr. BENNETT's land and to the S
on JOHN TRIDINE's land and on the sd FULWOOD's and to the N on vacant
land (at the time of the grant) and hath such shape...etc...marked
trees as plat represents..and by him (WILLIAM FULWOOD) by Indenture
of Release dated on or about 20 Dec. 1791 to his son WILLIAM FULWOOD
his heirs and assigns forever and by him transferred to NELSON GRAHAM
JR. his heirs and assigns forever..and now the sd NELSON GRAHAM JR
so by these presents Release unto the sd JAMES FULWOOD the same to
him his heirs and assigns...the other two parcels of land containing
280 acres more or less..that is to say, one Tract of 150 acres, the
other of 130 acres, adj. each other and was orig. granted to ROBERT
FULWOOD and by him transferred by Indenture of Release on or about
11 Mar. 1792 to WM. FULWOOD, JR. .... by him in same manner...to NELSON
GRAHAM.....now by sd GRAHAM to JAMES FULWOOD....the sd two parcels
or tracts lying in fork of Pudding Swamp on N side of Black River,
adj. lands of WILLIAM KENNEDY, NELSON GRAHAM & FULWOOD's Baroney..as
appears by plat annexed to deed of conveyance from sd ROBT. FULWOOD
to sd WM. FULWOOD, JR. ..shape, etc. plat represents...at this time
in Sumter Dist. Consideration: $500. Signed: N. GRAHAM (seal) Wit:
JAMES BURGESS, WM. SMITH & THOMAS ROSE. Proved by Rose bef. WM. KENNEDY,
J.P. 18 Feb. 1802. Rec. 30 Apr. 1802.

Pp 127-128: 14 July 1796. (Deed) THOMAS L. NORRIS & ANNA, his wife,
            Salem Co., S.C. to JAMES FULWOOD of same, the following
tract of land: 250 acres more or less in Camden Dist. situate on mouth
of Horse Branch and N side of Pudding Swamp..orig. granted to ROBERT
FULWOOD, ref. to two certain deeds hereunto annexed, ..with two separate plats.... Consideration: 75 pds sterling. Signed: THOS. L. NORRIS
(seal) & ANNA NORRIS (seal). Wit: ROBERT FULWOOD, JOHN FULWOOD & JOHN
CAPPS (by his mark). Proved by John Fulwood bef. G. COOPER, J.P. 12
Oct. 1796. Rec. 1 May ___?

Pp 128-130: 15 Sept. 1791. (Deed) SAMUEL NELSON, SR. of Clarendon Co.,
            Camden Dist., planter, and JANE, his wife, to SAMUEL EDGAR

Cont'd:
NELSON of the same place the following described tract of land: A certain plantation/tract of land containing 640 acres orig. granted to
the afsd SAMUEL NELSON, SR. also one other plantation of land containing 100 acres orig. granted to sd SAMUEL NELSON, SR. and one other
plantation/tract containing 100 acres orig. granted to JOHN GAMBELL
and from him transferred by Lease and Release to sd SAML. NELSON, SR.
all of which lands are situated in the fork of Black River and have
such shape, etc... as appears by plats duly rec'd. in Sec. Office of
the state afsd. ref. being had...... Consideration: 5 shillings sterling money. Signed: SAMUEL NELSON (seal) and JANE NELSON (seal) (by
her mark). Wit: JNO. MURRAY, JAMES NELSON & WM. POTTS. Rec. 12 May
1802. (Not proved).

Pp 130-132: 15 Sept. 1791. (Deed) SAMUEL NELSON, SR. of Clarendon Co.
          in Camden Dist., S. C., planter and JANE, his wife, to
SAMUEL EDGAR NELSON of the same place, the following tract of land:
A certain plantation/tract of 640 acres orig. granted to afsd. SAMUEL
NELSON, SR. also one other of 100 acres orig. granted to sd NELSON
and one other of 100 acres orig. granted to JOHN GAMBELL and from him
by Lease and Release to sd NELSON all of which are situate in fork
of Black River and etc.....(same as above). Consideration: 500 pds
current money. Signed: SAML. NELSON (seal) and JANE NELSON (seal) (by
her mark). Wit: JNO. MURRAY, JAMES NELSON & WM. POTTS. Rec. 12 May
1802. Proved by POTTS bef. WM. TAYLOR, J.P. 15 Sept. 1791.

Pp 132-133: 4 Mar. 1802. (Bill of Sale). SAMUEL NELSON, SR., Dist.
          of Sumter, S.C., one negro wench named Molera. Considera-
tion: 70 pds sterling. Signed: SAML. NELSON, SR. (seal). Wit: SAML.
E. PLOWDEN & MILES H. PLOWDEN. Proved by MILES PLOWDEN bef. WM. TAYLOR,
J.P. 11 May 1802. Rec. 12 May 1802. (This Bill of Sale to MARY NELSON,
same place).

Pp 133-134: 4 Mar. 1802. (Bill of Sale). SAMUEL NELSON, SR. of Sumter
          Dist., S.C. to SAMUEL EDGAR NELSON of sd dist. and state,
the following negroes: One negro fellow named John, one negro wench
named Dorenda, two negro boys named Billy and Dennis, three negro girls
named Binky, Rose and Aggy. Consideration: 700 pds sterling. Signed:
SAMUEL NELSON, SR. (Seal). Wit: SAML. E. PLOWDEN & MILES H. PLOWDEN.
Proved by MILES HAMPTON PLOWDEN bef. WM. TAYLOR, J.P. 11 May 1802.
Rec. 12 May 1802.

Page 134:   16 Aug. 1791. (Deed of Gift). SAMUEL NELSON, Clarendon
          Co., Camden Dist., S.C. to his son SAMUEL E. NELSON, the
following eleven negro slaves to wit: January, Primus, Frederick, Little
Derry, Alexander, Kate, Molly, Crissy, Cuffy, Sophy and Old Derry.
Consideration: Goodwill and natural affection. Signed: SAML. NELSON,
SR. (seal). Wit: JNO. MURRAY & DANL. CONYERS. Proved by GEO. HERIOT,
Esq. J.Q. of George town Dist. 23 Aug. 1792. Rec. 13 May 1802. (Orig.
rec. 5 Sept. 1791.)

Page 135:   13 Aug. 1791. (Deed of Gift) SAMUEL NELSON, Clarendon Co.,
          Camden Dist., S.C. to his daughter, MARY NELSON the follow-
ing six negro slaves to wit: Phebey, Peggy, Mitty, Letty, Stepney and
Juba. Consideration: Good will and natural affection. Signed: SAML.
NELSON, SR. (seal). Wit: JNO. MURRAY & DANL. CONYERS. Proved by MURRAY
bef. GEO. HERIOT, Esq. J.P. 23 Aug. 1791. Rec. 13 May 1802.

Pp 135-136: 20 Jan. 1801. (Deed) SAMUEL PAYNE of Kershaw Co., S.C.
          to ROBERT WHITE of same co., the following tract of land:
A plantation/tract containing 100 acres more or less, being part of
a tract of land containing 200 acres situate in co. of Claremont and
granted to WILLIAM HUX by grant dated 4 Sept. 1786, beg. on orig. line
that runs W at a corner made by covenant on a black jack and runs on
the sd line and corners at the orig. corner on a red oak and thence
runs on line that runs NW and corners on a red oak made by covenant
then runs NE and corners on a pine made by covenant - then runs SW
by a covenant line to the afsd black jack. Consideration: 20 pds sterling money. Signed: SAMUEL PAYNE (L.S.) Wit: BARNABAS PARTIN & THOMAS

Cont'd:
LEE. Proved by THOMAS LEE bef. DEV'X. BALLARD, J.P. 10 Oct. 1801. Rec.
13 May 1802.

Pp 136-137:   21 Jan. 1801. (Deed) JAMES WOODARD and SARAH his wife,
               of Sumter Dist., S. C., planter, to WYLEY FORT of sd
Dist. and State, the following described tract of land: 200 acres of
land being part of a tract of 300 granted to DENNIS MC CLENDON the
12th day of Sept. 1772, 100 acres of which was conveyed to the sd JAMES
REMBERT by WM. MC CLENDON, JOHN STONE & MARTHA his wife by conveyance
bearing date 13 Jan. 1786 the remaining 100 acres being a part of the
same tract was conveyed to the above JAS. REMBERT by WM. MC CLENDON
5 Oct. 1787 and hath such shape, form and marks as appear by a plat
thereof to the orig. grant annexed. Consideration: $275.00. Signed:
JAMES WOODARD (seal), SARAH WOODARD (seal) (by her mark). Wit: WILLIS
TURBEVILLE, DRURY CLANTON & ISAAC WOODARD. Proved by ISAAC WOODARD
bef. THOS. WILSON, J.P. Rec. 13 May 1802.

Pp 137-138:   21 Jan. 1802. (Deed) THOMAS WOODARD of Salem Co., S.
               C., planter, to WYLY FORD of same, the following tract
of land: All that land above the Road beg. at a post oak on the road
side in THOMAS WOODARD line and runs along to a corner pine and then
along sd line to the Road then up the road to the beg. to sd post oak,
containing 10 acres more or less lying and being in Salem County and
on the W side of sd road situate being part of the land where sd WOODARD
now lives. Consideration: 10 pds. Signed: THOMAS WOODARD (seal). Wit:
WILLIS TURBEVILLE, DRURY CLANTON & ISAAC WOODARD. Proved by ISAAC WOOD-
ARD bef. THOS. WILSON, J.P. 2 Feb. 1802. Rec. 13 May 1802.

Pp 138-139:   30 Apr. 1802. (Deed) WILLIAM BRACEY of Claremont Co.,
               S.C. to JOHN SINGLETON of Green Swamp of county and state
afsd., the following tract of land: 150 acres .. it being a tract of
land orig. granted to WILLIAM GARDENER on 7 June 1774, from him to
SARAH HOWARD from her to WILLIAM BRACEY, bounding S on lands vacant
when run, N on lands vacant when run, and on the other sides on lands
vacant when run having such marks, etc. as will more fully appear by
a plat hereunto annexed. Consideration: $300.00. Signed: WM. BRACEY
(seal). Wit: JNO. C. WALTER & JOLLY BRACEY. Proved by JOLLY BRACEY
bef. JOHN HORAN, J.P. 30 Apr. 1802. (Certified copy of orig. plat of
150 acres of land laid out for JOHN SINGLETON, son of ROBERT SINGLETON).
Rec. 14 May 1802.

Page 140:   9 Feb. 1801. (Deed of Gift). WILLIAM BROWN, SR. of Sumter
               Dist., S. C., planter, to his son, ROBERT BROWN of dist.
and state afsd. the following: A negro fellow by the name of Dudly
and one wench by the name of Denir, with her child by the name of Span-
igo and her increase hereafter. And also a negro girl by the name of
Tamor. Consideration: Love, goodwill and affection. Signed: WILLIAM
BROWN (seal). Wit: JOHN GUERRY, JR., PETER WIDEAU* GUERRY. Proved by
JOHN GUERRY, JR. bef. ABS. WILLIAM, J.P. 7 May 1801. Rec. 14 May 1802.
(*WIDEAU also spelled VIDEAU).

Pp 140-141:   12 Apr. 1802. (Deed) THOMAS WISE of Sumter Dist., S.C.
               to JAMES DAVIS of sd dist. and state, the following tract
of land: All that tract or plantation of land containing 500 acres
situate in the Dist. of Sumter bet. Santee and Black Rivers bounded
by lines running SW and NW by ROBERT DINGLE's land, NW by CHAPMAN's,
NE by the Frenchman's, SE & NE by FRANKLIN's and SE by THEAMS, and
hath such form etc. as plat represents ..granted to me by his Excellency
EDWARD RUTLEDGE. Consideration: 30 pds sterling. Signed: THOS. WISE
(by his mark) (seal). Wit: BENJ. DAVIS & GEORGE ANDREWS. Release of
Interest and Estate, also her right and claim of Dower in the above
premises, signed by MARY WISE (by mark) bef. WM. RICHBOURG, 12 Apr.
1802. Proved by GEO. ANDREWS bef. WM. RICHBOURG, J.Q. of the dist.
afsd, same date. Rec. 14 May 1802.

Pp 142-143:   26 Dec. 1790. (Deed) JOSEPH CORBETT of Orangeburg Dist.,
               S.C., to JAMES WEEKS, SR. of Clarendon Co., S.C. the
following tract: A certain plantation or tract of land containing 150
acres, situate in Dist. of Camden Clarendon Co. and hath such shape,

Cont'd:
form and marked trees as is represented in the plat annexed to the
grant thereof, granted to sd JOSEPH CORBETT 5 Dec. 1785 and on record
in Sec. office Book GGGG page 129, ref. thereunto being had will more
fully appear. Consideration: 5 shillings good and lawful current money
of sd state. Signed: JOSEPH CORBETT (seal). Wit: STEPHEN NIXON and
WILLIAM WEEKS. Not proven and no recording date.

Pp 143-145:   27 Dec. 1794. (Deed) JOSEPH CORBETT, of Orangeburg Dist.,
               State of S. C., to JAMES WEEKS, SR. of county of Clarendon
and state afsd., the following described tract of land: (Described
in above indenture of Lease bearing date the day next before the day
of the date of these presents). Consideration: 30 pds good and lawful
money. Signed: JOSEPH CORBETT (seal). Wit: STEPHEN NIXON & WILLIAM
WEEKS. Proved by WM. WEEKS bef. W. R. L. STOKES, J.P. for Clarendon
County. May 19, 1802. Rec. May 20, 1802.

Pp 145-147:   (Deed) Between WILLIAM REES and MARY his wife of S.C.,
               County of Craven in St. Marks Parish, planter of one
part, and AUSTIN SPEARS of the province, county and parish afsd. planter
of the other part, whereas in and by a certain grant bearing date the
12th day of June in the year of our Lord one thousand seven hundred
and sixty seven and in the the seventh year of his Majesties Reign
under the hand of his Excellency the Right Honourable Lord CHARLES
GREENVILLE MONTAGUE, Capt. Gen'l. and Governor in Chief in and over
the province of South Carolina, and the Great Seasl of the province
for that purpose appointed did give and grant unto WILLIAM REES a plantation or tract of land containing 200 acres in Craven Co. in St. Marks
Parish being formerly surveyed for the sd AUSTIN SPEARS, bounded on
all sides by vacant lands and hath such shape form and marks as appears
by a plat thereof to the sd grant annexed, as in and by the sd plat
and grant duly recorded in the Sec. office of sd province, ref. being
thereunto had may more fully appear. Consideration: 300 pds lawful
current money. Signed: WILLIAM REES (seal) and MARY REES (seal). Wit:
JAS. MC CORMICK, ISHAM REES. Proved by JAS. MC CORMICK bef. ANDREW
ALISON, Esq. (Sworn 21 May 1802.)

Pp 147-149:   (Deed) 8 Apr. 1791. Between MASON SPEARS of the state
               aafsd, Claremont Co. of the one part, Carpenter, and
JOHN BILLUPS of state of Virginia, Mecklinburg county, whereas in and
by a certain Grant dated 12 June 1767, under hand of his Excellency
Charles Greenville Montague, Esq., Gov. etc. and the great Seal for
that purpose, appointed did give and grant unto WILLIAM REES a plantation or tract of land containing 200 acres situate in Claremont Co.
granted to WM. REES, bounded on all sides by vacant land at time of
survey, hath such shape, etc. as appears by plat annexed to sd grant
duly rec. in Sec. office Book AAA, page 513, also one other plantation
or tract of 150 acres situate etc. in Claremont co. and state afsd.
bounding E partly on land of JOHN WHELER and WM. REES, all other sides
by vacant land at time of survey which sd grant is unto AUSTIN SPEARS
under the hand of his Excellency WM. BULL, Esq. Gov. etc. dated 1770
rec. in Sec. office Grant book FFF, page 5, ref. being had fully and
at large appear. Consideration: 1000 pds sterling money. Signed. MASON
SPEARS (seal). Wit: W. R. DAVIS & THOS. ANDREWS. Proved by Andrews
bef. WM. BRACEY, J.P. 9 May 1791. Rec. 21 May 1802. (The above 200
acres was sold and conveyed from WM. REES to AUSTIN SPEAR by Lease
and Release 9 & 10 June 1762. Orig. rec. 10 May 1791.)

Pp 149-151:   (Deed) 11 Sept. 1790. Between JOHN BILLUPS of Virginia,
               Mecklinburg Co. of one part, and MATTHEW JAMES of S.
C. Clarendon Co., whereas in and by a certain grant dated 12 June 1767
under hand of his Excellency Charles G. Montague, Esq., Gov. etc. ...a
grant unto WM. REES plantation/tract of 200 acres situate in Claremont
Co. granted unto WM. REES bounded on all sides by vacant land at time
of survey..such shape, etc. plat annexed to sd grant, rec'd. in Sec.
Office in Book AAA, page 513-also on other plantation/tract of 150
acres situate, being in Claremont co. and state afsd. partly on land
of JOHN WHELER and WM. REES, all other sides vacant land at time of
survey, which sd grant is unto AUSTIN SPEARS under hand of his Excellen-

Cont'd:
cy WILLIAM BULL, Esq., Gov. and dated 1770, duly rec'd. in Sec. Office
in Grant Bk. FFF, page 5, ref. had more fully, etc....the above 200
acres was sold and conveyed from WILLIAM REES to AUSTIN SPEARS by Lease
and Release, dated 9 and 10 June 1768 - now sold and conveyed from
MASON SPEARS, Executor of sd AUSTIN SPEARS to JOHN BILLUPS, (sd tracts
of land conveyed to JNO. BILLUPS contained 350 acres) and from BILLUPS
to MATTHEW JAMES, living as above mentioned. Consideration: 202 pds
2 shillings 6 pence sterling money. Signed: JOHN BILLUPS (seal). Wit:
HUGH C. BILLUPS & WM. BILLUPS. Proved by WM. BILLUPS bef. SAMUEL REILY,
J.P. 25 Apr. 1795. Rec. 21 May 1802. (The above 2 tracts of land conveyed to MATTHEW JAMES containing 350 acres, orig. rec. 28 Apr. 1795.)

Pp 151-153:   18 Mar. 1801. (Deed) MATTHEW JAMES, Clarendon Co., S.C.
               planter, to JOHN MURRAY of Claremont Co., SC the follow-
ing described tract of land: All that plantation, parcel or tract of
land, containing 350 acres, comprehending two orig. surveys or grants
adj. each other, situate in Claremont County, Sumter Dist., and on
which the sd JOHN MURRAY now resides, one containing 200 acres, orig.
granted to WILLIAM REES, on or about 12 June 1767 duly rec. in Sec.
Office, Grant Book AAA, page 573, the other tract of 150 acres orig.
granted to AUSTIN SPEARS 1770, duly rec. in Sec. Office Grant Book
FFF, page 5, which sd tract/tracts of land passed by divers conveyances to the above named MATTHEW JAMES party to these presents, as
may appear by a reference to Records of Claremont and Clarendon Counties
transferred to the Clerks Office of Sumter Dist. Consideration: 300
pds sterling money. Signed: MATTHEW JAMES (seal). Wit: ELIZABETH GOUL-
LIETTE and CHRISTOPHER MC CONNICO. Release of all interest and estate,
also her right and claim of dower signed by LETITIA JAMES, wife of
above named MATTHEW JAMES, bef. THOMAS N. JOHNSON, J.Q. Sumter Dist.
Proved by MC CONNICO bef. JOHN HORAN, J.P. 6 June 1801. Rec. 21 May
1802. (Orig. rec. 8 June 1801.)

Pp 153-154:   14 Jan. 1802. (Deed) WILLIAM SNELL of Claremont Co.,
               S.C. to JAMES HOWARD of state and co. afsd. the following
tract of land: A tract/plantation containing 1000 acres more or less
bounded by lines running NW and NE by MRS. ADKINS land and NEILSON's,
SE unknown, and THOMAS NIEL's (it laying on Gum Swamp and Wateree Swamp)
Consideration: 20 pds lawful money. Signed: WM. SNELL (seal). Wit.:
JOS. J. MARTIN & DAVID THOMPSON. Proved by Thompson bef. JOHN HORAN,
J.P. 8 June 1802. Rec. 10 June 1802.

Page 154:   9 June 1802. (Bill of Sale). J. B. VAUGHAN of the county
               of Claremont, State of S.C. to JOSEPH SINGLETON of same
county, one negro boy named Antony, aged about 13 years. Consideration:
$500. Signed: J. B. VAUGHAN (seal). Wit: ROBERT SINGLETON. Proved by
ROBT. SINGLETON bef. John Horan, J.P. 9 June 1802. Rec. 10 June 1802.

Pp 154-156:   7 May 1802. (Deed) RICHARD BRADFORD of Claremont Co.,
               planter, State of S.C. to JEREMIAH BROWN of county and
state afsd. 368 acres situate in Sumter Dist., state and county afsd.
on poly branch and Rocky Bluff Swamp and waters of Black River. Being
one half part of a tract of land orig. granted to sd RICHARD BRADFORD
signed by his excellency Wm. Moultrie, Gov. etc. and rec. in Sec. Office
in Grant Book OOOO page 576, ref. more fully appear by plat annexed.
Consideration: $600. Signed: RICHARD BRADFORD. Wit.: RICHARD MC KEWEN
and RICHARD BRADFORD, JR. Proved by RICH. BRADFORD, JR. bef. ABE WIL-
LIAMS, J.P. 7 June 1802. Rec. 10 June 1802. (Plat shows land of JOHN
PEEKS & ISHAM MOORE).

Page 156:   11 June 1802. (Deed) ZACHARIAH CANTEY of Kershaw Dist.
               in S.C., planter, to WILLIAM SAUNDERS, SR. of Sumter
Dist., sd state, the following described tract of land: All that tract
of land lying and being on Big Raften Creek, waters of Wateree River,
granted to ZACHARIAH CANTEY 4 Oct. 1794, containing 300 acres more
or less, bounded SW and SE by JAMES ROBINSON's, JOHN MELONE's, WILLIAM
WRIGHT's, and JAMES DULLEY's land; NW and NE by WILLIAM RICHARDSON,
SHERWOOD JAMES and land not known; a plat of same being annexed to
grant, ref. more fully appear. Consideration: $150.00. Signed: ZACH.

Cont'd:
CANTEY (seal). Wit: ALEX. MATHESON & DUNCAN MC RA. Proved by ALEX.
MATHESON bef. JAS. BROWN, J.P. 26 June 1802. Rec. 10 July 1802.

Pp 157-158:   20 Sept. 1791. (Deed of Gift) WILLIAM WESBURY of Clare-
                mont Co., S. C. to his cousins, JANE, WILLIAM, THOMAS,
MARTHA, RICHARD, SAMUEL, JOHN & JONATHAN (children of his uncle, JOHN
WESBURY and ELIZABETH WESBURY), three negroes, to wit: a fellow named
June, a boy called July, and a wench named Nan. (sd negroes kept to-
gether in possession of Aunt until JONATHAN comes of age, then divided)
Consideration: Natural affection. Signed: WILLIAM WESBERY (seal). Wit:
HENRY HAYNSWORTH, SARAH HAYNSWORTH & JOSHUA MC INTOSH. Proved by HENRY
HAYNSWORTH bef. THOS. HOPPER, J.C.C. 21 Sept. 1791. Rec. 10 July 1802.
(Orig. rec. 22 Sept. 1791.)

Page 158:   (no date) (Deed) ROBERT MACKEY of Claremont Co., S.C.
                to ELIZABETH WESBERY of sd county, the following described
tract of land: All that plantation or tract containing 83 acres situate
in the dist. of Camden and lying on Mins Branch, waters of the Wateree River granted to sd ROBERT MACKEY by grant dated 1 Sept. 1788; bounding NE by DAVID ROGER's land, NW by BENJAMIN FARGUSON's land, SW by
MILES LILLEY and LODWICK HUTSON's lands. Consideration: 20 pds sterling money. Signed: ROBERT MACKEY (seal). Wit: ROBERT SANDERS & WILLIAM
WESBURY. Proved by Sanders bef. John Horan, J.P. 11 Feb. 1801. Rec.
10 July 1802. (Orig. rec. 23 Feb. 1801.)

Pp 159-160:   8 July 1802. (Deed) ROBERT BATES and ELIZABETH BATES,
                his wife, late ELIZABETH WESBERY, widow, of Sumter Dist.
state afsd., TO ISAAC LENOIR and JAMES BARNES, of sd dist., planters,
the following described tract: A certain piece or parcel of land containing 83 acres situate on Mains Branch in Dist. of Sumter bounded
on lands of BENJ. FARGUSON, JAMES BATES & HENRY CLARKE, being the same
tract the sd ELIZABETH WESBERY purchased of ROBERT MACKEY. Also the
following household furniture: two feather beds and furniture, one
loom and gears, one cupboard and furniture, four iron potts, two tables
and one hand mill, the same to be held with the tract of land afsd.
in trust for the following uses and purposes, that is to say: if the
sd ROBERT BATES be the longest liver he holds the property during his
natural life, and in case the sd ELIZABETH BATES survive him she holds
the property during life, and our will and desire is that after both
our decease, the sd land and household furniture be equally divided
between the sd ELIZABETH's two youngest sons, SAMUEL WESBERY and JONA-
THAN WESBERY. Consideration: 20 shillings. Signed: ROBERT BATES (seal)
and ELIZABETH BATES (seal). Wit: WILLIAM MURRELL & WM. GERALD. Proved
by Murrell bef. John Horan, J.P., 9 July 1802. Rec. 12 July 1802.

Pp 160-161:   23 Feb. 1797. (Agreement) Between SAMUEL BENNET, JAMES
                BENNET, ESTHER BENNET, LEONORA BENNET, JAMES CANTEY,
JOHN BANISTER and PETER WILLIAMS, heirs of SAMUEL BENNET, deceased.
It was agreed upon by and bet. the above parties that their Rights
and Claims be referred and submitted to JOHN SINGLETON, ISAAC CONNOR
& RICHARD RICHARDSON, Esq., for an equal division and distribution
of sd property. Signed: JAMES CANTEY (seal), ESTHER BENNET (seal),
SAML. BENNET (seal), PETER WILLIAMS (seal), JOHN J. BANISTER (seal)
LEONORA BENNET (seal) (by mark), JAMES N. BENNET (seal). Wit: JNO.
SINGLETON, ISAAC CONNOR, R. RICHARDSON, JR. Proved by ISAAC CONNOR
bef. WM. TAYLOR, J.P., 13 Apr. 1801. Rec. 12 July 1802. Orig. rec.
18 Apr. 1801.

Pp 161-162:   13 Aug. 1791. (Deed of Gift) SAMUEL NELSON of Clarendon
                Co., Camden Dist., S. C. to his daughter, ELIZABETH NELSON
the following negro slaves, to wit: Judy, Sobina, Prince, Caesar, Mel-
izar, Sara and old Sara, and their increase. Consideration: Goodwill
and natural affection. Signed: SAML. NELSON, SR. (seal). Wit: JNO.
MURRAY & DANL. CONYERS. Proved by Murray bef. GEO. HERIOT, J.Q. 23
Aug. 1791. Rec. 26 July 1802. Orig. rec. 5 Sept. 1791.

Pp 162-163:   27 Jan. 1802. (Deed) DAN CARPENTER of Camden, S.C., mer-
                chant, to LEWIS PEOPLES of Kershaw Dist., S.C., planter,
the following described tract of land: Part of a tract of 900 acres,

Cont'd:
situate in Sumter Dist. on waters of Black River that is one fourth
part thereof containing 225 acres more or less the other three fourths
thereof being sold by me to WILLIAM DANIEL & THOMAS SMITH, also one
tract called the Piny Marsh tract containing 150 acres or so much thereof as is not taken by Biger Surveys also one other tract containing
100 acres more or less all granted to FREDERICK BELL. Consideration:
$54. Signed: DAN CARPENTER (seal). Wit: BENJAMIN HUTCHINSON & J. M.
SLUMP. Proved by Benj. Hutchinson bef. JAMES CLARK one of the Wardens
of Camden 2 June 1802. Rec. 26 July 1802.

Pp 163-164:   10 Oct. 1798. (Deed) HEZEKIAH REAMS, planter of S.C.,
                Claremont Co. to MOTT HANKES, of sd state, planter, the
following described tract of land: One afsd. containing 307 acres be
the same more or less lying on the N side of Rocky Bluff Swamp a branch
of Black River, that was orig. granted to JOHN CAUDLE, JR. 2 July 1787
and surveyed by FREDERICK BELL, Deputy Surveyor and certified for the
7th Oct. 1786, duly rec. in Sec. Office, Grant Bk. VVVV, page 83 and
examined by PETER FRENEAU, Secretary, and bounded NW on WILLIAM P.
BROWN's land, NE on EDWARD LOWNS, E. & S. on JOHN GIBSON's land, and
SW on JOHN TISDALE's lands, and hath such shape, etc. by plat of same
annexed to grant...Consideration: 60 pds good and lawful money. Signed:
HEZAKIAH REAMS (seal) and ELIZABETH REAMS (seal) (by mark). Wit: CHAS.
F. GORDON, WM. REAVES & ROBERT HENRY. Proved by WM. REAVES bef. JOHN
HORAN, J.P. 2 Aug. 1802.

Pp 164-165:   12 Dec. 1801. (Deed) JOSHUA JOSEPH HOWELL, of S.C., Sumter
                Dist., planter, to CORNISH NAVIE, of dist. and state
afsd., planter, the following described tract: All that plantation
where he now lives containing 300 acres it beginning W on a lightwood
stake corner and runs E N and corners E part N on a lightwood stake
bound on the N by land of GEORGE PAYNE, SR., runs from thence S by
E and corners on a red oak and bound on E by land sd to be the property
of JOHN LENOIR, it being part of the orig. tract from thence runs W
and corners on a pine bounds S on lands sd to be property of CARSON
SCOT & NATHAN NORTON, they being parts of the orig. tract from thence
runs E by N and corners on a lightwood Stake and binds NW on land of
afsd NATHAN NORTON from thence runs W and corners on the first mentioned lightwood stake and bind N on land granted to REUBEN BRASSFIELD
the afsd plantation or tract of land containing 300 acres, it being
a Moiety or part of a tract or tracts of land containing 4,900 acres
granted to DAVID REYNOLDS, deceased. (Granted 6 Nov. 1786, grant book
2222, page 149.) Consideration: $100. Signed: JOSHUA JOSEPH HOWELL.
Wit: ABNER MARTIN & BENJAMIN ROLLINS. Proved by Rollins bef. ABS. WIL-
LIAMS, J.Q. 12 Feb. 1802. Rec. 3 Aug. 1802.

Page 166:   26 Dec. 1800. (Deed) LEWIS MC COY of co. of Richmond,
                State of Georgia, to REDDEN MC COY of Claremont Co.,
S. C., the following described tract of land: All that tract containing
by estimation 100 acres, it being part of a tract containing 250 acres
orig. granted to ELIJAH MC COY, SR. the 23rd June 1774, which sd 250
acres of land is situate, etc. in Claremont Co., S.C. on S side of
the middle prong of Black River, bounded NE on JOHN TUCKER's lands,
NW on vacant lands, and the sd ELIJAH MC COY's land and other sides
by vacant land and hath such shape, etc. as plat annexed to grant represents, surveyed by NATHANIEL MOORE 11 Dec. 1772. Consideration:
$100. Signed: LEWIS MC COY (seal). Wit: JOHN BRANDON (by mark), ABRAHAM
TAYLOR & DAVID B. BUTLER, J.P. Rec. 3 Aug. 1802.

Pp 166-168:   9 Dec. 1792. (Deed) WILLIAM BARBER of Claremont Co.,
                S.C., planter, to REDDEN MC COY, planter, a certain plan-
tatioin containing by est. 285 acres, in dist. of Camden on Long Branch,
SW side of Black River, which land was granted unto the sd WM. BARBER
5 Feb. 1787, more fully described by plat of same annexed to grant.
Consideration: 33 pds. 5 sh. sterling money. Signed: WILLIAM BARBOUR
(seal). Wit: CHAS. F. GORDON & ELIJAH MC COY. C. COOPER, Atty. for
Bakers Barony. Proved by CHARLES FISHER GORDON bef. JOHN MC DONELL,
J.P. 28 Feb. 1795. Rec. 3 Aug. 1802. (Orig. rec. 3 Mar. 1801.)

Pp 168-169:   1 Jan. 1801. (Deed) STEPHEN MC COY, of Bullock Co., state

Cont'd:
                    of Georgia, to ELISHA MC COY of Clarendon Co., S. C.,
a tract of land containing by estimation 100 acres, it being part of
a 250 acre tract orig. granted to ELIJAH MC COY 23 June 1774; sd 250
acres being in Claremont Co., state afsd. on the south of Middle prong
of Black River, bounded NE on JOHN TUCKER's land, NW on vacant, and
the sd ELIJAH MC COY's land, and other sides by vacant land, more fully
described by a plat annexed to grant and surveyed by NATHL. MOORE,
7 Dec. 1772. Consideration: $100. Signed: STEPHEN MC COY (L.S.), NANCY
MC COY (no seal). Wit: ROBERT MC CALL, FRAN'S. MC CALL & LEWIS LANIER.
(Lanier a J.P.) (Not proven). Rec. 3 Aug. 1802. (Orig. rec. 3 Nov.
1801.)

Pp 169-170:   10 Jan. 1777. (Deed) ALEXR. ROBINSON, Executor for JOHN
               ROBINSON, of the Parish of St. Marks in province of S.C.,
planter, to MARTAIN HOWARD, of Prince Frederick Parish, in sd province,
tavern keeper, a tract of land containing 100 acres, situate on Wyboo
in St. Marks Parish, bounded on all sides by vacant land, more fully
described by plat and grant rec. in Sec. Office. Orig. granted to WIL-
LIAM CANTEY, 13 Feb. 1753, by JAMES GLEN, Capt. Gen. and Gov. in Chief
in and over the province of S.C. and purchased by JOHN ROBINSON, who
ALEXANDER ROBINSON is executor for. Consideration: 250 pds. Signed:
ALEXR. ROBINSON (seal). Wit: FRANCIS DROZE, BENJAMIN GUESS & JOHN MC
CARTNEY. Proved by MC CARTNEY bef. ROBERT DINGLE, J.P.C.C. 1 Sept.
1794. Rec. 5 Aug. 1802. (Orig. rec. 12 Jan. 1795.)

Pp 170-172:   10 Jan. 1777. (Deed) ALEXANDER ROBINSON, Executor for
               JOHN ROBINSON, of Parish of St. Mark in province of S.C.,
planter, to MARTAIN HOWARD of Prince Frederick Parish in sd province,
tavern keeper, formerly granted to JOHN ROBINSON, 3 June 1766, by his
Exc. WM. BULL, Esq., Lt. Gov. and commander in chief in and over the
province of S. C. Sd 150 acres being situate on Wyboo in St. Marks
Parish, bounded S on sd ROBINSON's land, N on ALEXANDER ROBINSON's
land, E on WILLIAM ROBINSON's land, and W on vacant land, more fully
described by plat and grant duly rec. in Sec. Office of sd province
for a consideration of: 350 pds. Signed: ALEXR. ROBINSON (seal). Wit:
FRANCIS DROZE, BENJAMIN GUESS & JOHN MC CARTNEY. Proved by McCartney
bef. Robt. Dingle, J.P.C.C. 1 Sept. 1794. Rec. 5 Aug. 1802.

Pp 172-173:   28 Mar. 1793. (Deed) MARTAIN HOWARD of Prince Frederick
               Parish, George Town Dist., State of S. C., planter, to
WILLIAM ROBERTSON of state afsd, Camden Dist., Clarendon Co., planter,
150 acres situate on Wyboo in St. Marks Parish, bounding on S on JOHN
ROBERTSON's land, on N by ALEXANDER ROBERTSON's land, on E by WM. ROB-
ERTSON's land, on all other sides vacant land, being a tract orig.
granted to sd JOHN ROBERTSON, and by his executor sold to above MARTAIN
HOWARD, 3 June 1766. Consideration: 100 pds sterling. Signed: MARTIN
HOWARD (by mark). Wit: AARON LITTELL. Proved by AARON LITTLE bef. CHAS.
F. LESESNE, J.P. Rec. 5 Aug. 1802.

Pp 173-174:   8 Mar. 1793. (Deed) MARTAIN HOWARD of Prince Frederick
               Parish, Georgetown Dist., S. C., planter, to WILLIAM
ROBERTSON, of state afsd., Camden Dist., Clarendon Co., planter, the
following described tract of land: tract containing 100 acres situate
in Clarendon Co., Camden Dist. on all sides vacant land when granted
to WILLIAM CANTEY dated 13 Feb. 1753 and by sd CANTEY sold to JOHN
ROBERTSON and by ROBERTSON's executorss to the afsd MARTAIN HOWARD.
Consideration: 57 pds. Signed: MARTAIN HOWARD (by mark). Proved by
AARON LITTLE bef. CHAS. F. LESESNE, J.P. 20 Aug. 1794. Rec. 5 Aug.
1795. Wit: AARON LITTELL, JOHN HOWARD & JOHN HICKSON. (Orig. rec. 12
Jan. 1795, now 5 Aug. 1802.)

Pp 174-176:   9 May 1801. (Deed) WILLIAM ROBERTSON of S. C., Sumter
               Dist., to JAMES DAVIS, state and dist. afsd. a tract/
parcel of land containing 100 acres, situate in Sumter Dist., on N
side of Santee River, butting and bounding on all sides by vacant land.
Orig. granted to WM. CANTEY by his Ex. JAMES GLEN, 13 Feb. 1750; also
a plantation/tract containing 150 acres in Sumter Dist. on N side of
Santee River, butting and bounding N on ALEXANDER ROBINSON's land,
to S of JOHN ROBERTSON's land, and on all other sides vacant land,

Cont'd:

orig. granted to JOHN ROBERTSON by his Exc. WILLIAM BULL, 13 June 1766 also a plantation or tract containing 200 acres situate on N side of Santee River on Peter's Swamp bounding on all sides on vacant land, granted to WILLIAM ROBERTSON by his Ex. BENJAMIN GUERARD dated 25 Jan. 1785. Consideration: 250 pds. Signed: WM. ROBERTSON (seal). Wit: ELIZ. DENNIS, WILLIAM DENNIS & JOHN ROWLETT. Release of all interest and estate, also right and claim of dower in within mentioned premises, signed by JANE ROBERTSON (seal-by her mark). Proved by JOHN ROWLETT bef. JOHN FRIERSON, J.Q. 9 May 1801. Rec. 5 Aug. 1802.

Pp 176-177:   25 Dec. 1785. (Deed) JEAN HAWKINS of St. Marks Parish and state of S. C., planter, to JAMES DAVIS of parish afsd, nephew of the sd JEAN HAWKINS, six acres and a half of land, being part of a tract that sd JEAN HAWKINS now lives on butting and bounding E on the sd land, and S and W on sd JAMES DAVIS' land, N on a branch of Wyboo or beard branch. Consideration: 35 sh. current money and natural love and affection. Signed: JEAN HAWKINS (seal). Wit: RICHD. COOPER, WM. BRUNSON, SR. & NATHL. DAVIS. Proved by BRUNSON bef. JNO. DICKEY, J.P. 14 Mar. 1786. Rec. 6 Aug. 1802.

Pp 177-179:   1 Nov. 1783. (Deed) SAMUEL CANTEY & EBENEZER BAGNAL, Executors of the Estate of JOSEPH CANTEY, deceased, and MATTHEW CANTEY, Exec. and joint heir to sd estate to Captain JAMES DAVIS of Camden Dist. Consideration: 5 pds sterling money. Two acres situate, on waters of Wyboo Creek a branch of Santee River in Craven Co. (being part of a tract granted to JOSEPH CANTEY by virtue of a grant bearing date 21 May 1772). Having such shape, etc. as plat in margin represents. Signed: SAML. CANTEY (seal), EBENEZER BAGNELL (seal) MATTHEW CANTEY (seal-by mark). Wit: SAML. MONTGOMERY, AARON WEBB & SAMUEL HODGKISS (by mark). Proved by MONTGOMERY bef. WM. MARTIN, J.P. 3 Apr. 1784. Rec. 6 Aug. 1802. (Plat shows land of JEAN HAWKINS & JAMES DAVIS).

Pp 180-181:   30 June 1784. (Deed) SAMUEL NELSON, SR. of Camden Dist., S. C., (Gentleman) and JEAN, his wife, to JAMES DAVIS of Camden Dist., state afsd, (gentleman). Consideration: 100 pds sterling. 150 acres in Craven Co. on N side of Santee River, bounded N on ELIZABETH WILLIAMS' and part on vacant land, to E on JAMES NOWIL's land, to S part on sd NOWIL's land and part on vacant land, to W on JOHN SMITH's land, which sd tract of 150 acres was granted to JOHN TROUP 31 Oct. 1765, conveyed by deed made by sd JOHN TROUP to MATTHEW NEILSON rec. in Sec. Off. which sd tract of land became the property of sd SAMUEL NELSON by the last Will and Testament of sd MATTHEW NEILSON, deceased, 12 Jan. 1771. Signed: SAML. NELSON, SR. (seal), JEAN NELSON (seal-by mark). Wit: JNO. GAMBELL, JOHN BAGNAL, & ISAAC BAGNAL. Proved by Jno. Gambell bef. JNO. DICKEY, J.P. 15 Dec. 1787. Rec. 6 Aug. 1802.

Pp 181-184:   26 Oct. 1785. (Deed) WILLIS WILLS, of the Parish of St. Marks in S. C., planter and LYDIA, his wife, to JAMES DAVIS, of sd parish and state, planter. Consideration: 1 sh. and 4 p. sterling. 400 acres of land, situate in Dist. of Camden on S prong of Black River on S side, bounded W on land laid out for ARTHUR WHITE and all other sides vacant lands; more fully described by a plat thereof to sd grant annexed. Sd tract of 400 acres was formerly granted to WILLIS WILLS, 5 Sept. 1785, under hand of his Exc. Wm. Moultrie, Esq., Gov. and Commander in Chief over sd state. Signed: WILLIS WILLS (seal) and LYDIA WILLS (seal). Wit: JNO. GAMBELL, ENEAS M. DEARMID & WM. BRUNSON, SR. Proved by Brunson bef. JNO. DICKEY, J.P. 14 Mar. 1786. Rec. 6 Aug. 1802.

Pp 184-185:   20 July 1788. (Deed) MATTHEW CANTEY and MARGRET CANTEY, his wife, to Capt. JAMES DAVIS of Camden dist., S. C. Consideration: 50 pds sterling money. 100 acres on waters of Wideboo Swamp, a branch of Santee River, in Craven Co. (being part of a tract granted to JOSEPH CANTEY by a grant bearing date 21 May 1772, and willed by sd JOSEPH CANTEY the father of MATTHEW CANTEY and JOSEPH his brother, to be equally divided between them, and after being done agreeable to his will, the E part of sd tract...more fully described by a plat on margin. Signed: MAT CANTEY (seal), MARGRET CANTEY (seal). Witness:

Cont'd:
EBENEZER BAGNAL, WM. BRUNSON, SR., SAML. REILY. Proved by BAGNAL bef.
Jno. Dickey, J.P. 15 Oct. 1788. Rec. 6 Aug. 1802.

Pp 185-186: 16 Apr. 1801. (Bill of Sale) ANDREW CALDWELL, Co. of
             Clarendon, S. C. to JAMES DAVIS, of Sumter Dist., S.
C. Consideration: $50 lawful money. One negro boy named Frank, aged
9 years. Signed: A. CALDWELL (seal). Wit: J. ROWLETT & DAVID REID.
Proved by JOHN ROWLETT bef. WM. TAYLOR, J.P. 5 Aug. 1802. Rec. 6 Aug.
1802. (Orig. rec. 10 Sept. 1801.)

Pp 186-187: 28 Jan. 1801. (Deed) CHARLES & SARAH AMONETT of Claren-
             don Co., S. C. to JAMES DAVIS of same place. Considera-
tion: 60 pds sterling. All that plantation or tract of land containing 200 acres more or less, situate on White Oak Branch E side of Santee
butting and bounding on all sides on vacant land at time of orig. survey; also 220 acres more or less which is part of a tract of 640 acres
orig. granted to sd AMONETT as also the tract of 200 acres was granted
to sd AMONETT. Signed: CHARLES AMONETT (seal), SARAH AMONETT (seal).
(by her mark). Wit: THOS. BUSHKIRK, WILLIAM SAVAGE (by mark). Release
of interest and estate, also right and claim of dower signed by SARAH
AMONET, wife of CHARLES AMONET,10 July 1801 bef. JAMES B. RICHARDSON,
Q.U. Proved by WM. SAVAGE bef. WM. TAYLOR, J.P. 6 Apr. 1801. Rec. 7
Aug. 1802.

Pp 187-188: 24 Apr. 1802. (Bill of Sale) HENRY CAPELL to JAMES DAVIS,
             Sumter Dist., S. C. Consideration: $390.00. A mulatto
boy named Boston, 13 yrs. Signed: HENRY CAPELL. Wit: THOMAS BOSHER
& WM. HUMPHREY, JR. Rec. 7 Aug. 1802. (Not proven).

Page 188: 30 Dec. 1790. (Deed) JANE HAWKINS of St. Marks Parish,
           Camden Dist., S. C. to BENJAMIN DAVIS, her nephew of
sd parish, dist. and state. Good causes and valuable consideration.
A dwelling house and manor plantation containing 293 acres and 1/2,
more or less, situate on branch of Wyboo, called Beards Branch in the
parish and dist. and state afsd. Signed: JANE HAWKINS (seal) (her mark).
Wit: JOHN FRIERSON, MARY MACKENETT & JAMES MC CAULEY. Proved by Frierson bef. JAMES MC CAULEY, J.P. 30 Dec. 1790. Rec. 7 Aug. 1802. (Orig.
rec. 9 Mar. 1791.)

Pp 188-189: 7 Apr. 1791. (Bill of Sale) JEAN HAWKINS of Camden Dist.,
             S. C., planter, to BENJAMIN DAVIS, of sd dist. and state,
planter. Consideration: 50 pds sterling money. One negro man named
Saser. Signed: JEANA HAWKINS (seal) (by mark). Wit: JAMES MC CAULEY
& MARY MACKENET. Proved by McCauley bef. ISAAC CONNOR, J.P. 16 Apr.
1791. Rec. 7 Aug. 1802. (Orig. rec. 15 June 1791.)

Pp 189-190: (no date) (Deed) JAMES NELSON of Sumter Dist., S.C.,
             to BENJAMIN DAVIS, SR. of sd dist. and state. Consider-
ation: 10 pds sterling. A tract of land containing 350 acres, situate
in Dist. of George-Town on Mount Hope, a N. branch of Santee - being
part of a tract of 710 acres orig. granted jointly unto BENJAMIN DAVIS
& JAMES NELSON by his Exc. Wm. Moultrie 6 Nov. 1786. Signed: JAMES
NELSON (seal). Wit: SAML. P. TAYLOR & SAML. E. NELSON. Release of all
interest and estate, also her right and claim of dower, in premises
above, signed by ISABELLA NELSON, wife of JAMES NELSON, bef. Wm. Taylor,
J.Q., 11 Feb. 1802. Proved by Saml. E. Nelson bef. Wm. Taylor, J.Q.
12 Feb. 1802. Rec. 7 Aug. 1802.

Pp 190-191: 9 May 1801. (Deed) JAMES DAVIS, Sumter Dist., S.C. to
             JAMES BRUNSON, son of WILLIAM BRUNSON, SR., of Sumter
Dist., state afsd. Consideration: 20 sh. A tract of land containing
100 acres situate in Sumter Dist., S. C. on E side of Santee River
on road to Nelson's Ferry, more fully described by a plat annexed,
granted to JAMES DAVIS by Wm. Moultrie, 1 Aug. 1785. Signed: J. DAVIS
(seal) and SH. DAVIS (seal). Wit: MICL. BIRCH, SAML. BENNETT. Release
of all interest, also right and claim of dower in premises above signed
by SUSANNAH DAVIS (seal) bef. JOHN FRIERSON, J.Q. 9 May 1801. Proved
by JAMES BENNETT bef. JOHN FRIERSON. Rec. 7 Aug. 1802.

Pp 192-193:   16 May 1801. (Deed) JAMES ALLEN PEARSON of Sumter Dist.,
               S. C. to MICHAEL BIRCH of sd dist. and state. Consider-
ation: 30 pds sterling. A tract of land whereon he now resides, con-
taining 400 acres known by name of Wyboo Swamp on N side of Santee
River in Sumter Dist., sd state, bounding on N on WILLIAM CANTEY, on
S by land of JAMES FRIERSON, SR., all other sides on vacant land, orig.
grant to WILLIAM PEARSON by his Exc. William Bull, A.D. 1765. Signed:
JAMES PEARSON (seal). Wit: JAMES DAVIS, JOHN ROWLETT & JOHN RHODUS.
Release of interest and estate, also her right and claim of dower to
above premises, signed by ELIZABETH PEARSON, wife of within named JAMES
ALLEN PEARSON, bef. JOHN FRIERSON, J.P. 16 May 1801. Proved by JAMES
DAVIS bef. JOHN FRIERSON, J.P. 15 May 1801. Rec. 7 Aug. 1801. (Orig.
rec. 10 Sept. 1801.)

Pp 193-194:   16 Sept. 1802. (Deed) THOMAS SUMTER of Sumter Dist.,
               S.C. to WILLIAM MURRELL of Stateburg, dist. and state
afsd., shopkeeper. Consideration: 175 pds sterling money. A parcel
of land containing 23 1/2 acres situate in Stateburg, dist. and state
afsd., bounding to E on the Main Road leading from Camden to Charleston,
to N on road leading through Stateburgh to Brisbanes Ferry, to S on
land belonging to the estates of THOMAS HOOPER and JOHN MACNAIR, deceased; and to W on land belonging to estate of JOHN MACNAIR, dec'd,
more fully described by a plat annexed. Signed: THOS. SUMTER (seal).
Wit: JOHN HAYNSWORTH & ROBERT PETTIPOOL. Proved by Haynsworth bef.
John Horan, J.P. 30 Sept. 1802. Rec. 5 Oct. 1802. Surveyed by JOSIAH
CANTEY.

Page 195:   19 Oct. 1802. Certificate signed by WM. BAY as follows:
               "the following to be the names of the twelve Negroes
settled by him and ANN, his wife on the children of WILLIAM RANSON
DAVIS, deceased, by deed to WADE HAMPTON and JOHN MAYRANT in trust
for the sd children, which deed was consumed in and with the Clerks
Office, see his affidavit in record Book A, page 19 - Appy, Mittee,
Bess, Suckey, Anna, Jenny, Hariot, January, Susannah, Jeffry, Sarah
and Letty." Bef. JOHN HORAN, J.P. Rec. 20 Oct. 1802. (Plat page 94:
land of Mrs. HOOPER, MC WAIR, THOMAS SUMTER).

Pp 195-197:   20 Mar. 1794. (Mortgage) WILLIAM MAYRANT of Claremont,
               S. C., planter, to BENJAMIN MAZYCK of Goose Creek, state
afsd. Consideration: 250 pds. The following negro slaves: Redriffe
and his wife Rachel, Daphne and her children Reddriffe and Charlotte
Tenor and her children Mulessa, Marcella, Suse, Kate and Robbin. Signed:
WM. MAYRANT (seal). Wit: SAM. FLEY. Proved by Fley bef. John Horan,
J.P. 23 Feb. 1795. Rec. 14 Dec. 1802. (Orig. rec. 23 Feb. 1795.)

Pp 197-198:   21 Mar. 1794. (Deed) WILLIAM MAYRANT to BENJAMIN MAZYCK.
               Consideratin: 5 sh. sterling money. "All that plantation
or tract of land lying and situated in the High Hills of Santee containing 400 acres, orig. granted to JOHN SHOVINOE, bounded at time
of orig. survey to the E on land granted to MOSES KNIGHTON and vacant
land, to the N on land granted to JOHN HOPE; to W on land granted
to JOHN JAMES and vacant land and to the S on vacant land, more fully
decribed by a plat. Signed: WM. MAYRANT (seal). Wit: SAML. FLEY and
PETER CROFT. Proved by Fley bef. John Horan, J.P. 23 Feb. 1795. Rec.
14 Dec. 1802. (Orig. rec. 23 Feb. 1795.)

Pp 198-200:   22 Mar. 1794. (Lease and Release via Mortgage). WILLIAM
               MAYRANT to BENJAMIN MAZYCK. Consideration: 250 pds. "All
that plantation or tract of land lying on High Hills of Santee, containing 400 acres orig. granted to JOHN SHOVINOE bounded at time of
orig. survey on E by land granted to MOSES KNIGHTON and vacant land,
to N on land granted to JOHN HOPE, to W on land granted to JOHN JAMES,
and vacant land, to S on vacant land." More fully described by a plat.
Signed: WM. MAYRANT (seal). Wit: SAML. FLEY and PETER CROFT. Proved
by Samuel Fley, Esq. bef. John Horan, J.P. 23 Feb. 1795. Rec. 14 Dec.
1802.

Pp 200-201:   1 Dec. 1802. (Mortgage) FLEMING WATKINS of Claremont
               Co., S. C. planter, to ELIZABETH MACNAIR of same, planter,
in consideration of $600.00.

398

Cont'd:
A certain negro man named Dick, 20 years old. Signed: FLEMING WATKINS
(seal). Wit: MARTHA A. G. ROBERTS. Proved by Mrs. MARTHA A. G. ROBERTS
bef. JOHN HORAN, J.P. 13 Dec. 1802. Rec. 15 Dec. 1802.

Pp 202-203:   20 Dec. 1802. (Mortgage) ANTHONY LEE of Sumter Dist.,
               S. C. to ELIZABETH MACNAIR of the dist. and state afsd.
Consideration: $600.00. A negro girl named Rachel, 10 years old. Signed:
ANTHONY LEE (seal) (by mark). Wit: JOHN M. ROBERTS & JOSHUA LEE. Proved
by Rev. JNO. M. ROBERTS bef. JOHN HORAN, J.P. 20 Dec. 1802. Rec. 21
Dec. 1802. (TIMOTHY LEE, executor of O. LEE has produced the mortgage.)

Pp 203-205:   23 Apr. 1789. (Deed) Honorable THOMAS SUMTER of the Vil-
               lage of Statesburgh in the Dist. of Camden and State
of S.C. to JAMES GREEN HUNT, Esq., Attorney at Law, of the same place.
Consideration: 175 pds sterling. Two lots of land each containing half
an acre, situate lying and being in the Village of Statesburgh opposite
a lot of land belonging to WILLIAM MURRELL, Esq. Signed: THOS. SUMTER.
Wit: A. BAY, CHAS. HARRIS & D. CONSTABLE. Proved by JOHN HORAN bef.
WM. MURRELL, Q.U., 20 Dec. 1802. Rec. 23 Dec. 1802.

Pp 205-206:   6 Aug. 1789. (Bill of Sale) JAMES GREEN HUNT, of Camden
               Dist. to GEORGE JOOR, of sd dist. Consideration: 200
pds sterling. Two lots of land each containing half an acre, situate
in the village of Statesburgh, in the dist. afsd. opposite a lot of
land belonging to WILLIAM MURRELL. Signed: J. G. HUNT (seal). Wit:
RIPLEY SINGLETON & A. BAY. Proved by RIPLEY SINGLETON bef. T. G. GUIG-
NARD, Mag. C.C. 8 Feb. 1790. Rec. 23 Dec. 1802.

Pp 206-208:   29 Nov. 1784. (Deed) ALEXANDER MOORE, Esq., Sheriff of
               Camden Dist., to General THOS. SUMTER of the dist. and
state afsd. Consideration: 100 pds sterling money. "Whereas JOHN ADAM-
SON and JAMES LESESNE of the Dist. and state afsd. were lately seized
of a certain tract of land containing 200 acres more or less orig.
granted to one PETER MATTHEWS and his heirs, lying, being and situate
upon the high hills of Santee in the state and dist. afsd. butting
and bounding on all sides on vacant land, and hath such shape form
and marks as the plat hereunto annexed represents ..and whereas the
sd JOHN ADAMSON and JAMES LESESNE on the 2nd day of Oct. in the year
1779 became indebted to Mr. JOSHUA LOCKWOOD in the city of Charleston
in the state afsd, Merchant, in the sum of 300 pds 9 shillings and
2 pence, sterling money, balance due to the sd JOSHUA LOCKWOOD from
the sd JOHN ADAMSON & JAMES LESESNE upon book amount." On the 4th day
of June 1784, judgment was obtained against sd JOHN ADAMSON and JAMES
LESESNE (also LESSENE) for the sum of 300 pds 9 sh. and 2 p. "Now this
indenture witnesseth that the sd ALEXANDER MOORE for and in consideration of the sd sum of 100 pds sterling money afsd to him in hand paid
at and bef. the sealing and delivery of these presents the receipt
whereof is hereby acknowledged, hath as far as he, as Sheriff of Camden
Dist., had a right, granted, bargained and sold and by these presents
doth grant bargain and sell unto the sd General THOMAS SUMTER his heirs
and assigns forever, all that tract of land bef. mentioned and described." Signed: ALEXANDER MOORE, Sheriff (Seal) of Camden Dist. Wit:
THO. BAKER and JAS. WITHERS. Proved by JOHN HORAN bef. WM. MURRELL,
Q.U.

(No p. no. given)
               24 July 1770: Pursuant to a warrant directed by JOHN
               BREMAR, Esq. D. Surveyor General, dated 6 Mar. 1770,
a tract of land containing 200 acres on the NE side of the Wateree
River in Craven Co. on the High Hills of Santee, was laid out unto
PETER MATTHEWS, more fully described by plat hereunto annexed. Certified by ISHAM MOORE, D.S. 24 July 1770. Rec. 24 Dec. 1802.

Page 209:   20 Nov. 1802. (Deed via Mortgage) JOHN MAYRANT of Sumter
               Dist., S.C. to THOMAS SUMTER, all of the sd dist. and
state. Consideration: 700 pds sterling. All that plantation/tract of
land containing 300 acres situate on the high hills of Santee near
to and to the E of the village of Stateburgh orig. granted to PETER
MATTHEWS and ISAAC HELTON. Further particulars may be had by reference

Cont'd:
to a deed of release from the sd THOMAS SUMTER to the above named JOHN
MAYRANT and the plat hereunto annexed. The house of the residence of
JOHN MAYRANT and 14 acres being part of two lots designated in the
plan of Stateburgh, on one of which the sd house stands are excluded
from the conditions of the above mortgage. Signed: JOHN MAYRANT (seal).
Wit: GEORGE BRASINGTON & MIDDLETON BELK. Proved by GEORGE BRASINGTON
bef. JOHN HORAN, J.P. 23 Nov. 1802. Rec. 24 Dec. 1802.

Pp 210-211:   28 June 1793. (Deed) HUBERD REES of Camden Dist., S.C.
               to HENRY LENUD of Georgetown Dist., sd state. Considera-
tion: 163 pds 2 s and 6 p sterling money. A tract of land containing
150 acres situate in the High Hills of Santee butting and bounded S
on lands belonging to OGLIVIE, N and E on lands belonging to JOHN WIL-
LIAMS, and W on lands belonging to Miss E. REMBERT; more fully described
by plat hereunto annexed. Signed: H. REES (seal). Wit: SAML. FLEY &
HENRY MAXWELL. Proved by FLEY bef. John Horan, J.P. 24 June 1793. Rec.
22 Jan. 1803. (Orig. rec. 1 July 1793.)

Pp 211-213:   28 June 1793. (Deed) JOHN WILLIAMS & EDITH, his wife,
               of Camden Dist., S. C. to HENRY LENUD of Georgetown Dist.
Consideration: 299 pds 1 s. & 3 p. sterling money. A tract of land
containing 275 acres situate upon the High Hills of Santee, butting
and bounding N and E on lands belonging to the sd JOHN WILLIAMS, S
on land belonging to OGLIVIE, MARTIN WILKINSON, deceased, and HUBERD
REES, W on lands belonging to Miss E. REMBERT, and more fully described
by plat thereof hereunto annexed. Signed: JOHN WILLIAMS (seal) and
EDITH WILLIAMS (seal). Wit: SAML. FLEY & HENRY MAXWELL. Proved by SAML.
FLEY bef. John Horan, J.P. (Orig. rec. 1 July 1793, and now 22 Jan.
1802.)

Pp 213-214:   7 Nov. 1794. (Deed) JOSEPH SINGLETON & ELIZABETH, his
               wife, of Camden Dist., S. C. to HENRY LENUD of the same
place. Consideration: 295 pds sterling money. A plantation or tract
of land containing 295 acres, - 220 acres of which was orig. granted
to JAMES BRUNSON, and 67 acres is part of a tract orig. granted to
JOHN DARGAN which sd tract of land is bounded to the NW by lands be-
longing to GEORGE JOOR, to the NE by lands belonging to the sd HENRY
LENUR, to the SE by lands belonging to OGLIVIE and HUBERD REES, and
S by lands late the property of BENJAMIN WARING; more fully described
by a plat hereunto annexed. Signed: JOSEPH SINGLETON (seal) and ELIZA-
BETH SINGLETON (seal) (by mark). Proved by SAML. FLEY bef. JOHN HORAN,
J.P. 5 Jan. 1795. Rec. 22 Jan. 1803. (Orig. rec. 5 Jan. 1795.)
Note: The above tract of land situate in the High Hills of Santee.
Late the property of the estate of ANDREW REMBERT, deceased. Release
of all manner of dower (not signed) by ELIZABETH SINGLETON, wife of
JOSEPH SINGLETON, of the High Hills of Santee, state afsd, bef. LAURENCE
MANNING & THOMAS HOOPER, Judges of the County Court of Clarendon County
in the State of S. C. Rec. 22 Jan. 1802. (Orig. rec. 5 Jan. 1795. Cer-
tified by ISHAM MOORE and RICHARD MOORE.)

Pp 214-216:   1 July 1794. (Deed of Gift) HENRY LENUD of Claremont
               Co., State of S.C. to HENRY LAUREN LENUD, his son, four
negro slaves, to wit: one wench named Lavinia and her child Lucy, one
other young wench named Hannah, and one boy named Saby. Consideration:
Natural Affection. Signed: H. LENUD (seal). Wit: SAML. FLEY. Proved
by Saml. Fley bef. John Horan, J.P. 1 July 1794. Rec. 1 July 1794 (originally) now 22 Jan. 1803.

Page 216:   1 July 1794. (Deed of Gift) HENRY LENUD of Claremont
               Co., S. C. to his daughter ELIZA LOVE LENUD, the three
following negro slaves, viz: one young wench named Juno, and two girls,
one named Jean and the other Phillis. Consideration: Natural Affection.
Proved by Saml. Fley bef. John Horan, J.P. 1 July 1794. Rec. 22 Jan.
1803.

Pp 216-218:   10 Dec. 1798. (Deed) THOMAS SUMTER of Claremont Co.,
               S. C. to JOHN JEFFERSON, of same place, the following
described tract of land: All that tract or parcel of land containing

400

Cont'd:
136 acres situate lying and being in the County and State afsd., on
the High hills of Santee and hath such form and marks buttings and
boundings as the plat thereof hereunto annexed do represents viz: its
beginning at a pine on the Seine road EPHRAIM ADAMS's line, and runs
with his line S 39 W ten chains and five links, to a pine, his and
JOHN ALLEN's corner; thence S 51 with sd JOHN ALLEN's line 13 chains
and 72 links to a stake his corner; thence S 39 W with line 28 chains
and 72 links to a pine, his corner; on FREDERICK ATKIN's line thence
S 53 E 20 chains and 10 links with sd ATKIN's line to a lightwood stake;
thence N 82 E 7 chains and 80 links to a sassafras saplin, my own line,
thence with my line S 82 E 22 chains and 70 links to a post oak on
the great road; thence N 7 W with sd road 30 chains, and 60 links to
a post oak; thence with the Seine road N 56 W 12 chains and 50 links
to a pine same road; thence N 51 1/2 W 16 chains to a black jack same
road; thence N 52 1/2 W 5 chains and 70 links to the beginning. Consideration: 10 s. sterling money. Signed: THOS. SUMTER (seal). Wit:
JOSEPH SYLVESTER & ROBERT ANDREWS. Proved by Robert Andrews bef. John
Horan, J.P. 30 Apr. 1799. Rec. 31 Jan. 1803. (Orig. rec. 1 May 1799.)

Page 219:   10 Feb. 1796. (Receipt) From THOS. HOOPER to MRS. JOHN
              JEFFERSON. Proved by SAML. FLEY and WM. MURRELL bef.
John Horan, J.P. 22 July 1799. Consideration: 18 pds for tract of land
sold THOS. HOOPER.

Page 219:   9 Apr. 1795. (Certificate) I do hereby certify that I
              have this day at the request of THOMAS HOOPER, Esq. sur-
veyed and laid off for JOHN JEFFERSON a tract of land containing 95
acres , three rods and 30 perches situate in county and state afsd.
on the NE side of the public road from Charleston to Camden on Dry
Swamp, waters of the Wateree River, more fully described by above plat.
Signed: JOHN CAIN, D.S. Rec. 31 Jan. 1803. (Orig. rec. 23 July 1799.)

Page 220:   10 Feb. 1796. (Bill of Sale) EDWARD PLOWDEN of Clarendon
              Co., S. C. to WILLIAM CROSKEY, all right, title and claim
to a negro girl named Murriah, formerly the property of WILLIAM TAYLOR.
Consideration: 5 pds. Signed: EDWD. PLOWDEN. Wit: WM. TAYLOR. Proved
by Wm. Taylor bef. WM. HUMPHREY, Clerk of the Court. 7 Apr. 1796. Rec.
11 Feb. 1803.

Pp 220-221:   2 May 1799. (Deed of Gift) HUGH OPRY of Claremont Co.,
              S. C. to GEORGE REABON, in trust for the use and behoof
of his wife, ANN ELIZABETH OPRY, the following slaves: two negro men
slaves named Tom and Prince; one negro woman slave named Hannah and
her future issue and increase; one feather bed, bedstead and furniture;
held in trust by GEORGE REABORN. Consideration: Love and Affection.
Signed: HUGH OPRY (seal). Wit: WM. MURRELL. Proved by Murrell bef.
John Horan, J.P. 3 May 1799. Rec. 4 May 1799. (now 11 Feb. 1803.)

Page 221:   2 May 1799. (Deed of Gift) HUGH OPRY of Claremont Co.,
              S. C. to his sons HUGH and ROBERT, "one negro girl named
Nanny and her future increase, and all my plantation tools, horses
and stock of cattle of every kind." "To my daughter, AGNESS, one negro
girl named Binah and her future issue and increase." Consideration:
Love, good will and affection. Signed: HUGH OPRY (seal). Wit: WM. MUR-
RELL. Proved by Wm. Murrell bef. John Horan, J.P. 3 May 1799. Rec.
4 May 1799 (now 1 Feb. 1803.)

Page 221:   Stock mark of WILLIAM BIRCHMORE, JR. recorded on 25 Feb.
              1803.

Page 222:   29 Aug. 1791. (Deed of Gift) SAMUEL NELSON of Clarendon
              Co., Camden Dist., S. C., planter, to WILLIAM POTTS and
SAMUEL EDGAR NELSON, for the support of his daughter, MARTHA POTTS,
the following six negro slaves: Satira, Nero, Damon, Sally, Hester
and Monday. Consideration: Good will and natural affection. Signed:
SAML. NELSON, SR. (seal). Wit: JOHN BAGNAL and WM. BRUNSON. Proved
by Wm. Brunson bef. WM. TAYLOR, J.P. Rec. 28 Feb. 1803 (orig. rec.
5 Sept. 1791.)

Pp 222-223:   12 Jan. 1795. (Bill of Sale) SAMUEL NELSON, SR. of Camden
               Dist., Clarendon County, State of S. C., to WILLIAM POTTS
of sd state, county and district, one negro girl named Bella. Consideration: 50 pds sterling. Signed: SAML. NELSON, SR. Wit: SAML. EDGAR
NELSON and JAMES NELSON. Rec. 28 Oct. 1803. (Orig. rec. 31 Oct. 1795.)

Page 223:   26 May 1796. (Deed of Gift) JOHN LOWDER and wife, SARAH
               LOWDER of the County of Claremont, State of S. C. to
JOB PERRY, their son, of the county and state afsd., the following
described tract of land: All and singular 300 acres of land with plantation and houses and orchards, and all household furniture and working tools and one negro man named Cesar, and all stock, cattle and
hogs and one horse and nothing of our present interest is to be expected
only one naked bed and two pewter dishes, and our support during the
mortal life of my beloved wife SARAH LOWDER and myself JOHN LOWDER
from JOB PERRY, his heirs or assigns. Consideration: Love, good will
and affection. Signed: JOHN LOWDER (seal) and SARAH LOWDER (seal) (by
her mark). Wit: SOLOMON THOMSON and ELIJAH PRICE and MARGARET PRICE
(by mark). Proved by SOLOMON THOMSON bef. JESSE NETTLES, J.P. 28 May
1796. Rec. 8 Mar. 1803. (Orig. rec. 18 July 1797.)

Page 224:   19 Apr. 1777. (Deed of Gift) JOHN PERRY, SR. of the parish
               of St. Marks, Craven Co., State of S. C., planter, to
his son JOB PERRY, of the same parish and county, planter, 300 acres
of land, one negro wench named Fibbe, and the half one one negro man
slave named Cesar. Consideration: Love, good will and affection. Signed:
JOHN PERRY (seal). Wit: WILLIAM GILLIAM, SILAS PERRY and PHIN'S. GIBSON.
Proved by WILLIAM GILLIAM bef. NATHL. MOORE, J.P. Also proved by PHIN'S.
GIBSON bef. WM. RICHBOURG, J.P. 24 Feb. 1798. Rec. 26 Jan. 1798 (orig.)
Now 8 Mar. 1803.

Pp 224-225:   3 Jan. 1798. (Deed of Gift) JOB PERRY, of the County
               of Claremont, State of S. C., planter, to his daughter,
MARGARET PRICE of the county and state afsd., 100 acres of land lying
and binding on both sides of Curry's branch in the county and state
afsd., which the sd JOB PERRY bought of ___ HELTON; more fully described
by a plat annexed to the sd land. Consideration: Love, good will and
affection. Signed: JOB PERRY (seal). Wit: JEMIMA PERRY and GEORGE PERRY
(by mark). Proved by JEMIMA PERRY bef. John Horan, J.P. 15 Jan. 1798.
Rec. 23 Jan. 1798. (Now 8 Mar. 1803.)

Pp 225-226:   27 Apr. 1801. (Deed of Gift) JOSIAH REAMES, of Claremont
               County, State of S. C. to his son JOSHUA REAMES, the
following goods and chattels, one feather bed and furniture, one pewter
dish, six pewter plates, one spinning wheel, three chairs and one table
and all other household furniture. Consideration: Natural love and
affection. Signed: JOSIAH REAMES (seal). Wit: JOHN MC DONELL and AZARIAH
REAMES. Proved by AZARIAH REAMES bef. JOHN MC DONELL, J.P. 27 Apr.
1801. Rec. 8 Mar. 1803. (Orig. rec. 7 Aug. 1801.)

Pp 226-227:   16 Dec. 1799. (Deed) JOHN RICHBOURGH of Clarendon County,
               state of S. C. to ASA RHAME and BRADLEY RHAME, as Guardian
for JESSE RHAME of the state and county afsd., all that plantation
or tract of land containing 240 acres more or less, situate lying and
being in the state and county afsd on roast hen and Wolf-branch, brances
of Sammy Swamp which is a branch of Black River, it being a tract of
land originally granted to JOHN RICHBOURGH, the third day of April
1786. More fully described by plat of same. Consideration: 40 pds sterling money. Signed: JOHN RICHBOURGH (Seal). Wit: JEREMIAH RHAME, JR.
and NATHL. RICHBOURGH. Proved by JEREMIAH RHAME bef. JAMES RICHBOURGH,
J.P. 15 Nov. 1800. Release of all interest and estate unto within named
ASA RHAME and BRADLEY RHAME, the premises above mentioned, also her
right and claim of dower (not signed) of SARAH, wife of the within
named JOHN RICHBOURGH, bef. THOS. N. JOHNSON, J.C.C. 16 Dec. 1799.
Rec. 19 Mar. 1803. (Orig. rec. 27 Nov. 1800.)

Pp 227-228:   27 June 1798. (Deed) JEREMIAH RHAME, SR. of Clarendon
               Co., State of S. C. to BRADLEY RHAME, for and in behalf
of ASA RHAME, son of the above JEREMIAH RHAME, both of sd county and

Cont'd:
state, a tract of land containing 100 acres, lying on the N side of
Big Pedee, being a tract originally granted to ERASMUS ROTHMAHLER,
on all sides vacant land at the time of the Grant and signed by his
Excellency THOMAS PINCKNEY, Esq., then Governor and Commander in Chief.
More fully described in record of Secretary's office book___ page ___.
Consideration: 5 pds sterling money. Signed: JEREMIAH RHAME (by mark)
(seal). Wit: STEPHEN NIXON and EMMANUEL HODGE (by mark). Proved by
STEPHEN NIXON bef. JNO. RIDGILL, J.P. 25 June 1798. Rec. 19 Mar. 1803.

Pp 228-229:   21 Dec. 1799. (Deed) BRADLEY RHAME and THIRZA RHAME,
                his wife, of Georgetown District, State of S. C., to
ASA RHAME, a certain tract of land containing 150 acres, being part
of a tract of 1550 acres granted to BRADLEY RHAME, 6th Feb. 1792; more
fully described by plat annexed to this deed. Consideration: 5 pds.
sterling money. Signed: BRADLEY RHAME and THIRZAH RHAME (by her mark).
Wit: JES DAVIS and JEREMIAH RHAME. Proved by JEREMIAH RHAME bef. JAMES
RICHBOURGH, J.P. 15 Nov. 1800. Rec. 19 Mar. 1803. (Orig. rec. 27 Nov.
1800.)

Page 229:   10 Nov. 1800. (Deed) BRADLEY RHAME and THIRZAH RHAME,
                his wife, of Georgetown Dist., State of S. C., to ASA
RHAME, a certain tract of land containing 246 acres, being part of
a tract of 1550 acres granted to BRADLEY RHAME 6 Feb. 1792; more fully
described by plat annexed to this deed. Consideration: 5 pds. sterling.
Signed: BRADLEY RHAME (seal) and THIRZAH RHAME (seal) (by her mark).
Wit: JES DAVIS and JEREMIAH RHAME. Proved by JEREMIAH RHAME bef. JAMES
RICHBOURGH, J.P. 15 Nov. 1802. Rec. 19 Mar. 1803. (Orig. rec. 27 Nov.
1800.

Pp 230-231:   15 May 1789. (Deed) THOMAS SUMTER of Camden Dist., State
                of S. C. to JOHN MACNAIR of sd district, a certain lot
of land whereon the store now occupied by JOHN MACNAIR and HENRY MAXWELL
now stands, bounded on the W by Main Street or road; on the S by lot
occupied by MRS. DANSBY; on the N by a lot occupied by LEONARD POWELL;
and on the E by lands belonging to the sd THOMAS SUMTER, sd lot being
one half acre; as also a lot of land bounded on the E by a street running in front of the lot possessed by WILLIAM MURRELL; on the S by
lands belonging to THOMAS HOOPER; on the W by lands belonging to the
sd JOHN MACNAIR; and on the N by lands belonging to sd THOMAS SUMTER;
sd lot supposed to contain about 2 acres of land. Consideration: One
hundred Guineas current money. Signed: THOMAS SUMTER (seal), by WILLIAM
MURRELL, his attorney. Wit: D. CONSTABLE and JOHN MORE. "Acknowledged
by the Grantor in Open Court on the ninth day of March 1790 and recorded
in Book No. 2, Folio 52." Signed: NAT ALEXANDER, Clk. C.C. Rec. 20
May 1803.

Pp 231-232:   1 Jan. 1803. (Sheriff's Deed) BENJAMIN BINEHAM, late
                deputy sheriff, Camden, to ELIZABETH MACNAIR, executrix
of the last Will and Testament of JOHN MACNAIR. Whereas, an action
was lately commenced in the Court of Common Pleas, in the State afsd.,
by MARY CLAYTON MILLER against ELIZABETH MACNAIR, Executrix of last
will and testament of JOHN MACNAIR, deceased; that the sd MARY obtained
a judgment, which was entered up in the office of the C. of C. on 22
June 1797. Thereupon a Fieri Facias issued against the Goods and Chattels, lands, etc. of the sd JOHN, at the time of his death for the
sum of 130 pds, which sd Fieri Facias was on the 24th June 1797 lodged
in the office of WILLIAM R. DAVIS, then sheriff of sd district; by
virtue whereof the sd WM. R. DAVIS did seize and take into execution
a certain lot, or parcel of land situate in the Town of Stateburgh
bounded on the E by and fronting on a street running in front of the
dwelling house of sd WILLIAM MURRELL; to the S by land belonging to
THOMAS HOOPER's Estate; to the W by lands which belonged to JOHN MACNAIR
in his life time; and on the N by lands lately bought by the sd WM.
MURRELL of THOMAS SUMTER. The sd piece or parcel of land being 105
feet wide in front and having the same width all the way back to JOHN
MACNAIR's land afsd., and supposed to contain about 2 acres. Sd Lot
was sold at public outcry on the first Monday in September 1797 to
ELIZABETH MACNAIR of Claremont Co., widow, for $5. As WILLIAM R. DAVIS

Cont'd:
was almost continually absent from Camden where his office was kept,
sd ELIZABETH MACNAIR settled with BENJAMIN BINEHAM, Deputy Sheriff
and did pay and satisfy him for the sd purchase of sd lot, the sd consideration money in full; and was to have titles from the sd WILLIAM
R. DAVIS, but sd DAVIS died suddenly without executing the same. Where-
fore BENJAMIN BINEHAM late Deputy Sheriff for the sd WILLIAM R. DAVIS,
did certify that while he acted as such sd ELIZABETH MACNAIR did fully
pay and satisfy him for the sd WM. R. DAVIS, the sd five dollars for
the sd lot of land, "and that she is entitled to and of right ought
to have and hold the sd premises with the appurtenances to her and
her heirs and assigns forever." Signed: BENJAMIN BINEHAM (seal), late
Deputy Sheriff, Camden. Wit: SAML. MATHIS & R. L. CHAMPION. Proved
by SAML. MATHIS bef. JAS. BROWN, J.P. 19 Jan. 1803. Rec. 20 May 1803.

Pp 232-233:   2 Jan. 1803. (Deed) ELIZABETH MACNAIR, of Claremont Co.,
                State of S. C., widow, to WILLIAM MURRELL, of same county
and state, merchant, a piece or parcel of land situate in the town
of Stateburgh, bounded to the E by and fronting on a street running
in front of the dwelling house of sd WM. MURRELL; to the S by lands
belonging to THOMAS HOOPER's estate; to the W by lands which belonged
to JOHN MACNAIR in his life time; and on the N by lands lately bought
by the sd WM. MURRELL of THOMAS SUMTER; the sd piece of land supposed
to contain about 2 acres more or less. Consideration: $40.00. Signed:
ELIZABETH MACNAIR. Wit: SAML. MATHIS & JOHN MILLER. Proved by SAML.
MATHIS bef. JAS. BROWN, J.P. Rec. 20 May 1803.

Pp 240-241:   19 Aug. 1799. (Deed) JOHN CHINA of Claremont Co., State
                of S. C., planter, to WILLIAM BRACEY of sd county and
state, a tract of land containing 150 acres, situate in Claremont Co.,
Nasty branch, waters of Black River, originally granted to JOHN HOLLA-
DAY on or about 28 Aug. 1767; (Secretary's Office Grant Book BBB, page
252), and was sold and conveyed to the sd JOHN HOLLADAY and SUSANNAH,
his wife, to the above named JOHN CHINA, by deed dated 28 Nov. 1797.
(Claremont County Court Book D, No. 4, pages 365-366). Consideration:
40 pds sterling money. Signed: JOHN CHINA (seal). Wit: ALEXANDER SIME-
SON, JOLLY BRACEY & MERRY BRACEY. Release of all interest and estate,
also all her right and claim of Dower signed by ANN CHINA, wife of
JOHN CHINA (by her mark). Proved by ALEXANDER SIMESON bef. JOHN HORAN,
J.P. Rec. 24 May 1803.

Pp 242-243:   1 Oct. 1799. (Deed) THOMAS ODIL of Claremont Co., State
                of S. C., to WILLIAM BRACEY, of the county and state
afsd., a tract of land containing 200 acres, situate in Claremont Co.,
Nasty Branch, Waters of Black River, sd tract of land originally granted
to THOMAS ODIL on or about 3rd day of Oct. 1785; bounding NW on land
granted to THOMAS MAPLES; NE on land granted to JOHN HOLLIDAY; SE on
land granted to MATTHEW SINGLETON. Consideration: 150 pds sterling
money. Signed: THOMAS ODIL (seal). Wit: ALEXANDER SIMESON & JOLLY BRAC-
EY. Release of all interest and estate, also all her right and claim
of Dower in the above mentioned premises, signed by ANN ODIL, wife
of THOMAS ODIL, bef. ISHAM MOORE, J.C.C. 15 Oct. 1799. Proved by ALEX.
SIMESON bef. John Horan, J.P. 26 Oct. 1799. Rec. 24 May 1803. (Orig.
rec. 6 Nov. 1799).

Pp 243-244:   5 Oct. 1799. (Deed) JOHN & THOMAS ODIL, of Claremont
                Co., State of S. C., to WILLIAM BRACEY, of county and
state afsd., a tract of land containing 150 acres situate in Claremont
Co., Nasty Branch, waters of Black River, sd tract orig. granted to
THOMAS ODIL, SR., left in his last Will and   Testament to be sold.
The above grant dated about June 1771. The above land when run on all
sides vacant; now bounding on lands run by THOMAS ODIL, JR. and MATTHEW
SINGLETON. Consideration: 105 pds sterling. Signed: JOHN ODIL (seal),
THOMAS ODIL (seal). Wit: ALEX. SIMESON & JOLLY BRACEY.

Page 244:   5 Oct. 1799. (Receipt) "Received of WILLIAM BRACEY by
                the hands of JOHN & THOMAS ODIL fifteen pounds each of
us, in full of our part of the within tract of 150 acres, formerly
the property of THOMAS ODIL, SR. Signed: JOHN CHINA, ALEXANDER POOL
(his mark), FLORA ODIL (her mark), SUSANA ODIL (her mark), and SOFIAS

404

Cont'd:
WALLACE. Proved by ALEXANDER SIMESON bef. JOHN HORAN, J.P. 30 Nov. 1799. Rec. 24 May 1803. (Orig. rec. 2 Dec. 1799.)

Pp 244-245: 11 Feb. 1797. (Deed) JOHN ODIL of Camden Dist., State of S.C., planter, to THOMAS ODIL, JR. of the co. and state afsd., planter, a plantation or tract of land containing 100 acres, being part of a tract of 200 acres granted to JOHN ODIL, by grant under the hand of his Excellency WM. MOULTRIE, dated 3 Oct. 1785, butting and bounding N on land granted to Col. SINGLETON, W on the remaining part of the 200 acres granted to sd JOHN ODIL; all other sides on vacant land at the time of the original survey. Consideration: 10 shillings. Signed: JOHN ODIL (seal). Wit: WILLIAM LINAM and MARK LINAM. Proved by WM. LINAM bef. JOHN GREENING, J.Q. 4 Apr. 1803. Rec. 24 May 1803.

(NOTE: the following pages are out of order; see previous page)

Pp 233-236: 20 Dec. 1789. (Deed of Release) JOHN HATFIELD of Claremont Co., S.C., Inn Keeper, to SIMON KINGSTON of co. and state afsd., the following described tract of land: All that plantation, parcel or tract of land, containing 300 acres, situate in the county and state afsd., bounding NW on lands of JAMES BRUNSON, NE on lands laid out for BENJAMIN MC KENNIES, the other sides by vacant lands (which sd plantation, parcel or tract was granted on or about 10 May 1773 to sd JOHN HATFIELD.) More fully described by a plat to the orig. grant annexed. Consideration: 100 pds sterling money. Signed: JOHN HATFIELD (seal). Wit: JAS. BRICKELL & ROBERT HATFIELD. Proved by ROBT. HATFIELD bef. J. G. GUIGNARD, M.C.C. Rec. 21 May 1803. (Orig. rec. 24 Apr. 1790.)

Pp 236-237: 10 Nov. 1789. (Deed) ISHAM MOORE and JOHN SINGLETON of Claremont Co., Camden Dist., S. C., planters, Executors of the Estate of MATTHEW SINGLETON, dec'd. to JOHN CHINEY, of same place, planter, a plantation or tract of land containing 100 acres, situate near Brunsons Swamp, a branch of Black River, in Claremont Co., being a part of a tract of 4,000 acres granted to MATTHEW SINGLETON 16 July 1784, under the hand of his Excellency, Gov. Guerard, butting and bounding S on land granted to JOHN ODLE, W on land laid out to THOMAS ODLE, N and E on the remaining part of the sd 4,000 acre tract granted to sd MATTHEW SINGLETON; more fully described by a plat annexed hereto. Consideration: 5 pds sterling money. Signed: ISHAM MOORE (seal), JOHN SINGLETON (seal). Wit: W. J. MC KENZIE, MATTHEW MOORE & THOS. ODIL. Proved by MATTHEW MOORE bef. WM. MURRELL, J.P. 15 Oct. 1790. Rec. 24 May 1803. (Orig. rec. 16 Oct. 1700.)

Pp 238-239: 10 Nov. 1789. (Deed) ISHAM MOORE & JOHN SINGLETON, of Claremont Co., Camden Dist., S. C., planters, Executors of the Estate of MATTHEW SINGLETON, deceased, to THOMAS ODLE, JR. of the same place, planter, a tract of land containing 100 acres, situate near Brunsons Swamp, a branch of Black River in Claremont Co., being part of a tract of 4,000 acres granted to MATTHEW SINGLETON 16 July 1784, by Gov. Guerard, bounding S on land granted to JOHN ODLE, all other sides on the remaining part of the sd 4,000 acre tract orig. granted to MATTHEW SINGLETON, more fully described by plat annexed. Signed: ISHAM MOORE (seal), JOHN SINGLETON (seal). Consideration: 5 pds sterling money. Wit: W. J. MC KENZIE, MATTHEW MOORE & JNO. CHINA. Proved by JOHN CHINA bef. JOHN GREENING, J.Q. 31 Mar. 1803. Rec. 24 May 1803.

Pp 239-240: 28 Nov. 1797. (Deed) JOHN HOLLADAY of Clarendon Co., S. C., planter, and SUSANNAH, his wife, to JOHN CHINA, of Claremont Co., state afsd., a tract of land containing 150 acres of land, situate in Craven (now Claremont) county on Nasty branch, bounding at the time of orig. grant, to the above named JOHN HOLLADAY on 28 Aug. 1769; on all sides on vacant land; more fully described by plat annexed to original grant. (Rec. in Sec. Office Grant Book BBB page 252). Consideration: 40 pds Sterling monoey. Signed: JNO. HOLLADAY (seal) and SUSANNA HOLLADAY (seal) (by her mark). Wit: SOLOMON

Cont'd:
BOND and JOHN HOLLADAY, JR. Proved by SOLOMON BOND bef. John Horan,
J.P. 15 Jan. 1798. Rec. 24 May 1803. (Orig. rec. 22 Jan. 1798).

Pp 245-246:   12 Mar. 1802. (Deed) THOMAS ODIL of Claremont Co., S.C.
              to WILLIAM BRACEY of co. and state afsd., a tract of
land containing 100 acres, situate in Claremont Co., Frog Branch, Waters
of Black River, sd tract of land being originally granted to MATTHEW
SINGLETON and conveyed to ISHAM MOORE & JOHN SINGLETON to the sd THOMAS
ODIL by lease, situate near Brunson Swamp, a branch of Black River,
and is a part of a tract of 1000 acres granted to MATTHEW SINGLETON
16 July 1784 under hand of Governor Guerard; bounding S on land granted
to JOHN ODIL, all other sides on the remaining part of sd 4000 acre
tract originally granted to MATTHEW SINGLETON, more fully described
by a plat hereunto annexed. Consideration: 150 pds sterling. Signed:
THOMAS ODIL (seal). Wit: THOS. BRUMBY & JOHN GREENING. Release of all
interest and estate, also her right and claim of Dower in the premises
mentioned, signed by ANN ODIL (by mark), wife of THOS. ODIL, 12 Mar.
1803, bef. JOHN GREENING, J.Q. Proved by JNO. GREENING bef. John Horan,
J.P. 23 Mar. 1803. Rec. 25 May 1803.

Pp 247-248:   12 Mar. 1803. (Deed) THOMAS ODIL of Claremont co., S.C.
              to WILLIAM BRACEY of same place, a tract of land con-
taining 100 acres situate in Claremont Co., Frog branch, waters of
Black River, which sd tract of land was orig. granted to JOHN ODIL
and conveyed by lease to THOMAS ODIL, it being part of a tract of 200
acres of land granted to JOHN ODIL, under hand of his Excellency Wm.
Moultrie, 3 Oct. 1785; bounding N on land granted to MATTHEW SINGLETON,
W on the remaining part of the 200 acres granted to sd JOHN ODIL, all
other sides on vacant land at time of orig. grant. Consideration: 150
pds sterling. Signed: THOMAS ODIL (seal). Wit: THOS. BRUMBY & JNO.
GREENING. Release of all interest and estate, also right and claim
of dower to the within mentioned premises, signed by ANN ODIL, wife
of within named THOMAS ODIL, bef. JOHN GREENING, 12 Mar. 1803 (by her
mark). Proved by JOHN GREENING bef. John Horan, J.P. 25 May 1803.

Pp 248-249:   12 Feb. 1797. (Deed) JOHN ODIL of Camden Dist., S.C.,
              planter, to THOMAS ODIL, JR., of state and county afsd.,
planter, "A certain plantation or tract of land being part of a tract
of 200 acres originally granted to JOHN ODIL, as appears by a Grant
under the hand of his Excellency Governor Moultrie, Esq., bearing date
3 October 1785, and under the great seal of the State; butting and
bounding N on land granted to Col. SINGLETON, W on the remaining part
of the 200 acres of land granted to JOHN ODIL, all other sides on vacant
land at the time of the original grant." Consideration: 50 pds sterling.
Signed: JOHN ODIL (seal). Wit: WILLIAM LINAM & MARK LINAM. Proved by
WM. LINAM bef. John Greening, J.Q. 4 Apr. 1803. Rec. 26 May 1803.

Pp 249-250:   6 May 1799. (Deed) THOMAS BRUMBY of Charleston, S.C.,
              Carpenter, to JOHN JORDAN of Claremont Co., S.C., a tract
of land containing 190 acres, being part of a tract of land granted
to THOMAS SINGLETON 11 Feb. 1773; more fully described by a plat thereof
annexed. Consideration: 30 pds sterling. Signed: THOS. BRUMBY (seal).
Wit: RICHARD MOORE & DANL. BRUNSON. Proved by MOORE bef. John Horan,
J.P. 30 Oct. 1799. Plat certified by R. DUNN, 5 Mar. 1799. Rec. 26
May 1803. (Plat shows BRUMBY's, Mrs. HUGER's and MOORE's land.)

Pp 250-252:   26 Nov. 1799. (Deed) JOHN JORDAN of Clarendon Co., S.C.
              to WILLIAM BRACEY of county and state afsd., a tract
of land containing 190 acres orig. granted to THOMAS SINGLETON 11 Feb.
1773, situate on the S side of Cane Savannah; bounding S on land of
THOMAS BRUMBY; W, NW and NE on land of ISHAM MOORE; more fully described
by a plat hereunto annexed. Consideration: 50 pds sterling. Signed:
JOHN JORDAN (by mark) (seal). Wit: ALEXR. SIMESON & JOLLY BRACEY. Release of all interest and estate, also all right and claim of dower
in premises above signed by CASSANDER JORDAN, wife of within named
JOHN JORDAN, bef. WM. MURRELL, J.C.C. (seal). 27 Nov. 1799. Proved
by ALEXR. SIMESON bef. John Horan, J.P. 30 Nov. 1799. Rec. 26 May 1803.
(Orig. rec. 2 Dec. 1799).

Pp 252-253:   30 Aug. 1799. (Deed) ISAAC GIDDENS of Clarendon Co.,
               S. C., planter, to WILLIAM BRACEY of Claremont Co., S.
C., a tract of land of 250 acres surveyed 3 Sept. 1771, situated on
the E side of Nasty Branch, more fully described by a plat hereunto
annexed. Consideration: $500.00. Signed: ISAAC GIDDENS (by mark), JEMIMA
GIDDENS (by mark). Wit: THOMAS GIDDENS (by mark) and PHILIP THOMSON.
Release of all interest and estate, also all right and claim of dower
signed by JEMIMA GIDDINS, wife of within named ISAAC GIDDINS, bef.
JOHN GREENING, J. Q. 15 Jan. 1801. Proved by THOMAS GIDDINS bef. John
Horan, J.P. 11 Sept. 1799. Rec. 26 May 1803. (Orig. rec. 6 Nov. 1799.)

Pp 253-255:   20 Oct. 1795. (Deed) HENRY PHILLIPS of Claremont Co.,
               S. C., planter, to WILLIAM BRACEY, SR. of sd county and
state, Merchant, certain tracts or parcels of land, containing 500
acres, it being in seperate grants, one survey of 300 acres granted
to JOHN HATFIELD in 1773, under the hand of Gov. WILLIAM BULL, bearing
date 10 May and conveyed from JOHN HATFIELD to SIMON KINGSTON, and
from sd KINGSTON to HENRY PHILLIPS; the above mentioned survey is situated on Cane Savannah, a branch of Black River; bounding NW on land
of JAMES BRUNSON, NE on lands laid out to BENJAMIN M. KENNIES, the
other side by vacant land when run out. Also 200 acres, it being part
of 400 acres lying on the land formerly belonging to JOHN HATFIELD;
NE on lands belonging to ABNER BROADWAY and vacant land, the sd 400
acres of land is to be equally divided, the sd WILLIAM BRACEY, SR.
is to have the 200 acres nearest adjacent to the land formerly of JOHN
HATFIELD's tract; the sd 400 acres was granted to HENRY PHILLIPS under
hand of Gov. WM. MOULTRIE, 6 May 1793. Consideration: 85 pds lawful
money. Signed: HENRY PHILIPS (seal). Wit: JOHN M. LANGSTAFF, RANDOLPH
SINGLETON & JOLLY BRACEY. Proved by JNO. M. LANGSTAFF bef. John Horan,
J.P. 20 Oct. 1795. Rec. 27 May 1803.

Pp 255-256:   14 Aug. 1800. (Deed) ABRAHAM PETTIPOOL of Claremont Co.,
               S. C., planter, to WILLIAM BRACEY of sd county and state,
277 acres, being part of a tract granted to MATTHEW SINGLETON 16 July
1784; more fully described by a plat annexed. Consideration: 155 pds
sterling. Signed: ABRAHAM PETTY POOL (his mark) (seal). Wit: ISHAM
MOORE & EZEKIEL EVANS. Release of all estate and interest, also all
right and claim of dower in the above premises, signed by SARAH PETTI-
POOL (by her mark), bef. JOHN GREENING, 28 Feb. 1801. Proved by EZEKIEL
EVANS bef. JOHN HORAN, J.P. 29 Aug. 1800. Rec. 27 May 1803. (Plat shows
land of ABRAHAM GIDDEN, THOMAS ODLE, THOS. ODLE, SR. & MATTHEW SINGLETON

Pp 257-258:   6 Nov. 1801. (Deed) ISAAC BRUNSON of Claremont Co., S.C.
               to WILLIAM BRACEY of the county and state afsd., 100
acres of land, being part of a tract containing 4000 acres granted
to MATTHEW SINGLETON 16 July 1784, bounding S on land granted to JOHN
ODIL, W on land laid out to THOMAS ODIL, N and E on the remaining of
the 4000 acre tract granted to MATTHEW SINGLETON; more fully described
by a plat hereunto annexed. Consideration: $400.00. Signed: ISAAC BRUN-
SON (seal). Wit: ISAAC BRUNSON, JR. & JOLLY BRACEY. Proved by Bracey
bef. John Horan, J.P. 29 Mar. 1803. Rec. 27 May 1803.

Pp 258-263:   14 Apr. 1803. (Marriage Settlement) ROBERT BRAILSFORD
               of the City of Charleston, State of S. C., Factor, and
ELIZABETH JAMES of St. Marks Parish, in the county of Clarendon, state
afsd., Spinister, to MATTHEW JAMES and DAVID DUBOSE, both of the Parish
of St. Mark, county of Clarendon, state afsd., a certain undivided
fourth part of the remainder of real estates, which were of the sd
JOHN JAMES, after certain specific devises of his sd lands to the two
sons of the sd JOHN JAMES, by his sd last Will and Testament, dated
7 Dec. 1787; also twenty negroes. Consideration: 5 shillings. Signed:
ELIZABETH JAMES (seal) and ROBT. BRAILSFORD (seal). Wit: JNO. C. WALTER
& CHAS. CONNORS. Proved by JNO. C. WALTER bef. John Horan, J.P. 17
May 1803. Rec. 7 June 1803.

Pp 263-266:   2 Nov. 1791. (Deed) Vestry and Church Wardens of the
               Episcopal Church at Stateburgh in Claremont County, to
MATTHEW JAMES of Clarendon Co., a tract of land containing 150 acres
more or less, situate in St. Marks Parish, adj. land belonging to the
Estate of JOHN JAMES, sd tract being granted to JOHN EVANS on 26 Mar.

Cont'd:
1756, by him conveyed to RICHARD RICHARDSON, deceased, on 20 Jan. 1759, and conveyed by sd RICHARD RICHARDSON and DOROTHY his wife to the Vestry and Church Wardens of St. Marks Parish on 18 Apr. 1764; more fully described by JOHN EVANS plat annexed to the original grant. Consideration: 5 sh. sterling. Signed: JOHN MACNAIR, WILLIAM REES, WM. BRACEY, GEO. JOOR, WM. MURRELL, C. W. ____, J. G. GUIGNARD, (all with seal). Wit: J. MURRELL & SAML. FLEY. Proved by Capt. Saml. Fley bef. John Horan, J.P. 24 May 1803. Rec. 7 June 1803.

Pp 266-267:   4 Jan. 1800. (Bill of Sale) HUGH OPRY of Claremont Co., S. C., to JOHN TEASDALE, SR., five negroes: Prince, Hanah, Binah, Bob and Nanny. Consideration: $600.00. Signed: HUGH OPRY (seal). Wit: PETER WORLEY, JACOB LACKEY. Proved by PETER WORLEY bef. CHARLES F. GORDON, J.P. 6 Jan. 1800. Rec. 7 June 1803.

Pp 267-268:   5 Nov. 1802. (Deed) RICHARD DEEN of Orangeburg Dist., S.C., planter, to MATTHEW OWEN of Sumter Dist., sd state, a tract of land containing 415 acres, more or less, being in Sumter Dist. on big Raften Creek; bounded W on THOMAS SINGLETON's land, N on JOHN COLLIN's land, NE on THOMAS JACKSON's land, SW on JOHN LENOIR's land, SE on vacant land. Consideration: 85 pds. Signed: RICHARD DEEN (seal) (by mark). Wit: DANL. GARTMAN, THOMAS GARTMAN & JACOB LITES (by mark). Release of all her interest and estate, also claim of dower in the within described land, signed by MARY DEEN, wife of RICHARD DEEN, bef. PHILIP GARTMAN, J.P. 5 Nov. 1802. Proved by JACOB LITES bef. Philip Gartman, 5 Nov. 1802. Rec. 8 June 1803.

Pp 268-269:   14 Jan. 1803. (Deed) LAURANCE & JUDAH FRANKLIN of Clarendon Co., Sumter Dist., S. C. to RICHARD GROOMS of state, dist. and county afsd., a tract of land situate lying and being in state, district and county afsd, containing 250 acres, it being the equal half of a tract of land containing 500 acres, orig. granted to sd LAURANCE FRANKLIN 4 Jan. 1796, bounding NW on DAVIS SHORTER's land, all other sides on vacant land, when surveyed; more fully described in plat to the orig. grant. (Secretary's Office Grant Book O No. S page 216). Consideration: 20 pds sterling. Signed: LAWRENCE FRANKLIN (seal), JULY FRANKLIN (seal) (by her mark). Wit: WILLIAM SAVAGE & JOHN RHODUS. Proved by WM. SAVAGE bef. JNO. RIDGILL, J.P. 18 Mar. 1803. Rec. 8 June 1803.

Page 269:   12 Jan. 1802. (Bill of Sale) JOHN J. CARTEY & NABOTH CARTEY, both of Clarendon Co., Sumter Dist., State of S. C., to BRADLEY RHAME, a negro boy named Willis, 15 yrs. Consideration: $85.00. Signed: JOHN J. CARTEY (seal) and NABOTH CARTEY (seal). Wit: JNO. SELBY & ASA RHAME. Proved by Asa Rhame bef. John· Ridgill, J.P. 20 May 1803. Rec. 8 June 1803.

Pp 269-270:   29 Sept. 1792. (Deed) ALBERT FORT of Darlington Co., S. C., planter, to BURWELL FORT of state and county afsd., planter, a tract of land containing 200 acres, situate near Raften Creek, beginning on DILLARD's survey, running SW to BRADLEY's line, NW to a corner pine, SW to a corner, then running N to a corner on Scrub oak, E to a corner stake running S, being a tract of 200 acres granted to ELIAS FORT 7 Sept. 1772. Consideration: 25 pds sterling. Signed: ALBERT FORT (seal). Wit: JOSIAH FORT & MILLS BARFIELD (by his mark). Proved by JOSIAH FORT bef. JESSE NETTLES, 12 Mar. 1793. Rec. 9 June 1803. (Orig. rec. 12 Mar. 1795.)

Pp 270-271:   12 May 1803. (Bill of Sale) AMEY HAMPTON of Sumter Dist., S. C., to JEREMIAH PITTS of sd dist. and state, Carpenter, six negro slaves, to wit: Peter, a fellow about 21 years of age; Peg, a wench about 16; Violet, a wench about 21; and her three children, Daniel, Lucy and Frank. Consideration: $1800. Signed: AMY HAMPTON (seal) Wit: WM. MURRELL. Proved by Murrell bef. John Horan, J.P. 2 June 1803. Rec. 9 June 1803.

Pp 271-273:   13 May 1803. (Mortgage) JEREMIAH PITTS of Sumter Dist., S. C., Carpenter, to AMEY HAMPTON, six negroes, to wit: Peter, a fellow about 21 years; Peg, a wench about 16 years; and Violet,

408

Cont'd:
a wench about 21 years, and her 3 children, Daniel, Lucy and Frank.
Consideration: $1800. Signed: JEREMIAH PITTS (seal). Wit: WM. MURRELL
and JOHN WILLIAMS. Proved by WM. MURRELL bef. John Horan, J.P. 2 June
1803. Rec. 9 June 1803.

Pp 273-274:   15 Dec. 1802. (Deed) NEEDOM KEEL of Clarendon Co., S.C.
               to JAMES JOHNSON of the co. and state afsd. a tract of
land containing 250 acres situate in Clarendon Co., and state of S.
C., in the fork of Black river, bounding SE on LOWN's lands, S on WIL-
LIAM TAYLOR's land, W and SW on REUBEN NICHOL's land, and on all other
sides on land belonging to the Estate of JAMES ROE, deceased; more
fully described by a plat thereof. Consideration: $312.00 sterling
money. Signed. NEEDOM KEEL (seal) (by his mark). Wit: SAML. E. NELSON
& ABRAHAM PIPPEN (by his mark). Release of all interest and estate,
also right and claim of dower in the premises above mentioned, signed
by ELIZABETH KEEL (by her mark), bef. WM. TAYLOR, J.Q. 23 Dec. 1802.
Proved by SAML. E. NELSON bef. Wm. Taylor, J.Q. 15 Dec. 1802. Rec.
9 June 1803.

Page 274:   4 Mar. 1799. (Receipt) Signed by W. R. DAVIS, Sheriff
               Camden Dist., to WILLIAM REES. Consideration: 80 pds
for two negroes, the property of JOHN MACNAIR, named Milly and Betty,
and sold by virtue of a mortgage to WILLIAM PRICE, etc. Proved by WM.
MURRELL bef. John Horan, 6 June 1803. Rec. 9 June 1803.

Pp 274-275:   12 Apr. 1787. (Deed) JAMES RICHBOURGH of St. Marks Parish
               in state of S. C. to RICHARD SINGLETON of sd state, a
tract of land containing 700 acres, in three plats, situate in the
Dist. of Camden on Jack Creek, waters of Santee River. The three plats
are divided as follows: One tract, 100 acres; one tract, 400 acres,
and one tract, 200 acres, all joining and granted to sd JAMES RICHBOURGH
Consideration: 300 pds good and lawful money. Signed: JAMES RICHBOURGH
(seal) and REBEKAH RICHBOURGH (seal). Wit: P. DARDELIE & HUGUES FOUR-
NIEU. Acknowledged by WILLIAM HUMPHREY, C.C. Rec. 10 June 1803.

Pp 276-277:   16 Mar. 1790. (Deed) WILLIAM RICHBOURGH, Sheriff of Clar-
               endon Co., Camden Dist., to THOMAS CASSITY of the dist.
and state afsd., planter, a tract of land containing 500 acres lying
on Jacks creek, whereon RICHARD SINGLETON now lives, orig. granted
to JAMES RICHBOURGH, the 500 acres afsd. was taken by virtue of an
execution to satisfy a debt due THOMAS CASSITY from RICHARD SINGLETON,
which sd execution was obtained in Clarendon Court 16 Feb. 1790; the
above land bounded S by CLAUDIUS RICHBOURGH's land, and to the N on
land granted to JOHN HUGHES. Consideration: 10 shillings sterling money.
Signed: WM. RICHBOURGH (seal), Shff. Clarendon Co., Wit: NATHL. RICH-
BOURGH & JOHN RICHBOURGH. Proved by JOHN RICHBOURGH bef. JAMES RICH-
BOURGH, J.P. 17 Mar. 1790. Rec. 10 June 1803.

Pp 277-278:   19 Dec. 1789. (Deed) RICHARD SINGLETON of St. Marks Parish
               of Clarendon Co., S. C. to MARY MAPLES of sd state, a
tract of land containing 200 acres, situate in Dist. of Camden, on
Jacks creek, waters of Santee river, bounded on the S by lands granted
to CLAUDIUS RICHBOURGH, and on the E by JAMES RICHBOURGH's land, and
all other sides vacant land. Consideration: 50 pds good and lawful
money. Signed: RICHARD SINGLETON (seal) and SARAH SINGLETON (seal)
(by her mark). Wit: JESSE CASSITY, WM. SIMS and THOS. CASSITY. Rec.
13 June 1803.

Pp 278-280:   27 Mar. 1790. (Deed) HENRY RICHBOURGH, JAMES RICHBOURGH
               and JOHN RICHBOURGH, Executors of the estate of CLAUDIUS
RICHBOURGH, deceased, of state of S. C., planter, to THOMAS CASSITY
of sd state, county of Clarendon, planter, 200 acres in Clarendon Co.
and state afsd., on Jacks Creek, in his actual possession now being,
by virtue of the last will and testament of the afsd. CLAUDIUS RICH-
BOURGH, deceased, and by legacy left to WILLIAM RICHBOURGH; sd land
being b unded on S and E by land belonging to JOHN RICHBOURGH; N by
and belonging to RICHARD SINGLETON; it being part of two tracts of
land, one granted to JOHN SULIVAN 12 Oct. 1771 (recorded Grant Bk 3

Cont'd:
K, page 97), the other tract granted to CLAUDIUS RICHBOURGH 19 Jan.
1765 (rec. in Grant Bk PP, page 314); more fully described by plat
hereunto annexed. Being part of two tracts of land belonging to the
estate of CLAUDIUS RICHBOURGH, deceased, out of which he laid off to
his son WILLIAM RICHBOURGH 200 acres in form of the plat on back of
indenture. Signed: HENRY RICHBOURGH, JAMES RICHBOURGH & JOHN RICHBOURGH,
(all with seal). Wit: GEORGE BRUNSON & HENRY WHITE. Consideration:
5 shillings. Proved by HENRY WHITE bef. THOS. N. JOHNSON, J.P. 26 Sept.
1791. Rec. 13 June 1803.

Pp 280-282:   23 Mar. 1793. (Deed) THOMAS CASSITY of Clarendon Co.,
               S. C., planter, to MARY MAPLES, widow, of same state
and county, planter, a tract of land containing 700 acres, being part
of four tracts, two of which were originally granted to JAMES RICHBOURGH
and transferred from him to RICHARD SINGLETON, one of 100 acres, 21
May 1764; bounded on the S by lands laid out for CLAUDIUS RICHBOURGH;
and on all other sides by vacant lands, also 400 acres granted to JAMES
RICHBOURGH, 3 Dec. 1771; bounded on S by lands belonging to JAMES RICH-
BOURGH and on all other sides by vacant lands; rec. in Book 4, No.
11, page 348, 14 Aug. 1772; also 200 acres being part of two tracts
of land, one granted to CLAUDIUS RICHBOURGH, the other granted to JOHN
SULIVAN; bounded SE by lands belonging to JOHN RICHBOURGH; and N by
lands of RICHARD SINGLETON; and hath such shape and form as the plat
of the indenture for same shall represent on the back of the deeds
from HENRY JAMES and JOHN RICHBOURGH to THOMAS CASSITY, one of the
tracts granted to JOHN SULIVAN 12 Oct. 1771, rec. in Grant Bk. 3:K,
page 97; the other to CLAUDIUS RICHBOURGH 9 Jan. 1765, rec. in Grant
Bk. PP?, p. 314; more fully described by plat annexed. Consideration:
200 pds sterling money. Signed: THOMAS CASSITY (seal). Wit: JAMES CASIDY
and RICHARD SINGLETON and NICKLES POUGHIN. Proved by JAMES CASIDY bef.
JAMES RICHBOURGH, J.P. 24 Mar. 1793. Rec. 14 Nov. 1803. (Orig. rec.
19 Mar. 1794.)

Pp 282-285:   21 Sept. 1793. (Deed and Bill of Sale) MARY MAPLES, of
               St. Marks Parish, Clarendon Co., S. C. to MATTHEW JAMES
and RICHARD SINGLETON, (husband of SARA SINGLETON), in trust for the
use and benefit of her sd grandchildren, RICHARD SINGLETON, JR., HIRAM
SINGLETON, MARY SINGLETON, JEHU SINGLETON & SARAH SINGLETON, children
of her daughter, SARAH SINGLETON; three tracts of land bought of THOMAS
CASSITY 23 Mar. 1793. All that tract of land containing 700 acres,
being part of 4 tracts (two of which were originally granted to JAMES
RICHBOURGH and transferred to RICHARD SINGLETON) and one of 100 acres
granted 21 May 1764; bounded on S by lands laid out for CLAUDIUS RICH-
BOURGH and on all other sides by vacant land. Also 400 acres granted
to JAMES RICHBOURGH 3 Dec. 1771; bounded on S by lands belonging to
JAMES RICHBOURGH and on all other sides by vacant land; recorded in
Book 4, No. 11, page 348, 14 Aug. 1772. Also 200 acres being part of
two tracts of land, one granted to CLAUDIUS RICHBOURGH, the other granted to JOHN SULIVAN; bounded SE by land belonging to JAMES RICHBOURGH
and N by lands of RICHARD SINGLETON, and hath such shape and form as
the plat of indenture shall represent on the back of the deeds from
HENRY JAMES and JOHN RICHBOURGH to THOMAS CASSITY, one of the tracts
granted to JOHN SULIVAN 12 Oct. 1771; recorded in Grant Bk 3K, p. 97,
the other to CLAUDIUS RICHBOURGH, 19 Jan. 1765; recorded in Grant Bk.
PP, p. 3 and 4, Also all that tract of land bought of RICHARD SINGLETON
by the sd MARY MAPLES, 19 Dec. 1789, containing 200 acres situate in
Dist. of Camden on Jacks Creek, waters of Santee River; bounded on
the S by land granted to CLAUDIUS RICHBOURGH; on the E by JAMES RICH-
BOURGH's land and on all other sides by vacant lands; also the following nine negroes: June, a fellow, Isaac, a fellow, Jack, a fellow,
Mindah, a wench, Sophy, a wench, Isabella, a wench, Dorcas, a girl,
Lucy, a girl, and Bob, a boy. Also fifty head of stock cattle. Consideration: 200 pds sterling. Signed: MATTHEW JAMES & RICHARD SINGLETON
(seal), MARY MAPLES (seal). Wit: WM. SIMS, JR. & THOS. CASSITY & JAMES
RICHBOURGH, SR. Proved by WM. SIMS, JR. bef. HENRY RICHBOURGH, 14 Feb.
1794. Rec. 17 June 1803. Receipt signed by RICHARD SINGLETON bef. JAS.
MASON, 4 Mar. 1790.

Pp 285-286:   22 June 1801. (Deed) ROGER DUNN & SYLVESTER DUNN, of

Cont'd:
State of S. C., District of Sumter, planters, to HENRY DUNN, of state
afsd., Dist. of Darlington, planter, 850 acres of land, viz: 150 acres
being part of 200 acres granted to WILLIAM ROBERTS 4 Nov. 1762, the
rest granted to SYLVESTER DUNN as follows: 400 acres, part of 690 acres
granted 3 Dec. 1787. 100 acres, part of 1000 granted 4 Nov. 1793. 100
acres, granted 16 July 1765. 100 acres granted 17 Dec. 1762. Bounding
N by CARTER's land, and a line from CHRISTMAS corner, a due E course
until it strikes Little Stoney Run and down sd run to JOHN REARDON's
Baroney line and down sd line to the run of Stoney Run and down sd
run to ALEXANDER's land and round on the W side of said land JAMES
CARTER's childrens land, and round that to the dividing line between
ROGER DUNN and the sd HENRY DUNN on the W side of Stoney Run until
it strikes WILSON's land and round that to FLEMING's land and around
FLEMING's land to CARTER's and round CARTER's to the sd pine corner
of CHRISTMAS. Consideration: $1000. Signed: ROGER DUNN (seal) and SYL-
VESTER DUNN (seal). Wit: SAMUEL NEWMAN & THOMAS SMITH. Proved by NEWMAN
bef. THOS. WILSON, J.P. 28 Dec. 1802. Release of all interest and estate
also right and claim of dower in the premises above mentioned. Signed:
G. COOPER, J.Q. on left, (not signed by SARAH DUNN and ELIZABETH DUNN,
wives of the within named ROGER DUNN & SYLVESTER DUNN.) 28 Dec. 1802.
Rec. 20 June 1803.

Pp 287-288:   5 June 1802. HENRY DUNN of S. C., Darlington Dist., plant-
               er, to JOHN DOUGLASS, Dist. of Sumter, Co. of Salem,
state afsd., planter, 460 acres of land, more or less, being parts
of different surveys joining each other, say a part of a survey for
JANE ROBERTS 27 Feb. 1754, and granted to WILLIAM ROBERTS 4 Nov. 1762
on Stoney Run, N side of Black River, then Craven County; bounded S
by THOMAS SMITH, JR. land when surveyed, a memorial of same being entered in the Aud. Gen'l. Office in Book G No. 7 page 18, 16 Dec. 1762,
containing 200 acres. Also part of a survey of 100 acres of land on
a N swamp of Black River, granted to SYLVESTER DUNN 16 July 1765, a
memorial of same entered in the Aud. office in Book G, No. 7, page
413, 1 Aug. 1765. Likewise part of a survey containing 100 acres, surveyed 24 Nov. 1757, and granted 20 Dec. 1765 to SYLVESTER DUNN, on
one of the N branches of Black River. The Moieties or parts of the
two surveys of 100 acres each granted to SYLVESTER DUNN, is by these
presents bargained to be held to the middle of the Swamp of Black River,
on the N or E side thereof, and the part or Moiety of the 200 acre
survey granted to WILLIAM ROBERTS as above, to be held on the W side
of big Stoney Run, from the edge of the sd swamp of Stoney Run, all
the land within the sd lines up excepting 15 feet square reserved by
WM. ROBERTS formerly, for burying place, also in the Moiety of 100
acres granted to SYLVESTER DUNN 1765 is a reserve of one acre square,
agreeable to the last Will and Testament of SYLVESTER DUNN, dec'd.
for the a burying place. The parts or Moieties of the three surveys
contain in the whole, 460 acres, more or less, (except as bef. excepted
for the burying places). More fully described by a plat annexed to
the grants of same.
N.B. MRS. JANET DUNN, widow of SYLVESTER DUNN, dec'd. to use and cultivate on the premises her natural lifetime, agreeable to the Will
of SYLVESTER DUNN. Consideration: $1000.00. Signed: HENRY DUNN (seal)
Wit: BENJ. DUBOSE & JOHN BARR. Release of all interest and estate,
also all right and claim of dower in the premises above mentioned,
signed ELIZA DUNN, wife of within named HENRY DUNN, bef. G. COOPER,
J.Q. 5 June 1802. Proved by JOHN BARR bef. THOS. WILSON, J.P. 20 Dec.
1802. Rec. 20 June 1803.

Pp 288-289:   5 Dec. 1802. (Deed) JOHN DOUGLASS of State of S. C.,
               Sumter Dist., Salem County, planter, to WILLIAM DIXON
of sd state, county and district, planter, 460 acres of land, more
or less, being parts of different surveys joining to each other as
follows viz: A part of a survey for JANE ROBERTS 27 Feb. 1754, and
granted to WILLIAM ROBERTS 4 Nov. 1762. Situated on Stoney run N side
of Black River bounded S by THOS. SMITH, JR.'s land when surveyed,
a memorial of the same being entered in the Aud. Office in Book G,
No. 7, p. 18, 5 Dec. 1752; containing in the survey 200 acres, also
part of a survey of 100 acres on a N branch of Black River granted

411

Cont'd:
to SYLVESTER DUNN, 16 July 1765. A memorial thereof being entered in
the Aud. Gen'l. Office in Book E, No. 7, p. 413, 1 Jan. 1765. Likewise
part of a survey containing 100 acres surveyed 24 Nov. 1763, and granted
the 20 Dec. 1765 to SYLVESTER DUNN on one of the N branches of Black
River the moieties or part of the two surveys of 100 acres granted
to SYLVESTER DUNN is by these presents bargained to be held to the
middle of the swamp of Black River on the N side thereof and the part
of moiety of the 200 acre survey granted to WILLIAM ROBERTS as above
to be held on the W side of Big Stoney Run from the edge of the sd
swamp of Stoney Runn all the land within sd lines up excepting 15 feet
square reserved formerly by WM. ROBERTS for a burying place, also in
the moiety of 100 acres granted SYLVESTER DUNN 1765 is a reserve of
1 acre square agreeable to the last Will and Testament of sd SYLVESTER
DUNN for a burying place the parts or moieties of the three surveys
containing/in the whole/460 acres except as bef. excepted the burying
places. Boundaries of the sd surveys will more fully appear by reference to the orig. plats annexed to the grant of same. MRS. JANET DUNN
having the privilege on the sd bargained premises during her natural
life to cultivate whatever part she may think sufficient to make a
support on agreeable to the last will and testament of Sylvester Dunn,
deceased. Also 200 acres of land being part of a survey of 632 acres
granted to SYLVESTER DUNN, 3 Dec. 1787. More fully described by orig.
plat and grant thereof in the Sec. office in Grant Book UUUU, page
492. Consideration: $1000.00. Signed: JOHN DOUGLASS (seal). Wit: JOSIAH
WILSON & WM. WILSON. Proved by WILLIAM WILSON bef. THOS. WILSON, J.P.
28 Dec. 1802. Release of all interest and estate, also right and claim
o dower in the above premises, signed by SARAH DOUGLASS, wife of the
named JOHN DOUGLASS, bef. GEORGE COOPER, J.Q. 28 Dec. 1802. Rec. 20
June 1803.

Pp 290-291:   28 Mar. 1803. (Deed) WILLIAM MONTGOMERY of Clarendon
              Co., Dist. of Sumter, S. C., planter, to JAMES BENNETTE
of sd dist. state and county, a tract of land containing 575 acres,
situate on the N side of Santee River on Butler's Creek Bay, waters
of Santee, butting and bounding due SW and NW on lands claimed by sd
WM. MONTGOMERY, NW on MRS. MARTHA MONTGOMERY's land, NE on vacant land,
and SE on Butler Creek Bay and WINDOM's land, agreeable to annexed
plat of same; being part of a 1900 acre tract surveyed 31 Dec. 1785
for WM. MONTGOMERY and granted 5 June 1786 to the sd WM. MONTGOMERY.
Consideration: 86 pds, 5 s. Signed: WILLIAM MONTGOMERY (seal). Wit:
DANIEL MC DONALD, WM. H. MOUSON, & WILLIAM HILTON. Proved by DANIEL
MC DONALD bef. JOHN FRIERSON, J.Q. Release of all interest and estate,
also all right and claim of dower in above described premises, signed
by MARTHA MONTGOMERY, wife of within named WILLIAM MONTGOMERY, bef.
JOHN FRIERSON, J.Q. 5 Apr. 1803. Rec. 8 July 1803. (Plat shows land
of JOHN WINDOM & WM. MONTGOMERY).

Page 292:   15 June 1803. (Deed of Gift) WILLIAM WILLIAMS of Claremont
            County, S. C. to his daughter, ESTHER LEONORAH WILLIAMS,
one negro girl named Phoeby, 8 yrs. Consideration: Good will and affection. Signed: WILLIAM WILLIAMS (seal). Wit: JAMES N. BENNETT. Proved
by Bennett bef. John Horan, J.P. 2 July 1803. Rec. 8 July 1803.

Pp 292-293:   10 Oct. 1800. (Deed) JAMES WEEKS, SR. of Clarendon Co.,
              S.C. to WILLIAM MOODY of same place, a tract of land
containing 100 acres, situate in the county afsd., which was granted
to JOSEPH CORBETT, under the seal of his Excellency WM. MOULTRIE, 5
Dec. 1785; beginning at a red oak, running N 50° W to a pine thence
N 40° E to a pine stake, thence S 50° E to a lightwood stake, the dif-
ferent courses to the beginning. Reference to Surveyor General's office
at Columbia will more fully appear. Consideration: 42 pds lawful money.
Signed: JAMES WEEKS & REBECCA WEEKS (seal). Wit: THOMAS MC ELVENE &
CHARLES CORBETT. Proved by Corbett bef. John Horan, J.P. 2 July 1803.
Rec. 8 July 1803.

Pp 293-294:   25 Sept. 1802. (Deed) WILLIAM REAVES of Claremont Co.,
              Sumter Dist., S. C. to ROBERT HENRY of sd district and
state, a tract of land by estimation containing 285 acres, 275 acres
of the sd tract of land was taken out of a 300 acre tract, orig. granted

Cont'd:
to WILLIAM P. BROWN, 25 Jan. 1785; also 7 acres taken out of a 230 acre tract that was granted to sd WM. P. BROWN, 2 July 1787, which sd 285 acres of land is situate in the Dist. and state afsd., bounding on land belonging to JOHN MC DONNELL; and on lands of SAMUEL MC COY; also on lands belonging to sd WILLIAM REAVES. Consideration: $300.00. Signed: WILLIAM REAVES. Wit: ISHAM CLARKE & ELIZABETH GORDON (by her mark). Proved by ISHAM CLARKE bef. CHARLES F. GORDON, J.P. 25 Sept. 1802. Rec. 9 July 1803.

Page 294:   7 Mar. 1803. (Deed) ROGER GORDON of Indian Town, George-
              town Dist., S. C., planter, to SAMUEL JAMES BRADLEY of
same place, a tract of land containing 100 acres, orig. granted to ROGER GORDON, late deceased, in 1761, and at the time of the survey, on all sides vacant land, on the W side of Black River, and on the E side of Scape hore, and on a late resurvey by JOHN MC DONNELL, Esq., are found to join lands of JOHN B. FRASER, Esq. of the afsd. county, more fully described by plat. Consideration: $150.00. Signed. ROG. GORDON (seal). Wit: CORNELIUS DIMPSY, JOHN SCOTT & ISABELLA COOPER. Proved by Dimpsy bef. G. Cooper, J.Q. 2 July 1803. Rec. 9 July 1803.

Pp 295-296:   28 Feb. 1803. (Deed) ROGER DUNN of Sumter Dist., Clare-
              mont Co., S. C., planter, to SAMUEL REMBERT of same place,
planter, a tract of land containing 640 acres, more or less, except what is taken by MEMBRANCE WILLIAMS's land, which was originally granted to TOMLINSON, as also about 5 acres of the lower end adj. the RICHARD-SON's land, as appears by an old line running into the land cornering on a pine, and running out and forming an angle (supposed to be NESBITT land), situate in the state and district afsd., on the waters of Black River, called Scape Hore in McGirt's Fork, bounding at the time on an original survey by a line running NE, by WILLIAM RICHARDSON's land, NW and SW by DANIEL CARTER's and WILLIAM BRUNSON's land; all other sides vacant, orig. surveyed for ELIZABETH BROWN (16 Aug. 1784) and granted by Wm. Moultrie, Gov. to PETER BREMAR, 5 June 1786, by him conveyed to ROGER DUNN, party to these presents, by deed dated 11 Dec. 1799, sd grant being recorded in Grant Book MMMM, p. 23. Also a tract of 150 acres, more or less, which was granted to JOHN BELTON, 14 Aug. 1775, as appears by plat annexed to orig. grant, situate in state afsd., on Scape hore swamp in McGirt's Fork, bounded on the NW side by land laid out for ROBERT CARTER; and on all other sides by vacant land at the time of the orig. survey, rec. in the Sec. Office in Book YYY, p. 445; sd land being conveyed by JOHN BELTON to JOHN ENGLISH, JR., 1 Mar. 1786, and by sd JOHN ENGLISH, JR., conveyed to ROGER DUNN, by deed dated 3 May 1799. Consideration: $3000.00. Signed: ROGER DUNN (seal). Wit: HENRY YOUNG, HUBERT REMBERT & SYLVESTER DUNN. Proved by HENRY YOUNG bef. ABSALOM WILLIAMS, J.Q, 3 June 1803. Release of all interest and estate, also all right and claim of dower in these premises signed by SARAH A. DUNN, wife of ROGER DUNN, 30 June 1803 bef. ABSALOM WILLIAMS, J.Q. Rec. 10 July 1803.

Pp 296-297:   14 May 1803. (Deed) JOHN GUERRY, JR. & PETER V. GUERRY,
              of Black River, S. C., planters, to SAMUEL REMBERT, plant-
er, a tract of land containing 700 acres, more or less, situate in Sumter Dist., S. C., waters of Black River, bounded by lines running SW 18° on ABIJAH REMBERT's land, SE 30° on JAMES REMBERT's land, NE 50° on SAMUEL REMBERT's land, NE on ROBERT BROWN, JR. and NW on SAMUEL REMBERT's land, being part of a tract of land surveyed 12 Sept. 1793, and granted by WM. MOULTRIE, Esq., 7 Oct. 1793 to JOHN GUERRY. Consider-ation: $1650.00. Signed: JOHN GUERRY, JR. (seal) and PETER V. GUERRY (seal). Wit: JOHN GUERRY & DANIEL D. ANDERSON. Proved by ANDERSON bef. ABSALOM WILLIAMS, J.Q, 10 June 1803. Rec. 10 July 1803.

Page 297:   14 May 1803. (Deed) ROBERT BROWN, JR. of Black River,
              S. C., planter, to SAMUEL REMBERT of same place, planter,
a tract of land containing 200 acres, more or less, situate in Sumter Dist., state afsd., bounded by lines running NE 20° on ROBERT BROWN's land, NW 40° on lands of SAMUEL REMBERT, NE on lands granted to JOHN GUERRY, SE on land of JOHN REMBERT, and on the E side of McGirt's Branch being part of a tract of land surveyed 12 Sept. 1793, granted by Wm.

Cont'd:
Moultrie, Gov. 7 Oct. 1793 to JOHN GUERRY. Consideration: $350.00.
Signed: ROBERT BROWN, JR. (seal). Wit: JOHN REMBERT & DANIEL D. ANDER-
SON. Proved by Anderson bef. ABSALOM WILLIAMS, J.Q, 10 June 1803. Rec.
11 July 1803.

Pp 297-298:   7 Sept. 1774. (Lease/Deed) SHADRACH POWELL, the Parish
               of St. Marks, Craven Co., S. C., to JOHN MOORE of the
province afsd., a tract of land containing 200 acres of land, lying
in the parish of St. Marks, bounding on all sides by vacant land. Consideration: 10 shillings lawful current money. Signed: SHADRACH POWELL
(seal). Wit: WILLIAM GILLAM, ROBT. MOSES and RICHARD BRADFORD. Rec.
11 July 1803.

Pp 298-300:   8 Sept. 1774. (Deed) SHADRACH POWELL and ELIZABETH POWELL
               his wife, of St. Marks Parish, Craven Co., S. C., to
JOHN MOORE of co. and state afsd., a tract of land containing 200 acres,
situate in Craven Co., on a N branch of Wateree River called Rafting
Creek, bounding on all sides by vacant land, more fully described by
a plat to sd grant annexed; orig. granted to SHADRACH POWELL by CHARLES
GREVELEY MONTAGUE, Gov. 3 Apr. 1772. Consideration: 1000 pds. Signed:
SHADRACH POWELL (seal) and ELIZABETH POWELL (seal) (by mark). Wit:
RICHARD BRADFORD, ROBT. MOSES & WILLIAM GILLAM. Proved by Bradford
bef. NATHL. MOORE, J.P. 8 Sept. 1774. Rec. 12 July 1803.

Pp 300-301:   14 Dec. 1799. (Deed) JOHN MOORE of Claremont Co., S.C.,
               to SAMUEL REMBERT of same place, a tract of land con-
taining (first mentioning 200 acres) granted to SHADRACH POWELL by
grant dated 3 Apr. 1772, and from him conveyed to sd JOHN MOORE, and
450 acres granted to sd JOHN MOORE, 5 Dec. 1785; more fully described
by plat annexed to sd grant. Consideration: 500 pds sterling money.
Signed: JOHN MOORE (seal). Wit: WM. WHITAKER & SAMUEL KIRKLAND. Proved
by WM. WHITAKER bef. DEVX. BALLARD, J.P., 1 Jan. 1800. Rec. 14 July
1803. (Orig. rec. 11 June 1800.)

Pp 301-302:   28 Feb. 1803. (Deed) SAMUEL REMBERT of Claremont Co.,
               Sumter Dist., S. C., planter, to R. DUNN of same place,
all that plantation or parcels of lands containing (first mentioning
200 acres) granted to SHADRACH POWELL grant dated 3 Apr. 1772, and
conveyed from him to JNO. MOORE; and 450 acres granted to JNO. MOORE
grant dated 5 Dec. 1785; more fully described by plat annexed. And
as the sd JNO. MOORE had previous to selling of or conveying of above
mentioned lands to sd SAMUEL REMBERT, sold to JOSEPH KNIGHTON a small
tract of land supposed to lie part of it in the E part of the above
named tract of 450 acres, on the S side of Raften Creek, the sd SAMUEL
REMBERT doth not agree to make good that part to the sd R. DUNN. Likewise 50 acres, more or less, it being part of a tract of 100 acres
orig. granted to ARTHUR RICHARDSON by grant dated 2 Apr. 1773, binding
N on the above mentioned tract of 450 acres, and resurveyed by Capt.
R. DUNN, 20 June 1800; more fully described by plat hereunto annexed.
Consideration: 500 pds sterling money. Signed: SAMUEL REMBERT. Wit:
HENRY YOUNG, HUBERD REMBERT & SYLVESTER DUNN. Release of all interest
and estate, right and claim of dower signed by LOUISA REMBERT bef.
ABSALOM WILLIAMS, J.Q., 30 June 1803. Proved by HENRY YOUNG bef. ABS.
WILLIAMS, 11 May 1803. Rec. 4 July 1803.

Pp 302-303:   14 Dec. 1799. (Deed) JOHN MOORE of Claremont Co., S.C.,
               to SAMUEL REMBERT of same place, a tract of land contain-
ing 800 acres, more or less, same being part of a tract granted to
JOHN MOORE, for 1000 acres, grant dated 4 Feb. 1793, lying in county
afsd., on Big Raften Creek, chiefly on the S side thereof. More fully
described by plat annexed. Consideration: 300 pds sterling money. Signed
by JOHN MOORE (seal). Wit: WM. WHITAKER & SAMUEL KIRKLAND. Proved by
Whitaker bef. Devx. Ballard, J.P., 1 Jan. 1800. Rec. 14 July 1803.
(Orig. rec. 11 June 1800.)

Page 303:   28 Feb. 1803. (Deed) SAMUEL REMBERT of Claremont Co.,
               S. C., to R. DUNN, of same place, a tract of land con-
taining 800 acres, more or less, being part of a tract of land granted

414

Cont'd:
to the sd JOHN MOORE for 1000 acres, grant dated 4 Feb. 1793, lying
in the county afsd., on Big Raftin Creek, chiefly on the S side thereof
and conveyed from sd JOHN MOORE to SAMUEL REMBERT 14 Dec. 1799; more
fully described by a plat hereto annexed. Consideration: $1000.00.
Signed: SAMUEL REMBERT (seal). Wit: HENRY YOUNG, HUBERD REMBERT & SYL-
VESTER DUNN. Release of interest and estate, right and claim of dower
signed by LOUISA REMBERT, wife of SAMUEL REMBERT, bef. ABSALOM WILLIAMS,
J.Q., 30 June 1803. Proved by YOUNG bef. Abs. Williams, 11 May 1803.
Rec. 15 July 1803.

Pp 304-305:   14 Dec. 1799. (Deed) JOHN MOORE of Claremont Co., S.C.
               to SAMUEL REMBERT of same place, a tract of land con-
taining 50 acres, more or less, being part of a tract of 100 acres
orig. granted to ARTHUR RICHARDSON, 2 Apr. 1773, lying on the N side
of Big Rafting Creek, binding on sd JOHN MOORE's 450 acre tract on
N side of same, beginning a covenant line at a hickory corner made
by the covenant, on the NE line of the same, and from the hickory corner
along the covenant line to a pine tree corner on the road leading from
the sd JOHN MOORE to Chamber's Mills, which sd line is a covenant dividing line between ADWELL ADKINSON and JOHN MOORE. Consideration: 50
pds sterling money. Signed: JOHN MOORE (seal). Wit: WM. WHITAKER &
SAMUEL KIRKLAND. Proved by Whitaker bef. DEVX. BALLARD, 1 Jan. 1800.
Rec. 15 July 1803.

Pp 305-306:   20 Oct. 1784. (Deed) JOHN EGAN of Moncks Corner Parish,
               S. C., to JOSEPH COMMANDER of St. Marks Parish, S. C.,
planter, 450 acres of land granted to CHARLES WOODMASON, 1 Aug. 1785,
situate in Craven Co. on S side of Lynches Creek, bounded NE part on
vacant land and part on JOHN CONNORS' land, NW part on the sd CONNERS
and part on vacant land, and the other two sides on vacant land, more
fully described by plat annexed to orig. grant. Consideration: 143
pds sterling current money. Signed: JOHN EGAN (seal). Wit: THOS. NEWMAN
& MARGARET EGAN. Proved by Newman bef. D. REESE, J.P., 5 Feb. 1790.
Rec. 16 July 1803.

Page 307:   8 Nov. 1791. (Deed) SIMON STUCKEY of Salem Co., S. C.,
               planter, to JOSEPH COMMANDER of sd co. and state, planter,
a certain tract of land, situate in the co. and state afsd., containing by estimation 100 acres, more or less, beginning at a white oak,
running NE 75° 38 Ch., from thence NW to a pine station running 15.
35° 25 Ch., thence NE 75° 38 Ch. to the main stream of Black River,
and from thence up the sd stream to the beginning corner, it being
part of a tract containing 200 acres, orig. granted to WILLIAM ROBERTS
as appears by plat annexed, ref. being had in the Sec. Office in Book
W. N 15, page 35. Sd tract being in the state and county afsd. on the
S side of Black River, granted to sd WILLIAM ROBERTS 2 Sept. 1775.
Consideration: 39 pds 13 sh. and 4 p. sterling money. Signed: SIMON
STUCKEY (seal) (by mark). Wit: JNO. DOUGLASS, THOMAS SMITH & EDMOND
STUCKEY. Proved by Thos. Smith bef. JNO. CASSELS, J.P., 31 Jan. 1800.
Rec. 16 July 1803. (Orig. rec. 12 Mar. 1800.)

Pp 307-308:   6 Feb. 1802. (Deed) ROGER DUNN, HENRY DUNN & SYLVESTER
               DUNN, of Sumter Dist., S. C. to JOSEPH COMMANDER, of
same place, a piece of land containing 203 acres situate on the SW
side of Black River, in dist. and state afsd., it being part of a tract
of 1000 acres granted to SYLVESTER DUNN, SR., 4 July 1792, bounding
by a line running NE by ROBT. WM. CARTER's land, NW and NE by the run
of Black River and RICHARD RATCLIFF's land, SW by JESSE COMMANDER's,
and SE by ROBT. BRISBAND's; more fully described by a plat hereto annexed. Consideration: $203.00. Signed: R. DUNN (seal), HENRY DUNN (seal),
SYLVESTER DUNN (seal). Wit: BENJAMIN DUBOSE, WILLIAM ROBERTS & JOHN
JS. BRADFORD. Release of interest and estate, right and claim of dower
signed by SARAH A. DUNN, ELISA DUNN & ELIZABETH DUNN, wives of the
within named ROGER, HENRY & SYLVESTER DUNN, bef. JNO. DOUGLASS, J.P.
16 Feb. 1801. Proved by WM. ROBERTS bef. Jno. Douglass, 10 Apr. 1801.
Rec. 17 July 1803. (Orig. rec. 17 Apr. 1801.)

Pp 308-309:   3 Dec. 1801. (Deed) JOHN DOUGLASS of Salem Co., Sumter
               Dist., S. C., planter, to JOSEPH COMMANDER, of same place,

Cont'd:
planter, 270 acres of land, more or less, being part of two surveys,
viz: 60 acres, more or less, situate on Black River in state, dist.
and county afsd., bounded NW and SW on WILLIAM CHRISTMAS' land, by
orig. conveyance, now RICHARD RATCLIFF's land, SE and NE on WILLIAM
ROBERT's land formerly, now STEPHEN DANIEL's land, as may appear by
having recourse to orig. plat and grant thereof, which was granted
to WILLIAM ROBERTS, 2 Sept. 1775, containing in the whole 200 acres,
the part of sd survey which is conveyed by these presents is situate
on E side of Black River, running in the lower line from the main stream
of Black River, reverse S 70 E out to a lightwood stake corner, from
thence to a pine N 20° W 24° to a corner, from thence to the white
oak corner, on the swamp S 75° W 12° from thence on the line running
N 15° W until its intersection with the stream or upper line of sd
survey containing in the whole part or moiety 60 acres, more or less,
including all the land on the E side of the main stream of Black River
within the lines of the sd 200 acres surveyed. Also a part or moiety
of land situate in the dist. and county afsd, on the E side of Black
River bounded N 20° W 38° on land granted to WILLIAM ROBERTS N 70°
W 309 on land now RICHARD ROBERTS, S 65° W 1572 on SYLVESTER DUNN's
land, S 72° E 93.50 on JOHN SMITH's land, N 2° W 9 on land now STEPHEN
DANIEL's and containing in the whole 210 acres, agreeable to a plat
thereof certified by ROGER DUNN, 21 Oct. 1793, it being part of a survey containing 1000 acres, granted to SYLVESTER DUNN, SR., containing
in both moieties 270 acres, more or less. Consideration: $250.00. Signed
by JOHN DOUGLASS (seal) and SARAH DOUGLASS (seal). Wit: LEWIS SMITH
& JOHN SMITH (by mark). Proved by Lewis Smith bef. John Douglass, J.P.
3 Dec. 1801. Rec. 17 July 1803. (Plat shows land of ROBT. WM. CARTER,
RICHARD RATCLIFF, JESSE COMMANDER, ROB BRISBAND.)

Pp 310-311:   17 May 1803. (Deed) ZACHARIAH NORWOOD of S. C., (Dist.
               not named), to JOSEPH COMMANDER of Sumter Dist., S. C.,
a tract of land situated on S side of Lynches Creek in Sumter Dist.,
containing 134 acres, more or less, being part of a 350 acre tract
granted to JOHN EGAN, 1 June 1767; the sd 134 acres being the lower
part of sd 350 acres; more fully described by plat annexed. Consideration: $200.00. Signed: ZACHARIAH NORWOOD (seal). Wit: EDM. BARRY bef.
JOHN HUGGINS, J.Q., 17 May 1803. Release of all interest, right and
claim of dower signed by ELIZABETH NORWOOD (by mark) bef. John Huggins,
J. Q., 18 May 1803. Rec. 18 July 1803.

Pp 311-312:   28 June 1802. (Deed) JOHN MC DONALD of Sumter Dist.,
               S. C. to JOSEPH COMMANDER of same place, a tract of land
of 100 acres, situate in sd dist., on Black River swamp, and hath such
shapes, forms and marks as is represented in this plat, hereunto annexed
which was orig. granted to WILLIAM CHRISTMAS, 19 Jan. 1773. Consideration: $300.00. Signed: JOHN MC DONALD. Wit: JONATHAN NEWMAN & JOEL
SMITH. Proved by Newman bef. John Huggins, J.P. Release of interest,
estate, right and claim of dower signed by ELIZABETH MC DONALD, wife
of JOHN MC DONALD, 20 June 1802 bef. John Huggins, J.P. of Dovington.
Rec. 18 July 1803.

Page 312:   Record of SARAH BROWN's stock and hog marks. Recorded
               28 July 1803.

               Record of WILLIAM MURRELL's stock mark. Recorded 28 July
               1803.

Pp 312-313:   4 June 1803. (Deed) WILLIAM VAUGHAN, SR., of Sumter Dist.,
               S. C., planter, to JOHN BRADFORD VAUGHAN, of same place,
planter, a tract of land containing 51 acres, situate in Claremont
Co., Dist. and state afsd., on or near Dry Swamp, comprehending part
of a certain tract orig. granted to DAVID NEILSON, and part of a tract
granted to sd WILLIAM VAUGHAN, SR., 7 Feb. 1803, recorded in Grant
Book G.B. XXX, No. 5, page 276, more fully described by plat certified
by JOHN J. BRADFORD, D.S., 2 May 1803. Consideration: $200.00. Signed:
WM. VAUGHAN, SR. (seal). Wit: LARKIN JENNINGS & HUGH MATTHEWS. Proved
by Jennings bef. John Horan, J.P., 11 June 1803. Rec. 2 Aug. 1803.
(Plat shows lands of Gen. THOMAS LEE, ANTHONY LEE, WM. VAUGHAN.)

Pp 313-315:   3 Nov. 1801. (Deed) HUBERD REES, Esq., Sheriff of Sumter
               Dist., S. C. to REDDEN MC COY, of same place: Whereas
JOHN TUCKER, deceased, of the state afsd., in his lifetime was seized
in his demesne as of fee or of and in some other good and lawful estate
of inheritance to him and his heirs and assigns forever, and possessed
of the plantation or tract of land containing 100 acres intended to
be herein more particularly mentioned and described. Whereas also the
sd JOHN TUCKER, dec'd. in his lifetime became indebted to the Estate
of PETER SINCLAIR, deceased, as by his obligation to PETER GAILLARD,
Executor to sd PETER SINCLAIR doth shew and whereas the sd PETER GAIL-
LARD did institute a suit against REDDEN MC COY, Adm. of the/said/JOHN
TUCKER, dec'd. in the Court of Common Pleas for the dist. of Sumter
which was holden at the house of JOHN GAYLE, and did in the sd Court
on 7 Nov. 1800 recover a judgment against the sd REDDEN for $140.50
for his debt. And also $39.96 for the costs and damages which he sus-
tained in and about proscution of his sd suit in that behalf whereof
the sd REDDEN MC COY was convicted as appears on record of sd Court.
The goods, chattels, houses, lands, etc. of REDDEN MC COY were levied
upon, and the sheriff did enter into and take into execution the afsd.
plantation, and after due notice same was sold at public outcry. The
following is a description of the land conveyed to REDDEN MC COY. "All
that afsd. plantation or tract of land containing 100 acres, more or
less, situate on Black River, in the Dist. afsd., granted orig. to
the sd JOHN TUCKER, deceased, bounded at the time of survey on all
sides by vacant lands." Consideration: $125.00. Signed: HUBERD REES
(seal), Shff. Sumter Dist. Wit: ULYSSES ROGERS & RICHARD BRADFORD.
Proved by Bradford bef. Charles F. Gordon, J.P. 1 Aug. 1803. Rec. 3
Aug. 1803.

Pp 315-317:   10 May 1788. (Deed) DANIEL CLARK of Claremont Co., S.C.,
               to JAMES CLARK, "part of an estate willed to me by my
brother, SAMUEL CLARK, deceased, which was the eighth part of his estate." Consideration: 50 pds sterling money. Signed: DANIEL CLARK (seal)
Wit: DRURY CLARKE, DAVID NEILSON & ISHAM CLARKE. Proved by David Neilson bef. WM. E. HERRING, J.P., 13 Mar. 1797. Rec. 3 Aug. 1803. (Orig.
rec. 18 Mar. 1797.)

Pp 316-317:   18 Apr. 1803. (Deed) ROBERT BROWN of Sumter Dist. on
               Black River, S. C. to CHARLES R. MC COY, "96 acres of
land, more or less, being part of a tract granted to ROBERT BROWN situated on Cowpen Swamp, a branch of black-river waters, Sumter Dist.
and state afsd., adj. SW on JOSEPH SPEARS, SE on EPAPHMODITUS HANKS,
SE & NW by ROBERT BROWN and NE by JOHN MC COY, granted to sd ROBERT
BROWN on 28 Feb. 1794 as will fully appear from the grant, signed by
PETER BREMAR, Surveying General in state afsd." Consideration: "of
the sum of forty six pounds thirteen shillings and four pence paid
to one MARTHA MC COY by RODGER MC COY of Sumter Dist. and state afsd."
Signed: ROBERT BROWN (seal). Wit: EPAPHRODITUS HANKS (by his mark)
and STEPHEN HANKS. Proved by EPAPHRODITUS HANKS bef. CHARLES F. GORDON,
J.P., 1 Aug. 1803. Rec. 3 Aug. 1803.

Pp 317-318:   16 July 1803. (Deed) HENRY CASSELS, JR. of Salem Co.,
               S. C., planter, to SAMUEL JAMES BRADLEY of co. and state
afsd., planter, a tract of 200 acres, orig. granted to ROGER BRADLEY
on the E side of Scape hore in the fork of Black River, on Long Branch
bounding E by JAMES ARMSTRONG & JOSEPH BURGESS land; N by MISS ARNOTT,
W by DAVID MC CLOUD and S by SAMUEL BRADLEY; more fully described by
a plat annexed. Consideration: $320.00. Signed: HENRY CASSELS, JR.
Wit: JOHN E. JAMES, SAMUEL BRADLEY, JR. & WILLIAM FALCONAR. Release
of all right and interest, also all her right and claim of dower in
above described premises, signed by AGNESS CASSELS (by her mark),
16 July 1803 bef. G. COOPER, J.Q. Proved by JNO. E. JAMES bef. G. Cooper
18 July 1803. Rec. 9 Aug. 1803.

Pp 318-319:   7 July 1803. (Deed of Gift) DAVID WITHERSPOON of Salem
               Co., S. C., planter, to his daughter, MATILDA WITHERSPOON
and to his son, JOHN STOREY WITHERSPOON and his son JAMES ADDISON WITH-
ERSPOON, the following property: "To my daughter MATILDA, a negro boy
named Isam, and a negro girl named Harriet, to my son JOHN STOREY,

417

Cont'd:
a negro boy named Nero, and a negro girl named Flora, and to my son
JAMES ADDISON, a negro boy named Jack and a negro girl named Wizoon."
Consideration: Love and natural affection. Signed: DAVID WITHERSPOON
(seal). Wit: SARAH LAVERTY & THOS. ROWSE. Proved by Thos. Rowse bef.
JOHN PERRY, J.Q., 7 July 1803. Rec. 9 Aug. 1803.

Pp 319-320:   4 May 1803. (Bill of Sale) JOHN B. VAUGHAN of Sumter
               Dist., S. C., to WILLIAM JONES of same place, three neg-
roes, viz: one woman named Cassey, and her two children - one a boy
named George, the other a girl named Sophey. Consideration: $600.00.
Signed: J. B. VAUGHAN. Wit: FURY CAMPBELL & BRADLEY RHAME. Proved by
BRADLEY RHAME bef. John Horan, J. P., 5 Aug. 1803. Rec. 9 Aug. 1803.

Page 320:   21 June 1800. (Bill of Sale) DAVID CEALTER, to MRS. LUCY
               JEFFERSON, a negro woman slave named Hannah and her mu-
latto child named Rhody. Consideration: $490.00. Signed: DAVID CEALTER.
Wit: JOHN HORAN. Proved by John Horan bef. JOHN MOORE, J.Q. 5 Aug.
1803. Rec. 9 Aug. 1803.

Pp 320-321:   24 Feb. 1803. (Deed) WILLIAM CARTER, Tanner, of Salem
               Co., Sumter Dist., S. C., to SAMUEL REMBERT of Claremont
Co., dist. and state afsd., planter, a tract of land containing 500
acres more or less in Mill Branch, waters of Black River, bounding
on all sides on vacant land at time of orig. survey; sd land being
granted on or about Aug. 14, 1775 to ROBERT CARTER, and by him conveyed
by his last Will and Testament to the above sd WILLIAM CARTER, party
to these presents. Signed: WM. CARTER (seal). Wit: EZEKIEL DUBOSE &
JOHN DUTART. Proved by Ezekiel Dubose bef. ABSALOM WILLIAMS, J.Q.,
2 Aug. 1803.

Page 321:   30 Mar. 1803. (Mortgage) HUGH CASSITY of Claremont Co.,
               S. C., to J. & M. BRACEY of same county, one negro fellow
named George. Consideration: $500.00. Signed: HUGH CASSITY. Wit: JOSEPH
WILLIAMS & ROBERT P. POOL. Proved by Robert P. Pool bef. John Horan,
J. P., 20 June 1803. Rec. 20 June 1803.

Pp 321-322:   9 June 1803. (Deed) ROYAL GIBSON & SAMUEL GIBSON, of
               S. C., to ROBERT DINGLE of same state, a tract of land
containing 100 acres, orig. granted to JOHN JAMES GIBSON by Benjamin
Guerard, Gov. 21 Jan. 1785; which land was bound at time of survey
on all sides by vacant land, and fell by heirship to the sd ROYAL &
SAMUEL GIBSON. Consideration: $200.00. Signed: ROYAL GIBSON & SAMUEL
GIBSON (seals) (by his mark). Wit: BENJA. RICHBURG and THOS. LOWDER.
Release of all interest and estate, also her right and claim of dower
in the above described premises signed by MARY GIBSON (by her mark)
(wife of the within named ROYAL GIBSON), bef. WM. RICHBOURG, J.Q. 10
June 1803. Proved by THOS. LOWDER bef. Wm. Richbourg, J.Q., 11 June
1803. Rec. 9 Aug. 1803.

Pp 322-323:   4 Apr. 1803. (Deed) WILLIAM RICHBOURG of Sumter Dist.,
               S. C., to BRADLEY RHAME of same place, a tract of land
containing 180 acres more or less, situate in Sumter Dist., S. C. on
Sammys Swamp, waters of Black River, bounded by lines running S & W
by GREEN's land, W by BENJAMIN HUGGINS, SE by SETH BONDS, which land
was orig. granted to sd WM. RICHBOURGH by grant dated 2 June 1794,
rec. in Grant Book L, No. 5. Consideration: 30 pds sterling money.
Signed: WM. RICHBOURG (seal). Wit: WM. HUMPHREY & JAMES GIBSON, JR.
Proved by WILLIAM HUMPHREY bef. WM. TAYLOR, J.Q. 4 Apr. 1803. Release
of all interest and estate also all her right and claim of dower to
the above described premises, signed by ELIZABETH RICHBOURGH (by mark),
wife of WILLIAM RICHBOURGH, 2 Aug. 1803 bef. WM. TAYLOR, J.Q. Rec.
16 Aug. 1803.

Page 324:   29 May 1803. (Bill of Sale) FRANCIS DANEY, JR. to JONATHAN
               BELL, one negro girl named Sarah. Consideration: $240.
Signed: FRANCIS DANEY, JR. (seal). Wit: WILLIAM OSTEEN & JEREMIAH RHAME.
Proved by JEREMIAH RHAME, JR. bef. WM. RICHBOURG, J.Q. 15 Aug. 1803.
Rec. 19 Aug. 1803.

Page 324:   8 Sept. 1803. (Dower) NAOMI WILLIAMS to THOMAS HALL.
                Release of all interest and estate, also all her right
and claim of Dower signed by NAOMI WILLIAMS, wife of JOSEPH WILLIAMS,
to the premises described, bef. JOHN MOORE, J.Q. Rec. 9 Sept. 1803.
(For deed alluded to see pages 24 and 25.)

Pp 324-325:   25 Feb. 1803. (Deed) JOHN CHESNUT of Camden, S. C., plan-
                ter, to JOHN BATES of Claremont Co., S.C. a tract of
land containing 100 acres, situate on both sides of the main road leading from Camden to Stateburgh, on or nearly adjoining Raften Creek,
on the E side of Wateree River, bounded to the N by lands belonging
to WILLIAM SANDERS; to the S by lands belonging to WILLIAM WRIGHT;
which sd tract of land was originally granted to the sd JOHN BATES,
and by virtue of an execution was conveyed by the Sheriff of Camden
District to the sd JOHN CHESNUT, 5 Nov. 1793. Consideration: 5 pds
sterling. Signed: JOHN CHESNUT (seal). Wit: BEN CARTER, JOSEPH BREVARD.
Proved by Ben. Carter 9 Apr. 1803, bef. JAS. BROWN, J.P.

Pp 325-326:   30 July 1803. (Deed) JOHN BATES, SR. of Sumter Dist.,
                S. C./, to ASBERY SYLVESTER of same place, a tract of
land containing by the original survey, 100 acres, situate in Claremont County, in sd District, on both sides of the public road, leading
from Camden to Stateburgh; originally granted to sd JOHN BATES on or
about 3 Feb. 1761; and passed by divers conveyances to JOHN CHESNUT,
and by him conveyed to the above named JOHN BATES by deed of release,
dated 25 Feb. (last) of record in the register's office of Sumter Dist.
Consideration: $200.00. Signed: JOHN BATES (seal). Wit: JOHN MOORE
& JOSEPH SYLVESTER. Proved by John Moore bef. John Horan, J.P. 15 Aug.
1803. Rec. 9 Sept. 1803.

Pp 326-327:   25 Feb. 1803. JOHN CHESNUT, planter, of Camden in S.
                C., to ASBERY SYLVESTER of Sumter Dist., S. C., planter,
a tract of land containing 500 acres, more or less, situate on the
E side of the Wateree River in the district afsd., bounded on the SW
by sd River; SE by land lately belonging to THOMAS SUMTER and on all
other sides by lands belonging to the Estate of THOMAS CASSITY, dec'd.,
excepting a small part of the sd tract, supposed to be about 3 acres,
which is now in possession of THOMAS SUMTER, sd tract of land having
been seized by the Sheriff of Camden by virtue of an execution against
JAMES BATES, and by the sd Sheriff sold and conveyed to sd JOHN CHESNUT
by deed dated 5 Nov. 1793. Consideration: $3000.00. Signed: JOHN CHES-
NUT (seal). Wit: BENJAMIN CARTER & JOSEPH BREVARD. Proved by Benj.
Carter bef. Jas. Brown, J.P. 9 Apr. 1803. Rec. 9 Sept. 1803.

Pp 327-328:   14 Mar. 1800. (Deed) ISHAM MOORE of Claremont Co., S.C.,
                planter, to ABRAHAM PETTYPOOL of same place, a tract
of land containing 300 acres, more or less, being part of a tract of
4000 acres granted to MATTHEW SINGLETON 16 July 1784; more fully described by a plat hereunto annexed. Consideration: 64 pds sterling.
Signed. ISHAM MOORE (seal). Wit: RICHARD MOORE & LEONARD MOORE. Proved
by Leonard Moore bef. John Horan, J.P., 3 Sept. 1803.

                Plat showing tract of 300 acres laid out for ABRAHAM
PETTYPOOL, adjoining lands of JOHN ODIL, THOS. ODIL, THOS. BRUMBY,
ISHAM MOORE & LYNN BROWN. Rec. 9 Sept. 1803.

Pp 328-331:   9 Sept. 1803. (Deed) THOMAS SUMTER of Claremont Co.,
                S.C., to SHADRICK ATKINSON of same place, a tract of
land containing 1000 acres more or less, orig. granted to Gen. THOMAS
SUMTER bounded as follows: beginning at WILLIAM MONTGOMERY's lower
s.westernmost corner, continuing up the sd Montgomery line to sd S.
ADKINSON's land, whereupon he now lives, thence up the sd line until
it intersects with a tract of 740 acres, sold by Gen. Sumter to the
sd Atkinson; thence to continue on sd line to the upper N.westernmost
corner; thence running a straight line to the middle of a 640 acre
tract on Tar coat granted to THOMAS COURTNEY which is DAVIS's corner;
thence down sd line to MARMADUKE ATKINSON's land; thence down the sd
line to THOMAS GRANT's land; thence down sd line to the sd SHAD. AT-
KINSON's mill tract sold to him by MR. HORAN and FLEY; thence to conti-

Cont'd:
nue on sd line to the NE corner; thence to WM. MONTGOMERY's S.western-
most corner, which is the beginning point. Consideration: 60 pds sterling. Signed: THOMAS SUMTER (seal). Wit: GEORGE BRASINGTON & RICHARD
BRADFORD. Proved by GEO. BRASINGTON bef. JOHN HORAN, J.P., 10 Sept.
1803. Rec. 12 Sept. 1803.

Pp 331-332:   9 Sept. 1803. (Bond) JAMES HAMILTON of District of Sumter,
                State of S. C., to THOMAS SUMTER, SR., of the Dist. and
State afsd. Consideration: 5740 pds. sterling money. Signed: JAMES
HAMILTON (seal). Wit: JAS. W. MURRELL. Proved by Murrell bef. John
Horan, J.P., 10 Sept. 1803. Rec. 12 Sept. 1803.

Page 332:   9 Sept. 1803. (Deed via Mortgage) JAMES HAMILTON of Sumter
                Dist., S. C. to THOMAS SUMTER, SR. of same place, a tract
of land containing 574 acres, situate in Sumter Dist. on Beach Creek,
waters of Wateree River, bounded by lines running NE and SE on lands
belonging to the Estates of THOMAS HOOPER and JOHN MACNAIR; SW on sd
THOMAS SUMTER, and a lot lately belonging to the Estate of JOHN C.
SMITH. Consideration: $2870.00. Signed: JAMES HAMILTON (seal). Wit:
J. S. RICHARDSON & JAS. W. MURRELL. Proved by Jas. W. Murrell bef.
John Horan, J.P. 10 Sept. 1803. Rec. 12 Sept. 1803.

Page 332:   4 June 1803. (Deed) ROBERT CASSITY of Sumter Dist., S.C.,
                to HUGH CASSITY of same place, a tract of land containing
295 acres, situate in the state and district afsd, on the public road
leading from Stateburg to Camden, on or near Gum Swamp, waters of the
Wateree River, which sd tract of land passed by divers conveyances
to the above named ROBERT CASSITY, more fully described by a plat of
same anexed to a deed of release from THOMAS SUMTER to HENRY CLARK,
SR. Consideration: $800.00. Signed: ROBERT CASSITY (seal). Wit: MERRY
BRACEY, JOS. WILLIAMS & ROBERT STAMPER. Proved by ROBERT STAMPER bef.
John Horan, J.P., 14 Sept. 1803. Rec. 15 Sept. 1803.

Pp 332-333:   11 June 1803. (Deed) HUGH CASSITY of Sumter Dist., S.C.,
                to RICHARD HAYNSWORTH of same place, a tract of land
containing 295 acres situate in the dist. and state afsd., on the public
road leading from Stateburgh to Camden, on or near Gum Swamp, waters
of the Wateree River, and was conveyed by ROBERT CASSITY to the above
named HUGH CASSITY, 4 June 1803. Rec. in the Register's Office of Sumter
Dist. Consideration: $1000.00. Signed: HUGH CASSITY (seal). Wit: TYRE
JENNINGS & JOSEPH ERWIN. Proved by Joseph Erwin bef. John Horan, J.P.,
15 June 1803. Rec. 15 Sept. 1803.

Pp 333-334:   1 Sept. 1803. (Deed) JOHN R. SPANN of Sumter Dist., S.C.,
                to RICHARD HAYNSWORTH of same place, a tract of land
containing 689 acres, situate in Camden (now Sumter) Dist. on the NW
side of the Wateree River, bounding at the time of the orig. survey
thereof to JAMES LANGLEY on the 15th day of Jan. 1793; W on land supposed to belong to ADAM B. BRISBANE: N on lands belonging to RICHARD
FURMAN & THOMAS WRIGHT; E on lands belonging to JOHN MACNAIR, ASBERY
SYLVESTER, WILLIAM BRACEY & SHERWOOD JAMES; and S on land laid out
to BATEMAN, and was sold and conveyed by the sd JAMES LANGLEY to the
above named JOHN R. SPANN by deed dated 3 July 1802. Rec. in the Register's Office of Sumter Dist., Book AA, page 66 and 67; more fully
described by plat annexed to the original grant. Consideration: $1200.00
Signed: JOHN R. SPANN (seal). Wit: WM. MURRELL & ULYSSES ROGERS. Proved
by Wm. Murrell bef. John Horan, J.P. 2 Sept. 1803. Rec. 15 Sept. 1803.

Page 335:   23 Aug. 1803. (Deed) GEORGE JOOR of Claremont Co., S.C.
                to JOHN SMYTH RICHARDSON of same place, Attorney at Law,
two lots of land containing one half acre each, situate in the village
of Stateburgh, bounding and measuring 105 feet front on a street leading by WILLIAM MURRELL's, and 420 feet on Turf Street, opposite to
a lot belonging to the sd WM. MURRELL, which sd lot or lots were conveyed by THOMAS SUMTER to JAMES GREEN HUNT, and by him to the above
named GEORGE JOOR, as may appear by record in the Register's office
of Sumter Dist., Book A, pages 203 to 207. Consideration: 100 pds sterling money. Signed. GEO. JOOR (seal). Wit: W. G. RICHARDSON and M.
M. HORRY. Proved by Richardson bef. Jno. Horan, 27 Aug. 1803.

Pp 336-337:   15 Sept. 1803. (Deed) WILLIAM MURRELL of Sumter Dist.,
               S.C., Merchant, to JOHN SMYTH RICHARDSON of same place,
Attorney at Law, a tract of land containing three acres & eight perches
more or less, situate in the village of Stateburgh, in the dist. and
state afsd., bounding to the N on the road leading through Stateburgh
to Brisbanes Ferry; to the W on land belonging to the sd WM. MURRELL;
to the S on lot belonging to sd JOHN SMYTH RICHARDSON and land belonging to the sd WM. MURRELL and to the E on what is called a street running with the Easternmost part of the lot whereon the sd WM. MURRELL
now lives; more fully described by a plat hereto annexed. Consideration:
$63.00. Signed: WM. MURRELL (seal). Wit: JNO. HAYNSWORTH & JAS. W.
MURRELL. Proved by Jas. W. Murrell bef. John Horan, J.P., 17 Sept.
1803. Rec. 21 Sept. 1803.

Pp 337-339:   14 Sept. 1803. (Deed) THOMAS SUMTER of the Dist. of Sumter
               in S.C., to JOHN SMYTH RICHARDSON of same place, the
following lots or pieces of land, to wit: one lot of land situate in
Stateburgh, in length 260 feet, in width 101 feet, more or less, bounded
on the E by the public road to Charleston; on the W by a lot now belonging to JNO. SMYTH RICHARDSON; N by MRS. MURPHY's lot; and on the
S by WM. MURRELL's lot, as marked in the plat annexed. Also one other
lot or piece of land, bounded on the E by WM. BRACEY's and the sd THOMAS
SUMTER's lots; on the W by the piece or slip marked N. 4; on the N
by the road to Brisbane's Ferry; and on the S by a part of MRS. MURPHY's
lot in length one hundred and sixty six feet and a half, in width 55
feet more or less, and marked in the plat hereunto annexed. Also the
two following pieces or slips of land, to wit: 1 piece marked No. 3
in the plat hereto annexed, in length 805 feet, more or less, in width
40 feet, more or less, bounded E by the road to Charleston; S by WM.
MURRELL's land; N by the lot first described, marked No. 1 and by
a lot now belonging to the sd JOHN SMYTH RICHARDSON; also one other
slip or piece of land, bounded N by the road to Brisbane's Ferry; and
running S bet. Lot No. 1, MRS. MURPHY's lot and lot marked No. 2 on
the E., and by slip marked No. 4 and the lot of JNO. SMYTH RICHARDSON
on the W, in length 511 and a half feet, in width 40 feet, and marked
No. 4 in a plat hereto annexed. Consideration: 50 pds. Signed: THOS.
SUMTER (L.S.) Wit: W. ELLISON and JOSHUA LEE. Proved by WILLIAM ELLISON
bef. John Horan, J.P., 17 Sept. 1803. Rec. 21 Sept. 1803. (Plat shows
land of WM. MURRELL, JOHN S. RICHARDSON, MRS. MURPHY, BRACEY & SUMTER).

Page 340:   18 May 1801. "Received this 18th of May 1801 of JOHN
               P. RICHARDSON the sum of two hundred pounds sterling
in part of a legacy left me by MRS. E. SINKLER's will and also 10 English Guineas and 1 French Guinea, received by the hands of Mr. CHARLES
CANTEY making Eleven pounds 18/11 in all two hundred and eleven pounds
18/11." Signed: THOMAS CLAY. Wit: CHARLES RICHARDSON & JNO. C. WALTER.

Page 340:   18 May 1801. "Received this 18th May 1801 of J. P. RICHARD-
               SON in addition the further sum of two pounds 6/9 to
that of two hundred and eleven pounds 18/11 for which the receipt is
given on the other side making in the whole two hundred and fourteen
pounds 5/8." Signed: THOS. CLAY. Wit: CHARLES RICHARDSON & JNO. C.
WALTER. (Both above receipts proved by Jno. C. Walter bef. John Horan,
16 July 1801.) Rec. 22 Sept. 1803.

Page 341:   19 May 1801. "Received this 19th day of May one thousand
               eight hundred and one of JOHN P. RICHARDSON the sum of
five hundred pounds sterling in full for the balance of a legacy to
which I am entitled under the last Will and Testament of the late MRS.
ELIZABETH SINKLER of Saint Stephen parish deceased." Signed: THOMAS
CLAY (seal). Wit: CHARLES RICHARDSON and JNO. C. WALTER. Proved by
Walter bef. John Horan, 16 July 1801. Rec. 22 Sept. 1803.

Pp 341-342:   11 Apr. 1801. (Bill of Sale or Mortgage) WILLIAM RICH-
               BOURG of Sumter Dist., S. C. to JOHN P. RICHARDSON of
same place, the following slaves: Dublin, Edny, Juby, Milly, Rachel,
Sarah, Jack, Mercury, Essex, January, Derry, Syphas, Rose, Betty, Grippa
and Leah. Consideration: 460 pds. Signed: WM. RICHBOURG (seal). Wit:
JAMES B. RICHARDSON & WM. N. RICHBOURG. Proved by Richardson bef. Jno.
Horan 16 Jul. 1801. Rec. 22 Sept. 1803.

Pp 342-343: 16 Sept. 1800. (Deed) THOMAS SUMTER, JR. of Claremont
Co., S. C. to JOHN PETER RICHARDSON of same place, a
tract of land containing 490 acres, situate in Camden (now Sumter)
Dist., Clarendon Co., being part of and taken out of the NE of a tract
containing 640 acres, granted to COMFORT STRANGE on or about 16 July
1784, duly recorded in the Sec. Office in Grant Book AAAA, page 24,
which sd tract of land was sold and conveyed by the sd COMFORT STRANGE
to THOMAS SUMTER by deed of lease and release dated 30 and 31 Aug.
1784, recorded in the Clerk's office of Claremont Co., Book A, pages
178 to 180; more fully described by record and plat annexed. Consideration: 100 pds sterling money. Signed: THOS. SUMTER (seal). Wit: SAML.
FLEY & JAMES THEUS. Proved by Saml. Fley bef. John Horan, 14 Oct. 1800.
Rec. 4 Oct. 1800.

Pp 343-344: 3 Oct. 1803. (Deed) WILLIAM MC KNIGHT of Sumter Dist.,
S. C. to AARON FRIERSON of same place, a tract of land
containing 1000 acres, orig. granted to Mr. ROBERT FULWOOD, situate
in the dist. afsd., on boggy gully, waters of Black River, including
Bull Head Bay, beginning at a lightwood stake corner, bounded on WILEY
BURROW's land; and running thence N 40 W 38 Chains to a pine corner;
thence running N 65 W ___ Chains to a lightwood stake corner; thence
running S 75 12 Chains to a pine corner; thence running N 75 W 17 Chains
to a red oak corner; thence running N 20 W 15 Chains to a pine corner;
thence running S 37 W 21 Chains to a lightwood stake corner; thence
running N 57 W 28 to a pine corner; thence running W 26 Chains to a
pine corner; thence runnins S 40 W 7 Chains to a pine corner; thence
running S 55 W 30 to a stake corner; thence running S 40 W 10 Chains
to a post oak corner; thence running S 56 E 5 Chains to a pine corner;
thence running S 16 Chains to a red oak corner; thence running S 30
E 10 Chains to a pine corner; thence running S 70 E 13 Chains to a
pine corner; thence running S 30 E 32 Chains to a pine corner; thence
running S 56 E 15 Chains to a pine corner; thence N 82 E 20 Chains
to a lightwood tree corner; thence running N 50 E 100 Chains to the
beginning. Consideration: $500.00. Signed. WM. MC KNIGHT. Wit: JOHN
RAWLLINS & CHRIS'R. T. WINDER. Proved by C. T. Winder bef. Wm. Taylor,
J.Q., 8 Oct. 1803. Rec. 14 oct. 1803.

Pp 344-345: 3 Oct. 1803. (Deed) WILLIAM MC KNIGHT of Sumter Dist.,
S. C., to AARON FRIERSON of same place, a tract of land
containing 637 1/2 acres, more or less, orig. granted to WILLIAM PARKER,
situate in the Dist. afsd., on the N and S sides of Black River Swamp,
being the tract of land on which the sd WILLIAM MC KNIGHT now lives;
beginning at a lightwood stake corner adj. JAMES MC KNIGHT's land;
and running thence NW 72° 67 Chains 50 to a lightwood stake and corner;
thence running S 69 W along a conditional line across Black River swamp
to the orig. line; thence SW along the orig. line to an open corner;
thence NE 72° 135 chains to the beg. corner, bounded on JOHN WITHER-
SPOON's land. Consideration: $1000.00. Signed: WM. MC KNIGHT (seal).
Wit: JOHN RAULINS, CHRIS. T. WINDER. Proved by Winder bef. Wm. Taylor,
J.Q. Rec. 14 Oct. 1803.

Pp 345-346: 3 Oct. 1803. (Deed) WILLIAM MC KNIGHT of Sumter Dist.,
S. C., planter, to AARON FRIERSON of same place, eleven
negroes, named as follows: Jack, July, Sylvia, Roger, Sabina, Pompey,
Rose, Moses, Flora, Susanah and Sam, also 1 sorrel horse and a bay
horse, which was bought from Mr. BEEN, also my stock of cattle, goats
and hogs, three featherbeds and furniture, with my household furniture
and crop of cotton and corn. Consideration: $2,150.00. Signed: WM.
MC KNIGHT (seal). Wit: JOHN RAWLLINS & CHRIS. WINDER. Proved by Winder
bef. Wm. Taylor, J.Q., 8 Oct. 1803. Rec. 14 Oct. 1803.

Pp 346-347: 24 July 1784. (Deed) ARCHIBALD HENSON of Camden Dist.,
S. C., Carpenter, to THOMAS SUMTER, of same place, Merchant, a tract of land containing 200 acres, situate in Camden Dist.,
Craven Co., on the N side of Santee River on both sides of the big
Branch of Jacks Creek; bounded on all sides by vacant land; and hath
such shape, form and marks as appear by a plat to the orig. grant annexed which sd grant was to ZACHARIAH DENNY by Charles E. Montague, Gov.
23 Jan. 1773, rec. in Sec. Office, Book NNN, p. 470, entered in the

Cont'd:
Aud. Office in Book M, No. 12, page 226. Consideration: 200 pds sterling money. Signed: ARC'D. HENSON (L.S.). Wit: FRANCIS PRINGLE & THOMAS ANDREWS. Proved by Thos. Andrews bef. WM. MURRELL, J.P, 22 Sept. 1785. Rec. 20 Oct. 1803.

Pp 347-349:   22 Oct. 1803. (Deed) THOMAS SUMTER of Claremont Co.,
                Sumter Dist., S. C., planter, to JOHN P. RICHARDSON, Esq., of same place, a tract of land containing 200 acres more or less, situate on Jacks Creek in dist. and state afsd., orig. granted to ZACHARIAH DENNY, 3 Jan. 1773; more fully described by plat annexed to sd grant. Consideration: $200.00. Signed: THOS. SUMTER (L.S.) Wit: JOHN MC DONNELL, GEO. BRASINGTON. Proved by George Brasington bef. John Horan, J.P. 28 Oct. 1803. Rec. 29 Oct. 1803.

Pp 349-350:   3 Aug. 1803. (Deed) WILLIAM RICHBOURG, SR. of the county
                of Claremont, Sumter District, State of S. C., to WILLIAM R. L. STUKES of same county and state, a tract of land containing 810 acres, lying on Bull Head Cypress and Home Branch, waters of Black River; binding NW on land surveyed for JOHN BRADLEY; SW on vacant land; SE on CHEVAN's land; and NE on JERDIN PERKIN's land, originally granted to sd WILLIAM RICHBOURGH, 5 Apr. 1802. Consideration: $200.00. Signed. WM. RICHBOURGH (L.S.) Wit: HUGH RICHBOURG & JOHN RIDGILL, JR. Proved by JOHN RIDGILL, JR. bef. JOHN RIDGILL, J.P. 4 Aug. 1803. Rec. 29 Oct. 1803.

Pp 350-351:;   3 Aug. 1803. (Deed) WILLIAM RICHBOURG, SR. of the county
               and state afsd., (Clarendon County, S. C.) to WILLIAM R. L. STUKES of the county and state afsd., a tract of land containing 552 acres, being the SE and upper part of a tract of land granted to the sd WM. RICHBOURG for 1000 acres, lying on Mill Branch and Kessing Branch and Sammy Swamp, waters of Black River. Consideration: $100.00. Signed: WM. RICHBOURG (L.S.) Wit: HUGH RICHBOURG & JOHN RIDGILL, JR. Proved by JOHN RIDGILL, JR. bef. JOHN RIDGILL, J.P. 4 Aug. 1803. Rec. 29 Oct. 1803.

Page 352:   14 Oct. 1803. (Bill of Sale) ANN SINGLETON to IRBY SINGLE-
                TON, a negro man named Peter, and a wench named Celey. Consideration: $1000.00. Signed: ANN SINGLETON. Wit: JAMES BRADFORD. Proved by James Bradford bef. John Horan, J.P., 4 Nov. 1803. Rec. 5 Nov. 1803.

Page 353:   22 Nov. 1802. (Bill of Sale) STEPHEN CADE of Marlborough
                county, S. C. to Captain SAMUEL BRADLEY of county and state afsd., a certain negro boy named Prince. Consideration: $345.00. Signed: STEPHEN CADE (L.S.) Wit: JOHN PERRY. Proved by John Perry. Rec. 24 Nov. 1803. (Received money from executors of PETER FITZ-PATRICK, who became security for sd STEPHEN CADE.)

Page 354:   12 Oct. 1803. (Bill of Sale) PARHAM SANDY KIRK, late
                of Orange County, N. C., to GEORGE CONLY, of Claremont Co., Sumter Dist., S. C., a certain negro woman slave named Fanny, 15 years. Consideration: $375.00. Signed: PARHAM S. KIRK (seal). Wit: WILLIAM WARDEN. Proved by William Warden bef. John Horan, J.P. Rec. 24 Nov. 1803.

Page 355:   Sheriffs sale day for the sd county to the best of my
                recollection in the month of Sept. Anno Domini 1799 I sold a tract of land as the property of JOHN CHANDLER containing 130 acres more or less, situate on Home Swamp, waters of Black River, and granted to the sd JOHN CHANDLER on 6 Mar. 1797 by virtue of an execution at the suit of BENJAMIN PERKINS, that the same was struck off to JOHN HORAN for the sum of $42.00 and that at his request I executed titles to JOHAM CLARK of Black River for the same. Given under my hand this 11th day of Nov. 1803. Signed: RICHARD MOORE. Wit: TALIFERO JAMES & JOHN HAYNSWORTH. Proved by Haynsworth bef. John Horan, J.P. Affidavit by John Horan that the deed within mentioned and the record thereof with his other papers were consumed on 27 Nov. 1801. Sworn to bef. CHAS. F. GORDON, J.P. Rec. 26 Nov. 1803.

Page 356:   14 Jan. 1796. (Deed) MARY SHEPHERD, Spinster, of Salem
                County, State of S. C., to JAMES REMBERT, of Camden Dist.,
S. C., planter, a tract of land containing 100 acres in Craven County
on the head of Black River; bounded SW on JOHN FLEMMING's land; all
other sides by vacant land at the time of grant. The sd land was orig.
granted on or about the 9th day of Sept. 1774. Consideration: 23 pds.
6 s. and 8 p. Signed: MARY SHEPHERD (L.S.) (by her mark). Wit: JOHN
MC FADDIN, WILLIAM BEARD & WILLIAM HAZELL. Proved by William Beard
bef. G. Cooper, J.P., 15 Jan. 1796. Rec. 27 Nov. 1803.

Page 357:   27 Aug. 1801. (Deed) JOHN FLEMMING, JR. of Salem County,
                S. C., planter, to JAMES REMBERT, SR. of Sumter Dist.,
S. C., a tract of land containing 300 acres, more or less, in Craven
County, on the head of Black River; bounded SW on SAML. CHRISMAS land
and all other sides on vacant land at the time of the original survey,
the sd land was granted on or about the 23rd day of June 1774 to JOHN
FLEMMING and by him conveyed by his last Will and Testament to the
above sd JOHN FLEMMING, JR. Consideration: $415.00. Signed: JOHN FLEM-
MING, JR. Wit: JOHN DUTART and ANN R. SMITH. Proved by John Dutart
bef. ABSALOM WILLIAMS, J.Q., 10 Nov. 1803. Rec. 27 Nov. 1803.

                       THE END OF RECORDS

                MISCELLANEOUS RECORDS - BOOKS 1 & 2
                PROBATE OFFICE - UNION COUNTY, S. C.

     Miscellaneous Records - Books 1 and 2 covers the period 1785 -
1800 and is bound into one volume which has been recovered and laminated by the South Carolina Archives. It is just exactly what it says
it is - various and sundry items were recorded such as mortgages, apprentice papers, powers-of-attorney, bills of sale for slaves, etc.,
and, most important, the Wills up to 1792. Will Book A, which is the
first Will Book, covers the period 1792 - 1815.

Page 1 is headed "Records of deeds, etc."

Page 1:   GABRIEL BROWN, SR. of Camden Dist., S. C., to Col. WILLIAM
                FARR of 96 Dist., S.C., 4 negroes named Selva, Chaney,
Jesse, and Dublin, for 200 pds. sterling. Dated 4/23/1785. Witnesses:
SAMUEL OTTERSON, J.P., and THOMAS BRANDON, J.P. Recorded 17 ___(torn
off).

Page 2:   WILLIAM JACKSON of Union Co., S.C. to Col. THOMAS BRANDON
                for 80 guineas, 1 negro woman named Racheal and 2 child-
ren. Dated 9/13/1785. Witnesses: JOSEPH JONES, GEORGE STORY, SR., and
WILLIAM McJUNKIN. Recorded 12/28/1785.

Pages 2-3:   DANIEL THOMAS "in consideration of the natural affection
                I have and bear to sister SARAH THOMAS and for other
good causes now hereunto moving have after the decease of my Father
and Mother DANIEL and CATHERINE THOMAS, Given, Granted and by these
presents do give and Grant unto the sd SARAH THOMAS" one negro girl
named Beck. Dated 12/29/1777. Witnesses: WILLIAM THOMAS & JAMES THOMAS.
Recorded 3/28/1786.

Pages 3-4:   MARY SCALES, widow, of Union Co., S.C., "hath put her
                son JOHN SCALES to LUZIANN PARLOR, widow" of Union Co.,
S.C. "to learn her art Trade and Mystery of Weaving and after the manner
of apprentice to serve her" for 14 years. The said apprentice shall
his said mistress faithfully serve, her secrets keep her lawful commands
every where gladly obey. He could not play cards, dice, or other unlawful games, could not "haunt alehouses or Taverns or play houses",
could not lend things to others, or contract matrimony during his term
of apprentice. The mistress was to teach the apprentice weaving, to
read, write, and cypher as far as the five common Rules in Arithmetick,
and to furnish him meat, drink, apparel, washing and boarding. Signed

                                424

Cont'd:
on 12/12/1785 by MARY (X) SCALES, LUZIANN (X) PARLOR and JOHN (X) SCALES
bef. WILLIAM KENNADY, J.P. Recorded 28 Mar. by order.

Pages 4-5:   East Florida - WILLIAM HENDRICKS of the province afsd.,
               appointed Col. THOMAS BRANDON of S.C. and MARGARET HEN-
DRICKS, jointly, to collect debts, transact business, etc., in S.C.
Signed at St. Augustine, Fla. on 5/27/1785. Witnesses: JAMES QUALL
and JOHN HENDRICKS. The witnesses swore to the signatures on 6/8/1785
in East Fla. bef. HENRY QUEAL(?), J.P. JOHN HENDRICKS swore to the
signature again on 8/8/1785 in Union Co., S.C. bef. CHARLES SIMS, J.P.
Recorded 3/30/1786.

Pages 5-6:   Col. WILLIAM FARR informed the Court that he had a bill
               of sale from THOMAS CROSBY for one negro woman named
Jane. Major OTTERSON made oath that he saw a bill of sale in the possession of Col. FARR with a copy, on the back, of sd CROSBY's oath
stating that sd slave was his rightful property and she was clandes-
tantly (sic) taken from him and that he never sold her to any person
but to sd WILLIAM FARR. No recording date.

Pages 6-8:   ?/13/1786 - SHADRICK LANDTRIP, planter, of State of S.C.,
               to AARON FINCHER, planter, of Union and state afsd.,
for 35 pds. 6 shillings sterling, chattel mortgage, (wagon and gears,
3 horses, 3 saddles, ... 2 cows and calves, 3 beds and furniture,
farm tools, etc.) to be paid by 10/13/1787. Witnesses: JAS. CAMPBELL,
JOHN (X) FINCHER, THOS. ELLIOT. No recording date.

Pages 8-10:   12/31/1785 - RICHARD BURGESS of Union Co., S.C. to Col.
               THOMAS BRANDON of same place, mortgage for 60 pds ster-
ling, on land and stock, plantation tools and household furniture,
to be paid by 2/1/1787. Witnesses: JAMES WOODSON and SARAH GIST. Recorded 6/26/1786.

Pages 10-12:   8/13/1786 - ALEXANDER CAINE of Brown's Creek, Union Co.,
               S.C. to ISAAC CAINE, same place, for and in consideration
of the natural love and affection which I have and bear unto my son
ISAAC CAINE, all goods and chattels, in what place soever the same
shall be found. Included 3 horses, 3 milch cows, plough, gears, saddles,
one field of corn, etc. Witnesses: JOHN EWART, HANCOCK (X) PORTER.
A schedule of the chattels given included with the deed. Recorded on
9/25/1786.

Pages 12-13:   9/11/1785 - WILLIAM WILSON of Union Co., S.C. with the
               consent of his mother LETTY WILSON, put himself appren-
tice to JOHN YOUNG, taylor (sic) of Union Co., to learn his trade for
period of 7 years. Signed by WILLIAM (X) WILSON, LETTY (X) WILSON &
JOHN YOUNG. Witness: WILLIAM SHAW. Recorded 9/26/1787 (86?).

Pages 13-14:   JOHN SMITH of Rutherford Co., N.C. to WILLIAM MILES of
               Chester Co., S.C. for seventy Guineas, one negro named
Rose and a certain still of eighty gallons and vessels. Dated 4/2/1785.
Witnesses: RICHARD SPEAKS & ROBERT MONTGOMERY. Recorded 9/27/1786(87?).

Pages 14-15:   HANNAH BROWN of Union Co., S.C. to WILLIAM FARR, same
               place, quit claim on all court actions, debts, accounts,
sums of money, damages, controverseys (sic), quarrels, demands, etc.
at law and in equity, from the beginning of the world to the day of
the date of these presents. Dated 9/14/1786. Witnesses: THOMAS BRANDON
& CHARLES SIMS. Recorded 3/21/1787.

Page 15:   3/7/1785 - Received of TEMPERANCE SAFOLD 250 pds. current
               money of Virginia for three negroes sold to her by THOMAS
WRIGHT. Witnesses: ADAM THOMSON & MATILDAY (X) WRIGHT. Recorded on
12/26/1786.

Page 16:   THOMAS POYTRIP, late of the State of Georgia, to WM.
               FARR, Esq. of Union Co., S.C., 2 negroes for 100 pds
sterling. Dated 1/19/1787. Witnesses: WILLIAM BECKHAM, GIBSON FOOTE

Cont'd:
and RICHARD FARR. Recorded 3/27/1787.

Page 17:   ROBERT LEVERETT of Union Co., S.C. to BARTHOLOMEW BROOKS
                for 45 pds sterling, 1 negro woman named Jude. Dated
3/19/1787. Witnesses: WILLIAM ROGERS and ROBERT LEVERETT, JR. Recorded
3/26/1787.

Pages 17-18:   ROBERT LEVERETT of 96 Dist., S.C. to WILLIAM ROGERS,
                same place, for 79 pds 15 shillings sterling, one negro
man named Jim and one still, putting ROGERS in full possession by delivering him one iron pot. Witnesses: JEREMIAH HAMILTON and JOHN MALONE.
Dated and recorded 3/26/1787.

Pages 18-19:   JOHN INLOW of 96 Dist., S.C. to JOHN JENKINS of Union
                Co., S.C. for 25 pds. sterling, 7 head of cattle, 2 feath-
er beds and furniture, and 5 head of hogs. Dated 8/15/1786. Witnesses:
DAVID HUDSON. Recorded 6/26/1787.

Pages 19-20:   HOLLAND SUMNER of 96 Dist., S.C. to Col. THOMAS BRANDON,
                same place, for 200 pds sterling, all household furniture
consisting of 5 feather beds and furniture, 32 pewter plates, 4 dishes,
6 basins, 2 chests, 2 tables, all stock of cattle (8 cows and all hogs
marked with a half-moon in each ear, about 30 head, and 5 brood horses),
all plantation tools and crops "now growing", and 4 negroes. He put
Col. BRANDON in full possession by delivering to him the beds and pewter. Dated 8/5/1784. Witness: JAMES WOODSON. Recorded 6/26/1787.

Pages 21-23:   Will of GEORGE MARTIN of 96 Dist., S.C., "being weak
                of body." Beloved wife SUSANNAH the use of 440 acres
on the waters of Gilkey's Creek, joining the land of JAMES MARTIN,
deceased, and REDARUS CLARK and ROBERT MONTGOMERY. Also the use of
3 negro men slaves named Stephen, Matt and Boson.. Also the use of
the rest of his estate during her natural life. After her decease,
"my two sons WYLY and RANDOLPH" to divide the 440 acres equally by
running a line from CLARK's line to the back line. The part that included CLARK's branch and joined ROBERT MONTGOMERY was to be WYLY's.
The other part for RANDOLPH. "To my reputed son JOSEPH JOHN" 400 acres,
including the place known as REUBEN's ponds. "To my daughter ANNE"
200 acres on Abitons (Abington's) Creek "including LEDBETTER's improvements." After wife died the three sons were to have the 3 slaves, and
the rest of the estate was to be divided equally between the three
sons and the daughter ANNE. Wife SUSANNAH and brother, PHILEMO MARTIN
named as executors. Dated 7/8/1785. Witnesses: JOHN HARRINGTON, RICHMOND
TERRELL, GEORGE PETTY and THOMAS PETTY. No recording date.

Pages 23-24:   DANIEL TRAMMEL, eldest son and heir at law of DANIEL
                TRAMMEL, deceased, to CHARLES SIMS, Esq., of Union Co.,
S.C., for 1,000 pds sterling - 7 negroes and their issue. Dated on
9/24/1787. Witnesses: JOHN EWART and WILLIAM BIRDSONG. No recording
date.

Pages 24-25:   Will of JOHN WATERS of Union Co., S.C., planter. Dated
                8/10/1786. His brother MOSES WATERS to receive 133 1/3
acres on Thickety Creek whereon the sd MOSES WATERS now lives. Also
to receive my wearing clothes and all the remainder of estate except
a negro fellow named Lewis, who was willed to my sister's son THOMAS
OWNBEY. If Lewis refused to go live with OWNBEY, Moses was to sell
him and give THOMAS OWNBEY the money. MOSES WATERS named executor.
Witnesses: JAMES TERRELL, THOMAS WRIGHT and SAMUEL SHIPPY. No recording date.

Pages 25-26:   THOMAS BRANDON of Union Co., S.C. to JAMES ADAMS McCOOL,
                for 1 guinea, 1 negro boy about 4 years old called Ab-
raham. Dated 9/24/1787. Witnesses: WILLIAM JOHNSON, JOSEPH HOWARD and
WILLIAM HUGHES. No recording date.

Pages 26-27:   Dated 11/10/1786 - JOHN STEEN of Union Co., S.C. to CHAS.
                MILES, same place, for 800 pds sterling, mortgage for

Cont'd:
6 months on 600 acres on Tickety Creek, joining JOHN THOMSON and FRANCIS
LATTIMORE, including the mill Shole. Witnesses: FRANCIS LATTIMORE and
PHILIP (X) SHAVOUS. Recorded 9/25/1787.

Pages 27-28:   Dated 7/27/1774 - JOHN NUCKOLS of Union Co., 96 Dist.,
               to JOHN DAVISON (also spelled DAVIDSON) same place, for
500 pds currency, 200 acres on the ridge bet. Thickety and Broad River,
formerly surveyed by WILLIAM McCOWAN and patterned (sic) by JAMES PAR-
VEST (PARVERT, PARROT?), Esq., Deputy Surveyor of North Carolina. Whereon sd JOHN DAVISON now lives. Bond for title. Witnesses: JAMES BROWN
and JOHN GILLIAM. To remain in effect until 9/25/1774. DAVISON paid
part on 8/13/1773(?) and paid it in full on 10/20/1774.

Pages 28-29:   Bill of Sale - WILLIAM THOMSON, planter, of Spartanburgh
               Co., S.C. to WILLIAM HENDLEY, planter, of Union Co.,
S.C., for 50 pds sterling, 1 negro girl about 8 years old named Suza.
Dated 12/1/1787. Witnesses: WILLIAM BOSTICK and RICHARD THOMSON. No
recording date.

Pages 29-30:   Dated 4/27/1786. ROBERT LINN of Union Co., S.C. to ADAM
               THOMSON, for 20 pds sterling, 3 cows and a calf, 1 mare,
one bed and furniture, 1 pot and pan. Witnesses: JOSIAH TANNER and
JAMES THOMPSON.

Pages 30-31:   Dated 2/14/1772 - JAMES HENRY of Barkley Co. and Amelia
               Township, bond to RICHARD HUGHES of Craven Co. for 500
pds current money. Witnesses: DAVID GEORGE and WILLIAM HARDWICK. HARD-
WICK swore to signature on 9/25/1787 bef. THOMAS BRANDON, J.P.

Pages 31-32:   Dated 10/22/1776 - JOHN STEEN of the Province of S.C.,
               am held and firmly bound unto, DAVID STOCKTON of Roane
Co., N.C. for 10,000 pds current money of S.C. To be paid by 11/1/1780.
Mortgage on 400 acres on Thickety Creek. Bound by ADAM GOUDELOCK, Capt.
JAMES STEEN and FRANCES LATIMORE. Including 100 acres granted to HENRY
SITMORE. Witnesses: JOHN NUCKOLS and JOHN THOMPSON. Recorded 25 Sept.
1787.

Pages 32-33:   Dated 10/10/1787 - GARLAND HARDWICK of Union Co., S.C.,
               deed of gift of 1 negro girl named Mariah to his niece,
NANCY HARDWICK TAYLOR, infant. If she died or had no issue, Mariah
to go to my sister, NANCY TAYLOR, her mother. Witnesses: WILLIAM HARD-
WICK, NANCY (X) DANIEL, MOLLY (X) HARDWICK. No recording date.

Pages 33-34:   Dated 3/28/1787 - Will of WILLIAM WOFFORD of Union Co.,
               S.C. Son ABSOLAM 1 shilling sterling; daughter ELIZABETH
RHODES - 1 shilling sterling; daughter HANNAH MERCHANT - 1 shilling
sterling; daughter MARY BRIAN - 1 shilling sterling; beloved wife ABI-
GAIL all the remainder of estate both real and personal whether in
this state or elsewhere, during her natural lifetime. After her decease
all of her part to go to my beloved daughter REBECAH. Daughter REBECAH
appointed executrix. Revoked all former wills. Witnesses: JEREMIAH
(X) WILSON, AMBROSE YARBOROUGH, THOMAS TOD. Signed: WILLIAM (W) WOFFORD.
No recording date.

Pages 34-35:   Dated 11/8/1787 - THOMAS BRANDON of Union Co.,S.C. to
               DANIEL WHITE for 30 pds, 1 negro girl 2½ years old called
Darkis. Witness: JEREMIAH GREGORY. No recording date.

Pages 35-36:   24 June 1789 - BENJAMIN GILBERT of Newberry Co., S.C.
               to JAMES BELL, Union Co., S.C., 2 horses, 2 saddles,
and 1 pair of saddle wallets, for and in consideration of the sd JAMES
BELL being Special Bail for JOHNATHAN GILBERT to WILLIAM SHAW, Esq.,
and costs of suit in the sum of fifty pounds sterling for the discharg-
ing and paying a sum of money due from sd GILBERT to WM. SHAW, Esq.
Witnesses: DANIEL JACKSON and THOMAS BRANDON. Signed by BENJAMIN GILBERT
and recorded 1 Oct. 1789.

Pages 36-37:   Dated 14 Aug. 1789 - Will of JAMES PRINCE of Union Co.,

Cont'd:

S.C., to my well beloved wife SICILY, one bay mare named Bounce, one bedstead, bed, and furniture, 3 pewter plates and one small dish, 2 cows and yearlings, one dutch oven, 2 iron wedges, one cotton wheel and cards, and 1 linen wheel, and to enjoy the benefits of my plantation during her natural life or widowhood. My loving son EDWARD all lands and tenements. Balance of estate to be divided equally among his children: RANCE, SICILY, JOICE, MARY RUTH, EDWARD..(2 childrens names have been torn off. One of those torn appears to be ELIZABETH - ____abeth). Wife and THOMAS GREER, SR. appointed Executors. Signed: JAMES (X) PRINCE. Witnesses: ELIJAH H. COOPER and THOMAS (X) WINN. Recorded 28 Sept. 1789.

Pages 37-38: Dated 10 Mar. 1787 - JOHN BRIGGS of Union Co., S.C., held and obliged to THOS. TOD of Spartanburgh Co., S.C. in the amount of 100 pds sterling. Conditions being that sd BRIGGS should pay TOD the amount of ten guineas by 25 Dec. next, rent for 2 plantations - one on which the sd JOHN BRIGGS now lives and another one which the sd TOD purchased of JOHN MARTINDALE. The rent of ten guineas to be paid in tobacco at the market price or waggoning at the common rates. Witnesses: PETER CHASTAIN and RICHARD BURGESS. Signed: JOHN BRIGGS. No recording date.

Pages 38-39: 10 Apr. (no year) - PHEBE WELLS, widow of ELIJAH WELLS, deceased, and LARKIN WELLS, heir of sd ELIJAH WELLS, dec'd., to GEORGE McWHORTER of Union Co., S.C. for 27 pds, 10 shillings Virginia money, all rights of possession to 100 acres on the south side of Pacolet River. According to a deed of conveyance made by JOHN STEEN to the sd GEORGE McWHORTER bearing date the 10th day of April 1788 - being possessed of sd land under the colour of sd JOHN STEEN's Title for 18 years past. Signed: PHEBY (X) WELLS and LARKIN (X) WELLS. Witnesses: JOHN McWHORTER, ABNER WELLS, GEORGE WELLS. Recorded 6/23/1788.

Pages 39-41: Dated 13 Oct. 1787 - Will of WILLIAM YOUNG of Spartan- burgh Co., 96 Dist., S.C. Wife and seven children to have his plantation on Enoree River where I no live, to live on and cultivate until youngest son named THOMAS comes of age. Wife MARGARET to have living off sd plantation as long as she lives. At her death or when THOMAS comes of age, plantation to be sold and proceeds divid- ed equally among his seven sons: SAMUEL, ADAM, WILLIAM, JAMES, JOHN, JOSEPH & THOMAS. The lands on Dorbins Creek in Laurens Co. to be sold to defray the expenses of educating children. Item - as I am entitled to an Estate consisting of thirty thousand pounds sterling in the West Indians (sic) which is now in the hands of Doctor ANDW. ARWIN(?), Esq., of the Island of Grannada which sum when got or any part thereof I give to be equally divided amongst my seven sons as afsd. Wife MARGARET YOUNG and Col. THOMAS BRANDON of Fairforest appointed executors. Signed: WILLIAM YOUNG. Witnesses: HUGH (X) McWILLIAMS, JEREMIAH (X) MOORE and IJORAH VINES (VIMS?). Appointed my well beloved brother in law ICHO____ QUAIL to be Guardian over above Executors and also over his children, beseeching him to do for them in all respects as if they were his own children. Recorded 25 Sept. 1788.

Pages 41-42: WILLIAM WHITE of Union Co., S.C., Administrator of CHRIS- TOPHER COLEMAN, deceased, gave power-of-attorney to THOMAS STRIBLING, JR., same place, to recover 3 negroes - a mother and 2 sons - to sign receipts for them, etc. Dated 9/6/1788. Signed: WILLIAM WHITE. Witness: CLAYTON STRIBLING. Recorded 9/26/1788.

Pages 42-43: Dated 6 Sept. 1788 - WILLIAM WHITE of Union Co.,S.C. to THOS. STRIBLING, JR., a bill of sale for the same 3 negroes named in above power-of-attorney, for 200 pds sterling. Wit- ness: CLAYTON STRIBLING. Recorded 9/26/1788.

Pages 43-44: Dated 8 Jan. 1789 - Will of JOHN HENRY KAYSER (also spell- ed KEISER in body of will) of Union Co., S.C., being sick in body...son AMERICUS MARERITUS KEISER to have 2 horses, 1 desk, working tools, household furniture and clothing. Appointed well beloved friend DANIEL WOODEN sole executor. Signed: JOHN HENRY KAYSER. Wit-

Cont'd:
nesses: W. WADLINGTON, JAMES CALDWELL and MARK LITTLETON. Recorded 3/23/1789.

Pages 44-45: Inventory of the Estate of Capt. JOHN HENRY KAYSER. He was a silversmith and clock and watch-maker evidently, since inventory includes items and tools relative to that trade. Also 2 horses, saddles, furniture, dishes, silver, etc. At the end of the inventory are two memos, both signed by JNO. HENRY KAYSER on 7 Jan. 1789, to the effect that he gave to HERMAN NEDERMAN certain silversmiths tools and to MARY CALLWELL (CALDWELL) for her services some cloth, a "chany" cannister, 1 mahogany box and a copper ladle. Memos are headed Newberry County, 96 Dist. No signatures are on the inventory of his estate - he may have listed the items himself and included the memos at the end. The will, inventory, and memos of gifts were all recorded 23 March 1789.

Pages 45-46: Dated 2/20/1788 - JOHN WEEDINGMAN, planter, of the County of Newberry, S.C. to WILLIAM HENDLEY, planter, of Union Co., S.C. for 60 pds sterling, 1 negro girl named Lucy about 11 years old. Witnesses: EZEKIEL STONE, JOHN (X) MORRIS, MANL. SMITH. Signed: JOHN WEEDINGMAN. Recorded 3/24/1788.

Pages 46-47: Will of AMBROSE YARBOROUGH of Union Co., S.C., Executors to make conveyances to JOHN BALIE, THOS. SCALES and JOHN-ATHAN PENNELL for the several pieces of land agreeable to my bonds, and take up the sd bonds. Beloved wife MARY all his estate whether in this state or elsewhere. After her decease, estate to be divided equally between my beloved children - ANN PINNELL, JEREMIAH YARBOROUGH, HUMPHREY YARBOROUGH, JOHN YARBOROUGH, and MARY YARBOROUGH. STEPHEN LAYTON and PETER PENNELL appointed executors. Dated 8/27/1788. Signed: AMBROSE YARBOROUGH. Witnesses: WILLIAM HENDLEY, ELIJAH (X) ALVERSON and THOMAS TOD. Recorded in Sept. 1788. (No day of the month given.)

Pages 48-50: Dated 8/31/1788 - Will of JOHN EWART of Union Co., S.C. "very sick", all debts to be paid. To my brother ROBERT EWART living in the Kingdom of Scotland, 524 acres on the waters of Broad River. To my brother MATTHEW EWART living in the Kingdom of Scotland, 150 acres...lying and joining to Union Court House formerly bought of JOSEPH JONES. Also to MATTHEW, 300 acres on Fannings Creek with a mill thereon. To my brother WILLIAM EWART living in the Kingdom of Scotland, 923 acres on Brown's Creek, a branch of Broad River. To my two trusty and well beloved friends THOMAS BLASSINGAME, Esq., and ANDREW TORRENCE, a negro girl called Dinah now living at THOMAS VANCE's. A negro man named Charles now in the possession of THOROWGOOD CHAMBERS, to be sold and money used at discretion of the executors. THOMAS BLAS-SINGAME, Esq. and ANDREW TORRENCE appointed executors. He very emphatically revoked all previous wills. Signed: JOHN EWART. Witnesses: WILLIAM MORGAN, ISAAC BOGAN and MOSES COLLYER. Recorded 23 Sept. 1788.

Pages 50-51: Dated 22 Oct. 1782 - JOHN JOURNEY, planter, of 96 Dist., S.C. "am held and firmly bound" unto JOSEPH EAST, of same place, for 5,000 pds lawful money of S.C., on 300 acres, as appears by the patent for which the sd JOSEPH EAST hath given his bond for six hundred pounds. Title to the land to be made unto sd EAST on 12/23/1783. Signed: JOHN (X) JOURNEY. Witnesses: ALEXR. MAC DOUGAL and JAMES CRAWFORD. Recorded 3/24/1789.

Pages 51-52: Dated 3/27/1789 - WILLIAM CLAYTON, planter, of Union Co., S.C., to THOMAS BLASSINGAME, Esq., for 70 pds sterling, a negro man named Cambridge. Bill of sale to be voided if CLAYTON paid to BLASSINGAME 9 thousand weight of Tobacco to cover 2 notes of February last. Cambridge was to continue to live with Clayton. Signed: WILLIAM CLAYTON. Witnesses: D. B. ROWNE(?) and ____(?) SUIT (?). (I cannot decipher the last witness's name). Recorded 3/28/1789.

Pages 52-53: Dated 6/8/1789 - WM. MERCHANT and HANNAH, his wife, to GEORGE HARLING, hatter, all of Union Co., S.C. for good will and affection and 20 pds lawful money of S. C., all goods and

Cont'd:
chattels consisting of a mare and colt, 1 feather bed and furniture,
3 cows, 2 calves, yearlings, hogs, etc. Signed: WM. MERCHANT and HANNAH
(X) MERCHANT. Witnesses: THOMAS PALMER, SR. and DUNCAN McCREVAN. Sworn
to bef. THOMAS BLASSINGAME, J.P., on 6/16/1789. Recorded 6/22/1789.

Pages 53-54: Dated 9/12/1783 - DAVID HOPKINS of Camden Dist., S.C.,
"am firmly bound unto NATHAN GLENN" of Cumberland Co.,
Va., for 1,000 pds sterling. Conditions being that DAVID HOPKINS was
to make a good title in fee simple to a tract of land lying above and
below the fishdam ford on Broad River the south side 250 acres known
as Feemster's land and 1,000 acres adj. the 250 acres bound by ISAAC
SIMPSON, GEORGE BELL, WILLIAM MOORE, the Widow HOLLINGSWORTH, THOMAS
SHOCKLEY, JOHN ARMSTRONG, and JUR. McFANSON (?), whenever he can obtain
a grant for the same. Signed: DAVID HOPKINS. Witnesses: ELIAS HOLLINGS-
WORTH, DANL. McKIE, WILLIAM (X) SMITH. WM. SMITH swore to signature
on 12/30/1789 bef. CHARLES SIMS, J.P. Recorded 12/30/1789.
                    (Note - DAVID HOPKINS was NATHAN GLENN's brother-in-
law. He moved to Chester Co. before the Revolution and lived right
across Broad River from the land mentioned in the above bond. NATHAN
GLENN and several of his sons and their families moved to Union Co.
circa 1789-90. DAVID HOPKINS evidently applied for a grant for NATHAN
in 1783 (the above bond). NATHAN was given a grant of over 900 acres
in the location described above. NATHAN GLENN and his sons served in
the Revolution from Virginia. CHARLES SIMS was also related to both
NATHAN GLENN and DAVID HOPKINS by marriage. JMC)

Pages 55-56: Dated 5/12/1784 - ISAAC EDMUNDSON, farmer, of 96 Dist.,
S.C., "am firmly bound unto my brother CALEB EDMUNDSON",
same place, for 300 pds sterling, obligation being that sd CALEB EDMUND-
SON shall have a good Right of Inheritance in an equal part of 700
acres on the North side of Enoree River. Signed: ISAAC EDMONDSON. Witnesses: JNO. WEEDERMAN and EDWARD MUSGROVE.

                    On 9/12/1789 CALEB EDMONDSON, JR. assigned all of his
right and title to the within bond to JOHN FINCHER. Signed: CALEB ED-
MONDSON. Witnesses: JAS. WOODSON, JOHN NIX and THOS. BISHOP. Thomas
Bishop swore to signatures on 9/25/1789 before CHARLES SIMS, J.P. Recorded 9/28/1789.

Pages 56-60: Dated 2/7/1784 - JESSE DOD of Arrensburgh (Orangeburgh)
Dist., S.C., a bond to PETER RENFRO of 96 Dist., S.C.,
in the amount of 286 pds 10 shillings and 8 pence sterling, on 300
acres on Tyger River waters in 96 Dist. To be paid by 2/7/1787. Witnesses: LEWIS GOLSON, J.P., JNO. GOLSON and LEWIS BOBO. In Abbeville
Co. on 5/27/1789 LEWIS BOBO swore to signature and delivery of bond
before JOHN MOFFRETT, J.P.

                    On 7/1/1788 PETER RENFRO assigned the bond and sold the
300 acres whereon ANDRW. TORRENCE now lives, to the sd ANDREW TORRENCE
for 120 pds sterling, stating that it has been bonded or obligated
by JESSE DODD of Orangeburgh Dist. Signed: PETER (X) RENFRO. Witnesses
were WM. (X) RENFRO and ARCHER SMITH. Again in Abbeville Co., Archer
Smith swore to signatures on 5/27/1789 before JNO. MOFFRET, J.P. No
recording date.

Pages 60-61: Dated 7/1/1789 - CALEB EDMONDSON of Union Co., S.C.,
appointed ANDREW TORRENCE and JOHN FINCHER his attorneys
to recover and receive all money, goods, chattels, etc. due the sd
CALEB EDMONDSON. Witnesses: JAMES WOODSON and SARAH GIST. James Woodson
swore to signatures on 9/28/1789 before CHARLES SIMS, Esq., J.P. Recorded 9/28/1789.

Pages 61-62: Dated 3/24/1789 - JOHN STEEN and NATHANIEL JEFFRIES of
Union Co., S.C., to JOHN TRIMMIER of Spartanburgh, S.C.
for 12 thousand weight of tobacco, 1 negro man named Jack. Witnesses:
JOHN HAILE and JAMES YANCEY, JR. Recorded 9/29/1789.

Pages 62-63: BENJAMIN CLARK to JOHN HAILE, both of Union Co. for 200
pds sterling, two negroes named Chance and Dezor, 137

Cont'd:
acres of land including the plantation and buildings where I now live,
3 horses, 4 cows, calves and all household furniture. Dated 5 Sept.
1789. Wit: RICHARD MITCHELL. Ack. by Clark on the same day before ZACHR.
BULLOCK, J.P. Recorded 29 Sept. 1789.

Page 63:   Dated 9 Mar. 1787 - ANN ROBINSON (also ROBERSON), Admx.
                of JOSEPH ROBINSON, dec'd., power-of-attorney to ROBERT
LUSK to recover a debt due by JOSHUA PETTY, adm. of JOHN NUCKOLS, dec'd.
Lusk authorized to sue or take any lawful way to recover the debt.
Wit: ROBERT SMITH and JOHN MONTGOMERY.

Pages 64-65:   RACHEL FORD to CUSHMAN EDSON, merchant, both of Union
                Co., for 25 pds 12 sh 7 p sterling, 2 beds and furniture,
1 doz. pewter plates, two pewter basons (sic), 2 pewter dishes, 3 cows
and calves, 3 horses, the whole crop on the premises, 1 pot, 1 dutch
oven, and 2 hogs. Dated 25 July 1789. Signed by RACHEL (X) FORE and
ARCHELEUS FORE. Wit: OBEDIAH TRIMMIER, GEORGE HENNING and JOHN BIRD-
SONG. Proved by John Birdsong, Esq. and recorded 2 Oct. 1789.

Page 65:   ARCHELOUS FORE to CUSHMAN EDSON, Merchant, both of Union
                Co., for 20 pds sterling, 3 mares (gives brand marks),
2 rifle guns, and a yearling heifer (gives brand mark). Dated 2 Oct.
1789. Wit: JOHN BIRDSONG and JOHN MURRELL. No recording date.

Pp 66-67:   EDWARD GOODE of Rutherford Co., N.C., to HERMAN HOWARD
                of Union Co., S.C., power-of-attorney to collect all
debts due GOODE from MARK JACKSON of the State of S. C. Dated 7 Dec.
1789. Wit: THOS. BRANDON and THOS. CROSBY. Recorded 28 Dec. 1789.

Pp 67-68:   ISAAC BROOKS of Chatham Co., N.C., power-of-attorney
                to WILLIAM BIRDSONG to recover by court of law or equity
from JAMES TERRELL a certain negro fellow named Jack, which negro JAMES
TERRELL unlawfully detained from sd ISAAC BROOKS. Dated 2 Nov. 1789.
Wit: JOHN MURRELL and SAML. MURRELL, both of whom proved the POA on
11 Nov. 1789 bef. THOS. BLASSINGAME, J.P.

Pp 68-69:   Appraisement Bill of the Estate of WILLIAM GREER, de-
                ceased. Includes livestock, farm equipment, pewter, kitch-
en equipment, 2 old Bibles and 1 Psalm Book, furniture, etc. Total
value 26 pds 1 sh 9 p. Dated 7 Dec. 1789 and signed by THOMAS VANCE
and WM. McJUNKIN. Vance and McJunkin were sworn in as appraisers of
the estate of the late deceased WILLIAM GREER by WM. KENNEDY, J.P.,
on 17 Dec. 1789 (?-error in date?)

Pp 69-70:   Dated 13 July 1789 - DANIEL JACKSON of Union Co., to
                Col. THOMAS BRANDON, as security for a mortgage for 40
pds 5 shillings sterling, all household furniture, livestock, bee hives.
If money paid in 2 years, mortgage null and void. Jackson was to deliver
1 mare to Brandon in lieu of the whole. Wit: JOHN BRANDON and CHRISTO.
BRANDON who proved the instrument on 15 July 1789 bef. HUGH MEANS,
J.P.
                A note at the bottom says that this same property had
been pledged on a bond and note to WM. SHAW for 18 pds 2 sh 11 p.,
bond dated 29 Mar. 1789, note dated 26 Dec. 1787, which Col. Brandon
has assumed to pay. Signed by DANL. JACKSON and W. SHAW. Recorded 29
Dec. 1789.

Pp 71-72:   JOHN SAUNDERS, carpenter, to LEWIS SAUNDERS, both of
                Union Co., for 56 pds current money, hath bargained,
sold and delivered in open market 2 horses, 2 cows and calves, 2 feather
beds and furniture, 2 dutch ovens, 2 iron pots, sundry carpenter tools
and plantation tools, 1 old wagon and gears, 1 pair chair wheels, 2
whip saws, and 300 weight of cotton, to him and his heirs forever.
Dated 3 Nov. 1789. Wit: JAS. TERRELL, HENRY (X) GIPSON, NATHAN (X)
GIBSON. Recorded 29 Dec. 1789. (Note: both Gipson and Gibson used.)

Pp 72-73:   JOHN FLINTON of Orrangburgh Co. (Orangeburgh) N.C. heir
                at law to EDWARD FLINTHOM, deceased, quit claim unto

Cont'd:
THOMAS FLINTHOM, RICHD. JENKINS, DANL. PRICE, & DANL. COMER, all manner
of action, causes of action, suits, bills, bonds, writings, obligations,
accompts...sum or sums of money, etc. from the beginning of the world
to this day. Dated 28 Nov. 1789. Wit: THOMAS BRANDON, J.P. and RICHARD
POWELL. No recording date. (Note - Orrangburgh Co. may be Orange Co.,
N. C.?)
        (Note: EDWARD FLINTHEM (FLINTON) lived in present-day Chester
Co., S.C. on Sandy River, as did also one DANIEL PRICE. Another DANIEL
PRICE owned land in Union Co., on Broad River but removed early to
Barnwell Co., S.C. Capt. DANIEL COMER lived in Union Co. and there
were JENKINS in both Chester and Union Counties. There are indications
in Chester Co. records that the FLINTHEMS came from North Carolina.)

Pp 73-74:   THOMAS HENDERSON of York Co., S.C., held and firmly bound
                to Mr. JOHN McCOOL of Union Co., in the penal sum of
100 pds sterling, which payment well and truly to be made, bond for
title to 227 acres in Camden Dist., S.C. on N side of Broad River,
Chester Co., being a tract conveyed by JOHN MONTGOMERY to the sd THOMAS
HENDERSON. Title to be made by 21 Nov. next ensuing. Dated 25 Mar.
1789. Wit: SETH ALDAY and JOHN LACKATURE (?LOCKHART?). Proved by SETH
ALDAY on 30 Dec. 1789 bef. JOHN BIRDSONG, J.P. No recording date.

Pp 74-76:   ADAM McCOOL of Chester Co., S.C. power-of-attorney to
                my trusty friend JOHN McCOOL of Union Co., S.C. to enter
upon the lands and tenements belonging to ADAM McCOOL by the last will
and testament of my father-in-law JAMES LOVE, deceased, to me and my
wife MARY, daughter of the sd JAMES LOVE, dec'd, to demand, sue for,
receive, etc., to bargain, sell, make title, etc. to sd lands. (Never
does state where the lands were located.) Dated 19 Nov. 1788. Wit:
THOS. BRANDON and JAS. BRANDON. Proved by Col. Thomas Brandon on the
same day bef. CHAS. SIMS, J.P. Col. Brandon stated that he saw ADAM
McCOOL, SR. sign, etc. No recording date.
        (Note: JOHN McCOOL of Union Co. was the son of ADAM McCOOL, SR.
of Chester Co. John was the only surviving executor of Adam, Sr.'s
will when Adam died in 1800, and Adam's estate file is located in Union
Co. records, though he stated in the will that he was "of Chester Co.".
According to local history, Col. Thomas Brandon's 1st wife, the mother
of all of his children, was ELIZABETH McCOOL, the daughter of ADAM
McCOOL, SR.)

Pp 76-78:   Dated 15(?) Feb. 1790 - ISAAC EDMONDSON of Union Co.,
                to JACOB DUCKETT of Laurince (Laurens) Co., S.C., sd
ISAAC EDMONDSON and JACOB DUCKETT were bound unto CALEB EDMONDSON,
father of the sd ISAAC EDMONDSON, in the sum of 500 pds sterling for
the support and maintenance of sd CALEB EDMONDSON during his natural
life. Isaac mortgages 500 acres whereon the sd Isaac Edmondson now
dwells on the N side of Enoree Rvier in Union Co., plus all the stock
of horses, kind, cattle, sheep, and swine, all the household goods
and utensils of husbandry, the property of him the sd Isaac Edmondson.
Mortgage given as security for the bond. Wit: JOHN PEARSON, JNO. (X)
TOWNSEND, SR., JAMES TOWNSEND. Proved by James Townsend by solemn affirmation (Quaker) on 17 Feb. 1790 bef. JOSEPH McJUNKIN, J.P. Recorded
21 Feb. 1790.

Pp 78-79:   ISAAC EDMONDSON of Union Co., S.C., power-of-attorney
                to JESSE DODD of same place, to ask, demand, sue for,
collect, etc. any sums of money of divers persons in afsd. state, due
to EDMONDSON and to prosecute a suit now commenced against Edmondson
by ROBERT MURRETT (MERRICK) of the State of Pennsylvania. Dated 26
Feb. 1790. Wit: WILLIAM (X) RAY and CALEB EDMONDSON. Proved by Ray
on 16 Mar. 1790 bef. John Birdsong, J.P. No recording date.

Pp 80-81:   The Will of JOSEPH JOLLY dated 15 Apr. 1778. I, JOSEPH
                JOLLY, Capt. of Ninety Six District living on Brown's
Creek, being sick in body.....Revoked all former wills. To beloved
wife MARY, her full thirds of her living, except his land, she to live
on the land during her widowhood. To son JOHN the land when he come
of age, likewise a good horse and saddle and 2 cows and my coat and

Cont'd:
jacket to my son JOHN. After wife's thirds taken out, all the remainder
of the estate except the articles above mentioned to be equally divided
among the rest of his children. Debts to be paid. Appointed Maj. THOMAS
BRANDON, BENJAMIN JOLLY and wife, MARY, to be Guardians to see that
Justice be done. Wit: JOHN BRANDON, RICHD. CRUCE and JAMES BOGAN. Proved
by all three witnesses on 25 Apr. 1778 bef. WM. KENNADAY (KENNEDY).
J.P. "...the within JOSEPH JOLLY, Capt., dec'd." Recorded 22 Mar. 1790.

Pp 81-83:   WILLIAM FARR of Union Co., to ELIAS HOLLINGSWORTH, Esq.
             of Newberry Co., S.C. for 2 pds sterling, quit claim
to 99 acres in Union Co., S side of Broad River, part of a larger tract
originally granted to THOMAS TRAMEL by Lord Chas. G. Montague (who
was Gov. of the Province of S.C.) in Nov. 1764. Bound by Broad River,
DANIEL TRAMEL's line, LOVE's back line. Dated 10 Nov. 1789. Wit: BERND.
GLENN, JOSEPH COLEMAN, HUMY (HUMPHREY) BATES. No recording date.

Pp 84-85:   SPENCER BRUMIT, planter to WILLIAM and DANIEL BRUMIT,
             all of Union Co., for 400 pds sterling, 6 negroes, to
wit, Davey, Bund(?), Sall, Sam, Old Cato and Young Cato. Also one horse
called Longtail, 14 head of cattle, with other goods and chattels,
etc. Dated 25 Oct. 1786. Wit: W. WADLINGTON and CHAS. LITTLETON who
proved the bill of sale on 22 Mar. 1790 bef. JOSEPH McJUNKIN, J.P.,
stating that he and WILLIAM WADLINGTON were the witnesses. Recorded
22 Mar. 1790.
     (Note: The witnesses WILLIAM WADLINGTON and CHARLES LITTLETON
lived in Newberry Co., S. C.)

Pp 85-87:   SPENCER (O) BRUMIT to WILLIAM BRUMIT, both of Union Co.
             for 50 pds current money of S. C., 3 negro women, viz,
Grace, Lavinia and Alis, and one bay mare with a blaze face. Dated
20 Mar. 1790. Wit: BERD GLENN and WM. MARTIN who proved the bill of
sale on 22 Mar. 1790 bef. Joseph McJunkin, J.P. Recorded 22 Mar. 1790.

Pp 87-89:   ELIAS HOLLINGSWORTH, Esq., of Union Co., to WILLIAM FARR
             of Unini Co., for 2 pds sterling, quit claim deed to
46 acres in Union Co., part of a larger tract originally granted to
WILLIAM LOVE by the Hon. Matthew Rowan, Esq., President of North Carolina, on 3 Sept. 1753. Bound by TRAMEL's line, LOVE's back line. quit
all claim from the date of the sd WILLIAM LOVE's grant to the end of
the world. Dated 10 Nov. 1789. Wit: BERND GLENN, JOSEPH COLEMAN & HUMP-
HREY BATES. Recorded 24 Mar. 1790.

Pp 89-92:   JESSE DODD, by his bond bearing date with these presents,
             is firmly bound unto ANDREW TORRENCE, both of Union Co.,
in the penal sum of forty thousand pounds of Inspected Tobacco with
conditions thereunder written for the payment of twenty thousand pounds
of tobacco delivered at Mr. DARBY's store and inspected by such person
or persons as he at that time has appointed for the inspection of his
tobacco, to be delivered on or before 1 Dec. 1792. To secure payment
of the 20,000 lbs. of tobacco DODD mortgages 300 acares on the ridge
between Tyger and Enoree Rivers, bound on all sides by vacant land,
formerly granted to WILLIAM RHOADS by grant dated 24 Aug. 1770. Also
included in the mortgage were 5 negroes, viz, Monmouth, Joe, Cloe and
her children. If the 20,000 lbs. of tobacco paid by 1 Dec. 1792, mortgage void. Dated 23 Jan. 1790. Wit: ARCHER HOWARD and NANCY (N) HOWARD.
Proved by Archer Howard on 24 Mar. 1790 bef. THOMAS BRANDON, J.P. Recorded 25 Mar. 1790.

Pp 92-93:   Last Will and Testament of WILLIAM BULLOCK of Union Co.
             Revoked all former wills. Bequeathed to his brother-
in-law NICHOLAS WATERS all worldly estate of whatever nature or property
and also appointed the sd NICHOLAS WATERS executor. Dated 16 Mar. 1787.
Wit: WM. WILLIAMS, JOHN PALMORE and EPHRAIM (X) PUCKET. (Does not give
proving or recording dates.)

Page 93:   REUBEN LANDRUM to OBEDIAH PRUIT, both of Union Co, bill
             of sale for 70 pds sterling for 1 negro woman named Selia
twelve years old. Dated 6 Feb. 1790. Wit: NICHOLAS KEATING and DANL.
PALMER. Recorded 28 June 1790.

433

Pp 94-95:   JOSEPH EDMONDSTON of 96 Dist., S.C. bond for title to
              HOSEA HOLCOMBE of same district and state, 100 acres
on a small branch of John's Creek, waters of Enoree River, bound by
ELENOR HOLCOME (sic) and vacant land, granted to RICHARD WICKERSHAM
on 20 Oct. 1772. When Edmondston gives Holcombe a "Lawful Conveyance"
and Holcombe pays Edmondston 200 pds currency, this bond null and void.
Dated 3 Aug. 1777. Wit: WILLIAM (W) SULLON (SUTTON?) and MARTHA (X)
RYAN. On 11 May 1779 Hosea Holcombe assigned "the within obligation"
to JOHN HOLCOMBE. On 1 Mar. 1787 JOHN (H) HOLCOMBE assigned it to WILL-
IAM WOOLBANKS with ARCHER SMITH as witness. No recording date.

Pp 96-97:   ROBERT MERRICK of Bucks Co., Pennsylvania, appoints my
              two trusty friends, GEORGE NORMAN and JAMES PARNELL,
both of Union Co., S. C. his attorney to convey deeds of conveyance
to JOHN TAYLOR of Union Co., to certain tracts: "my owld household
plantation as also one other tract adjoining GEORGE NORMAN's containing the one two and the other one hundred acres that which I bought
of MICHAEL PARKET, together with a strip of land adjoining EPHRAIM
SMITH's land so that the same on and down as far as the two hundred
acres tract first mentioned." All the land lying on John's Creek. Articles of agreement dated 4 Mar. now in possession of sd GEORGE NORMAN.
Also to convey to WILLIAM MARSHALL of Union Co. 140 acres that MERRICK
bought of JAMES PARNALL adjoining sd MARSHALL, WILLIAM MARTINDALE,
and others, according to an article now in possession of sd MASHALL,
"bearing date herewith." Dated 13 Mar. 1790. Wit: JOHN ADDINGTON, JAMES
DILLARD & THOMAS BRANDON. Proved by the solemn affirmation (Quaker)
of JOHN ADDINGTON on 22 Aug. 1790 bef. Thomas Brandon, J.P. Recorded
23 Aug. 1790.

Pp 98-99:   ESTHER (X) GRINDLE of Pendleton Co., S.C.., wife of JOHN
              GRINDLE, releases dower rights in a certain tract of
land sold by her husband JOHN GRINDLE to JOHN WATSON and ADAM CHISHOLM
by lease and release. Dated 11 May 1790. Certified on same date by
ROBERT ANDERSON, J.P. (who was of Pendleton Co.)

Pp 99-103:   Last Will and Testament of AARON JACKSON of Fairforest,
              Union Co., 96 Dist., S.C., who was "sick of body". Debts
to be paid. Beloved wife AGNES JACKSON, one horse, 2 cows, her bed
and bed clothes, saddle and household furniture to hold during her
natural life and at her death to be at her own disposal. She also to
have during her life the rents and profits arising from the plantation
to be rented out by the executors each year. Grandson AARON JACKSON,
son of WILLIAM JACKSON, 200 acres, the same tract on which "I now
live" after the death of wife AGNES JACKSON. If AARON dies before he
comes of age, the plantation to go to the next oldest son of above
named son WILLIAM JACKSON. Beloved friend JOHN WILSON, "now living
with me", one cow and if he lives with his Aunt the increase of the
sd cow to be disposed of by the executors and the proceeds applied
to his use most to his advantage. Grandson AARON JACKSON above named
to have one 2-year old heifer to be delivered to his father WILLIAM
JACKSON. The first heifer that she has to be the property of grand-
daughter AGNES JACKSON, sister to sd AARON. Son WILLIAM JACKSON, all
wearing apparel, saddle, handsaw, chisel and augur, also his note to
ARTHUR CRAWFORD dated 24 May 1784. All stock, tools, and farming equipment that remain to be sold by the executors by public vendue for use
of wife AGNES and the remainder afrer her decease to revert to the
heirs above mentioned. Wife AGNES to have during her natural life full
use of the house "in which I now live" with the spring house, outhouses,
etc. Grandson AARON JACKSON to have my broad axe. Outstanding debts
to be collected by the executors and used to pay debts and funeral
expenses, and the residue for the use of wife AGNES.
     Friend ARTHUR CUNNINGHAM and wife AGNES JACKSON to be executors.
Revoked all other wills. Dated 1 Sept. 1789. Signed by mark AARON (X)
JACKSON. Wit: JAMES McMULLIN and RICHARD THOMSON.
     Codicil: Gave to son WILLIAM JACKSON the privilege of clearing,
working, occupying and having the profits there from a parcel of land
of 30 acres "from the waggon road down on past his own house". He also
to have 3 yds. of blue cloth, 1 yd. of salom(?), 1 doz. benair(?) but-
tons, and one stick of mohair. Dated 5 Feb. 1790. Same witnesses as
will. Recorded 29 Sept. 1790.

Page 104:   ISAAC BRIGGS of Wilkes Co., Ga., power-of-attorney to
             Col. JAMES GIBBS of Union Co., S. C., to sell and convey
title to a certain tract of 730 acres in Wilkes Co., Ga. on Broad River
(in Georgia) granted to BRIGGS on 7 Apr. 1789. Not to be sold for less
than 1 shilling per acre. Dated 26 Mar. 1790. Wit: H. COSBRY(?) and
DANL. COMER. Recorded 29 Sept. 1790.

Pp 105-106: SAMUEL BISHOP of 96 Dist. to WILLIAM YOUNG, same place,
             for 500 pds current money of the Prov. of S. C., a negro
man slave named Mingo. Dated 11 May 1782. Wit: JAMES WOODSON and JACOB
DUCKET. Proved by James Woodson on 27 Sept. 1790 bef. Joseph McJunkin,
J.P. Recorded 1 Oct. 1790.

Pp 106-109: Will of JOHN BIRDSONG of Union Co., S. C. My son BATTLE
             BIRDSONG - 1 negro man named Obedeis, "and also I confirm
to him the Legacy that he recieved in Virginia which JOHN BIRDSONG,
my father, gave to me to the use of my son BATTLE and his heirs forever"
.....My son JOHN BIRDSONG - 1 negro boy named Dick and confirm to him
the sundry things he has already received. ...My son WILLIAM BIRDSONG
1 negro girl named Dilse and confirm to him the sundry things he has
already received from me. Likewise one rifle gun and my silver watch
to him and his heirs forever. ....My son HENRY BIRDSONG - 1 negro man
named Davy and after the death of my wife I give to him a negro man
named Tom, one horse named Panter, and one smooth-bore gun.....My well
beloved wife MARY BIRDSONG - I lend to her during life negroes Tom,
Phillaw, Rachel, Jude, and half the plantation with half the tools,
and liberty to clear and cultivate at her discretion any part of said
half with all the crop of tobacco excepted that shall be on the ground
at my decease; also, 2 feather beds and furniture, 4 cows and calves,
10 head of sheep, 20 head of hogs of her own choosing, 1 horse named
Lawer(?), a mare named Poll, with as much of the household furniture
as she requires. ....My son JESSE BIRGSONG - 200 acres of land with
half the plantatioin whereon I now live to possess at age 18 and after
the decease of his Mother to possess the whole 400 acres with all appurtenances thereunto belonging, on Fairforest Creek and the Waters
of the same. Also, one negro girl named Hesther, one horse colt named
Valiant, and one rifle gun.
     My daughter LUCY WADDLE - 1 negro boy named Moses.
     My daughter SARAH RAMSEY - 1 negro girl Jane.
     My daughter MARY DRAKE - 1 negro boy Daniel.
     My daughter REBECCA MINTER - 1 negro boy Jacob and all the money
          her husband is due to me on hand.
     My daughter ELIZABETH HOWARD - 1 negro girl Peggy with an order
          to JOHN MINTER for a feather bed and cow and calf.
     My daughter NANCY BIRDSONG - 1 negro girl Hannah, 1 feather bed
          and furniture, 1 mare cold named Peg, and 20 pds in cash
          to be paid when it is raised out of my estate.
     My daughter LIDDIA BIRDSONG - 1 negro girl Patience, 1 feather
          bed and furniture, 1 mare colt named Pleasant, and 25
          pds in cash when it is raised out of my estate.
     After just debts are paid, all money arising from my estate for
my two youngest daughters NANCY and LIDDIA BIRDSONG "and the rest if
any there be." The money to be kept at lawful usury till after the
death or remarriage of my wife, and then the wife's part to be divided
as follows (Tom excepted): LIDDIA BIRDSONG 2 parts; NANCY BIRDSONG
1 part; JESSE BIRDSONG 1 part; and WILLIAM BIRDSONG 1 part. "Divided
among the above named children Liddia, Nancy, Jesse, Henry and William
Birdsong, Henry to have a half a part."
     Sons WILLIAM and HENRY to be executors. Revoked all other wills.
Dated 21 Sept. 1790. Wit: JOSEPH WEST, RICHARD DAVIS, KINSEY WEST.
Proved in open court and recorded on 27 Dec. 1790.

Page 110:   BENAJAH THOMPSON to RAYNEY BALLEW, both of Union Co.,
             for 50 pds a negro woman named Tabb about 18 years old.
"One of her feet has but two toes on the foot." Dated 8 Oct. 1790.
Wit: THOMAS BLASINGHAM and WILLIAM ROUNTREE. Acknowledged in open court.

Pp 111-112: ISAAC EDMONDSON to JOHN FINCHER both of Union Co. bond
             for 500 pds sterling dated 26 Oct. 1789, mortgage on
350 acres in Union Co. formerly surveyed by BRYAN WHITE and joining

435

Cont'd:
land formerly the property of WILLIAM RHODES, Longshire, and land now
in possession of DAVID NORMAN. Wit: JAMES WOODSON and SARAH GIST. Proved
by James Woodson on 14 Apr. 1790 bef. Thomas Brandon, J.P. Recorded
28 Dec. 1790.

F I N I S of Book No. 1

Pp 113-114:   "Transcript of Book No. 2
              WILLIAM HEAILD of 96 Dist., held and firmly bound unto
              JOHN STILL, same place, for 100 pds sterling, dated 20
Feb. 1784. WILLIAM HAILD to make title to JOHN STILL to 100 acres on
the N side of Fairforest (Creek) joining JOHN HAILD and ZACHERY STEDHAM.
"On receipt of the bank Leaces" the obligation void. Signed. "WM. HAILD"
with witnesses: JACOB HAILD and MICHAEL DELONAH.

              JOHN (+) STILL assigned the Title Bond to ISAAC EDWARDS.
No date. Proved by JACOB HAILD on 5 Nov. 1790 bef. Thomas Brandon,
J.P. Recorded 7 Apr. 1791.

Pp 114-115:   Will of CALEB EDMONDSON of Union Co. "My body to be buried
              in a plain decent and Christian Manner" at the discretion
of my beloved wife. Funeral charges and debts to be paid.
       My wife JUDE EDMONDSON - plantation "where I now live", household
furniture, stock, plantation tools, and my negro fellow during her
life or widowhood.
       My three sons namely THOMAS, JOSEPH and CALEB EDMONDSON, to each
of them 1 shilling sterling money of Great Britain.
       After decease or remarriage of my wife, the remainder of the estate
to be sold and the money divided equally amongst my grandchildren,
the children of my children WILLIAM, ISAAC and CALEB EDMONDSON. If
my son WILLIAM should then be living, he to have an equal part with
my above mentioned grand children.
       My above mentioned legatees to have their legacies at Lawful age.
My friend JOHN CLARK to be executor. Revoked all other wills. Dated
4 Jan. 1791 (?-blurred). Wit: RALPH HUNT, CALEB SMITH, ANN (X) SMITH.
Recorded 6 Apr. 1791.

Pp 116-118:   Will of THOMAS (X) YOUNG of Brown's Creek, in 96 Dist.
              Dated 13 May 1777. "The Uncertain Estate of this Transi-
tory Life...." Revoked all former wills. Debts to be paid.
       My son WILLIAM YOUNG - 1 shilling sterling. Son GEORGE YOUNG -
1 shilling sterling. Wife CATERIN YOUNG - all estate, including land,
and all goods and chattels, debts, dues and demands. After her decease
the land to be given to my youngest son CHRISTOPHER YOUNG. Wife CATER-
INE YOUNG to be sole executor. Wit: THOMAS BRANDON, WM. KENNEDY, JOHN
BRANDON. Proved by Col. Thomas Brandon, William Kennedy and John Brandon
on 3 Feb. 1791 bef. Joseph McJunkin, J.P. Recorded 6 Apr. 1791.

       (Note: Descendants of THOMAS YOUNG, SR., state that his wife CATH-
ERINE was nee BRANDON, the sister of Col. THOMAS BRANDON, and that
the YOUNGs came from Pennsylvania with the BRANDON family. The YOUNGs
settled in both Union and Laurens Counties.)

Pp 118-120:   MARK (M) POWELL of Spartanburg Co., S.C. to SARAH GIST
              of Union Co., for 80 pds sterling, 1 negro woman named
Sall about 60 years old, now in possession of a certain JAMES MILLER
of Rutherford Co., N. C.; also, 1 negro woman named Patt about 35 years
old, and 1 negro girl named Eve about 13 years old, and 1 negro boy
named Jack about 8 years old, the last 3 now being in the possession
of ANDREW HAMPTON of Rutherford Co., N. C. Dated 3 Aug. 1791. Wit:
JOHN PEARSON, SARAH PEARSON, MARGARET HOLCOMB and JAMES WOODSON. Proved
by James Woodson on 6 Oct. 1791 before JOHN PEARSON, J.P. JAMES WOODSON
stated that he, JOHN PEARSON, SARAH PEARSON and MARGARET HOLDEN were
witnesses. Recorded 10 Oct. 1791.

Pp 120-121:   JOHN BENNET of Union Co. to Mr. WILLIAM DARBY for 5 pds
              sterling, 1 sorrel horse, about 13 hands high and about
6 years old. Dated 19 Feb. 1791. Wit: JAMES DARBY, JOHN HAM, WM. (X)

436

Cont'd:
SMITH. Proved by JOHN HAM on 6 Aug. 1791 before WILLIAM FARR, J.U.C.

Pp 121-123:   Will of JOHN HOPE of Union Co., who stated that he was
                'weak in body'. Beloved wife JEAN HOPE - 1 horse and
saddle and 1 bed and furniture worth 40 pds sterling, and 1/3 part
of the remainder of my estate, both real and personal, to her and her
heirs forever. She to remain on the premises during her pleasure.
    My six daughters, viz., JEAN HOPE, CATHRIN HOPE, AGNES HOPE, MARY
HOPE, MARGARET HOPE and REBECCA HOPE all the remainder of my estate
equally divided amonst them as they come to the years of Maturity.
If either of my daughters should die before maturity, her part to be
equally divided amongst the surviving heirs. Each child named to have
one negro, if there is a negro for each heir.
    Land to be kept so that wife JEAN will have sufficient estate
for the support of raising and schooling my children. When the youngest
child comes of age, land to be valued or sold and divided equally among
the surviving children. Wife JEAN HOPE and MOSES MEEK and CLEATON ROGERS
to be executors. Dated 2 July 1791. Wit: JAMES THOMPSON, WILLIAM Mc-
CULLOCK, NATHANIEL THOMSON. Recorded 5 Sept. 1791.

Pp 124-125:   Will of ZACHARIAH BULLOCK of Union Co., "being weak in
                body"..brother LEN HENLEY BULLOCK's four youngest daugh-
ters, namely, FANNY LYNE, LUCY, AGNES and NANCY BULLOCK, 50 pds sterling each, to be paid at the discretion of my executors.
    My brother LEN HENLEY BULLOCK of Warren Co., N. C., all the residue
of my estate of whatever nature.
    Executors appointed were the said LEN HENLEY BULLOCK, JAMES LYNE
of Grannville (Granville Co.), N. C. and my nephew RICHARD BULLOCK,
son of LEN HENLEY BULLOCK. Dated 10 Feb. 1791. Wit: ADAM POTTER, JOHN
LIPSCOMBE, WILLIAM LIPSCOMBE, JR. Recorded 5 Sept. 1791.

    (Note: The executors and legatees of LEONARD HENLY BULLOCK, de-
ceased, of Warren Co., N. C. were still disposing of the land that
belonged to ZACHARIAH BULLOCK, in the Pacolet River area of Union Co.,
as late as 1810-1812. See deeds recorded in Union Co. in Book K, p.
197; Book L, p. 11; Book L, p. 284. ZACHARIAH BULLOCK acquired this
land (1155 acres) when this area was still considered to be a part
of old Tryon Co. and Mecklenburg Co., N. C. This is a branch of the
same BULLOCK-RICE-HENLEY family that settled in Georgia. One WILLIAM
HENLEY lived in the same area of Union Co., and descendants of HEZEKIAH
RICE of Union Co. used the name BULLOCK as a middle name until the
1900's.

Pp 125-127:   Will of JOHN GEORGE of Union Co., who states that he
                is 'weakly and sickly in body'....Son, JOHN - plantation
whereon he now lives with all the land adjoining to it which I now
possess, 1 horse colt 2 months old, bay colored. Daughter, MARY - 200
acres on N side of Packolet (River) which she now possesses and 1 sorrel
colt. 1 head of cattle and my L(illegible) equally between son JOHN
and dau. MARY. Son THOMAS - plantation whereon I now live, 1 bay horse
6 years old. My wife - my gray horse, 4 cows, 4 calves and 1 bed and
furniture. N.B. The rest of the household furniture to be in her possession during her life or widowhood, then to be equally divided between
her and the children. Wife and son, THOMAS - all the rest of my goods
and chattels and personal estate, but out of the same to be decently
interred and funeral expenses paid by wife and son Thomas. If there
be any money it to be equally divided between wife and children. If
Thomas and his mother cannot agree in one house, sd Thomas is to furnish (her) with a cabin on the plantation, 40 bushels corn, 20 bushels
wheat, 200 weight of pork, and calf pasture during her life or widowhood. Also fodder for her stock. My brother-in-law JOHN JASPER and
my son JOHN to be executors. Dated 16 March in the year 1791 "according
to the English computation." Wit: JOHN JASPER, JOHN McWHORTER, CHARLES
HAMES. Recorded 6 Sept. 1791.

Pp 127-128:   JAMES OLLEPHANT of Union Co, 96 Dist., S.C., planter,
                formerly silversmith), bond to WILLIAM SHAW of Cambridge
in Dist. afsd., for 109 pds and 6 pence, signed and sealed on 28 March

Cont'd:
1791 at my plantation in said County of Union. If <u>OLIPHANT</u> pays SHAW
54-10-3 plus interest on or before 28 March 1793, the above obligation
void. Signed: <u>JAMES OLIPHANT</u>. ANDREW TORRANCE made oath that he was
well acquainted with the hand writing of JAMES OLIPHANT and that he
"verrily believes" this to be his signature. Dated 23 Sept. 1791. Recorded 29 Sept. 1791.

Pp 128-129:   Received of JOHN TAYLOR $200 and 1/3 of a dollar, part
               payment for 2 tracts of land on John's Creek and des-
cribed in an agreement now in the hands of GEORGE NORMAN, bearing date
4 March this instant. Dated 18 March 1790. No signature shown. Proved
by GEORGE NORMAN on his solemn affirmation (Quaker) who declared that
he saw ROBERT MERRICK sign and deliver the within receipt to JOHN TAYLOR
and that he signed as a witness. Affirmation dated 20 Aug. 1792 before
JOHN PEARSON, J.P. (Neither MERRICK's nor NORMAN's signature is on
the receipt as it was recorded.)

Pp 129-131:   Power-of-Attorney from ISAAC and SARAH (X) EADS, both
               of Frank Land (sic - Franklin) Co., Ga., to JAMES WHITE,
of Union Co., S. C. to sell and convey 183 acres on Tyger River bound
by the river on the N, S by WILLIAM NIX, W by DANIEL PRINCE, E by
land laid out for WILLIAM WHITE; also, 800 acres in Laurens Co. on
Enoree River near the mouth of Gilkers (Gilders) Creek, originally
laid out and granted to JAMES WHITE, deceased. Dated 1792 (month and
day omitted). Wit: ANDREW TORRANCE and WILLIAM WHITE. Proved by Andrew
Torrance on 4 Jan. 1792 before THOMAS BLASINGAME, J.P. Recorded same
day.

Pp 131-132:   SAMUEL YOUNG appeared before ZACHARIAH BULLOCK, J.P.
               and made oath with his hand on a certain white oak tree
that as a Deputy Surveyor of the Province of North Carolina in the
year 1750 by virtue of a Warrant from the Surveyor General of the last
mentioned Province, he marked the said white oak as a corner for the
said survey of land for JOHATHAN (sic) GILKIE and that the remaining
courses plotted according to the original plan made and annexed to
said GILKIE's grant or patent, and further deponent sayeth not. Dated
10 Dec. 1787. Signed: SAML. YOUNG and ZACHARIAH BULLOCK, J.P.

Page 132:   Bill of Sale and receipt from SAMUEL (X) TINDELL to C.
               R. EDSON for 10 pds sterling for a negro man named Stephen
and dated 3 May 1790. Wit: RICHD. FARR and LEWIS BOBO. Proved by Lewis
Bobo on 4 Jan. 1792 before Thomas Blasingame, J.P. Recorded same day.

Pp 133-134:   JOHN TOWNS, planter of Wilks Co., Ga., to WILLIAM FARR,
               Esq. of Union Co., S. C. release and quit claim forever
all manner of actions, suits, bills, bonds, accompts, mortgages, judg-
ments, etc. by Law or Equity which TOWNS ever had against FARR to the
day of these presents, 15 March 1792. Wit: WILLIAM POWERS and JAMES
VEALE. Proved in Union Co., by JAMES VEALE on 24 Mar. 1792 before CHAS.
SIMS, J.P. Recorded 4 Apr. 1792 by order of the Court.

Pp 134-135:   WILLIAM WHITLOCK to CUSHMAN R. EDSON both of Union Co.,
               for 30 pds sterling, mortgage on a negro boy named Stephen
(Stepney) about 9 years old, conditions being that if the above C.
R. Edson do stop a certain suit brought by the executors or administrators of the late JOHN McPHEARSON, deceased, in the County Court of
Union for 4000 wt. of tobacco and to pay the said WM. WHITLOCK 12 lbs.
of sugar and pay the above negro's taxes for 2 years or until the said
WHITLOCK pay the sd EDSON all the debts due EDSON & CO. or GRAFF &
CO. together with the afsd. debt due JOHN McPHEARSON, dec'd. with law-
ful interest, then the above bill of sale to be void, otherwise if
not reduced within 12 months to be in full force, debt to McPHEARSON,
dec'd., being 4000 wt. of tobacco. Dated 23 Dec. 1792 (sic). Wit: BEN
HAILE. Recorded 3 Apr. 1792.

Pp 135-136:   BENAJAH THOMPSON of Union Co. to JESSE FORE, for 30 pds
               sterling, 1 negro child named James. Dated 19 Dec. 1791.
Wit: CHARLES HAMES and J. CHESNEY. Proved by JOHN CHESNEY 2 Apr. 1792
bef. Thos. Blasingame, J.P. Rec. 3 Apr. 1792.

Pp 136-137: ANNA DORATHA MOORE of Union Co., to JOHN JEFFRIES of Union Co., for 5 shillings sterling, a negro girl named Jean. Dated 2 Apr. 1792. Signed: <u>ANATHORATHA</u> (X) MOORE. Wit: NATHANIEL JEFFERIES and ELENER JEFFERIES. Recorded 3 Apr. 1792. "Memorials sent for the aforesaid."

Pp 137-138: 96 Dist., S. C. Personally appeared JOHN HODGE and JOHN GRINDAL, SR., before J. THOMPSON, J.P. and deposeth and saith that they saw JOHN BECKHAM of 96 Dist. either in the year 1775 or 1776 sign, seal and deliver to WILLIAM HODGE of Pacolate River a lease and release for 400 acres, being the plantation whereon the sd WILLIAM HODGE now lives on S side of Packolet River, bound by ROBERT COLEMAN and THOMAS DRAPER. Dated 27 Aug. 1784. Recorded 3 Sept. 1792.

Pp 138-141: CHARLES SIMS of Union Co. to THOMAS BRANDON, as security for the payment of sundry notes, orders and book accounts, amounting to 200 pds sterling, negroes named Jenny, Gloster, Moses, Cager, George and Fanny, and all land, stock, and household furniture belonging to sd CHARLES SIMS. If the 200 pds plus interest paid by 1 Apr. 1793, mortgage void. Dated 1 Apr. 1792. Wit: JAMES BARRON, ROBERT GLENN and MARTHA M. BARRON. Proved by Mr. James Barron on 2 Nov. 1792 bef. WM. McCULLOCK, J.P. Recorded 8 Nov. 1792.

Pp 141-142: JAMES OLIPHANT, planter, of Union Co., 96 Dist. to JHN MONCRIEFFE, for 247-6-0 sterling, mortgage on 3 negro men named Sambo, Blue and Sokie, seurity on 2 notes of hand, one dated 12 Apr. 1784 for 74-11-0 sterling and one dated 1 Jan. 1785 for 103-15-11 sterling. If notes and cost of suit paid, the mortgage void. Negroes to continue in OLIPHANT's possession for 1 year until he fails in payment of the debt. Bill of sale (sic) sworn to bef. THOS. BLASS-INGAME, J.P. on 5 Aug. 1790. Recorded same day.

Pp 142-143: WILLIAM GIST to THOMAS STRIBLING and WILLIAM BUCKHANNON all of 96 Dist., S. C. bond for 10,000 pds lawful money of S. C., condition being that WILLIAM GIST do convey to STRIBLING and BUCKHANNON a certain tract of 450 acres on Brown's Creek joining HENRY LONG. Dated 1 Jan. 1779. Wit: GILES TURLEY who proved the bond on 28 June 1780 (year could be 1786) bef. THOMAS BRANDON, J.P. Recorded 4 June 1793.

Page 144: In consequence of my father ROBERT CHESNEY leaving me by deed of gift his remaining property and several horses cows and calves etc. I do promise to support him in his old age "in a decent comfortable manner until death shall call him hence." Dated 4 Aug. 1791. Signed: JOHN CHESNEY. Wit: JOHN HAILE who proved the instrument on 2 Mar. 1793 bef. BENJ. WOODSON, J.P. Recorded 4 June 1793.

Pp 144-145: Broad River, Fishdam, 12 Oct. 1793. SAMUEL M. THOMSON to RICHARD FARR & Co., bond for 30 pds sterling, mortgage on two likely cows and calves "now in my possession" - one late the property of JAMES JETER, the other late the property of JAMES C. YOUNG, also 1 bay horse late the property of <u>Mr.</u> (could be <u>WM.</u>) LOCKHART, also 1 gray horse late the property of PRESSLY WILLIAMS. Wit: WM. FARR and JOHN S. SIMS. Proved by JOHN SANDERS SIMS on 14 Oct. 1793 bef. CHARLES SIMS, J.P. Recorded same day by BEN HAILE, C.U.C. (Clerk of Union County).

Pp 145-147: 13 Sept. 1790 - DANIEL JACKSON of Wilkes Co., Ga., to THOMAS BRANDON of Union Co., S. C., for 60 pds sterling, for which the sd THOMAS BRANDON, Esq. stands bound with sd DANIEL JACK-SON unto MRS. SARAH GIST of county and state afsd (Union) by a judgment in the Court of Union, a negro man named Tobby. If JACKSON pays the judgment, this indenture void. Wit: ANDREW TORRENCE and JOHN MUR-RELL. Proved by Andrew Torrence in Union Co. on 8 Nov. 1791 bef. HUGH MEANS, J.P. Recorded 2 Nov. 1793 by BEN HAILE, Clerk.

Pp 147-149: ROBERT MERRICK, yeoman of Bucks Co., Pa. to JOHN TAYLOR of Union Co., S. C. bond for 500 pds sterling to be paid upon 25 Dec. next ensuing. Condition being that ROBERT MERRICK or his certain attorney, viz., GEORGE NORMAN and JAMES PENALL, any

Cont'd:
of them to make title to JOHN TAYLOR for 2 tracts of land on John's
Creek, 300 acres adjoining GEORGE NORMAN and others; also a certain
strip joining the 200 (sic) acre tract and EPHRAIM SMITH, the whole
being at this time in possession of sd JOHN TAYLOR, JOHN ALEXANDER
and GEORGE COMBS. If title made, above obligation void. Dated 19 Mar.
1790. Wit: JOHN PERSONS (PEARSON?) and JOHN ROBERDS. Proved in Union
Co. be JOHN ROBERDS by his solemn affirmation (Quaker) on 29 Oct. 1793
bef. ANDREW TORRENCE, J.P. Recorded 4 Nov. 1793.

Pp 149-151:   LOTT WOOD of Union Co., power of attorney to REUBIN GUT-
              TRIE of Maderson (Madison) Co., Kentucky, to handle all
business relevant to a "certain settlement and prescription" obtained
in sd LOTT WOOD's name lying in Maderson (sic) Co., Ky. Dated 11 Feb.
1794. Wit: WM. B. FARR, Acknowledged in person by LOTT WOOD bef. BEN-
JAMIN WOODSON, J.P. on 11 Feb. 1794. Recorded same day.

Pp 151-152:   Union Co., S. C. "Whereas JOHN HENDERSON, Esq. of Union
              Co. as Executor of the Estate of SOLOMON ALSTON, deceased
did receive sums of money due to the sd estate to the amount of about
1300 pds current money of Virginia which he the sd JOHN HENDERSON discharged in sundry bonds which were transferred to me LEMUEL JAMES AL-
STON as heir of the sd SOLOMON ALSTON, dec'd," LEMUEL JAMES ALSTON
hereby releases sd JOHN HENDERSON from any further claim by any person
claiming the sd debt of 1300 pds as afsd. Dated 30 Jan. 1794. Wit:
ANDREW TORRENCE who proved the release bef. BENJAMIN WOODSON, J.P.
on 28 Feb. 1794. Recorded 1 Mar. 1794.

Pp 152-153:   6 Mar. 1794 - BERTSEY (signed BETSEY) BROWN to JAMES
              FARR, both of Union Co., for value received (no amount
stated), bill of sale for 8 negroes, viz, one old wench named Luce,
one ditto named Amy, one boy named Stephen, one little boy named George,
one girl named Jobel, one boy named Isaac, one boy named Johnnie and
one named Moses. Wit: JOHN SALE and LEWIS DUTTIMS(?). Proved by JOHN
SALE on 11 Mar. 1794 bef. Charles Sims, J.P. John Sale stated that
he and LEWIS TEDLINS(?) witnessed. Recorded same day.

Pp 153-155:   THOMAS REDDER to JOHN McCOLLOUG (sic) both of Union Co.,
              for 10 pds sterling, "according to due form of law,"
mortgage on a bay mare, day bay, abuot 12 yrs. old, a 1 year old mare
colt and a sorrel mare 3 years old, and 5 head of cattle. WILLIAM MOUL-
TRIE, Gov. of S. C. to hold the sd mares, colts and cattle unto the
sd JOHN McCULLOUGH (also McCULLOCH), his heirs, assigns, etc. If THOMAS
REDER repays the 10 pds due by note plus interest from 15 May 1793,
by the last of July 1793, mortgage void. Dated 15 May 1793. Signed:
THOMAS (X) REDER (or RIDER). Wit: SAMUEL CLOWNEY, Proved by Clowney
in open court and recorded 1 Apr. 1794.

Pp 155-156:   Doctr. SAMUEL THOMPSON of Union Co. to ADAM POTTER, for
              7 pds sterling, mortgage on a negro boy named Harry,
age 8 years. If the 7 pds plus interest repaid by 1 July next, mortgage void. Dated 25 Feb. 1793. Wit: BEN HAILE and ANGELICA MITCHELL.
Proved by BENJ. HAILE on 9 May 1794 bef. JOHN HENDERSON, J.U.C. Recorded 12 June 1794.

Pp 156-157:   ADAM POTTER to THOMAS STRIBLING, JR., both of Union Co.
              power of attorney to ask, demand, sue for, recover and
receive the negro boy Harry about 9 yrs old. Any person having sd negro
in their possession and refusing to give him up to sd attorney, he
is authorized to take all lawful means for recovery thereof. Dated
11 June 1794. Wit: ANGELICA MITCHELL and REUBEN SAUNDERS, who proved
the POA on the same day bef. John Henderson, Justice. Recorded 12 June
1794.

Pp 158-159:   THOMAS (X) BALDWIN of Lawrence (Laurens) Co., S. C. to
              WALTER ROBERDS of Union Co., 1 sorrel mare branded G
on the near side, 2 2-yr. old colts branded SL on the near side, 8
head of cattle, all household furniture and the tract of land whereon
I now live with all farming utensils, for 20 pds sterling. Dated 1

Cont'd:
February 1793. Wit: JAMES ROBERDS, JOHN (X) ROBERDS, ISAAC (X) BALDWIN.
Proved by affirmation of JOHN ROBERDS (Quaker) before JOHN MARTINDALE,
J.P. on 9 April 1794. Recorded 13 Aug. 1794.

Page 159:   "JOHN DIXON 350 acres Mecklenburgh on Enoree joining
             above JOHN ODEL's land including his own improvements."
Included courses and distances. Land was on and across Enoree River.
Dated 26 Oct. 1767. Signed: WM. TRYON (Gov. of N. C.). JAMES GLASGOW,
Secretary of the State of N. C. certified the above to be a true copy
of the Record in the Secretary's Office. Dated 20 Oct. 1792. Recorded
30 Aug. 1794.

Pp 160-161:   JESSE DODD, planter, of Union Co. to AARON FINCHER for
              15 pds sterling, mortgage on one negro fellow named Mon-
mouth. If debt and interest paid by 1 Sept. 1794, mortgage void and
the negro fellow Monmouth shall be returned to sd JESSE DODD. Dated
3 Sept. 1791. Wit: MOSES COLLYER who proved the mortgage or bill of
sale on 5 Sept. 1794. Recorded same day. J.P.'s name not entered.

Pp 161-162:   FIELDS BLAKELY to WATSON CHISHOLM both of Union Co.,
              for 50 pds sterling, bill of sale for 1 negro boy named
Adam. Dated 31 Jan. 1794. Wit: WM. MITCHELL and JESSE MABERRY. Proved
by WILLIAM MITCHELL on 21 May 1794 bef. WM. L. McCULLOCK, J.P. Recorded
1 June 1794.

Pp 163-164:   JESSE DODD, planter of Union Co. to GEORGE GORDON & Co.,
              Merchants of Laurence (Laurens) Co., S. C., for 18 pds
17 sh 9 p sterling, mortgage on a certain negro wench named Dina about
20 years of age and her son named David about 1 year old. If money
plus interest repaid by 1 Jan. 1795, mortgage or bill of sale void.
Dated 13 May 1794. Wit: RICHARD BURGESS and AMBROSE RAY. Proved by
Richard Burgess on 31 May 1794 before Thomas Blassingame, J.P. Recorded
2 June 1794.

Pp 164-165:   JOHN (J) FINCHER of Union Co. assigns, releases and quit
              claims to JOHN MARTINDALE, same place, for 70 pds, all
his interest in a certain title bond by ISAAC EDMONDSON to JOHN FINCHER
of 500 pds penalty dated 20 Oct. 1789 and recorded in Book No. 1, page
87. Also authorized MARTINDALE to take the sd bond off the record or
change the same into his own name. Dated 27 Mar. 1793. Wit: JESSE DODD
and SAML. SIMPSON. Proved by Dodd on 5 June 1794 bef. ANDW. TORRANCE,
J.P. When the release was proved, SIMPSON's name was entered as "SAML.
SMITH." Recorded 2 June 1794. (Instrument was recorded before it was
proved if both of these dates are correct.)

Pp 166-168:   27 Mar. 1793 - MARGARET EDMONDSON, WALTER ROBERTS and
              DAVID SMITH to JOHN MARTINDALE, all of Union Co., bond
for 280 pds sterling. The above bounden MARGARET EDMONDSON, WALTER
ROBERDS and DAVID SMITH are to execute a deed to MARTINDALE for 350
acres between Tyger and Enoree Rivers, bound by lands laid out to CLOYD
LONGSHORE and JOHNATHAN NORMAN, originally granted to BRYAN WHITE.
Martindale to pay Margaret Edmondson or Walter Roberds 70 pds sterling.
If any of the parties fail in their obligation bond void. Signed: by
all three parties. Wit: JESSE DODD, JOHN (J) FINCHER and SAMUEL SIMSON
(sic). Proved by Dodd on 5 June 1794 before Andw. Torrance, J.P. Recorded 2 June 1794.

Page 168:   DANIEL HUGER of Richland Co., (S.C.) power of attorney
             to ABRAHAM NOTT, Esq., of Union Co., to sell, convey
or let any part of his lands in Union Co. and to recover all such sums
as may be due for lands already sold in the sd county and on Ready
River (probably refers to Reedy River in the Greenville-Pickens-Ander-
son-Laurens area). Dated 15 Aug. 1792. Wit: BEN HAILE. Proved in open
court and recorded on 2 Sept. 1794.

Pp 169-170:   HARMON ANDERSON of Union Co. to CHRISTOPHER JOHNSON of
              Chester Co., S. C. bond for 1000 guineas. Anderson to
give Johnson a deed or lease and release to 2 tracts of land: one on

Cont'd:
S side of Broad River, lying on the river, containing 216 acres; the other joining the above tract by a Land Grant and containing 200 acres. Wit: J. D. PUCKET, MESSER EAKEN and JAMES McCRAKEN. Proved in open court and recorded 1 Sept. 1794.

Pp 170-171:   WM. FARR of 96 Dist., S. C., bond to JOHN PETER SARTER for 500 pds sterling, dated 22 Jan. 1788, condition being that Farr to give John Peter Sarter title to that plantation he bought of ISAAC SAMPSON and PHEBE, his wife, the late wife of WILLIAM WRIGHT, deceased. Wit: MARK MITCHELL and THOS. STRIBLING. On 1 Sept. 1794 Stribling appeared before Thomas Blassingame, J.P. and made oath that he believed that the bond was signed by WILLIAM FARR, deceased, and that he was a witness to said bond. Recorded 2 Sept. 1794.

Pp 171-173:   DAVID SMITH, SR., to DAVID SMITH, JR., both of Union Co., for 10 pds sterling, one anvil, one bellows, 1 sledge and 1 hammer and other blacksmith tools. Dated 20 May 1794. Wit: JOHN TAYLOR and THOMAS LEE. Receipt for 10 pds sterling also recorded. Proved by the affirmation of JOHN TAYLOR on 29 Sept. 1794 bef. Thos. Blassingame, J.P. and recorded same day.

Pp 173-175:   ROBERT GREER, planter, to WILLIAM GREER, both of Union Co., bond for 500 pds lawful money, dated 19 Aug. 1788. Condition being that the sd ROBERT GREER, SR. is to give the sd WM. GREER title to 200 acres in Green Co., N. C. known by the name of ROBERT's place, on the North side of Nolychuky (Tenn.) Dated 17 Aug. 1788. Wit: BENJAMIN SAVAGE and JOSEPH HUGHES. Captain Joseph Hughes personally appeared before BENJAMIN WOODSON, J.P. on 3 Apr. 1793 and made oath that he was present and saw ROBERT GREER sign and deliver the within bond to WILLIAM GREER now deceased. On 28 Sept. 1793, BENJ. SAVAGE, JR. appeared before Woodson and made the same oath. Recorded with the above is a bond for 100 pds gold or silver from ISAAC TAYLOR which states that if he obtains a grant for Greers Island and tract of land containing 300 acres that he would "divide same equally quantity or quality or give the half of the value of sd tract to sd ROBERT GREER." Dated 7 Oct. 1793. Wit: JOSEPH RUYHUDSELL. Recorded 16 oct. 1794 by BEN. HAILE, Clerk.

Page 176:   JESSE DODD of Union Co. to AARON FINCHER for 80 pds sterling, one negro fellow named Joseph about 18 years of age. Dated 7 March 1794. Wit: JOS. C. GIST and JAMES WOODSON. Proved by Woodson on 15 Nov. 1794 before Thos. Brandon, J.C.C. Recorded 26 Nov. 1794.

Pp 177-178:   JOHNATHAN (X) HUMPHRIES of Union Co. mortgage to ALEXANDER McBETH & Co. as security for a note of 9 pds 12 sh 9 pence. Mortgage covers livestock, working tools (including a set of shoemaker's tools), and all household furniture. If note plus interest paid on or before 15 Nov. next, mortgage void. Dated 19 May 1794. Wit: BEN HAILE and WM. B. FARR. Proved by Ben Haile on 22 Jan. 1795 before ABRAHAM NOTT, J.P. Recorded same day.

Pp 178-180:   CHRISTOPHER JOHNSON of Union Co. to ALEXANDER McBETH & CO. as security for a bond dated 1 Jan. 1793 in the amount of 85 pds 11 sh and 1 pence sterling, mortgages a negro man Dick about 20 years old, negro man Isham about 18 or 19 years old, and a negro boy Matt about 10 or 12 years old. Dated 2 June 1794. Wit: BEN HAILE, who proved mortgage on 22 Jan. 1795 bef. Abraham Nott, J.P. Recorded same day.

Pp 180-181:   Note for 24 pds 7 sh and 3 pence sterling from HENRY HUEY to Messrs. ALEXANDER McBETH & Co. dated 26 May 1794, copied into the book, followed by a mortgage on several horses and cows plus the tract of land "whereon I now live," 162 acres originally granted to WILLIAM HUGHEY, on waters of Brown's Creek joining lands of McELROY and GEORGE HUEY. Mortgage dated 26 May 1794. Wit: BEN HAILE and WM. B. FARR. Proved by Haile on 22 Jan. ___.

Pp 182-183:   Note from W. HALL to ALEXANDER MAC BETH & Co. for amt.

Cont'd:
of 22 pds 14 shillings and 8½ pence sterling plus interest, being the balance of his account to January last. Dated 27
May 1794. Wit: BEN HAILE.
Mortgage on six head of horses to secure payment of above sum,
dated same day and signed by WM. HALL with BEN HAILE as witness. Proved
by Haile on 22 Jan. 1795 before Abraham Nott, J.P. Recorded same day.

Pp 183-184:   Note and mortgage from MC CORMICK (X) MC CAFITY to ALEX-
               ANDER MACBETH & Co. for 36 pds 8 sh and 3 p sterling,
dated 26 and 27 May 1794, mortgage on 332 acres on the waters of Buffalow Creek adjoining JONAS LITTLE, "whereon I now live." Mortgage signed
by MC CORMICH (X) MC CAFFERTY. Wit: BEN HAILE who proved mortgage on
22 Jan. 1795 bef. ABRAHAM NOTT, J.P. Recorded same day.

Pp 185-186:   Note and mortgage both dated 28 May 1794, from JOHN MARTIN
               to ALEXANDER MACBETH & Co. for 7 pds 8 sh and 1½ pence
sterling - mortgages certain livestock. Wit: WM. CUNNINGHAM, who proved
mortgage on 24 Jan. 1795 bef. Abraham Nott, J.P. Recorded same day.

Pp 186-189:   Power of Attorney from ROBERT MERRICK, SR. of Bristol
               Borough (sic), Bucks Co., Pa., to "my true and trusty
son ROBERT MERRICK, JR." of Bristol Borough, Pa., to demand sue for
and recover all rents, bonds, notes, debts, bills, etc. due ROBERT
MERRICK, SR. in Union Co., S. C. Power of Attorney dated 22 Dec. 1790.
Now ROBERT MERRICK, SR. continues said ROBERT MERRICK, JR. as his attorney to collect debts, demand, sue for, and recover all tracts of land
in the State of South Carolina and to sign deeds, leases, and lawful
conveyances for sd tracts of land, and "one or more attorneys under
him to constitute and at his pleasure to revoke." Dated 22 Dec. 1794.
Wit: SAMUEL HOLT and W. JOHN PHILIPS. Proved by Samuel Holt in Charleston Dist., S. C. on 16 Jan. 1795 bef. W. CUNNINGHAM, J.P. Recorded
in Union Co. on 18 Apr. 1795.

Pp 189-190:   JOHN HENDERSON, ADAM POTTER, HUGH MEANS and CUSHMAN R.
               EDSON, all of Union Co., bond for 1500 pds sterling to
the Treasurers of the State of S. C. and their successors, for JOHN
HENDERSON's appointment and performance as Sheriff of Union Co., dated
7 Apr. 1795. Wit: JOHN BLASSINGAME, J.U.C., and THOMAS BRANDON, J.U.C.
Recorded by order of the Court, 7 Apr. 1795 by BEN HAILE, Clerk.

Pp 190-191:   THOMAS JOHNSON and CHRISTOPHER JOHNSON to THOMAS STRIB-
               LING, JR., a negro mulatto fellow named Isham but common-
ly called and known by the name of John Nelson, formerly owned by RICH-
ARD JOHNSON of Virginia, to have and hold sd mulatto fellow Isham or
John Nelson for a term of four years. Dated 19 Mar. 1795. Wit: WM.
B. FARR, WM. HALL & ABM. NOTT, J.P. Recorded same day.

Pp 191-192:   "Whereas THOMAS JOHNSON & CHRISTOPHER JOHNSON, who have
               the legal right of disposing of me as their servant have
this day by their Bill of Sale, sold and delivered me to THOMAS STRIB-
LING for the term of four years, know ye that in consideration that
at the expiration of the above mentioned four years I am to be Liber-
ated from any further servitude for life. I do by this indenture bind
myself to serve and obey the said THOMAS STRIBLING honestly and faithfully, etc.....""An if I fail to serve him in manner above mentioned
then to become his absolute slave during my natural life." Dated 19
Mar. 1795. Signed by mark. Wit: ABM. NOTT, WM. B. FARR and R. SANDERS.

Pp 192-194:   DANIEL (X) ROBBINS of Union Co. to JOHN REID for 20 pds
               for a certain contract of work to be done by Robbins,
mortgage on "the yellow bay mare that I had of PAUL PEAK", certain
cows, calves, corn, fodder, furniture, kitchen equipment and all other
household goods. When the work is done then this "sale" is void. Dated
24 Dec. 1794. Wit: WM. REID who proved bill of sale on 12 June 1795
bef. BENJ. WOODSON, J.P. Recorded 15 June 1795.

Pp 194-196:   JAMES D. PUCKETT of Pinckneyville, late merchant, to
               GEORGE GORDON & ALEXANDER MORRISON, merchants of Lawrence

Cont'd:
(Laurens) Co., for 50 pds sterling, all book debts owing to me on account of goods sold by me when I lately kept store at Pinckneyville,
GORDON and MORRISON to have the right to exercise all such acts as
may be necessary to recover said debts. Dated 4 May 1795. Wit: DUGLASS
PUCKETT and JOHN M. GIST. Proved by Duglass Puckett on 9 Sept. 1795
before JOHN MARTINDALE, J.P. Recorded 19 Sept. 1795.

Pp 197-198:   State of South Carolina - THOMAS (T) SHOCKLY, late of
               Union Co., appoints his trusty friend Col. DAVID HOPKINS
his agent to sell a certain tract of land situated in Union Co. Referred to the original grant which shall be lodged in the hands of sd
attorney David Hopkins. Dated 26 Nov. 1788. Wit: WILLIAM GLENN and
SPILSBY GLENN. Proved by William Glenn on 11 July 1795 before CHRISTO-
PHER JOHNSON, J.P. Recorded 10 Aug. 1795.

Pp 198-200:   WILLIAM BRATTON, Esq., Sheriff of the District of Pinck-
               ney, was directed by a writ of Fire (sic) Facias dated
1 Nov. 1794 to levy the sum of 12 pds 13 sh 5 pence on the goods and
chattels of JAS. OLIPHANT, deceased, which ANDREW TORRANCE recovered
against the administrators of sd JAS. OLIPHANT, and also 10 pds 18
sh and 8 pence for costs in sd suit. Bratton levied on a certain negro
fellow called Mias lately the property of JAMES OLIPHANT, dec'd. and
after due advertisement, held a sale at public auction on 5 Oct. 1795
at Union Court House. GEORGE GORDON, merchant of Laurence (Laurens)
Co. was the last and highest bidder at 31 pds sterling. Bratton now
gives title to the sd negro Nias (both Mias and Nias in text) to GORDON.
Dated 5 Oct. 1795. Wit: THOS. STRIBLING and ANDW. TORRANCE. Proved
by Torrance on 7 Oct. 1795 bef. JOHN MARTINDALE, J.P. Recorded 4 Apr.
1796 by BEN HAILE, C.C.

Pp 200-202:;   PHILEMON WATERS and JAMES GIBBS to THOMAS HAYS, all of
               Pinckneyville Dist., bond for 100 pds sterling dated
30 June 1792. Conditions being that said Waters and Gibbs shall make
title to Hays for a tract of 151 acres located on Mitchell's Creek,
a branch of Fairforest, in Union Co., which land is said to have been
formerly the property of DANIEL PLUMER whose estate was confiscated
and sold by the commissioners of forfeited Estates. If Waters and Gibbs
make title by 31 Oct. next, the above obligation is void. Wit: RICHD.
HAYS and JOHN CAIN. Proved by RICHARD HAYS on 11 June 1796 before THOS.
BLASSINGAME, J.P. Recorded 17 June 1796 by Ben Haile, Clerk.

        (Note: DANIEL PLUMER of Union Co. was an officer in the Loyalist
Fair Forest Militia, Ninety Six Brigade, during the Revolution. When
the war was over his land was confiscated, and he removed to East Florida.)

Pp 202-203:   DANIEL JACKSON of Union Co., in the Dist. of Ninety Six
               bond to PHILEMON WATERS of Newberry Co., Ninety Six Dist.
in the sum of 100 pds sterling money of S. C., dated 6 May 1789. Condition being that said Daniel Jackson is to make title to said Philemon Waters on all Jackson's right, claim and title to a 150 acre tract
on Mitchell's Creek of Fairforest, which land is sd to have been formerly the property of DANIEL PLUMER whose estate was confiscated and sold
by the Commissioners of forfeited Estates. Wit: JOHN LINDSEY and W.
ANDERSON. Proved by WILLIAM ANDERSON, Esq., in 96 Dist. on 21 Nov.
1796 bef. W. C. WILSON (?), J.P. Recorded 6 Jan. 1797.

Pp 204-205:   29 Dec. 1795 - Nell, a negro woman who indentured her-
               self a servant to a MRS. ACTSON(?) for a term of years
and on her death was taken from her estate by Mr. WILLIAM DARBY of
Union Co. who sold her time to Mr. EDSON of sd place "who given me
free" on the 28th instant, now voluntarily binds herself for a term
of eight years unto CASPER RUGGLES EDSON, minor, of sd county, to serve
him or his guardian for sd time from the date above mentioned. RUGGLES
EDSON to pay her taxes during sd term. Signed by mark. Wit: CHRISTR.
JOHNSON and THOS. MAYBERRY. Acknowledged by "NELL alias BALUS" (or
BAKER) on 31 Dec. 1795 bef. THOS. BLASSINGAME, J.C.C. Proved on same
day by CHRISTOPHER JOHNSON who stated that NELL alias ELEANOR BALUS

Cont'd:
(BAKER, BAHES, BALNS?) signed. THOMAS BLASSINGAME, J.C.C. Recorded
31 Dec. 1796.

Page 206:   JOHN HENDERSON, OBEDIAH TRIMIER and WILLIAM CHISHOLM
              to THOS. W. CHISHOLM, bill of sale for one negro woman
named Fanny, she being part of the property of the Estate of DAVID
CHISHOLM, deceased, consideration being 25 pds sterling. Dated 6 Mar.
1797. Wit: HENRY FARNANDIS and WM. HENDERSON. Proved by Farnandis in
open court and recorded 3 June 1797.

Pp 206-207:   Certification by JOHN TOWNS that he had sold to Col.
              WILLIAM FARR 1 negro woman named Chloe and 1 negro boy
named Jack and 1 negro girl named Hannah for 650 pds consideration.
Dated 9 Feb. 1783. Wit: DL. McELDUFF, HANNAH GREEN FARR and RICHARD
FARR. Proved by Richard Farr on 2 Dec. 1797 before BEN HAIL, J.P. Recorded the same day.

Pp 208-209:   The Hon. JOHN MATTHEWS and H. RUTLEDGE, Esq., Judges
              in the Court of Equity in the State of South Carolina,
to WILLIAM ROUSE of Charleston, Tanner, greeting....Whereas JANE DARBY
and ELIZABETH DARBY, infants under the age of 21, viz, JANE twelve
and ELIZABETH eleven years of age, by their petition presented to this
Honorable Court on 5 July 1797 setting forth that they are minors and
for the reasons therein assigned prayed that the sd WILLIAM ROUSE might
be appointed their guardian, and all parties being present in court,
the sd WM. ROUSE excepted (sic) thereof and agreed to give security.
The judges impowered Rouse to take possession of property (lands, tenements, personal estate, etc.) to which the minors were entitled or
interested in, for the use of the sd minors. Dated in Charleston 18
Sept. 1797. Recorded in Union Co. 4 Jan. 1798 by order of the court.

     (Note: These young girls were probably the daughters of WILLIAM
DARBY, Merchant, who, according to THE FAIRFOREST STORY, History of
the Fairforest (Lower) Baptist Church and Community, by Vera Smith
Spears (1974), moved into Union Co. from the Charleston area of South
Carolina. He is buried in the cemetery of the old Fairforest Baptist
Church, and his tombstone states that he departed this life on 20 Aug.
1794, aged 45 years, and that he was "a native of Highworth, England,
in the county of Wilts. in England." He operated a store that was located near the old church.)

Page 210:   Received of WILLIAM WOOD 70 pds sterling for one negro
              man about 30 years old named Katow (sic). Dated 2 Oct.
1797 and signed by RICHD. FARR. Wit: CHRISTOPHER DeGRAFFENREID and
JOHN L. (or S.) SIMS. Proved by Sims on 2 June 1798 before WM. HOGANS,
J.P. Recorded the same day.

Pp 211-212:   ROBERT DENHAM of Aberville (Abbeville) Co., S. C., bond
              for title to JOHN BUCKHANNON of Fairfield Co., S. C.,
for 100 pds sterling for 200 acres on Packolet River originally granted
to JAMES CAMPBELL, the sd ROBERT DENHAM being the heir of the above
JAMES CAMPBELL. Dated 23 Nov. 1793. Wit: CREIGHTON BUCKHANNON who proved
the bond for title in Fairfield Co. on 10 Dec. 1798 before H. MILLING,
J.P. Recorded 13 Dec. 1798 in Union County.

Pp 212-213:   I do hereby sell and deliver to RICHARD COX all right
              and title to the thirds of land left to me by my husband
MAGNUS SIMONSON, and have received full satisfaction from him for the
same. Dated 27 Nov. 1797. Signed by ELIZABETH SIMONSON. Wit: RICHARD
FARR, WM. B. FARR and COLLINS JOHNSON who proved the "conveyance of
dower" on 30 Mar. 1799 in Union Co., Pinckney Dist., before J. P. SAR-
TOR, J.P. Recorded same day.

Page 214:   20 Nov. 1796 - We do give all our rights to a tract of
              land containing 100 acres that did belong to MAGNUS
SIMONSON, dec'd. in Union Co., S. C. about three miles of Fishdam Ford
adjoining JOSEPH HOLLINGSWORTH's land. We as his heirs do give to his
four youngest children, MAGNUS, GRACE, MARY and NANCY, the sd land

Cont'd:
to be divided agreeable to their father's will. Signed: JAMES BISHOP, STEPHEN BISHOP, HANNAH BISHOP, PHEBE BISHOP & MARY HOLLINGSWORTH. Wit: WM. HARPER, SALLY BISHOP & ASA BISHOP.

(Note: There is a line drawn all the way across the page between the above entry and the entry which follows. It is not clear that the following entry refers to the grantors named above.)

Pp 214-215:   Georgia, Hancock County - Certification by MARTIN MARTIN, Clerk of the Court of Hancock Co., that JOHN BAILEY, Esq., "who hath attested the annexed affidavit" is an acting J. P. of sd county. Dated 3 Oct. 1798. Certification by DAVID DICKENSON, Justice of Superior Court of Hancock Co., Ga., that MARTIN MARTIN, Esq., is an acting Clerk of Superior Court. Dated 3 Oct. 1798. Recorded in Union Co., 30 Mar. 1799.

Pp 216-217:   7 May 1799 - JOHN KERBY (or KIRBY), SR. of Union Co., S. C., to JOHN KERBY, JR. of Pitsylvania (sic) Co., Va., for 50 pds, 50 acres in Pitsylvania Co., Va., on waters of Sandy Creek on CANNON's line, up Pine Branch to MATHEW ORINDER's line, with his line to KIRBY's line, thence to the beginning. Wit: JOHN JEFFERIES, J.P. and H. MEANS, J.P. Recorded 3 June 1799.

Pp 218-219:   JOHN NUCKOLS, DAVIS GOWDYLOCK & CHARLES LITTLEJOHN, all of Union Dist., bond to the Treasurers of the State of S. C. for $700, dated 9 Jan.1800. Above named JOHN NUCKOLS was elected by the State Legislature Sheriff of Union Dist. This is a bond for his performance as Sheriff. Signed by JOHN NUCKOLS, DAVIS GOWDELOCK, WM. GOWDELOCK, CHAS. LITTLEJOHN. Recorded 10 Jan. 1800.

THE END

WILL BOOK A
UNION COUNTY, S. C. 1792 - 1799
UNION DISTRICT, S. C. 1800 - 1815

In the front of the book is the original index, and on the reverse side of the last page of that index is the last half-page of the will of CATHARINE YOUNG. The book has been rebound by the South Carolina Archives Department and this Will of CATHARINE YOUNG has been labeled by the Archives as "a continuation of a will beginning on page 235." The entries on this page will be included in the abstract of the Will of Catharine Young, the last Will in the book. Evidently the clerk who recorded Catharine's will ran out of pages in the book and recorded the last part of the will on the reverse of the index page.

Pp 1-2: State of South Carolina)   April Intermediate Court
        Union County   )   1792. 3rd day.

The LW&T of DAVID CHISHOLM, deceased, being proved in Open Court by the oaths of JESSE MABRY and JOHN BECKHAM, JR., who said they believed the said deceased to be in his proper senses, at the time of executing the said will. Ordered to be recorded.

DAVID CHISHOLM of Union Co., S. C., being weak and low in Body.

Funeral expenses and all just debts to be paid.

To my Father all the cash I have in hand together with what money I have lent out. Balance of estate to my Brothers and Sister to be disposed of and divided in the following manner: My negroes (to wit) Lewis and Fanny and her children to remain until my brother SAMUEL arrives to the age of ten years and then to be equally divided. All stock to be disposed of and the money to be divided equally amongst my Brothers and Sister.
(cont'd next page)

Friends JOHN HENDERSON and OBEDIAH TRIMMIER and my brother WILLIAM
to be executors. Dated 27 Dec. 1791.

Wits: CHARLES GREEN
      JESSE MABRY   /s/ DAVID (X) CHISHOLM
      JOHN BECKHAM, JR.

OBEDIAH TRIMMIER and WILLIAM CHISHOLM, appointed executors, came into
open court and took the oath prescribed by Law as executors, and also
gave bond and security.

Pp 2-3: LW&T of DAVID STOCKTON, deceased, proved in open court by the
        oath of ANGELICA MITCHELL, ordered to be recorded.

DAVID STOCKTON of Ninety Six Dist., Union Co., being sick, weak and
low. Disallowed all former wills.

Wife MARGARET STOCKTON to have one-half of estate, both real and personal, during her natural life, then to be given to my son BENJAMIN STOCK-
TON. Son BENJAMIN the remainder of estate, both real and personal,
forever.

Friend WILLIAM BUCKHANNON to be one executor, and he and son BENJAMIN
STOCKTON to "chuse" another person to act as executor. Dated 14 July
1791.

Wits: ANGELICA MITCHELL
      WM. DODGEN   /s/ DAVID STOCKTON
      THOMAS (X) HOLSEY

WILLIAM BUCKHANNON as executor came into open court and took the oath
according to Law.

Pp 3-6: April Intermediate Court 1792. 4th day.

LW&T of WILLIAM PLUMMER, deceased, proved in open Court by the oath
of JOHN STILES. Also came into open Court CHRISTIAN PLUMER the wife
of the sd WILLIAM PLUMMER, dec'd, and acknowledged said will to be
the LW&T of her husband WILLIAM PLUMMER, dec'd, which is ordered to
be recorded.

WILLIAM PLUMMER of Union Co., being in good health and of sound mind
and memory but calling to mind the mortality of my body.

Beloved wife all land and tenements so long as she shall live and remain my widow bearing my name.

My well beloved CHRISTIAN PLUMMER all household goods and personal
property, and all monies after just debts are paid and on condition
also that within twelve months after my decease she pay 30 pds sterling to MELON WOOD the son of PEGGA WOOD.

To the said MELON WOOD the sd sum of 30 pds.

After the decease of my wife CHRISTIAN PLUMMER or as soon as she shall
marry, all lands shall be immediately appraised by three honest Freeholders to be chosen by the executors. Land to be sold at Public Vendue
to the highest bidder and money to be divided as follows:

Beloved Sister REBECKAH MOORE - 25 pds sterling.

Balance of money to be divided into two equal parts and one part is
bequeathed to my beloved brother THOMAS PLUMMER living in Lancaster
Co., Pennsylvania. If he dieth, his eldest son to receive the legacy.

The other half of the money to be given to my loving brother DANIEL
PLUMMER, or if he decease before he receives it, I bequeath the same
money to his daughter ELENOR PRITCHETT.

All movable estate to remain with my wife CHRISTIAN until her decease,

Cont'd:
then it to be equally divided and one-half given to her brother, MOSES
COLLYER and the other half to my nephew ALEN COX or to his heirs.

Wife CHRISTIAN PLUMMER and trusty friends GEORGE HARLAN (Hatter) and
AARON FINCHER to be executors. Revoked all former wills. Dated 9 Aug.
1791.

Wits: JOHN STILES
      WILLIAM MORGAN   /s/ WILLIAM (W) PLUMMER
      JEMIMA MORGAN

CHRISTIAN PLUMMER and GEORGE HARLAND HATTER (sic - see previous page)
came into open court and entered into bond and took the oath as execu-
tors.
(Note: WILLIAM PLUMMER's brother DANIEL was an officer in a Loyalist
Militia regiment during the Revolution. When the war ended DANIEL left
S. C. and Union Co. deed records indicate that he refugeed to East
Florida.)

Pp 6-7: Intermediate Court 1792. 4th day.

LW&T of EDWARD SANDERS PORTER, deceased, being proved in open court
by the oath of NICHOLAS LAZARUS, ordered to be recorded.

EDWARD SANDERS PORTER of Union Co., weak in body. Revoked all other
wills. Debts to be paid.

Loving wife during the term of her widowhood this house where I now
dwell with all furniture, etc., all cattle, hogs, sheep, and one Bay
Horse named John. At her remarriage or death to be equally divided
among all my children.

Son - EDWIN PORTER - Bay Mare named Doe.
Son - EPAPHRODITUS PORTER - a "stalling" colt named Selah.
Two eldest sons LANDLOT PORTER and HANCOCK PORTER to be executors and
trustees for my wife and children.

Dated 1 Dec. 1791.

Wits: WILLIAM CAMPBELL
      JESSE (X) HOLCOM   /s/ EDWARD SANDERS (X) PORTER
      NICHOLAS (X) LAZARUS

Pp 8-9: April Intermediate Court 1793 1st day.

LW&T of DANIEL COMER, deceased, proved in open court by the oaths of
JAMES BELL and JAMES BRANDON and ordered to be recorded.

DANIEL COMER of Union Co, weak in body.

Debts to be paid. Balance of estate to be equally divided amongst my
surviving children, to wit: JOHN, THOMAS, DANIEL, SAMUEL, ANIS, JOSEPH,
FLETCHAL and MARY COMER, wife of THOMAS COMER and in her part what
she has already received of me to go in her part. "And JOHN something
the best part."

Col. THOMAS BRANDON and my son JOHN to be sole executors jointly, but
should Col. Brandon depart this life I appoint JAMES BELL in his stead.
Revoked all former wills. Dated 14 Feb. 1793.

Wits: JAMES BELL
      JAMES BRANDON   /s/ DANIEL (D) COMER
      SARAH SAVAGE
Col. Thomas Brandon and John Comer came into open court and took the
oath as executors.

Pp 9-12: April Intermediate Court 1793 1st day.

LW&T of JAMES HAWKINS, deceased, proven in open court by the affirmation

Cont'd:
of HENRY MILLHOUSE and THOMAS COX and ordered to be recorded.

JAMES HAWKINS of Union Co., being in health of body but calling to mind the uncertainty of life and being desireous of settling my affairs whilst life and health permits.

To be buried in plain decent Christian manner at the discretion of my beloved wife MARTHA HAWKINS. Funeral charges and just debts to be paid.

Wife MARTHA HAWKINS - 10 pds sterling a year during her life, five hundred weight Flower (sic) and three hundred weight of pork, grey mare called Jewel, her choice of one of the cows, the household furniture, and the privilege of "taking what fruit she wants for her own use on the place whereon I now live." After her decease what I have given her to be equally divided amongst my children.

My son ISAAC HAWKINS - 100 acres which was granted to JONATHAN HAWKINS.
My sons ISAAC and NATHAN HAWKINS - 40 acres which was granted to AMOS
       TIMS in the year 1774, sd tract to be equally divided between
       them.
My son JOHN HAWKINS - two tracts, one of 100 acres, the other of 180
       acres.
My son WILLIAM HAWKINS - 180 acres lying on the branches of Canes Creek
       joining land "laid for" GEORGE STRAWN.
My son JAMES HAWKINS - the plantation whereon I now live and another
       tract adjoining to it containing 170 acres.
Sons WILLIAM and AMOS HAWKINS - two-thirds of a 100 acre tract on the
       north side of Tygar River, adjoining land granted to one BEEKS.

All lands mentioned in this will except the first hundred acres which was granted to JONATHAN HAWKINS to be valued, and if any of my children shall have more than their share, they to pay to such of my children as have not had their share; for it is my will that my Estate be equally divided amongst them share and share alike.

The 100 acres whereon the mills are built and the mills and all the remainder of my estate either goods, chattels, money or credit, to be appraised by three men chosen by my executors and equally divided between my seven sons herein mentioned, except a legacy for my daughter MARTHA COOK of 180 pds sterling.

If any differences arise between any of the legatees, all differences to be determined in a friendly way by four honest men chosen by the Religious Meeting of the People called Quakers, and whoever will not stand to their Judgment shall receive no benefit by this will.

My sons ISAAC HAWKINS and JOHN HAWKINS to be executors. Dated 24th day of the Twelfth Month, 1790.

Wits: THOMAS COX
      RICHARD COX   /s/ JAMES HAWKINS, SENR.
      HENRY MILLHOUSE
Isaac Hawkins and John Hawkins, appointed executors, came into open Court and was qualified agreeable to Law.

Pp 12-14: 14 April Intermediate Court 1793   1st day.

LW&T of DANIEL PRINCE, deceased, proved in open Court and ordered to be recorded.

DANIEL PRINCE of Union Co., planter, being in good health but calling to mind the mortality of my body.

Beloved wife LYDIA PRINCE - one-third part of all my lands the place where I now live with one-third of all personal property after funeral expenses and just debts are paid and she shall hold the same during her natural life.
(cont'd next page)

449

My two sons WILLIAM PRINCE and JOSEPH PRINCE all lands and premises to be equally divided between them, provided they do pay in good trade 40 pds, that is, 20 pds apiece, to be equally divided, 10 pds sterling to JOHN PRINCE the eldest brother, and 10 pds sterling to my son RICHARD PRINCE, and 10 pds sterling to my son ISAM PRINCE.

Balance of estate to be appraised by three just men, Indifferent Freeholders, to be chosen by the legatees in this my will, and the amount so valued to be equally divided between all my children (viz) JOHN PRINCE, RICHARD PRINCE, ISAM PRINCE, WILLIAM PRINCE, JOSEPH PRINCE, ELIZABETH PRINCE, SARAH PRINCE, and CELIA PRINCE.

If any of the children should die without issue, their part to be equally divided between their surviving brothers and sisters legatees.

Friends SOLOMON WILSON and JOHN ADDINGTON to be executors. Dated 25 July 1791.
Wits: MOSES COLLYER
      WILLIAM MORGAN   /s/ DANIEL (D) PRINCE
      DARCAS (X) COLLYER
Solomon Wilson and John Addington appointed executors, came into open court and were qualified agreeable to Law.

Pp 14-16: 16 September Intermediate Court 1793. 2nd day.

LW&T of JOHN HARRINGTON, deceased, proven in open court by oaths of DRURY HARRINGTON and ABRAHAM GUITON and ordered to be recorded.

JOHN HARRINGTON of Union Co., in a sick and low condition.

Beloved wife FANNY all estate real and personal during life or widowhood. If she married or dieth before my children come of age, executors to "keep estate together and make the best they can of it" to raise and educate the children till they all come of age and then (and not till then) the estate to be equally divided amongst the children, male and female, in any manner that the major part of them shall agree upon.

Friends DAVID SMITH my son-in-law and NICHOLAS CORRY to be executors. Dated 12 Nov. 1792.

Wits: ABRAHAM GUITON
      JOSEPH MOORHEAD
      JOSEPH (+) GUYTON   /s/ JOHN (X) HARRINGTON
      DRURY HARRINGTON
David Smith, appointed executor, came into open court and took the necessary oath.

(Note: JOHN HARRINGTON's widow FRANCES married 2nd as his second wife, Col. ROBERT RUTHERFORD of Newberry Co., S. C. Col. Rutherford's first wife was DOROTHY BROOKS who was the mother of all his children. He moved from Virginia to Chatham Co., N. C., where he was a Justice of the County Court and a representative to the Third Provincial Congress which met at Hillsboro, N. C. in 1775. He moved to Newberry Co., S. C. ca 1780 where he was again a Justice of the County Court, elected to the House of Representatives in the State Legislature, Sheriff of Ninety Six Dist., and a large-scale planter.)

Pp 16-17: September Intermediate Court 1793. 3rd day.

LW&T of GEORGE CROSSLEY, deceased, proven in Open Court by the oaths of THOMAS LUMAR and JOHN STOKES and ordered to be recorded.

GEORGE CROSSLEY of Union County, being weak of body.

All my carpenter tools to be sold and the money applied to discharge of my debts, in addition to any other of my property that can be spared. Any debts owing in trade to be paid in trade.

All property to remain unsold in my beloved wife's possession to dispose of to my children as my children come of age, each child to have an

Cont'd:
equal part of my movable estate.

My wife to remain on my plantation as long as she remains a widow,
but if she should marry, land to be sold and the money divided equally
between my wife and children.

At my wife's death land to be sold and the then surviving heirs to
receive equal parts.
Wife LYDIA CROSSLEY and Col. THOMAS BRANDON to be executors. Dated
27 June 1793.

Wits: THOMAS LUMAR
      JOHN STOKES   /s/ GEORGE CROSSLEY
      JOHN BRANDON
LYDIA CROSSLEY and Col. THOMAS BRANDON came into open Court and were
qualified as executors.

Pp 18-19: April Intermediate Court 1794   7th day.

LW&T of WILLIAM HENDLEY, deceased proven in Open Court by the oath
of TURNER KENDRICK and ordered to be recorded.

WILLIAM HENDLEY of Union Co., being weak in body.

Beloved wife MARY whole estate both real and personal during widowhood.
And then I bequeath my land to my three sons to be equally divided.
Son JOHN FOSTER HENDLEY the lower part.
Son GEORGE HENDLEY the upper part.
Son WILLIAM HERROD HENDLEY the part that I now live on.

Three sons above mentioned also to have my two negro girls Loose and
Susey and their offspring, equally divided. Three sons also to have
balance of estate after just debts are paid.

Wife MARY and friends EDWARD TILMAN and WILLIAM McCULLOCK to be executors. Dated 27 Oct. 1793.

Wits: TURNER KINDRICK
      JOHN KINDRICK   /s/ WM. HENDLEY
      MARY McCULLOCK
MARY HENDLEY, EDWARD TILMAN and WILLIAM McCULLOCK, appointed executors,
came into open Court and were qualified as executors according to Law.

Pp 19-22: April Intermediate Court 1794. 7th day.

Presented in open Court a will said to be the LW&T of Col. WILLIAM
FARR, deceased, which was duly proven by the oath of Capt. WILLIAM
JOHNSON who said he believed the sd deceased to be in his proper senses
at the time, and ordered to be recorded.

WILLIAM FARR of Union County.

Daughter HANNAH GREEN McELDUFF - negro girl named Sarah that she has
         now in her possessioin, and also 1 shilling sterling.
Son RICHARD FARR - negro girl named Cheyney and negro boy named Will.
Step-daughter BROWN alias BETSY JETER - negro woman Hanner, negro girl
         Hager, negro girl Nan or Nance, and the household furniture and
         stock belonging to the house and plantation where she now lives.
Son WILLIAM BLACK FARR - negro boy named Ralph.
Son JAMES FARR - negro boy named Baalam.
Son THOMAS FARR - negro boy named Limrick.
Son JOHN POLASKIE FARR - negro boy named John.
Son TITUS GREEN FARR - negro boy named Monser.

After deceased or remarriage of beloved wife ELIZA TOLAFERRY FARR all
estate except my land to be equally divided between my eight children,
WM. B. FARR, JAS. FARR, THOS. FARR, JNO. P. FARR, TITUS G. FARR, ELENOR
THOMAS FARR, ANN KINCHELOE FARR and ELIZA FRANCIS (sic) FARR. All land

Cont'd:
to be equally divided between WM. B. FARR, JAS. FARR, THOS. FARR, JNO.
P. FARR, and TITUS G. FARR, at the death or intermarriage of my wife.

The labour of my negroes and produce of my lands to go to maintain
and school my eight children, WM. B., JAS., ELENOR T., THOMAS, JNO.
P., ANN K., TITUS G. and ELIZA F., and if any remainder, it to be yearly
divided between my five sons last named. Revoked all former wills.
Dated 31 July 1792.

Wits: WM. JOHNSON
      JOHN HAWKINS   /s/ WM. FARR
      BENJAMIN HAWKINS
N.B. - I the said WILLIAM FARR, Esq., do nominate RICHARD FARR, WM.
B. FARR, and THOS. STRIBLING, JR. as executors and beloved wife ELIZA
TOLIAFERRO FARR executrix. Same date and witnesses.

RICHARD FARR, WM. B. FARR, THOMAS STRIBLING, JR. and ELIZABETH TOLIA-
FERRO FARR, appointed executors and executrix, came into Open Court
and were qualified according to Law. Ordered that Letters Testamentory
with the Will annexed be granted to them.

        (Note: Col. WILLIAM FARR and his 2nd wife, ELIZABETH TOLIAFERRO
STRIBLING had a post-humus son, ROBERT GOODLOE HARPER FARR. This estate
went through Equity Court for settlement, and anyone interested would
do well to check the Equity case in its entirety. See also the National
Genealogical Society Quarterly, Vol. 55, No. 1, March 1967, for additional information on earlier generations of this family. The article
entitled "Crafford of New River, North Carolina" by Ellis Munson Goodwin (p. 21). Col. WILLIAM FARR married 1st the widow ELEANOR JETER
who was the mother of the first four children named in his will, RICH-
ARD, WILLIAM BLACK, JAMES and HANNAH GREEN (FARR) McELDUFF. The widow
JETER had at least one child by her 1st husband, the step-daughter
BETSY (JETER) BROWN named in Col. FARR's will. BETSY's husband, ____?
BROWN, was killed during the Revolution, and she received a pension
from the State of S. C. for several years after the Revolution.
        The balance of the children named in the will, as well as the
posthumus son were the children of Col. FARR's 2nd wife ELIZABETH STRIB-
LING who was the daughter of THOMAS STRIBLING, SR., who died in Pendle-
ton Dist. (Anderson Co. records), S. C., ca 1819, naming his daughter
ELIZABETH FARR in his will.)

Pp 22-24: April Intermediate Court 1794. 7th day.

LW&T of CHARLES CLANTON, deceased, presented and proved in open Court
by the oath of ABSOLEM PETTY. Ordered to be recorded.

CHARLES CLANTON of Union Co., Pinckney District, S. C., being weak
in body. Will was dated 15 Nov. 1793.

Debts to be paid. Well beloved wife to have her maintenance during
her natural life of the plantation which she now liveth upon, and one
featherbed with furniture, she to remain in quiet and peaceable possession of said house and plantation during her natural life.

My two sons SION CLANTON and STEPHEN CLANTON to have the two feather
beds and furniture now called theirs, one to each. Sons SION and STEPHEN
with the profits and other things to be mentioned to discharge the
debt which said plantation now lieth under, then said plantation to
remain unto the said SION and STEPHEN CLANTON and their heirs forever
upon the terms aftermentioned: First, all moveable property to be sold
and profits to go to pay said debt. After debt is paid, the plantation
of 437 acres, to be divided between my two sons SION CLANTON and STEPHEN
CLANTON, to be divided by the flat Branch on the north side of Thicketty Creek to the mouth of the branch, then straight across Thicketty
Creek to the line on the south side of Thicketty Creek, sd plantation
being the land I now live on.

Son SION CLANTON and JAMES PETTY to be executors.   (cont'd)

Wits: ABSALOM PETTY
     JAMES THOMPSON   /s/ CHARLES (+) CLANTON
     MILLINGTON LEDBETTER
SION CLANTON, appointed executor, came into open Court and was duly
qualified.

Pp 24-25: April Intermediate Court 1794. 7th day.

LW&T of JOHN HUGHEY, deceased, was proven in Open Court by the oath
of Maj. SAMUEL OTTERSON and ordered to be recorded.

Ninety Six District, Union County, S. C.
JOHN HUEY being very low and weak, do on 7 April 1792 make and publish
this my LW&T.

Loving wife - one-third of land and one-third of movable estate during
her widowhood, at her death or remarriage, to be equally divided between my sons THOMAS and JOSEPH.

Son THOMAS - one-third of land and one-third of movable estate.
Son JOSEPH - one-third of land and one-third of movable estate.
Sons JAMES, JOHN, SAMUEL, GEORGE and HENRY - each 10 shillings.
Daughters MARTHA and MARY - each 10 shillings.
Daughter HANNAH - 10 shillings and a cow and calf.

MARY HUEY my wife and THOMAS HUEY my son to be executors.

Wits: SAML. OTTERSON
     BENJAMIN GORDON   /s/ JOHN HUEY
THOMAS HUEY, appointed executor, came into open Court and was duly
qualified.

Pp 25-28: June Court 1794. 2nd day.

LW&T of FRANCIS DRAKE, deceased, proven in open Court by the oath of
JAMES THOMPSON, and ordered to be recorded.

FRANCIS DRAKE of Union Co., Pinckney Dist., S. C. "being weak in Body
and finding that Awfull Messenger of Death approaching," do this 18th
March 1794 make my LW&T.

Well beloved wife JOYCE DRAKE - negro wench Dinah, a girl called Nan,
a boy named Dembe, a girl named Fib, and one called Hester; also various
livestock, items of furniture, kitchen equipment, etc. (each item listed) and five hundred weight of tobacco during her lfe and she to dispose of them at her death to whom she pleases. She also to live on
and enjoy the profits from the plantation she now lives on as long
as she pleases, but if she leaves the plantation she is "not to have
no more wright to said Plantation in no manner." She also to receive
one-third of the crop made this year.

My son WILLIAM DRAKE - negro man Bob, negro Charles, 1 sorrel mare
     and a colt.
My daughter MARTHA HINTON - negro wench Cloe and negro named Quam.
My grandson ELIAS DRAKE - 200 acres of land on Gilkies Creek, formerly
     called Capt. NATHANIEL JEFFERIES'.
My grandson FRANCIS DRAKE - 1 black mare and $40.
"To JOHN PARHAM , grandson, and WILLIAM WALLACE" - the plantation of
     350 acres whereon I now live, also 200 acares called WILSON JOL-
     JY's joining the land whereon I live, sd land to be equally divid-
ed between them.
MATHEW HINTON, grandson - a bay horse called Darl, 2 cows and calves,
     and $10 in money.
JOSEPH HINTON, grandson - bay mare called Lub, 1 feather bed, 1 pot
     and Dutch oven, and $10 in money.
My granddaughter called MARGARET DRAKE, daughter of BRITTON DRAKE -
     1 feather bed and $20 in money, sd property to remain in the
     hands of the executors until she comes of age.

Remaining part of estate to be sold at vendue and the profits to be

Cont'd:
equally divided amongst all the above mentioned grandchildren.
My son WILLIAM DRAKE and my brother, RICHARD DRAKE to be executors.

Wits: JAMES THOMPSON
      NATHANIEL (N) GEFFERS   /s/ FRANCIS DRAKE
      WILLIAM THOMPSON
RICHARD DRAKE, appointed executor, came into open Court and was qualified according to Law.

Pp 28-29: June Court 1794. 2nd day.

LW&T of SAMUEL COOPER, deceased, proven in open court by JEREMIAH COOPER
and ordered to be recorded.

SAMUE, COOPER, of Union Co., and 96 Dist., "being in good health and
having to leave home." Dated 14 Feb. 1791.

Wife ELIZABETH COOPER - a plantation we now live on on Fairforest Creek
and also a plantation on Tygar River near Cook's Mill "which is sold
but knowing whether the man will have it or not, but if he take it
she is to (have) the price thereof." Also a wagon and 7 head of horses,
cattle, hogs, and also a plantation at mouth of Fairforest Creek which
DANIEL MELONE (is) living on, she may let DAVID COOPER have the sd
plantation or to give him 100 acres of the second quality of land a
horse, saddle and bridle valued at 20 pds. Wife ELIZABETH COOPER to
have remainder of effects such as tools and furniture, and she to be
sole executrix.

Wits: HANNAH (+) MULKEY
      JEREMIAH COOPER   /s/ SAMUEL (N) COOPER (LS)

ELIZABETH COOPER appointed executrix came into Open Court and took
the necessary oath as executrix.

Pp 29-31: September Intermediate Court 1794. 1st day.

LW&T of JOHN WILSON, presented in open court and duly proven by the
affirmation of REBECCA HILLHOUSE and HENRY MILLHOUSE, being qualified
to the same before a Justice. Ordered to be recorded.

JOHN WILSON of Union Co., S. C. To be buried at the discretion of my
wife.

Beloved wife DENAH (sic) WILSON, all movable property forever, provided
that she pay unto my son JEHU WILSON 5 pds sterling and likewise unto
my five daughters (viz) MARY SPRAY, PHEBE HAWKINS, ESTHER FURNAS, SARAH
HAWKINS and HANNAH WILSON the sum of 5 shillings to each of them.

My sons SETH WILSON and CHRISTOPHER WILSON 3 tracts of land containing
in the whole 464 acres, all adjoining the tract whereon I now live,
to be divided between them according to a line already run, they to
provide a comfortable living for my wife.

If any differences should arise between the legatees mentioned in this
will, all differences to be determined in a friendly way by four honest
men chosen by the Religious Meeting of the People called Quakers, and
whoever will not stand to their Judgment shall receive no benefit by
this will. Beloved wife to be executrix and sons JEHU and SETH WILSON
to be executors. Revoked all other wills.

Dated 7th day of the 5th month 1794.

Wits: HENRY MILHOUSE   JOHN WILSON (LS)
      REBECCA MILHOUSE
JEHU and SETH WILSON came into Open Court and were duly qualified as
executors.

Pp 31-33: September Intermediate Court 1794. 1st day.
(cont'd next page)

LW&T of THOMAS HENDERSON, deceased, proved by the oath of SAMUEL HARDY and ordered to be recorded.

THOMAS HENDERSON of Union Co. and Pinckney District.

Beloved wife - negro man Jinkins and negro woman Diner, and one mare during her widowhood. If she should marry or die before her children are raised, executors to use the negroes and mare for maintenance of her children, and after her youngest JINCY comes of age or marrys, then the negroes and mare to be sold for cash and the money equally divided between my children, to wit: ELIZABETH, POLLY, FANNY WORD, CISLEY and NANCY HENDERSON.
My daughter POLLY HENDERSON - negro woman Dise, 1 feather bed and furniture, 1 cow and calf.

To my five youngest children one shilling sterling each.

To my daughter ELIZABETH HENDERSON - negro woman Agg, 1 mare and colt, 1 feather bed and furniture, 1 cow and calf.

To my daughter CISLEY HENDERSON - negro girl Betty, 1 horse, 1 cow and calf and heifer.

To my daughter NANCY HENDERSON - negro girl Dol and a heifer.

To three of my grand Daughters (to wit) NANCY, JINCY and PEGGY WORD- negro girl Milly. Said negro girl Milly with her increase lent to my daughter FANNY WORD during her life and then to be divided between the above mentioned grand children.

I lend to my wife 2 cows and calves for her and her children's use.

I have already given what I intend to my two sons (to wit) NATHL. and WILLIAM HENDERSON.

To my daughter JUDY HALL - the balance of her grandfather DURVAN's estate.

If either of my daughters should die without marrying (viz) ELIZA, POLLY, CISLY and NANCY HENDERSON, then what I have given them shall be equally divided between the other three.

My son NATHL. HENDERSON and JOHN HENDERSON, son of DAVID HENDERSON, to be executors. Dated 26 May 1794.

Wits: MATTW. SIMS
      JOHN GEORGE   THOMAS (X) HENDERSON (LS)
      SAML. HARDY

NATHANIEL HENDERSON and JOHN HENDERSON appointed executors came into open Court and were qualified.

Pp 33-35: September Intermediate Court 1794. 1st day.

Presented in open Court the LW&T of THOMAS WRIGHT, deceased, which was proven by the oath of ANNER TAYLOR and WILLIAM WRIGHT and ordered to be recorded.

THOMAS WRIGHT of Union Co..."weak in body".

My two youngest children ELIZABETH and JOANNAH MORRIS - a certain part of my land from the Spring Branch to the dividing line between me and MOSES WATERS, on both sides of the Creek, to a small part of my land that I gave to my son WILLIAM WRIGHT, and on the south side to another part that I gave to my son-in-law ABRAHAM GOSSET.

Rest of thw whole estate to the sole possession of my wife during her widowhood unless my wife and Executors think fit to let any child in want have a part to be charged against their part at the Division of

Cont'd:
the Estate at my wife's death or marriage. Then my estate to be divided
equally between my nine children: WILLIAM, MARY, MATILDA, NANCY, DILLIE,
ABNER, SALLY, ELIZABETH, and JOANNER MORRIS WRIGHT.

WILLIAM BURT to be maintained as usual with my wife, and after her
death some of the children that he thinks fit to live with to take
him and everyone of the children to pay an equal part to maintain him.

Beloved wife and son WILLIAM WRIGHT to be executors. Dated 1 Dec.1787.

Wits: ANNER TAYLOR   THOS. WRIGHT (seal)
      WILLIAM WRIGHT

DYLLA WRIGHT and WILLIAM WRIGHT, appointed executors, came into open
Court and were duly qualified according to Law.

Pp 35-36: September Intermediate Court 1794. 1st day.

LW&T of JAMES GIBBS, deceased, presented in open court and proved by
oath of JACOB HOLMES and ordered to be recorded.

JAMES GIBBS, being sick and weak...

Land I live on to be divided among my three youngest boys, HIRAM to
have the plantation.

AGATHA my daughter to have one shilling sterling.

Land in Spartan (sic-Spartanburg) to be sold if I have not moveable
property enough to pay my debts.

Mr. JESSE CONNAL and my son ZACHARIAS to manage estate with my wife
until my three youngest sons come of age.

Wife to have her thirds of the Estate after debts are paid, but if
she marries, she to have no more than the Law allows her.

I desire to be buried in my own garden.

The negroes to be kept on the place until my small children are raised.
Then they to be valued, and them that keeps them to pay to the rest
of the children an equal part.

All of my children to have an equal part of my property but AGATHA.

My eldest son ZACHARIAS to have my Cool Spring land in Spartanburg,
if it does not have to be sold to pay my debts.

My son JOHN to have Negro Joe after the death of my wife and HIRAM
comes of age.

My daughter SUSANNAH to have a young negro if June ever has one, and
if she has more than one, the next to be for my son ZACHARIAS.

My son ZACHARIAS to make titles to all the land I have sold in Georgia
or elsewhere.

MARY MAYBERRY to be charged with all she has had. Signed 8 Aug. 1793.

Wits: AMOS MARTIN
      JACOB HOLMES
      ANDREW THOMSON   JAMES GIBBS (LS)
      MILLEY CONNELL
JESSE CONNELL, ZACHARIAS GIBBS and ANNE GIBBS, appointed executors,
came into open court and were qualified.

Pp 37-38: January Court 1795. 1st day.

LW&T of JOHN TAYLOR, deceased, proven by oath of JAMES MAY, JR. and

Cont'd:
ordered to be recorded.
JOHN TAYLOR of Union Co., S. C., Pinckney Dist., "being sick in body".

Derly beloved wife SUSANNA TAYLOR to have all my stock and household furniture to be at her disposal and for her proper use.

Wife SUSANNA TAYLOR and MOSES GUYTON to be executors. Revoked all other wills. Dated 20 Sept. 1794.

Wits: JOHN MITCHELL
      MOSES GUYTON   JOHN TAYLOR (LS)
      JAMES MAY, JR.
SUSANNAH TAYLOR and Maj. MOSES GUYTON appointed executors, came into open Court and took the oath of execution.

Pp 38-39: January Court 1795. 1st day.

LW&T of JEREMIAH COOPER, deceased, was proven by the oath of GABRIEL PHILLIPS, SR., and ordered to be recorded.

JEREMIAH COOPER of Orangeburgh District, S. C., being in good health but calling to mind the mortallity (sic) of my body.

To MARY RUNNELS 150 acres in Lawrence (Laurens) Co. adjoining ROBERT TWEEDY and Mr. WILSON. And also 10 pds sterling in money.

To my Dear Mother all the remainder of my money, notes and bonds.

To my sister HANNAH COOPER my bridle, 3 cows and calves, 15 head of sheep that is in the hands of ELIZABETH COOPER, and 150 acres of land adjoining DAVID SMITH and the land I bought of THOMAS HOLDEN.

To my brother JOSEPH COOPER 159 and 750 acres whereon HENRY HILL lives, my two silver watches, all my cloathing, and my surveying instruments, with 540 acres lying on Haddles Creek.

To my brother DAVID COOPER 600 acres on the north of Tygar River adjoining JOHN COOK's land and 594 acres on Beaver Creek waters.

To my cousin JEREMIAH PHILLIPS 1000 acres lying in Orangeburgh Dist. with the remainder of my land. Dated 11 June 1794.

Wits: GABRIL PHILLIPS, JR.
      GABRIL PHILLIPS, SR.   JEREMIAH COOPER Du(?) (LS)
      HANNAH (X) PHILLIPS

DAVID COOPER by permission of the court came into open court and took the oath as an executor.
      (Note: JEREMIAH COOPER and his brother SAMUEL COOPER (see his will earlier) were sons of WILLIAM, SR. and LYDIA (CLARK) COOPER who moved from Pennsylvania to the Tygar River-Fairforest Creek area of Union County before the Revolution. WILLIAM, SR. and LYDIA had a large family and were originally Quakers. However, WILLIAM, SR. and several of his older sons served in the Revolution and were evidently dismissed from the Quaker unity.)

Pp 40-42: January Court 1795. 1st day.

LW&T of ELIZABETH MILLER, deceased, proven by oath of EMANUEL HOLLUMS. Ordered to be recorded.

14 Dec. 1794. ELIZABETH MILLER of Union Co. being weak and sick of body...

To DENNIS MILLER my dearly beloved son, my plantation which I now live upon and all my effects, debts, goods and moveables.

Executors to be JOHN GREGORY and JEREMIAH GREGORY. Revoked all former wills. Wits: WILLIAM ADAIR & EMANUEL HOLLUMS. /s/ ELIZABETH MILLER.

Cont'd:
JEREMIAH GREGORY and JOHN GREGORY appointed executors, came into Open
Court and were dully qualified according to Law.

Pp 41-43: January Court 1795. 1st day.

LW&T of JAMES SIMS, deceased, was returned in Open Court by JOHN SANDERS
one of the Executors, was proven to the satisfaction of the Court by
the oath of CORNELIUS WILSON, and ordered to be recorded.

JAMES SIMS of Union Co., S. C. "being weak in body"...

To WILLIAM GILLIAM and NANCY, his wife, all the negroes and other estate
formerly delivered and now in their possession.

To PETER BRASELLMAN and DRUSILLA, his wife, all the negroes and other
estate formerly delivered and now in their possession.

To my daughter ANNE G. SIMS one negro woman Tabb and her five children,
namely, Milly, Fanny, Dilcy, Robin and Peter. If sd daughter should
die without lawful issue, the sd negroes and their increase to be equally divided among my five children, viz: DRUSILLA BRASELLMAN, MATTHEW,
JOHN, NATHAN and REUBEN SIMS, or their survivors.

Residue of my estate to remain in possession of my wife ELIZABETH under
the direction of my executors until my just debts are fully paid and
during her widowhood, to be delivered as a loan to either of my five
sons, as they may need, not to be removed beyond the limits of this
State, ever debarring the delivery of a slave to my son JAMES. After
the death or intermarriage of my said wife, all estate with the increase arising therefrom to be gathered together and appraised by three
Justices of the Peace of this county with the assistance of my Executors
which I give to be divided between my four sons MATTHEW, JOHN, NATHAN
and REUBEN SIMS, they paying to my son JAMES one-fifth part of the
appraised value of the slaves and one-fifth part of the residue of
such estate to be delivered to him. If either of my sons should die
without heirs lawfully begotten, their part to be equally divided between my two daughters DRUSILLA BRASELLMANN and ANNE GLENN SIMS and
the survivors of my said sons.

My wife ELIZABETH to be executrix and my friends PETER BRASELLMAN and
JOHN SANDERS to be executors. Dated 20 Nov. 1794.

Wits: JOSHUA KENWORTHY
      JOHN KENWORTHY   JAMES (X) SIMS (seal)
      CORNELIUS WILSON
ELIZABETH SIMS, PETER BRASELLMANN and JOHN SANDERS appointed executors,
came into open court and were duly qualified according to Law.

Pp 40-42: (cont'd) (Will Book A)
        (Note: JAMES SIMS was the son of MATTHEW and JEMIMA (GLENN) SIMS
of Newberry Co., S. C. who came to S. C. from Hanover Co., Va. after
the Revolution. Many years later this estate went through the Union
Co. Equity Court for division among the then living heirs, and this
Equity case gives much additional information on JAMES SIMS' children
and grandchildren.)

Pp 43-45: April Intermediate Court 1795. 6th day.

LW&T of AARON FINCHER, deceased, proved by the oath of HEZEKIAH RICE
and ordered to be recorded.

AARON FINCHER of Union Co., being very sick and weak in body...

To beloved wife MARY FINCHER the land and plantation whereon I now
live and my negroe boy Joe, together with every other part of my estate
until my yongest son JONATHAN PARKER FINCHER arrives at the age of
21 years.

Whole estate to be sold by the executors and the money arising from

Cont'd:
such sale to be equally divided between my wife MARY and all my children, namely, MOSES, HANNAH, TIMOTHY, AARON, MARY, SARAH, ARNOLD, JESSE, JOHN AND JONATHAN PARKER FINCHER.

My wife MARY, my son MOSES FINCHER, and my friend JOHN SANDERS to be executors. Revoked all former wills. Dated 6 Feb. 1795.

Wits: HEZEKIAH RICE
      THOS. BISHOP   /s/ AARON (X) FINCHER (seal)
      FRANCIS FINCHER

MARY FINCHER, appointed executrix and MOSES FINCHER, executor, came into open court and were duly qualified according to Law.

Pp 45-46: April Intermediate Court 1795. 7th day.

LW&T of JAMES THOMAS, deceased, proved in open court by the oath of JAMES TATE and ordered to be recorded.

JAMES THOMAS ...being sick and weak of body...

Loving wife to enjoy the land, plantation, and all personal and moveable estate during her widowhood in order to raise my children, and if she marry, or if she decease, my land to be sold and equally divided among my children. If my wife marry again, she to have an equal part in all my estate during her natural life and at her decease to be equally divided amongst my children. Balance of estate to be equally divided amongst my children at the discretion of my Trusty Friends WILLIAM THOMAS and REUBEN WILKS who I constitute to be executors. Dated 26 Sept. 1787.

Wits: WILLIAM WILLIAMS   /s/ JAMES THOMAS (seal)
      JAMES TATE
Postscript - My mother to have her living during her natural life.

WILLIAM THOMAS and REUBEN WILKS, appointed executors, were duly qualified in open court and letters granted them as executors according to Law.
    (Note: JAMES THOMAS lived on Neal's Creek and Broad River in Union County, and his brother, WILLIAM THOMAS, the executor lived just across Broad River in Chester County. REUBEN WILKS also lived in Chester Co., JAMES and WILLIAM THOMAS and their brother DANIEL, who died earlier in Union Co., were the sons of DANIEL THOMAS who died in Chester Co. about the time of the Revolution. There is much interesting information about this family in both Union and Chester counties, as well as in the old Ninety-Six District records and Camden District records. The family came from Virginia, according to Chester Co. deed records.)

Pp 46-47: September Intermediate Court 1795. 7th day.

LW&T of THOMAS LAYTON, deceased, proved by oath of JOHN GOODWIN and ordered to be recorded.

THOMAS LAYTON of Union County, S. C., very sick and weak of body.

To HUMPHRY BATES and ELIZABETH WELLS, wife of LEWIS WELLS, all my estate real and personal to be equally divided among them as they mutually and friendly agree.

Said HUMPHRY BATES to be executor. Revoked all former wills. Dated on 8 July 1795.
Wits: JOHN SANDERS
      JOSEPH McJUNKIN   /s/ THOS. (X) LAYTON (seal)
      JOHN (X) GOODWIN
HUMPHRY BATES, appointed executor, came into open court and took the necessary oath prescribed by Law.

Pp 47-48: At a called Court on Thursday, 14 October 1795.

LW&T of BENJAMIN HOLCOMB, deceased, proven in open court by the oath of ELIJAH H. COOPER and ordered to be recorded.

BENJAMIN HOLCOMB being sensible of the approach of Death...

To beloved wife ALICE one negro girl and the land and a necessary support for the rest of her lifetime or widowhood.

To RACHEL HOLCOMB the before mentioned negro girl named Pegge, one feather bed and furniture, one black mare and one cow and calf.

To JESSE HOLCOMB 8 pds sterling.
To SOLOMON HOLCOMB 8 pds sterling.
To my grand daughter FRANKY COMER 8 pds sterling and 1 feather bed and if she dies without an heir, then it to come to RACHEL.

Balance to be equally divided amongst all the children. Dated 12 August 1795.

Wits: ELIJAH H. COOPER   /s/ BENJAMIN (X) HOLCOMB
      MOSES YOUNG

Added notation: "left as Executor, ALICE HOLCOMB and NEVIL HOLCOMB."
"NEVIL HOLCOMB being appointed Executor in said Will was duly qualified according to Law."

Pp 48-49: September Intermediate Court 1795. 8th day. (Will Book A)
     (Note: This entry is out of line chronologically.)

LW&T of MAGNUS SIMONSON, deceased, proved by the oath of JOHN AUSTIN and BIRD BOOKER and ordered to be recorded.

MAGNUS SIMONSON of Union County, weak and sick of body...

To my daughters MARY HOLLINGSWORTH, LYDIA SIMONSON, ELENOR TEAGUE, HANNAH BISHOP and PHEBE BISHOP each 15 shillings sterling.

To my wife ELIZABETH SIMONSON one-third part of the land whereon I now live during her widowhood, and at her death to be divided as followeth:
To my daughter GRACE all the land on the north side of the creek.

To my son MAGNUS and my daughters MARYANNE and NANCY all the land on the south side of the creek, to be equally divided between them.
Horses, cattle, sheep, etc. to be equally divided between wife ELIZABETH and son MAGNUS and my daughters GRACE, MARYANNE and NANCY.

My son MAGNUS SIMONSON, ARTHUR THOMAS and RICHARD COX to be executors. Revoked all other wills. Dated 21 June 1795.

Wits: JOHN AUSTIN
      BIRD BOWKER   /s/ MAGNUS (X) SIMONSON (seal)
      NANCY (X) SCANE
MAGNUS SIMONSON and RICHARD COX, appointed executors, came into open court and took the oath prescribed by Law.

Pp 49-50: April Intermediate Court 1796. 4th day.

LW&T of ELIZABETH COOPER, deceased, proven by the oath of Capt. JOHN SANDERS and EZEKIEL FRAZER and ordered to be recorded.

ELIZABETH COOPER of Union County, S. C., being very weak and sick in body....

To the daughters of my brother, JOHN WORLY, my saddle and wearing appearal (sic).

After my just debts are paid, I bequeath to my said brother, JOHN WORLEY one-third part of my estate. (cont'd following page)

To RALPH HUNT, JR. the residue of my estate of every name or nature to him and his heirs forever.

The said RALPH HUNT, JR. and my friend Col. THOMAS BRANDON to be executors. Revoked all former wills. Dated 15 March 1796.

Wits: JOHN SANDERS
      EZEKIEL (X) FRAZIER   /s/ ELIZABETH (X) COOPER (seal)
      MARY HUNT
RALPH HUNT and Col. THOMAS BRANDON nominated executors came into open court and took the oath prescribed by Law.

Pp 50-52: April Intermediate Court 1796. 4th day. (Will Book A)

LW&T of JESSE PATTY, deceased, proven by the oath of JACOB WILLBRIGHT and JAMES PATTY, subscribing witnesses, and ordered to be recorded.

JESSE PATTY.."weak in body".

To my loving wife DELILAH the house I now live in with the clear gound inclosed with said house with the privilege of Timber to support the house, all household furniture, and one-third of the profits arising from the other part of the plantation to live and raise the children on during her life or widowhood. The whole of the estate that remains after the children come of age to be equally divided among my five children, namely, JOHN PATTY, JAMES PATTY, ZAROBABEL PATTY, MARY PATTY, JOSHUA PATTY.

To my son CHARLES PATTY 5 shillings.
To my son JESSE PATTY 5 shillings.
To my daughter DELILAH MULLINS one cow and calf.
To my two youngest sons ZEROBABEL PETTY and JOSHUA PETTY, all my land and plantation to be equally divided between them two when they both come of age. If either of them should die without heir, the other to have it, and also the two-thirds of the profits on the plantation till they come of age.

My loving wife DELILAH PETTY and my loving son JOHN PATTY and my trusty friend TURNER KINDRICK to be executors. Dated 9 Nov. 1795.

Wits: JACOB WILBRIGHT   /s/ JAMES PATTY (seal)
      JAMES PATTY

DELILAH PATTY and TURNER KINDRICK were qualified as executors.

Abstract of the Pension Record of WILLIAM ADDINGTON, wife DELILA, South Carolina, No. W 5598

WILLIAM ADDINGTON (signed by mark X) applied for a pension for his service in the Revolution on 30 May 1835 when he was living in Franklin, Macon Co., North Carolina. He signed his application before J. M. BRYSON, J.P. WILLIAM stated on oath that he was 75 years old when he applied.

He entered service as a volunteer in 1781 at the Old Block House at Fairforest, now Union Dist., S. C. under Capt. WILLIAM YOUNG, Col. BRANNON (BRANDON), Lt. Col. PHAIR (FARR?), and Maj. BENJAMIN JOLLEY. They marched to Ninety Six where the outfit was placed under Maj. Gen. GREEN. Ninety-Six Fort was in the hands of the British and Tories. When the seige was raised, they marched to Broad River, thence down the river to Sandy Run below Grandy, where they remained until an order came to march to the Eutaws. At this time, WILLIAM was discharged because of a wound received by the fall of a tree a few weeks before.

He volunteered again in August (year not recollected) under Capt. JAMES BRUTON at Prince's Fort, South Carolina, and marched to Kee Wee (Keowee) old fort under Col. BRANNON in pursuit of the Indians.

He re-entered a third time under Capt. YOUNG, received a commis-

461

Cont'd:
sion as Lieutenant, pursued the Indians through Georgia into North
Carolina on the Tennessee River, under Gen. PICKENS, Maj. BENJAMIN
JOLLY and Col. THOS. BRANNON. They killed three Indians on the Tennessee
River and one white man, took two Indians prisoner, and returned to
South Carolina.

He re-entered again by order of Maj. JOLLEY, having command of
the company, "the Captain (not named) not being out." They were sent
to Orangeburg to guard some ammunition, "from Santee," and marched
thence to Bacon's Bridge on Ashley River near Charlestown and remained
there six weeks.

WILLIAM had no documents or witnesses to prove his first claim,
which has no date, taken before JOHN LATHAM, Clerk, and M. FRANCIS,
D. Clk. of Macon Co., N. C. Included with his first claim are affidavits by JAMES KINSEY (or KIMSEY), a clergyman, and JAMES RUSSELL,
both residing in ADDINGTON's neighborhood, who believed that he was
74 years old and believed to be a soldier of the Revolution. His first
claim was turned down for lack of evidence.

He made a second application on 30 May 1835. By that time he
had received and annexed to his application an affidavit by WILLIAM
DOOD, and had heard of other witnesses living in the State of Georgia.
He received his pension.

In Union Co., Georgia, on 19 July 1849, DELILAH (X) ADDINGTON,
aged 83, appeared in court and applied for a pension, stating that
she was the widow of WILLIAM ADDINGTON, a pensioner of the United States
and a resident of Macon Co., N. C., which pension was before his death
transferred to Union Co., Ga....WILLIAM died on 8 Sept. 1845.

She further stated that she was married to sd WILLIAM ADDINGTON
on 22 Dec. 1784 (in one place the date is shown as 23rd Dec.) on Dun-
can's Creek, Newberry Dist., S. C., "by a regularly ordained minister
of the Gospel of sd State (of the Baptist Denomination) by the name
of ISAAC EDWARDS," and had in lawful wedlock thirteen children, to
wit:
JANE ADDINGTON, deceased, born in Jan. 1786
JOHN ADDINGTON, born 10 Nov. 1788
HENRY ADDINGTON, born in 1791
SARAH ADDINGTON, now SARAH HARRISON, born in 1793
WILLIAM ADDINGTON, born in 1795
MOSES ADDINGTON, born in 1797
JAMES ADDINGTON, born in 1799
MARCH ADDINGTON, born in 1802
DELILAH ADDINGTON, now DELILAH HUCKABY, born in 1804
MARTHA ADDINGTON, now MARTHA HICKS, born in 1806
POLLY ADDINGTON, now POLLY LOGAN, born in 1808
ELIZABETH ADDINGTON, now ELIZABETH CURTIS, born in 1810, and one child
who died in infancy, having no name.

DELILAH had no evidence to prove her marriage unless the statements of her children as to their ages would be sufficient. She requested that her certificate of pension, if approved, be forwarded
to WALTER R. WEBSTER, Crossville, Lumpkin Co., Ga.

Her application was dated 19 July 1849 and witnessed by ANDREW
YOUNG, J.I.C., by G. W. L.. MASHBURN, J.I.C., BANNISTER ALLGOOD, J.I.C.
and JONATHAN DUCKWORTH, J.I.C., who also certified that WILLIAM ADDING-
TON was a resident of that county before his death, and DELILAH, his
widow, was "a worthy and respectable person."

A certificate is attached, dated 2 June 1849 in Gilmer Co., Ga.
by JOHN ADDINGTON who stated that he was 60 years old on 10 Nov. 1848
and that he was the second child of WILLIAM and DELILAH ADDINGTON and
that WILLIAM was a pensioner who drew $33 or $34 per annum up to the
date of his death in Sept. 1845, leaving a widow DELILAH (mother of
sd JOHN) who married WILLIAM at or about the end of the Revolutionary

Cont'd:
War, about 1784. JOHN stated that he himself was married in Buncombe
Co., N. C. on 1 May 1808, "a few months after I was 19 years old."
His parents were married on Duncan's Creek, Newberry Co., S. C. and
lived together as husband and wife from his earliest recollection up
to the day his father died. He never had heard the legality of their
marriage doubted by anyone. Signed before ROBERT SMITH, J.P. who also
certified that JOHN ADDINGTON was "a worthy and respectable citizen
of this neighborhood."

DELILAH had applied previously on 2 Dec. 1848 in Union Co., Ga.
She gave the same statement with slight variations:
WILLIAM was a pensioner in Macon Co., N. C. until a short time
before his death, said pension transferred to Union Co., Ga....
They were married on Duncan's Creek, Newberry Co., S. C. within
3 miles of Enoree River.
They had 13 children, 10 of whom were alive within the last 18
months. Children then living (in Dec. 1848) were: JOHN, HENRY, WILLIAM,
MOSES, JAMES, and MARCH ADDINGTON, and MARTHA HICKS, DELILA HUCKABY,
MARY LOGAN and ELIZABETH F. CURTIS. Signed before GEORGE W. L. MASHBURN,
J.P. of Union Co., Ga.

In the file is a typed letter dated 11 April 1916 to Hon. WIL-
LIAM H. THOMPSON, U. S. Senate, that gives the same information. The
letter states that WILLIAM was a pensioner on an application dated
Dec. 1833 at which time he was 74. The letter was signed by G. M. SALTZ-
GABER, Commissioner.

END OF ABSTRACT

WILLIAM ADDINGTON was the son of HENRY ADDINGTON who stated in
his will that he was "of Union County." His will is on file in Union
Probate records (Box 1, pkg. 6) and was dated 1 March 1787 and entered
for probate on 3 Aug. 1787. In his will he names his wife SARAH ADDING-
TON, son WILLIAM ADDINGTON, son JOHN ADDINGTON, son JAMES ADDINGTON,
son HENRY ADDINGTON, daughter BETHTHENA McCLAIN, daughter MARTHA BRUTON,
daughter ELIZABETH ADDINGTON, daughter SARAH ADDINGTON, and daughter
CHARLOTA ADDINGTON who was the youngest daughter. He also named a grandson HENRY ADDINGTON. He appointed his son WILLIAM and trusty friend
JOHN ODELL as executors.
At least a part of the ADDINGTON family were members of the Quaker
Meetings in this area, and it would pay anyone interested in this family
to check Quaker records. Obviously, WILLIAM ADDINGTON left the Quakers
since he served in the Revolution. According to a descendant of WIL-
LIAM and DELILAH ADDINGTON, Delilah was a DUNCAN before her marriage
to WILLIAM ADDINGTON, probably the granddaughter of JOHN DUNCAN who
gave his name to Duncan's Creek in Newberry Co. where he settled ca
1750, one of the earliest settlers in that area.

Pp 52-53: Proved in Open Court by the oath of ADAM POTTER, Esq., the
LW&T of ADAM GOUDYLOCK, deceased. Ordered therefore that the same be
recorded.

In the name of God Amen - I, ADAM GOUDYLOCK of Union Co., S.C., planter,
being weak in body.....do this 24 Dec. 1793 make my LW&T.

To my well beloved sons DAVIS and WILLIAM GOUDELOCK - all the lands
belonging to me to be equally divided "between them two."

To my son DAVIS GOUDYLOCK - negro girl named Dinah.
To my daughter SARAH - negro girl named Balendar.
To my son WILLIAM GOUDYLOCK - negro man named Peter and a negro wench
    named Delphy, the sd WM. GOUDYLOCK to pay his sister SUSANNAH
    GOUDYLOCK 30 pds in good merchantable produce at Market Trading
    price within three years after my decease. Also to son WILLIAM
    my bed and furniture.
If my daughter SARAH should die without and heir of her body, the negro
    girl withher increase to be equally divided between my sons DAVIS
    and WILLIAM.

Cont'd:
So much of my movable estate to be sold as will pay all just Debts and purchase four Bibles at Charleston price to be worth 1 pd each. Remainder to be given to my son WILLIAM.

One of the Bibles to be given to my daughter, ANN SAFFOLD, one to my daughter ELIZABETH JOHNSON, one to my daughter PRUDENCE STOCKDEN, and one to my daughter HANNAH BLACKEY.

To my grand-daughter HANNAH STOCKDEN - 1 cow and calf.

Well beloved friends ADAM POTTER and THOMAS STOCKDEN to be executors.

Wits: JOHN BECKHAM, JR.
      ADAM POTTER   /s/ ADAM GOUDYLOCK
      SION CLANTON

Pp 54-55: June Court 1st day 1796.

Presented in Open Court the LW&T of THOMAS HARRIS, deceased, which was proved by the oath of RICHARD & THOMA HARRIS and ordered to be recorded.

In the name of God Amen - THOMAS HARRIS of Union Co., being very sick and weak in body...

Just debts and funeral expenses to be paid. Loving wife SALLY to have all estate both real and personal at her own discretion during her natural life, and for her to divide it amongst my children as she shall think fit at her death.

Wife SALLY HARRIS and trusty friend JAMES TOWNSEND to be executors. Revoked all former wills. Dated 2 Apr. 1796.

Wits: JAMES BENSON
      RICHARD HARRIS   /s/ THOMAS HARRIS
      THOMAS HARRIS
SALLY HARRIS and JAMES TOWNSEND, appointed executors, came into open court and took the oath prescribed by Law as Executors.

Pp 55-57: September Intermediate Court 1796 5th day.

LW&T of GEORGE NORMAN, deceased, proved before JOHN MARTINDALE, Esq. and ordered to be recorded.

"With an Awfull Reverence to the Great Almighty being," I, GEORGE NORMAN of Union County being weak of body....do make and publish this my LW&T.

Debts and funeral expenses to be paid.

My beloved wife MARGARET to keep possession and have the profits arising from my plantation and personal estate for her support during her widow-hood.

To my son ROBERT NORMAN all my land now in his possession, bounding on the east side of John's Creek, also 10 acres off the upper end of my field lying on weatern side of sd creek, which sd 10 acres (he my son ROBERT) is to have no use of during his Mother's widowhood without her consent.

My two sons THOMAS and JOHN, after the death or marriage of their Mother all my lands and improvements on the western side of John's creek, equally divided between them by two men appointed by my executors, they paying 15 pds sterling between them to my executors for the use of my son GEORGE.

Son GEORGE to have the privilege of his home with his Mother during her widowhood, and the 15 pds to be paid to him from time to time as his necessaties (sic) require, after the death or marriage of his Mother.

Cont'd:
If he should die before he receives his legacy, it shall be divided
equally between my said sons THOMAS and JOHN.

To my son JONATHAN - 5 shillings sterling.
To my son DAVID - 5 shillings sterling.
To my daughter ELIZABETH - 5 shillings sterling.
To my daughter JANE - 5 shillings sterling.
To be paid to each of them after the death of their Mother.
To my daughter LYDIA - 1 cow and calf after the death of her Mother
     or when my said wife may think proper.

Remainder and residue of estate, after death or marriage of my wife,
to be equally divided between my sons THOMAS and JOHN and my daughter
MARY, and fi either of them should die before that time, it to be divided between the other two.

My beloved sons JONATHAN and DAVID to be sold executors. Dated 28 Jan.
1794.
Wits: JOHN TAYLOR   /s/ GEORGE NORMAN
      JOHN NEDAMAN

Pp 58-61: December Court of Ordinary 1796. 3rd day.

Presented in open court the LW&T of WILLIAM LEE, deceased, which was
proved by the oath of HEZEKIAH RICE and ordered to be recorded.

In the name of God Amen - WILLAM LEE of Union Co., S. C., being weak
in body. Debts and funeral expenses to be paid out of personal estate.

To my son MICHAEL LEE - 60 acres, part of a tract of land containing
240 acres on Tygar River conveyed to me by SAMUEL CANNON, to begin
at the lower corner and extend up the River far enough to include 60
acres, to have for his use during his life and no longer, then to go
to my son THOMAS LEE and his heirs forever.

To my son JOHN LEE - 60 acres of the same tract of 240 acres, adjoining son MICHAEL, during his natural life and then to be divided equally
among the other boys, that is to say, if said JOHN does conform to
build and settle on said tract, otherwise it to "fall back" and be
equally divided among the other boys.

To my son JOSEPH - 60 acres of the same tract on the River above and
adjoining son JOHN, provided JOSEPH doth build, clear and settle on
said land.

To my son THOMAS - the remainder (60 acres) of above tract, above my
son JOSEPH LEE, with the houses, buildings, and other improvements
that he the sd THOMAS LEE hath done on sd tract.

To my above named three sons THOMAS, JOSEPH and JOHN, 245 acres, it
being the remainder of a 250 acre tract granted to me (the low land,
consisting of 5 acres more or less, being bequeathed as above) to be
equally divided between them, son THOMAS' share to include the dwelling
and improvements he now has made. Sons to be allowed to sell land with
approbation of the executors, provided they purchase other land with
the money they receive for above tract.

To my sons MICHAEL LEE and WILLIAM LEE, and to my daughters CATHARINE
BREED, JEAN HOWEL, OLVIAH FRAZER, SARAH BATES and NANCY JACKSON - 1
guinea each to be paid them 12 months after my decease, if demanded.

Personal property to be sold at public auction and proceeds to be divided equally between my three sons THOMAS, JOSEPH and JOHN LEE.

Trusty friends DRURY MURRELL and GEORGE HARLAN (hatter), and beloved
son THOMAS LEE to be executors. Dated 12 Sept. 1796.
Wits: JOHN STOCKES
      HEZ. RICE   /s/ WILLIAM (X) LEE
      WM. RICE

Cont'd:
(Note: WILLIAM LEE's son WILLIAM served in the Loyalist militia during the Revolution. When the war ended he was one of a group from Union County who removed to the Natchez area.

Pp 61-63: January Court 1797. 2nd day.

Presented in open court the LW&T of MARY FROST, deceased, which was duly proved by the oath of JAMES BENSON, SR. and ordered to be recorded.

In the name of God Amen - MARY FROST of Union County, South Carolina being weak in body....

Just debts and funeral charges to be paid with all convenient speed. All my goods and chattels to be sold except one "gound" (gown?) which I give to my daughter REBECCA FROST. And the proceeds of the sale to be divided amongst my children as follows, that is to say,
         To my son JOHN FROST one shilling.
         To my daughter SARAH WILLIAMS one shilling.
         To my daughter MARY FROST one shilling, if demanded.

Remainder to be equally divided between my four youngest children, namely, BARNET, ELIZABETH, RACHEL and WILLIAM, to be paid to them when they come of full age. Executors to have care of children and bind them to as good places as they can.

My brother JAMES BENSON and JESSE YOUNG and JAMES TOWNSEND to be executors. Revoked all former wills. Dated 25 Dec. 1796.

Wit: ELEANDER (X) BROWN
       JAMES (X) BENSON, SR.   /s/ MARY (X) FROST
       ELIZABETH (X) BENSON
JAMES BENSON and JAMES TOWNSEND, appointed executors, came into open court and took the oath prescribed by Law.

Pp 63-67: January Court 1797. 2nd day.

Presented in open court the LW&T of JOHN CLARK, late of Union County, deceased, which was proven by the oath of HENRY THICKPENNY witness thereto, and ordered to be recorded.

LW&T of JOHN CLARK of Union County...

To be buried in a plain, decent and Christian manner at the discretion of my beloved wife, and funeral charges and just debts to be paid.
To my son JOHN CLARK all my two tracts of land (290 acres) on Padgets Creek, provided and on condition that he pay to my son THOMAS CLARK 50 pds sterling when sd THOMAS CLARK shall arrive at age of 21 years.

To my son JOHN CLARK my Black Horse and my Great Bible.

To my son HENRY CLARK 200 acres which I bought of LAURENCE PEARSON, granted to him 7 Aug. 1791, on condition that HENRY or his heirs, executors, etc. convey to my son JONATHAN CLARK when he comes of age of 21 years, a certain parcel of land, part of the tract granted to CHARLES EMANUEL THIALL, bound by land granted to BARTHOLOMEW WOOD and CHARLES EMANUEL THIALL, the dividing line, sd WOOD's line.

To my beloved wife MARY CLARK as her Right of Dower, all that plantation whereon I now live granted to BARTHOLOMEW WOOD and given to me by my Father's will dated 22d day of 8th month, August 1793, with all appurtenances thereto belonging, for her support and the Family, during her natural life or widowhood, together with her bed and furniture, my Roan horse and my Roan mare, 4 cows, her choice of the stock, and certain furniture and farm equipment (itemized). At death or marriage of my wife, the land to be rented out by my executors and the profits thereof be for my son JONATHAN CLARK provided he be under age 21 and at that age to be given to him.

To my son JONATHAN CLARK when he arrives at age 21, the sd plantation

Cont'd:
whereon I now live as above said, together with all the tract adjoining
it containing 100 acres, granted to me 5 June 1786. If my wife MARY
his Mother be then living a widow, she to have during life or widowhood
the third part of the land and premises where she shall choose it.
When JONATHAN arrives at age 25, he is to pay to each of my daughters
then living the sum of 7 pds sterling in trade or property, and 20
pds sterling in trade or property to my son THOMAS CLARK.

Remainder of estate to be sold at 12 months credit, and the money arising from the sale to be disposed of as follows:
To my five daughters, namely, ELIZABETH, RACHEL, HESTER, MARY, and
RACHEL 5 pds each. If son JONATHAN should die before age 21, his part
to go to my son THOMAS CLARK. Balance of money, if any, from the sale
to be divided equally between my wife MARY and my son JONATHAN.

My two sons HENRY CLARK and JOHN CLARK to be executors and "my friend
JAMES TOWNSEND I leave in Trust to see my Will performed." Revoked
all other wills. Dated 9th day of the Ninth month called Sept. 1796.

Wits: WILLIAM MORGAN
      HENRY THICKPENNY   /s/ JOHN CLARK
      ISHM. PRINCE
HENRY CLARK and JOHN CLARK being appointed executors came into open
court and was qualified according to Law.

Pp 67-69: April Intermediate Court 1797. 3d day.

Presented in open court the LW&T of ISAAC GREGORY, deceased, which
was duly proved by oathes of NATHANIEL SANDAGE and JOSEPH TYREE and
ordered to be recorded.

In the name of God Amen - ISAAC GREGORY of Union Co., being weak of
body. Debts and funeral expenses to be paid.

I lend to my beloved wife ALSE GREGORY the house and plantation and
three negroes, viz, Bet, Peter and Adam, also my stock of every kind,
utensils of husbandry, and household furniture of every kind for her
sole and proper use during her natural life, and after her decease
the sd land and premises to be given to my son JARROD, his heirs and
assigns forever. My stock, implements of husbandry and household furniture to be divided in the following manner:
     One child's part to be divided equally among my following grand-
children, viz, SALLY GORDEN and WILLIAM, being children of my son BEN-
JAMIN, deceased, the remainder to be equally divided among my following children, JOHN, ROBERT, ELIZABETH, ISAAC, JERRAD and JEREMIAH.

To my son JOHN - one negro girl named Pat which he has now in his pos-
     session.
To my son ROBERT - negro boy Cato which he has now in his possession.
To my daughter ELIZABETH - negro woman Bet, with her youngest child
     named Sal, to her for her life and then to her children.
To my son ISAAC - negro boy Mark.
To my son JARRAD - negro boy Peter.
To my son JEREMIAH - negro boy Adam.
To my daughter SALLY - negro girl rose "which her mother MARGARET shall
     have in possession during her lfe and after her decease the wench
     and increase to her daughter SALLY."

My two sons ISAAC and JARROD to be executors. Revoked all former wills.
Dated 13 Aug. 1796.

Wits: NATHAN SANDAGE   /s/ ISAAC GREGORY
      JOSIAH TYREE
ISAAC GREGORY and GERARD GREGORY appointed executors, came into open
court and took the oath required by Law.

Pp 69-71: April Intermediate Court 1797. 3d day.

Presented in open court the LW&T of SUSANNAH BAILEY, deceased, which

467

Cont'd:
SUSANNAH BAILEY of Union County, District of Pinckney, being very sick
and weak in body....

To my daughter UNITY BAILEY 50 acres of land with the manner (sic)
plantation whereon I now live adjoining Pacolate River, together with
certain livestock, furniture, and kitchen equipment (listed).

To my daughter REACEY BAILEY 50 acres of land adjoining Pacolate River,
together with certain livestock, furniture, etc. (listed) which is
now in her possession.
To FRANCIS (sic) TOMLIN my daughter, my riding saddle and 1 spinning
wheel which makes up her full share with what she has already received.

To my daughter ANN RUNNELS - 1 shilling.
To my daughter RACHEL REDMON - 1 shilling sterling.
Dated 13 Nov. 1796.
Wits: JOHN CRITTENDEN
      PALMORE (P) KINDRICK   /s/ SUSANNA (+) BAILEY
      DREWSILLER (I) BAILEY
N.B. - Appointed JOHN BAILEY and GEORGE BAILEY sole executors. Same
date and same witnesses.
GEORGE BAILEY, appointed executor, came into open court and took the
oath required by Law.

Pp 71-72: April Intermediate Court 1797. 3d day.

The verbal will of ELIJAH H. COOPER, deceased, being duly proved by
the oaths of THOMAS GREER and SUSANNA COOPER, and a certificate thereof
presented to the court, it is therefore ordered to be recorded.

I do certify that ELIJAH H. COOPER called me into the waggon in which
he was going to the Pacolate Springs in his late illness on or about
8 Aug. 1796, and communicated to me the following words as near as
my memory will serve....

His debts to be paid and his wife to keep the children together with
the property they had and that the land should be for the three boys,
she nevertheless to enjoy a moity with the youngest her lifetime.

Certified 7 Jan. 1797.   /s/ THOS. GREER, SR.

On the 28th Dec. 1796 ELIJAH H. COOPER on his death bed told me the
following words, that it was his will that I should live on the place
as long as I lived and keep the children together in the best manner
I could with the little property he had, that there was a smuch due
him as would pay off all he owed, and that a certain tract containing
105 acres lying on north side of Tygar River should be his son JAMES's
part.

Certified by me the 9th Jany. 1797. /s/ SUSANA COOPER

SUSANA COOPER came into open court and was qualified as Executrix to
the above will of her husband ELIJAH COOPER, dec'd...

Pp 72-74: April Intermediate Court 1797. 3d day.

Presentede in open court the LW&T of NATHANIEL DAVIS, Esq., late of
this county, dec'd., duly proved by the oath of JAMES CALDWELL, SR.
and ordered to be recorded.

In the name of God Amen - NATHANIEL DAVIS of Union Co., Pinckney Dist.,
S. C., very sick and weak....

Lawful debts to be paid out of estate. Beloved wife ELIZABETH DAVIS
the plantation whereon I now live and as much of the tillable land
as she shall have need of, also one negro woman named Jane during her
natural life or widowhood, also one mare called Flint, one side saddle
and bridle, one feather bed and furniture.

Cont'd:
To my daughter MARGARET DAVIS - negro girl Phebe and one feather bed
    and furniture.
To my son JOSEPH DAVIS - negro girl Jane and one feather bed and furni-
    ture.
To my daughter SARAH DAVIS - negro named Phillis and one feather bed
    and furniture.
To my son NATHANIEL DAVIS - one negro boy named Cull(?) and one feather
    bed and furniture.
To my son EPHRAIM DAVIS - one negro girl named Hester and one feather
    bed and furniture.
To my son JAMES DAVIS - negro boy Abraham and one feather bed and furni-
    ture.
To my daughter ELIZABETH DAVIS - negro girl Celia and one feather bed
    and furniture.

My land to be equally divided among all my children as they come of
age, also the remainder of my personal property of whatever kind to
be equally divided among my children. If either of the afsd willed
negroes should die, the child or children so losing to be made out
of the estate.

Wife ELIZABETH DAVIS and friends JOHN VOLUNTINE and JAMES CALDWELL,
JR. to be executors. Dated 18 Jan. 1797.

Wits: JOHN (X) DAVIS
      W. WADLINGTON   /s/ NATHL. DAVIS
      JAMES CALDWELL, SR.
ELIZABETH DAVIS, executrix, and JOHN VOLUNTINE and JAMES CALDWELL,
JR. came into open court and took the oath prescribed by Law.

Pp 74-76: April Intermediate Court 1797. 3rd day.

Presented in open court the LW&T of HENRY CLARK, late of this county,
deceased, proven by the affirmation of FRANCIS FINCHER and ordered
to be recorded.

LW&T of HENRY CLARK of Union Co., S. C., being of sound well disposed
mind, and calling to mind the mortality of my body...

To be buried in plain, decent, Christian manner at discretion of executors, funeral expenses and just debts to be paid.

To my son JOHN CLARK all that tract of 150 acres whereon I now live,
the plantation which I bought of WILLIAM HENDRIX, provided that he
shall pay unto his five daughters the sum of 7 pds sterling a piece,
then the sd property to be to him and his heirs forever. Note the above
mentioned sums of money to be paid in good and sufficient property
when sd Legatees shall come to the age of twenty-two years, as they
shall agree.

All personal estate to be gathered together, with what can be collected
and appraised by two honest men chosen by my executors, then to be
equally divided between my two children JOHN CLARK and HESTER CAMPBELL,
to be exhibited (distributed?) among their children as they see cause.

To my grandson HENRY CLARK the upper tract of 100 acres which I bought
of CHARLES EMANUEL THEELY, "provided my rights hold the land," provided
that he pay 50 pds sterling to the children of JOHN CAMPBELL and HESTER
his wife as they come of age 22 years, equally divided amongst them.
If either of the legatees should die before reaching age 22, their
legacies to be equally divided among their surviving brothers and sisters.

If any disturbance should arise amongst any of my Legatees, it shall
be decided in a friendly and Christian way by four people, members
of the Monthly Meeting at Cane Creek of the Christian people called
Quakers, the same to be chosen by the sd Meeting. And he or she who
will not abide by their Judgment shall have no part in my estate.

Cont'd:
My son JOHN CLARK and my son-in-law JOHN CAMPBELL to be executors, and my friend ELI COOK to see my will performed. Revoked all former wills. Dated 22 day of the Eighth Month called August 1793.

Wits: FRANCIS FINCHER
      THOMAS BISHOP   /s/ HENRY CLARK
      RALPH HUNT
JOHN CAMPBELL, one of the appointed executors, came into open court and took the oath prescribed by Law.

Pp 77-79: June Term 1797. 1st day.

Proved in open court by the oath of SAMUEL HARDY the LW&T of JAMES BEUFORD, late of this county, deceased, and ordered to be recorded.

In the name of God Amen - I, JAMES BEUFORD of Union Co., S. C., "considering my age and frailty of body must expect er' long to make my final Exit from this World." Debts to be paid.

I lend to my beloved wife MARY BEUFORD 3 negroes, viz, Charles, Sue and Rose, during her widowhood. She also to choose, with advice and consent of the executors, for her exclusive use, such livestock, and household furniture, etc., as she and they judge to be sufficient to afford her a comfortable sustenance during her widowhood.

To my grand daughter JINCY PRIDE GLENN and to her heirs forever - 1
      negro named Ned.

All the rest of my estate, both real and personal, including those Negroes which I formerly lend to some of my children, to wit, my negro man Shinner lent to my son TAVINOR BIRD BEUFORD, Sal and her children lent to LELIAN PHILIPS, Lydda and her children lent to my daughter LUCY TUCKER, and also Daniel lent to my daughter MILDRED HUTT, with the rest of my estate both real and personal, the whole to be sold in such a manner that my children shall be the only purchasers, and the product of the sale to be equally divided between these my children, to wit, WARREN BEUFORD, PHEBE HARDY, MILDRED HUTT, LUCY TUCKER, LELIAN PHILIPS, TAVENOR BIRD BEUFORD, MARY WALKER or her heirs, AMBROSE BEUFORD or his heirs, to them and their heirs forever.

If any of the above named children to whom I have formerly lent negroes should fail to give up such negroes to my executors to be equally divided, then they shall be suffered to keep the said negroes, but shall be excluded from having any part of the rest of my estate.

At the decease of my beloved wife MARY BEUFORD all the estate then left to be divided as above.

To my son HENRY BEUFORD 12 pds cash which I formerly lent him, it to be his whole portion of my estate.

My two sons WARREN BEUFORD and TAVENOR BIRD BEUFORD and my wife MARY BEUFORD to be executors. Revoked all former wills. Dated 12 Dec. 1796.

Wits; SAMUEL HARDY
      PATRICK HENRY SIMS   /s/ JAMES BEUFORD
      JOHN BEUFORD
WARREN BEUFORD, TAVENOR BIRD BEUFORD and MARY BEUFORD, appointed executors and executrix, came into open court and took the oath required by Law.

Pp 79-80: June Term 1797. 2d day.

Proved in open court by the oath of THOMAS LEE the LW&T of DANIEL HOWELL deceased, and ordered to be recorded.

In the name of God Amen - I, DANIEL HOWELL of Union Co., being weak in body..Just debts, Doctor's bill and funeral charges to be first fully satisfied and paid.

To my son JOSEPH HOWELL all of my land, only beloved wife to have her maintenance out of said land during her widowhood.

Remainder of personal estate to my son JOSEPH and daughters SARAH LEE and ROSEANNER LEE and my wife, to be equally divided between them.

Trusty friends HUMPHRY BATES, JOHN LEE and JOSEPH LEE to be executors. Revoked all former wills. Dated 19 Dec. 1796.

Wits: THOMAS (X) LEE
      SARAH (T) LEE   /s/ DANIEL (X) HOWEL(L) (LS)
      REBECCA (X) SPICER

Pp 81-82: Court of Ordinary 4 November 1797.

Proved in open court by the affirmation of SAMUEL HUNT the LW&T of JAMES PARNELL, deceased, and ordered to be recorded.

Whereas I, JAMES PARNELL of Union Co., being sick and weak, do this 14 Oct. 1797 make this my LW&T. To be buried in a plain Christian manner at discretion of executors. Debts to be paid.

All my lands and plantation and mill to my two sons GEORGE and JAMES to be equally divided between them by my executors.

To said son GEORGE PARNELL my roane (sic) mare with corn and fodder
        sufficient to winter her this ensuing winter.
To my daughter ELIZABETH CAMPBELL my big iron pot and two young ewes.
All my bedding and furniture thereunto belonging to my three youngest
        daughters, namely, SARAH, EASTER and RUTH to be equally divided
        between them by their Aunt RUTH TOWNSEND when they come to age
        of 18 years.

Remainder of personal estate to be sold at public vendue and the money divided equally between SARAH, ESTER and RUTH after my 3 youngest children is schooled out of it to be paid to them as they come to age of 18 years.

Son GEORGE PARNELL and my brother-in-law JAMES TOWNSEND to be executors. Disannulled all former wills.

Wits; SAMUEL HUNT
      JOHN (T) TOWNSEND, SR.   /s/ JAMES PARNELL (LS)
      RUTH (S) TOWNSEND

Pp 82-84: January Term 1798. 1st day.

Proven in open court by oaths of ROBERT WOODSON, JAMES WOODSON, JAMES WHITLOCK and JEDUTHAN WOODSON the LW&T of TURNER ROUNTREE, late of this county, deceased, and ordered to be recorded.

In the name of God Amen - I, TURNER ROUNTREE of Union Co., S. C. of sound and perfect mind....

To my son WOODSON ROUNTREE - two negroes David and Gabril, two cows
        and one set of waggon wheels.
To my son WILLIAM ROUNTREE - eight negroes, viz., Lucy, Lewis, Sam,
        Jonas, Jane, Sarah, Jack and Chany, also all my land on both
        sides of Fairforest Creek with my houses, furniture, horses,
        cattle, hogs and sheep, but I lend to my wife all that I have
        willed to my son WILLIAM as long as she lives, then son WILLIAM
        to receive it.
I lend to my daughter MOLLY BLASINGAME - four negroes, viz., Phillis,
        Suck, Prince and Lucy, as long as she lives, then to be divided
        equally between her children. To my daughter MOLLY and her hus-
        band THOMAS BLASINGAME, 1 shilling each.
To my daughter SALLY BIRDSONG - one negro woman Dafny as long as she
        lives, then Dafny and her increase to be divided equally between
        her children. To my daughter SALLY and her husband HENRY BIRDSONG
        1 shilling each.

Cont'd:
My two sons WOODSON ROUNTREE and WILLIAM ROUNTREE to be executors. Dated 24 Dec. 1797.

Wits: ROBERT WOODSON
      JAMES WOODSON   /s/ TURNER ROUNTREE (LS)
      JAMES WHITLOCK
      JEDUTHAN WOODSON
WILLIAM ROUNTREE and WOODSON ROUNTREE appointed executors, came into open court and took the oath required by Law.

Pp 84-86: January Term 1798. 1st day.

Proved in Open Court by the oath of GEORGE HARLAN (Hatter), the LW&T of RENNEY BELUE, SR., late of this county, deceased, and ordered to be recorded.

In the name of God Amen - I, RENNEY BELUE of Union County, very sick and weak....

To my wife ANN $1 and whereas she has "left me in my Sickness and been gone sometime and has formerly Trangressed in such like manner and has practised dealing Greatly to my loss and disadvantage and for other good causes" I deny her being a wife to me and debar her from any claim on my estate including Dower or otherwise.

All estate real and personal to be sold and money divided equally between my nine children, namely, ZACHARIAH, RUBIN, SUSSAN, RENNEY, SARAH, JUDITH, ELIZABETH, JESSE and WILLIAM, to them or their heirs.

My three sons ZACHARIAH, REUBEN and RENNEY BELUE to be executors. Revoked all former wills. Dated 17 Dec. 1797.

Wits: GEORGE HARLAND
      WILLIAM MORGAN   /s/ RENNEY BELUE (LS)
      AGNES (X) HOLLAND
ZACHARIAH BELUE, REUBIN BELUE and RENNEY BELUE, appointed executors, came into Open Court and took the oath required by Law.

Pp 86-87: Court of Ordinary, 7 Feb. 1798.

LW&T of BENJAMIN JOHNSON, late of this county, deceased, proven by oath of PRESLEY WILLIAMS and ordered to be recorded.

In the name of God Amen - BENJAMIN JOHNSON being of sound memory but calling to mind the uncertainty of this life....

To my Dearly beloved wife MARY JOHNSON 1 feather bed that she has in possession, and 5 pounds sterling to be paid by executors on a horse or the like.

To my daughter LUCY MILLER 1 horse, bed and furniture, cow and calf.
To my daughter SARAH JOHNSON 1 mare colt, 1 feather bed and furniture, 1 cow and calf.
To my son JAMES JOHNSON 1 horse, saddle and bridle, 1 cow and calf, 1 feather bed and furniture.
To my daughter JUDITH JOHNSON (same items as above)
To my son WILLIAM JOHNSON (same items as above)

All household furniture, stock and tools to be sold and the money equally divided among all my children. If any of the above legatees should die without lawful issue, her part to be divided equally among the Residue of said Legatees.

To my son BENJAMIN's three children, FANNY, NANCY and ANSELM FINCH JOHNSON, 10 pds each.
My son CHARLES JOHNSON and DAVID JOHNSON and WILLIAM HOGANS to be executors. (Date left blank).
                      /s/ BENJAMIN JOHNSON (LS)

Cont'd:
N.D. - My old Negroe Woman Hannah to be free as she has been a faithful slave to me. 17 Nov. 1797.

Wits: PRESLY WILLIAMS
      DAVID WILLIAMS   BENJAMIN JOHNSON (LS)
      W. HOGANS
CHARLES JOHNSON and DAVID JOHNSON came into open court and took the
oath prescribed by Law.

Pp 88-89: June Term 1798. 1st day.
Proved in open court by the oath of ELIZABETH WEER, the LW&T of SAMUEL
TORBERT, deceased, and ordered to be recorded.

In the Name of God, Amen - SAMUEL TORBERT of Union Co., considering
the Transitory State of all human things.....

To my wife SUSANNAH TORBERT during her life, all estate, land, furniture, stock, tools, etc., and after her death, the whole of my plantation on Broad River with one other tract containing 90 aacres adjoining the same to my only son SAMUEL TORBERT.

After wife's decease, personal estate to be equally divided between
my three daughters, ANN HALL, ELIZABETH WIER and SUSANNAH LOGANS.

SAMUEL TORBERT, one of the executors appointed, came into court and
took the oath required.

Page 89: The voluntary examination of TABITHA PEARSON, HANNAH THICK-
PENNY and MARY SMITH on oath saith that on the evening of Sunday, 29th
Oct. last, they being present at the house of FRANCIS FINCHER and heard
REBECCA FINCHER who was then on her death bed direct her son FRANCIS
to destroy an Instrument of writing by way of a will and directed him
to give her daughter ELIZABETH her wearing apparel and also the clothing of her other daughters, to wit, HESTER's and REBECCA's, deceased,
and also directed him to pay said ELIZABETH 20 pounds. Deponents do
believe she was in her proper senses at the same time. Dated 3 Nov.
1797.

JOSEPH McJUNKIN, J.P.   TABITHA PEARSON
                                  HANNAH (X) THICKPENNY
                                  MARY (X) SMITH
Recorded 2 Jan. 1798.

Pp 90-91: June Term 1798. 4th day.

Proved in open court by the affirmation of JOHN BURGESS, the LW&T of
MOSES WELDON, late of this county, deceased, and ordered to be recorded.

MOSES WELDON of Union County, being sick and weak...To be buried at
discretion of beloved wife.

Wife MARY WELDON all estate after funeral charges and just debts paid,
either lands, goods, chattels or credits. She also to be sole executrix. Revoked all other wills. Dated 29 of the third Month called March
1798.

Wits: HENRY MILHOUS
      JOHN (X) BURGESS   MOSES WELDON (seal)
      OLIVE COOK
MARY WELDON as executrix, came into open court and took the oath prescribed by Law.

Pp 91-93: September Intermediate Court, 3rd day, 1798.

Proved in open court by oaths of MARSHAL WILBANKS and EDWARD PRINCE
the LW&T of SOLOMON WHITSON, deceased, and ordered to be recorded.

In the name of God, Amen - SOLOMON WHITSON of Union Co., (shoemaker),
indisposed in body....

Cont'd:
To my sons DAVID and WILLIS 250 acres adjoining WIAT WOOD's land to be equally divided.

To my sons JORDAN and SAMUEL 200 acres situated between above tract and the one hereafter mentioned to be divided between them.

To my other two sons SOLOMON and JOHN 311 acres adjoining WM. GIST's plantation, JOHN and SOLOMON to pay as conveniently and ability permits unto JORDAN and SAMUEL 15 pounds in horses or any good trade.

Rest of property both personal and real to beloved wife PHEBE whilst she liveth, and at the maturity or full age of my sons she to give a part of the horses, cows, hogs and sheep equally among my sons, retaining for her support 1 horse and 1 cow, also all household furniture to her only use and disposal. She to have (a home) on the plantation of SOLOMON and JOHN as long as she remains a widow. If she should marry again, she to have one good bed and furniture, all her pewter ware and all her such like necessaries.

Concerning 100 pounds Pennsylvaniaa money left by my Father for the support of my sister CLEMENT whilst she liveth and then to be confered to me, when recovered I will that to be equally divided between my children, sons and daughters, viz., 1st ANN; 2nd DAVID; 3rd MARY; 4th WILLIS; 5th JORDAN; 6th SAMUEL; 7th SOLOMON; 8th JOHN.

Wife PHEBE to be executrix and sons DAVID and WILLIS and son-in-law THOS. ROBARDS executors. Renounced all other wills. Dated 29th day of the Fifth month or May 1798.

Wits: WM. HENDMAN (HINDMAN?)
      MARSHAL WILBANKS   /s/ SOLOMON WHITSON (seal)
      EDWARD (P) PRINCE
DAVID WHITSON, WILLIS WHITSON and THOS. ROBERDS appointed executors came into open court and took the oath as such.

Pp 93-95: September Intermediate Court 3rd day 1798.

Proved in open court the LW&T of JAMES TOWNSEND, late of this county, deceased by the oaths of RALPH HUNT and JAMES DARBY and ordered to be recorded.

In the name of God, Amen - JAMES TOWNSEND of Union Co., being of perfect mind and memory....

To my loving wife MARTHA the plantation whereon I now live and all personal property after just debts are paid, for life or widowhood, and afterwards, if all my Daughters are not come of age, personal property to be sold and the money equally divided amongst my five daughters as they come of age.

All my lands to my two sons JOHN and ELI except what is above given to my wife MARTHA and at her death or widowhood it all to be divided equally between my two said sons, divided equally as to value, Friends ELI COK, JOHN COOK and JOHN TOWNSEND to lay out and divide the land to my Sons. If either son should die without issue, his part to my other son and he to pay one-half the value thereof to my daughters, and if either of my daughters die without issue, their part to descend to the other daughters.

Beloved friends ELI COOK, JOHN COOK and JOHN TOWNSEND to be executors. Dated 26 Jan. 1797.

Wits: RALPH HUNT
      JOSIAS DARBY   JAMES TOWNSEND (LS)
      JEREH. HAMILTON
ELI COOK and JOHN TOWNSEND, appointed executors, were qualified according to law.

Pp 95-97: Court of Ordinary met 13th October 1798.

Proved in open court the LW&T of GEORGE HARLAND, deceased, late of this county by oaths of SOLOMON SPANN and WILLIAM MORGAN and ordered to be recorded.

In the Name of God, Amen - GEORGE HARLAND of Union Co., being very sick and weak....

To my eldest son SAMUEL HARLAND 50 pounds sterling and my bay horse called hard times.
To my son GEORGE all my tract of land on Buffalow Creek.
To my son ISAAC my negroe boy named Paul.
To my son WILLIAM my negroe boy named Fitus and all that tract of land of 200 acres whereon I now live, with all things thereunto belonging, provided and on condition that he shall not hinder my wife REBECCA his mother from possessing the same, or as much as she shall require, during her natural life.
To my daughter SARAH BRANDON 10 pounds sterling.
To my daughter HANNAH 40 pounds sterling.
To my daughter ELINOR 40 pounds sterling.

Remainder of estate to be collected and the same to my beloved wife REBECCA and she to pay out of the same the several sums of money to my children above mentioned. Wife also to have my negroe girl Ester for life and after her decease Ester is bequeathed to my son ISAAC.

Wife REBECCA and my brother SAMUEL HARLAND and my son SAMUEL HARLAND to be executors. Revoked all former wills, legacies, etc. Dated 9 Sept. 1798.

Wits: SOLOMON SPANN
      JACOB HOLMES   GEORGE HARLAN (LS)
      WILLIAM MORGAN
REBECCA HARLAND and SAMUEL HARLAND, JR. were qualified as executors.

Pp 97-98: Words spoken by TURNER ROUNTREE before his death on 24 Dec. last before he signed his will, which will was afterwards signed, he said there is one thing which was not mentioned in writing his will that was some money a part of which was in the Desk and a part in the hands of JOHN PARHAM and that he intended that money for the payment of all his debts. We were witnesses to the will.

Dated 21 June 1798.   Signed: JEDUTHAN WOODSON
                                         ROBT. WOODSON
                                         JAMES WHITLOCK
Sworn by above men on the same day before THOS. BRANDON, J.U.C. Entered in Clerk's office 29 Oct. 1798.

Pp 98-100: April Intermediate Court 1st day 1799.

Proved in open court by the oath of JAMES BANKHEAD, the LW&T of ROBERT GOOD, deceased, and ordered to be recorded.

In the Name of God, Amen - ROBERT GOOD of Union Co., being indisposed in body. To be buried at the discretion of executors. Debts and funeral expenses to be paid.

To my dearly beloved wife ELIZABETH GOOD, a horse and saddle and her bed and furniture to be at her own disposal.

Lands and goods and chattels to stand as they are for support of my Family until the youngest child comes of age, and then to be valued and sold. Wife to have one-third during life or a child's part if she marries. "If she remains a widow, there will be but two-thirds of the Estate to divide amongst the children if not it is to be equally divided."

Wife ELIZABETH GOOD, JOHN BANKHEAD and JOHN MITCHELL to be executors. Revoked all former wills, legacies or executors. Dated 19 Jan. 1799.
Wits: HENRY GOOD, JAMES BANKHEAD, JAMES ADAMS /s/ ROBERT GOOD(LS)

Cont'd:
ELIZABETH GOOD and JOHN BANKHEAD, appointed executors, came into open court and took the oath according to Law.

(Note: ROBERT GOOD and his brothers, HENRY, THOMAS and JOHN, and his sister, NANCY (GOOD) FINLEY came to South Carolina ca 1771 from Cecil Co., Maryland..(See Deed Abstracts of Tryon, Lincoln & Rutherford Counties, North Carolina, 1769-1786, Tryon County Wills & Estates by Brent Holcomb (1976). They first lived in present-day York County near Bulloch's Creek Presbyterian Church. JOHN GOOD and NANCY FINLEY remained in York Co., but ROBERT and HENRY moved over into Union Co., where they lived on Broad River and Thicketty Creek in the area of Union Co. that was cut off to form a part of Cherokee Co. THOMAS GOOD is probably the same THOMAS who married MARY (POLLY) GORDON GILLHAM (daughter of EZEKIEL GILLHAM) and moved to Madison Co., Ill. ELIZABETH GOOD, widow of ROBERT in the estate above, and her four children, HUGH, HENRY, JOHN and MARYAN, moved to Rutherford Co., Tenn. HENRY, brother of ROBERT, died in 1821 and he and his wife SARAH are buried in Bulloch's Creek Church cemetery. They had no surviving children and HENRY's estate went through Equity Court for division between his widow SARAH and his brother THOMAS and his sister NANCY FINLEY and nieces and nephews, the children of his deceased brothers ROBERT and JOHN. Anyone interested in this family should check that case in Union Co. Equity records.)

Pp 100-102: In the name of God, Amen. WILLIAM BLACKSTOCK of Union Co., being of sound and disposing mind, memory and understanding publish this my LW&T this 19 Sept. 1788. Debts and funeral expenses to be paid.

To my beloved wife EUPHEMY and her heirs and assigns forever my new feather bed, one spoted (sic) coverlet, one blanket and 2 sheets belonging to the same, her wearing apparel, my young dark bay Pacing Mare, also all the cows my wife fetched me with their increase, the third part of this year's crop raised on my plantation, sheep, geese, all her yard and wool in the house, half my hogs, her side saddle and flax wheel, all kitchen furniture, 4 pewter and 3 earthen plates, all my spoons, knives and forks, 2 tin cups, one bread bowl, my New Testament, leather for 4 pairs of shoes, the dryed peaches and salt, the bolster of feathers, the straw baskets, 4 chairs, 5 quart bottles, the weaving loom and harness belonging to the same, my Barshear plow, 2 hoes, smoothing iron, and 2 axes, all the use of the plantation until May next.

To my daughter MARGRET BEARD my old feather bed with the pillow bolster and two blankets, one cow and calf, my big Pott, my bald horse, leather for 4 pairs of shoes.

To my daughter MARY BERD, the bed and cow and calf which I lent her, also one other cow and calf, 2 blankets, and my chest.

To my son WILLIAM 1 cow and calf, my Rifle gun, and 30 pounds sterling in good trade which my son JAMES must pay him out of the value of my plantation.

To my grandson JOHN BLACKSTOCK my big heifer and little ewe, my Silver Buckles, my Dutch plow, 1 pair pincers and his axe.

To my grand daughter RUTH BLACKSTOCK my yearling heifer.

To my son JAMES all the residue of my personal estate, also my plantation on which I now live and out of which he is to pay my Funeral charges and Just Debts, and also pay son WILLIAM 30 pds sterling in good trade above mentioned.
Son JAMES to be executor. Revoked all former wills.

Wits: WILLIAM CLAYTON
      THOMAS WHITE   /s/ WM. (D) BLACKSTOCK (LS)
      SAMUEL BELL

January Term 2 day 1799. The above will was proven in Open Court by

Cont'd:
oath of SAMUEL BELL and ordered to be recorded.

JAMES BLACKSTOCK appointed executor, came into Open Court and qualified
according to Law.
        (Note: The items devised in the above will give a good idea of
how out ancestors lived and the things that were important to them.
The Revolutionary Battle of Blackstocks wass fought on WILLIAM BLACK-
STOCK's farm in the western part of Union County.)

Pp 102-105: April Intermediate Court 1 day 1799.

Proved in Open Court the LW&T of JAMES BANKHEAD, late of this county,
deceased, by oath of JOHN RED and ordered to be recorded.

JAMES BANKHEAD of Union County, being weak and sick....

To my beloved wife ELIZABETH one half the plantation whereon I now
live known by MORES plantation, the Town lots excepted, also 4 lots
in Pickneyville, two of them on the northwest side of Trade St., and
near the Court House, the other two on Broad St. between the Court
House and Pacolet River opposite the public buildings.

To my beloved sons HUGH and JOHN BANKHEAD my old plantation on Broad
River now in their possession.

To my beloved son ROBERT BANKHEAD $20 in cash as I have paid him his
portion.

To my beloved son GEORGE BANKHEAD the remaining half of said Mores
Plantation whereon I live with the other half after the death of my
wife with the house and lot in Pinckney ville and 2 lots between the
said House and ARTHUR ROSSES (ROSS's).

To my daughter NANCY PLAXCO $5 cash her portion being paid.

To my beloved PATSY BANKHEAD (no relationship stated), the bay Horse
I bought of ARMSTRONG and side saddle, 1 bed and furniture, 1 cow and
calf.

To my beloved daughter BETSY BANKHEAD 1 horse and side saddle of value
of $60, to be paid at age or marriage.

To my beloved daughter MARY (same items as above)
To my beloved daughter JENNEY (same items as above)

The rest of my lotts (sic) in Pinckneyville to be disposed of at the
discretion of my executors as an addition to the Legacy of my daughters
BETSY, POLLY and JENNY.
Balance of personal estate for use of raising my youngest children.
I appoint my beloved wife executrix and my brother JOHN BANKHEAD and
my son GEORGE BANKHEAD executors. Dated 2 Feb. 1798.

Wits; JOHN REED
        HENRY KYLE   JAMES BANKHEAD (LS)
        JAMES KYLE
ELIZABETH BANKHEAD and JOHN BANKHEAD, appointed executors, came into
open court and took the oath according to Law.
        (Note: The extinct town of Pinckneyville was located on JAMES
BANKHEAD's farm in the northeast section of Union Co. It was the court
town for Pinckney District which covered Union, Spartanburg, Chester,
York and present-day Cherokee Co's. The BANKHEAD family migrated to
South Carolina from Maryland.)

Pp 105-106: April Intermediate Court 1st day 1799.

Proved in open court the LW&T of JAMES WOODSON, JR. late of this county,
deceased, by oaths of WILLIAM ROUNTREE and SAMPSON GOODWIN.

In the name of God, Amen - JAMES WOODSON, JUNIOR of Union Co. in a low state of health...

To my son GOODWIN WOODSON $100 cash.
To my daughters ELIZABETH WOODSON and NANCY WOODSON 1 feather bed, $25, and 1 cow and calf to each of them.
To my beloved wife ANNEY WOODSON 180 acres of land and residue of estate.

Wife ANNEY WOODSON to dispose of land at her death as she sees fit, balance of estate then to be divided equally among surviving children.

ANNEY WOODSON and THOMAS WOODSON to be executors. Dated 17 Jan. 1799.
Wits: WOODSON ROUNTREE
      JAMES WHITLOCK   JAMES WOODSON (seal)
      WILLIAM ROUNTREE
      SAMSON GOODWIN

THOMAS WOODSON, appointed executor, came into open court and took the oath according to Law.

Pp 106-108: April Intermediate Court first day 1799.

Proved in Open Court the LW&T of WILLIAM McJUNKIN, late of this county, deceased, by the oaths of ROBT. BEVEL, WM. HOLLINGSWORTH and THOS. VANCE and ordered to be recorded.

In the name of God, Amen - WILLIAM McJUNKIN, of Union Co., Pinckney District, being very sick and weak of Body...

To my beloved wife MARY one-third of movable estate and her living on the plantation while she remains a widow.

To my daughter NANCY - the Bay Mare colt.
To my son AQUILA HOLLINGSWORTH - one-half the land I now live on with one-half the tract down by NELSON's Mill with the Bay Mare. The other half to my son LANDLOT. The Grey mare and young horse to be kept to work the plantation and to help raise the family. Then the balance of the estate to be equally divided amongst all my children.

THOMAS VANCE and beloved wife to be executors. Dated 25 Jan. 1799.

Wits: ROBERT BEVEL
      WM. HOLLINGSWORTH   /s/ WM. McJUNKIN (seal)
      THOS. VANCE

THOMAS VANCE and MARY McJUNKIN, appointed executors, came into open court and took the oath.

Pp 108-110: In the name of God, Amen - RENNEY BELUE of Union Co., planter, being very sick and weak at present....

Enough property to be sold to pay debts and funeral expenses. Remainder of Estate, either Real or Personal, to my well beloved wife KEZIAH BELUE for her natural life for support and bringing up of my children. At her death remainder of estate to be divided equally between my children, namely: SARAH, ISABELL, LYDIA, GEORGE, ELIZABETH, REBECCA, ISAAC, JOSEPH and JONATHAN BELUE. If wife should have a child heir of my body, the same to have an equal share with the Brothers and Sisters above mentioned.

If wife should marry, all children under age to be put out to such convenient places as executors think best for the good of the children, and my said wife to have her bed and furniture and my Brown mare, and remainder of estate both real and personal, to be sold and the money used for the benefit of my children, equally divided amongst them as they come to the age of 21 years or marry.

My wife and my brother REUBEN BELUE to be executors. Revoked all former wills. Dated 29 October 1798.
(cont'd next page)

Cont'd:
Wits: JESSE LILES
      DANIEL CARRELL   /s/ RENNEY BELUE (LS)
      ZACHARIAH BELUE

KEZIAH BELUE and REUBEN BELUE, appointed executors, came into open
court and were qualified.

Pp 110-112: June Term 1799. 1st day.

Proven in open court by oaths of BRITTAN WILLIFORD and ISAAC WOFFORD
the LW&T of THOMAS HASELWOOD, late of this county, deceased, and ordered
to be recorded.

In the name of God, Amen - THOMAS HASELWOOD of Union County, weak in
body....

To my daughter PATTY BROWNING 1/4 of a dollar.
To my son LANCASTER HASELWOOD all my land except the house and planta-
tion where I now live which I give to my daughter MARY HASELWOOD.
To my daughter MARY HASELWOOD 1 feather bed and furniture.
To my daughter NANCY HASELWOOD 1 feather bed and furniture.
To my daughter SELAH HASELWOOD 1 feather bed and furniture.
To my daughter BETSEY HASELWOOD 1 feather bed and furniture.
To my daughter LUCY HASELWOOD 1 feather bed and furniture.

Rest of personal estate I lend to my wife during her natural life or
widowhood, and after her death or marriage to be equally divided among
my children, that is to say LANCASTER, MARY, SELAH, BETSEY, LUCY HASEL-
WOOD. My friends DAVID GOLIGHTLY and WILLIAM LANCASTER, JR. to be executors. Dated 13 Mar. 1799.

Wits: BRITTAN WILLIFORD
      ISAAC WOFFORD   /s/ THOMAS HASELWOOD (LS)
      SELAH WILLIAMS

Letters of Administration with above will annexed granted to MARY HASEL-
WOOD and LANCASTER HASELWOOD who gave bond for $1000 with JOHN LANCAS-
TER and MARK JACKSON securities.

Page 112: September Intermediate Court 1799.

Proved in open court the LW&T of JOSEPH HUGHES late of this county,
deceased, by oath of Col. JOSEPH HUGHES and ordered to be recorded.

21 July 1799. The desire of JOSEPH HUGHES on his death bed desired
that his brother THOMAS HUGHES should have his land which lies joining
said THOMAS. "My sister MARY" to have choice of his creatures and the
other creatures to be left to POLLY FLOYD. Remainder that is coming
to me from my Father's estate to be equally divided amongst the whole
of my brothers and sisters. Signed and delivered as my LW&T.

Wits: JOSHUA PALMERE
      JOS. HUGHES   /s/ JOS. (+) HUGHES
      WM. PAGE
Letters of administration with above will annexed granted to THOMAS
HUGHES who gave bond for $500 with JOSEPH HUGHES security and took
the oath prescribed by Law.

Pp 113-114: September Intermediate Court 1st day, 1799.

Proved in open court the LW&T of DANIEL NOHOR, deceased, late of this
county by oaths of JAMES JOHNSON and ROBERT McWRIGHT and ordered to
be recorded.

In the Name of God, Amen - DANIEL NOHOR of Union Co., (shoemaker)
very sick and weak in body..To be buried in decent Christian manner
at discretion of executors.

To JAMES NORHOR AND WILLIAM NORHOR 200 acres joining JAMES SAVAGE and

Cont'd:
ROBERT EADES to be divided equally by two honest men by paying JOHN
NORHOR 5 pds each when they come of age. Remainder of land to my wife
and family to (till?) my son JOSEPH NORHOR comes of age and then I
give it to him by paying JOHN NORHOR 5 pds.

To JAMES NORHOR the small bay mare at paying 4 pds to the estate at
delivery. The cow and yearling that I gave JOHN NORHOR I give him still.

Rest of personal property to be valued by three men and divided between my wife MARY NORHOR and ELIZABETH NORHOR and PEGGY NORHOR my
daughters, each of them equal share when they come of age. My wife
MARY NORHOR to have her share during her life or widowhood and my son
JOSEPH NORHOR to have it at the expiration of that time.

JOHN NORHOR, JAMES NORHOR and WILLIAM McWRIGHT to be executors. Revoked
all former wills. Dated 20 June 1799.

Wits: BENJAMIN WOODSON
      JAMES JOHNSON   /s/ DANIEL NOGHER (LS)
      ROBERT McCRIGHT

JOHN NOGHOR, JAMES NOGHOR and WILLIAM McCREIGHT, appointed executors,
came into open court and took the oath prescribed by law.

Pp 115-117: In the name of God, Amen...JOHN COLE of Union Co., enjoying
a small measure of health tho infirm in body, makes his LW&T.

To my son RICHARD COLE 150 acres, part of a 200 acre tract purchased
by me from JOHN WEINMAN, refers to original grant and deeds of conveyance, located on E side of the ready branch, to take in the improvement
made by sd RICHARD COLE, mentions folly branch.

To my daughter LUCY BAILEY 50 acres, the remaining part of the tract
above.

To my beloved wife MARY my lands, 2 negroes David and Judith, livestock, plantation tools, furniture, etc., for her support for life
or widowhood and at her marriage or death what remains to be sold and
the money equally divided to my children RICHARD, JOHN, ELIZABETH CAN-
NON, NANCY BAILEY, LUCY BAILEY and PHEBE YERBEY.

Wife MARY to be executrix and son RICHARD COLE executor. Revoked all
former wills. Dated 8 April 1799.

Wits; JAMES FOWLER
      JOSEPH WALKER   /s/ JOHN COLE (LS)
      SARAH (X) BAILEY

Proved 2 Sept. 1799 by JAMES FOWLER. MARY COLE and RICHARD COLE appointed executrix and executor, came into open court and took the oath prescribed by Law.

Page 117: Came THOS. RAY and ELIZABETH RAY and on their oaths say that
AMBROSE RAY on his death bed told them he had given to his son HOSEA
RAY 1/2 of his still and worm and cap, being the part be bought of
SAMUEL SIMSON in his lifetime - and always understood it was so from
the time HOSEA RAY begun to still with the still. And further says
not. Sworn to 2 July 1799. Signed by THOS. RAY and ELIZABETH (X) RAY
before THOS. BRANDON, J.U.S.

Pp 117-119: At a court of ordinary met on Monday, 28 Oct. 1799. Present
WM. KENNEDY and ANDREW TORRANCE, Judges. LW&T of JOSHUA BEUFORD, deceased, proved by oath of JOHN R. BEUFORD and ordered to be recorded.

In the Name of God, Amen - JOSHUA BEUFORD of Union Co., sensible of
the uncertainty and transient nature of this life....to my beloved
wife REBECCAH BEUFORD negro girl named Lucy, livestock, 1 bed and chest
and every other article which came with her as her portion from her

480

Cont'd:
parents, the whole of which to be hers and her heirs forever. Rest
of my estate to my two children ABRAM and ANNE, to remain in the hands
of my Father LEROY BEUFORD to be managed, occupied and disposed of
for the use of my said children. Father LEROY BEUFORD to be executor
and to act and transact for my children until they are legally capable
of transacting for themselves. Dated 15 Sept. 1799.

Wits: WM. WmSON (WILLIAMSON?)
      JOHN R. BEUFORD   JOSHUA BEUFORD (seal)

LEROY BEUFORD, appointed executor, refused to qualify. Ordered that
the goods and chattels and effects of the sd deceased be granted to
REBECCA BUFORD, wife of the sd JOSHUA BEUFORD, dec'd., and General
THOMAS BRANDON with the will annexed. Came REBECAH BUFORD into open
court and took the oaths required by Law and also gave bond of $2000
with Maj. SAMUEL OTTERSON and JOSIAH DARBY security. Recorded 28 Oct.
1799.

Pp 119-120: Court of Ordinary met on Sat. 16 Nov. 1799. Present - Judges
KENNEDY and TORRANCE.

LW&T of JOHN JASPER, late of this county, deceased, proved by oath
of JOHN FOSTER and ordered to be recorded.

29 Sept. 1799 - LW&T of JOHN JASPER, in a low State of Health. To my
beloved wife all Real Estate, goods and chattels, for her maintenance
during life or widowhood, no property to be made way with but such
as is necessary for her support, then to be divided equally among my
children now living, to wit, NICHOLAS, JOHN, RACHEL, ANNA, HANNAH and
CHARITY. To those of my children which are dead to them and their heirs
5 shillings. Son JOHN JASPER and son-in-law BENJAMIN COVENHOVEN to
be executors. Dated 29 Sept. 1799.

Wits: JOHN FOSTER
      BENJAMIN COVENHOVEN   /s/ JOHN (+) JASPER (seal)

JOHN JASPER and BENJAMIN COVENHOVEN appointed executors took the oath
prescribed by Law. Recorded 10 Nov. 1799.

The next page in the book is not numbered and contains the notation
"Record of Wills Probated before THOMAS BRANDON, Ordinary." Page numbers
start over with page no. 1.

Page 1: 1 April 1800 - LW&T of BENJAMIN WOODSON, deceased, proved by
the oath of JOHN MCDONALD and ordered to be recorded. In the name of
God Amen...BENJAMIN WOODSON of Union Co., weak in body...to my beloved
wife MARTHEW WOODSON eleven negroes, namely, Ben, Peter, Sal, Sam,
Hanno, Essie, Jacob, Esaw, Phillis, Jo and Jude; also all livestock,
furniture, tools, etc.

To my eldest brother's son - TALTON WOODSON $2.
To my brother - JAMES WOODSON $2.
To JOHN HUGHES, brother to my beloved wife MARTHEW WOODSON, all my
land, 200 acres in Union Co., to him and his heirs forever, but to
remain in possession of wife MARTHEW until her death.

Wife MARTHEW to be executrix with her brother THOMAS HUGHES. Revoked
all former wills. Dated 4 Nov. 1799.

Wits: THOMAS HUGHES
      WM. HUGHES   BENJAMIN WOODSON (LS)
      JNO. MACDONALD
MARTHA WOODSON and THOMAS HUGHES were qualified as executrix and executor. Recorded 19 Dec. 1800.

Pp 1-3: 31 March 1800. LW&T of ROBERT WALLACE, deceased, was proved
in the Ordinaries (sic) office by the oath of ANDREW TORRANCE, Esq.,
in order to be recorded.
      In the name of God, Amen..ROBERT WALLACE of Union Co., calling

481

Cont'd:
to mind the uncertainty of this life...To my son WILLIAM all my lands
in Union Co., also seven negroes, Harry, Long-Jude, old Judi (June?),
Sam, Millbry, Winn, Lowdin.

To my stepson JOHN PARHAM all my right, title and interest to a certain
tract of land on Cape Fear river in Chatham Co., N. C., which land
was granted by RICHARD CASWELL then Gov. of N. C. in 1780, sd land
adjoining lands now held by sd JOHN PARHAM in right of his Father JOHN
PARHAM, deceased; also I give to sd JOHN PARHAM a bay mare known as
the Hammar.

To my daughter MARTHA, 6 negroes, Sambo, Phebe, Phill, Sockey, Rose
and Peter.

To my daughter ELIZABETH 7 negroes, Will, Tom, Suke, James, Ellock,
Philis and Dembo.

To POLLY PINNELL only daughter of TABITHA PINNELL, 2 negroes, Young
Sambo and Myry (Mary?), to her and her lawful heirs begotten of her
own body, but in case she should die without such lawful issue the
afsd Sambo and Myry and their increase shall be equally divided between
my three children, WILLIAM, MARTHA and ELIZABETH or their heirs. Also
I give to sd POLLY PINNELL as her property without any restriction
a good feather bed and furniture and 10 pds sterling in cash, the cash
to be put out at interest or used for the benefit of the sd POLLY PIN-
NELL at the discretion of her mother TABITHA PINNELL.

All my lands lying in Granville and More (sic-Moore) Counties in N.
C. to be sold as soon as my daughter ELIZABETH reaches age 18 or marries
and the money to be equally divided between my 3 children WILLIAM,
MARTHA and ELIZABETH or their heirs, but in case my daughter ELIZABETH
should die before she marries or arrives at age 18, the lands to be
sold as soon as daughter MARTHA shall be of age 20 and not sooner and
to be equally divided between the 2 surviving children.

Household furniture to be as equally divided between my children WILLIAM
& MARTHA & ELIZABETH as can be done without selling the same. Residue
of the personal estate to be sold and money and debts due me to be
equally divided between my children WILLIAM, MARTHA & ELIZABETH, or
their heirs after paying debts due from me and paying what other gifts
or legacies I may have given.

My friends FRANCIS DRAKE and GEORGE HARLIN of Union Co., my son WILLIAM
WALLACE and WILLIAM DRAKE of Chatham Co., N. C., to be executors. (Date
of will left blank.)

Wits: SARAH DARBY
      WM. DARBY
      ANDW. TORRANCE   ROBT. WALLACE (LS)
      JAMES DARBY
WILLIAM WALLACE and GEORGE HARLIN duly qualified as executors. Recorded
19 Dec. 1800.

Page 3: 1 Apr. 1800. LW&T of EPHRAIM PUCKETT proved by oath of MARK
FOWLER and ordered to be recorded.

EPHRAM PUCKETT of Union Co., porely in body...
To my daughter CATHREN FOWLER 5 shillings sterling.
To my son EPHRAM PUCKETT and his heirs 5 shillings sterling.
To my daughter MARY BERY or her heirs 5 shillings sterling.
To my daughter HANNAH HANEY 5 shillings sterling.
To my beloved wife HANNA PUCKIT all my land and all personal property
that I now possess to dispose of according to her will and pleasure.

Trusty friends JEREMIAH LUCAS and ELES (sic-ELLIS) FOWLER to be executors. Dated 11 Apr. 1799.
Wits: WM. FOWLER
      ZACHARIAH (X) MABRY   EPHRIM (X) PUCKET (LS)
      MARK FOWLER

ELIS FOWLER was duly qualified as executor. Recorded 19 Dec. 1800.

Page 4: 31 March 1800. LW&T of CHARLES THOMPSON, proved by the oath of WILLIAM McCULLOCK, Esq., in order to be recorded.

In the Name of God Amen. CHARLES THOMPSON of Union Co. do this 23 Feb. 1795 make and publish my LW&T. I lend unto my beloved wife ELIZABETH during her widowhood all my estate real and personal. In case my wife ELIZABETH do marry, the personal estate to be equally divided amongst my wife ELIZABETH and my children that is now living with me. Each to have an equal part without having the personal estate sold.

To my daughter SUSANNAH to be paid at my decease 10 pds in property out of my personal estate.
At death or marriage of wife ELIZABETH all my lands to be equally divided between my three sons, namely, WILLIAM, JOHN and CHARLES, to them, their heirs and assigns forever.

Wife ELIZABETH to be executrix and son WILLIAM executor.
Wits: WM. McCULLOCK
      GEORGE PETTY   CHARLES (X) THOMPSON
      JOHN DUNBROW(?)
Recorded 19 Dec. 1800.

Pp 5-6: 16 Aug. 1800. LW&T of NATHANIEL DABBS proved by oath of TIMOTHY HAINEY in order to be recorded.
      In the name of God Amen...NATHANIEL DABBS of Union Co., planter, being very weak and sick...To my beloved wife ELIZABETH my land and plantation whereon I now live with 2 work mares, working tools, 3 cows and calves, hogs, one bell, furniture and kitchen equipment for her use and supplies during her natural life and after her decease, to be equally divided between my three youngest children, SAMUEL, JAMES and NANCEY.

To my beloved son JOHN DABBS a negro boy named Will. I lend to my beloved wife one negro girl named Lucy for her natural life and after her decease, she (Lucy) and her increase also to be divided equally between the above named 3 youngest children.
To my beloved son JOSIAH DABBS $100 in bonds and notes that is due my estate.
To my beloved son WILLIAM DABBS negro boy Frank.
To my beloved son NATHANIEL DABBS negro woman Fillis.
To my beloved son RICHARD DABBS $100 in notes and bonds due my estate with 2 cows and calves.
To my beloved son JESSE DABBS negro boy Harey.
To my beloved son ROBERT DABBS negro boy Abram.
To my beloved daughter MARY STRANGE negro girl Grace.
To my beloved son SAMUEL DABBS and JAMES DABBS my land and plantation whereon I now live after my wife's decease, one horse named Darby to JAMES and one colt that has but one eye to SAMUEL. The land to be divided equally according to quantity and quality. To my beloved daughter NANCEY DABBS negro girl Ann, 1 bed and furniture, 1 Bay filley and a good woman's saddle.

Wife ELIZABETH to be executrix and sons JESSE, NATHANIEL and WILLIAM DABBS to be executors. Revoked all other wills. Dated 16 Apr. 1800.
Wits: NANCEY (X) FOSTER
      TIMOTHY HANEY   NATHANIEL DABBS (LS)
      JOHN REED
ELIZABETH DABBS, JESSE DABBS, NATHANIEL DABBS and WILLIAM DABBS qualified as executrix and executors. Recorded 20 Dec. 1800 by JAS. WOODSON, Clerk for THOS. BRANDON, Ordinary.

Page 6: 11 Dec. 1800. LW&T of DANIEL McBRIDE was proved in the Ordinary's Office by oath of WILLIAM THOMSON and RICHARD THOMSON in order to be recorded.
      In the Name of God Amen...I, DANIEL McBRIDE of Union Dist., S. C. being weak of body...Debts and funeral expenses to be paid.
The plantation or tract of land on which I now live to be equally divided among three of my sons, viz, ISAAC, EPHRAIM and JOHN, ISAAC to

Cont'd:
have his part laid off joining the Tract he now owns, JOHN's to include
the new house, EPHRAIM to have the lower end.

My son HUGH, my son-in-law JAMES McMULLIN and my son-in-law ANDREW
THOMSON each to them to have one ginney.

My wearing apparel to be divided among my three sons, viz, ISAAC, EPH-
RAIM and JOHN. Remainder of movables to be sold and equally divided
among my five sons, viz, DANIEL, JAMES, ISAAC, EPHRAIM and JOHN.
My son ISAAC and RICHARD THOMSON to be executors. Dated 21 Nov. 1800.
Wits: JAMES McCORMACK
      WILLIAM THOMSON   DANIEL McBRIDE (LS)
      RICHD. THOMSON
ISAAC McBRIDE and RICHD. THOMSON duly qualified as executors. Recorded
20 Dec. 1800 by JAS. WOODSON, clerk for THOS. BRANDON, Ordinary.

END OF BOOK

UNION COUNTY, S. C. - DEED BOOK A

     The first settlers arrived in Union Co. around 1750. When the
Province of S. C. was divided into 7 Districts in 1768, Union was included in 96 District. In 1785 Old 96 District was divided into 6 counties, Abbeville, Edgefield, Newberry, Laurens, Spartanburg and Union.
County Court for Union Co. has been held in Unionville (now Union)
continuously since 1785 until the present. District courts were established in 1791, and Pinckneyville in upper Union Co. was named the
site of the Dist. Ct. House for Union, Spartanburg for Chester Co.
and most of York Co. Pinckneyville no longer exists, having been leg-
islated out of existence when the Court Districts were changed in 1798,
and courts were set up in each county. The Equity Court records that
pertained to Union Co. were moved from Pinckneyville to Union in 1799.
Evidently when the county court was established in 1785, people brought
in much earlier deeds to be recorded, and these were put on record
with no date at all, or in some instances, as you will notice, many
were recorded on one day (March 27, 1786). The changeover of the mone-
tary system of the State from pounds to dollars was accomplished in
1795. As you will notice, many of the tracts of land were N. C. grants.
The line between the two states was not completed until 1775, and there
was much confusion among the border counties. Some of the grants were
actually declared illegal, it is understood. The two states argued
over the boundry for many years, but finally settled their differences
in 1775 when the boundry was extended to the Georgia line. The deed
on pp 55-58 explains this very well, that is why so much of it was
copied.
     The upper portion of the County above Pacolet River was cut off
to make part of what is now Cherokee County. Therefore, all of these
deeds that refer to the area north of Pacolet River, which includes
Thicketty Creek and Gilkey's Creek, are in what is now Cherokee Co.
The exact date of this is unknown by the writer but it was on up in
the 1800's, after 1854, since an 1854 may show that area as still
part of Union County.

Pp 1-3:   2-12-1778, JOHN M. McWHORTER, planter, of 96 Dist., S.
     C., to JOHN GEORGE of 96 Dist., S. C., grant of 10-30-1765 by
Wm. Tryon, Lt. Gov. of N. C. to JOHN PORTMAN, 200 acres, which land
JOHN PORTMAN conveyed to JOHN McWHORTER on 9-20-1773, lying on both
sides of "Packolate" River. JOHN McWHORTER conveys to JOHN GEORGE only
the 83 acs. lying on the north side of sd river, for 300 pds current
money. Wit: ADAM POTTER, NICHOLAS JASPER, JOHN PORTMAN, SR. No recording date.

Pp 4-6:   9-15-1785, WM. EDMONDSON, planter, of Union Co., S. C.
     to SAMUEL TORBERT of same co. and state, 200 acs. on Brushy Crk.,
"the south side of Saludy", bounded on all sides by vacant lands when
granted. Tract granted by Benjamin Guerrard, Gov. of S. C. on 10-15-
1784, recorded in Secretary's office in Book AAAA, p. 125. Sold for

484

the sum of 50 pds current money. Wit: BENJN. LONG, WM. HENDLEY, JOSHUA PALMER. No recording date.

Pp 7-8:   12-2-1785, FRANCES McNAMAR of Rutherford Co., N. C. to
        CHARLES CLANTON of Union Co., S. C. for 100 pds sterling, 300 acs. "on the ridge between Tickety and Gilkie's Creeks," now in the actual possession of the sd CHARLES CLANTON, bound by JOSEPH COLLINS, MOSES COLLINS, EDMOND KENNEDY, WILLIAM JOLLY, CHARLES THOMPSON and JAMES MARTIN. Wit: JOHN EWART, ABSOM (ABSOLAM) PETTY, HANNAH McNAMAR. No recording date.

Pp 9-10:   6-2-1774, ROBERT LUNY OF "County Craven", Province of
        S. C., in 96 Dist., to GEORGE MARCHBANKS of same place, a tract of land granted to ADAM LOONY, father of ROBERT LOONY, who died intestate, by the Gov. of N. C., whereon GEORGE MARCHBANKS now lives. Wit: JOHN NUCKOLS, WM. MARCHBANKS. No recording date.

Pp 10-12:   4-8-1785, SAMUEL FARROW of 96 Dist., S. C. to WILLIAM
        BUCHANAN, same dist. and state, for 21 pds 8 shillings sterling, 150 acs. on a small branch of Broad River called Brown's Creek, being the north end of a tract of 450 acs. orig. granted to JOHN ELDER by patent dated Aug. 14, 1775, Secretary's office Book YYY, p. 450, and also recorded in Audts. Office, Book M, no. 15, p. 30, 11-20- 1775. Conveyed to SAMUEL FARROW by JOHN ELDER. Bound by WM. WILLIAMS, DANIEL HUGER's land, and THOS. STRIBLING. Wit: ALEX. McDOUGALL, THOS. STRIBLING. No recording date.

Page 13:   7-6-1785, WILSON ROGERS of 96 Dist., S. C. to JOHN THOMP-
        SON, JR. of Thicketty Creek, same state and dist., for 100 pds sterling, 100 acs. on west side of Broad River on a branch of Thicketty, known as STEPHEN JONES' branch, part of a grant of 243 acs. to sd WILSON ROGERS by the state of S. C. on 5-2-1785. Wit: JOHN THOMPSON, JOHN WOODS. Recorded 12-28-1786.

Pp 14-16:   8-30-1785, JOHN STEEN of Thicketty Creek, 96 Dist., S.C.,
        to FRANCIS LATIMORE, same dist. and state, for 500 pds sterling, 200 acs. on both sides of Thicketty Creek whereon sd FRANCIS LATIMORE now lives. Bound on north by DAVID STOCKTON. Wit: JOHN THOMPSON, MARY THOMPSON. No recording date.

Pp 17-18:   10-7-1785, WILLIAM HENDLEY and MARY, his wife, of Union
        Co., S. C. to JOHN REED, same state and co., for 30 pds sterling, part of a tract of land granted to sd WM. HENDLEY by the Gov. of the State afsd., on the west side of Broad River, adj. a tract granted orig. to HENRY CLARK and conveyed to JOHN FOSTER, and also a tract belonging to CUNNINGHAM, containing 48 acs. Wit: JOHN HANEY, EDWARD TILMAN, HENRY BAILEY. No recording date.

Page 19:   7-25-1778, DAVID GEORGE of 96 Dist., Province of S.C.,
        to WILLIAM WILLIAMS for 75 pds current money of S.C., a certain tract containing 600 acs. on the waters of Brown's Creek. Bound by STEPHEN MAYFIELD on one side. Wit: JNO. NUCKOLS, JAS. HARDWICK, WM. A. GEORGE. No recording date.

Pp 20-22:   5-12-1775, JOAB MITCHELL and MARY, his wife, of 96 Dist.,
        Prov. of S.C., to RICHARD HAWKINS, dist. and state afsd., for 250 pds current money of S.C., 300 acs. on Mill Creek, a branch of "Packolate" River, bound by ROBERT COLMAN on one side. Land granted to MITCHELL by Wm. Bull, Lt. Gov. of S.C. on 2-10-1775. Wit: CHRISTOPHER COLEMAN, ZACHA. BULLOCK, ISHM. SAFOLD. No recording date.

Pp 23-25:   12-8-1778, JAMES HARDWICK of 96 Dist., Prov. of S.C.,
        to FRANCIS POSSEY, same dist. and prov., for 175 pds current money, 100 acs. in Berkley Co., 96 Dist., on the south side of Broad River, on a branch called the Lower Fishdam, granted to ISAAC SIMONSON by Wm. Bull, Lt. Gov. of S.C. on 6-5-1770. Bound by lands granted to JOHN CLARK in a N. C. grant. Wit: DAVID GEORGE, REBECCA GEORGE, ABRAHAM GIBSON. No recording date.

Pp 26-27:   1-20-1775, ISAAC SIMONSON of 96 Dist., S.C. to JAMES

485

HARDWICK, same dist. and state, for 175 pds current money, same tract of 100 acs. described in preceding deed. Wit: DAVID GEORGE, THOMAS SHOCKLEY, JOHN DICKERSON. No recording date.

Pp 28-29:   4-9-1785, SAMUEL FARROW, planter, of 96 Dist., S.C. to THOMAS STRIBLING, 96 Dist., S.C. for 64 pds 14 shillings and 3 pence sterling, 300 acs. on branch of Broad River called Brown's Creek, orig. granted to JOHN ELDER on 8-14-1775, recorded in Sec.'s Office, Book YYY, p. 454. Wit: WM. BUCHANAN, ALEXR. McDOUGAL. No recording date.

Pp 30-32:   8-23-1785, FRANCIS POSSEY, 96 Dist., S.C. to CALEB GASSAWAY, 96 Dist., for 175 pds current money, 100 acs. on south side of Broad River, lower Fish Dam Creek, sd land granted to ISAAC SIMONSON by Wm. Bull, Lt. Gov. of S.C. on 6-5-1770. Bound by lands granted to JOHN CLARK by a North Carolina grant. Wit: WM. FARR, BENJ. HOLLINGSWORTH. No recording date.

Pp 33-34:   6-9-1785, CALEB GASSAWAY, NANCY GASSAWAY, his wife, Executrix of WILLIAM MOORE, deceased, and SUSANNAH MOORE, of 96 Dist., S.C. to BENJAMIN JOHNSON, same state and dist., for 2000 pds sterling, a tract containing 400 acs. on south side of Broad River, part of a larger tract of 1000 acs. granted by N. C. patent to JOHN CLARK on 9-3-1753. Wit: WM. FARR, CHARLES JOHNSON, MARY TAYLOR, JOSIAS WOOD. Signed by CALEB GASSAWAY, ANN GASSAWAY, SUSANNAH MOORE. No recording date.

Page 35:   11-6-1785, JOSEPH FRANKLING and MARY, his wife, of S.C., Union Co., to JAMES BEUFORD, same place, for 108 pds 6 shillings and 8 pence sterling, 75 acs. on Tiger River, granted to DAVID HOPKINS on 7-3-1775 by Charles G. Montague, Gov. of S.C. bound by THOMAS BIDDIE, MR. DUFF, Tiger River and land where JAMES BEUFORD now liveth. Wit: DAVID GEORGE, TAVERNOR-BIRD BEUFORD, JOSEPH TUCKER, ROBERT CRENSHAW. Receipt for money signed by MARYANN FRANKLIN & JOSEPH FRANKLIN. No recording date.

Pp 36-37:   1-26-1785, WILLIAM BRYON of 96 Dist., S.C. to JONATHAN PENALL, same place, 84 acs. part of 100 ac. tract granted to MARGARET McDOWELL on 9-12-1768 by Wm. Bull, Gov. of S. C. on Sugar Creek and Fairforest Creek, conveyed by MARGARET McDOWELL to PHILIP BRYON and inherited by WM. BRYON, for 20 pds sterling. The other 16 acs. sold to JOHN LITTLE to be laid off next to JOHN LITTLE's plantation. Wit: JAMES WOODSON, SR., SAMSON GOODWIN, JAMES WOODSON, JR. No recording date.

Page 38:   3-28-1786, JOHN STEEN and MARTHA STEEN, his wife, Union Co., S.C. to CHARLES MILLS, same place, for 400 pds sterling, 800 acs. on Thicketty Creek, granted by Mathew Rowan, President of N.C. on 9-3-1753. Bounded by granted lands. Wit: JAS. MARTIN, WM. GASTON & ROBERT LUSK. Rec. 3-29-1786.

Pp 39-40:   3-28-1786, ROBERT MONTGOMERY of Union Co., SC to JAMES MARTIN of same place, for 100 pds sterling, tract of land in Spartanburg Co., SC on Beaver Dam waters of Thicketty Creek, 213 acs. granted to ROBERT MONTGOMERY on 3-5-1786. Wit: WM. GASTON, ROBERT LUSK & THOROWGOOD CHAMBERS. Rec. 3-29-1786.

Pp 41-43:   3-26-1786, ADAM GOUDYLOCK, planter, and HANNAH, his wife, of 96 Dist., SC to Major CHARLES MILES and Co., Merchants, of 96 Dist., SC for 300 pds sterling, 300 acs. (except for a graveyard) bet. Packolate River and Thicketty Creek, granted to ADAM GOUDYLOCK on 12-6-1771 by Gov. of N. C. Wit: JAMES MARTIN, JOHN STEEN, DAVIS GOUDYLOCK. Rec. 3-29-1786.

Pp 44-47:   3-27-1786, ADAM GOUDYLOCK and HANNAH, his wife, of Union Co., 96 Dist., SC to ROBERT LUSK, same place, for 50 pds and 150 pds sterling, 200 acs. on the second Reedy branch of Thicketty Creek, granted to GOUDYLOCK on 12-24-1770 by Wm. Tryon, Gov. of NC. Wit: JAS. MARTIN, JOHN STEEN, CHAS. MILES. Rec. 3-29-1786.

Pp 48-51: 11-19-1785, EDWARD KENNADAY, late of 96 Dist., SC to
ROBERT LUSK, same place, for 650 pds old S.C. currency, 2 adj.
tracts containing 200 acs. on Thicketty Creek. Bound by FANING, JOS.
JOLLEY, JOHN JONES. Wit: WILLIAM COTTER, JOSEPH JOLLY, JOHN LUSK. No
rec. date. (EDMOND KENNADAY signed deed, may have moved from district.)

Pp 51-52: 7-13-1785, RYDARUS CLARK of Gilkey's Creek, 96 Dist.,
SC to JOHN FOSTER, 96 Dist., SC for 100 pds sterling, 31 acs.
(Abees) on S side of Broad River. Wit: JOHN EWART, RALPH ROGERS, RICHARD
THOMPSON. No rec. date.

Pp 52-53: 4-19-1784, JAMES LOVE of Camden Dist., SC to RYDARUS
CLARK of Gilkey's Creek, 96 Dist., SC for 100 pds current money,
31 acs. (Abees) on s. side of Broad River. Wit: CLAYTON ROGERS, ALEXR.
TOMB, HEZEKIAH LOVE. Rec. 3-27-1786.

Page 54: 2-29-1777, GEORGE GOWAN of N.C., to JOHN FOSTER of 96
Dist., SC, for 200 pds current money, a certain tract on E side
of Broad River near Lafferty's Creek, granted to GEORGE GOWAN on 11-
9-1774. Wit: JOHN NUCKOLS, RICHD. NUCKOLS. No rec. date.

Pp 55-58: 9-2-1773, HENRY CLARK, gentleman, and SARAH CLARK, his
wife, of 96 Dist., SC to JOHN FOSTER, same place, gentleman,
for 750 pds current money, 180 acs. - a certain grant bearing date
the 26th Oct. 1767, and in the 8th year of his Majesty's Reign....under
the hand of his Excellency William Tryon, Capt. General Governor and
Commander in Chief in and over the Province of North Carolina and the
Great Seal of the Province for that purpose appointed did give and
grant unto HENRY CLARK a plantation or tract of land containing 180
acs. situate laying and being on the west side of Broad River then
deemed Mecklenburgh County in the Prov. of N. C. but since the Continuation of the Boundary line of the sd Provinces lately run pursuant
to his Majesty's Instructions is in Ninety Six District in the Province
of South Carolina. Bound by LOVE and the River. Wit: SIMEOCK CANNON,
REYDARUS CLARK, WILLIAM LAUGHLIN. Rec. 3-27-1786.

Pp 59-60: 3-2-1786, CHARLES CLANTON of Union Co., SC to ABSOLAM
PETTY, same place, for 36 pds sterling, 100 acs. on the ridge
bet. Thicketty Creek and Gilkies Creek, part of a grant to FRANCIS
McNAMAR in 1774. Bound by MARTIN. Wit: JOHN EWART, STEPHEN CLANTON,
LYDIA CLANTON. Rec. 3-27-1786.

Pp 60-61: 2-28-1784, ELIS PALMER and ANN, his wife, of 96 Dist.,
SC to JOHN WHITE, same place, for 200 pds current money, 150
acs. on Brown's Creek of waters of Broad River, granted to WILLIAM
AKERIDGE in 1774. Wit: WILLIAM WILLIAMS, JOHN WHITE, DANIEL WHITE.
Rec. 3-27-1786.

Pp 62-63: 1-27-1783, WILLIAM SMITH of 96 Dist., SC to JOHN FOSTER
of same place, for 500 pds current money, 200 acs. on Minkum's
Creek, where WILLIAM SMITH formerly lived. Wit: DENIS DEMASSY, JOHN
McWHORTER, GEORGE McWHORTER. Rec. 3-27-1786.

Pp 63-64: 1-2-1779, RYDARUS CLARK and ANNA, his wife, of Camden
Dist., SC to JOHN FOSTER, of 96 Dist., for 2000 pds current money,
200 acs. on west side of Broad River, granted to CLARK, joining the
lines of sd JOHN FOSTER & NEAL McHESWICK, and LOVE. Wit: CLAIBOURN
GOOCH, WILLIAM ROGERS, CHARLES GILHAM. Signature attested to on 5-
22-1785. No rec. date.

Pp 65-66:; 12-29-1785, WILSON JOLLY and MARY, his wife, of Union
Co., SC to MOSES MEEK, same place, for 100 pds sterling, all
their interest in 150 acs. on south side of Broad River on Thicketty
Creek on Decks Branch. Wit: JOHN EWART, JOHN HOPE, JOHN BIRD. No rec.
date.

Pp 66-67: 12-29-1785, JOSEPH JOLLY, SR. of 96 Dist., SC to JOHN
HOPE, of Union Co., for 50 pds sterling, 73 acs. on south side
of Thicketty Creek, joining lands of sd JOHN HOPE and HUGH TAYLOR.
Wit: JOHN EWART, MOSES MEEK, AGNESS MEEK. No rec. date.

Pp 67-70:   10-27-1785, JAMES FANNIN of Thicketty Creek, 96 Dist.,
      SC to CHARLES THOMPSON of Gilkies Creek, 96 Dist., SC for 325
pds good and lawful money, 200 acs. on Gilkie's Creek, part of a 400
ac. N. C. grant to WILLIAM SIMS and JAMES FANNING. Wit: JOHN EWART,
LITTLETON MAPP, WILLIAM THOMPSON, JOHN LOVE. Rec. 3-28-1786.

Pp 71-72:   2-19-1786, ROBERT LOONEY of Broad River, York Co., SC
      to JOHN JEFFERIES of Gilkie's Creek, Union Co., SC for 50 pds
sterling, 600 acs. on Gilkie's Creek, orig. granted by N. C. patent
to SAMUEL GILKIE, conveyed by GILKIE to ADAM BICKISON, then to DAVID
LOONEY, then to the sd ROBERT LOONEY. Wit: JOHN ROSS, NATHL. JEFFER-
IES, MORNING MITCHEL. Rec. 3-27-1786.

Pp 73-74:   5-12-1785, MOSES GYTON to JOHN LEEK, both of Union Co.,
      SC for 500 pds sterling, 100 acs. on Abbington's Creek, granted
by patent to JACOB GARDINER on 12-9-1771, conveyed by GARDINER to ROBERT
WHITLEY on 7-23-1772, by him to MOSES GYTON on 12-6-1784. Wit: JAMES
PETTY, WILLIAM MOORHEAD, JAMES KENNEDY. Rec. 3-27-1786.

Pp 74-76:   9-5-1785, ROBERT MONTGOMERY, planter, and ISABEL MONT-
      GOMERY, his wife, of 96 Dist. SC to THOMAS KENNEDY, farmer, same
place, for 50 pds lawful money of Virginia, 201 acs. on west side of
Broad River, part of a 400 ac. tract, N.C. patent to WILLAM LOVE on
9-3-1753, conveyed by JOHN LOVE, heir to sd WILLIAM LOVE, to HENRY
SMITH, and from Smith to WILLIAM McMILLIN, from him to NATHANIEL GUYTON.
Wit: JAMES KENNEDY, JOHN LINDSAY, RYDARUS CLARK. Rec. 3-28-1786.

Pp 76-77:   10-24-1785, JACOB GARDINER to ISAAC PARKER, both of 96
      Dist., SC for 100 pds sterling, a tract containing 90 acs. on
the west side of Broad Rvier, joining land laid out to JACOB GARDINER,
whereon the sd ISAAC PARKER now lives. Granted to GARDINER under Great
Seal of Great Britain on 4-22-1767. Exempted JOHN MOSES' Patent in
description. Wit: MOSES GUYTON, JOHN MOORHEAD, JAMES STEVENSON. Rec.
3-27-1786.

Pp 77-79:   12-6-1784, ROBERT WHITLEY of State of Va., Co. of Montgom-
      ery, cordwinder, to MOSES GUYTON, Craven Co., SC for 400 pds,
100 acs., granted to JACOB GARDNER by patent on 12-9-1771, conveyed
to ROBERT WHITLEY on 7-23-1772. Joining ROBERT WILSON's line. Wit:
MARGARET SCOTT & MARY SCOTT. Rec. 3-27-1786.

Pp 79-80:   12-13-1779, MICHAEL CRAWFORD of _____ion (unreadable)
      Co., North Carolina, to LAURENCE EASTERWOOD of 96 Dist., SC for
500 pds current money, 200 acs. on South side of Packolate River above
the place where ZACHARIAH BULLOCK now lives in S. C. Granted to DAVID
PARKS on 2-23-1754 and regranted to MICHAEL CRAWFORD in South Carolina
in April 1775. Wit: JOHN GRESHAM & MARTHA THOMPSON. Rec. 3-29-1786.

Pp 80-82:   12-17-1785, JAMES TERRELL of Union Co., SC to MOSES QUALS,
      same place, for 300 pds, 134 acs. on Broad River in Union Co.,
SC granted to JAMES TERRELL on 1-21-1785, now in possession of MOSES
QUALS. Wit: ABNER ROBISON & JOHN ROBISON. Rec. 3-27-1786.

Pp 82-83:   3-9-1786, JOHN DUFF and DANIEL McELLDUFF of Union Co.,
      SC to STEPHEN CREANSHAW, same place, for 346 pds 10 shillings
sterling, 200 acs. on north side of Tygar River, bound by the river
and vacant lands. Granted to THOMAS McELLDUFF by James Glen, Esq.,
Gov., etc., on 2-7-1754. Wit: WM. FARR, THOMAS STRIBLING, JR. & W.
HARDWICK, JR. Signed "JOHN McELLDUFF and DAN. McELLDUFF". Receipt for
money from STEPHEN CRENSHAW STATES 200 acs. "known by the name of DANIEL
McELLDUFF's place, and was taken up by THOMAS McELLDUFF, his Grandfather."
Receipt signed JOHN McELDUFF. Wit: ROBERERT   CRENSHAW,   WM.   HARDWICK.
Rec. 3-27-1786.

Pp 84-85:   3-6-1778, JAMES CAMPBELL and MARTHA, his wife, of Craven
      Co., SC to JOHN HOPE, same place, for 330 pds sterling, 200 acs.
on both sides of Thicketty Creek. Granted to JAMES FANNING on 10-26-
1767. Wit: ROBT. MAYFIELD, WM. CASEY, EDMOND MAYFIELD. Wit. swore to
signatures on 8-5-1779. No rec. date.

Pp 85-86:   3-23-1786, LEWIS LEDBETTER and SARAH, his wife, of Union
    Co., SC to JAMES PETTY, same place, for 100 pds sterling, 200
acs. on a branch of Abbington's Creek, Union Co., part of a tract granted to SAMUEL GILKIE by the State of North Carolina. Bound by WILSON,
MARTIN and the sd LEDBETTER. Wit: GEORGE PETTY, JOHN HARRINGTON, JOHN
GILHAM. Rec. 3-27-1786.

Pp 87-88:   9-25-1785, ROBERT MONTGOMERY and ISABELL, his wife, of
    96 Dist., SC to JAMES KENNEDY, same place, for 50 pds current
money of Virginia, 89 acs. on south side of Broad River, formerly deemed
North Carolina, patented to WILLIAM McMILLIN on 9-26-1766 by Wm. Tryon,
Gov. of N. C. Wit: THOMAS KENNEDY, JOHN LINDSAY, RYDARUS CLARK. Rec.
3-28-1786.

Pp 88-89:   3-27-1786, JOHN WHITE and MARGARET WHITE, his wife, of
    Union Co., SC to WILLIAM MAYS, same place, for 500 pds sterling,
250 acs. in the fork of Broad and Tygar Rivers on the Lick Branch.
Bound by JOHN GASS and vacant lands. Granted to JOHN WHITE by Charles
Granville Montague, Gov. of S.C. on 2-12-1773. Wit: W. HARDWICK, JR.,
TAVINOR BIRD BEUFORD, EDWARD RAGSDALE. Wife signed by mark "PEGGY (X)
WHITE". Receipt for money, 150 pds current, signed 3-27-1785. No re-
cording date.

Pp 89-90:   2-8-1786, JOHN GOLIGHTLY of 96 Dist., to WILLIAM HEALD,
    same place, for 3 pds, 150 acs. in Craven Co. on Fairforest,
granted to JOHN GOLIGHTLY on 4-6-1773 by Wm. Bull, Lt. Gov. of S.C.
Bound by WILLIAM GIST, JAMES MEANS, HERRIF(?) and STEDHAM. Wit: ANNA
HOLLOWAY, JAMES GREEN, FREDARICK CROWDER. Recorded 3-29-1786.

Page 91:   8-21-1784, EDWARD McNEIL (also spelled McNEAL in same
    deed), of 96 Dist., SC to CHARLES SIMS, same place, for 1,000
pds sterling, 350 acs. on Tigar River, bound by the river and vacant
lands. Wit: Col. DAVID HOPKINS, ANDERSON THOMAS, WM. THOMAS. Recorded
3-31-1786.

Pp 92-93:   11-13-1784, RALPH ROGERS to HENRY SMITH, JR., 200 acs.
    on Gilkie's Creek, in 96 Dist., SC, granted to ARCHIBALD ROBISON
on 9-26-1766. Bound by JOHN WINN's land and JONATHAN GILKEY. Wit: SOLO-
MAN MANGHAM, JOHN HYNDMAN. Recorded 3-28-1786.

Pp 93-94:   3-1-1786, AARON HART, miller, of Union Co., SC. to Col.
    THOMAS BRANDON, same place, 100 acs. on south side of Fairforest
Creek, granted to sd HART by Lord Chas. Granville Montague, Gov. of
the Prov. of S. C., on 2-17-1773, bound by WILLIAM WOFFORD, Deputy
Surveyor's land, CHARLES KING, BENJAMIN GIST and land claimed by JOHN
LITTEL. Rec. in Grant Book OOO, p. 113. Consideration 50 pds sterling.
Wit: JOSEPH HUGHS, ROBERT WOODSON, JAMES WOODSON. Rec. 3-29-1786.

Pp 95-98:   2-1-1786, EDWARD HAYS and JEMIMA, his wife, to JOHN THOMAS
    a planter of Union Co., SC for 50 pds lawful money, 125 acs.
on a branch of Fairforest, called Buffalow's Branch not 5 feet broad
nor one deep, waters of Tygar River. Bound by EVAN THOMAS, JESSE FORE,
JOHN HAYES and JOSEPH THOMAS. Patent dated 3-16-1773, rec. 2-1-1775
in Book M, No. 13, p. 267. Wit: ELIJAH PALMER, URIAS PAULK, JOHN PAL-
MER, EVAN THOMAS & THOMAS PALMER. Rec. 3-27-1786.

Pp 98-102:   10-23-1778, ALEXANDER JOHNSON, and MARGARET, his wife,
    of Camden Dist., SC, carpenter and joiner, to JOSEPH GUYTON,
Camden Dist., SC, for 320 pds, 60 acs. on Abbington Creek, part of
a tract of 200 acs. granted to ROBERT WILSON by Gov. of N. C. on 12-
6-1771. Orig. thought to be in Tryon Co., N. C., now appears to be
in 96 Dist. in S. C. Conveyed by ROBT. WILSON to sd ALEX. JOHNSON.
Wit: JOHN BARNETT, HUGH ROGERS, ALEXANDER BROWN. Sworn to bef. JOHN
DRENNAN, J.P. of Camden Dist., SC on 10-24-1778. Rec. in Union Co.
3-27-1786.

Pp 102-103:   10-24-1785, THOMAS BISHOP of 96 Dist., SC, planter, to
    WILLIAM MARTINDALE, planter, same place, for 10 shillings sterl-
ing, tract of land containing 300 acs., except for 164 acs. now in

Cont'd:
possession of THOMAS DUCKET, on Enoree River in the fork of Broad River
and Saludy River. Wit: ROBERT BURNS, HENRY CLARK, JAS. CAMPBELL. No
recording date. This is a lease for 1 year (the previous year). The
release deed for this same transaction is on page 106 following.

Pp 104-105:   3-18-1786, JOSEPH LITTLE, planter, of 96 Dist., SC to
        BASIL WHEAT, same place, for 50 pds sterling, 150 acs. on branches
of Fairforest, bound by THOMAS GREIR's land, JACOB KEER (HEER, KERR?),
JOHN LITTLE, and JAMES AINSWORTH. Wit: JOHN HAILD, JONATHAN STOKES.
Rec. 3-27-1786.

Pp 105-106:   10-25-1785, THOMAS BISHOP and MARY, his wife, planter,
        of 96 Dist., SC to WILLIAM MARTINDALE, planter, same place, 300
acs. granted to WILLIAM RAGAN in 1763, conveyed by lease and release
by Ragan to THOMAS GORDEN, and by Gorden to THOS. BISHOP on 12-11-
1778. Grant recorded in Auditor General's Office in Book M, No. 13,
p. 557. Located on Enoree River, in fork between Broad and Saludy Rivers. Consideration of 71 pds, 9 shillings, sterling except for 164
acs. in possession of THOMAS DUCKET. Beginning point of survey near
Ragan's Shoals. Wit: ROBERT BURNS, HENRY CLARK, JAS. CAMPBELL. Rec.
3-28-1786. Note - This is the release deed for the lease on pp. 102-
103.

Pp 108-110:   3-27-1786, THOMAS BLASSINGAME, farmer, of 96 Dist., to
        BAZZLE (BASIL?) WHEAT, planter, same place, for 45 pds sterling,
150 acs. on waters of Dinia Creek, a branch of Fairforest. Bound by
BENJAMIN THOMPSON, WILLIAM VAUGHAN and vacant lands. Wit: NICHOLAS
KEATING, JAMES BLASSINGAME. Rec. 3-28-1786.

Pp 111-114:   3-21-1786, WILLIAM WOFFORD of State of N. C., to Col.
        THOMAS BRANDON, Union Co., SC for 100 pds, 150 acs. granted to
WM. WOFFORD on 2-13-1768 by Chas. Granville Montague, Gov. of the Prov.
of S. C. Grant rec. in Book H, No. 8, p. 440, 5-3-1768. Tract on both
sides of Fairforest Creek. Wit: W. SHAW, JAMES YANCY. No rec. date.

Pp 114-117:   3-27-1786, WILLIAM PEARSON and SARAH, his wife, of Union
        Co., SC to TOBITHA PEARSON, SR., same place, for 75 pds sterling,
tract now in her possession, 200 acs. on Padgett's Creek in Union Co.
said tract willed to WM. PEARSON by his father ENOCH PEARSON on 10-
30-1772; also, 80 acs. joining above tract, laid out by warrant of
JOHN HAYES'. Wit: ROBERT BURNS, WM. YOUNG, WILLIAM MARTINDELL. Rec.
3-27-1786.

Pp 117-121:   12-18-1783, JOSEPH BURSON and MARY BURSON, his wife,
        of the State of Georgia, to EVAN THOMAS, planter, of 96 Dist.,
SC for 400 pds, 150 acs. on a branch of Fairforest Creek, called Buffa-
low's Creek, granted to JOSEPH BURSON on 4-29-1768, rec. in Auditor's
Book H, No. 8, p. 450 on 7-1-1768. Wit: ISAAC BURSON, WM. NIX, WM.
LITTLE. Rec. 3-28-1786.

Pp 121-124:   2-7-1786, JOHN ELLIOT of 96 Dist., SC. to THOMAS HOBSON
        THOMSON, same place, for 130 pds sterling, 200 acs. on the south
side of Packolate River. Part of 2 tracts - 1 tract of 150 acs. granted
to JOHN GRINDALL by Gov. Bull on 3-1-1775, and 1 tract of 1888 acs.
granted to JOAB MITCHEL (no date of grant given). The 200 acs. was
conveyed to HENDERSON POTTER and thence to JOHN ELLIOT. Wit: ADAM POTTER
& NEWTON HOPKINS. Rec. 3-29-1786.

Pp 125-128:   7-20-1785, ARCHER SMITH of 96 Dist., SC to NEHEMIAH HOW-
        ARD, same place, for 300 pds current money, 100 acs., part of
a tract of 150 acs. granted to ARCHER SMITH in Aug. 1774 by Wm. Bull,
Gov. Wit: THOS. BLASSINGAME & JAMES HARRISON. Rec. 9-27-1785. (This
is the date as written.)

Pp 128-131:   12-15-1785, Col. THOMAS BRANDON, Union Co., SC to JAMES
        BELL, same place, for 100 pds sterling, 100 acs. on a branch
of Fairforest known as Shoaly Creek. Granted to GEORGE LEWIS on 2-
2-1773, conveyed by him to WILLIAM NOBLE, and from him to BRANDON.

Cont'd:
Wit: ZACHARIAH BULLOCK and JOHN BIRDSONG. No recording date.

Pp 131-133:   10-29-1785, JOHN LATTA and SARAH, his wife, of Chester
        Co., SC to ROBERT WALLACE of Chatham Co., N.C. for 114 pds 7
shillings S.C. money, 278 acs. in Union Co., SC on both sides of Sugar
Creek, a branch of Fairforest. Granted to JAMES MEANS on 11-18-1752,
plat and patent recorded in Secretary's Office of the State of North
Carolina. Wit: JOHN BIRDSONG, JAMES BLACKSTOCK, J. THOMAS, JR. No recording date.

Pp 133-134:   8-2-1770, JACOB BROWN of Berkeley Co., SC to JOHN MAYFIELD
        of same place, for 40 pds, 300 acs. in Tryon Co., N.C., on Brown's
Creek, a west branch of Broad River (now in Union Co., SC). Signed
by JACOB BROWN and RUTH BROWN. Wit: JOHN HAILE & WILLIAM GRANT. Rec.
6-27-1786.

Pp 134-136:   1-4-1786, NATHANIEL JEFFERIES of Gilkie's Creek, Union
        Co., SC to JOHN JEFFERIES, same place, for 200 pds sterling,
280 acs. on Gilkie's Creek, orig. granted to ZACHARIAH BULLOCK, and
conveyed by him to NATHANIEL JEFFERIES. Now in the actual possession
of the sd JOHN JEFFERIES. Wit: JOHN EWART, JONATHAN JONES, SARAH JEFF-
ERIES. Rec. 6-27-1786.

Pp 136-137:   5-10-1785, DANIEL McELDUFF of 96 Dist., SC to ROBERT
        CRENSHAW, same place, for 33 pds 6 shillings and 8 pence sterl-
ing, one tract of land (no acs. given) in the fork of Broad and Saluda
Rivers on Tygar River. Bound by lands laid out to WILLIAM HILL and
WILLIAM HARDWICK. Wit: DAVID GEORGE, JOHN CRENSHAW, EDWARD RAGSDALE,
JOSEPH TUCKER. Signed by DANL. McELDUFF & HANNAH McELDUFF. No record-
ing date.

Pp 137-140:   12-23-1785, THOMAS B. YOUNG, Gent., of Union Co., SC.
        to Col. THOMAS BRANDON, same place, for 100 pds lawful money
of S. C., 550 acs. on Buffalo Creek. Granted to THOMAS YOUNG on 1-
21-1785. Rec. in Sec. Office, Book ZZZ, p. 396. Bound by Col. BRANDON,
BOGAN, ROBERT WOODSON & ROUNTREE. Wit: JOHN McCOOL, ROBERT GREGORY.
Rec. 6-27-1786.

Pp 141-144:   1-1-1785. DANIEL PLUMMER of Saint John's River in East
        Florida to WILLIAM PLUMMER of 96 Dist., SC for 70 pds sterling,
220 acs. on Fairforest Creek, part of a 520 ac. tract granted to DANIEL
PLUMMER on 7-28-1775 by his Exc. William Campbell, Commander in Chief.
Wit: RENNEY BLUE and SHADRICK LAUDTRIP. Signture sworn to on 3-1-
1785 before THOMAS BRANDON, J.P. No recording date.

Pp 145-148:   10-30-1784, JOHN STEEN, SR. of 96 Dist., SC to FRANCIS
        DRAKE of North Carolina, for 126 pds sterling, 350 acs. on Grif-
fin's Branch of Thickety Creek in South Carolina, granted by North
Carolina patent to JOHN STEEN. Wit: JOHN HARRINGTON, WILSON JOLLY.
Signed by JOHN STEEN and MARTHA (X) STEEN. Recorded 6-27-1786.

Pp 148-150:   3-6-1780, WILLIAM WOFFORD of Lawson's Fork, 96 Dist.,
        SC to TURNER ROUNTREE of Fairforest, same dist. and state, for
1000 pds current money, 200 acs. including the dwelling house and plantation wheron the sd TURNER ROUNTREE now lives, part of a 500 ac. tract
granted to BENJAMIN GIFT (GIST?) on 7-15-1768, and conveyed by him
to WM. WOFFORD. Bound by NICHOL, VERNON, THOMAS COX, TINSLEY, Fairforest Creek, Woodson's Spring Branch, and CHARLES KING's land (now
claimed by Col. THOMAS FLETCHALL). Wit: JAMES WOODSON, SR., JAS. WOOD-
SON, JR. Rec. 6-27-1786. Note - Col. THOMAS FLETCHALL was one of the
most active Tory leaders in this area during the Revolution.

Pp 150-151:   3-6-1780, WILLIAM WOFFORD of Lawson's Fork, 96 Dist.,
        SC to ROBERT WOODSON of Fairforest, 96 Dist., SC for 1000 pds
current money, 50 acs. on Fairforest and Sugar Creeks, part of a 500
ac. grant to BENJAMIN GIFT (GIST?) described in the preceding deed.
Wit: JAMES WOODSON, TURNER ROUNTREE. No recording date.

Pp 152-156:   7-25-1770. MOSES STEVENS of Wilks Co., Ga., yeoman, to

Cont'd:
THOMAS BLASSINGAME, of 96 Dist., SC, gentleman, for 400 pds current money, 187½ acs., 1/2 of a 375 ac. tract granted to THOMAS MITCHELL
in 1752 by Nathaniel Rice, Esq., President of the Province of North
Carolina. Tract located in then Anson Co., N.C. now in 96 Dist., SC
on Mitchell's Creek on the south side of Fairforest Creek. Bound by
JOHN McDOWELL on one side. The 187½ acs. sold to MOSES STEVENS by Mitchell on 11-23-1765. Wit: BENJAMIN THOMPSON, WILLIAM THOMPSON. Signature
sworn to by WM. THOMPSON on 11-17-1777 before WILLIAM MOORE, J.P.,
96 Dist. No recording date.

Pp 157-158:   10-14-1775, JAMES VERNON to AARON HARLIN (no place of
residence given) for 50 pds current money of S. C., 50 acs. in
Craven Co. on a branch of Fairforest. Bound by JOSEPH BREED, MAGNESS
ARMOND. Granted 7-8-1774 and recorded in Bk. SSS, p. 485. Wit: JESSE
HAYES, MAGNESS ARMOND & GEORGE HARLIN. Signature sworn to by HARLIN,
1-4-1785 bef. JOHN BLASSINGAME, J.P. Rec. 6-27-1786.

Pp 158-159:   6-26-1786, OBADIAH HOWARD of Union Co., SC to JOSEPH
HOWARD, same place, for and in consideration of the love, good
will and esteem which I have and do bear toward my son JOSEPH HOWARD,
100 acs. on Shoaly Creek, a branch of Fairforest, part of a grant of
450 acs. to OBADIAH HOWARD, dated 6-23-1774. No witnesses. Acknowledged
in open court 6-26-1786. JOHN HAILE, Clerk of Court.

Pp 159-161:   7-9-1785, JOSEPH JONES, planter, of Union Co., 96 Dist.,
SC to JOHN McCOOL, Gent., same place, for 35 pds 14 shillings
and 3 pence, 200 acs. on both sides of the Ninety-Six Road, where sd
JONES now lives. Part of a 450 ac. grant dated 6-23-1774 to WALTER
HOLMES "in Berkeley County, in the fork bet. Broad and Saluda Rivers
on the drafts of Fairforest and Brown's Creek." Bound by GABRIEL ANDER-
SON and OBADIAH HOWARD and vacant lands. Grant rec. in Bk. QQQ, p.
591. Conveyed by Holmes to GEORGE CROSSLEY, SR., 200 acs. conveyed
by CROSSLEY to JOSEPH JONES. Wit: THOMAS BRANDON, J.P., DUNCAN McCREVAN,
JOHN BRANDON. Signed by JOS. JONES & SARAH JONES. No recording date.

Pp 161-164:   10-23-1785, WILLIAM FARR, Sheriff of Union Co., SC to
THOMAS BRANDON, Esq., same place, for 13 pds sterling, Sheriff's
sale of 100 acs. on the south side of Tygar River, which belonged to
DAVID ADAMS. Bound on one side by ARMEL FINCHER. Wit: JOS. HUGHS, THOS.
STRIBLING, JR. Rec. 6-26-1786. This sale was held to settle a debt
of 16 pds 8 shillings, which ADAMS owed BRANDON. Brandon was the high
bidder at the sale and got the land for 13 pds. All of this was done
on the basis of an English law passed by Parliament in 1731 to facili-
tate "recovery of debts in His Majesty's Plantations in America", even
though it was then 1785 and America had been independent for 10 years.

Pp 164-168:   1-23-1775, ELIZABETH RINCHARD, spinster, of Craven Co.,
S.C., to JOHN McPHERSON, yeoman, same place, for 100 pds, 100
acs. on Fish Dam Creek, on the southside of Broad River, bound by THOMAS
HOLLINGSWORTH, and vacant lands. Granted to ELIZABETH RINCHARD by Wm.
Bull, Lt. Gov. on 5-25-1774. Wit: WILLIAM STREIGHT & JOHN ARMSTRONG.
Rec. 3-27-1786.

Pp 168-172:   11-14-1785, THOMAS BRIGGS, son of JOHN BRIGGS of Edgecomb Co., North Carolina, and KATHERINE, his wife, Heirs at law
to JOHN BRIGGS, son of JOHN BRIGGS of Edgecomb, afsd., late of Enoree
in the Dist. of Ninety-Six and state afsd., deceased, of Spartanburgh
in the state afsd., to THOMAS TODD of Spartanburgh Co., 96 Dist., SC
for 80 pds sterling, 2 plantations, with the grist mill, formerly the
property of JOHN BRIGGS, dec'd., miller, of Enoree. 100 acs. in Spartanburgh Co. on north side of Enoree River conveyed by WILLIAM COX, deceased, late of Enoree, to JOHN BRIGGS, whereon JOHN BRIGGS did live
and where THOMAS BRIGGS and KATHERINE, his wife, does at present live.
Another tract of 100 acs. in Union Co., SC on the south side of Enoree
River, opposite to land surveyed for WILLIAM BRIGGS granted to JOHN
BRIGGS of Enoree afsd., dec'd. Wit: EDW. MUSGRAVE, THOMAS LAYTON. Rec.
3-28-1786.

Pp 172-176:   2-18-1786, JOHN WOOD, planter, and MARTHA WOOD, his wife

Cont'd:
of Spartanburgh Co., SC to JOHN McPHERSON, millwright, of Union
Co., SC for 100 pds sterling, 350 acs. granted to JOHN WOOD in 1770
on the south side of Fairforest Creek on Mitchell's branch. Wit: JOHN
GOLIGHTLY, JACOB HOLMES, WILLIAM WOOD. Rec. 3-29-1786. (One place in
deed the wife is called "Patty", but she signed by mark and "Martha".)

Pp 176-177:   3-24-1786, AARON FINCHER and MARY, his wife, of Union
          Co., SC to MOSES COLLIER, same place, for 5 shillings, 100 acs.
on Fairforest Creek, bound by WILLIAM PLUMMER on one side, part of
a grant dated 4-6-1765 of 300 acs. to ARCHIBALD GILLILAND. Conveyed
by Gilliland to JOHN IRVIN, by Irvin to JONATHAN PARKER on 2-26-1770,
now to MOSES COLLIER by the sd AARON FINCHER, Administrator to JONATHAN
PARKER, deceased. Wit: WILLIAM PLUMMER, MARY MUSGRAVE. Rec. 3-28-1786.

Pp 178-179:   3-24-1786, AARON FINCHER and MARY, his wife, of Union
          Co., to ANN COLLIER, EASTER COLLIER and MARY COLLIER, heirs of
BARNET COLLIER, deceased, same place, for 5 shillings, 100 acs. on
Fairforest Creek, adj. MOSES COLLIER's land. (Same description as above
deed.) Wit: WILLIAM PLUMMER, MARY MUSGRAVE. Rec. 3-28-1786.

Pp 179-182:   7-21-1785, NEHEMIAH HOWARD of 96 Dist., SC. to ARCHER
          SMITH, same place, for 300 pds current money, 100 acs. on Fair-
forest Creek, adj. a 200 ac. tract orig. granted to CASPER NAGLEY.
Sd 100 acs. is part of 150 acs. granted to NEHEMIAH HOWARD on 6-23-
1774 by Wm. Bull, Esq. Wit: JAMES HARRISON, THOMAS BLASSINGAME. No
recording date.

Pp 183-186:   5-25-1779, ALEXANDER WALKER of Camden Dist., SC on Sandy
          River, to RYDARUS CLARK of Gilkie's Creek, 96 Dist., for 500
pds current money, 100 acs. whereon the sd Clark now lives, on Gilkie's
Creek. Bound by PETER CULP, PHILIP WALKER and vacant lands. Wit: ROBT.
GOVRELL (or GORRELL), WILLIAM ROGERS, ANDREW HAMILTON. Rec. 3-28-1786.
Witnesses swore to signature on 8-2-1783.

Pp 186-191:   10-30-1785, JOHN BRANDON and MARY, his wife, of 96 Dist.,
          to WILIAM KENEDY, Esq., same place, for 600 pds, 260 acs. on
the west side of Broad River on Brown's Creek, joining land that JOHN
BRANDON lives on, below JOSEPH PEARSON's. Part of a tract granted to
BRANDON by a North Patent (North Carolina?) on 9-25-1766. Wit: THOMAS
VANCE, ELIAS HOLLINGSWORTH, EVAN THOMAS. No recording date.

Pp 191-193:   6-15-1785, ELIZABETH MARTIN to JOHN LITTLE (no county
          or state given) for 100 pds, 100 acs. part of a 200 ac. tract
on the north side of Sugar Creek in the fork between Sugar Creek and
Fairforest in Craven County. Bound by JAMES VERNER, MARGARET McDOWELL,
PHILIP BRIANT, JAMES FINLEY and by land run for North Carolina claimed
by NICHOLAS VERNON and by BENJAMIN GIST. Sd 200 acs. granted to JAMES
MARTIN on 7-26-1774 by Wm. Bull, Esq., and rec. in Book TTT, p. 243.
Wit: ROBERT WOODSON, SAMUEL CASE, JOHN SPRINGER. Rec. 9-25-1786.

Pp 193-194:   9-12-1786, GABRIEL BROWN, planter of Union Co., to RICHARD
          BARROT, planter of same place, for 50 pds sterling, 100 acs.
on Ned's Creek, bound by lands surveyed for BARTHOLOMEW BARKER, land
supposed to be PINCKNEY's, and by a creek called Meadow Branch, including the house where THOMAS SANDWICK now lives. Part of a 320 ac. grant
to GABRIEL BROWN dated 9-5-1785 by Wm. Moultrie, Esq., Gov. of S. C.
Wit: BATT BAKER, JAMES JETER, LEONARD BAKER. Rec. 9-25-1786.

Pp 195-198:   1-10-1785, AMBROSE RAY, planter, and ELIZABETH RAY, his
          wife, of 96 Dist., to ELIZABETH DUNCAN, same place, for 72 pds
current money, 200 acs. on the south side of Tygar River, part of a
350 ac. tract granted to EMANUEL STEVENS on 9-22-1768 by Wm. Bull,
then Gov. of S.C., bound by the river and vacant lands when granted.
Sd 200 acs. conveyed by Stevens to AMBROSE RAY. Wit: JAMES HARRISON,
WILLIAM YOUNG. Rec. 9-25-1786.

Pp 199-200:   10-14-1775, JAMES MARTIN to GEORGE HARLOW, hatter, for
          150 pds current money of S.C., 100 acs. in Craven Co., in the

Cont'd:
fork between Sugar Creek and Fairforest. Bound by JAMES VERNON, MARGARET
McDOWELL, PHILIP BRIANT, RUBEN LAWSON, land run for North Carolina
claimed by NICHOLS and VERNON, BENJAMIN GIST and JAMES FINLEY and JOHN
GOODWIN. Part of a 200 ac. grant to JAMES MARTIN, dated 7-26-1774 and
rec. in Book TTT, p. 243. One half of all gold and silver mines excepted.
Wit: GEORGE HARLIN, JAMES VERNON, EDWARD SPARKS. James Martin's signature sworn to by GEORGE HARLIN on 9-17-1784 bef. WM. KENEDY, J.P.
Rec. 9-25-1786. (This would be the same tract of land referred to in
the deed on pages 191-193.)

Pp 201-202:   12-2-1773, HUGH QUINN of Craven Co., Prov. of SC, to
        MOSES QUALLS, same place, for 200 pds current money, 150 acs.,
on the west side of Broad River, including an island in the river,
in Craven Co., patent granted to MANIN (MANNING?) GORE on 12-22-1768
and conveyed to sd HUGH QUINN. Wit: SAMUEL MORRIS, THOMAS MANING. From
Camden Dist., THOMAS MANNIN# swore to HUGH QUINN's signature by mark
on 3-8-1786 bef. EZEKL. POLK, J.P. Rec. in Union Co. on 9-25-1786.

Pp 202-208:   5-8-1775, JOSEPH ROBERTSON, gunsmith, and ANN ROBERTSON,
        his wife, of Craven Co., 96 Dist., to WILLIAM FAUCETT, same place,
for 750 pds, 300 acs. on the west side of Broad River, on Brown's Creek
above HUGH NELSON's land, granted to JOHN DAVIS on 9-25-1766 by Wm.
Tryon, Gov. of N. C., conveyed by Davis to GEORGE WALKER and by Walker
to the sd JOSEPH ROBERTSON. Wit: WILLIAM HUGHS, WILLIAM EDMONDSON,
JOHN McDONALD. Signature sworn to bef. JOHN NUCKOLS, J.P. on 5-10-
1775. Red. 9-25-1786. (ANN and JOSEPH's name spelled both ROBERTSON
and ROBINSON in the same deed.)

Pp 208-211:   1-1-1780, JOHN WOODS of Camden Dist., to DREWRY HARRINGTON
        of 96 Dist., for 400 pds current money, 174 acs. bet. Abbington
and Gilkie's Creeks, whereon the sd HARRINGTON now lives. Part of a
North Carolina grant to THEOPHELUS TEVER(?) joining JOHN MOOREHEAD's
land. Wit: JOHN MOOREHEAD, ABSOLM. PETTY. Rec. 9-25-1786.

Pp 211-213:   12-17-1785, MOSES QUALLS, miller, of Union Co., to JAMES
        TERRILL (also spelled TERRELL), planter, same place, for 150
pds, 150 acs. orig. granted to MANEN GORE by N. C. patent on 12-22-
1768, conveyed by Gore to HUGH QUIN, and by Quin to QUALLS. On the
north side of Broad River on the side of the island. Wit: ABNER ROBI-
SON, JOHN ROBISON, HENRY SMITH. Rec. 9-25-1786.

Pp 213-214:   1-18-1786, DANIEL LIPHAM of 96 Dist., to WILLIAM JINKINS
        of same place, for 107 pds sterling, a certain tract on Enoree
River, bound by the river, NATHANIEL DAVIS and WILLIAM WOOD. A South
Carolina grant to LIPHAM on 1-21-1785, rec. in Book CCCC, p. 297. Wit:
JOSIAH DARBY, BENJAMIN DARBY, WILLIAM ROGERS. Rec. 9-25-1786.

Pp 214-216:   9-25-1786, JOHN WHITE and PEGGY, his wife, of 96 Dist.,
        to HENRY MILHOUSE, same place, for 64 pds, 5 shillings and 8
pence and divers good causes and considerations, 2 tracts of land -
one tract of 100 acs. granted to WILLIAM PHILIPS in 1766 on Beaverdam
Creek, a branch of Tygar River. Another tract of 200 acs. granted to
sd JOHN WHITE in 1786, joining the above 100 ac. tract. Wit: ISAAC
COOK, JOHN COOK. Rec. 9-25-1786.

Pp 216-218:   9-7-1786, WILLIAM SMITH of Union Co. to WILLIAM LOCK-
        HART, same place, for 200 pds, 150 acs. on Broad River, orig.
granted by North Carolina to ISAM(?) PEOPLES, conveyed by Peoples to
MATTHEW RUSSELL, and from Russell to WILLIAM SMITH, SR. and from SMITH,
SR. to his son, WILLIAM by will. Wit: JAMES TERRELL, ABNER ROBISON,
HENRY SMITH. Signed by WILLIAM SMITH and MARTHA (X) SMITH. Rec. 9-
25-1786.

Pp 219-220:   5-15-1785, JEREMIAH ROUTH of Craven Co. to DANIEL JACKSON
        of same county, for 10 shillings sterling, one tract of land
in afsd. county, bound by BENJAMIN THOMPSON, JOHN WOOD, DANIEL CUMMONS,
AVERY BREED, MARY JACKSON and vacant lands. Granted to JEREMIAH ROUTH,
laid out by WILLIAM GIST to sd ROUTH. Wit: JOHN VERNON, MAGNAS ARMENT,
WILLIAM PLUMER. Rec. 9-25-1786.

Pp 220-222:   8-14-1786, GEORGE CROSLEY, SR. of the State of Georgia,
    to GEORGE CROSLEY, JR. of Union Co., SC for 100 pds sterling,
100 acs. on waters of Fairforest and Brown's Creek, part of a tract
of 450 acs. orig. granted by patent to WALTER HOLMES by Wm. Bull, Lt.
Gov. of S.C. Conveyed by Holmes to GEO. CROSLEY, SR. in 1779. Wit:
URIAS PAULK, EZEKIEL SPRINGER. Rec. 9-25-1786.

Pp 222-225:   11-9-1784, THEOPHILUS FAVOR of 96 Dist., to JOHN MOOR-
    HEAD, same place, for 25 pds sterling, 80 acs. on Abbington Creek
waters of Broad River, part of a 400 ac. tract granted to FAVER by
his Exc. JOSIAH MARTIN of N. C. on 12-8-1771. Laid off by JOSEPH ROBI-
SONO, Deputy Surveyor on 10-31-1772. Wit: WILLIAM MOOREHEAD and JOHN
MOOREHEAD. (Since the deed is to a JOHN MOOREHEAD, the witness could
possibly be another person of the same name, maybe father and son.)
Rec. 9-25-1786.

Page 226:   9-12-1785, WILLIAM GEORGE of Union Co. to WILLIAM SHARP,
    same place, for 50 pds sterling, 100 acs. in Union Co. bound
by the sd SHARP, RICHARD FAUCETT, WILLIAM SAVAGE, JOB HAMMOND and LOT
PORTER. Wit: RICHARD HUGHS, WILLIAM HUGHS, RICHARD FAUCETT. Rec. 9-
25-1786.

Page 227:   5-30-1752, JOHN HEIGLER to JOHN GORDEN, both of Barkley
    (sic) Co., for 25 pds current money of the Province of S.C.,
50 acs. bound by COLLIN's fences on NW, all other sides by vacant lands.
Granted by patent 1-9-1752 by James Glen, Esq., Gov. of S. C. Wit:
ABRAHAM ANDERSON, JEREMIAH WILLIAMS, HENRY AWBRY. Signature sworn to
by JEREMIAH WILLIAMS on 6-7-1752 bef. ANDREW BROWN, J.P. Recorded 9-
25-1786.

Pp 228-229:   8-24-1779, EDWARD NIXON, planter, and ELIZABETH, his
    wife, of 96 Dist., to BENJAMIN DARBY of Camden Dist., for 1000
pds S. C. currency, 200 acs. on the south side of Tygar River at the
mouth of Fishing Creek. Part of a tract granted by Matthew Rowan, Esq.,
President of the Prov. of North Carolina, to THOMAS GORDEN on 8-20-
1754, a memorial thereof is entered in the Auditor General's Office
of South Carolina in Book H, No. 8, p. 80, dated 8-4-1766. Plat included
with grant. Wit: JOSEPH FRANKLIN, ASA DARBY, THOMAS NIXON. Signature
sworn to by ASA DARBY on 5-16-1783 bef. JOHN HITCHCOCK, J.P. Recorded
9-25-1786.

Pp 229-230:   9-18-1786, SAMUEL POSTEN of the State of North Carolina
    Linkholm, planter, to RICHARD HUGHS, planter, of Union Co., SC
for 30 pds sterling, 125 acs. part of a grant of 250 acs. dated 10-
15-1772 by Charles Montague, Gov. of Prov. of S. C., to JONATHAN POSTON.
Tract located on west side of Broad River in Craven Co., bound by RICH-
ARD HUGHS' land, vacant lands and the river. The sd SAMUEL POSTON being
the heir of the sd JONTHAN POSTON, deceased. Wit: JOSEPH HUGHS, WM.
GILES, RICHARD FAUCETT. Rec. 9-25-1786.

Pp 230-231:   5-29-1786, JOHN HAM and wife MARY of Camden Dist., to
    BENJAMIN DARBY of 96 Dist., for 35 pds 5 shillings sterling,
50 acs. (part of a larger tract) on Tygar River adj. sd DARBY. Wit:
JOSIAH DARBY, DANIEL LIPHAM, SAMUEL (X) JINKINS. Rec. 9-25-1786.

Pp 231-233:   12-17-1785, DAVID PUETT and SARAH, his wife, of 96 Dist.,
    to BENJAMIN DARBY, same place, for 35 pds 5 shillings sterling,
and other considerations, 50 acs. on south side of Tygar River on Fishing Creek. Wit: JOSIAH DARBY, WILLIAM (X) JINKINS, SAMUEL (X) JINKINS.
Rec. 9-25-1786.

Pp 233-236:   1-2-1786, MARK MITCHEL of Washington Co., N. C. to MARHAR-
    SHALALBAZ LILE of Union Co., 96 Dist., for 40 pds sterling, 200
acs. on Mill Creek, part of a 300 ac. grant to JOAB MITCHEL by Wm.
Bull, Lt. Gov. of S. C. on 9-6-1775. Sd land falls to sd MARK MITCHEL
by Decent (sic) of Heir at Law to the sd JOAB MITCHEL, deceased. Bound
by THOMAS DRAPER, EDWARD PICKETT. Also stated in description, "my father
JOAB MITCHEL". Wit: JOHN HAILE, ADAM POTTER, PHILLIP SAUNDERS. Rec.
9-25-1786. (Note - The name of grantee copied exactly as written.)

Pp 236-239:   7-19-1786, ARTHUR SIMPSON and his wife (wife's name not
    given - neither did she sign deed) of 96 Dist., to ROBERT BARRON
and THOMAS BARRON, heirs of THOMAS BARRON, deceased, of same place,
for 100 pds sterling, 200 acs. on Jumping Run joining JAMES MACKELWAIN
(McILWAIN?) and ZACHARIAH BULLOCK. Granted to ARTHUR SIMPSON on 5-
4-1775 by Wm. Bull, Esq., Lt. Gov. of S. C. Wit: ADAM POTTER, DAVID
BROWN, SAMUEL SHAW. Rec. 9-25-1786.

Pp 239-240:   7-14-1786, VARDRY McBEE of Spartanburgh to PETER PETERSON
    of Union, 200 acs. joining GABRIEL PATRICK and LEWIS AKIN on
the north side of Abbington's Creek. Part of a tract of 535 acs. granted
to VARDY McBEE on 9-7-1785 by Wm. Moultrie, Gov. of S. C. Wit: DREWRY
HARRINGTON, JAMES PETTY, ISHAM SAFOLD. Rec. 9-25-1786. (Amount of com-
pensation not given.)

Page 241:   7-15-1786, VARDRY McBEE of Thicketty Creek, SC to JAMES
    PETTY of Abbington's Creek, for 10 shillings sterling, 112 acs.
on Abbington's Creek, Union Co., part of the same 535 ac. grant described in the deed above. Wit: DREWRY HARRINGTON, PETER PETERSON, ISHAM
SAFOLD. Rec. 9-25-1786.
    (Note - VARDRY McBEE was one of the "founding fathers" of Green-
ville, South Carolina.)

Pp 241-246:   2-7-1779, MATTHEW ROBISON, Eldest son and heir at law
    of DAVID ROBISON, late of Thickey Creek, S. C., deceased, and
IRBY DEWBERRY, Acting Executor to the last Will and Testament of the
sd DAVID ROBISON, of the one part, to WILLIAM SAFFOLD, planter, same
place, for 3400 pds current money of S. C., 266 acs. on Thickety Creek,
whereon DAVID ROBISON lived, being 2/3's of a tract granted to DAVID
ROBISON under a North Carolina grant, the other 1/3 reserved for Dower
lands "in possession of JAMES TERRELL." Bound by JOHN THOMPSON, vacant
lands, and the 1/3d Dower tract. Deed states that DAVID ROBISON died
in 1771. Wit: JOHN NUCKOLS, WILLIAM WILKINS, PHILEMON MARTIN. Signatures sworn to on 10-23-1782 bef. I. BERWICK, J.P. Rec. 9-25-1786.

Page 246:   8-16-1770, JOHN STEEN of Tryon Co., Prov. of N. C., bound
    unto ELIJAH WELLS, same place, for the sum of 500 pds current
money of S. C., condition being that ELIJAH WELLS had purchased a tract
of land containing 100 acs. on the south side of Packolate River, formerly owned by ROBERT BISHOP, for the sum of 6,000 net pounds of tobacco.
"If the sd JOHN STEEN refuses when the sd tobacco is paid to him to
make the sd WELLS or assigns a Good and Absolute Right to the above
mentioned land, then in this case the above Bond is good against him
the sd STEEN." Wit: MATTHEW GREGG, THOMAS SISSON. Rec. 9-25-1786.

Page 247:   8-15-1786, THOMAS TAYLOR, SR. of Union Co., SC to DAVID
    JOHNSON, sae place, for 100 pds sterling, 300 acs. in the fork
of Broad and Tygar Rivers. Sd tract was granted to Col. THOMAS TAYLOR
of the Congaree on 8-26-1774. Bound by JOHN BISHOP's land, THOMAS TAY-
LOR's land, land claimed by Mr. PINCKNEY and vacant lands. Wit: BENJ.
JOHNSON, SR., BENJ. JOHNSON, CHARLES JOHNSON. Rec. 9-25-1786.

Pp 248-251:   8-23-1786, WILLIAM HILL and DORCAS, his wife, of Edge-
    field Co., SC to ROBERT CREANSHAW of Union Co., for 100 pds ster-
ling, 100 acs. on Tygar River bet. Saluda and Broad Rivers. Orig. granted to TERRENCE CARRELL by Chas. Granville Montague, Gov. of S.C. and
conveyed by Carrell to WILLIAM HILL by lease and release bearing date
4-23-1774. Wit: EDWARD RAGSDALE, WILLIAM MAYS, SAMUEL MAYS. Rec. 9-
25-1786.

Pp 251-254:   7-27-1786, ARCHER SMITH, of Union Co., SC to THACKER
    VIVION, same place, for 20 pds sterling, 40 acs. on the north
side of Tygar River below the mouth of Duchman's (Dutchman's) Creek.
Part of a 640 ac. tract granted to WILLIAM COWAN (COWDEN?) on 9-3-
1753 by Matthew Rowan, Gov. of N. C. Sd tract since possessed and claimed by virtue of a purchase by MOSES WYLEY. Same tract also granted
to sd ARCHER SMITH by Wm. Bull, Lt. Gov. of S. C. on 10-14-1774. Wit:
BRITTAIN WILLERFORD, DANIEL JACKSON, BENJ. (X) HALCOMB. Rec. 9-25-
1786. Receipt signed 7-27-1785. (Mistake in date - deed 1786, receipt
dated 1785. Clerical error?)

Pp 254-255:   7-29-1786, THACKER VIVION of Union Co., to STEPHEN LAYTON
        of Greenville Co., SC for 5 pds lawful money of S.C., 100 acs.
on Tygar River, including the land whereon the sd STEPHEN LAYTON did
live. Part of a 200 ac. tract granted to VIVION on 8-1-1774 by Wm.
Bull, Lt. Gov. of S.C., situate as was then called Craven. Bound by
WILLIAM COWDEN, the river and vacant lands. Wit: JAMES HARRISON, ELIZA-
BETH HARRISON. Rec. 9-25-1786.

Page 256:   6-18-1785, LAURENCE EASTERWOOD of 96 Dist., to JOHN BECK-
        HAM, same place, for 100 pds sterling, 200 acs. on south side
of Packolate River above the place where ZACHARIAH BULLOCK now lives.
Granted by patent to DAVID PARK on 2-23-1754 and regranted to MICHAEL
CRAWFORD in South Carolina in April 1775. Wit: ADAM POTTER, JOHN BECK-
HAM. Rec. 9-26-1786.

Pp 257-258:   8-26-1786, JOHN STEEN, SR. and his wife MARTHA, of Union
        Co. to JOHN HOPE, same place, for 150 pds sterling, 300 acs.
on both sides of Thicketty Creek, including the mouth of Gilkie's Creek.
Bound by sd JOHN HOPE, and WILLIAM McCULLOCH. Wit: CHARLES MILES, JOSEPH
JOLLY, JAMES ARMSTRONG. Rec. 9-26-1786.

Pp 258-261:   9-19-1785, ISAAC CRYNE of 96 Dist., to WILLIAM McJUNKIN,
        same place, for 30 pds current money, 150 acs. on Brown's Creek,
a branch of Broad River. Orig. granted to MARY PROCTOR in April 1768,
by Charles Montague, Gov. of S. C. Wit: THOMAS BRANDON, SAMUEL PATTENT.
Rec. 9-26-1786. (Grantor's name shown as CRYNE in deed, but signature
apparently is CRUSE.)

Pp 262-263:   10-20-1785, JAMES WILKINSON of 96 Dist., to WILLIAM Mc-
        GOWIN of York Co., S.C., for 120 pds sterling, 200 acs. on the
south side of Broad River, upon which the sd JAMES WILKINSON now lives.
Part of a tract granted to HUGH QUIN by patent dated 10-26-1767. Bound
by the river and a path that leads to CURTIS CALDWELL's. Wit: MARGRET
BARRON and JOHN BARRON. Rec. 9-27-1786.

Pp 263-264:   11-1-1785, JOHN CORTHEN of Union Co., to WILLIAM McGOWIN
        of York Co., SC for 120 pds sterling, 200 acs. on the south side
of Broad River. Part of a tract granted to HUGH QUIN by patent dated
10-26-1767. Wit: MARGRET BARRON, JOHN BARRON. Rec. 9-27-1786.

Pp 264-265:   9-10-1786, ARCHER SMITH of 96 Dist., Union Co., to JAMES
        HARRISON, of the sd dist. and county of Granville, for 708 pds.
sterling money of the state afsd., a plantation containing 370 acs.
known by the name of Newmarket. Located on the waters of Fairforest
Creek. Bound by NEHEMIAH HOWARD, Estate of RALPH JACKSON, deceased,
WILLIAM BROWNIN and ROBERT WOODSON. Wit: THACR. (THACKER) VIVION, REUBEN
BELUE. Rec. 9-27-1786.

        (Note: The THACKER VIVION shown in these deeds in Union Co.,
S. C. is probably the same man shown in the Washington Co., Ga., Surveyor's Records, pages 445-448 of the Fall 1971 issue of GGM. He as
well as the WOODSON family is also referred to on pages 813-814-815
of the Nov. 1971 issue of the DAR Magazine.)

Pp 266-268:   7-12-1784, WILLIAM STEEN of 96 Dist., to JOHN McWHORTER,
        same place, for 50 pds sterling, 100 acs. on the south side of
Packolate River, now in his (McWHORTER's) actual possession. Granted
to STEEN by Wm. Bull, Lt. Gov. of S. C. on 2-10-1770. Wit: ADAM POTTER,
JESSE MABRAY, WM. HENDLEY. Rec. 9-27-1786.

Pp 269-272:   8-28-1786, ELENOR McWHORTER of Packolate River, 96 Dist.,
        Union Co., to DANIEL COVANHOVEN, same place, for 70 pds sterling,
50 acs. on the north side of Packolate River, where COVENHAVEN now
lives. Part of a 300 ac. tract granted to sd ELENOR McWHORTER by Wm.
Tryon, Gov. of Prov. of S.C. on 12-20-1766. Grant located on both sides
of Packolate River, then deemed Mecklinburgh Co., N.C. Wit: NICHOLAS
JASPER, GEORGE McWHORTER, JOHN McWHORTER. Rec. 9-27-1786.

Pp 272-274:   (There are 2 pages number 274 in the Book. This deed
includes all of the first one and part of the second page #274..JMC)

Cont'd:
7-12-1784, ELENOR McWHORTER of 96 Dist., to JOHN McWHORTER, same place, for 100 pds sterling, 200 acs. on south side of Packolate River. Part of a grant of 300 acs. dated 10-26-1767 to ELENOR McWHORTER by Wm. Tryon, Gov. of N. C. Wit: ADAM POTTER, WILLM. HENDLEY, JESSE MABRAY. Rec. 9-27-1786.

Pp 274-277: (Second page 274) 7-21-1786, JOHN PORTMAN of 96 Dist., to NICHOLAS JASPER, same place, for 60 pds sterling, 200 acs. on Little Sandy Run, a branch of Pacolate River. Bound on the north by CHARLES HAMES. Granted to PORTMAN on 5-1-1786 by Wm. Moultrie, Gov. of S.C. Wit: JOHN HENDERSON, JOHN BECKHAM, JR. and JAMES MOSLEY. Rec. 9-27-1786.

Pp 277-278: 4-18-1785, DUNCAN McCREVAN, planter of 96 Dist., to Capt. JOSEPH HUGHS, same place, for 55 pds 9 shillings and 3 pence sterling, 100 acs. on the south side of Broad River, bound on the west by RICHARD ADDES's land. All other sides by vacant land. Granted to DUNCAN McCREVAN on 1-21-1785 by Benjamin Guerrard, Gov. of S.C. Wit: DANIEL McMAY, JOHN McCREVAN, JOHN McCREVAN, JR. Signature sworn to by JNO. McCREVAN on 4-23-1785 bef. WILLIAM KENNEDY, J.P. Rec. 9-27-1786.

Pp 279-282: 8-29-1786, CHARLES JONES, SR., farmer of Laurens Co., S.C. and MARTHA, his wife, to JOHN FINCHER of Union Co., for 40 pds current money, 140 acs. on Fairforest Creek in Union Co. The lower part of a tract of 500 acs. granted to CHARLES JONES, SR. on 4-2-1773 by Wm. Bull, Esq., Lt. Gov. of S.C. Orig. grant bound by ZACHARIAH STEDHAM, JOSEPH BATES and DANIEL HUGER's land. Grant rec. in Book OOO, p. 366, Sec. Office. The 140 acs. sold to FINCHER bound by JOSEPH BATES, DANIEL HUGER's land and parts of the orig. grant claimed by WILLIAM GIST and HEZEKIAH RICE. Wit: GEORGE WHITMORE, CHARLES JONES & WILLIAM GRAY. Rec. 9-27-1786.

Pp 282-283: 1-24-1785, THOMAS BRANDON, Esq. of 96 Dist., to THOMAS YOUNG, same place, for 50 pds sterling, 140 acs. part of a 240 ac. tract granted to THOMAS BRANDON on 10-15-1784 by Benj. Guerard, Gov. of S.C., located on Fairforest Creek and bound by SHADRICK LANDTRIP, WILLIAM HAILE and vacant lands. Wit: JOHN McCOOLL, JAMES BELL & DUNCAN McCREVAN. Rec. 9-28-1785?

Pp 283-284: 5-17-1785, CHARLES JONES of 96 Dist. to HEZEKIAH RICE, same place, for 200 pds, 230 acs. part of a tract of 500 acs. on Fairforest Creek in Craven County, granted to JONES on 4-2-1773. Bound by ZACHARIAH STEDHAM, JOSEPH BATES & DANIEL HUGER's land. (Same grant referred to in deed on pp. 279-282). Wit: THOMAS BRANDON, J.P., WILLIAM GOLDSMITH, SHADRICK LANDTRIP. Rec. 9-27-1785?

Page 285: 5-14-1785, ADAM McCOOLL, blacksmith, of Camden Dist., to JOSEPH HUGHS, planter, of 96 Dist., for 28 pds, 11 shillings and 5 pence sterling, 100 acs. on west side of Broad River, bound by RICHARD HUGHS and DUNCAN McCREVAN, granted to ADAM McCOOLL on 5-21-1772 by Chas. G. Montague, Gov. of Prov. of S.C. Wit: JOHN HENDERSON, JOHN BIRDSONG(?) & THOMAS BRANDON. Rec. 9-28-1785?

Pp 286-288: 12-22-1785, Col. THOMAS BRANDON of Union Co., to THOMAS YOUNG, same place, for 50 pds sterling, 107 acs. part of a grant of 207 acs. on Morris Creek made to sd BRANDON on 1-21-1785. Grant and plat recorded in Sec. Office, Book ZZZ, p. 404. No witnesses. Rec. 12-26-1786.

Pp 289-291: 12-24-1785, Col. THOMAS BRANDON of Union Co., to JOHN BRANDON, same place, for 50 pds sterling, 125 acs. part of a tract of 550 acs. granted to THOMAS YOUNG on 1-21-1785, located on Buffalow's Creek. Grant and plat recorded in Bk. ZZZ, p. 396. The 125 ac. tract conveyed to THOMAS BRANDON by sd THOMAS YOUNG. Wit: ZACHA. BULLOCK, JOHN BIRDSONG. Rec. 12-26-1785?

Pp 292-296: 8-25-1770, EMANUEL STEVENS, planter, and LUCRECIA, his wife, of the Prov. of S.C., to WILLIAM LAWSON, planter, of same

Cont'd:
place, for the sum of one pound fifteen shillings lawful money of South
Carolina being equal in value to five shillings sterling lawful money
of Great Britain, 150 acs. on south side of Tygar River, part of a
grant of 350 acs. made to EMANUEL STEVENS on 9-22-1768, and recorded
in Bk. DDD, p. 436. Wit: SIMON MURPHY, JOHN HOWARD, NATHL. AUSTIN.
Signatures sworn to by SIMON MURPHY on 9-29-1770 bef. WILLIAM WOFFORD,
J.P. of Craven Co., S.C. Rec. 12-26-1785?

Page 297:   11-3-1774, JOSEPH ROBISON, Esq. of Craven Co., to THOMAS
        McGRUE, farmer, same place, a bond in the amount of 600 pds cur-
rent money of S.C., for 100 acs. in 96 Dist. on both sides of Abbington
Creek. Part of a tract granted to JACOB GARDNER. Joining land of ROBERT
WHITLEY. No witnesses.

        On 5-20-1777, THOMAS McGRUE assigned his interest in the bond
to ROBERT WHITLEY. Wit: MOSES GUYTON.

        On 12-6-1784, ROBERT WHITLEY assigned his interest in the bond
to MOSES GUYTON. Wit: MARGARET SCOTT. MARGARET SCOTT swore to MOSES
GUYTON's signature on 5-28-1785 bef. JOHN HAILE, J.P. Rec. 12-26-1785?

Pp 297-299:   2-21-1785, THOMAS YOUNG, Gent., of 96 Dist., to JOSEPH
        JONES, same place, for 14 pds sterling, 150 acs. part of a grant
of a tract of 450 acs. made to WILLIAM HOLMES by Wm. Bull, Esq., Lt.
Gov. of S.C. on 6-23-1774. Grant was in "Barkley" County in the fork
between Broad and Saluda Rivers on the Drafts of Fairforest and Brown's
Creeks. Bound by GABRIEL ANDERSON, OBEDIAH HOWARD, and vacant lands.
Grant recorded in Sec. Office, Book QQQ, p. 59. Entire tract of 450
acs. conveyed by HOLMES to GEORGE CROSLEY, SR. and 180 acs. of sd tract
conveyed by CROSLEY to the above named THOMAS YOUNG. Wit: HARRIS NICHOL-
SON, DUNCAN McCREEVAN & JEAN (X) CREEVAN (the "Mc" not shown.) Rec.
9-28-1785?

Pp 299-301:   1-31-1785, THOMAS TRAMMELL of Union Co., to Col. WILLIAM
        FARR, same place, for 100 pds sterling, 100 acs. on south side
of Broad River, bound by the river, DANIEL TRAMMELL, and vacant lands.
Orig. granted to the sd THOMAS TRAMMELL in Nov. 1767 by Lord Charles
Granville, Esq., Gov. of the Prov. of S. C. Wit: THOMAS STRIBLING,
JOHN PUTMAN, WM. GRANT. Rec. 9-27-1785?

        (Note: There is no explanation given in the Deed Book for the
fact that these last few deeds are recorded in 1785 instead of 1786,
even though they are in the middle of ones recorded in 1786. The clerk
either was a year late writing them in the book, or he simply made
a mistake when he wrote down the year. They were probably misplaced
and were a year late getting in the book..JMC).

Pp 302-303:   11-1-1786, WILLIAM JOHNSON, planter of Union Co., to
        CHARLES SIMS, Esq., same place, for 268 pds, 12 shillings, current
money, 280 acs. on the bank of Broad River. Part of a larger tract
conveyed by CALEB EDMONDSON to JOHN PEARSON. Wit: WARREN HALL, BERD.
(BERNARD) GLENN, WILLIAM GLENN. Rec. 12-25-1786.
        (Note: BERNARD GLENN and WILLIAM GLENN were brothers, sons of
NATHAN and LUCY COLEMAN GLENN. Nathan and several of his sons were
Revolutionary soldiers, serving from Virginia. They moved to S. C.
after the Revolution.)

Pp 303-304:   12-23-1786, THOMAS BRANDON, Esq., of Union Co., to CHRIST-
        OPHER YOUNG, same place, for 50 pds sterling, 100 acs. part of
a tract of 240 acs. granted to sd BRANDON on 10-15-1784, located on
both sides of Fairforest Creek, bound by WILLIAM HAILE's land, vacant
lands and SHADRICK LANDTRIP's Et. (Estate?). No witnesses. Rec. 12-
25-1786.

Pp 304-305:   12-22-1786, GEORGE CROSLEY, carpenter of Union Co., to
        ARTHUR BRANDON, same place, for 100 pds, 86 acs. on south side
of Shoaly Creek, a branch of Fairforest. Part of a tract of 172 acs.
granted to sd CROSLEY on 2-6-1786. Plat and grant rec. in Sec. Office,

Cont'd:
in Book GGGG, page 403. No witnesses. Rec. 12-25-1786.

Pp 306-307:   12-22-1786, GEORGE CROSLEY, carpenter of Union Co., to
    JAMES BELL, same place, for 100 pds sterling, 86 acs. on the
north side of Shoaly Creek, the other half of the tract described in
the next above deed. No witnesses. Rec. 12-25-1786.

Pp 307-308:   Dated Dec. 1786 (date incomplete), CHRISTOPHER BRANDON,
yeoman of Union Co., to THOMAS BRANDON, Esq., same place, for 100 pds
sterling, 100 acs. on Tygar River, granted to CHRISTOPHER BRANDON on
1-21-1785. No witnesses. Rec. 12-25-1786.

Pp 308-311:   3-2-1785, DANIEL OGLESBY to JAMES HOGGAT, for 150 pds
    lawful money of North Carolina, 350 acs. in S. C., 96 Dist.,
on a small river running into Broad River formerly called Collin's
River, now Innoree (Enoree) River. Tract was surveyed for MARY KING
and recorded in Sec. Office in S. C. Bound by the river and vacant
lands when surveyed. Wit: JAMES ROBERTSON, ELIJAH ROBISON, ZADOK (X)
BOUSSIER, THOMAS (X) CAING. Sale ack. by OGLESBY in court on 7-4-1785
and certified by ANDREW EWIN, Deputy Registrar of Davison County (North
Carolina?). Rec. in Union Co., S.C. on 12-25-1786.

Pp 311-312:   12-26-1785, GEORGE WILLIAM BRIANT, planter, and his wife,
    (name not given) of Union Co., S.C. to GEORGE HARLIN, hatter,
same place, for 15 pds sterling, 25 acs. on Sugar Creek, part of a
tract of 200 acs. granted to PHILIP BRIANT on 5-3-1773. Rec. in Sec.
Office in Book OOO, p. 486, and in Auditor General's Office in NN 12,
p. 376, on 8-16-1773. Descended to the sd WILLIAM BRIANT being the
Right and lawful Heir of the sd PHILIP BRIANT, deceased. Bound by JOHN
LITTLE, the creek and the original tract. Wit: THOMAS BRANDON, JOHN
MURRELL, WILLIAM WILSON, ARCHER HOWARD. Rec. 12-25-1786.

Pp 312-315:   11-13-1786, JAMES HOGGAT to MARLOW PRYOT (no county or
    state given) for 300 pds sterling money of S. C., 350 acs. in
Union Co., 96 Dist., S.C., which was surveyed for MARY KING, on a small
river called Collins River, now Enoree River, running into Broad River.
Wit: JOHN BLASSIGAME, THOMAS BLASSINGAME. Rec. 12-25-1786.

Pp 315-316:   10-4-1784, FRANCIS FINCHER of 96 Dist., to JOHN FINCHER,
    same place, for 5 pds sterling, 150 acs. on Armel's Branch, a
branch of Tygar River, bound on all sides by vacant lands. Granted
to CHARLES JONES on 8-19-1774. Wit: JAMES WOODSON, MARY (X) MUSGRAVE.
FRANCIS FINCHER's signature sworn to by JAMES WOODSON on 10-9-1784
bef. THOMAS BRANDON, J.P. Rec. 12-25-1786.

Pp 316-317:   10-4-1784, FRANCIS FINCHER of 96 Dist. to JOHN FINCHER,
    same place, for 10 pds sterling, 100 acs. on Fincher's Branch,
the south side of Tygar River. Bound by ARMOND FINCHER and vacant lands.
Granted to JAMES MITCHEL on 2-3-1775. Wit: JAMES WOODSON, MARY MUSGRAVE.
Signature sworn to as in above deed. No recording date.

Pp 318-319:   3-2-1770, MARY FEEMSTER, widow of Tryon, Prov. of N.
    C., to SAMUEL FEEMSTER, her son, planter, same place, 150 acs.
on south side of Broad River in Anson County at the time of the orig.
grant now in Tryon County. Bound by WILLIAM LOVE, Broad River and vacant
lands. Part of a 400 ac. tract granted to JOHN CLARK by Matthew Roane,
Pres. of Prov. of N. C. (no date). JOHN CLARK conveyed entire tract
to JOHN FEEMSTER, son of the sd MARY FEEMSTER. JOHN FEEMSTER sold 150
acs. to his mother, MARY FEEMSTER, but died without giving her a title.
In his last Will and testament, he ordered that his heirs give her
a true and lawful right. This 150 acs. now deeded by MARY to her son
SAMUEL FEEMSTER for love and affection and 35 shilliings. Reserved
the right to hold for her lifetime. Wit: ARCHD. ROBISON, THOMAS CROSBY,
SARAH ROBISON. Certified by EZEKIEL POL, Clerk of Court for Tryon Co.,
N. C. Recorded in Union Co., S.C. on 12-25-1786.

Pp 319-322:   12-25-1786, JOHN GRINDAL and HESTER, his wife, of Union
    Co., to JOHN WATSON and SAMUEL CHISHOLM, same place, for 300

Cont'd:
pds sterling, 3 tracts of land on both sides of Packolate River, including Grindal's Shoals and plantation adj. each other, containing
430 acs. in all. 250 acs. of above tract granted to JOHN GRINDAL by
Wm. Bull, Lt. Gov. of S.C., on 4-21-1775, 85 acs. granted to GRINDAL
on 12-22-1768 by Wm. Tryon, Gov. of N. C., 100 acs. bought from JAMES
HUEY on 4-2-1774. Wit: DAVID CHISHOLM, JESSE MABRY. No rec. date.

Pp 322-323:   4-2-1774, JAMES HUGHEY of Camden Dist., S.C. to JOHN
        GRINDAL of 96 Dist., S.C., for 100 pds currency, 100 acs. in
96 Dist., on the north side of Packolate River, joining the plantation
where GRINDAL now lives, and the place called Carrol's Shoals, including the several islands nearest the north bank of the sd River. Part
of a tract granted to JOHN CLARK and conveyed by him to JAMES HUGHEY.
Wit: ADAM POTTER, JOHN MOSLEY, CHRISTOPHER COLEMAN, J.P. No recording
date. (Grantor signed JAMES HUEY. This is the same tract referred to
in above deed.)

        (Note: Grindal's Shoal, referred to in these deeds, was a much
used crossing place before and during the Revolution. According to
local history, DANIEL MORGAN and his army camped here on JOHN GRIN-
DAL's farm for a week or so just before the Battle of Cowpens..JMC)

Page 324:   6-6-1785, FERDINAND HOPKINS of Camden Dist., S.C. to
        DANIEL LIPHAM of 96 Dist., for 100 pds former currency of S.
C. ..one certain tract in 96 Dist. on waters of Tygar and Enoree Rivers.
Orig. granted to sd HOPKINS by Benj. Guerrard, Gov. of S.C. on 1-21-
1785. Rec. in Book AAAA, p. 387. Plat dated 9-31-1784 attached to grant.
Wit: D. HOPKINS, VARDRY McBEE, NATHL. ABNEY, M.D. Rec. 12-25-1786.

Pp 325-326:   12-15-1786, Col. THOMAS BRANDON of Union Co., to CHRISTO-
        PHER BRANDON, same place, for 50 pds sterling, 300 acs. on south
side of Broad River on a fork of Brown's Creek. Orig. granted to JACOB
BROWN on 9-24-1754 by Matthew Rowan, Esq., Commander-in-Chief over
Province of North Carolina, laying and being in the County of Anson,
N. C. Conveyed by BROWN on 8-2-1770 to JOHN MAYFIELD, deceased, father
to WILLIAM MAYFIELD, now Heir at law. Sd WILLIAM MAYFIELD conveyed
to THOMAS BRANDON on 3-1-1785. No witnesses. Rec. 12-25-1786.

Pp 326-327:   9-15-1785, JOHN WIDAMAN, planter of Newberry Co., S.C.
        to GEORGE PURVIS, planter, of state afsd., bond for 2500 pds
old currency, 300 acs. on Fanning's Creek running thence to Broad River
including one mill, conditions being that sd WIDAMAN to give title
by lease and release by 10-15-1787. Wit: MICHL. DICKERT, MARGARET (X)
DICKERT. (Name also spelled WHEATMAN and WEATMAN but signed WIDAMAN).
on 10-22-1785, GEORGE PURVIS sold the 300 acs. (whereon I now live)
and assigned the bond for 2500 pds over to JOHN EWART of Union Co.,
for 30 pds sterling, in cash or tobacco to that value delivered in
Charlestown on or bef. the 30th day of Dec. next ensuing. Wit: JOHN
HOPE, JAMES HOPE. Rec. by order of the Court by JOHN HAILE, Clerk,
on 12-26-1786.

Page 328:   12-23-1786, WILLIAM COTTER and CATHERINE, his wife, of
        Union Co., to JAMES MARTIN, same place, for 100 pds sterling,
115 acs. on a branch of Thicketty Creek called McBee's Creek. Granted
to WILLIAM COTTER by Wm. Moultrie, Gov. of S.C. on 7-4-1785. Wit: ROBT.
LUSK, CHARLES MILES, THOMAS LUSK. Rec. 12-26-1786.

Pp 329-332:   10-16-1786, WILLIAM GAULT of Packolate, Union Co., S.C.
        to JOHN GEORGE of Union Co., for 71 pds, 8 shillings sterling,
100 acs. on south side of Packolate River. Part of a tract of 200 acs.
granted by patent to JOHN PORTMAN on 4-7-1767 by Wm. Tryon, Gov. of
Prov. of N.C., on both sides of Packolate River, then in Mecklenburgh
Co., N.C...Conveyed by PORTMAN to ROBERT McWHORTER for 13 pds, by Mc-
WHORTER to GEORGE McWHORTER on 11-3-1778, and by him to WILLIAM GAULT
on 4-5-1780. Wit: NICHOLAS JASPER, JOHN GEORGE, JR., JOHN PRIDMORE.
Rec. 12-26-1786.

Pp 332-334:   10-17-1786, JOHN McWHORTER of Packolate River, Union
        Co., to JOHN GEORGE, same place, for 40 pds old currency, 10

501

Cont'd:
acs. on the south side of Packolate River. Part of a tract of 300 acs.
on both sides of Packolate River granted by patent to ELEANOR McWHORTER
on 10-26-1767 by Wm. Tryon, Gov. of N. C. Grant located in what was
then Mecklenburgh Co., N. C. Conveyed by JOHN McWHORTER on 7-13-1784.
Wit: NICHOLAS JASPER, JOHN GEORGE, JR., JOHN PRIDMORE. Rec. 12-26-
1786.

Pp 334-337:   12-25-1786, ARCHER SMITH of 96 Dist., to JOHN PUTMAN,
          same place, for 50 pds currency, 200 acs. on north side of Tygar
River, granted to ANTHONY TOOMER on 5-5-1773 by Wm. Bull, Gov. of S.C.
and recorded in Sec. Office, Book OOO, p. 658. No witnesses. Rec. 12-
26-1786.

          (Note: There are 2 pages numbered 337 in the book. The deed above
ends on the 1st page 337, and the deed below begins on the 1st page
337 and ends on the 2nd 337.)

Page 337 (1 & 2): 11-27-1786, JOHN STEEN and MARTHA STEEN, his wife,
          to JOHN THOMPSON, JR., (no place of residence given for either
party), for 400 pds sterling, 284 acs. on Thicketty Creek, including
the mouth of Mincum's Creek, bound by MINCUM and HOWARD. The west end
of a tract of 375 acs. granted to JAMES BRIDGES by N. C. and conveyed
by him to WILLIAM TWITTY, and from him to WILLIAM TWITTY, JR. by heirship, and from TWITTY, JR. to sd JOHN STEEN. Wit: FRANCIS LETTIMORE,
JOHN GARDNER. Rec. 12-26-1786.

Pp 337 (the 2nd)-339: 12-5-1786, ABIGAIL PADGETT, spinster of St. Mat-
          thews Parish in Barkley (Co.) S.C. to RALPH HUNT, planter, of
S.C. for 32 pds 14 shillings and 3 pence sterling, 100 acs. on south
side of Broad River, on Padgett's Creek. Orig. granted to JACOB HOYLE.
Wit: JAMES ADDINGTON, JAMES BENSON. No rec. date.

Pp 340-341:   9-4-1783, JAMES GRAY of 96 Dist., to ROBERT WOODSON,
          same place, for 1000 pds current money, 150 acs. on the north
side of Fairforest Creek, bound by the creek, JAMES FINLEY's line,
now claimed by JOHN GOODWIN, and COX's line. Part of a 500 ac. tract
granted to BENJAMIN GIST on 7-15-1768, conveyed by him to WILLIAM WOF-
FORD, and the 150 acs. conveyed by WOFFORD to sd JAMES GRAY. Orig.
tract bounded by NICHOLS, VERNON, THOMAS COX, CHARLES KING, PHILIP
BRYON, JAMES FINLEY and vacant lands. Wit: GEORGE GRAY, WILLIAM WOOD-
SON, MARY GRAY. Rec. 12-27-1786.

Pp 341-342:   12-16-1783, WILLIAM GILHAM and JEAN, his wife, of 96
          Dist., to JOHN HAMILTON, of state afsd., (no county or dist.
given), for 300 pds current money, 81 acs. orig. granted to CHARLES
BARNS by Wm. Tryon, Gov. of N.C., on 4-20-1768, conveyed by heirship
to JOHN BARNS, then to BARBARA BARNS, then to MOSES and JACOB BARNS,
then to WILLIAM GILHAM. Wit: JAMES HAMILTON, JOHN HAMILTON, THOMAS
GOOD. JAMES HAMILTON appeared bef. FRAME WOODS, J.P. of Camden Dist.,
on 2-14-1785 and swore to WILLIAM and JEAN GILHAM's signatures. Wit.
named as JOHN HAMILTON, SR. and THOMAS GOOD. (Wife's name shown as
"JEAN" and "JANE" in deed, but she signed by mark "JEAN".)

Pp 342-344:   10-19-1779, ROBERT BISHOP and ELIZABETH, his wife of
          96 Dist., to WALTER HOLMES, for 500 pds current money, 130 acs.
on Buffalow Creek. Bound by WILLIAM BISHOP, THOMAS GREEN, OBEDIAH HOW-
ARD and ROBERT BISHOP. Part of a tract of 250 acs. in Craven County
on a branch of Fairforest called Buffalow Creek, surveyed for ROBERT
BISHOP on 4-4-1768 and rec. in Book III, p. 71. Signed by the Gov.
of S.C. on 7-12-1771. Wit: HENRY LONG, JAMES WOODSON, HENRY LIPHAM.
No recording date.

Pp 344-346:   8-2-1786, WILLIAM FARR of Union Co., to HENRY LONG, black-
          smith, same place, for 73 pds, 19 shillings, 4 pence, 317 acs.
on north side of Saluda on Brown's Creek, a branch of Broad River.
Bound by WILLIAM BUCHANNAN, WILLIAM WILLIAMS and JOHN WHITE. Granted
to WM. FARR, Esq. on 9-5-1785 and rec. in Grant Book FFFF, p. 54. Wit:
JOHN EWART, JOHN McCOOLL, JOHN HAILE. Rec. 9-29-1786.

Pp 346-347:   12-30-1786, JOSEPH JONES of Union Co., to JOHN McCOOLL,
    same place, for 81 pds 14 shillings lawful money of S.C., 150
acs. on the waters of Brown's Creek and Fairforest (Creek). Bound on
all sides by JOHN McCOOLL's land, being the remaining part of a tract
granted to WALTER HOLMES, conveyed by Holmes to GEORGE CROSLEY, SR.,
then by sd Crosley to THOMAS YOUNG, then to the sd JOSEPH JONES. Signed
by JOSEPH JONES and SARAH JONES. Wit: WM. KENEDY, JOHN BIRDSONG. Rec.
12-30-1786.

Pp 347-349:   2-15-1775, BRYAN WHITE and JUDITH, his wife, to AVERY
    BREED (no place of residence given) for 150 pds current money
of S.C., 200 acres in Craven Co. on a branch of Fairforest called Buffalow. Bound by JOSEPH BREED, ROBERT BISHOP and DAVIS PAULK. Granted
on 2-2-1773 by Lord Chas. Granville Montague, Gov. of Prov. of S.C.
Description excepted one-half of the gold and silver mines. Wit: RENNY
BELUE, RICHARD BRYAN, MARY BRYAN. RENNY BELUE swore to signatures in
1775 (no month or day given) in 96 Dist., bef. THOS. FLETCHALL, J.P.
Rec. 12-30-1786.

Pp 349-352:   1-1-1787, OBEDIAH HOWARD of Union Co., to ZACHARIAH BELL,
    SR., of same place, for 75 pds sterling, 150 acs. on Shoal Creek,
a branch of Fairforest, the plantation whereon JOHN SPRINGER now lives,
granted to OBEDIAH HOWARD on 6-23-1774. Signed by OBEDIAH HOWARD and
PRISILLA (X) HOWARD. Wit: JOHN EWART, JOHN McCOOLL, JOSEPH JONES. Rec.
3-26-1787.

Pp 352-353:   1-15-1787, JACOB BROWN of Washington Co., N. C., to JOHN
    JOLLY, of Union Co., S.C., for 40 pds sterling money of S.C.,
100 acs. whereon HANDCOCK PORTER now lives including the sd HANDCOCK
PORTER's plantation. Bound by JAMES BOGAN and vacant lands, on both
sides of Brown's Creek. Granted to sd JACOB BROWN by the Gov. of N.
C. in 1766. Wit: JOHN EWART, JOHN McCOOLL, JOHN MONTGOMERY. Rec. 3-
26-1787.

Pp 353-354:   2-5-1787, JESSE FORE, planter of Union Co., to THOMAS
    PALMER, planter of same place, for 15 pds sterling, 150 acs.
on Buffalow Creek, a small branch of Fairforest Creek. Bound by WOOD-
WARD, ALEXANDER McDOUGAL and JOHN PALMER. Granted by patent to sd JESSE
FORE on 5-1-1786 and rec. in Grant Book HHHH, p. 429. Wit: JOHN FORE,
ROBERT THOMPSON, HENRY CALAWELL, ABRAHAM JONES. Rec. 3-26-1787.

Page 355:   2-17-1786, EDWARD MUSGRAVE and ANN MUSGRAVE, his wife,
    of Laurens Co., S.C. to ROBERT CREANSHAW of Union Co., for 50
pds Virginia money, 100 acs. in Union Co., in the fork of Broad and
Saluda Rivers on the north side of Tygar River. Granted to EDWARD MUS-
GRAVE on 8-13-1766. Wit: EDWD. RAGSDALE, STEPHEN CREANSHAW, ANN MUS-
GRAVE. Rec. 3-26-1787.

Page 356:   12-28-1786, WILLIAM HILL and DORCAS HILL, his wife, of
    Edgefield Co., S.C. to EDWARD RAGSDALE of Union Co., S.C., for
200 pds sterling, 200 acs. in Union Co., on the SW side of Tygar River,
bound by THOMAS GORDON, FRANCES AUBREY, JAMES CALDWELL and vacant lands.
Granted to WILLIAM NOBLE on 4-21-1784 (error-should be 1774) by Wm.
Bull, Lt. Gov. of the Prov. of S.C. in the 14th year of His Majesty's
Reign. Wit: STEPHEN CRENSHAW, ROBERT CRENSHAW, FRANCIS CRENSHAW and
WILLIAM MAYS. Rec. 3-26-1787.

Pp 357-358:   3-25-1787, AVERY BREED of Union Co., to AARON HARLON,
    same place, for 30 pds sterling, 200 acs. on Buffalow Creek,
bound by JOSEPH BREED, ROBERT BISHOP and EPAPHRADITUS PAULK. Granted
to BRYAN WHITE on 2-2-1773, and conveyed by White to sd AVERY BREED
on 2-15-1775. No witnesses. No recording date. (Grantee's name also
spelled "HARLIN" in deed.)

Pp 358-359:   3-26-1787, JOHN HAILE of Union Co, to THOMAS BLASSINGAME
    of same place, for 100 pds sterling, 505 acs. on Mitchel's Creek,
waters of Fairforest. Granted by patent to sd HAILE in 1786 and rec.
in Book PPPP, p. 357. Wit: JOHN EWART. Rec. 3-26-1787.

Pp 359-360:   5-26-1787, JOHN HAILE of Union Co., to GEORGE HARLIN,

Cont'd:
    farmer of same place, for 10 pds sterling, 20 acs. on south side
of Fairforest Creek, part of a tract of 24 acs. granted by patent to
sd HAILE on 11-6-1785. Bound by sd HARLIN, VERNON, the creek and by
a road leading from Capt. THOMAS BLASSINGAME's to Union Courthouse.
Wit: JOHN EWART. Rec. 3-26-1787.

Pp 360-361:   11-13-1786, JAMES HALL of Union Co., to RICHARD PRUIT,
    of same place, for 10 pds current money, 100 acs. granted by
Wm. Moultrie, Gov. of S.C. (no location of land or date of grant given).
Wit: WILLIAM KENNEDY, NATHAN SANDAGE. Rec. 3-26-1787.

Pp 361-362:   11-13-1786, JAMES HALL of Union Co., to NATHAN SANDAGE,
    of same place, for 10 pds current money, 100 acs. in Union Co.,
granted by Wm. Moultrie, Gov. of S. C., (specific location or date
of grant not given). Wit: WILLIAM KENNEDY & RICHARD PRUIT. Rec. 3-
26-1787.

Page 363:   12-6-1786, THOMAS GORDON to JOHN McNEAL, both of the
    state of South Carolina and counties of Newberry and Union, for
5 pds sterling, 1/3 part of a 400 ac. tract on the south side of Broad
River, granted to THOMAS GORDON on 2-6-1786. Wit: W. WADLINGTON, ABEL
ANDERSON, ABRAHAM ANDERSON, ANAMANOS LILES. Rec. 3-26-1787. (Note:
The name of the witness seems to be spelled ANAMANOS LILES. However,
there was a gentleman by the name of ARAMANUS LYLES. The name is still
used in the LYLES family..JMC)

Pp 363-364:   12-6-1786, THOMAS GORDON to REBECCA NEAL, widow, both
    of the state of S.C., and counties of Newberry and Union, for
5 pds sterling, 2/3 of a tract containing 400 acs., on the south side
of Broad River, that is to say the one half of the sd two thirds to
her son, to wit, EDWARD McNEAL, the other to remain her property during
her life then to be the property of her other two sons ANDERSON McNEAL
and ABEL ANDERSON McNEAL. Orig. tract granted to THOMAS GORDON on 2-
6-1786. Wit: W. WADLINGTON, ABEL ANDERSON, ABRAHAM ANDERSON, ANAMANOS
LILES. Rec. 3-26-1787.

Pp 364-367:   9-5-1774, ROBERT McWHORTER, planter of the Prov. of S.C.
    to JAMES WOOD, Surveyor of Lawson's Fork, prov. afsd., for 40
pds current money, 500 acs. on south side of Packolate River. Granted
by patent to ROBERT McWHORTER on 8-19-1774. Wit: JAMES EDWARDS, JOHN
NUCKOLS, MATTHEW (X) ROBISON. Rec. 3-26-1787.

Pp 367-368:   1-29-1787, JOSEPH BREED and CATHERINE, his wife, of Wilkes
    Co., Georgia, to JOHN BIRGSONG, of Union Co., S.C., for 35 pds
sterling, 100 acs. on the east side of Fairforest Creek. Part of a
tract of 520 acs. granted to SAMUEL YOUNG in 1753, then laying in Anson
County, in the province of North Carolina, and lately Mecklenburgh,
and now, Tryon in the province of North Carolina. Conveyed by YOUNG
to DANIEL PLUMMER on 12-2-1764, and rec. in Mecklenburgh Co. Wit: GEORGE
HARLIN, JOB (X) SPRINGER, AVERY BREED. Rec. 3-26-1787.

Pp 368-369:   1-29-1787, JOSEPH BREED and CATHERINE, his wife of Wilkes
    Co., Georgia, to JOHN BIRDSONG of Union Co., S.C., for 30 pds,
14 shillings sterling, 100 acs. on east side of Fairforest Creek. Wit:
GEORGE HARLON, JOB (X) SPRINGER, AVERY BREED. Rec. 3-26-1787.

Pp 369-372:   2-1-1780, WILLIAM ORR, yeoman of 96 Dist., S.C. to WILLIAM
    RODGERS, yeoman of same place, for 410 pds current money, 200
acs. on Tygar River. Granted to THOMAS CURTIS by James Glen, Gov. of
Prov. of S.C. (no date of grant given). Conveyed by CURTIS to sd ORR
on 3-5-1775. Wit: ROBT. WILSON, SHARSHALL GRASTY, THOMAS COX. Signature
sworn to by ROBT. WILSON bef. JOHN CALDWELL, J.P. Rec. 3-26-1787.

Pp 373-374:   2-26-1787, LEWIS BOBO and SARAH BOBO, his wife, of Union
    Co., S.C. to DRURY MURRELL of same place, for 200 pds good money,
200 acs. on the Ninety Six road. Bound by EMANUEL STEPHENS, CALEB ED-
MONDSON, the 96 road, and the new road. Part of a tract of 700 acs.
granted to LEWIS BOBO on 7-30-1770 and rec. in Book FFF, p. 27, in

Cont'd:
Secretary's Office, "laying and being in the then Barkley County but now in Union County", on WOFFORD's and BARNET's branches, small branches of Tygar River. Grant bound by EMANUEL STEPHENS, RALPH JACKSON, and vacant lands. Wit: JOHN MURRELL, WILLIAM WILSON, SAMUEL MURRELL. Rec. 3-26-1787.

Pp 374-377: 2-23-1786, MARK JACKSON and ELIZABETH, his wife, of Union Co., 96 Dist., S.C., to PATRICK SHAW, same place, for 120 pds "old proclamation money Dollars at Six Shillings and Six pence Each," 200 acs. granted to MARK JACKSON on 4-21-1774 by Charles Greville Montague, Gov. of S. C., located in "Craven" Co. on Mitchel's Creek, a branch of Fairforest. Bound by AVERY BREED, SAMUEL JACKSON and vacant lands. Wit: JOSEPH EAST, SAMUEL NOBLET. Rec. 3-26-1787.

Page 378: 2-22-1787, FRANCIS POSEY to JOHN WOOD (no residence given) for 100 pds sterling, a tract of land in Union Co. on south side of Broad River. Part of a larger tract of 200 acs. orig. granted to AMOS TIMS on 7-26-1774 and recorded in Sec. Office in Book RRR, p. 506 and in Auditor Genl.'s Office in Book C.H.N. 13, p. 224, on 1-6-1775. Since conveyed by AMOS TIMS to JAMES TIMS and by JAMES TIMS to sd FRANCIS POSEY. Bound by WILLIAM ARMSTRONG, BENJAMIN HOLLINGSWORTH, sd POSEY, and the river. Signed by FRANCIS (X) POSEY and MILDRED (X) POSEY. Wit: JOSIAH WOOD, BENJAMIN (X) HOLLINGSWORTH, RUCKER (X) SMITH. Rec. 3-26-1787.

Page 379: 2-21-1787, FRANCIS POSEY of 96 Dist., to BENJAMIN HOLLINGSWORTH, same place, for 100 pds sterling, 100 acs. in Union Co. on south side of Broad River, part of the tract of 200 acs. described in the next above deed. Bound by Dr. NATHANIEL ABNEY and the other part of the original grant. Signed by FRANCIS POSEY (not by mark) and MILDRED (X) POSEY. Wit: JOHN WOOD, RUCKER (X) SMITH, JOSIAH WOOD. Rec. 3-26-1787.

Page 380: 2-1-1786, DAVID HOPKINS and MARY, his wife of Camden Dist., S.C., to JAMES SIMS of 96 Dist., S.C., for 50 pds sterling, 600 acs. according to a plat and grant, dated 1-1-1785, on the waters of Broad and Tygar Rivers. Bound by land formerly JOHN MARTIN's, THOAMS COX, MOSICK (?) SUTTIN, JOHN TOWN, EDWARD MUSGRAVE and Tygar River. Plat certified for 10-1-1784. Signed: D. HOPKINS & MARY HOPKINS. Wit: NATHAN GLEN, WM. ALEN BURTON, FERDINAND HOPKINS. Rec. 3-26-1787.

(Note: Col. DAVID HOPKINS moved from Virginia to Chester Co. (Camden Dist.) before the Revolution. His wife was MARY GLENN, sister of NATHAN GLENN (GLEN). JAMES SIMS was also related to the GLEN(N) family. The GLEN(N) family - several different sets of it - remained in Virginia until after the Revolution. Then they moved to Chester and Union Counties, settling near DAVID HOPKINS in Chester Co. and right across the Broad River in Union Co...JMC)

Pp 380-383: 3-10-1787, JOSEPH HOWEL, cooper of 96 Dist., S.C. to JAMES OLIPHANT, planter, of same place, for 10 pds sterling, 493 acs. on north side of Tygar River, part of a tract of 600 acs. granted to WILLIAM COWDEN by Matthew Rowan, Esq., Gov. of N. C., on 9-3-1753, and after Boundary line run between the two provinces, granted to ARCHER SMITH by Wm. Bull, Esq., Lt. Gov. of South Carolina, on 10-14-1774. Since purchased at a Sheriff's sale by sd ARCHER SMITH and conveyed to him by STARK (no first name given), Sheriff of 96 Dist. Conveyed by sd SMITH to above named JAMES OLIPHANT by lease and release dated 12-9-1786. Bound by Tygar River, the part of the 600 ac. tract that belongs to JAMES OLIPHANT, JEREMIAH BRASHERES, THACKER VIVION, CALEB LANSTONE & THOMAS WEAVER. Wit: BUCKNER (X) SMITH, RICHARD (X) BRIAN. Rec. 3-26-1787.

Pp 383-385: 4-15-1774, RALPH HUMPHREYS, Deputy Surveyor of Barkley Co., Orangeburgh Dist., to ISAAC HAWKINS, planter of Craven Co., 96 Dist., for 200 pds current money, 100 acs. on the south side of Tygar River, bound at the time of survey by vacant lands. Granted to HUMPHREYS on 6-7-1768. Wit: THOMAS WILSON & RANDELL ROBISON. Signature

Cont'd:
sworn to by RANDELL ROBISON on 11-23-1784 before THOMAS GORDON, J.P.
Recorded 3-26-1787.

Pp 385-386: 3-13-1787, JOHN McCOOLL of Union Co., to JOSEPH JONES
of same place, for 86 pds 14 shillings, 150 acs. on the waters
of Brown's Creek and Fairforest Creek. Part of a 450 ac. tract granted
by patent to WALTER HOLMES, conveyed by Holmes to GEORGE CROSLEY, SR.
by Crosley to THOMAS YOUNG, by Young to sd JOSEPH JONES and by Jones
to the sd JOHN McCOOLL. Now conveyed back again from the sd JOHN Mc-
COOLL. Wit: JOHN EWART, RICHARD FARR. Rec. 3-26-1787.

Pp 386-387: 3-27-1787, WILLIAM GRANT and KITTURAH, his wife of 96
Dist., S.C., to JOHN PALMER, same place, for 200 pds current
money and divers good causes and considerations, 100 acs. on the Middle
Fork of Brown's Creek. Granted to WILLIAM GRANT on 6-5-1786. Wit: JOHN
McCOOLL, JOHN GREGORY, DUNCAN McCREEVAN. Rec. 3-27-1787.

Pp 387-388: 10-25-1786, ISAAC CHAPMAN of Union Co., to BENJAMIN JONES,
same place, for 35 pds, 140 acs. on Gilkie's Creek, bound by
JOHN STEEN and WM. GILKIE. Granted to CHAPMAN on 9-28-1784. Wit: ISHAM
SAFFORD, WILLIAM (X) JONES, VARDY McBEE. No recording date.

Pp 388-389: 1-4-1786, GABRIEL BROWN, planter of Union Co., to JAMES
GASSAWAY, planter of same place, for 200 pds sterling, 220 acs.
on Ned's Creek in 96 Dist. Part of a tract granted to BROWN on 9-5-
1786. Bound by land supposed to belong to Mr. PINCKNEY and by Meadow
Branch. Wit: D. BROWN, JOHN GREGORY. Rec. 3-27-1787. (One of these
dates is in error. Otherwise, he was selling land before he received
the grant.)

Pp 389-392: 11-17-1786, ISAAC SAMPSON and PHEBE SAMPSON, his wife,
(and late wife of WILLIAM WRIGHT, deceased), of Union Co., to
WILLIAM FARR, same place, for 18 pds sterling, and for divers good
causes them there unto moving, 400 acs. granted to WILLIAM WRIGHT on
4-3-1786. Located on south side of Broad River. Wit: WILLIAM THOMAS,
JAMES CARR VEALE. No recording date.

Pp 392-393: 12-28-1786, WILLIAM GEORGE of Union Co., Heir apparent
and administrator of DAVID GEORGE, to WILLIAM WHITLOCK, same
place, for 100 pds sterling, 800 acs. part of a larger tract on Brown's
Creek of 2200 acs. orig. granted to the sd DAVID GEORGE by Lord Wm.
Campbell, on 7-21-1775. Rec. in Sec. Office, Book YYY, p. 239 and in
Auditor's Book M N 15, p. 1, on 11-8-1775. Bound by JOB HAMMOND, BORDEN,
ZACHARIAH GIBBS, JOHN MAYFIELD, CHRISTOPHER BRANDON, JOHN GORDEN, WIL-
LIAM McJUNKIN, HANDCOCK PORTER & WILLIAM WHITLOCK. Wit: JOB HAMMOND,
HANDCOCK (X) PORTER, WM. WOWSON (?), THOMAS ALBRITON (ALBURTON?). Rec.
3-27-1787.

Pp 393-394: 3-26-1787, TURNER KINDRICK of the State of S. C., to
WILLIAM HENDLEY of 96 Dist., S.C., for 100 pds sterling, 200
acs. on Packolate River, formerly laid out for JOHN WIDIMAN and conveyed
by him to TURNER KINDRICK on 3-24-1787. Granted (to WIDEMAN?) on 4-
28-1768, plat certified for on 5-27-1767. Bound by SAMUEL SMITH. Wit:
JOHN REED, WILLIAM REED, JOHN WIDEMAN (also spelled WIDDIMAN & WEADI-
MAN). Recorded 3-27-1787. (But signed WIDIMAN).

Pp 394-395: 3-24-1787, JOHN WIDIMAN of S. C., to TURNER KINDRICK
of 96 Dist., for 100 pds current money, 200 acs. on Packolate
River, granted to sd WIDIMAN on 4-28-1768 and certified for on 5-27-
1767. (This is the deed referred to in the next above deed). Wit: WIL-
LIAM REED, WILLIAM HENDLEY, JOHN REED. Rec. 3-27-1787. (In this deed,
JOHN signed name as WEEDIMAN.)

Pp 395-397: 1-10-1785, JOHN WEEDIMAN of the Settlement of the Dutch
Fork of Broad River, 96 Dist., S.C., to TURNER KINDRICK of the
Settlement of Packolate, 96 Dist., for 10 pds lawful money, 100 acs.
granted to WEEDIMAN on 12-24-1770. Located on Reedy Branch of Packolate
River. Wit: CHRISTOPHER (X) WEEDENMAN, ISAAC HOPE, ALEXANDER (X) KIND-
RICK. Rec. 3-27-1787.

Pp 397-400:   6-4-1776 (1774?), WILLIAM SISSON, planter of 96 Dist.,
          to JOHN WEEDINGMAN, miller, of same place, for 350 pds lawful
money of Prov. of S. C., 195 acs. part of a tract of 400 acs. granted
to sd WILLIAM SISSON on 5-5-1769 by Wm. Tryon, Gov. of N. C., on both
sides of Packolate River, in what was then Tryon Co., North Carolina.
Bound by STEPHEN SISSON and BISHOP's line. Wit: CHRISTOPHER (X) WEEDING-
MAN, GEORGE (X) MOORE, JOHN McDONALD. Rec. 3-27-1787. (Note: This is
a Lease and Release - year on lease is shown as 1776, and on release
on 1774. JOHN WIDIMAN's name, as usual, spelled several ways.)

Pp 400-401:   3-27-1787, JOHN McCOOLL, of Union Co. to THOMAS EVANS,
          same place, for 25 pds current money, 94 acs. granted to McCOOLL
on 2-6-1786. Wit: DUNCAN McCREEVAN, JOHN MARTIN. Rec. 3-27-1787.

Pp 401-404:   2-13-1787, WILLIAM FARR, High Sheriff of Union Co., SC,
          to AARON FINCHER, same place, to settle a judgment for 16 pds
7 shillings and 7 pence current money against DAVID FARMER, 150 acs.
o the south side of Fairforest Creek.
          Land was sold at auction on the order of the March Term of Court,
under old English law. Bid in by AARON FINCHER (who also instigated
the suit) for 18 pds 15 shillings. Wit: JOHN EWART, MOSES GUYTON. No
recording date.

Pp 404-407:   3-23-1787, MARK MURPHY, Union Co., to BIRD MURPHY, same
          place, for 50 pds sterling, 150 acs. part of a tract of 485 acs.
granted to SIMON MURPHY on 5-7-1774. Located on southwest side of Tygar
River, and bound by land laid out to EMANUEL STEPHENS ("now DUNKIN's"),
RALPH JACKSON, JOHN MacGARRITY, MOSES KIRTLAND, SION MURPHY and the
river. Wit: WILLIAM (X) LASSON (LAWSON?), SION MURPHY, RALPH JACKSON.
Signed by MARK MURPHY and HOLLY (X) MURPHY. Rec. 3-29-1787.

Pp 407-408:   6-20-1787, Col. THOMAS BRANDON, Esq., of 96 Dist., to
          ROBERT TALKINGTON, cooper, of same place, for 20 pds sterling,
100 acs. on the south fork of Brown's Creek, surveyed for HANDCOCK
PORTER on 8-19-1784 and granted to Col. THOMAS BRANDON at Charleston
on 3-5-1787. No witnesses. Rec. 6-26-1787.

Pp 408-409:   9-14-1786, JOHN PEARSON and SARAH, his wife, of Union
          Co., to WILLIAM JOHNSON, same place, for 400 pds sterling, 600
acs. on Broad River, conveyed to sd JOHN PEARSON by CALEB EDMONDSON
on 3-18-1783. Wit: BENJAMIN BURNS, JOHN TOWNSEND, MAHLEN(?) PEARSON.
Rec. 6-26-1787.

Pp 409-410:   6-27-1786, GEORGE LITTLE, gent., of 96 Dist. to JOSEPH
          LITTLE same place, for 250 pds lawful money, 100 acs. on Dining
Creek, a branch of Fairforest. Granted to GEORGE LITTLE on 9-23-1765
by Wm. Bull, Lt. Gov. of S.C. Recorded in Grant Book FFF, p. 171. Bound
on all sides by vacant lands when granted. Wit: JOHN (X) THOMAS, SAMUEL
(X) THOMAS. Rec. 6-26-1787.

Pp 410-411:   3-28-1787, WILLIAM WAFFORD and ABIGAIL, his wife, of
          Union Co., to THOMAS TOD of Spartanburgh Co., S.C. for 19 pds
sterling, 130 acs. on which we now live, on south side of Tygar River.
Bound by the river, AMBROSE YARBOROUGH, LEWIS BOBO and THOMAS WRIGHT.
Wit: JEREMIAH (X) WILSON and AMBROSE YARBOROUGH. Rec. 6-26-1787.

Pp 411-412:   12-28-1786, ANDREW JONES of Union Co., 96 Dist. to SAMUEL
          SHIPPY (also spelled SHIPPIE), same place, for 100 pds lawful
money, 50 acs. on south side of Thicketty Creek. Bound by STEPHEN JONES,
land formerly claimed by JOHN JOHNSON, but now JOHN THOMPSON's, and
vacant lands. Wit: THOMAS LITTLEJOHN, JOSHUA PETTY. Signed by ANDREW
JONES and ELIZABETH JONES. Rec. 6-26-1787.

Pp 412-413:   12-28-1786, ANDREW JONES of Union Co., 96 Dist. to SAMUEL
          SHIPPIE, same place, for 100 pds lawful money, a certain tract
on south side of Thicketty Creek, bound by ZACHARIAH BULLOCK and STEPHEN
JONES. Wit: THOMAS LITTLEJOHN, JOSHUA PETTY. Signed by ANDREW JONES
and ELIZABETH JONES. Rec. 6-26-1787.

Pp 413-415:   5-27-1783, JOSEPH BREED, planter of S.C. and CATY, his

507

Cont'd:
    his wife, to AVERY BREED, planter of 96 Dist., for 16 pds sterl-
ing, 150 acs. on waters of Fairforest Creek. Granted to JOSEPH BREED
on 6-23-1774. Signed by JOSEPH BREED and CATHERINE (X) BREED. Wit:
GEORGE HARLIN, JOB (X) SPRINGER, OBEDIAH HOWARD, THOMAS SCALES, ELIZA-
BETH (X) SIMMONS. Rec. 6-26-1787.

Pp 415-416:   4-2-1787, OBEDIAH HOWARD and PRISILLA, his wife of Union
    Co. to JACOB PAULK, same place, for 33 pds sterling, 150 acs.
part of a 450 ac. tract granted by letters patent to sd OBEDIAH HOWARD
on 2-2-1773. Located on Shoaly Creek, a branch of Fairforest. Wit:
JOHN EWART, JOHN McCOOLL, JOHN MARTIN. Signed by OBEDIAH HOWARD....
(PRISILLA did not sign). Rec. 6-26-1787.

Pp 416-417:   6-23-1787, POTTER INLOW of Union Co., to BENJAMIN JOHN-
    SON, JR., same place, for 100 pds sterling, a certain tract on
Cain's Creek. Granted on 2-6-1786 and recorded in Book FFFF, p. 481.
Bound on one side by JAMES HAWKINS. Wit: JOHN WOOD, JOHN HOGANS, JOSIAH
WOOD. Rec. 6-26-1787. (Grantor's name also shown in deed as "PETER",
but he signed "POTTER INLOW".)

Pp 417-418:   6-23-1787, THOMAS KENNEDY, farmer, and MARY, his wife,
    of 96 Dist., to JAMES KENNEDY, farmer, same place, for 100 pds
lawful money of Virginia, 107 acs. on west side of Broad River. Part
of a 400 ac. tract patented to WILLIAM LOVE on 9-3-1753. Conveyed by
JOHN LOVE, heir to the sd WILLIAM LOVE, to HENRY SMITH. 201 acs. conveyed by SMITH to WILLIAM McMILLIN. McMILLIN conveyed 94 acs. to NATHANIEL
GUYTON and this 107 acs. to KENNEDY. No witnesses. Rec. 6-26-1787.

Pp 418-420:   12-4-1786, JONATHAN PINNELL, planter, and MIMA, his wife,
    of Union Co. to JOHN LITTLE, planter of same place, for 33 pds
13 shillings Virginia currency, 84 acs. in the fork of Sugar Creek
and Fairforest, in a county formerly called Craven County but now called
Union County. Part of a 100 ac. tract granted to MARGARET McDOUGAL,
and conveyed to PHILIP BRIAN, deceased, and by the Death of the sd
PHILIP BRYON has descended by Heirship to WILLIAM BRYON, eldest son
and Heir at law to the sd PHILIP BRYON, deceased. Conveyed by WM. BRYON
to JONATHAN PINNELL. Said 100 acs of land granted to MARGARET McDOWELL
on 5-25-1768. Rec. in Book EEE, p. 91. One-half of gold and silver
mines excepted. Wit: WILLIAM LITTLE & SAMUEL LITTLE. Rec. 6-26-1787.

Page 420:   4-2-1787, DANIEL LIPHAM of 96 Dist., to WILLIAM RODGERS,
    same place, for 1 pd 8 shillings sterling, part of a tract of
40 acs. orig. granted to sd LIPHAM on 12-4-1786. Wit: PHILIP ANDERSON,
JOSIAS DARBY, ROBERT LIVERITT. Rec. 6-26-1787.

Pp 421-422:   6-22-1787, JOHN PALMER of Union Co., to EVAN THOMAS,
    same place, for 10 pds lawful money, 150 acs. part of a 392 ac.
tract granted by letter patent to sd JOHN PALMER on 4-4-1785, on Buffalow Creek, a branch of Fairforest. Bound by EDMOND HAYS land, HOLLAND,
sd THOMAS, and NUTT's branch. No witnesses. Rec. 6-26-1787.

Pp 422-424:   6-22-1787, JOHN PALMER of Union Co. to JOSEPH THOMAS,
    same place, for 20 pds sterling, 242 acs. the balance of the
392 ac. grant described in deed above. No witnesses. Signed by JOHN
PALMER and POLLY (PALLY?) (X) PALMER. Rec. 6-26-1787.

Pp 424-426:   6-12-1787, SAMUEL FEEMSTER and MARGARET, his wife of
    Chester Co., Camden Dist., S.C. to WILLIAM BECKHAM of Union Co.,
96 Dist., for 150 pds sterling, 150 acs. in Union Co. on south side
of Broad River above the Fishdam Ford. Bound by WILLIAM LOVE. The upper
part of a tract orig. granted by letters patent by the Gov. of N. C.
to JOHN CLARK, conveyed by Clark to JOHN FEEMSTER, by Feemster to his
mother, MARY FEEMSTER, "mentioned in his the sd JOHN FEEMSTER's last
Will and testament" (see deed on p. 318-319, Deed Bk. A), conveyed
by sd MARY on 3-12-1770 to sd SAMUEL FEEMSTER. Also conveyed by WILLIAM
FEEMSTER "son and heir at law of the sd JOHN FEEMSTER, dec'd." on 7-
29-1784 to the sd SAMUEL FEEMSTER (to clear title). Wit: WILLIAM FARR,
BENJA. JOHNSON. Recorded 6-26-1787.

Pp 426-429:   9-26-1777, WILLIAM FARR of 96 Dist., to WILLIAM HOLLINGS-
     WORTH, same place, for 150 pds current money, 196 acs. part of
a tract granted to WILLIAM FARR on 5-18-1773, on the south side of
Broad River on Lower Fishdam Creek. Bound by WILLIAM HOLLINGSWORTH,
WM. FARR and MAGNAS SIMONSON. Wit: DAVID GEORGE, BETSY JETER, JOHN
DICKISON. Rec. 6-26-1787.

Pp 429-432:   1-8-1787, JOHN HARDEN, planter, and ELIZABETH WALKER,
     Admx. of HENRY HARDEN, deceased, of Chester Co., S.C. to THOS.
BLASSINGAME, planter of Union Co., for 50 pds sterling, 135 acs. on
the south side of Sugar Creek, a branch of Fairforest, 1/2 of a tract
of 270 acs. orig. granted to JOHN HITCHCOCK. Wit: DANIEL PRUIT, OBEDIAH
PRUIT. Rec. 6-26-1787.

Pp 432-434:   1-8-1787, JOHN HARDEN, planter, and ELIZABETH WALKER,
     Admx. of HENRY HARDEN, dec'd., of Chester Co., to OBEDIAH PRUIT
planter of Union Co., for 50 pds sterling, 135 acs. the other half
of the tract described in the next above deed. Wit: THOMAS BLASSINGAME,
DANIEL PRUIT. Rec. 6-26-1787.

Page 435:   6-26-1787, Col. WILLIAM FARR, Sheriff of Union Co., to
     RICHARD COX, blacksmith, same place, for 200 pds sterling, 200
acs. part of a tract granted to Col. WM. FARR on 10-15-1784. Where
RICHARD COX now lives. Bound by THOMAS COX. Wit: BERD. (BERNARD) GLENN,
JOS. HUGHES, JOSEPH COMER. Rec. 6-26-1787.

Page 436:   4-27-1787, ELIJAH MAGUIRE, planter, of Union Co. to ROBERT
     SMITH, tailor, same place, for 50 pds lawful money, 200 acs.
on a branch of Hughes Creek, waters of Broad River, bound by JAMES
McCREACKING, ROBERT SMITH, and vacant lands. Granted to ELIJAH MAGUIRE
on 12-4-1786. Wit: WILLIAM HUGHES, JAMES McCREKEN, MERRY (or MARY)
McGUIRE. Rec. 6-26-1787. (ELIJAH signed "McGUIRE".)

Pp 437-439:   4-11-1787, NEHEMIAH POSEY of Union Co. to JOSEPH COMER,
     same place, for 50 pds, 100 acs. part of a tract of 400 acs.
granted to THOMAS COX on 2-20-1754 by Matthew Rowan, Gov. of N. C.,
located on the south side of Broad River on Cain's Creek. THOMAS COX
released entire tract to WILLIAM ARMSTRONG on 11-2-1773. Sd ARMSTRONG
sold 200 acs. to JOHN POSEY, including the dwelling house of the afsd
THOMAS COX. JOHN POSEY sold 100 acs. to NATHAN ARTHURBERRY on the SW
side of Cain's Creek. NATHAN ARTHURBERRY leased and released the 100
acs. to NEHEMIAH POSEY. Bound by JAMES HOGAN, ARMSTRONG, and the creek.
Wit: RICHARD COX, JAMES HAWKINS, JOSEPH HOLLINGSWORTH. Rec. 6-26-1787.

Page 440:   1-11-1787, JOHN HENDERSON, Esq. of Union Co. to JOHN
     HAILE, Esq., same place, for 150 pds sterling, 700 acs. on Big
Sandy Run. Wit: ZACHA. BULLOCK and ADAM POTTER. Rec. 6-26-1787.

Pp 441-442:   5-15-1787, THOMAS BRANDON, Esq. of Union Co. to ABNER
     CAIN, same place, for 9 pds sterling, 150 acs. on a small branch
of Padgett's Creek, a draft of Tygar River. Bound by land granted to
JOHN TOWNSEND, JOHN PEARSON, THOMAS PEARSON and vacant land. Granted
to sd THOMAS BRANDON on 3-5-1787 and recorded in Bk. RRRR, p. 293.
Wit: JOHN CAIN, JOHN TOWNSEND, JOHN PEARSON. Rec. 6-26-1787.

Pp 442-445:   4-20-1785, LAWRENCE PEARSON, planter, and LIDIA, his
     wife, of 96 Dist., to WILLIAM MARTINDALE, planter, same place,
for 5 pds sterling, 50 acs. part of a tract of 200 acs. granted to
JOHN McGARTHY on 8-19-1774. Located on Enoree River and bound by the
river, JAMES BOWMAN, THOMAS BISHOP, and vacant lands. Entire 200 acs.
sold by McGARATHY to ENOCH PEARSON and rec. in Sec. Office, Bk. SSS,
p. 140. Conveyed by will to LAWRENCE PEARSON. Wit: JOHN PEARSON, THOMAS
BISHOP, JESSE (X) YOUNG. Rec. 6-26-1787.

Pp 445-447:   6-23-1787, STEPHEN HOWARD, planter, and ELIZABETH, his
     wife, of Union Co. to GEORGE HARLIN, hatter, same place, for
20 pds sterling, 20 acs. on Fairforest Creek, bound by land granted
to WILLIAM PLUMMER now in possession of GEO. HARLIN, farmer, THOMAS
BLASSINGAME, JAMES VERNON and the creek. Granted to HOWARD 12-4-1786,
rec. Bk PPPP, p. 348. No wit. Rec. 6-26-1787.

Pp 447-448:   6-23-1787, STEPHEN HOWARD, planter, and ELIZABETH, his
    wife, of Union Co. to GEORGE HARLIN, hatter, same place, for
60 pds sterling, 80 acs. on Brown's Creek, waters of Fairforest, bound
by JOHN HAM, LACY McBEE, and THOMAS BLASSINGAME. Granted to Stephens
on 2-4-1786 and rec. in Book PPPP, p. 309. No witnesses. Rec. 6-26-
1787.

Pp 448-449:   4-4-1787, JACOB PAULK of Union Co. to ZACHARIAH BELL,
    same place, for 1 pd 1 shilling and 9 pence, one acre on the
NW of a tract of 150 acs. conveyed by OBEDIAH HOWARD to sd PAULK. Bound
by ZACHARIAH BELL, OBEDIAH HOWARD & JACOB PAULK and the Ninety-Six
Road. No witnesses. Rec. 6-26-1787.

Pp 449-450:   5-1-1787, CHARLES JONES, SR. and MARTHA, his wife, of
    Laurens Co., S.C. to JOHN FINCHER of Union Co., for 25 pds sterl-
ing, 67 acs. on the south side of Fairforest Creek. Part of a tract
of 500 acs. granted to sd CHARLES JONES on 4-2-1773, and recorded in
Book OOO, p. 366. Bound by the creek, JOSEPH BATES and HEZEKIAH RICE.
Wit: FRANCIS FINCHER, JOHN (X) BISHOP, HESTER (X) FINCHER. Rec. 6-
26-1787.

Pp 451-452:   4-21-1787, THOMAS BISHOP and MARY, his wife, of Union
    Co., to WILLIAM MARTINDALE, same place, for 5 pds sterling, 62
acs. part of a tract of 162 acs. to granted to Bishop on 3-6-1786 and
recorded in Grant Bk IIII, p. 5. Located on north side of Enoree River.
Wit: JESSE (X) YOUNG, DANIEL YOUNG. Rec. 6-26-1787.

Pp 452-453:   6-22-1787, LACY McBEE, planter, and ANN, his wife, of
    Spartanburgh Co., S.C. to HANNAH ARMENT of Union Co., for 40
pds sterling, 150 acs. granted to McBee by Wm. Bull, Lt. Gov. of S.C.,
on 10-28-1774 and recorded in Book FFF, p. 317. Located on Mitchel's
Creek, a branch of Fairforest, between Broad and Saluda Rivers. Wit:
H. WHITE, GEORGE HARLIN, RENNY BELUE. Rec. 6-26-1787.

Pp 454-455:   11-22-1786, THOMAS BISHOP, planter of 96 Dist., to WILLIAM
    YOUNG, same place, for 10 pds sterling, 50 acs. on east side
of Enoree River, bound by JAMES ADDINGTON, WILLIAM YOUNG, the river,
and vacant lands. Granted to sd Bishop by patent on 6th of March last
(3-6-1786). Wit: WILLIAM MARTINDALE, JR., SAMUEL BISHOP and WILLIAM
MARTINDALE, SR. Signed by THOMAS BISHOP and MARY (X) BISHOP. Rec. 6-
26-1787.

Pp 455-456:   5-24-1783, Deed of Gift. SARAH COOK, widow of 96 Dist.,
    for the goodwill and affection which I have and do bear towards
my loving grandsons GEORGE and JOHN COOK, 100 acs. including the house
and plantation whereon I now live. Wit: CHARLES BRANDON, JOHN COOK
& JOHN HAILE. Rec. 6-26-1787.

Pp 456-457:   5-2-1787, HANDCOCK PORTER, planter of Union Co. to LUZ-
    IANN (?) PARLOR (also PARLOUR), same place, for 20 pds sterling,
100 acs. on Tinker's Creek, granted to Porter on 3-5-1787 by State
of S. C. and recorded in Book SSSS (no page given). LUZIANN PARLOUR,
her heirs, etc. Wit: THOMAS BRANDON, ISAAC BOGAN, WILLIAM KENNEDY.
Rec. 6-26-1787.

Pp 457-460:   7-21-1786, DAVID FARMER, planter of Briar Creek in the
    State of Georgia, to WILLIAM NEWMAN, blacksmith of Union Co.,
S.C. for 100 pds sterling, 150 acs. on the north side of Tygar River
in the fork of sd river and Fairforest Creek. Bound by WILLIAM CURRY(?)
and DAVID FARMER, and vacant lands. Orig. granted to DAVID FARMER on
12-17-1772 by Charles Granville Montague, Gov. etc. of the Prov. of
S. C. and recorded in Bk NNN, p. 198. Wit: JAMES GIBBS, NELLY (X) WATSON
and WILLIAM YOUNG. Signed by DAVID (X) FARMER and ELIZABETH (X) FARMER.
Rec. 6-24-1787.

Pp 460-463:   7-1-1786, DAVID FARMER, gentleman of the State of Georgia,
    to WILLIAM NEWMAN, blacksmith of 96 Dist., S.C. for 100 pds cur-
rent money, 100 acs. bet. Tygar River and Fairforest Creek. Bound by
land laid out for DAVID FARMER and vacant lands. Granted to WILLIAM

Cont'd:
CURRY by patent dated 8-2-1768. Released unto the sd DAVID <u>FREEMAN</u>
the the sd WILLIAM CURRY by his Majesty's Patent bearing date as afsd.
Wit: JAMES GIBBS, NELLY (X) WATSON, WILLIAM YOUNG. Signed by DAVID
(X) FARMER and ELIZABETH (X) FARMER. Rec. 6-26-1787.

Pp 463-465:   1-22-1787, DAVID FARMER and ELIZABETH, his wife of Brier
        Creek in Georgia, to JOHN STOKES of Union Co., SC for 100 pds
sterling, 150 acs. on south side of Fairforest Creek, bound by WILLIAM
NEWMAN, WILLIAM HAILE and WILLIAM YOUNG, the sd JOHN STOKES and vacant
lands. Granted to DAVID FARMER on 12-17-1772 and recorded in Book NNN,
p. 199. Wit: WILLIAM YOUNG, PHILIP HALCOM (or HALEEM) and WILLIAM NEWMAN
and recorded 6-26-1787.

Pp 466-467:   4-18-1785, DUNCAN McCREEVAN, planter of 96 Dist., to
        Capt. JOSEPH HUGHES of same place, for 50 pds lawful money, 150
acs. on south side of Broad River, bound by JACOB BROWN, HUGH NELSON,
JOHN McDONNALD and WILLIAM HUGHS' land. Granted to DUNCAN McCREEVAN
on 1-21-1785 by Benj. Guerrard, Gov. of S.C. Wit: DANIEL McAULAY, JOHN
McCREEVAN and JOHN McCREEVAN, JR. Signature sworn to by JOHN McCREEVAN
on 1-23-1785 bef. WM. KENNEDY, J.P. No recording date. (Note: The date
the signature was sworn to is evidently an error. Otherwise, he was
swearing to the signature before the deed was dated.)

Pp 467-468:   9-20-1787, WILLIAM SMITH and JANE, his wife of 96 Dist.,
        to JOHN SMITH, same place, out of mere motion and paternal af-
fection, a certain tract on Swift Run, a branch of Tygar River. Part
of a tract of 305 acs. granted to sd WILLIAM SMITH on 11-7-1785 and
recorded in Bk FFFF, p. 300 in the Auditor's Ofcice. No witnesses and
no recording date.

Pp 468-469:   9-20-1787, WILLIAM SMITH and JANE, his wife of 96 Dist.,
        to JOSEPH SMITH, same place, out of mere motion and paternal
affection, part of the same tract described in the next deed above.
No witnesses and no recording date. (Note: Neither deed states that
JOHN and JOSEPH SMITH were the sons of WILLIAM and JANE SMITH, but
the paternal affection would indicate that they were.)

Pp 469-471:   9-1-1787, MERRY McGUIRE, planter of Union Co., to DRURY
        GOWING of Chester Co., SC, for 100 pds current money, 319 acs.
granted to sd Merry McGuire on 6-5-1786 by Wm. Moultrie, Esq., Gov.
of S.C. Located on south side of Broad River and bound by HUGHES' land,
Esquire BROWN, SAMUEL TALBOT, JOSEPH POLSON and vacant lands. Wit:
JAMES SAVAGE, JOSHUA PALMORE, WILLIAM (X) SHARP. No recording date.
Grantee's name also spelled GOWEN and GOING in the deed.

Pp 471-472:   8-7-1787, ARCHER SMITH, planter of Union Co., to GEORGE
        HARLING (also HARLAN), hatter, same place, mortgage for 3 years
for 75 pds, 8 shillings and 4 pence sterling, on 250 acs. bet. Tygar
and Enoree Rivers on Barnett's Branch. Granted orig. to JAMES OTTERSON
on 8-20-1767. ARCHER SMITH owned land by virtue of inheritance. Wit:
WM. YOUNG, GEORGE HARLAND, WILLIAM (X) PLUMER. Rec. 9-24-1787.

Pp 472-473:   8-20-1787, GEORGE BLANTON of Rutherford Co., N. C., to
        MATHEW COLDWELL (CALDWELL?) of Union Co., S.C. for 5 pds sterl-
ing, 200 acs. on Cherokee Creek, waters of Broad River. Wit: NATHANIEL
GUYTON, NATHAN LANKFORD. Rec. 9-24-1787.

Pp 473-475:   12-21-1787, JOHN STEEN, SR. to JOHN STEEN, JR. both of
        Union Co., SC, for 100 pds sterling, 400 acs. on both sides of
Thicketty Creek. Part of a tract granted to JOHN STEEN, SR. in 1775.
Bound by ADAM GOUDELOCK, DAVID STOCKTON, GIDEON SMITH. Wit: ABSALOM
PETTY, CHARLES CLANTON, JAMES STEEN. Rec. 9-24-1787. (Date of deed
evidently wrong, probably should be 12-21-1786.)

Pp 475-476:   2-2-1785, JOHN WEEDINGMAN of 96 Dist., to JOHN COLE,
        same place, for 60 pds sterling, 200 acs. on south side of Packo-
late River on Reedy Branch, including an improvement that JAMES McBEE
bought of CHARLES PARK. Wit: ISAAC HOPE, TURNER KENDRICK, PALMER O.

Cont'd:
KENDRICK. JOHN WEEDINGMAN signed the receipt for the money on 3-28-1787, before witnesses WILLIAM SISSON, REBECCA BROCK and JOHN REED.

Pp 476-477:   12-15-1781, HENRY GOOD of South Carolina, to ROBERT GOOD of the sd state, for 2,000 pds. currency, 162 acs. in 96 Dist. on south side of Broad River. Part of a tract that belonged to THOS. WADE and conveyed by him to sd HENRY GOOD. Above the mouth of Thicketty Creek. Wit: JOHN GOOD, THOMAS GOOD. Rec. 9-24-1787.

Pp 477-481:   6-21-1787, WILLIAM COLEMAN and MARY, his wife of Union Co., to NICHOLAS HARRIS, same place, for 40 pds sterling, 197 acs. part of a tract granted to JAMES McELWEAN and 500 acs. sold to sd WILLIAM COLEMAN by lease and release and recorded in Register's Office of S. C. in Book LN-4, pp. 265-269 on 9-12-1774. Evidently a North Carolina grant since it was thought to be in Mecklenburgh County on a branch of Fairforest on Mill Creek. (Now in Union Co., S. C.). Bound by ZACHARIAH BULLOCK's land, BENAJAH THOMAS and ARTHUR CUNNINGHAM. No witnesses. Rec. 9-24-1787.

Pp 481-483:   8-8-1787, JOHN PUTMAN, planter, and SARAH, his wife, of Union Co., to CLEMENTS MAGARITY (also spelled CLEMONS), and MICHAEL MAGARITY, same place, for 10 shillings sterling, 193 acs. part of a tract of 386 acs. on Sugar Creek, waters of Fairforest, granted to Putman on 3-6-1787 by State of S. C. To be divided equally between grantees. Wit: JOHN LITTLE, JONATHAN PENNEL. Rec. 9-24-1787.

Pp 483-485:   2-10-1785, JOHN FOSTER of Camden Dist., S. C. to GEORGE McWHORTER of 96 Dist., for 2,000 pds current money, 200 acs. on the west side of Broad River, joining JOHN FOSTR and NEEL McKISSICK, and vacant lands. Orig. granted to RYDARUS CLARK. Also, 31 acs. part of a tract granted to JAMES LOVE, bounded by the above tract, HENRY CLERK's line, GEORGE McWHORTER and JOHN REED. Wit: JOHN SMITH, JOHN CROW FOSTER, JAMES DARVID(?). Rec. 9-24-1787.

Pp 485-486:   7-29-1787, Col. THOMAS BRANDON of Union Co. to ROBERT WOODSON, same place, for 30 pds sterling, 200 acs. on north side of Fairforest, where SAMUEL GRAY lived. Bought by Brandon at public sale conducted by Col. WILLIAM FARR, High Sheriff of Union Co...part of a tract of 500 acs. granted to BENJAMIN GIST, conveyed by Gist to WILLIAM WOFFORD, conveyed by him to SAMUEL GRAY, then sold by Sheriff Farr at public sale. Wit: JOHN BRANDON, RICHARD LEATHAM, JAMES KINCAID. Rec. 9-24-1788.

Pp 486-488:   7-14-1787, THOMAS BRANDON, Esq., of Union Co. to MARY MAYFIELD, widow of same place, for 32 pds sterling, 185 acs. on waters of Brown's Creek. Part of a tract of 800 acs. granted to sd Brandon on 11-6-1786. Rec. in Grant Bk OOOO, p. 347. No witnesses. Rec. 9-24-1788.

Pp 488-491:   2-26-1787, THOMAS BEARDEN and ABBORZELA, his wife of Union Co., to RALPH JACKSON of same place, for 20 pds sterling, 100 acs. on a small branch of Tygar River. Bound by RALPH JACKSON and vacant lands. Granted to sd Bearden on 9-5-1785. Wit: THOMAS HUNT, JOHN BLASINGAME. No recording date.

Pp 492-493:   3-4-1778, FRANCIS WHILCHEL and MARTHEW, his wife of 96 Dist., to NICHOLAS CURRY, of same place, for 275 pds current money, 200 acs. on Abittony's(?) Creek. Orig. granted to JOHN McMILLEN by N. C. patent dated 1767. Sold by McMillen to Whilchel in 1773. Wit: GABRIEL PATRICK, PETER AKINS. Signature sworn to by GABRIEL PATRICK on 7-3-1778 bef. WILLIAM TATE, J.P. No recording date.

Pp 49-494:   7-25-1787, JOHN FOSTER and ELEANOR, his wife of 96 Dist., Greenville Co., S. C., to JOHN REED of 96 Dist., Union Co., for 466 pds, 13 shillings and 4 pence, 2 tracts - 310 acs. on the west side of Broad River, one laid out for JAMES LOVE and the other for J___ CLARK, granted to him by patent by the Gov. of N. C. and renewed to him by patent by the Hon. Wm. Bull, Lt. Gov. according to Order

Cont'd:
of Council in the South State dated 5-4-1775. Bound by river, LOVE,
JOHN McWHORTER, CLARK's old line and a corner on the Dreans of Packolate River. Wit: RICHARD THOMPSON, JOSIAH SMITH, MYHILL SMITH. No recording date. ELEANOR signed the deed as "NELLY FOSTER".

Pp 494-495:   3-24-1787, JAMES TERRELL of Union Co. to THOMAS WRIGHT,
        same place, for 31 pds sterling, 400 acs. on Thicketty Creek.
Bound by WILLIAM WILKINS and the sd THOS. WRIGHT. Granted to Terrell
by patent dated 1-1-1787. Wit: MOSES WATERS, JOSEPH HENDERSON. No recording date.

Pp 496-497:   2-13-1787, EPHRAIM CLARK and MARY, his wife, of 96 Dist.,
        to JOHN BANKHEAD, same place, for 178 pds, 15 shillings sterling,
200 acs. on south side of Broad River, bound by ADAM LOONEY, ROBERT
GOOD and the river. Granted by patent to ZACHARIAH BULLOCK on 4-20-
1768, and conveyed by him to sd EPHRAIM CLARK. Wit: HENRY GOOD, ROBERT
GOOD, JOHN ADAMS. No recording date.

Pp 497-498:   9-23-1785, WILLIAM LINDSAY of Spartanburg Co., S.C. to
        JONATHAN PENNEL of Union Co., for 30 pds sterling, 150 acs. on
Sugar Creek, waters of Fairforest. Bound by HENRY HARDEN, THOMAS ADAMS
and vacant lands. Granted to Lindsay on 1-1-1785. Wit: PETER PENNEL,
SAMUEL COSON. No recording date.

Pp 498-499:   Dated June __?, 1787, SAMUEL McJUNKIN of Union Co. to
        JOHN HOWEL, same place, for 50 pds sterling, 220 acs. on the
branches of Brown's Creek. Bound by JAMES BOGAN, GIDEON PORTER, WILLIAM
BRANDON. Granted to McJunkin on 6-5-1786 by Wm. Moultrie, Gov. of S.
C. Wit: JOSEPH McJUNKIN, THOMAS YOUNG. No recording date.

Page 500:   9-21-1780 (Note: Date may be wrong since the deed states
        "in the ninth year of the Independency of the United States"
which would make it 1785.) FRANCES HOLLAND and JOHN HOLLAND, his son,
to FRANCES (FRANCIS) WHILCHEL, for 60 pds, 200 acs. on Shoal Creek,
Saluda River, 96 Dist., S.C. Orig. granted to DOMINIO HOLLAND, soldier,
be a patent dated 1-21-1785. Wit: JAMES TERRELL, JOHN WILCHEL. No recording date.

Page 501:   8-27-1787, JOHN WOOD of Union Co. to WILLIAM HARRILL
        (also spelled HARREL) of Fairfield Co., S.C. for 50 pds, 50½
acs. in Union Co. on Broad River. Orig. granted to AMOS TIMS, conveyed
by Tims to FRANCES POSEY and by Posey to the sd JOHN WOOD. Wit: WILLIAM
HARRILL, THOMAS STOKES, JOSIAS WOOD. No recording date.

Pp 501-502:   5-4-1787, URIAH PAULK of Union Co. to JOSEPH REDIER,
        same place, for 40 pds, 10 shillings sterling, 200 acs. on the
waters of Fairforest Creek. Part of a tract of 500 acs. granted to
sd Paulk on 6-5-1786, and recorded in Grant Bk LLLL. Wit: DUNCAN Mc-
CREEVAN, JAMES BELL, HARESON BELL. No recording date.

Page 503:   Dated July __?, 1787, JOHN SAVAGE of Union Co. to Capt.
        JOSEPH HUGHS, same place, for 25 pds sterling, 100 acs. on Hughs
Creek, waters of Broad River. Granted to John Savage on 7-8-1774, by
Wm. Bull, Lt. Gov. of the Province, and recorded in Grant Bk. RRR,
p. 264. Wit: ISAAC GREGORY, WILLIAM HUGHS. No recording date.

Page 504:   7-21-1787, GABRIEL BROWN of Union Co. to Capt. JOSEPH
        HUGHS, same place, for 40 pds lawful money, 100 acs. on both
sides of Hughs Creek, a branch of Broad River. Bound by WM. HUGHS,
JOHN SAVAGE and vacant lands. Orig. granted to AGNES DOOD on 1-8-1771
by Wm. Bull, Lt. Gov. and recorded in Grant Bk. EEE, p. 479. Conveyed
by lease and release from sd AGNES DOOD to GABRIEL BROWN. Wit: JOHN
McCOOL, JOHN McDONALD, THOMAS BRANDON, J.P. No recording date.

Pp 505-506:   4-21-1787, WILLIAM MARTINDALE and MARTHA, his wife of
        Union Co. to DANIEL YOUNG, same place, for 50 pds sterling, 95
acs. on the north side of Enoree River. Part of a 300 ac. tract granted
to WILLIAM RAGAN and conveyed by him to THOMAS GORDEN who conveyed

513

Cont'd:
by him to THOMAS BISHOP. Bishop conveyed 115 acs. to sd WILLIAM MARTIN-
DALE on 10-25-1785. Near THOMAS DUCKET's ford. Wit: JOHN CAIN, JOHN
MARTINDALE, SARAH LAMB. No recording date.

Pp 507-508:   2-8-1787, SOLOMON MANGHAM, planter of Union Co. to WILLIAM
        TATE, JR., planter of same place, for 20 pds sterling, 103 acs.
on Minam's Creek, waters of Thicketty, waters of main Broad River.
Bound on one side by WILLIAM TATE, SR.'s line. Patent dated 1-21-1785.
Recorded in Charles Town in the Secretaries Office, Book CCCC, p. 133.
Wit: JAMES TERRILL, FRANCES WHILCHEL, JOHN JEFFERIES. Rec. 9-24-1787.

Pp 508-510:   4-21-1787, THOMAS BISHOP and MARY, his wife of Union
        Co. to DANIEL YOUNG, same place, for 50 pds sterling, 104 acs.
part of a tract of 160 acs. on the north side of Enoree River, granted
to THOMAS BISHOP on 3-6-1786, and recorded in Grant Bk. IIII, p. 5.
Wit: JOHN PEARSON, WILLIAM MARTINDALE, JESSE (X) YOUNG. No rec. date.

Pp 510-511:   2-6-1787, CHARLTON SHOCKLY, planter of Union Co., to
        WILLIAM BRUMMIT, planter, for 100 pds sterling, 100 acs. on Cain
Creek, waters of Tygar River. Orig. granted to THOMAS COX on 9-27-
1769 and rec. in Bk. CCC. Conveyed by Cox to VINCENT on 4-4-1776, by
Vincent to sd Shockley on 7-7-1785. Wit: JAMES SHOCKLY, SALATHEL SHOCK-
LY, THOMAS (X) SHOCKLY. Receipt signed on 2-26-1787. No rec. date.

Pp 511-513:   8-23-1787, JACOB EARNEST and AGNESS, his wife of Spartan-
        burg Co., S.C. to WILLIAM ADDINGTON of Union Co., for 30 pds
sterling, 147 acs. on the north side of Enoree River in the fork bet.
Broad and Saludy Rivers. Orig. granted to sd Earnest on 8-13-1766 and
rec. in Bk. AAA, p. 65. Wit: THOMAS BRANDON, JESSE (X) RIGHT, ALEXANDER
ALEXANDER. No rec. date.

Pp 513-514:   6-23-1787, WILLIAM COMBER of Union Co. to DANIEL COMBER
        a carpenter of same place, for 20 pds sterling, 220 acs. part
of a tract of 556 acs. granted to WM. COMBER on 2-5-1787, and located
on both sides of Shoally Creek, a branch of Fairforest. Bound by ISAAC
BOGAN, Col. THOS. BRANDON, CHRISTOPHER BRANDON and an old line run
by GEORGE SALMON. Wit: THOMAS BRANDON, ROBERT BELL, JOHN (X) NEAL.
No recording date.

Pp 514-515:   9-22-1787, JAMES ADDINGTON and REBECKAH, his wife of
        Union Co. to JOHN ADDINGTON, same place, for 20 pds sterling,
153 acs. on north side of Enoree River, granted to sd James Addington
on 12-5-1785, and rec. in Book GGGG, p. 178. Wit: JOHN PEARSON, RACHEL
(X) CLARK, SARAH PEARSON. No recording date.

Page 516:   9-25-1787, Col. THOMAS BRANDON of Union Co. to JOHN THOMAS
        of same place, for 30 pds sterling, 50 acs. including the improve-
ments where JAMES WOODSON formerly dwelt, part of a tract of 500 acs.
on Fairforest Creek, granted to BENJAMIN GIST on 7-15-1768. Benjamin
Gist sold the entire tract to WILLIAM WOFFORD. Wofford sold the 50
acs. to ROBERT WOODSON and he conveyed it to THOMAS BRANDON. Bound
by the creek, JAMES FINLEY's land possessed by JOHN GOODWIN, WOODSON's
spring branch, and the original tract. No wit. and no rec. date.

Pp 517-518:   8-16-1787, JOHN STEEN, SR. of Union Co. to WILSON JOLLY,
        same place, for 60 pds sterling, 200 acs. on waters of Gilkie's
Creek. Part of a tract of 400 acs. granted by patent to sd JOHN STEEN
on 1-21-1785. Wit: THOMAS BRANDON, JOHN EWART, NATHANIEL (X) JEFFRIES.
No recording date.

Pp 518-519:   9-25-1787, GEORGE CROSBY of Union Co. to JACOB HAILE,
        same place, for 20 pds sterling, 200 acs. on north side of Fair-
forest Creek on both sides of Haile's Branch. Granted 2-5-1787, surveyed
1-20-1786. (Does not state the name of the grantee.) No wit. and no
recording date.

Pp 519-522:;   3-10-1786, MATHEW ROBERSON and SUSANNAH, his wife of
        Unini Co. to JOHN WATERS (also spelled WATTERS), same place,

514

Cont'd:
for 180 pds sterling, 133 acs. on both sides of Thicketty Creek, part
of a tract of 400 acs. granted to HONAS BALUM from under the Great
Seal of North Carolina, and conveyed by him to JACOB WIDENER, and from
sd Widener to DAVID ROBERSON, deceased, and from sd Roberson, dec'd.
to MATHEW ROBERSON by heirship he being heir at Law to the sd DAVID
ROBERSON, afsd. dec'd. Bound by lands of THOMAS WRIGHT, JAMES ROBERSON,
THOMAS NUCKOLS, deceased, and vacant lands. Wit: JOHN THOMPSON, JOSHUA
PETTY. No recording date.

Pp 523-524: 7-31-1787, GEORGE NEWTON and URSULA, his wife of 96 Dist.
    to WILLIAM WILLIAMS, same place, for 200 pds current money, 518
acs. granted to sd George Newton in 1786, on the north side of Broad
River on the waters of Brown's Creek and Sandy Run, it being the tract
that ELLIS FOWLER now lives on. Bound by ISAAC WHITE, THOS. WILLIAMS,
JOHN WHITE. Rec. Grant Bk. GGGG, p. 467. Wit: JEPHTHA HOLLINGSWORTH,
JOHN WHITE, ELLIS (X) FOWLER. No rec. date.

Pp 524-525: 7-20-1787, JOHN STILL of 96 Dist. to THOMAS HARRELL,
    same place, for 50 pds sterling, 100 acs. on waters of Fairforest
Creek, granted by patent to sd JOHN STILL on 3-15-1771, recorded in
Auditor's Bk. KN 10, p. 448, and in Grant Bk. HHH, p. 21. Wit: JOSEPH
HUGHS, WILLIAM CLARK. Rec. 9-25-1787.

Pp 526-529: 1-9-1773, JOHN TOWNS and ALCIE, his wife (also spelled
    ALEE - signature evidently Alee) of St. Mark's Parish, Craven
Co., S.C. to WILLIAM HARDWICK, same place, for 230 pds current money,
250 acs. surveyed 11-14-1768 for JOHN HUGHS and granted to TOWNS by
Chas. G. Montague, Gov. of S.C. on 12-23-1771. Located on north side
of Tygar River and bound by EDWARD MUSGROVE, the river, and vacant
lands at time of survey. Wit: JAMES HARDWICK, THOMAS (X) BETTANY, RUTH
(X) BETTANY. JAMES HARDWICK swore to signature on 1-14-1773 bef. DAVID
GEORGE, J.P. Rec. 9-25-1787.

Pp 529-533: 6-27-1787, LARK WELLS, eldest son and heir at law of
    ELIJAH WELLS, deceased, of Union Co., to JOHN EWART, Clerk of
sd County, for 130 pds sterling, 130 acs. on both sides of Packolate
River, orig. granted to JOHN PORTMAN by North Carolina patent on 4-
27-1767. Conveyed by sd John Portman to sd Elijah Wells on 1-3-1769
and rec. in Clerk's Office of Mecklenburgh Co., N. C. at the January
Term 1769. Bound by the Widow McWHORTER's lands. Wit: THOMAS BALLOW,
ABNER WELLS, HEZEKIAH SALMON. Rec. 9-25-1787.

Pp 534-537: 4-1-1785, ARCHER SMITH, planter of 96 Dist., to JAMES
    OLIPHANT, planter of same place, for 80 pds sterling, 2 tracts
containing 150 acs. one on the north side of Tygar River, part of a
tract of 600 acs. granted to sd Archer Smith on 10-14-1774 by Wm. Bull,
Lt. Gov. of S.C., originally granted to WILLIAM COWDON on 9-3-1753
by Mathew Rowan, Gov. of N. C., bound by the river, THACKER VIVION,
Dutchman's Creek, and part of the orig. tract. The other tract included
in the 150 acs. was orig. granted on a Bounty Warrant by THOMAS BOON,
Esq. Lt. Gov. of S. C. to JACOB ELLISER on 12-7-1762, located on Dutchman's Creek, bound by sd 600 ac. tract, JOHN PEARSON and vacant lands
at time of survey. Wit: AMBROS RY (RAY), BURRILL BOBO. Rec. 9-26-1787.

Pp 537-539: 3-10-1777, WILLIAM BISHOP, farmer, and JANE, his wife
    of Craven Co., to JAMES JOHNSTON, farmer, same place, for 125
pds current money, 125 acs. on a branch of Fairforest called Buffalow
Creek, bound by THOS. GREEN, JOSEPH BREED and ROBERT BISHOP. Part of
a 300 ac. tract granted to WM. BISHOP on 2-2-1773, recorded in Bk.
13, p. 97 on 11-11-1774. Wit: JOHN BISHOP, AARON HARLON, JANE BISHOP.
Signed by WILLIAM (X) BISHOP and JANE (X) BISHOP. AARON HARLON swore
to signatures on 8-24-1787 bef. THOMAS BRANDON, J.P. No rec. date.

Pp 539-543: 9-7-1787, WILLIAM and ISAAC TRAMMELL of 96 Dist., SC
    to WILLIAM FARR, same place, for 1,000 pds. sterling, 200 acs.
on Broad River above Fishdam Ford, orig. granted to DANIEL TRAMMEL
(father to above named William and Isaac) on 3-4-1760 and rec. in Bk.
E, p. 15, on 5-2-1761. Bequeathed by DANIEL TRAMMEL by Will unto his

Cont'd:
two sons, the said William and Isaac. Wit: WILLIAM BECKHAM, RICHARD
FARR. Rec. 9-27-1787.

Pp 543-545:   11-3-1787, THOMAS BRANDON and ELIZABETH, his wife, of
        Union Co., S.C. to HEZEKIAH RICE, of the same place, for 25 pds
sterling, 67 acs. on the south side of Fairforest Creek. Formerly owned
by WILLIAM GUEST (a disaffected person to the American causes) and
confiscated and sold agreeable to a resolution of General Congress
of the United States. Wit: JOHN MONTGOMERY, JOHN SANDERS. Rec. 12-
24-1787.

Pp 545-546:   10-16-1787, JOHN FINCHER of Union Co., SC to JOHN SANDERS,
        of same place, for 100 pds currency, 140 acs. on the north side
of Fairforest Creek, bound by the creek, HEZEKIAH RICE, and land formerly patented by JOSEPH BATES, and land formerly laid out to DANIEL
HUGHS. Part of a tract granted to CHARLES JONES on 4-2-1773 and purchased by the sd FINCHER. Wit: CALEB FRAZIER, JOHN (X) CLARK. Rec.
12-24-1787.

 END OF DEED BOOK A

UNION COUNTY, S. C. - DEED BOOK B

Pp 1-2:   29 Oct. 1787, Col. THOMAS BRANDON of Union Co., SC to
        ROBERT GREGORY, same place, for 46 pds 10 shillings sterling,
150 acs. to the sd ROBERT GREGORY all that plantation where on he now
lives on the south side of Fairforest Creek, adj. WILLIAM YOUNG, THOMAS
HART and the creek. Part of a tract that Brandon bought from one JOHN
FLETCHAL and WILLIAM YOUNG. Wit: JOHN BRANDON, AARON HART, WOODSON
ROUNDTREE. No rec. date.

Pp 2-3:   25 Sept. 1787, ROBERT GREGORY of Union Co., to JEREMIAH
        GREGORY, same place, for 40 pds sterling, 100 acs. on Little
Brown's Creek, a branch of Broad River. Bound by vacant land, JAMES
HAWKINS, JAMES HENRY. Granted to sd ROBT. GREGORY on 5 May 1773 by
Wm. Bull, Lt. Gov. of S.C. Wit: THOMAS BRANDON,JAMES (X) MARLIN. Rec.
24 Dec. 1787.

Pp 3-4:   23 Oct. 1787, ROBERT WOODSON of Union Co., to JAMES WOOD-
        SON, JR., of same place, for 30 pds sterling, 150 acs. on south
side of Fairforest Creek. Part of a tract of 500 acs. granted to BEN-
JAMIN GIST on 15 July 1768 by Wm. Bull, Gov. Orig. grant bound by lands
granted to NICOLL & VERNON, BOXE's land, CHARLES KING's land, land
claimed by PHILIP BRYAN and JAMES FINLEY and vacant land. Plat and
grant recorded in Sec. Office in Bk. CCC, p. 238. BENJAMIN GIST conveyed
the entire tract to WILLIAM WOFFORD. Wofford conveyed 200 acs. to SAMUEL
GRAY, which tract was taken by execution or attachment at the instance
of Col. Thomas Brandon (confiscated?). Conveyed by Brandon to sd Robert
Woodson. Wit: THOS. BRANDON, THOMAS BLASSINGAME. Rec. 24 Dec. 1787.

Pp 5-7:   27 __? 1786, ROBERT STARK, late Sheriff of 96 Dist.,
        to DANIEL LIPHAM, for 100 pds current money, 200 acs. on the
ridge between Tyger River and Enoree River. Sheriff's sale to settle
a Judgement obtained by PAUL TOWNSHEN against THOMAS DUNLAP, debtor.
Public sale of land was held in May 1775, and DANIEL LIPHAM was high
bidder. Orig. grant was bound by PHILIP ANDERSON and vacant lands.
Wit: ROBERT STARK, JR., JAMES GUNNELL. Stark acknowledged signing and
delivery of deed to Daniel Lipham bef. ARTHUR SIMKINS, HUGH MIDDLETON
& WILLIAM ANDERSON, Esqs., "three of the Justices of Edgefield County",
on 8 Oct. 1787. Rec. in Union Co. on 24 Dec. 1787.

Pp 7-8:   15 Dec. 1787, JOHN McCOOLL of Union Co. to JOHN McKIBBINS
        of same place, for 14 pds sterling, lot no. 35 containing 1/2
ac. at Union Court House. Wit: THOMAS BRANDON, JAMES McCLURE. Rec.
24 Dec. 1787.

Pp 8-9:   21 Dec. 1787, JOHN McCOOLL of Union Co. to JOHN McKIBBINS

Cont'd:
    of same place, for 18 pds 14 shillings sterling, lot no. 31 con-
taining 1/2 ac. at Union Court House. Bound by public land of Union
Co. and sd JOHN McKIBBINS. Also, another lot, no. 20, containing 1/2
ac. bound by lot no. 32 belonging to sd John McKibbins. Wit: JOHN EWART,
THOMAS BRANDON. Rec. 24 Dec. 1787.

Pp 9-11:   15 Oct. 1787, JOHN McCOOLL of Union Co. to JOHN McKIBBINS,
        same place, for 30 pds sterling, 160 acs. on Tinker Creek. Part
of two tracts granted to sd John McCooll by letters patent. One tract
contained 406 acs. granted 1 May 1786. The other containing 1000 acs.
granted 4 Dec. 1786. Wit: WM. DALRYMPLE, JAMES McCLURE, ZACHARIAH BELL,
JOHN EWART. Rec. 25 Dec. 1787.

Pp 12-13:   14 July 1787, Lease and Release. LEWIS BOBO and SARAH,
        his wife, of Union Co. to CALEB EDMONDSON, same place, for 10
pds sterling, in his possession now being, 300 acs. on Wofford's and
Barnett's branches, waters of Tyger River. Part of a tract of 700 acs.
granted to sd Lewis Bobo on 13 July 1770 and rec. in Book FFF, p. 29
in the Sec. Office. Bound on one side by Lewis Bobo. Wit: ARCHER SMITH,
JAMES DUNCAN, son of ALEX. DUNCAN, and ANDREW TORRANCE. Rec. 25 Dec.
1787.

Pp 14-15:   8 Aug. 1786, HEZEKIAH GENTRY and CATARINE, his wife,
        of Edgefield Co., SC to JAMES HOGIN (also spelled HOGAN), of
Union Co., for 10 pds sterling, 197½ acs. in Union Co. on a branch
of Tyger River called Bogan's Creek. Bound by land granted to ISAAC
HOLLINGSWORTH. Granted to sd Hezekiah Gentry on 5 June 1786. Wit: JOHN
JENKINS, ROBERT LEVERILL, RIDGE (X) HOGINS. Rec. 25 Dec. 1787.

Pp 15-17:   22 Dec. 1787, JOHN McPHERSON and SARAH, his wife, of
        Union Co. to NATHAN GLEN, same place, for 160 pds sterling, one
tract of 150 acs. on Lower Fish Dam Creek. Orig. granted to JOHN HANNAH
on 4 Sept. 1753 by the Gov. of N. C. and regranted by Wm. Bull, Gov.
of S.C. on 6 Jan. 1775 to John McPherson, after states' boundary line
was run. Bound on one side by THOMAS HOLLINGSWORTH. Also, another tract
of 100 acs. on waters of Lower Fish Dam Creek, orig. granted to ELIZA-
BETH RINCHARD on 25 May 1774 by Lt. Gov. Bull of S.C. Wit: GEORGE HAR-
LAN, VALENTINE HARLING, JACOB HARLING. Rec. 25 Dec. 1787.

Pp 17-19:   13 Feb. 1787, WILLIAM FARR, Esq., Sheriff of Union Co.,
        to THOMAS BRANDON, Esq., same place, attorney for WILLIAM CUNNING-
HAM. Sheriff's sale of 100 acs. on Tyger River. Whereas Thomas Brandon
did on the 13th day of Dec. in 1775(?) obtain a writ of attachment
against the Estate of DAVID ADAMS, which was returned before the Justices of the County Court of Union in state afsd., on the 26th of Dec.
1785 executed on two tracts of land, one situate near Tygar River and
the other on Fairforest (Creek) by the sd William Farr, Sheriff, and
whereas the sd one tract situate on Tyger River containing 100 acs.
was conveyed by a certain THOMAS LANDTRIP to a certain THOMAS HOLDEN
and conveyed by the sd Thomas Holden to the afsd David Adams, ...he
the sd David Adams in and by his certain bond or obligation dated 26
Feb. 1777, became bound to JOHN CUNNINGHAM in the penal sum of 1,000
pds good and lawful money of sd late province now state afsd...? John
Cunningham assigned the bond to JESSE FINCHER. Sd bond became the right
of William Cunningham, who brought suit through his attorney Thos.
Brandon, Esq. by an action of debt. JOHN HAILE, Esq., Clerk of Court,
directed Sheriff Farr to sell the tract of 100 acs. on Tygar River
on 13 Feb. 1787. Sold for 16 pds sterling to Thomas Brandon, the high
bidder. Wit: JOHN EWART, CHARLES SIMS, WM. BECKHAM. Rec. 26 Dec. 1787.

Pp 20-24:   24 Dec. 1787, WM. FARR, Esq., of Union Co. to THOS. MILES,
        same place, for 6 pds current money of S.C., part of a tract
granted to sd Wm. Farr on 15 oct. 1784. Bound by RICH. COX, THOS. COX,
WM. HOLLINGSWORTH and NATHAN GLEN. Wit: WILLIAM HOLLINGSWORTH, RICHD.
FARR. No dower. Rec. 26 Dec. 1787.

Pp 21-22:   13 Oct. 1787, JOSHUA SAXON, planter of Laurens Co., SC
        to MOSES GUYTON, planter, of the state afsd. and co., for 1-
hundred pds lawful money of S.C., 150 acs. on Gilkie's Creek, a branch

Cont'd:
of Thicketty, waters of Broad River. Bound by JAMES BROWN and vacant
lands. Rec. in Grant Book SSSS, p. 202. Granted to sd JOSHUA SAXON
by Thomas Pinckney, Gov. of S. C. on 5 Mar. 1787. Now the condition
of the above conveyance is such that if hereafter there should appear
an older grant or Better Right and Title to sd tract, the conveyance
should not be binding on JOSHUA SAXON or his heirs. Wit: ANDREW ROGERS,
JOHN ROGERS. JR. No dower. Rec. 26 Dec. 1787.

Pp 22-23:   18 Sept. 1787, JOHN STEEN of Union Co. to GIDEON SMITH,
        son of GIDEON SMITH, deceased, same place, for 200 pds sterling,
200 acs. on both sides of Thicketty Creek, including the improvement
where MATHEW ROBERSON now lives and the improvement that GIDEON SMITH,
deceased, made where SAMUEL MONTGOMERY now lives. Orig. granted to
JOHN STEEN on 13 Oct. 1767 by Wm. Tryon, Gov. of N. C. JOHN STEEN conveyed the tract to GIDEON SMITH, dec'd., before his death, by lease
and release. Rec. in Sec. Office in N. C. Wit: THOS. WOODS, JOHN MOORE,
JOHN SMITH, ABRAHAM SMITH. Rec. 26 Dec. 1787.

Page 24:   10 Dec. 1787, WILLIAM KENNEDY of Union Co. to JOHN KENNEDY
        of same place, out of Natural Affection and Good Will, 135 acs.
on Brown's Creek, branch of Broad River. Orig. granted to sd WM. KENNEDY
on 6 Feb. 1786 by Wm. Moultrie, Gov. of S.C. and rec. in Grant Bk HHHH,
p. 71. Bounding on WILLIAM KENNEDY's land. No wit. or rec. date.

Page 25:   6 Oct. 1787, THOS. BRANDON of Union Co. to THOS. KENNEDY
        of same place, out of Natural Affection and Good Will, 100 acs.
including the forks of the great road leading to Charles Town. Part
of a grant dated 5 Feb. 1787, of 490 acs. on both sides of the Ninety
Six Road, to the sd THOS. BRANDON by Wm. Moultrie, Gov. of S.C., plat
and grant rec. in Grant Bk. QQQQ, p. 605. Wit: JOHN McCOOLL, JOHN BRAN-
DON, JEREMIAH GREGORY. Rec. 26 Dec. 1787.

Page 26:   4 Dec. 1787, Col. THOS. BRANDON of Union Co. to WILLIAM
        STEEN, JR., son of JAMES STEEN (no place of residence given),
for 50 pds sterling, 300 acs. on south side of Fairforest Creek. Bound
by the creek, NUCKOLS' old line, WILLIAM YOUNG, THOMAS GREER & ROBERT
GREGORY. Wit: DANIEL COMER, WILLIAM HEALD. Rec. 26 Dec. 1787.

Pp 27-29:   4 Sept. 1787, Lease and Release. JOHN HAMES of Union
        Co., to ROBERT GALT, same place, for 10 shillings (lease) and
7 pds. (release), 100 acs. all that plantation or tract of land that
he the sd HAMES now lives on, bet. Johny's Creek and Packolate River.
Part of a tract of 200 acs. orig. granted to HAMES on 21 Jan. 1786
by Benj. Guerard, Gov. of S.C. Wit: NICHOLAS JASPER, JOHN GEORGE, THOMAS
GEORGE. Rec. 26 Dec. 1787.

Pp 30-31:   26 Dec. 1787, THOS. BRANDON of Fairforest Creek in 96
        Dist., Union Co., to the County of Union "for the love and affec-
tion which he hath and beareth unto the sd County", two acres including the Courthouse and gaol of the sd county of Union, waters of Fairforest Creek. No wit. Rec. 26 Dec. 1787. (This is the land on which
the present Courthouse and jail is located..JMC).

Pp 31-32:   26 Dec. 1787, JOHN McCOOLL of Union Co. to JOHN YOUNG,
        tailor, same place, for 11 pds sterling, lot no. 58 at Union
Courthouse, containing 1/2 ac. Wit: JOHN EWART, JOHN HAILE. Rec. 26
Dec. 1787.

Pp 32-34:   27 Oct. 1786, PATRICK EARLY of Union Co. to THOMAS GREER,
        Esq., same place, for 5 guineas and other good causes and con-
siderations, 54 acs. on north side of Tygar River. Bound by the river,
sd THOMAS GREER and sd PATRICK EARLY. Part of a tract granted to EARLY
by a State Patent dated 21 Jan. 1785. Wit: THOMAS GREER, JR., JOHN
GREER, ANDREW THOMSON. Rec. 26 Dec. 1787.

Pp 34-35:   30 May 1787, JOHN BECKHAM, SR. of Union Co. to ROBERT
        THOMSON, same place, for 100 pds sterling, 200 acs. on south
side of Packolate River, bound on one side by the river, being the

Cont'd:
place where LAURANCE EASTERWOOD formerly lived. Wit: ADAM POTTER, JOHN
BECKHAM (JR.?). Signed JOHN BECKHAM. Rec. 26 Dec. 1787.

Pp 35-36:   26 July 1787, ISAAC BOGAN of Union Co. to Capt. DANIEL
        COMER, same place, for 30 pds, 150 acs. on Sholey Creek, branch
of Fairforest. The lower part of a 200 ac. tract granted to sd BOGAN
on 23 June 1774 by Wm. Bull, Lt. Gov. of. S.C. and rec. in Bk. QQQ,
p. 86, in the Sec. Office. Whereon sd DANIEL COMER now liveth. No wit.
Rec. 26 Dec. 1788. (Year should be 1787. Evidently an error since previous deed was rec. 26 Dec. 1787 and the second one following was rec.
24 Mar. 1788.)

Pp 36-37:   15 Dec. 1787, JOSEPH JONES of Union Co. to JOHN SPRINGER,
        same place, for 70 pds sterling, 346 acs. on Buffalow Creek,
branch of Fairforest. Granted by S. C. patent to sd JONES on 4 Nov.
1786. Signed by JOSEPH JONES & SARAH (X) JONES. No wit. No rec. date.

Pp 38-39:   20 Mar. 1788, JOHN GORDAN of Union Co. to CHRISTOPHER
        BRANDON, same place, for 30 pds sterling, 100 acs. part of a
450 ac. tract granted to sd GORDAN on 1 Oct. 1787 by Thos. Pinckney,
Gov. of S.C., on the waters of Brown's Creek on south side of Broad
River. Orig. grant bound by JOHN BRANDON, WM. MAJUNKIN (McJUNKIN),
and JOHN MAYFIELD. Plat and grant rec. in Sec. Office. No wit. Rec.
24 Mar. 1788.

Pp 39-40:   20 Nov. 1787, THOMAS SHOCKLEY, planter of Union Co.,
        to CHARLTON SHOCKLEY, planter of same place, for 100 pds sterling,
141½ acs. on a branch of Canes Creek. Bound by land laid out to Col.
HOPKINS and land laid out to ISAAC HOLLINGSWORTH. Granted to THOS.
SHOCKLEY on 5 May 1787 by the state of S. C. Wit: LALATHEL SHOCKLY,
JAMES (X) SHOCKLY, NOMI SHOCKLY. Rec. 24 Mar. 1788.

Page 41:   3 Feb. 1788, JOHN PALMORE and PATTEY, his wife, of 96
        Dist., to DANIEL HOLDER, same place, for 60 pds sterling and
divers good causes and considerations, 200 acs. on south fork of Brown's
Creek. Orig. grant to THOMAS BELL on 13 Feb. 1768. Wit: JESSE FORE,
EPHRAIM WELBORN. Signed: JOHN PALMORE. Wife PATTEY did not sign. No
recording date.

Pp 42-43:   22 Feb. 1788, THACKER VIVION of the State of Georgia,
        to JOHN LAYTON of Union Co., S.C. for 20 pds sterling, 125 acs.
part of a tract of 350 acs. granted to sd VIVION on 4 July 1785 by
Wm. Moultrie, Gov. of S.C., on north side of Tygar River. Bound on
one side by the balance of the orig. grant on which the sd VIVION formerly lived, PETER PENNELL's land and vacant land. Wit: NEHEMIAH HOWARD,
TURNER ROUNDTREE, JOHN HOWARD. No rec. date.

Pp 43-44:   26 Sept. 1787, JAMES HOGAN, JR. and CONNY, his wife,
        of Union Co. to JAMES HOGAN, SR. of same place, for 100 pds ster-
ling, 197½ acs. on Bogin's Creek, branch of Tygar River, bound SW by
land granted to ISAAC HOLLINGSWORTH. Orig. granted to HEZEKIAH GENTRY
5 June 1786 by S.C. grant. Wit: JOHN WOODS, JOSIAH WOOD, WILLIAM HOGANS,
JAMES (X) BANASTER. Signed: JAMES HOGINS and CONNY (X) HOGANS. Receipt
signed JAMES HOGINS, JR. Wit. to the receipt were H. HOGANS, JOHN WOOD,
JAMES (X) BANASTER. No rec. date.

Pp 44-45:   7 Mar. 1788, MATHEW SIMS of Newberry Co., SC to CHARLES
        SIMS, Esq., of Union Co., for the love and affection which he
hath and beareth unto his son the sd CHARLES SIMS, 125 acs. laying
and being in the State of Virginia, Hanover County, bounding on JOHN
GLEN's land, WILLIAM CHEEK's lands, DAVID HENDERSON's, CHARLES SIMS'
and CHARLES COLLEY's land. Wit: PATRICK HENRY SIMS, DAVID SIMS, JOHN
SANDERS. Rec. 24 Mar. 1788.

Pp 45-47:   27 Feb. 1788, PHILIP ANDERSON and ELIZABETH, his wife,
        of Union Co., to JAMES GUTHREY, same place, for 200 pds sterling,
250 acs. on south side of Tygar River, on Fishing Creek. Bound by sd
ANDERSON, DANIEL LIPHAM and vacant lands. Contains two tracts - one

Cont'd:
part orig. granted to RICHARD ANDERSON 11 Aug. 1774 by Wm. Bull, Lt.
Gov. of S.C., the other part granted to PHILIP ANDERSON 3 Apr. 1786
by Wm. Moultrie, Gov. of S.C. Wit: WILLIAM (X) JENKINS, SIMON (X) JENK-
INS, SAMUEL (X) JENKINS. Rec. 24 Mar. 1788.

Pp 47-48:   27 Feb. 1788, PHILLIP ANDERSON and ELIZABETH, his wife,
        of Union Co. to WILLIAM JENKINS, same place, for 50 pds sterling,
100 acs. on south side of Tygar River, bound by WM. ROGERS, the river
and vacant lands. Granted to PHILLIP ANDERSON 3 Apr. 1786 by Wm. Moultrie, Gov. of S.C. Wit: JAMES GUTHREY, SIMON (X) JENKINS, SAMUEL (X)
JENKINS. Rec. 24 Mar. 1788.

Pp 48-49:   29 Feb. 1788, WM. NEWMAN, blacksmith, of Union Co., to
        ARON FINCHER, planter, same place, for 16 pds 7 shillings and
9 pence sterling, 250 acs. bet. Tygar River and Fairforest Creek, on
the Main Road where DAVID FORMON did live formerly. A mortgage to be
paid by 25 Dec. 1788. Wit: FRANCES FINCHER, JOSEPH UNDERWOOD, VICE
(X) HOMES. Rec. 24 Mar. 1788.

Pp 50-51:   27 Nov. 1784, WILLIAM WHITE and BETTY, his wife, of 96
        Dist., to HANCOCK (also spelled HANDCOCK) PORTER, same place,
for divers good causes and considerations, and 30 pds sterling, 100
acs. on south fork of Brown's Creek, branch of Broad River. Bound by
LOT PORTER, WILLIAM McJUNKIN, WILLIAM GEORGE, & JAMES BOGAN. Formerly
the property of EDWARD NIXON. Wit: ISAAC SAMPSON, WILLIAM CAMPBELL,
ISAAC GREGORY. Wife BETTY signed by mark "ELIZABETH". WILLIAM CAMPBELL
and ISAAC GREGORY swore to signatures on 10 Dec. 1784 bef. THOS. BRANDON.
No rec. date.

Pp 51-52:   24 Feb. 1788, JOHN McCOOLL of Union Co. to CUSHMAN EDSON,
        same place, for 25 pds sterling, 2 lots at Union Courthouse con-
taining 1/2 ac. each, numbered 43 and 57, adj. on the south the Courthouse and gaol lots. Wit: JOHN BIRDSONG, THOS. BLASSINGAME. Rec. 24
Mar. 1788.

Pp 53-55:   11 Aug. 1785, Lease and Release. ABNER COLEMAN and SU-
        SANNAH, his wife, and WILLIAM COLEMAN, of Union Co., to NATHAN-
IEL GORDEN, same place, for 70 pds 14 shillings sterling, 100 acs.
on south side of Packolate River. Bound by COLEMAN and the Mill's Crk.
The Coleman's acquired the land by inheritance. No wit. Rec. 24 Mar.
1788.

Pp 56-57:   21 Mar. 1788, WILLIAM PLUMMER, planter, and CHRISTEN,
        his wife, of Union Co. to GEORGE HARLAN, hatter, same place,
for 53 pds sterling, 154 acs. on Fairforest Creek. One part thereof
being part of a tract containing 520 acs. orig. granted to SAMUEL YOUNG
by the Gov. of North Carolina and afterwards granted to DANIEL PLUMMER
by the Gov. of South Carolina on 28 July 1775. The remainder being
part of a tract containing 250 acs. granted to ALEXANDER McDANIEL by
Wm. Bull, Lt. Gov. of S.C. 22 Aug. 1771 and rec. in Auditor's Office
in Bk. L, No. 11, p. 53, 20 Sept. 1771. Bound by WILLIAM PLUMMER and
"the other GEORGE HARLAN's land", and Fairforest Creek. Wit: WILLIAM
MORGAN, GEORGE HARLAN, SARAH (X) BELUE. Signed WILLIAM (W) PLUMMER,
CHRISTEN PLUMMER. Rec. 24 Mar. 1788.

Pp 57-59:   21 Mar. 1788, WILLIAM PLUMMER, planter, and CHRISTEN, wife
        of Union Co., to GEORGE HARLAN, planter, same place, for 53 pds
sterling, 150 acs. on Fairforest Creek, part of the same tracts described in the deed next above and references to grantee's, etc. are
the same. Bound by the creek and land formerly called THOMAS MITCHELL's
land. Wit: WILLIAM MORGAN, GEORGE HARLAN, SARAH (X) BELUE. Signed:
WILLIAM (W) PLUMMER, CHRISTEN PLUMMER. Rec. 24 Mar. 1788.
        (Note: There were two men by the name of GEORGE HARLAN. One was
a hatter and is always referred to in the old deeds as George Harlan,
Hatter. The other one is referred to as "planter". Their name was also
spelled HARLIN, HARLING, HARLEN, etc...I do not know their relationship. These deeds are evidently to each one of them as grantees to
two different tracts of land...JMC)

Pp 59-60:   18 Feb. 1788, SHADRACH LANTRIP of Union Co. to SARAH
          GIST, same place, for 25 pds sterling, 150 acs. on both sides
of Fairforest Creek, branch of Tyger River. When granted was bound
by FRANCIS FINCHER, land then claimed by MICHAEL LEE and JOSEPH BAITS
(BATES), and vacant lands. Granted to LANTRIP by S. C. grant of 19
Aug. 1774. Wit: FRANCES FINCHER, AARON FINCHER, JOHN (X) FINCHER and
JAMES WOODSON. No rec. date.

Pp 60-62:   9 Aug. 1784, WILLIAM KENEDY of 96 Dist., to JOSEPH PEAR-
          SON (also spelled PIERCEN in deed), same place, for 32 pds ster-
ling, 100 acs. on the middle fork of Brown's Creek, south side of Broad
River. Bound by WILLIAM KENNEDY, SR., WILLIAM DAVIS, and vacant lands.
Granted by patent to the sd JOSEPH PEARSON (WILLIAM KENNEDY?), on 9
Aug. 1784 (this date is evidently wrong, since it is also the date
of the deed). Wit: CHRISTOPHER BRANDON, JOHN BRANDON. Signed by WILLIAM
(O) KENNEDY & ANN (O) KENNEDY. Rec. 25 Mar. 1788.

Pp 62-63:   15 Nov. 1787, JONATHAN GILKEY of Union Co. to SAMUEL
          GILKEY, same place, for 50 pds current money, 133 1/3 aacs. on
Gilkey's Creek, waters of Broad River. Orig. granted to sd JONATHAN
GILKEY by N. C. patent dated 31 Aug. 1753. POWERS (TOWERS?) LAMKIN
& WILLIAM LOCKHART are witnesses. Rec. 25 Mar. 1788.

Pp 63-64:   14 Dec. 1787, SAMUEL YOUNG of Rowan Co., N. C. to WILLIAM
          GILKEY of Union Co., SC, for 55 pds lawful money of the State
of Virginia and other considerations, two certain tracts in Union Co.,
lying together on both sides of Gilkey's Creek, each tract containing
300 acs., for a total of 600 acs. Granted to SAMUEL YOUNG by two patents
dated 27 Apr. 1767 and signed by Wm. Tryon, Gov. of N. C. Wit: WILLIAM
TATE, JONATHAN GILKEY. WILLIAM TATE, SR. attested to signatures on
24 Mar. 1788 bef. THOS. BRANDON, J.P. of Union Co. No recording date.

Pp 65-67:   14 Apr. 1773, Lease and Release. DANIEL PLUMMER, farmer
          and MARY, his wife, of Craven Co., North Carolina, (evidently
should be South Carolina) to STEPHEN WHITE, blacksmith, same place,
for 750 pds South Carolina currency, 200 acs. in Craven Co., South
Carolina, in the fork of Mitchel's Creek and Fairforest Creek. Bound
by JOSEPH BREED, SAMUEL JACKSON, the sd DANIEL PLUMMER, and vacant
lands. Granted to DANL. PLUMMER on 19 June 1772. Wit: ROBERT WHITE,
MARK GOODWIN, JOHN STEELE. ROBT. WHITE attested to signatures on 7
Mar. 1786 bef. Thos. Brandon, J.P. JOHN STEELE attested to signatures
on 27 Apr. 1786 bef. JOHN BIRDSONG. No recording date.

Pp 67-70:   10 May 1786, Lease and Release. WILLIAM HENDERSON of
          the State of South Carolina, to ABNER COLEMAN of 96 Dist., for
100 pds sterling, 135 acs. on Clark's Mill Creek, a branch of Packolate River. Bound by COLEMAN's line, the creek, and the School House
Branch. Part of a tract of 1,888 acs. orig. granted to JOAB MITCHEL
on 10 Feb. 1775 by Wm. Bull, Lt. Gov. og S.C. Entire tract conveyed
to WILLIAM HENDERSON. Wit: ABRAHAM SMITH, JOHN HENDERSON. Rec. 26 Mar.
1788.

Pp 70-71:   9 Feb. 1788, DANIEL WHITE of Union Co. to WILLIAM WILLIAMS
          of same place, for 10 pds sterling and divers good cause and
considerations, 150 acs. on a branch of the middle fork of Brown's
Creek. Bound by sd WILLIAM WILLIAMS', Col. FARR's land, and the Waggon
Road. Part of a tract granted to DANL. WHITE in 1787 and recorded in
Grant Bk. TTTT, p. 263. Wit: JOHN WHITE, JOHN PALMER, JANE (X) GILES.
Rec. 28 Mar. 1788.

Pp 71-72:   27 Oct. 1787, WILLIAM WILLIAMS of Union Co. to NICHOLAS
          WATERS, same place, for 46 pds. sterling, 170 acs. on south side
of Brown's Creek. Bound by Mr. LONG, Mr. HOLLENWORTH, and the creek.
Wit: EPHRAIM (X) PUCKET, ISAAC WHITE, CHARLES HUMPHRIES. Rec. 26 Mar.
1788.

Pp 72-75:   24 Dec. 1787, Lease and Release. THOMAS BLASINGAME, a
          planter and FANNY, his wife, of Union Co., to THOMAS PALMER,
planter of same place, for 5 pds lawful money, 55½ acs. on Sugar Creek,

Cont'd:
below the Ancient boundary line. The westward one-half of a tract of
111 acs. orig. granted to THOS. BLASSINGAME. At time of grant bound
by JAMES BETTERTON's land, the old line and vacant lands. Signed: THOS.
BLASINGAME, FRANCES BLASINGAME. No wit. Rec. 28 Mar. 1788.

Pp 76-79:   24 Dec. 1787, Lease and Release. JOHN HAMES of Union
          Co., 96 Dist. to WILLIAM HAMES, same place, for 7 (_?_ pds?),
100 acs. that the sd WM. HAMES now lives on. Part of a tract of 200
acs. granted by letters patent to JOHN HAMES by Benj. Guerard, Gov.
of S.C. on Johny's Creek, branch of Packolate River. Bound by ELENOR
McWHORTER and the orig. tract. Wit: NICHOLAS JASPER, JOHN McWHORTER,
ROBERT GALT. Rec. 28 Mar. 1788.

Pp 79-80:   22 Sept. 1787, ALEX'D. CANE of Union Co. to WILLIAM WHIT-
          LOCK, same place, for 25 pds sterling, 36 acs. on north fork
of Brown's Creek, bound by THOS. ALBRITTON, JOSEPH JOLLY, JAMES BOGAN
and sd WHITLOCK. Part of a tract granted to DAVID GEORGE and conveyed
by WILLIAM GEORGE, eldest son and heir at law also Administrator of
sd DAVID GEORGE, deceased, to sd ALEXANDER CANE. Wit: JOHN WHITLOCK,
THOS. ALBRITON. Signed: ALEXANDER CAIN. Rec. 28 Mar. 1788.

Pp 81-82:   28 Mar. 1788, JOSEPH McJUNKIN of Union Co. to DANIEL
          McJUNKIN, same place, for 100 pds, 150 acs. on both sides of
Tinker Creek, part of an old survey of 300 acs. Signed: JOSEPH McJUNKIN
and ANN McJUNKIN. Wit: JOHN CHESNEY, WILLIAM THOMAS, W. D. THOMAS.
WM. THOMAS and WILLIAM DAVIS THOMAS attested to signatures of Joseph
McJunkin and Anne, his wife on 29 Mar. 1788 bef. WM. KENNEDY, J.P.
No recording date.

Pp 82-83:   12 Jan. 1788, JOHN HEWY and MARY HEWY, his wife, of Union
          Co., to JOSEPH TUCKER, same place, for 155 pds current money
of Virginia, 150 acs. on north side of Tygar River bounded on a small
branch of Tygar River known as Duff's Branch, bound by DAVID HUDSON
when granted to JOHN HEWY by Lord Granville Montague, Gov. of S.C.
on 3 July 1772. Wit: SAMUEL OTTERSON, DAVID HUDSON and BIRD BEUFORD.
Rec. 28 Mar. 1788.

Pp 84-85:   28 Sept. 1787, JOHN McCOOLL of Union Co. to WILLIAM KEN-
          NEDY, same place, for 50 pds sterling, 109 acs. on waters of
Brown's Creek in the forks of the roads to Charles Town and Ninety-
Six, part of a tract of 1000 acs. patented to sd McCooll by Wm. Moultrie, Gov. of S.C. 4 Dec. 1786. No witnesses. Ack. in court 28 Sept.
1787, ordered to be recorded. (Note: The clerk evidently made an error
in copying since the deed contains one section of a deed from CHARLES
GLANTON to ABSALEM PETTY. JOHN McCOOLL signed the deed.)

Pp 85-87:   26 Aug. 1785, WILLIAM WOFFORD, ironmaster of Turkey Cove
          in Burk Co., N.C. to DANIEL LANGSTON and BENNETT LANGSTON, plan-
ters both of Spartanburgh Co., 96 Dist., S.C. for 100 pds sterling,
100 acs. on branch of Tygar River called the Dutchman's Creek, orig.
granted to STEPHEN HOLDEN, 3 June 1765 by Wm. Bull, Lt. Gov. of S.C.
Bounded then on all sides by vacant lands sd then to be in Berkley
County in the province of So. Carolina but now in Spartan-borough Co.
in the state of S.C. (Note: One Dutchman's Creek flows from Spartanburgh Co. into Union Co., then into Tyger River.) SPANN and BENNETT
(?) SPANN swore to signatures 23 Sept. 1788 in Union Co. bef. Thos.
Blasingame, J.P. No recording date.

Pp 87-92:   3 Oct. 1787, Lease and Release. ADAM GILCHRIST, merchant
          of Charles Town, to HENRY MILLHOUSE (also spelled MILHOUSE),
JOHN COOK and WILLIAM HAWKINS of Union Co., 96 Dist., on a branch of
Tygar River, planters, trustees named and appointed by the Congregation
of Friends of Cane Creek Meeting in sd dist. and state, for 10 pds
sterling, 372 acs. on drafts of Tinker Creek, waters of Tygar River.
Bound by vacant lands, WILLIAM SMITH, DAVID HARRIS & JAMES HALL. As
the sd congregation or society is not yet incorporated by Law they
cannot purchase lands and Tenements in their own names as a Corporated
Body it is therefore necessary that the Conveyance of Titles to sd

Cont'd:
lands be made in the name and names of Trustees appointed by sd congregation, to erect a place of worship and burying ground. Wit: H.
W. DeSAUSSURE and NATHAN HAWKINS. Rec. 23 June 1788.

Pp 92-93:   5 Apr. 1788, HENRY LONG and ANN his wife of Union Co.
     to WILLIAM WHITE, same place, for 46 pds, 13 shillings, 4 pence
current money of S.C. and other considerations, 200 acs. part of a
tract of 317 acs. granted to Col. WILLIAM FARR 5 Dec. 1785, sd HENRY
LONG and ANN his wife reserving to themselves 117 acs. Located on west
side of the Charles Town waggon road, adj. WILLIAM BUCKHANNAN, WILLIAM
WILLIAMS, JOHN WHITE, SR. and the sd WM. WHITE. Wit: WILLIAM DAWKINS
LANE, JOHN WHITE, DANIEL WHITE. Rec. 23 June 1788.

Pp 94-95:   21 June 1788, GEORGE McWHORTER of S.C., to JESSE PATTEY
     of Union Co., S.C., for 150 pds sterling, 231 acs. on west side
of Broad River, bound by McKISSICK, REED and the river. 200 acs. formerly laid out to REDARUS CLARK, and 31 acs. formerly laid out to JAMES
LOVE and HENRY CLARK. Signed: GEORGE McWHORTER, ELIZABETH McWHORTER.
Wit: JOHN McWHORTER. Rec. 23 June 1788.

Pp 95-96:   23 June 1788, WM. WILLIAMS of Union Co., to CHARLES HUM-
     PHRIES, same place, for 30 pds sterling, 100 acs. on a branch
of Brown's Creek. Bound by the waggon road, STRIBLING, and LONG. Part
of a tract granted to WM. WILLIAMS in 1775. Wit: WM. BUCKHANNAN, DANIEL
HOLDEN. Rec. 23 June 1788.

Pp 96-97:   10 Apr. 1788, JOHN STEEN of S.C., to GEORGE McWHORTER,
     of Union Co., for 70 pds sterling, 100 acs. on south side of
Packolate River about 1/2 mile above the Scull Shoals. Part of a tract
granted to ROBERT BISHOP, 2 Sept. 1765 by his Excellency William Tryon
(North Carolina). Wit: NICHOLAS JASPER, JOHN McWHORTER, ELISABETH (X)
McWHORTER. Rec. 23 June 1788.

Pp 97-98:   23 June 1788, WILLIAM BUCKHANAN and FRANCES, his wife
     of Union Co. to GAGE PUCKET, same place, for 20 pds current money
and other considerations, 113 acs. on head of Sandy Run, vacant lands
on all sides. Granted to Wm. Buckhanan 7 May 1787. Wit: WILLIAM WIL-
LIAMS, DANIEL HOLDEN. Rec. 23 June 1788.

Pp 98-99:   3 Feb. 1787, DANIEL LIPHAM of 96 Dist., to DAVID PUIT,
     same place, for 5 pds sterling, 100 acs. on south west side of
Tygar River, orig. granted to sd Lipham, 6 Nov. 1786 by his Excellency
Wm. Moultrie, Esq., recorded in Sec. Office, Grant Book QQQQ, p. 55,
with plat annexed. Certified 30 Nov. 1786. Wit: JOSIAS DARBY, JOSEPH
(X) HUEY, RANDELL (X) JENKINS. Rec. 23 June 1788.

Page 99:   18 June 1786, WILLIAM WILLIAMS of Union Co., to EPHRAIM
     PUCKET, for 15 pds sterling, 100 acs. on waters of Brown's Creek
bound by STEPHEN MAYFIELD, THOMAS WILLIAMS and the Creek. Wit: ISAAC
WHITE, ISOM PUCKET, JOHN WHITE. Rec. 23 June 1788.

Pp 100-101:   (A lease?) 20 June 1787 - Heading shows Spartanburgh
     Co., WILLIAM YOUNG and MARGARET, his wife, of Spartanburgh Co.,
to PETER BRASELMAN and CUSHMAN EDSON of Newberry Co., for 5 shillings,
209 acs. in Union Co., in the fork of Enoree and Tygar Rivers. Bound
by JAMES TOWNEND (TOWNSEND?), JAMES HAWKINS, WILLIAM TAYLOR, & JAMES
HILL. Granted to sd WM. YOUNG 7 Jan. 1787 by Thos. Pinckney, Esq.,
Gov. of S.C. Wit: SAML. JONES, LUTHER SMITH. Both witnesses swore to
signatures on 21 June 1787 in Laurens Co. bef. DANIEL WRIGHT, J.P.
Rec. in Union Co. 23 June 1788.

Pp 101-104:   12 Oct. 1784, Lease and Release. RICHARD CHESNEY, yeoman,
     and JANE, his wife, of Jammy's Creek in S.C., to JOHN GARRET,
millright (sic), of Enoree River, same state, for 30 pds current money
of S.C., 50 acs. on north side of Enoree River, bound by JACOB EARNEST,
the river and vacant lands. Granted to sd CHESNEY 29 Apr. 1768, by
Lord Chas. G. Montague, Gov. of S.C. Wit: ALEXANDER ALEXANDER, PAUL
(X) CASTLEBERRY, RANDEL (X) McDANIEL. Alexander attested to signatures

Cont'd:
on 23 Oct. 1784 before JAMES OLLIPHANT, J.P. of 96 District.

Pp 105-107:   14 Jan. 1788, Lease and Release. JOSEPH HUGHES of Union
        Co., to Col. THOMAS BRANDON, same place, for 272 pds 18 shillings
9 pence sterling, 251 acs. on north side of Fairforest Creek of Tygar
River. Bound by JOHN HAILD and vacant lands. The property of THOMAS
FLETCHALL and conveyed to the sd JOSEPH HUGHES by Lease and Release
by JOHN BERWICK, THOMAS WARING and JOHN EWING COLHOUN, being Commissioners of Forfeited Estates in the sd state. Rec. in Register's Office
in Bk. W, No. 5, pp. 342-343. (THOMAS FLETCHALL was a Tory.) Wit: BEN-
JAMIN WOODSON, JOHN BRANDON, JOHN MONTGOMERY. No rec. date.

Pp 108-111:   29 July 1786, Lease and Release. ROBERT COLEMAN, heir
        to ROBERT COLEMAN, deceased, of 96 Dist., to ABNER COLEMAN, same
place, for 100 pds sterling, 300 acs. on north side of Clark's Mill
Creek, being 1/2 of a 600 ac. tract owned by ROBT. COLEMAN, dec'd.,
who died intestate. Sd land falls by decent (sic) to ROBT. COLEMAN,
son of CHRISTOPHER COLEMAN as heir at law to the Real Estate of the
sd deceased. Bound by ROBT. COLEMAN, PETER COPLIN, WM. HODGE, ABNER
COLEMAN, the Mill Creek, and THOMAS DRAPER. Wit: JOHN HAILE, ZACHARIAH
BULLOCK, JOHN HENDERSON. Rec. 23 June 1788.

Pp 111-112:   13 May 1773, JOAB MITCHELL of the Co. of Craven, Prov.
        of S.C. to PETER COPELAND, of the Prov. of Virginia, for 100
pds currency of the State (S.C.), 150 acs. part of a 446 ac. tract
granted to sd JOAB MITCHELL by patent from the Gov. of North Carolina
26 Oct. 1767. Bound by JOAB MITCHELL on three sides. Wit: ZACHR. BUL-
LOCK, WM. HENDERSON, ADAM POTTER. Rec. 23 June 1788.

Pp 112-113:   23 Sept. 1786, JOHN WEEDAMAN of Newberry Co., SC to JOHN
        REED of Union Co., for 100 pds sterling, 100 acs. on Broad River
and both sides of Fannin's Creek, including the mill and plantation
formerly granted to ANN GOIN by Wm. Bull, Commander-in-Chief of the
Prov. of S.C. and since conveyed to BENJAMIN FERROR(?), Esq. to ROBERT
BAILEY, to sd JOHN WEDAMAN. Signed: JONANNES WEDAMAN. Wit: TURNER KEN-
DRICK, JAMES LINDSAY, WILLIAM LILES. A statement dated 28 Mar. 1787
was signed by REBECKAH BROCK and JOHN COLE to the effect that they
heard JOHN WEDAMAN ack. the deed as his own act. Another statement
signed by D. BROWN to the effect that "this deed was tendered to the
Court of Union Co. 28 Dec. 1786 and JAMES LINDSAY and WM. LILES as
evidence to prove it, but the Court refused to examine them or admit
it to record." Finally on 3 May 1788 WM. LILES was allowed to attest
to signatures bef. WM. McCULLOCH, J.P. and it was recorded on 23 June
1788.

Pp 114-115:   26 Oct. 1786, JOHN WEDAMAN of Newberry Co. to JOHN REED
        of Union Co., for 100 pds sterling, a certain tract on south
west side of Broad River, adj. on the lower side a tract of land granted
to ANN GOIN by patent and by deeds of conveyance to sd JOHN REED, and
on the upper side by GEORGE BALEY. This tract was granted to sd WEDA-
MAN by patent dated 20 Oct. 1772. Signed: JOHANNAS WEDINGMAN. Wit:
GEORGE PURVIS, DAVID (X) WEDINGHAM & WILLIAMSON LILES. REBECCAH BROCK
and JOHN COLE signed a statement on 28 Mar. 1787 stating that they
heard WEDINGMAN ack. the deed. DANL. BROWN signed the following statement: "This deed was tendered to Union Co. 26 Mar. 1787 and JOHN WED-
INGMAN ack. the same to be his Act and Deed but on a Supposition of
fraud the Court refused to admit same to Record." JOHN WEDINGMAN signed
a receipt 8 Mar. 1787 wit. by JOHN COLE and WM. SISSON. GEORGE PURVIS
attested to signatures on 3 May 1788 bef. WM. McCULLOCH, J.P. No rec.
date.

Pp 115-117:   1 Dec. 1787, SAMUEL SMITH and MARTHA his wife of Burke
        Co., Georgia, to ALEXANDER HAMILTON of Union Co., SC, for 70
pds sterling, 390 acs. on Packolate River, orig. granted to SAMUEL
SMITH in Mecklenburge Co., N.C., now in Union Co., S.C. 20 Oct. 1767.
Bound by GEORGE MOORE and the river. Wit: JAMES GRAHAM, CHARLES (X)
SMITH, LYDDA (X) SMITH. James Graham attested to signatures in Burke
Co., Ga. 1 Dec. 1787 bef. EDWARD WEATHERS, J.P. Charles Smith attested

Cont'd:
to the signatures in Union Co., S.C. on 18 Dec. 1788 before WM. KENNEDY,
J.P. Recorded 22 Dec. 1788.

Pp 117-118:   3 July 1788, JOHN McCOOL of Union Co., to JAMES McCLURE,
        same place, for 5 pds sterling, lot no. 46 containing 1/2 ac.
at Union Court House. Wit: JOHN EWART, JOHN McKIBBEN. Rec. 22 Dec.
1788.

Pp 118-121:   15 Sept. 1788, Lease and Release. WILLIAM WOFFORD of
        Burk Co., N. C. to JOHN HAMES of Union Co., S.C. for 25 pds ster-
ling, 200 acs. whereon he the sd HAMES now lives, on Little Sandy Run,
a branch of Packolate River. Granted to WILLIAM WILLIAMS 28 Apr. 1768
by Wm. Trion (Tryon), Gov. of N.C. and conveyed to WM. WOFFORD 11 Aug.
1770. Wit: CHARLES (X) HAMES, NICHOLAS JASPER. Rec. 22 Dec. 1788.

Pp 121-122:   15 Sept. 1788, SAMUEL BEAKS and SARAH his wife of New-
        berry Co., to WILLIAM HAWKINS, yeoman of Union Co., for 100 pds,
100 acs. in fork of Broad and Saluda River, on a branch of Broad river
called Tiger River. Sd tract granted to ANN MARGARETT REINGER on 22
Jan. 1759 by a bounty granted by his Exc. WILLIAM HENRY LYTTLETON,
Capt. General. Conveyd by ANN M. REINGER to ABRAHAM BEAKS by deed and
release dated 8 Mar. 1758 (Ann Margarett either sold the land before
she actually received her grant, or one of these dates is in error).
Sd tract since the decease of ABRAHAM BEAKS, "has fell to" SAMUEL BEAKS,
be being Heir at Law. Orig. grant rec. in Sec. Office, Book TT, p.
180, with plat attached. Wit: JOHN LINDSAY, JR., THOMAS LOFTON. John
Lindsay, Jr. attested to signatures 22 Dec. 1788 bef. BER. (BERNARD)
GLENN, J.P. Rec. 23 Dec. 1788.

Pp 123-124:   23 Dec. 1788, NEHEMIAH HOWARD, planter of Union Co. to
        ARCHER HOWARD, same place, for 20 pds sterling, 150 acs. on a
branch of Fairforest and Sugar Creeks, granted to NEHEMIAH HOWARD 23
June 1774 by Wm. Bull, Lt. Gov. of S.C. and rec. in Sec. Office in
Book QQQ, p. 579. Grant bound by RALPH JACKSON, PHILLIP BRYENT, WIL-
LIAM WOFFORD, ARCHER SMITH. No wit. Rec. 23 Dec. 1789 (88?).

Pp 124-127:   9 July 1788, Lease and Release. JOHN MARTINDELL and RACHEL
        his wife of Union Co. to THOMAS TOD of Spartanburgh Co., for
25 pds sterling, 190 acs. in Union Co. on north side of Enoree River
above the mouth of Frenchman's Creek. Part of a tract of 207 acs. orig.
granted to sd MARTINDELL 5 June 1786 by Wm. Moultrie, Esq. bound by
JOHN MARTINDELL (the tract on which he now lives), JOHN BRIGGS, Enoree
River, JOHN NEDDYMAN and vacant land. Wit: RICHARD BURGESS, ABSALOM
BOBO. Richard Burgess attested to signatures 23 Dec. 1788 bef. THOS.
BLASSINGAME, J.P. Rec. 23 Dec. 1788.

Pp 127-128:   29 Sept. 1788, JOHN MOLLINGS (also spelled MULLINGS,
        MOLLING) of Union Co., to JAMES HALL, same place, for 20 pds
sterling, 100 acs. on Brushecreek (Brushy Creek). Bound by Walter Road
(?) (WALTER ROADS?) and sd MOLLINGS. Part of a 300 ac. tract granted
to sd Mollings. Signed by mark JOHN (X) MOLLINGS. Wit: DAVID HARRIS,
JONATHAN HUMPHREYS. Humphreys and Harris attested to signatures 23
Mar. 1789 bef. JOSEPH McJUNKIN, J.P. Rec. the same day.

Pp 128-130:   26 Dec. 1787, GEORGE CROSSLEY of Union Co. to JOHN Mc-
        COOLL, same place, for 100 pds lawful money of S.C., 100 acs.
on waters of Fairforest Creek and Brown's Creek. Part of a tract of
450 acs. orig. granted by patent to WALTER HOLMES by Wm. Bull, Lt.
Gov. of S.C. and conveyed by deed in 1779 from Holmes to GEORGE CROSS-
LEY, SR. Conveyed by deed from CROSSLEY, SR. to GEORGE CROSSLEY, JR.
in 1786. Wit: SETH ALDAY, JOHN MARTIN. Alday and Martin attested to
signatures 23 Mar. 1789 bef. HUGH MEANS, J.P. Rec. same day.

Pp 130-131:   5 Mar. 1789, JOHN MULLINGS of Union Co. to PHILEMON BASS,
        same place, for 50 pds sterling, part of a tract of 260 acs.
except that part sold out of sd tract to JAMES HALL. (See pp 127-128
above). Granted to sd Mullings 6 Mar. 1786. Located on both sides of
Swift Run Creek, a water of Tyger River, bound by the waggon road and

Cont'd:
JAMES HALL. Signed by mark JOHN (X) MULLENS. Wit: WILLIAM BOSTICK,
WILLIAM HENDLEY, URIAH (?) MULLENS. Uriah Mullens swore to signatures
7 Mar. 1789 bef. WILLIAM KENNEDY, J.P. Rec. 23 Mar. 1789.

Pp 131-132:   20 Nov. 1788, GEORGE McCOLOGH and MARGARET his wife of
        96 Dist., to JOHN MASSEY of same place, for 20 pds sterling,
and other considerations, 100 acs. on waters of Fishdam Creek. Bound
by lands laid out to GEORGE IGLEBURGER and by JAMES BISHOP and vacant
lands. Signed GEORGE McCULLOCH and MARGARET (X) McCULLOCH. Wit: JAMES
CALDWELL, THOMAS (X) HARDY, WILLIAM MASSEY. Caldwell and Massey attested
to signatures 23 Mar. 1789 bef. HUGH MEANS, J.P. Rec. same day.

Page 133:   1 Jan. 1789. THOMAS BRANDON of Union Co., to JEREMIAH
        LUCAS, same place, for 50 pds sterling, 400 acs. part of a tract
of 1200 acs. granted to sd BRANDON 6 Nov. 1786. Bound by JUDAH CRAIN,
JOB HAMMON and sd BRANDON. Wit: WILLIAM CAMPBELL, WILLIAM CLAYTON.
Attested on same day bef. WM. KENNEDY, J.P. No rec. date.

Pp 134-135:   23 Mar. 1789, JOHN MARTINDELL and RACHEL his wife of
        Union Co. to JOHN GARRET of same place, for 37 shillings and
4 pence, 25 acs. adj. sd Martindell and the sd John Garret, and HENRY
ADDINGTON, JOHN ADDINGTON & WALTER ROBERTS. Part of a tract granted
to sd Martindell 29 May 1787 and rec. in Sec. Office Book QQQQ, p.
611. Wit: THOMAS HARRIS, PHEBEE (X) HUFF. Rec. 23 Mar. 1789.

Pp 135-137:   24 Jan. 1789, THEODOROUS PRIDMORE of Union Co. to NICOLAS
        JASPER, same place, for 9 pds, 93 acs. on Pacolate River. Bound
by ROBERT GALT, sd NICOLAS JASPER and CHARLES HAMES. Part of a S.C.
grant of 393 acs. to sd PRIDMORE 17 Jan. 1788. Wit: BENJAMIN COVENHOVEN,
JONATHAN PRIDMORE, JOHN STRANGE. Benj. Covenhoven swore to signatures
23 Mar. 1789 bef. WILLIAM McCULLOCH, J.P. Rec. same day.

Pp 137-138:   20 Jan. 1789, JAMES HILL, minister of the Gospel, and
        ANN HILL, his wife, both of Newberry Co., S.C. to LeROY BEUFORD,
yeoman, of Lunnenburg (sic) Co., Va., for 169 pds, 18 shillings, and
9 pence sterling, 2 whole tracts on SW side of Tiger River in Union
Co., one tract containing 250 acs. granted to WILLIAM DIXON and the
other tract of 100 acs. granted to HUGH DIXON by Wm. Bull, Lt. Gov.
of Prov. of S.C. Both grants dated 19 Mar. 1773. Wit: ED. RAGSDALE,
ROBERT (X) CRENSHAW, CHARLES JOHNSTON, BENJAMIN JOHNSON. Rec. 23 Mar.
1789.

Page 139:   20 Aug. 1787, JAMES SAVAGE of 96 Dist., to ELIJAH Mc-
        GUIRE, same place, for 20 pds lawful money, all the SE half a
tract containing 200 acs. granted 4 May 1775 to JOHN WEEDINGMAN by
Wm. Bull. Located on Fannings Creek. The sd 1/2 or 100 acs. conveyed
by Weedingman to JOHN McDONALD, and then to FREDERICK DAVIS, then by
sd Davis to James Savage. Division line begins at MARK KENT's black
oak corner. Wit: ROBERT SMITH, ROBERT CHAPMAN, RICHARD FAUCETT. No
recording date.

Pp 140-141:   14 Mar. 1789, JOHN LAYTON and SUSANNA, his wife of Spar-
        tanburgh Co., SC to ROBERT WHITE of Union Co., for 22 pds sterl-
ing, 175 acs. purchased by sd Layton from THACKER VIVION 22 Feb. 1788.
Located in Union co. and bound by THACKER VIVION, vacant lands and
PETER PINNIAL. (Note: PETER PINNIAL's name has been spelled other places
as PENNELL). Wit: STEPHEN LAYTON, HENRY BRAY. Henry Bray attested to
signatures in Union Co. on 23 Mar. 1789 bef. Hugh Means, J.P. Rec.
same day.

Pp 141-143:   31 Aug. 1773, JOSEPH PARK, carpenter, and RACHEL, his
        wife, of Craven Co., Prov. of S.C., to RICHARD SAY, cordwinder,
of Roan (sic) Co., Prov. of N.C., for 150 pds currency, 150 acs. in
the county of Craven in the Province of South Carolina on the waters
of Fairforest Creek joining the land JOHN PARK lives on. Bound by WIL-
LIAM MEANS and JOHN PARK. Granted to sd Joseph Park by royal patent
dated 16 Dec. 1769. Wit: SAMUEL THOMPSON, GEORGE PARK, JOSEPH PARK,
SR. Saml. Thompson swore to signatures 5 Mar. 1779 bef. Wm. Wofford.
Rec. 23 Mar. 1789.

Pp 143-144:   21 Mar. 1789, SAMUEL JACKSON to JORDEN JACKSON (no place
              of residence given), for 5 shillings sterling, 100 acs. it being
part of a tract of land granted from DANIEL JACKSON to SAMUEL JACKSON.
Bound by the waggon road, Reedy branch, AVERY BREED's land and DANIEL
PLUMMER's line. Excepted one-half of all gold and silver mines, and
contains the statement "SAMUEL JACKSON - doth agree with the sd JORDEN
JACKSON his heirs, etc....that he and they shall at all times hereafter peaceably and quietly possess and enjoy the sd parcel of 100
acs." Wit: DAVID HART & MARK JACKSON. Mark Jackson attested on 23 Mar.
1789 bef. WILLIAM McCULLOCH, J.P. Rec. same day.

Pp 145-148:   24 Dec. 1787, Lease and Release. THOMAS BLASSENGAME,
              planter, and FANNY, his wife, to DANIEL PALMER, planter, both
of Union Co., for 72 pds lawful money, 190½ acas. on Sugar Creek, a
branch of Fairforest. 135 acs. being one-half of an old North (Carolina?) survey of 270 acs. orig. granted to JOHN HITCHCOCK. The other
55½ acs. laying below the Ancient boundry line being the westward one-
half of 111 acs. granted to THOMAS BLASSENGAME. At the time of grants
bound by JAMES BETTERTON and vacant lands. Signed: THOMAS BLASSENGAIM
andFRANCES (X) BLASENGAIM. No wit. Rec. 24 Mar. 1789.

Pp 148-150:   14 Nov. 1787, FRANCES POSEY and MILLY, his wife, of Edge-
              field Co., to JOSEPH COMER, of Union Co., for 100 pds sterling,
100 acs. in the forks of Tyger and Broad Rivers on north side of Cain
Creek. Bound by the creek, WOOD's line, and RUCKER SMITH. Part of a
tract surveyed by SAMUEL YOUNG, Deputy Surveyor for THOMAS COX, granted
by his Honor Mathew Rowan (North Carolina) on 23 Feb. 1754, it being
the lower end of sd survey. Leased by sd THOMAS COX to WILLIAM ARM-
STRONG, and by sd Armstrong to JOHN POSEY, and from him to FRANCES
(FRANCIS) POSEY 31 July 1777. Signed: FRANCES POSEY and MILDRED (X)
POSEY. Wit: JOSHUA MARTIN, GEORGE (X) ROWDEN, RUCKER (X) SMITH. George
Rowden attested to signatures 13 Jan. 1789 bef. BERD. GLENN, J.P. Rec.
24 Mar. 1789.

Pp 150-151:   1 Nov. 1788, EUCLIDAS LONGSHORE and SARY, his wife, of
              Newberry Co., to JOHN FARROW, of Spartanburgh Co. for 500 pds
sterling, 250 acs. on Simmons branch, surveyed 20 Dec. 1776. Bound
by WILLIAM ROAD (RHODES?) and vacant lands. Granted to EUCLIDAS LONG-
SHORE 9 Sept. 1774 by the Hon. Wm. Bull (S.C.). Both Euclidas and Sary
signed by mark. "Sary" shown as "SARAH" in the attestation. Wit: LANDON
FARROW and RANDAL (X) DEPREST. Landon Farrow attested to signatures
in Spartanburgh Co. 12 Mar. 1789 bef. THOMAS FARROW, J.P. Rec. in Union
County on 24 Mar. 1789.

Pp 151-155:   19 Sept. 1787, Lease and Release. MARK LOVE, cooper,
              and SARAH, his wife, of Newberry Co., to SAMUEL SPRAY, also of
Newberry Co., the settlement of Bush River, for 165 pds sterling, 200
acs. in Union Co. on the NE side of Tyger River. Part of a grant of
250 acs. granted 10 Sept. 1765 by Wm. Bull, Gov. of S.C. to TERRENCE
CARRELL and conveyed by grant recorded in Sec. Office in Book LL, p.
413. WILLIAM ORE conveyed part of the tract to JAMES ORE, "and 200
acs. of sd lands fell to his only Heir, a daughter named SARAH, the
wife of MARK LOVE." Wit: JAMES LINDSEY and JAMES SPROULL. James Lindsey attested on 22 Sept. 1787 in Newberry Co. bef. JOHN LINDSEY, J.P.

Pp 155-156:   23 Mar. 1789, JOSEPH EAST to SAMUEL CLOUNEY (no place
              of residence given) for 90 pds current money of S.C., 300 acs.
in 96 Dist. on a branch of Fairforest Creek, bound on all sides by
vacant lands when first surveyed. Wit: JAMES YANCEY, JR. and SAMUEL
JACKSON. Yancey and Jackson attested to signatures on same day bef.
Thos. Blasengaim, J.P. Rec. 24 Mar. 1789.

Pp 156-157:   14 Oct. 1786, JOHN FOSTER of Greenville Co., S.C. to
              FRANCIS WHILCHEL of Union Co., for 100 pds current money of the
state of Virginia, 200 acs. in Union Co. on Mimcoms(?) Creek, waters
of Broad River. Orig. granted to NATHANIEL CLARK by JOSIAH MARTIN,
Gov. of N. C., conveyed by sd Clark to WILLIAM SMITH, from Smith to
sd FOSTER. Wit: JOHN CROW FOSTER, RICHARD THOMPSON and JOHN BEARD.
Proved by John Beard and rec. 25 Mar. 1789.

Pp 157-158: 9 Feb. 1787, JOHN McCOOL of Union Co. to SAMUEL CARGO, same place, for 50 pds sterling, lot no. 45 containing 1/2 ac. at Union Courthouse. Wit: JOHN McCIBBEN (McKIBBEN?) and ANDREW THOMPSON. Rec. 25 Mar. 1789.

Pp 159-160: 13 Dec. 1788, DAVID DIXON of York Co., S.C. to JOSEPH McJUNKIN of Union Co., for 300 pds current money, 300 acs. on both sides of Tinker Creek, a branch of Tyger River. Bound by THOMAS LANTRIP, SAMUEL McJUNKIN and vacant lands. Orig. granted to the sd DAVID DIXON by the Gov. of the Prov. of North Carolina and regranted to sd Dixon by Wm. Campbell, Gov. of South Carolina, on 14 Aug. 1775. Wit: SAMUEL (X) McJUNKIN, PHILIP (X) SHAVERTAKER. Samuel McJunkin attested on 27 Mar. 1789 bef. Thomas Blasingaim, J.P. Rec. same day.

Pp 160-163: 6 Mar. 1785, Lease and Release. TEMPERANCE SAFOLD, Executrix of the Last Will and Testament of WILLIAM SAFOLD, deceased, and ISHAM SAFOLD, eldest son of sd WM. SAFOLD, to THOMAS WRIGHT of Thicketty Creek, for 300 pds current money of Virginia, 266 acs. being 2/3's of a tract whereon DAVID ROBERTSON, deceased, formerly lived at his death. Located on both sides of Thicketty Creek. Bound by vacant lands, JOHN THOMSON, and 1/3 of the same tract whereon MATHEW ROBERTSON now lives. Wit: GEORGE MARTIN and AGATHA PETTY. Signed by TEMPERANCE (X) SAFOLD and ISHAM SAFOLD. Agatha Petty swore to signatures on 21 Mar. 1789 bef. ZACHARIAH BULLOCK, J.P. Rec. 27 Mar. 1789.

Pp 163-164: 2 Oct. 1773, JOAB MITCHELL of 96 Dist., Prov. of S.C., to SUSANNAH BULLOCK of Granville Co. in N.C., daughter of LEN HENLEY BULLOCK, for 150 pds, 300 acs. in 96 Dist. on both sides of Packolate River near Canols (Carrolls?) Shoals. Bound by GRINDEL and BECKHAM. Wit: ADAM POTTER, HENRY WHITE and CHARLES DRAPER. Adam Potter attested on 26 Nov. 1788 bef. WM. KENNEDY, J.P. Rec. 27 Mar. 1789.

Pp 164-165: 4 Aug. 1785, PETER JOHNSTON, Exec. of the Estate of JOHN KIRKONNELL, deceased, of Mecklenburg Co., N. C., to Major ZACHARIAH BULLOCK of Union Co., S.C. for 10 pds sterling, 200 acs. in Union Co. on north side of Pacolate River. Bound by ZACHARIAH BULLOCK and YOUNG's line. Wit: ADAM POTTER, WILLIAM COLEMAN and JOHN HAILE. Rec. 27 Mar. 1789.

Pp 165-167: 22 Sept. 1787, JOHN STEEN and his wife MARTHA, of Union Co., to JOHN THOMPSON of same place, for 25 pds sterling, 20 acs. on both sides of Thicketty Creek, and joins land which is now in the possession of JOHN THOMPSON and was conveyed to him by JOHN STEEN. Begins at a post oak marked by JAMES MARTIN, Deputy Surveyor. Part of 2 tracts granted to HOWARD and BRIDGES. Signed by JOHN STEEN and MARTHA (X) STEEN. Wit: WILLIAM STEEN & JOHN (X) WOODS. John Woods attested on 18 Oct. 1789 (error?) bef. WILLIAM McCULLOCH, J.P. Rec. 27 Mar. 1789.

Pp 167-169: 16 Dec. 1788, THOMAS FARROR, Esq., Sheriff of 96 Dist., S.C. to DANIEL BROWN and CUSHMAN EDSON, Esq's, for 32 pds sterling, the high bid on 638 acs. in Union Co. bet. the waters of Packolett River and Fairforest Creek. Bound by NICOLAS HARRIS, ARTHER CUNNINGHAM, JOHN THOMPSON, Major BULLOCK, DANIEL SHAW, EDWARD PICKETTS and vacant lands. Sold at public auction 22 Sept. 1788 by order of the Hon. HENRY PENDLETON, Esq., one of the associate judges of the Court of Common Pleas at Charleston, to pay a judgment against BENAJAH THOMPSON (who owned the land) in the case of BENAJAH SMITH vs. BENAJAH THOMPSON entered in the April term of court 1786. The suit was an action of trespass in the case for "the service and labour of a certain negro man named Sam, the property of the sd BENAJAH SMITH." Wit: JOHN HENDERSON and JOHN HAILE. Rec. 27 Mar. 1789.

Pp 169-171: 26 June 1788, PETER JOHNSTON of Rutherford Co., N.C., as Exor. of the Estate of JOHN KIRKONNELL, deceased, to BENJAMIN COVENHOVEN of Union Co., S.C., for 50 pds, 200 acs. on the north side of Pacolate River, granted to KIRKONNELL on 6 Dec. 1771 by JO___ (torn) MARTIN, Esq., Gov. of N. C., bound by the river and JOHN PORTMAN. At Peleats(?) Shoal. Wit: ZACHARIAH BULLOCK. Rec. 29 Mar. 1789.

(Note: The above lease and release is split - at the bottom of p. 171 is a note to see the bottom of page 173 for the remainder. The next deed begins on page 172.)

Pp 172-173: 23 Feb. 1789, ANDREW JONES and FEBY, his wife, of S. C., to WILLIAM LIPSCOMB, same place, for 130 pds, 150 acs. on Thicketty (Creek) in Union Co. Part of a tract granted to STEPHEN JONES. The sd STEPHEN JONES made a Deed of Gift to his son ANDREW JONES on 5 July 1770. Rec. in Brion Court, No. Carolina. Bound by JOHN NUCKOLS, SAML. SHIPPY, JOHN JOHNSTON's land that he sold to JOHN THOMAS, and JOHN THOMAS' land. Signed by ANDREW JONES (FEBY did not sign). Wit: WM. THOMAS, ROBERT ANDERS & JAMES WOOD. James Wood attested on 21 Mar. 1789 bef. ZACHR. BULLOCK, J.P. No rec. date.

(Note: Above is remainder of p. 173 and pp. 169-171 of Lease and Release above.)

Pp 174-175: 10 Oct. 1788, THOMAS SHOCKLEY of Union Co., to JOSEPH HOLLINGSWORTH, JR., same place, for 100 pds sterling, 183 acs. on lower Fishdam Creek. Grants 7 May 1787 by Thomas Pinckney, Gov. of S.C. (to SHOCKLEY?). Bound by the land held by JOHN ARMSTONG's heirs, ELIZABETH RINCHARD, Col. WILLIAM FARR, JAMES HAWKINS and vacant lands. Grant and plat rec. in Book TTTT, p. 230. Signed: THOMAS SHOCKLEY and CONEE (X) SHOCKLEY. Wit: NATHAN GLENN, RICHARD COX, JACOB HOLLINGS-WORTH. Richard Cox swore to signatures on 4 Apr. 1789 bef. Berd. Glenn, J.P. Rec. 22 June 1789.

Pp 175-177: 10 Feb. 1789, LEWIS LEDBETTER and SARAH, his wife, of Union Co. to JOHN CRITTENDEN (CRITENDEN), same place, for 100 pds Virginia money, 150 acs. on Abetin (Abbington's) Creek. S.C. grant to LEWIS LEDBETTER. Bound on one side by NICOLAS CURREY. Lewis and Sarah both signed, Sarah by mark. Wit: JAMES PETTY, SR., JAMES PETTY, and MARY (X) PETTY. James Petty, Sr. swore to signatures bef. William McCulloch, J.P. on 14 Mar. 1789. Rec. 22 June 1789.

Page 177: 22 June 1789, WILLIAM FARR, gentleman, of Union Co., to WILLIAM STEEN, JR., planter, same place, for the Love and good will and affection which I have and do bear to my loving friend WILLIAM STEEN, JR., a negro named Andrew. Wit: R. EDSON, THOMAS BRANDON, JAMES HOGINS. Rec. same day by order of the court, J. HAILE, Clerk.

Pp 177-178: 11 June 1789, JEDITHAN PORTER of Union Co. to JOSEPH HART, same place, for 5 pds sterling, 69 acs. part of a 119 ac. tract granted to sd JEDITHAN PORTER by letters patent on April 1788. On the S side of Broad River, branches of Sholey Creek. Bound by PAULK, GABRIEL, ANDERSON, & HOWARD. Wit: JOHN PALMORE and JOSHUA PAULK. Porter signed by mark. JOSHUA PALMORE and JOSEPH PAULK both swore to signatures on 22 June 1789 bef. JOHN BIRDSONG, J.P. No rec. date.

Pp 179-180: 11 June 1788, AARON FINCHER and MARY his wife and WILLIAM MORGAN and JEMIMA, his wife, to ESTHER INSCO all of Union Co., S.C. for 50 pds sterling, 300 acs. on waters of Fairforest, part of a tract of 500 acs. granted to JONATHAN PARKER on 11 Aug. 1774 by Wm. Bull, Lt. Gov. of S.C. (No adj. landowners given). Signed: AARON (X) FINCHER, MARY FINCHER, WILLIAM MORGAN & JEMIMA MORGAN. Wit: MOSES COLL-YER, WILLIAM (X) PLUMMER, CHRISTEN PLUMMER. Wm. Plummer and Moses Coll-yer swore to signatures 22 June 1789 bef. John Birdsong, J.P. Rec. same day.

Pp 180-181: 19 Feb. 1789, ANDREW JONES of the State of S.C., and formerly Union County, but now found Edisto River, to JOHN THOMP-SON of Union Co., for 150 pds sterling, 150 acs. on both sides of Thick-etty Creek where ADAM THOMPSON now lives. Conveyed to ANDREW JONES by deed of gift from his father, STEPHEN JONES. Bound on W by part (150 acs.) of the same tract in possession of the sd THOMPSON and SAMUEL SHIPPY, on E by land laid off to JOHN NUCKOLS now in possession of JOSHUA PETTY, on N by lands of sd THOMPSON, on S by PETTY and vacant land. Wit: SOLOMON MANGHAM, JOHN (X) WOOD, JAMES ROBINSON. All three wit. swore to signature on 27 Apr. 1789 bef. Thos. Brandon, J.P. In

Cont'd:
the attestation, THOMPSON is referred to as Capt. JOHN THOMPSON. Rec.
22 June 1789.

Pp 181-182: 5 Jan. 1789, JOHN MONTGOMERY to JOHN MALONE (no residence given) for 152 pds current money of S.C., 152 acs. on both
sides of Fairforest Creek, bound in the grant plat on all sides by
SHADRACH LANTRIP's land. Wit: DANIEL JACKSON, NANCY (X) MONTGOMERY,
MARGET MONTGOMERY. Daniel Jackson attested to signatures on 2 Mar.
1789 bef. HUGH MEANS, J.P. Rec. 22 June 1789.

Pp 182-183: 8 June 1789, WILLIAM MERCHANT and wife HANNAH, to GEORGE
HARLING (HARLAND), hatter, both of Union Co., for 20 pds lawful
money, 50 acs. whereon WILLIAM MERCHANT and HANNAH his wife now lives,
in the fork of Sugar Creek and Fairforest Creek, part of a tract formerly the property of PHILIP BRYANT. Bound by WM. PALMER, FIELDING CAR-
TER & WM. BRYANT. Wit: THOMAS PALMER, SR. & DUNCAN McCREVAN. Both wit.
attested on 16 June 1789 bef. Thomas Blasingame, J.P. No rec. date.

Pp 183-186: 29 Mar. 1770, JOHN NUCKOLS, miller, "on tiger river in
Trion County in the province of North Carolina" and JAMES VERNON,
planter, of "fairforest settlement" to WILLIAM WOFFORD, Esq., "lately
of the Settlement of Fairforest in the province of S.C. but now of
Losson's (Lawson's) fork in the county of Tryon and province of N.C.",
for 500 pds current money, 240 acs. part of a 640 ac. tract "on a branch
of Tiger River called fairforest" orig. granted to JOHN McDOWEL on
18 Nov. 1752 in Anson County, prov. of N.C. and conveyed by McDOWEL
to ROBERT HARRIS and by sd HARRIS to sd JOHN HUCHOL (NUCKOLS) and JAMES
VERNON. Nuchol and Vernon, finding the tract to be in S.C., petitioned
the Gov. and Council for it to be regranted in the Prov. of S.C. They
were given a S.C. grant by Wm. Bull, Lt. Gov. of S.C. on 17 July 1765.
A plat of the entire tract is in the deed book with the deed. Signed:
JOHN NICOLL & JAMES VERNON. Wit: JOHN EASLEY, ABRAHAM PENNINGTON, JAMES
MARTIN. John Easley attested on same day 29 Mar. 1770 bef. JOHN FORD,
Esq., J.P. in "Berkley Co." S.C. Rec. 22 June 1789.

Pp 186-187: 31 Jan. 1789, ALEXANDER HAMMELTON and wife JEAN (also
shown as JANE), of S.C., to WILLIAM HENDLEY of 96 Dist., Union
Co., for 10 pds sterling, 16 acs. granted to sd HAMMILTON 7 Apr. 1788,
plat annexed to grant certificate 31 Dec. 1787. Bound on SW by JOHN
WEDINGMAN and on all other sides by Pacolett River. Wit: TURNER KEN-
DRICK, JOHN LYLES, ALEXR. KENDRICK. Turner Kendrick attested to signatures on 22 June 1789 bef. CHARLES SIMS, J.P. Rec. same day.

Pp 187-188: 4 Feb. 1789, ALEXANDER HAMMILTON and JEAN his wife, of
S.C., to WILLIAM HENDLEY of 96 Dist., Union Co. for 50 pds sterling, 100 acs. on SW side of Pacolet River, bound by the river and
sd HENDLEY. Formerly granted to SAMUEL SMITH by State of N. C. and
also lately the same land has been laid out for sd HAMMILTON and granted
to him by Gov. of S.C. 7 Apr. 1788. Wit: TURNER KENDRICK, JOHN LILES,
ALEXR. KENDRICK. Turner Kendrick attested bef. Charles Sims, J.P. on
22 June 1789. Rec. same day.

Pp 189-190: 11 Mar. 1789, TURNER KENDRICK of S.C. to JOHN HENRY GEE
of 96 Dist., for 20 pds, 100 acs. the upper part of 390 acs grant-
ed to TURNER KENDRICK in 1787, cert. 22 Aug. 1786. Bound by RICHARD
COAL. On both sides of Ready Branch. Wit: JOHN LILES, JOHN GEE, JOHN
KENDRICK. John Gee attested bef. WM. HENDLEY, J.P. on 21 Mar. 1789.
Rec. 22 June 1789.

Pp 190-191: 20 June 1789, SAMUEL SCOTCHER of Edgefield Co., to JOSEPH
McJUNKIN, of Union Co., for 50 pds current money, 150 acs. on
Tiger Creek in Union Co., adj. HENRY MILLHOUSE, and granted to THOMAS
LANTRIP by a patent dated 22 Mar. 1769. Wit: JOHN LANDERS (SANDERS?),
and MASSA LANDERS. Attested on 21 June 1789 bef. Hugh Means, J.P. of
Union Co. Rec. 22 June 1789. (Samuel's signature may be either SCOTCH-
ER, SCOLEHER or SCHOCHER.)

Pp 191-193: 24 June 1788, JAMES OLIPHANT, planter of Union Co., to
the Hon. JOHN FAUCHERADE GRIMKIE one of the Assistant Judges

Cont'd:
of South Carolina, for 271 pds 17 shillings 6 pence sterling, 3 tracts
on the heds of Frenchman's and Coureton(?) Creeks, waters of Enoree
and Tiger Rivers, being particularly described in the foresd lease.
(Lease not recorded..JMC). Containing in all 750 acs., 2 tracts granted
to SAMUEL BELL 1 Nov. 1768 and 2 Feb. 1773 by Lord Chas. G. Montague
(S.C.) and conveyed by sd BELL to JAMES OLIPHANT and THOMAS TOD by
lease and release 14 and 15 May 1776. Thomas Tod conveyed his moity
thereof to sd James Oliphant by lease and release on 10 and 11 Dec.
1776. The third tract of 300 acs granted by Gov. Wm. Moultrie to James
Oliphant on 1 Aug. 1785. Wit: JAMES SMITH, JNO. (X) HACKER. James Oli-
pant signed a receipt for 250 guineas. James Smith attested on 22 Dec.
1788 bef. THOMAS HALL (HALT?), J.P. of Charleston Dist., S.C. Rec.
23 June 1789.

Pp 193-194:   8 May 1789, JOHN McCOOLL and wife JANE of Union Co.,
       to JOHN McKIBBEN of same place, for 7 pds, 3 lots at Union Court-
house, 1/2 ac. each, on the N side of Main St. Lots numbered 5,6, and
19. Wit: R. MITCHELL, JOSEPH MOSS. Rec. 23 June 1789.

Pp 194-196:   23 June 1789, JOHN BLASINGAIM, Esq., Sheriff of Union
       Co., to GEORGE McWHORTER of Union Co., for 18 pds 10 shillings
sterling, high bid at a sale held 13 Sept. 1788 of 100 acs. on Pacolet
River, about 1/2 mile above Skull Shoals. Orig. granted to ROBERT BIS-
HOP 2 Sept. 1765 by Wm. Tryon, Gov. of N.C. Tract was sold to levy
sum of 102 pds 18 shillings 7 pence against JOHN STEEN in the case
of WILLIAM FARR vs. JOHN STEEN in Dec. term of court 1786. Wit: WILLIAM
HENDLEY, WILLIAM KENNEDY. CHARLES MILES. Rec. 23 June 1789.

Pp 196-197:   13 Apr. 1789, HENRY LONG of Union Co. to ANN ROBINSON,
       same place, for 100 pds sterling, 200 acs. in Craven County on
the south side of Broad River on the waters of Hughes Creek. Granted
to HENRY LONG 14 Sept. 1774 by Wm. Bull, Gov. of S.C. Bound on all
sides by vacant land when surveyed. Wit: JOHN HAILE, JOHN BIRDSONG.
Henry Long signed by mark. No rec. date.

Pp 197-198:   5 Jan. 1789, DANIEL JACKSON to JOHN HIGH (no residence
       given), for 100 pds lawful money of S.C., 200 acs. on branch
of Mitchel's Creek, bound by BENJAMIN THOMPSON, JOHN WOOD, DANL. CUM-
MONS, AVERY BREED, MARK JACKSON and vacant land when first surveyed.
A plat annexed to a Grant dated 3 Oct. 1784. Wit: JAMES YANCEY, JR.,
EDWD. GOODE. Thomas Blasingaim, J.P. Rec. 23 June 1789. (JOHN HIGH's
name also spelled HIE.)

Pp 198-199:   6 Jan. 1789, Capt. DANIEL JACKSON to JOHN MALONE (no
       place of residence) for 150 pds, 300 acs. on Camp Spring Branch,
part of a tract granted to sd Jackson on 4 Nov. 1772, by C. G. Montague
(S.C.) bound by MARK JACKSON, sd DANIEL JACKSON, a branch and the waggon road. Wit: JAMES YANCEY, JR., MARK JACKSON. Thos. Blasingame, J.P.
Rec. 23 June 1789.

Pp 199-200:   23 Dec. 1788, ISAAC HAZE to WM. JACKSON (no place of
       residence) for 150 pds, 150 acs. part of a 350 ac. tract on Mitch-
el's Creek, a branch of Fairforest (Creek), bound by AVERY BREED, SAMUEL
JACKSON, vacant land, Capt. DANIEL JACKSON, and the creek. Granted
to MARK JACKSON, SR. from his Majesty, 21 Apr. 1774. Conveyed by Mark
Jackson to JACOB HAIZE and ISAAC HAIZE, heir of JACOB HAIZE, conveyes
it to WM. JACKSON. Signed by mark ISAAC (VI - his mark.) HAIZE. Wit:
DANIEL JACKSON, DANIEL HOLDER, FRANCES (X) STILES. Thos. Blasingaim ,
J.P. Rec. 23 June 1789.

Pp 201-203:   18 & 19 Oct. 1784, Lease & Release. THOMAS WARING, SR.
       and.....JOHN EWING COLHOUN, Comrs. of Forfeited Estates and Con-
fiscated Property in S.C., to DANIEL JACKSON, planter, of 96 Dist.,
highest bidder at a sale held on 18 Oct. for 5 sh. and 37 pds 15 sh.
current money of S.C., 150 acs. late the property of DANIEL PLUMMER,
located on both sides of Mitchels Creek, bound by THOMAS BLASINGAME,
STEPHEN WHITE, JNO. WOOD and vacant land. Wit: THOS. FARRAR, CHS. F.
L. SIMMONS. Signed by JNO. EWING COLHOUN & THOS. WARING, SR. Thos.
Farrar, Esq. attested to signatures before Thos. Blasingame, on 22

Cont'd:
July 1789. Rec. 22 June 1789. (Error?).

Pp 203-204:   7 Feb. 1788, CHARLES SIMS, Esq., and wife SEBELLOR, to
      THOMAS McDONNELL, both of Union Co., for 113 pds, 113 acs. on
Swift Run Creek, a branch of Tyger River, granted to the sd Chas. Sims
by Benjamin Guerard, Gov. of S.C. 21 Jan. 1785. Bound by AMOS COOK,
the SIMS line, SAML. OTTERSON, ELY COOK, & ISAAC COOK. Wit: WM. FARR,
WARREN HALL. Rec. 22 Sept. 1788.

Page 205:   7 Feb. 1788, CHAS. SIMS and wife SEBELLOR to THOS. Mc-
      DONNELL, both of Union Co. for 339 pds sterling, 399 acs. on
Tinker Creek, N side of Tyger River, granted to sd Chas. Sims 6 Feb.
1786 by Wm. Moultry (sic) Gov. of S.C., bound by AMOS COOK, land laid
out for KINGSBERRY, JNO. COOK, SAML. BURGESS and Tinker Creek. Wit:
WM. FARR, WARREN HALL. No rec. date.

Page 206:   22 Sept. 1788, CHARLES HAMES to JAMES McWHORTER, both
      of Union Co., for 20 pds sterling, 200 acs. on Little Sandy Run,
a branch of Pacolett River, orig. granted by S.C. to CHARLES HAMES,
21 Jan. 1785 and rec. in Book CCCC, p. 209. Wit: JOHN HAILE. Rec. 22
Sept. 1788.

Pp 206-207:   22 Sept. 1788, JOHN NIX to TULLY DAVITT, both of Union
      Co., for 30 pds lawful money, 104 acs. on Enoree River, granted
by letters patent, S.C. grant to sd JOHN NIX, in 1787 and rec. in Book
SSSS, p. 341. Bound by JAS. KENNEDY on one side and the river. Wit:
JAMES CRAWFORD, SAML. THOMPSON, JOHN D. YOUNG. Rec. same day.

Page 208:   15 Aug. 1788, JEPTHA HOLLINGSWORTH of Union Co. to HANCOCK
      PORTER for 30 pds sterling, 171 acs. granted by SC grant to sd
HOLLINGSWORTH, on 5 Dec. 1785. Bound by vacant land, DAVID BROWN, JOHN
MAYFIELD. Wit: LANDLOT PORTER, ROBERT (X) THOMPSON and JEDETHAN PORTER.
Rec. 22 Sept. 1788.

Pp 209-210:   15 Aug. 1788, JOHN GORDEN of Union Co. to HANCOCK PORTER,
      for 50 pds sterling, 341 acs. granted to sd GORDEN 5 Oct. 1787,
SC grant, bound by JOHN MAYFIELD, HOLLINGSWORTH, JOHN BRANDON. Wit:
LANDLOT PORTER, ROBERT (X) THOMPSON, JEDETHAN PORTER. Rec. 22 Sept.
1788. (No location of land given in the two preceding deeds.)

Pp 210-211:   31 Mar. 1788, MERY McQUIRE of Union Co. to JOHN McQUIRE,
      SR., same place, for 7 pds sterling, 100 acs. part of a tract
of 530 acs. granted to sd MERY McQUIRE 5 Mar. 1787, SC grant, the orig.
grant bound by JAMES McCRACEN, ROBERT GREER, JOHN WEEDINGMAN, CHAS.
SIMS, ROBERT SMITH. The 100 acs. sold by John "to be taken from the
ridge path called Mayfield's path down Mudy Branch" to an agreed on
point on Cudd's line. Wit: WM. BOWMAN, RICHARD HUGHES. Mery signed
his name as "MERRY McGUIRE". Rec. 22 Sept. 1788.

Pp 211-212:   20 Aug. 1788, ROBERT TALKINGTON (TARKINGTON?), of Union
      Co. to HANCOCK PORTER, for 20 pds, 100 acs. bound on one side
by the South Fork of Brown's Creek and all other sides vacant when
granted. This land had been surveyed for HANCOCK PORTER and granted
to Col. THOMAS BRANDON "in Charleston" on 5 Mar. 1787. Conveyed by
Brandon to the sd ROBERT TALKINGTON. Talkington signed by mark. Wit:
JEREMIAH GREGORY, JOHN HOWELL, JEDITHAN PORTER. Rec. 22 Sept. 1788.

Page 212:   22 Sept. 1788, JNO. McWHORTER of Union Co. to CHAS. HAMES,
      same place, for 100 pds sterling, 100 acs. on S side Pacolett
River, bound by GEORGE's line, the river, Johnny's Creek and including
the grist mill. Wit: JOHN HAIL. Rec. same day.

Pp 213-215:   31 Mar. 1788, Lease and Release. NATHANIEL JACKSON and
      wife SILLAH to JOSEPH KELLY of 96 Dist., Union Co., for 5 shill-
ings and 80 pds sterling current money of sd State, 200 acs in "Berkley
County southward of Tyger River", granted to JOHN McGARRITY by King
George III on 21 May 1772. At time of grant bound by the river and
land of MOSES KIRTLAND (KIRKLAND?). (Note: One MOSES KIRKLAND lived
on Saluda River and was a Tory officer in the Revolution)...all other

Cont'd:
sides vacant. Memorial of plat and grant rec. in the office of the
Auditor Gen. of sd state, Book L, No. 11, p. 347. Conveyed by sd McGAR-
RITY to JOSEPH WOOLBANKS and then to NATHANIEL JACKSON. Signed by NATH-
ANIEL JACKSON and by mark DREWSILLAH (X) JACKSON. Wit: JOHN NIX, JOHN
LAWSON, JOSEPH (X) NIX. Rec. 22 Sept. 1788.

Pp 215-216:   22 Sept. 1788, JOB HAMMOND of Union Co. to THOS. WILLIAMS
            of same place, for 20 pds, 100 acs. on the waters of Brown's
Creek and the plantation whereon the sd WILLIAMS now lives, as laid
out by CHAS. SIMS, D.S., and rec. in Grant Bk. MMMM, p. 454. Wit: JOHN
HAILE. Rec. same day.

Pp 216-217:   5 Nov. 1785, Lease and Release. JOHN NEWMAN and FRANCES,
            his wife, of Lawrence (Laurens) Co., to MOSES HAYNES of Union
Co. for 10 shillings and 10 pds 10 sh. 6 pence sterling, 100 acs. on
a branch of Tyger River called Cowdens Branch. Granted to ABSALOM WOF-
FORD 21 Apr. 1774 by Wm. Bull, Lt. Gov. of S.C., bound on all sides
by vacant land when granted. Conveyed by sd Wofford to John Newman.
Wit: LEWIS BOBO, WILLIAM HAYNES. JOHN & FRANCES (X), both signed. No
recording date.

Pp 218-219:   3 Apr. 1786 Grant, in Charleston, signed by William Moul-
            trie, Gov. and plat certified on 1 Mar. 1786 by ANDREW THOMSON,
D.S. and F. BREMAR, Sec'y. Gen'l. Grant to FRANCES BREMAR and PETER
FRENEAU, Esqrs., "as tennants in Common and not as Joint Tennants"
for 30 pds 3 sh 8 pence sterling, pd. "into the treasury for the use
of this state." 565 acs. surveyed for MARY ROBUCK 20 Oct. 1784, in
96 Dist., on N side of Tyger River, bound by MARY ROBUCK, ABSALOM LANGS-
TON, JOSEPH GOWEN, Tyger River. Following the plat and certification
is a transfer of the 565 acs. tract from Freneau and Bremar to Mary
Robuck, for 10 sh., dated 28 Mar. 1787. Wit: J. (I.?) MILLER, SAML.
HOPKINS, J.P. and JNO. BLASSENGAME. The final entry states "Treasury
Office, 29 Mar. 1787. Received by Discount on Indent No. 880 X the
sum of 13 pds 3/8 the consideration money within mentioned. 13 pds
3. 8." Signed by PETER BOCQUET, Comm. Sec'y. Office Rec. in Grant Book
SSSS, p. 228, and examined by Peter Freneau, Dy. Sec.

Pp 219-221:   12 & 13 Feb. 1788, Lease and Release. JEREMIAH BRASHEARS
            to ROBERT WALKER, both of Union Co., for 12 sh. and 20 pds. ster-
ling, 10 acs. part of a tract orig. granted to WILLIAM WOFFORD, SC
grant, on 24 Aug. 1770, on S side of Tyger River, bound by RICHARD
BRYANT, "a certain drean which separates it from the sd WM. WOFFORD's
land" and the river. Signed by mark by JEREMIAH & ELIZABETH BRASHIES.
Wit: HENRY BRAY, EZEKIAL (X) BROWN. Henry Bray attested 25 July 1788
bef. Thomas Blasengame, J.P. Rec. 23 Sept. 1788.

Pp 221-222:   6 Feb. 1790, JOHN McCOOL to THOS. BRANDON, Esq., both
            of Union Co., for 30 pds sterling, "two acres of land laying
at Union Court House called the Public Land of which the Afsd. Court
House and Gaol and Pillery stands"...for the Better Conveying and Se-
cureing the sd land..." Wit: WILLIAM DALRYMPLE, JOHN McKIBBEN, JAMES
McKIBBEN. McCool signed receipt on same day, and John and James McKibben attested on 8 Feb. 1790, bef. William Kennedy, J.P. Rec. 8 Feb.
1790.
            (Note: Thomas Brandon conveyed the land in the preceding deed
to Union Co. on 26 Dec. 1787, Deed Bk. B, pp. 30-31 (GGM 52-53, p.
208). It seems from the above deed that John McCooll also had an interest in the 2 acs. and that this deed was to clear the title to the
county.)

Pp 222-223:   20 Feb. 1788, SAMUEL PORTER of "Maclenburgh" Co., N.C.
            to WILLIAM PORTER of York Co., S.C. for 20 pds sterling, 100
acs. whereon MARTHEW PORTER formerly lived, in Union Co., S.C. on waters
of Abison's (Abbington's) Creek, on the W side of Broad River, near
two miles of sd river. The full contents of a N.C. grant to JACOB GARDI-
NER 22 Apr. 1767 and deed by sd Gardiner to BARNET BARNS 16 June 1770,
deed rec. in clerk's office of Tryon Co., N.C. at April term 1771 and
entered in public register of sd county on 20 July 1771, Bk. No. 5.

Cont'd:
Said land again deeded by BARNET BARNS to <u>MATHEW</u> PORTER on 1 Nov. 1771, proved in open court and rec. in clerk's office of Tryon Co., N.C. at April Term 1772 and entered in Book No. 6, on 11 May 1772. Sd land devolved by descent to the above SAMUEL PORTER he being oldest son of the above named MATHEW PORTER who died intestate in August 1783. Signed: SAMUEL PORTER. Wit: ROBT. KENNEDY, ABRAHAM ENLO & WILLIAM WALLACE. Robert Kennedy of York Co., attested to signatures on 26 Aug. 1788 bef. Wm. McCulloch, J.P. No rec. date.

Page 224:   23 Sept. 1788, JOHN McCOOLL to JOHN D. YOUNG, tailor, both of Union Co., for 13 pds sterling, lot #72 at Union Court House, adj. sd Young's lot #58, containing 1 3/4 acs. adj. Mr. EDSON's lot. Wit: ANDW. TORRENCE, WILLIAM CAMPBELL. Rec. 23 Sept. 1788.

Page 225:   Blank

Page 226:   23 Sept. 1788, JOHN HENDERSON, Esq., to JOHN JASPER, blacksmith, both of Union Co., for 100 pds sterling, 214 acs. on a branch of the E side of Big Sandy Run (a branch of Pacolet River) bound by JAMES MOSELEY on one side. Marked "Acknowledged." No wit. Rec. 23 Sept. 1788.

Pp 226-229:   2 Sept. 1785, Lease and Release. WILLIAM WOFFORD to THOMAS WRIGHT, both of Union Co. for 10 sh and 38 pds 5 p sterling, 200 acs. including the plantation where the sd Thos. Wright now dwells on the N side of Tyger River, adj. Wm. Wofford, LEWIS BOBO and the river. Part of a 300 ac. tract whereon Wm. Wofford now dwells...near to a branch by Bryant Mill, granted by the Prov. of S.C. to Wm. Wofford on 24 Aug. 1770, in the then called Craven Co., grant was bound on the N by Tyger River, on the S by Lewis Bobo, and all other sides vacant when laid out. Signed: WILLIAM (X) WOFFORD, ABIGALE (X) WOFFORD. Wit: THACKER VIVION, ROBERT WALKER, JR. Rec. 23 Sept. 1788.
(Note: There were two men by the name of WILLIAM WOFFORD, one lived on Fairforest Creek in Union Co., and later moved to Lawson's Fork in what is now Spartanburg Co. See pp. 183-86 in this book. The WILLIAM WOFFORD in the deed above lived on S side Tyger in what is now the Cross Keys area.)

Pp 229-230:   ___ Sept. 1788, SOLOMON MANGHAM to JOSIAH TANNER, both of Union Co., for 60 pds sterling, 140 acs. on N side of Thicketty Creek on a branch known as STEPHEN JONES branch. Granted by S.C. to sd Solomon Mangham. Wit: JNO. THOMPSON. Thompson attested to signature 23 Sept. 1788, bef. JOHN BIRDSONG, J.P. Rec. same day.

Pp 230-231:   28 July 1788, JAMES CAMPBELL of Abbeville Co., to ABRAHAM SMITH of York Co. for 130 pds sterling, 100 acs. in Union Co. on both sides of Gilkie's Creek on S side of Broad River, adj. RIDERIS (RYDERIUS) CLARK, RICHD. KELLEY, THOS. GIBBS, NATHANIEL JEFFERIES, WILSON JOLLY. Granted by S.C. to LEARD BURNS and conveyed from him to sd Campbell. Wit: JOSEPH FRENCH, JNO. HARRINGTON, PHILLIP (X) SHAVER. James Campbell signed a receipt for 5 sh. in full of the Consideration money. Harrington attested to signature in Union Co. bef. WM. McCULLOCH, J.P. Rec. 23 Sept. 1788.

Page 232:   2 Oct. 1787, JEAN McJUNKIN of the state of S. Carolina, to JOSEPH McJUNKIN of same, for 20 pds sterling, 40 acs. on Tinker Creek, a branch of Tyger River, granted to sd Jean McJunkin on 3 Apr. 1786 by Wm. Moultrie, Gov. of S.C. and rec. in Grant Bk. KKK, p. 133. Signed: JEAN (X) McJUNKIN. No wit. Rec. 23 Sept. 1788.
(Note: Major JOSEPH McJUNKIN, Revolutionary Soldier, stated in his Memoirs that he was born 22 June 1755, near Carlisle, Pa., son of SAMUEL McJUNKIN, a native of Ireland, and his wife ANN BOGAN of Pa. They moved to S.C. in 1775 and settled on Tinker Creek. JOSEPH McJUNKIN married ANNE THOMAS, dau. of Col. JOHN THOMAS. Joseph McJunkin died 31 May 1846, and his wife Anne, died 17 Mar. 1826, age 69. They are buried in the McJunkin Cemetery a few miles south of Union, S.C. off Hwy. 176. Joseph McJunkin's tombstone states that he was a ruling elder in the Presbyterian Church for 60 years.)

Page 233:   24 Sept. 1788, DUDLEY RED to RICHARD BERRY, both of Union
        Co., for 15 pds sterling, 40 acs. on S side of wagon road that
leads from Blackstock's to Pacolet. Part of a 250 ac. grant to THOMAS
FLETCHER, 100 acs. of which was conveyed to JOSEPH RED. Sd. Dudley
Red was heir at law of sd JOSEPH RED, dec'd. Tract of 40 acs bound
by JOHN RED, JOHN GOWAN. Signed by mark and noted "Acknow'd.". No wit.
Rec. 24 Sept. 1788.

Pp 233-234:   22 June 1788, ROBERT HENRY HUGHES of Laurence (Laurens)
        Co., to WALTER ROBERTS of Union Co. for 20 pds sterling, 100
acs. on Pagits (Padgett's) Creek, a branch of Tyger River. Bound on
S by WM. PEARSON, all other sides by vacant land. Entire tract granted
to sd HUGHES in 1787 by Wm. Moultrie, Gov. of S.C. Signed: ROBERT H.
HUGHES. No wit. Rec. 24 Sept. 1788.

Pp 234-235:   24 Sept. 1788, THOMAS BRANDON of Union Co. to JOB HAMMOND
        of same place, for 30 pds, a square 300 acs. part of a tract
of 1200 acs. granted to sd Brandon on 6 Nov. 1786, and rec. in Grant
Bk. 0000, p. 299. The 300 acs. bound by a part of sd grant that had
been conveyed to JUDAH CRAIN. No wit "Acknowledged." Rec. same day.

Pp 235-236:   26 Sept. 1789, NICHOLAS LAZERUS of Union Co. to JONATHAN
        PEEK, same place, 100 acs. granted to MARY GANTAREN in 1763 by
THOMAS BOONE, Gov. of S.C., and rec. Grant Bk. XX, p. 132. Sd. MARY
GANTEREN conveyed entire tract to JAMES BOGAN and Bogan to sd Lazerus.
Wit: DUNCAN McCREVAN, AUSTIN NEWMAN, THOMAS BRANDON. McCrevan attested
to signatures 26 Sept. 1789 bef. Thos. Brandon, J.P. Rec. 28 Sept.
1789.
        (Note: No explanation given for the various dates of recording
these deeds - 1789, 1788, one in 1790, 1788, and now back to 1789.
Perhaps Clerk John Haile got behind in his work and entered them all
in the book at the same time..JC).

Pp 236-237:   5 Sept. 1789, JOHN McCOOLL and JANE his wife to WILLIAM
        GOLDSMITH, both of Union Co. for 13 guineas, two lots numbered
18 and 4, 1/2 ac. each, now in his actual possession, adj. (north of)
the land whereon the Court House and Gaol now stand. Signed: JNO. Mc-
COOLL, JANE McCOOLL. Wit: JOHN BIRDSONG, JOHN MURRELL, HENRY BIRDSONG.
Rec. 28 Sept. 1789.

Pp 237-238:   25 July 1789, ISAAC EDMONDSON, farmer, to JNO. CAMPBELL,
        cordwinder, both of Union Co., for 191 pds sterling, 425 acs.
part of a 750 ac. tract on north side of Enoree River conveyed to sd
Isaac Edmondson by his father, CALEB EDMONDSON. The 425 acs. adj. the
river, the tract whereon Isaac Edmondson now lives, and sd Jno. Campbell. Wit: RALPH HUNT, JOHN HUNT, DAVID SMITH. Isaac signed his name.
On 27 Aug. 1789, John Campbell assigned all his right and title to
the deed and the tract of land to CALEB EDMONDSON, JR. John signed
his name. Wit. to assignment: JOHN PEARSON, SARAH PEARSON. On 12 Sept.
1789, CALEB EDMONDSON, farmer of Union Co., assigned his right and
title to JOHN FINCHER. Caleb signed his name. Wit: JAMES WOODSON, THOS.
BISHOP. RALPH HUNT attested bef. CHARLES SIMS, J.P. on 25 Sept. 1789.
No recording date.

Page 239:   7 Sept. 1789, WILLIAM SMITH to ISAAC COOK, both of Union
        Co., for 2 pds sterling, 50 acs. bet. the waters of Swift Run
and Otterson's Creek. Bound by ISAAC COOK and WM. SMITH. Signed by
mark and ack. No wit. Rec. 28 Sept. 1789.

Pp 239-240:   28 Sept. 1789, ARCHER HOWARD to JOHN PUTMAN, both of
        Union Co., for 10 pds sterling, 40 acs. on the branches of Sugar
Creek, part of a 150 ac. tract granted to NEHEMIAH HOWARD by the Gov.
of S.C. on 23 June 1774. Bound by ANTHONY TOOMMER's line, GILLEY's
spring branch, the Big Branch and RALPH JACKSON. Howard signed his
name and ack. No. wit. Rec. same day.

Pp 240-241:   28 Sept. 1789, WILLIAM COMER and SARAH his wife of Union
        Co. to JOHN COMER, same place, for 3 pds sterling, 100 acs. where
sd Jno. Comer now lives. Part of a S.C. grant dated 5 Feb. 1787 for

Cont'd:
556 acs. to WILLIAM COMER. Located on Shoaly Creek, a branch of Fairforest. Grant rec. in Grant Bk. PPPP, p. 647. The 100 acs. bound by
Capt. COMER's land and GEORGE CROSSLEY's land. Signed only by WM. COMER.
Wit: THOMAS BRANDON, JOHN McKIBBEN, NATHANIEL JACKSON. Rec. same day.

Pp 241-242: 2 Aug. 1789, MERY (MERRY) McQUIRE of Union Co., to CHARLES
     BROOKS, same place, for 20 pds sterling, 150 acs. part of a SC
grant of a 200 ac. tract to JOSEPH WILLIAMS on 4 Dec. 1786. Conveyed
to MERRY McQUIRE by ROBERT WILLIAMS, heir at law to the real estate
of sd JOSEPH WILLIAMS. Located on SW side of Broad River next below
the mouth of Fannens (Fanning's) Creek running to the mouth of Wilcatt
(Wildcat) Creek, bound by WILLIAM BOWMAN, Wildcat Creek and Broad River.
Merry signed his name. Wit: WILLIAM BOWMAN, JOHN REED, JAMES (his mark)
MORE. John Reed attested 4 Aug. 1789 bef. WM. HENDLEY, J.P. Rec. 28
Sept. 1789.

Pp 242-243: 10 Sept. 1789, JOHN BIRDSONG to ELISHA GREEN, both of
     Union Co. for 10 pds, 40 acs. on waters of Fairforest, part of
a tract of 70 acs., surveyed by John Birdsong on 7 Sept. 1784 and bound
by sd Birdsong's old corner near a path leading to Elisha Green's,
SAMUEL HARLING and Elisha Green. Further states that the sd John Birdsong had an indisputable Estate of Inheritance in fee simple in and
to the sd lands. Signed his name. Wit:THOS. BLASSINGAME, JNO. MURRELL.
Rec. 28 Sept. 1789.

Pp 243-244: 29 Apr. 1789, JNO. BECKHAM, SR. and ELIZABETH, his wife,
     of Union Co. to MOSES WRIGHT, same place, for 100 pds current
money, 70 acs. on north side of Pacolet River, the plantation where
WILLIAM MARCHBANDS formerly lived. Bound by JOSEPH COWEN and MOSES
WRIGHT, JOAB MITCHELL's orig. line, ZACHARIAH BULLOCK and the river.
Line marked by ZACH. BULLOCK, D.S. Both John and Elizabeth signed by
mark. Wit: MOSES WATERS, RICHARD WATERS. ZACHARIAH BULLOCK, J.P. Rec.
28 Sept. 1789. (Note: JOHN BECKHAM was a scout in the Revolution, served
in the South Carolina Militia.)

Pp 244-245: 24 Apr. 1788, THOMAS WRIGHT and DILLY WRIGHT, his wife,
     of S.C. to GEORGE TAYLOR, same place, for 50 pds sterling, 60
acs. on north side of Thicketty Creek, bound by JNO. THOMPSON, sd WRIGHT,
WILLIAM WRIGHT and Thicketty Creek. Part of a grant to (blank) PALUM
and conveyed by PALUM to JACOB WEDERNER, from him to DAVID ROBINSON,
deceased, to MATHEW ROBINSON by heirship, from him to WILLIAM SAFFOLD,
deceased, from the heirs of Saffold to Thomas Wright. Signed by Thomas
Wright and his wife Dillie (X) Wright. Wit: MOSES WATERS and RICHARD
WATERS. Zach. Bullock, J.P. Rec. 28 Sept. 1789.

Pp 246-248: 23 & 24 Dec. 1789, Lease and Release. JOHN McCOOLL and
     JANE, his wife of Union Co., to GRAAFF SEIBELS BRASELMAN of S.C.,
for 33 pds current money, 9 1/4 acs. (in their possession) joining
land that the sd Jno. McCooll now lives on, also 3 lots laid out at
Union Court House, 1/2 ac. each, no's. 43,57 and 71. Wit: RICHARD MITCH-
ELL, JOHN BECKHAM, JR. John and JEAN McCooll both signed their names.
Both wit. attested to signatures 24 Dec. 1789 bef. BERNARD GLENN, J.P.
Rec. 29 Dec. 1789.
     (Note: The business firm, GRAFF SEIBELS BRASELMAN CO., owned
a store in Union Village and were apparently engaged in land specu-
lation. They bought other lots in the village and also owned a large
tract of about 13,000 acs. in Spartanburg Co.)

Pp 248-250: 29 Dec. 1778, Lease Release (both dated same day), MOSES
     WINTERS to JONAS LITTLE, both of the Prov. of S.C., for 325 pds
lawful money of S.C., 200 acs. on a branch of Fairforest called Buffa-
low Creek not 5 ft. broad nor one deep. Bound by JOSEPH BURSON and
vacant land when granted to sd Moses Winters 11 Aug. 1774, rec. in
Sec. Office in Bk. RRR, p. 660, enrolled in Auditor Gen. Office. in
Bk. M, No. 13, p. 256, on 25 Jan. 1775. Wit: ALEXD. MAC DOUGALL, JONA-
THAN BURSON, SHARARD (X) HUDSON. McDougal attested to signature 29
Sept. 1789 bef. WM. KENNEDY, J.P. Rec. 28 Sept. 1789.

Pp 250-251: 27 Sept. 1789, Deed of Gift. ROBERT GREER, planter, to

536

Cont'd:
REBECCAH GREER, widow, both of Union Co., for 5 pds, 150 acs. on Huges
(Hughes) Creek, bound by JAMES McCRACHEN, BENJAMIN SAVAGE and vacant
land. Tract was granted to MERRY McGUIRE by S.C. grant on 2 Oct. 1786
and conveyed by him on 25 Oct. 1786 (to ROBT. GREER? - doesn't say).
REBECCA GREER to hold the land for her natural life, then land to fall
in equal proportion to ROBERT, MARY and CATRIAN, minors of WILLIAM
GREER, deceased. No wit. Ack. in open court and rec. 28 Sept. 1789.

Pp 251-252:   24 Sept. 1789, ROBERT LUSK, yeoman of Union Co., to JOHN
        HOPE, planter (no residence given), for 50 pds sterling, 200
acs. on Dick's branch of Thickity (Creek), bound by MOSES MEEK and
lands of sd Hope. Part of a 400 ac. tract granted to Lusk on 1 Aug.
1785. Wit: JAMES McADOO, JAMES JOLLY, MARY McCULLOCH. WILLIAM McCULLOCH,
J.P. Rec. 28 Sept. 1789.

Pp 252-253:   28 Sept. 1789, JOHN LITTLE to JOHN INGRIM, both of Union
        Co., for 14 pds sterling, 70 acs. on branchs of Sugar Creek,
a S.C. grant to JOHN LITTLE on 5 Feb. 1787. Ack. No wit. Rec. 28 Sept.
1789.

Pp 253-254:   24 Sept. 1789, THOMAS HARRIS and MARTHA his wife, to
        JOSEPH HARRIS, all of Union Co., for 5 pds sterling, 100 acs.
on John's Creek, north side of Enoree River. Granted to RICHARD HARRIS
13 Oct. 1772 and rec. in Book MMM, p. 444. Sd Thomas Harris, eldest
son of sd Richard Harris, was heir to the tract at the decease of Richard (Deed of gift?). Signed THOMAS & MARTHA (X) HARRIS. Wit: JOHN NEED-
ERMAN, JOHN MARTINDALE. Rec. 28 Sept. 1789.

Pp 254-256:   24 Sept. 1789, JOHN NEEDERMAN and JANE his wife, to JOHN
        MARTINDALE, all of Union Co., for 50 pds sterling, 76½ acs. on
Frenchman's Creek, including the mouth of the creek on N side of Enoree
River. Part of a tract of 100 acs. granted to sd John Neederman 15
Mar. 1771, rec. in Grant Bk. HHH, p. 31. Signed JOHN & JANE (X) NEEDER-
MAN. Jane also shown as JEAN. Wit: THOMAS HARRIS, JOSEPH HARRIS. Rec.
28 Sept. 1789.

Pp 256-257:   24 Sept. 1789, JOHN MARTINDALE and RACHEL his wife, to
        JOHN NEEDERMAN, all of Union Co., for 50 pds sterling, 86 acs.
on a small branch of Enoree River, granted to sd John Martindale 5
Feb. 1787, and rec. in Grant Bk. RRRR, p. 85. Signed JOHN & RACHEL
(X) MARTINDALE. Wit: THOMAS HARRIS, JOSEPH HARRIS. Rec. 28 Sept. 1789.

Pp 257-260:   4 & 5 1789, Lease and Release. WILLIAM CUNNINGHAM, car-
        penter of Charleston Dist., SC, son and heir at law to the real
estate   of JOHN CUNNINGHAM, dec'd., to JOHN REED, planter of Union
Co., 96 Dist., for 10 shillings and 5 pds sterling, 200 acs. in the
fork of Broad and Pacolet Rivers. Granted to JOHN WEEDINGMAN 28 Apr.
1768 by Gov. Tryon of N.C., then deemed to be in Mecklenburgh Co.,
N.C., but now in Union Co., S.C. William signed his name. Wit: JAMES
JORDON, JNO. CUNNINGHAM, WILLIAM KENNEDY. WILLIAM HENDLEY, J.P. Rec.
28 Sept. 1789.

Pp 260-262:   28 Sept. 1789, JOHN BLESINGAME, Sheriff of Union Co.
        to OBADIAH OLIPHANT, same place, for 8 pds sterling, 200 acs.
on S side of Thicketty Creek, highest and last bid at a public auction
to settle a case in which JOHN SAVAGE sued ROBERT LUSK for a total
of 8 pds, 16 shillings, 8 pence including the debt and court costs.
Wit: JOHN GEORGE RAINER & MOSES WATERS. Rec. 28 Sept. 1789.

Pp 262-263:   17 Aug. 1789, WM. NEWMAN and MARY his wife to JOHN STOKES,
        all of Union Co., for 100 pds current money, 250 acs. on the
branches of Fairforest Creek and Tyger River. Bound at present by lands
of FEDRICK CROUDER, THOS. BRANDON, Esq. and the sd JNO. STOKES and
THOS. GREER. Granted to WM. CURRY and DAVID FARMER by patents dated
2 Aug. 1768 and 17 Dec. 1772, rec. in Auditor's Office, Bk. A, No.
9, p. 120, and in Bk. M, No. 12, p. 163. Signed WILLIAM & MARY (X)
NEWMAN. Wit: JOHN SANDERS and AARON (A) FINCHER. Proved by Fincher
bef. Thos. Brandon, J.P. 5 Sept. 1789. Rec. 28 Sept. 1789.

Pp 263-264:   23 June 1789, GEORGE GOODWIN of S.C. county of Greevill
        (Greenville?) to JOSIAH GOODWIN and JOHN GOODWIN of state and
co. afsd., for love and affection of his sons JOSIAH and JOHN GOODWIN,
500 acs. in Union Co. bound by lines formerly called ARMSTRONG's, and
HOWELL and RUTH, agreeable to a plat and grant dated 13 Oct. 1772,
which contains 200 acs. Also, 100 acs. formerly the property of JOHN
POWELL and another tract of 100 acs., surveyed by JAS. CRAWFORD, both
adj. the 300 ac. tract. George signed his name. Wit: WILLIAM BIRDSONG,
JOHN BIRDSONG, JR. and DAVID (X) TRAIL. JOHN BIRDSONG, J.P. Rec. 28
Sept. 1789.

Pp 264-267:   22 & 23 Jan. 1773, Lease and Release. WILLIAM McMULLEN,
        planter, and ELIZABETH McMILLIN, his wife, of Craven Co., SC,
to NATHANIEL GUITON (GUYTON), blacksmith, same place, for 10 sh. and
298.8.9 current money of S.C., 94 acs. on W and S bank of mane (sic)
Broad River in Craven Co. including an island in the river, for a Fish-
ery. Part of a tract of 400 acs. granted to WILLIAM LOVE by the Gov.
of N.C. on 3 Sept. 1753, in then deemed Maclenburgh (sic) Co., N.C.
Entire tract of 400 acs. conveyed by JNO. LOVE, heir at law to WILLIAM
LOVE, to HENRY SMITH. Henry Smith conveyed 190 acs. of sd tract viz.
all that say (?) on the W and S side of Broad River unto WM. McMILLIN.
Grant and deeds rec. in Sec. and Reg. Offices in N.C. Wit: JOSEPH ROB-
INSON, J.P. of 96 Dist., MOSES WATKINS, ELIZABETH COCHRAN. Signed WIL-
LIAM McMILLIN, ELIZABETH (X) McMILLIN. Rec. 29 Sept. 1789.

Page 268:   19 June 1789, CHARLES HARRINGTON and PATIENCE HARRINGTON,
        his wife, of Union Co., to ROBERT RETHERFORD (RUTHERFORD), SR.,
of Newberry Co., SC for 50 pds sterling, 474 acs. on S side of Gilkie's
Creek, bound by ABSALOM PETTY, ROBERT LUSK, ROBT. MONTGOMERIE, SAML.
YOUNG and vacant land. Signed CHARLES (C) HARRINGTON. Wit: BENAJAH
THOMPSON, ABSALOM PETTY, JOHN HARRINGTON. PATIENCE (X) HARRINGTON released dower rights on 25 June 1789 bef. ZACH. BULLOCK, J.P. No recording date.

Pp 269-270:   19 June 1789, CHARLES HARRINGTON of Union Co. to ROBERT
        RETHERFORD (RUTHERFORD), SR. of Newberry Co., for 50 pds sterling,
500 acs. on a big branch of Gilkie's Creek, bound by JOHN STEEN and
all other sides vacant. Description states that CHARLES HARRINGTON
hath and Indefeasible Estate of Inheritance in and to the sd Premises.
Signed CHARLES (C) HARRINGTON. Wit: BENAJAH THOMPSON, ABSALOM PETTY,
JOHN HARRINGTON. PATIENCE (X) HARRINGTON released dower on 25 June
1789 bef. ZACHARIAH BULLOCK, J.P. Rec. 29 Sept. 1789.

Page 270:   3 July 1789, "To all to whom these Presents shall come
        Greeting..." CHARLES & PATIENCE HARRINGTON state that they have
sold for 50 pds sterling to ROBERT RETHERFORD, SR. 500 acs. in 96 Dist.
bound by LUSK's line and CHARLES HARRINGTON's line. Both CHARLES and
PATIENCE signed by mark. Wit: RICHMOND TERRELL, JOHN SIMS, JOHN HAR-
RINGTON. Zach. Bullock, J.P.

Pp 270-271:   3 July 1789, (Same type of instrument as that next above).
        CHARLES HARRINGTON & PATIENCE his wife have sold, for 50 pds
sterling to ROBERT RETHERFORD, SR., 292 acs. in 96 Dist. joining JOSEPH
GILLING, NATHL. GILLING, LEWIS LEDBETTER, MOSES GILLING and JOHN LEAK.
CHARLES & PATIENCE both signed by mark. Wit: RICHMOND TERRELL, JOHN
SIMS, JOHN HARRINGTON. Zach. Bullock, J.P.

Pp 271-273:   21 Mar. 1785, Lease and Release. HENRY MACHAN WOOD, "heir,
        etc." to JAMES WOOD, Esq., deceased, of 96 Dist., to ADAM POTTER,
same place, for 10 sh. and 100 pds sterling, 500 acs. on S side of
Pacolet River. Entire tract granted to ROBERT McWHORTER 19 Aug. 1774
by SC grant, and made over by lease and release to JAMES WOOD, Esq...
(Henry's middle name spelled variously as MACHAN, MEECHAN, MACHEN,
etc.) Signed H. M. WOOD. Wit: ISHAM SAFOLD, WILLIAM FOSTER, ALEXD.
WALKER. Isham Safold attested to signature on 17 Aug. 1789 bef. Zach.
Bullock, J.P. Rec. 29 Sept. 1789.

Page 274:   22 Nov. 1788, ADAM POTTER to JOHN and WILLIAM EASTER-
        WOOD, all of Union Co. for 60 pds sterling, 500 acs. on S side

538

Cont'd:
of Pacolet River in the counties of Union and Spartanburgh, the same
tract of land described in deed above. Bound by HAIL's line, ANGELICA
MITCHELL, JNO. KERCONNEL, MICHAEL CRAWFORD and the river. Adam signed
his name. Wit: JOHN STOVAL, GEORGE STORY, JR., JOHN MARTIN. Rec. 29
Sept. 1789.

Pp 274-277:   3 & 5 Feb. 1789, Lease and Release. WILLIAM CUNNINGHAM,
          carpenter of Charleston Dist., to JAMES LINDSEY, planter of Union
Co., 96 Dist. for 10 sh. and 90 pds sterling, 200 acs. in the forks
of Broad and Pacolet Rivers, a little above the joining of sd rivers,
bound SW by lands granted to JNO. CUNNINGHAM, NE by WILLIAM SHARP,
and other sides by Broad and Pacolet rivers. Orig. granted to DANIEL
THOMAS on 30 Oct. 1772 by S.C. grant and conveyed by him to JOHN WEED-
INGHAM. Conveyed by JOHN WEEDINGHAM and BARBARA his wife to JOHN CUNN-
INGHAM. The sd WM. CUNNINGHAM, son and heir at law of the Estate of
JNO. CUNNINGHAM, dec'd., now conveys entire tract to sd JAMES LINDSEY.
William signed his name. Wit: WILLIAM KENNEDY, JOHN CUNNINGHAM, JAMES
JORDON. Kennedy attested to signature 30 Sept. 1789 bef. WM. HENDLEY,
J.P. Rec. same day.

Pp 277-278:   26 May 1789, LEWIS AKINS of Lawrence (Laurens) Co., to
          JOHN HUGHES of Union Co. for 60 pds lawful money, 200 acs. on
Abiton's (Abbington's) Creek, waters of Broad River, bound by THOMAS
LOVELATTY (LOVELADY). Orig. granted to MARSHAL LOVELATTY by Wm. Tryon,
Gov. of N.C. and since regranted by Gov. Moultrie of S.C. by a plat
dated 17 Sept. 1785 and located by MARSHAL LOVELATTY on 13 Dec. 1774.
Akins signed his name. Wit: JAMES TERRELL, NICHOLAS CORRY, JONATHAN
GILKIE. Corry attested on 13 June 1789 bef. WM. McCULLOCH, J.P. No
recording date.

Page 279:   31 July 1786, VARDRY McBEE of Thicketty Creek, SC to
          LEWIS AKINS of Lawrence (Laurens) Co. for 5 pds sterling, 200
acs. on Abbington's Creek, bound by PETER PETERSON and JAMES PETTY.
Part of a tract of 532 ac. granted by state of SC to sd McBee on 7
Sept. 1785 and located by MARSHAL LOVELADY on 13 Sept. 1774. Wit: WIL-
LIAM WIER, ISHAM SAFOLD, SOLOMON MANGHAM, THOS. GORDON. Solomon Mangham
attested on 18 Apr. 1789 bef. Wm. McCulloch, J.P. Rec. 30 Sept. 1789.

Page 280:   11 May 1788, JEPTHA HOLLINGSWORTH and ANN his wife to
          WILLIAM WHITLOCK all of Union Co., for 200 pds sterling and divers
good causes, 320 acs. granted to sd Hollingsworth in 1785. Located
on the middle fork of Brown's Creek, waters of Broad River, bound by
JNO. MAYFIELD, WM. WILLIAMS and vacant lands when granted. Signed by
JEPTHA HOLLINGSWORTH, NANCY (X) HOLLINGSWORTH. Wit: WM. HUGHES, WM.
WILLIAMS, SAMUEL GORDON. No rec. date.

Page 281:   11 May 1788, WILLIAM WILLIAMS to WILLIAM WHITLOCK both
          of Union Co., for 100 pds sterling and divers good causes, 130
acs. on the middle fork of Brown's Creek, part of a tract of 200 acs.
granted to sd. Wm. Williams in 1768 at that time bounded on all
sides by vacant lands. Williams signed his name. Wit: WILLIAM HUGHES,
SAMUEL GORDON, JEPTHA HOLLINGSWORTH. No rec. date.

Page 282:   4 Nov. 1789, ISAAC McKISSICK and MARGRETT his wife of
          Union Co., 96 Dist., to JAMES BANKHEAD of Chester Co., Camden
Dist., for 60 pds sterling, 100 acs. on S side of Broad River, part
of a tract formerly "layed off for" ICHEBUD CLARK and being that tract
where ISAAC McKISSICK and wife formerly lived. Signed ISAAC McKISSICK,
MARGRET (X) McKISSICK. Wit: JAMES McGARITY, ROBERT (X) WALKER, WILLIAM
SPLEAN. Wm. Splean attested on 23 Dec. 1789 bef. Wm. Hendley, J.P.
Rec. 28 Dec. 1789.

Page 283:   28 Dec. 1789, JAS. BENDINGTON of Spartanburgh Co., SC
          to GEORGE HARLING (HARLAN) of Union Co., for 35.4.0 sterling,
100 acs. on the waters of Sugar Creek of Fairforest Creek in Union
Co., bound by land held by THOMAS PARMER and DANIEL PARMER, DAVID PRAET
(PRUITT?), and MILL SUMNER. Signed by mark, JAMES BEDDINGTON. Marked
ack. and rec. 28 Dec. 1789.

Pp 284-285: 10 Nov. 1789, JOHN GOODWIN, planter, to ROBT. WOODSON, planter, both of Union Co., for 50 pds sterling, 123 acs., 1/2 of a tract of 246 acs. on waters of Fairforest Creek, bound by Col. BRANDON, POLK, ARON HARLIN, BREED and GREY, and granted to sd GOODWIN by state of SC on 5 June 1786 and rec. in Grant Bk. IIII, p. 611. Goodwin signed by mark. Wit: JAMES WOODSON, JAMES WOODSON, JR., THOS. GITZENTANNER. Rec. 28 Dec. 1789.

Pp 285-287: 25 Nov. 1789 Lease and Release (both dated same day), MARLOW PRIOR to HARGROVE ARTHER (no places or residence given), for 10 sh. and 250 pds sterling, 350 acs. in Union Co., 96 Dist. which was surveyed for MARY KING and lying on a small river running into Broad River formerly called Collins River now Enoree River butting and bounding to the SE on sd river and on all sides by vacant land when surveyed. Plat lodged in the Surveyor Gen. Office of SC. Signed: MARLOW PRYOR. Wit: WM. GODBER, RICHD. BOLAN. Richd. Bolan attested on 8 Dec. 1789 bef. AMBROSE ARTHER, J.P. Rec. 28 Dec. 1789.

Pp 287-288: 20 Sept. 1789, ALEXD. McDOUGAL to THOS. STRIBLING, JR., for 80 pds sterling, 337 acs. on the branches of Buffalo and Brown's Creek. Bound by JESSE FOOR (FORE?) and ALEXD. McDOUGAL. McDougal signed his name. Wit: CORNELIUS DEMPSEY & THOS. STRIBLING, SR. Rec. 28 Dec. 1789.

Pp 288-289: 29 July 1789, ISAAC GREGORY, SR. to MARGARET GREGORY, both of Union Co., for 50 pds sterling, the one third part of 200 acs. on S side of Broad River on the S fork of Brown's Creek, a little above the waggon road. Entire tract orig. granted to sd Isaac Gregory on 20 (or 26) Oct. 1767 by Wm. Tryon, Gov. of N.C. The deed states that MARGARET GREGORY was the wife of BENJN. GREGORY, lately deceased, and was to hold the entire tract of 200 acs. during her lifetime. After her decease the whole tract, including her thirds, to go to her son WILLIAM GREGORY. If sd William should die without heirs, the land to fall to his sister SARAH. Isaac signed his name. Wit: JEREMIAH GREGORY, GERARD GREGORY. Rec. 28 Dec. 1789.

Pp 289-290: 25 Sept. 1787, JAMES JOHNSTON, farmer of Newberry Co., to AARON HARLAN, planter of Union Co., for 30 pds sterling, 125 acs. on Buffalow Creek, a branch of Fairforest Creek, bound by THOS. GREEN, JOSEPH BREED & ROBERT BISHOP. Part of a 300 ac. tract granted to WILLIAM BISHOP on 23 June 1774, SC grant, rec. in Book M, No. 13, p. 97 on 11 Nov. 1774. Sd 125 acs. was conveyed to sd JAMES JOHNSTON on 10 Mar. 1777. Signed JAMES JOHNSON. Wit: WM. MORGAN, JACOB HOLMES, JACOB HARLAN. Rec. 28 Dec. 1789.

Page 290: At the bottom of the page. The entire entry has been lined out. Dated 18 Dec. 1775 - JOAB MITCHELL of 96 Dist. to THOMAS DRAPER, same place, for 10 shillings, JOAB MITCHELL bargained and sold and by these presents.......the end.

Page 291: A plat or drawing showing the boundaries around the gaol of Union Co., N by JONES' field, E through sd village (of Union), S by EDSON's field, W to a stake N of the road. Surveyed "Agreeable to an act of the General Assembly of the State of S.C. for Granting Prison bounds to the unfortunate debtors of this State." Laid out in a circle with the Gaol as the center. No measurements given. Dated 26 Mar. 1790 and signed by JAMES MARTIN, D. Surveyor.

Pp 292-293: 16 Aug. 1787, JOHN NICOLL of Greenville Co., SC to AARON HARLAN, wheelwright of Union Co., for 60 pds sterling, 250 acs. on Fairforest Creek, a branch of Tyger River, being part of a 640 ac. SC grant to JNO. NICOLL and JAMES VERNON, dated 16 July 1765 and rec. in Book ZZ, p. 154. Bound on one side by the creek. Wit: THOS. BLASINGAME, JNO. (X) JONES. Rec. 29 Dec. 1789.

Page 293: 13 Sept. 1787, AARON HARLAN, SR., to SAML. HARLING, his son, for love and affection which he bears to his son SAML. HARLAN, 297 acs. whereon the sd Samuel Harlan now lives. Joining JNO. BIRDSONG's land which sd AARON HARLAN, SR. did purchase of M. AMMONS,

Cont'd:
adj. Fairforest Creek. Signed AARON HARLAN. Wit: WILLIAM BIRDSONG, JACOB HARLAN. Rec. 29 Dec. 1789.

Pp 293-295:   23 & 24 Dec. 1789, Lease and Release. JNO. McCOOLL and
     JANE (JEAN) his wife, of Union Co., to CUSHMAN EDSON, for 10
shillings and 10 pds current money, 3 lots at Union Court House, no.'s
44, 58 and 72, containing 1/2 ac. each. Signed by JOHN & JEAN McCOOLL.
Wit: RICHD. MITCHELL, JNO. BECKHAM, JR. Both Mitchell and Beckham attested on 24 Dec. 1789 bef. Berd. Glenn, J.P. No rec. date.

Pp 296-297:   22 June 1789, HUGH MEANS, Esq. to Col. THOMAS BRANDON,
     both of Union Co., for 100 pds sterling, 335 acs. on both sides
of Fairforest Creek, granted to sd Hugh Means by NATHL. RICE, then
Gov. of N. C., on 18 Nov. 1752. "....fell into the State of S. C."
and memorial entered in Auditor's Office (of S.C.?) 30 Nov. 1767. Wit:
CHAS. MILES, JAS. BELL. JAMES BELL attested on 3 July 1789 bef. JOSEPH
McJUNKIN, J.P. Rec. 29 Dec. 1789.

Pp 297-298:   29 Dec. 1788, Col. WILLIAM FARR to THOMAS MILES, both
     of Union Co, for 107 pds sterling, 461½ acs. on the branches
of Cain and lower Fishdam Creek. Bound by CLENDENON, BISHOP's land,
vacant land, LEVY HOLLINGSWORTH, JAMES HAWKINS, Col. FARR, and THOMAS
COX's land. Part of a larger tract granted to Farr by S.C. grant 3
Apr. 1786. Wit: HEZEKIAH RICE, WM. THOS. LINTON and JAMES THOMAS. Ack.
and attested by all 3 wit. Rec. 30 Dec. 1789.

Pp 298-301:   29 Jan. 1776 Lease and Release (both dated same day).
     WM. RHODES, cooper, and ELIZABETH, his wife, of Tyger River,
S.C., to JESSE DODD of Enoree River, same province (S.C.), for 10 sh.
and 500 pds current money of S.C., 300 acs. on a ridge bet. Tyger and
Enoree Rivers in Craven Co. Granted to sd Wm. Rhodes on 24 Aug. 1770
by Wm. Bull, Gov. of the Prov. of S.C. Bound on all sides by vacant
land at the time of the grant. Signed by WILLIAM (his mark) RHODES
and ELIZABETH (X) RHODES. (Name also spelled ROADS). Wit: THOS. DODD,
JNO. RHODES, ZILPHE (X) LINCH. Jno. Rhodes attested on 25 Dec. 1789
that he saw his father, William Rhodes, sign a release for the land
and that he believes the above to be his father's mark. Thomas Brandon,
J.P. John signed his name. Rec. 30 Dec. 1789.
     (Note: ELIZABETH RHODES was nee WOFFORD, the daughter of WILLIAM
WOFFORD whose will, dated 28 Mar. 1787, is recorded in Union Co., Box
1, pkg. 9.)

Pp 301-303:   5 Oct. 1789 Lease and Release (both dated same) JESSE
     DODD and MARY his wife, to ANDREW TORRENCE, both of Union Co.,
for 10 sh. and 100 pds sterling, the 300 acs. described in the deed
next above. Both Jesse and Mary signed their names. Wit: THOMAS BRANDON,
SAMUEL SIMPSON. Rec. 30 Dec. 1789.

Pp 303-304:   26 Nov. 1789, JNO. McCOOLL and JANE his wife to FREDRICK
     EISEN, blacksmith all of Union Co., for 60 pds sterling, 101½
acs. part of two tracts orig. granted to sd McCooll, one for 406 acs.
dated 1 May 1786 and the other for 1,000 acs. dated 4 Dec. 1786. No
location given. Signed by JNO. & JEAN McCOOLL. (Note: again she is
both JEAN and JANE). Wit: NATHL. JEFFERIES, CUSHMAN RUGGLES EDSON,
and JNO. WHITTICK. Thomas Blassingame, J.P. Rec. 30 Dec. 1789.

Pp 305-306:   17 Nov. 1789, JOHN McCOOLL and JANE his wife to JOHN
     WHITTICK, all of Union Co., for 50 pds sterling, 3 lots, 1/2
ac. each, no.'s 1, 15 and 30, joining the Courthouse land, JNO. Mc-
COOLL and JAMES TOSH. Also 4 acs. adj. the sd. numbered lots. 5½ acs.
in all. Wit: DANIEL HENNING, ROBT. POWELL. Thos. Blassingame, J.P. Rec.
30 Dec. 1789.

Pp 306-307:   16 Dec. 1787, JOSEPH JONES to JOHN EWART, both of Union
     Co., for 108.15.0 sterling, 150 acs. where I now live on the
waters of Brown's and Fairforest Creeks, Bound on all sides by land
belonging to JOHN McCOOLL, being the remaining part of 450 acs. orig.
granted to WALTER HOLMES, conveyed by Holmes to GEORGE CROSSLEY, SR.,

Cont'd:
then by Crossley to THOMAS YOUNG, by Young to sd JONES, by Jones to
sd JOHN McCOOLL, then by McCooll back again to sd JOSEPH JONES. Wit:
HENRY BAILEY, JACOB BROWN. Joseph signed his name. Rec. 30 Dec. 1789.

Pp 307-308: 2 Aug. 1789, MERRY McGUIRE and JANE his wife, to WILLIAM
    BOWMAN, all of Union Co., for 20 pds sterling, 154 acs. part
of a tract granted to ROBERT SMITH on 4 June 1787, conveyed by Smith
to Merry McGuire. On the waters of Fannenes (Fanning's) Creek and the
Wildcat (Creek), bound by CHARLES BROOKS (BROCK?), the Wildcat Creek,
the sedar (sic) Shoal tract, MARK THENT's (GHENT?) line, and sd Robt.
Smith. Merry signed his name and his wife signed by mark JEAN (X) Mc-
Guire. Wit: JOHN REED, CHAS. BRACK, JAMES (X) MOORE and JAS. LINDSEY.
CHARLES BROCK signed his name to the attestation on 28 Dec. 1789 bef.
WM. HENDLEY, J.P. Rec. 30 Dec. 1789.

Pp 308-309: 21 Dec. 1787, THOMAS BRANDON and ELIZABETH his wife to
    JOHN PALMER, all of 96 Dist., for 20 pds sterling and divers
good causes, one tract (no acreage given) on the S fork of Brown's
Creek granted to THOMAS BELL 15 Mar. 1768. No wit. Ack. and rec. 30
Dec. 1789.

Pp 309-310: 3 Feb. 1789, WALTER HOLMES, to JNO. McCOOLL, both of
    the State of S.C., for 100 pds sterling, 450 acs. granted to WALTER
HOLMES on 23 June 1774, in Berkley Co. in the fork bet. Broad and Saluda
Rivers, on the drafts of Fairforest and Brown's Creeks. Wit: JOHN Mc-
KIBBEN, ANDREW THOMPSON, DENNIS SPRINGER. Holmes signed his name. Wit.
to the receipt were AND. THOMPSON, SAML. CARGO. JOHN McKIBBEN attested
on 10 Mar. 1789 bef. Wm. McCulloch, J.P. and Jno. Birdsong, J.P. Andrew
Thompson attested on 17 Dec. 1789 bef. Thomas Brandon, J.P. Rec. 31
Dec. 1789.
    (Note: DENNIS SPRINGER moved to Lauderdale Co., Alabama before
1822, and other branches of the Springer family moved to Lawrence Co.,
Tenn. directly across the Alabama-Tennessee state line.)

Pp 310-311: 19 June 1789, JOHN McCOOLL and wife JANE to CORNELIUS
    DIMPSEY TAYLOR, all of Union Co., for 10 pds, 2 lots #7 and #31
at Union Courthouse, on N side of Main Street, containing 1/2 ac. Wit:
RICHD. MITCHEL, JNO. McKIBBEN. Rec. 31 Dec. 1789.

Pp 311-314: Lease and Release, dated 4 & 5 Dec. 1789. SAMUEL CARGO
    and wife MARGARET of Abbeville Co., SC to ALEXANDER MACBETH and
JNO. MONCRIEFFE (under the firm of Alexr. Macbeth & Co.) of Union
Co., SC, for 10 sh. and 50 pds sterling, lot no. 45 containing 1/2
ac. at Union Court House. Conveyed to Cargo by Jno. McCooll. Wit: JOHN
HENDERSON, JOHN HAILE, RICHARD MITCHELL. John Henderson, Esq., attested
bef. JOHN BIRDSONG, J.P. 16 Feb. 1790. MARGARET CARGO, wife of SAMUEL
CARGO, signed a dower release in Abbeville Co. bef. J. F. GRIMKE and
"Harper atto. at Law." No date. Rec. in Union Co. on 16 Feb. 1790.

Pp 314-315: 28 Dec. 1789, THOMAS BRANDON, Esq. and wife ELIZABETH,
    of Union Co. to ALEXR. MACBETH and JOHN MONCRIEFFE, Merchants,
for 30 pds sterling, lot No. 47, 1/2 ac. at Union Court House. Wit:
WM. DALRYMPLE, THOS. CABEEN, JOHN McCOOLL. Receipt for 8 pds sterling
signed by Brandon. Elizabeth signed dower release 21 Jan. 1790 bef.
Jno. Birdsong, J.P. Rec. 21 Jan. 1790.

Pp 315-317: 21 Jan. 1789 (error-later shown as 1790). JNO. McCOOLL
    and wife JANE to ALEXR. MACBETH and JOHN MONCREEFE (firm of Alexr.
Macbeth & Co.) all of Union Co., for 10 pds sterling, lot no. 33, 1/2
ac. at Union Court House. Wit: JNO. McKIBBEN, JAS. McKIBBEN, JNO. BIRD-
SONG. JANE McCOOLL (signed JEAN) signed dower release 21 Jan. 1790
bef. Jno. Birdsong, J.P. Rec. 16 Feb. 1790.

Pp 317-319: Lease and Release, 18 & 19 Dec. 1775. JOAB MITCHELL to
    THOMAS DRAPER both of 96 Dist., S.C., for 10 sh. and 100 pds
current money of SC, 100 acs. whereon EDWARD PICKET now lives, part
of a 300 ac. SC grant to sd JOAB MITCHELL, 6 Sept. 1774. Located on
Clark's Mill Creek of Pacolet River and orig. grant bound by EDWD.

Cont'd:
PICKET and THOS. DRAPER. Wit: PHILIP COLEMAN, EDWD. PICKET & EDWD.
WILLIAMS. Signed by mark JOAB (M) MITCHELL. Philip Coleman attested
on 2 May 1776 bef. CHRISTOPHER COLEMAN, J.P. No recording date.
   (Note: JOAB MITCHELL moved to Tennessee before the Revolution.)

Page 320:   29 Jan. 1790, JOHN HAM of Fairfield Co., to JOHN WHITE
      of Union Co., for 10 pds current money and divers good causes,
paid by the sd WM. WHITE, "confirm unto the sd WILLIAM WHITE", 50 acs.,
1/2 of a 100 ac. tract on Brown's Creek in Union Co., granted to WILLIAM
BOYD. Bound by JAMES BOGAN, WM. McJUNKIN and WM. WHITLOCK. "JOHN HAM
for himself and his heirs....and the heirs of EDWARD NIXON, dec'd."
to the sd WILLIAM WHITE. Wit: PHILIP ANDERSON, DAVID (X) PRUET. Rec.
22 Mar. 1790.
      (Note: Both JOHN and WILLIAM WHITE lived on Brown's Creek along
with DANIEL and ISAAC WHITE. EDWARD NIXON was an early landowner in
Chester Co., S.C.)

Pp 320-321:   5 Nov. 1789, RANDOLPH DEPRIEST to SARAH GIST, both of
      Union Co., for 10 pds sterling, 100 acs. on a small branch of
Enoree River, granted to sd Depriest on 3 Apr. 1786 by S.C. grant,
and grant and plat rec. in Sec. Office in Charleston. Bound by land
formerly claimed by JESSE DOOD, ____ LONGSHORE, HENRY ADDINGTON and
vacant land. Wit: JAMES WOODSON, JOSEPH GIST, WILLIAM GIST. Rec. 22
March 1790.

Pp 321-322:   28 May 1789, WILLIAM WHITLOCK to HANCOCK PORTER, both
      of Union Co., for 50 pds sterling, 13 acs. on the Old Main Wag-
gon Road to Love's Ford and bound by JOSEPH JOLLY, ALEXR. CAIN and
WILLIAM WHITLOCK. Wit: THOMAS HUGHES. Rec. 22 Mar. 1790.

Page 322:;   22 Mar. 1790, BENJAMIN DERBY (DARBY) to JEREMIAH HAMELTON,
      both of Union Co., for 100 pds sterling currency (sic) of S.C.,
140 acs. on waters of Tyger River, bound by HAMELTON's land, MATHEW
ANDERSON THOMAS, MARK LOVE, vacant land, BENJAMIN DERBY's land, and
GEORGE LYNAM's land. Part of a tract granted to DERBY by State of S.C.
5 Dec. 1785 and rec. in Grant Bk. GGGG, p. 242. Wit: PHILIP ANDERSON,
DANIEL LIPHAM. Ack. in open court 22 Mar. 1790.
      (Note: BENJAMIN and JOSIAS DARBY both lived on Tyger River. It
is stated in one instrument that they were brothers. They were related
to the DARBY family that lived in Chester Co., S.C. and there are indications that they moved to S. C. from Maryland.)

Page 323:   23 Sept. 1789, ISAAC HOLEMAN to GEORGE TAYLORS, both
      of Union Co., for 50 pds sterling, 139 acs. on N side of Thicketty
Creek, bound by TAYLORS' own land, BOVERSON(?) and THOMPSON. Surveyed
for HOLEMAN 4 Nov. 1788. Signed ISAAC (0) HOLEMAN and HANNAH HOLEMAN.
Wit: JOHN THOMPSON, WILLIAM STEEN. Thompson attested that ISAAC HOLE-
MAN and wife signed bef. Thos. Blasingame, J.P. 29 Sept. 1789. Rec.
22 Mar. 1790.

Page 324:   14 Mar. 1789, JOHN LANGLEY of Greenville Co., SC to IRBY
      DEWBERRY of Spartanburg Co., for 20 pds sterling, 150 acs. on
Quinton's Branch, waters of Broad River in Union Co., orig. granted
to SARAH ROBINSON, widow, by a patent dated 5 June 1786 and rec. in
Book KKKK, p. 627. Land became vested in the sd LANGLEY by marriage.
Land was now in Dewberry's actual possession. Wit: JAMES (X) ROBINSON,
WILLIAM CLAYTON. Robinson attested 13 July 1789 bef. Wm. McCulloch,
J.P. No recording date.

Pp 325-327:   2 & 3 Dec. 1784, Lease and Release. JAMES TIMS, JR.,
      yeoman, and PATTY, his wife of St. Mark's Parish, SC to JAMES
HAWKINS, planter, of 96 Dist., for 10 sh. and 35 pds sterling, 400
acs. on S side of Tyger River, bet. Tyger and Enoree Rivers, orig.
granted to AMOS TIMS, SR. on 26 July 1774 by Wm. Bull, Lt. Gov. of
S.C. Orig. bound by ZACHA. EASTES (also shown as EASTERS - should be
ESTES), bounty land and land claimed by EDWARD BIDDY. JAMES TIMS has
a "good sure perfect and indefeasible Estate of Inheritance." JAMES
and PATTY signed their names. Wit: J. PETER SARTOR, SPILSBY GLENN.

Cont'd:
SPILSBY GLENN attested on 22 Mar. 1790 bef. BERN. GLENN, J.P. Rec.
22 Mar. 1790.
(Note: AMOS TIMS lived in what is now Chester Co., S.C.)

Page 327:   6 Nov. 1789, PAGE PUCKET and REBECAH his wife to WILLIAM
      WHITE, all of Union Co., for 21 pds sterling and divers good
causes, 113 acs. on the head of Sandy Run, with vacant land on all
sides. Orig. granted to WILLIAM BUCKHANNON on 7 May 1787. Signed by
PAGE PUCKET only. Wit: WM. BUCKHANNON & SEJAZMOND STRIBLING. No attestation and no rec. date shown.

Pp 328-330:   29 & "thirteenth" (30th) May 1783, Lease and Release.
      DANIEL TRAMMEL to JAMES CARVEAL (this name should be JAMES KERR
VEALE), both of 96 Dist., for 5 sh. and 100 pds sterling, a tract (no
acs. given) whereon the sd DANIEL TRAMEL last dwelt, orig. granted
to sd TRAMEL on 24 Nov. 1767 by the Prov. of S. C., rec. in Sec. Office
in Book BBB, p. 365, memorial rec. in Aud. Office in Bk H, No. 8, p.
389 on 16 Feb. 1768. In Craven Co., 96 Dist. (sic) Signed: DANIEL TRAM-
MEL. Wit: NATHL. ABNEY, M.D., JAMES THOMAS and ARTHER THOMAS. James
Thomas attested on 30 May 1783 bef. WILLIAM FARR, J.P. Rec. 22 Mar.
1790.

Pp 330-331:   15 Jan. 1790, JOHN BLASINGAME, Esq., Sheriff of Union
      Co., to CUSHMAN EDSON of Union Co., for 20 pds sterling, high
bid at a public auction held 18 July 1789 to settle a case of debt
against SAML. JACKSON by THOMAS BLASINGAME, JR. for 26.18.2 sterling
in court held in Dec. 1788. Two tracts of land: one tract of 200 acs.
on Camp spring branch of Fairforest Creek, bound by JOSEPH BREED's
old line, now SAML. JACKSON's, Camp spring branch, the race path spring
branch, ready (Reedy) branch of Mitchell's Creek, AVERY BREED's line,
DANL. PLUMMER's line, part of a tract orig. granted to DANL. JACKSON
4 Nov. 1772; the other tract of 100 acs. on a branch of Fairforest
Creek, all sides vacant when surveyed, orig. granted to JOSEPH BREED
by S.C. grant 23 Oct. 1765. Signed JOHN BLASINGAME, late Sheriff of
Union Co." Wit: JOHN HAILE, RICHD. MITCHELL, THOS. BLASINGAME. Rec.
22 Mar. 1790.

Pp 331-332:   20 Jan. 1790, WILLIAM BLACKSTOCK, SR., planter and EU-
      PHENIA his wife, to WILLIAM EDWARDS, wheelwright, both of Union
Co., for 25 pds sterling, 196 acs. on Cowdon Creek, waters of Tyger
River, bound by WM. SMITH and lands laid off for THOMAS DUNLAP, all
other sides vacant. Granted to sd WM. BLACKSTOCK, SR. on 3 Apr. 1786
by State of S.C. Signed by WILLIAM (B) BLACKSTOCK, EUPHENIA (O) BLACK-
STOCK. Wit: JOHN SMITH, WILLIAM (X) SMITH. Rec. 22 Mar. 1790.

Pp 332-333:   10 Nov. 1788, JOHN LITTLE to THOMAS PALMER, both of Union
      Co., for 120 pds, 130 acs. - 100 acs. orig. granted to MARGARET
McDOWELL 12 Sept. 1768 by the Prov. of S.C. "in then named Craven Co."
in the fork bet. Sugar Creek and Fairforest, all sides vacant when
surveyed. Grant and plat rec. in Auditor's Office, Bk. I, No. 9, p.
248. The 100 acs. was conveyed to JOHN LITTLE in two tracts: one conveyed by WM. BRYANT to John Little having been conveyed by MARGARET
McDOWELL to PHILIP BRYAN, dec'd., the other parcel conveyed by JONATHAN
PINNIL to sd John Little. Also, 30 acs. part of a 100 ac. tract conveyed
to John Little by ELIZTH MARTIN - 130 acs. in all. Wit: WM. FARR, JAMES
WOODSON, WILLIAM STEEN. Proved in court by Wm. Farr and rec. on 23
Mar. 1790.

Pp 333-334:   13 Dec. 1789, JOHN LITTLE, planter, to THOMAS PALMER,
      SR., both of Union Co., for 120 pds sterling, 200 acs. on the
branches of Sugar Creek, part of a 223 ac. tract orig. granted to sd
LITTLE on 5 Feb. 1787 by S.C. grant and rec. in Grant Bk. RRRR, p.
1208 (sic). Wit: WILLIAM FARR, JAMES WOODSON and WM. STEEN. Rec. 23
Mar. 1790.

Pp 334-335:   24 Feb. 1790, THOMAS BISHOP to JOHN CAMBELL (also spelled
      CAMPBELL), both of Union Co., a mortgage for 180 pds sterling,
450 acs. which was conveyed by JOHN FINCHER to the sd THOMAS BISHOP.

Cont'd:
80 pds to be repaid "in Good trade" within 3 yrs. from date, the other
100 pds within 5 yrs. "to be paid in produce at Market price in Charleston deducting the expense of the carriage and Inspection with Lawful
Interest." If parties could not agree on the price of articles "they
shall be valued by two persons Indifferently Chosen at Trade price."
Mortgage void if sum repaid. Wit: JOHN ROBERDS, THOMAS ROBERDS, JOHN
PEARSON, who attested "by his solemn affirmation" (Quaker) on 23 Mar.
1790 bef. WM. KENNEDY, J.P. No rec. date.

Pp 335-336:   13 Feb. 1790, JOHN HUGHEY, JR. and ELIZABETH his wife
        to JAMES TOWNSEND, all of Union Co., for 70 pds sterling, 260
acs. on waters of Tyger River, orig. granted to sd HUGHEY 5 June 1786
and rec. in Grant Bk. MMMM, p. 30. JOHN signed his name, ELIZABETH
by mark. Wit: JOHN PEARSON, HARREL CAINE, RALPH CAMBELL (also CAMPBELL)
and Pearson attested by "his solemn affirmation" 23 Mar. 1790 bef.
THOS. BLASINGAME, J.P. No rec. date.

Pp 337-339:   19 & 20 Apr. 1785, Lease and Release. GEORGE TAYLOR to
        JOHN BLALOCK, JR., farmer, both of 96 Dist., for 10 sh. and 200
pds sterling, 640 acs. on both sides of People's Creek of Broad River,
including the road that leads to Cherokee Ford on Broad River. Entire
tract granted to sd GEO. TAYLOR by State of S.C. 21 Jan. 1785. Wit:
JOHN BLALOCK, SR. and JOHN FOSTER. George signed by mark (G). Blalock,
Sr. attested on 9 Oct. 1788 bef. JOHN LINDSEY, J.P. Rec. 24 Mar. 1790.

Pp 339-340:   24 Mar. 1790, JOHN McCOOLL and JEAN (JANE) his wife to
        THOMAS BLASINGAME, Esq., all of Union Co., for 26 pds sterling,
lot No. 60 at Union Court House, containing 1/2 ac. Signed by JOHN
McCOOLL only. Wit: WM. DALRYMPLE, SAML. JACKSON. Rec. 25 Mar. 1790.

Pp 340-341:   1 Sept. 1789, SHADRACH LEWELLING as heir apparent of
        MASHACH LLEWELLIN and RUTH LLEWELLIN, widow of MASHACH LLEWELLIN,
to WILLIAM MITCHELL, all of Union Co., for 100 pds sterling, 100 acs.
in the fork of Tyger and Broad Rivers, on Beaverdam branch of Tyger
River. Bound on SW by THOS. GORDON, all other sides vacant when sur-
veyed. Granted to JOHN COLTER (or COTTER) 15 Mar. 1771 by Prov. of
S.C. Signed by SHADRACH LEWELLIN & RUTH (X) LEWELLIN. Wit: JOHN JENKINS,
JOHN BIDDIE, THOMAS BIDDIE. Shadrach ack. conveyance 24 Mar. 1790 bef.
JOHN BIRDSONG, J.P. Rec. 25 Mar. 1790.

Pp 341-342:   11 June 1789, JEDUTHAN PORTER to ELIZABETH HOLMES, both
        of Union Co., for 5 pds sterling, 50 acs. part of a 119 ac. tract
granted to sd PORTER 7 Apr. 1788 and located on S side of Broad River
on branches of Sholey Creek, bound by lands of POLK, GABRIEL ANDERSON,
& HOWARD. The 50 acs. bound by PAULK and HOWARD. Signed by JEDUTHAN
(O) PORTER. Wit: JOHN PALMORE, JOSHUA PAULK, both of whom attested
on 23 June 1789 bef. JOHN BIRDSONG, J.P. No rec. date.

Pp 342-343:   27 Sept. 1787, ZACHARIAH BULLOCK of S.C. to JOHN STEEN
        and ROBT. STEEN, sons of WILLIAM STEEN, planter of Gilkie's Creek
Union Co., for 150 pds sterling, 250 acs. on both sides of Gilkie's
Creek, "being the plantation whereon the sd WM. STEEN now lives." Granted to BULLOCK by N. C. grant. Bound E by JOHN BIRD, S by vacant land,
W by land granted to sd Bullock, now the property of NATHL. JEFFERIES,
N by land supposed to be granted to SAMUEL GILKIE. Conveyed to John
and Robert Steen jointly. Wit: JOHN BIRD, JOSEPH JOLLY. John Bird attested 20 July 1788 bef. THOS. BRANDON and WM. McCULLOCK, Justices
of the Peace. Rec. 25 Mar. 1790.

Pp 343-346:   23 & 24 Feb. 1775, Lease and Release. GEORGE IGLEBERGER,
        planter to THOMAS CLANDENNAN, both of Craven Co., S.C. for 10
sh. and 500 pds current money, 300 acs. in "Craven Co. in 96 Dist.
on S side of Broad River on waters of Fishdam Creek", all sides vacant
when granted to sd IGLEBURGER 23 June 1774 by Prov. of S.C. George
signed GEORGE IGLEBURGER. Wit: ANDREW THOMAS, (illegible-German?) IGLE-
BURGER, JR. and WILLIAM HUTCHENSON who attested on 15th June that he
and ANDREW THOMAS saw GEO. EIGELBERGER (sign). WILLIAM HOUSEAL, J.P.
No recording date. (Note: Surname prob. should be EICHELBERGER.)

545

Pp 346-347:   22 Jan. 1787, EDWARD PRINCE to WILLIAM WOOLBANKS, both
        of Union Co., for 10 sh. sterling, 140 acs. part of a S.C. grant
of 640 acs. to sd PRINCE on 3 Apr. 1786, located on both sides of the
Sparkes Creek, a branch of Fairforest, bound on one side by GILBERD
PRINCE, all other sides vacant when granted. The 140 acs. bound by
sd EDW. PRINCE and sd WM. WOOLBANKS. Signed EDWARD (his mark) PRINCE
and ELIZABETH (X) PRINCE. Wit: JAMES WOODSON, SARAH (G) GIST, GILLUM
(X) WOLBANKS. Capt. JAMES WOODSON attested 7 Apr. 1789 that he, SARAH
GIST and WM. WOOLBANKS saw EDWD. PRINCE and his wife ELIZABETH sign.
THOMAS BRANDON, J.P.

Pp 347-348:   2 Apr. 1787, FRANCES POSEY to NEHEMIAH POSEY, for 100
        pds. sterling to him paid, 429 acs. in Union Co., on S. side
of Broad River on Cain Creek, part of a 529 ac. tract. Mentions a plat
of the 529 ac. tract. Bound by JAMES HOGAN & WILLIAM MOORE, no other
adj. landowners given. Signed by "FRANCES POSEY". Wit: BENJ. (B) HOL-
LINGSWORTH, RUCKER (R) SMITH, JOSHUA MARTIN. Mr. Martin "on his solemn
affirmation sayeth" that FRANCES POSEY as his act and deed signed on
14 Mar. 1789 bef. BERND. GLENN, J.P. No rec. date.

Pp 348-349:   2 Dec. 1788, WILLIAM HORREL and PRESILLAH his wife to
        GEORGE ROWDEN, all of Union Co., for 30 pds sterling, 50½ acs.
part of a tract of 200 acs. granted to AMOS TIMS 26 July 1774 by Prov.
of SC, on S side of Broad River below the Fishdam ford. Bound by WM.
ARMSTRONG, RICHD. GIVINS, Broad River, and vacant land at time of orig.
grant. The 50½ acs. lies bet. WOOD's tract and BENJ. HOLLINGSWORTH
land being part of the original. Signed by both WM. HORRELL and PRES-
CILLAH (X) HORRELL. Wit: NATHAN GLENN, JOSHUA MARTIN, JOSEPH COMER.
Comer solemnly affirmed on 13 Jan. 1789 bef. Bernd. Glenn, J.P. No
recording date.

Pp 349-350:   8 Dec. 1788, NEHEMIAH POSEY to GEORGE ROWDEN, for 100
        pds sterling, 300 acs. in Union Co. on Cain Creek, orig. granted
to FRANCES POSEY by State of S.C., and rec. in Book HHHH, p. 331, it
being part of a larger tract. Bound by JACOB HOLLINGSWORTH, a new line
made by NEHEMIAH POSEY and BENJAMIN POSEY, WM. ARMSTRONG. Signed NEHE-
MIAH (his mark) POSEY. Wit: BENJ. POSEY, JOSHUA MARTIN, WM. STEWART.
Joshua Martin solemnly affirmed 14 Mar. 1789 bef. Bernd. Glenn, J.P.
Rec. 25 Mar. 1790.

Pp 350-351:   8 Dec. 1787, THOMAS SMITH, yeoman of Richmond Co., Ga.,
        to WILLIAM HARDWICK of Union Co., S.C., for 28.10.0 , 50 acs.
in Union Co. in the fork bet. Tyger and Broad Rivers. Part of a larger
tract granted to JOHN GLASS by Prov. of S.C. Bound by the old Saludy
Road, "land I sold to JAMES BEUFORD," STEPHEN CRENSHAW. Thomas signed
his name. Wit: WILLIAM DAWKINS, JAMES TAYLOR, MOLLY (X) HARDWICK. Miss
MOLLY HARDWICK attested on 17 Mar. 1789 bef. Bernd. Glenn. J.P. Rec.
25 Mar. 1790.

Pp 351-352:   2 Sept. 1786, WILLIAM BRYAN, planter and GILEAD, his
        wife, to JOHN LITTLE, all of Union Co., for 10 pds, 37 3/4 acs.
being part of a larger tract, one part laying in a platt that formerly
belonged to MARGARET McDOWELL, and conveyed by lease and release to
PHILIP BRYAN, dec'd., has descended by Heirship to WM. BRYAN, eldest
son and heir at law to the sd PHILIP BRYAN, dec'd. The other part granted to PHILIP BRYAN, dec'd. and fell by heirship to WM. BRYAN. At the
time granted tract was bound by vacant land and JAMES MARTIN. MARGARET
McDOWELL's grant was for 100 acs. dated 25 May 1768, granted by Prov.
of S.C. and rec. in Auditor's Office , Bk. 1, No. 9, p. 240, 29 May
1769, also recorded in (grant) Book EEE, p. 91. PHILIP BRYAN's grant
of 200 acs. dated 2 Feb. 1773, SC grant, rec. in Aud.'s Off. Bk. M,
No. 12, p. 376, 16 Aug. 1773, Grant Bk. 000, p. 486. "One half of the
Gold and Silver mines excepted." Both WILLIAM and GILEAD signed by
mark. Wit: FIELDIN CURTIS, WM. ANDERSON. Both wit. attested 20 June
1789 bef. THOMAS. BRANDON, J.P. No rec. date.

Pp 352-353:   21 Aug. 1789, JNO. McKIBBEN and NANCEY his wife to JEAN
        (JANE) ROGERS, all of Union Co., for 2 pds., Lot No. 5 at Union
Court House, 1/2 ac. Signed JOHN McKIBBEN only. Wit: RICHARD MITCHELL.

Cont'd:
McKIBBEN signed a receipt the same day witnessed by JOHN BIRDSONG.
Recorded 26 Mar. 1790.

Pp 353-354:   4 Dec. 1789, CHARLES JONES of Newberry Co., to WILLIAM
        CLARK of Union Co., for 14.5.8 sterling, 100 acs. granted to
JONES on 16 Sept. 1774 by the Prov. of S.C., located on Morrishes (Morris') Branch, a fork of Fairforest. Grant rec. in Grant Bk. TTT, p.
138. Jones signed his name. Wit: SHADRACH LANTRIP, JAMES YOUNG, JOHN
(X) FINCHER. A receipt signed the same day was wit. by Lantrip, Fincher
and THOMAS YOUNG. Thomas Young and John Fincher attested on 23 Mar.
1790 bef. JOSEPH McJUNKIN, J.P.

Pp 354-355:   29 July 1789, ISAAC EDMONDSON, planter of Union Co.,
        to JAMES CAMPBELL (also CAMBELL), planter of Newberry Co., for
383 pds sterling, 350 acs., four surveys adj. each other, on NE side
of Enoree River, bound by JOHN ADDINGTON, Enoree River and land of
GEORGE McCLAIN's commonly known by the name of Edmondson's Place. It
mentions an orig. grant. Isaac signed his name. Wit: DAVID SMITH, CALEB
EDMONDSON, JOHN CAMPBELL. David Smith and Caleb Edmondson attested
on 20 Apr. 1790 bef. Joseph McJunkin, J.P. No rec. date. A pencil note
at end of the deed says "See also E-120."

        Deed Book E, pp 118-120, shows that on 28 Oct. 1797, JAMES CAMP-
BELL of 96 Dist. sold 425 acs. of this tract to JOHN FINCHER of Pinckney Dist. There was evidently some dispute about the title because
DAVID SMITH of Union Co. attested that ISAAC EDMONDSON sold the tract
to JAMES CAMPBELL; and CALEB EDMUNDSON of Pendleton Co., S.C. attested
that his brother ISAAC EDMUNDSON sold to CAMPBELL. Attestations dated
9 Sept. and 24 Oct. 1796, respectively. Note variation in spelling
of EDMONDSON/EDMUNDSON.

Pp 355-356:   7 Jan. 1790, WILLIAM FARR, Esq. to CALEB GASWAY, both
        of Union Co., for 100 pds sterling, 161 acs. bound by JNO. CLARK,
THOS. HOLLINGSWORTH, ISAAC SIMMISON. Part of a tract granted to WM.
FARR 18 May 1773 by Prov. of S.C. Wit: JAMES GUNNELL, GEORGE PATTERSON,
BERND. GLENN. James Gunnell attested 30 Mar. 1790 bef. Thos. Brandon,
J.P. Rec. 24 Apr. 1790.

Pp 356-357:   30 Mar. 1790, CALEB GASWAY (GASAWAY) to WILLIAM BECKHAM,
        both of Union Co., for 50 pds sterling, 60 acs. of the tract
in deed next above. The 60 acs. bound by sd Beckham, sd Gasway, and
BIRD BOOKER. Signed: CALEB GASAWAY. Wit: WILLIAM FARR, THOS. BRANDON,
GEORGE PATTERSON. Wm. Farr, Esq. attested 30 Mar. 1790 bef. Bernd.
Glenn, J.P. Rec. 24 Apr. 1790.

Pp 357-358:   13 Dec. 1789, JOHN BRANDON to THOMAS VANCE, both of Union
        Co., for 100 guineas, 140 acs. on Brown's Creek, part of a tract
of 300 acs. granted to BROWN 24 Sept. 1753 by Mathew Rowan, then Gov.
of the Prov. of N. C., "by a line run since now So. C.," on the main
fork of Brown's Creek. Sd 300 acs. conveyed by Brown to John Brandon
9 May 1763. Wit: CHRIST. BRANDON, DANL. JACKSON, DAVID KELLOUGH. CHRIS-
TOPHER BRANDON and DANIEL JACKSON both attested on 30 Dec. 1789 bef.
Thos. Brandon, J.P. Rec. 10 May 1790.

Pp 358-360:   27 Feb. 1790, JESSE DODD to JOHN FINCHER, both of Union
        Co., for 150 pds sterling, 300 acs., 100 acs. thereof granted
to ISAAC EDMONDSON, plat and grant rec. in Charleston; remainder of
the 300 acs. being part of a 750 ac. tract conveyed to sd EDMONDSON
by his father, CALEB EDMONDSON on 12 May 1784. Located on N side of
Enoree River. Both tracts conveyed to sd DODD on 23 Sept. 1789. Bound
by the river, JOHN ADDINGTON, other adj. owners not named. Jesse signed
his name. Wit: ANDW. TORRANCE, SAML. SIMPSON, who attested 24 Apr.
1790 bef. Thos. Brandon, J.P. Rec. 17 May 1790.

Pp 360-361:   23 Sept. 1789, ISAAC EDMUNDSON to JESSE DODD, both of
        Union Co., for 150 pds sterling, 300 acs., same tract referred
to in deed next above. Isaac signed his name. Wit: JOHN PEARSON, SR.,
JESSE YOUNG & SARAH PEARSON. Jesse Young attested on 28 Sept. 1789

Cont'd:
before Thomas Brandon, J.P. Rec. 17 May 1790.

Pp 361-362:   5 Feb. 1790, DANL. JACKSON to JOSEPH MEANS, no place
        of residence given, for 40 pds sterling, 50 acs. on S side of
Fairforest Creek, bound by the creek, sd Joseph Means, HUGH MEANS and
sd Jackson. Granted to sd Jackson by State of S.C. on 5 Mar. 1790,
and rec. in Grant Bk. TTTT, p. 65. Signed DANIEL JACKSON. Wit: SAMUEL
JACKSON & SAMUEL CLOUNEY (CLOWNEY). No rec. date.

Page 362:   5 Feb. 1790, SAMUEL JACKSON to JAMES MEANS, for 20 pds
        lawful money of S.C., 50 acs. on S side of Fairforest Creek,
bound by sd Mean's land and RACHEL MEANS. Granted to sd Saml. Jackson
by State of S.C. on 22 Feb. 1787. Signed SAML. JACKSON. Wit: MARK JACK-
SON, JR. & SAML. CLOUNEY. No rec. date.

Pp 363-364:   29 Mar. 1790, RENNY BALLEW, planter, to ZACHARIAN BALLEW,
        planter, both of Union Co., for 70 pds sterling, 100 acs. on
waters of Fairforest, bound by REUBEN BALLEW's dividing line, the original line, JONATHAN PARKER's land. Part of a 250 ac. tract granted to
sd RENNY BALLEW by Prov. of S.C. 5 May 1773 and rec. in Bk. 000, p.
484. Renny signed his name. Wit: WILLIAM MORGAN, MOSES COLLIER, WILLIAM
(W) PLUMMER. Plummer and Collier attested on 28 June 1790 bef. JOHN
BIRDSONG, J.P. Rec. 28 June 1790.

Page 364:   22 June 1790, ESTHER INSCO to HANNAH INSCO, daughter
        of sd ESTHER INSCO, both of Union Co., for love and affection,
100 acs. on waters of Fairforest Creek, part of a 500 ac. tract granted
to JONATHAN PARKER by the Prov. of S.C. 11 Aug. 1774. The 100 acs.
bound by PIERCE BUTLER's land called in the grant HUGHES land, and
the orig. line. Esther signed her name. Wit: MOSES COLLIER, RENNY BELEW,
WM. (W) PLUMMER. Plummer and Collier attested they saw Esther Insco
sign "the with Deed of Gift to Hannah Insco" on 28 June 1790 bef. John
Birdsong, J.P. No rec. date.

Pp 365-366:   29 Mar. 1790, RENY BELEW, planter, to REUBEN BELOEW,
        both of Union Co., for 20 pds sterling, 100 acs. on waters of
Fairforest, bound by JONATHAN PARKER's land, the old line, the dividing line of ZACHA. BELOW's land. Part of the 250 ac. grant to RENNY
BELEW referred to in the deed second above. Same wit's and dates.
        (Note: JONATHAN PARKER referred to in these deeds was deceased,
and according to Abstracts of Old Ninety-Six and Abbeville District
Wills and Bonds by Young, his estate was administered in old 96 Dist.,
by AARON FINCHER, WM. PLUMER & MOSES COLLYER in 1784.)

Pp 366-367:   10 Jan. 1789, JOHN HAMMELTON to JOHN BANKHEAD, both of
        S.C., for 20 pds sterling, 18 acs. in 96 Dist. on W side of Broad
River, part of a tract belonging to HAMMELTON, bound on one side by
the river. Signed JOHN HAMILTON. Wit: ROBERT GOODE, JAMES BANKHEAD.
Robert Goode attested in Union Co. 11 Dec. 1789 bef. WILLIAM HENDLEY,
J.P. No rec. date.

Page 367:   28 June 1790, RALPH JACKSON to JOHN PUTMAN, both of Union
        Co. for 20 pds sterling, 100 acs. on branches of Sugar Creek
granted to sd Jackson by Prov. of S.C. 16 Sept. 1774 and lying in Union
Co. Ralph Jackson signed his name. Wit: ANDREW TORRENCE, WILLIAM SMITH.
Rec. same day.

Pp 368-370:   4 & 5 June 1790, Lease and Release. JOHN HAILE and RUTH
        his wife to THOMAS DRAPER, SR. all of Union Co., for 1 shilling
and 100 pds sterling, 289 acs. all of a tract granted by the Prov.
of North Carolina to sd John Haile. Located on Clark's Mill Creek,
a branch of Pacolet River, about half-mile above where the old path
crossed which leads from Clark's Old Field on Pacolet to Fairforest.
Bound on one side by THOMAS DRAPER and including the plantation where
JOHN HAILE formerly lived on Mill Creek. Signed by both JOHN & RUTH
HAILE. Wit: RICHARD MITCHELL, JOHN BECKHAM, JR. Rec. 28 June 1790.

Pp 370-371:   20 Feb. 1790, ANDREW JONES planter and PHEBY his wife
        of Pendleton Co. to WILLIAM LIPSCOMB, JR. of Union Co., Pacolet

Cont'd:
River, for 130 pds Virginia money, 150 acs. on both sides of Thicketty
and Joneses Creek the N side of Thicketty, bound by NUCHOLS, SAML.
SHIPPEY & JOHN THOMPSON, it being 1/2 of a 300 ac. grant to JOS. JOHN-
STON. Andrew Jones signed his name, Phebe's signature not on deed.
Wit: PHILEMON MARTIN, JOHN SHIPPEY, SAML. SHIPPEY. Proved by Martin
7 Apr. 1790 bef. ZACHARIAH BULLOCK, J.P. Rec. 28 June 1790.

Pp 371-372:   13 Mar. 1790, WILLIAM MITCHELL and ELLENDER his wife
        of 96 Dist., to ISAAC COOK of same place, for 70 pds sterling,
100 acs. in the fork bet. Tyger and Broad Rivers on a small branch
of Tyger called Beaverdam Branch, bound SW by THOMAS GORDON, all other
sides vacant when granted to JOHN COULTER in 1771. Signed WILLIAM (X)
MITCHELL, ELLENDER (M) MITCHELL. Wit: WILLIAM HINDMAN, AMOS COOK, SETH
WILSON. Rec. 28 June 1790.

Pp 372-373:   3 June 1789, JOHN LITTLE, planter to FEDERICK (sic) JONES
        planter, both of Union Co. for 14 pds sterling lawful money of
S.C., 100 acs. part of a tract of 289 acs. granted to sd John Little
by the State of S.C. 7 Aug. 1786 and rec. in Bk. NNNN, p. 361. The
100 acs. bound by JOHN BLASINGAME, the orig. line, HAINSWORTH's branch,
JOHN LITTLE and WINNEFORD his wife, etc...John signed his name, Winne-
ford by mark (X). Wit: ELISHA BOND, WILLIAM ANDERSON, WM. (W) PLUMMER.
Proved by Plummer and Anderson 28 June 1790 bef. Thos. Blasingame,
J.P. Jno. Little signed a receipt on 3 June 1790. No rec. date.

Page 374:   28 June 1790, JOHN MURRELL, carpenter to ARCHER HOWARD
        planter, both of Union Co. for 10 pds sterling, 70 acs. granted
to John Murrell by the State of S.C. 2 Nov. 1789 in the fork bet. Tyger
and Fairforest Creek, bound by NEHEMIAH HOWARD, JAMES HARRISON & RALPH
JACKSON. Plat and grant rec. in Bk. A, No. 5, p. 124. Wit: ROBT. WALL-
ACE, ROBT. SMITH, STEPHEN HOWARD. Proved by all three wit. 28 June
1790 bef. John Birdsong, J.P. No rec. date.

Pp 375-377::   18 Dec. 1788, Lease and Release. JOHN BLASINGAME to THOMAS
        BEARDEN, both of Union Co. for 100 pds sterling, 300 acs. granted
to JOHN BLASINGAME, JR. 21 Jan. 1785 by S.C. grant, located on Salleys
Creek, waters of Fairforest, Union Co., bound NE and SW by LITTLEFIELD's
land, all other sides vacant. Signed JOHN & OBEDIENCE BLASINGAME, both
by mark (X). Wit: RALPH JACKSON, WM. BLASINGAME, HUMPHREY GRANT. Rec.
29 June 1790.

Pp 377-378:   4 Mar. 1785, WILLIAM JOLLEY and FRANCES his wife to WIL-
        LIAM McCULLOCH all of 96 Dist., SC, for 100 guineas, 200 acs
on the waters of Thickety and Guilkies Creeks, within a little of where
of sd creeks joins into one. Part of a grant to JOSEPH JOLLEY, SR.
in 1767 on N side of Thicketty Creek, bound by JOHN HOPE, the Thicketty Creek, ROBT. LUSK, JAMES BROWN and Guilkies Creek. WILLIAM & FRAN-
CES were "seized of a good sure perfect and indefeasible estate of
Inheritance" to the premises. Signed WILLIAM JOLLY & FRANCES (X) JOLLY.
Wit: JOSEPH JOLLEY, SR., JAMES JOLLEY & SARAH (X) JOLLEY. Proved by
James Jolley 18 Mar. 1790 bef. Wm. Hendley, J.P. Rec. 30 June 1790.

Pp 379-380:   24 Dec. 1789. JOHN McCOOL and JANE his wife to ALLEN
        HOLLAND, all of Union Co. for 100 pds sterling, 100 acs. on waters
of Fairforest and Brown's Creek, part of a 460 ac. grant to sd McCool
by letters patent 1 May 1786 by State of S.C. Mentions WALTER HOLMES'
line. Signed: JOHN McCOOLL (only). Wit: THOMAS BRANON (BRANDON), JOHN
BRANDON, HENRY HUGHEY. McCooll signed a receipt the same day wit. by
WM. DALRYMPLE & JNO. BRANDON. Plat drawn by BERND. GLENN, D.S. 21 Dec.
1789 also recorded. Rec. 30 June 1790.

Pp 380-381:   22 Sept. 1790. SHADRACH LEWALLEN as an heir apparent
        of MESHACK LEWALLEN, dec'd. and RUTH LEWALLEN to WILLIAM HARD-
WICK, all of Union Co., for 200 pds sterling, 250 acs. where GEO. HARD-
WICK now lives in the fork of Broad and Tyger Rivers on a branch of
Tyger called Bogan's Creek, bound by land laid out to BROWN, JAMES
SIMS, BRUMMET's land and ASHFORD. Granted to Meshack Lewallen by S.C.
19 Aug. 1774. Signed SHADRACH LEWALLEN, RUTH (X) LEWALLEN. Wit: M.
(or W.) HARDWICK, GARD. HARDWICK, GEO. HARDWICK. Rec. 27 Sept. 1790.

(Note: RUTH LEWALLEN (LLEWELLIN) was the widow of MASHACH LLEWELL-
IN and not SHADRACH's wife, as it might appear by a casual glance at
the preceeding deed. See Book B, pp. 340-341.)

Pp 382-383:   27 July 1790. WILLIAM LITTLEFIELD to LENARD SMITH both
        of Union Co. for 14.6.0 sterling, 100 acs. part of a 200 ac.
grant to THOMAS BROWN by S.C. 8 Sept. 1772, on a branch of Sugar Creek,
bound S by vacant land, E by JAMES BLASINGAME, N by Widow LITTLEFIELD,
W by THOMAS PALMER. Conveyed by Brown to WILLIAM WOFFORD and by Wofford
to WM. LITTLEFIELD, SR., dec'd., by death of sd WILLIAM LITTLEFIELD,
SR. descended by heirship to JOHN LITTLEFIELD, eldest son and heir
at law of sd Wm. Littlefield, dec'd. conveyed by John Littlefield to
WM. LITTLEFIELD, JR., and from him to LEONARD SMITH. William signed
his name. Wit: JAMES SAUNDERS, NICHOLAS KEALING (KEATING?). Rec. 27
Sept. 1790.

Pp 383-384:   10 Mar. 1790, CHARLES BROWNING, planter, and POLLY, his
        wife, to PETER LAURENCE, planter, both of Union Co., for 14 pds
sterling, 100 acs. on waters of Mitchell's creek of Fairforest, part
of a 614 ac. grant to sd Charles Browning 14 June 1787 by State of
S.C. and rec. in Bk. TTTT. Signed CHARLES BROWNING (only). Wit: JOHN
LITTLE, WILLIAM ANDERSON. Proved by both wit. 25 Sept. 1790 bef. Thos.
Brandon, J.P. Rec. 27 Sept. 1790.

Pp 384-385:   31 July 1790. FRANCIS WHILCHEL, SR. and FRANCIS WHEL-
        CHEL, JR. to JOHN JEFFERIES all of Union Co., for 106 pds, 150
acs. on S side of Gilkie's Creek, branch of Thicketty, waters of Broad
river. Granted by SC 21 Jan. 1785, plat thereof cert. 9 June 1784.
Does not state to whom granted. Signed by FRANCIS WHELCHEL, SR., FRANCIS
WHELCHEL, JR. and ANNY WHELCHEL. Wit: JAMES JEFFERIES, MATHEW (X) ROB-
INSON, JOHN LEFEVER (his mark). Rec. 27 Sept. 1790.

Page 385:   28 Nov. 1789. JAMES TOWNSEND and MARTHA his wife to JERE-
        MIAH O'CAIN, all of Union Co., for 5 pds sterling, 234 acs. part
of a 434 ac. grant to James Townsend 21 Jan. 1785 on waters of Tyger
River. Signed JAMES TOWNSEND, MARTHA (mark) TOWNSEND. Wit: JAMES CALWELL
(CALDWELL), RICHARD GIBSON, JAMES CALDWELL, JR. Receipt for 5 pds sterl.
this could be a deed of gift. No rec. date.

Page 386:   24 June 1790, JAMES CARVEAL (should be JAMES CARR VEALE)
        and LEVINA his wife to AMOS COOK, all of Union Co., for 65 pds
current money of SC, 140 acs. on Ned's Creek a branch of Broad River
on SW side of Broad River, part of a tract whereon JAMES CARVEAL and
LEVINA his wife now live. Signed JAMES CARVEAL, LEVINA (L) CARVEAL.
Wit: BENJ. HAWKINS, MARTHA (X) HAWKINS, THOMAS (X) MOORE. Rec. 27 Sept.
1790.
        (Note: JAMES CARR VEALE was associated with several Quaker fami-
lies in Union Co., and may have been of the Quaker faith himself. According to Goodspeed's History of Knox and Daviess Co's Ind., James
C. Veale took up land in Knox Co. in 1807 and operated a sawmill on
Veale's Creek in Veale Township. He disappeared from Union Co. records
about this same time - probably the same man. The HAWKINS family moved
to Daviess Co., Ind. about the same time. Other records show Veale's
name as JAMES CARR VEALE.)

Page 387:   THOMAS BRANDON, Esq., to THOMAS HIGHTOWER, both of Union
        Co. for 10 pds lawful money of S.C., 400 acs. whereon sd Thomas
Hightower now lives, part of a 1200 ac. tract granted to sd Thomas
Brandon 6 Nov. 1786 and rec. in Sec. Office, Book OOOO, p. 299. Wit:
JEREMIAH LUCAS, JOHN OSLING, THOS. WILLIAMS. Proved by John Osling
8 Mar. 1790 bef. CHARLES SIMS, J.P. Rec. 27 Sept. 1790. Deed dated
14 Aug. 1789.

Pp 387-388:   20 July 1790, WM. WILLIAMS, farmer to ISAAC WHITE , farmer
        both of Union Co., for divers good causes and 5 pds current money
of SC, 400 acs. bound by THOMAS WILLIAMS, a branch, lands of THOMAS
BRANDON, Esq., lands of SEMCOCK CANNON, Long's old road, JOHN WHITE,
lands surveyed for WM. FARR, Esq. Williams signed his name. Wit: WILLIAM
DAWKINS LANE, SAMUEL SMITH. Rec. 27 Sept. 1790.

Pp 388-389: "Sixth day of the Third Month or March" (Quakers) 1790,
     AMOS COOK and ELIZABETH his wife to JOHN COOK, all of 96 Dist.,
for 80 pds current money of S.C., 100 acs. in Union Co. on Tinker's
Creek, a small branch of Tyger River, waters of Broad River, in the
fork bet. Broad and Saludy Rivers, bound on SE by HENRY KINGSBERRY's
land, other sides vacant at time of orig. grant. Mentions plat annexed
to grant - does not say whether grant was issued by S.C. or N.C. but
does state that tract was granted to AMOS COOK in 1774. Amos signed
his name. Elizabeth by mark (X). Wit: WILLIAM HYNDMAN, JOHN WILSON,
MARY COOK. Rec. 27 Sept. 1790.

Pp 389-390: 30 Oct. 1789. JAMES WRIGHT of Laurens Co., to BAZEL WHEAT
of Union, for 57 pds current money, 130 acs. on Dining Creek, bound
at present by BENJ. HOLCOM's (HOLCOMB) land, JOSEPH LITTLE's land,
WM. BRANDON's land and the sd WHEAT's land. Part of 150 acs. granted
to BENJ. THOMPSON by patent 20 Aug. 1767. Wright signed his name. Wit:
WILLIAM WHITE, ABEL WHITE, SAML. SIMPSON. Rec. 27 Sept. 1790.

Pp 390-391: 22 Mar. 1790, THOMAS BLASINGAME, Esq. to JOHN HAM, planter
     both of Union Co., for 200 pds sterling, 400 acs. on Salley's
branch of Fairforest below the old boundary line, bound SE by McBEE,
NW by LITTLEFIELD, all other sides vacant. Granted to sd Thomas Blasingame by the State of S.C. 25 Jan. 1785 and rec. in Grant Bk. AAAA,
p. 380. THOMAS BLASINGAME and FRANCES his wife convey, etc. Signed
by Thos. Blasingame and FANNY (mark) BLASINGAME. Wit: AMOS MARTIN,
THOS. BLASINGAME, JR., JACOB HAM. Rec. 27 Sept. 1790.

Pp 391-392: 11 June 1790, THOMAS MILES to JOHN PETER SARTOR, both
     of Union Co., for 120 pds sterling, 461½ acs. on branches of
Kain (Cane) and Lower Fish Dam Creeks, bound by CLENDENAN, BISHOP,
vacant land, LEVY HOLLINGSWORTH, JAMES HAWKINS, Col. FARR and THOMAS
COX. Part of a tract granted to WM. FARR by State of S.C. 3 Apr. 1786,
conveyed by Farr to Miles 29 Dec. 1788. Miles signed his name. Wit:
WILLIAM SARTOR, WILEY (X) WRIGHT, ANNEY (X) SARTOR. ANNEY also shown
as ANN SARTOR. Wiley Wright attested by oath on 27 Sept. 1790 bef.
Wm. Kennedy, J.P. Rec. 28 Sept. 1790.

Pp 392-394: 14 May 1790. THOMAS MILES and ELIZABETH his wife to JOHN
     PETER SARTOR, both of Union Co., for 110.12.04 sterling, 300
acs. where the sd Thomas Miles now lives, commonly called the Cross
Roads. Part of a 640 ac. tract granted to Col. WM. FARR by State of
S.C. 15 Oct. 1784 and the 300 acs. conveyed by Farr to sd Thomas Miles
24 Dec. 1787. Bound by RICHD. COX, THOMAS COX, WM. HOLLINGSWORTH, NATHAN
GLENN, across the Ninety-Six Road. Thomas and Elizabeth both signed
their names. Wit: SUSANNAH UNDERWOOD, WILEY (X) WRIGHT, RD. (RICHARD)
COX. Proved by Wiley Wright by oath 27 Sept. 1790 bef. Wm. Kennedy,
J.P. Rec. 28 Sept. 1790.

Pp 394-395: 17 Oct. 1789, THOMAS BRANDON of Union Co. to JAMES JOHN-
     STONE (also JOHNSON) of Spartain (Spartanburg) Co., for 28 pds
sterling, 350 acs. part of a 2400 ac. grant to Brandon by State of
S.C. 3 Apr. 1787, rec. in Grant Bk. WWWW, p. 289. Located on waters
of Fannons (Fanning's) Creek, Sandy Run, and head of Portman's Creek.
The 350 acs. is on Fanning's Creek. Wit: ISHAM FOSTER, JEREMIAH LUCAS,
THOS. HIGHTOWER. Foster attested by oath 16 OCt. 1789 bef. Charles
Sims, J.P. Rec. 28 Sept. 1790.

Pp 395-396: 30 July 1790. WILLIAM FARR, Sheriff of Union Co, to HUM-
     PHREY BATES of Union Co. JOSEPH BATES owned 200 acs. which fell
by heirship to sd JOSEPH BATES, JR. by his father JOSEPH BATES, SR.,
deceased, bound on all sides by vacant land. In the Dec. term of Court
1789, HUMPHREY BATES obtained a judgment against JOSEPH BATES for 76.14.
5 sterling for damages and debt. On 1 Jan. 1790 the clerk of court
issued a writ of Fieri Facias directing the Sheriff to levy on the
goods, chattels and real estate of Joseph Bates for the sum of 76.14.5.
Joseph Bates' tract of land described above sold at public auction
27 Feb. 1790 and was purchased by Humphrey Bates for 75 pds sterling,
high bid. Farr makes title to Humphrey Bates. Wit: RICHARD MITCHELL,
ANDREW TORENCE, WM. COLEMAN. Ack. & rec. 28 Sept. 1790.

Pp 396-399:   25 Aug. 1777. Lease and Release. JOHN WOFFORD and MARY
        his wife to ISOM CLAYTON, all of Union Co, for 10 sh. and 250
pds current money of S.C., 300 acs. on Sugar Creek, waters of Fairforest. Bound by PETER RENFROW, JAMES McKOY, JAS. BETTERTON and vacant
lands. Entire tract had been granted to JOHN WOFFORD 17 Feb. 1773 by
the Gov. of S.C. Tract was now in actual possession of Isom Clayton.
Both John and Mary signed, Mary by mark (X). Wit: RALPH SMITH, ISAAC
BOGAN, WM. BRATCHER who attested by oath 10 Aug. 1790 bef. Thos. Brandon, J.C. Rec. 28 Sept. 1790.

Pp 399-400:   24 Jan. 1790, DAVID HOPKINS (error?) to RICHARD WATERS,
        BOTH OF Union Co., for 50 pds sterling, 190 acs. on both sides
of Polecatt Branch, bound by SAML. HENDERSON, bounded on CHARLES WOODS
being part of sd tract containing 498 acs. Mentions a plat and grant.
Sd DAVID ROBINSON renounced all claim, etc. to sd land for himself,
his heirs, etc. Signed by DAVID ROBINSON and JANE (X) ROBINSON. Wit:
JAS. HENDERSON, MOSES WATERS who made oath that David Robinson and
his wife Jane signed. Attestation made 29 Sept. 1790 bef. Thomas Brandon, J.C. Rec. same day.
        (Note: DAVID HOPKINS was a well-known deputy surveyor who lived
in Chester Co. and who owned land in both Chester and Union Co's. The
clerk who recorded the above deed may have had a "slip of memory" when
he entered DAVID HOPKINS' name - DAVID ROBINSON was evidently the grant-
or since he signed the deed.)

Pp 400-401:   21 Aug. 1790. JOHN LITTLE and WINNEFRED his wife to JAMES
        WOODSON, JR., all of Union Co., for 14 pds sterling, 30 acs.
on N side of Fairforest Creek, part of a 58 ac. tract lying on both
sides of Fairforest, bound S by land formerly claimed by SAML. GRAY,
W by JOHN LITTLE. Grant dated 17 Nov. 1785 and rec. in Charleston.
Fairforest Creek to be the dividing line. Both John and Winnefred signed.
Wit: JAMES WOODSON, SR., ROBERT WOODSON. Proved by Jas. Woodson, Sr.
on 29 Sept. 1790 bef. Thomas Brandon, J.C. Rec. 30 Sept. 1790.

Pp 401-402:   26 Dec. 1790. The release of a Lease and Release. JONATHAN
        PENNELL and MIMA his wife to ZACHARIAH NANCE, all of Union Co.,
for 100 pds sterling, 150 acs. on Sugar Creek of Fairforest, bound
by HARDEN's land, THOS. ADAMS and vacant land. Granted to WM. LINDSAY
by the State of S.C. 21 Jan. 1785, conveyed to THACKER VERNON (VIVION?)
and thence to JONATHAN PENNELL. Both Jonathan and Mima signed, she
by mark (X). Wit: NICHOLAS KEATING, HERMON HOWARD. Ack. 27 Dec. 1790.
No recording date.

Pp 402-403:   THOMAS PALMORE, SR., planter of Union Co. for love, good
        will and affection to his son WILLIAM PALMORE, planter same place,
130 acs. in fork bet. two roads, one of which leads through WOFFORD's
old field on Sugar Creek of Fairforest, the other leads to the lower
ford on sd creek, being part of a tract whereon the sd Thomas Palmore
now lives. Had been granted to JOHN LITTLE and conveyed by Little to
sd Thomas Palmore. Dated 10 May 1789. Wit: DUNCAN McCREVIN, DANL. PAL-
MORE, NICHOLAS KEATING. Ack. and rec. 27 Dec. 1790.

Pp 403-404:   10 Aug. 1790. CHARLES SIMS, Esq. to REUBEN WILKS, planter
        for 100 pds sterling, 100 acs. part of a tract which was laid
out to WILLIAM SIMS, bound by PINCKNEY's line on three sides, no other
adj. owners given. Charles Sims had apparently sold the land to Wilks
under bond for title in Nov. 1787 and was now giving him a deed. Signed
CHARLES SIMS & SEBELLOW SIMS who stated that she released her right
and dower with her husband Charles Sims. Wit: HUGH THOMAS, WM. HALL,
WM. WILLIAMS. Ack. in open court and rec. 27 Dec. 1790.
        (Note: SEBELLOW (ISABELLA) SIMS, wife of CHARLES SIMS, was ISA-
BELLA BOWLES before her marriage to Charles Sims. The SIMS and BOWLES
families moved to S. C. from Hanover Co., Va.)

Pp 404-405:   10 Aug. 1790, CHARLES SIMS, Esq. of Union Co. to ANN
        VEAL, same place, for 100 pds, 208 acs. the remainder of that
tract laid out for WILLIAM SIMS whereon GABL. BROWN formerly lived,
located on the N fork of Neel's Creek, bound on one side the tract
sold to REUBEN WILKS (see deed next above). Signed: CHARLES & SEBILLOW

Cont'd:
SIMS who released dower with her husband CHARLES SIMS. Wit: HUGH THOMAS,
WM. HALL, WM. WILLIAMS. Charles Sims signed a receipt on the same day
to Miss ANN VEAL. Ack. in court and rec. 27 Dec. 1790.

Pp 405-406:   4 Feb. 1790. THOMAS BRANDON to ABNER WELLS both of Union
        Co., for 30 pds sterling, 359 acs. on the main fork of Fannin's
Creek, part of a 2403 ac. S.C. grant to sd Col. Thos. Brandon dated
3 Apr. 1787, on waters of Fannin's Creek, Portman's Creek, and Sandy
Run, rec. in Grant Bk. WWWW, p. 289. Signed by THOS. BRANDON, J.P.
Wit: CHARLES SIMS, JOHN POPHAM, AUGUSTIN WOOD. Proved by Sims 12 Feb.
1790 bef. Thomas Brandon, J.P. Rec. 27 Dec. 1790.

Pp 406-407:   30 Oct. 1790, Col. WILLIAM FARR to JOHN UNDERWOOD, planter
        both of Union Co., for 40 pds current money of S.C., 100 acs.
on Lower Fishdam Creek, bound by CLENDENON's land, vacant land, MAGNESS
SIMESON's land, and Col. FARR's land. Part of a tract granted to Farr
by State of S.C. 3 Apr. 1786. Wit: RICHARD FARR, CALEB GASWAY. Receipt
shows 30 pds consideration. Ack. in open court by sd William Farr and
rec. 27 Dec. 1790.
        (Note: Col. WILLIAM FARR moved to the area that later became
Union Co., S. C., before the Revolution, from Mecklenburg Co., N. C.
and apparently was the same William Farr who was the son of RICHARD
FARR, SR., of the New River settlement of Onslow Co., N.C.

Pp 408-409:   28 Dec. 1790. JOHN McWHORTER to JOHN JASPER both of Union
        Co., for 45 Spanish dollars, 45 acs. on S side of Pacolate River
bound by the river and sd JASPER. Granted to sd McWhorter on 3 May
1790 by the State of S.C. Signed JOHN McWHORTER, ELIZ̲T̲H (her mark)
McWHORTER. Wit: ADAM POTTER, GEO. McWHORTER, PETER RAGSDALE. Rec. same
day.

Pp 409-412:   13 & 14 Aug. 1781. Lease and Release. JOHN McWHORTER
        of 96 Dist., SC to JOHN JASPER, same place for 10 sh. and 400
pds sterling current money of S.C., 120 acs. (also known as 121 acs.)
on S side of Pacolate River, whereon JOHN McWHORTER now lives, part
of a 200 ac grant to JOHN PORTMAN by Prov. of S.C. 13 Oct. 1765 and
conveyed by lease and release to sd McWhorter 21 Sept. 1775. Grant
was on both sides of Pacolate River. Signed JOHN McWHORTER, MARY (X)
McWHORTER (also McWHORTO̲R). Wit: NICHOLAS JASPER, BENJ. COVENHOVEN,
JOHN GEORGE. Receipt dated 30 Aug. 1781. Proved by Nicholas Jasper
29 Dec. 1781 bef. ROBERT LUSK, J.P. Jasper stated that John McWhorter
and his wife Mary signed.
        (Note: In the two deeds above, either one man named John McWhorter
had two wives named Elizabeth and Mary or there were two men named
John McWhortor. Re the JASPER family, the following letter appeared
in "The Union Daily Times", Union Co., S.C. several years ago, addressed
to the editor of the paper:
        This letter is in regard to the JASPER FAMILY, one of
Union County and my ancestors. I am now compiling another manuscript
and hoping to get in touch with any of the JASPER descendants living
in South Carolina.
        I have documented records of our immigrant ancestor up
to and including JOHN JASPER who went from Virginia to Union County.
The famous Sgt. WILLIAM JASPER was one of this family. My ancestor
was his brother, NICHOLAS JASPER who went to Kentucky.
        Whether I should ask you to place a notice in your paper
for my needs or just what should be done, I am not at all sure, but
the following are the needs:
        Records of descendants of RACHEL JASPER who married BEN-
JAMIN COWNOVER (COVENHOVEN) spelled both ways in documents, also descendants of NANCY JASPER, who married JAMES THOMAS MOSELEY, and CHARITY
JASPER, who married JOHN HAMES. These people all lived in Union Co.
prior to 1800.
                        Yours very truly
                        NANCY R. ROY
                        1174 East Main St., Sp. 52
                        El Cajon, CA 92021
        JOHN JASPER, SR. died in Union Co. in 1799 and named in his will
his wife (no name given) and "my children which are now living, to

Cont'd:
wit, NICHOLAS, JOHN, RACHEL, ANNA, HANNAH and CHARITY", as well as
"the Children that are dead, or their heirs."
     The son, JOHN, JR. died in 1811 without issue, leaving his estate
to his wife SUKY (SUSANNAH) JASPER, his brother NICHOLAS JASPER, nephew
JOHN JASPER, and nephew JOHN GEORGE. John's mother was still living
when he made his will in 1805 because he stated that his mother was
to be maintained and supported during her life.
     It is apparent from JOHN, JR.'s will that one of his sisters
married ____? GEORGE. There was a family with the surname GEORGE living
in Union Co. during this period.
     Sgt. WILLIAM JASPER, mentioned in Ms. Roy's letter, was a hero
of the Battle of Ft. Moultrie in Charleston harbor in 1776. He was
killed during the seige of Savannah later in the war.)

Pp 412-414:   20 Nov. 1790. JOSEPH PEARSON, planter, and ELIZABETH
          PEARSON, his wife of State of S.C., to JOHN and JAMES McKIBBIN
of co. and state afsd. (Union Co.?) for 60 pds sterling, 100 acs. lying
and being orig. in Craven Co. on the middle fork of Brown's Creek S
of Broad River, granted by letters patent to RICHD. BRANDON by Gov.
of Prov. of S.C., conveyed by sd Brandon to WILLIAM KENNEDY, and by
Kennedy to Joseph Pearson. Signed JOS. PEARSON & ELIZABETH (P) PEARSON.
Wit: WM. KENNEDY, CHRISTOPHER BRANDON. Proved by Wm. Kennedy 28 Dec.
1790 bef. Thomas Brandon, J.P. and rec. same day.

Pp 414-415:   1 Mar. 1785, WM. MAYFIELD, heir at law to JOHN MAYFIELD
          of Union Co., to Col. THOMAS BRANDON, same place, for 50 pds,
300 acs. granted to JACOB BROWN by Prov. of N.C., 24 Sept. 1754 and
conveyed to JOHN MAYFIELD by deed dated 2 Aug. 1770. Plat and grant
rec. in Sec. Office in N.C. Land was found to be in the state of S.C.,
96 Dist., Union Co., on the main fork of Brown's Creek below the Creek
Shoals. WM. MAYFIELD signed by mark. Wit: DUNCAN McCREVAN, CHARLES
(mark) CRAIN, JOHN McCOOLL. Rec. 28 Dec. 1790.
     (Note: The witness DUNCAN McCREVAN was the brother-in-law of
the witness JOHN McCOOL. Duncan McCrevan married JANE McCOOL, daughter
of ADAM McCOOL who lived in Chester Co., S.C. but whose will is filed
in Union Co. probably because his son JOHN McCOOL was executor and
John was living in Union Co. at the time.)

Pp 415-416:   "25 day of the Twelfth month" 1790. WILLIAM EDMONDSON
          to WALTER ROBERTS, both of Union Co., for 30 pds Virginia money,
100 acs. on the waters of Enoree River adj. JOHN ADDINGTON, JOHN GARROTT,
JOHN MARTINDALE, "and the plantation whereon the sd WALTER ROBERTS
now liveth." Signed by WILLIAM EDMONDSON & SARAH EDMONDSON. Wit: JOSEPH
ROBERDS, JOHN FINCHER who attested by oath 28 Dec. 1790 that Wm. Edmondson and wife signed. CHARLES SIMS, J.P. Rec. same day.

Pp 416-417:   28 Mar. 1791, WILLIAM SMITH, carpenter, to OLIVE SMITH,
          both of Union Co., for 15 pds sterling, 150 acs. part of a larger
tract granted to WILLIAM SMITH by the State of S.C. 3 Mar. 1788. Bound
by ISAAC COOK, JOHN WILSON, ELI COOK, NATHAN HAWKINS and land granted
to WM. SMITH. "OLIVE SMITH", her heirs, etc...." William signed by
mark(X). Wit: JOHN HAILE who proved the deed on same day bef. JOHN
PEARSON, J.P. Rec. same day.

Pp 417-418:   9 June 1789. SAMUEL PATTON to WILLIAM YOUNG, planters,
          both of Union Co., for 25 pds sterling, 100 acs. on Mitchell's
Creek of Fairforest, granted to sd Patton by the State of S.C. 6 Mar.
1786. Wit: ARTHER CUNNINGHAM, JOSEPH MEANES. Proved by Cunningham on
23 June 1789 bef. HUGH MEANES, Justice of the County. Rec. 28 Mar.
1791.

Pp 418-419:   6 Nov. 1790. MOSES GUITON to JOHN CRITTENDEN, both of
          Union Co., for 100 pds sterling, 169 acs. on Abiton (Abbington's)
Creek bound by JOHN ARNSTON. "LEDBETTER's now NICHOLAS CURRAY's line,"
JNO. LEEK. Surveyed in 1785 and granted in 1786 to sd Moses Guiton,
it being the same land as was transferred to the sd Guiton by bond
first from JNO. ROBINSON to me GREER, etc...MOSES GUITON and TABITHA
his wife doth covenent, convey, etc....Both Moses and Tabitha signed.
Wit: ISAAC PARKER, SAML. DAVIDSON, WILLIAM (X) TAYLOR. Proved by David-

Cont'd:
son on 6 Nov. 1790 bef. WM. McCULLOCH, J.P. Rec. 28 Mar. 1791.

Pp 419-420:   25 Nov. 1786, JOSEPH BREED of Wilks (sic) Co., Ga., to
          JORDON JACKSON of Union Co., S.C. for 15 pds sterling, 100 acs.
on a branch of Fairforest Creek, bounded on all sides by vacant land
(when granted?). Granted to JOSEPH BREED of 96 Dist. on 23 Oct. 1765
by " His Majesty". Signed JOSEPH BREED, CATHERINE BREED. Wit: DANL.
JACKSON, WILLIAM BREED, ANN (X) BRASEL (also spelled BRAZIL). Proved
by Jackson 17 Dec. 1790 bef. HUGH MEANES, J.P. Rec. 28 Mar. 1791.

Pp 420-421:   16 Mar. 1791. JOHN NEEL to JAMES MOORE, both of Union
          Co., for 10 pds sterling, 266 acs. on Simpson's Branch of Foster's
Mill Creek in the counties of Union and Spartanburgh. Bound by SAML.
SIMPSON, ROBERT HARRIS, GEORGE STORY, JOSEPH NESBITT & CRUCE. Signed
by mark. Wit: ADAM POTTER & WM. DALEFIELD. Rec. 4 Apr. 1791.

Pp 421-422:   8 Jan. 1791, ROBERT THOMPSON to JOHN EASTERWOOD both
          of Union Co. for 100 pds sterling, 200 acs. on S side of Paco-
late River, including the plantation whereon LAURENCE EASTERWOOD now
lives. Signed by mark. Wit: ADAM POTTER, THOMAS DEAN, NEHEMIAH NORTON.
Rec. 4 Apr. 1791.

Pp 422-423:   7 Dec. 1790, JOHN WHITE and MARGET his wife to WILLIAM
          WHITE, all of Union Co. for divers good causes but especially
for 20 pds current money of S.C., one tract of land on the middle fork
of Brown's Creek, granted to WILLIAM AKERRIDGE in 1774. (N half) (sic)
containing 150 acs. the sd JOHN WHITE and MARGET his wife reserving
to themselves 75 acs. on both sides of the creek adj. WM. WILLIAMS,
ISAAC WHITE and JOHN WHITE, SR. Signed JOHN WHITE & MARGET (X) WHITE.
Wit: JNO. WHITE, FANNY (X) WHITE, ISAAC WHITE. Rec. 4 Apr. 1791.

Pp 423-424:   26 Jan. 1791, JOHN WHITE, SR. and MARGET his wife to
          JOHN WHITE, all of Union Co., same consideration and description
(which is not clear) as in deed next above, 150 acs. - mentions a corner
not yet made but agreed upon...bound by WM. WHITE, WILLIAM WILLIAMS
and sd JOHN WHITE. Wit: DANIEL WHITE, ABNER WELLS. Rec. 4 Apr. 1791.

Pp 424-426:   1 & 2 Mar. 1791, Lease and Release. FRANCES BREMAR of
          Charleston City, S.C., Surveyor General to ADAM SCANE of the
waters of Broad River in sd state, farmer, for 5 sh. and 40 pds current
money of sd state, 200 acs. in Camden Dist., in the fork bet. Broad
and Tyger Rivers near the Fish Dam Ford. Surveyed for JAMES BISHOP
22 Nov. 1767 and granted to JOSEPH STEVENS (Soldier) 5 Sept. 1785 and
by him conveyed to sd Frances Bremar.."Now in ADAM SCANE's actual possession." Wit: PETER M. NEUFVILLE, JOHN HAWKINS. Rec. 4 Apr. 1791.
          (Note: The fact that FRANCIS BREMAR, the Surveyor General of
the State, signed this deed which states that the area in the fork
between Broad and Tyger Rivers was in Camden Dist. is indicative of
the confusion that existed in the minds of the state officials concerning the boundary lines of the up-country counties and districts.
In 1791 Union Co. had been in existence as such for 6 years and had
been in 96 Dist. since its beginning. It included the area in the fork
between Broad and Tyger Rivers from its beginning.)

Pp 426-427:   9 Apr. 1789, JOHN BENNET, planter, and MARY his wife,
          to JEHUE McPHEARSON, planter, all of Union Co., for 6 pds lawful
money of S.C. (no acreage given), part of a tract of 167 acs. on the
branches of Dutchman's Creek in Union Co. granted to John Bennet. Also
mentions a line dividing such tract. Grant bound by GEO. HARLING (HAR-
LAN), DAVID PREWIT, JOHN BENNET's old survey, and vacant land. "Set
our hands Apr. 9th 1790." Both John and Mary signed. Wit: JESSE SPANN,
JEREMIAH SPAN. Rec. 4 Apr. 1791.

Pp 427-429:   13 Dec. 1790. LEWIS BOBO and SARAH his wife to JAMES
          DUNCAN, son of ALEXANDER (this JAMES DUNCAN was always referred
to in this way), all of Union Co., for 15 pds, 15 acs. where STEPHEN's
line crosses the 96 Road. Part of a tract of 700 acs. granted to LEWIS
BOBO 13 July 1770 by Gov. of Prov. of S.C., located in then Berkley
Co. now Union Co. in the fork bet. Broad and Saludy Rivers on small

Cont'd:
branches of Tyger River called Wofford's and Barnet's Branches. Grant
bound by EMANUEL STEVENS, RALPH JACKSON, and vacant land. Grant rec.
in Book FFF, p. 27. LEWIS BOBO & SARAH (X) BOBO both signed. Wit: JES.
DODD, KINDRED BOBO. Proved by JESSE DODD 28 Dec. 1790 bef. CHARLES
SIMS, J.P. Rec. 4 Apr. 1791.

Pp 429-432:   22 & 23 Sept. 1777. Lease and Release. JOHN McMULLIN
        and AGNES his wife of 96 Dist., to JOSEPH GUITON of Camden Dist.,
for 10 sh and 400 pds current money of S.C., 119 acs. on Abiton's Creek
in 96 Dist. adj. ALEXR. WILKINS' line, and also 41 acs. being a part
of a tract of 200 acs. orig. granted to ROBERT WILSON and conveyed
by him to sd JOHN McMILLIN adj. the 119 acs. Receipt on the lease shows
consideration to be 10 shillings. The 119 acs. tract was part of a
tract of 510 acs. granted to SAMUEL GILKIE by Mathew Rowan, Gov. of
the Prov. of S.C. 11 May 1753, in Anson Co., N.C. on McDowell's Creek,
now called Abiton's (Abbington's) Creek, now since the continuation
boundary line appears to be in 96 Dist., S.C. Grant rec. in North Carolina. SAMUEL GILKIE conveyed to ALEXR. LOCKHART, Lockhart to ROBERT
WILSON, and Wilson conveyed 119 acs. to JOHN McMILLIN. Signed by John
McMillin and Agnes (mark) McMillin. Wit: HENRY SMITH, NATHL. GUITON,
WILLIAM SMITH who attested 24 July 1778 bef. ABRAHAM SMITH, J.P. of
the New Acquistion Dist., and Camden Dist. Rec. 4 Apr. 1791.

Pp 433-434:   20 Aug. 1790, JOHN BLASINGAME, Sheriff of Union Co. to
        JOHN HAILE, Esq., same place, for 13.10.0 sterling, high bid
at a public auction held on 10 Nov. 1788 to settle a case for debt
of 24.4.3 sterling against BRADLEY COLLINS by ROBERT LUSK, Sept. term
of court 1788, 400 acs. on both sides of Thicketty Creek, tract was
orig. granted to HUGH MOORE 27 Apr. 1768 and conveyed by sd Moore to
JOSEPH COLLINS 30 Aug. 1768 and rec. in "RICHARD LAMTON's Auditor Gen-
erals Office" on 2 Dec. 1772 in Bk. M, No. 12. Signed JOHN BLASINGAME,
Late Sheriff. Wit: JOHN HENDERSON, RICHD. MITCHELL. Ack. in open court
by sd John Blasingame and rec. 4 Apr. 1791.

Pp 434-437:   12 & 13 Jan. 1791, Lease and Release. JOHN WINN, Esq.,
        of Fairfield Co., SC had been given a power-of-attorney by the
Hon. DANIEL HUGER, Esq., 20 Jan. 1789, to sell certain tracts of land
belonging to Huger. Sd. John Winn, as attorney for Huger to JOHN WHITE,
planter of Union Co., for 10 sh. and 22 pds sterling, 125 acs. to be
laid out in a regular square, part of a 500 ac. tract orig. granted
to Daniel Huger 20 Jan. 1773, on waters of Brown's Creek. Bound on
E by WILLIAM WILLIAMS, all other sides by sd Huger's land. The 125
acs. to include the plantation whereon JOHN WHITE, JR. lived as shown
on the annexed plat (which is also recorded in deed book). Signed "JOHN
WINN for DANIEL HUGER." Wit: WM. WHITE, DANIEL WHITE. Proved in open
court and rec. 4 Apr. 1791.

Pp 437-438:   4 Apr. 1791. WILLIAM FARR, Sheriff of Union Co., to THOMAS
        COOK, same place, for 20.5.5. sterling, high bid at a public
auction held 1 Mar. 1790, 2 tracts belonging to ALEXANDER CHESNEY,
one of 100 acs. on a branch on N side of Pacolate River, bound by THOMAS
COOK, JOHN GRINDEL, ROBT. CHESNEY, & JAMES COOK, grant rec. in Bk.
TTT, p. 535; the other of 85 acs. on N side of Pacolate River, being
part of a tract granted to PETER HOWARD and sd to be since the property of ALEX. CHESNEY. Thomas Cook obtained a judgment against Chesney
for 17 pds 9 sh. 10 pence 3 farthings sterling and costs in the Mar.
term of court 1790. Clerk had issued a writ on 2 Feb. 1790 instruct-
ing the Sheriff to sell the lands, chattels, etc. of sd Alexander Chesney to levy the sum of 20.5.5. sterling against Thomas Cook. William
Farr, Late Sheriff make title to Thomas Cook. Wit: WM. KENNEDY, JOSHUA
PALMORE, THOS. STRIBLING. Rec. 4 June 1791.

Pp 438-440:   20 June 1789. WILLIAM WOFFORD of Lawson's Fork in Spart-
        anburg Co., SC to GEO. HARLAN of Fairforest, Union Co., for 60
pds sterling, 150 acs. on NE side of Fairforest Creek, bound by creek,
DAVISON, AVORY BREED and land granted to BENJAMIN GIST. Part of a 640
ac. tract orig. granted to JOHN McDOWEL (could be McDOWD) by N.C. grant
and falling in S.C. was regranted to JOHN NICOL and JAMES VERNON by

Cont'd:
the Prov. of S.C. Grants and plats rec. in both North and South Carolina. Sd 150 acs. was conveyed to sd WILLIAM WOFFORD 29 Mar. 1770 by
JAMES VERNON under "the firm of NICOL & VERNON." Wit: AARON HARLIN,
GEORGE HARLAN and WM. (X) PLUMMER. Proved in open court, rec. 4 Apr.
1791.
        (Note: There were two men named GEORGE HARLAN living in Union
Co., at the same time.)

Pp 440-441:   21 Oct. 1790. JAMES BANKHEAD and ELIZABETH his wife to
        JOHN HAYNEY, all of Union Co., for 100 pds sterling, 128 acs.
part of a tract granted to sd Bankhead 2 Mar. 1789 by State of S.C.
At the mouth of Pacolate River, S side, bound by JAMES FANNIN, HAMIL-
TON and SHARP. Signed JAMES BANKHEAD, ELIZABETH (X) BANKHEAD. Wit:
EDWARD TILLMAN, GEORGE BAILEY, HUGH BANKHEAD. Proved by Capt. Edw.
Tillman on 31 Mar. 1791 bef. WM. FARR, Justice. Rec. 4 Apr. 1791.

Pp 441-442:   27 Oct. 1790. DANIEL McPHEATORS of Rowan Co., NC to JOHN
        THOMPSON of Union Co., SC for 35.14.0, 180 acs. in Union Co.
on both sides of Thicketty Creek, part of a grant to DANIEL McPHEETORS
by Mathew Rowan, Gov. of N.C. bound by TANNER, SHIPPEY, NUCKOLS and
sd THOMPSON. Signed DANIEL McPHEETORS. Wit: DENNIS SULLIVAN, JAMES
McPHEETERS. Proved by Sullivan 27 Nov. 1790 bef. WM. McCULLOCH, J.P.
Rec. 4 Apr. 1791.

Pp 442-443:   25 Mar. 1791. BENJAMIN COWNOVER, farmer to WILLIAM JOHN-
        STONE, farmer both of Union Co., for divers good causes and 5
pds current money of SC, 200 acs. on Little Sandy Run (of Pacolet River).
Signed BENJAMIN COVENHOVEN. Wit: EPHRAIM (X) FOWLER, WILLIAM (X) JOHN-
STONE, THOMAS GEORGE. Rec. 5 Apr. 1791.
        (Note: See letter following the abstract of the deed on pp. 409-
412.)

END OF DEED BOOK B

YORK COUNTY, S. C. - DEED BOOK A
1786-1788

Pp 1-3:   DAVID JOHNSTON and his wife SARAH, MOSES SHELBY and his
        wife ELIZABETH, and ROBERT LEEPER, JR. and his wife JEAN, all
of York Co., Camden Dist., SC, to JAMES HAWTHORN of same, 26 Aug. 1785,
375 acs. on NW side of Catawba River, being part of grant to Col. THOMAS
NEEL, 31 Aug. 1774 by Gov. William Bull of SC. Wit: JOHN McCAW, WILLIAM
HOWE.
        (Note: JAMES HAWTHORN (1750-1809, commanded Col. WILLIAM HILL's
regiment at the battle of King's Mountain, and was first Sheriff of
York County. THOMAS NEEL (1730-1779, Member of S.C. Provincial Congress
1775-6; commanded New Acquisition District militia; was killed at Battle
of Stono, June 20, 1779.)

Pp 3-7:   THOMAS GILLESPIE, planter of Rowan Co., NC to JOHN McCAW,
        planter of York Co., SC, 15 Sept. 1785, 300 acs. granted in Anson
Co., N.C. (now York Co.) on S side of Catawba River on Humphrey's Creek
on North fork of Fishing Creek; granted to EDWARD BOYL and by him conveyed to THOMAS GILLESPIE, 16 Apr. 1759. Wit: DAVID JOHNSTON, ROBERT
JOHNSTON, JR.
        (Note: JOHN McCAW (1758-1825)

Pp 7-8:   JAMES HAWTHORN and his wife MARY, MOSES SHELBY and his
        wife ELIZABETH, ROBERT LEEPER, JR. and his wife JANE, all of
York Co., SC to DAVID JOHNSTON of same, 26 Aug. 1785, 404 acs. on NW
side of Catawba River, being part of grant to Col. THOMAS NEEL, 31
Aug. 1774 by Gov. Wm. Bull of S.C. Wit: JNO. McCAW, WM. HOWE.

Pp 9-11:   THOMAS GILLHAM, SR. of Craven Co., Camden Dist., SC to
        THOMAS GILLHAM, JR. of same, 25 Feb. 1780, 180 acs. on N side
of Broad River on waters of Bullocks Creek, being part of 380 acs.

Cont'd:
granted to THOMAS GILLHAM, SR., 26 Sept. 1766 by Gov. Wm. Tryon of
N.C.; beginning at WILLIAM SHEARER's corner and running to ISAAC LEAN-
EY's line, etc. Wit: EZEKIEL GILLHAM, WILLIAM BELL, ISAAC GILLHAM.

Pp 11-13:   DAVID NEEL, planter of Camden Dist., to JOHN McCAW, of
        same, 16 June 1781, 300 acs. of a grant of 400 acs. to DAVID
NEEL, 21 Apr. 1764 by Gov. ARTHUR DOBBS of N.C. (100 previously con-
veyed to ROBERT PATRICK), on N side of Crowders creek, adj. lands of
ROBERT LEEPER, WILLIAM HOWE. Wit: JOSEPH NEEL, DAVID JOHNSTON, ROBERT
JOHNSTON.
        (Note: ROBERT PATRICK served in Capt. PETER CLINTON's Company,
NEEL's Regiment.)

Pp 14-15:   GEORGE BLANTON of Tryon Co., NC to JOHN BARRON of Camden
        Dist., SC, 28 Feb. 1778, 200 acs. on which JOHN BARRON lives,
along the E side of Broad River; land formerly granted to EWINGS HATH-
LEY, 13 Oct. 1765, and conveyed to HUGH QUINN and by him to MERIARTER
SANDERS, 19 May 1769, and by him to GEO. BLANTON, 2 Dec. 1777. Wit:
THOMAS TATE, JOHN MAPP, FRANCIS TATE.

(Note: Skips to page 17)

Pp 17-19:   JAMES WILKINSON, planter of Union Co., SC to FRANCIS
        ADAMS of York Co., SC, 7 Oct. 1785, 200 acs. orig. granted to
MARTIN ARMSTRONG in 1768 and deeded to PETER KUYKENDALL and then to
WILKINSON; lying on a branch of Fishing creek, at SW corner of Indian
Land claimed by the Catawbas, adj. the Indian line and that of WILLIAM
MILLS. Wit: WILLIAM McGOWN, JOHN ADAMS, JAMES ADAMS, ELIZABETH ADAMS.
        (Note: FRANCIS ADAMS (1741-1826), member of the Second Provincial
Congress of South Carolina, 1775-1776.)

Pp 19-21:   ROBERT DICKEY of Chester Co., SC to ROBERT KENNEDY of
        York Co., 19 Aug. 1785, 100 acs. on Bullocks creek, bounded on
NW by DAVID PORTER's land, being full patent granted to ROBERT DICKEY
by Gov. Wm. Bull of S.C. 17 May 1774. Wit: WILLIAM WALLACE, JOS. SCOTT,
ABRAHAM ENLOE.

Pp 21-24:   THOMAS BROWN and his wife FRANCES ANNE of Turkey Creek,
        York Co., to GODFREY ADAMS of York Co., 11 June 1783, 100 acs.
on Turkey Creek, N side of Broad River, granted to DAVID EDWARD 18
Aug. 1763 by Gov. THOMAS BOONE of SC, transferred by David Edward &
his wife JANE, to THOMAS BROWN 12 Feb. 1767. Wit: JNO. McCAW, PETER
PETERSON.

Pp 25-26:   ROBERT ALEXANDER and his wife ALYSE of Craven Co., SC
        to JOHN and JOSEPH GABBIE of same, 24 Dec. 1772, 84 acs. on Fish-
ing Creek, adj. lands of WILLIAM WATSON, THOMAS SCOTT and ROBERT GABBIE.
Wit: FRANCIS TRAVERS, WILLIAM WATSON, MOSES FERGUSON.

Page 27:   JOHN PATTON, SR. of York Co., to ESTHER PATTON, 20 Mar.
        1786, bill of sale for one grey horse, three cows and calves
and other property. Wit: ALEXANDER GLASS, DAVID PATTON.
        Note: JOHN PATTON served in Capt. ANDREW LOVE's Company, Col.
THOMAS NEEL's Regiment of New Acquisition Dist. Militia.)

Page 28:   JOHN PATTON, SR. of York Co., to JANE PATTON of same,
        20 Mar. 1786, bill of sale for one grey horse and other property.
Wit: ALEXANDER GLASS, DAVID PATTON.

Page 29:   JOHN PATTON, SR. of York Co., to daughter MARGARET PATTON
        of same, 20 Mar. 1786, for natural love and affection deeds of
gift one negro man named Jasper, about 50 years of age and other property. Wit: ALEXANDER GLASS, DAVID PATTON.

Pp 29-32:   WILLIAM HAGGANS and his wife MARY of the Waxhaw and Meck-
        lenburg Co., N.C. to JOHN DRENNAN, yeoman, late of Pennsylvania,
24 Dec. 1765, 200 acs. in Mecklenburg on W side of Catawba River on
both sides of Twelve Mile Creek opposite the Catawba Indian Town and
adj. old grant to ROBERT McILHANEY, formerly granted to WILLIAM EDEY,

Cont'd:
18 Nov. 1752; deeded to ROBERT BARKLEY and then to HAGGINS, 10 Oct.
1765. Wit: ANDREW NUTT, ROBERT CROCKETT, SAMUEL THOMPSON.

Pp 32-34:   ROBERT DICKEY of Chester Co., SC to JOHN McNABB of York
            Co., 22 Sept. 1785, 150 acs. in York Co. on Beaver Dam fork of
Bullocks Creek, joining land formerly possessed by WILLIAM DAVIES and
now owned by DAVID PORTER, being patent granted by Gov. Wm. Tryon of
N.C. to WILLIAM DAVIES, 4 May 1769, sold by Davies to Dickey, 2 Oct.
1771. Wit: DAVID DICKEY, WILLIAM WALLACE, ROBERT KENNEDY.

(Note: Skips to page 39)

Pp 39-40:   JOHN STALLINGS of Camden Dist., SC to DEMCY WINBOURNE
            of same, 30 Oct. 1779, 100 acs. of PETER KUYKENDALL's new survey
on Fishing Creek and Milikins Branch. Wit: JESSE WINBOURNE, JOSIAH
STALLINGS.

Pp 40-41:   JOHN WALKER of Craven Co., SC to JAMES McNAIR of same,
            3 Aug. 1791, 120 acs. on head branch of Bullocks Creek and adj.
HUGH ALLISON's land. Wit: JAMES TEMPLETON, JEANE SHAW, SAML. WATSON.

Affidavits concerning title to land on which ROBERT KENNEDY lives.

ELISABETH BYERS, wife of Capt. WILLIAM BYERS of York Co., SC,
2 Feb. 1786, declares that in July 1780 NATHANIEL PORTER came to her
house then in North Carolina and gave her a pocketbook containing several papers including a patent with seal which he said were the deeds
to his land and asked her to give them to his brother DAVID PORTER
when she and her family went to Virginia, which she declares she did.
Test: DAVID LEECH, J.P.

EDWARD BYERS and ADAM MEEK, both of York Co., SC, 2 Feb. 1786,
declare that NATHANIEL PORTER when on his deathbed told them that DAVID
PORTER had the deeds to his land and that David was in Nathaniel's
debt which they understood was over and above the price of the land.
Test: DAVID LEECH, J.P.

SARAH PORTER of York Co., 2 Feb. 1786, declares that in 1778
her son DAVID PORTER was very sick and sent for his brother NATHANIEL
PORTER to come and get deeds to his land and that Nathaniel brought
them home and gave them to her and that she kept them until 1780 when
Nathaniel took them to North Carolina and gave them to ELISABETH BYERS
to take to his brother David when she went to Virginia, and that Nathaniel bought the land she lives on from David for 130 pds proclamation
money of North Carolina, giving to him a negro named Fortune valued
at 100 pds and the balance in money. Test: DAVID LEECH, J.P.

EDWARD BYERS of York Co., 11 July 1786, declares that sometime
after he returned from Virginia, the late NATHANIEL PORTER asked him
what his mother, ELISABETH BYERS, did with the deeds to his land, and
that he replied that he believed that she gave them to Nathaniel's
brother, David Porter. Test: JNO. MOFFETT, J.P.

JOHN McNABB, 10 July 1786, declares that once when on the premises of SARAH PORTER and ROBERT KENNEDY and his wife, he heard
NATHANIEL PORTER, now deceased, say concerning a negro in DAVID PORTER's
possession, "Fortune has made a good fortune for me as anybody, do
you think he has not, McNABB, when I got this land for him," and that
Nathaniel Porter told him that Fortune cost him 59 pds sterling in
Georgia, and that he had also heard David Porter say that he did not
know exactly how much land he had as he had sold part of it to Nathaniel
Porter, but that it had not been laid off. Test: FRS. ADAMS, J.P.
    (Note: WILLIAM BYERS was a member of the Second Provincial Con-
gress of S.C., 1775-1776, and commanded a company of horsemen in Col.
THOMAS NEEL's regiment of militia from New Acquisition Dist. 1775-
1779. EDWARD BYERS (1761-1832), Revolutionary soldier. Major ADAM MEEK
(1760-1807), of the Revolution and Sheriff of York County. Col. JOHN
MOFFETT (1742-1829) of the Revolution. JOHN McNABB (1748-   ) served
in Capt. WILLIAM BYERS' Company.)

Pp 42-44:   WILLIAM WALLACE, 10 July 1786, declares that in the summer
          of 1778 he was present when FRANCIS ADAMS, Esq., ran the line
bet. DAVID PORTER, formerly of Bullock Creek, and his brother, NATHANIEL
PORTER; that both were present and seemed to agree to the transaction;
that SARAH PORTER and ROBERT KENNEDY are in possession of the land
that fell to Nathaniel, and that he had repeatedly heard Nathaniel
say that he gave David a negro named Fortune as payment for the land.
Test: FRS. ADAMS, J.P.

Pp 45-46:   CHARLES MOORHEAD of Craven Co., SC to JOHN MOFFETT, of
          same, 14 Jan. 1779, 18 acs. on a branch of Bullocks Creek, joining
WILLIAM BYERS' line. Wit: JOHN WATSON, EDWARD MOORHEAD.
          (Note: EDWARD MOORHEAD (1744-1814) buried at Beersheba Presby-
terian Church.)

Pp 46-47:   GEORGE CUNNINGHAM of York Co., to JOHN EAKIN of same,
          21 Nov. 1785, 100 acs. on waters of Tools Fork of Fishing Creek,
adj. the Indian line, JAMES DUNCAN's, formerly JOHN DUNCAN's line and
the plantation on which Cunningham now lives. Wit: FRS. ADAMS, JOS.
BOGGS.

Pp 47-49:   JAMES ARMOUR and his wife JENNET of Craven Co., SC. to
          Rev. FRANCIS CUMMINS of same, 18 Nov. 1783, 260 acs. in Craven
Co. bet. Allison's and Beaverdam Creeks and on Camp Run branch, granted
to JOHN THOMAS and JOHN McCULLOCH in 1767. Wit: ADAM BAIRD, JAMES RAMSEY
& DAVID MOOR.
          (Note: Rev. FRANCIS CUMMINS of Bethel Presbyterian Church taught
young ANDREW JACKSON, future President of the United States.)

Pp 49-51:   WILLIAM BYERS and his wife ELISABETH of Craven Co., SC
          to HUGH ALLISON of same, 13 Feb. 1776, 320 acs. on the W side
of Catawba River and 99 acs. bounded on the NW by JOHN LAUGHLIN's land.
Wit: WILLIAM HALL, DANIEL McCLAREN, JOSIAH PORTER. Signed: WILLIAM
BYERS, ELISABETH (her X mark) BYERS.
          (Note: HUGH ALLISON (1746-) served in Capt. WM. BYERS' Company &
WILLIAM HALL (-1838) also served in same company.)

Pp 59-61:   THOMAS MORGAN and his wife MILISON to JOSEPH BOGGS, all
          of Craven Co., 21 Feb. 1782, two tracts on Fishing Creek; one
179 acs. patented 22 Apr. 1763 by CHARLES BEATTY and made over to THOMAS
MORGAN, bounded by lands of PETER KUYKENDALL and DEMSY WINBURN; the
other, 93 acs. patented by PETER KUYKENDALL, now in the possession
of JOSEPH BOGGS. Wit: JAMES YOUNG, JAMES YOUNG (JR.?), JANE YOUNG.

Pp 62-63:   JAMES LOCKHART and his wife ANN of Lincoln Co., NC to
          JOHN BERRY of Camden Dist., SC, 10 Nov. 1784, 400 acs. on head
waters of Fishing Creek, joining the Indian Territory, the plantation
of JOHN McWHORTER, and MILLIKIN's survey, now owned by JOHN STALLINGS,
SR., patented by WILLIAM MILLS, 4 Sept. 1753, in N.C. Wit: THOMAS CAR-
RELL, JOSEPH CARRELL, JOHN CARRELL.

Page 63:   ISABEL ASH of York Co., to ROBERT ASH of same, 22 May
          1786, bill of sale for a negro man named Tom. Wit: JNO. WALLACE,
JOS. PALMER.

Page 64:   ISABEL ASH to WILLIAM BURRISS 27 May 1786, bill of sale
          for one shilling paid in behalf of his wife MARY BURRISS, a negro
girl named Hannah. Wit: JAS. MITCHELL, JOS. PALMER.

Pp 65-66:   GEORGE ROSS and his wife SARAH of Camden Dist., to ALEX-
          ANDER MOORE, 1 Dec. 1785, 181 acs. on S side of Fishing Creek,
adj. lands of WILLIAM WALKER, WILLIAM IRWIN, also 31 acs. joining it,
being part of a tract on N side of creek that was in possession of
WILLIAM WALKER, dec'd. and now the creek is the line bet. the two places
but belongs to land on SW side of creek. Wit: JOHN ROSS, JAS. MARTIN.
          (Note: WILLIAM ERWIN/IRWIN (1734-1814); JAMES MARTIN (1752-1826)
was a captain in the Revolution.)

Pp 68-72:   HUMPHREY BARNETT and his wife ELISABETH of Craven Co.,

Cont'd:
        Camden Dist., SC to JOHN DARWIN of same, 15 Oct. 1782, 300 acs.
along the N side of Broad River and adj. lands of ELIZABETH YOUNG,
orig. granted to ZACHARIAH BULLOCK 28 Apr. 1768 by Gov. Wm. Tryon of
N.C. and transferred to GEORGE COWEN, then to ROBERT LOUGHRIDGE, then
to HUMPHREY BARNETT. Wit: WILLIAM GILLHAM, DENIS DEMPSY, ARTHUR DUDNEY,
WM. YOUNG.
        (Note: HUMPHREY BARNETT was a captain of a troop of light horsemen
and JOHN DARWIN served in the Revolution under sd HUMPHREY BARNETT.)

Pp 73-74:   ABRAHAM FLOYD and his wife EVE of Randolph Co., N.C.
        to HUGH QUINN of S.C. 4 Oct. 1785, 155 acs. on E side of Broad
River on both sides of Love's Creek, including CAMPBELL's improvement,
adj. lands of WOOD, FULTON, PRICE and FLOYD, granted to MATHEW FLOYD
by N.C. and conveyed to ABRAHAM FLOYD 9 Mar. 1781. Wit: GEORGE TAYLOR,
JOHN QUINN, PENNWELL WOOD, MICHL. HOGAN.
        (Note: ABRAHAM FLOYD (1755-   ) served under Capt. WILLIAM BYERS
and LT. JACOB BARNETT in Col. THOMAS NEEL's Regiment of Militia from
New Acquisition Dist. in the Cherokee Expedition of 1776.)

Pp 75-76:   RAINEY PHILLIPS of Abbeville Co., SC to JAMES MITCHELL
        of York Co., 20 Dec. 1785, 150 acs. on branch of Fishing Creek,
joining plantation now belonging to SAMUEL CARSON, ROBERT ASH, PHILIP
SANDIFER, WILLIAM ASH and THOMAS CLENDENIN; part of grant to BENJAMIN
PHILLIPS by S.C., 28 Aug. 1767. Wit: JOHN ABERNETHY, ROBT. GREER, BENJ.
PHILLIPS.
        (Note: PHILIP SANDIFER (1744-1817) and THOMAS CLENDENIN (1711-
1817.)

Pp 76-78:   HENRY WRIGHT of Craven Co. to ALEXANDER HENRY of same,
        27 Apr. 1774, 300 acs. on both sides of Crowder's Creek on TATE's
new line. Wit: WILLIAM HENRY, WILL. POLK. Proved by EZEKIEL POLK at
July Term 1786.
        (Note: ALEXANDER HENRY intercepted plea for aid sent by FERGUSON
to Lord CORNWALLIS just before the battle of King's Mountain. WILLIAM
POLK (1759-1835) last surviving field officer of the North Carolina
line in the Revolution, was offered the commission of a brigadier general by President Madison in 1812 but declined the honor. EZEKIEL POLK
(1747-1824) a member of the Provincial Congress of South Carolina and
Captain of a company in Col. NEEL's Regiment, was grandfather of President JAMES KNOX POLK.)

Pp 78-80:   JAMES HAMILTON of Camden Dist. to RALPH ROGERS of same,
        16 Nov. 1785, 100 acs. on Bullocks Creek, part of tract granted
to DANIEL RICHERSON. Wit: JAMES LINDSEY, ABRAHAM SMITH, CLAYTON ROGERS.

Pp 80-82:   MALCOLM HENRY of York Co. to JOHN GORDON of same, 11
        July 1786, 500 acs. "on head waters of Allison's Creek and Bul-
lock's Creek on both sides of the Waggon Road including the Plantation
whereon EZEKIEL POLK formerly lived," conveyed by EZEKIEL POLK to HENRY
WILLIAMS, to THOMAS RODEN, to JOHN BUIS and to MALCOLM HENRY. Wit:
JOHN LESLEY, JOHN GORDON.

Pp 82-84:   JOHN MILLER of York Co., to THOMAS MOORE of same, 7 Apr.
        1786, 150 acs. on waters of Crowders Creek, granted to WILLIAM
PATRICK 25 Apr. 1767. Wit: THOS. DAVIS, JOHN MOOR.

Pp 86-89:   JAMES HEMPHILL, planter, and his wife ALICE of York Co.,
        to WILLIAM DAVIDSON, planter of same, 13 June 1786, 67 acs.
on Fishing Creek, adj. to the Charleston Great Road and Widow CROFT's
land. Wit: JNO. McCAW, JOHN HEMPHILL.
        (Note: JAMES HEMPHILL (1749-1833) Revolutionary soldier.)

Pp 91-93:   SAMUEL GORDON and his wife MARY of Camden Dist., SC to
        WILLIAM and JOHN HOOD of same, 29 Nov. 1779, 50 acs. on both
sides of Clarks Fork of Bullocks Creek, the upper part of SAMUEL GORD-
ON's tract of 225 acs. deeded by JOHN DAVIDSON to GORDON, being part
of tract of 450 acs. granted to WILLIAM WRIGHT and bounded on W side
by JOSEPH CLARK's land and on the NE by the estate of ROBERT SWAN,

Cont'd:
who is deceased, sd lands conveyed to DAVIDSON by MOSES WRIGHT, heir
of WILLIAM WRIGHT; including mill where HOOD now lives. Wit: JAS. PINK-
ERTON, JOHN FULTON, ARCHIBALD BARRON.
    (Note: SAMUEL GORDON (1745-1798)

Pp 94-96:   WILLIAM BYERS, SR. of York Co., to HUGH ALLISON, JR.
        of same, 27 Sept. 1786, 99 acs. on head branches of Bullocks
Creek, bounded NE and SE by land granted to WILLIAM BYERS, NW by land
lately the property of WILLIAM LAUGHLIN, deceased, and NE by land formerly claimed by DAVID ADAMS. Wit: ALEXANDER ALLISON, EDWARD MOORHEAD,
J. BARNETT. Signed: WILLIAM BYERS.
    (Note: EDWARD MOORHEAD (1744-1814). Capt. JACOB BARNETT commanded
a troop of light horsemen during the War of the Revolution.)

Pp 96-98:   WILLIAM McADOW of Craven Co., to JAMES BARRON of same,
        23 July 1779, 550 acs. at Bullocks Creek, granted to WILLIAM
McADOW by S.C. in 1763, adj. land granted to ROBERTS and lands of FLIN-
TON and QUALES. Wit: WILLIAM BYERS, JAS. PINKERTSON, JAMES McADOW.
    (Note: JAMES BARRON was first Under Sheriff of York County. He
received ROBERT STEPHENSON's indent for Revolutionary War service.)

Pp 99-101:   ZACHARIAH BELL, SR. and his wife MARGARET of York Co.,
        to JAMES BARRON of same, 28 Sept. 1785, 100 acs. on N side of
Broad River, bounded on all sides by vacant land, surveyed for JOHN
CAMERON, 15 Mar. 1768. Wit: HENRY RAY, ISAAC GILLHAM.
    (Note: HENRY REA/RAY (1758-1842) served under Capts. JOSEPH BROWN,
JAMES JAMIESON, BARNETT and WILLIAM HANNA in the Revolution. ISAAC
GILLHAM served in Capt. ROBERT McAFEE's Company.)

Pp 101-103:   JACOB GARDNER and his wife MARY of Camden Dist. to WILLIAM
        SMITH of same, 19 June 1779, 100 acs. on N side of Broad River
about one mile from Smith's Ford, the place where JACOB GARDINER now
lives, granted to HENRY SMITH and conveyed to JOHN RUSSELL, JR. and
by him to THOMAS WADE, to WILLIAM MERRELL, to JACOB GARDNER. Wit:
JOHN SMITH, JONATHAN PICKENS, HENRY SMITH, JR.

Pp 104-106:   ROBERT SIMONTON of Rowan Co., NC to WILLIAM BERRY of
        York Co., SC 20 May 1786, 225 acs. on S side of Catawba River
on a branch of Rocky Allisons Creek, bounded by HUMPHREY CUNNINGHAM's
land, and tract granted to ROBERT SIMONTON by Gov. Matthew Rowan of
N.C., 25 Feb. 1754, and lands of Col. SAMUEL WATSON, ALEXANDER KENNEDY
and JAMES SIMRAL. Wit: FRAS. ADAMS, SAML. WATSON, ARCHIBALD BARRON.
    (Note: SAMUEL WATSON, Lieutenant Colonel; member of S.C. Provin-
cial Congress.)

Pp 106-107:   ROBERT SIMONTON, planter of Rowan Co., N.C. to WILLIAM
        BERRY, planter of York Co., 20 May 1786, 575 acs. on S side of
Catawba River and N side of Allisons Creek. Wit: FRAS. ADAMS, SAML.
WATSON, ARCHIBALD BARRON.

Pp 108-110:   ALEXANDER KENNEDY, saddler of Mecklenburg Co., N.C. to
        SAMUEL WATSON, SR., planter of York Co., 6 Oct. 1786, 180 acs.
on Allisons Creek being part of a grant by Gov. NATHANIEL RICE of N.C.
18 Nov. 1752 to ALEXANDER SIMRAL of Pennsylvania, then in N.C., but
now confirmed in the State of S.C., joining JOSEPH SIMRAL's line and
conveyed by JAMES SIMRAL to WILLIAM BERRY, which land was deeded to
ALEXANDER KENNEDY by JAMES SIMRAL, 6 June 1781. Wit: JAMES WATSON,
SAML. ROWAN, JOSEPH FORBES.

Pp 110-112:   ZACHARIAH BELL, yeoman, and his wife MARGARET of York
        Co. to JOHN FEEMSTER, yeoman of same, 7 July 1785, 94 acs. on
a tract of 500 acs. on waters of Bullocks Creek, granted to BELL 7
June 1774. Wit: THOMAS GILLHAM, GEORGE BLACK, ISAAC GILLHAM.

Pp 116-119:   ELIZABETH RIGGS of Camden Dist. to DAVID LEECH, tanner
        of same, 2 Aug. 1783, 120 acs. on Turkey Creek, parts of two
tracts granted by Gov. THOMAS BOONE of S.C., 20 Apr. 1763 to REYDERUS
CLARK and conveyed to JOHN RIGGS, the other granted to JOHN RIGGS,

Cont'd:
JOHN McKNITT ALEXANDER by Gov. Wm. Tryon of N.C., 20 Oct. 1767, being
property of ELIZABETH RIGGS by death of her husband, JOHN RIGGS; joining lands of DAVID LEECH, HUGH SIMPSON, THOMAS MORRIS, WILLIAM CLARK
and JOHN HILL. Wit: WILL. BOYD, HUGH SIMPSON, WM. BROWN.

Pp 119-122:   WILLIAM McCORKLE of Craven Co. to THOMAS ELLIOTT of same,
        22 Jan. 1776, 105 acs. on Twelve Mile Creek including the place
where THOMAS ELLIOTT now lives, along the various courses of Twelve
Mile Creek and the Steel Creek Waggon Road. Wit: WILLIAM NUTT, JOHN
WILSON, AGNES NUTT.

Pp 123-125:   ANDREW McCORKLE of Mecklenburg Co., NC to THOMAS ELLIOTT
        of Camden Dist., 16 Jan. 1781, 110 acs. along bank of Twelve
Mile Creek, ROBERT CROCKET's line, the Waggon Road and the Province
line. Wit: JNO. WILSON, THOS. DRENNAN.

Pp 126-128:   CHARLES MILLER, JR. to CHARLES MILLER, SR. both of Camden
        Dist., 25 Oct. 1779, 109 acs. on Twelve Mile Creek, and Millstone
Branch. Wit: JAMES CRAWFORD, JOHN WHITE, JOSEPH WHITE.

Pp 130-133:   MARY MORRIS of St. Marks Parish, Craven Co., SC to JAMES
        SMITH of same, 15 Oct. 1782, 250 acs. on Fishing Creek, granted
to MARY SMITH, 18 Aug. 1763 by Gov. Thomas Boone, S.C. Wit: HUGH WHITE,
SAMUEL LUSK, ELIZABETH McCLELLAND.

Pp 133-136:   JOHN MOORE of Craven Co., SC to JOHN SMITH, planter of
        same, 25 July 1777, 56 acs. part of grant of 800 acs. to GUYAN
MOORE by Gov. GABRIEL JOHNSTON of N.C., 3 Apr. 1752, then deemed in
Anson County, N. C. (now York County, S.C.) on main Broad River which
fell to JOHN MOORE, heir at law of GUYAN MOORE, and a part conveyed
to JOHN SMITH, on bank of river against an island. Wit: DANIEL SMITH,
GIDEON SMITH, JAMES STEEN.

Page 137:   Received of JOHN HILLHOUSE, three pounds for recording
        a set of deeds, 7 June 1774 from THOMAS MITCHELL and wife to
WILLIAM MINTER. Witnesses to deeds: WILLIAM HILLHOUSE, SR., HUGH NEEL
and wife.
        (Note: WILLIAM HILLHOUSE (1760-1848). Lord Cornwallis and the
British Army encamped on WILLIAM HILLHOUSE's plantation on Turkey Creek,
Jan. 16-19, 1781.)

Pp 138-139:   JOSEPH LANEY of Pennsylvania to DAVID and JANET WAUGH
        of S.C., 4 Nov. 1779, deed of gift of 150 acs. on Cowpen Branch
of Turkey Creek, granted to WILLIAM LANEY 26 June 1771, sd DAVID to
give to sd JANEY one-third value of land when he comes of age of 21.
Wit: WILL. MINTER, WILLIAM LANEY, JOHN WAUGH.

Pp 139-140:   ROBERT MONTGOMERY of 96 Dist. to ABRAHAM SMITH, planter
        of Camden, 3 Oct. 1785, one negro woman named Hannah, age 26,
and one negro girl named Rinah. Wit: HENRY SMITH, ISAIAH SHIPMAN, DAVID
SMITH.

Pp 140-142:   PETER JULIAN of Guilford Co., N.C. to JOHN HOFSTITLER
        of Lincoln Co., N.C. 5 May 1785, 125 acs. on N side of Broad
River on main fork of Kings Creek, joining tract granted to SAMUEL
FINLEY, 4 Sept. 1754, conveyed to JOHN MOORE, to PETER JULIAN. Wit:
WILLIAM ELLIS, JACOB HOFSTITLER.

Pp 142-144:   JOHN WALLACE, son of HUGH WALLACE, of York Co., Camden
        Dist., SC to EDWARD MELLON of Lincoln Co., N.C., 15 Dec. 1786,
200 acs. part in York County and part in Lincoln County, on waters
of Mill Creek, joining ROBERT LEEPER's and JAMES CRAIG's lines, granted
to WILLIAM DICKSON, 22 Apr. 1763, and conveyed from ROBERT HARRIS and
his wife MARGARET to JOHN WALLACE, 26 Nov. 1766. Wit: JOHN CLARK, JOHN
KINCAID.

Pp 144-146:   JONATHAN POTTS of N.C. to FRANCIS GILMORE of Camden Dist.,
        30 Dec. 1785, 300 acs. on both sides of Clarks Fork on E side

Cont'd:
of Broad River, granted to POTTS, 25 Apr. 1767, by N. C. Wit: JAS.
PINKERTSON, ROBERT STEPHENSON, JNO. SWANN.
(Note: ROBERT STEPHENSON (1756-1798) served in Capt. JACOB BAR-
NETT's and Capt. HUMPHREY BARNETT's Troop of Light Horsemen in the
Revolution.)

Pp 146-149:   WILLIAM HENRY of Camden Dist., to OLIVER and JAMES WALLACE
of same, 9 Jan. 1787, 150 acs. on branch of S fork of Fishing
Creek, granted to WILLIAM HENRY, 26 Oct. 1767, by N. C., joining CARR's
line, McCLAIN's line and ROBERT EWART's line. Wit: JOS. WALLACE, ALLEN
DOUDLE, WILLIAM DUNLOP.

Pp 149-151:   JOHN SMITH of Craven Co. to SAMUEL SWANN, JR., son of
ROBERT SWANN, late of Bullocks Creek, deceased, 29 Jan. 1776,
250 acs. on Watson's Branch of Broad River. Wit: JAMES POWELL, THOS.
WALLACE, WILLIAM McCULLOCH.
(Note: WILLIAM McCULLOCH, member of S. C. Provincial Congress,
1775-1776.)

Pp 151-153:   JOHN SWANN, son of ROBERT SWANN of York Co., to JAMES
WATSON, of same, 10 Feb. 1786, 200 acs. on both sides of Buck
Horn Fork of Bullocks Creek, being part of 400 acs. granted to WILLIAM
CLAYTON, 27 Apr. 1767, and deeded 20 July 1763, to sd ROBERT SWANN,
joining DICKSON's line, being lower part of sd 400 acs. next to ANDREW
COUNTRYMAN's plantation and JOHN CHAMBERS' plantation. Wit: JAMES MEEK,
HENRY DUNLOP, WILLIAM DUNLOP.
(Note: JOHN CHAMBERS (1742-1802) was badly wounded at Sumter's
Defeat on Fishing Creek, August 18, 1780.)

Pp 153-155:   WILLIAM McBRAYER, planter, and his wife MARTHA of Camden
Dist. to FRAME WOODS, planter of same, 30 Sept. 1779, tract on
N side of Broad River bounding on NE by land surveyed for ZACHARIAH
BELL, to SE by land surveyed by North-rights, to NW by land surveyed
for THOMAS FLETCHALL. Wit: WILLIAM ROGERS, ANDREW WOODS, MATTHEW ROGERS.
(Note: FRAME WOODS, member of the General Assembly of S. C.,
1776. THOMAS FLETCHALL was a notorious Tory in the Revolution.)

Pp 158-162:   DANIEL GREEN of 96 Dist., SC to BAGWELL BAILEY of Camden
Dist., 11 June 1784, 333 acs. on S side of Fishing Creek, joining lands of WOODS, PETER KUYKENDALL, JAMES YOUNG, and JAMES KUYKENDALL,
granted to ABRAHAM KUYKENDALL, 22 Apr. 1763. Wit: JESSE WINBORNE, JAMES
STALLINGS, BENJ. COOK.

Pp 162-164:   MARY HOGGE to JOHN HOGGE, blacksmith of York Co., 15
May 1786, 150 acs. on Bullock Creek, joining lands on N by CHARLES
STICE, on S by JOHN McKNITT ALEXANDER, being part of a grant to CHARLES
GILLHAM, 25 Apr. 1767. Wit: THOMAS GILLHAM, ROBERT KIRKPATRICK, JOSEPH
LEANEY.

Pp 165-166:   JOSEPH McKENZIE and his wife REBECCA of Camden Dist.,
to ELEANOR MOORE of same, 2 Jan. 1787, 63 acs. on the Camp branch
of Beaver Dam Branch of Crowders Creek, joining lands of DANIEL MURPHEY:
part of grant to JOSEPH McKENZIE, 6 Nov. 1786, and divided bet. DANIEL
MURPHEY and ELEANOR MOORE. Wit: ROBT. FARIES, WILLIAM ROBISON, JOHN
FARIES.

Pp 166-167:   JOSEPH McKENZIE and his wife REBECCA of York Dist., to
DANIEL MURPHEY, 2 Jan. 1787, 30 acs. on Camp branch of Beaver
Dam Branch of Crowders Creek, joining lands of JAMES CAMPBELL, BRADNOR
and being part of grant to JOSEPH McKENZIE, 6 Nov. 1786 by Gov. Wm.
Moultrie of S.C. Wit: ROBT. FARIES, WM. ROBISON, JOHN FARIES.

Page 168:   JAMES MARTIN of York Co., to JESSE DOUGLASS of same,
9 Jan. 1787, a negro girl named Darkus about 15 years of age.
Wit: JAS. MITCHELL, ALEXANDER FARIES, JNO. MARTIN.

Pp 169-174:   SAMUEL NESBIT, tailor, of Spartanburgh Co., 96 Dist.,
S.C. by a power of attorney from his brother JOHN NESBIT of Cum-

Cont'd:
berland Co., Penn., farmer, dated 19 Dec. 1777, to JOHN WATERS of York
Co., Camden Dist., S.C., carpenter, 2 Nov. 1785, 285 acs. on S side
of Catawba River on S fork of Fishing Creek in York (formerly Tryon
Co., N.C.) being upper half of tract formerly owned by WILLIAM ADAIR,
and now the plantation on which JOHN WATERS lives, being part of grant
of 570 acs. to ABRAHAM KUYKENDALL, 29 Mar. 1753, conveyed to WILLIAM
ADAIR 17 May 1754, and by ADAIR and his wife MARY to DAVID STERRET,
25 July 1769, and by STERRET and his wife RACHEL to JOHN NESBIT, 28
Apr. 1773. Wit: THOMAS SELMAN, CHAS. MOORE.

Pp 175-176: FRAME WOODS and his wife EDITH of Anson Co., N.C. to
        WILLIAM BOSTICK of Camden Dist., SC 7 Nov. 1785, tract on N side
of Broad River, bounded on NE by land surveyed for ZACHARIAH BELL,
on SE by land surveyed by North-rights, on NW by land surveyed for
THOMAS FLETCHALL. Wit: WM. SPLEAN, JOHN HAMILTON, MARGARET HAMILTON.

Page 177: BENJAMIN McKENZIE of York Co. to ALEXANDER GLASS of same,
        14 Nov. 1786, two cows and other property. Wit: JAMES GLASS,
JOHN THOMPSON.
        (Note: JOHN THOMPSON (1743-1795) is buried in Beersheba Churchyard)

Pp 178-181: PETER KUYKENDALL, SR. of Camden Dist. to WILLIAM BARRON
        of same, 28 Sept. 1779, 800 acs. on fork of Fishing Creek, adj.
lands of JAMES YOUNG, JOHN STALLINGS and being an inclusive tract,
having parts of different surveys in it - one granted to GEORGE CATHEY
by N. C. 3 Apr. 1753, and conveyed to PETER KUYKENDALL, 29 Jan. 1762
- an the other granted to PETER KUYKENDALL, 15 Nov. 1762 - and another
conveyed from ABRAHAM KUYKENDALL to PETER KUYKENDALL, 6 June 1768.
Wit: DEMSEY WINBOURNE, JNO. BLANTON, PHIL. SANDIFER.

Pp 182-185: ROBERT GILL, planter of Chester Co., to JOHN GILL and
        JOHN MILLS of same, 3 Apr. 1787, part of 600 acs. grant to ROBERT
GILL by Gov. Wm. Bull of S.C., 3 Feb. 1765, on Loves Creek, a branch
of Moores Creek, being orig. granted to WILLIAM LOVE by N. C., 3 Sept.
1753, and since purchased by ROBERT GILL. Wit: JAMES GILL, RICHD. MILES,
WM. MILES.
        (Note: ROBERT GILL (1720-1804) is buried in Fishing Creek Pres-
byterian Church cemetery in Chester Co., S.C.)

Pp 186-187: JOHN STANFORD, planter of Spartanburgh County, to JOHN
        BRIDGES, of York Co., 29 Mar. 1787, 300 acs. on Buffaloe Creek,
joining land BRIDGES now lives on, his upper line joining JAMES BRIDGES'
land on the W line, also GREEN's W line, granted to STANFORD, 24 Jan.
1785. Wit: JAMES BRIDGES, JAMES CONN, JOSEPH BRIDGES.

Pp 188-190: JOSEPH PATTERSON of York Co. to WILLIAM HARRIS of same,
        12 Feb. 1787, 226 acs. on both sides of Bullocks Creek in S.C.
(formerly N.C.) joining and lying bet. JOHN HARTNESS, JOHN ANDERSON,
WILLIAM McDOW, GUYAN MOORE and FULTON's lands; granted to JOHN RIGGS
25 Apr. 1767. Wit: SAMUEL BYERS, ALEXANDER PATTERSON, JOSEPH PATTERSON.
        (Note: WILLIAM HARRIS married ANN BYERS, daughter of DAVID BYERS.)

Pp 191-193: ROBERT McCURDY and his wife MARY of Camden Dist., to
        HENRY PLAXICO of same, 23 Dec. 1784, 150 acs. in S.C. (formerly
N.C.) on both sides of Beaver Dam Creek of Broad River, joining lands
of JOHN PARVIE, JAMES DARWIN; granted to McCURDY by Gov. JOSIAH MARTIN
of N.C., 14 Nov. 1771. Wit: GEORGE PLAXICO, WILLIAM GREER.

Pp 194-195: THOMAS WARREN of Rutherford Co., N.C. to JOHN BRIDGES,
        planter of Camden, 6 June 1782, 200 acs. adj. ROBERT HUMPHREY's
land; granted to NICHOLAS FISHER, 25 Apr. 1767, by Gov. Wm. Tryon of
N.C. Wit: WILLIAM TATE, JOHN CAMP.

Pp 198-201: JOHN BARRON and his wife MARGARET of York Co., to JOHN
        COPELAND of same, 18 Jan. 1787, 200 acs. granted 30 Oct. 1765
by Gov. Wm. Tryon of N.C. to EWINGS HATHLEY, along the E side of Broad
River near mouth of Buffaloe Creek, which fell into the hands of HUGH
QUINN and by him conveyed to MERIARTUR SANDERS, May 1769, and by his
heir BENJAMIN SANDERS conveyed to GEORGE BLANTON, Dec. 1777, and by

Cont'd:
him to JOHN BARRON on 28 Feb. 1778. Wit: JAS. WILSON, JOHN ROSS, MICHL. HOGAN.

Pp 201-203:   ROBERT BLAND, planter of 96 Dist. to JAMES DARWIN, planter
         of Camden Dist., York Co., 7 Oct. 1786, 300 acs. on Beaver Dam
Creek of Broad River, bounded NE on lands of JOHN RICHARDSON, SW on
ROBERT McCURDY and JAMES DARWIN; granted by Gov. of S.C. to ROBERT
BLAND, 21 Jan. 1785. Wit: JOHN DARWIN, HENRY PLAXICO.

Pp 203-205:   SAMUEL MORGAN, planter of York Co. to ABRAHAM GREEN,
         planter of same, 5 Feb. 1787, 75 acs. on E side of Buffaloe Creek
on which MORGAN lives; granted to JOHN TAGERT, 25 Nov. 1771, conveyed
to DRURY ROBISON, then to MORGAN. Wit: JAMES BRIDGES, THOMAS LOGAN,
JOHN MORGAN.

Pp 206-207:   WILLIAM McBRAYER and his wife MARTHA of York Co. to JOHN
         MORGAN, planter of same, 21 Feb. 1786, 300 acs. that McBRAYER
lives on, joining on NE side of ABRAHAM GREEN's land, formerly ABRAHAM
KUYKENDALL's on a branch on E side of Buffaloe Creek. Wit: JOS. CAMP,
SAMUEL MORGAN, BETH MORGAN.

Pp 207-209:   ABRAHAM KUYKENDALL and his wife, ELIZABETH of Tryon Co.,
         N.C. to THOMAS BRIDGES of Granville Co., N.C., 6 Aug. 1774,
333 acs. on both sides of Buffaloe Creek. Wit: MARTIN ARMSTRONG, JOHN
KUYKENDALL, JAMES BRIDGES.

Pp 211-214:   ANTHONY MORGAN, planter, and his wife, MARY of Camden
         Dist., to WILLIAM McBRAYER, planter of same, 22 Feb. 1786, 125
acs. granted by Gov. Wm. Tryon of N.C., 6 Dec. 1769, to EDWARD DICK-
SON, along the N side of Broad River in Tryon Co., N.C. (now S.C.).
Wit: JOS. CAMP, JOHN MORGAN, MARGARET MORGAN.

Pp 215-216:   JOHN ROSS of York Co. to JONATHAN SUTTON, of same, 17
         Jan. 1787, 200 acs. on main fork of Turkey Creek, being part
of grant to WILLIAM WATSON; and another tract of 100 acs. joining lands
of BRINSON. Wit: JNO. MARTIN, WILLEY S. BROWN.
         (Note: JONATHAN SUTTON (1753-1818).

Pp 217-218:   WILLIAM FERGUS of York Co., to JOHN VENABLE of same,
         12 Apr. 1787, 150 acs. on a branch of Turkey Creek, granted by
N.C., 22 Dec. 1768, to MATTHEW PORTER and conveyed to JAMES PORTER,
then to JAMES HOPE and then to WILLIAM FERGUS. Wit: ANDREW KERNAGHAN,
WILLIAM CARSON.
         (Note: JOHN VENABLE (1737-1808). WILLIAM CARSON (1760-1849).

Page 219:   JOHN McDOW, planter of Camden Dist. to WILLIAM GILLHAM
         of same, 14 Oct. 1785, bill of sale for negro wench and child
named Williba. Wit: THOMAS McDOW, WILLIAM McDOW, THOMAS GILLHAM.

Page 220:   JOHN McDOW, planter of Camden Dist. to JAMES and ARTHUR
         McDOW of same, 14 Oct. 1785, bill of sale for negro girl named
Jude. Wit: THOMAS GILLHAM, THOMAS McDOW, WILLIAM McDOW.

Pp 221-223:   JOHN DAVIDSON of Rowan Co., N.C. to SAMUEL GORDON, black-
         smith of Camden Dist., S.C., 3 Oct. 1774, 225 acs. on both sides
of Clarks Fork of Bullocks Creek, granted to WILLIAM WRIGHT, bounded
on W side by JOSEPH CLARK, on NE by land supposed to belong to ROBERT
SWANN, deceased, sd lands conveyed to DAVIDSON by MOSES WRIGHT, heir
of WILLIAM WRIGHT. Wit: EZEK. POLK, BENJ. BURGIN, NATHAN MENDENHALL.

Pp 223-224:   MATTHEW BIGGER of Craven Co. to SAMUEL McKEE of same,
         30 Oct. 1783, 281½ acs. adj. to N side of Crowders Creek, adj.
lands of THOMAS NEEL and WILLIAM HOWE. Wit: JAMES STAFFORD, JOSEPH
HOWE.
         (Note: JOSEPH HOWE was a member of the Second Provincial Congress
of South Carolina, 1775-1776.)

Pp 225-227:   PHILEMON MARTIN and WILLIAM HARTGROVE of Spartanburgh
         Co., Ninety Six Dist., to WILLIAM ALEXANDER of Camden Dist.,

Cont'd:
25 Jan. 1787, 200 acs. on N side of Broad River on branch of Bullocks
Creek, formerly granted by S.C. to WILLIAM HARTGROVE, 13 Aug. 1766.
Wit: HARRISON BELL, JOSEPH ALEXANDER, JOHN GILLHAM.
    (Note: JOSEPH ALEXANDER was a minister at Bullocks Creek Presby-
terian Meetinghouse, 1774-1801.)

Pp 227-229:   JAMES POWELL of Clarks Fork of Bullocks Creek, to JAMES
    DONNELLY of Kings Creek, 5 May 1787, 216 acs. on Burrels Branch
of Kings Creek. Wit: JNO. SWANN, MARY GORDON.

Pp 229-230:   JAMES POWELL of York Co. to THADDEUS REED of same, 1
    May 1787, 100 acs. on a branch of Wolfs Creek, a branch of Kings
Creek, he lives on; granted to POWELL by S.C., 16 Feb. 1787, and by
him conveyed to REED. Wit: JAS. HARBISON, DAVID ADAMS.

Pp 231-232:   JOHN McADOW of Camden Dist., planter, to WILLIAM McADOW
    of same, 14 oct. 1785, bill of sale for a negro wench named Venus
and two children. Wit: THOMAS GILLHAM, THOMAS McDOW, ROBERT McDOW.

Pp 232-233:: JOHN McDOW, planter of Camden Dist., to THOMAS GILLHAM,
    Esq. of same, 14 Oct. 1785, bill of sale for negro wench named
Hannah. Wit: WILLIAM McDOW, THOMAS McDOW, ROBERT McDOW. (Note: Appears
both as McADOW and McDOW.)

Pp 233-234:   DAVID RANKIN of Rowan Co., N.C. to HENRY WILLIAMS of
    Craven, 31 Oct. 1778, 320 acs. on the S side of Crowders Creek
and bet. JAMES HENRY's land and WILLIAM HENRY's land including the
mill. Wit: MOSES HENDRY, SUSANNA RANKIN, JAMES RANKIN.

Pp 235-237:   HENRY WILLIAMS, planter, and his wife ANN of Camden Dist.,
    to THOMAS JANES of same, planter, 23 Jan. 1779, 320 acs. on S
fork of Crowders Creek, bet. lands of JAMES HENRY (on sd fork), and
WILLIAM HENRY, including the mill. Wit: JOHN WILSON, JOHN BARBER, JAMES
GORDON.
    (Note: THOMAS JANES was a member of the Second Provincial Congress
of South Carolina, 1775-1776.)

Pp 237-239:   JAMES BARRON of Craven Co. to ALEXANDER BARRON of same,
    31 Dec. 1782, 97 acs. on waters of Bullocks Creek, being part
of grant to WILLIAM McDOW by S.C. in 1763 and made over to JAMES BARRON,
23 July 1779. Wit: JAS. PINKERTON, JAMES REED, SAMUEL BARRY.
    (Note: JAMES BARRON served 240 days as a horseman in Captain
BARNETT's Company during the Revolution.)

Pp 240-242:   JAMES BARRON of York Co, planter, to SAMUEL BARRY of
    same, planter, 16 May 1787, 67 acs. on Bullocks Creek, bounded
by lands of WILLIAM MINTOR, FLINTON, JAMES BARRON and ALEXANDER BARRON.
Being part of 250 acs. grant by S.C. to WILLIAM McADOW, 23 June 1779.
Wit: ALEXR. BARRON, WILLIAM McADOW.

Pp 242-244:   JAMES McCALLIN of Craven Co. to MATTHEW SMITH of same,
    18 Feb. 1780, 150 acs. on one of the branches of Fishing Creek
on BLEANY MILLS' line, granted to JOHN ELLIOTT, 25 Sept. 1766. Wit:
JAMES FERGUS, JOS. WALLACE.

Pp 245-246:   THOMAS DICKSON of Tryon Co., N.C. to WILLIAM HENRY, SR.,
    8 Aug. 1777, 88 acs. on W side of Catawba River and S fork of
Crowders Creek, joining FERGUSON's line and RANKIN's line. Wit: JOHN
CHITTIM, MALCOLM HENRY, WILLIAM HENRY.
    (Note: WILLIAM HENRY, SR. (1715-1819) had four sons at the battle
of Kings Mountain, 7 Oct. 1780. MALCOLM HENRY (1755-1840), son of WM.
HENRY, SR., was at battle of Kings Mountain. WILLIAM HENRY (1753-1807),
son of WM. HENRY, SR. was a major of militia at the battle of Kings
Mountain. EDWARD BYERS (1761-1832) was a legatee of his estate.)

Pp 247-250:   SAMUEL MOORE, planter and his wife MARY of Camden Dist.,
    to JESSE and JOHN MOORE (minors) of same, 3 Aug. 1785, 330 acs.
on Gumlog Branch of Fishing Creek, being a tract and part of other

Cont'd:
tracts granted to JOHN MOORE, SR. of Gumlog to which sd SAMUEL MOORE
became heir-at-law by sd JOHN MOORE dying intestate; JESSE MOORE to
have ½ of tract joining ADAM WILLIAMSON's line and JOHN MOORE that
½ joining SAMUEL RAINEY's line including dwelling house of JOHN MOORE,
SR., deceased. Wit: THOMAS BLACK, SAMUEL WILLIAMSON.
    (Note: SAMUEL MOORE (1756-1820) Revolutionary soldier.)
    (Note: SAMUEL WILLIAMSON (1759-1815), killed first Tory at Huck's
Defeat, Williamson's Plantation, 12 July 1780.)

Pp 250-253:   SAMUEL MOORE, planter and his wife MARY to NATHAN MOORE,
        planter of same, 3 Aug. 1785, 150 acs. on the E side of old Waggon
Road and on a dry branch leading into Gumlog Branch of Fishing Creek,
joining lands of JOHN MOORE and REBECCA KUYKENDALL; granted to JOHN
MOORE, SR., 25 Apr. 1767 and conveyed to SAMUEL MOORE, 2 Feb. 1777.
Wit: THOMAS BLACK, SAMUEL WILLIAMSON.

Pp 254-257:   DAVID LEECH, tanner, of Camden Dist., to JOHN MOORE,
        JR., planter of same, 14 May 1779, 126 acs. on both sides of
south fork of Fishing Creek, joining CHARLES BEATTY's land, being part
of grant to JAMES MOORE, 21 Dec. 1763, and conveyed to DAVID LEECH,
and now in possession of JOHN MOORE. Wit: JOHN McELHENNY, JR., JACOB
RICKARD.

Pp 257-259:   JOHN McKINNEY, planter of Rutherford Co., S.C. to JAMES
        SCOTT, planter of York Co., 27 Apr. 1787, 200 acs. granted by
N.C. to JOHN McKINNEY, 26 Sept. 1766, on both sides of GUYON MOORE's
Creek, bounded on N by lands on which MIREAH MARTIN lives, on E by
vacant land, on S by JOHN McKINNEY's, on W by SAMUEL BURNS. Wit: JAS.
PINKERTON, ABRAHAM SMITH, JAMES MILLER.
    (Note: SAMUEL BURNS (1754-1837) went with the army under Capt.
WILLIAM BYERS to Augusta, Georgia, 1779.)

Pp 260-261:   JAMES SCOTT and hiw wife ELIZABETH of York Co., to JNO.
        McKINNEY of Rutherford Co., N.C., 27 Apr. 1787, 250 acs. orig.
in Mecklenburg Co., N.C. (now York Co.) on waters of Bullocks Creek,
joining lands of JOHN RIGGS, FULTON and MOORE; granted to JOHN McKNITT
ALEXANDER by Gov. Wm. Tryon of N.C., 22 Apr. 1767, and conveyed to
JAMES SCOTT. Wit: ABRAHAM SMITH, JAS. PINKERTON, JAMES MILLER.

Pp 262-263:   WILLIAM TAYLOR, apprentice in Charlestown, bound to ZACHA-
        RIAH BELL of Craven Co., to make titles to 100 acs. Wit: JOHN
COUNTRYMAN, ANDREW PATRICK. Title of within bond assigned by ZACHARIAH
BELL to PATRICK ROBINSON, 11 Apr. 1787. Test: DUNCAN McCREEVAN.

Pp 265-269:   WILLIAM BARRON, gentleman of St. Marks Parish, Craven
        Co., to THOMAS CLENDENIN, weaver of same, 3 Dec. 1777, 200 acs.
on South Fork of Fishing Creek, orig. granted to JAMES ADAMS, 17 Apr.
1764 by Gov. THOMAS BOONE of S.C. and conveyed to BARRON, 14 Apr. 1772.
Wit: JOHN WALLACE, JOHN JOHNSTON, WM. CALLEY.
    (Note: WILLIAM BARRON served 40 days in 1781 as a horseman in
Capt. BARNETT's Company.)

Pp 269-271:   ABRAHAM BARRON of York Co. to JAMES HOGG of same, 17
        Nov. 1786, 200 acs. on waters of Turkey Creek on head of Ticer
Branch on both sides of Waggon Road including WILLIAM HILL's great
cowpen and along JOHN BRANDON's line. Wit: ABRAHAM ENLOE, HARRISON
BELL, ROBERT KENNEDY.

Pp 273-276:   JACOB DUNCAN, planter of Camden Dist. to JOSEPH HENDER-
        SON, planter of same, 27 Nov. 1784, 200 acs. above Crowders Creek
on Catawba River bounding NW on the river and MATTHEW BIGGER's land
and westwardly on DAVID JOHNSTON's land; granted 15 Nov. 1784 to JACOB
DUNCAN by Gov. BENJ. GUERARD of S.C. Wit: THOMAS McCORMICK, ARCHIBALD
McQUISTON, HUGH McQUISTON.

Pp 277-278:   WILLIAM SUMMERFORD, planter of York Co. to ARTHUR DUDNEY,
        planter of same, 24 Feb. 1787, 57 acs. on Beaver Dam Creek being
part of a 200 ac. grant to JOHN PERRY conveyed to ABRAHAM SUMMERFORD
and by him to WM. SUMMERFORD, adj. lands of PLAXICO and THOMPSON. Wit:

Cont'd:
THOMAS GILLHAM, J. BARNETT, HUMPHREY BARNETT.

Pp 279-280:   HUMPHREY BARNETT, planter of York Co. to FLOYD BOSTICK
and FRANCIS BROCK, planters of same place, 10 Sept. 1787, 200
acs. on waters of Bullocks Creek, granted to HUMPHREY BARNETT by Gov.
THOS. PINCKNEY of S.C. Wit: ARTHUR DUDNEY, WM. SUMMERFORD, JAMES PLAX-
ICO, J. BARNETT.

Pp 280-282:・ NATHANIEL CLARK and his wife AGNES of Camden Dist. to
SAMUEL DENTON of same, 8 Oct. 1774, 300 acs. on E side of Broad
River, granted to NATHANIEL CLARK, 25 Nov. 1771 by Gov. JOSIAH MARTIN
of N.C., joining lands of GUYON MOORE, PALMER & JONES, including part
of a S.C. grant dated 20 Apr. 1763. Wit: HENRY SMITH, JOHN MOORE, MARY
GARDNER.

Pp 282-284:   WILLIAM BARRON, planter and his wife OLIVE of New Acquisition Dist., to PHILIP SANDIFER, planter of same, 22 Apr.
1780, 240 acs. adj. lands of McNABB, THOMAS CLENDENIN, and ASH. Granted
to ANDREW McNABB. Wit: JNO. WALLACE, WM. CALLY, RICHD. BALL.

Pp 285-286:   SAMUEL WILLIAMSON and wife ANNA of York Co. to WILLIAM
BRATTON, gentleman of same place, 3 Jan. 1787, 60 acs. on waters
of South Fork of Fishing Creek which land was transferred from ADAM
WILLIAMSON to his brother SAMUEL WILLIAMSON. Wit: WM. MANAHAN, JAMES
REYNOLDS, JANE BRATTON.
(Note: Colonel WILLIAM BRATTON (1742-1815) commanded the militia
from New Acquisition District after the fall of Charleston, 1780.)

Pp 286-288:   SAMUEL WILLIAMSON and his wife ANNA to WILLIAM BRATTON,
3 Jan. 1787, 140 acs. on South fork of Fishing Creek, bounded
on N by SAML. WILLIAMSON's and his father, JAMES WILLIAMSON's land,
on E by SAMUEL MOORE's, on W and SW by DANIEL CROFT's, deceased, and
by WILLIAM BRATTON's land, including JAMES WILLIAMSON's old improvement. Wit: WM. MANAHAN, JAMES McREYNOLDS, JANE BRATTON.

Pp 289-290:   JACOB BARNETT, planter of York Co. to WILLIAM SMITH,
planter of same, 18 Sept. 1787, 100 acs. on waters of Bullocks
Creek, part of grant to JACOB BARNETT by Gov. Wm. Moultrie of S.C.,
2 Oct. 1786. Wit: CHAS. SMITH, JOSEPH FRENCH, JOSIAH SMITH. Signed:
J. BARNETT.

Pp 290-292:   JOHN FOSTER and his wife ELEANOR (NELLY) of 96 Dist.,
Greenville Co., to JOSIAH SMITH of Camden Dist., York Co., 26
July 1787, 470 acs. granted to GEORGE GOWAN, along the E side of Broad
River. Wit: RICHD. THOMPSON, MYHILL SMITH, JOHN REED.

Pp 294-297:   THOMAS COOK and his wife AMY of Camden Dist. to PHILIP
SANDIFER of same, 27 Jan. 1782, 170 acs. on S side of Fishing
Creek, part of grant to ANDREW WOODS, 31 Mar. 1753, and conveyed from
WOODS to JAMES STAFFORD and DANIEL ALEXANDER, 19 Sept. 1770, and by
them to JACOB WILSON, 17 Jan. 1774. Wit: DANIEL GREEN, BENJAMIN COOK,
ROBERT KILLOUGH.

Pp 297-299:   JOSEPH BOGGS, yeoman, and his wife MARY of Fishing Creek,
to THOMAS BOGGS of same, 4 Oct. 1787, 168 acs. of a tract on
which THOMAS BOGGS lives which was land that belonged to his deceased
father, JOSEPH BOGGS, SR., deeded to him by BENJAMIN PHILIPS, 21 Mar.
1768, on Fishing Creek, joining lands of JOHN HARDIN, WILLIAM DICKSON,
WILLIAM HEGERTE. Wit: WM. HANNA, ROBERT HANNA.
(Note: THOMAS BOGGS married ELIZABETH MASON in March 1784.)

Pp 299-302:   REYDERUS CLARK of Union Co., SC to DAVID LEECH of York
Co., 9 Oct. 1787, 150 acs. on both sides of Turkey Creek, adj.
to JOHN HILLHOUSE's land and the Charleston Waggon Road, granted to
REYDERUS CLARK by Gov. Thomas Boone of S.C., 20 Apr. 1763. Wit: W.
BRATTON, FRAS. ADAMS, JAS. WILLSON.

Pp 302-303:   DAVID LEECH and THOMAS GILLHAM, to REYDERUS CLARK, 9
Oct. 1787, bond of indemnity for 150 pds. W. BRATTON, FRAS. ADAMS.

Pp 303-305:   JOSEPH HARDIN, planter of Rutherford Co., N.C. to RICHARD
      WILSON of Craven Co., 27 Aug. 1777, 300 acs. on waters of Kings
Creek on South Fork of Jumping Branch including Glades below Whitakers
Mountain and near JOSEPH GREEN's path. Wit: JAMES WILLSON, THOMAS JENK-
INS.
      (Note: JOSEPH HARDIN and JOHN PATTON were executors of the Will
of JOHN STEPHENSON, who died in 1773.)

Pp 305-306:   DAVID NEEL of Mecklenburg Co., N.C. to ALEXANDER CAND-
      LISH of York Co., 9 Oct. 1787, bill of sale for a negro fellow
named Warley about 28 years of age. Wit: RICHARD HENRY, NATHANIEL IRWIN.

Pp 306-307:   DAVID NEEL to ALEXANDER CANDLISH, 9 Oct. 1787, bill of
      sale for negro girl named Esther about six years old. Wit: RICHARD
HENRY, NATHANIEL IRWIN.

Pp 307-309:   JOHN SMITH of York Co. to WILLIAM HILL, Esq., of same,
      10 Oct. 1787, 100 acs. adj. to Little Allisons Creek and the
Catawba Indian Land, part of grant to JOHN HALL and conveyed by him
to JOHN KIMBROUGH and by him to JAMES FERGUSON and by him to JOHN SMITH.
Wit: W. BRATTON, THOMAS GILLHAM.

Pp 309-311:   ROBERT DUNLAP and his wife ELIZABETH, to JOHN GALLAGHER,
      10 Nov. 1786, 146 acs. on S side of Allisons Creek, joining WIL-
LIAM McDOWELL's and Major TEMPLE's land. Wit: THOS. McCLURKEN, JOHN
BURNS.

Pp 312-313:   WILLIAM TEMPLE COLES of York Co., to JOHN RICE of same,
      2 Aug. 1787, 200 acs. (formerly in Tryon Co., N.C.) on Kings
Creek, being third part at the upper end of a 600 ac. tract. Wit: BERRY-
MAN SHUMATE, WM. LITTLE, WILLEY S. BROWN.

Pp 316-319:   ANDREW McNABB of Camden Dist., to WILLIAM BARRON of same,
      both planters, 6 Sept. 1777, 247 acs. bet. BENJAMIN PHILIPS'
land and branch of the South Fork of Fishing Creek; granted to ANDREW
McNABB by N. C., 6 Apr. 1753. Wit: PHIL. SANDIFER, ROBT. THOMAS.

Pp 319-323:   JAMES STAFFORD and his wife MARY and DAN ALEXANDER of
      Mecklenburg Co., N.C. to JOSEPH WILSON, late of York Co., 17
Jan. 1774, 400 acs. on a branch of Fishing Creek and joining GEORGE
CATHEY's land on S side; granted to ANDREW WOODS, 31 Mar. 1753, and
conveyed to JAMES STAFFORD and DAN ALEXANDER, 19 Sept. 1770. Wit: EDW.
GILES, GILBERT KENNEDY, JOHN WILSON.

Pp 323-326:   ALEXANDER HARPER and his wife MARTHA of Tryon Co., N.C.
      to ROBERT CARSON of Mecklenburg Co., N.C., 10 Aug. 1772, a tract
of land in Tryon Co., N.C. (now York Co.) on Susa Boles Branch of Turkey
Creek and next to JOHN KELLY's line; granted 22 Apr. 1767. Wit: JOHN
DENNIS, GEORGE SADLER.

Pp 326-328:   THOMAS RAINEY and his wife ANNE, BENJAMIN PHILIPS and
      his wife RACHEL, to WILLIAM BARRON, 12 July 1774, 175 acs. on
Turkey Creek, including improvements Philips bought of BULL and adj.
THOMAS KILLOUGH's line and WILLIAM BARRON's line; granted to THOMAS
RAINEY and BENJAMIN PHILIPS, 24 Dec. 1770. Wit: HENRY GOOD, ROBERT
GOOD.

Pp 320-330:   ROBERT CARSON and his wife MARGARET of Camden Dist.,
      to WILLIAM BARRON of same, 6 Jan. 1774, a tract whereon Barron
now lives, lying on Susey Boles' Branch of Turkey Creek and KELLY's
land; granted to ALEXANDER HARPER, 22 Apr. 1767. Wit: JOHN KELLY, JOHN
WALLACE.

Pp 331-333:   THOMAS GARVIN and his wife JANE of Camden Dist., to WILL-
      IAM BARRON of same, 19 Dec. 1777, 100 acs. on branch of Turkey
Creek and on both sides of sd creek; granted to DAVID VANCE by N.C.,
25 Apr. 1767. Wit: JESSE GLOVER, ROBERT GLOVER.

Pp 333-336:   DRURY GLOVER and his wife MARY of Camden Dist., to WIL-

Cont'd:
LIAM BARRON, 22 Dec. 1777, 200 acs. on a branch of the south fork of Turkey Creek on both sides of sd creek and joining lands of JAMES STEPHENSON, GARVIN; granted to <u>DREWRY</u> GLOVER by N. C., 15 May 1772. Wit: WM. CALLEY, JOHN CARSON.

Pp 337-339:   JOHN GREEN and his wife MARY of Camden Dist., to WILLIAM BARRON of same, 15 Sept. 1777, 100 acs. granted to WILLIAM GLOVER, bishop, 30 Oct. 1765, on W side of Turkey Creek. Wit: JOSEPH JEWEL, ISUM GLOVER.

Pp 340-342:   JACOB BARNETT, planter of York Co. to ADAM MEEK, planter of same place, 12 Sept. 1787, 500 acs. on Bullocks Creek where BARNETT now lives, it being the upper part of a grant to BARNETT by Gov. Wm. Moultrie of S.C. Wit: JAMES MEEK, EDWARD BYERS, WILLIAM PORTER. Signed: JACOB BARNETT.
        (Note: JAMES MEEK (1758-1819) brother of ADAM MEEK, married SUSANNA BYERS (1771-1844), daughter of Capt. WILLIAM BYERS. Meek commanded a company at Kings Mountain and was drowned in the Seneca River, 3 Mar. 1819, while on his way to attend a sale of public lands in Alabama.)

Pp 342-344:   PETER KUYKENDALL of Craven Co. to JAMES WILKINSON, SR. of same, 22 Dec. 1774, 200 acs. on Fishing Creek, beginning at SW corner of Indian line claimed by the Catawbas and with Indian line to WILLIAM MILLS' line, then with PETER KUYKENDALL's line to beginning. Granted to MARTIN ARMSTRONG, 22 Dec. 1768, and conveyed to PETER KUYKENDALL. Wit: JOHN GREEN, JAMES WILKINSON, JR.

Pp 344-347:   JOHN KUYKENDALL of Washington Co., N.C. to WILLIAM JENKINS of Camden Dist., 18 July 1782, 200 acs. on NW side of Kings Creek, joining and bet. STEPHEN PHILIPS', FREDERICK HAMBRIGHT's and PETER KUYKENDALL's lines. Wit: JONATHAN PRICE, SAMUEL WALLACE.
        (Note: FREDERICK HAMBRIGHT commanded a regiment at Kings Mountain)

Pp 347-349:   ROBERT McAFEE of Craven Co., to JAMES WILSON of same, 13 Sept. 1779, 500 acs. on both sides of north fork of Jumping Branch of Kings Creek, joining JACOB RANDALL's land, including JOHN HARDEN's improvement. Wit: JACOB RANDALL, THOMAS JENKINS, JACOB HOSSTATLER.
        (Note: ROBERT McAFEE was a member of S.C. Provincial Congress, 1775-1776.)

Pp 349-352:   JOHN SWANN, planter, son of ROBERT SWANN, deceased, of York Co., to JAMES PINKERTON, surveyor, of same, 30 Jan. 1787, for 250 acs. on Sirrates Creek in Spartanburgh Co., being half of 500 ac. tract in partnership betwixt JOHN SWANN and JAMES PINKERTON, deeds 150 acs. on waters of Clarks Fork of Bullocks Creek on Caldwell's and Gold's branches, and adj. CLARK's land, being the upper end of 300 acs. granted by N.C., 14 Nov. 1771 to ROBERT SWANN, dec'd. Wit: ROBT. PATTERSON, JOHN SMITH, JOS. CLARK.

Pp 352-354:   JOHN SWANN of York Co. to JAMES CLARK of same, both planters, 15 Jan. 1788, 150 acs. being one-half of a 300 ac. grant to ROBERT SWANN, by N.C., 14 Nov. 1771, on Clarks Fork of Bullocks Creek and on Caldwell's Branch, being the lower end of sd tract and adj. lands of JOHN THOMPSON and JOSEPH CLARK. Wit: ROBT. PATTERSON, JOHN SMITH, JAS. PINKERTON.
        (Note: JOHN THOMPSON (1743-1795), Revolutionary soldier.)

Pp 355-357:   JOSEPH WILSON of Craven Co., to THOMAS COOK of Bute Co., N.C., 8 Sept. 1774, 400 acs. on a branch of Fishing Creek joining GEORGE CATHEY's land on the S side; granted to ANDREW WOODS, 31 Mar. 1753, and conveyed to JAMES STAFFORD and DAN ALEXANDER, 19 Sept. 1770 and to JOSEPH WILSON, 17 Jan. 1774. Wit: BEN. COOK, DEMCY WINBORNE.

Pp 358-359:   Colonel WILLIAM HILL, Esq. of York Co., to JOHN GEE of same, 14 Nov. 1787, Lot No. 17 in the new town called by the

Cont'd:
name of Yorkville, adjoining Mr. BAILEY's on the northwest side of
Congress Street. Wit: CHRISR. BOLLING, ROBT. HILL, JOHN HENRY GEE.

Pp 359-361:   MARY HOGG of York Co. to THOMAS HOGG of Burke Co., NC.,
          25 Dec. 1787, 200 acs. on waters of Bullocks Creek, joining on
north lands of CHARLES STICE, and on south by land of JOHN McKNIT ALEX-
ANDER, being part of grant to JOHN HOGG, 19 Sept. 1770. Wit: WILLIAM
SCOTT, SAMUEL SCOTT, DANIEL HARSHA.

Pp 362-364:   JOHN HAMILTON of Lincoln Co., N.C. to JAMES MITCHELL
          of York Co., 9 Oct. 1787, 100 acs. on Fishing Creek; granted
to ROBERT McNABB and JOHN CARR, 25 Apr. 1767, and conveyed to HAMIL-
TON, joining lands of HUGH BRATTON, ADAMS, THOMAS RAINEY, LEECH and
JOHN MOORE. Wit: JOHN MARTIN, MATHEW RUSSELL, FRANCIS DOVER.

Pp 364-366:   JOHN BUIS of Craven Co., to MALCOLM HENRY of Lincoln
          Co., N.C., 8 Mar. 1781, 500 acs. on headwaters of Allisons Creek,
being part of three surveys lying on the Great Road and waters of Bullocks Creek. Wit: WILLIAM MOORHEAD, THOMAS JANES, WILLIAM HENRY.
     (Note: THOMAS JANES was a member of the Second Provincial Congress
of South Carolina, 1775-1776.)

Pp 366-369:   WILLIAM HARRIS and his wife ANNE of York Co., to JOHN
          MARTIN of same, 27 Oct. 1787, 250 acs. on both sides of Bullocks
Creek; granted to JOHN RIGGS by Gov. Wm. Tryon of N.C., 20 Apr. 1767,
and conveyed to THOMAS BRANDON, 4 Feb. 1769, and conveyed to JOSEPH
PATTERSON, 15 Mar. 1775, and to WILLIAM HARRIS, 12 Feb. 1787, joining
lands of JAMES HOPE and GIBSON. Wit: ABRAHAM SMITH, JAMES MARTIN, GEORGE
ROSS.
     (Note: Colonel THOMAS BRANDON, took part in battle of Ramsour's
Mill, made an attack on Tories at Stallings (York County) on 12 July
1780, and was at the battle of Musgrove's Mills, 19 Aug. 1780.)

Pp 370-372:   JOHN SWANN of York Co., to ROBERT CARSKADDEN of same,
          20 Aug. 1787, a tract on a ridge bet. the waters of Turkey Crk.
and Bullocks Creek, made over by deed to ROBERT SWANN, now deceased,
by ZACHARIAH BULLOCK. Wit: THOMAS WALLACE, JOS. WALLACE, JANE WALLACE.

Pp 372-375:   JOHN VINEYARD (Attorney for ISHMAEL VINEYARD, planter
          of York County), and JANE VINEYARD, to ROBERT SMITH of same,
12 Oct. 1787, 250 acs. consisting of 200 acs. granted to ISHMAEL VINE-
YARD by Gov. Wm. Tryon of N.C., 28 Apr. 1768 (then in Mecklenburg Co.,
N.C., now York Co.), joining JOHN KERNAHAN's land; and 50 acs. granted
to ISHMAEL VINEYARD by Gov. Josiah Martin, of N.C. on 14 Nov. 1771,
(then lying in Tryon Co., N.C., now York Co.), on waters of Turkey
Creek. Wit: JONATHAN SUTTON, JAS. HAWTHORN, JAS. MARTIN.
     (Note: JONATHAN SUTTON (1753-1818) Revolutionary soldier, was
buried at Beersheba Presbyterian Church.)

Pp 378-382:   THOMAS MOORE, planter of Chester Co., SC to JACOB BROWN
          of Winnsborough, S.C., 6 Oct. 1787, 600 acs. along N side of
Broad River on Beaver Dam Creek, known as "Beauty Spot", orig. granted
to GUYON MOORE by Gov. Matthew Rowan of N.C., 3 Apr. 1752, and willed
to his son JOHN MOORE, who died without children and intestate, which
land then decended to his oldest brother, JAMES MOORE, and was willed
by him to his son, THOMAS MOORE. Wit: D'd. HOPKINS, FERD. HOPKINS,
RICHD. MILES, J. G. HUNT.
     (Note: DAVID HOPKINS, colonel in the Revolutionary War.)

Pp 382-384:   WILLIAM HILL, of York Co. to ELIJAH BAILEY of same, plant-
          er, 8 Nov. 1787, Lot No. 16 in Yorkville on Congress St. adj.
to and on S side of the Court House lot. Wit: CHRISTOPHER BOLLING,
CALEB BAILEY, JOHN GEE.

Pp 385-387:   JOHN RICE of York Co. to JOHN GALLAGHER of same, 17 Jan.
          1788, 540 acs. granted to JOHN RICE, 2 Oct. 1786, on waters of
Bullocks Creek and Turkey Creek, adj. Widow HOGG's line. Wit: CHRISTO-
PHER BOLLING, DAVID McCALL, ROBERT SMITH.
                    END OF DEED BOOK A

287, William Sr.,287,
William,299,327,347,349,
Wm.,348, Wm.Jr.,292,
Wm.Sr.,292
BALDWIN, Caleb,037,038,
George,383, Isaac,441,
Thomas,440
BALDY, Anne,284, David,281,
282, Paul,283, S.,282,
Sarah,281,282
BALENTINE, Alexander,099,
Douogale,083, William,307
BALEY, George,524
BALIE, John,429
BALINGER, Edward,172
BALL, George,247, Isaac,017,
Richard,017, Richd.,569,
Trislena A.,264, William Jr.,
247, William,247
BALLANGER, Edward,128,143
BALLANTINE, Dugall,035
BALLARD, C.,294, Caroline,288,
Dev'x.,390, Dev.,369,
Devereaux,369, Devx.,414,
415, Jesse,185, Lewis,355,
Richard,214
BALLENGER, Edward,150,152,
158, Isaac,306
BALLENTINE, Edwin D.,005,
James A.,005, James D.,005,
Lemuel,005, Mary Ann,005,
Zacariah,005
BALLEW, Rayney,435, Renny,548,
Robert,327, Rueben,548,
Zachariah,548
BALLINGER, Edward,146,152,172
BALLOU, (& Co.),367
BALLOW, Thomas,515
BALNS(?), Eleanor,445
BALUM, Honas,515
BALUS, Eleanor,444, Nell,444
BANASTER, James,519
BANCKSTON, Elijah,088
BANDS, William,160
BANDY, Bryant,333, Jessie,051,
Phebe,333
BANISTER, John J.,393, John,
393
BANK, William,036
BANKHEAD, Betsy,477, Elizabeth,
477,557, George,477, Hugh,
477,557, James,025,086,089,
475,477,539,548,557, Jenney,
477, Jenny,477, John,086,
087,102,475,476,477,513,
548, Mary,477, Patsy,477,
Polly,477, Robert,477
BANKS, Albert E.,001, Betsey,
001, Charles,001,210,311,
Marie,001, Ransom,330,
Samuel,131, William,046
BANKSTON, Elijah,022
BANLEY, Thomas,299
BANNERS, Hugh,072
BANTON, Jedida,204, Lewis,198,
201,204,212,223,246
BAR, K.Eliz.,301
BARBER, James,110,112,121,
John,051,567, William,394
BARBOUR, Walter,315, William,
394
BARCHFIELD, James,236
BARE, Dl.,287
BARFIELD, Barrot Jr.,299,300,
Barrot,286,292,299,
Charles,299, Elisha,286,
292, Elizabeth,299, Furney,
299, Henry,299, Jas.,293,
299, Mills,408, Roger,287,
William,287, Winney,299,
Wm.,292,299
BARFOOT, Noah,286,292, Wm.,
292
BARIN, John,358
BARKER(?), Charlotte,342
BARKER, ,356, Bartholomew,493,
Benjamin,166, Elizabeth,
337, Jesse,250, Lewis,351
BARKLEY, Hugh,109, James,109,
110,112,114, Jas.,112,114,
120, Robert,559
BARKSDALE, Ann,200,225,
Nathan,211,214,216,

William,200,225,253, Wm.,
BARKSDDALE, Wm.,271
BARLOW, Elizabeth,306, John,
306,317
BARNDON, Thos.,537
BARNES, Caleb,103, Charles,
286,299, Chas.,293, Christian,
287, David,299, Dudley,313,
George,217, James,372,393,
Jas.,292, Jas.Jr.,292,
Joel,292, Jon.,236,
Nichodemus,103, Thos.,292,
Viney,293
BARNET(BARRET?), Nancy,350
BARNET, ,505, John,039,194,
224,236, Maradith,350,
Margaret,039, Rebecca,039,
Ruben,180, Seleter,225,
William,039
BARNETT, (Land),082, Ann,329,
Capt.,567,568, Elijah,329,
Elisabeth,560, Humphrey,
560,561,564,569, J.,569,
Jacob(Lt.),561, Jacob,562,
564,569,571, John J.,329,
John,489, Judy C.,329,
Mary,329, Melinda,329,
Rial,329, Rosannah J.,329,
Thomas,045
BARNETT, Thomas,329
BARNHILL, James,175
BARNS, Barbara,502, Barnet,
533,534, Charles,502,
Dudley,313, Jacob,502,
James,313, John,169,502,
Moses,502
BARR, John,411, Joseph,387
BARRAT, Nancy,307
BARRATT, Reuben,359, Sally,
359
BARRET, Lewis,346, Moses,185
BARRETT, Arthur B.,329,
Arthur,329, Benjamin,339,
David,339, Hannah,124,
John,339, Milton,339,
Reuben,124,136,139,146,
148,169,173, Sarah,329,
Thomas,307, William,339
BARRETTE, Reuben,170
BARRISON, Moses,189
BARRON, Abraham,568, Alexander,
567, Alexr.,567, Archibald,
562, Isaac,353, James,085,
439,562,567, John,497,558,
565,566, Margaret,565,
Margret,497, Martha M.,439,
Olive,569, Robert,496,
Thomas,496, William,565,
568,569,570,571
BARROT, James,353, Richard,
493
BARROTT, R.,182
BARROW, James,044,045
BARRY, Andrew,164, Edm.,416,
Samuel,567, Wm.,028
BARTAM, Charles,322
BARTELL, Jesse,287, Mary,286,
293,298, Peter,298, Philip,
298, William,298
BARTLETT, Elizabeth,260
BARTLY, ,370
BARTON(BURTON?), Jas.,207
BARTON, ,167, Absolom,005,
Augusta,335, B.,325,
Bailey A.,335, Bailey,346,
347,351,352,356,357,359,
Benjamin,131, Bevester,213,
Cloud T.,360, Daniel,360,
David O.,360, David,347,
360, E.H.,338, Eleanor,360,
Elias,360, Elizabeth,126,
Isaac,201
BARTON, Isaac,202,236, J.M.,
358, James,207, Joseph,193,
203, Josiah,203, Mary Jane,
339, Mary,338, Peter L.,347,
Peter,360, Samuel,221,
Thomas,126,131,134,
William E.,360, William,
126,131,326,352, Willoughby,
005, Winna,360, Wm.,347,359
BARTWISLE, Richard,311
BASCOM, Wm.Jr.,252

BASLIS, John,071
BASS, Bryan,286,293, Bryant,
298, Jethro,286,292, Jno.,
293, John,287,298, Jos.,293,
Joseph,286,298,387, Martha,
293,298, Philemon,525,
Robert,298
BASWELL, Tobias,292
BATEMAN, ,420, William,383
BATES, (Land),257, ,365,
Elizabeth,393, Flemming,
337, Henry,134, Humphrey,
433,551, Humphry,459,471,
Humy(Humphrey),433, James,
142,146,264,393,419, Jas.,
372, John Sr.,419, John,124,
132,384,419, Joseph Jr.,551,
Joseph Sr.,551, Joseph,498
BATES, Joseph,510,516,551,
Margaret,357, Polly,337,
Robert,393, Sarah,465,
Shelby,357, Shilvy,328
BATH, Daniel,287, Danl.,292
BATSON, Asbal,181
BATTEN, Richard,240, Richd.,
240, Richrd.,244
BAUGH, John Jr.,234, John,215,
220,227, William,226,234,
Wm.,215,234
BAUGHMAN, Samuel,252
BAUGHN, ,166
BAUX, Joseph,172
BAXLEY, Barnabas,287,299,
Thomas,287, Thos.,292
BAXTER, William,276
BAY, A.,399, Ann,371,398,
William,371, Wm.,398
BAYELY, Mary,089
BAYLEIGH, Jonas,299, Wm.,299
BEAKS, Abraham,525, Samuel,
525, Sarah,525
BEAL, ,151
BEALE, Mr.,142
BEALS, ,162
BEAM, Isaac,105
BEAN, Isaac,114, Robert,169
BEARD(?), James,222
BEARD, ,004, Elizabeth,307,
Hugh,192,219, James,192,
John,527, Jonas,001,
Margret,476, William,381,
424, Wm.B.S.,005
BEARDEN, Abborzela,512,
Edmund,164,166,175,
Richard,145, Thomas,512,549
BEASLEY, Jno.,272, Leanard,
250, Rebecca,005, William,
005
BEATEY, James,116
BEATTEY, James,109
BEATTY, Charles,560,568,
James,315, Jas.,112
BEATY, Catharine,359, James,
121,359, Joseph,352, Robert,
352, Robt.,348
BEAUFORT, (Col.),270
BEAVERS, Joseph,003, Lucinda,
003
BEAVERT, Wm.,348
BEAZLIE, Lenard,251
BECCKLEY, Jacob,015
BECK, William,061, Wm.,348
BECKET, James,113,120, Jas.,
113
BECKHAM, ,528, Elizabeth,536,
Jno.Jr.,541, Jno.Sr.,536,
John Jr.,446,447,464,498,
536,548, John Sr.,518,
John(Jr.?),519, John,439,
497,519,536, William,425,
508,516, Wm.,517
BECKWORTH, Henry,287,293,
Morning,299
BEDDINGTON, James,539
BEDENBAUGH, Daniel,005, Wm.,
003
BEDGEGOOD, (Rev.),279,
Nicholas,279, Rev.,281
BEDGEWOOD, (Rev.),281
BEDGGOOD, Mr.,282, Rev.,281
BEDGOOD, Nicholas(Rev.),281,
Rev.,282
BEE, Thomas,233

135,135,149,151,162,165,
168,175,185, Augustin,185,
Frances,143, Francis,143,
Geo.W.,325, George W.,354,
John E.,005, Malinda,325
BLACKBURN, Malinda,354,
Martha L.,005, Mary,185,
Matilda,325, Meredith,165,
Merideth,185, Nancy E.,005,
Ransome,005, Silvey W.,325,
Thomas,325,354, William,
307,320,354
BLACKBURNE, A.,156
BLACKERBY, Joseph,226,243,
245, Sarah,226
BLACKEY, Hannah,464
BLACKLEY, Jas.,349
BLACKMAN, David,286,299, Dd.,
293, Jno.,292, John,287,
299, Sol.,293, Solomon,286
BLACKSTOCK, ,168, Euphemy,476,
Euphenia,544, James,142,
165,178,326,352,476,477,
491, Jas.,347, John,230,
326,348,476, Levina,326,
352, Mrs.,352, Nehemiah,326,
Richard,326, Ruth,476,
Sarah,326, William,476,
477, Wm.(D),476, Wm.Sr.,544
BLACKWELL, ,132,140, Dan'l Jr.,
149, Daniel,151, Edmund,149,
Jacob,286, John,172,
Washington,354, Zachariah,
149
BLACLWELL, Jacob,293
BLADDON, Winney,005
BLAIN, Michael,092
BLAIR, ,325, Catharine,360,
George W.,004, George,347,
Hannah,358, James,033,044,
057,058,059,094,110,
Margaret,058,059, Martha,
004, Thomas,075, William,360
BLAKE, David,263, Jane Ross,
263, Jane,263, Peggy,263
BLAKELEY, Agnes,261, Martha,
261, Thomas,210
BLAKELY, Elizabeth,261,267,
Fields,441, James,248,
John,253, Jonathan,261,
Margaret,261, Robert,261
BLALOCK, Anderson,352,
John Jr.,545, John Sr.,309,
545, John,002,307, Lewis,309
BLANCHARD, Henry,287,292
BLANCHET, Jas.,299
BLAND, Edw.,055, Robert,566
BLANTON, George,511,558,565,
Jno.,565, John,017
BLASENGAIM, Frances,527,
Thomas,527
BLASINGAIM, John,531, Thomas,
528
BLASINGAME, ,130, Fanny,521,
551, Frances,522, J.,138,
152,160,172,173,174, James,
138,142,146,148,149,153,
160,171,172,173,550, Jas.,
147, John Jr.,549, John W.,
325, John,160,172,183,187,
512,544,549,556, Molly,471,
Obedience,549, Thomas,150
BLASINGAME, Thomas,438,471,
521,551, Thos.,438,522,530,
531,540,541,543,544,545,
549, Thos.Jr.,544,551, Wm.,
549
BLASINGHAM, Thomas,435
BLASSENGAME, Fanny,527, Jno.,
533, Thomas,527
BLASSIGAME(?), John,500
BLASSINGAME, James,135,143,
490, John,187,188,339,443,
492, Justice,190, Lucy E.,
339, Minyard(?),365, Robt.,
346, Thomas,429,430,441,
442,445,490,492,493,500,
503,504,509, Thos.,429,431,
439,444,490,509,510,516,
520,522,525,536
BLASSINGAMES, Fed,364
BLEAKLY, John,216
BLECKLEY, Jacob,083

BLEDIAS(?), (Land),257
BLESINGAME, John,537
BLEUK, Robert,077
BLEW, Archibald,299, William,
299
BLISITT, George,036
BLISSET, George,027
BLISSIT, George,097, Reason,
097, Stephen,097
BLITH, William,182
BLITHE, William,182, Wm.,182
BLUE, Wm.,293
BLUTHE, William,182
BLYTH, Absalom,159,181,350,
Absolam,163, David,181
BLYTHE, A.,366, Absalom,349,
Mack,364, William,182,185
BOATNER, Sally,333, Sarah,366,
367,368
BOATNERS, Jacob,375
BOATRITE, Daniel,299, Margt.,
299, Martha,299
BOBBET, Isham,185
BOBO, Absalom,204,220,525,
Absolum,209,250, Burrill,
515, Kindred,556, Lecil,255,
257, Lewis,430,438,504,507,
517,533,534,555,556, Sarah,
504,517,555,556, Solomon,
253, Spencer Jr.,220,
Spencer,217,244, Tillman,
257, William,252
BOCHER, Margaret,386
BOCQUET, Peter,533
BODIE, Ellen,005, Lucy,003,
Sophia,006
BOGAN, ,491, Ann,534, Isaac,
171,429,510,514,519,552,
James,433,503,513,520,522,
535,543, John,003, Rebacca,
003
BOGGS, A.M.,354, Aaron,330,
354, David H.,329,349,354,
Elizabeth,569, Garner,342,
J.N.,330, Jane,330,
John R.,330,352, Jos.,560,
Joseph G.,330,354, Joseph Sr.,
569, Joseph,560,569, Marcus,
363, Martha,330, Martin,330,
354, Mary,569, Mr.,359
BOGGS, T.Edward,363, T.G.,354,
361, Thomas G.,354,357,
Thomas,330,354,569,
William,328,330,360, Wm.,
BOGLE, James,292, Jas.,292
BOLAN, Richd.,540
BOLAND, John,005
BOLDING, Jonathan L.,354,
Jonathan,354
BOLDRIGHT, Thomas,287, Thos.,
293, William,287, Wm.,297
BOLDWRIGHT, Daniel,286, Dl.,
292
BOLING, Robert,253, Samuel,
196, Tulley,185
BOLLING, Chrisr.,572, Christopher,
572, Tully,185
BOLT, Abraham,244, Abram,251,
James,005
BOLTON, John,004, Robert,004,
Solomon,379
BOMER, George W.,325
BOMUN, Nathaniel,160
BOND, Elisha,549, Isam,061,
Iscm,068, Jas.,292, John,
068, Mary,107, Moses,013,
074, Seviller,068, Solomon,
405,406, Sovillen,061, Wm.,
231
BONDS, ,009, Betty,305,
Dudley,307,320, James,001,
John,252, Joice,305, Mary,
306, Menoah,305, Retter,305,
Richard,305,316, Sally,305,
Seth,418, William,150,305
BONER, John,112
BONEY, Jacob,109,112
BONFIELD, Miles,383
BONNER, Hugh,017
BONY, Jacob,106
BOOKER, Bird,460
BOOKS, James,305
BOON, Nathan,346, Sela,332,

Thomas,515
BOONE, Thomas,535,558,562,
568, Wm.,028
BOOTH, John,185,279,280,281,
Jos.H.,102, Joseph,083,
087,097, Sarah,278
BOOTHE, Joseph,036, Rhoda,283
BOOZER, Fredrick,310,312,
317,318, Henry,317
BORDEN, ,506
BOROUGHS, Jacob,337
BORROW, Robert,043, William,
043
BOSER, John,077
BOSHER, Thomas,387,397
BOSSART, Jacob,318
BOSTIC, (Estate),303, James,
300
BOSTICK, Floyd,569, Jas.,292,
William,427,526,565
BOURLAND, John,212, Mary,212
BOUSSIER, Zadok,500
BOVERSON(?), ,543
BOWDRY(BOWDY?), Sarah,278
BOWEN, ,254, Fredrick,185,
Isaac,185, J.B.,368,
John H.,342, John,280,284,
328,341,342,346,355,356,
357, M.D.L.,342, M.T.,342,
Martha,356, Milly,364,
Patsey,356, Rice,356,
Rolley,196, Rolly,217,219,
S.H.,342, Samuel H.,342,
W.F.,368
BOWEN, W.R.,342, William Sr.,
252, William,329, Wm.,271,
357
BOWERS, James L.,004, James,
001, Mary Ann,004, Mary,003
BOWIE, ,166, Alexander,005,
George,,270, John,135,137,
141,155,165,171, Maj.,158,
Sidney J.,005
BOWIN, Fredrick,185, Sarah,
117, William,117
BOWKER, Bird,460
BOWLES, (Family),552, Isabella,
552, John,219
BOWLIN, Edward,048
BOWLS, Elizabeth,233
BOWMAN, ,252, George,218,
Jacob,213,214,218,219,229,
240, James,509, John,214,
Matilda,354, Sarah,212,
218, Violet,358, William,
536,542, Wm.,532
BOWYER, Michael,017
BOX, Abraham,220, Edward,141,
234, Henry,211, John,196,
220,235,237, Joseph,132,
133,150,237, Margaret,259,
Robert Jr.,201, Robert,196,
201,214,220, Robt.,226
BOXE, (Land),516
BOYCE, Alexander,313, Alexr.,
255, Drury,191,210,228,
Elenor,214, John,255,256,
311,313,314, Thomas,204,
214,233
BOYD, ,009,234,258, Aaron,004,
Adaline,340, Agnes,109,
115, Andrew,109,115, Ann,
089,322, Anon(?),027,
Archd.,100, Archebald,076,
Archibald,097, Betsey,322,
Bradford,001, Catherine,
207,209, Charles,091,
Daniel,362, David,014,027,
083
BOYD, David,085,120, Geter Lewis,
346, Hannah,062, James Jr.,
272, James,078,109,209,253,
272,322,360, Jane Betsey,
322, Jno.,271, John H.,349,
John Jr.,388, John Sr.,322,
John,027,040,078,098,150,
209,219,220,255,274,318,
322,340, Ludy,004
BOYD, Margaret,014,027,322,
Margret,109, Martha,209,
Mary,346, Rachel,360,
Robert Jr.,346, Robert,002,
023,025,078,089,150,346,

Robt.,119,349, Rt.(?),361,
S.M.,030, Saml.,209,
Samuel,001,014,078,209,
259,273, Thomas,243,322,
346, Will,057
BOYD, Will,062, Will.,563,
William Sr.,274, William,
010,014,016,018,021,023,
024,027,039,050,053,054,
083,085,089,092,101,103,
104,144,207,209,243,322,
346,543, Wm.,072,074,075,
077,089,091, Wm.Jr.,273
BOYER, John,311
BOYERS, Frank,367, Sary,367
BOYKIN, John,246, William,067
BOYL, Edward,557
BOYLE, James,308, Wm.,073
BOYLES, Hugh,101, Martha,080,
William,080,101
BOYS(BOYCE), John,256
BOYS, John,249
BRACEY, ,421, J.,418, Jolly,
390,404,406,407, M.,418,
Merry,374,404,420, William Sr.,
407, William,374,375,390,
404,406,407,420, Wm.,391,
404,408
BRACHER, Laurence,158
BRACK, Chas.,542
BRACKEN, Thomas,047
BRACKENRIDGE, Thos.,325
BRACKFIELD, C.,051
BRADBERRY, Jesse,358
BRADDEY, Jno.,292
BRADDOCK, Francis,252
BRADDY, John,299
BRADEN, William,265
BRADFORD, C.D.,114, Chas.D.,
114, James,423, John J.,371,
416, John Js.,375,415, John,
370, Nathaniel,373, Richard Jr.,
392, Richard,392,414,417,
420, Robert,075,092
BRADLEY, (Line)408, ,092,
Abraham,124,162,173,173,
Annie,341, James(Dr.),004,
James,046,373, John,004,
287,292,298,423, Joseph,050,
052, Josiah Wm.,370,373,
Josiah,369, Matthew,370,
Mrs.,373, Nancy,267, Polly,
267, Roger,417, Saml.(Capt.),
423
BRADLEY, Saml.Jas.,413,417,
Samuel Jr.,417, Samuel,417,
Simeon,347, William,176,
Wm.,341
BRADNOR, ,564
BRADOCK, James,252
BRADY, Charles,234
BRAGG, Thomas,041,081
BRAILSFORD, Robert,407
BRAISHER, Aquila,136
BRAKEFIELD, Jacob,056
BRAKEN, Thomas,067
BRAMBLET, Enoch,216, Sandford,
216, William,216, Wm.,216
BRAMLET, Newton,243, William,
243
BRAMLETT, Nathan,231,239,247,
Reuben,231, Wm.,234
BRAMLETTE, Reuben,254
BRAMLING, Reuben,254
BRANDAWAY, Nancy,004
BRANDON, (Col.),461, ,490,
526, Arthur,499, Capt.,540,
Catherine,436, Charles,077,
510, Christ.,547, Christo.,
431, Christop.,506, Christopher,
500,501,519,521,554, Col.,
426, Elizabeth,432,516,542,
James,448, Jas.,432, Jno.,
549, John,045
BRANDON, John,394,431,433,
436,451,492,493,498,512,
516,518,519,521,524,532,
547,549,568, Mary,493,
Richd.,554, Sarah,475,
Thomas(Col.),428,448,451,
490,491,498,501,516,541,
Thomas,044,077,130,138,
150,424,425,426,427,431,

432,433,434,436
BRANDON, Thomas,439,443,461,
481,489,490,491,492,497,
498,499,500,507,509,510,
512,513,514,515,516,517,
524,526,529,535,536,541,
542,546,548,550,551,553,
554,572, Thos.(Col.),514,
532, Thos.(Maj.),433, Thos.,
051,052,176,431,432,442,
475,480
BRANDON, Thos.,483,516,518,
520,521,529,533,545,547,
550,552,553, William,150,
513, Wm.,551
BRANDT, C.,344, E.D.C.,344
BRANNON, (Col.),461, James W.,
339, Nancy E.,339, P.,272,
Thos.(Col.),462
BRANON(BRANDON), Thos.,549
BRASEL(BRAZIL), Ann,555
BRASELLMAN, Drusilla,458,
Matthew,458, Peter,458
BRASELLMANN, Drusilla,458
BRASELMAN, Graaff S.,536,
Graff S.,536, Peter,523
BRASHEARS, Jeremiah,533
BRASHER, ,136, Aquila,174,
175, Aquilla,175, Hanna,144,
Henry,175, John,174,175,
Laurence,143, Quella,175,
Samuel,175, Sarah,143,144,
175, Thomas,131,175,
William,141,144
BRASHERES, Jeremiah,505
BRASHIES, Elizabeth,533,
Jeremiah,533
BRASINGTON, Geo.,423, George,
370,400,420
BRASSFIELD, Reuben,394
BRASSWELL, Henry,286, Richard,
286, Tobias,286
BRASURE, Naomey,145, Thomas,
131,145, William,143
BRASWELL, Aaron,324, Allen,
324, Arthur,324,340, Betsey,
324, Cleveland,340, David,
324, Henry,292, James,324,
Marion,340, Nancy,324,
Perunia(?),340, Polly,324,
Richd.,293, Rutha,340,
Rutherford,324, Susan,324,
Thomas,340, Valantine,185
BRASWELL, Valentine,318,
William,324,340, Williams,
324
BRATCHER, John,268, Wm.,552
BRATT, Sarah,040
BRATTON, Hugh,572, James,078,
Jane,569, Robinson,112,
W.,569,570, William,444,569
BRAY, Henry,526,533, William,
346
BRAZEAL, Amanda,337, James,
337, Sarah,346
BRAZEALE, Samuel P.,334,
Sarah Ann,334
BRAZELMAN, Peter,320
BRAZER, James,186
BRAZIER, John,178, Samuel,268,
Sarah,185, Thomas,185
BRAZIL, William,323
BRAZZELMAN, Peter,312
BRAZZLE, Richard,154,155
BREADY, Robert,058
BREAKFIELD, Jacob,095
BREASHER, ,136
BREASUR, Thomas,175
BREAZEAL, Gambrell,335
BREED, ,540, Avery,494,503,
504,505,508,527,531,544,
Catharine,465, Catherine,
504,508,555, Joseph,492,
503,504,508,515,521,540,
544,555, William,555
BREITHAUGHT, Christian,004,
Sarah L.,004
BREMAN, R.,065
BREMAR, D.S.,533, F.,159,533,
Frances,533,555, Francis,
555, John,399, Peter,413,417
BREMER, Joseph,345
BRESHER, John,136

BREVARD, Jno.,069, Joseph,049,
069,419
BREWER, Acry,299, Asa,287,
292, Benjamin,268, D.,292,
David,287,299, Elizabeth,
333, James,333, Joseph,332,
Nedom,304, Needham,287,292
BREWSTER, Ann,208, Anne,208,
William,208
BRIAM, William,255
BRIAN, Mary,427, Philip,508,
Richard,505
BRIANT, (Wife),500, Geo.Wm.,
500, James,125, Jesse,080,
302, Philip,493,494,500,
Richard,124, Smithy,299,
William,500
BRICE, William,286
BRICKELL, Jas.,405
BRIDGES, ,528, Benjamin,134,
175, Francis,292, James,502,
565,566, John,565, Joseph,
173,565, Thomas,134,153,
566, William,152
BRIGGMAN, H.D.,344
BRIGGS, Isaac,435, Jane L.,
357
BRIGGS, John,207,211,428,492,
525, Katherine,492, Myra L.,
357, Robert H.,351,357,
Thomas,492, William,492
BRIGHT, Charity,221, James,
206,208,221, Sarah,221
BRIGMAN, Thos.,300
BRINSON, ,566, John Sr.,373
BRISBAND, Rob,416, Robt.,415
BRISBANE, Adam B.,420
BRISCO, Nathan,060
BRISON, James,225, John,225
BRISTER, William,166
BRITAIN, Jean,058, William,
026,044,045,058,068
BRITAINS, William,018
BRITIAN, Jean,048, William,
048
BRITTON, Thomas G.,287,
Thomas,088
BROACH, Abner,293
BROADWAY, Abner,407
BROCK, C.H.,361, Charles,542,
Elias,005,209,230, Elizabeth,
341, Francis,569, Frederick,
171, G.,340, George,140,
236, Hannah,005, James(Dr.),
005, James,171, John,005,
Rebecca,512, Rebeccah,524,
Rebeckah,524, Silas,166,
Thomas,140
BROCKMAN, Henry,241
BRODEY, John,220
BROOK, Ursula,260
BROOKS, Elisha Sr.,311,
Bartholomew,426, Charles,
536,542, Dabney,156,
Dorothy,450, Elisha Jr.,
311, Elisha,319, Frances,
237, George,194,236, Isaac,
431, James,003,175,220,307,
Jesse,307, Joab,309,
Mariah,260, Mary,127,
Peter,127,199
BROOKS, Peter,213,220, Roger,
219, Sarah,213, Susanna,220
BROOM, John,118
BROTHERTON, Esther,196, John,
196
BROWN, ,009,033,282,451,501,
547,549, Abner,185, Agnes,
020, Alexander Jr.,012,016,
040, Alexander Sr.,036,040,
098, Alexander,011,012,013,
016,025,027,036,040,051,
098,101,489, Allmon,211,
Andrew,495, Ann(?),190,
Ann,049,175, Anne,284,
Barlett,199
BROWN, Bartlett,199,216,231,
Benjamin,199,245,246,
Bertsey(Betsey),440,
Betsy Jeter,452, Catherine,
051,101, Christopher B.,299,
Clairborn,260, Coalman,224,
Coleman,205, D.,506,524,

BURRISS, David,219, Mary,560,
William,015,560
BURROW, Wiley,422
BURROWS, William,205
BURSON, Isaac,490, Jonathan,
536, Joseph,490,536, Mary,
490
BURT, Frances,351, Francis,
351,354, William,456
BURTON, Aaron,322, Allen,019,
020, Benjamin,019,020,
Caleb,002, Joseph,203,237,
303, Thomas,306, Walthall,
019, Wm.,002,210, Wm.Alen,
505
BURTS, Rachel,315
BURTZ, Joshua,351,355,
Levi(Lewis?),351, Michael,
351
BUSBY, Barth.Austin,118,
Nimrod,107, Thomas,322
BUSH, Daniel,124,132,160,161,
Eliz.(Chadwick),005,
Elizabeth,004, George,309,
John H.,309, Lewis,004
BUSHKIRK, Thos.,397
BUSHOP, Boling,249,255
BUTLARS, ,181
BUTLER, Aaron,312, Abner S.,
139, Abner Smith,139, Agnes,
312, Benjamin,201, Capt.,
352, David B.,394, Elias,
293,299, Elizabeth,335,
Jno.,292, John,287,299,
Leurese,299, Lucretia,287,
292, Nancy,004, Nathan,287,
Peter,335, Pierce,238,244
BUTLER, Pierce,548, Robert,
300, Saml.,299, Steph.,293,
Stephen,287, Thomas,004,
William,286,287, Wm.,299,
Wm.Jr.,293, Wm.Sr.,292
BUTT, Elizabeth,333, Jacob,
353, John Sr.,346
BUTTLER, Abner Smith,139
BUZARD, Rudolph,311
BUZBY, Charity,121, Nathaniel,
121
BUZHARDT, Anna Mary,311,
Jacob,311,318, John,311
BUZZARD, Jacob,310
BYERLY, Gosper,121
BYERS, Ann,565, David,565,
Edward,559,567,571,
Elisabeth,559, Elizabeth,
560, Samuel,565, Susanna,
571, William Sr.,562,
William(Capt.),559,561,
571, William,559,560,562,
568, Wm.,560
BYNUM, James,160
BYRAM, Jesse,356, Nancy,356
BYRD, Benj.,254,273, Benjamin,
238, Patrick,381, Zachariah,
385
CA--YTON, B.J.,183
CABAN, Thomas,063
CABEEN, Thomas,098,101,102,
Thos.,542
CABINESS, Thomas,090
CADE, Stephen,423
CADWELL, James,164
CAHOON, Thomas,196,219
CAHUNE, Thomas,240
CAIN, Abner,509, Alexander,
522, Alexr.,543, Arrington,
299, Bat.,299, Candas,347,
John,370,401,444,509,514,
Larry,300, Moses,336,
William,299
CAINE, Alexander,425, Harrel,
545, Isaac,425
CAING, Thomas,500
CAKIN, James,087
CALAWELL, Henry,503
CALCOT, Christop.,293, James,
287, Samuel C.,287
CALCOTE, (Estate),300, James,
293, John,299
CALCUT, (Est.),299
CALDWELL(?), Mathew,511
CALDWELL, (Families),007, ,
198,207,321, A.,397, Andrew,
397, Capt.,217, Curtis,497,

Dan,005, David,318,328,
Eleanor,318, Eliz.A.,262,
Elizabeth,223, Hugh,308,
James Jr.,469,550, James Sr.,
468, James,134,138,147,243,
262,310,313,316,318
CALDWELL, James,429,503,526,
550, Jane,326, Jas.,270,
Jean,223, John Jr.,318,
John Sr.,318, John,047,
094,194,198,201,207,217,
223,233,236,256,261,262,
316,319,504, Joseph,306,
Margaret,050,316, Mary,193,
Moses,223, Patrick C.,262,
Robert,077
CALDWELL, Robert,316,318,
Samuel,050,052,097,238,
308, Susannah,318, William,
195,200,201,204,218,243,
249,258,306,313,315,318,
Wm.,138,215,219,224,270,
Wm.Thos.,200
CALHOUN, Ann,328, Fanny,360,
John Ewing,195, John,043,
217,347,359, Lucinda,003,
Ruthy,360
CALL, John,308, McHugh,299
CALLAHAM, John B.,003
CALLEY, Wm.,568,571
CALLOWAY, Joseph,170, Massey,
005, Melton,005, Nancy,170,
Thomas,170
CALLWELL(CALDWELL), Mary,429
CALLY, Wm.,569
CALMES, Thomas B.,002,
William,315
CALVIN, James,062, Job,313,
John,048,062
CALWELL, James,550
CAMBELL, Alexander,053, James,
547, Jane,149, John,053,
544, Ralph,545
CAMBERT, (Land),070
CAMBRIDGE, John M.,246,
John W.,238
CAMERON, Duncan,147, Izabel,
119, James,117, John,562,
Simeon,106,116,119, Simon,
116, William,320
CAMMACK, David Sr.,117
CAMMERON, Duncan,268
CAMMILL, John,230
CAMMOCK, David,106
CAMOCK, David,106
CAMP, Benj.,222, Benjamin,238,
239,268, Bradford,127,244,
Burrell,268, Elizabeth,239,
Harden,129, Hardin,141,
Hosea,169, James,268,
Jeams,183, John Jr.,183,
John Sr.,184, John,151,
565, Jos.,566, Joseph,185,
239, Langley B.,003, Mary,
169
CAMP, Nathan,230,238,268,
Sterling,268, Thomas Jr.,
268, Thomas,127,151,170,
Thos.,169,184, William,185,
268, Wm.W.,003
CAMPBELL, (Estate),303, ,
222,224,561, Alexander,074,
076,100, Angus,200,216,217,
219,220,221,224,228,229,
235,236,237,238,257, Ann,
287,293, Archd.,293,299,
Archibald,287, Catharine,
299, Cathe.,293, Danl.,299,
David,121,299, Duncan,148
CAMPBELL, Duncan,287,293,299,
Dunklin,139,222, Edward,
287,293, Elizabeth,315,471,
Fury,418, Hester,469, Hugh,
299, James(Rev.),076, James,
074,100,287,445,488,490,
534,547,564, Jane,136,167,
Janet,096, Jariat,309,
Jas.(Rev.),074, Jas.,293
CAMPBELL, Jas.,299,425,490,
Jean,140, Jenny,140,
Jeremiah,299, Jno.,293,
535, John,010,126,176,199,
215,277,469,470,544,547,

Joseph,309, Levi,299,
Lidia,293, Lord Wm.,506,
Martha,488, Mary,222,
Peter,287,293,299, R.,272,
Ralph,545, Richard,121
CAMPBELL, Richd.,111, Robert,
258, Sarah,056,309,314,
William,309,314,448,520,
526,534, Wm.,299
CAMPFIELD, John,232
CAMRON, Duncan,184, Lavender,
293, Nepsey,293, Simon,110,
Thomas,029
CANDLISH, Alexander,570
CANE, Alex'd.,522, Alexander,
522
CANEY, Thos.,294
CANNING, (Land),256
CANNON(?), Richard L.,359
CANNON, (Line),446, Carter,
328, Daniel,005, David,312,
318, Elijah,328,346,349,
Eliz.C.,310, Elizabeth,310,
480, Ephraim,313,314, Isaac,
310,321, James,310,313,328,
356, Jane,349, John R.M.,
339, John,199,226,252,253,
258,277,309,310,320
CANNON, Kiziah,310, Lyda,310,
Lydia,311, Malinda A.,349,
Martha,349, Mary,310,
Rachel,360, Robert,152,
153, Russel,169, Russell,
129, Sam.,362, Samuel,308,
309,310,311,465, Semcock,
550, Simcock,129,159,163,
173, Simeock,487, William,
199
CANNON, William,310,328
CANON, Ransom,349
CANSLER, Ann,361, Elizabeth,
361, F.H.,361, John M.,361,
John Sr.,361, John,329,
361, Thomas M.,361, William,
329,361
CANTELEW, Lewis,187
CANTEY, Charles,421, James,
378,393, John,378, Jos.,387,
Joseph,387,396, Josiah,398,
Margret,396, Martha,378,
Mat,396, Matthew,396,
Samauel,396, Sarah,378,
William,378,395,398, Wm.,
395, Zach.,378,393, Zachariah,
378,392
CANTRAL, Moses,325, Ruth,325,
Stephen,172
CANTRELL, Elizabeth,352, John,
339, Mary,339, Micajah,339,
Moses,327, Nancy,353,
Statin,339, Stephen,152,
William,339
CANTY, Zachariah,225
CANTZEN, Moses,073
CAPEHART, B.W.F.,354, Bartley W.F.,
325, John,170,332,344
CAPELL, Henry,397
CAPPELMANN, E.,345
CAPPS, John,388, Matt,181
CAPS, Wm.,293
CARGIL, ,252, Cornelius,198,
202,249,257, Elizabeth,204,
John A.,204, John,205,
Thomas,199,204,205,249
CARGILE, Cornelius,234,237,
238, John,234,239, Sarah(Wid.),
234
CARGILL, (Family),264,
Cornelius,241,242,246,247,
John Jr.,194,234, John,194,
213,242, Keziah,194, Magnis,
282, Magnus,284,285, Sarah,
241,285, Thomas,213,239
CARGO, Margaret,542, Saml.,
542, Samuel,528,542
CARLE, John,313
CARMICHAEL, Abraham P.,002,
Archd.,299, Archd.M.,293,
Archibald,287, B.John,287,
Daniel Sr.,287, Dl.,293,
Dougal C.,293, Dougal Jr.,
293, Dougald C.,287,
Dougald Sr.,293, Dugal Jr.,

287, Dugal Sr.,287, Duncan Jr.,
287, Duncan Sr.,293
CARMICHAEL, Duncan,287, Jno.,
293, Jno.Sr.,293, John,287,
Mary,322, Neale,299, Neil,
293, Neill,287,293, William,
322
CARNE, Elizabeth,358, Jesse,
355, Thos.William,358
CARNER, Absalom,136
CARNES, John F.,259, P.,150,
Th.P.,138, Thos.P.,122,
William,257
CARNEY, Absalom,168, Absolum,
182, Sarah,168
CARNS, John Danl.,166
CARPENTER, Bauston,141, Dan,
393,394, Dennis,185
CARR, (Widow),102, ,564,
Chas.,056, David,013,
James,070,072,078, Jane,
366, John,152,572, Wm.,349
CARRADINE, J.B.,345
CARREL, Dennis,090, Thomas M.,
186
CARRELL, Cain,028, Daniel,479,
Dennis,085,086,091,101,
104, John,560, Joseph,560,
Richard,028, Sarah,086,
104, Terrence,496,527,
Thomas,560, Willie,078,
Willis,028,080
CARRIL, Dennis,028
CARROL, Richard,028,223
CARROLL, ,094, Dennis,037,
Richard,028, Wm.Thos.,183
CARRON, Henry,124
CARRUTH, ,187
CARSEY, Elijah,251
CARSKADDEN, Robert,572
CARSON, Elizabeth,035, James,
019,020, John,035,038,039,
069,083,098,571, Margaret,
570, Rachel F.,329, Robert,
570, Samuel,561, William,
020,566, Wm.,348
CARTEE(CARTER?), F.,339
CARTEE, Frasier M.,339
CARTER(MCCARTER?), Chas.,299
CARTER, (Land),411, ,009,380,
382, Ben,419, Ben.,419,
Benj.,419, Benjamin,054,
222,419, Betty,235, Bety,
246, Daniel,413, Elisha,222,
Elizabeth,035,105,311,312,
Fielding,530, Frederick,
388, Geo.,105, George,105,
241,243,246,299, J.,166
CARTER, J.,171, Jacob,023,
055, James,235,241,246,411,
Jas.Mc.,299, Jesse,130,
132,155,156,160,164,171,
172,173,178,179,180,181,
184,185,186,187,190, Jessie,
144,145, John Jr.,235,246,
John,013,014,023,047,105,
202,211,235,241,351, Joseph,
241
CARTER, Joseph,246, Josiah,
287,293, Margaret,241,246,
299, Rachel,235, Randel,035,
Richard,235,241,246,
Robert,162,202,235,241,
246,413,418, Robt.Wm.,415,
416, Samuel,035,105,
Shadrack,311,312, Stephen,
299, T.,219, Thomas Sr.,246,
Thomas,241
CARTER, Thos.,212, William,
122,382,418, Wm.,418
CARTEY, John J.,408, Naboth,
408
CARUTHERS, James,003
CARVEAL, James,544,550
CARVER, Amanda Jane,333, Ara,
333, Asa,333, Harriet,332,
John,358, Willis,332
CARY, ,065, James,346,
Winchester,334
CASE, Jno.,293, John,287,
Samuel,493
CASEN, Ann,243, William,243
CASEY, Abner,311, Charity,165,

167,219, Eliz.(Mrs.),005,
Isaac,131, Jacob,160,
Levi(Gen.),005, Levi,132,
165,219, Mary,165,236,
Randolph,160,165,167,176,
215,219,220, William Jr.,
236, Wm.,488
CASIDY, James,372,410
CASISY, James,372
CASITY, Chas.,372, Hugh,372,
Peter,223, Thos.,372
CASON(?), Mary,236
CASON, Ann,222, Benjamin,222,
243, Cannon,111, H.,041,
John Jr.,249, John,249,
Thomas,205,210,236,249,
William Jr.,205, William,
205,207,208,222,243,249,
Wm.Jr.,207,236,249
CASSELL, Ephraim,336, Fanney,
336, John,336, Marion,336,
Mary,336, Nathaniel,336,
Samuel H.,336, Zelia A.,336
CASSELLS, James,309
CASSELS, Agness,417, Benjamin,
385, Henry Jr.,417, Jno.,
369,370,373,380,385,415
CASSIDY, James,384
CASSITY, Charles,372, Hugh,
372,374,418,420, James,372,
Jesse,409, Peter,227,229,
Robert,420, Thomas,372,
374,409,410,419, Thos.,372,
384,409,410
CASTLE, John,326, Milley,326,
Nancy,353
CASTLEBERRY, Paul,523
CASWELL, Richard,482
CATE, William,193
CATER, John,369
CATES, Joshua,218
CATHEY, George,565,570,571
CATHRON, Alexander,319
CATO, William,121
CATON, John,061, Katherine,
061
CATWELL, Adam,173
CAUBLE, Mr.,366
CAUDLE, John Jr.,394
CAVE, Sarah,245, Thomas,245
CAWTHON, Chesley,349
CEALTER, David,418
CEMP, Hardin,153
CERD(?), John,091
CERTER, Benjamin,092
CHADLER, John,247
CHADWICK, ,004, Elias,005,
Elizabeth,004, John,005,
William,005
CHALMERS, Alexander,316,
Alexr.,316, David,316,
Jane,316, Matthew,316,
William,316
CHAMBERS, ,325, Adam,311,
Jacob,384, James,358, Jane,
260, John,042,076,081,082,
358,360,564, Lamech,358,
Mansfield,260, Margaret,
260, Martha,260, Polly,260,
Rachel,260, Spencer,360,
Thomas,018, Thorogood,319,
Thoroughgood,317, Thorowgood,
429
CHAMBERS, Thorowgood,486,
William,260
CHAMBLESS, Mary,283,285
CHAMBLIN(?), D.,357
CHAMBLISS, John,283
CHAMPION, R.L.,404
CHANCE, Eliz.,293, Elizabeth,
287
CHANDLER, ,169, Abednego,172,
Agnes,184, Ann,308,316,
Big John,184, Daniel,172,
David,185, George,373,385,
Iseral,249, Israel,005,
Isreal,316, Jeremiah,137,
140,156,168,184, Jess,124,
Jesse,128,131,141,154,165,
166,167,185, Jno.,185
CHANDLER, Jno.F.,185, Joel,
127,165,183,184,268,
John F.,185, John Jr.,184,

John,169,184,185,423,
Jonathan,316, Josiah,268,
Little John,184, Shadrac,
167, Shadrach,131,141,
Shadrack,128,167,184,
Shadrick,184, Solomon K.,
268, Timothy,184
CHANDLER, William,167,174,
175,305, Wm. Chandler,305,
Zechariah,268
CHAPMAN, (Land),390, ,009,
219,506, Archibald,321,356,
Benjamin J.,337, Benjamin P.,
337, Benjamin,005,353,354,
Caroline,334, Chevis M.,
005, Cyntha J.,337, Daniel J.,
334, Delilah D.,321,
Delilah,322, Elijah,321,
Eliz.Carolina,005, Eliza A.,
337
CHAPMAN, Elizabeth,333,353,
356, Enoch,334,356, George J.,
337, George,337,356, Giles,
308,319,340, Isaac A.,333,
Isaac,506, Israel,340,
Isreal,333, Jacob,003,331,
333,340, James,334,356,
Jane,321, Jeremiah,356,
Joel,333,340, John W.,337
CHAPMAN, John,184,208,255,
268,327,346,359, Joseph Sr.,
355, Joseph,206,219,310,
315,321,355,356, Joshua,331,
333,340,359, Marcus,005,
Margaret,333, Marmaduke J.,
321, Mary Ann,003, Mary,321,
Miles,334, Nancy,321,
Nathaniel,255, Polly,355
CHAPMAN, Rachel,331,333,
Rebecca,353, Robert H.,321,
Robert,088,526, Saml.,322,
Samuel,310,315,321,322,
340,342,359, Sarah,308,337,
Stephen R.,005, W.A.,337,
William,088,121,310,321,
322, Wm.,322
CHAPPEL, John,113,115,122
CHAPPELL, Thomas,247
CHAPPLE, John,109,113
CHARLES, Joel,135,191, Oliver,
185, Rachel,311, Sarah,170
CHARMICHAEL, Danl.,299,
Dugal Jr.,299, Dugal,299,
Duncan,299, John,299,
Malcom,299, Michael,299,
Neal,299, Neale,299
CHARVIN, Claudias,028,030,
Claudius,044,100
CHASTAIN, ,341, A.M.C.,341,
Abner D.,341, Abner,325,
341, Abraham,131, Alcy,367,
Edward,336, Feeby,333,
Jacob,330, James,186,
John B.,341, John,333,341,
Jos.Tilmon,341, Lucinda,
341, Martha L.,341, Mary M.,
341, Nancy R.,341, Nelson,
341
CHASTAIN, Peter,428, Rachel L.,
341, Rowland,341, Sarah A.,
326, Susan,341, Temperance,
341, Tilman,341, Washington P.,
341, William,341, Wm.,349
CHASTEEN, Abner,163, Abraham,
154
CHASTIEN, Abner,159
CHASTIN, James,186
CHEEK, Allias(Ellis),195,
William,519, Wm.,216
CHERRY(?), ,342
CHERRY, David,349, George,075,
102, Jennett,075, John,050,
Lettuce,050, Robert,018,
050, Sarah,284, William,283
CHESLEY, Daniel,292
CHESNEY, Alexander,556, Jane,
523, John,438,439,522,
Richard,523, Robert,439,
Robt.,556
CHESNUT, Alexr.,108, Esther,
102, James,115, John,102,
372,419
CHESNUTT, Alexander,116

CRAFORD, Alexander,057
CRAFT, Edward,CRAFT, Edward,015
CRAG, Elizabeth,059
CRAGE, James,053,196
CRAIG, Archibald,276, Elias F.,
265, Elihu,265, Elizabeth,
040,096, Geo.,096, George,
011,016,040,096,098,104,
James,114,116,249,276,306,
563, Jane,276, Jas.,114,
119, John,167, L.C.,344,
Lucinda,355, Mary,217,
Samuel,050,058,101, Thomas,
342
CRAIG, William,217,242,248,
249, Willm.,112, Wm.,112,
234,271
CRAIGE, John,196
CRAIN, Charles,177,554,
Elizabeth,332, Hezzia,367,
John,176, Judah,526,535,
Judeth,176, Judith,177,
Samuel,176, William,176
CRAMER, G.,343, G.H.,345,
G.H.D.345
CRANE, Charles,176,178, Eliza,
337, Hizzey,367, John,177,
178, Judeth,176, Judith,178,
Nancy,178, Nansey,176,
Suana,176, William,178,355
CRANES, Charles,176,177,
Judeth,176, Judith,177
CRANFORST, Christian,343
CRANFROST, Christian,343
CRANSHAW, Jesse,016
CRAWFORD, Alexander,072,104,
105, Andrew,101, Arthur,434,
Bennett H.,004, David,178,
Eliza Eliz.,003, Gadi,287,
Hardy,287,293, Henry,056,
James G.,287,293, James Sr.,
287, James,075,076,429,532,
563, Jas.,293,299,538, John,
272, Joseph,204
CRAWFORD, M.,299, Michael,488,
497,539, Moses,183, Stephen,
287, William,268
CREAMER, Absolem,189,190
CREANSHAW, Robert,496,503,
Stephen,488,503
CREATH, William,082
CREEL, James,299
CREELE(?), Agnes,283
CREELE, James,285
CREEMER, Absalem,190, Absalom,
124, Absolum C.,189
CREEVAN, Jean(Mc.?),499
CREIGHTON, Hugh,315
CRENSHAW, ,322, Abner(Dr.),
005, Anderson,005, Charles,
312,314,315, Francis,503,
J.L.,365, Jesse,336, Jincy,
336, John,491, L.M.,334,
Martha,334, Nathan,242,
Roberert(?),488, Roberert,
488, Robert,486,491,503,
526, Stephen,503,546
CRESWELL, Elihu,257,258,271,
347,351, Henry H.,351,
James,218,309,351, R.,271,
Robert H.,347, Robert,257,
351, Robt.,270,272, Sarah,
351
CRIB, ,299, Dempsey,299,
Eliz.,293, Elizabeth,299,
John,299, Thos.,293
CRIBB, Elizabeth,287
CRIDER, Daniel,183
CRIMKIE, John F.,530
CRISP, J.H.,002, John Rodgers,
256, Mancil,216, Mansil,218,
237,248, Mansill,218,
Margret,245, Sarah,256
CRISSEY, Jas.,293
CRITENDEN(?), ,529
CRITTENDEN, John,468,529,554
CRO(W?), Jacob,234
CROCHER, Jacob,078
CROCKER, (Family),264, ,
252, Jacob,005,080, James,
284,285
CROCKET, Robert,563
CROCKETT, (Family),265,

Robert,559
CROFFORD, David,187
CROFT, Daniel,569, Edward,057,
Peter,398, Widow,561
CROGIN, Hannah,148,149,
Thomas,148
CROME, James A.,002
CROMER, Andrew,323, Christian,
005, Hilliard,005, Phillip,
005, Simon,005
CROOK, Joshua,059, Samuel,024,
Solomon,059, William,042,
048
CROOKS, Hugh,256
CROSBY, ,425, Abner,348,
Frances(Mrs.),348, Francis,
348, George,514, John,053,
Mrs.,348, Richard,026,090,
Thomas,026,287,425,500,
Thos.,293,431, William,053
CROSKEY, William,401
CROSLEY, ,499, George Jr.,495,
George Sr.,495,499,503,
506, George,499,500
CROSS, Samuel,097, Viney,356
CROSSLEY, Geo.Sr.,492,
George Jr.,525, George Sr.,
525, George,450,451,536,
541, Lydia,451
CROSWELL, Gilbert,384
CROUDER, Fedrick,537
CROW, Francis,359, Isaac,335,
William,353
CROWDER, Fredarick,489, John,
268, Stephen,186
CROWTHER, Isaac,309
CRUCE, ,555, Richd.,433
CRUICKSHANKS, George,275
CRUIES(?), Isaac,171
CRUKS, Hugh,249
CRUMLEY, Benjamin,315,
Catherine,315, Charles,315,
Hannah,314,315, James,002,
315, Jemina,315, John,314,
Rachel,315, Samuel,315,
Sarah,315, Thomas,315,
Wm.Smith,002
CRUMPTON, Alexr.,108,111,113,
115,121, John,197
CRUPTON, Nome(?)Mrs.,366
CRUSE, (Isaac?),497
CRYNE, Isaac,497
CUGAN, John,062
CULBERTSON, Celia,146, Jas.,
222, Josiah,146, Robert,214,
216,222,248
CULP, ,089, Agnes,096,
Augusteen,019,082, Augustine,
096, Augustus,072, Ausben,
076, Austin,081,082,093,
Benjamin,022,062, Gasper,
067, Henry,011,019,040,072,
096,098, Jacob,096, John Jacob,
102, John,022,081,092,093,
Peter,012,013,014
CULP, Peter,057,062,092,098,
493
CULPEPPER, Ann Eliz.,005,
Henry,299, John,005,
Joseph B.,005
CULWELL, Samuel,084
CUMMINGS, David,287, Dd.,293,
Elizabeth,003, Hiram,003,
James,236, John,256,257
CUMMINS, Francis(Rev.),560,
Terry,169
CUMMONS, Daniel,494, Danl.,
531
CUNINGHAM, ,258, Andrew,199,
216,217,220, Ann,194,195,
202, David,247, Elizabeth,
217, George,244, James,217,
228,248, Jas.,220, John,206,
249, Margaret,229, Mary,244,
Matthew,258, P.,223,249,
Pa.,241, Patrick,194,195,
202,207,212,215,227
CUNINGHAM, Patrick,229,238,
241,245,248, Robert,200,
Sarah,195, Thomas,192,193,
227,238,243,244, Widow,253
CUNNELL, James,516
CUNNINGHAM, ,182,485, Andrew,

191, Arther,528,554, Arthur,
434,512, Elihu,262, Francis,
216, George,560, Henry L.,
001, Humphrey,562, Jacob,
262, James,192, Jane,262,
Jno.,226,539, John,005,
043,168,182,192,236,517,
537,539, Joseph S.,299
CUNNINGHAM, Joseph,262,
Margaret H.,001, Margaret,
262, Patrick,227, Polly,262,
Robert F.,001, Robert,249,
Sally,262, Samuel,272,
Thomas,226, W.,443,
William,191,537, Wm.,443,
539, Wm.D.,001
CURB, ,321
CURBEY, Jesse,188, John,188,
Susanah,188
CURBY, Alesebeth,188, Frances,
188, Francis,188
CURETON, ,009, Fred S.,001,
Thomas T.,001
CURRANCE, Cisy,199
CURRAY, Nicholas,554
CURREY(?), Stafford,109
CURREY, Green,109, Nicolas,
529, S.,109, Stafford,117
CURRY(?), William,510
CURRY, Anne,061, Bestore,061,
Daniel,061, David,061,299,
Gavin,113,115, John,061,
Mary,061, Nathan,250,252,
Nicholas,512, Staffd.,047,
Stafford,113,115, William,
511, Wm.,537
CURTIS, Elizabeth F.,463,
Elizabeth,462, Fieldin,546,
Joshua,155, Naman,359,
Thomas,504
CUSAAC, Adam,299, Joseph,300
CUSACK, Adam,287,293, Jos.,
293, Joseph,287
CYTON, Moses,488
D'SURRENCY, Jacob,278,279,280
DABBS, ,009, Elizabeth,483,
James,483, Jesse,483, John,
483, Josiah,483, Lucy,003,
Nancey,483, Nathaniel,483,
Richard,483, Robert,483,
Samuel,483, Silas,003,
William,483
DACUS, Nathaniel,325
DALEFIELD, Wm.,555
DALEY, James,185
DALRYMPLE, Ann,217,253,
George,205,217,236,
Sophronia C.,002, Thomas,
229,253, Thos.Jr.,253,
William,231,253,533, Wm.,
517,542,545,549
DALTON, Dorcas J.,342, L.R.,
342
DANEY, Francis Jr.,418
DANIEL, Beverly,182, Chesley,
294, Ezekel,288, John Jr.,
240, John Sr.,231,240, John,
288,294,300, Nancy,427,
Nelly,176, Reuben,166,182,
Reubin,187, Rewbin,187,
Ruben,182, Stephen,380,
416, William,134,300,380,394
DANIELS, William,194,380
DANNAHOO, Cornelius,236
DANNELLY, Ann W.(?),293
DANNER, Jacob G.,005
DANOL, Morgan,346
DANSBY, Isaac,121, Mrs.,403
DARBY, Asa,051,495, Benjamin,
494,495,543, Elizabeth,445,
Family,543, Honor,283,
James,436,474,482, Jane,
445, Josiah,481,494,495,
Josias,474,508,523,543,
Mr.,433, Nancy,006,
Nicholas,174, Owen,283,
Peggy,283, Sarah,482,
William,436
DARBY, William,444,445, Wm.,
482
DARCUS, Lucretia,340
DARDELIE, P.,409
DARGAN, John,378,379,400,

David,195,347, Edward,566,
Elizabeth,350, James,347,
Jas.,348, John,023,347,
360, Joseph,347, Liney,347,
Martin,325, Michael,021,
029,036,094, Michial,010,
Polly,347, Robert,347,360,
Samuel H.,021,025,355,
Sarah,010
DICKSON, Simpson,347, Thomas,
567, William B.,350,
William Jr.,028, William,
028,347,563,569, Wm.,028,379
DIE, Abraham,023
DIEL, Martin,238
DILL, Archeybel,168, Stephen,
146
DILLARD, (Survey),408, Ann,
208, Anna,256, Frances,120,
Francis,111,112, George,
249,255,256, James Jr.,024,
James,024,026,076,090,208,
211,221,222,253,255,259,
434, Jas.,136, John,253,
254,255,256, Major,111,120,
Margaret,358, Mary,211
DILLARD, Mary,221, Percilla,
076, Samuel,208,221,222,255
DILLEN, Wm.,294
DILLIN, William,288
DILLINGHAM, A.,163, M.,182,
Michael,159
DILLON, Joshua,288
DILLS, Archibald,124
DILWORTH, Benjamin,329,352,
Catharine,329, Elizabeth,
329, Frances,329, George,
327,329, Mary,329, Rebecca,
329, Robert,329
DIMPSY, Cornelius,413
DINGLE, Mary,388, Robert,385,
386,387,388,390,395,418
DINING, John,131
DINKINS, Asa,371, Thomas,085,
William,371
DINNING, John,131
DIXON, Abel,384, David,528,
Hugh,526, John Jr.,249,
John,441, Michail,010,
Michial,010, Sarah,010,
Starling,310, William Sr.,
268, William,268,411,526
DNEDY, Mary,193, Thomas,193
DOBBINS, Jesse,320, Keziah,
005, Washington,005,
William,320
DOBBS, Arthur,076,558, Hugh,
075,076
DOBY, Martha,005, Susan,005
DOD, Jesse,430
DODD, ,433, Jesse,430,432,
433,441,442,541,547,556,
Mary,541, Thos.,541,
William,213
DODDS, Samuel,122
DODGEN, James,311, Nancy,356,
Olleman,311, William,311,
312, Wm.,447
DODSON, John,334
DOEG, Thomas,129,158, Thos.,
158
DOGGETT, Chatten,149
DOGGETTE, Thomas,185
DOGWOOD, Thomas,149
DOHERTIE, George,220
DOHERTY, Samuel,117
DOLHRON, Joseph,332, Malinda A.,
332
DOLTON, John,183
DOMENY, Henry,147
DOMINICK, ,009, David,002,
Henry,002, James F.,002
DOMMON, J.S.,078
DONAHOE, Wm.,219
DONAHUE, John,202
DONAL, Elizabeth,214
DONALD, Alexander,025,027,
John,074,095
DONALDSON, Wm.,074
DONILLY, Thos.,075
DONNAHOE, Wm.,215,220
DONNAHOW, Cornelius,220, John,
220,233, William,220, Wm.,

220
DONNELLY, Ann W.,287, James,
567
DONOHOE, Cornelius,227,
Elizabeth,227, John,227
DONOL, David,346
DONOLD, James,074
DOOD, Agnes,513, Jesse,543,
William,462
DOOLITTLE, Joseph,198
DORAH, John,233
DORAN, ,262, Peter,063
DORAW, Mary,262, Nancy,262
DORCEY, Cornelius,103
DOROUGH, David,250, James,244,
Wm.,244
DORRAH, ,262, David,250
DORROH, James,213, John,226,
William,244
DORROUGH, James,238
DORSET, Joseph,192,238
DORSETT, James,243,244,
Joseph,243,244, Thomas,243,
244
DORSEY, David,331, Elisha,331,
John Jr.,331, John,331,
Mary,331, Polly,331,
William,206,331
DORTCH, S.D.,360
DOUDLE, Allen,564
DOUGHARTY, James,036,091,
John,026,036, Saml.,108,
115, Samuel,115
DOUGHERTY, Agey,031, Agnes,
031, Charles,162, James,132,
165,167, John,027,030,031,
101
DOUGHTREY, James,013
DOUGHTY, Joseph,146
DOUGLAS, ,021, James,144,209,
305, John,185,305,313,321,
380, Joseph,103, Lyda,321,
Mary,305
DOUGLASS, Anne(Mrs.),281,
Anne,278, James,080, Jesse,
564, Jno.,415, Jo.,370,380,
384, John,411,412,415,416,
Philip,278,279,281, Sarah,
412,416
DOUGLESS, (Land),068
DOUTHET, James,355
DOUTHIT, Davis,350, H.B.,368,
James,169, John Jr.,169
DOVER, Francis,572
DOWDLE, Sally,268, Sarah,189,
190
DOWDY, Lemuel,347
DOWIS, John,334,354, Sarah,
334
DOWLING, John,382
DOWNES, Rachel,278, Walter,
278,279,280,282, William F.,
261
DOWNEY, ,254, John,077
DOWNIN, James,245
DOWNING, Andrew,082, James,
226,230, John,033,062
DOWNS, Allen,327, Alse,327,
Betsey,322, David,322,
James,322, Jane,198, John,
282,322, Jonathan,131,190,
191,193,198,200,205,213,
217,221,222,224,225,227,
229,236,238,245,246,248,
250,252,259,271,272,
Jonathon,202,250, Jos.,227,
272, Joseph,190
DOWNS, Joseph,196,197,198,
205,227,237,243,245,273,
Joshua,205,219,226,228,
238,248, Justice,190, Mary,
322, Nancy,322, Sarah,283,
322, W.D.,271, Walter,282,
284, William F.,256,258,
William,185,246,250,256,
Wm.,257, Wm.F.,259
DOWTHIT, Silas,350
DOWTY, Joseph,146
DOYAL(DIAL), H.,218
DOYAL, Haistings,207, Hasten,
210, Jane,359, John,359,
Rebecca,210
DOYALL, Haisten,207,209

DOYEL(DIAL), Haisting,209
DOYLE, James A.,358, James,
361, John,031,311, Mary,311,
Susan,333, William,031,
Wm.,348
DOYLEY, Daniel,380
DOZER, Ann,288, Benjamin,287,
Elias,287, James,287, Jas.,
293, William,287, Wm.,293
DOZIER, Ann,294, Elias,293
DRAKE, Britton,453, Edmond,
207, Elias,453, Francis,453,
454,482,491, Joyce,453,
Margaret,453, Mary,435,
Richard,454, William,453,
454,482
DRAPER, ,238, Charles,528,
Thomas Sr.,548, Thomas,439,
495,524,542,548, Thos.,540,
543
DREGGARS, Mary,387, William,
387
DREGGERS, Ephraim,294, Isaac,
294
DRENNAN, John,489,558, Thos.,
563
DRENNON, Jas.W.,348, John,274
DREW, Ann,294, William,197,
Wm.,212,220
DRIGERS, Isaac,300
DRIGGARS, Mary,387, William,
387
DRIGGERS, Avis,300, Eliz.,294,
Elizabeth,288, Thomas,288,
300, Thos.,294, Tilley,300
DRIGGINS, Ephraim,288, Isaac,
288
DRNAL, Nick.,162
DROGERS(?), Hizzy,367
DROZE, Francis,395
DRUMMON, Benjamin,234
DRUMMOND, Nathaniel,235
DRUMMONS, James,347
DUBOSE, Benj.,411, Benjamin,
415, Danl.,380, David,407,
Ezekiel,418
DUCKET, Jacob,204,435, Sally,
259, Thomas,203,490,514
DUCKETT, Jacob,203,432,
Josiah,311, Josias,005,
Mary,006, Sarah,267,
Thomas(Capt.),006, Thomas,
DUCKWORTH, Jonathan,462
DUDGENS, ,243
DUDLEY, Col.,269
DUDNEY, Arthur,561,568,569
DUE, John,287
DUFF, Denis,173, Dennes,182,
Dennis,128,129,151,156,
163,169, Elizabeth,163,
John,488, Mr.,486, Wm.R.,
354
DUFFIELD, Anthony,091
DUGAN, Jacob,083, Thomas,012,
015,306,313
DUGANS, Elizabeth,115,
Richard,115
DUGGANS, Elizabeth,116,
Richard,116
DUGGAW, ,375
DUGGINS, Elizabeth,107,
Richard,107
DUGLAS, John,132
DUKE, Abraham,328, Harriet,
337, Inz,071, John,078,
Robert,071, Robt.,078
DUKES, Aaron,117, Hardiman,
253, Keiton,288
DUKINSON, Robert,191
DULIN, Lod,147
DULLEY, James,392
DULOE(?), A.,366
DUMAS, David,266, Emeline,266,
Matilda,266, Nancy,266,
Nehemiah,266, Polly,266,
Robert,129, Stephen,121
DUNAGAN, Joseph,128,149
DUNAVANT, William,114, Willm.,
107
DUNAVEN, Willm.,114
DUNAVON, William,106
DUNBROW(?), John,483
DUNCAN, ,009, Alex.,517,

Alexander,555, Amos,003,
311, David,334, Delilah,463,
Eliz.(Mrs.),008, Elizabeth,
493, George,179, Jacob,016,
083,568, James,216,517,555,
560, Jaocb,568, Jesse,178,
179, John C.,334, John,002,
179,311,463,560, Jonathan,
083
DUNCAN, Jonathan,089, Joseph,
173, Martha,007, Mary,178,
179, Nathaniel,329,334,
R.B.,357, Rachel,309,
Robert,129,152,174,180,
William,006
DUNGA, (Family),091
DUNGAN, Ann,091, Jacob,016,
091, Jonathan,089,091,
Nancy,091, William,091
DUNHAM, Robt.,294
DUNIGAN, Joseph,149
DUNIVAN, William,116
DUNKIN, Amos,311, James,179,
Jesse,178,179
DUNKINS, Samuel,310
DUNKLIN, Elizabeth,174, Jeams,
184, John,174,202, Joseph,
124,125,131,146,147,165,
174,183,184,186, Samuel,250,
William,185
DUNKLING, Joseph,148
DUNKLINN, Joseph,184
DUNLAP, David,192,227,
Elizabeth,209,570, John,
115,230,266, Margaret,230,
Robert,003,005,027,073,
201,209,570, Samuel,062,
194,214,250, Thomas,516,
544, Widow,195,197, William,
216,218,226,231,242,255,
258, Wm.,214,216,257,270,
271,272,323
DUNLAY, Robert,027
DUNLOP, Henry,564, William,
564
DUNN, Allen,264, Andw.,110,
Andw.Sr.,116, Elisa,415,
Eliza,380,411, Elizabeth,
411,415, Henry,380,411,415,
Janet(Mrs.),411,412,
Joseph,139,155, R.,406,
414,415, Roger,410,411,413,
415,416, Sarah A.,413,415,
Sarah,411, Sylvester Jr.,
380
DUNN, Sylvester Sr.,380,415,
416, Sylvester,380,410,411,
412,413,414,415,416
DUNNAGAN, Joseph,149, Thomas,
149
DUNNAM, John P.,298
DUNNAVAN, Willm.,112
DUNNIVANT, Wm.,116
DUNOSE, Guard,109
DUPRE, Benj.D.,348,351,352,
C.P.,349, Cornelius P.,358
DURANT, Henry,369, Sarah,369
DURBOROW, Benjamin,200
DURHAM, Benjamin,353, Carter,
333, Charles Jr.,353,
Charles,342,349,351,353,
Chas.,348, Daniel,325,346,
347,348,349,353, Elizabeth,
333, Ellis,342, Fell,338,
Hannah,333,366,367, Isaac,
342, Jeremiah,353, Jerry,
346, Joel,346,354, John,342
DURHAM, Jos.,118, Joseph,333,
353, Joshua,119,121,
Lucinda,342, Malinda,333,
366,367, Mary Ann,342, Mary,
353, Nathaniel,188, Polly,
353, Rachel,342, Sally,268,
Sarah C.,338, William O.,
342, William,333
DURKEE, N.,274
DURRAM, Arthur,211, Aurthor,
241, Stephen,241
DURRETT, ,004, Benj.,005,
Thomas,001,005
DURROM, Arthur,206
DURROW, Arthur,233
DURRUM, MArgaret,211, Mary,

211
DURVAN, ,455
DUTARGUE, Lewis,219
DUTART, John,418,424
DUTTIMS(?), Lewis,440
DUTTON, Daniel,129,133,150,
Jeremiah,125,133,134,139,
146,153,173, Sarah,125,139,
153
DUTY, Richard,227,229,238
DUVAL, Lewis,197, Terissia,
197
DUVALL, Benjamin,185, J.,253,
Lewis,136,192,222,238,240,
Terresa,222, Theresey,136
DWYER, Samuel,382
DY, Abraham,023
DYAL, Edward,247
DYCHE, John,156,163,168
DYCK, John,145
DYE, Abram,024, Elisha,024,
Henry,070, John,070,074,
Richard,024
DYER, Thomas,071
DYES, Thomas,017,022
DYKES, John,185
DYSON, Daniel,315,318, James,
317,320, Margaret,318,
Thomas,323
EADDY, Henry,288,294, Samuel,
288
EADENS, Samuel,353
EADES, Robert,480
EADS, Isaac,438, Sarah,438
EADY, Henry,304
EAGERLIN, Dorothy,294, Henry,
294
EAGERTON, Charlotte,300,
Dorothy,288, Geo.,294,
George,288, Mary,300,
William,288,300, Wm.Jr.,
288,294, Wm.Sr.,294
EAGOR, Adam,070
EAKEN, Messer,442
EAKENS, David,024
EAKIN, Alexander,058, John,
560, Lewis,197, Samuel,225
EAKINS(AKINS), Samuel,195
EAKINS, Alexander,105, David,
023, Elizabeth,105, Jane,
207,249, Lewis,228, Robert,
105, Samuel,207,249,
Thomas Jr.,105, Thomas,047,
105
EARGLE, Joseph,006
EARL, John,352, Samuel Sr.,
176
EARLE, (Doc.),333, ,165, B.,
155, B.J.,183, Bayles,179,
180,183, Baylis Jr.,128,
Baylis,125,127,128,133,
140,143,151,163,184,332,
Damaris,163, Elias,128,
129,131,139,150,152,158,
176,179,180,186,353, Gaylie,
127, J.B.,156,157, J.Baylis,
151
EARLE, Jno.,157, John Baylis,
156,157, John Jr.,128,129,
John,128, M.P.,353,
S.C.Thompson,002, Samuel Sr.,
138, Samuel,128,129,131,
135,136,138,157,160,162,
163,173,176,183, Thos.P.,179
EARLY, Patrick,518
EARNEST, Agness,514, Jacob,
514,523
EASEN, James,185
EASLEY, Anne,164, John,160,
530, Millington,137,162,
Saml.,146, William,162
EASLY, Anne,164
EAST, Isham,230, Joseph,429,
505,527, Josiah,208,210,
Shadrach,221, Thomas,208,
William,209,221, Wm.,216,
Wm.Jr.,221
EASTERLING, Jas.,300
EASTERWOOD, John,538,555,
Laurance,519, Laurence,488,
497,555, William,538
EASTES(EASTERS), Zacha.,543
EASTES, Charles,154,162

EASTLAND, Elijah,006, Ezekiah,
006, Thomas,006,144
EASTON, John,078
EATON, Lewis,334, Mary,334
EAVES, Mark,088
EAYLOTT, Arch,057
ECTOR, John(Mrs.),002
EDDY, Saml.,294
EDENS, Alexander,330,341,
Allen R.,341, Crafton Alex,
341, Elijah C.,341, James M.,
341, John M.C.,341, Margaret,
341, Mary,341, Peggy,341,
Pinkney N.B.,341, Samuel S.,
341, Samuel,330,341,
Sarah A.,341, Warren D.,
341, William J.,341,
William,330
EDENS, William,341, Williama E.,
341
EDEY, William,558
EDGAR, Edward H.,349, William,
075
EDGE, Little,334, Manerva,334
EDGEHILL, Thomas Jr.,204,207,
Thomas Sr.,207, Thomas,195,
201,207,209,225,233,235
EDGER, Adam,072,075, William,
117
EDMONDSON, ,432, Caleb Jr.,
430, Caleb,430,432,436,499,
504,507,517,535,547, Isaac,
430,432,435,436,441,535,
547, Joseph,436, Jude,436,
Margaret,441, Richard,353,
Sarah,554, Thomas,436,
William,436,494,554, Wm.,
484,554
EDMONDSTON, Joseph,434
EDMONSON, ,186
EDMUNDSON, ,547, Caleb,430,
Calen,547, Isaac,430
EDMUNSON, John,283
EDSON, & CO.,438, ,540, C.R.,
438, Casper Ruggles,444,
Cushman R.,438,443,541,
Cushman,431,520,523,528,
541,544, Mr.,444,534, R.,
529, Ruggles,444
EDWARD, David,558, James,034,
Jane,558
EDWARDS, Abel,280,282,284,
285, Catharine,285, Catherine,
282, Charity(Mrs.),282,
Charity,278, Cullin,294,
David,300, Edmund,123,170,
175, Edward,232, Elizabeth,
170, Isaac,204,436,462,
James,217,248,504, Jane,
195, Jerred,036, John S.,006
EDWARDS, John S.,346, John,
092,105,123,208,217,225,
232,282,284,285, Joshua(Rev.),
278, Joshua,092,278,280,
281, Josiah,045, Judith,204,
Leah,181, Lylleton,006,
Mark Sr.,027,034, Mark,049,
Martha,204,284,285,
Mary(Mrs.),285, Mary,217
EDWARDS, Mary,225,227,229,
278, Mr.,278, Peter,191,
Richard,249,288,300,
Richd.,294, Robert,280,
Saml.,294, Samuel,288,
Sarah,278,282,285, T.,179,
180,184, Tho.,180, Thomas Jr.,
181, Thomas,179,180,181,
183,184,278,282, Thos.,179,
184, William Jr.,282
EDWARDS, William,285, Wm.,544
EGAN, John,415,416, Margaret,
415
EGGER, James,105, William,105
EGGNEW, George,052
EICHELBERGER, (?),545
EICHLEBERGER, (Capt.),006,
George,001, John Jr.,006,
John,310
EIGELBERGER, Geo.,545
EISEN, Fredrick,541
EKANS, Alexander,045
ELAIN, Martin,068
ELAM, George,101, Martain,058,

Martin,056,101
ELDER, John,485,486
ELIOTT, Nancy,190
ELLAGE, John,182
ELLENBURG, Wm.,348
ELLIMAN, Amey,306, Catherine,
306, Elizabeth,306, Enos,
306, Hannah,306, John,306,
319, William,306,319
ELLIMON, Abner,319
ELLIOT, Daniel,056, Ebenezer,
056, George,305, John,490,
Lucy,204, Thomas Jr.,196,
Thomas,196,204, Thos.,425
ELLIOTT, Allen R.,345,
Archebald Jr.,075,076,
Archebald,075,076, Archibal,
017, Archibald Jr.,085,
Archibald Sr.,085, Archibald,
011,012,013,017,022,039,
044, Clarissa D.,332,
Daniel,058, Ebenezer,058,
George,190,306, Hugh,108,
109,112
ELLIOTT, James,103,108,109,
112, Jas.,117, Jean,073,
John,103,349,567, Nancy,
189, Robert,072,073,103,
Sarah,013,017, Thomas Jr.,
235,248, Thomas Sr.,235,
Thomas,248,268,563,
Thos.Jr.,221, Thos.Sr.,221,
William,011,013,016,017,
040,052
ELLIOTT, William,076,239, Wm.,
349
ELLIS, Benjamin,023,025,072,
124, Gideon,337,348,349,
351,353,354, Joel,331,
Sarah,341, Shadrach,383,
Simon,138, Underhill,383,
384, William,349,563
ELLISER, Jacob,515
ELLISON, Agnes,340, Edmond,
318, Elizabeth,179, Joel,
334,338, John,069, Robert,
377, W.,421, William,226,
421, Wm.,112
ELLOT, Nancy,190
ELMORE, Abigail,313, Elijah,
002, Giles,001, J.A.,250,
254,255,256,257,259,273,
James C.,256, John A.,226,
238,249,259, John Archer,
213,253, John,195,232,313,
Joseph,313, Mary,313,
Mathias,308, Rachel,313,
Ridgeway,313, Steven,313,
William,311
ELMORE, William,313, Wm.,300
ELOM, Martin,048
ELROD, Anne Q.D.,336, Elijah J.,
336, Frances E.,336,
Franklin W.,336, George C.,
336, J.A.,336, John C.A.,
336, Mary N.,336, Quincey D.,
336
EMBRIE, Wm.,039
EMBRY, W.,033,051,052,
William,046,047, Wm.,032
EMER, Dr.,042
EMERY, Elijah,332, Sarah,332,
W.,032, Wm.,077
EMMERSON, Robert,351
ENDSLEY, Andrew,191,204,206
ENGLISH, Alexander,098, James,
105, John Jr.,413
ENLO, Abraham,534
ENLOE, Abraham,558,568
ENLY, W.,063
ENTREIKEN, John,256
ENTREKIN, Elizabeth,208, John,
208,218
ENTRICAN, Thomas,253
ENTRIKEN, Thomas,002
EOFF(?), Isaac,011
EOLL(?), Isaac,011
EOLLY, Isaac,011
EPTING, Monroe J.(Rev.),002
ERASTUS, Widow,347
ERLS, Elias,185
ERSKINE, Hugh,361, Jane,361
ERVIN & GIBSON, ,294

ERVIN, Hugh,294, James R.,288,
294, James,294, Jennie,337,
John,288,294,337
ERWIN, George,339, Isaac,339,
John B.,339, John,339,
Joseph,420, Nancy,339,
Thomas,339, William,339
ERWIN/IRWIN, Wm.,560
ESLEY, Thomas,178
ESTES(?), Zacha.,543
ESTES, Asa,172, Charles,129,
183, William,090,092
ETHERIDGE, Joseph,002, Sarah,
003
EUSTICE, Lydia,281
EVAN, ,174, John,021
EVANS, (Estate),304, ,151,
Abel,278,279,282,285,
Agnes,021,037, Anne,284,
Benjamin,313, Burwell,369,
D.,099,148,151,159, D.R.,
112,151, Daniel,178
EVANS, David R.,109,137,151,
David Read,112,148,151,
David Reed,168, David Reid,
151, David,148,278,280,281,
282, Eleanor(Mrs.),281,
Eleanor,278,279, Elizabeth,
037,049,278,282,284,285,
Enoch Jr.,283, Enoch Sr.,
283, Ezekiel,373,407,
Garner,361
EVANS, George,117, Hannah,037,
057,278,280, Isaac,312,320,
John Jr.,282,285, John,018,
021,037,057,092,126,169,
278,285,326,348,407,408,
Josiah J.,270, Josiah,272,
285, Lydia,283, Margaret,
278,285, Martha,278,280,
283,285, Mary,037,049
EVANS, Mary,104,283,285,
Milly,326, Nathan,292,298,
Owen,018,021,037,054,083,
104, Philip,278, Phillip,
178,185, Poley,176, Richard,
015,018,021,049,090,093,
104, Samuel,278,281, Sarah,
283, Stephen,384, Thomas Jr.,
278,283, Thomas,255,278
EVANS, Thomas,281,282,285,
288,294,300,507, William,
100, Wm.,148
EVATT, Hundley,328,349,354,
James A.,354, James H.,335,
Joseph G.,356, Marilda,335,
Mary,325, Thomas,349
EVELEIGH, Mary,232, Nicholas,
204,232, Richd.A.R.,233,
Thomas,233
EVENS, John Jr.,154, John,143,
154
EVERITT, Benjamin,043
EVINS, Isaac,023, John,021,
167
EWART, John,039,425,426,429,
485,487,488,491,501,502,
503,504,506,507,508,514,
515,517,518,525,541,
Matthew,429, Robert,429,
564, William,429
EWIN, Andrew,500, Hugh,288,
James,166, Thomas,231
EWING, John,110, Robert,110,
Samuel,210, Thomas,196,
208,215,246,254, William(LS),
110, William,110,112,196,
Wm.Jr.,110
EXUM, (Estate),300, Benj.,294,
Benjamin,288, Delilah,288,
Mary,300, Robert,288,
Robt.,294, William,288,
Wm.,294
FADEY, W.,344
FAGAN, Henry,224
FAGEN, C.,343, C.H.,343, H.,
343,344
FAGIN, H.,343, Henry,236
FAIR, ,366, E.Y.,006
FAIRBAIRN, Jas.,274
FAIRBURN, James,257
FAIRESS, John,034
FAIRFOREST, Story(Book),445

FAKES, Margaret,220, Thomas,
194,220,247, Thos.Wm.,206,
207,247, Wm.,220
FALAS, Sary,111
FALCONAR, William,417
FALCONER, John,214,248
FALIS, Elizabeth,116
FALKONER, Elizabeth,214, John,
214
FANING, ,487
FANNIN, James,488,557
FANNING, James,488
FANT, C.H.P.,345, James,358
FAOX(?), Martha,281
FARDO, George,241
FARE, William,433
FARGASON, Elizabeth,056,
Robert,056
FERGUSON, ,065, Benj.,393,
Benjamin,393, Elizabeth,
056, James Jr.,044, James,
034, John,034,044, Mary,034,
Pleasant Wm.,034, Robert,
056, Widow,057
FARIES, Alexander,564, John,
564, Robt.,564
FARIS, Hector,185, Levi,185,
William,178,226
FARISS, William,128,172
FARMER, David,507,510,511,
537, Elim,360, Elizabeth,
510,511, Frederic,131,
Frederick,191, Josiah,358
FARNANDIS, Henry,445
FARR(?), (Lt.Col.),461
FARR, (Col.),553, ,186,
Ann K.,452, Ann Kincheloe,
451, Col.,425,521,541,551,
Eleanor,452, Elenor T.,452,
Elenor Thos.,451, Eliza F.,
452, Eliza Francis,451,
Eliza Tolaferry,451,
Eliza Toliaferro,452,
Elizabeth,452, George W.,
331, Hannah G.,452
FARR, Hannah Green,445, James,
440,451,452, Jas.,451,452,
Jemima,331, Jno.P.,451,
452, John Polaskie,451,
Richard Sr.,553, Richard,
426,439,445,451,452,506,
516,553, Richd.,438,445,
517, Robt.G.H.,452, Thomas,
235,451,452, Thos.,451,452
FARR, Titus G.,451,452,
Titus Green,451, William(Col.),
424,445,451,452,523,541,
553, William,425,433,437,
438,442,451,492,499,502,
506,507,508,509,512,515,
517,529,531,544,547,551,
553,556, Willis,274,
Wm.(Col.),551, Wm.,425,
439,442,452
FARR, Wm.,486,488,517,532,
544,550,551,557, Wm.B.,440,
442,443,445,451,452,
Wm.Black,451
FARRAR, ,162, Field(Capt.),
174, Thomas,122,126,138,
140,141,162,163,167,171,
Thos.,531
FARREL, David,058
FARRELL, Thomas,040
FARRIS, Caleb,067, John,067,
Thomas,076,077, William,
077,210,230
FARRISE, James,185
FARRISS, William,043
FARROR, Thomas,528
FARROW, (Land),150, ,253, Eli,
313, Jean D.,313, John,196,
206,217,231,253,527, Landon,
527, Leony,313, Liney,318,
Rebecca,003,153, Samuel J.,
313, Samuel,259,485,486,
Sarah,313, Sydney,313,
Thomas,153,162,206,231,
312,313,318,527, Thos.,182
FARROW, William Jr.,312,
William,313
FAUCETT, Richard,495,526,
William,494

FAUGOURSON, James,180, Thos.,
180
FAULKNER, John,150
FAUST, ,182
FAVER, ,495
FAVOR, Theophilus,495
FAYSSAUX, Ann,227, Peter,227
FEAGAN, (Land),258
FEAMSTER, Joseph,015
FEARES, John,034
FEARISK, John,045
FEARNES, Henry,274
FEARSON, Sarah,283
FEATHERSON, Lewis,261
FEATHERSTONE, Sarah,056, Sera,
053
FEAWELLS, George,286
FEE, Robert,082
FEEMSTER, John,500,508,562,
Joseph,102, Margaret,508,
Mary,500,508, Samuel,120,
121,500,508, William,120,
508, Wm.,120
FEENSTER(?), James,049
FEGAN, George,250
FEIGAN, Henry Sr.,251
FEIGEN, Henry,251
FELDER, S.,194
FELTMAN, Frederick,311, Jacob,
006, Mary,006, Theodores,311
FEMSTER, Joseph,052
FENNALL, Seth,039, Steth,039
FENNEL, F.G.,336, H.J.,336,
Hardy H.,336, Martha,336,
337, W.J.,336,337, William M.,
336
FENNELL, Fielding,357, Hardy,
353, Steth,040
FENNESTER, Joseph,049
FERCUAHARD(?), Wm.F.,216
FERGERSON, Williama(?),130
FERGUS, James,567, William,
566
FERGUSON, (Land),095, (Line),
567, ,561, Abraham,074,104,
Adam,068, Agnes,073,074,
Andw.,348, Benj.Sr.,369,
Benjamin,369, Caty,133,
Charles,255,257,268, David,
315, Elizabeth,097, Henderson,
234, J.G.,341, James Sr.,
012, James,021,037
FERGUSON, James,068,073,074,
330,570, Jas.,347,350, John,
021,094,095,097,332,348,
350,351,355, Johnson,316,
Joseph,369, Judge G.,350,
Margaret,369, Mary Ann,001,
Molly,316, Moses,369,372,
558, Paul,060,101, Peggy,
133, Robert,012, Samuel,022
FERGUSON, Samuel,052,097,
William,021,076,133, Wm.,
001,062, Wm.H.,001
FERNANDEZ, William,006
FERREL, Anne,278, James,300,
Wm.,278
FERRELL, Elizabeth,118,
Rebecca O.,294, Robert,118,
Wm.,073
FERROR(?), Benjamin,524
FIELD, John Sr.,350, Joseph A.,
325,332
FIELDING, Elizabeth,059, Isam,
059, Isom,040
FIELDS, B.W.,332, Betty Ann,
226, Elizabeth,337, James M.,
332, Jeremiah,332,349,
John D.,332, John,226,231,
Rahab,332,350, Wm.C.,350
FIFER, John,319, Samuel,265
FIGS, Martha,319
FILES, Reubin,184
FILLER, George,147
FILLSON, Alexander,273
FILMORE, Benjamin,256
FILPOT, Robert,221
FILPOTT, Robert,183
FILSON, Williama,137
FINCH, Joey(Dr.),261
FINCHER, ,498, Aaron,425,441,
442,448,458,459,493,507,
521,529,537,548, Armel,492,

Armond,500, Arnold,459,
Elizabeth,473, Frances,520,
521, Francis,459,469,470,
473,500,510,521, Hannah,459,
Hester,473,510, Jesse,459,
517, John(J),441, John,425
FINCHER, John,430,435,459,
498,500,510,516,521,535,
544,547,554, Jonathan P.,
458,459, Mary,458,459,493,
529, Moses,459, Rebecca,473,
Sarah,459, Timothy,459
FINDLEY, Charles,203,237,
Elijah,203, Hezekiah,332,
James Jr.,348, James,222,
227,233,324, John M.,332,
John,241,324,334, Joseph,
332, Martha,332, Paul,258
FINDLY, Hezekiah,332, John,
020
FINELY, Patrick(?),063,
William,063
FINKLEA, Alex,294, Alexr.,291,
Charles,085,291,300, Chas.,
294,298, Elias,291, Jno.,
294, John Sr.,288, John,288,
300, Thomas,085,288, Thos.,
294, Willis,300
FINKLEY, Abner,300, Charles,
300, Willis,300
FINLEY, Ann,313,317, Anne(Mrs.),
002, Elenor,317, Howard,139,
Hugh,317, James,279,313,
317,319,493,494,502,514,
516, John,120,143,200,243,
337,351, Margaret,317, Mary,
317, Nancy,476, Patrick,063,
Paul,252, Robert,317,
Samuel,563, Thomas,139
FINNEY, (Land),257, James,240,
Manasah,254, Manassa,259,
Robert,247
FINNIE, Menasah,254
FINTLEY, ,157
FISH, Ann,310, Joseph,310
FISHER, Anice,178, Elizabeth,
178, James,144,178, John,
178, Micam,051, Nicholas Sr.,
178, Nicholas,137,144,178,
565, Peggy,178, Thomas,178
FISHR, James,137
FITS, Reuben,184, William,184
FITTS, Reuben,185, Reubin,185,
Wm.,185
FITZ, William,184
FITZ-PATRICK, Peter,423
FITZGERALD, Ambrose,160,352,
Dudley,352, Eli,347,352,
Garret,327,352, Margaret,
327, Mary Anne,283, Michael,
283, Thomas,353
FLADGER, Henry,288,294
FLANAGAN, Reuben,212,215
FLANAGIN, Averilla,221,
Reuben,242, Reubin,221
FLANNEGAN, Reuben,316
FLEETWOOD, John,097
FLEMING, (Land),411, Elizabeth,
380, James,273, John,082,
083, Robert,273, Robt.,110,
111
FLEMING, Samuel,204, William,
255
FLEMMING, John Jr.,424, John,
424
FLENEGAL, Elizabeth,285
FLENEGALD, Elizabeth,283
FLETCHAL, John,516
FLETCHALL, Edward,052, James,
038,052,085, Thomas,052,
085,099,491,524,564,565,
Thos.,503
FLETCHER, Hugh,300, Thomas,
535
FLEWELLING, Thomas,204
FLEY, ,419, Sam.,398, Saml.,
400,401,408,422, Samuel,371,
374,377
FLIMTHEM, Edward,084
FLIN, John,373,375
FLINN, George,019,249
FLINT, Thomas,288,300, Thos.,
294

FLINTHEM(FLINTON), Edw.,432
FLINTHEMS, ,432
FLINTHEN, Edward,062, John,
062
FLINTHOM, Edward,431, Thomas,
432
FLINTON, ,562,567, John,431
FLIPPE, William,181
FLIPPO, Anne,173, William,173,
Wm.,158
FLIPPS, William,145
FLITCHALL, James,025
FLOID, James,189, Matthew,014
FLOWERS, Ann,288,294,300,
Bennet,288, Bennett,300,
Bennit,294, Nathan,300,
Rachel,288,294
FLOYD, ,004, Abraham,561,
Agnes,120, Charles,001,
Eve,561, Jack,006, James Jr.,
190, James,189,190, Jas.,
190,215, Jasper,190, John,
006,190,315, Lee,189,190,
Mathew,561, Milley,189,
Polly,479, Richard,190,
Richd.,190, Ruth,355,
Solomon,355
FLOYD, William,190
FOARD, Elisha,307, G.,116,
Gardner,116,122, Sarah,307
FOCHEE, Nathaniel,201
FOLKS, Joel,300, William,300,
374
FONDREEN, John,016
FONDRREN, John,021
FOOTE, Gibson,425, Newton,003
FOOTS, George Jr.,076,
George Sr.,076, George,076,
John,076, William,076
FOR(FORE?), Jesse,540
FORBES, Joseph,562
FORBUSH, John,180
FORD, Agatha,003, Ann,181,
Anna,312, Arasmus,181,
Archeleus,431, Charles,300,
Daniel,003,123,124,163,
170, Elisha,201,206,215,
Emsmus,182, Francis,300,
Frederick,043, Gardner,106,
114, Genny,181, George,288,
294, Isaac,181, James,306
FORD, James,312, Jas.,294,
Jesse,123,124,170,182,288,
294,300, John,126,128,131,
134,145,148,152,156,161,
163,164,170,176,181,190,
288,294,300,306,530, Jos.,
294, Joseph,288, Leah,181,
Levi,181,182, Linna,181,
Mary,034,288,294,300,
Milly,189
FORD, Nancy,163, Nathaniel,
109, Neal,300, Polley,181,
Preserved,288,294,300,
Rachel,306,431, Steph.Sr.,
294, Stephen Sr.,288,
Stephen,131, Thomas,086,
Tressia,181, Verlinda,181,
William,034,086,181,182,
300, Wm.Jr.,034, Wm.Sr.,034,
Wyly,390
FORD, Zadock,003
FORE, Archeleus,431, Archelous,
431, James,300, Jesse,438,
489,503,519, Joel,294, John,
503, Mary,288, Rachel,431,
Richard,288, Richd.,294
FORES, Joel,300, John,300,
Wm.,300
FOREST, Richard,165
FORESTER, James,143, Solomon,
143
FORGASON, James,056
FORGESSON, James,037
FORGUSON, Abraham,012,
Charles,185, James Sr.,012,
James,012, Robert,012
FORISTER, Jane,341, William,
341
FORKNER, James,349
FORMON, David,520
FORREST, James,138, John,154
FORRESTER, James,176

FORRISTER, Elizabeth,176,
Hardy,176, James,176, John,
176
FORSHEE, Benjamin,255
FORT, Albert,408, Burwell,408,
Capt.,112, Elias,369,408,
Gardner,112, Josiah,408,
Wyley,390
FORTNER, (Old Lady),363,
Arminda,362, Charlotte,363,
David,168, George,363,
James,363, Jasper,363
FOSTER, "Nelly",513, ,159,
165, Crojiah(?),235,
Eleanor(Nelly),569,
Eleanor,512,513, Frances,
175, Geo.Singleton,128,
George S.,175, George,175,
Henry,367, Isham,134,153,
551, James H.,175, James Hocket,
175, Jane,367, Jas.McDuffie,
367
FOSTER, John C.,175, John Crow,
128,175,512,527, John,128,
139,154,175,195,481,485,
487,512,527,545,569, Josiah,
175,182, Martha,367, Mary,
121,367, Millie,367, Nancey,
483, Nancy,175, Newton,367,
Robert S.,175, Robert,121,
Robt.S.C.,175
FOSTER, Sarah,283, William,
538
FOSTR(?), John,512
FOUNTAIN, James,334, Littleton,
355, Mary M.,334, Paul,152,
153,171, Richard,234,
Simpson L.,334, Stephen,
153, Wildey,334, William M.,
006, Wm.M.,008
FOURINGRISER, Zr.,312
FOURNIEU, Hughes,409
FOUSHEE, Benjamin,240
FOWLER, Andrew,264, Bidy,324,
Cathren,482, Charles,264,
Coleman,329, Debby,231,
239, Eles(Ellis),482, Elis,
483, Eliz.,351, Ellis,515,
Ephraim,557, George,249,
Henry,251, Isaac,239,
James,035,038,480, Jesse,
292, John,259,324,325,351
FOWLER, Jonathan,351, Joshua Jr.,
325, Joshua Sr.,351, Joshua,
325,351, Josiah,267,325,
346,351, Mark,482, Mary Teague,
001, Nancy,265,351, Newton,
267, Patsey,267, Richard,
231,239, Robert,061, Sally,
351, Sarah,267, Thomas,325,
351, W.,271
FOWLER, William,194,205,249,
257,266,268,288,325,351,
Wm.,300,482
FOX, John,004, Philip,081,
Phillip,058,060
FOXWORTH, Abel,288,294,300,
Absalom,294, Absolem,288,
Eliz.,294, Henry,288,294,
300, Jesse,288,294, Jno.,
294, Job,288,294,300, John,
288,300, Joseph,300, Steph.,
294, Stephen Jr.,288,
Stephen,288,300
FRACHURE, Ransom,359
FRAKES, Thomas,316
FRANCIS, M.,462
FRANKLAND, Thomas,028
FRANKLIN, (Land),390, ,069,
Ann,083, Edman,156, Edward,
031,158, Esen,084, Isham,
090,164, John,026,037,039,
041,048,050,058,063,069,
081,083,084,090, Joseph,486,
495, Judah,408, July,408,
Laurance,408, Lawrence,387,
408, Mayann,486, Morning,058
FRANKLIN, Mourning,063,083,
Nancy,057,070, Owen,031,
Priscillar,069, Rachel,031,
S.D.,081, Thomas B.,041,
083,084, Thomas Baker,027,
Thomas,026,027,058,083,

084, Thos.B.,027,077,081,
Thos.Baker,025,026,039,
048,049,070,081,084,090,100
FRANKLIN, Thos.Baker,104
FRANKLING, Joseph,486, Mary,
486
FRANKLYN, John,015,016,038,
Persills(a),015, Thomas B.,
016,041, Thomas Sr.,015,
Thomas,015,016
FRANKS, Jane(Mrs.),267,
Marshall,210,212,214,248,
255, Nehemiah,192,197,202,
203,206,210,211,212,214,
216,248, Robert,210, Samuel,
210,214
FRANKSZ, ,248
FRASER, Alex.,232, Alexr.Jr.,
232, Bethshaba,357, James,
027,044, John B.,413,
Margaret,359, Pingue H.,359
FRASHER, Wm.,348
FRASIER, James,049
FRASUER, Bethsheba,327,
Samuel,327
FRAZER, Ezekiel,460, Olviah,
465
FRAZIER, Caleb,516, Ezekiel,
461, James,169,170
FREDERICK, Geo.,348
FREDRICK, Francis,072
FREE, Jacob,319
FREEMAN, Alexander,324, Anne,
122, Bennett,341, Benton,
346,350, David,511, Elizabeth,
325, Fanny,324, Francis,324,
Harris Sr.,122, Harris,109,
112, James Jr.,122, James,
107,342, Jane,113,324, Jas.,
165, Jeptha,337, John,324,
Joseph,310
FREEMAN, Mark,223,325,346,
351, Mary J.,342, Mary,198,
324, Readin,353,358, Reden,
346, Reeves,109,112, Rev.,
122, Robert,198,223, Sally,
324, Starkey,300, Westly,
324, Wiley,324, William,198,
300,324
FREIZER, Elizabeth,089,
Samuel,089
FRENCH, John P.,268, John,128,
154, Joseph,534,569, Samuel,
153, William,130
FRENEAU, Peter,159,394,533
FRIERSON, Aaron,422, James Sr.,
398, John,396,397,398,412,
Moses Gordon,374
FROST, Barnet,466, Edward,345,
Elizabeth,466, John,107,
108,115,466, Judith,107,
115, Mary,466, Rachel,466,
Rebecca,466, Robert Sr.,
090, Robert,060,061,062,
068, Ruth,060,061, William,
466, Wm.,294
FRYER, Geo.W.,006, Matilda,
006, Robert,254, William,300
FULCHOR, Francis,139
FULLER, (Family),265, (Land),
250, A.,360, Alfred,360,
Archibald,260,262, Daniel,
253, George W.,330, George,
237,251,258, Isham,260,
Isreal,260, Jane,330,
Jones J.,262, Jones(Capt.),
262, Jones,260, Kitturah,
262, Maryann,260, Peter,260
FULLER, Richard,156, Shadrack,
283, William,262
FULLERTON, Samuel,219
FULLHORN, Francis,139
FULLINGTON, William,077
FULLWOOD, Robert,384,385,
Robt.,385, Thomas,385
FULTON, ,568, John,562, Land,
565, Thomas,073,273,
William,259,273
FULWOOD, James,388, Robert,
085,388,422, Robt.,385,
William,388, Wm.Jr.,388
FUREY, Martha(Mrs.),003
FURGASON, William,056

FURGURSON, Braham,077
FURGUSON, Abraham,014,
James Sr.,014, James,014,
033,068, John,033,068,
Meham,068, Robert,014,015,
Samuel,058, W.,067,
William,058,068, Wm.,082
FURLOU, William,232
FURMAN, (Rev.),284, Rev.,285,
Richard,420
FURNACE, Joseph,322
FURNAS, Esther,454, Joseph,
318
FUTHERTON, Robert,068
FUTRILL, Jos.,294
FUTTERTON, William,068
GA, ,057
GABBIE, John,558, Joseph,558,
Robert,558
GABLE, William,353
GABRIEL, ,529
GADDES, Jas.,300, William,300
GADDY, Ithamar,294, Ithamer,
288,300
GAFFORD, Michael,233, Thomas,
195,199,209,233
GAFFY, Charles,214
GAGE, James,274
GAGGAN, George,306
GAILLARD, Isaac,227,229,
Peter,417, Tacitus,227,
229, Theodore,320
GAINERS, Isaac,056
GAINES, Catherine,260, Edmund,
260, James,348, Margaret,
260, Nancy,352, Robert,348,
352,357, Sarah,260, Simeon,
351,352
GAINS, (?),254, (Land),251,
James,349, Nancy,351,
Richard,313, Stephen,250
GALAGLY, Joseph,236
GALAHER, Lawrence,045, Peter,
277
GALAKER, Lawrence,092
GALBRETH, Joseph,028
GALE, James,288, Leuraney,294,
Miriam,294
GALLAGHER, John,570,572
GALLAHER, Lawrence,067
GALLAWAY, Barring,341,
Evelina B.,341
GALLEGLY, Wm.,223
GALLIKER, John,103
GALLMAN, Christina,318, John,
307,318
GALLOWAY, Alexander,111,116,
Anna,305, Elizabeth,305,
Jean,305, John,305,
Margaret,305, Martha,305,
Mary,313, Peter,305,313,
Wm.F.,349
GALT, Robert,518,526
GAMBEL, Robert,113, Robt.,383
GAMBELL, James,383, Jno.,396,
John,389
GAMBLE, David,259, George,259,
James Jr.,222, James Sr.,
222, James,259, Robert,220,
William,259,384
GAMBLIN, John,164
GANTAREN, Mary,535
GANTEREN, Mary,535
GANTT, Alexander,334, Allaman,
250, Caroline,334, John,334,
Nicey,334, Norman,252,
Richard,277, William,334
GARDENER, John,288, Stephen,
288
GARDINER, Jacob,488,533,562
GARDNER, ,144, Jacob,137,144,
488,499,562, John,502, Mary,
562,569, Steph.,294
GARDON, Thomas,305
GARE, James,144
GARETT, Enoch,249
GAREY, Benjamin,263, Charles,
229, Doratha,267, Dorothy,
263, Jacob,252, John Sr.,
316, Joshua,263, Rachel,263,
Thomas,267, William J.,252,
William,252,263
GARLINGTON, Jno.,270,271,272,

John,261,267,275
GARMANY, George W.,002, Nancy,
006, William,006
GARMON, Adam,258
GARNER, H.M.,330, James,275,
John,213,214,330,356, Mary,
330, R.T.,330, Richard,372,
Sarah J.,330, Sarah,330,
Starling,330,357, Sturdy,
185, Susan,202,256, Thos.,
107, William R.,330,
William,349,353
GAROTT, Daniel,372
GARRATTE, James,052
GARRAWAY, Robert,288, Robt.,
294
GARRET, Dickerson,185, Edw.,
227, Edward,226,243, John,
222,523,526, Thomas,055,060
GARRETT, Anna,211, Bluford,
339, Charles,261, Edward,
256, Elizabeth,339,340,
Enoch,211,256, Franklin,
339, Hannah,261, Harrison,
339, John Sr.,211, John,208,
211,256, Joseph,211,256,
Levi,256, Martha,339,
Milton,339, Nicholas,169,
257, Nicules,257
GARRETT, Rebecca,261, Silas,
208,211, Stephen,339,
Thomas,256, Warren,339
GARRIOT, John,309
GARRISON, David,183,185,
James,158, Thos.,215
GARROTT, John,554
GARTHER, Thomas,070
GARTMAN, Danl.,408, Philip,
408, Thomas,408
GARVEN, Frederick,349
GARVIN, ,571, Aaron,362, F.N.,
332,335,341,354,360,
Frederick N.,353,354,360,
Genl.,365, Green S.,335,
Greenbery,354, Jane,570,
Thomas D.,335, Thomas,222,
334,354,359,570
GARY, ,009, Charles Jr.,313,
Charles,221, George,502,
Isaac,320, Jacob,256,
John H.,006, John Jr.,308,
John,319, Thomas,319,
William,268,312, Wm.,006
GASAWAY, Coleman,349, Daniel,
349, Hannah,349
GASKIN, Ezekiel,380
GASQUE, Absalem,288, Absalom,
294,300, Archd.,294,
Archibald,288, Elly,300,
Henry,288,294,300, John,
288,294,300, Saml.,294,300,
Samuel,288
GASS, John,489
GASSAWAY, Ann,486, Caleb,486,
Henry,333,353, Ira,333,
James,333,506, John,333,
Rachel,333, Thomas Jr.,349,
Thomas,360, Wesley,333,
William W.,358, William,
333, Wm.,359, Wm.G.,036,
Wm.W.,359
GASTIN, Jas.,190
GASTON, Alexander,010,096,
097, Alexr.,094, David,010,
Ebenezer,070, Hugh,010,
036,094,097, James Love,088,
James,010,080,087,088,
John Jr.,070, John,010,
012,018,070,071,072,074,
077,078,087, Joseph Jr.,010,
Joseph,010, Margaret,077,
Martha,010
GASTON, Martha,036, Mary,054,
097, Mathew,076, Robert,068,
092, Thomas,080, William,
010,036,037,038,040,043,
045,068,077,087,088, Wm.,
059,072,073,189,486
GASWAY, Caleb,547,553
GATES, Edmund,260, John,243,
312, Theney,001
GATHER, John,074, Thomas,070,
073,074,085

GAULT, William,501
GAUNT, Nebo,217, Zebulon,208,
217
GAUNTT, Isreal,310, Z.,310,
Zimri,310, Zinuri,309
GAYLE, Billups,371, Jno.,378,
John,378,379,417
GEAN(DEAN?), John,181
GEARIN, Abigail,329,361,
Jacob,361, John,329
GEE, John Henry,530,572, John,
530,571,572
GEER, Deborah,283, John,284,
285
GEFFERS, Nathaniel,454
GEILLOTT, George,163
GENT, John,222
GENTRY, Catarine,517, Hezekiah,
517,519
GEORGE, (?),554, (Line),532,
B.A.(Mrs.),259, Bernice A.,
223, David,114,427,485,486,
491,506,509,515,522, James,
353, John Jr.,501,502, John,
437,455,484,501,518,553,
554, Mary,437, Needom,352,
Rebecca,485, Thomas,437,
518,557, William,495
GEORGE, William,506,520,522,
Wm.A.,485
GERALD, Benjamin,377,378,
Elizabeth,377,378, Gabriel,
377,378, William,378, Wm.,
393
GERRAL, Margt.,294
GERRALD, Gabriel,316
GERRET, Thomas,034
GEVIN, John,099
GHENT(?), Mark,542
GIBBS, Agatha,456, Anne,456,
Hiram,456, James(Col.),435,
James,444,456,510,511,
John,456, Susannah,456,
Thomas,159,163, Thos.,159,
534, Wm.Hasel,384, Zachariah,
506, Zacharias,456
GIBREATH, Alexander,315,
George,315, Jesse,315,
John,315, Mary,315,
William,315
GIBS, Cannon,300
GIBSON, ,572, Abraham,022,
485, Abram,022, Absalom,332,
Benjamin,367,368, David,
300, Elijah,022,333,
Elizabeth,326, George,333,
Gideon,290, Gurdin,301,
Henry,431, Hiram,332,359,
Isaac,117, Jacob Sr.,312,
Jacob,107,112,119, James Jr.,
418
GIBSON, James,193, Jane,387,
Jeremiah,326, John Jas.,
418, John,022,288,294,394,
Jordan,294, Jos.Sr.,119,
Joseph,122,367, Levi,287,
Martha G.,366, Martha J.,
367, Mary,418, Nancy,333,
367, Nansey,367, Nathan,431,
431, Phin's.,402, Polly,333
GIBSON, Richard,550, Robt.,
113, Royal,418, Samuel,418,
Steph.,294, Stephen,119,
289, Thomas,354,367,368,
W.H.,367, Wm.,107
GIDDEN, Abraham,407, Edward,
248
GIDDENS, Abraham,384, Edward,
238, Isaac,407, Jemima,407,
Thomas,407
GIER(?), J.,150
GIFT(GIST?), Benjamin,491
GILASPIE, Green B.,325
GILBERT, ,004, Abram,001,
Alexander,151, Benjamin,
427, Bookter,006, Catharine,
177, David,006, John,250,
Johnathan,427, Thomas,006,
William,253, Wm.,212
GILBERTS, ,005
GILCHRIST, Adam,522, James,
048, William,277
GILES, Edw.,570, Jane,521,

Wm.,495
GILHAM, Allen,362, Charles,
487, Jane(Jean),502, Jean,
502, John,489, Sam,363,
Thomas,566, William,149,
152,502
GILKEY, Jonathan,489,521,
Samuel,521, Wm.,521
GILKIE, Jonathan,438, Jonathan,
539, Samuel,488,489,545,
556, Wm.,506
GILL, Agnes,038, Archibald,
059,100, Elizabeth(Mrs.),
176, Elizabeth,155, Geo.,
061, George Jr.,025, George,
016,017,100,101, Hannah,003,
J.,152, James,015,027,028,
097,100,102,565, John Sr.,
102, John,015,016,038,102,
565, Jos.,176, Joseph,176
GILL, Joseph,177, Mary,097,
Robert Sr.,016, Robert,011,
015,016,017,059,060,075,
085,195,565, Sarah,015,016,
102, Thos.,003
GILLAM, Allen,362, Harris,211,
215, John,094, Robert,002,
William,414
GILLELAND, James,268
GILLESPIE, Thomas,557
GILLEY, ,535, Susanna,375
GILLHAM, Charles,564
GILLHAM, Ezekiel,476,558,
Isaac,562, John,567,
Mary(Polly) G.,476,
Thomas Jr.,557, Thomas Sr.,
557,558, Thomas,562,564,
566,567,569,570, William,
GILLIAM, ,009, Ann,308, David,
306, Frances,319, Hannah,
308, Harris,202,319, Isaac,
558, James,320, Jemina,306,
John,308, Joshua,224,234,
319, Mary W.,003, Mary,224,
308,318, Nancy,458, Peter,
002, Robert B.,003, Robert Jr.,
316,319, Robert Sr.,318
GILLIAM, Robert,134,164,224,
William,262,308,310,318,
402,458, Wm.C.,262
GILLIAN, John,046
GILLIHAM, Wm.,182
GILLILAND, Lemuel J.,336,
Archibald,493, David,333,
336, Elijah H.,333, Emily C.,
333, Henrietta J.,336, J.,
257, James A.,333, James,
333,347, Jean,141, John R.T.,
336, John,172, Lemuel J.,
336, Mary Ann,333, Nancy A.E.,
336, Nancy E.,336
GILLILAND, Richard T.,336,
Robert,123,141,273,
Robt.Jr.,171
GILLING, Joseph,538, Moses,
538, Nathl.,538
GILLIS, Angus,300
GILLISON, Israel,348, Isreal,
357, James,143, Jonathan,348
GILLISPIE, William,204
GILLMAN, Edward,285
GILLS, John Jr.,055
GILLSTRAP, Delilah,353,
Ephraim,339, Louisa,339,
Patsey,353
GILLY, Charles,178
GILMER, R.A.,333
GILMORE, Francis,563
GILSTRAP, Ann,347, Anne,324,
348, Bright,356, Hardy,324,
347, James,324,348, John,
324,347,348, Peter,324,
William,334
GIPSON, Henry,431, Jacob,112,
John,019, Nathan,431,
Stephen,113
GISSEL, H.,343,344
GIST, Benjamin,489,493,494,
502,512,514,516,556,
John M.,444, Jos.C.,442,
Joseph,543, Sarah(Mrs.),
439, Sarah,425,430,436,521,
543,546, William,254,439,

489,494,498,543, Wm.,474
GITTY, Ann,008
GITZENTANNER, Thos.,540
GIVEN, William,051
GIVENS, Samuel,102, Wm.,052
GIVIN, William,013,014
GIVINS, Richd.,546
GLADEN, Samuel,106
GLADNEY, Agnes,106, Agness,
117, Hugh,106, James,106,
Joseph,106, Mary,106,
Patrick,106, Richard,027,
028,029,092,106,117, Samuel,
106,117, Thomas,106,109,
Thos.,113, Thos.Jr.,113
GLAISHER, John,108
GLANTON, Charles,522
GLASGO, Archibald W.,313,
James,313, John,313,
Margaret,313, Mary,313,
Rachel,313, Robert,313
GLASGOW, Archibald,317, James,
441, John,317, Robert,317
GLASS, Alexander,558,565,
James,565, John,546, Sarah,
305, Thomas Jr.,006, Toby,
305, Vincent,209
GLAUS, Johannes,344
GLAUSS, John,344
GLAWN, Elizabeth,288
GLAZER, John,109
GLAZIER, A.,318, All(?),213,
John,112,116, Margaret,318
GLEEN, James,066, John,320,
Mr.,065,066, Robert,090
GLEN, David,272, Francis,243,
James,386,395,488,495,
John,519, Nathan,505,517
GLENN, (Family),505, ,004,
065, Alexander,175,179, Ann,
305, Anna,329, Ber.(Bernard),
525, Berd,433, Berd.(Bernard),
499, Berd.,509,527,541,
Bern,544, Bernard,053,317,
509,536, Bernd.,433,546,
547,549, D.W.,349, Duke W.,
329, Frances,254
GLENN, Francis,275, James Jr.,
024, James,034,053,064,257,
305,329, Jean,305, Jemima,
458, Jincy Pride,470, John,
206,305, Joseph,242,
Lucy(Coleman),499, Margaret,
305, Mary,305,505, Nathan,
064,430,499,505,529,546,
551, Noble,329,347,349
GLENN, Robert,086,329,439,
Spilsby,444,543,544,
Thomas,034,062, Tyra,239,
Warren,329, William,305,
329,444,499
GLIDE, James,185
GLOVER, Benjamin Jr.,309,
Drewry,571, Drury,570,
George,060,100, Isum,571,
Jesse,570, Mary,570,
Robert,019,060,570,
Susanah,016, Susanna,023,
William,571
GLOW, George,334, Rhoda,334
GOAD, William,095
GODBER, Wm.,540
GODBOLD, (Estate),300,
Abraham,288, Abrm.,304,
David,288, Dd.,294,
Hugh G.,300, Jacob,294,
Stephen,288,300, Thomas Jr.,
288, Thomas Sr.,288, Thomas,
304, Thos.,288,294,300,
Thos.Jr.,294, Thos.Sr.,294
GODFREY, Amy,006, Richard,288,
Richd.,294, Wm.,288
GOGGANS, Abram,006, Burr,001,
Daniel,006, George,306,
308,311, Lucinda T.,006,
Matilda,003, Samuel,006,
Sarah Ann,008
GOGGINS, George,195
GOIN, Ann,524
GOING, ,511, Drury,042,072,
077, Isaac,072, Job,042,072
GOINGS, Drury,073,074, Job,
073

GOLDEN, Anthony,218, John,189,
Rubin,189, Sallie,101,
Sarah,101
GOLDING, ,252, Anthony,258,
John,258, Reuben,305,308,
Richard,198
GOLDSMITH, William,498,535
GOLIGHTLY, David,479, John,
489,493
GOLLIFIN, Martin,166
GOLLITHAN, Martin,167, Nancey,
167
GOLLOTHAN, Martin,166,167,
Nancey,167
GOLORSHEEN, Martin,163
GOLSON, Jno.,430, Lewis,430
GOOCH, Claibourn,487
GOOD, ,165, Elizabeth,475,
476, Henry,475,476,512,513,
570, Hugh,476, John,476,
512, Mackerness,237,
Mackness,212, Magnneese,
235, Mary(Polly) G.,476,
Maryan,476, McNees,215,
221, McNeese(Old),230,
McNeese,225,230, Nancy,476,
Richard,163
GOOD, Robert,475,476,512,513,
570, Samuel,237, Sarah,476,
Thomas,476,502,512
GOODDEN, William,180
GOODE, ,145, Edna,310, Edward,
431, Edwd.,531, Jemina,310,
Jno.,145, John,176, M.,
235, Mac Neese,196, Mackernuss,
236, Mackneese,198, McNeese,
206, Rebekah,128, Richard,
128,145,156,163, Richd.,145,
Robert,548, Samuel,237,
310, Thomas,176
GOODEN, Crafford,126
GOODIN, George,142
GOODLETT, Ann,181,182, D.,
180,180,181, David,179,180,
Jas.,181, John,154,158,
160, Mr.,187, Richard,181,
Robert,126,144,154, Wm.,144
GOODLEY, (Land),144, David,
187
GOODMAN, (Widow),244, Beauforte,
262, Claborn,223, Clabourn,
223, Claburn,223, Duke,262,
James,138,262, Mariah,209,
Nancy,237, Overton,134,
Samuel,215, Sarah,262,
Thomas,323, Timothy,237,
William,204, Wm.,216
GOODMON, Overton,153
GOODRICH, Mr.,182
GOODWIN, Abel,283, Ann(Mrs.),
186, Charles,004,209,
Craffford,165, Crafford,
126,135,136, Crawford,125,
Ellis M.,452, Frances,186,
Francis,182, George,135,
136,538, Giles,264, James,
244, Jesse,207, John,137,
191,196,198,201,216,217,225
GOODWIN, John,230,235,459,
494,502,514,538,540, Jos.,
145,160,186, Joseph,177,
186, Josiah,538, Julius,006,
L.,182, Mariah,206, Mark,
521, Mary Ann,264, Mrs.,178,
Rachel,216, Robert Jr.,212,
Robert Sr.,212, Robert,198,
203,235, Sampson,477
GOODWIN, Samson,478,486,
Uriah,178, William,136,
179,186
GOODWYN, Frances,178, Jesse,
171, Jno.,172, John,151,
162,168,171, Jos.,162,163,
Joseph,178, William,162
GOODYEAR, John,294,300, Lovet,
301, William,288, Wm.,294,
300
GOOLEY, Robert,140
GOOLSBY, Burgess,243, James,
205
GOOSWIN, John,197
GORDAN, Frankey,185, John,169,
519, Samuel,155,169,

Thomas Sr.,309,315, Thomas,
313
GORDEN, Jno.Jr.,070, John,495,
506,532, Nathaniel,520,
Sally,467, Thomas,490,495,
513
GORDIN, John,073, Ruth,073
GORDON, (Land),250, ,444,
Adam,214,255, Benjamin,203,
453, Charity,308, Charles F.,
377,413,417, Chas.F.,394,
408,423, Chas.Fisher,394,
Elizabeth,203,216,377,413,
George,246,259,441,443,
444, James,098,567, John C.,
330, John,048,156,208
GORDON, John,561, Mary,214,
561,567, Nathan,256,
Nathaniel,255, Roger,413,
Samuel,157,539,561,562,
566, Thomas(Maj.),203,
Thomas,216,250,378,379,
503,504,506,549, Thos.,539,
515, Thos.Sr.,307
GORE, (?),144, Aron,057,
Eleazar,061, Eleazer,050,
068, Elijah,080, Elisha,056,
Elizabeth,068, Frances,061,
James,020,026,041,048,056,
062,068,069,080,085,093,
170, Jamse M.,035, Jas.Mannen,
137, John A.,080, John Ashford,
061,081,085, John,085
GORE, Joshua,055,068,264
GORE, Manen,494, Manin(Manning?),
494, Mannin,020,056, Mannon,
097, Mary,085, Thomas,037,
038,061,069
GOREE, ,006,009, Claiborne,
006, Claudius,006, Edward,
311,314, Ephraim,006,
James Lyles,006, James,006,
John Sr.,316, John,316,
317,319, Joseph,316, Josiah,
319, Judith,006, Nathan,006,
Sarah,316, Silas,006
GORELY, Ayers,248, Ayres,242
GORES, ,004
GORLEY, Hugh,112
GORMAN, Wm.,057
GORRELL, Agnes,031, Ralph,043,
Robert,031,041,043, Wil,031
GOSE(?), ,057
GOSSET, Abraham,455, John T.,
336
GOTTIER, Francis,137,155,
Isabella,137
GOUD, Wm.,300
GOUDELOCK, Adam,427,511,
Davis,463, William,463
GOUDY, Ayres,200, James,387
GOUDYLOCK, Adam,463,464,486,
Davis,463,486, Hannah,486,
Sarah,463, Susannah,463,
William,463,464
GOUGH, George,168, William,
148
GOULD, William,314
GOULLIETTE, Eliz.,392
GOULY, Ayres,206
GOURLEY, Hugh,112
GOVRELL, Robt.,493
GOWAN, George,487,569, Mack,
364
GOWDELOCK, Davis,446, Wm.,446
GOWDY, Robert,239
GOWDYLOCK, Davis,446
GOWEN, ,511, Allen,132,134,
146, Jno.,162,164, John,125,
133,134, Joseph,533, Major,
174, Thomas,180,183,184,
Thos.,179,180
GOWING, Drury,511
GOWLEY, John,214
GRACE, George,186
GRADON, Elizabeth,008
GRAFF, & CO.,438
GRAHAM, Alexander,334, Andrew,
075,098,102, Arthur,369,
David,259,275, James,051,
103,309,369,524, Jesse,309,
Joel,309, John,309,
Margaret,075, N.,388,

HAGEN(HOGAN?), Jas.,256
HAGEN, David,256
HAGEWOOD, Benjamin,346
HAGGANS, Mary,558, William,
558
HAGGINS, ,559
HAGIN, Benj.,071, Thomas,289
HAGINS, Thomas,301, Thos.,295
HAGOOD, B.,335,347, Benj.,348,
Benjamin,330,355,357,
Eliz.D.,006, J.E.,341,343,
344,345, James E.,343, Jeff,
363,364, Mark,006
HAGOON, J.E.,343
HAGUE, ,094
HAIL, (Line),539, Ben,445,
Joab,182, John,301,532,
Robert,301, Thomas,103,
105, Thos.,055
HAILD, Jacob,436, John,436,
490,524, William,436, Wm.,
436
HAILE, ,504, Ben,438,439,440,
441,442,443,444, Ben.,442,
J.,529, Jacob,514, John,
289,430,439,491,492,495,
499,501,502,503,509,510,
517,518,524,528,531,532,
533,535,542,544,548,554,
556, Ruth,548, William,498,
499,511
HAINE, George,166, Marget,166
HAINEY, Timothy,483
HAINS, George,133, Ruth,358
HAINSWORTH, ,549
HAIR, Agnes,311, Anna Mary,
311, Barbara,311, Catherine,
311, Hettie Jr.,311, John,
311, Margaret,311, Mary,311,
Matthais,311, Molly,311,
Peter,311, Rachel,311
HAIRGROVE, Geo.,295, George,
289, Jno.,295, John,289
HAIRGROVES, Newel,301
HAIRSTON, Thomas,208
HAIS, John,030
HAISE, Milly,190
HAIZE, Isaac,531, Jacob,531
HAKKUMS, John,198
HALBERT, William,145,245, Wm.,
141
HALCOM, Philip,511
HALCOMB, Benj.,496, Elisha,
268
HALE, Capt.,174, Jno.,295,
Joseph,159, Robt.,298, Wm.,
295
HALFACRE, Barbara,318,
Elizabeth,318, Henry,318,
Jacob,318
HALL(HALT?), Thomas,531
HALL, ,004, Abigail,322,
Acquila,246, Acquila,196,
215, Allen,301, Ambrose,244,
Ann,473, Caroline,335,
Clementine,006, Daniel,335,
David,154,155,348, George,
354, Henry,354, Hugh,347,
352, James,202,504,522,525,
526, Jesse,354, Jno.,322
HALL, John W.,006, John,112,
206,214,217,220,225,226,
570, Joseph,099,205,244,
Judy,455, Mary,354, Merry,
149,187, Nancy,006,111,354,
Nathaniel Sr.,214, Nathaniel,
214, Robert,194,204,214,
Ruth,335,354, Saml.,349,
Samuel,006,322,325, Sarah,
335
HALL, T.J.,335, Thomas,354,
372,419, Warren,499,532,
William,024,025,040,195,
225,289,326,335,354,560,
Wm.,211,221,348,443,552,
553, Z.,334, Zachariah,335,
354,356
HALLMAN, John,029
HALLSEL, George,117
HALLUMS, Nero,362, William,
252,360
HALMAN, John,029
HALSELL, Benjamin,099, Thomas,

099
HALSEY, Edward,062, James,210,
Mary,099, Thomas,099
HALTON, Lewis,323
HAM, Jacob,551, John,152,436,
437,495,510,543,551, Mary,
495, Phebe,152, Thomas,134
HAMBLETON, Edley,325, Hance,
102, James,095,217,324,
John,066,185,301, L.J.,336,
Lilles(L),066, Lilles,066,
Mary,025, Patrick,036,056,
Robert,222, Saml.,074,
Samuel,066, Wm.,301
HAMBRIGHT, Frederick,571,
L.B.,351
HAMBY, Hambleton,353, John,
172, Malissa,339, Samuel,
355, Thomas M.,339, William,
172,353, Wm.M.,352
HAMELTON, ,169, Jeremiah,543,
John,185, Lewis,185
HAMES, Charity,553, Charles,
437,438,498,525,526,532,
Chas.,532, John,518,522,
525,553, William,522
HAMILTON, (Family),263, ,
557, Alexander,198,214,219,
234,248,327, Alexr.,524,
Andrew,148,352,353,357,
493, D.K.,360, David L.,357,
David Sr.,327,357, David,
092,328, Frances D.,289,
Frances,289, Hance,097,
Henry,199,216, James,111,
112
HAMILTON, James,120,217,251,
420,502,561, Jane,327,328,
357, Jean,122, Jereh.,474,
Jeremiah,426, Jno.,294,
John Sr.,502, John,288,
502,548,565,572, Lemuel G.,
342, Lidia,295, Major Andw.,
357, Major David K.,357,
Margaret,357,565, Mary,361
HAMILTON, Patrick,041,042,
Peter,122, Robertson,276,
Samuel,042,276, Sarah J.,
339, Sarah,111,112,120,
Temperance,186, William,
275,289,306
HAMLETON, Samuel,034
HAMMELLTON, Wm.,295
HAMMELTON, ,548, Alexr.,530,
Jean(Jane),530, John,548
HAMMET, John,124
HAMMILTON, ,530, Alexaner(?),
530, Jean,530
HAMMON, Job,526
HAMMOND, Frances,355, Job,495,
506,533,535, Lar(?),230,
Leroy,230, Peter,160,
Susannah,331, William,003
HAMMONDS, William,160
HAMPTON, Amey,408, Amy,408,
Andrew,436, Ann,311,
Benjamin,315, Charles,060,
Ellen,307, John,002,115,
140, Nathan,198, R.,140,
Sarah,198, Wade,115,371,
398, William,371,383
HAMRICK, A.W.,006
HANAN, Agnes,111,112, James,
111, Robert,111,112
HANCOCK, (Widow),245, Eliz.(Mrs.),
004, Hester,002, Jesse,004,
Lana(Dr.),006, Porter,520,
Richard,211
HAND, John,200, Jonathan,023,
024, Robert,219, Robt.,219
HANDCOCK, Porter,520
HANE & BERK, ,198
HANES, John,358, Lidian Ann,
358, Susannah,358
HANEY, Hannah,482, John,485,
Thomas,082, Timothy,483
HANING, Daniel,312
HANKES, Mott,394
HANKS, Epahroditus,417,
Epaphmoditus,417, James,
289, Luke,206
HANNA, (Son of Wm.),257,
Agnes,101, Anna,077,

Barnett,562, J.,257, James,
006,024,089,097,101,216,
242,250,256,257, John,006,
216,242,256, Margaret,242,
Mary,216, Robert,140,216,
251,569, Robt.,217, Samuel,
256,257, Thomas,101,
William,006
HANNA, William,204,242,250,
251,301,562, Wm.,213,216,
257,569
HANNAH, Agnes,027, John,517,
Mary,027, Richard,289,
Robert,197,246,306,322,
Widow,197
HANNER, Robert,156
HANNERS, Richard,301, Rilhard,
301
HANSON, Thompson M.,353
HARADIMAN, Uriah,316
HARBENSON, Ann,083
HARBERSON, Mary,083, Robert,
083
HARBIN, ,359, John,329,
Joseph,340, Matilda,359,
Morgan,347,352, Nathanicl,
090, Polly,329, T.W.,326,
Thomas W.,347,350,352,355,
356, Thomas,359, Thos.,347,
355, Thos.W.H.,335
HARBISON, James,098, Jas.,567,
Mary,035, Matthew,098,
Patrick,036,089
HARBOUR, Walter,310
HARBROUGH, John,112
HARBRY, John,112
HARDEN, (Land),552, Clary,243,
Green,349, Henry,088,243,
509,513, John,259,509,571
HARDGROVES, Chris.,309
HARDIMAN, James,315
HARDIN, (Land),095, Eliza,340,
John,047,332,569, Joseph,
340,570, William,038
HARDING, Henry,222
HARDWICK, Gard.,549, Garland,
326,427, Geo.,549, Hansel,
092, Hasel Jr.,078, Hasel Sr.,
086, Hasel,095, Hazel,012,
018,020,050,055,062,078,
101, James,040,085,086,485,
486,515, Jas.,078,485, Lucy,
326, M.(W.?),549, Mary,018,
Molly,427,546
HARDWICK, W.Jr.,488,489,
William,427,491,515, Wm.,
488,546,549
HARDY, (?),209, Christopher,
199, Phebe,470, Saml.,455,
Samuel,455,470, Thomas,314,
526
HARELSON, Josiah,295, Ruth,
288
HARGISS, Abraham,134,138
HARGROVE, Anne,283,286
HARILL(HARREL), Wm.,513
HARISON, Carter,178
HARKEY, Catharine,335, Josiah,
335
HARLAN, Aaron Sr.,540, Aaron,
540,541, Geo.,555,556,
George,448,465,472,475,
517,520,557, Jacob,540,541,
Joseph,257, Mrs.,255,
Saml.,540, Voluntine,262
HARLAND, Elinor,475, George,
472,475,511,530, Hannah,475,
Isaac,475, Rebecca,475,
Samuel Jr.,475, Samuel,475,
William,475
HARLEE, Thos.,294
HARLEN, ,520, Elizabeth,258
HARLIN, ,504,520, Aaron,492,
503,557, Aron,216,540, Geo.,
509, George,482,492,494,
500,503,504,508,509,510
HARLING(HARLAN), Geo.,511,539
HARLING, ,520, Geo.,555,
George,429,530, Jacob,517,
Joseph,257, Saml.,540,
Samuel,536, Valentine,517
HARLINGS, Mrs.,255
HARLLEE, David S.,301, Thomas,

301
HARLON, Aaron,503,515, George,
504
HARLOW, George,493, James F.,
077, John,077
HARLSTON, John,232
HARMAN, Alram,301, Shoecraft,
289,295, Thomas,289, Thos.,
295
HARMON, Crafts S.,301, Daniel,
301, Godfrey,314, Jacob,314,
John,314, Mary,314, Thomas,
314, William,314
HARP, James,044,045
HARPER, Alexander,193,194,
203,214,227,228,231,232,
237,570, Daniel,075, Danl.,
067, Jas.,110, John,024,
Joshua,156, Margaret,038,
Martha,570, Mary,284,
Robert,038,093,098,134,
William,059, Wm.,082,446
HARRALSON, Hugh,290
HARREL, (Est.),298, David,301,
Jas.,301, Jesse,301,
Josiah T.,301, Levi,301,
Matthey T.,301, Stephen,
301, Zephaniah,301
HARRELL, David,289, Dd.,295,
Ephraim,289,295, Jacob,289,
295, Jas.,295, Jesse,295,
Lewis Sr.,295, Lewis,289,
295,304, Thomas,515
HARRELLEE, Thomas,289
HARRELSON, Jesse,289,295
HARRILL, Hugh,296, William,
513
HARRILSON, Hugh,301
HARRINGTON, Charles,538,
Chas.,538, Drewry,494,496,
Drury,450, Fanny,450,
Frances,450, Jno.,534,
John,426,450,489,491,538,
Patience,538
HARRIS, Alexr.,348, Ann,565,
Anne,572, Benjamin,003,
252, Braddock,250, Carter B.,
331, Catherine,215, Chas.,
399, Clough,202,306, David,
329,522,525, Dorcas,331,
Frances,193, J.H.,137,
J.P.,357, James,002,144,
331, John,121,218,250,254
HARRIS, John,258,331,348,
Joseph,537, Little Berry,
201, Littleberry,306,
Lucinda,331, Lud,003,
Lurany,329, Margaret,563,
Martha,537, Mary,201,306,
Micajah,313, Moseby,306,
Nathaniel,306,331, Nathl.,
348, Nicholas,512, Nicolas,
528, Nimrod,316
HARRIS, Rebecca,306, Richard,
306,348,352,354,464,537,
Richd.,348, Robert,530,
555,563, Sally,464, Samuel,
088,201,247,306, Sarah,331,
Shadrack,348, Thomas,211,
464,526,537, William,193,
194,210,258,565,572
HARRISON, Elizabeth,166,497,
George,153, H.,356, James,
135,144,145,147,149,157,
163,165,166,167,169,170,
172,490,493,497,549, Jas.,
190, John M.,263, John T.,
356, John,185,189,190,349,
356, M.,159, Martin,328,
350,360, Matilda,356, Mr.,
365
HARRISON, Nancy,360, Naomi,
356, Oliver,360, R.,114,
Reuben,112,114,120,153,
Reubin,107, Robert,153,
156,171,356, Sarah,462,
Shadrach,360, Thomas,356,
360, William,263
HARRY(?), Sarah,284
HARRY, David Sr.,279, David,
278, Eleanor,278, James,278,
280, John,278, Mary,280,
Naomi,278, Thomas,278,282,

285
HARSHA, Daniel,572
HART, (Rev.),281, Aaron,489,
516, Ann,013, Benjamin,116,
120, Catherine,309, Celia,
004, Cristen,159, David,527,
Joseph,529, Michael,039,
Oliver(Rev.),281, Rev.Mr.,
281, Thomas,003,516
HARTGROVE, William,566,567
HARTH, John,058
HARTLEY, George,312
HARTMAN, Henry,345
HARTMANN, H.,345, Henry,345
HARTNESS, John,565
HARTSFIELD, Fredk.,295,
Fredrk.,289
HARVEY, Alexr.,118, Charles,
196,222,223,247, James,112,
198,209, Jas.,112, Jno.,112,
Joel,196, John,112,120,
210,214, Little Berry,198,
247, Mary,214, Philemon,204,
210, Sarah,204, Widow,215
HARWELL, Ambrose,295
HARWICK, Hasel,081
HASE, John,030
HASELWOOD, Betsey,479,
Lancaster,479, Lucy,479,
Mary,479, Nancy,479, Selah,
479, Thomas,479
HASKET, Sarah,310
HASKETT, Thomas,313
HASLEDEN, Wm.,295
HASLIP, Robt.,148
HASSELTON, (Estate),300
HATCHELL, Jno.,295, John,301
HATCHER, Edy,118, Felt,268,
Fleming,268, Nancy,268,
Thomas,268, William,118
HATFIELD, John,405,407,
Robert,405, Samuel,375
HATHCOCK, John Sr.,379,
Meshack,370
HATHLEY, Ewings,558,565
HATTER, George Harland,448
HATTON, Francis,324
HAUGH, Martin,318
HAVARD, John,006, Mary,006
HAVEN, John,143
HAVIS, Jesse,111,112,113,116,
120, John,112
HAWKINS, Amos,449, Benj.,550,
Benjamin,452, Eaton,141,
175, Family,550, Isaac,449,
505, Jacob,324, James,448,
449,508,509,516,523,529,
541,543,551, Jane,397, Jean,
396,397, Jeana,397, John,
449,452,555, Jonathan,449,
Joshua,135, Josiah,135
HAWKINS, Martha,449,550,
Nathan,449,523,554, Peter,
006,314, Phebe,454, Pinck,
175, Pink,141, Pinkey,153,
Richard,485, Sarah,454,
William,086,176,309,323,
449,522,525, Wm.,086
HAWTHORN, James,557, Jas.,572,
Mary,557
HAWTHORNE, James,132
HAYES, David,077,357, Elisha C.,
348, Henry,128, James,037,
Jesse,492, John,037,038,
039,041,042,489,490, Wm.,348
HAYETT, James,185
HAYMAN, James,112
HAYNAN, Agnes,112, Agness,120,
James,112,120, Robert,112,
Robt.,120
HAYNES, Hiram,352, Melvina,
002, Moses,533, Sheriff,347,
348, Thomas,019, William,533
HAYNEY, John,557
HAYNS, George,137
HAYNSWORTH, Henry,393, Jno.,
421, John,398,423, Richard,
420, Sarah,393
HAYS, Barbara,327, Benj.,295,
Benjamin,289,301, David,
088,327, Drury,288,295,301,
Edmond,508, Edward,489,
George,167, Henry,128,

Hester,301, James,040,288,
289,301,315, Jane,330, Jas.,
295, Jemima,489, Jesse,301,
John,019,030,033,041
HAYS, John,042,093,094,095,
Jos.,295, Joseph B.,301,
Joseph Sr.,301, Joseph,196,
288,301, Mary,093, Milly,
190, Newton,288,298,
Pennesso,040, Richard,444,
Richd.,444, Thomas,444,
William,288,330, Wm.,298
HAYWORTH, Gee,305
HAZE, Isaac,531
HAZELDEN, Wm.,288
HAZELL, William,424
HAZLIP, Robert,148
HEAD, Ann,067, Benjamin,326,
Daniel,079, George,019,
035,085,091, Henry,085,086,
091,326,348,356, James,085,
086,091, John,199,213,
Katharine,326, Mary,231,
326, Richard,090,091,104,
William Sr.,014,054,231,
William,014,079,213,219,
Wm.,229
HEAD, Wm.Jr.,229
HEADEN, William,127
HEAILD, William,436
HEALD, William,489,518
HEARD, Stephen,002, Thos.,182
HEART, Ann,022
HEATH, (Col.),270
HEATON, Benjamin,310
HECKLIN, Arthur Jr.,043
HEDDEN, Elisha,327, Elizabeth,
327,328, George,327, Jacob,
327, Jeffrey,327, Joel,328,
Joseph,327, Katharine,327,
Maria,327
HEDRICK, Peter,269
HEDSON, Obediah,282
HEER, Jacob,490
HEGERTE, William,569
HEIGLER, John,495
HEIRS, Wm.L.,002
HELLAMS, Constant,211, David,
210, John,207,210,211,
William Sr.,211, William,
209
HELLER, Catherine,312, John,
312
HELSEY, Robt.,063
HELTON, ,402, Isaac,399
HEMBREE, William,185
HEMPHENS, John,229
HEMPHILL, A.,053, Alice,561,
Andr.,054, Andrew,012,030,
032,033,034,051,053,058,
071,075,086,087,103, Andw.,
052,055,088,089,110, Andwr.,
056, Isbell,058, James Sr.,
051,058, James,051,561,
John,087,095,561, Jon'a.,
051, Jonathan,092, Robert,
034
HEMPHILL, Robert,081
HENDERS, Nancy,341
HENDERSON(?), ,341
HENDERSON, (Land),259, ,
004, Ann,317, Anna,068,
Caroline,007, Charles,213,
Cisley,455, Cisly,455,
David,148,455,519, Edward,
050,061,068,076, Eliza,455,
Elizabeth,055,329,455,
Frances,058,059,098,
Francis,068,074,075,104,
Hannah,317
HENDERSON, Hopkin,295,
Hopkins,289, Isaac,144,
James (Capt.),193, James,
124,132,144,148,160,161,
167,195,204,215,228,247,
259,357,361, Jas.,552,
Jincy,455, John,006,013,
133,134,144,220,268,275,
329,361,440,443,445,447,
455,498,509,521
HENDERSON, John,524,528,534,
542,556, Joseph,513,568,
Mary Ann,209, Mary,220,

Benjamin,460, Brent,476,
Elisha,227, Hosea,266,
James,250, Jesse,460,
Jonathan,142, Joseph,250,
Joshua,251, Margaret,436,
Nevil,460, Rachel,460,
Solomon,460, Zachariah,237
HOLCOMBE, (Col.),329, Elvira,
342, Hosea,434, John,434,
Joseph,193, R.E.,342,
William,355,357,359
HOLCOME, Elenor,434
HOLCUM, James,254, Joseph,203,
254
HOLDEN, Catharine,340, Daniel,
523, Francis,365, Isaac,325,
Jno.,295, John,289,301,
328,356, Joseph,301, Joshua,
333, Keziah,333, Margaret,
436, Richard,340, Stephen,
522, Thomas,231,457,517
HOLDER, Daniel,519,531, Mary,
176
HOLEBROOK, William,149
HOLEMAN, Hannah,543, Isaac,
543, John,028
HOLEN, Richard,251
HOLIDAY, William,272
HOLINGSWORTH, Jos.Jr.,529
HOLLADAY, John Jr.,406, John,
404,405, Susannah,404,405
HOLLAMS, William,138
HOLLAND, ,009,508, Abram,002,
Agnes,472, Allen,549, B.F.,
330, Badale,259, Benjamin,
338, D.T.,333, Dominico,352,
Dominio,513, Elizabeth,333,
Frances,513, Jacob,350,
James,289, Jas.,295, Jese,
187, Jesse,187, John,513,
Mary,328,354, Richard,251
HOLLAND, Richard,254, Robert,
350, Sarah,354, Thomas,259,
W.,354, W.T.,333, Waymon,
259,349, Weymon,354
HOLLEMS, ,138, Emanuel,168,
James,168, William,137
HOLLENWORTH, Mr.,521
HOLLEY, James,273, Jas.,272,
Marshall,324, Parthmia,324
HOLLIDAY, John,404
HOLLING, Aaron,249
HOLLINGSWORTH, ,532, Abraham,
218, Ann,336,539, Aquila,
478, Benj.,486,505,546,
Clinton,340, David,228,
307, Elias,308,336,430,433,
493, Elis.,053, Eliz.R.,340,
Evaline,336, Eveline,336,
Geo.,201,237, George,218,
230, Isaac,216,230,309
HOLLINGSWORTH, Isaac,517,519,
Jackson,352, Jacob,529,
546, Jas.J.,354, Jeptha,154,
155,157,176,515,532,539,
John,230, Jonathan,216,
228, Jos.,445,509, Levy,541,
551, Mary,278,283,285,446,
460, Nancy,486,539, Saurah(?),
336, Susanna,216, Thomas,336
HOLLINGSWORTH, Thomas,517,
Thos.,492, Valentine,278,
279, Warren,336, Widow,430,
William,309,336, Wm.,478,
509,517,551
HOLLIS, Burwell,111,112,115,
James,111,112,114, Sarah,
112,115, Sary,111, William,
115
HOLLOWAY, Anna,489, Lewis,004,
Thomas,004
HOLLUMS, Emanuel,457
HOLMAN, (Land),101
HOLMES, ,499, David,122,
Elizabeth,545, Jacob,456,
475,493,540, John Bee,232,
Solomon,101, Walter,492,
495,502,503,506,525,541,
542,549, William,499
HOLMS, Joseph,244
HOLSEY, Edward,054, Thomas,
447
HOLSTON, Asa,004, Caroline,

004, Eliza,004, Emily,004,
Mary,004
HOLT, Samuel,443
HOLZEN, John,102
HOMEA, Abner,349
HOMER, Wm.E.L.,006
HOMES, David,113,117, Vice,
520
HONE, Judey,188
HONEA, Abner,326, Mary,364
HONEYCUT, Wm.B.,347
HONEYCUTT, John,185
HOOD, ,562, Ellender,220,
Enoch,346, John,348,561,
Morgan,225, Mr.,252,
Robert,227, William,561
HOOKER, Matilda,256
HOOKS, Dorcas,288,295
HOOPER, ,136, Bety,171, James,
160,172, Jn.,340, John,154,
158, Mrs.,398, Ob.,144,155,
160, Obadiah Jr.,155,
Obadiah,130,142,144,148,
154,158,159,168,171,
Richard,171, Stacy,130,
Thomas,172,398,400,401,
403,404,420, Thos.,401,
William,137
HOOPER, William,144
HOOPS, Henry,343, Hinnerich,
343
HOPE, Agnes,437, Cathrin,437,
George,159, Isaac,506,511,
James,501,566,572, Jean,437
HOPE, John,225,398,437,487,
488,497,501,537,549,
Margaret,437, Mary,437,
Rebecca,437
HOPKINS, (Col.),270, Col.,519,
D'd.,572, D.,062,064,066,
067,501, David BS,049,
David(Col.),444, David,012,
013,024,027,035,044,046,
049,053,062,063,064,066,
067,068,079,086,088,090,
099,105,106,159,169,430,
486,489,505,552,572,
Davis(Capt.),052
HOPKINS, Davis,034, F.,062,
Fer.D.,044, Ferd.,572,
Ferdenan,062, Ferdenn,053,
Ferdinand,025,027,064,065,
066,086,088,090,105,501,
505, Fred,056, Frederick,
088, John,049,084, Mary,027,
088,105,505, N.,062, Newton,
062,064,065,066,490, Saml.,
533
HOPKINS, Washington,027,062
HOPPER, Jane,316, Thos.,393
HOPSON, William,176
HORAN, Jno.,374,375,376,378,
379,381,382,386,421, John,
370,371,372,373,374,378,
379,380,381,390,392,394,
398,399,400,401,404,405,
406,407,408,409,412,416,
418,419,420,421,422,423,
Mr.,419
HORLBECK, Daniel,345
HORN, Hardy,289,298,301,
Nathan,288
HORNADAY, John,138
HORREL, Presillah,546,
William,546
HORRELL, Prescillah,546, Wm.,
546
HORRY, M.M.,420, Sarah,284
HORSKINS, John,378
HORTON, H.O.,366, John,185,
Manurva,340, Rachel,332,
Thomas,340
HOSSTATLER, Jacob,571
HOUPTE, Christian,310, Mary,
310
HOUSE, Dennis,351, Thomas,103
HOUSEAL, William,310, Wm.F.,
006
HOUSEL, William,545
HOUSTEN, Elinor,089, William,
089
HOUSTON, J.D.,002, James,001,
013,098,102, Mary A.,001,

Saml.,148, William,006
HOUZE, Samuel,369
HOWARD, ,502,528,529,545,
Absalom,346,347, Anna,335,
Archer,433,500,525,535,
549, Catherine,336, Elizabeth,
435,509,510, Herman,431,
Hermon,552, Isaac,352,
J.B.,362, James,392, Jas.,
120, John J.,328, John Jr.,
253,254, John,210,240,395
HOWARD, John,499,519, Joseph,
426,492, Lemuel A.,336,
Martain,395, Martin,395,
Nancy(N),433, Nehemiah,490,
493,497,519,525,535,549,
Obadiah,492, Obediah,499,
502,503,508,510, Peter,137,
142,556, Priscilla,508,
Prisilla,503, Richard,289
HOWARD, Richd.,295, Sarah,390,
Stephen,347,509,510,549,
Tilman,335
HOWE, Joseph,566, William,557,
558,566, Wm.,557
HOWEL(L), Daniel,471
HOWEL, Abner,180, Francis,180,
Franciss,180, Hannah,278,
280, Jean,465, John,513,
Joseph,505, Lydia,283,
Philip,280,281
HOWELL, ,538, Daniel,470,
John,532, Joseph,471,
Joshua Jos.,394, Thos.,043,
W.,043, Wm.,043
HOWERTON, James,259
HOY, Quinton,111,120
HOYLE, Jacob,502
HOYT, William,289
HROIS(?), Jesse,109
HUBBARD, John B.,363, Polly,
331
HUBBS(?), Willama,214
HUBBS, Elizabeth,237, William,
237, Wm.,230
HUCHOL(NUCKOLS), John,530
HUCKABY, Delilah,462,463
HUDDLESTON, James,214, Jane,
246, Jean,214, William,214,
246
HUDGENS, Ambrose Jr.,192,276,
Ambrose,226, Joanna,226,
William,262
HUDGINS, Ambrose Jr.,204,238,
264, Ambrose Sr.,193,
Ambrose,204,205,222,264,
Nancy,263, Patsey,263,
Patsy,263
HUDSON, (Estate),300, ,009,
371, Abraham,139, Alex.,295,
Amanda L.,337, Burrel,179,
184, Cinner,136, David,088,
426,522, E.H.,337, Eleanor,
284, Elizabeth,180, F.J.,
337, Forest,179,180,184,
Forrest,179,180,183,
Frankey,180, Franky,180
HUDSON, George,075, Hall,283,
Hannah,383, Henry,180, Is.,
288, Jannett,301, Jas.,294,
Jno.,295, John M.,337,
John,002,180,289, Joseph,
180, Kener,158, Kerner,123,
Lunceford,139, Margaret,
337, Mary,283, Noakana,136,
Obadiah,284,285, Pleasant,
128
HUDSON, Pleasant,139, Richd.,
295, Robert,006, Sarah Elizabeth,
002, Sarah,136, Sary,123,
Sharard,536, Thomas,180,
W.M.,337, William,006,075,
Wyatt,337
HUETT, Charles,253, John,253
HUEY, George,442,453, Hannah,
453, Henry,442,453, James,
019,037,062,090,094,104,
453,501, Jas.,035, John,453,
Joseph,453,523, Martha,453,
Mary,453, Samuel,453,
Sarah,037, Thomas,453
HUFF, ,365, Lucy,007, Phebee,
526, Rebecca,009

John E.,417, John S.,259,
John,372,374,375,383,388,
398,407, Jos.,365, Josiah,
283, Letitia,392, Lucinda,
342, Malachi,301, Margaret,
283, Martha,331, Matthew,391
JAMES, Matthew,392,407,410,
Mr.,278, Philip,278,
Rebecca,283,284,285,374,
Rebekah,374, Rev.,285,
Samuel,374, Sarah,278,280,
283,285, Sherwood,392,420,
Stephen,268, Tabitha,281,
284, Talifero,423, Thomas,
278,282,285, Thos.,295,
Vincent,331
JAMES, Vincent,359, William D.,
320, William,278,279,280,
281,283,284, Wm.,280,
Wm.Jr.,279
JAMESON, Gardiner,100,
Gardner,076, James,075,
Joseph,075, Robert,034,
074,075,076,100, William,
JAMIESON, Frances W.,323,
James,562, John,323
JAMISON, Alexander,109,
Frances W.,322, Gard'r.,
040, Henry,144, James,323,
John,322, Robert,024,
William,325,329,336
JANES, Thomas,567,572
JARNAGAN, Willis,301
JARR, J.Thomas,184
JARRARD, James,027
JARRELL, Margaret,289
JARRETT, Martha(Key),004
JARRIS, John,060
JARROTT, Debux,347
JASPER, Anna,481,554, Charity,
481,553,554, Family,553,
Hannah,481,554, John Jr.,
554, John Sr.,553, John,437,
481,534,553,554, Nancy,553,
Nicholas,142,481,484,497,
498,501,502,518,522,523,
525,553,554, Nicolas,526,
554, Rachel,481,553,554
JASPER, Suky(Susannah),554,
William(Sgt.),554, Wm.(Sgt.),
553
JAUNTT, Zebulan,307
JAYNES & SHELON(?), ,365
JEAMS, Stephen,183
JEAN, William,145
JEANS, Alexander,270, Catharine,
350, Elbert P.,006, James A.,
006, William,348
JEE(?), Wm.C.,343
JEFFERAS, George,129
JEFFERIES, James,194, John,
488,491,514, Nathaniel,491,
Nathl.,488,534,545, Sarah,
491, Thomas,194
JEFFERSON, John(Mrs.),401,
John,400,401, Lucy(Mrs.),
418
JEFFRIES, Elener,439, James,
550, John,439,446,550,
Nathaniel,430,439,514,
Nathl.,541
JEMISON, ,182
JENKIN, Ashford,054
JENKINS, ,432, Abner,335,
Alvin,332, Anderson,335,
358, Andrew,332, Ara A.,333,
Archibald E.,332, Clayton,
330,333, David,314,317,
Eliza,332,335, Elizabeth,
333, Francis,332,335,357,
358, George M.,333, Isaac,
314, J.M.,332, James G.,333
JENKINS, Jesse,314,332,
John M.,332,333, John,004,
426,517,545, Lovicy C.,332,
Macajah,127, Mary Jane,333,
Mary,335, Micajah,268,
Michager,184, Micigh,183,
Nancy,332, Randell,523,
Richard,052, Richd.,432,
Samuel,520, Simon,520,
Stewart,335
JENKINS, Thomas,019,020,025,

027,039,040,041,046,052,
127,136,147,149,152,185,
268,332,335,570,571, Thos.,
036,066,348, Thos.Wm.,377,
Uriah,333, William,046,
309,317,332,520,571, Wm.,
056,058,066
JENNINGS, ,009, Hiram,001,
John,001, Larkin,416,
Miles,138, Sarah,001, Tyre,
420
JETER, Andrew,096,097, Betsy,
451,452,509, Eleanor,452,
James,439,493
JETT, James,156, John,148,
161,171
JEWEL, Joseph,571
JEWELL, Ratcliff,192
JILES, William,176
JINKINS, Samuel,495, Thomas,
085, William,494,495
JINNINGS, Miles,149
JINNINS, Miles,149
JOEL, Ratcliff,196
JOHN, Griffin,281, Griffith,
278,281, Margaret,278
JOHNS, James,333, Jeremiah H.,
337, Nancy,333, Rebecca,337,
Samuel,178, T.,333
JOHNSEY, Jno.,077
JOHNSON, ,006, Alex.,489,
Alexander,053,081,489,
Allen,265,301, Andrew F.,
292, Andrew,164, Ann,305,
Anna,265, Anselm Finch,472,
Benj.,295,496, Benj.Jr.,
295,508, Benj.Sr.,496,
Benja.,508, Benjamin,261,
301,309,472,473,486,526,
Charles,472
JOHNSON, Charles,473,486,496,
Christopher,441,442,443,
444, Christr.,444, Clementine,
006, Collins,445
JOHNSON, Daniel,308, David,
120,472,496, Eddy,283,286,
Ede,176, Elizabeth,007,
464, Fanny,265,472, Frances C.,
006, Francis(Mrs.),005,
Francis,295, Gardner,301,
George,315, Gressebe(?),
282, Gresset,285,286,
Henrietta,265, James,195,
223
JOHNSON, James,259,301,309,
409,472,480,540,551, Jas.,
295, Jesse,259, John,252,
255,258,274,507, Jonathan,
195,220,229,238,242,243,
258,274, Joseph,006,306,
Joshua,006, Judith,472,
Lewis,265,295,301, Margaret,
489, Mary,472, Matilda,006
JOHNSON, Matthew,250, Nancy,
472, Peggy K.(Mrs.),003,
Peter,055, Richard,301,
443, Robert,312,353, Saml.,
295,301, Samuel,120,121,
Sarah,301,308,472, Sherod,
295, Thomas N.,392, Thomas,
224,443, Thos.N.,402,410,
William P.,242, William(Capt.),
451
JOHNSON, William,054,250,253,
258,265,426,472,499,507,
Wm.,223,452, Wm.P.,238
JOHNSTON, ,110,380, Alex,048,
Alexander,021,022,313,
Benjamin,289, Charles,526,
David,349,380,557,558,568,
Ellender,312, Ferdelia,335,
Frances,289, Gabriel,563,
James,047,236,289,312,515,
540, John,006,060,067,080,
162,214,306,529,568
JOHNSTON, Jonathan,242, Jos.,
549, Lewis C.,289, Lewis,
289, Matthew,097, Michael,
127,142,161,171,312, Nelly,
313, Noblelo,162, Peter,528,
Robert Jr.,557, Robert,335,
340,381,558, Robt.,376,
Samuel,289, Sarah,557,

Seth,015, Thomas N.,377
JOHNSTON, Thomas N.,378,379,
Thomas,378, Thos.N.,377,
378,386, William,313,313,
Zeph.,052
JOHNSTONE, Burr(Dr.),006,
James,551, John F.(Dr.),
006, John,075,077, William,
557
JOINER, William,122
JOLLEY, (Maj.),462, Benjamin,
461, Frances,549, James,549,
Jos.,487, Joseph Sr.,549,
Sarah,549, Wm.,549
JOLLY, A.Jos.,295, Benjamin,
433,462, Frances,549, James,
325,349,537, John,349,432,
433,503, Joseph Sr.,487,
Joseph(Capt.),433, Joseph,
289,432,487,497,522,543,
545, Margaret,328, Mary,432,
433,487, William Sr.,328,
William,289,350,356
JOLLY, William,485,549,
Wilson,453,487,491,514,
534, Wm.,295
JONENS(?), Anne,341
JONES, ,240,540,569, Abraham,
503, Abram,253, Ada Crain,
244, Adam Cr.,155, Adline,
341, Andrew,125,131,141,
166,167,507,529,548,549,
Ann,136,240, Anne,278,
Aron,258, Barsheba,011,
047, Ben,211, Benja.,164,
Benjamin,185,193,194,506,
Bersheba,011
JONES, Bethsheba,060,104,
Bryan,289,295, Cabel,191,
192, Catharine,019, Charity,
230, Charles Sr.,498,510,
Charles,052,211,498,500,
510,516,547, Daniel,258,
Darling,112,114,233, David,
278,289,295,301, Edward,229,
278,285, Eleanor,278, Elias,
331
JONES, Elijah,112,113,115,
117, Elizabeth,166,201,225,
351,507, Feby,529, Federick,
549, Frederick,289, Freeman,
006, George,274, Griffith,
278, Harrison Sr.,003,
Harrison,003, Harry,336,
Harvey,337, Jabez,346,347,
359, Jacob,222,223,247
JONES, James,181,185,289,341,
350, Jas.,295, Jesse,289,
295, Jno.,540, Joel,348,
John D.,295, John G.,295,
John P.,003, John,155,159,
160,165,178,179,185,187,
191,192,196,199,216,220,
230,231,233,238,242,246,
251,265,278,279,289,295,301
JONES, John,331,346,487,
Jonathan Jr.,060, Jonathan,
011,016,018,019,047,054,
060,074,079,104,491, Jos.,
492, Joseph P.,005, Joseph,
047,060,079,255,353,424,
429,492,499,503,506,519,
541,542, Lewis,230, Malinda,
339, Malissa R.,006,
Marmaduke,206
JONES, Martha,278,498,510,
Mary A.E.,336,337, Mary Ann,
005, Mary J.,341, Mary,005,
155,278,283,284,285,335,
Nathan,289,295, Peter,059,
060,092,094,095,137, Pheby,
548, Philip,349, Ralph,119,
Rebecca,007,319, Reuben,
289, Richard,003,228
JONES, Richard,351, Robert,
331, Robt.,295, Sally,242,
Saml.,523, Samuel P.,199,
203, Samuel,319,352, Sarah,
341,492,503,519, Stephen,
485,507,529,534, Thomas F.,
275, Thomas H.,301, Thomas Jr.,
226, Thomas,067,122,200,
219,221,242,243,248

KINGSTON, Simon,405,407
KINLOCH, Cleland,371
KINMAN, Abner,266, Melton,266,
  Quiton,266, Sarah,266,
  Thomas,257, Winnefred,266
KINNEY, Alexander,018
KINSEY, James,462
KIRBY, (Line),446, Archibald,
  304, Elizabeth,176,189,
  Francis,188,189, John,189
KIRK, Elizabeth,263, James,
  224,260, John Sr.,263, John,
  224,260, Parham S.,423,
  Parham Sandy,423, Sarah,260
KIRKCONNELL, John,055
KIRKENDALL, Abraham,029,030
KIRKLAND, Ambrose,115, Capt.,
  107, Jesse,108, Moses,196,
  532, Samuel,414,415,
  William Jr.,049, William,
  050,095, Wm.,118, Zachariah,
  095
KIRKONNELL, ,528, John,528
KIRKPATRICK, Alexr.,275,276,
  Andrew W.,327, James,072,
  Jas.,118, Mary,327,328,
  Mr.,025, Robt.,564, Thomas,
  102,277, William,075, Wm.,
  071
KIRKSEY, Christopher,349,
  Robert,349, Silas,354,
  William,349
KIRTLAND, Moses,219,507,532
KIRTON, Henry,301, Philip,301,
  302
KITCHEN, Charles,070,073,074,
  Frances,074, John,073,074,
  Josiah,082, Wm.,132
KITCHENS, Ann,040
KITCKINGS, Charles,034
KITIOT, Jenet,189
KITTET(?), Jenet,189
KIVELL, Aga,247, Benjamin,223,
  Thomas,247
KLEINBECK, Gesina(Mrs.),332,
  J.D.,332, John H.,332
KLENBECK, Eliza,332, Gesina(Mrs.),
  332, J.D.,332, Juliana,332
KLINBECK, John M.,332
KNECHT, A.M.,345, Martin,345
KNIGHT, Benjamin,120, Benjn.,
  120, Ephraim,255, Thomas,342
KNIGHTON, Joseph,414, Moses,
  398
KNIGTON, Moses,398
KNOWLAN, Sari,068
KNOWLAND, Phillip,068, Samson,
  068
KNOWLING, Philip,084
KNOX, Elizabeth,018, Frances,
  357, Hugh,015,016,062,083,
  084,090,093,097,101,
  James Sr.,351, James,012,
  018,020,050,054,056,057,
  062,067,071,072,074,075,
  077,079, Jane,101, Jarnl.,
  073, John Jr.,072, John,015,
  016,060,070,347,351, Robert,
  028
KNOX, Samuel,019,095, William,
  018
KOLB, Hermon,061, Sarah,283
KOONE, Adam,007, Martha,007,
  Silas,007
KOONROD, Peter,056
KUMBALL, Fedr.Jr.,071
KUYKENDALL, Abraham,564,565,
  566, Elizabeth,566, James,
  564, John,566,571, Peter Sr.,
  565, Peter,558,559,560,564,
  571, Rebecca,568
KYLE, Catherine,330, Eliza,
  330, Henry,330,477, James,
  270,330,477, John,330,
  Laughlin,330, Mathew,330,
  Robert,330, William,330
KYSER, George,007
LA GRONNE, Frederick,317,
  Susannah,317
LACEY, ,087, Col.,053, Edw.,
  032,063, Edw.D.,041,
  Edward Jr.,055, Edward,011,
  016,021,026,029,031,035,

039,040,041,042,043,046,
  052,053,055,059,086,095,
  098,100, Jane,011,043, Mary,
  289,295, Reuben,031,
  Samuel Jr.,046, Samuel,038,
  045,046
LACEY, Samuel,084, W.H.,153,
  158, William,157,164, Wm.,
  212, Wm.H.,132,158
LACKATURE, John,432
LACKEY, Jacob,408
LACY, Edward,053, James,103,
  Stephen,269, W.H.,127,129,
  Wm.B.,007
LADD, James,363, Polly,355,
  William,355
LADER, W.,345
LADEY, W.,344
LAFERTY, Andrew,160
LAFFEN, James,223, Rhoda,223
LAFFERTY, Andrew,150,160,
  John,157,160,172, Patrick,
  130,133,134,135,150,154,
  155,162
LAFFOON, William,162, Wm.,158
LAGRANNE, Adam,310
LAGSTON, Joseph,190
LAIN, Ausburn,302, James,302,
  John,174, Thomas,302
LAIRD, Elizabeth,051, Lodowick,
  051, Messay,057, Robert,051,
  066, William,051
LAKE, ,009, Ann,321, Benjamin,
  321, Elisha,187, Enoch M.,
  002, Thomas,002,305,307,
  309,319
LAKES, ,005
LAMANDS, James,038, Martha,
  038, Robert,038
LAMAR, Elizabeth,352, John,
  004,007, Thomas,352
LAMB, David,168, Sarah,514
LAMBERT, Elizabeth,302, Henry,
  289,295, Hugh,289, William,
  302
LAMKIN, Powers,521, Towers(?),
  521, William,004
LAMPLEY, Anne,283, Martha,283,
  Susannah,284
LAMTON, Richard,556
LANCASTER, John,479, Wm.Jr.,
  479
LANCE, John,067,105
LAND, John,032,247, Thomas,
  056,070, William,055,336
LANDERS, Ezekiel,078, John,
  185,530, Massa,530
LANDRETH, Emily C.,331, R.P.,
  331
LANDRITH, Thomas,354
LANDRUM, Reuben,433
LANDRUN, Robert,071
LANDTRIP, Shadrick,425,498,
  499, Thomas,517
LANE, James,289,304,316, Jas.,
  295, Mary Ann(Mrs.),307,
  Mary Ann,316, Osborne,289,
  295, Thomas,289,295,316,
  William D.,307, William,
  316, Wm.Dawkins,321,523,550
LANEY, Janey,563, Joseph,563,
  William,563
LANG, Feribe,283,284, Sarah,
  283,284,285, William,282,
  284,285
LANGBEY, James,099
LANGFORD, ,004, Anne,319, Asa,
  319, Henry,135,136,142,143,
  168, Jacob,319, John,185,
  319, Robert,174, William,
  319, Winnefred,319, Wm.B.(Dr.),
  007
LANGLEY, ,186,543, Carter,148,
  James,420, John,543,
  Joseph,148
LANGSBEE, Elizabeth,018,019,
  James,018,019
LANGSBEEY(?), ,011
LANGSBEY, James,011
LANGSBY, Elizabeth,018,019,
  James,018,019,047
LANGSTAFF, Jno.M.,407,
  John M.,407

LANGSTON, Absalom,533, Asa,
  175,251, Bennett,522,
  Daniel,522, Fanny,175,
  Henry,191, James,011,175,
  348,349,353, Jechoniah,175,
  Jechonias,129,175, Jesse,
  175, John,164,171,174,175,
  180, Joseph,135,141,164,
  175,179, Levi,175, Mary,179,
  180
LANGSTON, Mary,184,191,
  Ragland,164,180,190,
  Samuel,175, Solomon,175,
  230,257, William,175
LANIER, Lewis,395
LANKFORD, Nathan,511, Robert Jr.,
  186
LANKSTON, Solomon,257
LANSTONE, Caleb,505
LANTRIP, Shadrach,521,530,
  547, Thomas,528,530
LANYARD, Richd.,212
LARKFORD, Thomas,185
LARSON, Jesse,131
LASHLEY, Sarah,320, William,
  320
LASLAY, Rosanna,327, William,
  327
LASSON(LAWSON?), Wm.,507
LATHAM, Anthony,355, George,
  355, James,355, John S.,337,
  John,462, Robert,341,
  Sinkler,355
LATHEM, James,329,356, John,
  355
LATHIN, Robert,113
LATIMORE, Frances,427,
  Francis,485
LATTA, John,013,022,044,076,
  348,491, Sarah,076
LATTIMORE, Francis,427
LATTO, John Sr.,053
LAUCHLAN, Cuery,296
LAUDTRIP, Shadrick,491
LAUGHLIN, John,560, William,
  487,562
LAUGHON, Mary,107, Samuel,107
LAUGHRIDGE, James,272, Robert,
  130
LAURENCE, James,351, Peter,
  550
LAURENS, James,355
LAUY, Edward,073
LAVENDER, Robert,007
LAVERTY, Sarah,418
LAW & TURNER, (Family),263
LAW, Saml.Jr.,270
LAWING, George,260, Jas.H.,
  271
LAWLESS, Michael,212
LAWLEY, Elisha,327, Frances,
  327
LAWRENCE, A.,273, Elisha,354,
  James,345,354,355
LAWS, Robert,381, Rose,381,
  Spencer,269
LAWSIN, James,187
LAWSON, John,533, Riley,336,
  Ruben,494, William,498
LAXON, Jesse,153
LAY, Charles,347, David,347,
  James,025,327,328,356,
  John James,347, Nancy,347,
  William,347
LAYSON, Lewis,250, William,
  214
LAYTON, John,519,526, Mary B.,
  311, Milly,311, Stephen,429,
  497,526, Susanna,526,
  Thomas,459,492
LAZARUS, Nicholas,448
LAZERUS, Nicholas,535
LE GRONNE, George,007, John,
  007, Robert,312, Rudolph,312
LEA, Edmond,037, Edmound,078,
  Emound,078, Nancey,078,
  Nancy,078, Onra,063
LEABERRY, Moses,072,073
LEACH, James M.,359, John,289,
  295,302
LEAGE, Joseph,330
LEAGUE, Edmund,127, Elisha,
  325, Jacob,253, Joab,152

LEAK, James,181, John,538
LEAKE, Bryant T.,003, Dorcas(Mrs.),
003, John,003, Martha,003
LEANEY, Isaac,558, Joseph,564
LEAR, Jacob,268
LEARWOOD, Edmond,219, Edmund,
198
LEASON, ,254
LEATHAM, Richard,512
LEATHERS, Benjamin,349,
Elijah,326, Mary,349,
Melinder,326, Nimrod Jr.,
349, Nimrod,325,332,346,
347,348,349,356, Ruth B.,332
LEATHS(?), James,164
LEAVELL, Richard,316, William,
316
LEDBETTER, ,426,489,554,
Atty.,368, Lewis,489,529,
538, Millington,453, Sarah,
489,529
LEE, ,009, Abart,040, Ambrose,
048,049, Anthony,399,416,
Edmond,050, Edmund,043,
050, Elliott,039, Gilla,337,
Harriet,333, Honorias P.,
007, James C.,333, James,
185,289,302, Jared C.Jr.,
007, Jas.,295, Jesse,376,
John Jr.,289, John,028
LEE, John,029,208,295,302,
465,471, Jonathan,354,
Joseph,080,465,471, Joshua,
399,421, Lazarus Jr.,289,
295, Lazarus Sr.,289, Mary,
190, Michael,465,521, O.,
399, Owin,058, Randolph,348,
Reuben,337, Roseanner,471,
Sarah,471, Stephen,117
LEE, Thomas(Gen.),416, Thomas,
208,289,389,390,442,465,
470,471, Timothy,399,
William,057,465,466
LEECH, ,572, D.,164, David,
559,562,563,568,569
LEEK, Jno.,554, John,488
LEEMAN, James,351
LEEPER, Jane,557, Jean,557,
Robert Jr.,557, Robert,558,
563, William,289
LEESLAND, William,099
LEESTER, George,117, Sarah,
117
LEFEVER, John,550
LEFFAN, James,222,247
LEGARE, J.G.(Mrs.),002,
John Giradeau,002
LEGETT, Absalom,295, Dd.,295,
Henry C.,295, Jas.,295,
Jesse,295
LEGGETT, Abner,289,302, Ebby,
302, Elias,289, James,289,
Jesse,289,302, Rebecca,302
LEGGIT, Abner,295
LEGIA, H.,344
LEGRAND, John,360, Thomas,364
LEGRONE, John,323, Margaret,
323
LEGROON, John,323
LEHALF, Daniel,099
LEILA, C.F.,344
LEISTER, George,106, Sarah,
106
LEITNER, Geo.,001
LELLAN, McDaniel,302
LEMBY, Peter,035
LEMMON, Robert,021,022
LEMMOND, Robert,022, Unity,
022
LEMON, James,069, Robert,031,
070, Samuel,272
LEMOND, Robert,021
LEMONDS, Robert,085,086
LEMONS, Robert,035
LEMPRIER, Clement,091
LENARD, Hannah,351, John,078,
351
LENDERMAN, Henry,182
LENDHART, R.,336
LENNARD, John,047,069
LENOIR, Isaac,372,373,393,
John,394,408
LENOX, Wm.,071

LENUD, Eliza Love,400
LENUD, Henry Lauren,400,
Henry,400
LENUR, Henry,400
LEOFFEL, Georg,345, George,
345
LEONARD, Davice,042, David,
059, John,008,043,071,087,
094,325, Samuel,326, Thomas,
042,059,326,356, William,326
LESENE, Jos.M.,183
LESESNE, Chas.F.,386,387,395,
J.W.,183, James,399,
Jos.W.,183
LESLEY, Abraham,346, David,
340, Elizabeth,340, James,
159, John,561, W.A.,338,
William,346, Wilson,352
LESLIE, Geo.,051
LESLY, David,330, John,357
LESSENE, James,399
LESTER, ,009, Abner,323,
Alfred,007, Allen,323,
Frances,244,245, Francis,
209, George D.,323, James Sr.,
007, Jane,310, Peter,001,
007,310, Samuel,323, Smith,
007, William R.,323
LETIMORE, Francis,502
LETTRELL, ,269
LEUREY, Henry,333, Sarah,333
LEVERAL, (Land),258
LEVERETT, Robert,426, Robt.Jr.,
426
LEVERILL, Robert,517
LEVESTON, David,245, Joseph,
245
LEVIN, Christopher,061
LEVISTON, George,214, Martin,
307
LEVY, Zodic,002
LEWALLEN, Meshack,549, Ruth,
549,550, Shadrach,549
LEWELLING, Shadrach,545
LEWERS, Samuel B.,256, Sophia,
256, Thos,272, Thos.,270,
271,272,273
LEWERY, Michael,007
LEWIS, (Land),068, ,154, A.N.,
375, Abner,332, Andrew F.,
358, Benj.,229,271,295,
Benjamin,229,245,256,257,
289, Betsy,364, Cader,302,
Charles,326, Crawford,208,
David,013,040,098,245,
Elisha,289,295, Elizabeth,
127,326, F.,136, George,012
LEWIS, George,180,490, Hizzey,
366, Hugh,125,127,133,
Isaac P.,320, Isaac,289,
295, Isiah,182, J.O.,338,
352, Jacob,229,245,335,347,
James,289,308, Jas.,295,
Jas.O.,348, Jas.Overton,
350,352, Jesse P.,350, Joab,
347, Joel,289,295, John E.,
350
LEWIS, John,127,130,132,134,
135,144,145,146,148,151,
156,162,205,229,269,313,
324,364, Jon.,295, Jonathan,
289, Kizzie(Mrs.),368,
Kizzie,367, Lindamira,350,
Mary,308,313,332, Mills,
295, Phebe,320, Prior,302,
Priscilla,205, Rebecca,007
LEWIS, Richard,176, Ruth,289,
295, Stephen,308, Susan M.,
350, T.(?),024,025, T.,040,
126,127,130,138,142,
Tarleton,355, Thomas,026,
035,053,123,127,130,132,
133,134,137,144,151,154,
155,162,168,169,170,171,
205,269, Vincent,132,137,
141,154
LEWIS, Vincent,155,162,
William,007,020,021,102,
Wm.,082
LICON, Thomas,257
LIDE, Anne(Mrs.),284, Anne,
285, Elizabeth,283, Mary,284
LIGEN, Woodson,003

LIGHT, Jacob,161
LIGHTNER, Barbara,115, Caty,
115, Christian,115, Eliz.,
115, George,115,117,122,
John,114,115,117, Mary,115,
Philip,115
LIGON, (Land),257, Francis(Mrs.),
368, Joseph,255, Thomas,257,
William,255,258
LILE, Marharshalalbaz,495
LILES, Anamanos,504, Jesse,
479, John Sr.,307,309, John,
308,530, Joseph,337, Salina,
337, William,524, Williamson,
309,524, Wm.,040,524
LILLEY, Miles,393, Thomas,372,
373
LILLY, Moses,369, Thomas,369
LILY, Moses,369, Thomas,369
LINAM, Mark,405,406, William,
405,406
LINCECUM, Sarah,087
LINCH, Joseph,254, Mary,154,
William,154, Zilphe,541
LINDERMAN, Henry,122,147,
John,147
LINDLEY, David,007, Elizabeth,
201, James,201,219,235,246,
Polly,007, Thomas,201,259,
William,264
LINDLY, Simon,128
LINDSAY, ,009, Abraham,199,
David,090, Elce,306,
Elizabeth,306, James,306,
524, John Jr.,525, John Sr.,
306, John,199,306,307,488,
489, Lydia,308, Morn(Mrs.),
122, Moses,306, Samuel,306,
Thomas,306, William,513,
Wm.,552
LINDSEY, Alsea,323, Caleb,323,
David,311, Elizabeth,323,
Fama,323, Humphrey,327,
James M.,323, James,208,
313,323,527,539,561, Jas.,
542, John,003,138,216,323,
327,444,527,545, Joseph C.,
323, Josephh G.,323,
Samuel,308, Tabitha,323,
William,007
LINDSEY, Winney,007
LINLEY, James,224, John,185
LINN, James,117,122, John,057,
078, Robert,098,427,
William,204
LINNIN, John,070
LINSEY, John,185
LINTON, Wm.Thos.,541
LINVALL, Lewis,320
LINVILLE, Lewis,007
LION, Unis,053
LIPHAM, Daniel,494,495,501,
508,516,519,523,543, Henry,
502
LIPPELMAN, Jacob,310
LIPSCOMB, William,529, Wm.Jr.,
548
LIPSCOMBE, John,437, William Jr.,
437
LITES, Jacob,408
LITON, Wm.Thomas,061
LITTEL, John,489
LITTELL, Aaron,395
LITTLE, Aaron,395, Archibald,
012, Charles,271, David,271,
F.,214, Frederick,214,224,
237, George,507, James,195,
198, Jno.,549, John,486,
490,493,500,508,512,537,
544,546,549,550,552, Jonas,
443,536, Joseph,490,507,
551, Samuel,382,508,
William,197
LITTLE, William,253,508,
Winneford,549, Winnefred,
552, Wm.,490,570
LITTLEBURY, ,090
LITTLEFIELD, (Land),549, ,
551, John,550, Widow,550,
Wm.,550, Wm.Jr.,550,
Wm.Sr.,550
LITTLEJOHN, Charles,446,
Thos.,507
LITTLETON, Charles,125,133,

147, Chas.,433, Mark,007,
429, Solomon,144,170
LIVELY, Jane,359, John,359,
Mark,359, Rachel,359,
Thomas Sr.,359
LIVERITT, Robert,508
LIVINGSTON, John Jr.,310,
John,310,312,317, Thomas,
185, William,233
LLEWELLIN, Mashach,545,550,
Ruth,545,550
LLOYD, Charles,255, Robert,
279, William,253
LOCK, Sarah,283
LOCKART, Aaron,077, Andrew,
048,073, Aron,072, John,077
LOCKHARD, Andrew,022
LOCKHART(?), John,432
LOCKHART, Alexr.,556, Andrew,
087, Ann,560, James,560,
Mathew J.,265, Thomas,265,
William,494, Wm.(?),439,
Wm.,521
LOCKLEEN, Cutridge,152
LOCKWOOD, Joshua,399
LOCOOK, William,382
LOCQUERT, Andrew,073
LOCQUERTS, Aron,072
LODEN, Eliza,334, John E.,334
LOFTIN, Eli,002
LOFTON, Daniel,320, John,309,
Thomas,252,525
LOGAN, Joseph(Rev.),127, Mary,
463, Patrick,114,119, Polly,
462, Ryars,127, Thomas,196,
216,566
LOGANS, Susannah,473
LONAM, Olive,312, Rosannah,
312, Samuel,312, Squire,312
LONG, ,523, Ann,523, Benjn.,
485, Capt.,377, George,318,
Henry,439,502,523,531,
Jacob,318, Jas.,107,
Jemima,335, Jno.,293,374,
John Jr.,122, John,042,
072,289, Mesiah,335,
Michael,318, Mr.,521, R.,
375, Reuben,371,374,376,
379,388, Robert,232
LONG, Robert,254, Robt.,271,
William B.,335, William,067
LONGESBAY, James,058
LONGLEY, Carter,150
LONGRIDGE, Jas.,274
LONGSHORE, ,543, Cloyd,441,
Euclidas,527, Sarah,527,
Sary,527
LONRIE, Elizabeth,060, Saml.,
060
LONUM, Samuel,311
LOONEY, A.J.,350, Adam,513,
David,488, Margaret,350,
Mariam,350, Martin L.,350,
Robert,488
LOONY, Adam,485, Robert,485
LOOPER, Arminda A.,331,
Arminda,331, Daniel,326,
331, Elender P.,331,
Elizabeth,331, J.Perry,342,
James Perry,336, Jemima,
358, Jeremiah,326, Joyce,
331, Margaret,342, Mary,332,
Matilda,336, Rachel,332,
Samuel,331, Solomon Jr.,
331, Solomon Sr.,331
LOOPER, T.P.,362, Temperance,
336, Thomas P.,336, Wm.Anderson,
336
LOOPO, William,302
LORD(LAND?), Samuel,012
LORD, Sarah,023, William,023,
036
LORTON, J.L.,350, J.S.,360
LOTT, John,013
LOUGHON, Saml.,115
LOUGHRIDGE, Robert,561
LOURIMORE, John,295
LOVE, (Back Line),433, (Line),
433, ,487,513, Andrew,558,
Benjamin,040, Hezekiah,487,
Isaac,234,236, Jack,047,
James Jr.,037, James,037,
038,432,487,512,523, Jane,

036, Jas.,077, Jno.,538,
John Jas.,038, John,036,
037,038,045,488, Mark,527
LOVE, Mark,543, Mary,432,
Mathew,240, Richard,040,
Robert,007, Sarah,527,
Thos.B.,348, Willam,488,
William,037,040,044,045,
433,488,500,508,538,565
LOVEL, William,132
LOVELADY, Marshal,539, Thomas,
539
LOVELAND, R.,325
LOVELATTY, Marshal,539,
Thomas,539
LOVELESS, Bartin,348, William,
259
LOVELL, David,132
LOVING, Christopher Jr.,055
LOVINGS, Christopher,018
LOW, Jesse,356, John Ma(T?L?),
190, Nathaniel,356, Philip,
356
LOWDEN, Jesse,376
LOWDER, John,402, Sarah,402,
Thos.,418
LOWE, John S.(Mrs.),007,
William,201
LOWERY, Edward,120, Isom,022,
Patrick,316, Samuel,054
LOWHAN, Mary,121, Samuel,121
LOWN, (Land),409
LOWNES, (Land),382
LOWNS, Edward,394
LOWRANCE, Edward,089
LOWREY, Isom,022, Patrick,314
LOWRIE, Saml.,033,034, Samuel,
069,092
LOWRIMORE, John,289
LOWRY, Isom,022, Samuel,029,
Thomas,140
LOWTHA, Anne,283
LOWTHER, Charles,282,285
LUCAS, Alice,283,285, Jeremiah,
141,482,526,550,551, John,
129,133,142,146, Sarah,129
LUKE, (Land),257, Alex.,259,
Alexander,257,259,273,
Alexr.,254, Celete,283,
Charlotte,005, Elizabeth,
283, John,254,259,273,
Joseph,282,284,285, Samuel,
256, William,283
LUMAR, Thomas,450,451
LUMPKIN, James,004
LUNDY, Nathaniel,004
LUNSFORD, S.,182
LUNY, Robert,485
LUPO, Wm.,295
LUPTON, Joseph,315
LUSK, (Line),538, James,067,
181, John,208,487, Nathan,
356, Robert,033,081,082,
431,486,487,537,538,553,
556, Robt.,501,549, Samuel,
021,067,082,100,563, Thomas,
501
LYALL, Beverly,152
LYLE, (Ford),096
LYLES, ,004,009, Ann Rachel,
337, Aramanus,504, Aromanus,
115, D.L.,335, Elizabeth,
111,115,117, Ephm.,117,
Ephraim,003,111,115,
Ephriam(Capt.),007,
Fanny Debbs(?),337, Henry,
317, James(Col.),007, James,
006, John Bell,337, John,
530, Joice,316
LYLES, Jonah,337, Letty A.,
337, Martha Ann,335, Mary,
335, Nancy J.,337, Nancy,
317, Samuel,335, Sarah,151,
William,111,117, Williamson,
307, Willm.,115
LYNAH, James(Dr.),380
LYNAM, George,543
LYNCH, ,166, John,269, Mary,
154,155, Nathaniel,336,341,
Rebecca,341, William,131,
154,155,156,166,181,186,
Wm.,134,190
LYNE, James,437

LYNN, James,113, Joseph,036,
152
LYON, John,062, Joseph,040,
098, William,208
LYONS, Joseph,241,271
LYTTLETON, Wm.Henry,525
MABERRY, Jesse,441
MABRAY, Jesse,497,498
MABREY, Danl.,121
MABRY, Jemima,263, Jesse,263,
446,447,501, Zachariah,482
MAC ELROY, ,143
MACBETH, Alexander,443,542,
Alexr.,542
MACDONALD, Jno.,481
MACDOUGAL, Alexr.,429
MACDOUGALL, Alexd.,536
MACE, John,289,302
MACEPHE, James,187
MACGARRITY, John,507
MACGUIRE, Elijah,509
MACHAN(MAHAN?), James,212
MACHEN, ,152, Grace,177,
Henry,123,149,170,174,177,
182, John,177,187, Mary,177,
Thomas,177
MACHIN, Henry,146
MACHON, John,242
MACKELWAIN, James,496
MACKENET, Mary,397
MACKENETT, Mary,397
MACKEY, James,071, Robert,393,
William,141
MACKLER, Thomas,099
MACNAIR, Elizabeth,379,398,
399,403,404, John,398,403,
404,408,409,420
MACUIRE, Elijah,509
MADDEN, Ann,243, David,243,
E.,361, Ezekiel,354,
George,226,243,249,252,
John,252,258, Michael,134,
Nancy J.,339, Nancy,243,
Thomas E.,339, William,252
MADDOX, Benjamin,257, Nathl.,
257, Posey,356, William,249
MADIN, John,258
MADOKS, Benjamin,257
MAGBY, Nelly,327, Samuel,327
MAGEE, Robert Henry,207
MAGINIS, ,157, Solomon M.,157
MAGULLOU(?), Molly,212
MAHAFFEY, Hannah,212, Martin Jr.,
242, Martin,210,212,242,269
MAHAFIE, (Land),102
MAHAFY, ,163, Hugh,252
MAHAN, Archibald,172, Edward,
054
MAHERG, John,267, Nancy,267
MAHON, Bailey,217, Joseph,168,
170,171
MAHORN(MAHON?), Jos.,252
MAIBEN, Col.,269
MAIRS, Lewis,296
MAJOR, Elijah,035, John,354,
Sarah,310
MAJORS, Dl.,296
MAJUNKIN, Wm.,519
MAKFIELD, Robin,059
MALIN, ,145, Elizabeth,133,
134, John,133,134
MALLIN, ,145, Elizabeth,145,
John,145
MALONE, ,009, Booth,144, John,
426,530,531, Robert,369,
374, William Sr.,311,
William,002,057,313,374
MAN, Francis,223, James,232,
John,232, Page,223, Robert,
232, Susanna,232
MANAHAN, Wm.,569
MANGHAM, Solomon,489,514,529,
534,539
MANGUM, John,315, William,315
MANING, Levi,311, Thomas,494
MANLEY, John Jr.,213,226,
William,237
MANN, George,323, James,306,
John,306, Manasse,306,
Robert,306, Susannah,306,
Sussannah,306
MANNING, John,289,296,302,
Laurence,400, Levi,313,

MCCALLA, David,020,021,068,
James,047, Mary,020,021,
Samuel,321, Thos.,080
MCCALLAS, David,056
MCCALLE, (Land),255
MCCALLIE, Margaret,311
MCCALLIN, James,567
MCCANCE(?), Samuel,027
MCCANCE, Samuel,044
MCCANE(?), Samuel,027
MCCANE, James,123
MCCANN, Edward,007, J.L.,357,
Robert,357, Robt.,381,
T.H.,360, Thomas H.,353,360
MCCANNON, John,098
MCCANTS, Jane,379, John,378,
379, Thomas,379
MCCAREY, James,271, John,265,
Nancy,265
MCCARLEY, John,137, Samuel,
137, Thomas,275
MCCARLY, John,348
MCCARMAIG, John,289
MCCARREL, Thomas,153,163
MCCARRELL, Thomas,178, Thos.,
140
MCCARRIL, Thomas,162
MCCARTER, Frasier,339, James,
021,037, Moses,015, Peter,
299
MCCARTHY, John,509
MCCARTNEY, Jain,024, Jane,014,
John,395
MCCARTY, Moses,052
MCCAUGHRIN, S.J.,007
MCCAULEY, Henry,114, James,
397, John,370
MCCAULLEY, Henry,119
MCCAW, Ann,025, James,029,
184,190, Jno.,557,558,561,
John,557,558, William,025
MCCAY, John,295,379
MCCELVEY, John,212
MCCENAHAN, Jno.,058
MCCENNELL, John,071
MCCLAHAN, John,338
MCCLAIN, ,564, Beththena,463,
George,547
MCCLAMERY, John,013
MCCLANAHAN, Catherine,266,
James,210,213,228, John,
219,266, Margaret,266, Mary,
266, Robert,266,349, Sarah,
266, William,266
MCCLAND, Robert,060
MCCLANNAHAN, James,210, John,
196, Wm.,252
MCCLAREN, Daniel,560
MCCLAUGHLIN, ,161
MCCLEAHAN, John,104
MCCLEAN, John,296,299
MCCLEARY, George,254, Joseph,
254
MCCLEHENA, James,035, William,
035
MCCLELAND, John,097,098,
Rebecca,098, Robert,097,098
MCCLELLAND, Eliz.,563,
Margaret,317
MCCLENDON, Dennis,390, Wm.,
390
MCCLERKIN, James,192, Thomas,
192
MCCLIHIN(?), James,035
MCCLIKINA, James,035
MCCLINTOCK, Agnes,250, James,
059,205,242, John Sr.,252,
John,194,205,242, Margaret,
263, Nancy,263, Robert,222,
246, William,050
MCCLOUD, David,379,417, James,
162, Jas.,299, John,299
MCCLUER, Alexr.,255, David,
233, Ellinor,245, James,029,
245, William,251
MCCLUR, David,232
MCCLURE, Charles,013,016,346,
353, 353, David,320, Easter,348,
Esther,348,364, Hugh,050,
052,060,093, Hus.,079,
James Sr.,028, James,001,
011,015,016,019,027,028,
029,030,052,054,101,250,

348,352,516,517,525, Jane,
027, Jean,029, John,015,016
MCCLURE, John,054,095, Mary,
054, Mrs.,364, William,015,
016
MCCLURKEN, Samuel,207, Thomas,
206,243, Thos.,570
MCCLURKIN, (Land),250, Janet,
257, Saml.,215, Samuel,209
MCCOLL, Jane,077, John,077
MCCOLLOUG, John,440
MCCOLLUM, Elizabeth,002,
George,002, James,351
MCCOLOGH, George,526, Margaret,
526
MCCOLPIN, Elizabeth,055, John,
062, Nancy,062
MCCOLPINE, John,056
MCCOMBS, Ann,090, John,055,
090
MCCONEY, Samuel,148
MCCONNELL, Margaret,075,
Samuel,317
MCCONNICO, Christop.,392, Wm.,
377
MCCOOL, A.,045, Adam Jr.,077,
Adam Sr.,432, Adam,017,
036,044,045,077,432,
Elizabeth,432, Gabriel,317,
J.,140, Jane,549, Jas.Adams,
426, Jean,077, John,017,
077,218,432,491,492,498,
513,525,528,533,549, Joseph,
077,177, Mary,432
MCCOOLL, Adam,498,554,
Jane(Jean),541,542, Jane,
531,535,536,541,542,554,
Jean(Jane),545, Jean,536,
541, Jno.,541,542, John,040,
502,503,506,507,508,516,
517,518,520,522,525,531,
533,534,535,536,541,542,
545,549,554
MCCORKLE, Andrew,563, William,
563
MCCORMACK, Drewsella,385,
James,484, Jno.,180, John,
385, Maxwell,272, Shadrack,
385
MCCORMICK, Jas.,391, Thomas,
568
MCCORY, James,106
MCCOSH, John,222
MCCOUN, Moses,071
MCCOWAN, William,427
MCCOWEN, Alexander,067
MCCOWN, Alexander,020,045,
092,103, Alexr.,104,
Alexr.Sr.,052,053, Frank,
046, Hugh,105, James Jr.,
046, James Sr.,046, James,
054,104,105, John,020,045,
052,070,071,092, Mary,046,
Moses,046,069, Robert,105,
Samuel,105, Sarah,053
MCCOY, ,144, Allis,339,
Annice,339, Charles R.,417,
Chas.,370, David,137,324,
Elijah Sr.,394, Elijah,394,
395, Elisha,395, Elizabeth,
324, Emaline(?),339, Henry,
267, James,339,381, John,
384,417, Laurence,339,
Lewis,394, Martha,417,
Nancy,395
MCCOY, Redden,394,417, Rodger,
417, Samuel,413, Stephen,
394,395
MCCRACEN, James,532
MCCRACHEN, James,537
MCCRACHIN, ,224
MCCRACKEN, Arthur,311, James,
311
MCCRACKIN, Eliz.(Mrs.),007,
James,007, William,338
MCCRADY, Caroline,265, Jane,
265, Mary,265, Sarah,265
MCCRAE, Elizth.,299
MCCRAKEN, James,442
MCCRAREY, Robert,216
MCCRARY, ,004, Ann(Mrs.),007,
Isaac,214, James,007, Jane,
205, John,068,069,070,087,

205,213,255, Mary,206,
Robert,205,206, Thomas,007,
258,259, Thos.,259
MCCRAY, John,299, Thomas,254
MCCREACKING, James,509
MCCREARY, George,251,254,259,
J.,082, John,042,054,059,
082,083,087,088,090,104,
Jos.,254, Matthew,214,
Robert,134,236, Samuel,088,
Thomas Sr.,259, Thomas,236,
257,258,259, Thos.,259,
Thos.Jr.,236, Wm.,119
MCCREDY, Wm.,271
MCCREEVAM, Duncan,507
MCCREEVAN, Duncan,499,506,
511,513,568, John,511
MCCREIGHT, David,040, James,
057,109, Jos.,109, Matthew,
057, William,480
MCCREKEN, James,509
MCCREMAN, Archd.,296
MCCRERY, ,217
MCCREVAN, Duncan,430,492,498,
530,535,554, Jane,554, Jno.,
498, John Jr.,498, John,498
MCCREVIN, Duncan,552
MCCRICH, Samuel,255
MCCRIGHT, Robert,480
MCCRIMMON, Archd.,290
MCCROREY, John,095,096,
William,113
MCCRORY, William,115,117, Wm.,
106,117
MCCRUTH(?), David,020
MCCUAGE, John Jr.,296, John,
295
MCCUAIGUE, John,289
MCCUARIGUE, John Jr.,290
MCCULLEY, Ephraim,077, John,
075, Margaret,077, Thomas,
072,074,077, Thos.,075
MCCULLOCH, Alexander,017,
George,526, James,017,
John,440,560, Margaret,526,
Mary,537, William,497,527,
528,537,549,564, Wm.,524,
534,539,555,557
MCCULLOCK, Mary,461, William,
024,437,451,483, Wm.,439,
483,545, Wm.L.,441
MCCULLOUCH, Wm.,542
MCCULLOUGH, Alexander,012,
James,012, John,050,076,
440, Joseph,185,274, Rutha,
002, Samuel,076,321,
William,274, Wm.,083
MCCULLUM, McKeneth,384,
Samuel,346
MCCURDY, Mary,565, Robert,565,
566
MCCURLEY, Robert,226, Roland,
227, Rowland,199
MCCURRY, John,078
MCDADE, Andrew,183
MCDANEL, Thomas,077
MCDANIAL, J.H.G.,368
MCDANIEL, Alexr.,520, Daniel,
282, Edward,094, Elizabeth,
215,355, Henry,330, Intyre,
300, J.H.G.,368, James,290,
Jas.,301, John,290, Mary,
212, Matthew,224, Mr.,368,
Randal,290,296,300, Randel,
523, Sally,260, Sara A.F.,
007, Sarah,278
MCDANIEL, Sarah,290,296,300,
Thomas,210,213,215,226,
230,249, Thos.,348, William,
201,250,260, Wm.,296
MCDANNEL, Charles H.,304
MCDARVELL, William,308
MCDAVID, Andrew,182, David,
150,172,198, James,150,238,
243,244, John,238, Jonathan,
257, Penellabb,244, William,
226
MCDAVIT, William,256
MCDILL, David,021, John,021,
087,089,102, Samuel,089,
092, Thomas,089
MCDOAL, Jane,247
MCDONALD, (?),079, Chas.,121,

Daniel,019.412. Donald,092,
Eliza,348. Elizabeth,416,
Flora,289,296, Hugh,025,
John,022,089,269,416,481,
494,507,513,526, Jon,039,
Mary,215, Mida,071,
Middleton,071, Nancy,348,
Thomas,207,228, William,019
MCDONALD, William,043,048,
094,201, Wm.,071,219
MCDONELL, John,394,402,
Rodrick,118
MCDONNALD, John,511
MCDONNELL, John,370,373,383,
413,423, Thomas,532
MCDOUGAL, Alexander,503,
Alexd.,540, Alexr.,486,
Margaret,508, Moses,348
MCDOUGALD, Danl.,300
MCDOUGALL, Alex.,485
MCDOW, ,567, Arthur,566,
Elizabeth M.,357, Elizabeth,
331, James,566, John,566,
Margaret A.,357, Margaret,
331, Samuel,353, Thomas,566,
William H.,331, William P.,
331, William,357,565,566,
Wm.H.,357, Wm.Pinkney,357
MCDOWALL, Jno.,112, Patrick,
235
MCDOWD, John,556
MCDOWEL, Alexander,193, John,
530,556
MCDOWELL, Alex.,212, Alexander,
121,204,214, Andrew,096,
Archabald,067, John,122,
492, Joseph,350, Malinda,
337, Margaret,486,493,494,
508,544,546, Mira Eliz.,350,
Patk.,215, Patrick,002,
227, William,310,570
MCDUFFEE, Alexr.,290,300,
Duncan,300
MCDUFFIE, Alex.,296, Ann,296,
Danl.,300, Duncan,296
MCDUGAL, John,290
MCEACHIN, Gilbert,296
MCEAHERN, Christopher,300,
Gilbert,300
MCECHAIN, Gilbert,290
MCELBRAY, John,185
MCELDUFF, Daniel,488,491,
Danl.,491, Dl.,445,
Hannah G.,452, Hannah Green,
451, Hannah,491, John,488
MCELHANNY, William,144
MCELHANY, Alexander,136
MCELHENEY, Alex.,164
MCELHENNEY, James,128,129,151
MCELHENNY, ,140, Alexr.,136,
James,134,150,151,152,
Jas.,161, John Jr.,568,
Margaret,152, Marget,150
MCELHENY, John,162
MCELLDUFF, Daniel,488, Thomas,
488
MCELLELLY, John,011
MCELLERY, Elias,181
MCELLOW, John,131
MCELREY(MCELROY), John,189
MCELROY, (Mrs.),335, ,243,
442, David,211,216, Fanney,
169, James,169,171,174,175,
John,143,152,160,166,183,
184,186,190,191,192,195,
197,216
MCELVANY, Andrew K.,348
MCELVEEN, William,384,385
MCELVENE, Thomas,412
MCELVY, Andw.K.,348
MCELWEAN, James,512
MCFABIN, John,072
MCFADDEN, Ann,012, Cander,044,
Elisha,111, Elizabeth,044,
Gay,056, Isaac,044,058,
John,015,048,056,063,087,
Mary,048,063, Ralph,044,
056, Robert,033,044,056,
245, William,012, Wm.,012
MCFADDIN, Conrad,097, Elisha,
120, John,083,424, R.,374,
Robert,083,369, Thomas,381
MCFADEN, Ester,070, John,069,

070,094, Mary,069, Robert,
069,070, William,012
MCFADIN, John,073, Wm.,073
MCFANSON, Jur.(?),430
MCFARLAN, James,017
MCFARLIN, (I.or J.?),012,
James,016
MCFARNOS, Thos.,228
MCGAHA, Farrell,348
MCGALMERY, John,105
MCGARA, James,070
MCGARATHY, ,509
MCGARITY, Clements,512,
Clemons,512, James,539,
Michael,512, Patrick,086,
William,074,086
MCGARRAH, James,072
MCGARRITY, ,533, John,532
MCGAUGHEY, Alexander,079,
James,051,079, Jean,051,
Jennet,051
MCGEE, Benjamin,352, Elizabeth,
356, John,069,244, Solomon,
356, Williama,117
MCGIBBEN, John,528
MCGIFF, Patrick,080
MCGILL, James,243
MCGILLERAY, Mr.,239
MCGILVERY, John,301
MCGIN, Daniel,201
MCGINES, ,182
MCGINNEY, John,387
MCGIRTT, Daniel,372
MCGLADERY, David,211,216,221,
Sam,253
MCGLAMARY, John,024,025
MCGLAMERY, John,021,105
MCGLAMORY, John,053
MCGLAUCHLIN, Joseph,161
MCGOMERY, William,087
MCGOWAN, Jon,274, William,272
MCGOWIN, William,497
MCGOWN, William,558
MCGRAW, David,116,119
MCGREW(?), Thos.,126
MCGRIFF, Pat'k.,048, Pat,011,
032,046,069, Patrick(Col.),
011, Patrick,021,025,026,
041,059,073,084, Thomas,025,
056
MCGRUE, Thomas,499
MCGUFF, Pat.,055
MCGUIRE, Elijah,526, Jane,542,
Jean,542, Merry(Mary),509,
Merry,511,532,537,542
MCHARGE, Archibald,249
MCHARRY(?), Robert,010
MCHENRY, Alexr.,112
MCHESWICK, Neal,487
MCILHANEY, Robert,558
MCILWAIN(?), ,496
MCINAGARD, Alex.,296
MCINNIS, Daniel Jr.,289,
Daniel Sr.,289, Daniel,290,
Malcolm,301, Malcom,295,
Miles,301, Murdoch,301,
Neill,290,301
MCINTIRE, John,289, Malcom,
289
MCINTOSH, ,373, Alexr.,280,
Jane(Mrs.),281, Joshua,393,
Martha,278, Peter,371
MCINTYRE, Daniel,300, Danl.,
301
MCIVER, Caty,284, Evander,283,
301, Roderick,280, Sarah,284
MCJUNKEN, Jane,154
MCJUNKIN, Ann,522,534, Daniel,
157,159,163,522, Jane,162,
Jean,534, Joseph,157,432,
433,435,436,459,473,513,
522,525,528,530,534,541,
547, Landlot,478, Mary,478,
Nancy,478, Robert,336,
Rose,336, Samuel,513,528,
534, William,424,478,497
MCJUNKIN, William,506,520,
Wm.,431,519,543
MCJUNKINS, Jean,145
MCKAIN, Alexr.,121, J.,108,
James,121
MCKANAN, John,082
MCKANN, Rob.,071

MCKANON, John,082
MCKAY, Daniel,290,301, Dl.,
295, Jesse,383, John,295,
301, Jonathan,104, William,
073
MCKEBBIN, J.W.,270
MCKEE, Daniel,002, Elivira E.,
334, J.A.,334, Michael,002,
Samuel,566, Thomas,135
MCKELLER, Daniel,301, John,
301, Peter,289,301
MCKELVEY, Henry,261, Hugh,072
MCKELVIE, John,259
MCKELVIN, John,380
MCKENNEY, Hannah,072, John,
066
MCKENNIES, Benj.,405
MCKENNY, John,072, Wm.,072
MCKENY, Johnsn.,107
MCKENZEN, Benj.,187
MCKENZEY, Reuben,187,188
MCKENZIE, Benjamin,140,565,
John,225, Joseph,564,
Kenneth,350, Rebecca,564,
Robert,289, W.J.,405
MCKENZIL, John,301, Robert,
301
MCKBOWN, (?),105
MCKEWEN, Richard,392
MCKEWN, John,077
MCKIBBEM, John,542
MCKIBBEN(?), John,528
MCKIBBEN, ,547, James,533,
Jas.,542, Jno.,542,546,
John,525,531,533,536,542,
546, Nancey,546
MCKIBBIN, James,554, John,554
MCKIBBINS, John,516,517
MCKIE, Daniel,315, Danl.,430
MCKINEY, ,155, Eliksander,134,
William,026
MCKINLEY, Daniel,301, John,
301
MCKINNEY, Alexr.,155, Alice T.(?),
338, Benjamin,236, Charles,
328, David,328,351, Elizabeth,
353, Fountain,359, James,
328,351, Jesse,328,355,
Jno.,568, John C.W.,338,
John W.,338, John,093,236,
355,568, Jon.,169, Jonathan,
381, Joseph,021
MCKINNEY, M.A.E.,338, Mary,
333,340,381, Patrick,021,
Preseton,328, Samuel,017,
018,157, Sarah C.,338,
Thomas,333, Vesta K.,338,
William,039,042,073,082,
Wilson,158,328
MCKINNIE, Bernie,004
MCKINNY, William,073,096
MCKINSEY, Robt.,296
MCKINSTREY, Thos.,119
MCKINSTRY, Thos.,119
MCKINZE, ,221
MCKINZEY, Reuben,187
MCKINZIE, Salley,187
MCKINZY, John,221
MCKISSACK, Archd.,290
MCKISSICK, ,523, Isaac,539,
Margaret,539, Neel,512
MCKITRICK, James,265, Lucretia K.,
265, Robert,265
MCKNIGHT, (Land),251, ,250,
Abigail,269, Andrew,228,
Big Andw.,185, James,422,
Jas.,384, John,253,
William,422
MCKOWN, Alexander Sr.,054,
Alexander,052,053, Elizabeth,
054, Hugh,048, James,048,
053, Nancy,053
MCKOY, James,552
MCLAIN, Daniel,215,227
MCLARRY(?), Robert,010
MCLAUGHLIN, James,212, Jno.,
273, John,254
MCLAURIN, Daniel,289, Danl.,
302, John,289,296, Neill,
289,290,296,302
MCLEAN, Daniel,210, Duncan,
290,296, John,290, Malcom,
290, Mary,210

Delilah,290,296, Hugh,004,
516, Jno.,294, John,288,
Robert,198
MILAM, John Jr.,260, John,206,
209,221,222,244, Nancy,244,
Sarah,260
MILCOLLUM, Newman,057
MILDREDGE(?), Amos,117
MILES(?), Charles,013, James,
013
MILES(MILLS?), John,013
MILES, ,009, Charles,014,486,
497,501,531, Chas.,426,541,
David,289,313, Dd.,296,
Elizabeth,551, James,014,
015, Jesse,289,296, John,
013,014,015,062,100,102,
Richard,013,014,026,052,
100, Richd.,045,565,572,
Samuel,313, Thomas,541,551
MILES, Thos.,517, William,013,
014,015,052,053,062,102,
313,350,425, Wm.,031,565
MILHOUS, Henry,473
MILHOUSE, ,522, Henry,454,
494, John,310, Rebecca,454
MILICAN, Joseph,089
MILL, Jno.,071, John,032
MILLAN, William,029
MILLEN(?), ,William,041
MILLEN, Hugh,099, W.,041
MILLER, (Mrs.),254, ,033,196,
Abraham,039, Alexander,084,
Andrew,029, Ann,013,
Anthony,230, Archabald,325,
Archibald,347,349, Archible,
346, Catharine,359, Catherine,
318, Charles Jr.,563,
Charles Sr.,563, Charles,
021,023,029,041,079
MILLER, Charles,100,101,253,
Dennis,457, Elias,290,296,
Elisha Jr.,359, Elisha,359,
Elizabeth Sr.,015, Elizabeth,
015,079,100,101,359,457,
Fanny,359, Gardiner,100,
Gardner,075, Geo.,348,
George,121,303,346, Hamon,
251, Henry,029, Isaac,353
MILLER, J.(I.?),533, Jacob Sr.,
259, Jacob,251,254, James,
079,100,101,116,217,242,
259,436,568, Jane,359, Jean,
121, Jinney,121, John,010,
019,100,121,159,205,236,
259,347,361,404,561, Josiah,
100, Josias,015, Laura E.,
336, Lucy,472, Margaret,075
MILLER, Margaret,359, Martha J.,
336, Martha,217,380,
Mary Clayton,403, Mary,029,
Michael,129,146,162,
Nathaniel,145,290, Parker C.,
359, Polly Ann,364, Polly,
359, Richard,290, Richd.,
296, Robert L.,335, Robert,
015,029,052,057,060, Sally,
359
MILLER, Saml.,296, Samuel,015,
147, Thomas,079,100, Thos.,
015, William,022,023,027,
029,040,066,075,098,111,
122,256,290,302, Wm.,296
MILLES, William,041
MILLHOUSE, Henry,449,454,522,
530
MILLIGAN, Joseph,089, William,
277
MILLIKEN, ,560
MILLIN, ,029, Charles,029,
Hugh,058, Robert,078
MILLING, David,144, H.,106,
445, Hugh,058,075,084,117,
119, Jno.,140, John,144,196
MILLINGS, William,020,021
MILLNER, Richard,250
MILLNOR, Richard,250,252
MILLS, Alexander,256,261,267,
Amanda,006, Bleany,567,
Charles,486, Chas.,273,
David,267,302, J.,024,
James,252, John Jr.,017,
022,035,036,051,055,090,

100, John Sr.,022, John,011,
012,015,018,021,032,034,
035,038,058,060,062,066,
076,078
MILLS, John,079,081,094,099,
100,105,565, Mary,038,105,
261, Nancy,261,267, Priscilla,
267, William,261,267,350,
558,560,571, Wm.,007,348
MILLSAP, Elizabeth,356
MILLWEE, James,245
MILWEE, James,200,222, John,
214, Margaret,222, William,
209,214,222,227, Wm.,211
MINARD, Jacob,250,251
MINARY, John,193
MINCUM, ,502
MINER, Jacob,251
MINIS, James,024,025
MINNES, James,063, William,
063
MINNIS, George,080
MINTER, John,435, Rebecca,435,
Will.,563, William,045,
052,102,105,563
MINTERS, William,015
MINTOR, William,567
MIRACLE, James,323
MIRES, John,302
MISKELLY, Sarah,035
MITCHEL, Ephriam,046, George,
168, Harris,007, Henry,185,
James,500, Joab,490,495,
521, Joseph,033, Macklin,
251, Mark,495, Morning,488,
Nancy,107, Polly,007,
Richd.,542, Sally,007, Wm.,
007, Wm.A.,002
MITCHELL, (Family),264,265,
Angelica,440,447,539, Asa,
269, Benjamin,075,083,092,
098, David,103, Elias,103,
105, Ellender,549, Ephraim,
088,214, G.W.,331,357,
Henry,184,185, Hepsabeth,
102,103, Isaac,195,319,
Isaiah,105, Isiah,103,
James,045
MITCHELL, James,051,099,290,
561,572, Jas.,560,564, Joab,
193,485,524,528,536,540,
542,543, John B.,317, John,
110,201,216,373,457,475,
Joseph,093, Lewis,306,
Mark,442, Mary,485, Mason,
185, Nancy,107, Nimrod,229,
Patrick,243, R.,531,
Richard,431
MITCHELL, Richard,536,542,
546,548,551, Richd.,541,
556, Ricnd.,544, Stephen,
383, Susannah,092, Thomas,
102,103,105,492,520,563,
William,545, Wm.,216,441,
549
MITCHEN, Henry,172
MITCHERSON, Wm.,191,228,237,
240
MITCHISON, William,197
MITCHUM, John,143
MITCHUSON, William,193,197
MITCHUSSON, Wm.,136
MOATS, Daniel,082
MOBBERLY, William,046
MOBERLEY, John,014,043
MOBERLY, John,030,078
MOBLEY, ,090, Biggers,118,
Darkey,118, Edward,117,
Elizabeth,078, John,118,
Mary,117,118, Samuel Sr.,
117, Samuel,117,118
MOBS(MOTES?), Jesse,223,
Mourning,223
MOFFET, James,073
MOFFETT, ,061, Barbara,311,
Jno.,559, John,559,560,
William,102
MOFFIT, Gabriel,145
MOFFRET, Jno.,430
MOFFRETT, John,430
MOLIN, John,132,160,161,163
MOLLIN, (Eliz.),145, ,145,
Elizabeth,144, John,144

MOLLINGS, John,525
MOLLOW, John,181
MOLTON, John,181
MOLTRIE, William,381
MONAGHON, Barbara,280
MONAHON, Daniel,280
MONCREEFE, John,542
MONCRIEFFE, Jhn.,439, Jno.,
542
MONOCHON, Barbaray,278,
Daniel,278
MONRIEFFE, John,542
MONRO, Robert,277
MONROE, Johnson,156,172
MONTAGUE, Charles G.,414,
Chas.E.,383, Chas.G.(Lord),
010, Chas.G.,391
MONTGOMERIE, Robt.,538
MONTGOMERY, Charles Sr.,110,
Hugh,034,038,103, Isabel,
488, Isabell,489, James,023,
094,096,191,205,212,214,
219,227,232,234,236,238,
306, Jas.,219, John T.,340,
John,038,431,432,503,516,
524,530, Marget,530,
Martha(Mrs.),412, Martha,
412
MONTGOMERY, Mary A.,340,
Mary E.,340, Nancy,530,
Robert,130,425,426,486,
488,489,563, Saml.,396,
Samuel,518, Thomas,340,
352, William,412, Wm.,420
MONTOMERY, William,419
MONTRU, William,375
MOODY, ,122, Barfield,302,
Benjamin,388, Bennet,328,
Charles Sr.,290, Charles Sr.,
290, Chas.Jr.,296, Chas.Sr.,
296, Didner,185, Dinah,136,
175, Esther,296, Hannah,328,
Irvin,302, Isham,302,
James,290,302, Jesse,136,
159,175,290,296, Jessie,143
MOODY, Lucinda,328, Martin,
328, Robert Jr.,290, Robert,
290,302, Robt.,296, Roger,
302, Tapleigh,302, Tapley,
290,295, Theop.,296, Thomas,
290,302, Thos.,296, Wiley,
351, William,412
MOON, (Dr.),320, A.A.H.,338,
B.B.,329, Narcissa,329
MOOR & WHITE, ,190
MOOR, B.B.,329, David,560,
James,128,149, John,561,
S.,258, William,249
MOORE, ,066,185,406,568,
Agnes,326,355, Alexander,
016,057,208,399,560, Allen,
179, Anathoratha,439,
Andrew B.,271, Anna D.,439,
Barbara W.,263, Barbara,
263, Benjamin,223,227,229,
Burt,325,356, Chas.,565,
Curtis,219,220, Daniel(Negro),
379
MOORE, Daniel,002, David,131,
356, Davis,185, Dick(Negro),
379, Dolly(Negro),379,
Dorothy Jr.,066, Dorothy,
066, Eleanor,564, Elijah,
002, Elish,179, Eliza,263,
Elizabeth,102,355, Else,
240, Frances,235, Francis,
235, George,070,507,524
MOORE, Guyan,563,565, Guyon,
568,569,572, H.,132,
Harriet,263, Henry,007,
Hugh,132,163,556, Hughey,
356, Isham,392,399,400,404,
405,406,407,419, James,043,
049,090,138,149,157,355,
542,555,568,572, Jason Jr.,
164, Jason,164, Jeremiah,428
MOORE, Jesse,567,568, Jno.,
414, John A.,355,357,
John Jr.,568, John L.,302,
John Sr.,568, John,057,
138,312,313,318,319,370,
371,382,414,415,418,419,
518,563,567,568,569,572,

O'NEAL, Abajah,206, Abijah,
201,206,228,312,313, Anne,
201, Henry,201, Hugh,201,
206,207,225,228,233,321,
322, James,105, John,210,
224,320, Mary,200, Patience,
207, Thomas,105,249,
William,200,201,228
O'NEALL, ,009,322, Abijah,307,
Edward,007, Henry,263,264,
307, Hugh,001,307,309,320,
322, John,307, Mary,307,
Rebecca,007, Thomas,007,
William,263,264,307,309
O'NEL, Hugh,201,206, William,
237
OAKLEY, Sarah,367
OATES, Fanny,111,120, Samuel,
111,120
OATS, Samuel,111, Zachariah,
296
OBANNON, Joseph,149,159, Wm.,
215
OBRIANT, Jesse,080, Jessee,
059, Lessley,078
OBROYAND, Jesse,080, Lessley,
078
ODAM, Archibald,302, Levi,302
ODEAR, Benjamin,164, Catherine,
164, James,164
ODEL, John,203,204,441
ODELL, Ellenor,314, John E.,
357, John Jr.,314, John,203,
267,314,356,463, Martha,314,
Rignal,314, Ruth,314,
Thomas,314, William,329,
354, Wm.,354
ODIL, Ann,404,406, Flora,404,
John,404,405,406,407,419,
Susana,404, Thomas Jr.,404,
405,406, Thomas Sr.,404,
Thomas,404,406,407,419,
Thos.,406
ODLE, John,405, Thomas,405,
407, Thos.Sr.,407
ODLES, James,322
ODOM, Archd.,296, Levi,290,
296
OGILVIE, ,400, John,114
OGLESBY, ,500, Daniel,500,
Labard Sr.,309
OGLETHORPE, Hanna,081, John,
081
OKLEY, Sarah,367
OLDS, William W.,004
OLIPHANT, James,197,438,439,
505,515,530,531, Jas.,444,
Obadiah,537, Robert,216
OLIVER, Aaron,296, Alfred,302,
Elijah,158,172, Ely(?),161,
James,007,353, Jilson,354,
355, John C.,007, John,185,
Levina,302, Reacy,302,
Rhisa,296, Sarah,355,
Susan Sarah,003, William,
348,349,354
OLLEPHANT, James,437
OLLIPHANT, James,524
OLLIVER, Aaron,290, Rhesa,290
ONEAL, Abijah,220, Henry,219,
John,213,215, Thomas,078,
Wm.,222
ONEALL, Ann,215, Charles,215,
Hugh,215, John,221,
Patience,215, Rachel,215,
Ruth,215, Thomas,215, Wm.,
220
OPRY, Agness,401, Ann Eliz.,
401, Hugh,401,408, Robert,
401
ORE, James,527, William,527
ORINDER, Mathew,446
ORPHAN, Dudley,108
ORR(?), Patterson,359
ORR, Charles,075, Chas.,058,
066, Cunningham,351,358,
J.L.(Col.),183, J.L.,185,
John,057,075, William,075,
504, Wm.,288,294
OSBORN, Daniel,255, Edward,
204,205,264, James,325,357,
Jas.,357, John,199, Ruthy,
264

OSBORNE, Daniel,195, William,
209
OSBURN, Jeriah,237, John Sr.,
237, John,221
OSDILL, Daniel,156
OSLING, John,550
OSTEEN, William,418
OTTERSON, James,511, Major,
425, Saml.,453,532, Samuel(Maj.),
481, Samuel,424,453,522
OTWELL, Benjamin,185
OVABY, Meshac,272
OVERBY, Meshack,247
OWEN, John,028,079,169,290,
296,323, Lewis,360, Matthew,
408, Robt.,079, William,290
OWENS(?), John,082
OWENS, ,009, Andrew,232,
David,323, Eliza Eliz.,003,
Esther,302, James M.,003,
Jane,302, John,069,185,
266,269,333,359, Jonathan,
251, Joshua,201,202, Lucy,
290, Michael,370, Nancy,258,
Penelope,302, Peter,104,
Phillip,290, Richard,269
OWENS, Robert,056,082,095,
Sarah,266, Shade,302,
Solomon,302,304, Thomas,
185,269,323, William,252
OWENSON, Andrew,232
OWIN, David,036, George,183,
John,036
OWINGS, Ann,246, Elizabeth,
215, John,199,257, Richard,
246, Richd.,211, William,257
OWINS, Andrew,204, Archibald,
257, Butler,215, John,195,
196,203,211,221,222,290,
Joshua,236, Phillip,296,
Richard,215, Shadrach,290,
Shadrack,296, Sol.,296,
Solomon,290, Wm.,296,
Wm.Jr.,296
OWNBEY, Thomas,426
OWNES, ,009
OXNER, Henry,312, Jacob,312
OZBON, Daniel,255
OZBURN, Daniel,197,230,237,
Edward,193,247, John Sr.,
237, John,237
PACE, Burrell,340, Hannah,340,
Nathaniel,088, Nathl.,373
PACKARD, C.,352
PADEN, James,018,023, Samuel,
178
PADGET, Benjamin,352
PADGETT, Abigail,502, Ephraim,
099, Nelopy,003, Penelope,
003
PAGAN, James,016
PAGE, Abraham,302, Elizabeth,
247, Hester,002, James,232,
John D.,302, John F.,302,
John,178,290,297, Jos.,297,
Joseph,290,302, Nathaniel,
373, Pendleton,320, Robert,
247, Solomon,290,297,302,
Thomas,290,302, Thos.,297,
William,178,290
PAGE, Wm.,002,297,302,479
PAGIT, Abraham,068
PAIN, Elizabeth,302, Richard,
174, Thomas,188,189
PAINE, Jeremiah,288, John,186
PAISLEY, (Family),265, Thomas,
290, Thos.,297
PALMER, ,569, Ann,487,
Benjamin,351, Daniel,527,
Danl.,433, David,290,
Dd.Jr.,297, Dd.Sr.,297,
Elijah,489, Elis,487, Jo,
014,015, Jo.,029,055, Joe,
078, John,320,489,503,506,
508,521,542, Jos.,560,
Joseph,070, Joshua,485,
Polly(Pally?),508
PALMER, Thomas Sr.,430,544,
Thomas,489,503,521,544,
550, Thos.Sr.,530, Timri,
320, W.,045, William,291,
Wm.,287,293,530, Wm.Sr.,297
PALMERE, Joshua,479

PALMORE, Danl.,552, John,433,
519,529,545, Joshua,511,
529,556, Pattey,519,
Thomas Sr.,552, William,552
PALMOUR, Benjamin,351
PALUM, ,536
PANNEL, David,352
PANNELL, Andrew,099, Andw.,
122, Benjamin,122, Thomas,
122, William,122
PANTON, William,239, Wm.,239
PARHAM, Elizabeth,482, John,
453,475,482, Martha,482
PARIS, Richard,138
PARISH, Gideon,282, Henry Stone,
206, Henry,380, Stone,206
PARK, Charles,511, David,497,
George,526, Hugh,102,
James,271,273, John,526,
Joseph,526, Rachel,526
PARKER, (Land),256, Abel,269,
Charity,199, Elmer O.,557,
Francis,185, Henry,207,
212, Ichabald Sr.,291,
Ichabod,297,302, Isaac,488,
554, James,193,248, John(Dr.),
200, John,046, Jonathan,493,
529,548, Jos.,297, Robert,
186, Thomas,248, William,422
PARKER, Wm.,381
PARKET, Michael,434
PARKINS, Daniel,313,315,317,
Thomas,364
PARKS, Andrew,240, Barbara,
119, Charles,227, David,488,
James,099,223, Samuel,119,
Thos.,271,273
PARLOR, Luziann(?),510,
Luziann,424,425
PARLOUR, Luziann(?),510
PARMER, Daniel,539, Elizabeth,
267, Frederick,178, Isaac,
306, James,267, Saraith,306,
Thomas,539, William,306
PARNALL, James,434
PARNELL, Easter,471, Ester,
471, George,471, James,434,
471, Ruth,471, Sarah,471
PARRIS, Margaret H.,001,
Robert H.,001
PARRISS, John,034
PARROT(?), James,427
PARROT, Charles,196
PARROTT, Charles,215, Daniel,
339, Elizabeth,339, Jerry J.,
339, Levina,339, Melissa,
339, Milly,339
PARSON, (Land),257, Major,125,
Samuel,254
PARSONS, (Estate),303, Alcey,
205, Edmund,327, Elizabeth,
327, Joseph,205,218, Lucy,
133, Major,145, Martha,133,
Matilda,335, Samuel,218,
335, Sarah,133, W.J.,334,
350, Wm.J.,355
PARTAIN, Benjamin F.,001,
James,364, Sarah,001,
Speer,001
PARTIN, Barnabas,389
PARVERT, James,427
PARVEST, James,427
PARVIE, John,565
PASMORE, Jos.,297
PASSMORE, Joseph,290,302
PASSON, Major,142
PASSONS, Elizabeth,125
PASSONS, Major,125,169,172
PATE, Saml.R.,302
PATRICK, Andrew,568, David,
044,045, Gabriel,496,512,
Jesse,385, John,385,
Robert,558, William,044,
045,561
PATT, John,090,091
PATTENT, Samuel,497
PATTERSON, (Land),256,
A.L.(Mrs.),002, Alexr.,565,
Clary,349, Cynthia,347,
David,051,087,095, Dudley R.,
349, Dudly,327, George,547,
James,128,138, John,138,
256,274, Jos.,565, Joseph,

PIPPEN, Abraham,409
PIRCHARD, Isaac,057
PIRELE, Michael,141
PITMAN, Abner,291, Hardy,290,
  296, John,182, Saml.,296,
  Samuel,290
PITMON, Phoebe,326
PITS, ,206
PITT, Thomas,079
PITTMAN, Noah,297
PITTS, Abner,007, Ann,312,
  Aron,213, Benjamin,249,
  Charles,264,327,348,
  Christian,311, Christina,
  314, Daniel,008,311,
  Drayton,007, Ephraim,263,
  Jeremiah,408,409, John,251,
  Magy,327, Nancy,007,
  Obediah,007, Permelia,007,
  Reuben,007
PITTS, William,206,213
PLANT, Stephen,219
PLAT, Jas.G.,302
PLATHRO, Mary,278
PLATT, Daniel,290, Dl.,297
PLAXCO, Nancy,477
PLAXICO, ,568, George,565,
  Henry,565,566, James,569
PLEDGER, Elizabeth,283, John,
  282,284,285,286, Joseph,283,
  Phebe,283, Sarah,283,286
PLINES, Chr.,220, Christopher,
  219,236
PLOWDEN, Edward,401, Miles H.,
  389, Miles Hampton,389,
  Saml.E.,389
PLUMER, Christian,447, Daniel,
  444, William,494,511, Wm.,
  548
PLUMMER, Christen,520,529,
  Christian,447,448, Daniel,
  447,448,491,504,520,521,
  527,531, Danl.,544, Mary,
  521, Thomas,447, William(W),
  448, William,447,448,491,
  493,509,520,548, Wm.(W),548,
  Wm.,529,549,557
PLUNCKET, Richard C.,265
PLUNCKETT, James,313
PLUNKETT, ,206, Robert,206
PLYNAS, Christopher,215
POE, Richard,331,347
POER, David,325,353, Emila,
  325, Frances,325,353,
  James M.,325,353
POKE, William,123
POL, Ezekiel,500
POLAND, Anne,284, Jane,278,
  280,281, Mrs.,281
POLK, ,540,545, Ezek.,566,
  Ezekiel,561, Ezekl.,494,
  James Knox(Pres.),561,
  Will.,561
POLLACK, James,245
POLLARD, B.Sr.,183, Benj.Jr.,
  182, Benjamin,146,147,182
POLLARD, Richard,210,324,
  William,185,229,257,258,
  Wm.,146
POLLEY, John,088
POLLOCK, Ann,232, Elizabeth,
  210, James,232, John,210
POLSON, Joseph,511
PONDER, Hezekiah,054, James M.,
  331, Thomas,146
POOL, ,326, Abraham,378,
  Alexander,404, Elizabeth,
  008, Gabriel,008, George,
  258, John P.,384, Miriam,
  326, Nancy,009, Robert P.,
  418, Seth Petty,220,
  William,320
POOLE, Adam,002, Elizabeth,
  007, Robert,254, William,
  159, Wm.,007,159
POOR, David,353
POPE, Charles,186, George(Rev.),
  008, Harriet,009, Hum.,177,
  Le Roy,003, Maria,008,
  Susannah,307
POPHAM, John,553
POPLIN, William,186
PORTER, Alexander,041,

Basel S.,350, David,067,
  558,559,560, Edw.Sanders,
  448,448, Edwin,448,
  Epaphroditus,448, Gibson,
  347, Gideon,513, Hancock,
  425,448,532,543, Handcock,
  503,506,507,510, Isiah,016,
  James,347,566, Jeams,183,
  Jedethan,532
PORTER, Jedithan,529,532,
  Jeduthan,545, Josiah,015,
  028,560, Landlot,448,532,
  Lot,495,520, Margaret,095,
  Marthew,533, Mathew,534,
  Matthew,566, Nathaniel,559,
  560, Saml.,165, Samuel,015,
  533,534, Sarah,559,560,
  Thomas,050, Thos.,271,272
PORTER, William,533,571
PORTERFIELD, Chas.,250, John,
  256,257,319, Sarah,319
PORTMAN, John Jr.,126,127,
  John Sr.,484, John,137,
  154,176,484,498,501,515,
  528,553, Margaret,126,127
POSEY, Benjmain,546, Frances(?),
  527, Frances,185,513,527,
  546, Francis,505,527, John,
  509,527, Mildred,505,527,
  Milly,527, Nehemiah,509,546
POSSER, William,291
POSSEY, Francis,485,486
POSTEN, Samuel,495
POSTON, Daniel,291, Dl.,297,
  Eli,291, Eli.,296, Francis,
  291,296,302, Hugh,291,296,
  Jas.,297, Jno.Jr.,296,
  John Sr.,296, John,291,
  Jonathan,495, Saml.,302,
  Samuel,495, Thomas,291,
  302, Thos.,296, William,291
POTEET, Tobias,130
POTES, Jeremiah,093
POTTER, Adam,437,440,443,463,
  464,484,490,495,496,497,
  498,501,509,519,524,528,
  538,553,555, Henderson,490,
  Miles,379
POTTS, ,564, James,051,
  Jeremiah,100, Jonathan,563,
  Martha,401, William,401,
  402, Wm.,374,389
POUGHIN, Nickles,410
POUNCEY, Sarah,283,285
POW, Ann,008, Mary,009,
  Rebecca,009
POWEL, Benjamin,195,239,
  Dempsey,302, James,251,
  Jas.G.,302, Jordan,302,
  Martha,195,239, Robt.,302,
  Samuel,194,211
POWELL, Abraham,353, Abram,
  326, Allen,351, Almon,347,
  Almond,326, Benjamin,239,
  Davis,038, Elizabeth,414,
  George,318, Henry,206,
  Isom,038, James,254,564,
  567, John,205,206,538,
  Jordan,297, Jordon,290,
  Joseph,038,361, Leonard,
  403, Manuel,038
POWELL, Mark,436, Mary,120,
  121,219, Nicholas,291,
  Polly Ann,333, Reuben,251,
  254, Richard,432, Robert,
  291,312,316,333, Robt.,296,
  541, Sally,353, Samuel,194,
  225, Sarah(Mrs.),008,
  Shadrach,414, Thomas,120,
  121, William,120,121,354,
  Wm.,219
POWER, Drewery,331, Harriet O.,
  331, James G.,331, James,
  349, John,194,197, Mariah,
  331, Mary L.,331, W.L.,331,
  William,258, Zachariah,328
POWERS, Elizabeth,278, James,
  348,349, John Jr.,297,
  John W.,302, John,290,297,
  Mrs.,340, William,438
POYTRIP, Thomas,425
PRAET(PRUITT?), David,539
PRALL, John,080

PRATA, Sye,119
PRATER, (Land),256, Aaron,331,
  Delila,009, Jeremiah,331,
  John,249,327,331,349,
  Joseph,331, Josiah,331,
  Margaret,327,328,357, Mary,
  206, Middleton,239, Philip,
  331, Thomas,331, William,206
PRATHER, Amos,242, Basil,221,
  Bazel,221, Bazell,221,
  Bazzel,222, Braswell,306,
  Brice,208,221, Elizabeth,
  361, John,242, Josiah,213,
  Martha,242, Middleton,248,
  Priscilla,221, Verlinda,203
PRATOR, Bazzel,212, Josiah,
  212
PRATT, Jennet,088, John P.,
  008, John,019,020,026,041,
  042,048,052,062,069,073,
  074,075,077,079,080,081,
  083,084,085,086,087,088,
  089,091,093,101, Leonard,
  020,042, Lydia,088, Sarah,
  020,062, Thomas,069
PRAYTOR, Middleton,240
PRESCOT, Ephraim,373
PRESSLEY, Mary(Mrs.),008
PRESSLY, Jane(Mrs.),002
PRETHRO, Mary(Mrs.),281
PREWET, Bright,166
PREWITT, David,555
PRICE, ,561, Alfred,364,
  Benj.,297, Daniel Sr.,019,
  Daniel,019,028,062,432,
  Danl.,432, Edmd.,297,
  Edmund Jr.,290, Edmund Sr.,
  290, Edmund,297, Elijah,373,
  402, Henry,297, Jenny,215,
  John,035,302, Jon.,297,
  Jonathan,290,571, Margaret,
  215
PRICE, Margaret,230,402,
  Margret,215, Mary,215,
  Nathl.,297, Robert,126,
  Ruth,215, Sarah,215,
  Thomas W.,350, William,103,
  201,215,230,290,302,409,
  Wm.,247, Wm.S.,297, Wm.Sr.,
PRICHARD, John,136
PRIDE, Wm.,173
PRIDMORE, ,526, John,501,502,
  Jonathan,526, Theodorous,
  526
PRIEST, Alexr.,302
PRINCE, Celia,450, Charles,
  340, Daniel,438,449,450,
  Edward,428,473,474,546,
  Edwd.,546, Elizabeth(?),
  428, Elizabeth,450,546,
  Gilberd,546, Henry,126,
  140,150,152,154,168,172,
  Isam,450, Ishm.,467, James,
  427,428, Jean,126, John,165,
  340
PRINCE, John,346,450, Joice,
  428, Joseph,450, Lydia,449,
  Margaret,340, Mary Ruth,
  428, Mary,136,142,162,
  Narcissa,340, Patty,122,
  Rance,428, Richard,450,
  Robert,122,126,127,130,
  132,136,140,142,145,149,
  151,153,154,156,162,169,
  Robt.,158
PRINCE, Rutha,340, Sarah,340,
  450, Sicily,428, William,
  340,450
PRINGLE, ,229, Francis,423,
  John,229
PRIOR, Marlow,540
PRISCOUT(?), John,035
PRISOCK, Adam,323, Caty,323,
  David,323, Frederick,323,
  Geo.,323, John,323, Molly,
  323, Rosannah,323, Sally,323
PRITCHARD, Isaac,095, Simon,
  290,297
PRITCHART, Isaac,024, Jean,
  024
PRITCHET, Simon,302
PRITCHETT, Elenor,447
PRITTEET, (Land),133, Tobias,

137

PRO, Peter,269
PROCTER, Robert,068
PROCTOR, (Land),255, Edward,
316, Frederick,291, Fredk.,
297, Henry,316,318, Jesse,
290,291,297,302, Margaret,
316, Mary,497, Phillip,316,
318, Robert,232, Samuel,316,
319
PROSSER, John,302, William,
302, Wm.,296
PROUD, John,222
PRUDE, John Jr.,222, John Sr.,
222, John,206, Margaret,222,
William,221,222
PRUET, David,543
PRUIT, Daniel,509, David,021,
062,083,092, Obediah,433,
509, Richard,504
PRYOR, Marlow,540
PRYOT, Marlow,500
PUCKET, Douglas,227, Ephraim,
433,521,523, Ephrim,482,
Gage,523, Isom,523, J.D.,
442, James,238, John,250,
251, Major,250, Page,155,
544,544, Rebecah,544
PUCKETT(?), Richard C.,265
PUCKETT, Alexander,266,
Andrew,266, Benjamin,270,
Charles,246, Cheatiam,246,
Douglas,246, Duglass,444,
Ely,246, Ephraim,482,
Ephram,482, J.,271,
James D.,443, James,234,
247, Jno.,273, John,246,
266, Martha,234, Mary,246,
247, Richard,247
PUCKETT, William,266, Wm.,266
PUCKIT, Hanna,482
PUGH, Azariah,314, David,308,
Ellis,314, Isaac,315,
Jesse,314, John,029,036,
045,061,086,087, Mr.,281,
282, Rev.,281, Richard,201,
244, Samuel,087, Thomas,314,
William,231,242,314
PUIT, David,523
PULLEY, C.B.(Mrs.),259,
Charles B.(Mrs.),202
PULLIAM, John,327, Wm.,224
PUNCH, Nichs.,290
PURCELL, John,207
PURKLE, Barbara,146, Michael,
146
PURSE, William,227,235,241,
Wm.,229
PURSELL, John,243
PURTLE, Michael,123
PURVIS, George,044,501,524,
John,232
PUTMAN, John,499,502,512,535,
548, Sarah,512
PUTT, Samuel,245
PUTTETS(?), Ely,166
PUTTIT, Tobias,126
PYLAND, George,369
PYLANT, Edward,369
PYLE, John Jr.,143, John Sr.,
143,185, John,138,143,170,
171,175, Mary A.,174, Mary,
174, Nicholas,186, Sameul,
174, William,185
PYLES, Abner,217,225,270,
John,147,159, Reuben,200,
206, Reubin,217,218,225,
S.E.,218, Samuel,159
PYNIAN, Stokes,353
QILKS, Abner,057
QUADDELBUM, John Jr.,318
QUADDLEBAUM, ,009
QUAIL, Charles,201, Icho--(?),
428
QUALES, ,562
QUALL, James,425
QUALLS, ,494, Moses,494
QUALS, David,178, Moses,488
QUARLES, David,353, Elizabeth,
007, Hubbard,353, John Jr.,
353, John,351, R.G.,007,
Robert,353, William G.,007
QUARLS, David,150

QUEAL(?), Henry,425
QUEEN, Mary,328, William,328
QUIN, Hugh,494,497
QUINN, Hugh,494,558,561,565,
John,561, Thomas,275
RABB, ,110, Elizabeth,110,
James,120,240, Jas.,114,
Robt.,114,119
RABKIN, Sarah,326
RABUN, John,175
RABURN, Elizabeth,284, Sarah,
284
RACKLEY, Adaline,340,361, B.,
361, Eliza C.,361, James,
340, Jesse,349, John L.,340,
John,340, Lewis,361,
Mahaley C.,340, Mahla C.,
361, Malissa,340, Mary,340,
361, Redden,340, Reden,329,
361, Thomas,340,361,
Warren B.,340,361, William,
361
RACKLEY, Winney E.,361,
Wm.Benson,340
RAE, Ann,294
RAFFIELD, William,376
RAGAN, John,259, Lucy,203,
William,203,204,490,513
RAGEN, James,055
RAGLAND, Samuel,308, William,
308
RAGLIN, Benj.,139
RAGSDAIL, David,243
RAGSDALE, ,171, Ed.,526,
Edmund,184, Edward,489,
491,496, Edwd.,503, Peter,
127,184,192,243,553, Thomas,
243
RAIBRES, Widow,258
RAINER, John Geo.,537
RAINES, Phalba,340, Stephen,
340
RAINEY, Anne,570, Benjamin,
193,197,199,203,207,212,
214,228,237,245, Bethiah,
228, Bithiah,122, Genj.,122,
John,196,234, Rebecca,009,
Samuel,568, Sarah,122,197,
203, Saray,197, Thomas,570,
572, William,009,050,080,
095,196,244
RAINY, Thomas,008
RALSTON, David,208
RAMAGE, Jane,233, Jean,233,
John,233,321, Mary,008,
321, Robert,008,321
RAMMEL, Daniel,544
RAMSAY, Robert,150
RAMSEY, Alexander,349, Alexr.,
348, Elizabeth,160, James,
017,035,560, John,042,
Robert,123,157,160, Sarah,
435
RANDALL, Jacob,571
RANDOLPH, Hugh,053,056,111,
121
RANDON, Thomas,542
RANEY, Benjamin,170, John,049,
Mary,063, William,049,055,
063
RANKIN, (Line),567, David,567,
James,567, Sarah,356,
Susanna,567
RANKINS, John,361
RANSON, John,277, William,277,
Wm.,276
RANY, John,234
RAPLEY, Richard A.,232,233
RAST, John,038
RATCLIFF, Joel,196, Jowell(Joel),
210, Richard,415,416
RATLIFF, James,369, John,370,
Richard,370, William,385
RATTERUY(?), Alexr.,033
RATTERY, John,079
RAULINS, John,422
RAVEN, Elizabeth,233
RAWLES, Esther,004, Martha,
004, Thos.H.,004
RAWLLINS, John,422
RAWLS, William,291, Wm.,297
RAY, ,168, Ambrose,441,480,
493, Elizabeth,480,493,

Francis,071,077,106,
Gilbert,297,303, Henry,249,
253,562, Hosea,480, John,
095,201, Thos.,480, William,
131,166,207,432
REA, Henry,097, William,166,
207, Wm.,166
REA/RAY, Henry,562
REABON, George,401
REABORN, George,401
READ, Joseph B.,346
READEN, John,057
READER, Ann Mary,318, Daniel,
249, David,249
READY, John,217
REAGWAY, John,185
REAMES, Azariah,402, Joshua,
402, Josiah,402
REAMS, Elizabeth,394, Hezakiah,
394, Hezekiah,394
REARDON, John,411
REASONOVER, Joseph M.,302
REAVER, Thomas,061
REAVES, Benj.,096, Benjamin,
094,096,097, Charles,291,
302, Chas.,297, Mary,096,
097, Moses,034,038, Thomas,
020, Wiley,356, William,094,
096,097,412,413, Wm.,394
RECE, Hezekiah,130
RECTOR, Lewis,179,184
RED, ,009, Dudley,535, Fields,
319, James,003, John,477,
Joseph,535, Susannah,319
REDDER, Thomas,440
REDDING, Joseph,216
REDDISH(?), Mary,108
REDDISH, George,118
REDER, Thomas,440
REDFORD, John,024
REDIER, William,513
REDING, Joseph,206
REDMAN, John,228
REDMON, James,207, John,207,
Rachel,468
REECE, Absalom,349, Absolem,
349, David,163, Eph.,178
REED, ,523, Avory,556, Caty,
507, George,163, Isaac,157,
164,170, James,567, Jane,
202, John,101,157,169,170,
186,359,477,483,485,506,
512,524,536,537,542,569,
Jonathan,202,235, Joseph,
144,152,157,165,169,170,
186,234,507, Mary,186,
Nathaniel,152
REED, Nathaniel,157,183,
Nathl.,152, Thaddeus,567,
William,144,155,506
REEDER, ,009, A.P.,330,
Amanda F.,359, Andrew P.,
359, Benjamin F.,359,
Catherine,266, Joel,359,
Jonathan,326,347,348,350,
352, Joshua,308,309,316,
Lewis W.,359, Mary Teague,
001, Patsey,266, Samuel C.,
359, Samuel,353, Thomas C.,
001, Thos.Milton,359
REES, Ephraim,128, H.,371,
379,381,382,386,400, Huberd,
371,379,380,382,385,400,
417, Isham,391, Jean,313,
John,313, Mary,391,
William,391,392,408,409,
Wm.,375,391
REESE, ,009, Anna,381,
Charles M.,350, D.,415,
Elizabeth,306, Ephriam,126,
George,355,381, Harrison,
001, Nancy,126, Rachel,360,
Solomon,306
REEVE, Abraham,011
REEVES, Moses,103, Thomas,122,
Wiley,335
REID, ,009, Abner,004,
Absalom,346, Ambrose,325,
354, Andrew,269, Clayton N.,
353, David,397, Elizabeth A.,
326, Elizabeth,322, F.M.,
353, George B.,347, George,
244, Henry,269, Isaac,157,

ROBINSON, ,366, Abner,494,
Alexander,097,395, Alexr.,
112,395, Allen,313, Amos,
348, Ann,431,494,531, C.E.,
365,366, Chas.E.,365, David,
536,552, Gerrard,156,
Henrietta,336, Isabella,
200, Isaiah,156, James,003,
058,392,529,543, Jane,552
ROBINSON, Jno.,222,554,
John M.,173, John,057,061,
080,167,180,207,211,221,
222,245,269,346,348,357,
395,494, Joseph,349,431,
494,538, Margaret,222,
Martha,113, Mathew,536,
550, Patrick,568, Peter,041,
042,353, Randolph,307,
Richard,191
ROBINSON, Richard,192,220,
Robert Jr.,057, Robert,020,
Sarah,113,313,543, Suffias,
307,309, Thos.,053, William,
345,395, Willis,361,380,
Wm.,349
ROBINSON-MOONEY, ,366
ROBISON(?), Joseph,495
ROBISON, Abner,488,494,
Alexander,110,116, Alexr.,
112, Archd.,500, Archibald,
489, David,496, Drury,566,
Elijah,500, James,109,113,
115, John,110,116,488,
Joseph,499, Margret,109,
Matthew,496,504, Peter,042,
R.,203,215, Randell,505,506
ROBISON, Richard Jr.,203,
Richard Sr.,203, Richard,
203,215,219, Robert,017,
Sarah,500, William,564,
Willis,380
ROBLYRS(?), Ann,279
ROBUCK, Mary,533
ROCHELL, James,112,114,117,
119, Margaret,113,114,
Margret,117
ROCHESTER, Jon.W.,329,
William,328
RODDEY, David,094,110
RODEN, Greenberry,040,057,
079, James,079, John,040,
073,079, Mary,014,059,079,
101, Thomas,011,014,020,
030,031,068,073,079,081,
084,090,093,097,100,101,
103,561, William,030,059,
078,079
RODGERS, A.(Andrew),202,
A.Jr.,271, Abner(Capt.),
259, Abner,256,271, Alexander,
195, Andrew Jr.,197,199,
204,235,237, Andrew Sr.,192,
214,273, Andrew,193,199,
205,212,214,217,232,236,
239, Ann,192, Charles,157,
160, Isaac,212,224,250,
J.Jr.,271
RODGERS, James,245,248,252,
Jane,219, Jeanne,192, Jno.,
224,230, John Jr.,257, John,
157,192,193,197,198,202,
203,204,211,212,213,215,
216,217,219,220,222,224,
225,226,229,230,240,248,
250,251,252,253,254,255,
258, Letty,212, Margaret,197
RODGERS, Margret,213, McNeese,
269, Patty,245, Robt.,297,
Thomas,212,219,251,
William H.,235, William,
153,192,213,214,253,504,
508, Wm.,219, Wm.Jr.,251,
Wm.T.,213
RODGILL, Jno.,387
ROE, Ann,288, Cynthia,324,
James,409, John H.,346
ROEN, John,194
ROGER, David,393
ROGERS, ,009,371, Alexander,
089, Amelia,172, Andrew,018,
193,518, Arthur,018,
Buttrick,072, Charles,157,
172, Clayton,071,072,487,

561, Cleaton,437, D.Joseph,
291, Daniel,093,095, Dew,
291,297, Due,303, Eli,291,
297,303, Ethelred,297,
Frances,085
ROGERS, G.Thos,291, Gassaway,
314, Henry,303, Hugh,489,
Isaac,072, James,116,278,
282,285,355, Jasper,076,
100, Jean(Jane),546,
John Jr.,518, John Sr.,297,
John,003,037,078,157,248,
291,297,303, Jos.,297, Lot,
291,297,303, Martha,278,
Mary Ann,003
ROGERS, Matthew,564, Nicholas,
279, Noah,303, Philip,303,
R.Joseph,291, Ralph,487,
489,561, Riddin,303,
Robert Jr.,291, Robert,291,
Robt.,297, Saml.,297,
Samuel,291, Sarah,072,
Silas,291,297,303,304,
Susanna,182, Thomas A.,320,
Timothy,291
ROGERS, Timothy,297,303,
Ulysses,379,386,417,420,
William,426,487,493,494,
564, Wilson,485, Winney,007,
Wm.,520
ROINS, Levi,147
ROLAND, Christopher,237,
Ezekial S.,250, Ezekiel,
228,248, Ezikial,255,
Jemina,305, John B.,309,
Reuben,309
ROLINS, Albert,147
ROLLINS, Benjamin,394
ROLLYN, Anne,282
ROLSTON, Isaac,141, Robt.,141
ROOK, Nathaniel,216
ROPER, Aaron,349,350, Absalom,
336, Benj.,349, Benjamin,
350, Cazzy,350, Chas.,350,
Delila,358, Frederic,303,
Gideon,337, Harrison,336,
Jacob,350, John H.,350,
John,291,297,303, Keziah,
350, Louisa,336, Malinda,
330,336, Marcus,336,
Mary E.,340
ROPER, Mary Jane,341, Melinda,
333, Meredith,350, Nancy,
350, Reuben,349, Samuel E.,
336, Sarah,350, Susan,336,
Susannah,350, Tilmon,349,
Toliver,340, Tyre L.,330,
Tyre,341, William,327
RORK, Hugh,123
ROSAMOND, James,207,231, John,
155
ROSE, George,231, Thomas,369,
388
ROSEBOROUGH, Alexander,052,
076, Alexr.,022,106, Jno.,
113, John,113
ROSIER, Chloe,302, Fanny,312,
Wm.K.,302
ROSS, ,249, Arthur,477,
Catharine,283, David,175,
200,256,257, Elenor,253,
Francis,192,243,246,
George F.,337, George,142,
167,169,199,205,231,246,
271,273,560,572, Harriet,
337, Isabella,227, James,
149, Jesse A.,337, Jesse,
337, John Jr.,337
ROSS, John,127,161,167,168,
169,171,179,277,337,488,
560,566, Lunsford M.,337,
Margaret,202,203,216, Mary,
337, Melissa,337, Michael,
304, Richard,337, Robert,
191,192,202,214,216,269,
275, Robt.,203,212,218,
Sarah M.,337, Sarah,560,
Thomas,303
ROSS, Thos.,297, Wiley,337,
William L.,337, William,
129,196,232
ROSSBOROUGH, Alex.,117
ROTHEL, Caleb,348, Catharine,

365, Clayborn,326,365,
Delilah,326, William,325
ROTHER, William,325
ROTHMAHLER, Erasmus,403
ROTTENBERRY, Wm.,101
ROUNDTREE, Turner,519,
William,250, Woodson,516
ROUNTREE, ,491, Turner,471,
472,475,491, William,435,
471,472,477,478, Woodson,
471,472,478
ROUSE, Shepard,369, William,
445
ROUTH, Jeremiah,494
ROWAN, Mathew,039, Matthew,
017,433, Saml.,562
ROWAND, Chas.Elliott,091,
Elliott,091, Harriett,091,
Robert,091,092
ROWDEN, George,527,546
ROWE, Benjamin,243, John,205
ROWEL, Anna,352, David C.,303,
Elizabeth,303, Julity,352,
Martha,302, Wm.,279,303
ROWELL, David C.,297, David Jr.,
291, David Sr.,291, David,
291,303, Dd.,297, Dd.Jr.,
297, Dd.Sr.,297, Jacob,291,
297, Valentine Jr.,291,297,
Valentine Sr.,297, Valentine,
291, Voluntine,303, Wm.B.,
303
ROWLAND, Thomas,181
ROWLETT, J.,397, John,396,
397,398
ROWNE(?), D.B.,429
ROWSE, Thos.,418
ROY, Ms.,554, Nancy R.,553,
Susannah,186, Thomas,186
ROYSTON, John C.,312
ROZER, Jimima,291, William,
291, Wm.,297
ROZERS, Elis,291
ROZIER, Jemima,297
RUBLE, Mary,310, Peter,310,
Samuel,310, Susannah,310
RUCK, William,240
RUCKS, William,243,247, Wm.,
220,223
RUFF, Christian,312, David,
318, Elizabeth,318, George,
307,318, John H.,314, John,
314
RUGELY, Henry,225
RULE, Wm.,368
RUNALDS, James,164
RUNNELLS, Joseph,258
RUNNELS, Ann,468, David,291,
Mary,457
RUNNILS, Dd.,297
RUNNOLDS, Martin,104
RUNOLDS, John,071, Martin,071
RUSELL, Charles,249
RUSH, John,107, Susannah,107
RUSHING, Keziah,262
RUSK, John,326, Joseph,327
RUSSEL, Betty,113, Edmond,092,
George,143,180, James,002,
Jeremiah,134, Jerry,176,
Margaret,113, Martha,217,
Robt.Jr.,353
RUSSELL, Abner,325,328,
Edmund,054, George,168,
326, Henry,328, James,002,
113,169,227,328,462, Jean,
168, John Jr.,562, John,125,
176,186,349, Malinda,328,
Margaret A.,002, Mary,002,
Mathew,572, Matthew,494,
Patrick,362, Polly,003,
Robert,002
RUSSELL, Rosannah,307,
Susannah,137, Thomas,003,
William,113,136,137, Wm.,
113,168
RUSSELLS, Mary,002
RUST, Joseph,359
RUTH, ,538
RUTHERFORD, Dorothy,450,
Elizabeth,078, Frances,450,
Griffith,078, Robert Sr.,
538, Robert,231,304,307,
450, Robt.Sr.,538, Thomas,

002

RUTLEDGE, (Land),381, Charles,
246, Edward,232,390,
Frederick,246, H.,445, J.,
246, John Jr.,246, John Sr.,
246, John,232,246,382,
Wm.Z.,250
RUYHUDSELL, Joseph,442
RY(RAY), Ambros,515
RYAN, James,192,196,197,198,
243, John,232, Martha,434
RYLEY, Ann,230, Catren,306,
James,185, John,242,
Patrick,147,230,242
SADLER, George,011,040,073,
570, Isaac,046,071, John,
036,045,046,221,226, Mary,
036,045,046, Thomas,257,
William,036
SAFFOLD, Ann,464, William,496,
536
SAFFORD, Isham,506
SAFOLD, Isham,496,528,538,
539, Ishm.,485, Temperance,
425,528, William,528
SAINT, Thomas,112,122
SALE, John,440
SALLYERS, Levi,186
SALMON, (Land),139, ,153,161,
Elizabeth,159,181, G.,127,
182, Geo.,156,158,159,162,
163,169,174,181,182, George,
124,125,126,128,137,140,
142,148,149,150,153,158,
159,161,163,168,171,173,
181, Hezekiah,515, William,
200
SALMONS, George,169
SALSE, John,092
SALTZGABER, G.M.,463
SALVADORE, Joseph,232
SALYER, Levi,185
SAMFORD, Fatha,182, James,146,
147,172, Thomas,146
SAMPLE, John,247, Nathaniel,
013
SAMPLES, ,009, Wm.,003
SAMPSON, Isaac,442,506,520,
Phebe,442,506
SAMSON, John,092
SANDAGE, Nathan,467,504,
Nathaniel,467
SANDEFUR, Peter,053,056
SANDERFUR, Elizabeth,070,
Philip,070
SANDERS(?), John,530
SANDERS, ,009, Benjamin,565,
Edward,147, Ezekel,014,
Ezekial,032, Ezekiel,033,
034,050, Ezekl,032, Geo.,
161, George,169,382,383,
James,062,355, Jas.,348,
John,137,150,221,222,291,
297,307,458,459,460,461,
516,519,537, Mary,317,
Meriarter,558
SANDERS, Meriartur,565,
Michael,308,319, Nathaniel,
303, Patrick,331, R.,443,
Robert,393, Susannah,331,
Thomas,032,203,228,291,
303, Thos.,297, William,257,
383,419, Wm.,348, Wm.Jr.,372
SANDFORD, Barack J.,360,
William,360
SANDIFER, Burrell,086,104,
Phil.,565,570, Philip,561,
569, William,023
SANDRIDGE, Richard,141
SANDWICK, Thomas,493
SANFORD, Asa,352, Henry,003,
John,130
SARAGIN, Jonathan,223
SARGANT, Henry,348
SARGEANT, Henry,354
SARGENT, Darais,317, Henry,
354
SARTER, John Peter,442
SARTOR, Ann,551, Anney,551,
J.P.,445, J.Peter,543,
John Peter,551, William,551
SATERWHITE, Thomas,100
SATTERWHITE, Barlett Sr.,314,

Bartlett,310,315,320,
Drury,008,320, Elizabeth,
320, Francis,320, Jemina,
310, John Sr.,318, John T.,
310, John,002, Narcissa,320,
Rebecca,310, Susanna,320,
Theresa C.,320, Theresa,
008, Thomas,008,320
SAUNDERS, James,550, John,431,
Lewis,431, Parthenia,261,
Phillip,495, Reuben,440,
Robert,038, Robt.W.,261,
Thomas,014, Thos.,047,
Wm.Sr.,392
SAVAGE, ,153,154, Anthony,263,
Benjamin Jr.,442, Benjamin,
442,537, Eli,126, James,479,
511,526, John,247,513,537,
Sarah,448, William,167,
171,178,180,206,397,408,
495, Wm.,387
SAWYER, Archibald,260,
Eliza(Mrs.),008, Polly,008,
260, William,008, Willis,
291,297
SAXON, ,009, Alexander G.,002,
B.H.,271,273, Benjamin T.,
008, C.,275, Charles,191,
192,193,195,206,209,219,
222,229,245, Chas.,233,
Hugh,1⌒2, James,135,136,
143,202,209,211,212,215,
Jesse,139,148, John,210,
215,231,259, Joshua,169,195
SAXON, Joshua,205,211,227,
242,517,518, Judith,193,
210,219, Lewis,191,193,194,
195,196,197,198,202,203,
207,209,210,212,213,214,
215,218,219,220,227,229,
238,239,242,244, Samuel,193,
202,204,209,213,216,219,
Sarah,213
SAY, Richard,526
SAYER, Robert,218
SC, ,005
SCALES, John,424,425, Mary,
424,425, Thomas,508, Thos.,
429
SCANE, Adam,555, Nancy,460
SCHAFFERT, Ludwick,344
SCHAFFROTT, Ludwig,344
SCHOCHER, Samuel,530
SCHOPPERT, Phillip,008
SCHRODER, Jacob,350
SCHROEDER, Jacob,332
SCHUMPER, Jacob,197
SCHUMPERT, Amos K.,008, Jacob,
008, John I.(Dr.),008
SCOGGINS, Humphrey,140
SCOLEHER, Samuel,530
SCOT, Carson,394, Nathan,059,
Robert,252
SCOTCHER, Samuel,530
SCOTT, Arthur,052, Benj.,117,
122, Benjamin,117, Charity,
370, Edward,186, Eli,291,
297,303, Elizabeth,568,
James,186,370,568, Jean,
052, Jesse,292, John,185,
186,413, Jos.,558, Lewis,
291,297, Margaret,224,488,
499, Margret,221, Mary,488
SCOTT, Patience,292, Pharoah,
291,297, Rebecca,283,
Robert,013,185,210, Samuel,
195,572, Thomas(Capt.),270,
Thomas,558, William,115,
314,572, Wm.,113
SCRIMSHAW, John,269
SCRIVEN, James(Col.),270
SCROGGINS, Humphrey,139,144
SCROGIN, Barton,126,140,
Hannah,148,149, Humphrey,
144, Thomas,148,149
SCRUGGS, Jeffery,226, Jesse,
235
SCURRY, Patrick,315
SEABOR, James,143
SEABORN, Geo.,177, James,123,
132,136,159,163,170,185,
186, Jas.,185,187
SEABORNE, James,158

SEAGO, Benjamin,356
SEAL, Anthony,111, Enoch T.,
035, Enoch,111, James Sr.,
122, Jas.,113
SEALE, James,113
SEALEY, John,062
SEALY, John,039,062,074,
Peter,074, Samuel,074
SEAMATER, William,053
SEARCY, Jeremiah,233
SEATON, Samuel,327
SECO, Benjamin,326
SEEBA, C.F.,344
SEEBER, C.F.,343
SEEBREE, Mary,103
SEELEY, Elender,032,033,
Peter,032,033, Sarah,032,
033
SEELY, Jane,051, John,051,
Peter,051, Samuel,051,
Sarah,051
SELBY, Jno.,408
SELMAN, Thomas,565
SEMPLE, Nathan,066
SENTS(?), Ch.,163
SEOF(?), John,035
SERGEANT, Henry,328
SERVICE, John,010
SERVIS, John,024
SERVISE, John,054
SETZLER, ,318
SEYMORE, Henry,248
SHACKELFORD, Francis,291,297,
John,291,297, Mary Ann,240,
Mary,240, Richard,240,
Richd.,237,262, Sept.Jr.,
297, Steph.Sr.,297, Stephen J.,
291, Stephen Jr.,291,
Stephen Sr.,291
SHADDOCK, Samuel,373
SHADEA, Pleasant,258
SHADRICK, William,082
SHADRIT, William,059
SHAN, David,056
SHANKLIN, Edw.Henry,350,
Joseph D.,354
SHANKS, Geo.,297, George,291,
303
SHANLEY, William,224, Wm.,221
SHANNON, David,117, John,106,
116, Thomas,090, Thos.,117
SHARP, ,557, Aaron Allen,073,
James,047,048,056,075,
John,351, William,047,048,
067,075,176,495,511,539
SHARPE, William,034
SHARPLIN, Jas.,369
SHATEEN(?), Abraham,166
SHATEEN, Abraham,129
SHAVE, William,237
SHAVER, Phillip,534
SHAVERTAKER, Philip,528
SHAVOUS, Philip,427
SHAW, ,438, Agnes,116, Daniel,
112,114,116,303,528, Haley,
305, Jeane,559, John,070,
Leanard D.,186, Nancy,112,
114, Patrick,505, Patty,305,
Rebecca,305, Robert,008,
243, Samuel,496, W.,431,
490, William,013,050,085,
186,223,231,303,425
SHAW, William,427,437, Wm.,
182,431
SHAWFF, William,055
SHEAD, William,327
SHEARER, William,558
SHEARLY, Jacob,307, Ursley,
307
SHEETS, Nicholas,062
SHELBY, Eliz.D.,008, Elizabeth,
129,557, Joseph,303, Moses,
129,557, William,303
SHELER, Susan,335, Thos.,335
SHELL, ,009, Henry W.,002,
Stephen,001
SHELLY, Noah,291,297,303,
Philip,291, Phillip,297,
Steph.,297, Stephen,291,
William,291, Wm.,297
SHELTON, Nanna,134, Robert,
194,215, Samuel W.,009,
Sarah,317

Lemuel,358, Margarett,185,
Martha,332,358, Mary,074,
281,283, Mathew A.,543,
Molly,311
THOMAS, Mr.,188, Mrs.,280,
Permelia,002, Rebecky,351,
Reuben,266, Roan,291,298,
Robt.,570, Saml.,348,
Sampson,282, Samuel,009,
348,507, Sarah,330,424,
Susannah,054, Tristan,283,
W.D.,176,522, Wiley,351,
William D.,136, William,
066,067
THOMAS, William,079,090,240,
280,281,291,316,424,459,
506,522, Wm.,079,172,221,
222,281,298,489,529, Wm.D.,
164,165, Wm.Davis,164,522
THOMASON, Betsy,184, Elizabeth,
257, John,238, Mourning,222,
238, William,222,238,239,
251, Wm.,222,238,257
THOMB, Samuel,274
THOMBS, Samuel,357, William,
357
THOMLEY, Thomas,312
THOMPKINS, David C.,337,
David,340, Mary,340,
Thomas,337
THOMPSON, ,004,255,529,543,
557,568, Abraham,314,322,
Absolam,164, Adam,331,529,
Alexander,119, And.,542,
Andrew,164,528,542,
Benajah,435,438,528,538,
Benj.,551, Benjamin,490,
492,494,531, Charles,314,
349,483,485,488, Charlotte,
325, David,119
THOMPSON, David,392, Elijah,
325,346, Elizabeth,119,303,
483, Ethalind,325, Fleming,
350, Green,109, Henry,001,
Hugh,231, J.,439, James,
119,185,231,291,303,325,
346,351,427,437,453,454,
Jas.,297,348,349, Jean,164,
Jno.,534,536, John Jr.,485
THOMPSON, John Jr.,502,
John L.M.,326,350, John W.,
291,297, John(Capt.),530,
John,104,119,291,298,303,
325,427,483,485,496,507,
515,528,529,543,549,557,
565,571, Jonah,187, Joseph,
162,176,211,256,257, Joshua,
325,346
THOMPSON, Keziah,317, Lewis,
034,291,298,303, Louisa,325,
Mark,174, Martha,488, Mary,
211,325,346,485, Neill,291,
298, Nicholas,120, Rebecca(Mrs.),
009, Richard,128,175,487,
513,527, Richd.,569, Robert,
020,503,532,555, Saml.,298,
303,532
THOMPSON, Samuel,291,440,526,
559, Sarah,315,346, Steph.,
297, Stephen,291, Susannah,
483, W.,182,267, Waddy,320,
Wady,182, William H.,463,
William,069,116,119,159,
234,325,454,483,488,492,
Wm.(Capt.),064, Wm.,492
THOMSON, Adam,425,427, Andrew,
456,484,518,533, David,114,
119, Elizabeth,114, George,
134, James,231, Jane,201,
John,427,528, Joseph,317,
Lusia,175, Nathan,378,
Nathaniel,437, Nicholas,
112,113, Philip,407,
Richard,317,427,434,483,484
THOMSON, Robert,518, Samuel M.,
439, Samuel,099, Solomon,
378,402, Thos.Hobson,490,
William,009,106,427,483,
484, Willm.,112
THORN, Edmund,352
THORNBURG, James W.,001,
Mary Ann,001
THORNTON, Job,009, John,216,

228, Martha,009
THORP, Aaron A.,118
THURSTON, James,243
TIDWELL, Jno.Sr.,112, John,
111,117
TIGER, David,242
TILLER, Edward,139, Wilie,252,
William,139
TILLEY, Edmond,103
TILLISON, Ananis,348
TILLMAN, Edward,557, Mary(Mrs.),
005
TILLOTSON, Annanias,348
TILMAN, Edward,451,485, Glus,
019, Jesse,019
TIMMON, Simmeon,291
TIMMONS, Alexr.,303, Isaac,
298,303, John Jr.,291,298,
John Sr.,291,298, John,303,
Jud.,303, Saml.,297,303,
Samuel,291, Simeon,298,
Wm.,291,297
TIMMS, Amos,048,068,086,093,
Fanny,068, Hollis,078,085,
086,090,093,100, James,049,
085,093,095,099,100,103,
105, Jesse,062, John,048,
Joseph,035,048,068,081,
090,104, Patty,049,099,100
TIMS, Amos Sr.,543, Amos,012,
013,449,505,513,544,546,
James Jr.,543, James,013,
505,543, Joseph,056, Patty,
543
TINCH, Nancy,356
TINDALL, Assa,072, Robert,047
TINDEL, Robert,047
TINDELL, Samuel,438
TINDSLEY, ,224, Betty,225,
Elizabeth,218, Menoah,204,
Prestings,218
TINKER, James,198
TINKLER, Jno.D.,058
TINLER, (Land),096
TINNEY, John,147
TINSLEY, ,491, Cornelius,194,
Elizabeth,194, Frances,262,
Golding,308, James,237,
308, Manoah,216, Matilda,
262, Philip,236, Sarah,194,
Widow,213
TIRBELLEE, John,303, Solomon,
303
TISDALE, John,394, William,
124
TISDEL, William,124
TISDELL, William,131
TOD, Thomas,172,427,429,507,
525,531, Thos.,428
TODD, (Land),255, Andrew,271,
275,276, Charlotte R.,006,
James,252,253,258,361,
John,210,230,272, Margaret,
214,224,237, Nathan,255,
Patrick,273, Robert J.,009,
Robert,210,214,230,252,
Sam'l,271, Samuel,270,271,
272, Thomas,145,198,255
TODD, Thomas,257,492, William,
361
TOLAND, Ann,311
TOLBERT, John C.,004, John,
002, Mary,002, William,194,
269
TOLLAND, James,275
TOMB, Alexander,088, Alexr.,
487
TOMBS, Alexander,042, David,
042
TOMESON, John Sr.,269, L.D.,
269, Wm.Jr.,269, Wm.Sr.,269
TOMLIN, Francis(F),468
TOMLINSON, ,413, John,096,
Moses,191
TOMPKINS, John B.,337,
Joseph J.,337, Mary E.,337,
Sarah A.,337, Thomas J.,009
TONEY, Timothy,124,161
TOOD, Robert J.,009
TOOMBS, Robert,248
TOOMER, Ann,323, Anthony,323,
502
TOOMMER, Anthony,535

TORBERT, Samuel,473,484,
Susannah,473
TORIANSON, Peter,150
TORRANCE, ,481, Andrew,444,
480,481,517, Andw.,441,444,
482,547
TORRANXE, Andrew,438
TORRENCE, Andrew,003,429,430,
433,439,440,541,548,551,
Andw.,430,534
TOSH, James,541
TOURELL, Francis,276
TOWERS, Benjamin,244, Isaac,
243,244, L.,333, Leonard,
347,355,358,359,360,
William,165
TOWLES, Joseph,317, Oliver,
201
TOWN, John,505
TOWNEND, James,523
TOWNS, ,515, Alcie(Alee),515,
G.F.,366, John,438,445,
515, W.,174, William,160,161
TOWNSAN, Benjamin,244
TOWNSEN(D), Amphlilada,183,
Benjamin,183, Light,166,
167, Sight(Light),183,
Thomas,166
TOWNSEN, Thomas,184
TOWNSEND(?), ,523
TOWNSEND, Benjamin,184, Eli,
474, James,432,464,466,467,
471,474,545,550, Jno.Sr.,
432, John Sr.,471, John,474,
507,509, Martha,474,550,
Repentance,191,192, Ruth,
471, Thomas,183,184,291,
Thos.,298
TRAIL, David,538
TRAINUM, Catherine,341, David,
184, George W.,341, Jeremiah,
331,341, John W.,341,
Willis,341
TRAMEL, (Line),433, Daniel,
433,544, Thomas,433
TRAMMEL, Daniel,426,515
TRAMMELL, Daniel,499, Isaac,
515, Thomas,499, William,516
TRANELL, William,515
TRANUM, William,185
TRAP, Thos.,111
TRAVERS, Arthur,095, Francis,
558, Mark,001
TRAVERSE, Daniel,061, Sarah,
061
TRAWELKS(?), George,283
TRAWICK, Wm.,298
TREAWEEK, William,291
TREAWICK, Geo.,298
TREEWEEKS(?), Lydia,284
TREPHENEY, ,188
TRIBBLE, Robert C.,335
TRIBLE, Jeremiah,264
TRIDINE, John,388
TRIMBLE, Hugh,192
TRIMIER, Obediah,445
TRIMMIER, John,430, Lucy,346,
Marcus T.,352,355, Obadiah,
347, Obediah(Col.),346,
Obediah,431,447, Selina,346
TRION, William,015
TROTTER, Eliza,333, Elizabeth,
333, Isiah,346, J.R.,334,
James,347,359, John,214,
222,227,234,244, Rebecca,
347, Robert,347
TROUP, John,396
TRUSELL, William,026
TRUSSEL, Daniel,084, William,
058,063,083
TRUSSELL, James,015,041,042,
John,042, William,015,063
TRYON, William(Gov.),021,
William,017, Wm.,018,441
TUBB(?), Peter,218
TUBB, George,124,132,138,161,
James,132,138,142,153,161,
178, John,132,138,142,149,
Mary,178, William,130,136,
140, Wm.,132
TUCKER, Joel,003, John,394,
395,417, Joseph,486,491,
522, Lucy,470, Mary,188,

Moses,536,562,566, Nancy R.,
264
WRIGHT, Nancy,456, Nathan,309,
Phebe,442,506, Randle,087,
Rich.,063, Ruth,283,284,
285, Sally,456, Sarah,214,
Thomas,420,425,426,455,
507,513,515,528,534,536,
Thos.,271,272,456, Wiley,
551, William,264,309,352,
371,392,419,442,455,456
WRIGHT, William,506,536,561,
562,566, Wm.G.,003
WRING(?), Benjamin,052
WYAT, Richart,083
WYATT, David,094, Richard,102,
Thomas B.,126
WYER, John,170
WYLEY, John Castle,353, Moses,
496, William,068, Wm.,034
WYLIE, Isabella,095, James,
010,056,059,096,102, Joel,
094, Peter,010, Sarah,056,
Saray,056, William,010,
025,095
WYSE, Fred,002, Frederick,009
YAGER, Ezekiel,253, Jesse,253,
John,253, Lewis,253
YANCEY, ,225, Ambrose,226,
James Jr.,139,141,430,527,
531
YANCY, James Jr.,137,152,
James,490
YARBEY(IRBY), Wm.,256
YARBOROUGH, (?),209, Ambrose,
427,429,507, Humphrey,429,
Jeremiah,429, John,429,
Mary,429, Rachel,108,
Richard,099, Thos.Griggs,
108, Thos.Grigs,108, Wm.,107
YARBROUGH, George W.,004,
John Sr.,050,051, John,246,
William,051
YATES, Thomas,200
YEARBY, Isham,189,190
YELDELL, Wm.,004
YELVERTON, Jesse,292,298,304,
John,292,298,304, Nathn.,
304, Zadoc,304, Zadock Jr.,
292,298, Zadock,292,298
YERBEY, Phebe,480
YONGUE, Wm.,116
YORK, John,199, Jonathan,250
YORKE, Thomas,242
YOUNG, (Line),528, ,009,182,
223,254, Abner,253, Abram,
002, Adam,428, Agnes,263,
Amy(Miss),363, Andrew,462,
Ann,192,193, Anna,348,358,
Archibald,208, Augustus,
003, Caterin,436, Caterine,
436, Catharine,446, Catherine,
436, Christopher,436
YOUNG, Christopher,499,
Clarinda,329, Daniel,510,
513,514, Elender,032,033,
Elizabeth,262,561, Ezekial,
159, Ezekiel,158, George,
259,267,329,436, Hannah,124,
Hanner,162, Henry G.,276,
Henry,413,414,415, Hugh,
226, Jacob,267, James C.,439
YOUNG, James Jr(?),560,
James Sr.,262, James,009,
016,063,075,077,153,192,
193,199,208,209,213,215,
219,221,227,230,235,258,
262,263,330,345,348,358,
365,428,547,560,564,565,
Jane,560, Jas.,271, Jean,
045, Jesse,466,509,510,514,
547, John Adam,307
YOUNG, John D.,532,534,
John Jr.,133,135,141,174,
John Sr.,177, John,033,
063,133,141,153,162,174,
177,186,205,208,223,244,
245,269,329,425,428,518,
Jos.,226, Joseph,001,207,
226,245,346,428, Kitturah,
262, Lucy,262, Margaret,003,
428,523
YOUNG, Mary,208,245, Moses,

460, Nancy,009, Pauline,010,
Philip,356, Rebecca,347,
Richard,329, Robert Jr.,
249, Robert,009,199,206,
207,209,213,223,245,250,
252, Robt.,253, Sam,253,
Saml.,438,538, Samuel,003,
147,177,254,428,438,504,520
YOUNG, Samuel,521,527,
Susannah,281, T.W.,099,
Thomas B.,491, Thomas Sr.,
436, Thomas,267,428,436,
491,498,499,503,506,513,
542,547, Washington,348,
William A.,365, William(Col.),
523, William,020,032,033,
063,097,133,135,137,141,
169,174
YOUNG, William,192,203,214,
237,254,263,306,428,435,
436,493,510,511,516,518,
554, Wm.(Capt.),461, Wm.,
174,490,511,561
YOUNGBLOOD, Ann,353, Berena,
009, Manly,009, Meely,336,
Simeon,336,353, William,336
YOW, Dempsey,332, Demsey,326,
Jane,350
YOWELL, James,358
ZACHRA, Alexr.,351
ZEIGLAR, Wm.,009
ZIMMERMAN, ,321
ZUBER, Conrad,312, Leonard,
312, Uriah,318